"第三届数字时代出版产业发展与人才培养国际学术

数字出版与出版教育
（第三辑）

ShuZi ChuBan Yu ChuBan JiaoYu（Di San Ji）

主　　编　黄先蓉　罗紫初
副 主 编　张美娟　练小川　朱静雯
编委成员（以姓氏笔画为序）
　　　　　方　卿　王　清　王晓光　朱静雯　吴　平
　　　　　吴永贵　沈　阳　张美娟　罗紫初　练小川
　　　　　姚永春　徐丽芳　黄先蓉

高等教育出版社·北京
HIGHER EDUCATION PRESS　BEIJING

图书在版编目（CIP）数据

数字出版与出版教育. 第 3 辑，"第三届数字时代出版产业发展与人才培养国际学术研讨会"论文集/黄先蓉，罗紫初主编. —北京：高等教育出版社，2012.3
ISBN 978－7－04－027024－2

Ⅰ. ①数… Ⅱ. ①黄…②罗… Ⅲ. ①电子出版物－出版工作－国际学术会议－文集 Ⅳ. ①G237.6－53

中国版本图书馆 CIP 数据核字（2012）第 008533 号

策划编辑 曹 园 责任编辑 阳化冰 郭治学 封面设计 王 洋 版式设计 范晓红
插图绘制 尹文军 责任校对 刘 莉 责任印制 刘思涵

出版发行	高等教育出版社	咨询电话	400－810－0598
社 址	北京市西城区德外大街 4 号	网 址	http://www.hep.edu.cn
邮政编码	100120		http://www.hep.com.cn
印 刷	北京外文印刷厂	网上订购	http://www.landraco.com
开 本	787mm×1092mm 1/16		http://www.landraco.com.cn
印 张	40.75	版 次	2012 年 3 月第 1 版
字 数	970 千字	印 次	2012 年 3 月第 1 次印刷
购书热线	010－58581118	定 价	116.00 元

Proceedings of the 3rd International Conference on
Publishing Industry and Publishing Education in the Digital Age

Digital Publishing and Publishing Education
(Volume 3)

Editors-in-chief   Huang Xianrong   Luo Zichu

Vice Editors-in-chief   Zhang Meijuan   Lian Xiaochuan   Zhu Jingwen

Editorial Staff   Fang Qing   Wang Qing   Wang Xiaoguang
                         Zhu Jingwen   Wu Ping   Wu Yonggui   Shen Yang
                         Zhang Meijuan   Luo Zichu   Lian Xiaochuan
                         Yao Yongchun   Xu Lifang   Huang Xianrong

高等教育出版社·北京
HIGHER EDUCATION PRESS   BEIJING

第三届数字时代出版产业发展与人才培养
国际学术研讨会

The 3rd International Conference on

Publishing Industry and Publishing Education in the Digital Age

Wuhan University, People's Republic of China

第三届数字时代出版产业发展与人才培养国际学术研讨会

一、主办、承办和协办单位

主办单位

武汉大学（中国）

佩斯大学（美国）

承办单位

武汉大学信息管理学院

佩斯大学出版系

武汉大学信息资源研究中心

国家新闻出版总署武汉大学高级出版人才培养基地

协办单位

中国出版科学研究所

龙源期刊网

湖北省新闻出版局

湖北长江出版传媒集团

湖北省编辑学会

武汉大学出版社

荆楚网

腾讯·大楚网

二、组织机构

顾问委员会

李　健　武汉大学党委书记，教授，博导

顾海良　武汉大学校长，教授，博导

斯蒂芬·弗莱德曼　美国佩斯大学校长，教授

谢红星　武汉大学副校长

蔡学俭　湖北省新闻出版局原局长

彭斐章　武汉大学资深教授，博导

马费成　武汉大学教授，博导，信息资源研究中心主任

学术委员会

主席

罗紫初　武汉大学信息管理学院教授，博导

谢尔曼·拉斯金　美国佩斯大学出版系主任，教授，佩斯大学出版社社长

委员

迈克尔·希利　美国（谷歌）图书版权登记处（BBR）执行主任，美国佩斯大学大卫·派克特聘荣誉教授，国际标准书号管理局主席，国际数字对象标识（DOI）基金会主任，美国书业研究会前执行主任

乌苏拉·劳腾堡　德国埃朗根—纽伦堡大学图书学系主任，教授

A. H. 范德韦尔　荷兰莱顿大学图书与数字媒体研究系教授

郝振省　中国出版科学研究所所长，武汉大学兼职教授

周百义　湖北长江出版传媒集团总编辑

陈传夫　武汉大学信息管理学院院长，教授，博导

吴　平　武汉大学教务部部长，教授，博导

方　卿　武汉大学信息管理学院副院长，教授，博导

黄先蓉　武汉大学信息管理学院出版科学系主任，教授，博导

组织委员会

主任委员

张儒芝　湖北省新闻出版局局长

黄泰岩　武汉大学副校长

王建辉　湖北省长江出版传媒集团董事长，武汉大学兼职教授

陈庆辉　武汉大学出版社社长

谢尔曼·拉斯金　美国佩斯大学出版系主任，教授，佩斯大学出版社社长

陈传夫　武汉大学信息管理学院院长，教授，博导

委员

苏珊·丹齐格　美国 DailyLit 网站创始人和首席执行官，美国佩斯大学出版系顾问委员会委员

柯尔斯顿·D. 桑德伯格　美国佩斯大学出版系兼职教授，哈佛商学院出版社前高级编辑

练小川　美国佩斯大学兼职教授

徐德欢　湖北长江出版传媒集团出版产业部部长

万　智　湖北长江出版传媒集团综合部部长

钱建国　武汉大学校长办公室主任

卢江滨　武汉大学国际交流部部长

沈壮海　武汉大学人文社会科学研究院常务副院长，教授，博导

吴　平　武汉大学教务部部长，教授，博导

郭明磊　武汉大学人文社会科学研究院副院长

宋朝阳　武汉大学人文社会科学研究院副院长

姜星莉　武汉大学人文社会科学研究院副院长

穆广菊　龙源期刊网副总裁、总编辑
阎思甜　荆楚网总编辑
谢湖伟　腾讯·大楚网总编辑
何　皓　武汉大学出版社副社长
董有明　武汉大学信息管理学院党委书记
李　纲　武汉大学信息管理学院副院长，教授，博导
方　卿　武汉大学信息管理学院副院长，教授，博导
王新才　武汉大学信息管理学院副院长，教授，博导
黄先蓉　武汉大学信息管理学院出版科学系主任，教授，博导
朱静雯　武汉大学信息管理学院出版科学系副主任，教授，博导
徐丽芳　武汉大学信息管理学院出版科学系副主任，教授，博导

秘书长

方　卿　武汉大学信息管理学院副院长，教授，博导

秘书组

组长

黄先蓉　武汉大学信息管理学院出版科学系主任，教授，博导

成员

徐丽芳　武汉大学信息管理学院出版科学系副主任，教授，博导
张美娟　武汉大学信息管理学院出版科学系教授，博导
王晓光　武汉大学信息管理学院出版科学系副教授

宣传组

组长

胡　伟　武汉大学信息管理学院党委副书记

成员

王　清　武汉大学信息管理学院出版科学系副教授
吴永贵　武汉大学信息管理学院出版科学系教授
沈　阳　武汉大学信息管理学院出版科学系教授
姚永春　武汉大学信息管理学院出版科学系副教授

会务组

组长

朱静雯　武汉大学信息管理学院出版科学系副主任，教授，博导

成员

赵金利　武汉大学信息管理学院党政办公室主任
查　荔　武汉大学信息资源研究中心办公室主任
严冠湘　武汉大学信息管理学院实验中心副主任
居森林　武汉大学信息管理学院学生工作办公室
宗　建　武汉大学信息管理学院研究生教学与科研管理办公室
钱宏宇　武汉大学信息管理学院党政办公室
余良珍　武汉大学信息管理学院党政办公室

前　言

随着信息技术在出版领域的广泛应用，国际出版业正在经历一场前所未有的数字革命。2009 年，我国数字出版产业的总收入达到 799.4 亿元，比 2008 年增长了 50.6%；国际知名网络书店亚马逊网站的电子书销量也一度超越印刷图书，成为 2009 年圣诞节最热销商品。2010 年 4 月，美国苹果公司推出出版界翘首以待的 iPad 平板电脑，头三个月销量就超过 300 万台，国际出版传媒界无不为之震动。

移动互联网、智能手机、电子阅读器等各种新兴媒介的出现和蓬勃发展，不仅加快了传统出版业的转型，也推动了各类新型数字出版业务的发展。面对日益澎湃的数字出版浪潮，出版业遇到了前所未有的挑战与机遇。如何进一步加快传统出版机构的数字化转型步伐，推进数字出版产业链健康成长，实施出版高等教育改革，培养现代出版业急需人才，保证出版产业可持续发展，已经成为当代出版人和出版教育工作者亟待思考和广泛探讨的重要议题。为此，武汉大学、美国佩斯大学和新闻出版总署武汉大学高级出版人才培养基地决定联合举办"数字时代出版产业发展与人才培养国际研讨会"。

前两届研讨会得到了中外出版界与出版教育界同仁的热烈响应，并引起了社会各界广泛关注。近两年来，国际数字出版领域的发展日新月异，为了交流与探讨数字时代出版产业和出版教育的最新成果与未来发展思路，"第三届数字时代出版产业发展与人才培养国际学术研讨会"于 2010 年 10 月 19—20 日在武汉大学隆重召开并获得圆满成功。

本次大会以特邀作者撰文和公开征文的方式征集会议论文，共收到 260 多篇自由投稿。经过组委会筛选，我们选用了 90 篇文章编辑成为会议论文集，其中，由外国专家撰写的论文 8 篇，来自国内出版界、学术界的论文包括：宏观出版类 11 篇、学术出版与开放存取类 10 篇、出版教育类 10 篇、数字期刊类 5 篇、出版社数字化转型类 13 篇、出版信息交流类 5 篇、出版营销类 7 篇、国际出版类 9 篇、移动出版与电子书刊类 12 篇。

由于时间等原因，本会议论文集在一些方面难免存在错讹和不规范之处，恳请读者批评指正。

编者
2010-12-12

目　录

学术出版与开放存取

出 版 教 育

数 字 期 刊

出版社数字化转型

出版信息交流

出 版 营 销

国 际 出 版

移动出版与电子书刊

Opening Speech

Sherman Raskin

（Director, Professor, M. S. in Publishing, Pace University）

（美国佩斯大学出版系主任谢尔曼·拉斯金教授致辞）

sDear Colleagues,

We were last in Wuhan in November 2008 for the Second International Conference on Publishing Industry and Publishing Education in the Digital Age. As I stated in 2008, digitalization and technology continue to change the publishing industry. iPod, Kindle, the Nook and the Sony Reader grow in popularity. On-demand books also continue to grow in popularity, and Jason Epstein's Espresso Book Machine continues to print and trim books in minutes. Digital files are retrieved and transmitted by the Internet and printing, page logging, and cutting are performed in a continual process.

More readers are turning to iPhones, smartphones and electronic books to retrieve information and major questions to ask are the following: What is the future of books as we know them today? How far will the technical revolution take us? This is a challenging time to work in publishing and digitalization presents the industry with new opportunities. The publishing industry and publishing education can only advance if we address these issues with confidence and creativity.

And so, we meet again at Wuhan University in 2010 to participate in the Third International Conference on Publishing Industry and Publishing Education in the Digital Age, a conference sponsored by Pace University, Wuhan University and General Administration of Press and Publication (GAPP). The last conference, in November 2008, covered numerous interesting subjects such as "Digital Publishing Technology and the Global Liquidity Crisis", "E-books in Theory and Practice: Anticipating the Year 2020", "Marketing in an Increasingly Digital World", "Electronic Publishing in Germany" and "Reading in the Digital Age".

In 2010, the digital challenge is growing quickly and in the past two years since we last met digitalization has made huge gains in the publishing industry. In the next two days, we will discuss these changes and attempt to look into the future and understand where the industry will be in 2012, the year of the next digital conference. During the next two days scholars, publishing executives and publishing professionals will discuss how digitalization will alter the way that we conduct the business of publishing and publishing education. Today is a special day for Pace University, Wuhan University, GAPP, and the United States and China.

With the support of Professor Liu Binjie, Administrator of GAPP, Dr. Chen Chuanfu, Dean of the School of Information Management of Wuhan University, and Stephen Friedman,

President of Pace University, we have organized the third conference on digital publishing, inviting publishers and publishing educators worldwide to participate.

The conference is essential as technology changes the face of the industry and alters methods to disseminate information. Most importantly, the conference symbolizes the mutual cooperation between Pace University and Wuhan University. We began this process in the academic year 2003—2004 when Dr. Xu Lifang and Dr. Fang Qing served as research scholars at Pace University. They met educators and publishing professionals to learn about the publishing industry in the United States. Their visit was unique and gave us opportunity to share ideas.

One year later Dr. Huang Xianrong, presently Chair of the Publishing Science Program at Wuhan University, was in residence at Pace. Dr. Huang was instrumental in establishing an agreement of mutual understanding between Pace University and Wuhan Universities. In the fall 2007, Dr. Zhu Jingwen spent six months in New York. Her focus was the magazine industry in the United States. Last year, Dr. Yao Yongchun visited New York and her specialty was children's book publishing.

Pace University is proud of our strong ties with Wuhan University. We are honored to participate as a cosponsor of the conference and pleased to have Pace faculty in attendance. We are very proud to have Michael Healy, the David Pecker Distinguished Professor of Publishing at Pace University, present the keynote address. He has served in the book industry for more than 25 years and has spent most of his time in senior editorial, sales and distribution roles in publishing. Professor Healy presently serves as the Executive Director of the Book Rights Registry (BRR) which will be the lead body in the administration of the Google Book Settlement. The BRR will represent authors and publishers in the administration of their digital assets.

President Stephen Friedman extends his congratulations to all participants and looks forward to a long and productive relationship between Pace University and Wuhan University. Most unique is the mutual cooperation between these two prestigious institutions.

Seeking Permanence in a Time of Turbulence

——An Overview of Recent Trends and Developments in U. S. Digital Publishing and Bookselling

Michael Healy

（Google Book Rights Registry）

Abstract：All aspects of book publishing are being disrupted by digital technology. The disruption started more than forty years ago, but its effects have been felt with particular intensity in trade publishing in the last few years since the advent of e-readers and the pervasiveness of inexpensive Internet access. Technology has allowed some of the traditional functions of book publishers to be usurped by other individuals and organizations and this is provoking a debate about what it is that publishers contribute distinctively to the value chain. Traditional roles and responsibilities are shifting and this is likely to intensify in the future.

Keywords：Publishing　Bookselling　E-books　Digital books　Digital publishing

混乱时代里的永恒：美国数字出版和书籍销售的近期发展趋势

迈克尔·希利

（谷歌图书版权登记处）

摘要：数字技术对图书出版的各个方面都带来了扰乱。四十年前这种扰乱就已开始，但在最近几年，由于电子阅读器和廉价互联网的普及，它对大众出版的影响愈加激烈。技术已经导致图书出版商的部分传统功能被其他领域的个人和组织取代。这种现象引起了关于出版人对价值链有何贡献的激烈讨论。出版人传统的角色和责任正在发生改变，未来这种变化将更加剧烈。

关键词：出版　图书营销　电子书　数字图书　数字出版

Before I begin my presentation I want to thank those here at Wuhan University and my friends at Pace University in New York for the opportunity to be here today. It's a privilege to be in China at a time of such profound change and to be given the opportunity not only to share with you some of my experiences of how that change is transforming the American book industry, but also to learn how Chinese publishing and bookselling are responding to developments that are truly global in their significance and impact.

The remarks I want to share with you today are based on two very simple observations. Observation Number One: there's only one conversation being conducted today in the American book world: the conversation about digital technology and its impacts on the publishing and bookselling industries. In conferences and seminars, in blogs, tweets, and discussion lists, the talk is exclusively of digital technology and how it is influencing the ways in which books are commissioned, developed, edited, produced, marketed, priced, sold, and consumed. It is reasonable to ask why this conversation is being conducted with such intensity right now. After all, digital publishing itself is nothing new. In fact it's at least 40 years old if you choose to trace its origins back to the inception of Project Gutenberg back in 1970. For much of the intervening time, technology has been quietly transforming many facets of publishing, especially academic and scientific publishing, starting with periodicals more than 20 years ago. I suggest there are two answers to my question — why is the debate as intense and all consuming as it is right now? First, the debate is being led by the trade publishing sector, which is not only by far the largest and most influential in the U. S. industry, but also the sector that attracts the most prominent news coverage in the wider general media. Second, the debate within trade publishing coincides with the convergence of all the conditions necessary for the radical transformation of the publishing and bookselling industries: ubiquitous, low-cost, and high-speed access to the Internet; the rapidly declining costs of hardware and bandwidth; the evolution of technical standards for the development of e-books and other digital content; the development of low-priced reading devices; the maturity of a new generation of readers that is much more technically sophisticated than its predecessors; and the growing interest and participation of powerful, global interests in the book industry (notably Google, Apple and Amazon). I will be talking about many of these conditions in a little more detail during my presentation but before doing so let's talk about my second observation.

Observation Number Two is this: whenever you listen into the conversation about the impact of digital technology on U. S. publishing and bookselling, beneath the superficial discussion lies one recurring theme. Conversations that seem to be ostensibly about pricing, about copyright, about digital rights management, about royalties, on closer inspection turn out to be conversations about the same thing: they're about survival; they're about re-defining what it really means to be a publisher or to be a bookseller at a time when cheaper technology seems to put within the reach of everyone the tools that used to make publishers unique and distinctive. In other words, all these conversations are about permanence and that's why I chose to call this talk Seeking Permanence in a Time of Turbulence.

The sales of digital books in the United States, which I would argue are impressive given how new the marketplace is, are themselves not yet sufficiently significant to explain the intensity of the conversation now underway about the future of publishing and bookselling in the U. S. In the twelve-month period ending June 30, 2010 retail sales of trade e-books were approximately $550 million. [1] Total book sales in the trade sector in the same period were approximately $11 billion[2] suggesting that digital books now account for approximately 5% of all trade sales. If there is any temptation to dismiss the significance of digital books on the basis of these retail sales numbers or on the proportion of total sales that they represent, it's important to stress the growth rates behind these numbers. The annual figure of $550 million I quoted a moment ago was only $185 million the year before, indicating a three-fold increase in twelve months. And let's not forget these figures have been achieved in an industry that didn't even exist three years ago. It is of course impossible to say the e-book industry started on any one particular date, but as far as the trade book industry is concerned I tend to place its foundation to the time of the launch of the first Amazon Kindle in December 2007. If you agree with me that this is a reasonable starting point, I think you'll agree that the growth from zero to $550 million in fewer than three years is not inconsiderable. The growth is especially impressive when you appreciate that unit sales of printed books across all sectors in the United States have been flat for many years and that much of the revenue growth enjoyed by publishers in that same period has been achieved by price increases rather than in genuine growth in the number of books sold. (See Tables 1—3)

Table 1   U. S. book industry 2007—2010: dollar and unit sales (all sectors)

All sectors	2007	2008	2009	2010
Dollar (Millions)	39,936	40,321	41,040	42,028
Units (Millions)	3,127	3,079	3,101	3,169

Table 2   U. S. book industry 2007—2010: dollar growth rate (all sectors)

Growth rate (revenue)	Percent
2007—2008	1.0%
2008—2009	1.8%
2009—2010	2.4%
CAGR 2007—2010[3]	1.7%

Table 3   U. S. book industry 2007—2010: unit growth rate (all sectors)

Growth rate (units)	Percent
2007—2008	−1.5%
2008—2009	0.7%
2009—2010	2.2%
CAGR 2007—2010	0.4%

Based on current sales figures for e-books in the trade sector, most industry commentators are comfortable saying that digital sales today represent between 5% and 10% of total sales for the largest trade publishers. Consensus among commentators is more elusive when it comes to projections from this base. The more cautious observers suggest that it will take a further five years for digital sales to reach 25% of trade publishers' total revenue, with less conservative commentators projecting that the number will be 50% in the same time period. The numbers don't matter. What matters, and what everyone can readily agree upon, is that there is an appetite and a steadily maturing market for digital books, evidenced not only by these sales numbers but also by other indicators such as the fact that more than 3 million Kindles have been sold since launch. There is clear consumer enthusiasm for the product, and 2010 has been the breakthrough year, the year in which digital books have gone into the mainstream and ceased to be exclusively for the early adopters or the tech pioneers. Much of the consumer enthusiasm that I'm referring to here has been stimulated by an equal (if not greater) measure of enthusiasm on the part of book publishers and booksellers, enthusiasm matched by considerable investment. When I last looked at Amazon's e-book store, they were offering 420,000 titles for the Kindle in every conceivable genre (plus at least 700,000 public domain titles). For a device launched fewer than three years ago, this is a remarkable gesture of support by publishers in the future of reading on digital devices. Amazon's success has, of course, led to a proliferation of dedicated e-book reading devices. We've seen the Sony E-Reader, the Barnes & Noble Nook, the COOL-ER, the Astak, the EZ Reader, the BeBook and the IRex. And this is just a list of the most well-known brands, a list joined earlier this year by Apple and its iPAD. Just as Amazon's Kindle has spawned many imitators, the Amazon e-book store has attracted a multitude of competitors. Kobo, the service formerly known as Shortcovers and owned principally by the Canadian bookseller, Indigo, claims to have 2 million e-books available on its website. Barnes & Noble speaks of more than a million titles on its site. None of this seems remarkable until we stop to think that none of this existed three years ago. An entirely new business has been born in less than three years, developed by a 500-year-old industry that has traveled a significant distance in a very short time. In the journey, many publishers, large and small, general and specialized, appear to have discovered a willingness to embrace change and new ways of looking at their products, their customers and their markets, and to face up to what they see as the inevitable disruption ahead. Everywhere we look there are signs of innovation, experimentation and success, and everyone ought to find this very encouraging.

While it's easy to see that a sense of optimism, enthusiasm and energy pervades in the U. S. book industry today, it's easy also to detect fear, uncertainty and anxiety. Why?

Some of the anxiety is explicitly commercial. In other words, as the proportion of digital sales increases, will the total business (physical plus digital) decline? Book publishers and retailers are well aware of what happened as the music industry made its transition from one based almost entirely on physical products (vinyl records and CDs) to one based almost entirely on digital products (downloads). The decline in total sales was precipitous. In one year alone (2008 to 2009), unit sales of physical products fell more than 18%. Some of this decline was of course offset by a corresponding increase in unit sales of digital products (9.6%), but the overall dollar effect was a year-to-year revenue decline of 12.3%. [4] In case you're thinking I have deliberately focused on one especially difficult year for the music industry, it's even more instructive to look at sales and licensing revenue in the U. S. music industry over the past decade which fell from

$14. 6 billion in 1999 to $6. 3 billion in 2009. [5] While influences other than changes in consumer behavior are clearly at work here — including recessionary influences and piracy — the most important influence (the significance of which has not been lost on the book industry) is that sales of digital music have not come close to compensating for the very steep decline in CD music sales in the same period. Book industry executives and analysts appreciate of course that the patterns and dynamics of the two industries are very different, but they watch the steep revenue decline in the music industry over 10 years, they watch the almost total disappearance of record stores from the U. S. retail scene in that same period, they watch the impact of piracy on music sales and the proliferation of legitimate free music services, and they are left feeling anxious about how best to manage the transition from physical to digital.

While there is a very legitimate concern among book industry executives about future revenues, and while there have been very well-publicized efforts to reverse what appeared to many to be an unstoppable decline in the price of e-books, most executives do not expect to see in the near future anything like the very dramatic decline in revenues that the music industry has witnessed in the past decade. The real concern is for the longer term, for the next 10 or 20 years, a period in which prosperity (or even survival) will depend on publishers and booksellers being able to demonstrate their continuing relevance and discovering what it is that is unique and distinctive in the services they offer readers and book buyers going forward.

The concerns about continuing relevance are partly stimulated by a growing awareness that the ways in which readers consume content (much of which in the past was delivered in traditional printed books) may change radically if social and technological developments mature as expected. One of the most important of these developments is the accelerating shift to mobile computing platforms. Data traffic on mobile devices (and mobile in this context means not just cell phones but data cards used for Internet connectivity in laptops and other devices) is already growing at an exponential rate. According to Cisco, data traffic has grown globally at a rate of 160% in the past year alone and today it is estimated that 90 petabytes of data are exchanged each month. That's the equivalent of 23 million DVDs full of data being exchanged on mobile devices every month. By 2014 it is estimated, again by Cisco, that 5 billion personal devices will be connected to mobile networks. Gartner, a highly respected analyst of the computer and telecommunications industries, goes further in its predictions, saying that by 2014 there will be 6. 5 billion mobile connections and 90% penetration of the global population. If accurate, these predictions mean that mobile devices will far outpace PCs as the favored means of retrieving and sharing data over the Internet. Many book industry commentators believe that these figures ought to provoke a process of careful reflection in the minds of every CEO of every publishing company in the U. S. , a process that ought to begin now given that we're talking about conditions that are likely to prevail in less than four years time. Today most content emerging from publishing houses is prepared, designed, and optimized for consumption in traditional book form. The fact that an increasing proportion of that content is delivered, purchased and read as e-books doesn't change that fact. E-books today in almost all cases are simple digital facsimiles of traditional books. In a world in which almost the entire global population chooses to connect to a global information network using mobile devices and in which those devices gradually push aside PCs as the means of accessing information consumed for the purposes of education, leisure, news, and professional development, publishers need to give urgent thought to how their content is commissioned, edited, and formatted. This is especially true for publishers with significant markets outside the U. S. where dedicated e-reading devices may be considered too expensive and where it's much more likely that mobile phones will be the reading device of choice. The simple replication of traditional formats for distribution in digital form is not going to be an option. There are welcome signs that some (and especially the largest) publishers are preparing for these conditions and that investments are being made in the necessary systems to support the tagging of content for exploitation in new and different forms. There is also evidence among some publishers of a growing appreciation of the "book as application" prompted by the success of Apple's App Store. However, today that is probably true of relatively few publishers and that many are "betting the farm" that traditional models of editorial and production will persist well into the future. There is some sense in this calculation. After all, almost no commentators speak of the complete disappearance of the printed book over the course of the next 10 years, but it may be critically important for publishers to re-engineer their editorial and production processes to support businesses that are primarily digital and secondarily printed rather than (as now) primarily printed and secondarily digital.

And it's not just traditional means of content preparation and production that will need to be addressed urgently. What commercial partnerships and business models will be appropriate in a setting in which more and more traditional book content is distributed for consumption on mobile devices? Many commentators suggest it is difficult to see a role for traditional book retailers in such a model and possibly even for some of today's leading Internet booksellers such as Amazon, whereas opportunities for partnerships between publishers and companies like Apple and Nokia look promising. And what happens to traditional pricing models in such an environment? Conventional pricing models— $15 for a trade paperback, $25 for a trade hardcover, $100 plus for a college textbook—these models are already under extraordinary pressure. The well-publicized dispute between Macmillan and Amazon earlier this year in which the publisher successfully forced the retailer into an agency model rather than the traditional wholesale model was an effort to reclaim control of retail pricing and to force e-book prices for the Kindle up from what was dangerously becoming a norm of $9.99. This confrontation between publisher and bookseller was more than a simple dispute about who has the power in the supply chain or who owns the consumer. Many saw it as a battle to hold onto a disappearing business model, a struggle to maintain in the digital age a commercial model designed for the pre-digital age. New companies are emerging with radically different pricing and business models. One example is Flatworld Knowledge, whose business model is to give digital textbooks away for free and to build a business model on value-added services. Traditional book pricing models may be under strain and may come under even greater strain in the future as conventional models of delivery and consumption change, but that's not to say that content free at the point of the consumption will become a dominant model.

Free may be an appropriate price point for some types of content, particularly genres that are likely to attract significant sponsorship—travel guides, recipes, and other forms of content with mass consumer appeal. Other forms of content will have no difficulty in the future attracting premium prices, but many publishers are beginning to reflect on what it means for traditional pricing models when content is consumed in snippets or chunks and in a world of continuous connectivity via mobile platforms. Will we see finally the emergence of book rental models similar to what has been tried successfully with movie and TV services? To some extent, it's here already with services such as DeepDyve offering a rental model for access to scholarly articles. It's possible we will see the App Store filled with books priced at free and 99 cents all through the way to high-priced premium content. We may see in the relatively near future consumers demanding educational and professional content delivered to their cellphones or their cable TV via subscription packages for a monthly fee instead of paying what they perceive to be inflated prices for books, only part of which they need or use. Publishers are becoming increasingly aware that consumers, at least those in the U.S., have a proven track record of being willing to pay more and more for access, and less and less for content. Americans' spending on newspapers and magazines has fallen 40% in the past 10 years to $61 per person per year. In the same period, spending on Internet access has quadrupled to $222 per year, phone bills have risen 25% to $1,127 per year and cable TV bills have risen 57% to $401 per year. Americans appear more than willing to pay for access to content, but having access and then being expected to pay for the content itself appears to be a step too far for many.

As publishers anticipate these wider developments—technological, demographic, and commercial—they recognize the need for change in their businesses. They recognize that the traditional processes and systems used to prepare and produce content, the skills of editorial and production staff, and the partnerships that have supported those functions will have to change. They recognize that traditional book pricing models will have to be re-thought. They recognize that the conventional ways in which books have been publicized and marketed will have to be changed in a world in which consumers rely on social media tools such as Twitter and Facebook for information and recommendations. They recognize that traditional bookstores are disappearing fast, that the chain booksellers will inevitably consolidate and shrink, that the independent sector will continue its inexorable process of decline, and that as their traditional retail partners recede it will be necessary to re-invent themselves, moving from the B2B model that has sustained them for well over 100 years to a new B2C model. The awareness among many publishers of the need for change is undeniable, as is their willingness to change and to invest resources in support of that change. But for even the most far-sighted publishers, the ones most willing to change, to re-invent, and to invest, a difficult question arises, a question that has to be answered before any long-term, strategic change can be contemplated: what will it mean to be a book publisher in the future? What are the attributes, skills, and functions that will distinguish a book publisher in the future and that will protect them from the scale of disruption that has threatened so many industries—from newspapers to music, from stock broking to insurance. What will define a book publisher?

Where is the permanence in all this turbulence?

It takes no imagination to recognize that the publisher's traditional production functions— printing, packaging, and binding — will largely disappear in the transition to a more digital industry, but the delegation of most of those functions to specialist companies was already complete before the onset of e-books. What functions does that leave? Commissioning content, editing, marketing (in the widest sense), and selling.

The commissioning of content, the process of identifying and nurturing authorial talent, and the application of skills and experience to the editing of a manuscript— processes that collectively can be summarized as curation — is the place which many book publishers identify as being the enduring and permanent "value add" that they offer.

Some have suggested that the principle of curation will save publishing— the idea that publishers act as arbiters of quality, authoritative gatekeepers carefully distinguishing the diamond hidden in the carbon, and that book buyers value that function. There is a lot of value in the idea of curation, but if publishers, and especially trade publishers, hope to avoid the worst effects of Internet-inspired disruption by claiming unique powers of curation they may be mistaken. Why? For many, the Internet has disrupted the whole principle of curation itself. Whatever your particular interest might be — science fiction, carpentry, stamp collecting — you can be sure somewhere on the Internet there is a thriving community of experts who share your passion. Each of these communities has its own thought-leaders, its own tastemakers, its own curators, who help define for the community what is interesting, what is authoritative, what is topical, what is fashionable. Publishers may in the future perform a curator-type role in these Internet communities. In fact, many commentators have argued strongly that general trade publishers have no future unless they re-invent themselves as leaders of, or at least as service providers to, Internet communities built around specific subjects and disciplines, much as O'Reilly Media has tried to do in computer science or Harlequin has in romance fiction. This is all perfectly possible, but it's difficult and it cannot be achieved simply by pointing to the past and to a role conferred on it when everything about the business of publishing was different. Whatever curatorial role publishers feel they had in the past has to be earned anew in an entirely different setting. Few will doubt that it can be earned or that it will be easier to earn in some parts of the publishing industry than in others. If you look along the list of the top 10 publishers globally, what is so striking is how successful many of them have been in re-inventing themselves as digital destinations for authoritative content in the professional, academic and educational space. Companies like Pearson Education, Thomson Reuters, and Reed Elsevier have all been remarkably successful in re-inventing themselves in the digital age while maintaining their brands as arbiters of excellence. All of these companies were once titans of traditional book and journal publishing and all of them appear to be prospering producing content today that you won't find in any conventional bookstore. How have they achieved this? It certainly helps to have such high brand recognition among corporate and library subscribers from which continuing revenue streams are more assured than they are from the fickle individual book buyer. But we ought not to lose sight of the foresight of these companies several years ago to see the direction in which their consumers and technology were heading, the willingness to invest heavily in the infrastructure necessary to achieve the change in strategic direction, and their relentless innovation with new business and delivery models. These are qualities I suggest trade publishers would do well to analyze if they can be emulated in their own sectors.

One further challenge associated with relying on curation as the publisher's distinctive attribute is the fact that many of the most successful authors don't require a publisher to perform the curation function for them. The commercial success that such authors enjoy, the level of "brand awareness" they have among their readers, and the marketing and promotional tools to which they now have direct access via the Internet, have led some of them to question not only the publisher's curatorial function, but all the other functions as well. In a recent high-profile example, the business author Seth Godin announced that he would not use a conventional publisher for his future books. While relatively few authors have the fame, recognition, and success that make such a move possible, many publishers will be concerned that some of their most profitable and well-known authors will have access to the tools that prompted Godin's move and more importantly already have the leadership status in their respective communities to make such a move possible and viable.

It is in the areas of marketing and selling that publishers arguably face the biggest transitional challenge. With the exception of library sales, publishers have traditionally sold to intermediaries — notably booksellers and wholesalers — and direct commercial contact with readers has been minimal. As the number of physical bookstores in the U. S. declines, whether through consolidation of the major chains or the disappearance of independents, publishers are finding themselves in the uncomfortable situation of becoming increasingly dependent on a very small number of powerful customers. This poses a threat which, combined with the opportunities that technology affords to reach consumers directly via the Internet, has led many major publishers to identify the transition from B2B to B2C as being the most significant challenge facing them in the immediate future. The CEO of Random House, the U. S.'s largest publisher, made this point very clearly in an interview only last month. [6] The difficulties of making this change can hardly be overstated. How many U. S. publishers have imprints that are in any way consumer brands? How many publishers have the contact details of their customers? The difficulties involved have so far not inhibited trade publishers from developing online bookstores on their website or from direct marketing using many of the social media tools used as a matter of course in other industries. These are relatively easy steps to take, but the task of moving a business from one whose success has depended on a few hundred retailer relationships to one whose survival depends on perhaps millions of reader relationships is a formidable one, and large trade publishers are no doubt grateful that they probably still have a few years in which they can continue to rely on retailers as their primary means of reaching readers. And with publishers selling books directly, with booksellers like Amazon and Barnes & Noble establishing their own publishing operations, and with many best-selling authors now choosing to self-publish and sell their own books, the blurring of roles in the book industry looks set to continue.

While it is right to emphasize the difficulties publishers will face as they look to identify what distinctive functions they will perform in the future and as they work to move towards being more reader-centered, it ought also to be emphasized that in sectors such as science, technology and medicine publishers have made important advances in these directions and look to be managing the transition with some success. For general trade publishers, the transition may be much more difficult, leading some to predict that they will become an even more endangered species than they are today and that we will see considerable consolidation among the major trade houses in the intervening period. Success for former general trade publishers will depend on how smoothly they re-invent themselves as community leading content providers in specialized, vertically organized niches. Publishers overall will have moved from a book-centered outlook and digital will be the primary format, with printed books being a secondary format except for particular distinctive subjects and niches.

As they plot their course and try to navigate their companies in the years ahead, book publishers will be watching very closely the reading behaviors of a generation of consumers very different from the one that preceded it. A generation continuously online; a generation whose members are routinely connected to one another via communities of interest; a generation with few and rapidly shifting brand loyalties; a generation with different attitudes to the authority and credibility of content; a generation prepared to pay, but increasingly familiar with free; a generation highly sophisticated in its ability to source the content it wants and demanding about how and when that content should be presented; a generation used to mixing text, audio and video; a generation used to mixing content from multiple sources — from friends, community members and strangers; from old and new authorities; from formal and informal sources.

It is in relation to these new consumers— and their different behaviors and expectations — that publishers will have to re-define their role and value. The scale of the challenge is immense, but publishers have time in which to confront it and exemplars of success elsewhere to guide them.

For booksellers in the United States, the challenges are more immediate and the overall situation more dangerous. Today, the U. S. book market has two large retail book chains and the future of one of these (Borders) appears to be in jeopardy. The independent bookstores look likely to continue their steady decline as they find it increasingly difficult to compete with the range and the discounts offered by Amazon and the discounts offered by supermarkets. Amazon's dominance in the online sale of physical books looks set to continue. As sales of e-books grow, the leading booksellers like Barnes & Noble and Amazon (and Indigo in Canada) have invested heavily to establish themselves as destinations for e-book buyers. Not only have they created online bookstores containing hundreds of thousands of e-book titles, but they have also launched proprietary e-reading devices such as the Kindle and Nook, and are reporting considerable success in selling the devices. It remains to be seen whether these single-purpose reading devices will endure as more affordable, multi-purpose, and constantly connected devices (the iPad and its successors) reach the marketplace. What is already clear is that the arrival of Apple and Google (with its long awaited Editions service) is likely to transform the competitive landscape of bookselling, not just in the U. S. but elsewhere. This transformation will be realized by booksellers equipped to provide digital book content immediately and flexibly, in ways consumers can use without restrictions — any content, any time, on any device and in any format.

An industry that has evolved relatively gently over 500 years is entering a phase of its development that will be anything but gentle. The signs of turbulence are already visible to everyone, though how turbulent the conditions will be is still unclear. There will be casualties, as there always are when change of this magnitude happens. But there will be vibrancy, experimentation and innovation at every turn, and throughout the process there will be readers looking (as they always have) for content that informs, educates, delights and stimulates them — and creative entrepreneurs finding new ways to ensure they get it. It's already an extraordinary time for our industry and it will only get more extraordinary as time goes on. Thank you.

Notes

[1] Source: the International Digital Publishing Forum

[2] Source: the Book Industry Study Group

[3] CAGR means Compound Annual Growth Rate — the year-on-year growth rate over a specified time

[4] Source: RIAA 2009 Year-End Shipment Statistics

[5] Source: Forrester Research Forecast/RIAA: http://money. cnn. com/2010/02/02/news/ companies/n apstersic_industry/

[6] http://www. idealog. com/blog/

Author

Michael Healy, the former executive director of Book Industry Study Group, the chairman of international committee who revise international standard book number, the first executive director of Google Book Rights Registry.

作者简介

迈克尔·希利，美国（谷歌）图书版权登记处（BBR）执行主任，国际标准书号管理局主席，国际数字对象标识（DOI）基金会主任，前美国书业研究会执行主任。

E-Books and E-Readers on the German Book Market: Current State and Future Developments

Ursula Rautenberg

(Erlangen-Nürnberg University, Erlangen)

外国专家

Abstract: The lecture overviews the current state of the e-book market in Germany, especially the spread of e-reading devices in Germany and the market volume of e-books. It points out the most important market drivers and market barriers, and concludes with a forcast for 2015.

Keywords: E-book E-reader Electronic publishing Multi-channeling bookstore

德国图书市场上的电子书及电子书阅读器
——现状及未来发展

乌苏拉·劳滕堡

(德国埃朗根—纽伦堡大学 埃朗根)

摘要：本文概述了德国电子图书市场的现状，重点论述了德国电子阅读设备的传播和电子图书的市场容量。文章指出了电子图书和电子阅览器市场的最重要驱动力和市场壁垒，最后本文对 2015 年的电子图书和阅览器的市场状况进行了预测。

关键词：电子图书 电子阅读器 电子出版 多渠道书店

Dear colleagues, dear students,

First of all I would like to thank Dean Chen and my dear colleague, Chair Huang Xianrong, most cordially for the kind invitation to Wuhan and to this conference. As previously at the conferences in 2006 and 2008, I would like to talk about a current trend in the German book market. The topic is:

E-Books and E-Readers on the German Book Market: Current State and Future Developments.

1 Online behaviour of the Germans

Approximately 50 million Germans — this is about 66% of the population — of all ages and social classes have Internet access. About 20. 1 million people of these — this is 58. 5% — are interested in books according to a new study on the online behaviour. [1] Here we find a significant potential for the online distribution of printed books and e-books as well as audio books. In online retail trade, (printed) books are even one of the most popular products: in 2009, 14. 9 million people bought books online. [2]

2   Trade with e-books and e-readers

However, a special challenge for publishers, intermediaries and general book retailers is the distribution of electronic books. Databases as well as e-books and retrodigitalizations of reference and science books have been an established and profitable area for several years now, but e-books aiming at a broad public is a new phenomenon on the German market. It became evident at a stroke in 2009 that e-books will also take hold in fiction and non-fiction. By e-books I mean the digital version of a book which is distributed through electronic sales channels. It is meant to be used with mobile devices like laptops, smartphones, tablets and special e-readers, but can also be saved and read on a PC.

The e-book is ready to break out of its niche at the time when special terminals (e-readers) for reading electronic books (e-books) are introduced. These e-readers were brought onto the market first in the USA and a short time later also in Europe and Germany. Sony introduced its e-reader in spring 2009. At this time these special readers were noticed by public and press for the first time. In October 2009 the Kindle was released which offers E-ink technology, integrated wireless access and a shop system. Since then, at short intervals new models by a growing number of new suppliers have entered the market. These new e-readers provide different equipment features as well as a wide range of functions, usability and display technology; prices differ from low up to a high triple-digit range. A further highlight was the market launch of the iPad by Apple in May 2010 which was hyped by press and marketing. In September, the IFA — the consumer electronics show — in Berlin brought many new e-readers and tablets. The Frankfurt Book Fair in October 2010 has also confirmed the beginning market penetration of the e-book. But only the sales figures will show whether e-readers and tablets will become such strong market drivers in Germany as they are expected to be.

Certainly remarkable is the fact that a leading German bookshop chain — Thalia — has introduced its own e-reader on the IFA in Berlin: the Oyo. The distribution of e-books by the Oyo is part of a new strategy: the multi-channeling bookshop. This is an attempt to face the risk that the stationary book trade could fall out of the distribution chain of e-books and e-content. The first branches to carry out this multi-channeling concept have already been opened:

— Anchoring multimedia elements in store design to present Internet content from www. thalia. de via special terminals for customers;

— Selling e-reader Oyo and e-books at point of sale;

— Diversification with computer games in a separate games-shop.

Following this short introduction I would like to present some data and forecasts to you. I refer mainly to a new study "E-Books in Germany" which was published on behalf of PricewaterhouseCoopers in September 2010[3] and besides this to relevant trade data.

3 Market volume

Unlike in the USA there are no concrete sales figures for e-books in Germany at the moment. The German Booksellers Association speaks about an estimated turnover of about 0.4% (40 million Euros) for electronic books related to total turnover in book trade. This is calculated using the number of e-books sold from 2009 until spring 2010 and an average download of eight e-books per reader. [4] In 2010 we could probably find a turnover of 50 million Euros and 0.5%.

A dynamic development similar to that in the USA can not be observed in Germany and most of the European neighbouring countries. For comparison: in the USA the turnover with e-books was $313 million in 2009 — that is an increase of 177 percent compared to 2008. The major publishers of popular books have estimated their share of turnover with e-books at. 3% to 4% and expect a duplication in 2010. [5] The latest figures show that the rapid development continues: in July 2010 the turnover of e-books in the USA was $40.8 million which means an increase of 150.2 percent from the previous year, June 2009.

In general there are the following reasons for the much slower development in Germany: according to new customer surveys the German readers still attach great importance to the sensual experience of reading and the haptics and optics of the printed book. Digital reading is widely accepted for obtaining information as well as in education and training: 60% of specialist information already is called for digitally. [6] However, reading for entertainment is still restricted to the printed book. Another reason for the restraint of the consumers is related to the different structure of the book trade in the USA and Germany. Here we find a dense network of more than 4,000 stationary book shops not only in major cities but also in small and medium-sized towns. These shops invite the public to come in and browse, and every book which is not in stock can be ordered within 12 hours from one of the book wholesalers. The German readers and buyers of books are used to a great shopping convenience. Therefore the e-book does not need to fill in gaps in supply with books.

What are the most important opportunities and risks in the e-book market? In the study by PricewaterhouseCoopers I mentioned before, 40 interviews with experts were evaluated. The following notes are based on the analysis of these interviews.

4 Market drivers: which developments promote the mass market?

(1) Attractive and affordable terminals (e-readers and tablets) with improved screen technology and integrated shopping function

There is now a great range of e-readers and tablets available on the German market which is, however, confusing for most consumers (huge price differences, a significant number of suppliers, different equipment and performance ranges). As in the Netherlands and Great Britain only a few devices were sold compared to in the USA: 50,000 to 80,000 readers.

(2) A wide range of new popular titles and bestsellers published as e-books in 2009 most bestsellers in German are available as e-books for the first time.

There is an urgent need for action to improve the selection on offer. Today a strong impetus comes from the major publisher groups of popular books like Random House in Munich. *Libreka* ! — a platform established by the German Booksellers Association which includes small and medium-sized companies and publishers as well as book stores in the chain of distribution — has not been successful so far. Platforms held by intermediaries from outside the book sector (Ciando for example) have been successful for some time in the area of reference and science books.

(3) Additional content and fast updating especially in the sector of reference books

The electronic reference book could be enhanced by additional content; the benefits of updating is obvious here. Experts think there is no need in the sector of books read for pleasure.

5   Market barriers: why are fiction e-books still only a small market niche?

(1) Readers are too expensive. Prices have been falling since July 2009 but are still in the region between 100 and 300 Euros. Prices must be lower than 50 Euros if the readers want to be successful with a broad audience. Thalia has been selling the Oyo since October for a price of 139 Euros.

(2) The number of different formats is too high, although EPUB as an open standard and PDF for reference books seem to have caught on.

(3) Rigorous digital rights management: it is too complicated to register on some platforms for buying e-books. Further negative restrictions are: the indirect route of the e-book which has to be downloaded on PC first as well as the restricted possibility to give it to your friends.

(4) The readers are too technically complex; they should be easier and more intuitive to handle also for the less technically-able users.

(5) The prices for e-books are too high. Respectively the consumers think the prices are too high compared to the print products. The major publisher groups in fiction market (Holtzbrinck, Random House in the paperback sector) offer their e-books for the price of the cheapest print edition.

(6) We find different VAT rates: there is a reduced VAT rate of 7% for printed books but the full VAT rate of 19% for electronic books. The e-books by de Gruyter, an important scientific publisher, are offered on the platform Reference Global even for a higher price compared to the printed edition because of the higher VAT rate.

6   Forecasts for 2015

Experts believe that e-books will be accepted as an additional format beside hard covers and paperbacks in Germany, but its market share will increase slower compared to the internation rate:

(1) Digital books will have a 6.3% share of turnover in the fiction sector; from 2010 to 2015 this is a cumulated increase of 77%, though coming from a very low starting point.

(2) 2.4 million Germans will own an e-reader in 2015 and buy eight e-books on the average.

（3）12 million will own a tablet but the reading of e-books on these devices will remain a niche application.

You see: The e-Book market in Germany is starting to gain momentum but forecasts are still restrained.

Hartmut Ostrowski— chairman of Bertelsmann AG and one of the most powerful media manager in Europe — said in an interview in September 2010:

"Printed books will still be there in 50 years."

Thank you for your kind attention.

Notes

[1] Börsenblatt. Wochenmagazin für den Deutschen Buchhandel [Weekly magazine of the book trade in Germany]. 177 (2010), issue 35, 2.9., p. 18.

[2] Buch und Buchhandel in Zahlen [Books and book trade in numbers]. Published by the German Booksellers Association e. V. Frankfurt am Main 2010, p. 8.

[3] Müller, Christina/Spiegel, Stefan/Ullrich, Franka: E-Books in Deutschland. Der Beginn einer neuen Gutenberg-Ära? Published by PricewaterhouseCoopers in September 2010.

[4] Roesler-Graichen, Michael: Hochrechnungen ohne Sicherheitsleine. In: Börsenblatt. Wochenmagazin für den Deutschen Buchhandel [Weekly magazine of the book trade in Germany]. 177 (2010), issue 35, 2.9., p. 35.

[5] Sambeth, Frank: E-Book-Markt USA — Aktuelle Entwicklungen und Ausblick. Vortrag Publisher's Forum Berlin, 27. 4. 2010; based on data of the American Association of Publishers (AAP).

[6] E-Books in Deutschland, p. 32.

Author

Ursula Rautenberg, professor of Erlangen-Nürnberg University (Germany), ursula.rautenberg@ buchwiss. uni-erlangen. de.

作者简介

乌苏拉·劳滕堡，德国埃朗根—纽伦堡大学图书研究中心主任，教授，ursula. rautenberg@ buchwiss. uni-erlangen. de。

E-Books: Discovery vs Invention

Adriaan H. van der Weel

(Leiden University, the Netherlands)

Abstract: There are other important aspects to e-books than the technological and socio-economic ones that are most frequently discussed as we watch how readers adopt or reject them. Like all technology, e-books (and e-book uptake and resistance to e-books) need to be studied as a socio-technical phenomenon. That is to say, e-books do not just represent a technological invention, but also a process of social discovery. Likewise, the stakeholders are not just the manufacturers of the hardware and software, various parties in the book trade and authors, but they include also government and, perhaps most badly neglected, the users.

Keywords: Discovery Invention E-book Social acceptance

电子书：发现与发明

A. H. 范德韦尔

（莱顿大学　荷兰）

摘要：对于电子图书而言，当我们观察读者如何接受或摒弃它们时，除了最经常讨论的技术和社会经济因素外，还有更为重要的其他因素。像所有的技术一样，电子图书（以及对电子书的采纳和拒绝）需要被作为一项社会技术现象来研究。也就是说，电子图书不仅仅代表了一种技术创新，也是一种社会发现过程。同样，利益相关者不仅仅是软硬件生产商、图书贸易中的各参与方及作者，还包括政府以及最常被忽略的用户。

关键词：发现　发明　电子书　社会接受

The phonograph was invented by Thomas Alva Edison as a device for recording and replaying speech. However, as a dictaphone this recording technology was destined for a future that was decidedly marginal compared to the runaway success of music recordings. Invention may present an answer to a problem, question or demand or simply to curiosity. However, the inventor can never predict the way the invention will be used. Inventions are frequently used for a different purpose than the inventor had in mind. Invention is a technological act, but the invention's actual uses and usefulness usually remain to be discovered. All technology can therefore be called a social construction.

Invention is a deliberate process of technological design by an inventor. Discovery on the other hand is a gradual, unintentional and social process. Because the development of technologies occurs in an interplay between technological invention and social discovery, the study of the social acceptance of technology requires a socio-technical approach. This certainly also applies in the case of e-books. E-book acceptance is slow, and has been slow for a long time. In a very rough estimate, e-book acceptance statistics are currently as follows:

Country	proportion of book sales (%)
U. S.	5
China	2
Netherlands	1. 5

A comparison with two modalities other than text—music and video/film—makes these figures especially pregnant. Music has been available for public consumption in a digital form (from CDs via downloads to streaming) since the 1980s. Worldwide music is now consumed almost exclusively in a digital form. Similarly, moving images (film/video) have been available in a digital form (from DVDs via downloads to streaming) since the 1990s. Again, like music, film and video are consumed everywhere virtually exclusively in digital forms. However, though text was first digitised as early as the 1940s, after more than sixty years books, newspapers and magazines are still mostly consumed in analogue forms.

In his book *Books in the Digital Age* John Thompson identifies the following factors in e-book resistance (Thompson, 2005):

(1) Hardware is "expensive and awkward to use".

(2) There are too many formats to choose between, and they are incompatible.

(3) The ownership of digital rights is not clear.

(4) Publishers and retailers set prices too close to those of print books, higher than the "perceived value" of e-books.

Taking our cue from this list two chief advances since 2005 may be identified. Firstly there has been the widespread adoption of E-ink technology, which uses a reflective reading surface (for example, Amazon's Kindle in the U. S. , the iLiad by iRex Technologies in the Netherlands and the Han Wang reader in China). This has actually improved acceptance somewhat, but mainly among dedicated older readers. Secondly, there has been the introduction of the iPad in 2010. However, the iPad is not properly speaking an e-book reading device. Not only does it have a backlit screen, which is by many people regarded as more tiring on the eyes than a reflective screen, it comes out of the box without reading software.

Not surprisingly the effects of these two technological advances have been modest. The rate of uptake is rising, but only marginally. According to John Thompson the factors in e-book resistance remain the same as in 2005 (Thompson, *Merchants of Culture*, 2010). Analysis of these factors shows firstly that all are either technological (1 and 2) or socio-economic (3 and 4) by nature. Secondly they concern the interests of a limited number of stakeholders only: hardware and software manufacturers (1 and 2) , the book trade (3 and 4) , and , marginally , authors (3) .

If e-book acceptance is to be improved , it will be necessary first of all to identify *all* stakeholders. Besides hardware and software manufacturers , the book trade and authors , these also include government and users. Secondly it will be necessary to identify their interests. This results in the following list of stakeholder—interest combinations :

(1) *The hardware/software manufacturing industry* has an interest in maximising profit , which may be translated into an interest in speeding up user uptake through technological improvements of hardware , functionality , ergonomics , as well as marketing ;

(2) *The book trade* (in terms of the *process* and infrastructure as well as the resulting *product*) has an interest in economic solutions (suitable business models , value chains and pricing) and copyright (and DRM to protect its interests) ;

(3) *Authors* have economic as well as cultural interests ;

(4) *The government* (in terms of policies) has an interest in regulation of the media , especially in terms of international competitiveness , cultural diversity and access-concerns in which the promotion of reading and literacy feature prominently ;

(5) And finally *the users* (in their guise as readers and/or buyers) have a wide range of interests. They will want to use e-books for the dissemination of culture and knowledge , for relaxation , for teaching , and so on. Most importantly , they will demand that e-books have minimally the same functionality in this regard as printed books. Ultimately they hold the key to the acceptation of new technology.

Secondly , it is necessary to extend the areas of research from the heavy emphasis on the technological and socio-economic aspects of e-book resistance (represented by device hardware and software manufacturers and the book trade) to include the larger social , and more particularly the socio-cultural perspective represented by the user.

Taking into account the user perspective is not straightforward. As a socio-cultural perspective it is a great deal more difficult to identify and represent than the goal-oriented technological and socio-economic perspectives of hardware and software manufacturers and the book trade. This is precisely because the users represent a process of discovery , which is , as we have seen , a gradual , unintentional and social process. Discovery , in other words , cannot be programmed ; it simply takes time. Problems include the fact that users have no agenda of their own , and that they are not necessarily even aware of the (potential) issues that might affect them. It is , for example , notoriously difficult to canvass users about functionalities that have not yet been designed or at least described. In that sense user surveys are more suitable for soliciting evaluations of existing technological solutions ; they tend to fall short of unearthing the potential uses that , as it were , lie waiting to be discovered in the technology.

This difficulty is further complicated by the fact that user's attitudes to e-books are affected by cultural values that remain largely implicit. In Bourdieu's terms , books represent symbolic as well as economic social capital. In its nature this symbolic capital is extremely hard to calculate and make operational in any models. Moreover, it is likely that most users, if they are aware of the existence of any such symbolic value at all, would have difficulty in voicing their appraisal of it.

Having recognised these complications and challenges, however, a historical perspective can be helpful in solving them. A historical perspective allows recognising and describing socio-cultural aspects of earlier developments. Equally, this will help to recognise much of the symbolic value attached to (paper) books and reading. The symbolic capital represented by books can be of enormous value: books are frequently regarded as part of people's identity. People want to be seen to be reading (or thought to be reading, for example by buying) particular books. So far the visibility of books has of course always depended on their physicality, which has given them a presence. The fact that this visibility is very much diminished in the case of e-books may well be a significant factor hampering e-book uptake.

It is understandable for that reason that people are loth to give up the presence of physical books in their lives. The history of the book as a text technology is long and deeply embedded in our culture. What books have come to represent cannot easily be replaced. It would therefore seem urgent to find a way to attach symbolic meaning to books and reading in the digital realm in the same way as we have been doing in the analogue world for so many centuries.

Web resources

http://www.idpf.org/doc_library/industrystats.html

For further reading

A longer version of this paper appears in *Logos*: *Journal of the World Book Community* 21: 3-4 (2010).

Author

Adriaan H. van der Weel, Professor of Book and Digital Media Studies at Leiden University, Netherlands

作者简介

A. H. 范德韦尔，荷兰莱顿大学图书与数字媒体研究系教授。

Discovering Digital Communities:
Connecting with Book Buyers in Their Natural Habitat

Susan Danziger

(Pace University, New York)

Abstract: Digital communities are beginning to transform the way that books are discovered and sold. By understanding the different types of communities, how to build successful communities, and the behaviors of individuals within particular communities, publishers (and authors) have an opportunity to build successful new business models not based on traditional and threatened retail relationships.

Keywords: Digital community Social media Book publishing Digital publishing Book selling

发现数字社区：在图书消费者的聚集地寻找商机

苏珊·丹齐格

（佩斯大学 纽约）

摘要：数字社区正在改变发现和购买图书的方式。通过了解社区的类型、如何建立成功的社区以及特定社区内的个体行为，出版商（和作者）将有机会不依赖传统的、面临威胁的图书零售关系建立新的成功的商业模式。

关键词：数字社区　大众传媒　图书出版　数字出版　图书销售

I would like to first thank the University of Wuhan, Prof. Sherman Raskin and all of you here for allowing me to come and share my thoughts and visions for the future with you today. If I were speaking to a group of students, academics or book professionals in the United States, I would ask them whether they are tweeting[1] about my talk, if they've checked into Foursquare[2] and if they plan to blog about this event when they get home tonight. If not, I would let them know in no uncertain terms that they are missing a huge opportunity to become a leader in their chosen community, to connect with their particular audience and to become a trusted authority. In fact, the future of publishing lies in leading communities, understanding and connecting with readers, and creating trusted and engaging environments in which large numbers of books can be sold.

1　What are communities?

Traditionally, communities have been known to be groups of interacting people living in a common location. Since the advent of the Internet, the concept of community of course no longer has geographical limitations since people can virtually gather regardless of physical location. Online communities come in many different forms: they can gather around a particular common interest (e. g. poetry), connect by virtue of being a particular gender or age (e. g. teen girls), be in a particular location (e. g. Wuhan University), share a particular trait (e. g. mothers), or merely share a general interest in connecting with one another (e. g. Facebook). They can have leaders or be leaderless, meet offline or only online, and gather (whether online or off) every day or at only one moment in time for a specific purpose.

There are several distinct types of communities in which potential book buyers can gather. The first is a "community of readers"; that is, a community of individuals who like to read particular types of books such as science fiction or romance. A second type of community is a "community of interest". These communities consist of people of like interests (such as pregnant women or those who eat Thai food) who because of their interest may happen to buy books in large numbers. And then there are communities that have publishing value. These communities are so distinct that they lend themselves to being wonderful book subjects. For instance, The Happiness Project, a community that focuses on what makes people happy, translated to a New York Times No. 1 bestselling book. And similarly, "Sh * t My Dad Says" records what a 74-year-old father says; the associated Twitter stream now has almost 2 million followers and the related book has become a No. 1 New York Times bestseller which was recently made into a television series.

2　Communities in historical context

Communities led by publishers are a relatively recent phenomenon. Previously, in the late 20th/early 21st century, trade publishing was generally organized "horizontally"; in other words it was organized in a way that made it easier and more efficient to publish in lots of different subject areas. Large general trade publishers such as Random House, HarperCollins and Simon & Schuster would typically publish books in thousands of different subject areas that would appeal to completely different audiences. Although these publishers were organized by imprints, few such imprints focused on individual subjects that appealed to the same readers; the same imprint could publish literary fiction, science fiction, and "chick lit", each of which tends to appeal to a different readership or community. At the time, publishers' biggest customers were large bookstores such as Barnes & Noble, mass market stores such as Wal-Mart and wholesalers such as Ingram. As such, it was best to publish books that appealed to a wide range of audience that in turn would appeal to the different outlets. In fact, it was often detrimental for publishers to publish works in the same subject area since retailers or wholesalers would take only a limited number of books on the same subject.

Publishers are now beginning to understand the value of focusing on individual subjects and creating vertical imprints created around specific areas of interest (e. g. science fiction, pregnancy and happiness). In this context, communities of readers, communities of interest and even communities of publishing value[3] can be established (or existing ones exploited) which allow like-minded people to connect and discuss issues common to their communities.

Under the old model[4], there was little direct communication between publishers and their readers. In fact, when I worked at Random House in the 1990s, there was widespread concern that retailers (which were the primary channel for selling Random House's books) would be upset and threatened by any move made by Random House to interact and engage directly with readers. As a result, Random House, wary of alienating their key retailers, deliberately refrained from any such direct communication with readers.

Publishers are now beginning to understand the importance of building direct and sustained connections with readers. That is why Marcus Dohle, the CEO of Random House (the world's leading trade publisher) has recently remarked, "We have to change from being a B2B company to B2C over the coming years. "[5] By this, he meant that he intended to transition his publishing company to being one whose primary relationships would be with consumers or readers rather than with other businesses such as retailers. Dohle then qualified his statement by remarking that he was "convinced that publishers have to become more reader-oriented in a marketing and trend finding/setting way rather than in a direct to consumer selling way. " Although Dohle is correct that publishers need to learn to market directly to readers, I believe that publishers need to learn to sell directly to readers as well regardless of the short term risks that this move poses for their relationship with retailers; this is particularly true since book retailers and traditional book selling outlets are shrinking.

3   Importance of communities versus audience

A particularly interesting question is whether there is a difference between communities and audience. Communities consist of actively engaged individuals whereas audiences are generally passive. Since a publisher's ultimate goal is to grow audience that can buy its books (whether directly from publishers or via retailers), publishers can create and use communities as a tool for engagement that increases the size of its audience. That is, by creating a community, publishers are engaging potential customers who can then be made aware of publishers' books. What's particularly interesting about communities is that a relatively small number of engaged users in a community can create content, "user-generated content", that doesn't need to be created by the publisher. And since one of the major challenges for communities is to keep content fresh and vital — key for "spectators" which far outnumber "creators" in a community (as discussed later[6]) — such user-generated content helps maintain interest in the community and grow the overall audience.

4   Building successful communities—but by whom?

Who is in the best position to create such vertical communities? On the surface it may appear that publishers are in a unique position to create these communities; they have a large backlist that can be tapped to enrich a site with content, they specialize in editing (and often creating) first-rate content — at least for books — which could translate to the creation of a premiere site, and they have in-house teams of professionals that can devote time to establishing an engaging community. However, others would argue that building communities require different skills that publishers need to learn and that authors may be in a stronger position to create engaging communities. Authors can create premiere content that is naturally focused, have a driving personality that can generate interest; and depending on their own schedules, may have more time to devote to nurturing their communities. I would argue that since few people have experience in developing online communities and given that this is a new space for everyone with new community tools being developed on a daily basis, almost anyone with passion and dedication can build and lead a strong community.

5 Benefits of communities

By creating and serving communities of readers, publishers have been able to reduce costs and at times increase sales of books as well. For instance, in the late 20th/early 21st century, each time a new book was published, a new audience for that book needed to be established by the publisher. As such, marketing budgets, especially for lead titles, were often exorbitant. In order to reach a particular book's intended audience, publishers needed to spend money on expensive advertising in newspapers and magazines and participate in expensive co-op programs to obtain shelf space at retailers.

Publishers can capitalize on the same audience from book to book by creating and nurturing new online communities. Publishers no longer need to rely on expensive advertising or co-op programs with booksellers but rather can market directly to their own lists of readers. In fact, by building their own audiences, publishers can ultimately cut out wholesalers or retailers completely (or, the very least, use them less and less). As such, rather than paying e. g. 40% to retailers to act as middlemen, publishers no longer need to pay this fee and thus can keep more of the revenue from the sale of a book. And since the number of book retailers is shrinking, publishers in any case need to find other outlets for the sale of its books. In other words, by building and investing in communities, the publisher can take responsibility for its audience, an audience it once allowed retailers to control exclusively, and thereby in many cases keep more of the revenue.

One prime example is a particular self-help author who published his first book with Random House and sold only a few thousand copies. The author then moved to Hay House Publishers, which specializes in self-help books and developed an in-house email list of hundreds of thousands of readers of self-help books. Marketed to Hay House's existing community of self-help enthusiasts, the author's second book sold several hundred thousand copies. [7] This illustrates well the significant sales advantage available to publishers who have invested in cultivating direct relationships with members of the community that publishers are trying to lead.

Communities also provide publishers with direct feedback about their books. Previously, the only feedback publishers received from readers was via sales reports from big retailers such as Barnes & Noble or from such independent sources as Nielsen BookScan. Such reports only told publishers how many copies of books were sold; a publisher had little other information on why a book might or might not have sold a certain number of copies or which features a reader liked or disliked. With online communities, publishers have a huge opportunity to obtain feedback from readers on publishing decisions, including which kinds of books to publish, thoughts on particular chapters or manuscripts, and even preferred cover designs.

6 Examples of book-related communities

U. S. 's leading trade publishers have clearly got these messages and have begun to create communities in a number of interesting ways. Harlequin, the leading romance publisher, has established a bustling eHarlequin community of 300,000 members by rewarding loyalty and encouraging participation in its community. Early releases of books as well as large discounts on books are available to community members. eHarlequin also encourages engagement by tapping members of its community to write Harlequin books and even features a forum for potential writers on its site. One particularly creative initiative involved hosting a Secret Santa[8] in which the publishers organized an exchange of Christmas ornaments by its readers. [9] By setting up a system for readers to send Christmas ornaments to each other in the mail, the publisher is encouraging engagement, connecting readers with one another, and offering cost-free, tangible rewards to participants.

Another example of an active community created by a publisher is Tor. com, which was created by the science fiction imprint of Macmillan (one of theU. S. 's large trade publishers). This science fiction community hosts conversations posted by its readers, releases chapters on its site prior to book publication, offers free books for members who leave comments to blog posts, and offers podcasts, which include the audio of stories as well as recent topics from Tor's blog.

Other publishers have gone a step further. Rather than taking a book-centered approach, these publishers have created a community around a particular subject matter, with the sale of books seemingly secondary to the community. For instance, Chelsea Green created a community[10] for "the politics and practice of sustainable living". Articles and information about the subject matter are prominent while the sale of books is certainly not obvious. In fact, on the front page of chelseagreen. com, there is only a small indication via an "Our Books" tab that the website was created by a publisher or that books are sold on the site. And certain articles make no mention and include no link to buy a related book. By not appearing too commercial, the publisher is hoping that environmental enthusiasts, the core audience for its books, will become engaged with its community. That is, publishers believe that by not creating such an explicitly commercial site, the audience will believe the community to be more authentic and as such participate more, which in turn may result in higher book sales.

Lark Crafts is doing the same with jewelry, that is, they use their books as a springboard for developing their craft community[11]. Larkcrafts. com features blogs about topics related to their books (e. g. a blog post about jewelry pop-up shops in Japan) mingled with book-giveaways and information from their backlist and frontlist titles.

Although such community stimulus initiatives have been interesting, there are other, even more creative ways that publishers can engage their communities and creatively reward participation. For instance, book projects on Kickstarter[12] include such rewards as receiving a signed edition of a particular book, an acknowledgement in the book itself, dinner with the author, or even being literally drawn onto the book cover (as in the case of a manga). In one particular project that involved a bookstore, certain individuals were rewarded by being able to select books that would be permanently stocked at the store, or even control the selection of books on a particular bookshelf. One could easily see publishers rewarding active readers who help determine a book's title by including them in a book's acknowledgements, allowing active readers to determine featured books on a publisher's website or even having one of the book's principal characters named after an active reader.

Publishers could also capitalize on today's popularity of online games. [13] For instance, similar to Foursquare, publishers could create different digital badges that could be displayed on readers' profiles to reward certain behavior. Readers could earn online badges by completing certain books, attending particular book signings or writing a number of book reviews.

7   Rules for establishing successful communities

The establishment of successful communities relies on certain principles that encourage growth and continued participation. These rules include:

- Audience first
- Authenticity /Trusted Source
- Acknowledgment

The first rule is that the audience always comes first. That is, the interests of a community member or visitor to a site should be paramount to any decision made about the site or service. If a visitor has a good experience, the visitor may become loyal to the site, potentially become more engaged in the community and spread word about it to his/her friends. In fact, a prime indicator of whether someone has a good experience and is loyal to the site is whether he/she would recommend the site to his/her friends. [14] And these recommendations are critical for virally spreading the word about a particular site. This is precisely why effective customer service (e. g. with knowledgeable and responsive online support) has been called "the new marketing". [15]

The second key to establishing successful communities and connections with readers is being authentic and becoming a trusted source. Being authentic includes avoiding sock puppets[16] and letting members of a community know that the website is sponsored by a particular publisher. If a community or site becomes a trusted source, people may follow its recommendations and make purchases accordingly.

According to Figure 1, trust that leads to purchases is built most effectively by recommendations from known individuals.

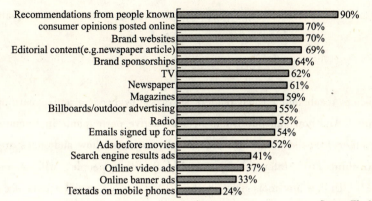

Source: The Nielsen Company

*E.g.90 percent of respondents trusted "completely" or "somewhat" recommendations from people they know

Figure 1   Degree of trust in the forms of advertising (April 2009)

Martha Stewart Living Omnimedia has made a conscious effort to become a trusted source on the web by acting like a good friend rather than a traditional formally branded company. Effective tools deployed have been sending out seasonal greetings such as "Happy New Year" or simple reminders such as "Don't forget to set your clocks ahead one hour tonight!" By being a trusted friend, Martha Stewart has been extremely successful at selling products (including books) she recommends or has created.

Cory Doctorow, a bestselling science fiction author, has also used the power of trust to create a vibrant community that successfully sells books. He created Boing-Boing[17] that features quirky facts, videos and images and has millions of followers; interestingly enough, it's a site unrelated to Doctorow's own writing. Given that Cory's followers trust his opinion, whenever a book is mentioned, whether it's his own or someone else's, books are purchased on his site (via Amazon's affiliate program). As such, although Boing-Boing is not meant to be a bookseller, it sells over 25,000 books each year. Given that the author, Cory Doctorow, was able to create a successful, engaging online community, it again raises the question whether authors, or, in the case of Martha Stewart, branded companies, may be in as good if not better position than publishers to create such engaging communities.

The third key to establishing successful communities is acknowledging readers' contributions. That is, publishers need to make a concerted effort to monitor and engage its readers in conversations — and even better, to act on readers' suggestions. That in turn assures readers that not only are the accounts genuine (rather than set up by an entity pretending to be the publisher) but also, even more important, that readers' suggestions are valued. Publishers can use a number of online tools (including search. twitter. com) to follow re-tweets, respond to comments, and thank those who link to, tweet about or mention a publisher's content. Mark Hurst, the founder of Good Experience, sends a personal note welcoming anyone who joins his community or tries out one of his tools. And Melanie Notkin, founder of savvyauntie. com, sends a personal note each time someone opts out of her community. She lets that person know how sorry she is that they have left the community and invites them back any time they like. Hurst and Notkin both explain that such personal notes are effective tools in maintaining citizenship and loyalty to their communities. [18]

8   Tools for successfully creating community

How can publishers reach and engage readers so that they become active participants in a publisher's community? And how can publishers become active participants in communities controlled and built by others? Social media has dramatically impacted how audiences are reached. By 2014, nearly two-thirds of all Internet users, or 164.9 million people, will be regular users of social networks. [19] Unlike any tools used in the 20th century, social media occurs in real time, which means that publishers have the opportunity to engage readers numerous times during a day and immediately respond to any comments or suggestions. There is a myriad of different social media tools that are transforming the way publishers can interact with online communities. These tools include blogs, Twitter, social networks such as Facebook and Ning, video on YouTube, photo applications such as Flickr and Twitpick, forums and forum replies, comments through Disqus[20], as well as bookmarking and sharing.

Media companies have successfully used such tools to create large followings. They have found that by using a spokesperson to whom people can relate —or better yet, a celebrity that personifies a company — social media can be extremely powerful. For instance, Martha Stewart Living Omnimedia consciously uses the person, Martha Stewart, to be the face and personality behind the company; she now has over two million Twitter followers. Anytime status updates with photos of her or information about her whereabouts are posted, there is great interest. Publishers and authors can learn from these personality-driven successes. That is, as previously discussed, authors could use their personalities to create brands that drive interest and audiences to their books. Similarly, publishers could appoint spokespeople to be the human face behind their companies. In fact, Knopf, an imprint of Random House, uses a photograph of Alfred J. Knopf, long dead, as its avatar on Twitter.

DailyLit[21], the leading publisher of serialized books, has developed and used online and social media tools to virally spread the word about its service. For instance, it implemented an "Invite a Friend" feature that allows people to easily invite their friends to sign up for a book on DailyLit. DailyLit also integrated with Twitter which allows readers to automatically tweet books they've started to read, books added to their "to read list" or contributions to DailyLit's forums.

Other online tools available to publishers include Meetup[22] that could be used to organize book clubs. Publishers could create built-in audiences for author tours and discussions, use these forums to obtain feedback on future releases, and in turn could reward readers by providing them with free books.

9   Understanding the readers

To build successful online communities and use tools effectively, it is critical for publishers to understand the significance of the demographics of its audience. In fact, an entire discipline called "social technographics" has been created to study how the Internet is used by people of different ages, gender and regions. [23] A social demographics profile includes as Figure 2: A "creator" is at the top of the chain and at least once a month either publishes a blog or online article, maintains a web page, or uploads videos or audios to sites such as YouTube. A "critic" reacts to other content online, posts comments on blogs or in forums and posts ratings or reviews. There are also "collectors" who save URLs and other information; "joiners" who maintain profiles on social networking sites; "spectators" who consume what others create (e. g. blogs, videos and reviews); and those who remain inactive. By understanding the percentage of readers who tend to be creators versus spectators, a publisher can alter its use of social media to best fit the needs of its community. For instance, a publisher that is trying to reach women aged 35 ~ 44 will realize that women in this demographic are far more likely to be spectators than creators. As such, rather than posting questions to be answered, such publishers may be better off posting articles of interest.

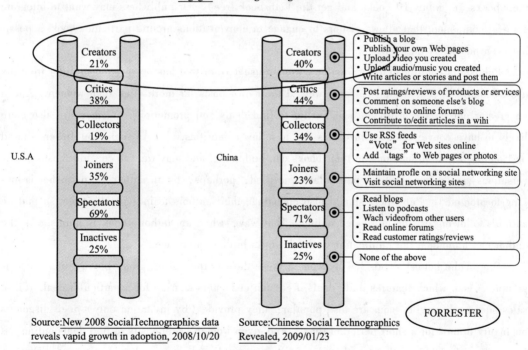

Figure 2　A Social demographic profile

In metropolitan China, as of March 4, 2009, 40% of the people surveyed were "Creators". [24] The engagement in China via social media in fact surpasses the use of social media in the United States.

In China, three groups were found to use social media very heavily: young adults, online shoppers and the middle class. This means for publishers in China that use of social media on their websites could be particularly effective, for instance, if it were targeted at young adults.

In the United States, [25] the online buying habits of women and how women use the digital space are critical to understanding how publishers can create engaging online communities. Although women make up less than half of the Internet population, they are the key drivers of online purchases. [26] In fact, with respect to the purchase of products related to entertainment, including books, women are responsible for 61% of all such purchases. [27]

The average woman in the United States spends 20% more time on retail sites than men, and women are particularly concerned with finding bargains. [28] In fact, women are more likely to shop online only when there are sales [29] and also are more likely to sign up for loyalty and incentive programs. [30] And not surprisingly, social media attracts a strong female audience. [31] According to comScore Plan Metrix, almost 56% of adult women say they use the Internet to stay in touch with people. It should be noted that in the Asia-Pacific region, women spend 20% of the total time online on "social" sites, with half of their time spent on social networking sites. This is still greater than 17% of the total time spent on social sites by men in Asia-Pacific.

Publishers can use such information as they develop their own communities. For instance, publishers may want to highlight sales on their sites' home pages or create incentive programs for their books (e. g. buy 10 books and get the 11th book free). Or publishers may want to integrate a social component that allows visitors to engage in conversations around particular books, possibly even hosted by authors.

Publishers could also learn from how women use Twitter that has been found to differ from the use by men. [32] For instance, men tweeted their own posts far more often than women. And a far greater percentage of women use Twitter to find deals and promotions. Women are also more likely to have conversations with others and to follow celebrities. [33] As such, publishers should be tweeting where promotions on their books can be found, and may want to consider hosting conversations via Twitter around a particular topic (led, perhaps, by an author the publisher is looking to promote). Publishers should also encourage their authors to individually tweet so that an author's following can be cultivated online. That way, when an author's book is published, the author can announce the publication and sale to its built-in audience.

One of the hottest trends led by women these days is the rise of group buying sites such as groupon. com which features daily deals if enough customers sign up for a particular deal. Flash sales sites such as gilt. com are also popular; they provide (by invitation only) deep discounts on luxury brands for a short period of time. And given women's propensity to find deals online, it is not surprising that another trend in the retail sector is digital coupon clipping sites. [34] That is, coupon clipping refers to finding certificates or coupons (traditionally found in newspaper inserts) which represent certain savings or discounts for particular products or services. Digital coupon clipping sites have simply moved this activity online.

Publishers could imitate these initiatives by bringing "special sales" to the general customer. That is, if enough customers sign up to buy a particular number of books, each customer could buy the book at a deep discount. Similarly, a huge discount on a particular author's books could be made available to active online fans for 36 hours. Or a coupon-clipping site for books could be created.

10　Conclusion

According to Seth Godin, a bestselling author and marketing professional, at present there is a short window of opportunity to establish and become leaders of individual digital communities. Godin estimated in 2009 that this period will last five years, and if a person or company does not claim to lead a particular community in that time, someone else (or other some entity) will claim that community. [35] I would argue that the window is now narrowing and is in fact three years rather than five.

A key question still remains whether authors need publishers to build communities. That is, it may be true that an author could implement the "B2C" model him/herself. In fact, Godin has recently announced that he is not renewing his publishing agreement but rather is leaving to become a self-published author. More and more authors like Godin who have large followings and who have established their own communities of readers may soon realize that they do not need publishers that lack communities of readers for these authors' books.

As such, it behooves publishers to act quickly to develop and stake their claim to particular vertical communities. Publishers can capitalize on their in-house staff and creativity and, develop engaging content which can, in turn, help publishers make informed decisions, reduce costs and ultimately increase sales for their books. But publishers must act now.

Notes

[1] "Tweeting" is a verb representing the use of Twitter.

[2] Foursquare is a social media tool that uses a gaming component to check into places in real time and share a person's whereabouts with friends.

[3] Grammar Girl, found at grammargirl. com, is an example of a publisher-led community (in this case, Macmillan) that created an online property that then translated into an interesting book program.

[4] End of 20th century, beginning of 21st century.

[5] Conversation that Mike Shatzkin, consultant to the publishing industry, had with Marcus Dohle in August, 2010 as recorded in Shatkin's blog (found at www. idealog. com) on September 6, 2010.

[6] See section on Understanding the Readers.

[7] Per Mike Shatzkin, in presentation to The Publishing Point on December 10, 2009. See associated video here: www. publishingpoint. com.

[8] Secret Santa is a Western Christmas tradition in which members of a group are randomly assigned other members to whom they anonymously give a gift.

[9] See: http://community. eharlequin. com/forums/cafe-social/cafe-social-ornament-exchange-2010.

[10] Chelsea Green's community can be found at chelseagreen. com.

[11] Lark Crafts's community can be found at larkcrafts. com.

[12] Kickstarter (found at kickstarter. com) is a funding platform for creative projects by artists, writers, designers, filmmakers and others.

[13] It should be noted that there are two demographic groups that drive the Games category: young males (of whom there are more) and older females, that is from 45 to 55 plus (who spend more time playing games). Source: comScore "Women on the Web: How Women are Shaping the Internet", June, 2010.

[14] The "Net Promoter Score" is a management tool that can be used to gauge the loyalty of members of a community. It asks the question: "How likely is it that you would recommend our company to a friend or colleague?" It was developed by Fred Reichheld, Bain & Company and Satmetrix and introduced in 2003 Harvard Business Review article "The One Number You Need to Grow".

[15] Conversation with Lane Becker, the founder of GetSatisfaction, October 1, 2008. See: http://radar. oreilly. com/2008/10/ustomer-service-is-the-new-mar. html.

[16] "Sock puppets" are online identities used for purpose of deception within an online community. For instance, a sock puppet may pretend to be an avid science fiction reader in a science fiction community but in fact is hired by a publisher to make the community seem more active.

[17] Found at boingboing. com.

[18] Per conversation with Mark Hurst and Melanie Notkin on July 22, 2010.

[19] Source: "Social Network Demographcis and Usage" in report by eMarketer released on August 24, 2010.

[20] Disqus is a service for blog comments; it enables bloggers to make the conversations on their blogs more interactive and manageable.

[21] Found at dailylit. com.

[22] Found at meetup. com.

[23] Source: *Groundswell: Winning in a World Transformed by Social Technologies* by Charlene Li and Josh Bernoff (of Forrester Research). Harvard Business Press, 2008.

[24] Forrester Report on "Chinese Social Technologies Revealed", January 23, 2009, updated March 4, 2009.

[25] Per the comScore report released in June, 2010, the United States has the largest e-commerce in the world.

[26] Although women in the United States make up just half of the Internet population, women spend 58% of all dollars generated from e-commerce. In February, 2010, 12.5% of women Internet users made online purchases (as compared with 9.5% of men). And in February, 2010, women accounted for 49.8% of the population but made 61.1% of online purchases. Source: comScore Report on "Women on the Web: How Women are Shaping the Internet", June, 2010.

[27] Refers to U. S. consumers (comScore e-Commerce Report, February 2010).

[28] Source: comScore Report on "Women on the Web: How Women are Shaping the Internet", June, 2010.

[29] Source: comScore Report on "Women on the Web: How Women are Shaping the Internet", June, 2010.

[30] Source: comScore Report on "Women on the Web: How Women are Shaping the Internet", June, 2010.

[31] Female audience comprises 64% of use of social media. Source: emarketer. com/Mintel Corporation.

[32] Source: comScore's April, 2010 U. S. survey.

[33] These findings are indeed borne out by Martha Stewart's two million Twitter followers.

[34] 42% of women (vs. 34% of men) listed coupons as being one of the three online cost savings methods most important to them. Source: comScore Report on "Women on the Web: How Women are Shaping the Internet", June, 2010.

[35] Delivered in a talk to The Publishing Point, September 24, 2009. See associated video at www. publishingpoint. com.

Author

Susan Danziger is the Founder and CEO of DailyLit. She is also on the M. S. in Publishing Advisory Board for Pace University.

作者简介

苏珊·丹齐格，美国 DailyLit 网站创始人和首席执行官，美国佩斯大学出版系顾问委员会委员。

Publisher's Dilemma: From Penguin Books to E-Books

Xiaochuan Lian

(M. S. in Publishing Program, Pace University, New York)

Abstract: A "dilemma" refers to a situation where one faces two or more choices, of which none is practically acceptable. This paper uses the "Innovator's Dilemma" theory to describe the challenge posted by the e-book to trade publishers. According to the "Innovator's Dilemma" theory by Harvard Business School professor Clayton Christensen, there are two types of technologies: sustaining technology and disruptive technology. Sustaining technologies make established companies stronger and more competitive, while disruptive technologies would topple established companies, because, when facing disruptive technologies, the good management which made the established companies successful in the first place would in turn make it difficult for them to adopt the new technologies. This is the "innovator's dilemma". Disruptive technologies initially appear at the bottom of a market and underperform sustaining technologies, but continuously improve and relentlessly move "up market", eventually displace established competitors. For trade publishers, the innovation of Penguin paperbacks 75 years ago was a sustaining technology, so the publishing industry was able to leverage the technology and became stronger. The Kindle and e-books, however, represent disruptive technologies, and present book publishers the kind of dilemma which brought down Encyclopedia Britannica, the music industry, and currently threatens the newspaper and magazine industries.

Keywords: Innovator's dilemma Disruptive technology Sustaining technology E-Book Penguin Books

出版社的困境：从企鹅丛书到电子图书

练小川

(佩斯大学出版系 纽约)

摘要："困境"是指某人面临两个或多个选择，其中每一个选择都无法被接受。本文用哈佛商学院教授克莱顿·克里斯滕森创立的"创新者的困境"理论来描述大众出版业因电子图书而面临的挑战。根据"创新者的困境"理论，技术分为两种："维持性技术"和"颠覆性技术"。维持性技术使成功的公司更强大、更具竞争力；而颠覆性技术将毁灭那些成功的公司，因为当成功的公司面临颠覆性技术的时候，那些使之成功的先进管理方法会反过来阻止这些公司采用新的、颠覆性的技术。这就是"创新者的困境"。颠覆性技术往往始于低端市场，功能效率劣于维持性技术，但是颠覆性技术不断改善，无情地蚕食高端市场，最终将颠覆那些强大的竞争者。对于大众出版业来说，75年前企鹅平装书的创新代表的是维持性技术，所以大众出版业采用这个创新后变得更加强大。但是亚马逊的 Kindle 阅读器以及电子书代表的是颠覆性技术，使大众出版业面临着一个"困境"，这个"困境"已经颠覆了《大英百科全书》和音乐产业，现在正在威胁报刊行业。

关键词：创新者的困境　颠覆性技术　维持性技术　电子书　企鹅丛书

July 30, 2010 was the 75th birthday of Penguin Books. In the same month, book publishing industry reached another milestone: sales of Amazon Kindle e-books surpassed hardcover sales on amazon. com. Jeff Bezos, CEO of Amazon, predicts that "we will surpass paperback sales in the next 9 to 12 months. Sometime after that, we'll surpass the combination of paperback and hardcover". [1] This is a stunning development, considering that Kindle is only 33 months old.

But publishing industry is in no mood to celebrate this e-book milestone as they did for the Penguin birthday. People in the traditional publishing can't help but wondering, in the next few years, what kind of market will the Penguin march into?

Both Penguin Books and Kindle represent revolutions in book publishing, but the Penguin revolution was different from the Kindle revolution in that the former was a paper-based revolution. As a result, the impact of Penguin Books and Kindle on the publishing industry is very different.

1　Penguin Books

In the 1930s, hardcover books in Britain were marketed as luxury goods for elite readers, they were expensive and available only in bookstores, most people couldn't afford to buy and read a hardcover book. Cheaper paperbacks did exist, but they were printed on cheap, yellowing paper with flimsy bindings and mostly for genre fictions such as romances, mysteries, westerns and adventures, none of them were considered serious literature. No reputable publisher and bookseller would engage in the lowbrow paperback business.

In 1935, Allen Lane, a director of book publisher The Bodley Head, was desperately trying to save his company from bankruptcy. One weekend, after visiting Agatha Christie, Allen was browsing a newsstand at a train station, wanted to buy a book to read on the train back to London. The newsstand only had paperbacks of reprinted Victorian novels, pulp fictions and magazines. Suddenly, Allen realized that there was an unmet market for contemporary literature, and it might save his company if he could fill the need by publishing contemporary literature in inexpensive paperback format, distributing them through newsstands, train stations and chain stores, rather than just bookstores.

Allen named his new business Penguin Books, as an imprint of The Bodley Head, and planned to use the chain store Woolworth as his main distribution channel. Since most items sold at Woolworth were priced at sixpence, Allen priced his Penguin paperback at sixpence a copy as well.

The first 10 Penguin books were published in August 1935; they were all reprints of contemporary literature, including *A Farewell to Arms* by Ernest Hemingway, *The Mysterious Affair at Styles* by Agatha Christie and *The Unpleasantness at the Bellona Club* by Dorothy L. Sayers. At sixpence, one Penguin paperback was only one fifteenth of the price of a hardcover book.

The price was so low that no other publishers would want to compete with Penguin Books. Publishers, authors and bookstores were resentful, fearing Allen's innovation would harm the hardcover business and disrupt the publishing industry. George Orwell, the author of *1984*, warned at that time, "The Penguin Books are splendid value for sixpence, so splendid that if other publishers had any sense they would combine against them and suppress them."[2]

But readers embraced these inexpensive paperbacks. In the first four days on sale, the initial list of 10 Penguin titles sold some 150,000 copies. In the first year, three million copies were sold. By 1937, there were 100 Penguin Books titles in print, and every new title had a first printing of at least 50,000 copies. At the end of three years, 17 million Penguin Books titles had been sold. Thanks to inexpensive Penguin paperbacks, book-reading was no longer a luxury reserved for the upper and educated classes.

Penguin Books revolutionized the publishing industry through the combination of pricing (costing only 1/15 of the typical hardcover), distribution (chain store) and design (inexpensive paperback with serious content). It turned out that this "paperback revolution" didn't disrupt the book industry at all; instead, Penguin Books opened up a new market for all publishers without killing the old hardcover business. Every publisher adopted paperback technology. In the end, the book publishing industry became stronger and more prosperous. Today, paperback is a profitable format for all publishers; more than 600 million paperbacks are sold annually worldwide.[3]

2　The Kindle

The impact of Kindle and e-books will be different because they are not paper-based.

A book has two components: content and container (or rendering device). In the paper-book world, the container/rendering device is paper, the content and the container are one piece and can't be separated. Publishing a book is to put content on paper; reading a book is to read content on paper. Since content can't be separated from container, book publishers have absolute control of the finished product in both content and rendering device. This control gives publishers the power of gatekeeper in the book ecosystem: from editorial to wholesale to retail.

With Kindle and e-books, the content and container are separated. Technically, the content of an e-book is just a binary file with a bunch of 0s and 1s; readers will need a rendering device to convert the binary codes into readable content. The rendering device can be a desktop computer, a laptop, a smart phone, an e-book reader (Kindle, Nook, and Sony), an iPad, or paper (via Print on Demand). In the digital age, publishers still have control of content in the form of digital files but no longer have control of the container and rendering device, which are now controlled by non-publishers such as Amazon, Apple, Sony, Barnes & Noble and

Google. As a result, publishers' power of gatekeeper is cut in half. (Interestingly, STM publishers still control both their digital files and rendering devices which are mainly databases; therefore, digital technology is strengthening, not weakening STM publishers' market position.)

With Penguin Books, publishers were competing with a fellow book publisher; with Kindle and e-books, publishers are competing with technology companies (Barnes & Noble is not a technology company but has decided to become one. On March 18, 2010, Barnes & Noble appointed 39-year-old William Lynch as its new CEO, who is from the IT and e-commerce industry with no publishing and book-selling experience whatsoever. In a CNBC interview that day, Lynch announced that he'll lead the transformation of Barnes & Noble to "a digital and technology company"[4]).

The question now is whether traditional trade publishers can adopt the e-book innovation and come out stronger as they accomplished with the innovation of Penguin Books. Will Kindle and e-books augment or disrupt traditional book publishing? No one has an answer yet, but all signs so far have pointed to an industry-wide disruption by Kindle and e-books, that's why the Kindle milestone is worrisome to most publishers. If the future of publishing is more e-books and less paper books, then the impact on trade publishing from Kindle and e-books may well be disruptions, instead of enhancements.

3   The Innovator's Dilemma Theory

Kindle and e-books represent a different technology from the one represented by Penguin paperbacks.

In his book *The Innovator's Dilemma*, Harvard Business School professor Clayton Christensen defines a technology as a way "by which an organization transforms labor, capital, materials and information into products and services of greater value"[5]. Every company — from Amazon to Penguin — employs technology to deliver value to its customers. A brick-and-mortar bookseller like Barnes & Noble employs a particular technology to procure, present, sell and deliver books to its customers, while an online bookseller like Amazon employs a different technology. "The concept of technology therefore extends beyond engineering and manufacturing to encompass a range of marketing, investment, and managerial processes. *Innovation* refers to a change in one of these technologies."[6]

Prof. Christensen classifies technologies into two types: "sustaining technologies" and "disruptive technologies".

"Sustaining technologies" are new technologies that improve performance of existing products, which are valued by the mainstream customers in major markets. Most new technologies are sustaining technologies, they can be incremental or radical, but even the most radical sustaining technologies rarely threaten the established firms or incumbents, which are usually the leading innovators in sustaining technologies.

"Disruptive technologies", on the other hand, are new technologies that make products cheaper, simpler, smaller and more convenient to use. Initially, disruptive technologies underperform existing products in mainstream markets and are dismissed by established companies, but disruptive technologies have other features that are valued by some niche customers. Disruptive technologies often promise lower profit margin than sustaining technologies, therefore require a new concept of product value. From sustaining technologies' point of view, disruptive technologies tend to "devalue" existing products.

Disruptive technologies create a dilemma for established companies: these companies become industry leaders because of their good management and competency, but paradoxically, when facing a disruptive technology, the same competency and sound management become obstacles that prevent these companies from adopting the disruptive technology. Because of this dilemma, when competing in sustaining technology, established companies or incumbents win; when competing in disruptive technology, newcomers win.

Prof. Christensen calls this phenomenon "the Innovator's Dilemma", which is due to the fact that a leading company's capability in dealing with sustaining technology is also the company's incapability in dealing with disruptive technology.

4　Sources of a Company's Capabilities

According to the "Innovator's Dilemma" theory, a company's capabilities come from three sources: a company's resources, processes and values.

① Resources

Resources are people, equipment, product design, brand, information, cash, and relationships with suppliers, distributors, and customers. Resources are assets and can be changed readily — they can be hired and fired, bought and sold, depreciated and enhanced. Abundant and high-quality resources give a company better chance to meet the challenge of disruptive technologies. However, Prof. Christensen points out, two companies can have similar resources but the outcomes from those resources may be very different — "because the capabilities to transform inputs into goods and services of greater value reside in the organization's processes and values"[7].

② Processes

Processes define how an organization transforms its resources into products and services. According to Prof. Christensen, a firm's processes include not just manufacturing processes, but also product development, procurement, market research, budgeting, planning, employee development and compensation, and resource allocation. Processes can be "formal" and "informal". "Formal processes" are explicitly defined, documented and consciously followed. "Informal processes" are habits and routines evolved over time, employees follow informal processes unconsciously. Informal processes constitute the culture of a company.

Processes are designed to do specific tasks. When people use a process to do a work for which it was designed, the work is likely performed efficiently. But when the same process is used to do a very different task, the process appears to be slow and inefficient. In other words, a process that defines the capability in doing certain tasks also defines the inability in accomplishing other tasks.

Disruptive technology requires changes in a company's processes, but to ensure consistency and efficiency of the business, the company's processes, by their very nature, are meant not to change. That is the dilemma established companies are facing when they try to adopt disruptive technologies.

③ Values

A firm's values are the standards used by the management to set the firm's priorities — whether a project is attractive or unattractive; whether a market segment is important or not important; whether an idea for a new product is attractive or marginal. Values dictate management to invest or not invest in new products, services, and markets. In the meantime, a company's values also define what a company cannot do. Values are reflections of a company's cost structure and business model; a company must adhere to its values in order to make money. For example, if the structure of a company's overhead costs requires it to achieve gross profit margins of 40% , it will not be interested in products that promise gross margins below 40% . This means that such a company — even with its vast resources — would be incapable of successfully commercializing products targeting low-margin markets. At the same time, another company, whose values are based on a very different cost structure, may succeed in the very same low-margin product.

The resources-processes-values framework is the reason why established firms cannot deal with disruptive technologies successfully. The disruptive technologies offer lower profit margins and are not valued by a company's mainstream customers; disruptive technologies are incompatible with established company's processes and inconsistent with its values. In other words, the processes and values in an established firm give it an advantage in sustaining technologies, but the same processes and values also make it difficult for the firm to adopt disruptive technologies, even though the firm has ample resources. But the danger for established companies is that, while disruptive technologies initially under-perform sustaining technologies and are shunned by mainstream consumers, they will improve over time and "relentlessly moves 'up market', eventually displacing established competitors". [8]

5   How to Deal with Disruptive Technology?

According to Prof. Christensen, companies have three options to obtain capabilities of adopting disruptive technology.

5. 1   Acquire a different company whose processes and values are a close match with a disruptive technology

When the purpose of the acquisition is to obtain some unique processes and values that the acquiring company doesn't have, such as unique ways of working and decision-making, developing, making and delivering new products in a specific fashion, then the acquiring company should not integrate the purchased company into the parent organization. "Integration will vaporize many of the processes and values of the acquired firm. " Prof. Christensen points out, "The best strategy in this case is to let the business stand alone, and the parent company infuses its resources into the acquired firm's processes and values. "[9]

5. 2   Try to change the processes and values of the current organization

Some companies try to change internal processes and values in order to adopt disruptive technology. It's easy for companies to hire people with new skills, license new technologies, but it's very difficult to change existing processes and values. Prof. Christensen points out, "When disruptive change appears on the horizon, companies need to assemble the capabilities to confront the change before it has affected the mainstream business. In other words, they need an organization that is geared toward the new challenge before the old one, whose processes are tuned to the existing business model, and has reached a crisis that demands fundamental change. Because of its task-specific nature, it is impossible to ask one process to do two fundamentally different things. If a company needs to do both types of tasks simultaneously, then it needs two very different processes. And it is very difficult for a single organizational unit to employ fundamentally different, opposing processes. "[10]

5. 3   Establish an independent organization and develop the new processes and values that are required to adopt a disruptive technology

When a company's processes and values make it incapable to adopt disruptive technologies, the company should set up a separate organization to experiment with the disruptive technologies. It is very difficult for a company whose cost structure is tailored to compete in high-end markets to be profitable in low-end markets as well. When a threatening disruptive technology requires a different cost structure in order to be profitable and competitive, then an independent organization with new processes and values is required. The business at the spin-out organization should be completely separate from the parent company; it cannot be forced to compete with business in the parent company for resources.

6   A Case of the Innovator's Dilemma: *Encyclopaedia Britannica*

No case can better illustrate the "innovator's dilemma" than the demise of *Encyclopaedia Britannica*.

In the encyclopedia market, *Encyclopaedia Britannica* is the best known brand and was once the gold standard of the industry. Britannica's strong brand came from its resources, processes and values.

6. 1   Resources

In the late 1980s, Britannica differentiated itself from the rest of the market as a luxury brand, with an excellent reputation as the world's most comprehensive and authoritative encyclopedia. Britannica boasted 44 million words on half a million topics, written by leading scholars, including more than 80 Nobel laureates. It was every scholar's dream to write for Britannica. The strong brand made Britannica one of the most profitable reference publishers in the U. S.. In 1991, the entire U. S. encyclopedia market was approximately $1. 2 billion, Britannica dominated the industry with sales of $650 Million[11].

6.2　Processes

The production cost of one set of *Encyclopaedia Britannica* was only $250, while the retail price per set was $1,500 to $2,000 depending on the binding. Britannica was strictly relying on door-to-door direct sale and had one of the best direct-sale force in the world. Britannica employed over 2,300 salespeople in 1989; each salesperson could earn $500 to $600 commission per sale.

6.3　Values

Britannica's internal market research revealed that a typical encyclopedia owner opened his or her volumes less than once a year, so Britannica believed that encyclopedias were "sold, not bought", and a door-to-door sales force was indispensable. As a sales-driven organization, Britannica's senior executives were mostly coming from sales; as a result, the company became very sensitive to the mood and morale of the sales force.

In the summer of 1985, Britannica was approached by Microsoft for a partnership to publish a CD-ROM encyclopedia. Microsoft offered to pay a royalty for nonexclusive rights to use Britannica's contents, with an advance and an guaranteed minimum payment. Britannica refused, fearing it might lose its "most valuable asset". The president of Britannica asked the Microsoft manager to guess what that asset was. "The encyclopedia's contents?" the manager ventured. "No, it's my salespeople." If Britannica salespeople learnt that a competitor was going to market a new encyclopedia with identical contents in CD-ROM format that could replace the printed volumes, they would quit Britannica immediately. No salespeople means no Britannica [12].

For Britannica, a cheaper CD-ROM encyclopedia was just a toy, such a product would not fit Britannica's prestigious brand, couldn't generate the $500 commissions for the sales force, and therefore was incompatible with Britannica's business processes and values. Britannica already controlled the high end of the encyclopedia market, charged the highest price premium among encyclopedia publishers, and enjoyed strong and stable profits. One former Britannica employee noted that "anyone who messed with the goose that laid the golden egg would have been shot". [13]

In 1993, Microsoft launched its own CD-ROM encyclopedia *Encarta* for a retail price of $99. The contents of Encarta were licensed from a third-rate product called the *Funk & Wagnall's New Encyclopedia*, plus some public domain video and audio materials. The majority of copies were bundled with PCs and given away by manufacturers to promote the sale of computer. *Encarta* presented a value mismatch: the marginal cost of *Encarta* CD-ROM was $1.50 per copy, while the marginal cost of *Encyclopaedia Britannica* was $250, plus $500 to $600 for sales commission. With the same price of a set of print *Encyclopaedia Britannica*, customers could get a computer and the *Encarta* encyclopedia. For families wanted to give their children an advantage at school, *Encarta* plus a computer was a much better deal. The result of this value mismatch was a complete disruption of Britannica: in 1993, Britannica sold 117,000 sets of hardcopy encyclopedia, but in 1996, the sales dropped to 55,000 sets, and its revenue had dropped to $325 million in 1996 from 1991's $650 million. In January 1996, after 18 months trying to find a buyer,

Britannica was sold to a Swiss banker for a mere $135 million, less half of its book value, and the famed door-to-door sales force was dismantled.[14]

Ironically, Britannica was an early innovator and a leader in the electronic encyclopedia business. In 1981, under an agreement with database publisher Mead Data Central, the first digital version of the *Encyclopaedia Britannica* was created for the Lexis-Nexis database service. In 1989, Britannica created the first multimedia CD-ROM encyclopedia, *Compton's MultiMedia Encyclopedia* (the first DOS based, text-only CD-ROM encyclopedia was *Grolier's Academic American Encyclopedia* in 1985). In 1994, the company developed *Britannica Online*, the first encyclopedia for the Internet, which made the entire text of the *Encyclopaedia Britannica* available worldwide. That year the first version of the *Britannica* on CD-ROM was also published.[15]

Britannica acquired this digital capability by chance. Most Britannica's digital innovations were created by a small group of IT professionals, who came from a technology firm named Del Mar Group. Britannica hired Del Mar Group to develop its CD-ROM encyclopedia *Compton's* in 1988, and purchased the company in 1990. The Del Mar technicians joined Britannica's software division Compton's New Media, and later formed another small unit called Advanced Technology Group. This unit was located in California, 1,723 air miles away from Britannica's Chicago headquarters, and to a large extent was left alone, which was the main reason why the Advanced Technology Group was able to experiment freely with new digital initiatives.[16]

While the California unit was busy churning out new products, the senior management at Britannica tried hard to fit these innovations into Britannica's existing processes and values and hoped they would enhance its lucrative print encyclopedia business, these efforts ultimately failed, as the "Innovator's Dilemma" theory would predict.

6.4   Why Britannica on Lexis-Nexis failed?

In 1981, Britannica made its encyclopedia available and searchable on Mead Data Central's Lexis-Nexis database. Why would Britannica allow its contents appear in Lexis-Nexis? Robert McHenry, former editor-in-chief of *Encyclopaedia Britannica*, recalled, "I have no information regarding how or by whom this decision was made. It seems clear that this venture was deemed acceptable because Lexis-Nexis, running on a proprietary network and used at significant cost by professional researchers, posed no threat at all to home field sales. One might even guess that it even provided a handy riposte to those who might criticize Britannica for failing to engage the electronic field. Just to make very, very sure that there would be no effect on (print) sales, users who accessed *Britannica* on Nexis were denied the ability to print out articles."[17] Britannica made it very clear to Mead Data Central that any non-business subscribers, specifically schools, libraries or individuals that were subscribers to Lexis-Nexis' other content retrieval services, were not allowed to subscribe the electronic encyclopedia.[18] The encyclopedia on Lexis-Nexis ended in the late 1980s when the original data having aged considerably, Lexis-Nexis needed more current content but was unwilling to bear the cost of parsing the data into the appropriate format.

6.5   Why *Compton's MultiMedia Encyclopedia* failed?

Britannica acquired *Compton's Encyclopedia* in 1961, which was an encyclopedia for young readers. Britannica used the *Compton's* exclusively as an add-on to aid sales of *Encyclopaedia Britannica*. The editorial cost of maintaining *Compton's* was treated as a promotional expense of the *Encyclopaedia Britannica*. After rejecting Microsoft's proposal, Britannica decided to use *Compton's* content in its own CD-ROM experiment. The Britannica's sales force would not allow a CD-ROM *Encyclopaedia Britannica*, but the management figured that these salespeople would have no objection to using the *Compton's* name and content in electronic products. Britannica issued *Compton's MultiMedia Encyclopedia* in 1989, which was called by *Business Week* as "one of the top ten new products of the year". [19]

Britannica treated the *Compton's* as a sustaining technology to support the print sale. Salespeople gave the *Compton's* disk away to buyers of a print *Encyclopaedia Britannica*, but standalone *Compton's* CD-ROM would cost $995. This way, sales force would view the CD-ROM as a "sales closer", not a threat to the traditional way of direct sale. As a standalone CD-ROM product, however, *Compton's* content didn't have the breadth and depth to justify the $995 price tag. In 1993, Britannica decided not to make a long-term investment in this product, and sold the *Compton's* business to Chicago Tribune for $57 million. [20]

6.6 Why *Britannica* on CD-ROM failed?

The first version of the *Britannica* on CD-ROM was issued in 1994 to compete with *Encarta* and priced at $995. However, the sales force rebelled. Even with such a high price premium over *Encarta*, the CD-ROM version could not generate the $500 commission the sales force was receiving from the print sale. To gain support from its sales force, Britannica eventually decided to make the *Encyclopaedia Britannica* CD-ROM a free add-on to the print version, and the CD-ROM was only available from the salespeople. If someone wanted to buy the CD-ROM without the print edition, the price would be $1,500. In the meantime, Microsoft's *Encarta* CD-ROM was selling at $99 or less. Soon Britannica had to drop the price of the CD-ROM to $995 in 1995 and to $200 in 1996, but it was too late and the company itself was sold in 1996. [21]

6.7 Why *Britannica Online* failed?

The *Britannica Online* was also developed in 1994, and became the first encyclopedia for the Internet in the world.

According to Robert McHenry, *Britannica Online* was a great success with its intended market: colleges, universities and libraries; some hundreds of institutions in the United States signed up. In the fall of 1995, *Britannica Online* was available to individual subscribers as well, but it failed to penetrate the consumer market as hoped by the company management. "One chief reason, no doubt, was that at the institutional level no other encyclopedia could hope to match Britannica's reputation or performance; while for many consumers, looking for homework assistance for younger students, there were credible competitors, especially those that were supplied freely with that newest of apparitional goods, the home PC." [22]

The concern of Britannica management was always about the sales force, and the focus was on developing a consumer CD-ROM version of Britannica that the sales force could accept, meaning to price the CD-ROM at the same level of the print version. As a result, *Britannica Online* was not considered by senior management to be the future of the company and had to compete with the CD-ROM and print version for resources. In 1996, Britannica was in serious financial trouble, and could no longer make major investment for *Britannica Online*. The head of the Advanced Technology Group left in 1999, the California office was closed in 2001. [23]

7 The Publisher's Dilemma

"Microsoft and the dawning of the CD-ROM presented a company like Britannica with an awful choice: it was damned if it replaced its premier product with technology that dramatically lowered production costs and thereby angered its sales staff — but it was damned too, as it found out painfully, if it did not cooperate in the development of the new medium." [24] This was the "innovator's dilemma".

When it was *Encarta's* turn to face the dilemma — the faster, cheaper, simpler and more convenient Internet and Wikipedia, Microsoft chose not to fight but simply discontinued the *Encarta* business.

The "innovator's dilemma" that has crippled the music industry is currently threatening the newspaper and magazine industry. Now Kindle and e-books are presenting similar dilemma to book publishing industry.

Notes

[1] Volume of Kindle Book Sales Stuns Amazon's Jeff Bezos, *USA Today*, July 29, 2010. http://www.usatoday.com/tech/news/2010-07-29-amazon29_VA_N.html.

[2] http://www.penguin.co.uk/static/cs/uk/0/aboutus/aboutpenguin_companyhistory.html.

[3] http://us.penguingroup.com/static/pages/publishers/adult/penguin.html.

[4] http://www.huffingtonpost.com/2010/03/19/barnes-noble-ceo-on-amazo_n_505802.html.

[5] Clayton M. Christensen, *The Innovator's Dilemma*. Harvard Business School Press, 1997. Page 8.

[6] *Ibid*.

[7] *Ibid*. Page 163.

[8] http://www.claytonchristensen.com/disruptive_innovation.html.

[9] Clayton M. Christensen. *The Innovator's Dilemma*. Havard Business School Press, 1997 Page 172.

[10] *Ibid*. Page 175.

[11] Josh Kopelman, *Shrink a Market*! http://redeye.firstround.com/2006/04/shrink_a_market.html.

[12] Randall Stross, *The Microsoft Way*. Addison-Wesley Publishing Company, Inc., 1996. Page 80.

[13] Shane Greenstein and Michelle Devereux, *The Crisis at Encyclopaedie Britannica*, case study, Kellogg School of Management, Northwestern University, 2006.

[14] *Ibid.*

[15] *History of Encyclopaedia Britannica and Britannica Online*. http://corporate. britannica. com/company_info. html.

[16] Robert McHenry, *The Building of Britannica Online*. http://www. howtoknow. com/ BOL1. html.

[17] Robert McHenry, *The Building of Britannica Online*. http://www. howtoknow. com/side-bar2. html.

[18] William F. Achtmeyer, *Encyclopaedia Britannica*, *Inc.* (A), Tuck School of Business at Dartmouth, case No. 2-0007.

[19] Robert McHenry

[20] Shane Greenstein and Michelle Devereux

[21] Josh Kopelman

[22] Robert McHenry

[23] *Ibid.*

[24] Randall E. Stross. Page 80-81.

Author

Xiaochuan Lian is currently serving as Senior Staff Associate and an adjunct professor in the M. S. in Publishing Program at Pace University.

作者简介

练小川，美国佩斯大学出版系兼职教授。

Re-imagining Business Publishing: A Balance of Technology and Expertise

Kirsten D. Sandberg

(Pace University, New York)

Dedicated to the late Coimbatore Krishnarao Prahalad

Abstract: This lecture explores the impact of six forces on business publishing within a knowledge economy. The author posits that technological innovation is more important to individual consumers whereas editorial expertise is more important to groups. Specifically, business publishing will become important to the knowledge management function within organizations. The need for this function is growing, and publishers have an opportunity to expand their role from purveyors of products to providers of services that capture institutional memory and organizational learning.

Keywords: Dominant logic Knowledge economy Intellectual property Value chain Digitization Commoditization Groundswell Experienced goods Infrastructure Globalization Fiercening of capital Purpose brand

商业出版的再思考：科技与专业知识的平衡

柯尔斯顿 D. 桑德伯格

（佩斯大学　纽约）

摘要：本文探讨了六种力量对知识经济时代商业出版的影响。作者认为技术创新对个体消费者是重要的，但是编辑技巧对团队更重要。具体来说，商业出版对组织机构的知识管理功能变得不可或缺。随着组织知识管理需求的增长，出版商拥有了一个将自身角色从产品供应商向机构记忆和组织学习服务提供商拓展的机会。

关键词：主导逻辑　知识经济　知识产权　价值链　数字化　商品化　风暴　体验性商品　基础设施　全球化　资本膨胀　目的品牌

Thank you, ladies and gentlemen, for the great honor of sharing a set of ideas with you today. Thank you especially to my generous and honorable hosts and to my estimable colleagues at Pace University, Professor Sherman Raskin and Professor Xiaochuan Lian. I am very grateful and pleased to join you and your important guests.

I am also very grateful to my mentors and authors, particularly those at the Harvard Business

School Publishing Corporation. They taught me more than I deserve to know. The one who changed my thinking and inspired me the most is the late C. K. Prahalad, one of the world's most influential business minds.

Over dinner in 2009, Dr. Prahalad and I were discussing a new project that I wanted him to write. Its working title was "Change Your Dominant Logic and Change the World: A Humble Call to Action." He defined "dominant logic as top management's cognitive orientation and collective mental mapping that influenced the company's strategic direction."[1] He argued, as he always did, that, "The only way to change the world is to change how we think about it." Then he diagnosed the problem, "Our individual and collective ideologies, our life experiences good and bad, our business success...are now holding your company hostage from its future."[2] Dr. Prahalad went on to add, "The larger problem is that you have no idea what you actually think as a group, what assumptions you are making about your business."[3] In essence, the very ideas that established our incumbency in a market or an industry are now preventing us from seeing what he called "weak signals", leading indicators of change that cannot yet be scientifically validated but that warrant our attention until we understand their meaning. Only then, can we dismiss these signals as idiosyncrasies, or modify our current assumptions, or develop all new assumptions.[4]

In the spirit of C. K. Prahalad, I am here today to surface some assumptions about the nature of business publishing, so as to expand its role in the **knowledge economy**, an economy wherein a company's only sustainable competitive advantage will depend upon its ability to create, manage and deploy its own knowledge in a marketplace of ideas and expertise. More specifically, I am here to suggest that the process of business publishing is critical to the knowledge management function within corporations, that the need for this function is growing, and that publishers have an opportunity to expand their role not just as purveyors of educational products but as providers of services to the corporate world as corporations devote more resources to capturing organizational learning. In pointing out what I believe to be weak signals, I will call upon other authors, ideas and examples from my 20 years in business publishing.

Now it is a fortuitous time to challenge our thinking because the global economic downturn is stirring up all sorts of opportunities. I will do so throughout the rest of my talk by exploring these fundamental questions, "What value are we really creating?" "What is the appropriate unit of analysis?" and "How and for whom are we creating this value?" in the context of fast moving changes in the industry, due to a set of unstoppable and irreversible forces at work. Those forces are:

- The digitalization and dis-integration of assets
- The commoditization of assets and brands
- The groundswell of personal publishing and promoting
- The infrastructuring of content
- The globalization of markets for knowledge and expertise
- The fiercening of capital

1 Core assumptions

First, let us ask ourselves the fundamental questions. What value are we really creating? What is the appropriate unit of analysis? The publishing establishment tends to think primarily in terms of an economic **product**, the contents of which take various forms: the dictionaries and textbooks on the business-related subjects of economics, finance and accounting, and trade books such as John Naisbett's *Megatrends* and McKinsey & Company's professional guide to *Valuation*. For each category, the industry measures and reports year-over-year books sales by unit and dollar value. In 2009, for example, the Academic-Professional segment rebounded by 21%, and the Scientific-Technical-Medical segment, by 9%. [5] As of June 2010, Professional was up 11.4% over last year. [6] In a recent survey of book-buying behavior, roughly a third of the 9,300 participants stated that they bought books for business or professional purposes and for educational or self improvement; and 33% of those who used electronic readers, did so during work breaks or while commuting. [7] Positive signs of an economic recovery perhaps, but not necessarily of value creation in business publishing.

When it comes to value, business publishers also talk in terms of **copyright**, a specific type of **intellectual property**, defined by the World Intellectual Property Organization as "creations of the mind...used in commerce" [8]. They believe that the economic benefits of their product are derived from and protected by an **intellectual property rights system**, an earmark of a robust knowledge economy, and so they spend much time negotiating and carefully drafting the initial **publishing contract**. This process of negotiation is vital because it sends weak signals about changes in the economic importance of certain rights, in the roles of publisher and author, and in publishing practices in so far as they create value. For example, in the last decade, debates have been heated over the definition of digital (electronic) rights, the implementation of those rights, the meaning of the phrase "out of print," and the relevance of the distinction between retail sales and direct sales over the Internet. Authors have also argued over the need to submit their manuscripts on paper rather than as digital files, and some even still insist on promises of full-page advertisements in printed newspapers. Most recently, a major dispute erupted between a renowned literary agent, Andrew Wylie, and the world's largest publisher, Random House, over the royalty rates on sales of the electronic books of classic manuscripts by such important authors as Saul Bellow and Vladimir Nabokov.

By and large, these debates signal changes to the publishing **value chain**. I am borrowing the phrase loosely from the strategy guru Michael E. Porter, who describes the value chain as a series of activities that creates value for customers, starting when an author begins conducting research and concluding when the customer has actual content in hand. [9] In this value chain, the typical business publisher performs a subset of activities, supported by layers of human resources, finance, information technology and procurement:

- Editorial: These activities include acquisitions of copyright, coaching of the author, and development, copy-editing, proofing, design and production of manuscript.

- **Sales & Marketing**: These activities include advertising, promotions and publicity of the manuscript and its author, merchandising of actual products, and licensing of copyrights to third parties.

- **Operations & Logistics**: These activities include sourcing raw materials for manufacturing, warehousing, fulfillment and distribution of products.

For many business publishers, the decision to publish a book depends on whether the projected sales volume of the hardcover edition during its first year in print will generate an acceptable level of **return on investment** (ROI), and the **profit-and-loss statement** (P&L) puts the fixed costs of performing these legacy activities front and center. Production costs are generally high, not unlike the big budget of a blockbuster movie. For example, Feng Xiaogang spent 135 million Yuan (approximately USD20 million) to create his latest film, *Aftershock*, and those costs are sunk costs: Mr. Feng cannot recoup them if no one watches his film. [10] But now that he has produced it, the cost of **reproducing** it is low and marginal. "Once several firms have sunk costs necessary to create the product, competitive forces tend to move the price toward marginal cost, which is the cost of producing an 'additional' copy" [11], write Carl Shapiro and Hal R. Varian, [12] authors of the international bestseller, *Information Rules*. In the traditional print value chain, "books that cost hundreds of thousands of dollars to produce can be printed and bound for a dollar or two" [13].

The publishing contract and the P&L statement are critical to our discussion because, more than any other signal document or spreadsheet, they institutionalize the assumptions that publishers are making about their business in terms of the necessity and the costs of editorial, marketing and sales, and operations and logistics activities. They define and establish measures of economic success. Publishers are reluctant to revise them and loath to abandon them altogether. All changes in the industry are viewed as changes to the sacred contract and the P&L statement, and not as unstoppable and irreversible forces at work, for which no definitions or measures yet exist. In the rest of my presentation, I will review the major forces, their impact on incumbent publishing practices, and some weak signals of the future of business publishing.

2 Digitization of Assets

The first force is the most obvious but perhaps the least understood. It is **digitization**, the rapid technological advance of computer power and speed, enabling far more of us to do far more connecting and computing at a far lower cost. "Essentially, anything that can be digitized — encoded as a stream of bits — is information," say Professors Shapiro and Varian. "Baseball scores, books, databases, magazines, movies, music, stock quotes, and web pages are all *information goods*" [14], and you can trade them as quickly as investors can trade commodities on the stock exchange.

For book editors, the implications are both exciting and terrifying. Exciting, because now you can sell a book in pieces; you can sell each chapter and each piece of art separately; you can make the charts and tables in the art program interactive, allowing readers to input their own data. You can embed hyperlinks to original source material, to audio, video and other websites. The possibilities are almost endless. Unfortunately, neither the publishing agreement nor the P&L statement — nor your job description nor incentive structure, for that matter — allows you any room for experimentation.

The implications of digitization are terrifying because, unlike coffee beans or barrels of oil, your product is digital: even though you still have high sunk costs to create it, it now costs nothing to reproduce. If consumers can search the Internet and find comparable content for free, your high-cost product has quickly become a no-value commodity. No copyright laws will protect you from consumers' unwillingness to pay for business content according to your traditional value chain.

3 The Commoditization of Value

That is what **commoditization** does: it drives down the differentiation among assets, the purchase price of those assets, and ultimately the profit margin that those assets generate. Commoditization can also drive down the value of publishers themselves. Consider the mechanism of the manuscript auction, whereby a literary agent auctions off the rights to an author's work usually to the highest bidder among the publishing houses — not unlike one of Sotheby's auctions of fine art and cultural icons. To get the potential blockbuster that every other publisher wants, the winner often sinks hundreds of thousands, sometimes millions, of dollars in advances and makes costly commitments to the author regarding marketing and promotions and costly concessions to the agent as to which intellectual property rights the winner can actually exploit. This buying behavior underscores the commercial publishers' lack of **unique** value-adding services and author support. We might forgive publishers for obsessing over all the aspects of their business that digitization affects, such as production, sales, marketing, distribution and the other activities that puts a manuscript into a consumer's hands. But we cannot forgive their neglecting to cultivate author talent and to hone their own editorial expertise in guiding authors through the dis-integration of the book as a discrete format, so as to become sought after and known for their superior author services. Institutional shareholders have been unforgiving as well, putting intense pressure on publicly-owned publishers "to increase shareholder value", as Wall Street investors frequently say, or at least to generate a profit greater than what the owners would get if they invested their money in an interest-bearing bank account instead. There are few substantial distinctions among their contracts and P&L statements. And so, from an author's viewpoint, the primary point of differentiation among commercial publishers is the level of advance that they are willing to pay.

Consider this not-so-weak signal: at the end of August 2010, Seth Godin, author of the best-selling business book *Purple Cow* and eight others all published by Portfolio, an imprint of Penguin-Pearson PLC, announced that he will begin publishing and selling his own books. [15] Mr. Godin is an entrepreneur: ten years ago, he founded **Squidoo**, a free online publishing platform that he uses to inform his fans of his travel plans and speaking engagements. He already creates and manages digital marketing campaigns for his books, and he once packaged books for others.[16] Going forward, Mr. Godin will hire his own editor to ensure the quality of his manuscripts, and he will leverage social media to promote and possibly to sell digital versions of his books. He can do so because his weblog ("blog") attracts an estimated over 438,000 people. Over 67,000 people have befriended him on Facebook, and over 43,000 people follow him on Twitter. That means that he has a direct relationship with nearly half a million potential book buyers. Clearly, this author needs neither a traditional publisher nor its value chain.[17]

4　The Groundswell of Personal Publishing, Promotion & Consumption

From a consumer's standpoint, there is little distinction among publishers as well: readers rarely pay attention to which publisher's brand occupies the spine of their favorite book. They focus instead on the author if they want fiction, and on the subject matter if they want non-fiction.[18] That segues nicely into what Charlene Li and Josh Bernoff of the independent research company, Forrester Research, call a groundswell. The dictionary definition of groundswell is "an obvious change of public [support or action] that occurs without leadership or overt expression"[19] which Li and Bernoff attribute to the rapid mass adoption of social media such as Facebook.com and Twitter.com. It derives some of its force from the principle that information goods are what economists call experienced goods with a social life: you must experience them to determine their utility, and thus their value, to you. To some extent, all new products and services are experienced goods; you really do not know whether you will prefer the Apple iPhone 4 over Huawei Technologies' Ideos smartphone until you try them. To help consumers make decisions under uncertainty, anyone in the business of experienced goods has historically provided "free samples" or "trial runs" so that prospective buyers could experience them and determine their value before buying.

But the actual product or service is its own best marketing. If you value the experience, then you tell your friends. If you hate the experience, you still tell your friends. Who cares what the publisher says about a book? Or about its editorial staff? And so I expand the definition of groundswell to include the obvious change of the mass public's buying, selling, creating and collaborating behavior, evidenced by the growth of peer-to-peer and business-to-business commerce sites such as Mǎ Yún's Alibaba.com; the upsurge of massively multiplayer online role-playing games (MMORPGs) such as Blizzard Entertainment Company's World of Warcraft, which enables an estimated 11.5 million players, half of whom come from Asia, to engage each other virtually;[20] and the proliferation of "personal publishing" platforms such as Blogger.com and Wordpress.com, "self-publishing" services such Author Solutions, Inc, and various academic consortia on open innovation, defined as "the use of purposive inflows and outflows of knowledge to accelerate innovation",[21] such as the Open Publishing Lab, "a cross disciplinary center, based in the Rochester Institute of Technology's School of Print Media, that focuses on researching new methods of content creation and developing innovative applications to publish across various media".[22] Large social networks benefit from positive feedback loops: the strong gets stronger, partly because consumers value widely-used technology.[23]

5　The Infrastructure of Information

That leads us to **infrastructuring**, which derives its force from the economic principle, that all **content** (information, text, video, audio and software) requires an **infrastructure** (electronic hardware and communications services) in order to be consumed. Content and infrastructure "are inexorably linked", Dr. Shapiro and Varian remind us. All software needs hardware. [24] Acting upon that intelligence has made technology companies like Amazon. com and The Apple Company dominant players in publishing. Referring to the iPad, author and management guru Gary Hamel wrote, " 'Old media' had 10 plus years to figure out the whole ' [electronic] ' thing — and mostly failed. Now it [is] Steve Jobs' turn. That [is] (mostly) a good thing...But still, you [have] to feel sorry for the incumbents. " [25] The inaction of the retail brands, Barnes & Noble and Borders, has weakened their market value: digital commodities do not require retail real estate. The infrastructure, on the other hand, requires land for housing the data centers and computer servers that underpin the knowledge economy. Perhaps publishers and book chains should instead convert their retail space and warehouses into technology training facilities and server farms, that is, large collections of computer servers maintained under one large roof? (No, not yet: Borders recently announced that it will open Build-a-Bear Workshops within select Borders stores, where books will supplement the experience of customizing one's own stuffed animal.) [26]

One business publisher who understood very early that information and infrastructure go hand in hand is Michael Bloomberg, founder of Bloomberg LP, a source of financial information goods for professionals. The Bloomberg news organization consists of "2,300 news and multimedia professionals at 146 bureaus in 72 countries", the news production of which Bloomberg can reproduce across its network of print, radio, television and digital media formats. Bloomberg combines proprietary hardware, software, information technology services, enterprise solutions and customer support. Its hardware, fondly dubbed "The Bloomie" terminal, brings the experience of stock exchange trading floor to the desktop, and runs Launchpad 2010, Bloomberg's "real-time platform for news, security monitors, charting, technical analysis and connecting with peers in the industry". In specially designed training facilities at its headquarters in New York City, "Bloomberg University" maintains a curriculum of workshops free to Bloomie subscribers, employees and student interns on how to use its hardware and software features and functions. It already has a strong presence in business schools, seeding its future market, and many campuses offer special courses or library assistance in learning to use The Bloomie. Expanding on its community, Bloomberg will be producing "invitation-only, in-person gatherings that combine world-class editorial programming with peer-to-peer networking".

The breadth and the depth of its business content and its interface's capabilities enable it to serve a variety of individual, professional and corporate clients with different bundles of goods and services, ranging from "free to the public" to premium pricing. [27] Few business publishers have the IT innovation capabilities to replicate the quality, complexity and sophistication of

Bloomberg's infrastructure: customer lock-in is high — there are approximately 287,500 sites that subscribe to Bloomberg Professional, [28] and their costs of switching from The Bloomie to another information system would be high. McGraw-Hill recently sold its flagship *Business Week* magazine to Michael Bloomberg's eponymous company, just as Bloomberg was selling its entire business book list to John Wiley, a publisher of scientific, trade, professional and educational books and ancillaries. [29]

And so now, when writing book proposals, negotiating publishing contracts and making publishing decisions, we must think in terms of developing an **information system**, that provides expertise, accommodates flexibility, functionality and connectivity, and results in both Copyright and Invention. [30]

6   The Globalization of the Market for Ideas

Next, let us factor in the **globalization** of the markets for capital, customers, labor and information. Globalizing services, manufacturing and operations has added some two billion people to the workforce and enables firms to hire, compete with and sell content and advisory services to anyone in the world. After the dot. com boom and bust of 2000 — 2001 and the growing shortage of skilled workers due in part to personnel retirement, western companies raced to rationalize production, most evidently by moving manufacturing to China, services to India and research to both of those countries. [31] Given the pace at which developing countries can expand the knowledge sector of their economy, the global need for business content will increase, particularly in China. I have heard publishing executives complain that they cannot recoup their investment, let alone make a profit, in markets that lack a fully developed and enforced intellectual property rights system. But, as Professor Hamel pointed out, mainstream incumbent publishers are not innovating as well as technology companies in markets that do have such a system.

Zhao Shuming of Nanjing University's School of Business describes China's remarkable progress, "The dominant industry of the whole society is being transformed from resources- and energy-consumption-based to knowledge- and intellectual-based." [32] According to Zhao, "During the past decade, China has placed more importance on reforming and modernizing its information and communication technology (ICT) sector than any other developing country…China's Ministry of Information Industries predicts that the ICT industry will continue to grow about 20% annually, or around three times the growth rate of [China's gross domestic product]." [33] What is more, "the current leadership under President Hu Jintao and Premier Wen Jiabao continues to devote massive material and political resources to what it called 'informatization' as a key strategic element for advancing [national] goals." Between now and 2014, industry analysts expect the Chinese publishing market to grow by 18.6%, whereas the United States publishing market is expected to increase by only 6.3%. [34]

Equally important, these developing knowledge economies will become rich sources of new and different business content. Managers in the U. S. will appreciate the practical stories of Chinese executives who are creating value outside state-owned enterprise, and the experiences of entrepreneurs such as Cài Wénshēng, a "top angel investor in the Internet business…an influential blogger with more than 850,000 followers on sina. com's Twitter-like service, and a sought-after speaker at industry conferences". [35] He recognizes that "mimicking is a necessary learning process"; imitation can lead to innovation. Chinese "start-ups can continue to make money out of copying U. S. product model…But to succeed in the long term, they [must] need to innovate to give them a broad appeal to the Chinese masses" and to build world-class brands. [36] How they innovate and build world-class brands will be of immense interest to managers around the world.

7 The Fiercening of Capitalism

Finally, let us factor in what Walter Kiechel, the former editor-in-chief of *Fortune* magazine, describes as "the **fiercening of capitalism**", where fame and fortune flow to those folks who have the best ideas, "almost always ideas sharp with a purpose, namely, to solve a problem bedeviling a company". [37] (I myself do not think that getting paid for solving problems is exclusive to capitalism.) Mr. Kiechel was talking specifically about the business of management consulting, dominated by such partnerships as McKinsey & Company, Bain & Company, and the Boston Consulting Group. In Mr. Kiechel's critically acclaimed new book, *The Lords of Strategy*, the publishing process becomes critical to communicating, socializing and realizing these ideas in business. That is why many consulting firms publish their own periodicals aimed at corporate clients, such as the McKinsey Quarterly and Booz & Company's *Strategy + Business*. That is also why large technology companies have internal publishing organizations: IBM Inc. publishes its Redbooks, and Microsoft Inc. has its Press. And that is why information-rich organizations such as Gallup Inc. and American Express Inc. have grown their publishing programs significantly in recent years. They are using the publishing process not simply to educate customers but also to capture organizational knowledge.

That, in my opinion, is what made Harvard Business School Publishing so successful. For those of you who are not familiar with the organization, please allow me to give you a brief overview. First, Harvard serves three distinct but complementary sets of customers — business educators, corporate training professionals, and individual managers, in both consumer and business-to-business markets. Second, it is what Professor Clayton M. Christensen, author of the seminal business book The Innovator's Dilemma, calls a purpose brand, a brand that is "tightly associated with the job" that customers are hiring it to do. [38] The job that its customers hire it to do, its "idea sharp with purpose", is "to improve the practice of management worldwide". Third, to serve its customers, Harvard publishes content in at least five formats: academic case studies, articles in the journal *Harvard Business Review*, chapters in books, weblogs on its website, and interactive training and development ("T&D") tools, all of which can be distributed and consumed in print or on a digital device such as Apple's iPad or Amazon's Kindle. In response to globalization, it opened its first international office in Mumbai, India, in 2009.

Finally, even though Harvard considers itself a trade publisher, its editorial process is more rigorous than that of commercial business presses. As an executive editor there, I put each manuscript through editorial development, peer review, editorial board review and manuscript revision. I also screened authors carefully, not just for their ability to sell their own books but also for their knowledge of business history and their ability to teach me something new; and I judged each manuscript's sales potential as well as its place in the business literature. Where did the idea originate? How did it build upon its predecessors? What research or practical experience informed the author's argument? What were the key findings? Could I develop it for multiple audiences, formats and platforms? How well would it **backlist**? That is, what was the idea's shelf-life? Above all, how would it improve the practice of management worldwide?

Consultants, academics and corporate executives who wanted to be taken seriously for their ideas and their expertise, valued such high standards and specific criteria. As more of the global economy shifts to knowledge-based enterprise, the demand for this capability will grow. When asked, "Which…areas of activity offer the greatest potential for productivity gains over the next 15 years?" 43% of the 1,600 CEOs and managers surveyed identified **knowledge management** as the activity with the most promise. [39] Dr. Zhao of Nanjing University concurs, "How to apply existing knowledge to create sustainable competitive advantages is the new challenge faced by corporations…[They] will need to provide value-added service for more diversified customers, which requires them to have stronger capabilities in communication, knowledge acquisition, knowledge creation and knowledge transmission" [40] — the very skills of the best business editors, journalists and academic authors.

But, within corporations, the process of generating, coordinating, codifying, transferring and applying knowledge in business contexts, perhaps internally at first, and then commercializing and going to market publicly with it, must remain more impartial and rigorous than those used by the marketing department to generate customer brochures or by the human resources department to produce employee newsletters. I see it as a complement to the research and development department and as a source of content for marketing and HR. Which publishers are better prepared to begin offering such editorial services to corporations, independent of their commercial operations? I think that John Wiley, Elsevier BV and the University of Chicago Press, to name a few, have established their expertise through their high-ranking refereed publications: they understand how to administer editorial and licensing processes according to professional standards, not just to market tastes.

As so I leave you with a question: **what is the job that your customers are hiring you to do**? Remember that readers are hiring you for one job, authors are hiring you for another, and whoever pays your salary, for yet another. Remember that their needs are changing, thanks to the forces of digitization, commoditization, the groundswell, infrastructuring, globalization and the fiercening of capital. And remember that the tools that you use right now to make decisions may be blinding you to coming opportunities. Will you compete on technological innovation, providing customers with tools and applications? Or will you compete on the innovation of expertise, providing customers with services for capturing what they know? Or some combination of content and infrastructure?

We must conduct more research on the relationship between the publishing industry and the knowledge management of organizations, on the nature of publishing relative to other formal knowledge management systems that are already used within corporations, and on the deployment of trained editors and authors in non-publishing industries. You have an opportunity to expand your role not just as purveyors of educational products but as providers of services that capture organizational learning. Thank you for allowing me to share these ideas and for listening so patiently to me. Thank you again, my hosts and colleagues, for this opportunity to speak. I welcome your questions and comments.

Notes

[1] Richard A. Bettis and C. K. Prahalad, *The Dominant Logic: A New Linkage between Diversity and Performance*, Strategic Management Journal, Vol. 7, No. 6 (Nov. -Dec. , 1986). Pages 485–501.

[2] C. K. Prahalad, *Change Your Dominant Logic, and Change the World: A Humble Call to Action*. Working proposal. Revised 11 May 2009.

[3] Ibid.

[4] C. K. Prahalad, *Weak Signals Versus Strong Paradigms*, Journal of Marketing Research, Vol. XXXII (August 1995), Page 3.

[5] Jim Milliot, *Chains, Fiction, Paperback Ruled in* 2009: *New Bowker Study Finds Bookstore Chains Sold the Most Books Last Year*. Publishers Weekly 257. 32 (2010): 3+. Expanded Academic ASAP Web. 12 Sept . 2010.

[6] *AAP June sales report*. Publishers Weekly 257. 34 (2010): 6. Expanded Academic ASAP Web. 12 Sept. 2010.

[7] Verso Digital, 2010 *Survey of Book-Buying Behavior*, presented at American Booksellers Association Annual Book Exposition America, May 2010. http://www. versoadvertising. com/beasurvey/.

[8] "IP is divided into two categories: Industrial property, which includes inventions (patents), trademarks, industrial designs, and geographic indications of source; and Copyright, which includes literary and artistic works such as novels, poems and plays, films, musical works, artistic works such as drawings, paintings, photographs and sculptures, and architectural designs. " World Intellectual Property Organization (WIPO) is a specialized agency of the United Nations. http://www. wipo. int/about-ip/en/. Accessed 10 Sept. 2010.

[9] In his article *From Competitive Advantage to Corporate Strategy*, Michael E. Porter grouped these into primary activities that include inbound logistics, operations, outbound logistics, marketing and sales, and after-sales services; and support activities that include facilities and systems, human resource management, technology development, and procurement. Boston, Massachusetts: Harvard Business Review, May-June 1987.

[10] Alexandra A. Seno, *Blockbuster from China*, Wall Street Journal Online, July 22, 2010.

www. wsj. com. Accessed August 18 ,2010.

[11] Carl Shapiro and Hal R. Varian, *Information Rules*: *A Strategic Guide to the Network Economy*. Boston: Harvard Business School Press, 1998. Page 24.

[12] In 1997, I had the great good fortune of acquiring the rights to this manuscript. Both authors are professors at the University of California at Berkeley. Carl Shapiro is currently on leave from his University post to serve in the Antitrust Division of the U. S. Department of Justice. Hal R. Varian is an emeritus professor and now Chief Economist of Google.

[13] Shapiro and Varian, *Information Rules*. Pages 2-3.

[14] Shapiro and Varian, *Information Rules*. Pages 2-3.

[15] Jeffrey A. Trachtenberg, *Author to Bypass Publisher for Fans*, Wall Street Journal, August 24, 2010. http://online. wsj. com/article/. Accessed August 24, 2010. Data on Seth Godin's Facebook page and Twitter account come from his pages on those sites, Facebook. com, and Twitter. com, accessed September 10, 2010.

[16] A book packager is a professional who assembles content for an author or a publisher or even a corporate brand such as American Express. I was considering Mr Godin's proposal to package American Express's Personal Income Tax Guide for HarperCollins.

[17] The great irony is that publishers would bid for manuscript as if it were high art, but be forced to sell it as an information commodity. We all know that buy high/sell low was never a sustainable investing strategy.

[18] Verso digital, *2010 Survey of book-buying Behavior*, presented at American Booksellers Association Annual Book Exposition America, May 2010.

[19] Definition attributed to *Webster's Revised Unabridged Dictionary* (1913) by the online dictionary, Die. net. http://dictionary. die. net/ground% 20 swell. Accessed September 10, 2010. The definitions found in *Webster's New World College Dictionary* (Cleveland, Ohio: Wiley Publishing, Inc. , 2010) and in The *American Heritage® Dictionary of the English Language*, 4th edition (Boston: Houghton Mifflin Harcourt Publishing Company, 2010) are comparable.

[20] Statistics from MmorpgRealm, an online source of gaming news, owned by 21st Century Gaming Entertainment. Inc.. www. mmorpgrealm. com. Accessed 12 Sept. 2010.

[21] Henry Chesbrough, Executive Director of the Center for Open Innovation, Adjunct Professor, Haas School of Business University of California, Berkeley, and author of the book, *Open Innovation*: *The New Imperative for Creating and Profiting from Technology* (Boston: Harvard Business School Press, 2002). Quotation is from the Center for Open Innovation's website http://openinnovation. haas. berkeley. edu/. Accessed 30 April 2010.

[22] http://opg. cias. rit. edu/about. Accessed 10 Sept. 2010.

[23] Shapiro and Varian, *Information Rules*. Page 224.

[24] Shapiro and Varian, *Information Rules*. Page 2.

[25] Gary Hamel, 48 *Hours With Apple's iPad Management* 2. 0: *A look at New Ways of Managing*. Wall Street Journal Blogs. http://blogs. wsj. com/. Accessed April 5 ,2010.

[26] http://www.borders.com. Accessed September 1,2010.

[27] All quotations sourced from www.bloomberg.com. Accessed September 10, 2010.

[28] *Bloomberg Set to Roll-out Launchpad 2010*, InvestmentNews, 2010. www.investmentnews.com. Accessed 12 Sept. 2010.

[29] *Bloomberg and Wiley Announce Exclusive Book Publishing Alliance*, Wiley press release. Hoboken, New Jersey: 12 March 2010.

[30] "Invention" refers to the other category of intellectual property, "Industrial property, which includes inventions (patents), trademarks, industrial designs, and geographic indications of source". World Intellectual Property Organization.

[31] John Houghton, *The Future of the Profession*, Information Outlook, June 2009. v13 i4. Page20 (4). Special Libraries Association. 2009.

[32] Zhao Shuming, *Application of Human Capital Theory in China in the Context of the Knowledge Economy*, The International Journal of Human Resource Management, Vol. 19, No. 5, May 2008. Page 802

[33] Ibid. Page 804.

[34] China's and the U.S. markets are expected to reach USD21.7 billion and USD 53.3 billion respectively by 2014, according to Datamonitor PLC, *Publishing Industry Profile: China* and *Publishing Industry Profile: United States*, both released in June 2010.

[35] Li Yuan, *China's Unlikely Internet Success Story*, 29 August 2010. Chinese edition of The Wall Street Journal Online. http://cn.wsj.com/gb/index.asp. Accessed English version 10 September 2010.

[36] Ibid.

[37] Walter Kiechel III, *The Lords of Strategy: The Secret Intellectual History of the New Corporate World*. Boston, Massachusetts: Harvard Business Press, April 2010. Page 11.

[38] Clayton M. Christensen, Scott Cook, and Taddy Hall. *Marketing Malpractice: The Cause and the Cure*. Harvard Business Review, Dec. 2005, Vol. 83 Issue 12. Page 79.

[39] Economist Intelligence Unit, *Foresight 2020 Survey of 1,600 CEOs and Managers*, 2006.

[40] Zhao Shuming, *Application of Human Capital Theory in China in the Context of the Knowledge Economy*, The International Joural of Human Resource Management, Vol. 19, No. 5, May 2008. Page 803.

For further reading

[i] Porter, Michael E., *Competitive Strategy: Techniques for Analyzing Industries and Competitors*, Free Press, New York, 1980.

[ii] Shapiro, Carl, and Hal R. Varian. *Information Rules: A Strategic Guide to the Network Economy*, Harvard Business School Press, Massachusetts, Boston, 1999.

[iii] Li, Charlene, and Bernoff, Josh, *Groundswell: Winning in a World Transformed by Social Technologies*, Harvard Business Press, Massachusetts, Boston, April 2008.

[iv] Chesbrough, Henry. *Open Innovation: The New Imperative for Creating and Profiting from*

Technology, Harvard Business School Press, Boston, 2002.

[ⅴ] Kiechel Ⅲ, Walter. *The Lords of Strategy*: *The Secret Intellectual History of the New Corporate World*, Harvard Business Press, Massachusetts, Boston, April 2010.

[ⅵ] Christensen, Clayton, and Johnson, Curtis W., and Horn, Michael B., *Disrupting Class*: *How Disruptive Innovation Will Change the Way the World Learns*, McGraw-Hill, New York, 2008.

[ⅶ] Davenport, Thomas H., and Prusak, Laurence, *Working Knowledge*: *How Organizations Manage What They Know*, Harvard Business School Press, Massachusetts, Boston, 1998.

[ⅷ] Nonaka, Ikujiro and Takeuchi, Hirotaka, *The Knowledge-Creating Company*: *How Japanese Companies Create the Dynamics of Innovation*, Oxford University Press, New York, 1995.

Author

Kirsten D. Sandberg, Adjunct faculty, MS in Publishing, Pace University, New York, kirstensandberg@ rocketmail. com.

作者简介

柯尔斯顿 D. 桑德伯格，美国佩斯大学出版系兼职教授，哈佛商学院出版社前高级编辑，kirstensandberg@ rocketmail. com。

Using the Kindle DX E-reader in the Classroom: Is It an Effective Teaching Tool?

Manuela Soares

(Pace University, New York)

外国专家

Abstract: This paper analyzes the Pace University experiment with Amazon—using the Kindle DX in a Pilot Program. Other universities also participated in the study, including Princeton, Case-Western and the University of Virginia. These schools gave out Kindle DX e-readers to selected faculty, who used them to teach a variety of graduate and undergraduate courses. Would the Kindle DX enhance the learning experience for students?

Keywords: Amazon Apple iPad Barnes and Noble Nook E-books Entourage edge E-readers Kindle DX Marketing Pace University Publishing Sony

在课堂上使用 Kindle 阅读器
——这是一个有效的教学工具吗？

曼维拉·苏亚雷斯

（佩斯大学　纽约）

摘要：本文分析了佩斯大学与亚马逊联合开展的一个使用 Kindle DX 的实验项目，普林斯顿大学、凯斯西储大学以及弗吉尼亚大学也参与了此项研究。这些学校给选定的教师提供了 Kindle DX，他们使用这些设备教授了多种研究生和本科生课程。Kindle DX 会提升学生的学习体验吗？

关键词：亚马逊　苹果 iPad　巴诺书店　电纸书　随从边缘　阅读器　Kindle 阅读器　市场营销　佩斯大学　出版　索尼

1　Introduction

A central question in education has always been — How can we help students learn? In the past, teachers and professors have used different media, including computers, overhead projection, video presentations, PowerPoint presentations and films to enhance the learning experience and stimulate students.

The answer to the question is more complex in the digital age as technology introduces many new and innovative hardware and software. We now ask ourselves: do the new digital technologies help or hinder the educational process?

Universities have long been the incubators of great ideas, making college campuses the perfect place for Amazon to experiment with its latest DX e-reader in 2009. At the time, Amazon's e-reader was just one of several e-readers available on the market, but the new DX was larger and had a larger screen, but it also had something that the others didn't — limited web browsing capability.

As e-book sales continued to rise, many in the industry have speculated that print books would become a thing of the past. The university setting, where students routinely carry heavy and expensive textbooks, seemed a logical place in which to work with a captive group of consumers.

In May of 2009, Pace University Provost Geoffrey Brackett partnered with Amazon and other universities in the Kindle DX Pilot Project to explore the possibilities of using the Kindle DX in the classroom.

An article in the May 7, 2009, *New York Times*, *Amazon Introduces Big Screen Kindle*, announced the new larger screen Kindle DX, "Speaking to a crowd of journalists, Amazon employees and business partners at Pace University in Manhattan, Jeffrey P. Bezos, Amazon's chief executive, said the new Kindle was a step in the direction of a long-dreamed-of 'paperless society'." (Stone, Rich, 2009)

The article also quoted Pace University's Provost at that time, Geoffrey Brackett:

"Geoffrey Brackett, the provost of Pace, said the university would distribute the new Kindles to about 50 students and compare them with 50 studying the same material using traditional textbooks, to see differences in how the two groups learn."

"Mr. Brackett said he expected the university to split the cost of the Kindles with Amazon but said whether the students would get the devices on loan or as a gift had not been determined." (Stone, Rich, 2009)

Shortly after the conference, the university invited faculty members from a range of disciplines, both graduate and undergraduate, to submit proposals for using the Kindle DX in the classroom. Four professors were ultimately chosen.

2　Participants

These four professors reflected the diversity and richness of the Pace graduate and undergraduate programs.

(1) Faculty

Graduate Nursing — Dr. Joanne Singleton (Lienhard School of Nursing)

Graduate Publishing — Professor Manuela Soares (Dyson College of Arts and Sciences)

Undergraduate Marketing — Dr. Karen Berger (Lubin School of Business)

Undergraduate Biology — Professor Erica Kipp (Dyson College of Arts and Sciences)

In preliminary discussions with the other faculty members in the Pilot Program, we all agreed that the Amazon Kindle could be an incredible asset to teaching. It seemed especially important in my own course — Marketing Principles and Practices (PUB 634) in the MS in Publishing Program. In the increasingly digital world of publishing, marketing strategies have been changing dramatically. Social media and social networking, blogging, podcasts, apps, widgets, downloads and other methods of utilizing digital technology and the Internet are common new marketing methods with yet unrealized potential. As a result, trade book publishers have had to radically alter their marketing methods in order to reach readers. The growing use of e-book readers, not just to read books, but to download magazines, newspapers and other printed matter, has been changing the ways in which publishers, agents and authors conduct their business.

(2) Students

Twenty students were selected at random to participate in the Marketing course in the MS in Publishing program. At the same time, two other sections of the course were being taught without the Kindle. The original intent was to use the same textbooks and course materials in all three of the Marketing classes and compare the results. However, the textbooks and methods by which these other courses were taught were different from my Kindle course, so there were no valid comparisons to be made between the courses, since there was no real control group. Would a control group have mattered? In this instance, probably not.

(3) Preparation

In anticipation of the fall semester, a Faculty Forum was held in Charlottesville, Virginia, at the University of Virginia's Darden School of Business on August 9 and 10, 2009. At the Forum, several professors from Pace, University of Virginia and Case-Western met with representatives from Amazon to review the Kindle DX and discuss our teaching methods.

Amazon made sure that as many of the e-textbooks as possible were downloaded to our Kindles prior to the conference. Most of the faculty had already received their Kindle DX before the Virginia conference so we could familiarize ourselves with the device.

Amazon provided information about navigating on the Kindle DX and promised dedicated staff to answer any and all questions from students and faculty during the pilot semester.

The general consensus of the faculty at the conference was that students would have immediate benefits from using the Kindle:

- A completely digital classroom
- Immediate access to relevant content
- Easy to transport textbooks to class
- An opportunity to be in the forefront of digital technology

As a professor, these were also benefits to me. My intention was to use the Kindle myself as I directed my students in its use for course projects in and out of the classroom. Another benefit to students was that Amazon would make all of the textbooks I had chosen for the Marketing course available for free. They included:

- *The Age of Engage: Reinventing Marketing for Today's Connected, Collaborative, and Hyperinteractive Culture* by Denise Shiffman

● *Publicize Your Book (Updated) : An Insider's Guide to Getting Your Book the Attention It Deserves* by Jacqueline Deval

These books were automatically uploaded onto the student Kindles prior to the start of the semester. A third textbook I had previously used and felt was important for the course was not originally available on the Kindle. However, as a result of our experiment, *The Complete Guide to Book Marketing* by David Cole, became available as an e-book and we were able to use it on the Kindle.

Students who had been chosen to participate in the Kindle Pilot Program were notified by an e-mail sent by their respective professors before the start of the fall semester . Students were also informed that they would have to sign an agreement that outlined that the Kindle was a loan for the semester and that it was to be returned at the end of the semester in December. Students had to agree that they were responsible for the device if lost, stolen or damaged. The cost of the Kindle DX at the time was a retail price of $489. However, defective Kindles would be replaced through the User Services Computer Labs. There was also an option to purchase the Kindle at the end of the term for a reduced cost to be determined later.

While the Marketing textbooks were uploaded onto the student Kindles for free, every student had to have an Amazon account prior to the start of the semester in order to access the books. However, if a student wanted to add any other (non-course-related) content to the Kindle, they had to purchase it themselves. Students were instructed on how to open an account.

Students could get the Kindle directly from Pace University's IT department at One Pace Plaza in Manhattan, or they could wait for the first class of the semester, when the IT department would distribute the Kindles to the students and answer any issues they might have regarding use of the device.

Just prior to the fall semester, on September 4, 2009, Pace University posted this explanation for the Kindle pilot on their website:

Why is Pace doing the Kindle DX pilot?

Digital readers are becoming more common with both faculty and students using them for personal reading. It is an obvious choice that we look to see if course material already in e-book format can be easily converted for successful teaching and learning. Users of digital readers cite the convenience, portability and large storage capacity as compelling reasons for their use in courses. With a Kindle DX, one can easily carry a year's worth or more of course readings in a lightweight device, can search for content, and can annotate, bookmark or highlight readings. Pace is excited to be part of this pilot which will help forecast the future use of the digital reader in higher education.

The general Pace student's reaction was positive:

Although I do not currently own a Kindle, I can see it being a great alternative to textbooks! I am very excited to see what the actual outcome will be.

great idea!

Looking forward to possibly working with a Kindle instead of 100 textbooks!

There were additional expectations about the Kindle as well. The cost of paper and the waste of paper has been an issue in institutions and businesses for some time. Many hoped that the e-readers would contribute significantly to saving paper costs.

"The Kindle DX (for "deluxe") is searchable and portable, a plus for students accustomed to toting heavy backpacks. But there is another reason that some institutions jumped at the chance to try it out: the technology could substantially reduce their use of paper. " (Peters, 2009)

3   Teaching methods

Incorporating the Kindle into the syllabus and exploring the new technology along with my students was a great opportunity for me to experiment with the latest e-reader and work with the largest book retailer in the U. S.

In addition to reading their textbooks on the Kindle DX, students were also assigned to download articles on a weekly basis from *Publisher's Weekly*, *The New York Times* and other publications with relevant material that I brought to their attention.

Students were instructed to bring their Kindles to class and to discuss the text they had highlighted or commented on in each week's reading.

Though the course was taught in the classroom, students also had access to a Blackboard site for the class. Blackboard is an online teaching platform used by Pace University and others, where assignments can be posted and students can participate in online Discussion Boards. A Discussion Board was created in Blackboard where students could post their experiences and questions about using the Kindle.

Students also browsed through the Amazon bookstore and used the Kindle's limited web capabilities.

In every class meeting, students had the opportunity to discuss using the Kindle to market trade books and to develop marketing plans that incorporated the growing use of e-books in today's consumer market. These in-class discussions were interesting and insightful, and having the Kindle in the classroom allowed students to work with the device in a group setting, which illustrated both the Kindle's advantages and limitations.

One consistent question from students was the publication dates for Kindle e-books. Would publishers allow e-books to be released simultaneously with the hardcover editions or delay them? Both strategies had been tried by publishers with varying results. At the time, publishers were delaying publication of the e-book by weeks and even months, hoping to protect the sale of the hardcover edition. However, it became increasingly clear as the semester progressed that the most popular strategy would have to be a simultaneous release, since publishers found that if e-books were not available along with the hardcover, pirated e-books soon appeared on the market. In fact, e-book piracy was already a major concern for publishers.

"It's exponentially up," said David Young, chief executive of Hachette Book Group, whose Little, Brown division publishes the "Twilight" series by Stephenie Meyer, a favorite among digital pirates. "Our legal department is spending an ever-increasing time policing sites where copyrighted material is being presented. " (Rich, 2009)

Students brought articles to class about e-books, e-book pricing and costs, e-book timing, and e-book bestsellers. They also researched publishing web sites to see what social media marketing was taking place and how, if at all, e-books were being promoted.

In addition to their reading, students had several guest speakers throughout the semester, including Rosa Perez, e-sales director at Routledge and Executive Editor Keith Kahla from St. Martin's Press. Students were also required to attend the first David Pecker lecture given by Michael Healy, Executive Director of the Book Rights Registry, who had recently been appointed David Pecker Visiting Distinguished Professor of Publishing at Pace University for the 2009 — 2010 academic year. As Executive Director of the Book Rights Registry, Mr. Healy will oversee the database organization for all digitalized works that are part of the Google settlement, once a final agreement has been reached.

Each of the guest speakers discussed the role of the e-book and how it affected the entire industry as well as their particular publishing companies and specific departments. It was clear from our guest speakers and from the weekly newspaper, magazine and journal articles that students were sharing that the use of e-readers and the sales of e-books were quickly becoming an important and integral part of the publishing landscape.

4 Evaluations

While students were happy to have three of their textbooks conveniently located in one relatively light device, they complained most often about the limitations of the note-taking and highlighting capabilities on the Kindle DX. In a regular print textbook, students were able to flip easily back and forth through the pages. The button navigation (a joystick or 5-way controller to move the cursor) on the Kindle DX made this harder to do. Most students also found it difficult to transfer data between the Kindle and their PC or Mac. Though they could annotate their Kindle notes and highlights on their computers, many complained that they had difficulty interfacing between the Kindle and their computers.

According to an article at UPI. com:

"Students at Pace and other schools have found it hard to find an electronic equivalent of highlighting text with yellow magic marker. Taking notes is more difficult, and students in class have a harder time finding the same portion of text for group discussion." (UPI, 2010)

Another problem was the absence of page numbers on the Kindle DX. Instead, there were "location" numbers listed at the bottom of the e-book page. Of course the reason for using location numbers instead of page numbers was clear — with variable type size capabilities, the amount of text on any given "page" would change. However, students found that instead of being able to use the book's index, they had to search the entire book for passages they wanted to reference.

An article in Inside Higher Ed quoted the experience of students at Case-Western:

"... in addition to grumbling about ' implementation of underlining, annotation, and bookmarking', [students] found it disorienting that the Kindle did not mark texts by page numbers in the same way as their bound counterparts, which made it difficult for them to follow along in class when professors kept instructing students to turn to a particular page. Their most frequent complaint, according to a summary provided to Inside Higher Ed, was that they could not "flip" randomly through pages of a text — echoing the comments of some Princeton students who missed the ability to easily "skim" texts. (Kolowich, 2010)

Another issue was the fact that although students had all three textbooks loaded onto their Kindles, they couldn't have all three open at once.

"The students also wanted it to be easier to navigate among annotated pages, and wished there was some way to impose a coding system for annotations, similar to how some students use differently colored highlighters to organize their annotations in bound books. Indeed, highlighting and note-taking went hand in hand with another feature students on multiple campuses considered important: navigation. Students did not like being unable to have multiple texts open at the same time." (Kolowich, 2010)

Many of these same problems were being experienced by the other schools in the Pilot Program. The University of Virginia's Darden School of Business also reported difficulties with the device. In a statement posted on the university's web site, Michael Koenig, Darden's director of MBA operations, said that while Amazon had "created a very well-designed consumer device for purchasing and reading digital books, magazines and newspapers. It's not yet ready for prime time in the highly engaged Darden business school classroom."

The Darden statement went on to say:

"The concern with the electronic reading devices is that they are too rigid for use in the fast-paced classrooms of the Darden School where the Socratic method and case-based pedagogy means students have to be nimble. 'You must be highly engaged in the classroom every day,' says Koenig, and the Kindle is 'not flexible enough…It could be clunky. You can't move between pages, documents, charts and graphs simply or easily enough compared to the paper alternatives.'"

Students also found the limited browser capability frustrating. It simply wasn't robust enough for students accustomed to accessing the internet through their computers. Added to this problem was the battery life of the Kindle. With the wifi disabled, students found that they didn't have to recharge very often. However, with the wifi capability on, the Kindle quickly lost battery power within a few days even when the device wasn't being used.

Another issue was the resale value of their e-book — which was nonexistent. Regular print editions, though often costly, could be sold at the end of a semester. Students investigated and found that e-books, even e-textbooks, were usually slightly less expensive than the print edition. However, there was no resale value to the e-book.

"…What does bother me about the Kindle's DRM is the fact that once you download a book, it is permanently bound to your Kindle account. The new Kindle lets you share the content if you own multiple units and Amazon says it will make Kindle content available on other devices. But what you cannot do is sell, trade or give away the book when you are done with it." (Wildstrom,

2009)

While students recognized that e-books were changing the publishing world daily, they still found print editions easier to use. While they appreciated the free aspects of the Kindle DX-free chapter downloads, limited free access to books in advance (as part of a book promotion), and the many free public domain books available, they were still reluctant to give up their print editions. The general consensus was that while the e-reader was more convenient, they still preferred print. Yet, they also argued about the convenience of having so many books available in one device and ultimately, could agree that for entertainment purposes, the e-reader had merit.

Several students in the class worked for trade publishers and had been given a Sony e-reader by their companies. These students reported that though smaller, the Sony e-reader was more convenient to use in terms of downloading Word documents and content other than e-books.

Twice during the semester students were asked to respond to a questionnaire and evaluate their experience with the Kindle DX. Amazon correlated the data and produced an analysis of the results.

When the device was first announced the previous May, some industry pundits had already predicted the failure of the Kindle DX to capture the college market:

"Amazon announced its most recent Kindle device this week: the Kindle DX. Though it's almost identical to the original Kindle, this newer model is marketed for use with textbooks and for reading periodicals. While this seems to give the impression that Amazon has presented a more practical solution for college students, it's likely that the everyday pupil will reject this new device." (Vaknin, 2009)

In an article in The Arizona Republic, Amazon responded to the criticism of the Kindle DX:

"Amazon spokeswoman Stephanie Mantello said in an e-mail that the pilot programs have been effective in gathering feedback. The company is always looking at ways to improve the student experience, she said." (Ryman, 2010)

At the end of the semester, students were offered the opportunity to purchase their Kindles at roughly half of the retail price. Two students out of the twenty in the class took advantage of the offer.

5 Conclusion

Was the Kindle DX Pilot Program a failure? Students clearly found that the Kindle DX was too expensive and did not provide enough convenience for the price.

So are all e-readers unsuitable for a university environment? Developing an e-reading device for students is a goal for many companies. Students would benefit from a device that allowed them to carry multiple heavy textbooks in one handy device and also connect them to the Internet, allow them to take notes and to upload and download files with ease.

That brings us to the most important question — What type of device would be best suited for university students and professors?

In January 2010, just a month after our Pilot Project with the Kindle was completed, Apple

Chief Executive Steve Jobs announced the upcoming release of the new Apple iPad. In April 2010, the new iPad was released and was an instant success with consumers even with a high ticket price. Apple sold over 3 million of the devices in 80 days (Hansen, 2009). This next generation of e-reader appeared to have much more appeal for consumers.

Unlike the Sony e-reader, the Kindle and the Barnes and Noble Nook, the iPad does not use e-ink technology, which means that it is harder to use in direct sunlight. While e-ink may be easier to read in bright sunlight, it limits any color capability and allows only gray scale, which for reading straight text, is usually fine. The Nook overcomes this limitation by adding a smaller color screen to their e-ink e-reader so readers can view graphics and book covers.

Another interesting difference between all of these devices is their compatibility with libraries. The New York Public Library makes e-books available to patrons through the Internet. The e-Pub and PDF e-books that the library uses work with most computers and with the Sony e-reader, Barnes and Noble Nook and several other devices, but are not compatible with the Amazon Kindle, Kindle DX and iPad.

The iPad combines many of the features of smart phones and tablet computers into one device. It allows users to read e-books and e-zines, watch videos, play games, take notes, surf the Web, and much more in full four-color on an almost 10-inch (9.7 inch) screen. While it may have problems in direct sunlight, like a computer, it's easily read without any other light source.

The iPad has some of the same features as the Kindle DX including screen size (9.7 inches). The iPad and the Kindle DX allow for rotating the screen for either horizontal or vertical reading. The biggest difference is the LED-backlit screen for the iPad, which Kindle uses in ads for their device, showing two readers, one with a Kindle, reading easily in bright sunlight-and the other reader with an "unknown" device, not being able to do so.

The iPad is also able to show "enhanced" books, i.e., e-books with embedded video and audio and images, which gives it a distinct advantage over the Kindle DX, which can only show static text and image. And there are also over 1,000 Apps that have been developed for the iPad.

The other major difference is in the keyboard. The Kindle uses a button keyboard with small raised keys, while the iPad uses a pop-up screen keyboard with larger keys.

The cost of an e-reader ranges widely depending on the size of the device, memory and capabilities. The Kindle has several versions with retail prices of $139 for the basic version to $389 for the DX. Sony has three e-reading devices that range in price from $179 (Pocket) to $229 (Touch), and the Barnes and Noble Nook ranges from $149 to $199, depending on the features. The Apple iPad is much more expensive, starting at $499 for the 16 GB version and rising to a whopping $699 for the 64 GB edition.

So which device will be most appealing to students? The four-color capability of the iPad, the integration of audio and video, and the tablet components included in the device make it an appealing tool for college use, even with the high retail price.

Several universities, Pace included, began using the iPad in the Fall 2010 semester. The

Chronicle of Higher Education reported that Reed College (one of the Kindle Pilot schools) as well as the University of Maryland and North Carolina State would be "test-driving" the new iPads.

"We are going to—to the extent that we can—make the iPad study as parallel to the Kindle DX study as possible," said Martin D. Ringle, chief technology officer at Reed College, in an interview. "If I were to predict, I would say that the results are going to be dramatically different and much better—and they're going to point the way to what role this technology is going to play in higher education." (Young, 2010)

However, the iPad is not the only device that incorporates these features. There are other e-readers currently being marketed that will compete with both the Kindle DX and the Apple iPad.

One e-reader that stands out and that was developed specifically for college use was released in early 2010 — the Entourage Edge. Combining attributes of both a tablet PC and an e-reader, this hybrid reader uses e-ink, yet also has four-color capability. This combination or "hardware mash-up" of e-reader and laptop has great appeal in the college market.

Although the Edge has the same size screen as the DX and iPad, it weighs considerably more (3 pounds versus 1.5 pounds for the iPad and 1.11 pounds for the DX), no doubt as a result of having a tablet computer as well. Prices for the Edge are comparable ($549). Yet the tablet computer adds a considerable advantage—two devices in one. This trend will most likely continue, since it provides users with benefits from two devices into one portable package.

"Coupling screens together so that we can thumb through textbooks alongside live commentary on the Web is only the beginning." (Zimbalist, 2010)

One major issue for using e-readers at colleges and universities is the availability of content. Software developers are working with publishers such as McGraw-Hill and Houghton-Mifflin to create textbooks that work with a variety of devices (Trachtenberg, 2010).

This key element is the future of e-books and e-readers on campus. A new company, Inkling, is working on creating a more interactive textbook (Bilton, 2010). According to their website:

"Inkling titles are redesigned to take advantage of the power of mobile devices like iPad."

"Unlike a traditional book, they're dynamic, social, interactive and easy to carry around. Our list of titles continues to grow every semester, so if you don't see your book featured, we're probably working on it."

Working with Apple, this new company is creating new applications that will enable students to:

• Interact with other students (and professors) by sharing and commenting on specific sections of text and allowing other students to add their own comments.

• Take interactive quizzes embedded in the text.

• View certain graphics as 3-D images, from any angle.

The ability to search text, change the size of the type and highlight text can be done on the

Kindle DX and the iPad. However, Inkling adds another dimension to their downloads—the ability to purchase individual chapters.

In Fall 2010, the University of Alabama and Seton Hill University began using the Inkling textbook app. The founder and chief executive of Inkling said in an interview that "the company wants to offer a textbook experience that moves far beyond simply downloading a PDF document to an iPad." He added that "Professors are really excited about the ability to leave notes for the class in specific areas of the book and to also see commentary from their students." (Bolton, 2010)

The cost factor of the e-reader remains an issue for most college students. If the costs for textbooks in a typical year are roughly $1,000 for students, then adding a $500 device could be prohibitive—depending on the retail price of the textbooks in the e-book format. If the cost of a digital book is less than the print edition, then owning an e-reader might make financial sense, especially if students can purchase one chapter of a book at a time.

So what device is best suited to the university student and professor? As mentioned earlier, a device that allows students to upload and download files with ease, that connects them to the Internet, that allows for robust interactivity with their books, and is multi-purpose—a device that can handle audio, video, as well as social networking, games and web browsing.

Some of these capabilities already exist in today's e-readers, but like a lot of technology, innovation is a daily occurrence. The e-readers of the future will be better, as will the e-textbooks available for these devices. Prices should also be cheaper as more and more companies compete for this market and as the development costs are amortized. Another factor will be how future students embrace the new technology. According to a new study by Scholastic:

About 25% of the children surveyed said they had already read a book on a digital device, including computers and e-readers. 57% between ages 9 and 17 said they were interested in doing so.

Only 6% of parents surveyed owned an e-reader, but 16% said they planned to buy one in the next year. 83% of those parents said they would allow or encourage their children to use the e-readers. (Bosman, 2010)

Although we have seen the future and it is digital, another finding in the Scholastic study was interesting:

"Many children want to read books on digital devices and would read for fun more frequently if they could obtain e-books. But even if they had that access, two-thirds of them would not want to give up their traditional print books."

Perhaps these two formats will be able to coexist comfortably in the future, but it is a certainty that the move to e-readers has only just begun. It is my firm belief that print will continue to fascinate and engage readers, but the benefits for students, teachers, parents and general consumers of having one digital device that is easy to use, lightweight and versatile is too compelling to ignore. Which device a consumer chooses will depend on the user's preferences and requirements. The Kindle DX may not have fared well in the Pilot Program, but it heralded a new age of e-reader in the college market.

Selected bibliography

[1] Bilton, Nick. Replacing a Pile of Textbooks With an iPad. New York Times, August 23, 2010. http://bits. blogs. nytimes. com/2010/08/23/replacing-a-pile-of-textbook-with-an-ipad/.

[2] Bosman, Julie. In Study, Children Cite Appeal of Digital Reading. New York Times, September 29, 2010. http://www. nytimes. com/2010/09/29/books/29kids. html.

[3] Hansen, Kristena. Apple Sells 3 Million iPads in First 80 Days. Los Angeles Times, June 22, 2010. http://articles. latimes. com/2010/jun/22/business/la-fi-ipad-20100623.

[4] Kolowich, Steve. Highlighting E-Readers. Inside Higher Ed, February 23, 2010. http://www. insidehighered. com/news/2010/02/23/ereaders.

[5] Paul, Ian. Interactive Textbooks Headed to iPad, Report Says. PCWorld, February 3, 2010, http://www. pcworld. com/article/188427/interactive _ textbooks _ headed _ to _ ipad _ report_says. html.

[6] Peters, Sara. Universities Turn to Kindle — Sometimes to Save Paper. New York Times, July 30, 2009. http://green. blogs. nytimes. com/2009/07/30/universities-turn-to-kindle-sometimes-to-save-paper/.

[7] Rich, Motoko. Print Books Are Target of Pirates on the Web. New York Times, May 12, 2009, http://www. nytimes. com/2009/05/12/technology/internet/12digital. html? _ r = 2&partner = rss&emc = rss.

[8] Ryman, Anne. Profs: Kindle No Threat to College Textbooks. The Arizona Republic, July 6, 2010. http://www. azcentral. com/business/articles/2010/07/06/20100706amazon – kindle-school-textbooks. html.

[9] Stone, Brad and Rich, Motoko. Amazon Introduces Big–Screen Kindle. New York Times, May 7, 2009.

[10] Trachtenberg, Jeffrey and Kane, Yukari Iwatani. Textbook Firms Ink E-Deals for iPad. Wall St. Journal, February 2, 2010. http://online. wsj. com/article/SB1000142405274870 3338504575041630390346178. html.

[11] UPI. com. Kindle Not Ready for Campus? July 6, 2010. http://www. upi. com/Top_News/US/2010/07/06/Kindle-not-ready-for-campus/UPI-44741278442364/.

[12] Vaknin, Sharon. E-textbooks vs. Kindle DX: What Will College Kids Pick? CNET News, May 8, 2009. http://news. cnet. com/8301-17938_105-10235937 – 1. html.

[13] Wildstrom, Stephen. How Do I Sell My eBook: Kindle, Rights Management, and First Sale. Bloomberg Business Week, February 11, 2009. http://www. businessweek. com/the_thread/techbeat/archives/2009/02/hwo_do_i_sell_m. html.

[14] Young, Jeff. Kindle Failed Tests at Several Colleges. Will iPads Do Better? The Chronicle of Higher Education, April 19, 2010. http://chronicle. com/blogPost/Kindle-Failed-Tests-at-Several/23253/? sid = wc&utm_source = wc&utm_medium = en.

[15] Yun, Wonpyo. U. releases Kindle Pilot Data. The Daily Princetonian, February 22, 2010. http://www. dailyprincetonian. com/2010/02/22/25262/ .

[16] Zimbalist, Michael. Imagining a World of Hardware Mashups. New York Times, February 8, 2010. http://bits. blogs. nytimes. com/2010/02/08/imagining-a-world-of-hardware-mashups/? scp = 2 & sq = entourage% 20edge&st = Search.

Author

A full-time faculty member at Pace University's MS in Publishing Program since 2004, Manuela Soares has worked in both magazine and book publishing. Most recently she was the Managing Editor for the Scholastic Trade Book Group (overseeing the hardcover imprints, including the first five Harry Potter books) and previously she was a Senior Editor at Rizzoli. Her published works include a story in the anthology Teen Flash, to be published by Persea Books in 2011, as well as *The Joy Within-A Beginner's Guide to Meditation* with Joan Goldstein (Simon & Schuster), *One Hand Clapping-Zen Stories for All Ages* with Rafe Martin (Rizzoli), *Butch/Femme* (Crown Publishing), *A Reading Guide to a Wrinkle in Time* (Scholastic Bookfiles), *Heart Throbs: The Best of DC Romance Comics* (pseudonym Naomi Scott, Fireside Books), *ESP McGee and the Dolphin's Message* (pseudonym Jesse Rodgers, Avon Books), etc.

作者简介

曼维拉·苏亚雷斯，美国佩斯大学出版学系教授。

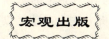

图书定价的经济学分析

陈 昕

（上海世纪出版集团 上海 200001）

摘要：本文运用现代经济学的理论和方法对图书商品的属性进行分析，并深入探究其价格形成的内在机制。本文指出图书商品具有低价格弹性、高收入弹性和正外部性等经济属性；在分析图书市场基本特征的基础上，采用相应的定价模型对图书定价策略进行综合分析；认为图书市场存在一定的垄断性，三级价格歧视和跨期价格递减是图书市场的基本定价机制，图书市场容易出现生产过剩。本文还论述了欧美国家的图书定价模式及其对我国的借鉴意义。

关键词：图书定价 需求弹性 外部性 定价机制 定价模型

Economic Analysis of Books-pricing

Chen Xin

（Shanghai Century Publishing Group，Shanghai，200001）

Abstract：With the theories and methods in modern economics，this article analyses the intrinsic attributes of books and lucubrates in the mechanism of book- pricing. As a commodity，the price elasticity of books is low，while the income elasticity is high，and books generate positive externalities. Based on the analysis of book market's basic characters，this article also uses corresponding price model to analyze the book-pricing strategy comprehensively. The consideration is that the book market is monopolistic；third-degree price discrimination and calendar-spread price digression are the basic book-pricing mechanism；overproduction of book market is common. At last，there is a brief introduction of American and European book-pricing model and its reference value for China.

Keywords：Book-pricing Elasticity of demand Externality Mechanism Models

　　现代经济学告诉我们，价格是其研究的核心问题，所有经济规律的后面都有价格规律在发挥作用，纷繁复杂的经济现象背后的运行机制、规律和法则都会直接或间接地反映在价格变化上。本文将从图书价格这一最显性的现象入手，运用相关的经济学理论和方法，对图书商品的内在属性进行分析，并深入探究其价格形成的内在机制。

　　在研究图书价格时，特别要分清的是经济学分析方法和社会学分析方法的区别。社会学更多的是以问卷调查的主观感受（比如读者是否普遍感到书价很高）作为立论的依据并展开相应的分析。经济学中关于商品价格的分析则是以供给—需求分析方法为基础，以实际价格和均衡价格的偏离度作为衡量价格的标准尺度。而商品的经济属性又是其价格波动的基础，各种因素总是通过供求关系的变动对商品的价格水平发生作用，不同经济属性的商品，其对同样的供求关系变动的反应程度是不同的。因此，本研究报告把图书商品经济属性的分析作为图书定价问题研究的起点。

1 图书商品的经济属性分析

商品的经济属性可以用弹性指标进行具体量化，该指标能够对商品价格、收入与需求关系进行一般性的描述。图书的需求价格弹性直接影响出版厂商的定价决策，图书的收入弹性则直接反映消费者对图书商品的非必需性需求。而更为重要的是，图书作为"传达思想和文化的工具"，具有与其他商品不同的特殊属性，在赋予图书较强垄断性的同时，也显示出其信息产品的特性，以及较强的正外部性。

1.1 性质1：图书是低价格弹性商品

在经济学中，商品需求的价格弹性是指在其他商品价格不变、收入也不变的条件下，某一商品价格变动百分之一而引起的该商品需求量变动的百分比。价格弹性反映的是商品的需求量对价格变动的敏感程度，弹性越大，则需求量对价格的变化越敏感，反之则越迟钝。价格弹性对商品定价有重要的影响，如果商品的价格弹性较高，则厂商更倾向于采取低价策略，因为此时商品需求量增加的幅度将超过价格下降的幅度，从而提高厂商的收入。表1给出了不同需求价格弹性下厂商的定价决策。

表1 需求的价格弹性（E）和销售收入

弹性 价格决策	E>1	E=1	E<1	E=0	E=∞
降价	收入增加	收入不变	收入减少	同比例于价格的下降而减少	既定的价格下，收益可以无限增加，厂商不会降价
涨价	收入减少	收入不变	收入增加	同比例于价格的上升而增加	收益会减少为0
最佳决策	降价	两可	涨价	涨价	不变

对图书价格弹性的实证研究表明，图书属于缺乏弹性的商品，即E<1。根据美国著名经济学家斯蒂格利茨《经济学》一书中的测算，美国图书市场的需求价格弹性为0.34[1]；而国内研究人员对中国图书市场1990—1998年的需求价格弹性的研究表明，这一时期中国图书的价格弹性一直稳定在0.40左右[2]。显然对于图书这样的低价格弹性商品，厂商一般会采取涨价策略来提高销售收入。

需要说明的是，就其一般性而言，图书属于缺乏价格弹性的商品，但对于不同类型的图书，其价格弹性可能会有较大的差异，甚至不排除某种图书有较高的价格弹性。比如教材的价格弹性较低，但教辅书的价格弹性则较高；专业图书与大众图书相比，后者的价格弹性较高；而大众图书中内容雷同、风格相差无几的图书，比如大众食谱、养生健康等生活类图书，则往往会有更高的价格弹性。

1.2 性质2：图书是高收入弹性商品

商品需求的收入弹性是指在价格不变的条件下，消费者收入变动百分之一时该商品需求量变动的百分比。当比值大于1时，则称该类商品富有收入弹性，或收入弹性较高；当比值小于1时，则称该商品缺乏收入弹性，或收入弹性较低。收入弹性大于1，意味着该商品消费量增加的幅度将超过收入增加的幅度；收入弹性小于1，则该商品消费量增加的幅度将小于收入增加的幅度。在经济学中，该指标用来衡量某种商品需求量的变动对收入变动的反应程度，它是反映商品经济学特性的一个重要指标。

收入弹性值在0与1之间的商品，一般又可称为必需品，它是维持人们日常生活所不可缺少的商品。在收入增加时个人对该商品的需求会相应增加，但增加的幅度会小于收入增加的幅度。

收入弹性大于1的商品，又可称为超必需品，它对于个人的基本生活而言不是必不可少的，而是可有可无的。正因为如此，该类商品往往需要消费者有较高的收入。这类商品一般包括奢侈品、品牌商品、定制商品以及一些个性化服务等。

据美国学者的测算，图书商品的收入弹性为1.44[3]；而国内的研究表明，中国图书市场在1990—1998年间的收入弹性在1.03～1.49之间[4]。虽然不同类别图书的收入弹性存在差异，但一般而言，可以认为图书需求的收入弹性较高，属于一种较弱的超必需品。[5]

1.3 性质3：图书有较强的垄断性

图书具有相当程度的垄断性。其垄断性主要来自图书的版权，一本书一般只能由一家出版社出版，从而保证了该书在市场上的唯一性。当然，进入公共领域的无版权的书可能除外，同样一本书可以存在多个版本相互竞争。尽管如此，不同出版社的品牌、信誉度、出版质量等因素仍然可以增强其垄断性。

图书的垄断性还来自其"内容产品"的特性。正如不同书法家写同一幅字，不同画家画同一幅画，被认为是不同的作品，彼此之间不能相互替代一样，图书也同样存在这一特点。同样类型、同样内容的图书，由于作者写作风格、表达方式、结构框架、思想深度等方面的不同，也会产生很大的差异性，更不用说不同内容、不同类型的图书了。差异化高的商品，被其他相近产品所替代的可能性则越小，从而增加了图书的垄断性。在适当抽象的情况下，任何一本图书都是一种唯一的产品，不会受到其他图书的竞争，因此从产业组织角度而言，图书的出版社可以视为一个垄断者，可以充分运用价格歧视的定价策略。

1.4 性质4：图书是一种信息产品

图书是一种信息产品，其提供消费的本质是知识和信息内容，因此可以将其归纳为"内容为王"的产品。而近年来，图书出版社也更多地将自身定位为内容提供者。图书作为信息产品，其价值是复杂劳动的一种凝结，也反映了生产者多年来知识资本的累积。

所有的信息产品在生产技术上都具有如下的特点，即生产的固定成本很高，但边际成本却很低。也就是说，信息产品一旦生产出来，再生产一份的成本非常低，其成本主要来自前期投入的固定成本。对于完全数字化的信息产品，比如软件、数字音像产品等，其边际成本几乎等于零。

我们知道，在价格理论中，边际成本是决定产品价格的一个重要因素。对于一般商品而言，边际成本随着产量的增加会逐渐上升，但对于信息产品，其边际成本往往与产量无关（比如软件，边际成本恒等于零），或者随产量的增加而下降（比如图书）。关于这一点，我们以后的分析中还会涉及。

1.5　性质5：图书具有较强的正外部性

当个人或厂商的一种行为直接影响到他人或社会，却没有支付相应成本或得到相应的补偿时，就出现了外部性。[6]外部性意味着个人或厂商没有承担其行为的全部后果。如果外部性为负，意味着他人或社会的福利受到了损失，但行为人或厂商却没有支出相应的成本，比如污染、吸烟、乱丢垃圾等；如果外部性为正，意味着他人或社会的福利有了增加，但行为人或厂商却没有得到补偿，比如发明、公共绿地、教育等。从经济学角度而言，负外部性的产品相对社会合理需求而言总会生产得太多，而正外部性的产品则会相对生产不足。因此，对于有外部性的产品而言，市场竞争机制和价格机制会存在一定程度的"失灵"，需要政府作为一种外部力量介入，以"矫正"外部性产品的产量与社会需求之间的差距。

作为文化和知识载体的图书，主要承担传递和普及知识与信息的功能，因此，它是一种典型的正外部性产品。一本书的价值绝不能等同于出版一本书的成本或销售一本书的价格。读书的人越多，对于社会而言，整体收益也便越大。也就是说，销售一本书的同时，出版社的收益与社会整体收益是不对等的，后者要远高于前者。但从图书内部来看，不同种类不同性质的图书的外部性是有差异的，相比较而言，普及知识型的、科普教育型的、专业知识型的、提供信息类的图书的正外部性要大一些，而纯粹娱乐消遣性的图书其外部性要小得多，或者没有。当然我们也应该看到另一种情况，即内容不健康、不科学的图书还会具有负的外部性。因此，对于那些社会效益很高而私人效益较低，即正外部性较强的图书品种，政府应该通过各种非市场手段，比如补贴、直接生产、减税等，来刺激市场的实际生产量增加以弥补市场提供的不足；而对于那些外部性较弱，私人收益同社会收益背离较小的品种，可以交由市场，按市场经济的法则来提供。

2　对图书垄断性的再考察

图书具有垄断性是本研究报告的一个基本结论。经济学意义上的垄断是指产品具有差异性，不容易被其他产品所替代。这种性质越强，则其垄断性就越强。图书具有较高的差异性在上文已有所论及，这里重点考察在信息技术革命的背景下，图书产品的可替代性问题。

信息载体的技术革命很容易对纸质图书产品形成替代。随着数字技术的发展以及公共图书馆的普及，知识信息的载体日益增多，传统纸质图书的替代方式也越来越多，主要包括电子图书、图书馆以及复印类图书。

2.1　电子图书

电子图书对纸质图书的替代作用可从以下两个方面进行分析：

其一，从整体而言，电子图书作为一种新的阅读方式和手段正逐渐成势，其存在和发展必然会挤占和侵蚀传统的纸质图书市场，但挤占和侵蚀的程度要受消费者阅读习惯的制约。从目前的发展情况看，这种挤占并未普遍发生，原因是目前的读者主体是在纸质图书的熏陶下成长起来的，阅读习惯难以在短期内改变。对于在数字技术时代成长起来的读者，有可能会更偏爱电子图书，或者说至少不会排斥电子图书。到那时，电子图书的替代作用将会表现得更加充分。这种替代性将对读者群产生细分作用，即把读者划分为偏爱纸质图书的读者和偏爱电子图书的读者，前者的购买对象仍然以纸质图书为主。在这种情况下，一个可预见的趋势是，纸质图书的市场将会减小，但图书的价格会比现在更高。

其二，对于以传递信息和知识为主的图书，比如各种年鉴、研究报告、专业类图书、教材和教辅图书，电子图书无疑对纸质图书形成更强的替代，这种现象目前已经表现得很充分了。但受版权的制约，这类图书的电子版和纸质版往往归同一家出版社所有（正如我们经常看到的那样，欧美出版巨头一般都拥有这类图书两种版权）。此时出版社会在两种产品之间进行平衡，制定更为复杂的定价策略。我们看到的现实是，在美国，专业类电子图书的价格并未由于低廉的边际成本而大幅度降低，这是版权唯一性所导致的图书垄断性的结果。可以这样说，图书产品（不论它是电子图书还是纸质图书）的价格更多地是由需求方决定的。在这种情况下，尽管电子图书对纸质图书形成替代，但对纸质图书价格的影响却是不确定的，既可能推升纸质图书的价格，也可能抑制其价格。

2.2　公共图书馆

图书馆的出现与发展是现代文明社会进步的表现之一。图书馆对图书价格的影响主要表现在以下两个方面：

其一，一般来说，图书馆是一个稳定、庞大且对价格不敏感的购书群体。国外数据及经验显示，与其他购书群体相比，图书馆购书有以下特点：图书馆购买的图书印数大多都在 5 000 册或以下；购书主要以精装本为主；其购书渠道主要是大型代理商或出版社直销方式，尤其是专业和学术类图书。上述特点也直接促成了图书馆成为购买高价位图书的重要群体，例如，1996 年—2002 年美国图书馆购书平均每册费用一直高于美国国内图书平均价格，2002 年美国图书馆购书平均每册费用高于其国内图书平均价格 11.38 美元。

其二，图书馆的存在也对读者群作了进一步的细分。在图书馆网络十分发达的情况下，图书潜在消费者中对价格较为敏感的人群会从市场直接购书转为到图书馆借书，而保留下来的在市场中购书的消费者基本上都是对图书价格不敏感的群体。因此，图书馆的存在可能会降低图书的销售量，但却会推升图书的市场价格。从发达国家的实际情况来看，图书馆的大量购书是图书出版业繁荣的重要基础。比如对于小印数、高定价的图书，如果没有图书馆市场的支持，很可能就根本不能出版。

2.3　复印类图书

由于中国版权意识和保护措施起步较晚，在很长一段时间，对图书，主要是大学教材以及专业图书没有严密的版权保护措施，存在着大规模复印的现象。图书作为内容决定型商品，大量的复印类图书成为大学教材及专业图书的替代品，从而减少了人们对正版图书的需求，降低了图书的销售量，并对图书价格形成一定的抑制作用。可是，在版权保护良好的市场，尽管纸质图书会受到多种方式的替代，但并没有影响到图书的垄断性，因而也不会影响到图书价格的形成机制。

3　图书定价的微观经济学分析

企业所处的市场特征直接影响到企业的定价行为，因此，图书出版业的市场特征是我们分析图书定价的基本前提。在明确这一前提后，我们将采用相应的定价模型，对图书的定价策略进行综合分析。

3.1 图书出版业的市场特征分析

经济学通常按照市场竞争的差异程度将市场分为四种类型：完全竞争市场、完全垄断市场、寡头垄断市场、垄断竞争市场。其中，完全竞争市场和完全垄断市场是两种极端状态，而寡头垄断市场和垄断竞争市场处于上述两者之间，市场结构较为复杂，兼具垄断与竞争两种特点。据吴赟的研究，现实中的出版业市场结构主要表现为垄断竞争和寡头垄断两种形态（详见表2），这也印证了我们上文得出的性质3的判断。本研究报告主要从图书具有垄断性这一特征出发对图书微观定价机制展开分析。

表2　出版业市场的类型和特征

市场类型	厂商数量	产品差异程度	企业对价格的控制程度	进出行业的难易程度	出版市场实例
完全竞争	许多	完全无差别	没有	很容易	出版业无此情况
垄断竞争	许多	有一定的差别	一些	比较容易	大众出版、教育出版、专业出版市场
寡头垄断	几个	差别很小或没有差别	一些	相当困难	教育出版、专业出版市场
完全垄断	唯一	产品是唯一的且无相近的替代品	极大，但通常受管制	几乎不可能	部分政府出版物、部分专业出版物市场

资料来源：吴赟：《垄断竞争和寡头垄断条件下的出版市场分析》，《出版科学》2009年第2期。

3.2 图书垄断企业对不同市场的定价行为分析：三级价格歧视策略

根据性质3，我们可以认为图书出版企业具有一定垄断力量，因此可以运用垄断定价模型解释图书定价行为。为了简化分析，假设图书市场可以分隔为两个子市场，高收入人群市场和低收入人群市场，或者是价格敏感型市场和价格不敏感型市场。这两类市场分别有不同的需求曲线（如图1所示），其中 D_1 表示高收入人群和价格不敏感人群的需求曲线，价格弹性用 E_1 表示；D_2 表示低收入人群和价格敏感型人群的需求曲线，价格弹性用 E_2 表示。

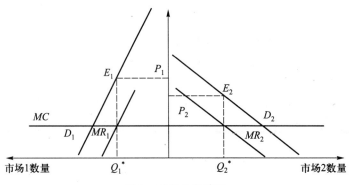

图1　三级价格歧视

对出版企业而言，市场1代表了其稳定的消费者，并且也往往是消费的主体。向这类消费者销售图书的交易成本较低。而市场2则代表了不稳定消费者，其消费行为容易受到价格、收入、替代产品和竞争产品的影响。因此，出版企业向这类消费者销售图书的交易成本较高。垄断企业此时可以对上述两个市场分别采取不同的价格来获得最大利润，这就是"三级价格歧视"策略。在实践中，图书是一个容易采取"三级价格歧视"策略的市场，比如在英美等国的图书市场上，出版商在推出昂贵的精装书同时，也生产广受欢迎、价格低廉的大众市场纸皮书。另外，三级价格歧视策略在时装、电影等商品上也屡见不鲜。

根据利润极大化条件 $MR_1 = MR_2 = MC$，可以确定出两个市场上的价格分别是 P_1 和 P_2，并且有如下的等式：

$$P_1/P_2 = (1-1/|E_2|)/(1-1/|E_1|)$$

该等式意味着出版企业应该在价格弹性较低的市场制定较高的价格，在价格弹性较高的市场制定较低的价格，因此有：

$$P_1 > P_2$$

从社会福利的角度而言，"三级价格歧视"会改善部分消费者的社会福利，这已为微观经济学理论所证明。比如在某种情况下，市场2的需求曲线位于图1的 MR_2 的位置。此时如果出版企业不采取价格歧视，则市场价为 P_1，这意味着市场2中的消费者将没有能力购买图书，从而退出图书市场，也就是说对于这部分消费者而言，图书的价格显得太昂贵了。显然，这对出版企业和低收入消费者而言都是一种福利损失。而在实行"三级价格歧视"策略的情况下，市场2的消费者面对的价格将是 P_2，该群体购买 Q_2^* 数量的图书，从而提高了消费者和出版企业双方的福利水平。

3.3 图书耐用品垄断企业的跨期动态定价：递减价格序列

在上面的分析中，我们只考虑了图书定价的静态情形，而垄断企业一般都持有动态的定价观点，即为了将来的利润可能会牺牲一点当前利润。我们知道图书是一种耐用品，购买了耐用品的消费者，一般不会再次购买同一商品。也就是说，每位消费者对同一本图书只会购买一次。因此，对出版企业而言，今天的图书销售就降低了明天的市场需求。在此情况下，为了获得最大利润，企业会采取逐渐降低图书价格的策略。这一策略同样可以视为是一种"三级价格歧视"，与前文分析不同的是，这里并不是按对价格的敏感程度来划分市场，而是按对时间的敏感程度划分市场。

我们首先建立一个能够说明主要观点的简单的两阶段模型。假设垄断企业在时期 T_1 制定价格 P_1，则估价超过 P_1 的消费者会接受该价格。在时期 T_2 开始时，垄断企业只能面对剩余的需求，后者由估价小于 P_1 的消费者构成。这样垄断企业试图制定较低的第二阶段价格。假设第二阶段是垄断企业销售的最后阶段，则企业会根据剩余的需求制定 T_2 时期的垄断价格，即 P_2（显然 $P_2 < P_1$）。如果引入企业与消费者的博弈，即如果消费者在时期 T_1 知道垄断企业事后在时期 T_2 会降价，则消费者的购买行为会发生一定程度的改变。那些估价高于 P_1 并且急需得到该图书的消费者仍然会接受价格 P_1，而估价低于 P_1 的消费者，以及估价高于 P_1 但并不急于得到该书的消费者则不会购买，因为他通过等待可以得到更低的价格。因此，对未来价格的预期降低了时期 T_1 的需求。扩展到多阶段模型，我们发现，在给定企业行为下，并且给定企业和消费者合理预期下，企业采取的最优策略

是递减价格序列的形式，即在离散时间 $T=1$，2，$\cdots t$ 期内，均衡价格逐级递减，有：
$$P_1 > P_2 > \cdots > P_t$$
在实践中，这种定价策略往往以"打折"的形式表现出来。这也就意味着，对于在时期 T_1 以后才购买图书的消费者而言，时期 T_1 的价格 P_1 有点昂贵了。

3.4 图书产品市场过剩分析——生产技术视角

价格理论主要研究的是价格和产量的关系，考察产量的决策对于我们深刻全面地了解图书出版业的价格形成机制同样有重要意义。我们知道，图书出版业是一个容易生产过剩的产业，国际和国内均如此。从价格理论来说，均衡价格对应的是均衡产量。也就是说，在这一价格下，市场正好出清，产品既不会出现过剩，也不会出现不足。如果市场不能出清，则一般认为该市场的价格高于均衡价格。

但对于图书这样的信息产品，这一观点需要做一定的修正。上文性质4的分析表明，图书是一种固定成本很高，而边际成本很低的产品。在市场需求确定的情况下，企业将生产 Q^* 的图书，将价格定在 P^* 的水平上，市场将全部出清，如图2所示。

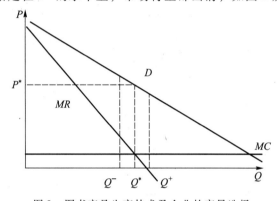

图2 图书产品生产技术及企业的产量选择

但是在需求不确定的情况下[7]，企业不可能准确地知道市场需求曲线 D，只能根据经验和预期进行一个估计，下文将证明，企业总是倾向于多生产一些图书。

现假设企业预期的需求水平是 D，此时价格是 P^*，而产量是 Q^*。

情形一：企业选择在此基础上多生产 ΔQ 的产量，即达到 Q^+ 水平，此时企业既可能获得一个更高的收益，但也面临着产品积压的风险。此时，企业的

收益 $\Pi_1 = (P^* \times Q^+) - MC \times Q^+$

损失 $S_1 = MC(Q^+ - Q^*) = MC \times \Delta Q$

情形二：企业选择在此基础上少生产 ΔQ 的产量，即达到 Q^- 水平，此时企业既可能获得一个较低的收益，但也面临着没有充分获得利润的风险。此时，企业的

收益 $\Pi_2 = (P^* \times Q^-) - MC \times Q^-$

损失 $S_2 = (P^* - MC) \Delta Q$

比较情形一和情形二，可以看出，Π_1 总是大于 Π_2，也就是多生产可能获得的收益总是大于少生产。而对于图书商品而言，由性质4有，其边际成本非常低，即 $(P^* - MC)$ 总是大于 MC，甚至于远远大于 MC，这也就意味着，S_1 总是小于 S_2，即企业多生产的损失要小于少生产的损失。

因此，对出版企业而言，其最优策略是在预期需求水平的基础上多生产一定数量的图

书产品。如果每一家出版社都倾向于多生产一个 ΔQ 的话，则整个出版行业就会多生产 $N \times \Delta Q$（N 是出版社的数量）的数量，这就意味着产能过剩。

这个性质对于理解图书出版业有重要的意义。首先，它表明出版业总是容易出现过剩，国际和国内经验也一再表明，这一结论是符合实际的。其次，它也表明，此时的产量过剩是企业的一种最优策略，并不意味着实际价格高于均衡价格。

综合上述理论分析，可以得出如下结论：

结论一，图书市场存在一定的垄断性，而垄断市场中形成的价格要高于完全自由竞争市场中形成的价格，或者说，价格与成本之间存在较大的差额。

结论二，三级价格歧视和跨期价格递减是图书市场的基本定价机制。

结论三，图书市场容易出现生产过剩。

4 图书定价的不同模式：欧美国家的经验

从世界图书出版业来看，图书定价存在固定价格体系和自由价格体系两种不同的模式。固定价格体系是指对图书价格实行统一定价的制度，即规定图书价格由出版社定价，并在固定位置明确标示，任何图书销售机构都不得擅自加价或减价销售图书；而自由价格体系是指图书以自由价格在市场销售的定价制度，出版社通过周密的成本核算后，以一定的折扣批发给中间商，只要能保证正常运营，零售商可以自由定价销售。

目前图书自由价格体系主要以美国、英国为代表，图书固定价格体系以德国、法国、西班牙为代表。两种模式都有国家层面和行业层面的理念及规则为支撑。即使在同一定价模式下，由于不同国家历史、文化和法律的不同，定价模式的应用和认可程度也各有特色，并且在不断地发展和演变。例如表3给出的主要固定价格体系国家，其图书定价就有两种形式：一种是法律形式，德国、法国、西班牙、葡萄牙、希腊等都通过立法规定图书按定价销售，违反价格法将受到制裁；另一种则是商业协议形式，丹麦和挪威等国执行的就是定价协议。

表3 欧美主要国家图书固定价格和自由定价体系表

固定价格体系		固定价格体系	自由价格体系
立法形式	制定年份	协议形式	
法国	1981		美国、英国、比利时、塞浦路斯、捷克、爱沙尼亚、芬兰、冰岛、爱尔兰、拉脱维亚、立陶宛、波兰、瑞典、瑞士等
德国	2002	丹麦	
奥地利	2000	匈牙利	
希腊	1997	卢森堡	
意大利	2001	挪威	
荷兰	2005	斯洛文尼亚	
葡萄牙	1996		
西班牙	1975		

资料来源：Doris Stockman：Free or fixed prices on books-patterns of book pricing in Europe, *The public*, vol. 11（2004）4, pp. 49–64.

比较而言，在自由价格体系下，零售企业对最终销售价格具有较大自主权，而出版企业对最终销售价格的控制力较弱。因此，我们通常可以看到零售企业对价格弹性较高的图书品种，比如大众图书，通过打折降价等手段提高销售量，以获取更大的经济利益。而在固定价格体系下，出版企业对价格的控制力则较强，可以更好地通过定价策略来维护自身的利益，特别是对那些有一定特色的小众图书出版企业而言，更有利于其维持长期经营。

值得关注的是固定价格体系对图书定价的具体影响。固定价格制实际上是一种在垂直产业链中常常使用的转售价格维持制（resale price-maintenance，简称 RPM），即出版社事先定好价格并打印在书上，一般情况下必须按打印在图书上的价格销售。产业组织理论的研究认为，在 RPM 定价方式下，出版商、批发商（代理商）、零售商很容易达成合谋。在下列情况中，出版社可能会提高图书定价：第一，中间环节的不确定性。一个典型的不确定性是出版社不知道中间环节有多长，出版社此时会按照最坏的可能性来确定图书价格，因此更倾向于制定一个高价格。第二，中间环节的垄断性。如果中间环节的企业具有垄断实力，在瓜分行业利润的谈判中，就具有更强的谈判能力，从而能够得到更多的折扣。面对这样的发行结构，出版社只能通过抬高图书定价，来保证自己和下游其他环节的利润水平不受影响。第三，面临销售和退货等风险，在此情况下，出版社也会通过提高图书定价来消化部分风险。

上述两种价格运行体系不仅对图书的实际价格会产生一定的影响，而且也对图书的产业组织带来影响。在固定价格体系下，中小出版社可以很好地保护自身的利益，而在自由价格体系下，由于出版社失去了对价格的控制，因此很容易陷入恶性竞争之中，中小出版社很容易成为牺牲品。以英国为例，英国在 20 世纪末取消了图书固定价格体系而改为自由价格体系后，图书销量巨增，不少新书五折甚至四折销售，中小书店纷纷倒闭，中小出版社被出版集团并购。至 2006 年，大众市场 52.9% 的份额已经被阿歇特、兰登书屋、企鹅和哈珀·柯林斯这四大出版集团所掌控。与之形成鲜明对比的是，在将固定价格体系立法并严格实施的德国，中小出版社依然活跃，最大的 15 家出版社只控制着 30% 的市场份额。

需要说明的是，一个国家或地区究竟采取何种图书定价制度，是由这个国家或地区出版产业的成熟程度以及市场结构和竞争环境乃至于文化安全所决定的。英国最近一百多年来图书定价制度的演变颇能说明这个问题。19 世纪末，英国出版业发行商之间的竞争加剧，导致低价倾销现象相当普遍，不少发行商因此破产，销售渠道不断萎缩，进而影响了整个出版业的健康发展。在这种情况下，1897 年，英国出版商协会和发行商协会签署了图书固定价格协议（Net Book Agreement），并于 1900 年 1 月在获得英国作家协会认可后正式实施。这项制度的主要规定有三点：（a）出版商有权（但非必须）给所出版的图书制定价格，即出版商可以决定图书是否以固定价格形式销售；（b）销售商必须按固定价格销售，其回报是从出版商那里获得一定的折扣；（c）销售商如果违反制度，所有参与签订图书固定价格协议的出版商将停止向其供应图书。这项制度在英国实行了近百年的时间，它有力地解决了英国出版产业发展之初市场秩序失范所产生的严重问题，推动了英国出版业的快速发展。任何制度安排都可能产生正的和负的外部性问题。随着英国出版产业的不断成熟，固定价格体系负的外部性问题开始显现，这主要表现为出版商或发行商之间所形成的垄断行为，抑制了竞争的开展，进而不利于消费者和社会福利的提高。于是，英国出版业于 1997 年中止了这项实行了近百年的制度，改行自由价格体系。[8] 十多年过去了，一些学者的跟踪研究结果表明，实行自由价格体系对英国出版业发展的总体影响还算是正面的，尽管对此英国出版业内部存在不同的看法。

还需要指出的是，任何一种制度安排均可能有正负两个方面的影响，对它的选择是利弊权衡的结果。问题在于，当我们选定某一种制度安排后，并不意味着我们不应该采取一定的措施来抑制它的负面影响。美国出版业的做法值得我们思考。在自由价格体系下，美国一般不限制书店对读者的售价与折扣，但同时不允许出版社对不同规模的书店提供不同的供货折扣，以避免大型连锁书店以进货规模优势获得优惠的进货折扣，从而对小书店形成不公平竞争。[9] 这就在一定程度上保证了美国出版业有一个较为合理的书店布局和结构。

注释

[1] 参见斯蒂格利茨. 经济学（上）[M]. 北京：中国人民大学出版社，2000：91

[2] 参见王广照. 向更高的境界迈进——用产业组织理论分析中国出版业 [J]. 出版广角，2003（5）

[3] 参见 E·爱斯菲尔德. 微观经济学：理论与应用 [M]. 上海：上海交通大学出版社，1988：156

[4] 参见王广照. 向更高的境界迈进—用产业组织理论分析中国出版业 [J]. 出版广角，2003（5）

[5] 中小学课本的情况除外，其价格的制定主要由行政手段控制

[6] 参见斯蒂格利茨. 经济学（上册）[M]. 北京：中国人民大学出版社，2000：138

[7] 作为微观经济组织的出版机构，在实践中决定供给量时通常是凭经验判断，出版产品的本期（当前出版周期）价格并不一定由本期产量决定，出版产品的本期价格也不一定能决定下期（下一出版周期）产量。一种图书的总印数主要受其读者群规模大小的影响，而与定价的关系并不明显。这一特点在传统出版领域表现尤为明显。印刷史研究专家柴瑞特（David Zaret）曾针对出版业供给的风险性指出："印刷文本的经济学更多涉及计划、风险和其他市场行为等。印刷者只能依靠不确定的市场需求来估计生产数量。" 参见 David Zaret. Origins of Democratic Culture：Printing, Petitions, and the Public Sphere in Early-Modern England [M]. Princeton, New Jersey：Princeton University Press, 1999, P.136, 转引自吴赟. 试论出版机构供给行为的经济学机理 [J]. 出版科学，2008（2）

[8] 参见周正兵. 英国百年净价图书制度及其启示 [OL]. [2010-06-20]. http://brand.bookdao.info/Default.aspx

[9] 参见郝明义. 现阶段我们需要定价销售制的理由 [N]. 中国图书商报 2010-10-15.

参考文献

[1] ［法］泰勒尔. 产业组织理论 [M]. 北京：中国人民大学出版社，1997

[2] ［法］贝纳西. 不完全竞争与非市场出清的宏观经济学：一个动态一般均衡的视角 [M]. 上海：上海人民出版社，2005

[3] 平新乔. 微观经济学十八讲 [M]. 北京：北京大学出版社，2003

[4] 蒋殿春. 高级微观经济学 [M]. 北京：经济管理出版社，2000

［5］陈昕．中国出版产业论稿［M］．上海：复旦大学出版社，2006

［6］陈昕．美国数字出版考察报告［M］．上海：上海人民出版社，2008

［7］郝振省．2007—2008中国出版业发展报告［M］．北京：中国书籍出版社，2008

［8］史东辉，王利明，董宝生．中国图书出版业的产业组织分析［M］．南宁：广西人民出版社，2008

［9］吴赟．文化与经济的博弈：出版经济学理论研究［M］．北京：中国社会科学出版社，2009

［10］魏龙泉．纵览美国图书出版与发行［M］．中国经济出版社2007年版。

［11］宋木文．亲历出版30年——新时期出版纪事与思考［M］．北京：商务印书馆，2007

［12］陈悟朝．定位图书流通［M］．北京：中国书籍出版社，2005

［13］成致平．中国物价五十年：1949—1998［M］．北京：物价出版社，1998

［14］新闻出版总署计划财务司．中国新闻出版统计资料汇编（2005）［M］．北京：中国劳动社会保障出版社，2006

［15］中国出版年鉴（1987—2008）［M］．北京：中国书籍出版社

［16］中国图书年鉴（1996）［M］．武汉：湖北人民出版社，1999

［17］中国图书年鉴（1998）［M］．武汉：湖北人民出版社，2001

［18］封延阳．浅谈商品需求价格弹性与图书的定价策略［J］．科技与出版，2001（6）

［19］唐要家．序列加成的可维持性与图书高价格［J］．财经问题研究，2007（5）

［20］周蔚华．中国图书出版产业的供求分析［J］．出版经济，2002（9）

［21］周建华．定价策略：出版社利润增长的动力源泉［J］．大学出版，2002（4）

［22］魏玉山．图书价格比较研究［J］．传媒，2004（3）

［23］乌苏拉·劳腾伯格、安欣．德国电子出版业当前总体趋势及未来的发展［J］．出版科学，2009（1）

［24］李武，肖东发．2000年以来英国图书出版业发展特征和趋势研究［J］．出版发行研究，2008（12）

［25］禹继来．从数字看我国农村图书市场现状［J］．出版广角，2007（7）

［26］王薇．透视法国出版业经济政策［J］．出版参考，2008（9）

［27］史海娜．国外出版产业价值链转型模式分析［J］．编辑之友，2008（3）

［28］甄西编译．首次欧盟25国图书出版调查分析［J］．中国编辑，2005（4）

［29］李实，岳希明．中国城乡收入差距世界最高［J］．理论参考，2005（4）

［30］陈昕．发达国家图书出版产业发展经验的借鉴及比较［J］．出版商务周报，2007（8）

［31］渠竞帆．欧美两种价格体系出版面貌迥异［J］．中国图书商报，2007（11）

［32］周正兵．英国百年净价图书制度及其启示［OL］．［2010-06-20］．http://brand.bookdao.info/Default.aspx

［33］2008开卷读者调查报告——读者水涨、阅读船高［N］．出版商务周报，2009-04-22

［34］理想的学术出版与学术出版的理想［N］．文汇报，2010-03-27

［35］陈昕．图书市场呼唤中盘雄起［N］．中国图书商报，1996-11-13

［36］ 最新中国新闻出版产业数据大势 ［N］. 中国图书商报，2010-07-27

［37］ 韩成，周中华. 中美电子书市场分析与比较：商业模式制胜数字出版产业 ［N］. 中国新闻出版报，2010-08-26

［38］ 郝明义. 现阶段我们需要定价销售制的理由 ［N］. 中国图书商报，2010-10-15

［39］ Doris Stockman. Free or fixed Prices on Books-patterns of Book Pricing in Europe ［J］. The public，vol. 11（2004）4，pp. 49-64.

［40］ K. Clay，R. Krishnan，E. Wolff and D. Fernandes. Retail Strategies on the Web：Price and Non-Price Competition in the Online Book Industry ［J］. The Journal of Industrial Economics，Vol. 50，No. 3（Sep，2002），pp. 351-367.

作者简介

陈昕，上海世纪出版集团总裁、董事长。

数字时代专业出版的主体意识及其数字化选择

敖 然

（电子工业出版社　北京　100036）

摘要：当前，数字出版已成为我国出版界最热门的话题。在数字时代，传统出版业面临着巨大的挑战，专业出版领域在数字化出版环境中也面临着许多棘手的问题。本文从如何认识数字时代专业出版的主体意识和怎样把握数字出版特征这两方面入手，就战略层面和技术层面探讨了破解专业出版数字化困境的方法，最后强调了人才因素在数字化进程中的重要作用。

关键词：专业出版　数字时代　主体意识

Sense of Subject on Professional Publishing & Choice of Digitalization

Ao Ran

（Publishing House of Electronics Industry，Beijing 100036）

Abstract：Nowadays，digital publishing has become the most popular topic in China's publishing industry．In the digital age，traditional publishing is facing huge challenges．Professional publishing is also faced with many difficult problems in the digital publishing environment．This paper starts with how to understand the consciousness of professional publishing in the digital age and how to grasp the characteristics of digital publishing，discusses the way to break the dilemma of digital professional publishing and attaches the importance to the talent factor in the digital process in the last．

Keywords：Professional publishing　Digital Age　Consciousness

　　本文根据专业出版单位在数字时代面临的具体情况，谈谈对数字化环境下的专业出版的几个问题的看法。

1　如何看待传统出版产业数字化生存环境

　　"数字出版"无疑已成为我国出版界最热的话题，新闻出版总署统计数据表明，截至2009年年底，我国广泛意义下的数字出版产业生产总值已超过 779 亿元人民币，不论是生产总值还是增长率大大超过传统出版产业。如果我们以比较有把握的数据来分析也可以得到相似的结论，比如以"数字出版"为关键词在清华同方知网上作全文检索，检索到

2007 年全年的记录条数为 1 453 条，2008 年是 1 829 条，2009 年是 2 775 条，数字出版文献量也呈现快速增长态势。

但如何理解数字出版，其在我们专业出版领域的含义、特征和实现途径确实是我们目前面临的一个棘手问题。按照国内外较为成功的数字出版模式来看，服务学术研究的高端学术出版和提供休闲娱乐的大众文学出版都找到了较为可行的商业模式。基于技术平台服务和信息集成服务的所谓"数字出版"也有了成功的先行者，请注意我说的是"所谓的'数字出版'"并加了引号，因为严格来讲，后者并不是出版，它们并不拥有数字内容的资产主权，它们是为传统出版数字化转型提供技术平台和信息咨询服务的。

上述以知识生产和服务流程为代表的数字出版融合只是我们传统出版面临的困境之一，而电信网、计算机网和有线电视网三大网络逐步融合导致的知识及其服务呈网状的扩散则令我们面临更大的危机。

2　如何认识数字时代专业出版的主体意识

我们理解的数字出版应该包括一个复杂的编辑环节。在我们国家，这个编辑环节具有很强的政治性、思想性、科学性、创造性和选择性，也就是说我们传统出版企业必须承担文化发展过程的设计、组织、选择、引领和优化功能，这是我们的基本要求，就是在向数字出版转型的过程中也无法放弃的，我想我们专业出版工作者尤其应该坚持。

由于体制、资金、人才以及相对封闭导致传统出版在数字出版产业发展过程中处于非常不利的地位，内容被无偿使用、投资得不到有效保护、专业人才匮乏等一系列的问题使得很多人怀疑传统出版还能不能在数字时代生存、发展。

事实上，传统出版业是科学交流体系的源头，是数字资产的主权单位，是文献信息系统的上游，理所当然应该成为数字出版产业的主角和决定力量。传统出版尤其是专业出版业者不能满足于所谓内容提供商的角色和功能，所谓出版产业链重新分工、数字出版新的商业模式等似是而非的论断否定了传统出版产业在数字出版时代的主体地位，带来了网络盗版横行、产业后劲乏力、出版业者茫然等现实问题。

目前，利用电子社的品牌和资源优势，我们正和一部分技术服务商和渠道服务商探讨新的数字出版商业模式，我们强烈呼吁管理部门、产业界和学界认真研究上述政策模糊给我国出版产业带来不利影响。

3　如何把握数字时代专业出版的基本特征

数字出版风头正劲，Kindle 的出现引爆了电子书产业大战，iPad 似乎想要一统江山，好一派"乱花渐欲迷人眼"，致使传统出版业者很难确认自己的角色和方向。在数字时代，知识高度聚合、服务完全定制。所以，依传统出版的观点来看所谓的数字出版，我们认为必须包应含三个基本要素：一是知识生产者必须采用信息网络对知识进行采集、编辑和标识。二是知识发行者必须建立数字版权保护和认证管理体系。三是知识使用者可以通过信息网络与发行者建立交流和反馈。

专业出版不可能像大众出版那样可以由作者自助的方式完成出版全过程，严格的同行评审和完善的编辑加工手段仍然是传统出版业者的利器，同时我们的编辑力量和专家队伍可以更好地利用数字技术和网络技术带给我们的便利。事实上，依托互联网和知识采集、标识、制作和发布工具，作者和编辑可以更好地互动、选题策划手段更加丰富、专家评审更加科学，内容可以得到更好的组织，读者可以得到更好的体验。

专业出版必须紧密结合专业和行业优势，充分尊重用户对知识服务的个性化需求。在信息社会分工服务体系没有完全建立之前，传统出版业者应将自己视为数字知识的生产和服务提供商，知识生产和服务的主体必须统一，这两个功能缺一不可！

4 如何破解专业出版面临的数字化困境

伴随着我国信息产业的飞速发展，我们所在的专业出版领域也经历了一个高速发展的时期。但信息技术确实也是一把双刃剑，在快速地推动社会转型的同时，也对一切不适应其发展规律的事物予以否定。我们的专业出版如何不被数字化和网络化趋势所湮没已成为一个迫在眉睫的问题。我想体制改革、流程再造和人才战略将是专业出版社破解目前的数字化困境的必要手段。

事实上，出版体制的改革和创新已成为专业出版社转型发展的核心因素。出版体制改革的原则在于坚持出版工作的正确导向，坚持把社会效益放在首位，努力实现社会效益和经济效益的统一。目的是在我国建立出版的现代企业制度，形成有效率、有活力、有竞争力的企业管理体系。

从战略层面上来看，考虑到出版业涉及的意识形态属性以及国家文化安全。我们建议在建立出版的现代企业制度过程中，政府给予出版产业以更大的政策、财税和资金方面的支持，学界开展更多有针对性的理论研究。

从技术层面上来看，由于个人计算机及字处理软件的广泛应用，作为图书产品的各种原始文档和图片都可以在计算机上来创建、修改、校对、存储、复制并通过互联网传递，同时知识的海量聚合又需要对其进行高度的结构化，读者需求的可定制化还必须确保知识服务的有效性。所有这些必须通过协同知识创作、编辑和服务等出版要素，建立标准、共享和开放的数字出版流程来实现。传统出版基于出版物编辑、生产、发行建立的成熟的业务流程，在数字时代和互联网环境下必须予以有步骤和彻底的变革。产业界应该更加积极地进行探索。

不管是体制创新还是流程再造，人才因素永远是体制创新和流程再造的决定性力量。对于数字出版的发展趋势，我们的看法是需兼顾两种出版形式长期共存的现实，依据社会的不同需求，采取实用的出版方式，而不是一味追求数字化。在这一过程中，真正的数字出版人才必须秉持坚定的出版责任意识，必须具有适应网络社会发展的创新精神，必须具备扎实的专业出版领域知识，必须熟练掌握知识生产和服务过程的数字化工具。希望我们的出版教育体系注重对人才的基础知识和基本技能的培养。

今天，我们谈到了专业出版在数字时代面临的两个问题的四个方面，即如何坚持专业出版的主体意识和把握数字出版的特征要求。不当之处，请批评指正。我们相信，以体制改革为契机，适时变革出版业务流程，发挥复合型人才在数字出版过程的核心作用。传统出版业者在数字时代依然可以独占鳌头！

作者简介

敖然，电子工业出版社社长、党组书记，武汉大学信息管理学院出版科学系兼职教授。

出版改革与出版社改制

王建辉

（湖北长江出版传媒集团　武汉　430070）

摘要：随着我国社会主义市场经济体制的逐步完善，文化体制改革的进一步推进，出版改革势在必行。具体而言，就是指出版社改制。出版社改制应该以实现国有企业转变为公司制企业为核心，产权和人员则是改制的焦点所在，而不同性质的出版社的转变类型各不相同。在后转企改制时代，出版改革除了实现从传统出版到现代出版的转型，还要加快发展方式的转变，同时紧抓社会效益和经济效益，为读者奉献好书，为人类留下经典。

关键词：出版改革　出版社改制　后转企改制时代

Publishing Reform and Press Restructuring

Wang Jianhui

（Hubei Changjiang Publishing Group，Wuhan，430070）

Abstract：Along with the gradually perfecting of socialist market economy system and the further promoting of the cultural system reform，publishing reform becomes imperative. Exactly，it refers to press restructuring. Press restructuring should center on the transformation from State-owned enterprises to company. Property and personnel is the focus of the restructuring. However，different kinds of presses bring about different reforming style. In the post-reforming age，publishing reform should not only change from traditional style to the modern style，but also accelerate the transformation of development mode. At the same time，press should grasp social benefits and economic benefits tightly and provide classic books for readers.

Keywords：Publishing Reform Press Restructuring post-reforming age

　　这个题目是武汉大学出版系的老师给出的，我按照自己的理解来做答卷，也和各位出版专业的专职教师交流。出版的研究向来就有两条路数，学术的路子和实践的路子，或者叫学院派与实战派。各位可以说是学院派的，我是把两者结合起来的路数，因为这样的结合是我的长项，学术的操练与实践的经验，在我都还有那么一点。这里讲的如果学术性不够，那就算是给在座各位提供一点思路和素材。

1　出版改革

出版改革是文化体制改革的一个组成部分，以 2009 年 4 月新闻出版总署颁布的《关于进一步推进新闻出版体制改革的指导意见》为标志，中国出版改革的思路基本确定。

1.1 出版改革的必然性

这一场改革并不是凭空而来的，要认识其必然性。其一，国家实行社会主义市场经济，大的经济体制发生变化，要求它所有的子系统必须纳入这个体系，新闻出版业也不能例外了。其二，出版业发展的需要。这一次的文化体制改革有理论的依据，就是两分开的理论，即公益性的文化事业与经营性的文化产业要两分开。对于出版业就是要把出版业的主体部分作为产业来发展，产业的基本细胞必须企业化，产业是企业的集群，不能不对组织细胞进行变革。其三，出版业的现状长期是企业不像企业，事业不像事业，旧的生产关系严重束缚生产力的发展。早改早主动，不改革没有出路，成为行业的共识，我们从改革以后的发展可以反证改革的必要性。长江出版集团改革前点资产 20 亿元，现在 80 亿元。对于改革的意义，人们并不是认识很清楚的，有两种提法，从早期一些出版社提出的"企业化管理，事业化运作"，到现在又有所谓"企业化经营，事业化管理"，可见一些人依然不理解出版改革中出版社改制的意义。

出版改革的最大的意义，是从根本上改变了中国出版的整体格局，由事业一统天下转到了企业。有两个巨大的成果，一是理论成果，让我们对于出版的意识形态性有了正确的认识。我们过去总是强调出版的意识形态性，原来意识形态与是事业还是企业可以无关，用企业的办法也可以做意识形态。这一次改革让我们突出了出版的产业性，原来出版的产业性也是基本属性之一。二是实践成果，这一场改革大大地解放了生产力。

1.2 任务书、路径图和时间表

出版改革由三项组成：任务书、路径图和时间表。通常的表述只有后两者。

（1）任务书。任务书包括两部分：一是管办分离，解决政府管理部门既当裁判员又当运动员的问题；二是把事业改为企业。就第一个任务说，管办分离后，办的这部分改革比较到位，作为政府部门的附属机构的出版单位，向市场经济中的自主经营主体转变的改革目标基本实现，而管的这部分改革还不怎么到位。管理体制束缚的结果，导致出版社在经营上、甚至是改革上受到阻碍。就第二个任务说，转企的工作内容主要从五个方面体现，即注销事业单位法人，核销事业单位编制，进行企业工商登记，与在职职工签订劳动合同，职工按企业办法参加社会保险。

（2）路线图。路线图是进行文化体制改革怎么做的路径。我把"转企—改制—上市"称为中国文化体制改革的逻辑进程。这是一种高级的逻辑进程，因为并不是每一个出版单位或出版集团都要走完这个逻辑进程。

为什么要转企，为什么要改制，为什么要上市，每一个为什么都可以做成一篇大文章。如为什么上市？从国家来说，文化这几年大发展，可谓朝阳产业，但在资本证券市场上文化产业还是个薄弱环节，没有形成板块，去年还是十五六家，后来增加了几家，国家鼓励文化产业上市。对企业来说，也有必要。我常对集团的员工说，上市"最重要的是，集团通过完成上市的基础性工作，使全体员工充分认识到转企改制上市的意义，配合并投身转企改制上市，集团的企业形态更为成熟，发展站到了新的起点"。这一段话里说到了两个方面，一方面上市带来的变化首先是在观念上的，对原事业单位旧观念的冲击是强大的；另一方面更是重点，即在公司形态的变化，上市大大提升了企业的形态，因为上市公司是企业的一种高级形态，上市公司的十二字要求"规范运作，信息披露，持续盈利"，是对这些变化的一种表述，由这一点带出经营管理以及人力资源等许多的变化。

（3）时间表。我国的出版改革从 2003 年试点开始，2006 年在试点单位改革的基础上扩大试点。在 2008 年的时候人们还说，改革没有时间表，但到 2009 年就不同了，因为有关部门要求到 2009 年底地方出版社必须全部转制到位，2010 年底 148 家中央部委出版社必须完成转企。

在 2010 年全国"两会"期间，财政部发布了《关于 2009 年中央和地方预算执行情况与 2010 年中央和地方预算草案的报告》（以下简称《报告》）。其中明确，中央财政部安排文化体育与传媒支出 314.49 亿元，积极支持文化体制改革，重点推进中央各部门 148 家经营性出版社转企改制等文化事业的发展。这一政策既是 2010 年底完成转企改制的总体目标的时间安排，也是保障措施。

2 出版社改制

如果说出版改革是一个宏观问题，那出版社改制则可以说，既是一个微观问题，也是个宏观问题。微观问题是指单个出版社改革的具体问题，宏观问题是说许多出版社改制有相似之处，可以相互借鉴。

2.1 改制的核心

改制是比转企更进一步的要求，改制的核心内容是把国有企业改成公司制企业。国有企业与公司制企业是有很大区别的。公司制是现代企业制度的一种有效组织形式。公司法人治理结构是公司制的核心。我国国有企业实施公司制改造是一项重大的企业制度变革。我国公司立法要解决的一个主要问题，就是如何规范国有企业公司制度改革，把握产权清晰、权责明确、政企分开、管理科学的具体要求。国有企业改制为公司是为了建立现代企业制度，是发展社会化大生产和市场经济的必然要求，是国有企业改革的方向。在社会主义市场经济日臻完善的过程中，会有相当一批国有企业实行规范的公司制改革。

国有企业改建为公司，并非只是企业名称的转换，实质上是一次企业制度的创新，是企业面向市场的一次深刻的改革。因此，必须依照法律、行政法规规定的条件和要求，转换经营机制，有步骤地清产核资（界定产权、清理债权债务、评估资产），建立规范的内部管理机构。坚持转换经营机制，这是公司制改革的关键；坚持做到产权清晰，这是公司制度的本质要求，也是现代企业制度的基本特点；坚持建立规范的公司法人治理结构，这是衡量规范的公司制改革的最重要的标准。这些是对国有企业怎样改制为公司的具体要求。

以上是从一般意义上说。具体到出版单位的转企，可能更具体也更复杂。因为出版单位原来还是事业单位，一下子从事业单位跳到公司制企业，这有好处也有难处。难处是出版单位还不是一个成熟的国企，好处是加快了改革的步骤。出版单位在转企的基础上改制，技术处理上有两个问题，一是分步走或并步走，都是好的选择，多数是选择了并步走；二是在治理结构上采用执行董事制较为合适。

2.2 焦点问题

改到深处是产权，改到难处是人员，是当下中国所有体制改革的症结所在。

（1）产权问题。产权是企业制度的基础，现代企业制度的核心之一。在改革前，出版单位的产权是有许多问题的。一是产权总量不清楚，二是产权不清晰，三是产权迷失，有严重者个人借去土地证变为私人。湖北长江出版传媒集团在改制中对土地房产的清理达90%，虽然很高，但还有一部分没办法完善。出版社过去的出资人实际是长期缺位的，中央各部门出版社改制曾经也面临着亟待解决的难题，即转企后企业的出资人是谁，国有资产的监管由谁来负责。地方出版社的出资人是出版集团，出版集团的出资一般是省级财政。中央出版单位的出资人是谁？看来应该是财政部。此次《报告》的发布也解决了这一问题，现在各部门出版社改制道路已并无大障碍。

（2）人员问题。人员是出版企业生产力的首要因素，但一旦改起来人成了最难办的问题。一是出版单位普遍人员偏多，尤其是辅助人员偏多的现象更为普遍，改制后人往哪里去？二是对现有人员如何做到改制后反差不要太大，一个是身份差，一个是待遇差，身份差主要是一个观念问题，指的是由事业单位到企业的落差，待遇差则是一个利益问题，主要是社保与医保的建立与完善。

2.3 改制的不同类型

主要是依据原来出版社的类型而带来改制的不同类型。地方出版社是一类，大学出版社是一类，中央部委出版社可算一类。作为一类，他们有一些相似性或共同性。地方出版社走在改革的前面，因为实施主体一般是出版集团，地方出版社跟着走就是；大学出版社改制相对容易，因为它的人员比较好办，多数高校出版社人员退休后是退到学校，给出版社解决不少难题，也因为相对容易也容易出现假改；中央部门出版社的改制相对较为复杂，多数部委出版社原来是一些部委的人员与资金的"蓄水池"，又有部委的背景，市场化程度差，单独生存能力差，积极性不高，而实施主体又不好厘清很可能是出版社自身，其原来的主管部门基本上不懂出版社改制问题，对原主管部门来说出版社改制也是一个很边缘的问题，诸种原因使中央部委出版社改制改起来不易。部委出版社单个改制效果不会好，因此最好的途径是扎堆捆绑，或与地方出版集团联合。

3 后转企改制时代的出版走向

从2010年起，出版改革先于整体的文化体制改革逐步进入了后转企改制时代。我比较早地注意到并使用了这一个词：转企改制后时代。就全国而言，还是转企改制进行时，有一种提法，"向面上铺开，向纵深发展"。"向面上铺开"是把这样的改革推进到中央部委出版社与大学出版社等，但就地方出版集团而言，作为这一轮改革的先锋，已提前进入转企改制后时代，这也是"向纵深发展"的一种含义。我个人认为，这个后转企改制时代可能会有三五年时间，也许更长一点，改革处于相对平稳期。在这个转企改制后时代如何做出版，是我们出版人面临的重要课题，不然就会改完也就没事可做了。

3.1 后转企改制时代还改什么

改革无止境。还改什么，我想是两条：

（1）从传统出版向现代出版的转型

从传统出版转向现代出版，只有到了后转企改制时代才是一个真命题。在我看来，现代出版有三个标志，即现代技术手段，现代企业制度，现代经营体系。这三个方面都要强力推进，才是向现代出版的转型。其中以现代企业制度为后转企改制时代进一步改革的重点和难点。从某种意义上说，改革要继续推进，继续推进的含义是建立起现代企业制度，破与立的结合，"破"了之后要有"立"，立就是现代企业制度。现代企业制度在我们这个行业里可能还没有破题。建立现代企业制度比转企更难，转企难在观念，建立现代企业制度难在观念与管理的双推进。现代企业制度是一种新型企业制度，它适合现代市场经济体制，以完善企业法人制度为基础，以有限责任制度为保证，以公司企业为主要形态，以产权清晰、权责分明、政企分开、管理科学为基本特征。出版企业距离建立起现代企业制度的要求还很远。

（2）加快发展方式的转变，转变就是改革

改是为了发展，"立"的另一层意思就是以发展立身。没有发展，所有的改革都会站不住脚。发展比改革难，改革与发展同时抓比单抓一个难。发展要有思路，要有举措，思路与举措并重。思路决定出路，思路决定方向，举措提供保障。我曾有一篇文章，对文化体制改革与后转企改制时代的有关问题，包括中国出版发展各有道路，制度革命比技术革命更为重要，上市是企业管理形态飞跃等，提供了意见，这里不多说。

发展方式的转变，知难行不易。转变什么，怎样转变，都不是一蹴而就的。其一，依靠教材教辅的方式要转变。其二，依靠传统出版的方式要转变，转向现代出版。其三，小作坊的生产经营方式要转变，转向集团集约化。其四，线性的发展方式要转变，转向"三跨"裂变式发展。

3.2　骨干出版企业做强做大问题

中国的出版管理机构在 2009 年提出，未来几年要形成六七个资产与销售双过百亿的骨干出版企业。这可以说是国家发展出版产业的一种战略考虑，是中国出版体制改革的逻辑发展。2010 年我国政府的有关部门又响亮地提出建设世界出版强国，从六七个"双百亿"骨干文化企业到出版强国，应该是发展思路的一种巨大进步。

（1）建设六七个骨干文化企业是可能的

现状是基本上没有合格的骨干文化企业。在中国出版业有一个现象，就是政府太强势，而企业不强。就经济的一般规律而言，政府强势的地方一般企业不强。在新闻出版领域也存在这样一个问题。所以中国目前没有太强势的出版企业，中国前十位的出版集团（企业）仍不足以在市场上形成强大的支配力量。

"双百亿"规模在工业企业中是很平常的事，在出版企业里确实不容易。但在未来出现几个是有可能的。双百亿不是目标，仅有几个"双百亿"，还是不能在世界出版之林中占有较好的位置，体现出版强国的地位。"双百亿"应该只是中间层级的目标。

怎样才能做到"双百亿"，单靠自身的发展是很难做到的。因为对多数出版社而言，现有的规模都太小，要靠重组与兼并。

（2）争创"双百亿"，也是中国出版业的一次重新洗牌

在转制中完成"双百亿"骨干文化企业的构建，其意义就是崛起中国的文化骨干企业。对格局的影响，一是中国"双百亿"出版企业尤其是"双百亿"集群将引领出版业的潮流与方向，得到政府更多的青睐与政策倾斜；二是直接带来骨干文化企业与非骨干文化企业的博弈，影响中国的出版格局。如同媒体说的，"不管怎样，大家都不愿在新一轮的竞争中落在人后，一些有实力的出版单位，特别是一些出版集团的老总们都会去盘点一下自己的家底，测算一下自己距'双百亿'距离的远近，思忖一下自己是否有进入这'六七家'的实力与后劲。"

国家正在着力打造国家级的出版集团，如中国出版集团、中国教育出版传媒集团等。

在出版集团的第一轮发展中，可以说地方出版集团独领风骚，离"双百亿"的目标最近。随着国家扶持战略的改变，中国出版集团与骨干文化企业的格局将会发生巨变。

3.3　永远不改的是社会效益与经济效益的结合

（1）出版业永恒的主题

从历史的情况看，新世纪的出版人依然是文化的传人，文化是代有传人的，并不因为时过境迁而中绝。在中国出版人的血脉里，文化责任是一种永不言弃的担当。当然商业利益毕竟也是我们不能放弃的，在转企之后更是如此。

从现实的情况看，做到文化责任与商业利益两者的结合，是我们出版业永恒的主题，是我们这一行区别于别的行业的所在，我们从事了这一职业，就要承担把这两者很好地结合起来的使命。

（2）社会效益与经济效益如何有机统一

我讲几个观点。一是始终坚守文化责任与商业利益相结合的整体理念。只有把握好我们的行业本身的特征，才能做好我们的工作。二是在具体运作中尽可能地把两者糅合到一起。我本人在长江出版集团所走的路子，就是用把两者糅合到一起的办法来做的，你分不清哪是商业利益，哪是文化责任，它是一个统一体。三是姑且提出一种"钟摆理论"。可以根据运行的需要而采行不同的侧重，或这边摆一下，或那边摆一下，总体上达到一种平衡，文化责任与商业利益的平衡。四是始终抓住发展不放。一心一意谋发展，解决一切问题的锁钥在发展，也只有发展才能找到让文化责任与商业利益并行不悖的途径。

（3）永恒的奉献只能是读者心目中的好书

市场上永远都以产品说话，对于出版业来说也就是好的图书。读者不关心你这个出版集团或出版社赚了多少钱，这与读者无关，金钱只与股民有关。当读者与股民合一的时候，他既关心你出了什么好书，也关心你赚了多少钱。但我们现在的命题不在这，而在你是一个读者。读者关心什么，那自然是好的图书。出版社以什么立足，也是图书。出版集团何以名之，也是图书做得如何。所以，一年当中安排一些什么好书，应当是出版集团与出版社的老总首先要关心的事情。

我曾经提出过一个命题，就是我们搞文化体制改革以来，我们提出产业大发展以来，出好书是多了，还是少了？想来这个问题是有一定的尖锐性的，我不知道有没有人或者部门做过这样的统计。当然我不会要具体的数据与结果，只是想提醒我们的同行或者有关的管理部门重视这个问题。对于出版业来说，不是拿金钱奉献给读者，永恒的奉献只能是读者心目中的好书，尤其是世代留传的好书，可以成为经典的好书。

改革使中国出版业走上了发展之路。中国出版界正在为建设世界出版强国而努力，希望这种努力获得更为丰硕的成果。

作者简介

王建辉，湖北省长江出版传媒集团董事长，武汉大学兼职教授。

编辑思想的实践性探讨[*]

吴 平

（武汉大学信息管理学院 430072）

摘要：编辑思想是编辑实践反映在编辑者意识中经过思维活动而产生的结果，因而具有浓厚的实践特性。文章从以下四个方面进行了阐述：编辑思想者也是出版实践者，编辑思想与编辑工作发展同步，编辑思想是编辑工作本质的反映，使编辑工作不断创新是编辑思想的灵魂。

关键词：编辑思想 编辑工作 实践

Ananalysis on Practical Characters of Editorial Ideas

Wu Ping

（School of Information Management，Wuhan University，Wuhan，430072）

Abstract：Editorial ideas are results of the thinking of editors，which have characters of practice. The paper explains this from the following four aspects，editors are also publishing explorer，editorial ideas develop with editorial activities，editorial ideas are the essence of editing，and the spirit of editorial ideas make the editing innovate continuously.

Keywords：Editorial ideas Editing Practice

编辑思想是思想的一个侧面，思想所具有的属性与特点，编辑思想也都有。如，思想具有依附性，依附于事实而存在；思想具有逻辑性，是思维的运动过程；思想具有抽象性，可在某一类或几类事实的共同属性中总结概括出规律性和本质属性；思想具有历史性，是长时期历史沉积的结果，对众多事物的认识都带有共性……但从某种意义上来说，编辑思想的实践性更加明显，因为编辑思想是编辑实践反映在编辑工作者的意识中经过思维活动而产生的结果。它可以是历史中某个编辑或某位从事编辑出版活动者的思想，也可以是某一时期编辑出版主流意识和编辑出版成果的集中体现。

1 编辑思想者也是出版实践者

我国古代第一个既有编辑思想又编定成"书'的人是孔子，他以"述而不作，信而

* 该项目为教育部 2007 人文社会科学研究基金项目，项目编号：07JA870003。

好古"[1]为宗旨，编定六经，成为历史上最早的编辑家。汉代"槐市"的出现，证明书籍已有了社会流通形态，尽管那时获取书籍的方法还只是手抄石刻。公元 7 世纪，中国发明了雕版印刷术。11 世纪，活字印刷术诞生，印本书大量出现，开创了书籍出版的新时代。15 世纪 50 年代，德国人谷登堡开始以机械的方法用铅活字印刷图书，为出版业指明了工业化方向。随着印刷术的普及，图书在社会上的流传越来越多，民众阅读、收藏书籍越来越便利，出版走向成熟。就在出版技术、手段、数量不断进步、发展过程中，编辑思想也越来越丰富，编辑思想者也越来越多，他们伴随着书籍的出版而产生，伴随着出版实践而发展。

编辑思想多指编辑个体的思想，但同时也包含有社会、国家的出版思想，个体的编辑思想必须服从社会、国家的出版方针和政策。国家的出版政策由个体编辑思想与实践来落实与体现。由于编辑个体、社会、国家对出版活动表现出不同的需要，因此，个体编辑意志必须服从国家出版思想；同时，国家出版思想也要依赖个体编辑思想、社会出版思想来反映，并最终在出版内容和形式上表现出来。

编辑思想来源于人类编辑出版活动，也形成于人类编辑出版活动，它不以人的意志为转移，编辑个体意志对国家出版活动整体编辑思想的形成具有反作用。一般来说，编辑个体意志与国家出版政策保持一致时，编辑出版事业比较顺利与和谐；编辑个体意志与国家出版政策不统一时，如果政府允许其代表作品出版，个体意识会十分强烈。如果政府不允许出版，个体编辑思想要么熄灭，要么处于潜伏期伺机而动，它的发展和运动服从于全局编辑出版活动。编辑思想与出版环境同步，编辑个体与社会、国家环境呈和谐运行状态时，出版冲撞就小；反之，出版矛盾则大。

凡思想家往往是研究思想、思维和思考模式并且形成思想体系的人。凡编辑思想家大多从事编辑出版工作，且具有以下共同特征：

(1) 有深厚的知识积淀；

(2) 有很强的观察分析出版历史、现状、总结活动规律的能力；

(3) 思维活动广泛、深刻，结论相对正确；

(4) 编辑理论与出版实践统一；

(5) 观点或思想的代表作品流传广泛，影响深远，经得起历史的考验。

有鲜明而正确的编辑思想者遵循事实，尊重读者，并能用编辑作品、出版作品的方式表达思想内容。编辑思想集前人对编辑出版活动的认知和实践经验于体系框架中，为出版事业的发展提供指导。人类出版文明发展史，也就是不断总结和吸取编辑出版思想精华的过程，在这一过程中编辑出版文化及人类文明得到不断发展。

2　编辑思想与编辑工作同步发展

思想是人们经过逻辑思维后产生的对自然与人类社会的种种判断。正确或不正确的思想都来自于现实世界。实践是人同客观环境发生的主动交流。人通过实践产生了大量的信息，经过认知能动后形成了思想。编辑思想是一种理性认识，是编辑思维活动的结果，是编辑出版客观存在在编辑意识中的反映所形成的相对稳定的观念。编辑出版活动历史与现实决定编辑思想，符合编辑出版客观事实的是正确的编辑思想，对编辑出版活动的发展起促进作用；反之，是错误的思想，对编辑出版事业发展起阻碍作用。编辑思想来源于实践。

  编辑思想伴随编辑工作产生而产生。中国编辑工作源远流长。殷商时代，有典有册，即有人已经在从事编辑整理简策的工作。孔子编辑"六经"便是以"仁"作为指导思想的核心，对鲁、周、宋、杞等国的文献资料进行取舍，主张"不语怪、力、乱、神"，删去芜杂荒诞的篇章；认为"攻（治）乎异端（杂学），斯害也已"，排斥一切反中庸之道的议论，宣扬儒家学派的理论主张和价值观念，编辑思想十分鲜明。实际上，伴随着中国学术、文化的发展，编辑工作也得到不断发展。汉代司马迁《史记》中的十表八书，便是编辑工作的结晶。记载战国时期政治斗争风云变幻的《战国策》，具有很强的艺术感染力与重要的史料价值，它是刘向根据流行的《国策》、《国事》、《短长》、《事语》、《长书》、《修书》等，整理校订、精选汇集而成的。《战国策书录》就是一份著名的"编辑报告"。南朝梁昭明太子萧统与门下许多文人经常讨论篇籍，商榷古今，并编撰完成了《文选》。在《文选序》中专门说明了其编选的原则和方法编排的标准是"凡次文之体，各以汇聚。诗赋体既不一，又以类分。类分之中，各以时代相次"、"事出于沉思，义归乎翰藻"，"不收经、史、子三部类的文章"[2]，对后世文学的发展很有影响。其后，李阳冰为李白编《草堂集》，李汉为韩愈编《昌黎先生集》，刘禹锡编《柳宗元文集》，元稹编《白香山集》，杜牧编《李贺集》，他们的编辑思想大多是出于倾慕和纪念性质的。而司马光精研历史，在长达19年的时间里编成了《资治通鉴》。这项工程是司马光与他人一起完成的，有人评论他们是"一个小而精的编辑部"，"是专职的编辑"。

  "南宋而后及至明代，雕版印刷盛行，商品经济发达，手工业城镇中书市坊铺兴起，出现了受聘于书铺的编辑，明末苏州冯梦龙、吴兴凌蒙初等即是代表。真正的近代职业编辑，在清末戊戌维新运动时及其后，才活跃于学术文化界，成为一种自由职业者。他们中间著名的人物有梁启超、谭嗣同、唐才常、樊锥、章太炎、蔡元培、张元济等。"[3]1902年2月8日，继《清议报》后，梁启超创办的《新民丛报》（半月刊）在日本横滨正式出版发行。在创刊号上，梁启超以"中国之新民"的笔名发表了脍炙人口的《新民说》，强调"新民为今日第一急务"，大力鼓吹人们都要摆脱封建奴性，树立独立、自由和爱国家、爱民族的思想，激励人们都要具有"自尊"、"进步"、"利群"以及"进取冒险"等奋发图强、积极向上的精神，并非明确说明却真真切切地阐述了《新民丛报》的编辑思想。之后，《新民丛报》果然成为辛亥革命前维新派的重要刊物。尽管后趋保守并于1907年8月停刊，但它在初期激进的言论所介绍的西方资产阶级思想政治学说对中国知识界产生的影响却是不容忽视的，发行量曾高达一万四千份。

  编辑思想与编辑方法是密切联系在一起的。在出版中采用什么指导思想决定了用什么编辑方法。杜佑的《通典》，记述了唐天宝以前历代政治、经济、礼法、兵刑等典章制度，全书200卷，内分九门，子目1 500余条，约190万字，规模十分宏大。上自《史记》八书、《汉书》十志，下至晋、宋、齐、魏、隋书诸志，并参照了《隋官序录》、《隋朝仪礼》、《大唐仪礼》、《开元礼》、《太宗政要》、《唐六典》等典制政书，确立了中国史籍中与纪传体、编年体并列的典制体，开辟了史学著述的新途径。《通典》的编辑思想十分明确，就是要揭举先代"政治之大方"，为唐朝统治者提供"龟镜"。《通典》在"经邦济世，治国安民"的编辑思想指导下，将食货典12卷列为九门之首；将原地理志的内容改编为州郡典；在食货典中增加"轻重"子目；把原属地理志的人口内容收入食货典，单开"历代盛衰户口"之目；同时，另增边防典。这些类目的增减、先后安排都体现了他"经邦济世"的编辑思想。

编辑思想没有最终目标，它不是一种产物，是一个过程。编辑工作也没有终结，而且不断会遇上新的挑战，编辑思想应使自身更加完善，更理性的反映编辑出版客观现实，并利用规律解决现实中的编辑工作问题。

3　编辑思想是编辑工作本质的反映

编辑思想来源于编辑实践，随着编辑实践的发展而发展，编辑思想同时也指导编辑实践，促进编辑实践的发展。编辑思想的实质即反映编辑实践规律，并指导编辑工作思维的成果。正如王建辉先生十多年前所言，"编辑思想是一定时期和一定范围内从事编辑工作的主导思想，它是编辑工作在人的头脑中的能动的意识反映，是关于编辑工作各方面和环节的一系列见解观点，是编辑个体与出版社集体基本素质修养、学识作风、方针策略、事业理想、图书结构以及意图指向等的综合的和最高的体现，是编辑工作的本质反映。"[4]编辑工作是出版的中心环节，是在作者提供材料的基础上依据出版原则、印制条件等对原稿选择、审阅、加工、传播等一系列工作进行的总体设计。总体设计即策划。策划，离不开编辑思想。成功的策划是编辑思想作用的结果，失败的策划也是对编辑思想的验证。

概括编辑工作，其实质也就是对作品出版及其传播所做的总体设计。编辑思想贯穿编辑工作全程，既体现在前期选题策划、中期审稿加工印制，也体现在后期对产品的宣传与反馈。以某一文学汇编本为例，选择什么题材、收录哪些作家哪些时期创作的哪些作品都需要明确的编辑思想，只有编辑思想确定了之后，所有的选择方案及素材才能确定。《史记》是我国第一部纪传体史书，是一部以人物为中心的包含百科知识的50多万字的通史。全书包括"本纪"12篇，"表"10篇，"书"8篇，"世家"30篇，"列传"70篇。从黄帝到汉武帝时代，悠悠3 000年历史聚汇，既有明主贤相、忠臣义士，也有游侠货殖，民间普通百姓，社会全貌尽揽一体。成就这部气势恢宏传世之作的原因多种，但自始至终体现如一的是该书的编辑思想，后人可在《报任安书》和《太史公书》中清晰地观察到，这就是司马迁的"原始察终，见盛观衰"[5]、"考之行事，稽其成败兴坏之理"、"究天人之际，通古今之变，成一家之言"……实质上，司马迁"究天人之际，通古今之变"、"以拾遗补艺，成一家之言，厥协《六经》异传，整齐百家杂语，藏之名山，副在京师"[6]的最终目的还是要"稽其成败兴坏之理"，为现实政治服务。而对"成败兴坏之理"的探讨也成就了他"一家之言"。

在这部历史编撰中，司马迁取众家之长成一家之言，本纪、表、书、世家、列传五种体例成纪传体通史体裁，为后人提供了一种重要的历史编撰范式。赵翼《廿二史札记》云："司马迁参酌古今，发凡起例，创为全史，本纪以序帝王，世家以记侯国，十表以系时事，八书以详制度，列传以志人物，然后一代君臣政事贤否得失，总汇于一编之中。自此例一定，历代作史者，遂不能出其范围，信史家之极则也。"《史记》全篇文献可分成两部分：正文在前，主为人物生平描述，以代表性事件或逸事衔接交杂而成；正文之后专为作者的评论或感想，常以"太史公曰"起头，或述作者个人经历，或对人物予以评价，或叙收集资料之来源，但主要以评论题材人物的性格与行事为主，以此呼应"究天人之际"的写作目的。

4　使编辑工作不断创新是编辑思想的灵魂

编辑工作的本质是以不断出版优秀作品来满足读者精神文化食粮的需要，即编辑工作创新。创新也是编辑思想的灵魂。

20世纪30年代，随着新文学第一个十年的过去，具有新锐眼光的出版家赵家璧请蔡元培先生作总序，组织编选人作导言编纂出版了《中国新文学大系》，各卷名称目及导言人依次为：《建设理论集》、胡适，《文学论争集》、郑振铎，《小说一集》、茅盾，《小说二集》、鲁迅，《小说三集》、郑伯奇，《散文一集》、周作人，《散文二集》、郁达夫，《诗集》、朱自清，《戏剧集》、洪深，《史料·索引》、阿英。该书对"五四"文学革命至1927年间新文学理论的发生、宣传、争执以及小说、散文、诗歌、戏剧诸方面系列尝试取得的成绩进行了整理、保存、评价。"创"和"闯"是赵家璧编辑思想的直接体现。所谓"创"就是"从无到有"的创造性劳动的编辑思想。在这种思想指导下，众多作家的劳动将设想变成具有独特面貌的现实。所谓"闯"是指作家送来的稿件，只要与编辑思想相一致就大胆实践。《中国新文学大系》的成功表明编辑思想和作家创作同等重要，在编辑活动中具有同等重要的意义。1933年，赵家璧先生又推出了轰动文坛的"良友文学丛书"。他的编辑目标用今天的话来说就是：书籍内容与外在形式均创一流。为此，他向鲁迅、茅盾、巴金等当时一批一流的著译家约稿，别出心裁地用软布面精装外加套色彩印包封，上印作者像。这一创新再次引起强烈反响。再加上以廉价著称的"一角丛书"，及时地介绍了很多译著到中国来等举措，使"良友"崭露头角。赵家璧先生的确是位具有远见卓识的编辑思想家。

历史事实不断证明，实践性是编辑思想的属性，编辑实践是编辑思想的出发点，也是落脚点。当代编辑出版工作正值现代化、国际化、信息化、网络化交互发展之际，注重编辑思想，充分发挥编辑主体的作用，使现代编辑出版实践焕发出勃勃生机，尤其具有深远的历史和现实意义。

注释

[1]《论语·述而》，转引自吕思勉，《中国文化思想史》（下）第507页。

[2] 李瑞良，中国出版编年史（上卷），福建人民出版社2004年版，第150页。

[3] 引自百度百科"编辑"词条。

[4] 王建辉、魏世弟，编辑思想是编辑工作之魂，《编辑之友》1992年。

[5]（汉）司马迁，《史记》卷一百三十《太史公自序》，上海古籍出版社1997年版，第2503页。

[6]（汉）司马迁，《史记》卷一百三十《太史公自序》，上海古籍出版社1997年版，第2503页。

参考文献

[1] 刘国进，中国上古图书源流，北京：新华出版社，2003.

[2] 何根海，汪高鑫，中国古代史学思想史，合肥：合肥工业大学出版社，2004.

[3] 曹之，中国古籍编撰史，武汉：武汉大学出版社，2006.

［4］黄永年，黄永年古籍序跋述论集，北京：中华书局，2007.

作者简介

吴平，武汉大学信息管理学院教授，博士生导师。

宏观出版

An Exploratory Study of the Choice Behaviour on E-Books for Readers

Yu-Kai Huang   Rurng-Shueei Wahn

(Nanhua University, Taiwan, China)

Abstract: This paper is intended to investigate the effects of using e-books in reading. According to the case study, 392 valid questionnaires were collected. From the analysis through binary logit model, the findings indicated that the pricing, occupation and the weekly online time would pose significant influences to selection behavior. According to the parameter calibrated value, market share for the book was about 65% and that for the e-book was about 35%. Direct elasticity for both the book in paper and e-book were −0.031 and −0.382 respectively; and it was obvious that the impact to market share from e-book sales price would be larger. Cross elasticity for book in paper and e-book were 0.035 and 0.193 respectively; and it was obvious that the price rising for the book in paper had less impact to the market share of e-book; nonetheless, the price rising for e-book would influence more on the market share for book in paper. From the findings for this research, readers were more susceptible to books than e-books. If the advantage of e-books can be maintained, including massive amount of e-books and reader with powerful performance, the design for the screen presentation more in tune with notebook and the e-books equipped with reader, in addition to enhancement to the payment method, then with the advantage from e-book pricing, it can effectively raise the market share for e-book.

Keywords: E-books Choice behavior Logit model

读者选择电子书行为影响因素初探

黄昱凯   万荣水

(中国台湾   南华大学)

摘要: 本文旨在探讨影响读者选用电子书的因素及其对选择行为所造成的影响。本研究共回收了392份有效样本，经过二元Logit模型分析，发现电子书价格高低、职业与每周上网时间等因素对于读者的选择行为有显著影响。校准后的参数显示纸本书市占率约为65%，电子书的市占率约为35%。纸本书与电子书的直接弹性分别为−0.022与−0.351，可见电子书价格变化对市占率影响较大。纸本漫画书与电子漫画书的交叉弹性分别是0.031与0.177，可见纸本书价格上涨对电子书的市占率影响较小，电子书价格上涨对纸本书影响较大。本研究表明学生对于电子书的接受度高，如果能继续保持其优势，包括出版数量庞大的电子书，推出功能强大的阅读器，在版面设计上更适于做笔记，为电子书捆绑阅读器，改善付费方式，并辅以电子书的价格优势，必能有效地提高电子书的市场占有率。

关键词：电子书　选择行为　Logit 模型

宏
观
出
版

1. Introduction

Digital technology has provided a new paradigm for our society and changed our lives through interaction with the Internet. As an efficient and flexible sales channel, companies can use auction sites to liquidate unwanted inventory, as well as to assist in pricing new products, acquiring new markets for low margin items, and reaching markets that would be too costly using traditional distribution methods. Consumers can surf on the e-books, browse the information and compare prices of diversified merchandise. The development of e-book is an efficient business model that enables new relationship between readers and publishers. E-books stores are becoming more important for online or offline readers. Because of the short development history of e-books reading behavior, there are few studies about the e-books. This paper had two aims: one is to examine the factors influencing the choice behaviour of e-books; the other is to describe a way in which a logit model is used to develop a marketing strategy for e-books choice behavior in the publishing market.

2. A brief review of e-books

Due to rapid innovation and development in information technology, people are no longer satisfied by traditional means of learning and obtaining knowledge. Thus, e-book is bound to become the new trend in reading in the future. An e-book is an ELECTRONIC book — a file containing all the information that a hard book would contain. An e-book (short for electronic book and also known as a digital book, e-book, and e-Book) reader is an electronic device that is designed primarily for the purpose of reading digital books and periodicals and may uses e-ink technology to display content to readers. The main advantages of these devices are readability of their screens in bright sunlight and long battery life. E-book has been a very hot topic recently since the success of Kindle from Amazon, which combines the three key characteristics: (1) a reader that is suitable for reading e-Book content, (2) wireless communications for simplicity and convenience, and (3) a rich and attractive content line-up. The trend of e-book has extended to outside of the most matured U. S. market into other parts of the world. Figure 1 shows the wholesale electronic book sales.

With e-books, you are paying for the information the e-book contains and not for anything other than that, such as impressive dust jackets or expensive colors printing or leather binding. E-books are often treated much more like computer programmers by the publishers in that you can receive free upgrades of future editions as well as free replacement copies should your copy get lost or wiped by accident, for example. As e-book technology advances and these readers are becoming ever cheaper and ever more sophisticated, you can expect within the next couple of years to

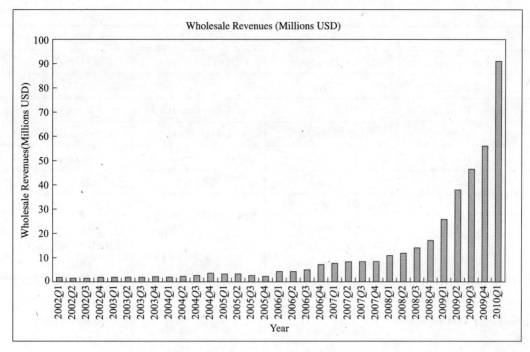

Figure 1. Wholesale Electronic Book Sales[1]

be able to add all your e-books into an electronic library that you can carry with you and search for any title, any chapter or even a specific word within seconds. [2]

E-books are preferable because usually they are searchable, modifiable and enhanceable (Anderson-Inman & Horney, 1999). By searching key words, readers can easily locate an e-book on the Internet. When reading an e-book, readers may usually adjust the font size and reading speed or even add notes to meet personal needs. Various types of embedded resources, such as translational, illustrative or instructional resources, can promote readers' comprehension. The attractive animation and vivid narration in the e-books can benefit readers in understanding the text and enhancing their reading motivation. Table 1 compares three different kinds of e-book reader devices (Amazon Kindle, Barnes & Noble Nook and Sony Portable Reader) that use e-paper.

Table 1. E-book Reader Devices

Brand name	Amazon Kindle	Barnes & Noble Nook	Sony Portable Reader
Model	Kindle 3G+WiFi	Alex	Touch Edition PRS−650
Manufacturer	Hon Hai Precision Industries	Spring Design	Sony
Picture			

Brand name	Amazon Kindle	Barnes & Noble Nook	Sony Portable Reader
Dimensions	190×122×8.5 mm	96×126×13 mm	168×119×9.6 mm
Weight	247g	343g	215g
Screen Technology	E-ink Pearl	E-ink Vizplex	E-ink Pearl
Power	L-P 1750mAh	L-P 1530mAh	Li-Polymer 940mAh
OS	Linux 2.6.26	Android 1.5, Linux 2.6.27	Linux
Memory	4GB Flash	2GB Flash	2GB Flash
Supported Formats	Kindle (AZW), PRC, PDF, HTML, DOC, TXT, MP3, Audible, JPEG, GIF, PNG	PDF, EPUB, eReader, PDB, JPEG, GIF, PNG, BMP, MP3	BBeB (LRF/LRX), PDF, EPUB, TXT, RTF, JPEG, BMP, GIF, PNG, MP3
Supported DRM Formats	AZW and TOPAZ (Kindle only)	eReader (EPUB/eReader), Adobe ADEPT (EPUB/PDF)	Marlin DRM (BBeB), Adobe ADEPT (EPUB/PDF)
Content Partners	Amazon	B&N eBooks	Random House, Simon & Schuster, HarperCollins, Libri.de, Thalia.de, Thalia.ch

3. Methodology

Choice behavior can be characterized by a decision process, which is informed by perceptions and beliefs based on available information, and influenced by affect, attitudes, motives and preferences. The logit model is based on the notion that an individual derives utility by choosing an alternative. The *utilities U* are latent variables and the observable *preference indicators y* are manifestations of the underlying utilities. The utilities are assumed to be a function of a set of *explanatory variables X*, which describe the *decision-maker n* and the *alternative i*. The resulting utility equation can be written as (Emmanuel *et al.*, 2002):

$$U_{in} = V(X_{in}; \beta) + \varepsilon_{in} \tag{1}$$

where U_{in} is the utility of alternative $i[i=1, \cdots, j_n]$ for decision-maker n $[n=1, \cdots, N]$ (U_n is a vector of utilities for decision-maker n); X_n is a vector of explanatory variables describing alternative i and decision-maker n (X_n is a matrix of explanatory variables describing all alternatives and decision-maker n); β is a vector of unknown parameters; V (called the systematic utility) is a function of the explanatory variables and unknown parameters β; and ε_{in} is a random disturbance for i and n (ε_n is the vector of random disturbances, which is distributed $\varepsilon_n \sim D(\theta_\varepsilon)$, where θ_ε are unknown parameters).

Decision-maker n chooses i if and only if $U_{in} \geqslant U_{jn}$ for all $j \in C_n$, where C_n is the set of I_n

alternatives faced by n. The choice probability equation is then:

$$P(i \mid X_n; \beta, \theta_\varepsilon) = prob[U_{in} \geqslant U_{jn}, \forall j \in C_n].$$ (2)

The utility of alternative i prefer the utility of alternative j in individual, k can be showed as follow:

$$U_{ik} > U_{jk} \quad i, j \in A_k \quad i \neq j$$

The utility function of U_{ik} can be showed as follow:

$$U_{ik} = V_{ik} + \varepsilon_{ik}$$ (3)

The probability choice behavior model can be showed as follow:

$$\begin{aligned}
P(i \mid A_k) &= P(U_{ik} > U_{jk}, \forall j \in A_k) \\
&= P(V_{ik} + \varepsilon_{ik} > V_{jk} + \varepsilon_{jk}, \forall j \in A_k) \\
&= P(V_{ik} - V_{jk} > \varepsilon_{jk} - \varepsilon_{ik}, \forall j \in A_k)
\end{aligned}$$ (4)

It assumed that all of the disturbances are independently and identically distributed (IID) and have the same Gumbel distribution, the GMNL model as follow:

$$P(i \mid A_k) = \frac{e^{V_{ik}}}{\sum_{J_k = 1}^{J_k} e^{V_{jk}}}$$ (5)

where J_k denotes the number of alternative A_k.

4. Data and analysis results

The data for our study are collected from an online survey (see Figure 2). During the survey of two-week period, in the final survey we retrieved 392. Among the sample data, more than 66.9% of respondents are female, 64.2% are 18 – 29 years old. More than 69.4% of the respondents are unmarried. In terms of education level, 66.8% of respondents are educated at the college / university level. In terms of income level, more than 28.1% makes less than NT $30,000 per month. More than 49.7% of respondents live in northern Taiwan. Furthermore, about 34.8% of the respondents are students. About 77.9% of the respondents have three years or more experience in online shopping when they fill in the questionnaire.

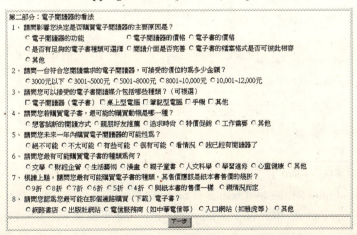

Figure 2. Questionnare web site

Discrete choice analysis assumes that decision-makers select the alternative with the highest utility. Thus, the utility of an alternative includes a deterministic portion which is a function of the attributes of the alternative and characteristics of the decision-maker and a random component which represents unobservable components of the utility function. The characteristics variables of participants are socioeconomic variables, like gender, age, marital status, education level, monthly income level, area and occupation. In this research, we use the binary logit model to analyze items that influence customers in choosing the e-books or book (a novel of Harry Porter). This choice set of e-books or book is shown as Figure 3. The choice model is estimated using the NLOGIT 3.0 software and the Maximum Likelihood method. All estimates have plausible signs (except the dummy for marital status, education, area and occupation in the model for respondents). The costs were combined with income variables in various ways. The estimated coefficients for the binary logit model are shown in Table 2.

E-books   Book

Figure 3. The choice set of e-books or book

Table 2. The Estimation Results of Binary Logit Model

Variable	Model Structure Binary Logit Model		
	Coefficient	t-value	P-value
Constant (e-books)	−0.18387	1.16761	0.24297
Attributes of respondents			
Weekly online time	1.079	1.820 **	0.068 *
Price (e-books)	−0.682	−2.131 **	0.016 *
Income	1.832	−2.115 **	0.016 *
Dummy for Area-of-Southern Taiwan	−0.751	−1.807 **	0.007 *
Dummy for Occupation-of- Professional	0.263	1.672 **	0.037 *
Observations		392	
Log-likelihood		−431.902	
"Rho^2" w. r. t. 0		0.136	

** t-value >1.645; * p<0.1.

The likelihood ratio for the best results of binary logit model is 0.136. That means the variables which have significant effect on the binary logit model have powerful explanation. And the calibration results reveal that: The variables for gender, age, marital status, and education can be removed, because their estimates are clearly insignificant now. The variables for area have a positive impact on e-books choice behavior: People living in southern Taiwan prefer to choose books to e-books. Professional and high weekly online time has a positive impact for choosing e-books.

In this study we present the application results of applying the choice behavior. These results are compared to actual outcomes. We also report the results of policy simulation runs in which one variable is changed and everything else is assumed to remain constant. All simulation results reported here are obtained using the binary logit model (final column in Table 2). Below are the outcomes for simulations in each of which a single (policy) variable is changed. The model system has been used for the following policy runs: a 10% (30%) increase (decrease) in the e-books (books). The main outcomes for this system are in Table 3. The results are expressed as percentage differences relative to the base run. These results therefore give predictions of the impact of the respective policy measures only. The choice behavior model itself is sensitive to changes in price. For e-books and books, to decrease 10% of price construct will increase the market share by 1.848% and 2.121%. If e-books decrease 30% of price construct will increase the market share by 5.367%.

Table 3. Simulation Results for Different Price Policies

		E-books	Books
Base		35.53%	64.47%
E-books			
	Price ↑10%	34.88% (↓1.832%)	65.12 % (↑1.832%)
	Price ↑30%	32.86% (↓5.783%)	67.14 % (↑5.783%)
	Price ↓10%	33.47 % (↑1.848%)	66.53% (↓1.848%)
	Price ↓30%	35.27 % (↑5.367%)	64.73 % (↓5.367%)
Books			
	Price ↓10%	37.66% (↓2.121%)	62.34 % (↑2.121%)
	Price ↓30%	35.24% (↓6.434%)	64.76% (↑6.344%)

Next, we analyze elasticity issue using by the results of logit model. The Price elasticity[3] of demand measures the percentage change in quantity demanded caused by a percent change in price. As such, it measures the extent of movement along the demand curve. The cross elasticity of demand or cross-price elasticity[4] of demand measures the responsiveness of the demand for a good to a change in the price of another good. It is measured as the percentage change in demand for the first good that occurs in response to a percentage change in price of the second good. According to the (6) and (7), the direct elasticities for both the book in paper and e-book were −0.031 and −0.382 respectively; and it was obvious that the impact to market share from e-book sales price would be larger. Cross elasticities for book in paper and e-book were 0.035 and 0.193 respectively; and it was obvious that the price rising for the book in paper had less impact to the market share of e-book; nonetheless, the price rising for e-book would influence more on the market share for book in paper.

5. Conclusions and limitations

In the booming of e-book industry, many of Taiwan's IT firms benefited from the global hardware demand of e-readers since Taiwan has the core upstream technology and reader device innovation along with OEM capability. However, the e-book industry hasn't fully developed yet in Taiwan. There is not a firm like Amazon who provides a total solution to customers. The uncertain business model and unclear positioning of industry players also dragged down the development of e-book industry.

According to analysis results, market share for the book was about 65% and that for the e-book was about 35%. Direct elasticity for both the book in paper and e-book were −0. 031 and −0. 382 respectively; and it was obvious that the impact to market share from e-book sales price would be larger. Cross elasticity for book in paper and e-book were 0. 035 and 0. 193 respectively; and it was obvious that the price rising for the book in paper had less impact to the market share of e-book; nonetheless, the price rising for e-book would influence more on the market share for book in paper.

From the findings for this research, even readers were more susceptible to book than e-book (a case of novel of Harry Porter), but we think that if the advantage of e-books can be maintained, including massive amount of e-books and reader with powerful performance, the design for the screen presentation more in tune with PC, notebook and the e-books equipped with reader, in addition to enhancement to the payment method, then with the advantage from e-book pricing, it can effectively raise the market share for e-book.

Our data are all focused and gathered in Taiwan, so the conceptual framework proposed by us is suitable for Taiwanese people. But consumers with different culture may not be explained by this conceptual framework. Future research can collect samples from other regions and compare the difference.

Notes

[1] http://www. publishers. org/

[2] http://www. lucythewonderdog. com/whatisanebook. htm#where

[3] The formula used to calculate the coefficient cross elasticity of demand is:

$$E_d = \frac{P}{Q_d} \times \frac{dQ_d}{dP} \tag{6}$$

[4] The formula used to calculate the coefficient cross elasticity of demand is:

$$E_{XY} = \frac{\dfrac{\Delta Q_{dX}}{Q_{dX}}}{\dfrac{\Delta P_y}{P_y}} = \frac{\Delta Q_{Xd}}{\Delta P_y} \cdot \frac{P_y}{Q_{Xd}} \tag{7}$$

Reference

[1] Lynne A. I. , Mark A. H. . Supported E-text: Assistive Technology through Text Transformations. Reading Research Quarterly, vol. 42, 2007 (1): 153-160

[2] Emmanuel G, Hyungsik R. M. . A Note on the Nonstationary Binary Choice Logit Model, Economics Letters, vol. 76, 2002: 267-271

Acknowledgment

We would like to thank Kitty Li (Hong Kong) for her support throughout.

Author

Yu-Kai Huang: Assistant Professor, Institute of Publishing and Culture Enterprise Management, Nanhua University.

Rurng-Shueei Wahn: Associate Professor, Institute of Publishing and Culture Enterprise Management, Nanhua University.

作者简介

黄昱凯,南华大学出版与文化事业管理研究所助教。

万荣水,南华大学出版与文化事业管理研究所副教授。

宏观出版

数字时代出版业资本运营

徐建华　梁浩光　卢正明

（南开大学商学院　天津　300071）

摘要：随着我国出版业改革的深入推进，资本运营作为有效的发展手段，已经被更多的出版集团广泛运用。如今在数字时代背景下，国内外环境对现代出版业的资本运营提出了更高的要求。本文从出版业资本运营的概况出发，对资本运营的必要性、发展模式、风险防范与策略进行分析，以期为学界和业界的研究与实践提供一定的参考。

关键词：数字时代　出版业　资本运营

Publishing Capital Operation in Digital Age

Xu Jianhua Liang Haoguang Lu Zhengming

(School of Business Nankai University, Tianjin, 300071)

Abstract: With the development of China's publishing industry, Capital operation is widely used as an effective development way by more publishing group. On the background of Digital period, the environment of internal and abroad claims for more requisition. On the base of analysis on the general situation of publishing capital operation, this article makes an analysis on the following aspects: necessity of publishing capital operation, its development mode, risk prevention and its strategy. In order to card the current conditions of China's publishing capital operation, and to serve as an reference for the research and practice of the Schools and Industry.

Keywords: Digital period　Publishing industry　Capital operation

时下，无论是出版理论界还是产业界，关心最多、探讨最多的莫过于数字出版问题。根据新闻出版总署发布的《2009年新闻出版产业分析报告》，中国数字出版业2009年年产值达799.4亿元，首度超越传统出版业。2006年以来的年均增长率超过55%，大大高于其他行业增长率。[1]数字出版的迅速发展，表明我国出版业的转型成效初显，出版业的总体格局在技术进步的带动下，已发生深刻改变。

数字出版近年内将成为国际出版界竞争的主战场，因此，搭建数字资源管理平台、构建数字出版产业链、培养数字出版人才队伍、开拓数字产品国内外市场等，日益成为我国现代出版企业关注的焦点。而这些经营策略的实施，在很大程度上依赖于出版企业的资本运营。可以毫不夸张地说，当今出版业的发展、壮大，离不开资本运营；完成新闻出版总署提出的"双百亿"目标，更得依靠资本运营。尤其是国资委近期以来国有资产证券化的思路已非常明显前提下，面对这场国有资产的财富盛宴，出版业绝不应该缺席。

1　出版业资本运营的内涵

对出版业资本运营内涵的表述，在当今出版业，可谓"仁者见仁，智者见智"，只有学者的认识较为一致，主要集中在以下几个方面：

第一，出版业资本运营的对象是其可经营性资产，包括生产要素和资本形态；

第二，出版业资本运营的方式包括合资经营，吸收合并，投资、控股、参股、产权转让、收购、兼并、租赁和上市融资等；

第三，出版业资本运营的核心与本质是实现资本的保值、增值。

据此，我们认为，出版业资本运营是资本运营在出版产业的具体运用，主要指出版企业将拥有的各种生产要素和资本形态，通过兼并、收购、参股、控股、租赁、股份化、上市等多种途径，进行优化配置，实现最大限度的增值。出版企业所拥有的各种有形资产和无形资产，都可视为资本，都可通过资本运营的方式，实现价值增值。

2　出版业资本运营的必要性

实施资本运营是我国当今出版业的必要选择，这种必要性主要表现在以下几个方面：

2.1　资本运营是出版业进一步融资的需要

我国出版业现阶段正处于数字出版飞速发展时期，对资本的需求量越来越大。主要体现在：

首先，现代出版，尤其是数字出版的产业链延伸，体现了越来越强的资本效应，即大投入，高产出；小投入，无产出。为了将出版业做大、做强，需要有大资本的支持。

其次，我国出版业在实现产业化、集团化的过程中，必须有大量资金的投入。

第三，激烈的市场竞争，使得出版业面临新的整合，为了避免被市场淘汰，维持生存和发展，出版单位就必须有强大的资本实力做后盾。

第四，出版单位日常经营中的诸多环节，如数字出版体系的建设、出版信息化建设、现代化物流中心的建立等，都需要大量的资金支持。

当今出版业在数字出版和现代出版产业链构建中所面临的巨大资金缺口，单靠出版单位自身的积累是很难实现的，只有充分依托资本运营，达到以少量国有资本控制大量社会资本的目的。

2.2　资本运营是出版业提高经营水平的需要

在我国出版业传统的经营方式中，编辑处于整个出版流程的中心环节，出版单位的经营管理措施几乎都是围绕编辑来制定和实施的，这在一定程度上导致了出版活动与市场需求的分离。随着我国出版业市场化、产业化的推进，必须将资本运营作为出版单位经营的核心，才能使其适应市场经济运行的需要。此外，通过资本运营，可以将出版企业现有资本进行优化配置，发挥最大作用；也可以盘活闲置的可经营资产，发挥其现实效用，避免资源的浪费；还可以挖掘潜在资本和无形资本，发挥品牌优势，使其创造新的价值和经济效益，从而达到整体资本增值。

2.3　资本运营是出版业应对国际挑战的需要

资本运营作为现代企业的一种先进经营方式，已被国外出版企业所普遍采用。由于发达国家市场经济已确立多年，因此，其出版企业在市场竞争中很早就运用多种资本运营方式来发展和壮大自己，积累了丰富的资本运营经验。随着我国出版业对外开放力度的逐步加大，国外出版企业必然会凭借其雄厚的资本实力，通过多种资本运营手段，如兼并、收购、集团化等来获取我国本土的出版资源，拓展业务领域，扩大自己的经营范围和影响力。在他们通过资本运营觊觎我国出版市场的情况下，我国出版单位必须变革陈旧的经营方式，有效实行资本运作。我国出版单位只有尽快熟悉、掌握和应用资本运营，通过各种适宜的资本运作手段盘活资本、实现价值增值，才能使国内出版单位在短期内提升竞争力，应对外资的挑战。

2.4 资本运营是出版业集约化发展的需要

国内出版业虽然有一些出版企业随着出版产业化的推进，取得了较好的经济效益，拥有一定规模的资产。但还有很多出版企业由于长期受垄断体制的影响，观念陈旧、管理粗放、人才缺乏，不重视资本的运用，不懂得资产的开发，造成了资本的严重浪费和闲置。为了更好地促进当今出版产业的发展，就必须通过资本运营，盘活存量资产，加速资本的流动，达到最优配置，实现经营的集约化。

3　出版业资本运营的模式

出版业资本运营的模式是出版业资本运营的核心内容，对出版业的资本运营活动有直接的指导意义。尽管说法不一，如"出版业资本运营的形式"、"出版业资本运营的方式"、"出版业资本运营的内容"、"出版业资本运营的路径"等，但其所指代的内容是一致的。

长江出版传媒集团公司王建辉先生的观点值得关注，他认为，出版业的资本运营方式大致有三种类型："一种是出版业内部资产重组，即对企业的资产进行剥离、置换、出售和转让；一种是通过出版企业间进行合并、托管、收购、兼并、分立以及风险投资的行为，以实现资本结构或债务结构的改善，为实现资本运作的根本目标奠定基础；一种是发行股票和债券、配股、增发新股、转让股权、派送红股、转增股本、股权回购等。"[2]

无论采取哪种资本运营模式，我们认为，出版业都应该注意以下几点：

其一，结合出版业宏观管理目标的特殊性进行资产组合；

其二，整合产业链，实现价值链；

其三，在政策允许范围内，引入多元化股权结构；

其四，整合上游和下游相关优质资源，形成规模经营。

4　出版业资本运营的风险与规避

安全性是出版业资本运营的一个基本要求。由于当今我国出版产业环境的不确定性和复杂性，出版业在进行资本运营的过程中，会遇到各种不确定因素和风险。因此，出版业在开展资本运营的实践中，要对其将面临风险的类型与风险的规避有一个充分而全面的认识，只有这样，才能够做到万无一失。

从资本运营的方式来看，出版业资本运营的风险主要分为内部运用型资本运营风险和外部交易型资本运营风险。由于两种资本运营的方式不同，在运营过程中可能遇到的风险也就不同。下面结合具体的风险类型谈谈资本运营风险规避的主要方法。

4.1 内部运用型资本运营的风险与规避

出版业内部运用型资本运营主要指通过对资本使用价值的有效运用，实现资本增值，即在出版经营过程中合理有效地运用资本，不断地开发新产品，采用新技术，以提高资本的效率和效益。[3]在这个出版经营的过程中，出版企业由于面临的各种不确定性会引发利润变动、国有资本流失、支付困难、甚至破产的风险。具体而言，内部运用型资本运营风险又可具体划分为政策风险、市场风险、产业风险和理念风险。

4.1.1 政策风险及规避

政策风险主要是指由于国家政治因素、政策因素和基础法律模糊所造成的不确定性给企业的资本运营带来的风险。政策是出版业资本运营过程中不可回避的问题。出版业与国家的文化、宣传、舆论和意识形态等方面密切关联，是受国家政策管制较多的行业。我国现行体制决定了现在各行业所进行的一切改革都必须在政策的指导下缓慢推进，出版业资本运营的开展，从某种意义上，也是得益于政策的放松，政策导向可以说是我国出版业资本运营的基本特点。但由于出版业资本运营过程中政策的不确定和模糊，以及某种程度的探索性，因此，极有可能遭遇政策风险。对于这种类型的风险，出版业可以从以下几个方面进行规避：

（1）加强党的领导，充分研究我国政府现行的法规、条例与政策文件；

（2）坚持编辑业务与经营业务相分离；

（3）确保国有资本控股。

4.1.2 市场风险及规避

我们在谈论资本运营的时候，更多地是从外部扩张的角度去分析的，没有把重点放在具体产品与项目的合作上。但是资本运营并不是空中楼阁，必须建立在具体产品运营上，否则就会失去其存在的基础。

虽然我国图书出版产业总的市场空间很大，但是现在各种性质的资本在逐利性的驱动下想方设法进入图书出版产业，图书出版产业领域的竞争异常激烈和残酷。另一方面，我国的图书出版市场发展却并不成熟和规范，整个市场十分复杂和难以把握，这在一定程度上就加大了市场的风险。对于这种类型风险，出版业可以从以下几个方面进行规避：

（1）对市场动向进行实时监测；

（2）对资本进入门槛进行准确评估[4]；

（3）把握最佳的资本运营时机。

4.1.3 产业风险及规避

产业发展有其自身的规律，它本身所蕴涵的复杂性与不确定性也会给资本运营带来风险。当这个产业表现很好时，就有更多的资本进入；当这个产业表现不好，资本就会出现外流。对于我国出版业而言，在产业表现不尽人如意的情况下，如果资本没有及时退出，运营主体就面临损失的风险。

对这一类型风险进行规避，运营主体的单个力量往往很难改变整个产业的命运，所以对于出版业而言，最好的规避就是资本运营前的产业分析与判断，提高其在这一领域进行资本运营的警惕性。出版企业可以主要从以下两个方面对产业环境进行分析：

（1）出版产业：发展的现状与前景；

（2）相关产业：对出版产业发展的影响。

4.1.4　理念风险及规避

资本运营是一种经营理念、模式和战略，它的引入，能开拓出版业经营者的思路，使其经营活动更为活跃。但由于出版业经营者对资本运营的概念以及作用的认识存在一定偏颇，与资本运营的本质涵义和作用有一定的距离，为即将开始的资本运营埋下潜在的风险，最终可能导致资本运营未能起到应有效果。面对这种情况，风险规避的方法主要有：

（1）资本运营要为"主业"经营服务，树立核心竞争力意识；

（2）全面认识资本运营，充分挖掘各种类型的资本价值。

4.2　外部交易型资本运营风险与规避

外部交易型资本运营主要指通过资本市场进行交易，实现资本增值，包括股票的发行与交易、企业产权交易以及企业部分资本买卖等。[5] 在外部交易型资本运营方式的选择中，不同的融资方式和融资环境会给企业带来不同的风险。外部交易型资本运营的风险又可以具体划分为信息风险、扩张风险、管理风险和金融风险。

4.2.1　信息风险及规避

信息风险是指在资本运营前期，由于运营主体对资本运营对象缺乏全面的了解，在没能完全掌握真实、有效信息的情况下，就贸然做出资本运营的决策，以致降低了资本运营的成功率。[6]

出版单位在对是否要进行资本运营、采取哪种运营方式、资本运营中另一方的选择，以及资本运营的赢利和成本估测问题进行决策时，需要有科学的分析和充足的信心作为依据。但由于"信息不对称"这一现象的客观存在，使得出版单位在进行资本运营的过程中可能会因为信息不足而作出错误的决定。这里尤其需要提醒出版单位注意的是会计信息风险。在实施合资、合作、兼并收购等资本运作时，必然会涉及对另一方资产、效益、经营的评估，而这种评估，很大程度上取决于对方披露的财务报告。因此，出版单位的资本运营必须建立在对运营对象、运营环境、运营条件的调查和充分了解的基础之上，从而避免决策失误。对信息风险的规避主要有以下方面：

（1）积极主动地去获取有效信息；

（2）注重所获取信息的可靠性与权威性；

（3）充分掌握资本运营对象的市场价值。

4.2.2　扩张风险及规避

出版企业要想做大、做强，必须进行一定的扩张；但是扩张并不是随意的，而要考虑到主业与辅业的关系、一元化与多元化的关系。这些关系处理不当，就会给资本运营带来风险，我们称之为扩张风险。在扩张风险中最为典型的就是由于出版企业过于看重规模扩大，一味地追求规模的扩张，而忽视专业实力的打造，采用多元化来分散风险的做法受到冷落，从而产生资本运营的风险。面对这种情况，风险规避的方法主要有：

（1）相关产业扩张办法：确保扩展业务与主业的相关性；

（2）核心产业扩张办法：确立核心产业的支撑地位；

（3）非相关产业扩张办法：相关产业与非相关产业协调发展。

4.2.3　管理风险及规避

出版企业若采用兼并、收购方式进行资本运营，就必须防范管理风险，即出版企业同被并购企业在理念、文化、管理、制度等多方面存在差异，从而导致并购后出版企业的管理活动不能进入正轨，存在内部排斥和消耗。[7]

并购后的资产重组绝不是简单的实物资产的重组过程，它既包括生产要素的重新组合，还包括运行机制、企业文化的融合，同时还涉及与政府关系、与竞争对手关系的重新调整和定位。这些方面如果处理不好，出版企业不仅不能获得规模经济效应、财务协同效应、市场份额协同效应以及经验共享互补效应等并购效果，甚至还会受到被购并进来的新企业不良业绩的拖累，而影响自身的发展。对管理风险的规避主要应做到以下两个方面：

（1）认真思考发展定位和经营需要，有目的地进行资本运营；

（2）仔细考察合作对象，防止乱收购、乱兼并等行为的发生。

4.2.4　金融风险及规避

外部交易型资本运营很多情况下是和金融市场的支持分不开的，而金融市场本身的不确定性会直接给企业的资本运营带来风险。对于出版企业来说，资本市场的影响力度更大，因为股份化、上市、参股、收购等诸多融资方式都是与资本市场相联系的，可以说完善、健全的资本市场是出版业进行有效资本运营的重要条件。而货币市场，由于利率的完全市场化还需要一个很长的过程，出版企业通过银行贷款进行资本运营的风险较小，但是随着银行利率的充分市场化，这个风险不得不引起重视。

对于这一类型风险的规避，出版业可以考虑以下几个方面：

（1）以资本市场的资本运营为主；

（2）积极拓展融资手段；

（3）实现资金投向的多元化。

5　出版业资本运营的战略

我国出版业所面临的数字环境以及资本运营的现实挑战，需要宏观层面的指导与规划来给予解决。因此，在资本运营的实践过程中逐渐形成具有特色的宏观战略，对于当今出版业可持续发展来说至关重要。

5.1　改制上市运营战略

运用股改上市这种资本运营手段，在国外出版业已经有相当长的时间，许多知名的出版商在这方面都拥有悠久的历史并取得了辉煌的成就。国内出版业在股票市场运作方面的探索虽然才刚刚开始，但成绩显著。随着我国上海新华传媒、四川新华文轩、辽宁北方联合出版传媒等一批大型出版发行企业的上市，刺激了更多的出版企业投身到改制上市的行列之中，为数字时代背景下出版业资本运营开辟了广阔的天地。

出版业通过股改上市进行资本运营，通过公开招股，不仅可以获得持续稳定的资金支持，同时，上市过程中的脱胎换骨的打造和历练，可以帮助他们建立起真正的现代企业制度，实现规范化运作，有利于出版业的制度创新。此外，通过股票市场运作，可以激活其无形资产，盘活可经营性资产，发挥自身的品牌优势，使其整体资产增值，并通过从股票市场筹集资金，将经营风险部分地转移和分散给了投资者，实现了风险的社会化，提高了出版产业的抗风险能力。

5.2　数字化运营战略

在 2009 年我国的数字出版产业中，数字期刊收入 6 亿元，电子书收入 14 亿元，数字报（网络版）收入 3.1 亿元，网络游戏收入 256.2 亿元，网络广告达 206.1 亿元，手机出版（包括手机音乐、手机游戏、手机动漫、手机阅读）达到 314 亿元，总产值达 799.4 亿元。网络游戏、网络广告和手机出版成为数字出版产业名副其实的三巨头。我国数字出版产业在短短几年内产值实现了跨越式发展，年均增长率超过 55%，可谓突飞猛进。数字出版产业产值屡创新高的同时，呈现出手机出版异军突起，数字技术加快创新、阅读终端不断升级，政策引导加强等产业发展特点，这些都为数字出版的产业化发展提供了坚实的基础。因此，数字化应该成为中国出版业发展的核心战略之一。

数字化运营战略的核心是构建数字出版产业链。其主要包括内容创造、网上平台、无线下载传输和数据处理、终端产品等几个环节，让内容、平台、终端三位一体，最终实现数字化、产品化、平台化和规模化。同时，商业模式应多样化，最后走出自己的路。

5.3 无形资本运营战略

出版业无形资本运营，是出版企业依据其所拥有的无形资本的特殊性，对无形资本进行管理、维护和经营，实现无形资本的保值、增值，进而获取收益的全部过程。[8] 出版业要利用好无形资本具有不可复制性的优势，实现无形资本价值的最大化。特别是在当前数字化大发展的环境下，出版业更要确立相应的无形资本运营战略，进而达到出版资本价值整合的战略目标。因此，出版业应该从战略高度积极进行无形资本运营的探索和创新。

数字时代，我国出版业无形资本大致可划分为四大类型：权利类无形资本、市场类无形资本、人力资本和制度资本。其中，权利类无形资本包括出版专营权、专有出版权、名称权、商标权、专利权和经营秘密；市场类无形资本包括关系资本、声誉和合同；人力资本包括编辑人力资本、职业经理人力资本和领导者人力资本；所谓制度资本就是制度作为投入要素，参与图书的生产和销售等过程，并因而取得"利润"分享的机会，依靠与出版企业家签订的合约得到"收益"的权利。由此可见，现代出版业无形资本的内涵和外延相当广泛，出版业要想做大、做强，就需要各出版企业从战略高度予以重视，研究、开发、维护和发展无形资本，积极进行无形资本运营的探索和创新。

从宏观上我们认为，以下几个方面应该引起出版业的重视：

一是树立无形资本运营意识，做好无形资本运营规划；

二是科学地进行无形资本评估；

三是重视出版业无形资本的保护；

四是实施多种运行战略，包括总体战略和专门战略。

5.4 "走出去"资本运营战略

打造国际一流的出版传媒企业，实施国际化发展是通向未来的必由之路。现代出版业要充分利用好国内、国外两种资源、两个市场，拉动产业发展。中国出版业作为对外传播中华文化的重要渠道，加强国际传播能力的重任在肩。同时，要打造出国际一流的出版传媒企业，也必须形成并不断提高国际竞争力。近几年来，我国出版业"走出去"步伐正在加快，版权引进与输出的逆差已经大幅度缩小，但总体上并不乐观。

我国出版业走出去，包括版权"走出去"、产品"走出去"和实体"走出去"三个方面。

在版权"走出去"与产品"走出去"方面，出版企业要不断加大外向型选题的开发力度，整合海外资源和合作渠道，发挥整体品牌优势，主动策划外向型选题，积极进行版权输出和成品图书出口。

　　在实体"走出去"方面，要开创条件在海外办实体，实施国际本土化战略。这既能贴近国际社会的实际和受众，又有利于有效进入国际主流市场；既可以将原有驻外业务代表处改制成为公司，以增强其经营活力，也可以控股海外出版机构，开展出版国际营销；同时，整合与利用好原来存在欧美的专销中国图书的"红书网"，也是一种不错的选择。以中国出版集团为例，2007 年以来建立了中国出版（巴黎）公司、中国出版（悉尼）公司、中国出版（温哥华）公司。去年，这三家公司出版的法文、英文图书将近 70 种，通过海外渠道进入西方主流市场。中国出版（悉尼）公司因市场表现突出，已跻身澳大利亚图书中盘商 A 级供货商名录。2010 年，中国出版集团公司已与韩国熊津出版公司合资建立中国出版（首尔）公司，与英国查思出版社合资建立中国出版（伦敦）公司，与香港凤凰卫视控股有限公司在香港合资建立凤凰出版有限公司。同时还先后在美国纽约、圣地亚哥地区合资开办了两家新华书店，目前在海外的独资、合资出版发行公司及销售网点已达 27 家。可见，在当前环境下，中国出版业在"走出去"方面大有可为。

6　小结

　　进入数字时代以来，国际上一些大企业相继破产或陷入困境，其中一个共性的原因就是过度扩张，盲目并购，大量资本投资于低效的领域。而目前，我国一些中央企业也存在过分追求规模扩张，低效资本占用过多，资本使用效率不高的现象。为了限制非主业投资，国资委于 2007 年推行经济增加值考核试点，提出中央企业全面实行经济增加值（EVA）考核，对企业非经常性收益将减半计算。这种考核方式无疑是一场"管理革命"，目的是有效抑制央企的投资冲动，鼓励企业加大科技创新投入，引导中央企业做强主业、控制风险、优化结构。

　　面对这种新的变化，出版业资本运营将面临更大的挑战。在数字时代背景下，今后我国出版业将呈现出怎样的竞争格局，资本运营在其中居于何等地位，将发挥什么作用，我们拭目以待。

注释

[1] 数据来源：《2009 年新闻出版产业分析报告》，新闻出版总署 2010 年 7 月发布。

[2] 王建辉. 出版业的资本运作. 出版发行研究，2008（8）.

[3] 夏永乐等. 资本运营理论与实务. 东北财经大学出版社，2010.

[4] 陈相雨. 我国图书出版产业资本运营的风险规避研究. 南京师范大学硕士学位论文，2005.

[5] 夏永乐等. 资本运营理论与实务. 东北财经大学出版社，2010.

[6] 陈相雨. 我国图书出版产业资本运营的风险规避研究. 南京师范大学硕士学位论文，2005.

[7] 徐建华. 现代出版业资本运营. 中国传媒大学出版社，2006.

[8] 徐建华. 现代出版业资本运营. 中国传媒大学出版社，2006.

参考文献

[1] 陈相雨. 我国图书出版产业资本运营的风险规避研究. 南京师范大学硕士学位论文, 2005.

[2] 徐建华. 现代出版业资本运营. 中国传媒大学出版社, 2006.

[3] 夏永乐等. 资本运营管理理论与实务. 东北财经大学出版社, 2010.

[4] 赵婧. 从辽宁出版传媒上市看中国出版业资本运营之道. 中国集体经济, 2007 (12).

[5] 樊士德. 我国传媒产业体制改革与资本运营战略的探索. 四川大学硕士学位论文, 2005.

[6] 季峰. 从国际经验看我国出版业资本运营的模式选择及认识误区. 出版发行研究, 2008 (12).

[7] 黄进. 中外传媒资本运营比较研究. 山东大学硕士学位论文, 2005.

[8] 王建辉. 出版业的资本运作. 出版发行研究, 2008 (8).

[9] 程旭, 徐丽芳. 我国图书发行集团资本经营的路径选择. 大学出版, 2009 (1).

[10] 叶思遏. 我国出版传媒整体上市及资本运营研究——对传媒改革路径再思考. 浙江大学硕士学位论文, 2009.

[11] 崔丹. 试析中国传媒产业资本运营——以辽宁出版集团为例. 兰州大学硕士学位论文, 2008.

[12] 唐溯, 陈敬良. 上市转身：出版企业决胜资本市场的战略. 出版发行研究, 2009 (9).

作者简介

徐建华，南开大学商学院教授、博士生导师。

梁浩光，南开大学商学院信息资源管理系研究生。

卢正明，南开大学商学院信息资源管理系研究生。

数字技术环境下的出版产业发展战略

甘慧君　刘玲武

（武汉大学信息管理学院　武汉　430072）

摘要：数字化浪潮风起云涌，出版业发展道路上机遇与挑战并存。虽然出版业近些年来在数字化道路上取得了一定的成就，但依然存在着诸如版权、人才、意识的问题。如何在新的环境下制定适合出版产业的发展战略，谋求出版产业新的发展成为目前研究的重点。本文通过波特五力分析法，试图对我国的数字出版产业竞争现状进行系统的梳理与分析，在运用SWOT分析法对出版产业内外的优势、劣势，机会、威胁进行分析基础上，对我国出版产业发展提出一些建议举措，以期增强出版产业的核心竞争力，应对新技术环境带来的挑战与威胁。

关键词：出版产业　竞争现状　SWOT矩阵　战略建议

Study on the development strategy of publishing industry under the digital environment

Gan Huijun Liu Lingwu

（School of Information Management，Wuhan University，Wuhan，430072）

Abstract：The surging wave of digital publishing has put publishers into a position in which challenges and opportunities coexist. There is no denying that publishing industry has made great achievement in recent years，but the problems like talents，understanding and copyright still exist. How to make the right development strategy in new circumstances to stimulate the development of publishing industry has got public attention. This paper starts from the current competitive status of publishing industry by using the Michael Porter's Five Forces Model，and then attempts to raise some suggestions on the basis of SWOT Matrix Model，so as to strengthen the core competitiveness of publishing industry to face the challenges and threats in digital environment.

Keywords：Publishing industry　Competitive status　SWOT matrix　Strategic suggestions

1　数字环境下出版产业的竞争现状

根据迈克尔·波特的竞争战略理论，一个产业内部竞争状态是由五种竞争作用力共同决定的。如图 1 所示，这五种竞争力分别是：进入威胁、替代威胁、买方议价能力、供方议价能力和现有竞争对手之间的竞争。通过对五种基本竞争力的分析可以看出出版产业所面临的竞争形势：内有出版企业间的竞争，外有替代品与技术商的威胁。

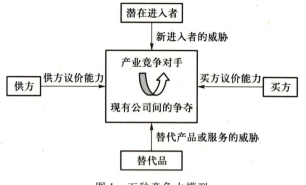

图1 五种竞争力模型

1.1 进入威胁

随着国家政策的放宽与数字出版的兴起，民营资本可以在国家政策允许范围内进入出版领域，网络图书又不再受到书号的限制，可以说，出版产业的竞争对手已由行业内转向行业外，出版产业面临的竞争更加激烈。

1.2 数字产品竞相出炉

技术的日新月异使得图书的替代品在近几年来以多种形态、多种载体竞相出现，如手机电子书、数据库等新兴产品形态，MP4 播放器、PDA 阅读器等便携的产品载体。这些以满足读者个性化需求为目的的各类产品已在出版物市场上占据了半壁江山。另据我国第七次国民阅读调查结果显示，在接触过数字化阅读方式的国民中，91% 的读者阅读电子书后就不会再购买此书的纸质版。

1.3 买方议价能力

处于产业链中游的技术运营商具有技术优势，可以直接后向整合，从而取得对内容的控制权。而产业链下游的读者需求越加个性化，而且通常可直接从网络上获得一部分免费的内容资源，这对基于内容销售的传统出版业也形成了一定的冲击。

1.4 卖方议价能力

虽然出版形态发生了变化，但内容资源的主导地位与作用并未发生改变，因此版权成为出版社及技术商们竞相争夺的资源，尤其是拥有畅销书版权的作者，可供其选择发表方式的增多，发表渠道的增加，提高了其对稿费和版税的议价能力。

1.5 行业内竞争

从出版业市场集中度来看，我国出版业内尚未形成规模较大或掌握话语权的大型出版企业，企业规模均等偏小而且多为综合性出版社，因此产业秩序不易建立，经常会引起跟风出版或恶性价格战。这样容易导致同质化，致使出版业在读者心目中的形象下降，引起业内恶性循环。

2 数字技术环境下出版产业的 SWOT 分析

从上面的分析可以看出，出版产业面临着越来越大的竞争压力，应对数字技术环境带来的挑战与威胁，就必须对自身的优势、劣势与外部的机会、威胁有较为清楚的认识。只有这样，才有利于在激烈的竞争中扬长避短。

2.1 优势（Strength）分析

出版资源丰富。在新的数字技术环境下，传统出版社的最大优势就在于其长期积累的丰厚的出版资源，包括丰富的内容资源、资深的作者队伍以及专业的编辑策划人员。网络的信息是海量的，但其中包括很多垃圾信息、无用信息甚至是有害信息，而最终受众所需要的只是正确的符合自身需求的资源。如何对庞大的内容信息进行筛选、分类以及校对，这就需要专业的编辑人员。

2.2 劣势（Weakness）分析

2.2.1 出版业市场意识薄弱，出版网站建设力度不够

长期以来，出版单位作为事业单位，竞争压力不足，导致出版业人士对市场反应不够灵敏。在早期与作者签订合同时，数字版权并未被签下。在借助网站推广自身方面，也有些不足之处。随着数字化的深入发展，网站已经成为读者了解出版社的一个重要窗口，通过网站读者可以了解企业文化、可供书目信息或者直接在网站购买产品。目前，有近80%的出版社建立了自己的网站，但却疏于原创内容的建设与后期的及时更新。出版社网站内容多是信息搬家，一般是在版书目信息与单位介绍的集合，而且出版社一般都在推出新书后才会更新其网站内容。据2007年11月《全国出版社网络出版调查问卷》显示，近2/3的出版社网站只是起到宣传作用，并不具备电子商务平台的功能。另外一些开展网上购书的出版社，由于支付手段单一，价格并不占优，也很难吸引读者注意力。

2.2.2 数字版权问题严重，数字标准不统一

中文在线董事长童之磊在2007年举行的第二届中国数字出版博览会上说："目前从事数字出版的网站约1 400多个，但是其中只有4.3%的内容真正拥有版权，大多数是盗版。"

网络传播使得著作权侵权极为便捷与隐蔽，简单的复制粘贴就可以完成完整作品的再次传播。对网络运营商来说，大批量地把纸质内容扫描上网就可获得大量利润；对读者来说，可能本身并未认识到在网上享受免费资源会是一种侵权行为；对出版单位和作者来说，网络侵权面临着取证难，找到侵权人难等困难，对这种得不偿失的官司纠纷，出版社与作者往往忍气吞声，这样使得网络侵权更为嚣张。

纵观数字出版业的各个环节，元数据的标准化、编码的标准化、作品格式的标准化等都尚未统一。方正的CEB、书生的SEP、超星的PDG、中文在线的OEB、万方的PDF、知网的CAJ这些版式互不兼容，出版社必须制作每一版式标准的文本供读者选择，这必然会增加出版社的技术成本。[1]而读者也必须使用不同的阅读器来阅读相应文本，这将在一定程度上增加成本开支，从而使出版社在无形中流失部分客户。

2.2.3 商业模式不清晰，数字产业链缺乏合作

商业模式是指为实现客户价值最大化，把能使企业运行的内外各要素整合起来，形成一个完整的、高效率的、具有独特核心竞争力的运行系统，并通过最优实现形式满足客户需求、实现客户价值，同时使系统达成持续赢利目标的整体解决方案。[2]简单来说，商业模式包括企业的目标定位、分销渠道、赢利模式等。我国出版产业目前存在自身定位不清，商业模式模糊等问题，导致出版单位在向数字出版领域发展时找不到赢利点，不愿为此投入资金、人才和物力，因此在数字出版领域处于弱势地位。

商业模式不清晰，导致我国数字出版产业链分工不明确，各环节缺乏有效的交流与合作。目前，数字产业链主体由著作权人、出版社、网络运营商、技术提供商以及图书消费

者组成。处于产业链上游的著作权人与出版社对数字出版的积极性不高，著作权人对数字出版的收益分配不了解，出版社害怕会影响纸质书销售往往不会提供新书的内容信息；处于产业链中游的网络运营商及技术提供商往往身兼数职，不仅提供技术、产品与服务，还参与到作品的内容创作与销售等环节中，在整合数据方面也存在着较大的相似性；在产业链下游，消费者可以便利地从网上获取资源，不愿为电子图书付费。

2.2.4 数字化出版人才储备不足

与传统出版业不同，数字化出版人才不仅需要具有深厚的学术背景，还应具有一定的计算机技术知识，对数字出版物的制作流程和数字化管理也要有一定的了解。而从目前看来，这种复合型人才奇缺，从事数字出版方面工作的大多是 IT 人员，传统出版人参与较少，这就使得网络出版在专业性、严谨性、规范性方面有所缺失。而传统出版单位又不注重培养与引进既懂出版又懂技术的复合型人才，使得出版产业在面临数字出版时显得准备不足。

2.3 机会（Opportunity）分析

2.3.1 政府开始关注，数字出版政策陆续出台

近些年来，为了推动数字出版产业健康有序的发展，政府出台了一系列相关政策，如2006 年 5 月中共中央办公厅、国务院办公厅印发的《2006—2020 年国家信息化发展战略》及随后颁布的《国家"十一五"时期文化发展规划纲要》、《文化产业振兴规划》都提出要加快推进我国数字出版的发展，并将其作为今后发展文化产业的重点。在微观领域，政府也做了大量工作，从规范互联网著作权行政执法行为的《互联网著作权行政保护办法》到保护著作权人权益的《信息网络传播权保护条例》，从鼓励优秀电子出版物的《国家电子出版物评奖办法》到 2010 年国务院常务会议提出的推进三网融合等，无一不说明政府对数字出版的关注与重视。可以看到，文化部、工业和信息化部、广电总局、新闻出版总署等多部门都出台了与数字出版相关的文件。虽然目前我国并没有一部专门性质的数字出版法律，但这些政策对数字出版行业起到了良好的规范与引导作用，形成了一个比较良好的支持数字出版的法律政策环境。

2.3.2 国民阅读率和数字阅读率呈上升趋势

中国互联网络信息中心（CNNIC）发布的《第 25 次中国互联网络发展状况统计报告》显示，截至 2009 年 12 月，我国网民规模达 3.84 亿，同时中国手机上网用户也达2.33 亿人。如此庞大的受众为数字出版的发展提供了广阔的市场。另从中国出版科学研究所历年发布的《全国国民阅读与购买倾向抽样调查报告》中可以看到，从 2007 年开始国民阅读率开始呈上升趋势，数字阅读率也从 1999 年的 3.7% 上升到了 2009 年的24.6%。

2.3.3 高新技术的发展

高新技术的发展，使得出版社应用新技术更为方便，阅读载体的设计也更加人性化与便捷化，数字阅读方式逐渐被大众所接受。

2.4 威胁（Tnreat）分析

其他行业介入出版领域。早在 20 世纪 90 年代中后期，技术商就开始了他们的数字化征途，从技术研发到内容平台，凭借强大的资金力量和对技术的掌控，技术提供商及原创网络平台已在很大程度上介入了数字出版市场，并建立了可赢利的商业模式，出版单位在

数字出版领域面临着被边缘化的危险。如起点中文网直接与作者签约，通过网络平台发布作品供读者阅读，直接绕过出版社，拥有了大批受众。

通过对我国出版产业的整体分析，根据 SWOT 分析法列出 SWOT 矩阵，得出在新的技术环境下我国出版产业应采取的总体发展战略（见表 1）。

表 1　我国出版产业的 SWOT 分析矩阵表

内部能力 / 外部因素	优势 S 出版资源丰富	劣势 W 1. 出版业市场意识薄弱，出版网站建设力度不够 2. 数字版权问题严重，数字标准不统一 3. 商业模式不清晰，数字产业链缺乏合作 4. 数字化出版人才储备不足
机会 O	SO	WO
1. 政府开始关注，数字政策陆续出台 2. 国民阅读率和数字阅读率呈上升趋势 3. 高新技术的发展	在编、印、发等多个环节上应用新技术	1. 通过法律与技术双重手段防范著作权侵权，规范数字出版环境 2. 政府与出版社应加强出版教育与专业技术培训的投资力度，高校应重视相关课程的设置
威胁 T	ST	WT
其他行业介入出版领域	明确自身定位，形成品牌优势	与技术商或网络运营商形成战略合作关系

3　新技术环境下的出版业发展战略

通过 SWOT 矩阵分析可以看出，目前应采取如下措施以实现出版产业的稳定可持续发展。

3.1　在编、印、发等多个环节上应用新技术

数字技术的飞速发展使得新技术应用到出版业的各个领域中：编辑工作的网络化、印刷流程的科技化、发行手段的数字化都是新技术应用的表现，这些不仅提高了工作效率，缩短了出版周期，也为出版社提供了多种赢利方式。在编辑选题方面，编辑可以通过网络，了解到目前的热门话题以及选题的出版情况，还可以通过网络互动，吸引读者对某一选题进行事先讨论，评估此选题的可行性，了解读者对内容定价等信息，无形中也为图书做了事先宣传。在编辑加工方面，开发多种产品形态来满足读者多样化的需求，如社会科学文献出版社的皮书系列、高等教育出版社的在线学习系统等。在印刷环节，对于小众书、古籍可以提供按需印刷服务，在节约资源的同时，也可使作品做到永不绝版。在营销发行方面，通过技术系统来管理图书发行业务、统计销售信息；利用搜索引擎、论坛、博客、自身网站等来宣传推广产品；通过在网络上与读者即时交流，了解读者对图书的意见，并及时改进等，以人性化服务，方便读者为目标，这样才能有效地吸引读者、促进销售。

3.2 明确自身定位，形成品牌优势

我国出版业应明确自身定位，专注于自身特色优势进行出版，对拥有自主版权的产品进行全方位深度开发，增加产品的附加值，以拓展其市场空间。另外可借鉴行业内已形成的赢利模式，结合自身实际进行产品全方位开发，比如在教育出版领域，以在线课程、评估系统为主要赢利模式；大众出版方面则侧重于个性化定制、电子书；专业出版则在在线期刊论文数据库上有良好的发展。出版社只有充分利用自己的内容优势，做大做强，形成品牌优势，才能在产业链上占据主导地位。

3.3 通过法律与技术双重手段防范著作权侵权，规范数字出版环境

版权问题是发展数字出版的难点与重点，版权问题不解决，就谈不上数字出版产业的健康有序发展。因为网络技术的发展和新产品形态的产生，导致数字版权领域在面临许多新问题、新情况时找不到相应的法律依据，这就需要我国的相关法律法规在实践中不断完善，政府也应加强版权立法和司法保护，还可培育专业的维权组织，通过普及版权知识、提供法律咨询、收集侵权证据、协助行政机关执法等对著作权人的利益加以保护。同时，数字水印技术与数字版权保护技术的应用也为版权保护提供了必要保证。

3.4 政府与出版社应加强出版教育与专业技术培训的投资力度，高校应重视相关课程的设置

随着数字出版的进一步发展，对人才的需求将会越来越大。因此需要政府、高校与出版社共同努力，加大对出版教育的重视与投资力度，以产学研相结合的模式培养企业型人才。同时政府与业内应提供一些在职在岗培训，提高从业人员的素质与技术水平。如高等教育出版社下设的畅想书院，通过面授、网络课程相结合的方式对编辑、业务人员进行数字化培训。另外高校在课程设置上，应加大数字技术应用课程的比例，重视实践教学环节，培养实用型人才。

3.5 与技术商或网络运营商形成战略合作关系

数字出版前期投入较大，传统出版企业因为资金问题，一般都难以独立承担内容与技术全产业链的投入与开发，因此利用自身内容与品牌优势，与技术提供商或网络运营商进行合作或并购是实现优势互补的一个良好的途径。一些国际传统出版商在向数字化转型过程中，往往会采用与技术提供商合作或并购的方式进行，如哈珀·柯林斯出版集团选择与Newstand 进行合作，并为此拥有其 10% 的股份；约翰·威立并购布莱克维尔和 Whatson-when 以进军数字出版；桦榭美国公司通过收购 Jumpstart 来完成其网上广告销售；培生教育出版集团收购了"电子大学"来扩大网络教育出版等。[3]

注释

[1] 张雪思. 传统出版数字化进程中的难题［J］. 青年记者. 2010（1）：69.

[2] http://wiki.mbalib.com/wiki/% E5% 95% 86% E4% B8% 9A% E6% A8% A1% E5% BC% 8F［OL］. 2010-5-19.

[3] 陈晓宏. 传统出版向数字出版转型的思考［J］. 中共福建省委党校学报. 2009（1）：91.

作者简介

甘慧君，武汉大学信息管理学院 09 级出版发行学硕士。

刘玲武，武汉大学信息管理学院 09 级出版发行学硕士。

中国出版业"走出去"：跨国经营的文化风险分析
——以跨文化传播为理论视角

潘文年

（安徽大学新闻传播学院　合肥　230039）

宏观出版

摘要：中国出版业正在走向世界，但是文化差异使我国出版业的跨国经营面临一定的文化风险。本文采用跨学科研究方法，借鉴跨文化传播和国际经济学相关理论，从基本内涵、产生根源、主要形式、影响过程以及防范措施五个方面分析了中国出版业跨国经营中的文化风险。进而认为这种文化风险根源于文化差异，存在着不同的表现形式，对跨国经营有着阶段性影响，可以通过一定的方法进行防范。

关键词：出版业"走出去"　跨国经营　文化风险　跨文化传播

"Going Out" of Chinese Publishing Industry: An analysis of the Cultural Risk of Multinational Businesses
——From the theoretical perspective of inter-cultural communication

Pan Wennian

（School of Journalism and Communication，Anhui University，Hefei，230039）

Abstract：Chinese publishing industry is "going out", but cultural divergence makes the multinational businesses facing cultural risks. This paper adopts the method of interdisciplinary, references the related theory of inter-cultural communication and international economics theory, analyzes the cultural risks of Chinese publishing industry in multinational business from five aspects：the basic meaning, production origin, major forms, influence process and preventive measures. This paper holds a view that the cultural risks come from cultural divergences, and there are different forms of its expression. This has a phasic effect on multinational business, but it can be regulated through some methods.

Keywords："Going out" of Chinese publishing industry　Multinational business　Cultural risk Inter-cultural communication

1 引言

中国出版业正在"走出去"。[1]这种"走出去"是国内出版企业"利用自身比较优势和竞争优势进行跨国经营走向国际图书市场的一种过程"[2]，实质"是国内出版企业的一种跨国经营活动"[3]和跨文化传播行为，最终目的是促进中国图书、中国文化走向世界，实现中外文化的共融与共生。但是，文化背景的巨大差异使这种跨国经营面临文化风险，直接影响跨国经营的总体目标和出版业"走出去"的实际成效。那么，这种文化风险具有怎样的内涵和特点？根源何在？中国出版业跨国经营中会遇到哪些类型的文化风险？这些文化风险又是如何影响跨国经营的？如何对这种文化风险进行防范？本文拟以跨文化传播为理论视角对这种文化风险的诸多问题进行探讨，以期对已经、正在和即将"走出去"的中国出版企业有所帮助。

2 中国出版业跨国经营文化风险的基本内涵

跨文化传播理论认为，跨文化传播是个体、组织身处不同区域、不同文化背景之下而"遭遇不同文化信仰与价值观的一个过程，因此必然会产生文化冲突"[4]，导致文化风险。中国出版业"走出去"之后，通过海外新建和跨国并购这两种基本模式[5]设立的海外出版分支机构处于一个与国内完全不同的文化环境之中，这种"文化的差异性有可能导致来自不同文化背景的人与人之间的文化冲突"[6]和文化误解，从而影响甚至危及到跨国经营目标的实现。这种由文化差异而导致的风险是一种典型的文化风险。因此，中国出版业跨国经营的文化风险是指国内出版企业通过新建、并购方式设立的海外出版分支机构在跨地域、跨民族、跨国体、跨政体以及跨文化的经营管理过程中，由于不同区域、不同民族、不同组织、不同个人的文化差异而导致的文化冲突使跨国经营的实际效益与预期效益发生偏离的可能性。它有两层涵义，一是国内的海外出版分支机构在异国经营时由于与东道国文化背景不同而产生的文化冲突导致的文化风险；二是在一个海外出版分支机构内部，由于员工个人分属不同文化背景的国家而产生的文化冲突导致的文化风险。这种风险有四个基本特点：第一，客观性。它是客观存在、无法回避的，从根本上说这一特点来源于不同区域、不同国家之间客观存在的文化差异。第二，双效性。它一方面可以使海外出版分支机构跨国经营的目标受阻，另一方面又可以成为一种积极因素和诱发优势，可激发企业活力、促进企业创新，加快经营目标的实现。第三，复杂性。这一特点来源于文化内涵的丰富性、复杂性，主要表现为文化风险复杂多样、形式各异且不断变化和发展。第四，可控性。它与其他类型的风险一样，同样能够被识别和控制。

3 中国出版业跨国经营文化风险的产生根源

中国出版业"走出去"进行跨国经营意味着这部分出版企业的经营活动已由一种文化背景进入了与本国文化完全不同的另外一种文化背景。而文化是一个群体在价值观念、信仰、态度、行为准则、风俗习惯等方面所表现出来的区别于另一群体的显著特征[7]，正是文化在群体上的差异性这一客观存在，使这种经营活动遭遇各种各样的陌生理念、陌生行为和处事方式，进而影响到预期效益，跨国经营的文化冲突和文化风险由此而生。可见，中国出版业跨国经营文化风险的根源在于"不同文化之间的差异"[8]，具体体现在：

（1）权力距离感差异。人类学家南达和沃姆斯曾指出，"权力是这样一种能力，它做出并施行影响着一个人自身生活的决定，控制其他人的行为"[9]。权力距离感则是指社会对权力在社会、组织或个人中不平等分配的接受程度。当国内出版企业在权力距离感比较大的文化背景下（如墨西哥）进行跨国经营时会发现此类地区的企业中往往存在着严格的等级观念，管理者有着较大的权威，且难以接近，与员工之间的感情距离较大；在权力距离感较小的文化背景下（如奥地利、丹麦、以色列等）进行跨国经营时，会发现此类地区的企业中等级观念较薄弱，上下级之间的感情差距较小，下属容易接近并敢于反驳上司。

（2）不确定性回避差异。跨文化传播之"不确定性回避理论"[10]假设，"当陌生人相遇时，他们最关心的事情是对在相互关系中自己和其他人行为的不确定性的减少或可预见性的增加"[11]。根据这一理论，所有的人在与他人接触的情况下都需要了解自己，同时也要去了解别人，以减少、回避每一次新的相遇中存在的不确定性。[12]不同文化背景的组织或个体对这种不确定性的回避截然不同，跨国经营的文化风险也各不相同。如希腊、比利时属于强不确定性回避文化，这些地区的组织或个人在维护现有的信念和行为规范时，不能容忍不同的观点，在企业中（包括出版企业）表现为组织内部制度严格，职责明确，原则性强，力求高度一致，但决策迟缓、行为谨慎、创新不足、灵活性缺乏；新加坡、加拿大则属于弱不确定性回避文化，这些地区有着较为宽松的氛围，允许、鼓励个人或组织提出不同的思想和观点，敢于冒险、勇于创新。

（3）个人主义和集体主义差异。不同文化背景之下的组织或个人所体现的个人主义与集体主义倾向存在着很大的差距，这种差距构成了跨国经营与跨文化交流中文化风险的重要诱因。如美国文化体现了典型的个人主义倾向，这种文化背景下的社会结构较为松散，组织或个人只关心他们自己以及最亲近的亲属，与此无关者显得较为漠视；而委内瑞拉、哥伦比亚则属于集体主义倾向较为明显的文化类型，这种文化背景下的社会组织结构较为严密，个人具有强烈的集体主义意识，希望内部群体能够时刻关心自己，同时自己也对内部群体充满热情，绝对忠诚。

（4）功利主义和人文主义差异。不同的文化引发的功利主义和人文主义倾向各不相同，不同文化背景下的组织或个人由于各自所属文化中的功利主义和人文主义倾向的不同，在相互交往、进行跨文化交流时必然会导致文化风险，这种情况在中国出版业的跨国经营中也不可能例外。功利主义偏于强烈的文化背景之下，组织或个人非常注重挑战、收入、进取、利益，具有强烈的成功欲和被认可欲；而人文主义偏于强烈的文化背景之下，组织或个人较为强调团结、平等、互助，注重营造良好的工作环境、人文环境，提供相应的就业保障，个人或组织取得成就的标志是良好的人际关系和宽松、愉悦的生活、工作环境，工作压力较小，个体的自由度较高。

此外，政治文化导向、民族性格、民族思维模式及处理问题的模式的不同，以及沟通的误会、文化的误读、文化符号系统的不同理解等也都会导致程度不同的文化风险。

4 中国出版业跨国经营文化风险的主要形式

文化差异使中国出版业"走出去"的跨国经营面临文化风险，这种文化风险的形式主要有以下四种：

（1）沟通交流型风险。不同的文化具有不同的语言表述方式和沟通交流模式，文化差异的存在使得不同文化间的人们在跨文化交流时由于对同一信息理解出现差异，从而经常发生误解和沟通交流困难进而引发文化冲突[13]，导致文化风险。中国出版业海外出版分支机构在进行内部企业管理和外部图书营销时，由内部员工文化背景的差异和外部市场文化环境的不同而引发的文化沟通误会和文化沟通障碍导致沟通失败的风险，即为沟通交流型文化风险。

（2）种族优越型风险。"种族优越感是指一个人认为自己的文化优于其他任何文化的观念"[14]，它存在于每一种文化之中。但是，"当它被用来排斥他人、提供诋毁性评价的基础以及拒绝改变时就变得有害"[15]，导致文化风险。海外出版分支机构跨国经营时的种族优越感主要表现为相信自己国内的经营管理模式优于海外合作者而采取与国内相同的方式进行跨国经营管理；不能在图书的内容和形式上进行适当改造以适应海外特殊文化背景下读者的需求；将海外跨国经营的利润全部转回国内而不再对东道国的图书出版领域进行追加投资；让在国内出版界做得很好但却没有跨国经营管理经验的管理者充任海外出版分支机构的要职等。

（3）企业管理型风险。国内的海外出版分支机构在异国进行跨国经营管理时，面对的是不同的文化环境以及具有不同文化背景的企业员工。而不同的文化有不同的企业认知、管理理念、管理模式和管理风格，一种文化支配下的管理理念和管理风格不能被另一种文化所理解和接受的现象在跨国经营中时有出现；不同文化背景的管理人员之间以及编辑人员、营销人员之间也存在着一定的交流障碍，难以建立有效的协调关系。这些都使得海外出版分支机构在内部管理上要花费更多的精力和成本，管理效率明显降低，产生海外出版分支机构的管理型风险。

（4）商务惯例型风险。此类风险是指国内的海外出版分支机构在海外与合作伙伴进行商务合作时，由于商业习惯、交流方式的差异而导致合作失败以及不同的文化对特定事物或现象的不同判断和理解而导致的营销失败的风险。如西方很多国家的出版公司可以接受打高尔夫球时洽谈业务，但日本的出版公司洽谈出版业务时却从不这样做；德国人习惯于把商务活动和家庭生活区分开，德国的出版公司很少在下午五点以后还洽谈业务，而日本出版公司的工作时间却持续到日落或更晚的时间。

根据我国海外出版分支机构组织内部不同种类文化差异性大小和容忍度的高低（可以用相关的特征变量进行测度，篇幅所限，这里从略），我们可以把跨国经营中的上述文化风险构造成图1所示的评估矩阵，大致判断出海外出版分支机构跨国经营文化风险的大小。

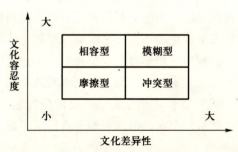

图1　文化风险评估矩阵

图1中，"相容型"文化风险是指海外出版分支机构组织内部核心成员与其他成员的文化差异性小而文化容忍度大的一种风险类型。这种情况下，机构组织内部的文化适应程度高，核心成员能非常有效地发挥文化协同作用，跨文化经营的文化风险小。"模糊型"

文化风险是指海外出版分支机构组织内部两类成员间的文化差异性大、容忍度也大的一种风险类型。这种情况下，组织内部核心成员由于同时接纳两种甚至数种完全不同的文化类型而导致文化确定感的一时丧失，存在着一定的跨文化经营风险。"摩擦型"文化风险是指海外出版分支机构组织内部两类成员间文化差异性小、容忍度也小的一种风险类型。这种情况下，组织内部两类成员间的文化基本相容，但存在着局部冲突，跨国经营的文化风险较小。"冲突型"文化风险是指海外出版分支机构组织内部两类成员间文化差异性大、容忍度小的一种风险类型。这种情况下，海外出版分支机构会由于激烈的文化冲突而极易产生灾难性的后果，文化风险很大。

5　中国出版业跨国经营文化风险的影响过程

中国出版业"走出去"进行跨国经营的过程实际上也是两种或多种文化相互交流、融汇的过程，通常分为吸引、冲突、交汇和融合四个阶段[16]，相应地，文化风险对跨国经营的影响会经历以下四个阶段：

（1）潜伏时期。海外出版分支机构处于多种文化交汇的吸引阶段时，文化风险对跨国经营的影响则处于潜伏时期。这时，海外出版分支机构组织内部不同文化背景的员工被完全不同的文化所吸引，对发展前景充满美好期待，对待文化差异的态度也比较乐观，有时甚至忽视了这种文化差异可能带来的不利后果。这一时期，人们对异国文化的热情可能使他们忽略了跨文化交流过程中文化差异导致的一些小问题，但这并不意味着文化冲突、文化风险不存在。相反，这种冲突和风险一旦爆发，将会给跨国经营带来严重后果。

（2）爆发时期。海外出版分支机构的跨文化交流由文化交汇的吸引阶段进入冲突阶段时，文化交汇程度的不断加深使不同文化之间的差异得到确定和放大；同时，民族文化优越感的存在也极易使海外出版分支机构中不同文化之间相互怀疑甚至排斥，致使组织内部不同文化之间产生激烈碰撞。这时，不同文化背景的员工多以自我为中心，理解、沟通、信任和体谅的缺乏使彼此之间产生困惑、矛盾以致激烈的冲突和对抗，文化风险也相应地由潜伏时期进入爆发时期。这一时期，文化风险的爆发导致的文化误解、文化冲突将打击海外出版分支机构跨国经营的信心，动摇和阻碍经营决策的制定和执行。文化风险引发的各种问题如得不到及时有效的解决，将对跨国经营的目标产生不利影响。

（3）缓和时期。海外出版分支机构的跨文化交流进入文化交汇阶段时，机构内部不同文化背景的员工开始从彼此排斥、拒绝、不认同、不接受向理解、谅解、尊重以及对其他文化的认同转变，人们处理事情更加谨慎，也能够以理解、体谅、迁就的态度去分析出现的矛盾和冲突，能在相互比较中互相学习、取长补短，文化风险也由爆发时期转而进入缓和时期。这一时期，不同文化背景的员工能够以更加理性的态度对待文化冲突和风险，开始更多地进行自我审视，同时也积累和掌握了一定的应付和处理文化风险的经验和方法。文化冲突和文化风险虽然依然存在，但激烈和严重程度明显降低，对跨国经营的不利影响也趋于弱化。

（4）创新时期。海外出版分支机构进入文化交流的融合阶段时，不同形态的文化或文化要素之间相互结合、相互吸纳、相互渗透、相互塑造，直至融为一体。这一时期，机构内部不同类型的文化发挥各自不同的优势，通过不断的融合创新，不断孕育、形成独具特色的新文化。文化差异的客观存在非但不会给海外出版分支机构的跨国经营带来文化风险和消极影响，反而会发挥机构内部跨文化优势，给这种跨国经营产生积极、有利的影响，使分支机构的跨国经营更加得心应手，圆满甚至远超预期地实现经营目标。

需要指出的是，国内出版企业"走出去"从事跨国经营的时间先后不一，那些从事跨国经营时间较长的出版企业可能对这种文化风险有较为明显的体会，而那些刚开始从事跨国经营的出版企业对文化风险的体会可能不甚明显，对它们而言文化风险或许只是初现端倪，但这并不意味着上述四个影响阶段的不存在，随着这种跨国经营的不断深入，文化风险的影响阶段将会逐次展开；同时，海外出版分支机构跨国经营时的文化交汇过程并不是不同文化的简单相加，而是你中有我、我中有你，冲突中有融合、融合中有冲突。相应地，文化风险对海外出版分支机构跨国经营的影响过程也不是截然分开的，而是伴随着文化交汇的发展相互共存、相互融合、相互交叉、相伴而行。

6 中国出版业跨国经营文化风险的防范措施

中国出版业"走出去"跨国经营的文化风险不管显露与否，始终都是客观存在的。因此，已经、正在以及准备"走出去"从事跨国经营的出版企业都需要对此有清醒的认识，制定好防范措施。

6.1 文化观念的正确树立

海外出版分支机构的跨国经营处于一个多元文化的背景之下，需要经营者、管理者树立正确的文化观念。首先，海外出版分支机构中充斥着各种类型的文化，它们之间只有差异之分，而无好坏之别。经营管理者需要放弃文化偏见，用一种客观中立的眼光来观照不同类型的文化，尽可能地去发现每一种文化的优势，力求取长补短。其次，跨文化的基本含义体现在两个方面：一是理解"己文化"，理解自己民族文化的内涵、模式、优缺点的演变，促成文化关联观念的形成和文化自我意识的觉醒，这势必有助于获得判断"己文化"和相关"他文化"之间客观存在的类同和差异的参照系；二是理解"他文化"，这种理解需建立在文化移情的基础之上，要求人们在一定程度上摆脱自身本土文化的约束，并借助组织内的其他文化来反观自己原来的文化，同时又能够以一种超然的态度来对待"他文化"，而不是简单、盲目地落入另一种文化俗套之中。再次，海外出版分支机构需要在文化共性认识的基础上，以求同存异为原则，在机构内建立一种共同的文化观、经营观，达到强有力的文化认同，支配和统领整个跨国经营活动，减少机构内的文化摩擦和文化冲突。

6.2 文化差异的正确理解

防范文化风险需要对文化差异进行正确理解。首先，文化差异是非好坏的辩证理解。海外出版分支机构的文化差异大，发生文化冲突的可能性也大；但如能恰当利用，差异越大的文化相结合所产生的正面增值效益的可能性也越大。国外一些跨国经营成功的大型出版公司都不是没有文化差异的公司，而是偏爱文化差异、能有效管理和利用这种差异使之产生巨大增值效应的出版公司。因此，管理者需要以一种中立的、不含偏见的态度对待文化差异和合作伙伴之间的误解，减少文化冲突。其次，文化差异的准确识别。美国人类学家爱德华·赫尔把文化区分为正式规范、非正式规范和技术规范三个范畴。正式规范性文化是指人的基本价值观和是非的判断标准，能自觉抵制来自外部的企图改变它的强制力量，它导致的文化风险一般难以规避；非正式规范性文化是指人们的生活习惯和日常习俗，它引起的文化冲突和文化风险可以通过较长时间的文化交流来克服和规避；技术规范性文化是指那些通过技术知识的学习而获得的文化范畴，很容易进行改变，引起的文化冲突和文化风险通过适当措施基本可以规避。

6.3　风险控制的工具选择

海外出版分支机构跨国经营控制文化风险的工具主要有以下三种：第一，风险回避。指海外出版分支机构进行跨国经营时，主动回避高风险的投资东道国、高风险的跨国经营项目、高风险的国际化方式，进行低风险选择。如当所出版的图书内容、形式不符合当地读者的阅读习惯、阅读口味而受到市场冷落时，应果断改变生产经营方向、更换图书的经营品种以回避经营风险；由于种种原因不能或无法改变经营方向时，应及时把生产经营的地点转移到合适的地方去以回避经营风险；当图书生产经营活动（包括图书内容的选择、封面版式的设计及图书营销活动开展等）与当地的文化习俗不符、存在潜在的文化风险时，应设法通过管理方法和经营方式的改变以规避可能出现的文化风险。第二，风险转移。指海外出版分支机构在进行跨国经营遭遇文化风险时设法通过合适的方式把风险转移至别处，如与当地出版公司、发行公司进行合资、合作经营，以与当地的合作伙伴共同分担风险损失；把可能引发文化冲突、导致文化风险的领域或项目主动向保险公司投保以转移可能出现的文化风险。第三，风险分散。指海外出版分支机构跨国经营时，在图书项目策划、图书品种开发和图书市场开拓上采取多样化的投资策略，分散和降低跨文化经营中的文化风险，如上述投资项目的国别多样化、国际经营形式的多样化和灵活化以及投资项目本身的多样化，进行高风险项目和低风险项目的适当搭配，以便高风险项目遭遇失败出现损失时通过低风险项目给予适当弥补。

6.4　跨国经营的文化培训

这种培训内容主要包括：第一，"他文化"培训。通过语言培训、研讨会、书籍、课程、网站、模拟演练等方式对当地民族文化及被并购之前的当地原出版公司的文化进行培训，包括"他文化"的认识和了解、语言学习、跨文化交流的技巧及文化冲突的处理等，缩小管理人员与员工间及其相互之间可能存在的文化距离；第二，文化适应性培训。对拟被派往海外从事跨国经营的经营管理人员进行文化适应性培训，以获取应对其他文化的技能，如派他们到海外短期工作或出差，以亲身体验不同文化的差异和冲击；或者留在国内设法使其与不同文化背景的人相处，等等。第三，文化敏感性培训。主要是训练员工对海外出版分支机构所在地的当地文化特征的分析能力，掌握当地文化的精髓，弄清当地文化决定当地人行为方式的原因，以使员工更好地应对不同文化的冲击，减轻他们在不同文化背景下的苦恼、不适应感及挫败感，促进不同文化背景的员工之间的交流和理解，避免对当地文化形成偏见。第四，跨文化沟通及文化冲突的处理能力培训。主要是建立和开辟各种正式与非正式、有形与无形的跨文化沟通组织和沟通渠道。

6.5　机构文化的整合交流

海外出版分支机构是一个多元文化的结合体。不同类型的文化、不同文化背景的员工交织在一起，彼此之间的冲突和摩擦难以避免。因此，需要在机构内适时进行有效的跨文化整合和跨文化交流。

跨文化整合是指海外出版分支机构中不同类型的文化相互吸收、融合、调和而趋于一体化的一种过程。常见的文化整合策略主要有：第一，适应型文化整合。海外出版分支机构为了适应所在地的文化背景，主动适应东道国文化，自愿被东道国文化所同化而产生的文化整合策略。第二，征服型文化整合。海外出版分支机构利用自身文化优势，采取以我为主的文化策略设法改造机构内的当地文化而形成的在跨国经营中能起主导作用的文化整合策略。第三，融合型文化整合。海外出版分支机构在跨国经营中采取文化创新的办法，融合机构内不同类型文化之长、各种文化相互借鉴取长补短而形成的文化整合策略。

跨文化交流则是指海外出版分支机构中不同文化背景的员工相互交流的一种情境。首先，管理人员可以有目的、有计划地组织各种正式与非正式的集体和小组活动，以加强沟通、消除偏见。这一方面可引导机构内他文化背景的员工积极、主动地融入当地的文化、生活环境；另一方面也可为来自不同地区、具有不同文化背景的员工提供相互了解对方文化、价值观、对事物的不同理解和表达观点的不同方式创造条件。其次，鼓励机构内不同文化背景的员工之间建立个人友谊，这是机构内成效较为明显的一种跨文化交流方式。再次，海外出版分支机构的管理者在经营决策的讨论过程中，要充分尊重不同文化背景的员工的意见的表达，避免文化歧视，强调文化差异的存在对于跨国经营的价值；应设法激发不同观点的提出，通过真诚的交流、讨论让员工理解他人观点的形成过程，帮助员工正确理解和对待文化差异，并通过目标的实现或问题的解决来彰显文化差异的价值，在员工之间塑造一种良好的文化共识和文化氛围。

7 小结

以上论述表明，中国出版业"走出去"进行跨国经营是在完全陌生的文化背景下进行的，文化差异的客观存在使这种跨国经营面临文化风险。这种文化风险对跨国经营的影响是渐次的、阶段性的，有其产生的根源和表现形式，可以通过一定的措施进行防范。需要指出的是，由于国内出版企业"走出去"跨国经营的时间先后各不相同，对跨国经营文化风险的体会也会不一样。先期"走出去"的出版企业可能对这种文化风险有着较为明显的切身体会，而近期"走出去"的出版企业则可能尚未明显感觉到这种文化风险及其影响的存在。但是，这并不意味着这种文化风险不存在，它们只是暂时没有充分暴露而已，或处于休眠状态，或处于蛰伏时期，一旦爆发将令人措手不及。因此，已经、正在和即将"走出去"进行跨国经营的国内出版企业需要对这种文化风险有一个较为全面的、清醒的认识，树立风险防范意识、提高风险应对能力，只有这样才能使中国出版业真正地、稳健地"走出去"，融入世界出版的大潮之中。

注释

[1] 如 2002 年 7 月，中国外文局与香港联合出版集团合资组建了我国在美国本土建立的第一家出版机构——长河出版社；2007 年 4 月，中国青年出版社在英国成立伦敦分社；2007 年 9、10 月间，中国出版集团公司在纽约、悉尼和巴黎陆续新建了海外分公司；2008 年 7 月，人民卫生出版社美国有限责任公司正式成立；2008 年 8 月，中国出版集团公司与美国百盛公司在纽约共同投资开设了海外第一家新华书店分店等，而国内出版企业最早"走出去"进行跨国经营则始于 20 世纪 90 年代。

[2] 潘文年：论我国政府在出版业"走出去"中的角色. 国际新闻界, 2009（6）

Pan Wennian. "On the Roles of the China Government during the 'Going out' of Chinese

Publishing Industry". *Journal of International Communication*, 2005（2）（in Chinese）

［3］潘文年. 中国出版业"走出去"：出版行业组织的作用分析. 出版发行研究，2010（2）.

Pan Wennian. "the 'Going out' of Chinese Publishing Industry：the Analysis of the Publishing industry organizations "effect". *Publishing and Issue Research*, 2010（2）.（in Chinese）

［4］常燕荣. 论跨文化传播的三种模式. 湖南大学学报，2003（5）

Chang Yanrong. "three Models of Intercultural Communication". *the School Paper of Hunan University*, 2003（5）.（in Chinese）

［5］潘文年. 中国出版企业海外市场投资模式比较分析. 中国出版，2009（2）

Pan Wennian. "the Comparative Analysis of the Investment Modes of Chinese Publishing Enterprises Overseas Markets". *China Publishing Journal*, 2009（2）（in Chinese）

［6］［7］唐晓华，王伟光. 现代国际化经营. 北京：经济管理出版社，2006：315-381。

Tang Xiaohua, Wang Weiguang. "Modern Internationalization Management". Beijing：the Press of Economics and Managemen, 2006：315-381.（in Chinese）

［8］顾天辉，张光宝，李丽，吕超. 文化风险与企业国际化. 技术与创新管理，2009（1）

Gu Tianhui, Zhang Guangba, Li Li, LV Chao. "Cultural Risk and Enterprise Internationalization". *Technology and Innovation Management*, 2009（1）.（in Chinese）

［9］S. Nanda & R. L. Warms. *Cultural Anthropology*. 6th ed. （Belmont：CA：Wadsworth, 1998）：226

［10］C. M. Berger & R. J. Calabrese. "Some Explorations in Initial Interaction and Beyond". *Human Communication Research*, 1（1975）：99-112

［11］C. M. Berger & R. J. Calabrese. "Some Explorations in Initial Interaction and Beyond". *Human Communication Research*, 1（1975）：100

［12］［美］拉里·A·萨姆瓦，理查德·E·波特著. 闵惠泉，王纬，徐培培等译：跨文化传播. 第四版. 北京：中国人民大学出版社，2004：267

［America］Larry A. Samovar：*Communication Between Cultures*, 4th Edition. Beijing, the Press of People's University of China, 2004：267（in Chinese）

［13］单波，石义彬. 跨文化传播新论. 武汉：武汉大学出版社，2005：43

Shan Bo, Shi Yinbin, *the New Analysis of Intercultural Communication*, Wuhan, the Press of Wuhan University, 2005：43（in Chinese）

［14］S. Nanda & R. L. Warms. *Cultural Anthropology*. 6th ed. （Belmont：CA：Wadsworth, 1998（6）

［15］F. M. Keesing. *Cultural Anthropology：The Science of Custom*. New York：Holt, Rinehart, & Winston, 1965：45

［16］Lillian H. Chaney, Jeanette S. Martin. *Intercultural Business Communication*. 第 2 版（影印版）. 北京：高等教育出版社，2002.

Lillian H. Chaney, Jeanette S. Martin, *Intercultural Business Communication*. 2th ed, Beijing，Higher Education Press，2002

作者简介

潘文年，博士，安徽大学新闻传播学院副教授、硕士生导师。

宏观出版

数字出版与信息网络传播对社会的影响

那 欣

（东北财经大学出版社　大连　116025）

摘要：数字化根本地改变了体现人的本质特征的信息生产、传播方式，并进而改变了人类的生产、生活方式，把人类带入高度信息化的社会，尤其对传统出版业、传统印刷业、传统发行业、和大众文化生活将产生重大影响。本文将从这四个方面论述数字出版与信息网络传播对社会的影响，并提出：出版业界应将更多目光转向数字出版，一方面数字出版本身具备潜力，另一方面国家对数字出版高度重视和支持。最后，网络与生俱来的特质，使得数字出版相对于传统出版，具有极大的优越性。

关键词：数字出版　信息传播　电子出版物　影响

Digital Publishing and Information Network Transmission of Social Impact

Na Xin

（Dongbei University of Finance and Economics Press，Dalian，116025）

Abstract：As the digitizing fundamentally changes information production，transmission modes which representing the characteristics of human nature，it surely will transform the mode of production and human life styles and bring the human into the highly information-oriented society. In publishing filed，significant impact would be brought about on traditional publishing industry，traditional printing industry，traditional distribution industry and public cultural life particularly because of it. This paper will discuss the influence of digital publishing and information network transmission from the upper four aspects and give the advice that digital publishing should be put on more attention for the reasons that on the one hand，the development of digital publishing is promising；On the other hand，more attention and policy support is given to digital publishing by government；Finally，digital publishing shows great superiority compared to traditional publishing.

Keywords：Digital publishing　Information dissemination　E-publications　Impact

21 世纪的人类社会以前所未有的速度进入数字化时代。信息技术的发展将人类带入了一个全新的信息社会和一个全新的知识经济时代。如果说纸与笔、阅读与书写是人类社会传统的信息传播模式，那么集声、光、电于一身，聚音、字、像于一体，汇采、传、授于一线的另一种模式，即计算机与网络的新型信息传播模式——信息的网络传播将展现在我们的面前。

信息传播是影响社会发展的重要因素。作为传播信息的重要媒介——电子出版，尤其是网络出版，在信息传播中占有重要地位，由于数字化根本地改变了体现人的本质特征的信息生产、传播方式，并进而改变了人类的生产、生活方式，因此，它必然带动社会整体的变迁，把人类带入高度信息化的社会，对传统出版业和大众文化生活将产生重大影响。

1 数字出版对传统出版业的影响

数字出版是人类文化的数字化传承，它是建立在计算机技术、通讯技术、网络技术、存储技术、显示技术等高新技术基础上，融合并超越了传统出版而发展起来的新兴出版产业。数字出版在出版的整个过程中，将所有的信息都以统一的二进制代码的形式存储于光盘、磁盘等介质中，信息的处理与接收则借助计算机或其他终端设备进行。它强调内容的数字化，生产模式和运作流程的数字化，传播载体的数字化和阅读消费、学习形态的数字化。下面我们就数字出版下的产物电子出版物与传统出版物的区别作如下阐述：

（1）阅读的方式不同。电子出版物的阅读需要利用计算机或者其他的电子阅读工具。

（2）海量存储。数以千计的文学作品只需几张光盘便可容纳，"坐拥书城"对每个人来说都轻而易举。

（3）长久保存。电子出版物中的信息是数字化的记录，只要妥善保管，信息将长久保存，不会像纸质图书随着时间的流逝而变得字迹模糊、色彩黯淡。

（4）发行渠道不同。电子出版物的发行渠道呈多样化。可以通过软件销售商出售，也可以通过与电子计算机硬件捆绑销售；还可以通过互联网传输，用户经网上付费后下载。

（5）版本更新灵活、方便、快捷。出版物内容的更新只需修改电子文档，内容增减不影响版面，页码重新排列可以瞬间完成，这是纸质出版物无法办到的。

（6）复制成本低廉。批量复制光盘成本很低，相比印刷图书的成本就高得多。

由于电子出版物的特点较传统出版物有明显的优势，对传统出版物形成很大的冲击，使其面临着严峻的挑战。

在电子出版刚刚起步初期，出版社并没有感受到多大的压力，只希望它能给出版社带来新的经济增长点。相关阅读调查显示，阅读传统出版物的人数在以每年12%的速度下降，而阅读新媒体的人数则以30%的速度在增长，特别在年轻人和知识分子人群中表现尤为明显，而他们正是媒体市场未来消费的主力，数字出版的发展趋势已毋庸置疑。数字出版，特别是互联网出版已经形成强劲的发展势头，正日益影响和改变着人们的阅读习惯、消费结构和认知倾向，这些变化给传统出版业造成了巨大影响。虽然电子出版物不可能完全取代纸质书刊，但网络作为一种新载体，我们对它不能漠然视之。我们应及时进行战略上的调整，把传统出版物同数字出版有机地结合起来，如果传统出版社转型数字出版步伐缓慢，在未来的市场竞争中必将处于不利地位。

目前基于互联网的数字出版业仍处于起步阶段，未来的发展空间相当大，已知和未知的商机还相当多。这得益于互联网应用技术的不断改进和提高，也得益于宽带的进一步普及和3G技术在移动通信领域的应用。与此同时，随着网民数量和宽带用户的快速增长，互联网应用终端也将重新整合，这些都将极大地刺激互联网信息产业包括出版产业新一轮的竞争和发展。

2　数字技术对传统印刷业的影响

数字出版将极大地冲击传统书刊印刷行业。面对新技术的挑战，从 20 世纪 80 年代起，传统的印刷行业已经经历了一个数字化的发展进程。如今，印刷行业不仅仅是人员加设备的组合，在印刷生产的每一个环节，无论是软件还是硬件，都融入了数字技术，步入了文字、图像数字化，图文合一数字化的进程。过去的一些落后的工艺技术已经被淘汰。印刷行业的数字化过程为其自身的发展开拓了新的天地，同时也为包括网络出版在内的电子出版奠定了坚实的基础，为制作网络出版的电子书提供了庞大的数字化资源。

随着信息和知识更新的加快，电子书等网络出版物将迅速增长，纸质图书的出版也将会向多品种、小批量、短周期发展。因此，"按需印刷"将成为市场的需求。面对网络时代，印刷业必须调整、更新观念。尽管现在传统印刷方式还占有一定优势，但随着数字印刷技术的不断完善和成本下降，数字印刷将会逐渐成为主流，传统印刷方式将受到巨大冲击。因此，从现在开始，传统的书刊印刷行业必须面对现实，加快信息化以及数字化印刷的进程。

3　数字技术对传统发行业的影响

传统的纸质出版物——图书是一种"小商品"：品种多、定价低、交易频、市场广；同时，图书生产相对集中，交易相对分散，自然形成了供求在时间和空间上的巨大矛盾。为解决这种矛盾，超大型书店、超大型批销中心等不断出现，但仍然不能解决问题。而随着网络传播技术和电子商务技术的进步，网上书店有了很大的发展，任何地方的任何读者，可以在任何时间在计算机终端上通过因特网看到全国甚至世界各地的图书信息，并实现订购。全国各地的书店，可以通过网络及时了解最新的出版动态，并找到最理想的供货商，就供货等问题在网上及时沟通，还可以由网络提供及时的市场动态分析，从而更好地通过市场分析指导图书的生产与采购行为。这样，图书通过网络实现了从市场到流通，再到生产的良性循环，比建设超大书店、批销中心要更加节约资源，并能取得更广泛的成效。这既是网络公司进入书刊发行业的重要途径，又是对传统零售书店的挑战，对传统的书刊零售业构成了强烈的冲击。

在数字出版时代，出版社在发行过程中的主动地位也将大大加强。传统发行业将面对来自各个方面的挑战。发行业要适应网络出版并期望取得发展，就一定要主动迎接挑战，加强数字化建设，只有尽快建立能实现纸质图书和电子书兼容销售的电子商务平台，才能使出版发行在数字化时代立于不败之地。

4　数字出版对大众文化生活的影响

4.1　数字出版改变了阅读方式

数字出版将会改变人们的生活，最大的改变就是阅读方式，纸质图书将被边缘化。电子出版物的出现，使得传统的书刊阅读方式受到了挑战。手机出版和移动存储设备（电子书）的数字出版由于其特有的便捷性和成本逐渐降低而被广大年轻人和高端用户所接受。人们可以通过计算机或便携式电子阅读器，实现传统阅读方式所不能做到的大信息量包括文字、声音、图像于一体的，能快速进行全文检索的阅读。

电子出版的数字化产品，由于可以全文检索，读者能够快速获得需要的信息，极大地提高工作效率。阅读文献资料数据库类、工具类的电子出版物，检索的优势可得到淋漓尽致的发挥。

汉王科技股份有限公司董事长刘迎建在参加 2009 年法兰克福国际书展之际，这样描述汉王电子书的海外发展前景："站在全世界的角度看，数字化出版几年前就很热。但自从电子阅读屏幕成为成熟产品，以及亚马逊和汉王等企业获得成功后，整个数字化出版产业的脉络才呼之欲出。可以说，电子书将是未来十年的一场巨大革命，它将彻底改变人们的生活。"

4.2　数字出版和信息网络传播技术使现代远程教育得以快速发展

随着电子出版技术以及信息网络传播技术尤其是高速宽带网技术的普及，依托于信息网络传播的现代远程教育得到了快速发展。远程教育是学生与教师、学生与教育组织之间主要采取多媒体方式进行系统教学和通信联系的教育形式，是将课程传送给校园外的一处或多处学生的教育。它是随着现代信息技术的发展而产生的一种新型教育方式。计算机技术、多媒体技术、通信技术的发展，特别是因特网（Internet）的迅猛发展，使远程教育的手段有了质的飞跃，成为高新技术条件下的远程教育。

数字技术可以有效地发挥远程教育的作用。远程教育是一种相对于面授教育的师生分离、非面对面组织的教学活动。这是一种跨学校、跨地区的教学模式，其特点是：学生与教师分离，采用特定的传输系统和传播媒体进行教学，信息的传输方式多种多样，学习的场所和形式灵活多样。与面授教育相比，远距离教育的优势在于它可以突破时空的限制，提供更多的学习机会，扩大教学规模，提高教学质量，降低教学成本。基于远程教育的特点和优势，许多有识之士已经认识到发展远程教育的重要意义和广阔前景。以电子信息技术为基础的现代远程教育，必将使教育领域产生深刻变革，促进教育现代化。它将突破传统教育时空的限制，扩展教育资源，推进教育大众化和终身化。它以覆盖面广，全方位为各类社会成员提供教育服务的优势，对人力资源开发产生强大的推动作用；它将会推动我国信息产业发展，进一步扩大信息产品和信息服务的需求，促进优秀软件的开发和应用，带动一批高新技术产业的发展和高校科研成果的转化，成为国家信息产业发展以及整个经济社会发展的新的增长点，推动知识经济的形成和发展。

数字出版被公认为 21 世纪出版业的发展方向。随着数字技术的不断发展，出版业界将目光转向数字出版，这一方面来自于数字出版本身所具备的潜力，另一方面则来自于国家对数字出版发展的高度重视和政策支持。此外，由于网络与生俱来的特质，使得数字出版相对于传统出版，具有极大的优越性，孕育了美好的前景。

变者，天下之公理也。数字出版的方兴未艾正让出版人见证了又一次出版业的变革。创新及应用是数字出版发展的根本动力，自主创新已经成为我国数字出版发展的核心推动力。作为数字出版的内容生力军，我国传统出版业要积极适应新的内容传播方式，根据内容资源的特点进行有效配置和开发，致力打造多元传播格局中的强势地位，加快数字化转型步伐。

参考文献

[1] 曲辰晨. 传统出版的数字化作为及定位策略 [EB]. http://www.epuber.com/? p = 2713#_.

[2] 王晓光. 数字出版时代的跨媒介转移出版战略研究 [EB]. http://www.epuber.com/? p = 2713#_.

[3] 任殿顺. 中国出版业数字转型的困境与出路 [EB]. http://www.epuber.com/? p = 2713#_.

[4] 寇晓伟, 武强. 数字出版带来了什么 [EB]. www.qklw.com.

作者简介

那欣，东北财经大学出版社一级校对。

浅析湖北省数字出版产业发展存在的问题及对策

赵 丹

（武汉大学信息管理学院 武汉 430072）

摘要：本文从产业分布、主体构成、准入门槛、网络管理、版权纠纷、人才资源六个方面分析了湖北省数字出版产业发展中存在的问题，并指出加快湖北省数字出版产业发展应从以下六个方面着手：提高认识、加强领导，推进创新、整合资源、塑造品牌，建立奖励和资助机制，设立数字出版园区，培育大型数字出版企业，培养专业化、国际化的人才队伍。

关键词：数字出版 产业 问题 对策

Problems and Countermeasures of Digital Publishing Industry in Hubei Province

Zhao Dan

（School of Information Management, Wuhan University, Wuhan, 430072）

Abstract：This paper analyzes six specific problems of digital publishing industry in Hubei province, that is the industrial distribution, the composition of the investors, the entry threshold, the administration of networks, copyright disputes, talent resources. And then the article points out that in order to accelerate development of digital publishing industry in Hubei we should pay more attention to the following six aspects: raise the awareness, enhance the capacity of leadership, bring forth innovation, marshaling resources, build brands, establish encouraging and assisting systems, build industrial park for digital publishing, nurture large-scale digital publishing company, cultivate specialization and internationalization talents.

Keywords：Digital publishing Industry Problem Countermeasures

数字出版在我国虽然起步较晚，但是发展很快，目前已经形成了网络图书、网络期刊、网络地图、网络视频、网络音乐、网络教育、网络游戏、手机出版等新业态。湖北的数字出版起步较早，曾与北京、上海一起，同属我国三大数字出版策源地和活动中心之一。武汉城区积聚了大批数字出版人才和企业，培养出了华中地区最大的数字创意产业园，形成了一定的产业规模和明显的产业优势，为发展数字出版奠定了良好的基础。

湖北现有湖北日报传媒集团、湖北长江出版传媒集团、知音传媒集团、长江日报传媒集团、武汉出版集团等7家大型出版、报业集团，14家图书出版社、22家音像电子网络出版机构，每年出版图书 7 000 多种，电子音像出版物 1 000 余种；现有报纸 131 种，期刊 402 种。湖北报纸、杂志出版规模大、数字化进展快，音像电子出版稳步发展。网络游戏开发企业数量较多，仅武汉市的网游开发制作公司就达 20 多家，动漫产业主要集中在武汉，发展比较快。2009 年湖北省的动漫（包括网游、手机动漫、网络动漫、CD 动漫以及部分书刊动漫）制作出版产值规模估计在 8～10 亿元（不含衍生工业产品产值），部分企业年销售收入超过 1 亿元。

随着信息技术的快速发展和新闻出版体制改革的不断深化，湖北省数字出版及其相关产业发展既面临着机遇与挑战，也面临着诸多问题和现实困难。

1 湖北省数字出版创业发展中存在的问题分析

1.1 数字内容产业分布集中，发展不平衡

湖北省从事网络出版的单位或机构，基本上都集中在武汉地区，其他地区由于经济水平相对落后，传统出版产业基础薄弱，互联网普及程度和应用水平不高，网络出版这种新的出版方式基本上没有启动，导致了网络出版发展的地域失衡，制约了湖北省网络出版的发展规模和速度。

1.2 数字出版主体构成复杂，监管困难

在当前从事互联网出版业务的网站中，存在着经营主体资格不明确的问题。有的网站是湖北省传统出版单位创办的，经营主体明确，对它们的监督管理比较容易开展；有的网站是民营企业或者个人投资出资创办从事互联网出版活动的。目前湖北省取得新闻出版总署颁发的《互联网出版许可证》的单位只有 10 家，而省内有上百家单位在从事互联网出版活动。这种情况造成网络出版单位投资主体的构成比较复杂，导致互联网出版管理部门监管困难，容易产生管理上的漏洞。

1.3 网络出版主体市场准入门槛过高

目前，我国网络出版主体市场准入门槛过高，特别是对民营网络出版企业的网络出版权控制较严。湖北省还没有取得网络出版权的民营企业，包括立得空间技术有限责任公司这样数字技术含量很高的全国知名企业，申报网络出版权已经半年了，还没有获得批准。而一些出版单位尽管拥有网络出版机构资质，但没有开展网络出版业务。

1.4 互联网管理存在政出多门、多头管理的现象

目前，国内互联网管理部门立法监管虽然已有了长足进步，但对网络出版的监管仍然存在着政出多门、多头管理的现象，严重制约了网络出版的发展。据调查，著名的门户网站网易目前已办理的牌照有 10 个之多，分别为：ICP 许可证、互联网新闻刊登许可证、网络出版许可证、互联网广告刊登许可证、药品信息刊登许可证、医疗服务信息刊登许可证、网络文化经营许可证、教育信息刊登许可证、BBS 经营许可证、移动短信经营许可证等，其中还不包括网络游戏经营许可证。这些许可证分别出自不同的管理部门，一方面，无形中增加了企业的审查手续和运行成本；另一方面，这些许可证许可范围在很多方面存在交叉，也给管理部门的日常管理带来许多问题。因此，很多网络出版单位呼吁各管理部门切实做到归口管理，简化手续，最好由一个机构出面统筹，然后将涉及的问题分解至相应的部门办理，以切实促进网络出版产业健康发展。

1.5 版权问题比较突出

一直以来，网络作品的侵权问题十分突出，侵权官司不断，许多网站未经授权，擅自使用他人作品的情况经常发生。虽然新修订的著作权法及其实施细则和《信息网络传播权保护条例》已明确了作品的"网络信息传播权"，但由于目前网络作品的稿酬或版费缺乏相应支付标准，而网站、出版社和作者对稿酬或版费的标准分歧较大，导致不少网站常常是"先斩后奏"。此外，关于网络内容暂时复制权的问题，如何界定一直争论不休。

1.6 数字出版复合型人才缺乏

与传统出版相比，数字出版有着全新的出版环境，编辑收集信息、选题策划、约稿、编辑加工、校对以及排版，甚至发行等环节都将在网络上进行，出版工作越来越多地与互联网相关联，从而对网络出版从业人员的技能和整体素质提出了更高的要求，这使得出版业的发展不但需要有新的出版理念，而且对于能够驾驭数字出版和跨媒介出版的人才的需求也日益强烈。《互联网出版管理暂行规定》第二十一条对实施网络出版的责任人提出了明确要求，要求从事网络出版工作人员具有较强的网络知识即计算机操作能力、信息识别能力和较丰富的出版工作经验。而在现阶段，网络出版机构所拥有的人才资源要么局限于前者，要么局限于后者，能够满足出版业发展需要的复合人才非常匮乏，尤其是从事网络出版的研发、营销、管理的人才更是奇缺，不能完全满足网络出版业发展的需要。

2 加强湖北省数字出版产业发展的对策

2.1 提高对数字网络出版的认识、加强对数字网络出版发展的组织领导

应充分认识发展数字网络出版的重要性、紧迫性，认识它对经济社会的推动作用。相关政府部门应加强对数字与网络出版事业和产业发展的领导，要把发展、壮大数字与网络出版产业作为增强湖北省综合竞争力的重要组成部分，纳入经济社会发展的总体规划。在管理机构及人员、项目建设经费、税收、融资等方面提供强有力的支持。抓好重点工程和平台建设，加大对网络出版资源的引导，确保社会主义先进文化占领主导阵地。

2.2 推进科技创新，整合数字出版资源，塑造数字出版品牌，着眼于做大做强湖北数字出版产业

应鼓励有条件的图书、报刊、音像电子出版等相关单位从事网络出版，充分发掘和整合现有的出版资源，在网络文化建设上得到延伸和发挥，扩大湖北网络出版文化产品的社会影响力。应重视网站的出版功能建设，整合湖北的网站资源，打造名牌网站。大力发展网上图书馆、网上博物馆、在线数据库等。大力发展一批从事教育软件和文化娱乐软件开发制作的专业公司。大力发展高科技娱乐产品、音像动漫、游戏软件等数字化新品。重点将湖北武汉建成中西部教育软件和文化娱乐软件开发基地和生产基地。

2.3 建立数字出版奖励、资助机制和政策，鼓励原创，引导数字出版健康发展

（1）设立面向数字出版的专门奖项，每年或者定期对本省范围内的数字出版物进行评审。对优秀的数字出版作品、出版人才和出版社或者公司进行奖励。

（2）设立湖北数字网络出版文化产业发展基金或者从其他基金中设立数字网络出版发展专项基金，为数字网络出版产业提供资助、政策贷款或者贷款补助。凡具有重大原创性，或者宣传湖北历史文化，或者重大产业价值的项目均可以申请。优先鼓励原创民族游戏以及湖北历史文化题材的作品。

2.4 设立数字出版园区，探索园区式数字出版管理机制和模式

（1）数字网络出版具有技术集成性、平台支撑性、内容集成性，适合园区式的发展模式。数字出版园区具有开发成本低、产业集中度高、易于管理和服务等特点。

（2）依托出版集团、传媒集团或者通信公司等大型企业或者基础性公司建设数字与网络出版园区。

（3）设立数字出版园区管理服务中心，负责园区内企业技术平台搭建、数字出版项目申报审查、数字出版人员培训和指导、日常管理服务等工作。

2.5 择优引入和孵化，培育大型数字出版传媒企业

第一，对省内经营规模大、营运状况好、资质好能力强、管理有序、服从管理部门指导的出版机构以及其他企事业单位，要纳入日常出版监管和扶持的体系，进行孵化。从湖北省现有的动漫、网游、网站、数据库、音像、手机读物等新型出版物的制作发行企事业单位中，确立一批骨干单位作为"数字出版孵化单位"，纳入数字出版的日常管理体系，按照正式出版单位的要求对其进行指导、培训和管理，纳入日常的统计范围，待条件成熟时，优先审批其相关出版权。鼓励其上市融资，做大做强。

第二，通过引资、引智和引入优质内容资源等方式引入国内外的优势出版传媒企业到湖北落户。

2.6 培养人才、壮大队伍，造就专业化、国际化的数字网络出版队伍

第一，培养和用好高层次文化技术人才。支持企业培养和吸引创新人才，加快数字出版及网络文化人才教育培训，坚持选拔优秀人才到省外或国外进修、观摩、学习深造。第二，培育和完善数字媒体与网络文化人才市场，建立数字网络出版专业人才交流平台，促进人才合理流动。第三，积极主动地吸引国内外优秀的数字网络出版人才到湖北发展，为他们提供发展空间，提升湖北省数字网络出版业的竞争力。第四，完善人才激励机制。建议制定以鼓励数字网络文化建设为重点的湖北省优秀文化人才奖励办法，设立湖北省优秀文化人才奖励专项基金，对有突出贡献者进行重奖。深化分配制度改革，探索建立以知识产权、无形资产、技术要素等参与收益分配的新路子。

作者简介

赵丹，武汉大学信息管理学院 2009 级出版发行硕士研究生。

基于"钻石模型"的我国数字出版产业优劣分析

祝桂丽

（武汉大学信息管理学院　武汉　430072）

摘要：近年来，世界各国都在争相发展数字出版产业，尽管我国的数字出版产业发展迅猛，但是面对激烈的国际市场竞争，我国的数字出版产业依然面临严峻的考验。本文试结合迈克尔·波特的"钻石模型"，分析我国数字出版产业发展的优势与劣势，认为复合型人才匮乏、产业链不完善以及出版单位战略定位不明是制约我国数字出版产业发展的主要因素。

关键词：钻石模型　数字出版产业　产业链

Diamond Model-based Analysis of the Digital Publishing Industry's Advantages and Disadvantages in China

Zhu Guili

（School of Information management，Wuhan University，Wuhan，430072）

Abstract：In recent years，various countries are competively developing digital publishing industry. Our country's digital publishing industry development is quite swift，but，given the intensive international market competition，our country's digital publishing industry still faces severe test. This article analyzes the development's advantages and disadvantages based on Diamond Model. The article argues that the inter-disciplinary talent's deficiency，the industrial chain's imperfectness as well as unclarity of publishing institutes' strategic positioning are the main factors that restricts the development of our country's digital publishing industrial.

Keywords：Diamond model　Digital publishing industry　Industrial chain

近几年我国先后公布的《国民经济和社会发展"十一五"规划纲要》、《中长期科学技术发展规划纲要》和《国家"十一五"时期文化发展规划纲要》以及2009年国务院通过的《文化产业振兴规划》等均将发展数字出版产业作为国家文化建设、出版传媒产业发展、国家竞争力提升的重要战略，这为数字出版产业发展提供了良好的政策环境。且在人们阅读习惯发生巨变的今天，对数字出版产品的需求会逐步增加，这也为数字出版产业提供了良好的发展机遇。如何把握机会，使我国数字出版产业成为带动经济进一步复苏的新亮点是亟待解决的问题。

美国经济学家迈克尔·波特的"钻石模型"阐述了一个产业乃至一个国家要想在竞

争中立于优势地位需要具备的四个关键性因素：要素条件、需求条件、相关支持产业、企业战略与组织结构。对于我国数字出版产业而言，要想把握机遇，加快发展，培养竞争优势同样需要从上面四个条件入手。

1 我国数字出版产业的发展现状

随着数字技术的进步，传统出版物正不断向数字化方向发展。内容的传播已经不仅仅是传统的媒体传播形式，基于互联网进行数字内容传播的形式也逐渐成为主流之一。国外数字内容产业发展迅速。据国际数字出版论坛（IDPF）的销售统计数据，2007 年美国全年电子图书渠道销售额同比 2006 年增长 23.6%。有报道称韩国 2006 年电子书的销售额已达 1 400 亿韩元，约合 1.44 亿美元。

近年来，随着经济的高速发展，以及互联网技术和移动通信技术的提高和应用普及，国民阅读习惯和环境的明显变化，我国的数字出版产业在短短几年内产值突飞猛进，实现了跨越式发展，呈现出以产值屡创新高，手机出版异军突起，电子阅读器风生水起，数字出版赢利模式不断创新等的发展特点。

据统计，从 2000 年电子书这种新兴出版形态在我国萌芽开始，数字出版产业至今已形成产值超过 500 亿元的产业规模。中国的数字出版在近 10 年内的发展突飞猛进。2006 年数字出版产业达 213 亿元，2007 年达 362.42 亿元，2008 年达 530.64 亿元。2009 年我国数字出版产业的产值达 799.4 亿元，是 2006 年产值的 3.75 倍，比 2008 年增长 50.6%，年均增长率超过 55%。其中数字期刊收入 6 亿元，电子书收入达 14 亿元，数字报（网络版）收入达 3.1 亿元，网络游戏收入达 256.2 亿元，网络广告达 206.1 亿元，手机出版（包括手机音乐、手机游戏、手机动漫、手机阅读）则达到 314 亿元。网络游戏、网络广告和手机出版成为数字出版产业名副其实的三巨头。[1]

2 基于"钻石模型"的我国数字出版产业优劣势分析

2.1 优势

2.1.1 阅读习惯的改变带来广阔的市场需求

任何一种产品、一个产业要想获得持续的发展空间，首先一个前提是有足够的市场需求作为基础保障，迈克尔·波特也同样将需求条件作为钻石模型中不可或缺的条件。

传统的阅读习惯使不少人依恋于纸媒读物，他们普遍不适应电子屏幕显示，认为网上传播的内容不太可靠。但年轻一代对无纸作业和阅读逐步适应甚至依赖，纸媒读物一统天下的局面被打破，这已是不争的事实。

我国网民数增长迅速，截至 2008 年 6 月已达 2.53 亿人，一年间增加了 9 100 万人，年增长率为 56.2%。互联网逐步向各层次的居民扩散。体现互联网娱乐作用的网络音乐、网络影视、网络游戏等排名靠前，我国互联网市场娱乐功能占据主要地位；即时通信高居第二位，体现了中国互联网鲜明的本土特色；网络新闻的排名依旧很高，更新博客/个人空间比例迅速提高，互联网新媒体的地位更加突出。认为互联网对工作/学习有很大帮助的网民占 93.1%，尤其是娱乐方面，认为互联网丰富了网民的娱乐生活的比例高达 94.2%。而同时期，中国手机用户已达到 6 亿，手机网民数达 8 000 万人，增量可观。

此外，2010 年 4 月中国出版科学研究所发布的第七次全国国民阅读调查结果显示，

2009 年我国 18—70 岁国民中，接触过数字化阅读方式的国民比例达 24.6%，比 2008 年增长了 0.1 个百分点。其中，有 16.7% 的国民通过网络在线阅读，比 2008 年增加了 1 个百分点；有 14.9% 的国民接触过手机阅读，比 2008 年增长了 2.2 个百分点。另外，有 4.2% 的国民使用 PDA/MP4/电子词典等进行数字化阅读，与 2008 年持平；有 2.3% 的国民用光盘读取，比 2008 年减少了 1 个百分点。值得注意的是，2009 年，有 1.3% 的国民使用其他手持电子阅读器进行数字化阅读，比 2008 年增加了 0.3 个百分点，增幅为 30%。除光盘读取这一数字化阅读方式有所衰退和 PDA/MP4/电子词典读取没有变化外，其他数字阅读方式的接触者规模都有一定程度的增长，网络在线阅读和手机阅读是数字化阅读方式中的主流。

同时，在接触过数字化阅读方式的国民中，有 52.1% 的读者表示能够接受付费下载阅读，这一读者群体能够接受的一本电子图书的平均价格为 3.45 元。调查显示，在接触过数字化阅读方式的国民中，91.0% 的读者阅读电子书后就不会再购买该书的纸质版，另有 9% 的读者表示阅读电子书后还会购买该书的纸质版。[2]

在阅读习惯的变化中，年轻人和知识分子人群表现尤为明显，他们将逐渐成为数字出版物市场未来的消费主力。

2.1.2　数字技术不断创新

迈克尔·波特认为，高级生产要素包括现代通讯、信息、交通等基础设施，这些要素对获得竞争优势具有不容置疑的重要性。

近两年来，以搜索引擎、移动终端、电子阅读器等为主的数字出版技术创新日新月异，数字阅读终端产品不断升级，新型阅读方式不断涌现。在移动终端方面，以 Symbian（赛班）和 WindowsMobile（WM）最新版移动操作系统支持的智能手机，以及苹果公司等推出的基于新型移动操作系统的 iPhone 手机，不仅备受手机制造商和移动运营商关注，也为用户提供了更加完备的体验。2009 年被称为"电子书年"，亚马逊在美国推出的电子阅读器销售了 40 万台，带动了自身网上书店数字化图书的销售。

数字技术的不断创新和应用为数字出版产业的发展提供了根本保证，促进了数字市场的进一步发展。

2.2　劣势

2.2.1　缺乏复合型的数字出版人才

钻石模型认为，高级生产要素需要先在人力和资本上大量和持续地投资，而作为培养高级生产要素的研究所和教育机构，本身就需要高级的人才。越是高端的产业越需要专业生产要素，而拥有专业生产要素的企业也会产生更大的竞争优势。

目前，我国数字出版人才严重匮乏，各出版单位主要由计算机专业背景的人员从事数字出版，而这些人员缺乏出版专业知识。传统出版人员虽具有相应的出版专业知识，但对数字出版物的制作以及数字出版业的信息化商业运作模式不了解，这就造成了数字出版成本过高、机会把握不准、难以真正实现赢利。

而且我国对数字出版的准备仍然严重不足，我国的出版教育与数字出版产业严重脱节。这其中的主要原因是数字出版企业在实践操作中应用的数字技术是由国外一些公司提供支持的，而出版企业本身对国内已有出版专业的高校信任度不高，缺乏合作，并且由于高校老师多是转自其他专业，导致与业界的联系较为薄弱，使数字出版教育与业界发展不能同步，因此造成严重的产、学、研结合的断裂，为以后的发展中由于人才水平的参差不齐所带来的一系列问题埋下了隐患。[3]

由此，我国的数字出版产业急需一批对传统出版流程和数字技术及经营管理都比较熟悉和精通的人才。

2.2.2 缺少相关支持产业，数字出版产业链不完善

钻石模型认为，一个优势产业不是单独存在的，它一定是同相关强势产业一同崛起，与上下游产业是一种密切合作的关系。而一个良好的产业生态，应该在企业群落内形成一个合理的分工链条，这个链条上的每个环节都有自己专注的领域，合起来才能形成整体优势。

完整的数字出版产业链应该包括以下方面：（1）创作数字化，即写作多媒体化；（2）编辑数字化，实现无纸编辑；（3）出版数字化，多元化出版（电子纸的应用、按需印刷方式等），满足不同需求偏好、不同层次的读者；（4）发行数字化，实现网上发行，网上发行不再是过去传统出版时从出版社向读者的单向流动，而是基于互联网的读者与作者、读者与出版社的双向多向交流，是为读者、作者的更深层次服务；（5）标识数字化，把一二次文献同步制作、报道与发行，实现社会性的标准化与规范化；（6）管理数字化，流程管理与内容管理融为一体，在操作的每个环节上都可以浏览所涉及的内容，不仅令出版全过程可控，改善编辑的工作强度，提升出版质量和效率，而且为随机修改带来无可比拟的灵活性。

但单纯从目前我国数字出版的产业链状况来看，产业链的各个环节发展很不平衡。在产业链上游，内容缺乏，没有形成规模化的数字内容的制作能力，而且数字厂商对数字出版的期待过高，但传统出版单位的态度却相对漠然。在产业链的中游，由于格式标准不统一，几家数字出版技术解决方案提供商的数据整理雷同，重复开发浪费较大，方正的CEB、超星的PDG、书生的SEP、Adobe的PDF、万方数据的PDF、知网的CAJ，各自都有自己的一套格式，不利于行业内容的交换和整合。在产业链的下游，分销领域渠道单一，电子图书等的营销过于依赖机构消费者，甚至存在恶性竞争。因此到目前为止，B2C领域的爆发式增长仍然是数字出版商业模式最大的期望。但从总体上来说，我国尚未形成有机的产业链和适当的赢利模式，难以产生规模经济效应。

2.2.3 战略定位不明，缺乏统一的标准

我国大部分出版企业在数字出版方面的定位不准确，其定位要么很大，要么很小，没有找准在产业链条中的定位。是做内容提供商、内容服务商还是数字出版商或发行商？对于这些，出版企业自身或者尚不清楚，或者目标宏大却难以实现。一方面，出版单位作为内容提供商，大多缺乏从全局性战略的高度来实施数字出版产业的内容构建和市场布局，以为与技术商展开了合作，并成立了数字出版部、网络部、信息中心或创办了网站，就意味着跨入了数字出版产业的行列。实际上，这既不等于传统出版与数字技术的全面转型，也不代表内容生产与销售方式的全面对接。另一方面，出版单位所建立的网站大多局限于本版图书信息发布，基本没有甚至无法进行交易，而再往下又不知还要投入多少，看不到回报将有多大，从而导致数字出版产业发展资金的投入严重不足。

此外，数字出版标准化问题长期得不到解决，已成为制约我国数字出版快速发展的瓶颈之一。在互联网领域，中文标准严重缺失，4 000项国际标准中只有3项由中国制定；

除了互联网基础性标准，数字出版产业的标准化还包括出版元数据的标准化、网络出版的标准化、出版物流系统的标准化等。然而，我国目前数字出版的技术系统和装备系统缺乏行业的总体标准，缺乏统一的标准和文本格式，数字技术提供商内部垂直系统多，难以关联和复用，无法敏捷应对用户需求的变化；数字技术提供商之间缺少统一的标准和相应的对接机制，难以互联互通、强强联合、共享客户资源，从而形成产业竞争优势。

3 我国数字出版产业的发展对策

3.1 走"产学研"互动培养之路，为数字出版产业提供后备人才

如何培养适应数字出版的复合型高素质创新人才，既是出版界也是教育界一直关注的关键问题。据了解，2010 年，国务院学位办批准设立了出版硕士专业学位，各校开始面向产业应用的专业硕士培养。此前，北京大学、武汉大学、北京印刷学院等全国 100 多所院校已开设了有关数字出版的专业方向和相关课程，约 40 所院校开设了电子出版、数字传媒、多媒体出版等数字出版教育课程，形成了一定教育规模。同时，约 30 所院校设立了数字出版课程。上述学校的人才培养目标主要是适应数字出版产业发展需要，培养既懂现代数字传媒技术，又懂文化艺术表现形式，既懂数字信息技术的应用，又懂内容和艺术设计，以多媒体出版物、网络出版物的内容编创、艺术设计和制作为特色的应用型、创新型数字化出版人才。[4]

而数字出版又是应用性比较强的学科，这需要高校创立校内实践创新体系。高校要为教学体系提供充足的项目创新实践机会，要挖掘专业内部资源，强化实践教学资源的开发。如建立导师指导制，为学生在校内校外竞赛、毕业设计或者参与社会项目提供专业的帮助与指导；利用实习基地的优势引导校内学生进行项目参与或创新活动；通过一些大型培训机构进行合作，来提升对于学生培养教育方式更新，并且创造、接受一些社会项目引导一部分有能力学生参与实践；组织学生参加各类有关的竞赛，拨发一定的创业基金鼓励学生自主创新和创业，开设工作室、创办社团、创办刊物、设立和经营网站等。利用学校已有的社会资源，指导优秀学生到出版社去实习学习，并且高校还要借助自身其他学科优势，采取跨学科联合培养的方式对学生进行全方位的培养。通过加强实践创新教育培养出符合产业发展要求的复合型人才。

3.2 发展相关产业，构建数字出版产业链

目前在我国的数字出版产业发展过程中，版权问题已成为我国数字出版业健康发展的瓶颈。为此国家应尽快更新相关的法律法规，让数字出版业也得到法律的有效保护，促使市场能得到有效的运作。

此外，出版单位还应根据自身的资源条件，专注于自己的领域，选择适当时机，融入有利于自身发展的出版产业链，形成整体优势。把握出版产业数字化的规律性特征，不断创新思维方式，调整竞争策略，实现出版产业做大做强。打破出版、传媒、网络、电子、电信等行业的界限，不断创新商业模式，将产业链扩展至电视、电影、游戏等一系列领域，抓住一切有利时机，寻求出版、印刷、旅游文化等商机，延长出版物的产品线，实现内容资源价值的最大化，拉动出版主业和多元产业的发展。

为了进一步开拓数字出版产业的市场需求，还可以通过报纸、广播电视、互联网等加大对数字出版产业的宣传力度，摒弃数字阅读是年轻人的专属的观念，深入挖掘成年人的

市场。

3.3 明确战略定位，制定统一的技术标准

数字出版单位要找准在产业链中的定位，无论是做内容供应商、数字内容服务商、数字出版商还是数字发行商，都应该更新观念，从自身定位考虑，遵循统一的标准，为共同缔造合理公平的数字出版产业链而努力。

目前国内很多出版社开始重视数字化出版的发展，都想在数字出版中分一杯羹。但我国数字出版的各环节技术标准还不统一，大多数数字出版单位都拥有自有的一套格式和浏览工具，这在一定程度造成了出版资源的浪费，也不利于数字出版产业整体竞争水平的提高。因此，可以建议新闻出版总署加大对数字出版技术标准化的研究力度，有效整合各类现存的标准，或制定出新的符合市场规律的技术标准。而技术提供商之间可以通过互联互通、强强联合、共享客户资源等方式寻求合作，制定符合产业发展的行业标准，建立一个统一的互动操作平台，通过不断沟通协作与改进，形成自身的产业竞争优势，为数字出版产业的发展提供完善的技术基础与良好的技术服务。[5]只有建立统一的技术标准，实现数据标准化与资源共享，才能有效地降低成本，优化资源配置，更好地促进数字出版产业链的健康有序发展。

注释

[1] 2010 中国数字出版产业年度报告发布 [EB/OL]. 中国出版网 http://news.xinhuanet.com/newmedia/2010-07/22/c_12360171.htm, 2010 年 07 月 22 日

[2] 第七次全国国民阅读调查显示：数字化阅读持续增长 [EB/OL]. 温州网 http://news.66wz.com/system/2010/04/19/101859271.shtml, 2010 年 04 月 19 日

[3] 张淑芳. 传统出版单位数字出版人才匮乏问题 [J]. 中国出版，2009 年第 6 期

[4] 杨晓芳. 数字出版人才培养亟待升级 [J]. 中国新闻出版报，2008 年 11 月 12 日

[5] 余琛，赵雪芹. 我国数字出版产业链问题分析 [J]. 现代商贸工业，2008 年第 4 期

作者简介

祝桂丽，武汉大学信息管理学院 2009 级出版发行专业硕士研究生。

资源、技术与共享：数字出版的三种基本模式*

方 卿

（武汉大学信息管理学院 武汉 430072）

摘要：经过数十年的探索，数字出版已形成了三种基本的成功模式。它们分别是基于内容资源的模式、基于数字技术的模式和基于开放共享理念的模式。其中，基于内容资源的模式，主要包括高端内容资源、原创内容资源和集成内容资源等三种实现形式。基于数字技术的模式主要包括阅读终端技术、出版平台技术和数字权利管理技术等三种实现形式。基于开放共享理念的模式包括开放存取仓储和开放存取期刊两种实现形式。

关键词：数字出版 出版模式 内容资源 数字技术 开放共享

Content, Technology & Sharing: Three Basic Models of Digital Publishing

Fang Qing

（School of Information Management， Wuhan University， Wuhan， 430072）

Abstract：After decades of exploration， digital publishing has formed three basic models of success. They are content-based model， technology-based model and the model based on open sharing of ideas. The content-based model includes three basic forms， which are high-end content resources， original content resources， and integration of content resources. The technology-based model involves terminal technologies of reading， publishing platform technologies and digital rights management technology. The model based on open sharing of ideas consists of open-access repositories and open-access journals.

Keywords：Digital publishing Publishing model Content Digital technology Sharing

数字出版是当今出版领域的高频词汇。然而，在我国，出版业界、学界和管理层，对数字出版可谓情感复杂，明知数字出版代表着出版业的发展方向，却又苦于找不到适合自

---

* 本文为国家自科基金项目"开放存取数字期刊学术质量评价与控制研究"（70873094）的中期成果。

己的数字出版发展模式。近些年来，我国各类出版企业在数字出版方面投入的人、财、物力不可谓不多，然而，真正在该领域获得较好赢利的却并不多见。那么，问题到底出在什么地方呢？应该说，从世界范围来看，经过近 30 余年的发展，数字出版在不少地方已获得巨大成功，科学有效的数字出版模式业已形成。我们认为，我们的一些出版企业对这些业已形成的成功模式缺乏足够的了解和认知，这正是导致其难以成功的根源。那么，数字出版到底有哪些成功模式呢？本文将给予简要分析。

1　基于内容资源的数字出版模式

众所周知，出版属内容产业范畴。内容资源是出版产业赖以生存和发展的基本要素。传统出版业如此，数字出版也不例外。纵观世界出版业，我们可以了解到，大多数在数字出版领域获得成功的企业都是基于其独特的内容资源而立于不败之地的。无论是世界顶级出版商励德·爱思唯尔（Reed Elsevier）、施普林格（Springer Verlag），还是本国的中国知网、盛大文学等均系以内容资源制胜的数字出版企业。需要强调的是，内容资源对传统出版和数字出版有着完全不同的意义。在传统出版业中，只要能够占有独特的内容资源，一般都能够获得成功。而数字时代的情况则不同，仅仅有独特的内容资源是远远不够的。我们的研究发现，数字时代出版企业基于内容资源获利的实现途径主要有以下三种。

第一，大量占有高端内容资源。所谓高端内容资源主要是指学术出版领域中各学科领域的一流学者产出的创新性学术成果。在学术或专业出版领域，这类高端内容资源具有极高市场价值。谁占有了这类内容资源，谁就占领了学术或专业出版的制高点。一些顶级学术或专业出版商，如励德·爱斯唯尔、施普林格等，之所以能够实现从传统出版向数字出版的"华丽转身"，在数字技术条件下仍然能够获得丰厚的回报，主要应该归因于其对这类高端学术内容资源的大量占有。当前我国学术或专业出版领域存在的许多问题，如产业集中度相对较低，学术内容资源的占有较为分散；学术或专业出版商品牌知名度较低，难以有效吸引高端内容资源，此类内容资源大量流向国外品牌知名度高的学术或专业出版商。高端内容资源的分散和流失，使得我国学术或专业出版只能建立在依靠低端内容资源的基础上。显然，这正是我国学术或专业数字出版难以获得成功的主要原因。

第二，充分获取原创内容资源。内容的创新是出版的生命，充分获取原创内容资源则是数字出版获得成功的又一个重要实现途径。这一模式在商业出版领域业已获得巨大成功。盛大文学正是实践这一模式的典范。盛大文学首席版权官周洪立先生之所以能够代表中国在法兰克福书展 TOC 国际讲堂宣讲数字出版，应该说正是因为"盛大"所创立的基于原创内容资源的数字出版运营模式所获得的巨大成功。盛大文学以"原创文学网站"为定位，自创立以来陆续收购了起点中文网（www.qidian.com）、起点女生网（www.qdmm.com）、晋江文学城（www.jjwxc.net）、红袖添香网（www.hongxiu.com）、榕树下（www.rongshuxia.com）、小说阅读网（www.readnovel.com）和潇湘书院（www.xxsy.net）等 7 家原创文学网站，成为我国原创文学的第一品牌。科学的定位与有效的市场运作，使得"盛大"几乎垄断了我国网络原创文学市场。原创内容资源的充分获取奠定了"盛大"在数字出版市场的领头羊地位。

第三，内容资源的高度集成。"规模效应"对数字出版有着特殊的意义，无论是学术出版、专业出版、大众出版还是教育出版，内容资源的高度集成都有利于形成"赢者通吃"的局面。对于数字出版企业而言，如果不能集成一定规模的内容资源，往往难以为网络读者所关注，并形成自己的品牌。以学术期刊出版为例，我国数以千计的专业学术期刊虽然大多都有自己的网站，但是真正有影响的却寥寥无几。然而，集成了众多学术期刊的"中国知网"、"重庆维普"和"龙源期刊"学术期刊数字出版平台却能够独树一帜，成为我国学术与专业出版市场领导者。"知网"、"维普"与"龙源"现象，充分说明内容资源的高度集成是数字出版的一种重要实现途径。

2 基于技术创新的数字出版模式

出版业产生与发展的历史表明，出版是一个高度的技术依赖型行业。出版业的每一次重大进步都与出版关联技术的发展密不可分。造纸术、活字印刷术、激光照排技术的出现都极大地促进和推动了出版产业的发展和进步。数字出版，与传统出版的本质区别同样也是源于出版技术手段的进步。以信息处理与传播为核心的数字技术的进步给传统出版业带来了巨大的影响，催生了今天的数字出版业。因此，以数字技术为突破口，通过数字出版技术的创新，同样可以形成具有良好竞争力的数字出版发展模式。从目前的情况看，基于技术创新的数字出版模式大致不外乎基于阅读终端技术、数字出版平台技术和数字版权管理技术的三种基本实现途径。

第一，基于阅读终端技术的数字出版。由于电子书阅读器之类的阅读终端是数字内容"落地"的基本手段，因此，阅读终端技术的创新与电子书阅读器的开发必然成为数字出版产业中最具活力的竞争领域。2006 年，索尼公司在美国投放了首批电子书终端——Reader 阅读器；2007 年，亚马逊公司推出了 Kindle 阅读器。据市场研究公司 Forrester 估算，2009 年美国电子阅读器销售量约 300 万台，而 Kindle 系列更是占据 60% 的份额。在电子书阅读器市场日益火爆的背景下，2010 年 4 月苹果公司又推出了新一代替代产品 iPad 系列平板电脑。截至 2010 年 6 月 21 日，iPad 上市 80 天，共销售了约 300 万台，且短期内每台 iPad 约下载 2.5 本书籍。由于其对电子阅读器阅读功能的较好替代性，再次将阅读终端领域的竞争推向高潮。在国内，电子阅读器市场同样发展迅猛。国内最早介入电子阅读器市场的是汉王科技。2009 年，"汉王"卖出了近 30 万套电纸书，成为国内该市场毫无争议的霸主。目前，我国涉及电子阅读器开发与生产的企业数量众多，而且不少传统出版企业也纷纷加入到这一行列，但是，真正具有市场影响力的仍然只有汉王科技。

在基于阅读终端技术的数字出版实现方式中，特别需要强调的是，技术固然重要，但它还必须与内容资源实现有效结合。阅读终端技术开发商，如果不能与内容出版商合作，不能在数字版权控制上获得主动权，仍然难以单纯依靠技术控制市场。索尼公司 Reader 阅读器在与亚马逊 Kindle 阅读器的较量中败下阵来的事实就是亚马逊在版权资源上较索尼公司有更大的优势所致。从这个意义上讲，阅读终端技术开发商应该尽力寻求与内容开发商的合作。

第二，基于数字出版平台技术的数字出版。数字技术的进步在相当程度上重构了出版业务流程，建立适应当代数字技术的出版流程是数字出版发展的关键所在。正如美国参数技术公司（PTC）大中华区高级业务经理王霞女士所指出的："应用数字出版的最成功的一点，就是能够把技术平台建立起来，完成第一步。第二步就是企业的应用能够深度挖掘，用业务不断地影响和完善技术平台。"[1] 从世界范围来看，Adobe 公司应该是实践此类数字出版方式的领导者。目前，Adobe 正在 Adobe ® Creative Suite ® 5 和 Omniture ® 技术的基础上构建一个开放的、综合性的"数字出版平台"（Digital Publishing Platform）。该平台通过提供应用、技术和服务支持，让内容出版商能够方便地将他们的内容转化为数字出版物，包括杂志、报纸、书籍和其他出版物，并把内容发布给最为广泛的读者，让顾客可以直接消费这些数字内容。该数字出版平台的首次应用是，2010 年 6 月《连线》（Wired）杂志发布的 WIRED iPad 版。得益于新颖的动画效果和阅读体验，售价 4.99 美元的 iPad 版《连线》杂志在 App Store 里获得了良好的销售业绩，自发布以来几乎已经占据付费应用排行榜首位近一周时间。[2][3] 事实上，国内外一些成功的数字出版商在数字出版平台的搭建上都走到了同行企业前面。

第三，基于数字版权管理技术的数字出版。数字内容产品的版权保护是数字出版发展中一个难以回避的现实问题。因此，围绕数字内容产品的版权保护，为数字出版商与发行商提供开发并提供数字版权管理技术与服务支持必然成为数字出版产业发展的一个重要环节。不仅像微软、苹果、方正等大型 IT 企业纷纷建立自己的 DRM 解决方案，诸如 Verimatrix、Widevine 等独立小公司以及贝塔斯曼等出版企业也同样专注于 DRM 技术的研发。

需要指出的是，当今数字版权管理的重点仍然主要集中在流媒体的数字版权保护方面，与数字出版直接相关的电子文档的版权保护尚未受到足够的重视。正如唐潇霖所指出的："目前国外大公司试图抢滩的基本是在流媒体 DRM 市场，因为这涉及未来音乐、电影等更广阔的消费领域。电子文档的数字版权保护……还并未引起广泛关注"，"虽然电子图书、电子期刊不如数字音视频产品的规模巨大，但它也将在 2015 年发展成为一个上百亿元规模的市场。"[4] 因此，我们完全有理由相信，从数字版权管理这一环节介入数字出版仍然存在着巨大的市场空间。

3　基于开放共享理念的数字出版模式

数字技术的进步不仅改变了传统出版产业的经营与运作方式，而且还在相当程度上对传统出版的某些理念也提出了严峻挑战。兴起于 20 世纪 90 年代的开放存取出版（Open Access Publishing）正是数字出版理念的一种创新，它从根本上颠覆出版企业通过出版物产品销售获利的传统范式，确立起了出版产品与服务全方位"开放"、"共享"的全新出版理念。

Open Access 这一英文术语，有开放存取、开放获取、开放共享、开放访问、开放近取、开放近用、开放阅览、公共获取等不同的译法。[5]2002 年 2 月 14 日发布的《布达佩斯开放存取倡议》（Budapest Open Access Initiative，BOAI）提出了迄今为止仍被广泛接受的关于"开放存取"的定义，即开放存取是指论文可以在公共网络（Public Internet）中免费获取，它允许所有用户不受经济、法律和技术限制地阅读、下载、复制、散发、打印、搜索或超链接论文全文，允许自动搜索软件遍历全文并为其编制索引，允许将其作为软件的输入数据，允许有关它的任何其他合法用途。有关论文复制和传播的唯一限制，亦即版权在该领域的唯一作用，就是承认作者的署名权、作者对作品完整性的控制权以及作品被正确地引用。

1987 年，美国锡拉丘兹大学研究生 Michael Ehringhaus 创办《成人教育新视野》（*New Horizons in Adult Education*），1991 年创办的《E 期刊》（*Ejournal*），1989 年创办《公共存

取计算机系统评论》（*The Public-Access Computer Systems Review*）等，可以看作是开放存取出版的早期实践者。此后，开放存取期刊出版得到迅猛发展。2010 年 10 月 12 日，瑞典伦德大学（Lund University）图书馆主办的开放存取期刊目录 DOAJ（Directory of Open Access Journals）正式收录的开放存取期刊竟达 5 511 种之多。可见，开放存取出版业已成为一种重要的数字出版形态。

开放存取尚处于发展的初期，其实现途径也还处于发展过程中。芬兰学者 Bo-Christer Björk 将开放存取总结为实施开放存取期刊（open access journals）、主题仓储（subject-specific repositories）、机构仓储（institutional repositories）以及作者的个人主页等 4 种方式。在这 4 种开放存取方式中，"作者的个人主页"离现代出版的概念尚有较大差距；"主题仓储"和"机构仓储"则只具备了现代出版的部分属性，如将研究成果"公诸于众"等，但却不具备现代出版的产业属性；"开放存取期刊"几乎具备了现代出版的全部要件，完全可以看作是数字出版的新业态。我们认为，开放存取期刊和开放存取仓储是开放存取出版的两种基本实现形式。

第一，开放存取期刊。开放存取期刊是开放存取出版的主要实现形式，它是指不向读者或其所属机构收费的学术期刊[6]。只有当一种学术期刊能够满足 BOAI 对开放存取的定义，即读者可以任意地"阅读、下载、复制、散发、打印、搜索或超链接论文全文"，才被认为是开放存取期刊。当前有影响开放存取期刊很多，如 PLoS 系列（Public Library of Science）、BMC 系列（BioMed Central）等，这些专业期刊的影响因子在同类期刊中都稳居前列。

开放存取期刊采用与无线电台和电视台类似的收入模式：有兴趣传播内容者支付生产成本，而每一个拥有适当装备的人都可以免费接收内容。因此，开放存取期刊的收入一部分来自主办机构或学会的津贴；一部分来自论文的版面费，该费用可能由作者自己支付也可能由作者所属机构支付。当前的开放存取期刊中有 47% 的期刊是收取版面费。[7] 例如，PLoS 系列采用的就是收费出版模式。表 1 是 PLoS 系列期刊每篇论文的发表费用。

表 1　PLoS 系列 OAJ2010—2011 年的收费标准

序号	刊名	收费标准
1	PLoS Biology	US$2900
2	PLoS Medicine	US$2900
3	PLoS Computational Biology	US$2250
4	PLoS Genetics	US$2250
5	PLoS Pathogens	US$2250
6	PLoS ONE	US$1350
7	PLoS Neglected Tropical Diseases	US$2250

第二，开放存取仓储。开放存取仓储包括主题仓储和机构仓储两种形式。主题仓储可以看作是研究资料的并行出版，这些资料也许是为学术会议或者传统印刷型期刊而编写的，但是预先在仓储中发布。这有利于更快也更加高效地传播科学研究结果。通常在十分看重出版速度，而且在互联网兴起以前就有交换预印本传统的学科领域更容易产生主题仓

储。通常的做法是由作者将论文手稿上传到主题仓储中，这样可以大大地降低维护成本。仓储的管理者一般对上传过程不加干预，只剔除完全不相关的材料。仓储中的论文可以先于其正式出版时间很久就被全球的读者看到。这对于像计算机科学这样发展迅速的学科来说是十分有利的。目前全球最著名的主题仓储是 1991 年 8 月美国洛斯·阿拉莫斯国家实验室（Los Alamos）的 Paul Ginsparg 建立的电子印本仓储（e-print Archiving）arXiv。物理学家在论文正式发表以前将文章的数字版本张贴上去。仓储不接收只提交文摘而没有全文的文章。2001 年后康奈尔大学取代美国国家科学基金会（National Science Foundation）和能源部成为主要的资助、维护和管理者。同时它也由理论高能物理领域的预印本共享仓储转变为涉及物理学、数学、非线性科学、计算机科学和数量生物学（Quantitative Biology）等学科的电子印本仓储，并提供 358 597 篇预印本文献[8]。研究人员按照一定的格式将论文进行排版后，通过 FTP、Web 和电子邮件等方式按学科类别上传至相应的库中。arXiv 电子印本仓储没有任何先决条件决定某一论文能否进入仓储，也没有任何评审程序，任何人都可以把自己的论文放上去，也可以免费下载其中的论文。不过同行可以对仓储的论文发表评论，与作者进行双向交流。论文作者在将论文提交到 arXiv 电子印本仓储的同时，也可以将论文提交给学术期刊。如果论文在期刊上正式发表，在仓储中相应的论文记录中就会加入正式发表论文的期刊的卷期信息。面向用户，仓储提供完全免费的基于学科的分类检索服务。arXiv 电子印本仓储的建立和发展，在加快科学研究成果的交流与共享，帮助研究人员追踪学科的最新研究进展和避免重复研究工作等方面都发挥了重要作用。创建于 1997 年的 CogPrints 则是另一个较为著名的主题仓储，它涵盖心理学、神经系统科学、语言学和计算机科学的相关领域[9]。另外，中国的奇迹文库等都属于这一类型[10]。

　　与主题仓储和开放存取期刊相比，机构仓储是一种较晚出现的开放存取途径。但是大学及其图书馆显然更有能力保证长期而且系统地存取学术资料，因此机构仓储是第三种非常重要的开放存取出版渠道。机构仓储可以收录大学本身的工作文档和学位论文，当然从更长远的角度来看，关键是要能够较为系统地存取大学的优质新产品，如会议论文、期刊论文，等等。对于大学来说，机构仓储本身就是一个出色的营销宣传工具。此外，如果大学仓储能够加入开放存取的合作编目和索引服务，就更加有助于扩大大学在全球范围内的影响。因此，对于在互联网时代必须重新调整和制定其出版政策和图书馆政策的大学院校来说，机构仓储的建设将是它们长远战略目标的一个重要组成部分。[11]全世界有许多机构建立了机构仓储，它们通常使用由南安普顿大学开发的免费软件 eprints. org。通过它可以创建与 OAI 协议兼容的文档，它们就能够被 Google 等软件准确定位并搜索到。早期的机构仓储有麻省理工学院的 Dspace，南安普顿大学的 TARD 等。阿姆斯特丹大学的 Digital Academic Repository（DARE）则是通过图书馆联盟或者其他组织连接起来的国际性网络。2005 年则被认为是大学建立机构仓储最为活跃的一年，许多大学宣布正式支持开放存取，也有一些大学出台了相关的政策[12]。

　　开放存取仓储虽然只具备了现代出版的部分要件，尚不能看作是严格意义上的数字出版，但它在学术传播中所发挥的效用，与学术或专业出版并无二致。我们相信，它所倡导的开放、共享的理念对传统学术或专业出版的影响必将进一步深化。

注释

[1] 王霞. 国际数字出版平台技术及发展 http://www. chuban. cc/rdjj/2010sznh/zlt/

201007/t20100720_74329. htm

［2］Adobe 数字出版平台 http://article. yeeyan. org/view/44140/108464

［3］Adobe 宣布数字出版平台，针对 iPad 等设备 http://www. cnbeta. com/articles/112691. htm

［4］唐潇霖. 守护数字文档　数字版权管理：一个商业难题 http://news. xinhuanet. com/newmedia/2006-07/07/content_4805798. htm

［5］莫京. 关于 Open Access 译名的建议. 科学术语研究，2005（2）

［6］Directory of Open Access Journals. http://www. doaj. org/articles/about

［7］方卿，徐丽芳. 开放存取运动及其研究进展《海外人文社会科学年度发展报告》武汉：大学出版，2007

［8］P. Ginsparg. Electronic publishing in science. Paper presented at a Conference held at UNESCO HQ, Paris, 19-23 February, 1996, during session *Scientist's View of Electronic Publishing and Issues Raised*, 21 February, 1996. http://arXiv. org/blurb/pg96unesco. html

［9］http://cogprints. org/

［10］http://www. qiji. cn

［11］Bo-Christer Bjork. Open Access to scientific publications：an analysis of the barriers to change?. *Information Research*, 2004, Vol. 9 No. 2. http://informationr. net/ir/9-2/paper170. html

［12］Peter Suber. Open access in 2005. Welcome to the SPARC Open Access Newsletter, 2006（93）. http://www. earlham. edu/~peters/fos/newsl

作者简介

方卿，管理学博士，武汉大学信息管理学院教授、博士生导师、副院长。

科技论文开放存取经济生存途径及发展前景[*]

黄先蓉 林姿蓉

（武汉大学信息管理学院 武汉 430072）

摘要：在科技论文的传统订购出版模式下，出版机构用读者的订阅费支付成本并获利，而在开放存取出版模式下，读者免费访问成为开放存取出版的巨大经济挑战。目前开放存取出版单位或机构对出版费用的运作模式各执己见，其经济生存大致有作者支付出版费、有关机构支付年度成员费、政府或基金资助、从期刊订购费中挪出部分费用、借用 OA 资料以及 OA 仓储来增加广告收入、对其他附加产品收取费用等。开放存取已获得许多国家、政府和科研机构的关注与支持，其实践渐获佳绩、运作规模渐次扩大、资源持续快速增长，具有良好的发展前景。

关键词：科技论文 开放存取 经济生存

The Economic Viability and Development of Scientific Paper Open Access

Huang Xianrong Lin Zirong

（School of Information and Management, Wuhan University, Wuhan, 430072）

Abstract: Publishing institutions pay costs and get profits from readers' subscription fee in the traditional subscription publishing mode of scientific paper, while in OA mode, free Internet access brings economic challenges to publishing. At present, OA publishing units holds different opinions on the operation pattern of publishing costs, the way OA publishers economically survived depends on the publication fee author pays, annual membership fee from relevant institutions, financial aids from government or funds, part of journal subscription fee, the corresponding advertising revenue with the increase of OA data or OA storage and charging fees for additional products, etc. OA publishing has received great attention and support from lots of counties, governments and scientific research institutions, it presents better outcomes, expanding operation scale, rapidly increasing resources, which means a bright future.

Keywords: Scientific paper Open access Economic viability

---

* 本文为教育部科技发展中心"网络时代的科技论文快速共享研究资助项目——面向科技论文网络共享的版权保护研究"（项目编号：2008113）的成果之一。

科技论文是人类科技文明成果的集结、整理、研究与陈述，对科技发展有着极其重要的推动作用。长期以来，科研工作者发表论文的重心多在积累学科上的专业及知识，以广泛传播和推进学科专业发展为目的。科技论文除了在上述学术领域里有着众所周知的社会效益外，在规模经济效益上，也有其特殊性。

19世纪中期，出版商开始进入市场，但获利状况并不显著。20世纪60年代，随着世界著名的《科学文献索引》（The Science Citation Index，SCI）的出现，核心期刊在经济上的特性表现得越来越突出，此时，图书馆也将SCI所收录的期刊视为馆藏的重要期刊。商业型出版商开始意识到潜藏的营利机遇。随后，学术期刊价格的成长相对限制了相关研究人员获取资源等所必需的出版物。

在网络化的今天，与学术研究密切相关的各项软件、硬件交流平台随之建立，这些都积极、快速促进了科技文明成果的传播。开放存取（Open Access，OA）的出版模式，便是在此基础上应运而生的。OA的出现，就面对期刊出版效益及市场挑战而言，在一定程度上提供了另一种选择和机制。

为了得到更多学术出版机构的支持并实现可稳健发展的需求，开放存取的运作模式必须讲求一定的生存条件与能力，甚而从中获利，以作为可持续发展的重要基础。

开放存取式的出版模式借助网络技术及资源平台运作，虽费用大为降低，但其运行经费是否有力支撑仍是保障其运行状况的重要因素。为了让有限经费、资源广泽所有的开放存取出版机构，许多机构除了积极争取政府、基金会等经费的支持外，也需依托商业运作模式，想方设法弥补经费上的不足，这事关开放存取出版模式与此类交流形态的生存条件与发展，值得我们进一步关注。

1　科技属性及科技论文开展概说[1]

随着科学知识的日益增长、交流，科学技术也不断发展。其中，担负科学知识的传播、记述、积累等重要功能的科技论文是科技进步、发展、发达的重要基础，也是科学知识进步的产物。因此，能快速地向科学研究者提供系统化且有整合功用的科学知识，对于科技时代的推进是相当重要且必要的。以下，我们就科技特有的属性可探知，科技论文等文献的积累及开展，具有重要的传承使命和意义。

第一，科技论文是通过科学的研究方法产生的客观知识，并且经过科学的实验证明与自然现象的观察有其一致性。因此，记录客观知识的科技论文具有"客观性"。

科技论文的创建与发表，都是对现有客观知识的进一步扩充与提炼。也由于客观的科学知识是持续积累的，因此，科技论文每新增一篇，或是某议题内涵的延伸与扩充，或是其见解的提升与淬炼，或是重新定义该知识及追踪修订。

第二，科学的真相是无国界的，它不受时间、环境、文化、语言或政治等种种因素的影响，通过科学客观实验证明所获知的结果，不会因上述表象或媒介条件而有所差异，由于真相是恒定不变的，因此，科技知识在其本质上具有"普遍性"。

科学知识通过科技论文等发表形式、各种形式的传播，包括文字转译等过程，即可将各种自然科学的文献、情报等知识传送至任何地域，供科学研究人员来撷取及利用。因此，科技论文有系统的积累，是科学研究者不断研究与突破的重要基础及辅助力量的来源。

第三，科技论文等形式是科学知识的"公共"记录，在一定条件的限制或约束下，它是允许被任何对象利用及交流的，因此，科技知识具有"公共性"。

由于科技知识是由其自身的文献资料来积极维持及扩充的，因此，便利及快速的检索条件，相关的软硬件设备、配套措施等，都起着关键性的作用。而 OA 出版模式的出现，在很大程度上便是扮演、支撑着这样的角色。

2　传统出版与开放存取出版模式比较

从传统订购的出版模式转变到开放存取的出版模式面临着许多挑战，为了进一步探讨开放存取出版模式的经济生存条件，我们首先就这两种模式的出版流程做简单比较：

出版流程	1. 研究者投稿	2. 投稿至期刊	3. 制作	4. 读者获取
传统出版模式	一般不支付审稿费用	学术期刊 （审稿、组织同行评审）	出版、印刷、发行	付费订阅
开放存取出版模式	支付审稿费	开放存取期刊 （审稿、组织同行评审）	网络传播	免费访问

在传统订购期刊的出版模式下，出版机构通过发行、销售，用读者的订阅费来支付"审稿、组织同行评审"及"出版、印刷、发行"等成本，并在此过程中获利。而在开放存取出版模式下，固定成本与传统模式基本相同，由于没有读者订阅费用的收入，因此，如何弥补经费缺口，成为开放存取出版的巨大挑战。目前在两种出版同时存在的过渡时期，图书馆和研究机构需要支付双重费用，包括开放存取的发布费用及传统出版的订购费用[2]。

然而随着学术期刊的年度订阅价格的大幅增加，图书馆和研究机构渐感难以承担，此外，存放空间需求也是个不容忽视的问题。图书馆除了不断追加经费来因应期刊价格的成长外，并希望通过"大宗订购"（Big deals）及联盟打折等手段，以减少支出。在这种传统的订购模式下，出版商为了谋求自己的利润，对图书馆订购的期刊不断地提高价格，图书馆不但丧失了主动权，且时而被迫停订一些重点文献，从而形成了科技期刊价格的恶性循环[3]。

近年来，学术期刊订购价格高涨已成为学术界关心的一个重要问题，以美国为例，自1986 年至 2004 年间，学术期刊的订阅费用共成长了 220%[4]。面对期刊价格持续大幅增长，图书馆和研究机构渐感难以承担：图书馆不得不通过停订部分期刊和减少图书订购预算来应付；国际上许多大型科研机构也对"价格增长、注册许可、捆绑式政策、讨价还价策略"等接连发出不满的声明。

3　各界对开放存取出版费运作模式的观点

在讨论开放存取经济生存条件前，我们试就开放存取出版机构对出版费用的运作模式，提出其观点。

3.1　STM 出版商

STM 出版商（即指 Science、Technology、Medicine）强调目前期刊的高出版费用，如对电子技术的大量投资和开发新学科领域的出版物等，他们向"作者支付出版费"模式的经济有效性提出挑战[5]。认为 OA 期刊若非提高作者的版面费用，则应另寻找可替代性的经费来源以支撑其长期发展。

此外，出版商认为，OA 的出版模式偏重作者的论文发表，而非重视对其进行过滤或评价。并认为其出版模式的最终目标是，发表大量的论文以获取更多的利润。因此，期刊的评价质量将受到威胁，即意味着学术标准的降低和同行评审的终结。

3.2 非营利型出版商及学会

多数非营利出版商、学术学会虽也指责商业型出版商提高期刊价格过多，其"大宗订购"的行为是促进了期刊价格的提高，但他们也同时认为论文于出版后的 6～12 个月开放存取没有必要[6]，并进而预测，若期刊被迫采取 OA 模式，除了威胁到传统期刊的生存外，并将影响到依靠订购收入的科学学会的发展。

3.3 图书馆馆员及其学会、协会

世界各国图书馆馆员向来要求改变目前的出版系统，他们除了认同 OA 的观点外，许多组织学会也在 2003 年参加了信息获取联盟，致力于敦促政府阻止期刊出版商以垄断为目的的兼并。他们认为，在出版商寻找可替代的期刊出版模式的同时，OA 模式还是能为公众提供更多所需信息的重要通道。

许多图书馆馆员对作者支付出版费的经营模式提出质疑，并想得知 OA 模式是否能够缓和期刊价格的危机[7]？但其改由作者支付高额出版费的模式，将使得他们的机构支付的出版费要比目前的订购模式多出许多。因为许多学会、协会往往会利用出版期刊的收入来开展学术活动，加上 OA 模式本身即存在着不平等，如发表论文少的营利型机构将会得到免费的期刊论文，而学术型的机构则将承担作者大部分的出版费用。

3.4 研究人员及其机构

研究者在期刊上发表论文的主要目的是为了使其研究成果或观点得到认可，并提升或维护其学术声望，或顺利申请到研究经费，故而促使他们支持 OA 的出版模式。然而，对于自行支付出版费，许多作者也持不同意见：

（1）认为网络出版物的学术影响力仍远不及印刷版出版物。

（2）英国联合信息系统委员会（The UK Joint Information Systems Committee，JISC）完成的一项研究证实，多数科技作者赞同 OA 期刊能够扩大其论文读者群的观点，且大多数（81%）的研究人员愿按照机构要求自行存档。然而，由于多数机构是请求而非强行规定研究者将其论文自行存入其机构的数据库；再者，由于时间压力及版权法疑虑等因素，许多人仍不愿意将其论文存入其机构的数据库，导致许多议题难以在其领域找到合适的 OA 期刊[8]。

学术团体、研究机构、政府部门等组织，声称他们对其学术论文拥有合法权利，并可限制其作者将版权转让给出版商，此种做法将迫使出版商接受 OA 的出版模式，并允许作者自行存档或将其论文发送到类似 PubMed Central（在线公共知识仓库，PMC）等数据库[9]。

4 开放存取的经济生存途径

在 OA 出版模式削减了使用者的订购费后，科技论文出版的整个运作过程的经费支撑

点何在？以下，我们尝试着从各种途径来思考。

4.1　途径一：作者付费

由作者为自己研究成果来支付出版费用，这是目前 OA 期刊出版最主要的资金来源，运用也最为广泛。作者付费模式是针对传统读者付费模式而言，即作者为出版自己的研究成果需要支付一定的出版费用，并为读者提供免费服务。作者支付的出版费主要用于同行评审、专业制作、提供文摘和索引服务、以电子和印刷两种形式发行等。目前约有 47% 的 OA 期刊出版采用此种收费方式，例如发展最好的先驱代表：商业性的学术出版机构——英国的生物医学出版中心（BioMed Central，BMC）及非营利性的出版机构——美国的科学公共图书馆（Public Library of Science，PLoS）。

（1）BMC。BMC 是英国一家非营利的学术出版商，提供免费的经讨同行评审的生物医学领域的开放存取期刊。目前已经拥有 186 种开放存取期刊，收录的范围涵盖了生物学和医学的所有领域，任何人可以通过网络来查阅这些期刊上的文献，但发表论文的作者需支付一定金额的"论文处理费用"，如对于被发表的论文每篇收取 580 美元的评审费用（另有 10 多种高质量期刊收取更高的评审费用）[10]。

（2）PLoS。PLoS 采用新的商业模式来运行开放存取期刊，用户可以从网上免费获取 PLoS 的所有出版物，并可以不受限制的使用、传播和复制。PLoS 对被发表的论文每篇收取 1 250 美元至 2 500 美元不等的出版费用，主要用于支付同行评审费用、编辑费用、期刊生产费用和期刊论文在线储存和维护费用[11]。但是，PLoS 明确提出，出版与否的关键并非决定于出版费用的支付能力，而是论文质量的水平。

据统计，36% 的作者表示出版社没有收取出版费，25% 的作者用研究经费来支付，8% 来自于部门经费，9% 来自于其他机构的经费，仅有 4% 是由作者自己来支付出版费[12]。

开放存取期刊所收的费用差异很大，部分 OA 期刊的评审费用或出版费用更高，面对高昂的出版费用，这些作者该如何支付呢？部分机构开始采取了相应措施：如健康信息网络存取计划（HINARI）是开放社会机构（OSI）和世界卫生组织（WHO）联合举办的大型出版项目，他们对人均国民生产总值低于 1 000 美元的国家提供免费的在线访问；对人均国民生产总值低于 3 000 美元的中等水平国家也提供一定的优惠[13]。对于来自发展中国家或缺乏研究经费的作者，PLoS Biology 承诺降低甚至免除其出版费用。另外，开放社会机构（Open Society Institute，OSI）基金会也宣布赞助计划，来自发展中国家的科研人员可申请基金，以用于发表在 PLoS 期刊上的出版费用。

4.2　途径二：会员制

有关机构可以通过支付年度成员费来免除该单位作者的发表费，是开放存取期刊目前的第二大获利途径。如英国所有大学都是 BMC 的机构会员，英国的大学研究人员在 BMC 开放存取期刊发表文章都是免费的。BMC 现有的机构会员超过了 100 家，其机构会员的年度会费在 1 500 至 7 500 美元之间。会员制可依据顾客的不同性质将其区分为数种类型。

（1）BMC。将会员区分为预付费会员、季度后付费会员和支持者会员三种会员资格，每种会员享受不同程度的折扣。

（2）PLoS。根据所缴纳的年度费用将会员制分为个人会员制和机构会员制两类，并依其不同级别发表文章则可享受相对应的折扣，甚至免费。

由于 OA 出版可让科研机构以更便利及免费的方式获取资料，相较于传统出版模式下，需支付大量订阅费而言，会员费用还是比例很小的一部分。

4.3 途径三：政府或基金资助

大多数的科学研究机构皆有来自国家财政上的支持，尤其在自然科学的领域，并都设立了自然科学研究基金等来资助科学研究者来推广 OA 计划。

（1）政府资助。建立政府资助机制是进行学术出版及交流不可或缺的重要环节。英国政府委员会给开放存取出版提出了 82 项建议，并提供了强有力的资助，包括资助所有英国大学的知识仓库、资助大英图书馆保存数字形式的学术资料，并要求所有政府提供资助的研究都必须有 OA 文档，此外还为资助无法付费的 OA 作者设立了一个基金会等[14]。

（2）基金资助。基金资助主要是科研资助机构基金和私立基金，是开放存取出版运动兴起的经济先行力量。例如：布达佩斯开放存取计划（BOAI）得到了开放社会机构（Open Society Institute）基金会的承诺，连续 3 年以每年 100 万美元的赞助资金支持该计划的实施。2002 年 PLoS 得到来自摩尔（Gordon and Betty Moore）基金会 900 万美元为期 5 年的捐款，而于翌年 10 月创建了第一份全文同行评审期刊《PLoS Biology》[15]。BMC 得到英国惠康（The Wellcome）基金资助经济上有困难的研究者，支付在 BMC 上出版科技论文所需的费用。

（3）其他。一些开放存取期刊还获得了各种形式的非现金赞助，如自愿工作的人员、办公空间、电脑硬件和软件的使用、网站设计和运行、法律和会计等。

4.4 途径四：图书馆、学术单位运作机制

此途径是指从大学、图书馆、科研机构等学术单位的期刊订购费中，挪出部分费用，以支持学术协会的开放存取出版。由于这些学术单位之间合作较为密切，有资源及条件来解决有关同行评审、出版、索引和文档处理等诸多问题。科研资助机构可借鉴 Howard Hughes 医学研究所等机构做法，为科技研究者在 OA 期刊上发表论文提供经费支持，并承诺对其研究人员在 OA 期刊上发表的论文支付出版费用[16][17]。

学术出版与学术资源联盟（SPARC）即是此种运作模式的先驱。SPARC 系由美国研究图书馆协会发起的非商业化学术出版合作交流体系，目前成员已超过 300 家，参与者包括教育单位、图书馆及研究机构，他们通过一系列的研究、宣传和技术活动等，组织并动员和支持学术单位等机构来支持开放学术刊物，并努力摆脱出版商控制，出版非商业的学术刊物。

4.5 途径五：广告收入

在纸本期刊时代，欧美国家许多学术期刊的广告收入占期刊总收入的 40% 至 90%，是期刊赖以生存及维持发展的重要经费来源。2004 年，Google 和 Yahoo 也开始借用 OA 资料以及 OA 仓储来增加自身的可用性、访问量和广告收入。此后，ProQuest/Bepress 和 BMC 也开始着手向大学外包此类出版任务，并提供开展和维护学院仓储的服务。

（1）BMC。BMC 针对自己 OA 期刊的学科类型，在其网站上运行广告，是成功的典范。它将广告分为两块进行招商，一来吸引生命科学方面的读者，二来吸引医学领域的广告客户。BMC 对在其网站上运行的广告，一次点击收取 5 美元，一年的广告收入可达上百万美元[18]。

（2）PLoS。PLoS 网站上所有网页下方都提供广告链接，以吸引更多的广告来增加经

费来源。但 PLoS 要求所刊登的广告必须得到出版者的认同。同时，不接受药品和医疗器械广告。

4.6 途径六：附加服务

尽管读者可以免费获取 OA 期刊的论文，但其他附加产品也会收取费用，如：

（1）订阅费。如 BMC 即针对其 Faculty of 1000 系列产品（知名专家之评价意见）收取订阅费，并就部分印刷版和电子版共存的期刊以及期刊重点部分文章收取订阅费等[19]。

（2）链接费。即查阅特定文章所收取的链接费，如 BMC 提供文献的校阅和评价、协助查询的软件等所收取的费用。

（3）其他。如提供提醒服务（alert services）、网站定制服务（site customization）、相应格式的文献增值服务、向书店销售刊物的复制件系列增值服务等。

此类附加服务，一则可使读者更便利地利用期刊，二则也增长期刊出版商的收入。对于营利性的出版公司来说，OA 的运作所带来的商机是无限的[20]。

5 开放存取的发展前景

开放存取运动发展已有相当时日，虽现今仍处于传统学术期刊的垄断操控状态，但其发展速度是有目共睹的。开放存取的出版模式虽仍存在相当问题亟待解决，然而，由于科研人员在发表研究成果时，多数人并非看重经济利益，而是期待借由快速、便利的传播模式，助其学术成果的相互交流、应用与增长。因此，开放存取模式对学者及快速累积学术成果来看，是有利的。基于此，在有关政策制订及执行成果上，已有了相当不错的成效。

5.1 开放存取政策与进展渐获支持

现今开放存取已获得许多国家和政府、科研机构等有关部门在法律和政策上的积极关注与支持，推行相关政策以来，已具一定成效：

（1）2004 年 8 月 24 日，美国公共利益组织发起成立纳税人自由获取联盟 ATA（Alliance for Taxpayer Access）支持纳税人的钱资助的研究成果的公共存取。

（2）2004 年 12 月，美国国会通过国立卫生研究院（National Institutes of Health，NIH）拨款法案；并于翌年 2 月 3 日，正式发布公共存取政策；接着，在 2008 年 4 月 7 日，强制性实施的公共存取政策正式生效。该政策内容指出：受 NIH 资助开展研究而产出的经同行评审的最终版本论文，均应开放存档至指定的 NIH 的文档库 PubMed Central 内，并在发表后至多 12 个月内可供公众免费获取[21]。

（3）2005 年 7 月，英国资助研究的主要公共基金机构——英国研究委员会，正式批准并公布论文"开放存取"的新规定：从 2005 年 10 月起，所有接受英国 8 个研究机构资助的研究人员都应尽可能早地将他们的论文放入免费的公共数据库。据称，该项政策将覆盖英国 50% 受资助的研究人员。

继上述美英两国之后，许多学术工作者、媒体以及政府所属等机构，也开始呼吁各国政府应更积极强化其执行力。迄今为止，澳大利亚、加拿大、法国、德国、荷兰、印度、挪威、苏格兰以及瑞士等国家，已为开放存取提供了有力的政策支撑。

5.2 开放存取实践渐获佳绩

在开放存取运动的推动下，许多学术期刊正逐渐放宽对作者的限制，允许作者将自己的科研成果放到个人主页或开放知识库内以共享，因而，机构知识库也得以快速成长。此

166

学术出版与开放存取

外，也有不少知名大学宣布使用开放存取出版模式来发表研究成果。如：

（1）美国。康奈尔大学的 Euclid、加州大学的 eScholarship 机构知识库、佛罗里达州立大学的 D-Scholarship 等。

（2）英国。诺丁汉大学主持的由 20 所大学共同参与的开放存取知识库的项目——SHERPA（Securing a Hybrid Environment for Research Preservation and Access）。

（3）荷兰。国家存储 DARE（Digital Academic Repositories）由荷兰 17 所大学和国家图书馆、荷兰自然科学和艺术科学皇家科学院、荷兰科技研究所等多家单位共同发起的分布式开放存取系统计划，支持各个大学建立自己的开放存取系统，并支持全世界范围的自由获取。该计划由荷兰国家政府提供资金支持。

5.3 开放存取的运作规模渐次扩大

开放存取运动开展以来，在部分出版商、大学、相关资助机构，以及作者本身的积极参与后，开放存取非但未减少传统学术期刊的订购量，反而吸引部分出版商积极参与，如试行作者选择的 B2C 和 C2C 复合模式，甚至将内部的某期刊完全转成开放存取模式。

此外，由于开放存取对于提升作者的影响力度和机构的知名度起了一定的作用，故而，也促使一些大学和资助机构开始统一执行开放存取政策。

5.4 开放存取资源持续快速增长

为了适应科研成果的快速增长及传播上的需求，由开放存取方式所获取的资源、开放存取机构库存储的文献，也随着开放存取期刊的投稿量、新建的开放存取机构库、新建的或转型的开放期刊的快速增长而迅速增加，不论从参与运动的单位、人数，还是从资源成长来看，其发展的规模都将不断扩大。

5.5 开放存取的影响力渐增

开放存取运动正蓬勃开展，有关议题也被热烈地讨论着，可以预见，这种新型出版模式将备受关注，其对科研工作者、出版商、图书馆，以及科研等相关机构等，将持续产生深刻及重大的影响[22]。

6 小结

目前科研期刊提供开放存取的比例虽仍小，且该部分的运作多依靠作者支付出版费或基金会等机构所提供的资助来支撑，然而随着电子出版系统的不断提升及相关出版软件的应运而生，开放存取出版模式在其数字化、网络化、便利化，以及更低廉的出版成本等有利因素下将获得更大的优势，读者只需通过网络便可迅速地获得完整的科研学术成果；而出版者、作者在思考经济生存条件及促进科研学术发展等层面上，这类出版模式的积极开展必将直接或间接地促进开放资源的循环利用及增长。对于此种"作者付费出版，读者免费使用"的运行模式，其中仍蕴含着其他种种可能性，这些都有待我们进一步关注、思考、探索及检验。

注释

[1] 蔡曙光. 科学文献的特点和结构. 贵图学刊, 1993（1）：30-31

[2] 蔡焰辉. 开放存取学术出版模式经济可行性分析. 图书馆学刊, 2008（5）：34

[3] 杜海洲, 宋金燕, 杜云祥, 刘娜. 开放存取模式的发展及其影响. 现代情报, 2008

（11）：14

［4］ Kranich，N. The Information Commons：A Public Policy Report，NYU School of Law. 2004，18

［5］ Frank M，Reich M，and Ra'anan A. A not-for-profit publisher's perspective on open access［J］. Ser Rev. 2004，30（4）：28-7

［6］ Sber P. Welcome to the SPARC Open Access Newsletter，issue #93（January 2，2006）［EB］. http：//www. earlham. edu/~peters/fos/newsletter/01-02-06. htm（visit on Dec. 12. 2009）

［7］ Anderson. R. Author disincentives and open access［J］. Ser Rev. 2004，30（4）：288-91.

［8］ Swan A，Brown S. Open access self-archiving：An author study（May 2005）［EB］. http：//cogprints. org/4385/（visit on Dec. l2. 2009）

［9］ 杜海洲，宋金燕，杜云祥，刘娜. 开放存取模式的发展及其影响. 现代情报，2008（11）：15-18

［10］ Frequently asked questions about BioMed Center's article-processing charges［EB/OL］. http：//biomed central. com/info/authors/apcfaq（visit on Dec. 12. 2009）

［11］ Publication Fees for PLoS Journals. http：//www. plos. org/journals/pubfees. html（visit on Dec. 19. 2009）

［12］ 曾丹. 开放存取期刊模式的研究. 高校图书情报论坛，2007（3）：54

［13］ 乔冬梅. 国外学术交流开放存取发展综述. 图书情报工作，2004（11）

［14］ 李敬平. 网络环境下学术资源的开放存取运动. 科技情报开发与经济，2005（13）

［15］ 李武，刘兹恒. 一种全新的学术出版模式：开放存取出版模式探析. 中国图书馆学报，2004（6）

［16］ Frequently asked questions about BioMed Center's article-processing charges［EB/OL］. http：//biomedcentral. com/info/authors/apcfaq（visit on Dec. 12. 2009）

［17］ 刘兹恒，李武. 试析 OA 期刊发展中各利益关系方的作用. 数字图书馆论坛，2007（4）：56

［18］ John Willinsky，Scholarly Associations and the Economic Viability of Open Access Publishing. Journal of：Digital Information，Volume 4，Issue 2（2003）

［19］ 牛晓宏. 浅谈学术期刊开放存取出版的营利模式. 知识经济，2009（2）：178-179

［20］ 蔡焰辉. 开放存取学术出版模式经济可行性分析. 图书馆学刊，2008（5）：35-36

［21］ 参见 NIH 网站说明：http：//www. nih. gov/（2010-8-13 访问）

［22］ 肖冬梅. 版权的争取、让渡、保留及其对公众信息权利的保障——关于学术资源开放存取模式的思考. 中国图书馆学报，2006（4）：94

作者简介

黄先蓉，女，武汉大学信息管理学院教授，博士生导师。

林姿蓉，女，武汉大学信息管理学院 2008 级博士研究生。

开放获取期刊的分布研究[*]

徐丽芳

（武汉大学信息管理学院　武汉　430072）

摘要：本文通过对 DOAJ 收录的 5 278 种 OA 期刊的地理、学科、语种、创刊时间以及出版机构等分布规律的分析，发现 OA 期刊的发展得到了整个学术出版社群的广泛支持，并呈现出一种持续增长的良好发展态势。与我国科技发展水平以及学术出版现状相比，我国 OA 期刊出版发展相对落后，需要引起政府、学界以及出版界的高度重视。

关键词：开放获取　OA 期刊　分布规律

Research on the Distribution of Open Access journals

Xu Lifang

（School of Information Management, Wuhan University, Wuhan, 430072）

Abstract：Through the analysis of distribution regularity of 5278 open access journals embodied by DOAJ in geography, discipline, language, first publication time and publishing agencies, this paper finds that the development of OA journals received wide supports of the whole academic press group and it shows a good trend of continuous growth. Compared with our country's technology development level and academic press situation, OA journals's development in China relatively falls behind, it should be highly valued by government, academic circles and publishing circles.

Keywords：Open access　OA journals　Distribution regularity

1　引言

开放获取期刊（Open Access Journals，以下简称为 OA 期刊）诞生的目的是旨在解决"学术期刊传播危机"，所以其一出现就受到整个学术出版社群的广泛关注。所谓开放获取期刊，按照开放获取期刊目录（Directory of Open Access Journals，DOAJ）的定义，是指"采用资助模式（Funding Model）出版的、不向读者或其所属机构收取任何使用费用的学术期刊"。[1] 它同时认为只有当一种期刊能够满足《布达佩斯开放获取宣言》（*Budapest*

---

* 本文为 2009 年度国家社科基金项目"开放获取学术资源分布与集成研究"（09CTQ024）以及"中央高校基本科研业务费专项资金资助"项目成果之一。

Open Access Initiative，BOAI）对开放获取的定义，即读者可以任意地"阅读、下载、复制、散发、打印、搜索或超链接论文全文"时，才可以被认为是开放获取期刊。然而，由于种种原因，OA 期刊起初的发展并不顺利，直到 20 世纪 90 年代的中后期，才出现大规模的 OA 期刊出版活动[2]。经过十多年的蓬勃发展，OA 期刊不仅实现了期刊种类和资源数量的快速增长，而且其学术质量也得到了迅速提升和广泛认可。如 Björk 等人（Bo-Christer Björk et al，2010）指出 2008 年全球出版的全部学术论文中，以 OA 期刊形式出版的论文占 8.1%[3]；而劳伦斯（Steve Lawrence）则在 2001 年就指出开放获取可以显著增加论文的学术影响力[4]。与 OA 期刊迅猛的发展速度相比，OA 期刊的利用效率似乎不太理想。造成这种现象的原因是多方面的，其中读者对 OA 期刊的分布情况缺乏了解是主要因素之一。因此，有必要对 OA 期刊的分布情况进行详细分析与研究，以掌握其分布现状和揭示内在的分布规律，进而提高对其的开发与利用效率，而这也正是本文研究的意义之所在。

2　OA 期刊的分布研究

由于收录标准的不同，开放科学目录（Open Science Directory，OSD）、Open J-gate 以及开放获取期刊目录（Directory of Open Access Journals，DOAJ）等主要 OA 期刊名录所收录和登记的 OA 期刊数量也存在巨大差异。其中 DOAJ 以"OA 期刊必须采用诸如同行评议、编辑审议等质量控制机制[5]"这一相对较为严格的条件为收录标准，因而其收录的 OA 期刊数量相对较少。例如，截至 2010 年 8 月，DOAJ 收录的 OA 期刊仅有 5 278 种[6]，而在 OSD 上登记的 OA 期刊则高达 13 000 余种[7]。众所周知，OA 期刊最令人诟病的缺点之一就是部分 OA 期刊由于缺乏必要的质量控制机制而得不到学术质量上的保证，从而造成读者失去对其利用的欲望与信心。也正因如此，本文以 DOAJ 收录的 5 278 种 OA 期刊为研究样本，对 OA 期刊的地理、语种、学科、出版机构等分布情况进行分析与研究，以揭示其分布规律。

2.1　OA 期刊的地理分布

通过对 DOAJ 中 OA 期刊的相关出版信息整理发现，5 278 种 OA 期刊分布在 108 个国家或地区，说明开放获取运动已经得到了世界上多数国家或地区的响应。但是，统计数据也表明 OA 期刊在国家或地区之间的发展非常不平衡。其中，排名前 20 位的国家出版了 4 155 种 OA 期刊，占全部期刊的 78.72%；排名后 60 位的国家或地区出版了 265 种 OA 期刊，仅占期刊总数的 5.02%，有 33 个国家或地区仅出版 1~2 种 OA 期刊。在排名前 20 位的国家中（参见表 1），高居第一的美国出版 1 114 种 OA 期刊，占期刊总量的 21.11%，这与美国作为全球第一大期刊出版者的地位相吻合。而巴西、印度、土耳其、罗马尼亚、智利、哥伦比亚、墨西哥、波兰、委内瑞拉、阿根廷等 10 个发展中国家也进入前 20 名，则可能与巴西、智利、墨西哥等这些发展中国家试图通过开放获取提高其科学研究的显示度的政策有关[8]。如果不考虑香港、澳门、台湾的数据，中国仅出版 16 种 OA 期刊，这与中国作为期刊出版大国的地位极不相称。究其原因，则可能与我国科技界对开放获取期刊的认知程度不高有关。有资料显示，我国科技界有 94.5% 的人不了解开放获取期刊[9]。

表 1　OA 期刊出版种类排名前 20 国家

排名	国家	OA 期刊种数	排名	国家	OA 期刊种数
1	美国	1 114	11	智利	111
2	巴西	472	12	法国	101
3	英国	423	13	日本	101
4	西班牙	299	14	哥伦比亚	97
5	印度	221	15	澳大利亚	95
6	德国	193	16	墨西哥	84
7	加拿大	162	17	波兰	80
8	土耳其	144	18	委内瑞拉	78
9	意大利	129	19	瑞士	70
10	罗马尼亚	112	20	阿根廷	69
合计					4 155

如果将 108 个国家或地区按照欧洲、亚洲、北美洲、南美洲、大洋洲和非洲等各大洲进行归类统计可以发现，OA 期刊在各大洲的发展也不平衡（参见表 2）。其中，欧洲国家出版了 2 129 种 OA 期刊，占期刊总数的 40.34%，排名第一；北美洲由于美国和加拿大两个 OA 期刊出版强国的存在而排在次席，共计出版 1 414 种 OA 期刊；巴西等 10 个南美洲国家共出版了 852 种 OA 期刊，排名第三；亚洲共出版了 635 种 OA 期刊，排在第四位，其中印度、日本、巴基斯坦和伊朗四个国家分别出版了 221、101、68 和 65 种 OA 期刊，是亚洲 OA 期刊的主要出版国；澳大利亚和新西兰两个大洋洲国家出版了 163 种 OA 期刊，排在第五位；非洲国家仅出版了 85 种 OA 期刊，排名最后。也就是说，OA 期刊在非洲的发展非常缓慢，这与该地区的科技发展与出版水平相对落后有关。

表 2　OA 期刊在各大洲的分布

地区	国家/地区数量	期刊数量	比例
欧洲	42	2 129	40.34%
北美洲	13	1 414	26.79%
南美洲	10	852	16.14%
亚洲	26	635	12.03%
大洋洲	2	163	3.09%
非洲	15	85	1.61%
合计	108	5 278	100%

2.2　OA 期刊的学科分布

由于 DOAJ、Open J-gate 等 OA 期刊收录平台都有各自的学科分类标准和方式，因而其 OA 期刊的学科分类情况也不尽相同。例如 Open J-gate 就将其收录的 OA 期刊划分为农业与生物科学、艺术与人文科学、生物医学、基础科学、工程与技术以及社会与管理科学等六大学科门类进行管理；而 DOAJ 则将其期刊划分为农业与食品科学、艺术与建筑学、社会科学、化学等 17 个大的学科门类。本文在进行 OA 期刊的学科分布研究时，根据 OA 期刊的出版现状，参照《中国图书分类法》的分类标准将 DOAJ 中的 OA 期刊划分为 19 个学科门类进行分类研究（参见表 3）。需要说明的是，由于许多 OA 学术期刊属于跨学科的交叉性期刊，本文在统计分析时将参考期刊在 DOAJ 中所属学科进行重复统计，因此本部分的最终统计期刊总量可能会多于 5 278 种。

表 3　OA 期刊的学科分布情况

学科名称	所属学科大类	OA 期刊	比例
医药与卫生	自然科学	1 506	23.74%
文化、科学、教育与体育	人文社会科学	664	10.46%
工业技术	自然科学	576	9.08%
生物科学	自然科学	538	8.48%
社会科学	人文社会科学	481	7.58%
数理科学与化学	自然科学	415	6.54%
哲学	人文社会科学	313	4.93%
农业科学	自然科学	284	4.48%
天文学与地球科学	自然科学	280	4.41%
历史与地理	人文社会科学	234	3.69%
政治与法律	人文社会科学	224	3.53%
文学	人文社会科学	194	3.06%
语言与文字	人文社会科学	136	2.14%
经济	人文社会科学	114	1.80%
艺术	人文社会科学	111	1.75%
综合性学科	人文社会科学	97	1.53%
环境科学	自然科学	87	1.37%
自然科学总论	自然科学	72	1.13%
交通运输	自然科学	19	0.30%
合计		6 345	100%

从表 3 中可以发现，除了军事、航空与航天等少数学科外，DOAJ 中的 OA 期刊涵盖了包括医药与卫生、工业技术、生物科学、社会科学、哲学、艺术等 19 个学科领域。其中，医药与卫生、工业技术、生物科学以及文化、科学、教育与体育领域的 OA 期刊数量较多，占期刊统计总量的 51.76%；交通运输、自然科学总论、环境科学等领域的 OA 期刊数量较少，仅占总量的 4.33%。也就是说目前 OA 期刊在各学科之间的发展不均衡，存在较大差异。如果从自然科学和人文社会科学两大学科门类进行分析可以发现，在人文社会科学领域共出版 2 568 种 OA 期刊，占 OA 期刊总量的 40.47%；在自然科学领域共出版了 3 777 种 OA 期刊，占总量的 59.53%，与目前两个学科学术期刊所占比例基本相似。

也就是说，从总体来看目前 OA 运动在人文社会科学和自然科学之间发展相对均衡。

2.3 OA 期刊的语种分布

OA 期刊是否采用国际通用语言出版将会直接影响其利用效率，因此有必要对 OA 期刊出版语种的分布情况进行分析，以方便读者在掌握其分布规律的基础上提高对 OA 期刊的利用效率。分析发现，5 278 种 OA 期刊一共采用英语、西班牙语、葡萄牙语、法语等55 种语言出版（参见表4）。其中英语为第一大出版语言，有超过80%的 4 401 种 OA 期刊采用英语为出版语种，这与英语作为全球通用学术出版语言的地位紧密相关。西班牙语和葡萄牙语分别被 1 028 种和 601 种 OA 期刊采用，排在第二和第三位，说明这两个语种在 OA 期刊领域具有一定的影响力。分析其原因，主要与巴西、智利等南美洲国家以及西班牙等国家或地区的 OA 期刊均采用西班牙语和葡萄牙语为出版语言有关。如巴西出版的472 种 OA 期刊中有 408 种采用葡萄牙语，155 种采用西班牙语；西班牙出版的299 种 OA 期刊有 248 种采用西班牙语出版；阿根廷出版的 69 种 OA 期刊中有 66 种采用西班牙语出版。汉语作为全球使用人数最多的语言，在 OA 期刊出版领域仅有 24 种期刊采用，说明汉语在 OA 期刊领域影响力较小，这主要与国内 OA 期刊数量较少有关。

表4 OA 期刊的语言分布情况（前10位及汉语）

排名	语言	期刊数量	比例
1	英语	4401	83.38%
2	西班牙语	1028	19.48%
3	葡萄牙语	601	11.39%
4	法语	411	7.79%
5	德语	241	4.57%
6	意大利语	151	2.86%
7	土耳其语	87	1.65%
8	加泰罗尼亚语	58	1.1%
9	俄语	53	1%
10	克罗地亚语	52	1%
14	汉语	24	0.45%

如表5所示，在是否采用多语种出版方面，有超过70%的 3 847 种 OA 期刊采用英语、西班牙语等单一语言出版模式；采用多语种出版模式的期刊仅有 1 431 种，占全部期刊的27.12%。在采用多语种出版模式的期刊中，大部分是采用 2 ~ 3 种语种出版，且语种大多为英语与期刊所属国家或地区的母语。另外，有40.9%的人文社会科学领域 OA 期刊采用多语种出版模式，比自然科学领域20.49%的统计数字几乎高出 1 倍，说明人文社会科学领域的 OA 期刊更喜欢采用多语种出版模式。

表 5 OA 期刊的多语言出版情况

采用语言种数	期刊种数（种）	比例
1	3 847	72.88%
2	926	17.54%
3	318	6.03%
4	104	1.97%
5	51	0.97%
6	19	0.36%
7	4	0.08%
8	5	0.09%
仅标注多语种	4	0.08%
合计	5 278	100%

2.4 OA 期刊的创刊时间分布

分析 OA 期刊的创刊时间不仅可以反映 OA 期刊的增量情况，而且可以大体反映 OA 期刊的发展情况。表 6 的数据表明 OA 期刊的创刊数量按年呈总体上升趋势，说明 OA 期刊的发展呈现出稳步增长的良好状态（由于统计时间关系，2010 年数据仅计算到统计时间为止）。1987 年锡拉丘兹大学研究生 Michael Ehringhaus 创办的免费同行评阅电子期刊《成人教育新视野》（*New Horizons in Adult Education*）被认为具备现今 OA 期刊的全部要素[10]，因而可以认为 1987 年是现今 OA 期刊的诞生日期。然而从表 6 中可以发现在 1987 年—1994 年长达 8 年的 OA 期刊发展初期，OA 期刊的发展似乎并不太顺利，每年仅平均新增 20 余种 OA 期刊。究其原因可能和读者对 OA 期刊的认知程度有关，因为期间半数以上的 OA 期刊或中途夭折，或每年只出版几篇文章[11]。1999 年公共医学中心（PubMed Central，PMC）的诞生是 OA 运动发展历史上的重要事件，它不仅标志着政府对 OA 运动的支持，而且促使 OA 期刊在新世纪得到了高速发展。因此，可以认为 1995 年—1999 年间为 OA 期刊的成长期，其间每年平均新增 133 种 OA 期刊。进入新世纪后，随着 OA 运动得到越来越多来自政府、机构、学者等的支持，OA 期刊实现了高速发展，每年新增期刊的数量高达 407 种。另外，数据还显示 1987 年以前出版的 OA 期刊有 141 种（最早的 OA 期刊为 1874 年创刊的《蛾：昆虫学杂志》*Psyche：A Journal of Entomology*，但并不能说明 OA 期刊诞生于 19 世纪，因为这些期刊大多是由传统订阅型期刊转变而来）。

表 6 OA 期刊的创刊时间分布

创刊时间	创刊种数	创刊时间	创刊种数
2010 年	189	2006 年	426
2009 年	447	2005 年	463
2008 年	488	2004 年	392
2007 年	502	2003 年	354

创刊时间	创刊种数	创刊时间	创刊种数
2002 年	334	1993 年	39
2001 年	349	1992 年	18
2000 年	316	1991 年	19
1999 年	166	1990 年	26
1998 年	174	1989 年	17
1997 年	158	1988 年	15
1996 年	124	1987 年	4
1995 年	83	1987 年以前	141
1994 年	34	合计	5 278

2.5 OA 期刊的出版机构分布

分析 OA 期刊出版机构的分布情况，不仅可以发现 OA 期刊出版市场的竞争情况，而且可以了解大学、协会、科研机构等参与 OA 期刊出版的实际情况。表 7 数据反映 5 278 种 OA 期刊分别由 3 151 家机构或个人出版，说明各种出版机构积极投身于 OA 运动，参与出版 OA 期刊。但是，数据也同样表明 OA 期刊出版市场集中程度不高，属于一种分散竞争型市场。因为数据表明，3 151 家出版机构或个人平均每家仅出版 1.68 种 OA 期刊，其中有 2703 家机构或个人仅出版一种 OA 期刊，有 249 家出版机构仅出版 2 种 OA 期刊，共占出版机构总数的 93.68%；同时，Bentham Open、公共医学中心（BioMed Central）以及 Hindawi 出版公司（Hindawi Publishing Corporation）等出版 OA 期刊较多的前 8 家机构仅出版 836 种 OA 期刊，占 OA 期刊总量的 15.84%，小于美国经济学家贝恩和日本通产省对产业集中度的划分标准。该标准认为如果产业中前 8 家企业的市场份额总和小于 20%，则该产业市场属于分散竞争型市场。这一方面说明 OA 期刊出版市场行业进入壁垒低，众多出版机构或个人的参与利于产业繁荣；另一方面也说明现有 OA 期刊出版机构的竞争能力相对较弱，有利于出版机构实现高速成长。Bentham Open、公共医学中心以及 Hindawi 等出版机构在 OA 期刊产业的脱颖而出便是明证。

表 7 OA 期刊的出版机构分布

创刊数量	出版机构	期刊数量	创刊数量	出版机构	期刊数量
1	8（个人）	8	7	10	70
1	2 695	2 697	8	8	64
2	249	498	9	11	99
3	56	168	10	5	50
4	36	144	11	7	77
5	22	110	12	5	60
6	13	78	13	3	39

创刊数量	出版机构	期刊数量	创刊数量	出版机构	期刊数量
14	4	56	32	1	32
15	2	30	44	1	44
16	1	16	48	1	48
17	1	17	62	1	62
19	2	38	71	1	71
20	1	20	185	1	185
25	1	25	189	1	189
26	2	52	205	1	205
28	1	28	合计	3 151	5 278

另外，如表 8 所示在 OA 期刊的出版机构类型分布方面，包括 BMC 等机构在内的一般出版机构出版了 2 408 种 OA 期刊，占期刊总量的 45.62%；而学院、大学、学会、协会、科研机构、基金会、政府等出版机构以及个人则总共出版了 2870 种 OA 期刊，占 OA 期刊总量的 54.38%，显示了这些非赢利性出版机构对 OA 期刊出版的支持力度，尤其是一些基金会不仅向 OA 期刊出版机构提供资金支持，有的还直接参与出版 OA 期刊。在统计过程中还发现包括 Elsevier，Blackwell，Springer 等在内的部分国际著名商业性 STM 出版商也纷纷参与 OA 期刊出版活动，说明开放获取运动目前得到了整个学术出版社群的广泛认同和支持。

表 8　OA 期刊出版机构类型分布

出版机构类型	出版 OA 期刊数量	比例
一般出版机构	2 408	45.62%
学院、大学	1 649	31.24%
学会、协会	756	14.32%
科研机构	352	6.68%
基金会	74	1.4%
政府	31	0.59%
个人	8	0.15%
合计	5 278	100%

3　结论

总体来说，5 278 种 OA 期刊由 108 个国家或地区的 3 151 家出版机构或个人出版，并得到整个学术出版社群的支持，但 OA 期刊在学科和地区之间的发展较为不均衡。OA 期刊在医药与卫生、文化、科学、教育与体育、工业技术、生物科学等领域发展较好，而在交通运输以及环境科学等领域发展缓慢；同时，OA 期刊在欧、美等发达国家发展较好，在非洲等不发达地区发展非常落后，而包括巴西、阿根廷等国家在内的部分发展中国家则以 OA 运动为契机，大力发展 OA 期刊出版，并取得了较为丰硕的成果。另外，OA 期刊出版市场属于分散竞争型市场，有利于产业的繁荣发展。

在 OA 期刊的出版语种和出版时间分布方面，5 278 种 OA 期刊共采用 55 种语言出版，其中英语作为全球通用学术出版语言被 4 401 种 OA 期刊采用，西班牙语和葡萄牙语分别被 1 028 种和 601 种 OA 期刊采用，排名第二和第三位；与自然科学领域相比，人文社会科学领域的 OA 期刊更多地采用多语言出版模式。从 OA 期刊的出版时间分布来看，目前 OA 期刊的发展版可以分为萌芽期、成长期和高速发展期三个阶段，呈现一种持续增长的发展态势。

与国外 OA 期刊出版产业的快速发展相比，我国 OA 期刊的出版相对落后，目前仅有 16 种 OA 期刊被 DOAJ 收录，且采用汉语为出版语言的 OA 期刊也仅有 24 种，这与我国的科技发展水平与学术出版现状极不相符，需要引起我国整个学术出版社群的重视。

注释

[1] Definitions：Open Access Journal ［OL］. http://www. doaj. org/doaj? func = loadTempl &templ = about［2010-08-20］

[2] 徐丽芳. 数字科学信息交流研究 ［M］. 武汉：武汉大学出版社，2008 （7）：64

[3] Bo-Christer Björk，Patrik Welling，et al. Open Access to the Scientific Journal Literature：Situation 2009 ［J］. *PloS ONE*. 2010，Vol. 5 （6）：e11237.

[4] Steve Lawrence. Free Online Aavailability Substantially Increases a Paper's Impact ［J］. *Nature*，2001 （411）：521.

[5] Selection Criteria ［OL］. http://www. doaj. org/doaj? func = loadTempl&templ = about ［2010-08-22］

[6] http://www. doaj. org/ ［2010-08-22］

[7] http://www. opensciencedirectory. net/ ［2010-08-22］

[8] Estrada-Mejía，Catalina，etc.. The Guest for Visibility of Scientific Journals in Latin America ［J］. *Learned Publishing*，2010，Vol. 23 （3）：237-252

[9] 王应宽. 中国科技界对开放存取期刊认知度与认可度调查分析 ［J］. 中国科技期刊研究，2008 （5）：753-762

[10] 徐丽芳. 数字科学信息交流研究 ［M］. 武汉：武汉大学出版社，2008 （7）：44

[11] Alison Wells. Exploring the development of the independent，electronic，scholarly journal ［D］. MSc in Information Management. 1998/1999. http://panizzi. shef. ac. uk/el-ecdiss/edl0001/abstract. html［2010-08-22］

作者简介

徐丽芳，博士，武汉大学信息管理学院教授、博士生导师。

如何提高科研人员对 OA 知识库的使用意愿
——基于用户接受的研究视角

李 武

（上海交通大学媒体与设计学院　上海　200240）

摘要：基于量化研究数据并结合焦点小组和专家咨询研究结果，本研究提出了 OA 知识库建设主体提高科研人员对 OA 知识库使用意愿的八条策略建议，包括：在功能定位方面，坚持 OA 知识库信息传播功能的同时适当发挥其学术评价功能；在技术操作方面，加强互操作标准化建设，改善使用界面，简化存储流程；在质量控制方面，采取适当的学术质量控制措施；在版权管理方面，确保论文首发权，并向作者加强版权知识教育工作；在宣传推广方面，针对不同年龄、职称和学科的科研人员开展差异化工作。

关键词：开放存取　OA 知识库　用户接受　对策研究

How to Improve Researchers' Intention to Use OA Repositories as Authors
——From the Perspective of User Acceptance

Li Wu

(School of Media and Design, Shanghai Jiao Tong University, Shanghai, 200240)

Abstract: Based on the findings of a previous empirical study and the following focus group and expert consultation, this paper brings forwards eight suggestions for OA Repositories to improve researchers' intention to self-archive their papers into OA Repositories. They include but not limited to the following items: strengthening inter-operability among different OA Repositories, improving the users interface and simplifying archiving procedures within a certain OA Repository, adopting proper measures to guarantee the papers' qualities and copyrights, and promoting OA Repositories in differentiation strategies according to the different subjects and groups.

Keywords: Open access   OA repositories   User acceptance   Strategy analysis

1　引言

以 arXiv. org 的创建为起点，OA 知识库已有 18 个年头的发展历史了，在数量上已有了质的飞跃。但是，与 OA 知识库的倡导者和建设者的热情形成鲜明对比的是，科研人员本身的不使用行为现象非常突出，[1]尤其是作为作者身份的科研人员不愿意将自己的研究论文存储在 OA 知识库中。针对这一现象，笔者基于用户接受视角，首先以 UTAUT（Unified Theory of Acceptance and Use of Technology，技术接受和使用整合理论）为基础，参考学术传播的相关理论和先导访谈的文本内容分析结果，[2]构建了研究科研人员接受 OA 知识库影响因素的理论模型；[3]然后根据该理论模型设计量表，就影响科研人员接受 OA 知识库的相关因素开展了问卷调查。[4]同时，利用同一份问卷，笔者对科研人员对 OA 知识库的认知程度和使用行为也开展了同期调查。[5]

通过对 447 份有效样本的数据分析，研究发现影响科研人员将后印本（postprint）存储在 OA 知识库的因素有四个，按其重要性分别是：职业发展期望、操作努力期望、使用焦虑和政策导向；而影响科研人员将预印本（preprint）存储在 OA 知识库的因素则有五个，按其重要性分别是：使用焦虑、长期保存期望、职业发展期望、政策导向和技术优势期望。通过深入分析，研究还发现这些影响因素与科研人员"使用意愿"之间的关系在不同程度上受到性别、年龄、身份/专业技术职务和学科等控制变量的干扰。同时，通过考察科研人员对 OA 知识库的认知程度和使用行为现状，研究发现了解开放存取的中国科研人员人数在逐渐增加，但仍有将近 30% 的科研人员对开放存取"完全不了解"，将近 80% 的科研人员从未利用 OA 知识库存储过学术论文。

作为后续工作，本研究将阐述上述量化研究的策略意义。具体而言，本研究在上述量化研究的基础上，探索影响 OA 知识库建设主体促进科研人员将自己的研究论文存储在 OA 知识库中的因素，排除阻碍科研人员将自己的研究论文存储在 OA 知识库中的因素，从而提高科研人员对 OA 知识库的使用意愿。有两点需要说明，一是本研究对 OA 知识库的界定与之前研究完全保持一致——"存储学术研究成果、并为用户提供全文免费阅读和使用的数字文档库"，而研究中涉及的"学科知识库"和"机构知识库"也特指基于开放存取原则的"OA 学科知识库"和"OA 机构知识库"。二是本研究在分析策略的时候聚焦于 OA 知识库建设主体，即基于 OA 知识库建设主体立场分析相关策略，而没有涉及其他利益关系主体（比如科研资助机构和科研管理部门等），其目的是希望本研究所提出的对策更具有针对性和操作性。

2　研究方法

本研究结合了焦点小组法和专家咨询法。

在利用 SPSS 软件完成了对 447 份有效问卷的数据分析后，本研究采取焦点小组法对该研究结果进行了讨论，时间为 2009 年 4 月 15 日，地点为北京大学新闻与传播学院，参与人员为该学院编辑出版学方向的教员和研究生，人数为 12 人。焦点小组讨论持续约 2 个小时，基本程序是：首先，由研究者介绍数据分析结果，约 15 分钟；然后，由参与成员讨论这些研究结果的策略意义，约 1 个小时 15 分钟；最后，研究者汇总众多成员的观点并让成员予以确认和补充，约半个小时。

在随后的半个月内，研究者走访了四位专家，包括（按走访时间先后排序）：奇迹文库负责人季燕江先生、清华大学图书馆信息参考部郭依群副研究馆员、中国科学院图书馆学科咨询部主任初景利教授以及厦门大学图书馆馆长萧德洪研究馆员。基本程序是：首先，向专家简要介绍数据分析结果（事先已经发送了电子邮件）；其次，结合焦点小组的讨论结果征求专家的意见，包括专家介绍各自单位在建设 OA 知识库过程中为了提高科研人员的使用意愿所采取的主要措施。专家访谈的时间长度不一，长则两个多小时，短则 45 分钟左右。

3 研究结果

3.1 准确定位 OA 知识库的信息传播和学术评价功能

研究表明，"政策导向"与科研人员的"后印本使用意愿"和"预印本使用意愿"都有显著关系（p<0.01，p<0.01）。根据研究界定，"政策导向"包括三个行为主体，科研人员的所在单位、科研资助机构以及传统期刊出版机构。换言之，科研人员所在单位和科研资助机构对 OA 研究成果是否认可对科研人员的使用意愿有着重要影响。不同学者对 OA 知识库在学术传播系统中的功能定位有不同的看法。为了充分利用信息传播技术的优势，同时保证学术传播其他功能的继续有效运作，有学者提出了学术传播的功能分化理论，比如 Phelps 建议将信息传播与学术评价相分离。宋丽萍博士则明确提出了网络环境下的以多渠道功能分化为主导的体系结构，该体系结构将学术传播划分为交流和评价两个部分。其中，交流部分以内容提供为主，完成传播职能；而评价部分通过同行评审的质量控制，完成奖励和认可职能。[6] 也有学者提出了融交流和评价为一体的思想，以 Tim Broday 和 Stevean Harnad 等人为代表。他们在一篇题为"开放文档环境的数字化计量服务"论文中以 CiteBase 为例，将其作为可能出现的奖励中心替代模式。[7] Citebase 通过监控 arXiv 的记录以及实际使用情况，通过点击率和被引率等事后监控指标弱化传统同行评审机制，将内容传播和计量奖励功能融为一体。

在综合考虑根深蒂固的学术评价传统和科研人员实际需求的前提下，本研究建议 OA 知识库建设主体对 OA 知识库在学术传播体系中所要扮演的角色要有相对明确的定位：原则上以信息传播为核心功能，同时在一定程度上也要对正式学术评价发挥适当的修正和补充作用。首先，OA 知识库在学术传播系统中要重点发挥信息传播的核心功能。具体来说，OA 知识库既要使读者容易地检索到自己所需的研究资源，又要使作者最大程度地传播自己的研究成果。而学术评价功能主要仍然由学术期刊来承担，OA 知识库应该允许并鼓励作者将预印本继续提交给传统期刊以完成学术评价功能。当然，在具体形式上可以有所创新，overlay 期刊的出现可以说是一种富有创新意义的举措。[8] 其次，考虑到目前科研人员的信息存储行为在很大程度上受制于现有学术评价制度这一客观事实，本研究建议 OA 知识库建设主体与科研人员所在单位和科研资助机构进行协商，说服他们在考核科研人员的科研业绩或者制定项目审批标准的时候，将科研人员存储在 OA 知识库中的论文的被点击次数和下载量等数量指标作为对传统学术评价指标的有益补充。

3.2 从技术角度加强 OA 知识库的互操作标准化建设

研究发现，"职业发展期望"对于科研人员的"后印本使用意愿"和"预印本使用意愿"都有显著的影响（p<0.001，p<0.001），而且"职业发展期望"是众多促进科研人员的"后印本使用意愿"影响因素中权重最大的一个（Beta = 0.265，p<0.001）。正如研究界定的，"职业发展期望"主要是指科研人员希望提高自己研究成果的被引率。相对于传统出版，开放存取的核心特征就是"读者免费获取"，可以提高论文的被引率。[9][10][11][12] 但是论文被他人引用还有一个重要前提，即资源容易被发现和检索。

因此，为了满足科研人员对OA知识库的这种"职业发展期望"，从OA知识库建设主体的角度出发，本研究建议首要任务就是加强OA知识库的互操作标准化建设，实现不同OA知识库之间和OA知识库与其他数字资源库之间的无缝链接和统一检索。因为只有这样，读者才能"一站式"地检索到这些分布在不同物理位置的OA知识库资源，而这正是读者阅读和引用文献的基本前提。

目前厦门大学学术典藏库和中科院力学研究所机构知识库的平台建设都基于DSpace系统。从2007年1月开始，美国密歇根大学数字图书馆产品服务（University of Michigan Digital Library Production Service）OAIster对厦门大学学术典藏库进行元数据收割，将其纳入数据提供成员。DSpace是由美国麻省理工学院图书馆与美国惠普公司联合开发的开放源码软件，该软件既应用了OAIS参考模型，又遵循了OAI-PMH协议。OAIS参考模型从整体上高度概述了数字信息资源保存系统的参与者、职责、信息模型、功能以及服务等，可以为OA知识库在共享机制中的长期访问提供一个可资借鉴的框架。而OAI-PMH协议在OAIS参考模型提供长期访问的基础上又为OA知识库的共享提供了标准接口，使用户可以通过服务提供方提供的统一检索界面进行检索，进而将OA知识库纳入到数字信息资源共享体系之中。但是，我国目前大多数OA知识库（包括国内三大学科OA知识库）都没有考虑到不同OA知识库的互操作检索问题，这样导致的直接结果就是每个OA知识库都是一个"信息孤岛"，从而不能真正发挥OA知识库的信息传播功能。

在具体操作上，OA知识库建设主体可以采用目前在国际上被广泛应用的开源代码软件。据OpenDOAR的统计数据表明，[13]DSpace和EPrints是目前最为流行的两大OA知识库建设软件，其中在OpenDOAR收录的1538个OA知识库中，应用DSpace软件的OA知识库高达488个，占32%；而应用EPrints软件的OA知识库也达到了260个，占17%。与DSpace一样，由英国南安普顿大学开发的EPrints软件同样也遵循OAI-PMH协议，目前也有多种语言版本。本研究建议国内的OA知识库建设主体可以重点考虑采纳DSpace和EPrints这两种软件。在选定了具体的软件后，OA知识库建设主体还需要加强对这些软件的本地化设置和界面汉化工作，具体流程和步骤可以参考厦门大学基于DSpace构建机构知识库的本地化实践工作和上海交通大学机构知识库系统的设计与开发工作。[14][15]

3.3 改善OA知识库的使用界面，简化论文存储流程

研究发现，"操作努力期望"与"后印本使用意愿"有显著影响（p<0.001）。也就是说，科研人员是否愿意将论文的后印本存储在OA知识库中与OA知识库的操作难易程度直接相关。Key Perspectives Ltd于2004年开展的作者自存储行为调研报告也得出了类似的结论，[16]该研究表明在实施过程中碰到的技术问题是导致科研人员不愿意实施自存储的原因之一。20%的被调查者认为在第一次将论文存储在OA知识库中存在或多或少的技术问题，23%的被调查者报告说第一次将论文存储在OA知识库时花费了一个多小时的时间。为此，在技术方面，本研究建议OA知识库建设主体不仅需要加强后台的互操作标准化建设，而且也需要改善OA知识库的使用界面，尤其是要简化论文存储流程和最大程度地减少用户输入信息的工作量。

为了实现技术上的互操作功能，OAI-PMH协议为不同OA知识库的资源共享提供了标准接口，而互操作性同时还得需要标准化元数据做支撑。标准化元数据包含两个层面的含义：元数据的内容和形式。前者是指规定哪些元数据是必须提供的，目前对网络资源的

揭示往往采用通用的 Dublin Core 的 15 种非限制性元数据。后者是指元数据输入格式是否标准，如果元数据输入格式不符合规范或者存在拼写错误的话，就不能体现提交内容的属性与特性，那么就无法使用户检索到该资源。提供内容完整和形式规范的元数据固然会提高资源的建设质量和检索效果，但同时也无疑会增加用户存储的负担。本研究建议 OA 知识库在保证基本的数据质量的同时最大程度地减少用户输入信息的工作量。

具体来说，本研究提出以下三个小技巧供 OA 知识库建设主体参考。其一，允许根据用户的个人注册信息自动生成部分元数据信息，包括作者姓名、单位和通讯地址等，这种做法无疑减少了用户的信息手工输入量。这个方面可以借鉴中科院各研究所建立的机构知识库，它们的存储步骤非常简单，而且还可以通过增加字段对已有的数字化数据进行相互导入或导出。其二，提供自动格式转换和拼写纠错功能。比如对于后印本的发表年月格式，系统会自动地将其转化为系统默认的格式。其三，提供即时保存信息功能，这主要是防止因系统异常或用户因突发情况中止提交过程而导致信息丢失。

3.4 实施适当的学术质量控制措施，确保论文的首发权

研究发现，"使用焦虑"与科研人员的"后印本使用意愿"和"预印本使用意愿"都有显著关系（p<0.001，p<0.001），而且"使用焦虑"是众多阻碍科研人员的"预印本使用意愿"影响因素中权重最大的一个（Beta = −0.499，p<0.001）。为此，OA 知识库建设主体必须采取措施消除科研人员在决定是否将论文（尤其是预印本）存储在 OA 知识库时所存在的顾虑和担忧，包括对论文质量的担忧、对论文首发权的担忧以及对在线评审有效性和公正性的质疑。

相对于传统期刊而言，OA 知识库并不实施严格的同行评审或编辑部评审工作（主要是指存储预印本，对于后印本的存储不存在质量的重新评审问题），这是对传统出版流程的一大革新，但也存在不足之处。为此，本研究建议 OA 知识库建设主体在质量控制方面采取中间道路，具体做法可以将事先控制和事后控制进行有机结合。事先控制可以借鉴 arXiv. org 的"认可系统"。为了保证收录论文的学术质量，arXiv. org 于 2004 年开始实施"认可系统"，也就是说，首次提交论文的作者要得到来自一位 arXiv 已有用户的批准（来自著名机构的知名学者除外）。[17] 首先，arXiv. org 赋予来自著名机构的知名学者和先前的活跃用户批准权（判断是否活跃的标准是前三个月到前五年期间提交论文的数量）。提交者能够容易地在 arXig. org 网站上找到某个学科领域内具有批准资格的科研人员，然后通过电子邮件征求对方的意见。通常而言，批准人一年可以批准一名新用户，而系统保留撤销批准人的审批资格的权力。在获得批准后，用户就可以在 arXiv 中上传论文了，系统也根据其今后的表现决定是否赋予该用户批准他人的资格。

事后控制就是典型的"先发表后评审"机制。"先发表后评审"机制在很大程度上借鉴了开放同行评审制度的做法，这种做法最早是由 Gordon W. Hewes 等人提出，[18] 后来引起了 Harnad 的极大兴趣，他不仅以此思想为指导创建了 BBS 刊物，而且为了更好地利用网络优势来支持和维护开放同行评审的做法，他又与其他人一道创建了纯电子期刊 Psy-coloque。[19] 从理论上讲，"先发表后评审"机制充分利用了网络平台交互性特点，评审过程相对快速和透明，但也可能会存在"网络话语污染"问题。为了保证在线同行评审意见的公正性，本研究强烈建议 OA 知识库对注册用户实施严格的实名制，要求作者存储论文和读者发表评论之前必须以真实的个人信息注册为正式用户，但可以保留通过计算机终

端使用虚拟身份发表评论的权利。这种做法不仅有利于消除科研人员对在线评审意见的公正性的质疑，同时也有利于保护用户的基本隐私权。当然，上述的做法主要是针对学科知识库而言的，机构知识库由于其注册用户来自本机构或联盟机构成员，对提交论文的质量相对比较好控制。

另外，研究也表明科研人员在决定是否提交存在论文的时候有害怕论文被他人剽窃的顾虑。为此，本研究建议 OA 知识库建设主体提供论文首发权证明服务，同时也提供反剽窃服务。具体来说，OA 知识库必须严格记录并在需要的时候为作者提供提交和存储论文的时间证明，为可能会发生的首发权纠纷提供确凿的证据。同时，OA 知识库还应该利用同行监督和反剽窃技术及时发现剽窃行为，保证原创作者的权益。对于发现有严重剽窃现象的作者，实施惩罚措施，比如撤销该论文的存储并在网站上发表谴责申明。这两点的具体做法均可借鉴中国科技论文在线，该网站可为发表论文的作者提供论文发表时间的证明打印服务，同时制定了"在线发表科技论文的学术道德和行为规范"，并在网站首页设置"学术监督"栏目，公布发现存在学术作假或者学术剽窃的论文。[20]

3.5 加强版权知识宣传，并代表成员与出版机构进行版权协商

研究表明，"政策导向"与科研人员的"后印本使用意愿"和"预印本使用意愿"都有显著关系（p<0.01，p<0.01）。正如上面提到的，在研究界定中，"政策导向"包括三个行为主体：科研人员的所在单位、科研资助机构以及传统期刊出版机构。而传统期刊出版机构的政策特指以下两种情况：一是将预印本存储在 OA 知识库是否会影响论文被期刊的录用，二是将后印本存储在 OA 知识库是否会招致期刊的反对。目前论文出版的惯例通常是一旦论文被期刊录用，论文的版权往往由作者转交给了出版者，比如 Kaufman-Wills Group 对 ALPSP、美国医学院协会、HighWire 出版社和 DOAJ 所拥有的 495 家期刊进行了调查，结果发现除 DOAJ 外，绝大部分期刊都要求作者签署版权转让协议，其比例分别为 40.3%、87.9%、66.7% 和 14.4%。[21] 而在认知方面，科研人员对论文的版权政策的认识也都模糊不清。根据本次调研，36% 的科研人员表示对上述第一种情况不清楚，而40.3% 的科研人员表示对上述第二种情况不清楚。

因此，本研究建议 OA 知识库建设主体在版权方面需要加强以下两个方面的工作。其一，在科研人员当中普及和加强版权知识的宣传工作。根据 ROMEO 的统计分析，截至2009 年 1 月底，允许将论文预印本进行自存储的期刊和出版机构分别是 3228 份和 59 家，占统计总数的 31.68% 和 12.5%，而允许论文后印本进行自存储的期刊和出版机构则是6440 份和 253 家，占统计总数的 63.2% 和 53.6%。[22] 通过宣传可以让科研人员了解这些期刊和出版机构的政策，在一定程度上打消科研人员在 OA 知识库中存储论文时存在的"害怕破坏与期刊的关系"的顾虑。其二，代表个体科研人员与出版机构协商，争取作者对论文的自存储权利（或更多的相关权利）。在具体策略的应用上，一方面 OA 知识库建设主体可以考虑以联盟的形式与传统出版机构直接沟通，采用联盟的形式不仅有助于提高自己的谈判砝码，而且能节省大量的时间和精力。另一方面，OA 知识库建设主体可以考虑资助相关研究项目、请求相关权力部门和利用相关媒体机构开展研究和舆论引导工作。

3.6 制定强制性后印本存储政策，并允许用户撤销预印本

研究发现，"组织机构影响"与科研人员的"后印本使用意愿"和"预印本使用意愿"都没有显著关系，而"长期保存期望"与科研人员的"预印本使用意愿"有着显著

的负相关关系（Beta＝−0.226，p<0.001）。根据讨论结果，科研人员的"使用意愿"与"组织机构影响"没有存在显著影响很有可能是因为这种来自组织机构（包括所在单位、科研资助机构和科研管理部门）的影响只是一种建议或者倡导，并没有实质上的引导作用或者约束作用。已有研究对用户在强制性和自愿性两种情景下的自存储行为进行比较分析，研究表明，在 1~2 年内，如果没有强制性要求，机构知识库自愿进行存储的论文数量只有 15%，而如果实施强制性要求，存储论文数量则达到 100%。[23] 而"长期保存期望"与科研人员的"预印本使用意愿"之所有呈现显著的负相关关系，则很有可能是因为科研人员担心 OA 知识库对存储论文的"不可撤销"规定与期刊录用文章的前提规定存在一定的冲突，即部分期刊决定录用文章的时候会要求作者将原先存储在网络上的版本给予删除，而往往 OA 知识库都要求作者一旦将论文存储在 OA 知识库中，就不能撤销了。

基于这两点研究发现和讨论分析，对于机构知识库来说，本研究建议应与所在单位进行充分沟通，建议实施后印本强制性自存储政策。在国际上，自存储政策也在从鼓励层面走向强制层面，包括美国卫生研究院和哈佛大学等著名机构。[24][25] 在具体做法上，本研究建议可以借鉴中科院国家图书馆机构知识库。该机构知识库明确规定了"国家科学图书馆员工已正式发表在各种学术期刊和会议论文集的研究论文在正式发表后，存缴人必须立即在 1 月内将作品的最终出版版本或定稿最终版本存缴到该机构知识库中"。[26] 这种做法可以有效地提高科研人员的参与度，尤其是在科研人员不熟悉 OA 知识库潜在优势的情况下。对于预印本，不管是机构知识库还是学科知识库，本研究建议都应该允许科研人员在适当的时候给予撤销全文，但为了保证资源建设的连续性和完整性，在实际实施过程中保留撤销论文的元数据信息，并注明相关的撤销信息以及录用原文的期刊题名和卷期（若该撤销论文已被期刊录用）。

3.7 针对不同人群灵活地开展宣传和推广服务工作

研究发现，开放存取概念在科研人员当中有所普及，但是仍然有相当部分的科研人员对开放存取和 OA 知识库并不了解，因此 OA 知识库建设主体在加强自身建设的同时需要大力开展宣传和推广工作。根据罗杰斯的创新扩散理论，创新的扩散总是一开始比较缓慢，创新事物要在一个社会系统中继续扩散下去，首先必须有一定数量的人采纳这种创新事物。通常，这个数量是目标人群总人数的 10%～20%。创新扩散比例一旦达到临界数量，扩散过程就进入快速扩散阶段。[27] 因此，OA 知识库需要重点攻克这 10%～20% 的人群，为了顺利完成这一任务，本研究建议在策略上有所倾向，包括确定重点推广对象以及确定具体推广形式和主要推广内容。

根据研究结果，在读博士研究生和讲师/助理研究员这两个群体在决定是否使用 OA 知识库的时候在很大程度上受到"人际关系影响"（p<0.05，p<0.05），即他们身边的导师和同行的建议和行为对他们有很大的导向作用。另外，根据拉扎斯菲尔德的两级流通理论，在信息传播过程中，存在不同的人群，其中"舆论领袖"是指那些传递信息给舆论追随者的人群，并在信息传播中发挥了重要的中介和导向作用。[28] 可以说，在接受 OA 知识库过程中，教授/研究员和副教授/副研究员扮演了"舆论领袖"的角色。因此，在重点人群选择方面，本研究建议以教授/研究员和副教授/副研究员这两个群体为主。OA 知识库建设主体只要成功说服教授/研究员和副教授/副研究员接受 OA 知识库，那么在读博士研究生和讲师/助理研究员这两个群体也就很有可能受其影响而加入到使用者之列。

另外，研究还发现，教授/研究员和副教授/副研究员这两个群体在决定是否使用 OA 知识库的时候不受"人际关系影响"，并且更重视"职业发展期望"（低年龄组：Beta = 0.351，t = 6.985，p < 0.001；高年龄组：Beta = 0.622，t = 7.738，p < 0.001）。所以在具体宣传形式方面可以重点考虑直接开展演示会或推介会，比如与学术会议主办方合作，利用学术会议这一平台开展相关宣传活动。在具体的推广内容方面，由于科研人员更加在意的是使用 OA 知识库带来的对职业发展的优势，并不十分在意该系统的使用难易程度，所以在介绍 OA 知识库的时候，应重点介绍 OA 知识库相对于传统出版的核心功能，介绍 OA 知识库在保证论文质量和确保论文首发权所做的努力。同时要重点强调使用 OA 知识库能给科研人员带来的潜在好处，包括有助于提高他们的论文被引率和提高他们在同行中的知名度等。另外，也可以采用电子邮件直销策略，定期向教授/研究员和副教授/副研究员这两个群体发送邮件，内容除了向他们介绍 OA 知识库的基本功能和核心特征外，还可以特别提供存储论文的利用率通报服务。

3.8 充分意识到学科差异，针对不同学科开展差异化工作

研究结果进一步证实了来自不同学科的科研人员在信息利用和信息发布行为方面存在显著差异。从认知程度和实际使用的角度来看，来自图书情报领域的科研人员比来自其他任何学科的科研人员更加熟悉开放存取，而来自物理领域的科研人员利用 OA 知识库存储研究论文的行为较其他任何学科都要普遍。从大的学科角度来看，除了图书情报学之外，来自社会科学和人文艺术的科研人员对 OA 知识库的认知程度不如来自自然科学领域的科研人员那么高，其实际使用行为也不如后者普遍。因此，学科知识库建设主体一方面需要明确自己的学科覆盖范围，可以考虑优先发展物理、数学、计算机和工程学等学科领域的 OA 资源建设。但对于这种单学科的建设，必须要突出自己的特色，否则很难与 arXiv. org 等成熟的 OA 知识库竞争内容资源。对于确定需要建设综合性学科知识库或者机构知识库而言，则需要加强对来自社会科学和人文艺术领域的科研人员的宣传工作。

相对于其他学科，来自人文艺术领域的科研人员认为自己的"后印本使用意愿"和"预印本使用意愿"均受"配合条件"的影响（p < 0.05，p < 0.05）。因此，本研究建议在针对来自人文艺术领域的科研人员在宣传 OA 知识库的时候，不仅要强调 OA 知识库的核心特征和使用 OA 知识库所带来的潜在好处，同时也应该突出说明 OA 知识库所提供的使用配套服务，包括提供在线帮助、实地培训以及专人帮助服务。另外，通过对学科与"使用意愿"的方差分析，研究发现来自化学领域的科研人员对 OA 知识库的"使用意愿"是最低的，这非常出乎本研究的预期，但却与国外的相关研究发现基本吻合。[29][30]因此，本研究建议 OA 知识库建设主体应该特别针对来自化学领域的科研人员开展调研，系统地了解他们信息发布行为特点和学科传统文化，找出问题所在，以便制定有效的宣传策略和开展相应的建设工作。

4 结论

基于量化研究数据并参考焦点小组和专家咨询结果，本研究提出了 OA 知识库建设主体提高科研人员接受 OA 知识库的使用意愿的八条策略建议。总结起来，包括以下几个方面：

（1）在功能定位方面，坚持 OA 知识库信息传播功能的同时适当发挥其学术评价

功能；

（2）在技术操作方面，加强互操作标准化建设，改善使用界面，简化存储流程；

（3）在质量控制方面，采取折中路线，实施适当的事先和事后学术质量控制措施；

（4）在版权管理方面，确保论文首发权，并加强作者的版权知识教育工作；

（5）在宣传推广方面，针对不同年龄、职称和学科的科研人员开展差异化工作。

本研究结合量化研究和质化研究结果提出了 OA 知识库建设主体提高科研人员对 OA 知识库使用意愿的策略建议，具有一定的实践指导意义。一方面，这些策略建议囊括政策、技术和管理等各个维度，为开展具体工作提供了系统的分析框架，反映了 OA 知识库建设主体需要从各个不同的角度加强实践工作。另一方面，这些策略建议又非常具体细致，具有很强的可操作性。就加强 OA 知识库的宣传工作来说，不同于类似研究中口号式的提法，本研究明确了重点宣传对象、具体宣传形式和主要宣传内容。因此，合理应用本研究的策略建议无疑将有助于提高科研人员利用 OA 知识库的参与热情，从而在一定程度上有效地解决 OA 知识库在发展过程中碰到的内容获取这一瓶颈问题。但本研究也存在诸多不足之处，其中最为明显的便是没有分别针对学科知识库和机构知识库提出对应的策略建议。另外，本研究关注的是科研人员接受 OA 知识库的影响因素，相应的对策分析也是试图解决这种基于个体层面的影响因素。但是，OA 知识库的采纳和扩散还取决于机构层面的相关因素，比如机构固有的文化传统和原先的组织结构等。这个问题对于机构知识库的建设来说更为突出，也是对策研究过程中必须要重点考虑的地方。今后类似的研究应该对这些问题加以明确界定和深入分析。

注释

[1] Philip M. D. & Matthew J. L. Institutional Repositories：Evaluating the Reasons for Non-use of Cornell University's Installation of DSpace. D-Lib Magazine. 2007，13（3/4）. [2009-5-2]．http：//www. dlib. org/dlib/march07/davis/03davis. html.

[2] 李武，杨琳. 科研人员接受 OA 知识库的影响因素分析——一项基于先导访谈的探索性研究. 大学图书馆学报［已录用，待发］.

[3] 李武，卢淑静. 构建科研人员接受 OA 知识库的影响因素的理论模型. 情报理论与实践. 2010（2）：73-76，20.

[4] 李武. 科研人员接受 OA 知识库影响因素的实证研究. 中国图书馆学报. 2010（3）：57-66.

[5] 李武，卢振波. 科研人员对 OA 知识库的认知程度和使用现状分析. 图书情报工作. 2010（10）：58-62.

[6] 宋丽萍. 基于网络的学术信息交流体系研究［博士学位论文］. 北京：中国科学院，2006.

[7] Brody, T. etc. Digitometric Services for Open Archives Environments. In：European Conference on Digital Libraries 2003. Norway：Trondeim，2003：207-220.

[8] Magnus Enger. The concept of 'overlay' in relation to the Open Archives Initiative Protocol for Metadata Harvesting［硕士学位论文］. Tromso，Norway：University of Tromso，2005.

［9］ Lawrence S. Free online availability substantially increase a paper's impact. Nature. 2001, 411 (521). ［2009-5-12］. http://www. nature. com/nature/debates/e-access/Articles/lawrence. html.

［10］ Harnad, S. & Brody, T. , Comparing the Impact of Open Access (OA) vs. Non-OA Articles in the Same Journals. D-Lib Magazine. 2004, 10 (6). ［2009-5-6］. http://www. dlib. org/dlib/june04/harnad/06harnad. html.

［11］ Kurtz, M. J. Restrictive access policies cut readership of electronic research journal articles by a factor of two, Harvard-Smithsonian Centre for Astrophysics. 2004. ［2009-5-15］. http://opcit. eprints. org/feb19oa/kurtz. pdf.

［12］ Brody, T. etc. The effect of Open Access on Citation Impact. In：National Policies on Open Access (OA) Provision for University Research Output：an International meeting. Southamtpon：Southamtpon University, 2004.

［13］ OpenDOAR. Usage of Open Access Repository Software. ［2009-6-2］. http://www. opendoar. org/onechart. php? groupby = r. rSoftWareName&orderby = Tally%20DESC& charttype = pie&width = 600&height = 300&caption = Usage%20of%20Open%20Access% 20Repository%20Software%20-%20Worldwide.

［14］ 陈和等. 基于 DSpace 构建机构仓储的本地化实践. 现代图书情报技术. 2007 (3)：13-17.

［15］ 唐兆琦. 基于 DSpace 的机构仓储应用研究 ［硕士学位论文］. 上海：上海交通大学，2008.

［16］ Key Perspectives Ltd. Open Access self-archiving：an author study. 2005. ［2009-3-20］. http://www. jisc. ac. uk/uploaded_documents/Open%20Access%20Self%20Archiving - an%20author%20study. pdf.

［17］ arXiv. org. The arXiv endorsement system ［2009-3-24］. http://arxiv. org/help/endorsement.

［18］ Gordon W. Hewes. Primate Communication and the Gestural Origin of Language. Current Anthropology. 1973, 14 (1/2)：5-24.

［19］ 师曾志. 基于知识增长的电子期刊质量控制研究 ［博士学位论文］. 北京：北京大学，2001.

［20］ 中国科技论文在线 ［2009-5-13］. http://www. paper. edu. cn/index. php.

［21］ Kaufman-Wills Group. The Facts About Open Access ［2009-5-15］. http://www. alpsp. org/ngen_public/article. asp? id = 200&did = 47&aid = 270&st = &oaid = -1.

［22］ Open Access and Institutional Repositories with EPrints. Journal Policies-Summary Statistics So Far. ［2009-3-18］. http://romeo. eprints. org/stats. php.

［23］ Sale, Arthur. Comparison of IR content policies in Australia. First Monday. 2006, 11 (4). ［2009-5-12］. http://www. firstmonday. org/issues/issue11_4/sale/.

［24］ National Institutes of Health Public Access. NIH Pubic Access Policy Details. ［2009-6-12］. http://publicaccess. nih. gov/policy. htm.

［25］ Faculty of Arts and Sciences, Regular Meeting. VIII-5. ［2009-7-25］. http://www.

fas. harvard. edu/ ~ secfas/February_2008_Agenda. pdf.

［26］ 中国科学院国家科学图书馆机构知识库服务网格 ［EB/OL］. http://dspace. llas. ac. cn/guiter? id＝3.

［27］ 罗杰斯著. 辛欣译. 创新的扩散. 北京：中央编译出版社，2002：10-37.

［28］ 巴兰等著，曹书乐译. 大众传播理论：基础、争鸣与未来（第 3 版）. 北京：清华大学出版社，2004：132-135.

［29］ Lawal, I. Scholarly Communication：the Use and Non-Use of E-Print Archives for the Dissemination of Scientific Information. Science and Technology Librarianship. 2002 （Fall）. ［2009-5-15］ http://www. istl. org/02-fall/article3. html.

［30］ Key Perspectives Ltd. Open Access self-archiving：an author study. 2005. 5. ［2009-3-20］ http://www. jisc. ac. uk/uploaded_documents/Open% 20Access% 20Self% 20Archiving -an% 20author% 20study. pdf.

作者简介

李武，博士，上海交通大学媒体与设计学院助理研究员。

开放获取学术资源分布研究综述[*]

刘锦宏

（武汉理工大学文法学院　武汉　430070）

摘要：开放获取学术资源分布是指 OA 资源在地理、学科、语言等不同维度上的数量表现。本文主要从对 OA 资源的介绍，OA 期刊、OA 仓储以及其他 OA 资源的分布研究四个方面，对 OA 学术资源的分布研究进行综述。国内外学者目前主要从 OA 期刊、OA 仓储以及学术博客等层面，对 OA 资源的地理、学科、语言、出版频率、出版机构等分布情况展开研究，以揭示 OA 资源的分布规律。从总体看，OA 资源的分布较为失衡，OA 资源大多集中在北美和欧洲等发达地区，以及科学（Science）、技术（Technology）与医学（Medicine）等学科领域。

关键词：开放获取　学术资源　OA 期刊　OA 仓储

Researches Review of Open Access Academic Resources Distribution

Liu Jinhong

（School of Arts and Law，Wuhan University of Technology，Wuhan，430070）

Abstract：Open access academic resources distribution is OA resources' quantitative performance in geography，discipline，language and other different latitudes. This paper reviews the researches on OA academic resources distribution from four major aspects：a brief introduction of OA resources，OA journals distribution research，OA repositories distribution research and other OA resources distribution research. At present，domestic and foreign scholars focus on the researches on OA resources' distributions in geography，discipline，language，publishing frequency，publishing organization and other aspects to reveal the distribution discipline from OA journals，OA repositories，academic blog and other levels. Overall，OA resources' distribution is unbalance，OA resources are mainly concentrated in North America，Europe and other developed areas and in science，technology，medicine and other discipline fields.

Keywords：Open access　Academic resources　OA journals　OA repositories

＊ 本文为 2009 年度国家社科基金项目"开放获取学术资源分布与集成研究"（09CTQ024）以及"中央高校基本科研业务费专项资金资助"项目成果之一

1 引言

一般来说，学术资源可以通过"金色道路"（Gold Road）和"绿色道路"（Green Road）两种方式[1]实现开放获取。所谓"金色道路"是指资源通过开放获取期刊（Open Access Journals）出版的方式实现开放获取，而"绿色道路"则是指资源通过"自我典藏"（Self-archive）方式实现开放获取。而自我典藏是指作者将其作品存放于开放式的个人主页、机构仓储或学科仓储等网络平台上，供读者开放使用的一种行为。根据 Marie E. McVeigh 的统计，在 Web of Science 2003 年收录的期刊中，有超过 55% 的期刊和 65% 的论文被允许以适当的方式进行自我典藏，实现开放获取[2]。目前，包括爱思唯尔（Elsevier）、施普林格（Springer）等国际著名出版商在内的、越来越多的出版机构允许作者以自我典藏方式典藏其期刊论文。随着作者"自我典藏"行为的盛行以及 OA 期刊数量的快速增加，OA 学术资源的数量也在不断地增长。如根据 Bo-Christer Björk 的统计，在全球 2008 年出版的全部学术论文中，20.4% 的论文实现了开放获取。[3]如今，在遍布世界各地的 1 841 个开放获取仓储[4]和 13 000 余种 OA 期刊[5]中，出版和典藏了大量的学术论文、学术专著、研究报告、实验数据以及教材教案等学术资源供读者开放使用。

然而，OA 学术资源的急剧膨胀不仅给 OA 学术资源的组织与管理工作带来很大冲击，而且也给 OA 学术资源的利用效率造成很大影响。因此，关于 OA 学术资源的分布研究在一开始就成为学者关注的研究重点之一。所谓 OA 学术资源分布是指 OA 学术资源在地理、学科、语言等不同分布维度上的数量表现。从目前 OA 学术资源分布研究的现状来看，研究者主要从 OA 期刊、OA 仓储、个人主页等层面，展开对 OA 学术资源的地理、学科、语言等分布规律的相关研究。

2 OA 期刊的分布研究

虽然 L. Rich 和 J. Rabine 早在 2001 年就通过对学术图书馆网站的重复访问情况进行调查研究，揭示了电子期刊不断变化的存取情况[6]，D. Rosenberg（2002）总结了非洲在线期刊的学科范围和发展状况以及非洲学术期刊目录和文摘的免费服务情况[7]，但直到开放获取期刊目录（Directory of Open Access Journals，DOAJ）于 2003 年 5 月第一次对 OA 期刊的定义作出了学界公认的界定，认为只有"采用资助模式（Funding Model）出版的、不向读者或其所属机构收取任何使用费用的学术期刊才可以被认为是 OA 期刊[8]"后，学者们才真正开始展开对 OA 期刊分布规律的研究。

研究 OA 期刊的分布规律，首先要确定 OA 期刊的研究样本。一直以来，开放获取期刊目录（Marie E. McVeigh，2004；Jutta Haider，2005；马景娣，2005；刘辉，2006 等）、乌利希期刊指南（Jutta Haider，2005；潘琳，2006；陈传夫等，2007 等）、Open J-gate（黄如花等，2009 等）、非洲期刊在线（Daisy Ouya，Pippa Smart，2006 等）等期刊目录或指南经常被研究者们用作 OA 期刊分布研究的样本库。他们通过数据筛选、对比查重等分析方法，确定作为研究样本的 OA 期刊数量及名录相关信息，进而对 OA 期刊的地理、学科、语言等分布规律展开研究。

2.1 OA 期刊的地理分布研究

自从开放获取期刊被 ISI 的《期刊引用报告（Journal Citation Reports，JCR）》（2002

年版）首次收录后，关于 OA 期刊被 Web of Science 收录情况的讨论就从来没有停止过。Marie E. McVeigh[9]（2004）认为 OA 期刊必须是采用同行评议机制出版的、供读者免费使用的电子期刊，并以此为标准从 DOAJ、J-STAGE 以及 SciELO 中筛选了 1 190 种 OA 期刊，与 Web of Science 中收录的 9 000 种期刊进行对比研究，发现有来自不同国家或地区的 239 种 OA 期刊被 Web of Science 收录。研究还发现，与 Web of Science 中大约 90% 的期刊由北美和西欧国家出版商出版不同的是，239 种被 Web of Science 收录的 OA 期刊中，北美和西欧（包括英国）地区出版的 OA 期刊虽然排在第一位，但仅占 43%，亚太地区出版的 OA 期刊约占 33%，中、南美洲地区出版的 OA 期刊约占 14%，东欧地区出版的 OA 期刊约占 8%，中东和非洲地区最少，仅占 2%。分析其原因，与这些地区出版机构的 OA 出版态度有关。在欧洲和北美地区，只有不到 2% 的期刊采取 OA 出版模式，而亚太地区和中、南美洲地区则分别有 15% 和 40% 的期刊采取 OA 出版模式。

作为一种能够迅速提高研究成果显示度（Visibility）的新型出版物，OA 期刊的出版受到巴西、印度、智利等发展中国家的极大重视。2005 年 5 月的一份统计数据[10]表明，在全球全部学术期刊出版数量排名前 25 位（国家后括号中的数字为排名）的国家中，有中国（5）、波兰（10）、印度（12）、俄罗斯（15）、巴西（20）、埃及（23）和捷克（25）七个发展中国家；网络学术期刊出版排名前 25 位的国家中，仅有中国（4）、俄罗斯（11）、巴西（15）、印度（18）、墨西哥（24）和波兰（25）六个发展中国家，而在 OA 期刊出版领域，排名前 25 位的国家中有包括巴西（3）、印度（5）、智利（9）、委内瑞拉（10）、巴基斯坦（14）、波兰（17）、墨西哥（17）、土耳其（18）、中国（19）、捷克（21）和克罗地亚（22）在内的 11 个发展中国家，其中，巴西、印度、智利和委内瑞拉分别进入前十位。另外，根据 DOAJ 的统计，有 18% 的卫生科学（Health Sciences）、26% 的生物学（Biology）和生命科学（Life Science）OA 期刊是由拉丁美洲和加勒比海地区国家的出版机构出版。在巴西、印度、智利等发展中国家高度重视的同时，欧、美等发达国家也没有忽视 OA 期刊的发展。从欧、美等发达国家或地区出版的 OA 期刊数量来看，其所占 OA 期刊总量的比例呈增长态势，已由 2006 年的 65.53%[11]增长到 82.17%[12]。其中，美国出版的 OA 期刊数量已由 DOAJ 首次发布时近 100 种增长到如今的 1 114 种[13]。

随着 OA 运动的快速发展，OA 期刊受到越来越多国家和或地区的重视。出版 OA 期刊的国家或地区的数量迅速增长，已由最初的几十个国家或地区增长到如今的 108 个[14]国家或地区。但 OA 期刊在各大洲的发展很不均衡，其中欧洲和北美洲 OA 期刊发展较好，出版的 OA 期刊数量也较多，中、南美洲，亚洲和大洋洲 OA 期刊发展相对平稳，非洲 OA 期刊发展相对落后，出版的 OA 期刊数量最少。如截至 2007 年 8 月[15]，被 DOAJ 收录的 OA 期刊中，38.86% 的期刊由西班牙、法国等欧洲国家或地区出版，24.02% 的期刊由美国、加拿大等北美洲国家或地区出版，21.34% 的期刊由巴西、阿根廷等中、南美洲国家或地区出版；11.97% 的期刊由印度、巴基斯坦、中国等亚洲国家或地区出版，2.83% 由澳大利亚和新西兰两个大洋洲国家出版，0.98% 的期刊由南非、埃及等非洲国家或地区出版。如今，在 DOAJ 收录的 OA 期刊中，由欧洲、北美洲、亚洲、大洋洲和非洲国家或地区出版的 OA 期刊的比例有所上升，分别为 40.34%、26.79%、12.03%、3.09% 和 1.61%，而中、南美洲出版的 OA 期刊的比例有所下降，由 21.34% 下降到如今的 16.14%[16]，表明 OA 期刊在中、南美洲增长的势头有所减缓。

另外，印度（Leila Fernandez，2006；Ghosh，2007；Fayaz Lone，2008 等）、巴西（C. H. Marcondes，L. F. Sayao，2003；J Esanu，P Uhlir，2004 等）、南非（胡德华，尹加帮，陶雯. 2007）、克罗地亚（J. Stojanovski，J. Petrak，B. Macan，2009 等）等国家或地区的 OA 期刊的发展与分布情况以及论文的开放获取情况也引起研究者的关注。如 C. Hajjem 等人（2005）通过研究发现美国和法国出版的论文中均有 13% 的论文实现了开放获取，英国对应的数字为 10%，日本和德国均为 7%[17]。研究者还发现这些国家或地区的政府及科研机构对 OA 运动的大力支持以及试图通过开放获取提高研究成果显示度的目的，是这些国家或地区 OA 期刊实现快速发展的主要原因[18]。

2.2　OA 期刊的学科分布研究

2003 年 10 月在德国柏林召开的"科学与人文知识开放获取会议"（Conference on Open Access to Knowledge in the Science and Humanities）签署了《柏林科学与人文知识开放获取宣言》（*Berlin Declaration on Open Access to Knowledge in the Sciences and Humanities*），鼓励包括人文社会科学领域在内的科学家以开放获取方式出版科研成果。从此，开放获取期刊覆盖的学科范围从自然科学领域向人文和社会科学领域延伸。然而，从总体上看，OA 期刊在不同学科之间的发展不均衡，自然科学领域的 OA 期刊数量明显多于人文和社会科学领域的 OA 期刊数量，其中自然科学领域 OA 期刊数量占 64.64%，而人文社会科学领域 OA 期刊数量仅占 35.36%。具体来说，如果将截止到 2009 年 3 月出版的 12 531 种 OA 期刊按照 DOAJ 的学科分类标准，即按照健康科学（Health Sciences）、社会科学（Social Sciences）、工业技术学（Technology and Engineering）、生物生命科学（Biology and Life Sciences）等 17 个学科进行分类统计的话，可以发现健康科学、工业技术学、生物生命科学、农业食品科学（Agriculture and Food Sciences）、地球及环境科学（Earth and Environmental Sciences）、化学（Chemistry）、数学与统计学（Mathematics and Statistics）、物理和天文学（Physics and Astronomy）、科学概论（Science General）等 9 个自然科学学科出版的 OA 期刊所占的比例分别为 21.73%、12.77%、8.83%、6.18%、4.96%、3.42%、2.67%、2.45% 和 1.63%，合计 64.64%；而包括社会科学、商业与经济学（Business and Economics）、法学与政治科学（Law and Political Science）、语言与文学（Languages and Literatures）、历史与考古学（History and Archaeology）、哲学与宗教（Philosophy and Religion）、艺术与建筑学（Arts and Architecture）以及综合性学科（General Works）在内的 8 个人文和社会科学学科则分别出版了 19.5%、3.97%、3.30%、2.81%、1.79%、1.75%、1.36% 和 0.88% 的 OA 期刊[19]。

研究者在分析 OA 期刊的总体学科分布情况的同时，还从化学（M. Baker，2006；Antony J. Williams，2008. etc. al.）、生物医学（Mamiko Matsubayashi. etc.，2006）、计算机科学（倪娟，2008）、图书馆学（谭从容，2007）等单一学科层面分析 OA 期刊的分布情况。例如在计算机科学领域，114 种 OA 期刊不仅涉及计算机理论、多媒体、信息系统、硬件、软件工程、人工智能、计算机图形学、信息安全等多个计算机分支学科，而且还涉及图书情报学、社会学、数学、化学、经济管理科学等其它多个学科[20]。另外，研究者还发现不同学科实现开放获取论文的比例也存在差异。如在 1992—2003 年间出版的、被 SSCI 和 SCI 收录的社会学、生物学、经济学、商业学、管理学、心理学、保健学、教育学、政治学和法学等十个学科的论文中，分别有 16.0% 的社会学论文、15.0% 的生物学论文、13.5% 的经济学论文、9.0% 的商业学论文、7.0% 的管理学论文、7.0% 的心理学论文、6.2% 的保健学论文、5.3% 的教育学论文、5.3% 的政治学论文和 5.0% 的法学论文实现了开放获取[21]。相似的研究还发现，在 2001—2002 年出版的哲学、政治学、电气与电子工程学和数学四个学科论文中，有高达 69% 的数学论文实现了开放获取，排名第二的电气与电子工程学中有 37% 的论文实现了开放获取，而政治学和哲学则分别有29% 和 17% 的论文实现了开放获取[22]。造成开放获取在不同学科之间发展不均衡的原因则是多方面的，其中最主要的原因是不同学科的研究者对开放获取认识和接受程度的不同。

2.3　OA 期刊的其他分布规律研究

研究者在对 OA 期刊的地理和学科分布规律进行研究的同时，还对 OA 期刊的出版语种、出版机构、创刊时间、出版频率等分布规律进行了研究，以揭示 OA 期刊的发展状况。在 OA 期刊的出版语言方面，有 82.6% 的 OA 期刊都采用英语这个全球学术通用语言作为出版语种；由于西班牙语和葡萄牙语在巴西、阿根廷、智利等南美洲国家和西班牙、葡萄牙等部分欧洲国家被广泛使用，因此分别有 17.6% 和 8.1% 的 OA 期刊使用它们作为出版语种[23]。而在多语种出版方面，有 27.12% 的 OA 期刊采用多语种出版方式[24]，以提高 OA 期刊的利用效率。在 OA 期刊的出版机构方面，包括爱思唯尔、施普林格在内的众多出版机构和个人的积极参与促进了 OA 期刊的快速发展。调查发现[25]有 2 382 家出版机构参与出版了 3 354 种 OA 期刊，平均每家出版机构出版 1.4 种 OA 期刊，其中有2 111家出版机构仅出版一种 OA 期刊；英国的生物医学中心（BioMed Central）、美国的Internet Scientific Publications L. L. C. 公司等是 OA 期刊的主要出版机构。

在 OA 期刊的创办时间方面[26]，20 世纪 90 年代中期以前，年出版的 OA 期刊种数均在 100 种以下，其中最多为 1995 年达 86 种，累计出版 OA 期刊种数达到 355 种；20 世纪90 年代后期以来，年出版的 OA 期刊种数突破 100 种，其中最多为 1998 年达 167 种，至1999 年累计出版 OA 期刊种数达到 962 种；进入 21 世纪，年出版 OA 期刊的种数突破 200种，其中最多为 2007 年达 417 种，截至 2009 年 7 月，累计出版 OA 期刊种数达 4 254 种。而在 OA 期刊的出版频率方面[27]，OA 期刊采用多种出版频率进行出版，其中 22.44% 的OA 期刊为季刊，21.39% 的 OA 期刊为半年刊，21.86% 的 OA 期刊为不定期刊，7.24% 的OA 期刊为年刊，表明 OA 期刊的稿源数量比较缺乏。

3　OA 仓储的分布研究

作为 20 世纪 90 年代兴起的新兴的学术信息交流与共享模式，开放获取仓储（Open Access Repositories）在近 20 年的发展中取得了辉煌的成绩。截至 2010 年 9 月，在开放获取仓储目录 Open DOAR（the Directory of Open Access Repositories）上登记的 OA 仓储有1 650个[28]，在开放获取仓储记录 ROAR（the Registry of Open Access Repositories）上登记的 OA 仓储有 1 850 个[29]，在开放获取仓储目录 Celestial（Archives Registered in Celestial）上登记的 OA 仓储有 1 970 个[30]。然而，在 OA 仓储发展的前十多年，OA 仓储的增长非常缓慢，直到 2005 年 2 月左右全球 OA 仓储总数突破 400 个以后，OA 仓储的数量才呈现出一种爆发式的增长[31]。与此同时，研究者开始重点关注于 OA 仓储分布规律的研究，并从地理、语言、学科、类型等方面详细分析 OA 仓储的分布特征。

3.1　OA 仓储的地理分布研究

关于 OA 仓储的地理分布规律研究，研究者主要从两个方面展开研究。一是分析全部 OA 仓储在洲和国家层面上的数量分布；二是分析不同国家的 OA 仓储发展和分布情况。从 OA 仓储的发展来看，其在全世界的分布非常不均匀。由欧洲和北美国家建设的 OA 仓储数量最多，占到全球 OA 仓储总量的 80% 左右，其他地区国家仅占 20% 左右。在 930 个由 47 个国家建设的 OA 仓储中，由美国建设的 OA 仓储高达 260 个，占仓储总量的 28%，紧随其后的是德国、英国、澳大利亚、荷兰、法国、日本和加拿大，分别建设了 12%、11%、6%、5%、4%、4% 和 3% 的 OA 仓储，余下的其他 39 个国家建设了 27% 的 OA 仓储[32]。如果按照欧洲、北美洲、亚洲、澳洲、南美洲和非洲进行统计分析的话，可以发现在全球 1 250 个 OA 仓储中，欧洲国家或地区建设了 599 个 OA 仓储，占仓储总量的 47.92%；北美洲国家或地区建设了 366 个 OA 仓储，占总量的 29.28%；亚洲国家或地区建设了 138 个 OA 仓储，占总量的 11.04%；澳洲建设了 73 个 OA 仓储，占总量的 5.84%；南美洲国家或地区建设了 55 个 OA 仓储，占总量的 4.40%；非洲国家或地区建设了 19 个 OA 仓储，数量最少，仅占总量的 1.52%[33]。OA 仓储这种地理分布的不均匀性，与世界文化与科技发展的世界版图有一定程度的一致性。

另外，C. A. Lynch（C. A. Lynch & S. Costa，2005）、S. B. Ghosh（S. B. Ghosh & A. Kumar Das；L. Fernandez，2006）、B. R. Bravo（B. R. Bravo & M. L. A. Díez，2007）、M. van Deventer（M. van Deventer & H. Pienaar，2008）等人分别介绍了美国、印度、西班牙、南非等不同国家或地区的 OA 仓储发展和分布情况。美国网络信息联合会（the Coalition for Networked Information，CNI）在 2005 年春季所做的关于美国机构仓储（Institutional Repository）的发展状况的一项调查发现，在美国 250 个具有博士学位授予权的研究性大学中，有近一半的大学已经建设了机构仓储；在回答没有机构仓储的大学中，有 88% 的大学表示将开始建设机构仓储或以某种方式参与其他仓储系统[34]。在印度建设的 20 个 OA 仓储中[35]，有 18 个仓储为印度的研究学会、研究协会、研究中心或实验室建设，仅有 2 个仓储为大学建设；在建设平台方面，有 15 个平台采用 DSpace 软件，有 5 个平台采用 EPrints 软件；另外，20 个仓储收藏着大量有关天体物理学、图书馆学、管理学、农业技术、航空等众多学科的研究论文、研究报告、会议论文、学位论文等相关资料，供读者使用。与印度不同的是，在南非的 10 个 OA 仓储中有 7 个是由大学建设，且多为机构仓储，收藏着大量与建设机构有关的学习、研究等相关资料[36]。与南非相类似，西班牙的 OA 仓储也大多为大学建设，在 12 个 OA 仓储中有 9 个为大学建设，并涵盖多个学科领域的科学信息[37]。

3.2　OA 仓储的学科分布研究

与 OA 期刊大多仅出版单一学科科研成果不同的是，OA 仓储尤其是机构仓储大多可以提供多学科内容收藏和检索服务。按照 OA 仓储的学科分布来看[38]，有一半左右的 468 个多学科仓储（Multidisciplinary）收录的学科种类十分全面，而一些工程类、农业类专科院校以及主题仓储通常覆盖少数几个学科。如果将 OA 仓储按照仓储数量高低进行排列，各学科的排列顺序依次为：计算机科学与 IT 技术、保健与医学、自然科学、历史与考古学、技术总论、社会科学总论、商业与经济学、地理与区域研究、图书馆与信息科学、法律与政治学、生物学和生物化学、物理与天文学、数学与统计学、生态与环境学、教育学、化学与化工、艺术与人文科学总论、工艺美术与表演艺术、机械工程与材料、哲学与宗教、语言与文学、地球与行星科学、电子与电气工程、农业与食品以及兽医学、心理学、管理与计划、建筑学和工民建。除了科学、医学和技术等学科外，历史和考古学也处于领先地位，表明这些科学领域的学者能够与时俱进，紧跟技术创新的潮流，积极参与OA 运动与实践。

研究者还对图书情报学（A Coleman，2005；朱玉奴，田稷，2007）、生物医学（Mamiko Matsubayashi 等，2006）、化学（A. J. Williams，2008）、语言与文学（夏笑吟，2009）等学科领域的 OA 仓储的发展和分布情况进行了详细研究，以提高资源的利用效率。2006 年统计的 46 个图书情报学 OA 仓储[39]分别由美国、英国、法国、德国、巴西、加拿大、澳大利亚、芬兰、荷兰、意大利、印度、西班牙、南非、葡萄牙、墨西哥、纳米比亚等 16 个国家建设。在语言支持方面，有 80% 的 OA 仓储支持英语，其中 50% 以上OA 仓储仅支持英语。在文献收藏方面，意大利的 E-LIS 收录文献最多，达到 4 414 条，其他仓储收藏的文献从几十条到几百条不等。A. J. Williams 则详细介绍了化学领域 OA 仓储的分布和发展情况，并对该领域的 PubChem、eMolecules、DrugBank、SureChem 等仓储的发展情况和使用方法进行了特别介绍，以方便读者利用[40]。

3.3　OA 仓储的其他分布规律研究

在 OA 仓储的语言分布方面，大部分 OA 仓储均采用多种语言，但作为国际学术通用语言的英语仍然是 OA 仓储的首选。与 OA 期刊语言西班牙与和葡萄牙语排在第二和第三位的分布规律不同的是，德语和法语排在 OA 仓储采用语言的第二和第三位，西班牙语和葡萄牙语分别排在第四和第九位。如根据 Z. A. Wani 等人的统计[41]，1 250 个 OA 仓储共采用 45 种语言，有 21 种语言仅被 1～3 个仓储采用。在采用频率较高的语种中，依次为英语被 1 069 个仓储采用，德语被 151 个仓储采用，法语被 82 个仓储采用，西班牙语被81 个仓储采用，日语被 70 个仓储采用，汉语被 16 个仓储采用，排在第十位。如果将 OA仓储划分为机构仓储、学科仓储、混合仓储和政府仓储四种类型，1 250 个仓储中包含1 001个机构仓储，166 个学科仓储，58 个混合仓储和 25 个政府仓储。由此可见，机构仓储具有较好的发展前景。

4　其他 OA 资源分布研究

除了 OA 期刊和 OA 仓储外，学术博客、个人主页、个人网站、维基、学术论坛、RSS 种子等公共网络也分布着作者收藏的大量 OA 资源供用户开放使用。为此，研究者从不同的角度对学术博客、个人主页、个人网站等 OA 资源的分布情况进行分析，以提高这些 OA 资源的利用效率。科学网（http://www.sciencenet.cn）博客作为国内最大的学术博客群在 2007 年成立后发展迅速，受到研究者的积极关注。2009 年 3 月的一项抽样调查发现[42]，科学网博客中 40.2% 的博文属于与科学无关的原创性文章，32.6% 的博文属于与科学有关的原创性文章，27.2% 的博文属于转载文章。与科学相关的原创性博文中，15.4% 的博文讨论科学普及，10.7% 的博文进行学术讨论，7.3% 的博文讨论教育培养，7.0% 的博文分析科研体制，2.5% 的博文记录了学术活动，分别有 0.9% 的博文讨论学术道德和科研方法。在学术博客点击率方面，科普小说的点击率最高，平均点击率为 3 784

次，以下依次为科学文化、科学家故事、常识和专业知识，分别为 2 971 次、2 865 次、1 311次和633 次。数据表明，与科学文化等内容相比，专业知识的吸引力相对较弱。

在学科博客研究方面，虽然我国的教育博客发展迅速，取得了一定的成绩，但教育博客也存在地区分布差异较大、学生博客和班级博客缺乏以及教育博客在各教育阶段分布不均匀等缺点。根据马秀峰等人[43]2005 年 9 月的统计，在具有代表性的 16 个教育博客群中，大部分分布在华东沿海省市；在博客数量方面，小学博客站点和博客人数在数量上有明显的优势，高中博客数量较少；另外，教师博客是教育博客的主要组成部分，学生博客数量很少。另外，国外的图书情报学博客起步较早，发展较快。根据统计[44]，740 个图书情报学博客的影响力存在较大差距，大部分博客被链接次数较少，仅有 8 个博客被链接超过 200 次，其中 The Shifted Librarian 博客（http://www. theshifledlibraian.com）的被链接 886 次，位居第一。在博客更新频率方面，能够在 24 小时之内进行更新的图书情报学博客仅为 149 个，占 20.1%，在一周内进行更新的博客为 262 个，占 35.4%；有超过 40% 的博客更新周期长达一周以上，有的甚至超过一年。在博客创办者类型方面，有 370 个博客由组织创办，318 个博客由个人创办，52 个博客由团队创办。

总之，随着 OA 运动的进一步深入，作者的自我收藏意识将更加突出，收藏在个人主页、学术博客、学术论坛等公共网络上的 OA 资源将持续增长，OA 资源的分布也将更加分散。因此，研究者在做好 OA 期刊和 OA 仓储等 OA 资源分布规律研究的同时，也应重视对作者个人主页、个人网站、学科博客、学术论坛等 OA 资源的研究，以揭示其分布特点和规律，进而进行开发与利用。

注释

［1］ Jean-Claude Guédon. The "Green" and "Gold" Roads to Open Access：The Case for Mixing and Matching ［J］. *Serials Review*，2004（30）：315–328.

［2］ Marie E. McVeigh. Open Access Journals in the ISI Citation Databases：Analysis of Impact Factors and Citation Patterns ［R］. Thomson Corporation，2004（10）：1.

［3］ Bo-Christer Björk，Patrik Welling，et al. Open Access to the Scientific Journal Literature：Situation 2009 ［J］. *PloS ONE*，2010，Vol.5（6）：e11237.

［4］ Welcome to the Registry of Open Access Repositories ［OL］. http://roar. eprints. org/ ［2010–08–28］.

［5］ http://www. opensciencedirectory. net/［2010–08–28］.

［6］ Linda A. Rich，Julie L. Rabine. The Changing Access to Electronic Journals：A Survey of Academic Library Websites Revisited ［J］. *Serials Review*，2001，Vol. 27（3/4）：1–16.

［7］ D. Rosenberg. African Journals Online：Improving Awareness and Access ［J］. *Learned Publishing*，2002，Vol. 15（1）：51–57.

［8］ Definitions：Open Access Journal ［OL］. http://www. doaj. org/doaj? func = loadTempl &templ = about［2010–09–2］.

［9］ Marie E. McVeigh. Open Access Journals in the ISI Citation Databases：Analysis of Impact Factors and Citation Patterns ［R］. Thomson Corporation，2004（10）：1–25.

［10］ Haider，Jutta. The Geographic Distribution of Open Access Journals ［OL］. http://arizona. openrepository. com/arizona/handle/10150/105894 [2010-09-04].

[11] [27] 陈传夫，王云娣. 开放存取期刊的分布及获取策略研究. 中国图书馆学报，2007（6）：82-87.

[12] [25] 罗爱静，胡德华，刘双阳. OA 期刊的分布规律研究 [J]. 数字图书馆论坛，2009（6）：1-12.

[13] [14] [16] [24] 根据 DOAJ 数据库数据统计所得，统计日期：2010-09-05.

[15] 崔新琴. 开放存取期刊的地理分布状况分析 [J]. 图书馆建设，2008（7）：52-54.

[17] [21] C. Hajjem, S. Harnad, Y. Gingras. Ten-Year Cross-Disciplinary Comparison of the Growth of Open Access and How It Increases Research Citation Impact [J]. *IEEE Data Engineering Bulletin*, 2005（28）：39-46.

[18] C. Estrada-Mejia, C. Forero-Pineda. The Quest for Visibility of Scientific Journals in Latin America [J]. *Learned Publishing*, 2010, Vol. 23（3）：237-252.

[19] 孙波，黄颖. 国内外开放获取期刊现状调查 [J]. 图书馆学研究，2010（4）：98-101.

[20] 倪娟. 计算机类开放存取期刊资源的调查分析 [J]. 图书馆学研究，2010（12）：91-93.

[22] Kristin Antelman. Do Open Access Articles Have a Greater Citation Impact? [J], *College & Research Libraries*, 2004, Vol. 65（5）：372-382.

[23] 潘琳. 开放存取期刊的来源、分布与质量分析研究 [J]. 山东图书馆季刊，2006（2）：104-108.

[26] 王景文，黄晓鹂. 基于《开放存取期刊列表》的 OAJ 出版研究 [J]. 图书馆理论与实践，2010（3）：36-39.

[28] http://www. opendoar. org/ [2010-09-06].

[29] http://roar. eprints. org/ [2010-09-06].

[30] http://celestial. eprints. org/ [2010-09-06].

[31] http://roar. eprints. org/cgi/roar_ graphic?cache=396598 [2010-09-06].

[32] [38] 徐丽芳. 数字科学信息交流研究 [M]. 武汉：武汉大学出版社，2008（7）：247-248.

[33] [41] Z. A. Wani, S. Gul, J. A. Rah. Open Access Repositories：A Global Perspective with an Emphasis on Asia [OL]. http://www. white-clouds. com/iclc/cliej/cl27WGR. htm [2010-09-06].

[34] C. A. Lynch, S. Costa. Institutional Repository Deployment in the United States as of Early 2005 [J/OL]. *D-Lib Magazine*, 2005, Vol. 11（9）. http://www. dlib. org/dlib/september05/lynch/09lynch. html [2010-09-06].

[35] S. B. Ghosh, A. Kumar Das. Open Access and Institutional Repositories — a Developing Country Perspective：a Case Study of India [C]. *Word Library and Information Congress*：*72nd IFLA General Conference and Council* 20-24 August 2006, Seoul, Korea.

[36] M. van Deventer, H. Pienaar. South African Repositories：Bridging Knowledge Divides [J/OL]. 2008, Issue 55. [2010-09-06] http://www. ariadne. ac. uk/issue55/vande-

venter-pienaar/.

［37］ B. R. Bravo & M. L. A. Díez. E-science and Open Access Repositories in Spain ［J］. *OCLC Systems & Services*, 2007, Vol. 23 （4）: 363–371.

［39］ 朱玉奴，田稷. 图书情报学开放存取知识库的对比分析 ［J］. 情报资料工作，2007 （3）: 62–65.

［40］ A. J. Williams. A Perspective of Publicly Accessible: Open-access Chemistry Databases ［J］. *Drug Discovery Today*. 2008, Vol. 13 （11/12）: 495–501.

［42］ 黄晓慧，詹琰. 科研人员博客的科普内容研究: 以科学网博客为例 ［J］. 科普研究，2010 （2）: 24–29.

［43］ 马秀峰，李庆玲. 教育 Blog 应用现状调查与分析 ［OL］. http://itc. qrnu. edu. cn/ mxf/lunwen/blog% E7% 8E% B0% E7% 8A% B6% E8% B0% 83% E6% 9F% A5. pdf ［2010–09–08］.

［44］ 赵景明，张福学. 国外图书情报学博客的定量分析 ［J］. 图书馆理论与实践，2008 （5）: 84–86.

作者简介

刘锦宏，博士，武汉理工大学文法学院新闻传播系教师。

学术信息开放存取出版政策研究

牛晓宏

（黑龙江大学 哈尔滨 150080）

摘要：学术信息开放存取出版的可持续发展需要科学合理的政策体系来规范和保障。本文首先分析了开放存取出版政策的必要性，制定开放存取出版政策有利于增强机构和个人对开发存取的认同、推进我国开放实践项目的展开、促进开放存取相关立法的早日出台、拓展学术信息资源传播共享的范围。其次，分别对美国、英国、芬兰、印度、乌克兰等国外开放存取政策介绍分析。最后，本文对我国制定学术信息开放存取出版政策提出建议：由国家制定宏观层面的开放存取政策、由科研机构及科研资助机构制定强制性开放存取政策、由出版机构制定自愿性开放存取政策。

关键词：开放存取 开放存取出版 开放存取政策

The Research on Open Access Publishing Policies to Academic Information

Niu Xiaohong

（Heilongjiang University，Harbin，150080）

Abstract：Scientific and rational system of policies is needed to govern and protect sustainable development of open access publishing on academic information. Firstly, it is pointed out of the paper that open access publishing policies is necessary. Establishing open access publishing policies is conducive to enhancing the identification in open access of institutions and individuals, promoting the development of open practicing project, accelerating the relevant legislation on open access publishing, expanding the scope of sharing academic information. Second, this paper introduces and analyzes open access policies in the United States, Britain, Finland, India, Ukraine and other oversea countries. Last, some suggestions for open access policies of academic information which are suitable for China are proposed：to establish the macroscopic policies of open access by the government, to set up the mandatory policies by research institutions and research funding organizations, to build voluntary policies by publishing agency.

Keywords：Open Access Open Access Publishing Open Access Policy

开放存取出版模式促进了网络环境下学术信息资源的广泛传播与共享。随着开放存取出版理念和技术研究的成熟，国际上有关学术信息开放存取出版的实践和研究正在如火如荼地开展着。为了规范和指导学术信息开放存取出版的健康持续发展，各国政府和相关机构都非常重视开放存取政策的研究和制定。

1 制定学术信息开放存取出版政策的必要性

1.1 增强机构和个人对开放存取的认同

取得科研人员和相关机构的认可，是开放存取出版模式被采纳和接受的前提条件。尽管学术信息开放存取出版带来了一种全新的学术信息交流和出版模式，但由于观念上和经济上的原因，一些机构和个人对开放存取模式持有怀疑和抵制的态度。通过开放存取政策的制定与颁布，能够提高科研人员、科研机构和出版机构等对学术信息开放存取出版的认同，从而扫除一些机构和个人对待开放存取观念上的障碍。

1.2 推进我国开放存取实践项目的展开

与目前国际上开放存取出版实践项目的蓬勃发展相比，我国的开放存取出版实践还很落后，只有少数的学术期刊和科研机构实行了开放存取出版。这与我国目前在开放存取出版领域缺乏相关的政策指导有着一定的关系。如果由国家和相关机构制定开放存取出版政策，就可以表明我国政府和相关机构鼓励并支持学术信息开放存取的态度，必然会使越来越多的科研人员、科研机构、科研资助机构、出版机构接受并积极参与开放存取实践项目的探索。同时，对于已开展开放存取实践的项目来说，有了政策上的支持，必然能发挥出更大作用。

1.3 促进开放存取相关立法的早日出台

政策是法规制定的依据和指导，法规是政策得以实现的重要保证。法规与政策相比可以更加强制性地保证学术信息的开放存取出版。随着开放存取政策体系的逐渐完善，必然会促进开放存取相关立法的早日出台，反之，开放存取法规的出台也会促进开放存取政策的实现。目前，国外已有一些国家在开放存取政策实践的基础上制定了开放存取法规，例如乌克兰颁布的强制开放存取法规，再如美国为强制性实施开放存取而颁布的 CURES 法案和 FRPAA 法案。

1.4 拓展学术信息资源传播共享的范围

制定学术信息开放存取出版政策的最终目的是为了促进我国学术信息资源的开放存取，从而实现学术信息资源的最广泛传播与共享。通过政策所具有指向性、强制性和监督性，必然能够促使更多的科研成果和学术信息资源以开放存取的模式出版，从而让更多的公众可以方便地利用互联网发布和获取所需的信息，同时也使得科研成果等学术信息资源得以更加广泛地传播，一定程度上消除数字鸿沟的影响。

2 国外学术信息开放存取政策分析

开放存取政策是由欧美发达国家率先制定并实施的，例如美国、英国、芬兰等国家，随后印度、乌克兰等发展中国家也相继制定了的开放存取政策。

2.1 美国的开放存取政策

美国 NIH 公共获取政策是最具有代表性、影响最广泛的开放存取政策。美国国家卫生学会（National Institutes of Health，简称 NIH）从 2004 年开始就着手制定开放存取政策，经过一年多的调研，在广泛征求多方的意见和建议及基础上，于 2005 年 5 月开始正式实行开放存取政策；2007 年 7 月美国众议院批准了该项政策的提案，使得该政策更具强制性；2009 年 3 月美国总统奥巴马签署了美国 2009 年综合拨款法案，其中就包括了将 NIH 的开放存取政策永久化的规定。NIH 政策要求所有接受 NIH 资助的科研人员都必须在科研论文正式出版 12 个月内，将经过同行评审的科研论文的终稿以电子版的形式提交到 PubMed Central 数据库中，以提供给公众免费获取。[1] NIH 政策是由科研资助机构制定的，但该政策得到了美国政府机构的认可和支持，其对其他国家或机构相继制定出更加合理的开放存取政策起到了重要的借鉴作用。

2.2 英国的开放存取政策

英国的开放存取政策主要是由科研资助机构制定的。英国研究理事会（Research Councils UK，简称 RCUK）是第一个要求对其资助产生的科研成果实施强制性开放存取的公共资助机构，RCUK 开放存取政策要求所有接受资助的科研人员必须将最终出版的期刊论文或会议论文存储在相应的开放存取仓储中。[2] 目前 RCUK 的六个成员机构已经制定并颁布了各自的强制性开放存取政策。这些政策要求所有由公共资助的研究成果必须广泛、快速、有效地提供给公众开放获取。

2.3 芬兰的开放存取政策

芬兰教育部为推动芬兰开放存取的发展，成立了开放存取科学出版委员会（Open Access Scientific Publishing Committee，简称 OASP）并提出了《促进芬兰科学出版领域开放存取建议》报告，表明了芬兰开放存取的基本政策[3]。具体政策包括：（1）高等教育机构和科研机构建立或合作建立必要的开放存取仓储，以方便科研人员将自己科研成果提交到开放存取仓储内，提供给公众开放获取；（2）鼓励科研人员将自己的论文提交到开放存取仓储中，使仓储中科研论文的数量可以得到快速积累。芬兰教育部还分别对科研资助机构、高等教育机构和科研机构、期刊和学术团体、图书馆、芬兰教育部制定了有针对性的具体的开放存取政策。虽然芬兰还没有决定在国家层面上对开放存取采取强制态度，但是强调了从国家宏观层面考虑科研信息自由获取的重要性。[4]

2.4 印度的开放存取政策

印度政府在 2006 年先后制定和颁布了两个国家开放存取政策——《国家开放存取最优政策》和《发展中国家的国家开放存取政策》，其目的都是为了实现科研成果的开放存取。《国家开放存取最优政策》内容包括[5]：（1）获得全额或部分政府基金资助的科研论文，在被同行评审期刊接受出版以后，将论文电子版存储到开放存取仓储中；（2）鼓励获得政府资助的科研人员在已有的、适合的开放存取期刊上发表论文，政府可以提供出版费用；（3）鼓励获得政府资助的科研人员尽可能保留所发表论文的版权。《发展中国家的国家开放存取政策》与《国家开放存取最优政策》相似，取消了对科研人员保留发表论文版权的政策，增加了鼓励获得政府资助的科研论文在存储之后就立即提供开放存取的政策[6]。印度的《发展中国家的国家开放存取政策》是在《国家开放存取最优政策》基础上制定出来的，更具有普遍适用性，适合于所有发展中国家采纳。

2.5 乌克兰的开放存取政策

乌克兰的第一个开放存取政策是在 2005 年 2 月举办的"开放存取学术交流研讨会"时起草制定的。该政策主要包括以下内容：（1）保证公众获取信息知识的权力并保证知识产权制度不妨碍公众获取知识；（2）鼓励研究机构和高等教育机构参与开放存取实践；（3）由国家资助开放存取相关研究，并为研究机构和高等教育机构创建并维护开放存取仓储提供国家财政和技术支持。2006 年 11 月，为保证公共资助研究的开放存取，乌克兰国家基础研究基金授权国际复兴组织（IRF）对该开放存取政策进行了补充。在开放存取政策实施的基础上，乌克兰政府出台了开放存取法规，从 2007 年 1 月开始对获得公共资金资助的科研人员实施强制开放存取，并计划在档案馆、图书馆、博物馆、科研机构等具备开放存取条件的地方建设开放存取仓储。[7]虽然受到政治危机的影响这项开放存取法规在实施的过程中被迫终止了，但乌克兰政府对于学术信息开放存取所制定的政策和法规值得借鉴。

3 构建我国学术信息开放存取出版政策的建议

依据国外开放存取政策制定方面的经验，我国学术信息开放存取出版政策体系应该由国家相关行政主管部门、科研资助机构、科研机构、高校、出版机构分别制定的开放存取政策共同组成，具体应从以下几方面进行。

3.1 由国家制定宏观层面的开放存取政策[8]

笔者首先主张由国家制定宏观层面的开放存取政策，其原因如下。第一，国家政府的支持是开放存取得以广泛开展的强大推动力，越来越多的国家制定并颁布了开放存取政策，对开放存取产生积极的影响，纵观全球开放存取出版发展较好的国家，全都是由国家政府认可或出台了开放存取政策。第二，推动一个国家学术信息资源开放存取的发展，仅仅依靠几个机构制定几个政策来实现是远远不够的，只有由国家有关部门从宏观角度考虑制定出覆盖面广泛的国家开放存取政策，再由开放存取各相关机构根据国家政策再制定出具体实施政策，并将这些政策整合后形成一个政策体系，才能使开放存取政策真正地发挥作用，才有利于国家对学术信息资源的开放存取进行宏观的规划与管理。也只有从宏观角度考虑制定出的政策，才具有全局性和前瞻性，才有利于未来学术信息资源开放存取出版的可持续发展。第三，从目前已有的一些开放存取实践来看，由于缺乏政策上的统一规划与管理，呈现出学术信息资源分布与发展的不平衡、不稳定等问题。另外，政策的不统一还导致了学术信息资源开放存取实践过程中出现冲突与矛盾。因此，有必要从国家宏观管理层面上制定学术信息开放存取出版政策体系。

我国制定国家层面的宏观开放存取政策的具体内容可以参考印度的《发展中国家的国家开放存取政策》，该政策应由国家政府相关部门统一制定，供我国所有的组织机构共同遵守，其主要作用是为全国各级组织、机构制定相关政策提供宏观指导。因此该政策不必非常具体，但要表明我国支持学术信息开放存取出版的态度。学术信息开放存取出版主要是通过开放存取期刊和开放存取仓储实现的，因此国家开放存取政策要分别针对开放存取期刊和开放存取仓储制定。我国在开放存取期刊的实践建设上，一方面要在政策上鼓励创建新的开放存取期刊，另一方面通过相关政策的指导逐渐实现传统学术期刊向开放存取期刊的转化。在开放存取仓储的实践上，既要通过政策鼓励指导各科研机构、科研资助机构、大学创建可实现各自学术信息资源自由存储的机构仓储，同时，也要重视各学科领域学科仓储的建设，而不同机构的分工与合作需要通过国家宏观政策的指引与协调来实现。

国家开放存取政策的一项重要内容，就是在现有的学术评价体系中承认开放存取出版物的学术价值，即发表在开放存取期刊上的论文和在传统期刊上发表的论文一样，在科研成果认定时同样予以认可。国家还应通过政策支持开放存取基础设施（包括开放存取期刊、开放存取仓储）的建设，具体体现为建设经费由政府全部或部分资助。

另外，国家还应出台学术信息开放存取出版的技术支持政策。目前网络上学术信息自存储的格式和标准是多样的，随着开放存取出版资源数量的增长，按照统一的技术标准对学术信息资源进行开放存取，可以保障开放存取出版的可持续发展，这就需要通过国家或机构制定统一的技术支持政策来保证实现。

3.2 由科研机构及科研资助机构制定强制性开放存取政策

科研资助机构、科研机构和高校应在国家宏观政策的指导下，依据本机构的特点制定各自的开放存取政策，规范所资助科研人员或机构成员的权利和义务。国外现行的开放存取政策中既有强制性政策，也有自愿性政策。依据国外的经验，强制性开放存取政策好于自愿性开放存取政策，例如美国 NIH 的开放存取政策，起初是自愿性的开放存取政策，但执行起来效果并不好，但 2007 年在国会立法授权下，从 2008 年起对受资助者改为实行强制性开放存取政策，实行效果良好，促进了开放存取出版的广泛实施。因此，为了保证学术信息开放存取出版在我国的广泛开展，我国的科研资助机构、科研机构和高校等，应制定和实施强制性开放存取政策，要求相关机构和个人必须在规定的时限内执行，否则将不再对这些机构或个人提供资助。

如科研资助机构在各自的开放存取政策中可以强制性的要求所有受到本机构资助的科研成果必须开放存取出版，以提供给更多的公众免费获取和共享学术信息资源。科研机构和高校则可以强制性的要求本机构的科研人员将所有的科研成果提交在本机构的开放存取仓储中。目前已经实施强制开放存取政策的高校包括：麻省理工学院、哈佛大学文理学院、俄罗斯科学院中央经济与数学研究所、土耳其中东理工大学等。[9] 拥有丰富教学资源的高校，还应制定鼓励教学资源的开放存取的政策，即教学课件资源的开放存取。

同时各机构还应根据自己机构的特点或所属学科的特点制定不同的版权保护政策。版权保护政策不仅鼓励获得政府资助的科研人员尽可能保留所发表论文的版权，还支持所有作者在与出版机构签署版权协议时不要转让版权，或至少保留自己在开放存取仓储中自存取作品的权利。

3.3 由出版机构制定自愿性开放存取政策

学术信息开放存取出版的发展同样需要出版机构的政策支持。与科研资助机构制定的强制性政策不同，出版机构制定的开放存取出版政策更多的应该是自愿性的政策。出版机构应提供出多种出版模式的选择，由作者选择是否以开放存取的模式出版自己的科研成果，或者选择以哪种开放存取的方式出版自己的科研成果。

对出版机构而言，需要通过相关政策来规定论文正式发表后，提供开放存取的时间期限，例如 6 个月或 12 个月。另外，出版机构还要通过技术支持政策来保证其学术信息资源的长久保存问题。虽然出版机构不需要制定强制性的开放存取政策，但是出版机构应该根据国家宏观政策的指导方向，积极鼓励学术信息的开放存取出版。

注释

[1] NIH Public Access Policy Details [EB/OL]. http://publicaccess.nih.gov/policy.htm.

［2］付晚花，肖冬梅. 英国 RCUK 开放获取政策及其分析. 图书馆杂志，2009（4）.

［3］Recommendations for the promotion of open access in scientific publishing in Finland ［EB/OL］. http://www. minedu. fi/export/sites/default/OPM/Julkaisut/2005/liitteet/opm_250_tr16. pdf.

［4］Turid Hedlund，Ingegerd Rabow. Open Access in the Nordic Countries-a State of the Art Report. ［EB/OL］. http://nordbib. net: dynamicweb. dk/Files/Filer/Documents%20for%20download/Open_Acces_in_the_Nordic_Countries_Hedlund_Rabow_Nordbib. pdf.

［5］Subbiah Arunachalam. Open Access-Special session at the 93rd Science Congress ［EB/OL］. https://arl. org/Lists/SPARC-OAForum/Message/2713. html.

［6］Workshop on Electronic Publishing and Open Access ［EB/OL］. http://www. ncsi. iisc. ernet. in/OAworkshop2006/pdfs/NationalOAPolicyDCs. pdf.

［7］Iryna Kuchma. Developing National Open Access Policies：An Ukrainian Case Study ［EB/OL］. http://elpub. scix. net/data/works/att/135_elpub2007. content. pdf.

［8］牛晓宏，马海群. 开放存取的国家宏观政策体系建设研究. 出版发行研究，2008（4）.

［9］李麟. 稳步发展的开放获取事业. 中国图书馆学报，2008（5）.

作者简介

牛晓宏，博士，黑龙江大学信息管理学院讲师。

学术出版与开放存取

维基百科编辑机制分析

王京山[1]　廖小珊[2]

（1. 北京印刷学院　北京　102600；2. 中国新闻出版报社　北京　100122）

摘要：维基百科作为世界上最大的 wiki 系统，具有独特的编辑机制，它具有操作简易、支持协作、灵活多样的编辑方式。但在其信息编辑过程中也存在一些不足和问题，如编辑过程无序，编辑标准欠严谨，编辑结果不具备权威性等。维基百科利用 wiki 技术，不断更新其编辑机制，使维基百科成为多人协同知识生产模式的重要代表之一。在 Web2.0 的环境下，维基百科体现了自身强大的优势与发展态势。多人协同知识生产模式已经成为互联网分工合作产生巨大成果的典范。活跃在维基百科中的无数参与者，将自己的知识以网页为主要载体，以信息为传播方式，汇集成丰富的信息资源库。维基百科正是全体参与者不断创造与编辑的结果。

关键词：维基百科　编辑机制　协同

Analysis of Editing Mechanism in Wikipedia

Wang Jingshan[1] Liao Xiaoshan[2]

（1. School of Publishing Communication and Management in Beijing

Institute of Graphic Communication，Beijing，102600

2. China Press and Publication News，Beijing，100122）

Abstract：As the world's largest wiki system，Wikipedia has its own editing mechanism，its editing mode is easily operated，cooperation supported and flexible. However，there are problems and shortcomings in its editing process，such as editing process disorder，edit standard owed and edit results don't have authority. Wikipedia using wiki technology，the editors update，collaborative knowledge wikipedia become more important representative of production mode. Under the Web2.0 environment，wikipedia reflects their powerful advantages and development trend.

Keywords：Wikipedia　Editing mechanism　Cooperation

作为目前世界上最大也最有名的 wiki 系统，维基百科利用 wiki 技术，通过网络用户的参与迅速发展，目前已经涵盖了人类所有知识领域。维基百科自 2001 年 1 月 15 日开始建设，就表现出了相当惊人的发展速度，当年 9 月就达到了 1 万个条目，一年后维基百科拥有了 2 万多条目，平均每月增加 1 500 条。到 2006 年 3 月，英文维基百科已拥有 100 多万条目，接近有 233 年历史的《大英百科全书》的条目数。截至 2009 年 8 月，维基百科条目数第一的英语维基百科已有 290 万条条目，而全球所有 266 种语言的版本共突破 1 300 万条条目，总登记用户也超越 1 800 万人，总编辑次数更超越 7 亿次。与此同时，维基百科的国际化道路发展也非常迅速，2001 年 5 月，13 个非英语维基百科版本计划开始实施，很快覆盖了几乎所有的主要语种。

维基百科的迅速发展，离不开其独特的信息编辑机制。维基百科上的信息内容可能与传统出版信息的编辑没有太大的出入，但是，维基百科利用 wiki 技术，当原有的载体与新的技术相结合时，整个过程就会发生变化，显示出巨大的差异。

1 维基百科具有独特的编辑机制

维基百科允许大众的广泛参与，其内容允许第三方不受限制地复制、修改与再发布，它开辟的是一种全民参与的信息创作与智慧分享模式。据美国麻省理工学院的一项统计，一条随便加入维基百科的不良信息会在平均 1.7 分钟内被删除。而据 IBM 的一个研究小组最近发现，维基百科遭遇的多数破坏活动 5 分钟内就能修复。这都归功于维基百科独特的信息编辑方式。

1.1 操作简易的编辑形式

Wiki 系统用简单的格式标记来取代 HTML 的复杂格式标记，对于使用者而言，所用即所得，这种所用即所得的简易性一方面体现在维基百科信息的生产上，另一方面更体现在信息的编辑上。维基百科有一个专门的编辑手册，里面对于编辑的操作有非常详细的介绍。用户对维基百科内容的编辑十分容易。例如，对于页面的编辑，用户只要点击页面上方的"编辑本页"或者右侧的"编辑"链接即可以修改本页面；或者点击"讨论本页"然后再点击"编辑本页"来讨论该页面，点击后就可以看到一个包含那个 wiki 页面的可编辑的文字区域。然后先将文字复制到文字编辑器，再使用维基百科规定的格式编辑并检查，再复制粘贴回编辑页面中的文字区。这种简易的操作，对于维基百科参与者来说，只要能懂基本的电脑知识，能识字，就没有任何技术上的难题。

1.2 支持协作的编辑规范

维基百科里的一篇文章往往由上百人审查，而且是在不断讨论的基础上接受检验。维基百科中每个会员都可以修改维护页面。由于维基百科没有专门的审核机制，为了保证维基百科上信息更新的正确性与有效性，就更加要求每个成员必须具备较高的道德精神。对于维基百科来说，它的条目永远处于不断的更新状态中，它的条目永远没有最正确的，只有更正确的。

当然这种完全良性的写作是一种理想的状态，对于一些刻意的破坏活动，维基百科也做了一些规范。比如维基百科通过保留网页每一次变动的数据，从而使恢复页面十分方便，用户也可以与管理员对话，那么信息完善的过程就更加顺利了。

1.3 不断更新的编辑内容

传统的互联网信息发布主要采用网站集中发布模式（Server/Browser），一般用户只能浏览信息而不能随意发布信息。传统印刷出版物，信息一旦发布出来就意味着信息已经打印出来，再来编辑和修改就非常麻烦，并且成本也很大。维基百科采用 wiki 技术为核心技术建构，任何人都可以随时对内容进行修改，这种可擦写的页面从技术上保证了维基百科信息编辑的历时性。同时，维基百科上的信息没有版权限制，所有文本内容在 GNU 自由文档许可证下发布，GNU 自由文档许可证（GNU Free Documentation License）是一个版权属左（copyleft，或称"著佐权"）的内容开放的版权许可证。

维基百科上的内容没有最终的版本，自条目的最初创作者创作开始，维基百科上的信息就会不断接受编辑与修改。借助于网络，任何反映社会科学技术文化新动向的概念、词汇都会在第一时间被全球热心的作者补充进去。就维基百科这个整体而言，其内容每天都在不断变化，这种变化既包括修改，也包括新增内容。因此，维基百科信息的编辑是一个历时性的过程。

1.4 灵活多样的编辑制度

尽管维基百科上的信息人人都可以编辑，但是并不是说所有一经编辑的东西都能保留下来。正如上面所分析的，维基百科的编辑是一个历时性的过程，任何显而易见的错误和问题都会得到或早或晚的解决与更正。

实际上，维基百科是个民主制、精英制、独裁制的混合。维基百科上通常大部分的内容由一般维基人讨论、修改，一般为民主的形式。维基百科的系统里同时有资深的维基人担当管理员，负责清除破坏及封锁的恶意破坏者的账户。非常敏感的议题，则由吉米·威尔士最后把关。

为了防止可能存在的一些恶意的破坏和捣乱者，wiki 的群体社区会发挥作用，管理员和每个人都可以行使自己的权利，比如将删除帖子甚至封闭其 IP 的提议发布在公告栏上，让大家投票，一周后决定其去留。同时，对一些重要信息，为了防止被修改和删除，系统管理员可以对某些特定的页面进行"保护"，使其不能随意修改。wiki 是一个网上信息数据库，每次修改的信息都会被记录下来，并且可以恢复。维基百科信息编辑的多样性真正体现和保证了"让更多的眼睛发现更多的错误"。

2 维基百科编辑机制存在问题分析

技术上的优势，让维基百科信息的编辑具有更大的优势和特征，但是正如矛盾是普遍存在的一样，维基百科在具有这些优势的同时也存在着一些问题。这些问题有些是优势运用不当造成的，有些是优势运用过头造成的，而有些则是事物发展过程中由不完善到完善必经的阶段。

2.1 编辑过程无序

维基百科信息编辑的简易性，使得人人都可以参与编辑，这一方面对于信息内容的愈辩愈明有好处，对于信息内容的正确性最终走向有引导作用，但是另一方面，这种低门槛的编辑很容易造成信息编辑过程中的无序性。

在维基百科编辑过程中，这种无序有些是人为故意造成的，有些是人为无意造成的。据业内人士介绍，真正恶意操作的倒不是太多，更多的问题出在用户测试和做练习时，并不会造成显著的影响，但也有一些人利用维基发布网络广告。出现类似的问题，维基百科能通过技术和惩罚的办法对恶意破坏者进行警告，同时恢复编辑前的数据。但是，这都只是事后的补救措施，这种无序的信息编辑方式会给维基百科带来很大的负面效应。

在维基百科上，类似清空页面及加入冒犯性图像的内容能在很短的时间内纠正，但是有些破坏行为并不能得到及时地更正。尤其是一些知名度不高的条目，这些编辑过程中的故意破坏性行为可能会持续很长的时间。例如，有位用户曾经在英文版的 Martin Luther

King Day 条目中加入极端种族主义的内容，这些内容差不多四个小时候后才被更正。

2.2 编辑标准欠严谨

维基百科把自身定位为"网络百科全书"，针对这种"伟大的"定位，这与人们头脑中固有的定义还是有距离。McHenry 的批评者指出维基百科把自己定为一部百科全书是错的，因为该词意味具有一定水平的权威性及问责性，一部公开供人编辑的参考作品是不可能做到的。McHenry 更说："对一般使用者来说，一篇维基百科条目可能埋藏着看不见的混乱及不确定性。他或者从 Google 找到一篇维基条目，看到它是一部宣称是'百科全书'的东西的一部分，而这个词蕴含了可靠的意思，可是除了传统百科全书自己以外，一般用者根本不知道传统百科全书是如何达致可靠性的。"

其实这种批评也不无道理，对于百科全书，《中国大百科全书·新闻出版》卷定义为："概要介绍人类一切门类知识或某一门类知识的工具书。供查检所需知识和事实资料之用。但也具有扩大读者知识视野、帮助系统求知的作用。它是一个国家和一个时代科学文化发展的标志。"而针对维基百科中的条目来说，维基百科的整个编辑过程是不严谨的。虽然为了确保资料的正确性，维基百科要求贡献者查核所引述的参考来源，但是事实上，许多条目没有提供参考来源以引证文中内容。与传统印刷书籍编辑过程的"三审三校"相比，维基百科的编辑甚至偶尔会有某种涂鸦的性质，整个过程都不严谨。

并且，对于维基百科上信息优劣的判断，在编辑过程中很多时候是凭着编辑者的感觉。比如，以学者语气写成的破坏性内容不易被察觉，因为它"写得好"及符合该条目的风格。如果某人加入一行说某名人"终日放屁"，它会被快速删除，不过一个以学者语气写成的关于其"胃胀气"的破坏性段落却在英语维基百科的人物传记中存在了超过一个月。对于这种编辑过程中欠严谨的做法，专栏作家 Sujay Kumar 评论说："虽然维基百科宣称大多数破坏在 5 分钟内移除，一些假信息仍然无人察觉，一个说 Larry King（美国电视节目主持人）有不受控制的胃胀气的假东西就存在了 1 个月。"

2.3 编辑结果的非权威性

信息编辑的无序与欠严谨就暗含了维基百科作为一部网络百科全书与传统的权威百科全书的巨大差距。对于维基百科上的信息，人人都是编辑，并且只要用户认为已有的条目内容有欠妥的地方或者不完善的地方，都可以按照自己的意愿去编辑。截至 2009 年 8 月，维基百科总登记用户超越 1 800 万人，而这些志愿者中当然不乏某一领域的专家或者学者，但是更多的是一些玩家，学生或者普通的喜欢新鲜事物的网民，他们可能对于某一事物有自己的看法，但是距离百科全书编辑的标准还相差很远。

威尔士称维基百科条目的编辑是一个达尔文的进化过程，在该过程中内容通过反复的修改和编辑逐条改善。每一个维基百科文章平均被编辑 20 次，新的条目被编辑的次数就更多了，在编辑的过程中，维基百科有时会爆发"编辑战"，维基百科的用户们再三颠覆其他人的修改，在这些比较罕见的情况下，是由维基百科的正式员工作出一个最终的判断。然而，现在，维基百科的正式员工只有 23 人，要依靠着 23 人来对无所不包的内容作一个决定性的最终判断，并让人信服，还是有点差强人意。

根据《中国大百科全书·新闻出版》卷对于百科全书的定义，"百科全书是一个国家和一个时代科学文化发展的标志。"维基百科中的信息包罗万象，关于打喷嚏都会有详细的介绍，这种条目信息的无所不包性一方面会丰富维基百科的内容，增强它的亲和力；另一方面却降低了它的权威性。

2.4 编辑制度的无计划性

传统的印刷版百科全书都遵循严格的"三审三校"制，对于某些特殊且重要的内容为了保证其正确性，还会增加校对的次数。同时，对于编辑的整个过程，传统百科全书都会有一个完整的时间表，在编辑过程中一般都会严格遵循时间表开展编辑的工作。与此相比，维基百科的编辑制度就缺乏计划性。

维基百科因为所有的条目都是维基百科用户根据个人的认识与爱好添加上去的，从信息的生产上来说就维基百科就具有随意性与无计划性。这种生产上的随意性首先就决定了后期信息编辑过程的无计划性。在编辑的过程中，对于维基百科条目，人人都可以参与编辑，编辑的主体是广泛而随意的，并且平均一个维基百科信息条目会被编辑 20 次，新的热门的条目则会更多。对编辑的主体和客体而言，整个编辑过程中也是无计划的。有时一个条目可能被频繁地编辑，有时一个条目可能很长时间都无人问津，这取决于维基百科参与者的兴趣以及编辑的对象。维基百科信息编辑的无计划性还体现在对信息编辑的时间上。因为维基百科编辑主体的无计划性，编辑客体的无计划性，维基百科信息编辑的时间也就只能是无计划的，维基百科是一个时时都可编辑的在线网络百科全书。维基百科上的条目处于不断的编辑状态中，确切地说没有最终的版本形式，对于每个编辑阶段想要达到的效果与状态在开始编辑时，维基百科参与者可能有一定的想法与意图，但是每个条目最终的编辑效果与编辑走向都是处于无计划状态的。

3 维基百科编辑机制的完善发展

维基百科作为一部在线的百科全书，其创始人吉米·威尔士在阐述维基百科的政策和目标时表示："维基百科是一个百科全书网站，是对人类知识的摘要和总结。我们的目标是为世界上每一个人免费提供人类的所有知识。"其中，维基百科的编辑机制对于维基百科目标的实现具有重要的意义，加强和完善维基百科的编辑机制显得异常重要。

3.1 吸纳更多维基百科的参与者

维基百科的参与者是群体传播的主体，这个群体传播的主体包括维基百科信息的编撰者，也包括维基百科信息的阅读者。维基百科信息的编撰者是维基百科信息的阅读者，但是阅读者是一个更广的范围，并且阅读者也极有可能向编撰者转变。在吉米·威尔士阐述的目标中"为世界上每一个人免费提供人类的所有知识"，他把世界上的每一个人都视为维基百科的目标阅读者，这是一种目标，也是一种野心。

为了吸纳更多的维基百科参与者，维基百科应该加大对自身的宣传，让更多的人能知晓，只有在大家知晓的情况下，人们才会对你的产品与内容产生一定的兴趣。宣传的方式可以多种多样，既可利用传统的宣传方式，比如广告、公关活动等，也可以结合自身的特点，充分利用互联网超链接的特征，增加进入维基百科的入口。同时，对于已经知晓维基百科的那部分人应该努力增强维基百科对他们的黏性，让他们视维基百科为他们日常生活中的百科全书。

3.2 提高维基百科信息的质量与数量

维基百科利用先进的 wiki 技术，用户可以在 web 的基础上对 wiki 文本进行浏览、创建、更改，与 html 文本相比更便捷更容易。这种技术上的"低门槛"有利于增强参与者的积极性与主动性，有利于维基百科数量的增加。对于一个立志于"为世界上每一个人免费提供人类的所有知识"的网络百科全书，说到底还是一个"内容为王"的产品，可以说，维基百科信息条目的数量能为维基百科"撑门面"，维基百科信息条目的质量才是真正为维基百科"树品牌"的根本。

大英百科全书总编辑曾把维基百科说成是一个"公共厕所"。但是，2005年12月《自然》杂志刊登一篇文章，专门对维基百科和大英百科全书的准确性进行了对比——在随机选择的各40篇文章中，维基百科错4处，大英百科全书错3处，差别不大，这样的抽查引起了业界的一片关注。虽然大英百科全书的支持者此后指出，《自然》杂志的这种随机性抽查使得结果具有很大的偶然性，几乎全部错误，丝毫没有科学性与权威性，在研究过程中"偏袒"维基百科；但《自然》杂志却不肯轻易低头，拒绝了大英百科全书的指控，并称其研究十分公正。支持维基百科的相关研究者也指出，问题的关键在于维基百科的信息已经得到了更正，而大英百科全书的错误却依然存在。

对于维基百科来说，"百年老店"大英百科全书是榜样也是竞争对手，要想与之进行竞争，依靠先进的技术，数量上的优势很容易达到，而信息质量的提升才是关键。

3.3 不断提高维基百科编辑过程的规范性

维基百科信息传播的过程复杂而频繁，如果没有一套严谨而行之有效的系统规范整个传播过程，那么就很容易陷入混乱。至今为止，对于维基百科的一些批评性的话语很多都是对维基百科编辑过程不规范的指控。例如对于文献来源的可疑性是对学术不规范的指控，对于隐私的过多关注的批评是对道德不规范的关注，对于版权争议的批评是对职业操守不规范的提醒，等等。对于维基百科在群体传播过程中的不规范，在开始的时候一种随意性会促成事物的迅速发展，但是当发展到一定的程度需要继续发展时，发展到一定规模需要继续膨胀时，这种不规范带来的随意性就会造成发展过程中的混乱。

维基百科作为生产内容、提供信息的在线百科全书，其编辑过程就是对信息的再加工过程。提高维基百科编辑过程的规范性，可以提高编辑的效率，可以保证信息编辑的有序性，也能保证产出信息的质量。一般的群体规范的维持是通过群体内的奖惩机制来保证与实现，维基百科可以借鉴一般群体规范维持的措施，结合自身的特点，探索出有序规范适合自身的奖惩机制。

4 结语

在Web2.0的环境下，维基百科体现了自身强大的优势与发展态势。维基百科是多人协同知识生产模式的重要代表。多人协同知识生产模式是一种全新的知识生产模式，它利用互联网传播平台，推动网络用户自由使用、共享网络信息资源，达成工具、程序、信息、知识、文化思想的共享，最终大幅度提高知识生产的效能。通过网络用户的协同行动，可以在较短时间内生产出高质量、大容量的信息，这是传统的个人创作、出版发行的知识生产模式所不可比拟的。虽然维基百科存在这样那样的问题，但是在只用了3年的时间，便通过全球志愿者的协作便产生了150万篇文章，我们已经看到了多人协同知识生产模式旺盛的生命力。多人协同知识生产模式的意义或许已经不仅仅是一部部网上的作品，而是已经成为互联网分工合作产生巨大成果的典范。活跃在维基百科中的无数参与者，将自己的知识以网页为主要载体，以信息网络为传播方式，汇集成丰富的信息资源库。而维基百科影响力的实现，是全体参与者不断创造与编辑的结果。可以说，唯有提高维基百科信息编辑的质量，维基百科才能向前更快发展。

参考文献

［1］何筠红．在线共享的自由百科全书［J］．新世纪图书馆，2006（4）：40-42．

［2］朱玉强．维基百科：分享知识的自由百科全书［J］．农业图书情报学刊，2006（1）：118-11．

［3］张妍．维客：一种群体的书写方式［N］．计算机世界，2006-03-27．

［4］McHenry，Robert．The Faith-Based Encyclopedia Blinks［N］．TCS Daily，2005-12-14．

［5］Sujay Kumar．Oh，the wonderful world of Wikipedia［N］．The Daily Illini，2007-04-13．

［6］维基百科．Wikipedia：政策［EB/OL］．2005-09-25/［2009-10-10］．http://zh．Wikipedia.org/Wiki/政策．

作者简介

王京山，博士，北京印刷学院副教授。

廖小珊，硕士，《中国新闻出版报》编辑、记者。

PLoS——十年缔造的网络科技出版强者[*]

温 宝

（武汉大学信息管理学院 武汉 430070）

摘要：截至 2010 年，国际著名的网络科技期刊出版者 PLoS（Public Library of Science）已经成立了十个年头。这十年中，PLoS 从一家一般性的公益性质的支持开放存取的仓储机构，逐步发展成为目前拥有 8 本国际知名生命科学与医学期刊的优秀国际出版者，并独树一帜建立起了 条多种类、多形式的赢利渠道，作为 家非营利性质的出版商却成功地实现了收入盈余。正因如此，它的发展策略和编辑、发行、经营模式都值得我们研究分析和借鉴学习。本文从 PLoS 的发展策略、编辑策略、发行策略、经营策略等方面出发，在探究 PLoS 取得辉煌成绩的原因的同时，寻找其发展经验对我国网络科技期刊的启迪。

关键词：PLoS 网络 科技期刊 出版商

PLoS：A Strong Network Publisher of Technology Created in a Decade

Wen Bao

（School of Information Management，Wuhan University，Wuhan，430070）

Abstract：As of 2010，PLoS（Public Library of Science），the world's leading network journals publisher of science and technology has been established 10 years. In this decade，PLoS developed from a Non-profit general storage facility which supported for open access to an excellent publishing company which owns eight internationally renowned journals of life science and medical. In the same time it established more than one type of unique，multi-channel form of profit. As a non-profit publisher，it has successfully achieved the revenue surplus. So its development strategy and editing，distribution，management patterns are worthy of our research and analysis. In this paper，we will analyze PLoS's development strategy，editorial strategy，distribution strategy and business strategy at the same time，in order to explore the reason PLoS achieving brilliant results and find the enlightenment to the publishing of network scientific and technical journals of China.

Keywords：PLoS Network Technology journals Publisher

* 此文系 2008 年度教育部科技发展中心网络时代的科技论文快速共享专项研究资助课题"网络科技期刊出版模式研究"（项目编号：2008117）的成果之一。

2009 年下半年，科学公共图书馆[1]（Public Library of Science,简称PLoS）隆重推出期刊 PLoS Currents——这是它继 PLoS Biology、PLoS Medicine、PLoS Computational Biology、PLoS Genetics、PLoS Pathogens、PLoS ONE、PLoS Neglected Tropical Diseases 后建立的第八种可以免费获取全文的生命科学与医学领域的期刊，该刊在第一期凭借由顶级病毒专家筛选的 4 篇关于甲流的论文迅速获得了业界的关注，从此 PLoS 又多了一名有力的新成员。在这样 8 位有力成员的支持下，PLoS 顺利地走进它成立以来的第十个年头——2010 年。在过去的十年中，PLoS 从最开始的一般性的支持开放存取的仓储机构，逐步发展成为拥有 8 本国际知名生命科学与医学期刊的开放存取出版者，这样骄人的成绩无疑是由多方面铸就的。

1 明确的发展定位和目标

PLoS 于 2000 年由生物医学科学家哈罗德·瓦尔缪斯、帕克·布朗和迈克尔·艾森在美国创立，是一家由众多诺贝尔奖得主和慈善机构支持的非营利性学术组织。PLoS 一直将自己定位于开放存取的倡导者和支持者，但它在成立之初并没有将自己定位于出版者，而是鼓励和号召科技和医学领域的期刊出版机构通过在线公共知识仓库（如 PubMed Central）为研究人员提供文献全文的免费获取。2001 年 PLoS 认识到，更为有效和实际的开放存取方法应该是自己创建提供免费存取的高质量 PLoS 期刊。于是，在 2002 年 11 月份收到 Gordon and Betty Moore 基金会的 900 万美元的赞助后，PLoS 招募工作人员成立了期刊编辑部，并相继建立了在国际上达到顶级水平的 8 种期刊。目前 PLoS 已通过 www.plosjournals.org 出版了数以千计的经过同行审查的论文和数以百计的导读、论文、辩论、故事，以及科学和医学课题，逐步成长为开放存取出版的中坚力量。[2]

事实证明，PLoS 在开放存取目标的实现上已经获得很多成就——目前所有 PLoS 的论文都存储在免费的公共文档库 PubMed Central 中，使用者可立即免费在线获取，并可根据创作共享许可协议（Creative Commons Attribution License，简称 CCAL）进行再传播和再利用。

2 完备的组织结构

在组织机构上，PLoS 建立了组织理事会，并设立了首席执行官。PLoS 为其出版的 PLoS Biology、PLoS Medicine、PLoS ONE 三种期刊分别设立了期刊部门，为其他期刊设立了总部门——PLoS 期刊群部门（PLoS Community Journals Team）。除此之外，PLoS 还分别设立了财政部门、战略联盟与发展部门、IT 网络部门、出版部门、市场部门和产品部门。每个部门都有相关的领导者或负责人管理部门相关事宜，建立起了相对完备的组织机构。

3 完备的编审模式

PLoS 的编审模式由以下几部分构成：

（1）灵活的投稿系统

PLoS 要求作者在投稿前在 PLoS 投稿平台阅读投稿指南，在其七种期刊里选择自己文章最适合的期刊。之后就可以进入相应 PLoS 期刊的在线投稿系统（online manuscript submission system）进行投稿。

PLoS 鼓励作者自由地阐述自己的想法，一般不接受在其他媒体发表过的文章。除要求稿件必须是用英语写作外，在稿件的页数、图片、表格等方面均不设硬性限制。

（2）因刊而异的同行评议制度

PLoS 期刊均由专业编辑、资深科学家、医生与国际编委会密切合作来管理运行。采用传统学术期刊的同行评议和编辑审查等质量控制机制，对刊载论文的学术质量进行严格控制。PLoS 期刊（如 PLoS Biology）的退稿率一般高达 90%，明确说明作者付费并没有影响该刊的论文取舍标准。

PLoS 的八种期刊中，只有挂靠在 GooGle 网站下的 PLoS Currents（《PloS 潮流》）收录未经评审的热门研究论文，但它每期都邀请高水平的稿件筛选人。美国国立卫生研究院（NIH）网站为此设立了专门的文章"档案"。PLoS 主席 Harold Varmus 就此项目解释说："该项目的期望是这些论文稍后能发表在同行评议期刊上。"而另一本期刊 PLoS One 则采用一种"轻度"同行评审（"light" peer-review）系统，它发表任何在方法学上合理的文章，靠版面费增加收入。除 PLoS Currents 和 PLoS One 外，PLoS 期刊发表的每一篇论文都必须严格履行专业和学术编辑密切合作的高质量的同行评审程序。在该评审体系中，担任学术编辑的科学家进行专业学术与技术把关，经验丰富的全职专业编辑负责使评审程序公开和连贯一致。

（3）多样化的互动系统

PLoS 开放存取的特点除了免费之外就是对普通读者的充分照顾，它的每篇论文都会附带有一篇供非专业人士阅读的大纲，某些论文还会附带关于该领域的入门性质的简介。如此一来，即使是难度颇深的研究，普通大众也能明其要旨。此外，PLoS 期刊的文章一旦出版，读者就可以通过"notes"选项注释部分文本，并可以通过"comments"选项进行全文评论，或通过五星评分系统选项（5 star rating system）对文章进行洞察力、可信度、系统性、总质量等方面的评分。

为了促进与临床实验相关的学术信息的传播和交流，PLoS 还建立了一个交流社区——PLoS Hub。PLoS Hub 把很多临床实验方面的开放存取的文献收集在一起，是该领域的信息窗口。PLoS Hub 允许对同一个课题有兴趣的人们在社区分享他们的意见和知识，最终建设一个充满活力的互动社区。在 PLoS Hub，从收稿到发稿一般只需要三周的时间，而且出版费用更低廉。PLoS 还建了官方博客提供最新的学术进展信息，并允许读者留言评论实现交流互动。

（4）人性化的版权政策

按照传统期刊的做法，作者将版权转让给出版者，人们再花钱订阅或付费访问，不仅付费更多而且剥夺了大部分人的访问权，包括纳税人的访问权，阻碍了文献的广泛传播与充分利用。而 PLoS 采取的版权政策是创作共享许可协议，允许作者拥有其文章的版权。作者不需要与 PLoS 签订版权转让协议，可以保留发表在 PLoS 期刊上的论文的版权，但 PLoS 要求作者根据创作共享许可协议，授权任何人可以下载、再利用、重印、修改、传播和/或复制 PLoS 期刊的文章，只需正确引用文献来源和致谢原始作者。[3]

4 多形式多渠道的收入模式

随着 PLoS 的日益发展，其对慈善资助的依赖度逐渐降低，而是更多的偏向于依靠出版费用、广告费用、会费、赞助商资助来维持发展。PLoS 在 2007 年取得 348.6 万美元年收入的基础上再接再厉，2008 年取得了 614.2 万美元的年收入，增长 76.2%。目前 PLoS 已建立了相应经济机制以保持自己在经济上的独立性。从 PLoS 的经营收入模式方法来看，PLoS 当属一家非营利的赢利楷模。PLoS 的收入来源具体有以下几种：

（1）利用 PLoSOne 和 PLoS Current 实现赢利

PLoS 的经营策略之一即依靠低质量论文的大批、廉价出版来资助和养活少数的高质量旗舰期刊。PLoSOne 和 PLoS Current 则是其实现这一目的所利用的两本期刊。采用"轻度"同行评审系统的 PLoSOne 发表任何在方法学上合理的文章，其仅 1 250 美元的版面费使得稿源充沛。在 2007 年第一个全年运作中，PLoSOne 共发表 1 230 篇文章，带来 154 万美元的版面费，约占全年收入的一半。相比之下，2007 年发表了 321 篇文章的 PLoS Biology 收入不到这一数字的一半。从 PLoSOne 尝到甜头的 PLoS 在 2008 年 8 月建立了 PLoS Current，PLoS Current 的最大特色是不经同行评审，讨论目前最热门和最流行的生命科学与医学领域的热门课题，[4]为科学家们提供一个观点、数据、结论聚集的集散地，便于科学家尽快的交流心得体会。由于无需同行评审，因此，并不影响文章在其他专业期刊上的发表。照这样的发展趋势下去，PLoS Current 将成为 PLoS One 后 PLoS 新的摇钱树。

（2）向作者收取出版费用

PLoS 期刊采用的是非传统的商业模式，依靠向作者或研究资助者对每篇发表的文章收取一定的费用来回收开放存取的成本。PLoS 制定的对接受发表文章的处理费标准一般是每篇 1 350 美元至 2 900 美元，各个期刊有所不同，近年来收费标准也在不断变化。

随着财政状况不断严峻，PLoS 在 2006 年大幅提高了所有期刊的版面费，顶尖的 PLoS Biology 和 PLoS Medicine 从 1 500 美元涨到 2 500 美元。2007 年和 2008 年 PLoS 的论文处理收入高达 839.9 万美元。PLoS 对研究论文以开放存取形式发表的成本进行了详细的核算，结果得出每页、每篇研究论文和每期的生产成本分别为：74.05 美元、869.75 美元和 8 697.50 美元；加上电子文稿的版面处理加工，每篇论文的生产成本为 1 069.75 美元，每期的生产成本为 10 696.50 美元。

因为 PLoS Biology 追求高质量，只发表全球该领域最好或最重要的研究成果，这就意味着其刊稿率退稿率高达 90%。专家估计，90% 多的退稿率（退稿不收费），退稿的处理费分摊到已发表的文章上会使每篇发表论文的成本非常高，远高于 1 500 美元。耶鲁大学的细胞生物学家，同时担任 The Journal of CellBiology 主编的 Ira Mellman 指出，"实际（出版）成本是 PLoS 估算成本的 4 ~ 6 倍"，所以 PLoS 仅依靠从发表论文的作者收取的费用还不足以维持出版高质量的期刊。

尽管如此，对于那些没有机会获得基金或机构支持来支付出版费用的作者，PLoS 会对他们实行费用免除和优惠政策，大幅度减少或免除发表费。同时，来自 PLoS 机构会员单位的作者也有资格要求给予发表费优惠的待遇。开放社会研究所（OSI）支持发展中和过渡性国家的大学成为 PLoS 机构会员，PLoS 鼓励所有作者了解更多有关可获得资金支付发表费，包括通过他们的机构、基金代理机构和政府支付他们的出版费用。

（3）融资收入

向作者收取出版费是 PLoS 医学的重要收入来源，此外慈善事业捐助，赞助商赞助等也构成收入的其他部分。

PLoS 在成立之初就接受了来自于 Gordon and Betty Moore Foundation 为期 5 年共 900 万美元的基金资助，并在 2006 年 5 月又追加了为期 18 个月共计 100 万美元的赞助；[5] 同时还受 Sandler Family Supporting Foundation，the Irving A. Hansen Memorial Foundation，The Open Society Institute（OSI）和 The Joint Information Systems Committee（JISC）等机构的资助；同时，PLoS 还接受来自于社会的赞助。但 PLoS 有权选择接受还是拒绝捐助，并不受捐助者影响保持稿件变身的独立性。

（4）会员费收入

PLoS 收取来自于个人、大学及其他机构的个人会员与团体会员会费，并为其提供服务。PLoS 基于个案谈判鼓励和吸引财团会员。PLoS 也鼓励研究基金代理机构代表其研究者和受资助者成为会员，也欢迎支持开放存取宗旨的组织成为会员。

① 针对个人会员

按照分类与提供服务的级别不同，PLoS 对个人会员收取的会员费也不同，有从 25 美元到 1 000 美元六个级别。个人会员费一定程度上弥补了 PLoS 期刊出版成本。但 PLoS 同时规定，个人会员捐助者不会对期刊的编审决定产生影响，会员提交的论文在同行评审过程中不享受特殊待遇，论文的发表费也不享受任何折扣。[6]

② 针对机构会员

目前 PLoS 的机构会员主要来自北美（147 个，其中美国 144 个）、欧洲（11 个）、澳洲（1 个）、非洲（1 个）。许多大学是 PLoS 的机构会员，有的大学中的学院也单独成为机构会员。这些机构会员的会费为 PLoS 提供了经费支持，帮助 PLoS 创造了一个可持续的和综合的开放存取出版系统。PLoS 机构会员交纳会费后可以享有会员论文发表费优惠、补充订阅期间期刊的印刷版、拥有 PLoS 会员专栏等权利。

（5）其他收入

PLoS 愿意同致力于开放存取地方任何团体（科学/学术团体，医生，患者的宣传，教育组织）和任何发布商合作，协助他们进行开放存取计划并收取一定费用。虽然 PLoS 的开放存取期刊可以免费使用，但印刷版本用户是要付费购买的。单册期刊购买费用为 45 美元。

此外，PLoS 收入还包括广告收入和出版业其他部门的收入。

5 PLoS 的多渠道发行模式

所有在 PLoS 期刊发表的文章，自发表之时起就被存储在期刊网站上，同时完整的文章内容将被立即存储在 PubMed Central 中。文章的图表与全文可以在期刊网站和 PubMed Central 通过关键词、作者、主题、卷期数等多种标准搜索查询。PLoS 也将致力于同其他机构合作在世界各地建立类似的文档库来存储论文。

TOPAZ 是另一个 PLoS 期刊存储平台。TOPAZ 是一个建立在 Fedora 服务框架上的内容开源建模和存储架构，也是一个开源存储库，Mulgara 则是一个开放源码语义数据库。TOPAZ 的目标是提供一个出版平台，以促进科学和医学界期刊从订阅型转向基于网络的开放存取型。TOPAZ 随着 PLoS ONE 的启动于 2006 年 12 月首次在公众面前亮相。目前，PLoS 的七种期刊已经全部可以在 TOPAZ 平台获取。

此外，PLoS 还允许任何第三方如图书馆、机构或个人等建立 PLoS 期刊文章的档案库，只要根据开放存取的原则使文章可免费获取即可。

6 结论

从 2000 年到 2010 年，PLoS 正好诞生并成长在开放存取出版日新月异发展的时间段里，因此它的成长也是国际开放存取出版成长之路的浓缩。从 PLoS 的发展经历中我们可以看出，开放存取正向着规模化、现代化、赢利化的主要方向发展。伴随着科学技术和经营理念的变革，OA 出版界一定还会涌现出更多像 PLoS 这样，将崇高理念和现实赢利完美结合的出版者。

注释

［1］PLoS 官方网站［OL］：www. plos. org. 2010-01-10.

［2］王应宽. 开放存取期刊出版：PLoS 案例研究［J］. 出版发行研究：2006（5）.

［3］OA White Paper：publishing open access journals［OL］. http://www. plos. org/.

［4］GrantAwarded［OL］. http://www. plos. org/downloads/progress_report. pdf.

［5］黄先蓉，罗紫初等主编. 数字出版与出版教育［M］. 北京：高等教育出版社，2009（4）.

［6］刘锦宏，顾轩. 网络科技期刊收入模式研究［J］. 出版科学：2009（5）.

作者简介

温宝，武汉大学信息管理学院硕士研究生。

Study on China Internet-based Academic Journals Digital Publishing Modes

Shen Xiangxing[1] Li Xiangdong[1] Yang Yuan[1] Yan Guanxiang[1] Shen Chong[2]

(1. School of Information Management, Wuhan University, Wuhan, 430072

2. College of Information Science & Technology, Hainan University, Haikou, 570228)

学术出版与开放存取

Abstract: The research takes three fundamental Internet Academic Journals (IAJ), which are China National Knowledge Infrastructure (CNKI), Chongqing VIP Information Co., Ltd. (VIP) and Beijing Wanfang Data Co., Ltd. (WFD), as subjects to discuss digital publishing mechanism innovations for China's science information communication system. After introducing main Internet environment, comparing journal characteristics and explaining publishing & operation modes of the IAJs, the paper analyses important issues such as redundant contents, digitalization issues, illegal journals, standards construction, copyright and benefit sharing, etc. By learning from research practices and open access, a new benefit sharing and copyright management mode based on the Third Party Agency (TPA) is proposed. Future IAJs operation modes are also discussed from the view of scientific research innovation and the art platform construction.

Keywords: China Publishing mode Internet academic journals Digital library Standard Illegal journals

中国互联网学术期刊数字出版模式研究

沈祥兴[1] 李向东[1] 扬漾[1] 严冠湘[1] 沈重[2]

(1. 武汉大学信息管理学院 武汉 430072

2. 海南大学信息科学技术学院 海口 570228)

摘要：本文以国内有代表性的 CNKI，重庆维普和万方数据三家互联网学术期刊 Internet Academic Journal (IAJ) 为研究对象，探讨我国科学交流系统中，基于数字出版的机制创新问题。在介绍互联网主要环境、比较和说明三大 IAJ 基本特征、典型出版经营模式之后，从现行模式中对收录内容重复、买卖论文和非法期刊、标准建设问题、版权和利益分配管理等方面存在的问题进行分析；通过借鉴开放获取模式和研究实践中的成果，提出基于第三方机构的利益分配和版权管理模式的解决方案，从创新型科学研究服务和建设创新型发布平台的不同角度，讨论了 IAJ 今后的运行模式。

关键词：中国 出版模式 网络学术期刊 数字图书馆 标准 非法期刊

1 Introduction

Science information communication is one of the most important stakeholders in digital publishing. In practice the information carrier plays a vital role while the traditional science information communication theory is based on the understanding of carrier's function. For example, H. Menzel's "Information Communication Process" theory divides the process according to information carriers and A. Mikhailov's "Science Information Communication" theory defines books, journal literatures and other paper carriers as the foundation for constructing science information communication system. [1] Each theory emphasizes that information carriers are the possibilities for science information communication. Traditional science information communication system, which was independent in form of printed publications, has gradually adapted to the coexistence with digital publications such as electronic books, IAJs, etc.

Digital publishing refers to publications published using digital technology. As digital technology evolves with the development of computer hardware and software as well as communication technology, digital publishing has developed from early stage electronic publishing, desktop publishing, web publishing and network publishing to today's Internet publishing. Regardless the names, such publishing is a succeeding publications of books, journals, newspapers and magnetic medium publications including audio and video tapes, which is a brand-new cultural production and transmission mode. Supported by digital technology and carried by computer networks, digital publishing brings about a revolutionary transformation of traditional publishing forms and patterns. [2]

Of various forms of digital publications, IAJ which shares traditional printed journals properties is a major tool in science information communication system. In this research the typical CNKI IAJ is taken by us as the main form of digital publishing to discuss mechanism innovation issues in China.

2 Status Quo of IAJs in China

2.1 *Network Environment of IAJs in China*

Two backbone networks, the China Education & Research Network (CERNET) and China Science & Technology Network (CSTNET) were constructed by the China state, [3] as shown in Figure 1 with a description on geographical topology. The two networks are now managed by the Ministry of Education and Ministry of Science and Technology separately. The construction, operation & maintenance and service update of the two networks are undertaken by leading institutes such as Tsinghua University and Chinese Academy of Sciences respectively. In 1996, the two networks were officially listed as two of four China backbone infrastructure networks by the China state council.

CERNET was finished construction in 1994 and is the first nationwide Internet backbone network in China. At present, the transmission speed of CERNET's main stream is up to 2.5 – 10Gbps and that of its local substream is up to 155Mbps – 2.5Gbps. The network covers more than 200 cities of 32 state provinces including autonomous regions and Hong Kong special administrative region. It physically possesses over 30,000 km optical fiber with independent international outreaching throughput exceeding 5G. Ten regional centers and 38 provincial nodes are in operation with one central network center located at Tsinghua University, Beijing. The giant network also links more than 2,000 universities, educational institutions and scientific research units serving over 20 million users, which becomes a fundamental and indispensable educational information platform in China. [4]

CSTNET was established in 1989 as a scientific research network of Chinese Academy of Sciences and national public network. The transmission speed up of CSTNET's main trunk is up to 2.5 Gbps and that of its local substream is up to 155Mbps-2.5Gbps. The inter-network data exchange rate between CERNET and CSTNET is up to 2Gbps while CSTNET's international outreaching throughput exceeds 4.5G. Similar to CERNET, the network also covers 30 provinces, autonomous regions and Chinese Taiwan. The domestic backbone network is composed of 13 distributed city sub-centers including Beijing, Changchun, Shenyang, Shanghai, Guangzhou, Chengdu and Lanzhou, making itself another basic scientific information platform in China. [5]

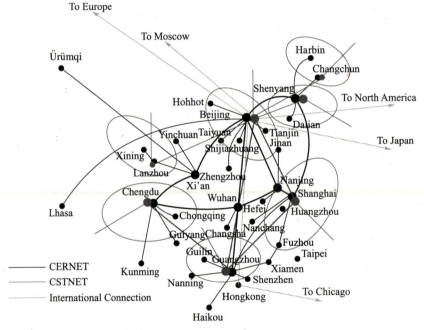

Figure 1   Topology of CERNET and CSTNET

2.2 *Development of IAJs in China*

In 1989, Chongqing VIP issued the earliest academic digital journal in China in the form of floppy disk. In 1996, a large-scale integrated Chinese academic Journal (CD Edition) was developed by China Academic Journals Electronic Publishing House (CAJEPH) which marks the beginning of journal digital publishing in China. In 1997, WFD & company established the first technology information World Wide Web (WWW) website. The company focused on the association between the digital publishing and Internet. In June 1998, Chinese Academic Journal (CD Edition) was officially listed on the web. The Chinese academic Journal Full-Text Database marks an important milestone and initiates a new era of IAJ publishing in China.

The National Knowledge Infrastructure and its application such as knowledge based economy, as the fourth main infrastructure after energy, transportation and telecommunication, were identified and agreed in different degree by America, Britain and other developed countries governments. Increasing attention has also been paid to China National Knowledge Infrastructure (CNKI) in China. Under the leadership of the Ministry of Education (MOE), the Ministry of Science and Technology (MST), General Administration of Press and Publication (GAPP) and other ministries or commissions of China, relying on the support from libraries, information service centers and almost all Chinese academic journal editorial boards (CAJEB), Tong Fang Knowledge & Network Technology Co. Ltd. (TKNT) has developed CNKI as a national development project with several Internet editions, which promotes Chinese IAJs to an advanced level in terms of literature volume and data collecting technologies.

The three IAJs — VIP, CNKI (TKNT) and WFD — so far have effectively collected printed journals into respective electronic journal databases by cooperating with printed journal editorial boards. These databases are formal and serialised Internet publications with electronic journal serial numbers approved by the GAPP. Every CAJEB is administrated by competent departments under one of the ministries or commissions under the China State Council which disburse funds to pay editorial staff's salaries and daily operation expenditures. In order to protect intellectual property right, coordinated by the GAPP and the ministries and commissions, the three organizations established copyright monitoring systems with various types of CAJEBs to mutually reuse resources between databases, which forms the basic science information communication mode based on Chinese IAJs as shown in Figure 2.

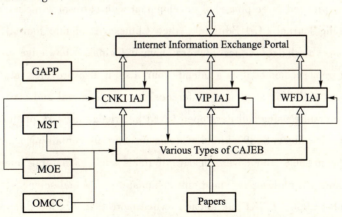

Figure 2   IAJ science information communication modes

2.3   *Status Quo of Construction of Chinese IAJ Literature Database*

After more than 20 years development, Chinese IAJ literature database market has been divided and shared by VIP, CNKI and WFD with other small-sized specialized literature databases. China now owns totally 9,468 kinds of Chinese journals.

VIP's Chinese scientific and technical journals full-text database collects more than 20 million published papers in over 8,000 kinds of domestic journals, which are divided into eight special areas: social sciences, natural sciences, engineering technology, agricultural science, medicine and hygiene, economy and management, educational science, and library and information science. It is also an important strategic partner of Google, and one of the largest cooperative Chinese content websites of Google Scholar. However, the website itself does not present any English interface, as shown in Table 1.

Table 1. Internet database of three major Chinese academic journals

Content	VIP database	CNKI database	WFD database
IAJ site	http://www.cqvip.com/	http://www.edu.cnki.net	http://www.wanfangdata.com.cn/Default.aspx
IAJ mirror site	http://vip.hbdlib.cn/	http://cnki2.lib.whu.edu.cn/kns50/index.aspx	http://g.wanfangdata.com.cn/Default.aspx
Site location	Chongqing	Beijing	Beijing
Product	CSTNET non-backbone network node	CERNET backbone network node	CSTNET backbone network node
Date	1989—	1994—	1997—
forms	Web version Mirror version CD-ROM version	Web version Mirror version CD-ROM version	Web version Mirror version CD-ROM version

CNKI has experienced three phases of development with corresponding name changes: earlier Chinese Academic Journal (CD Edition), then Chinese Academic Journal Network and currently a brand new knowledge service platform named China's Knowledge Resources Database (CKRD). Apart from accommodating academic journals, it also provides Internet publishing for a series of databases including academic conference papers, doctoral and master's theses, newspapers and other literature using self-developed CNKI knowledge network platform for management and data retrieval. It collects 8,893 kinds of domestic journals containing more than 23.45 million of full-text documents, and covers nearly all fields such as natural sciences, engineering technology, agriculture, philosophy, medicine, humanities, social sciences, etc, as shown in Table 1. By October 2006, CNKI had already owned more than 17,000 different customers covering universities, research institutions and government organizations. It is also subscribed and frequently used by university libraries outside China such as Harvard University library and Oxford University DL, and large-scale public libraries like National DL of Singapore. [6] CNKI is therefore identified as one of the most representative IAJs in China.

WFD's Chinese digital journal group specialized in eight categories with more than 100 subitems: philosophy, politics and law, social sciences, economy and finance, education, science, culture and art, fundamental sciences, medicine and hygiene, agricultural science and industrial technology. It includes 6,065 kinds of domestic journals and more than 12.9 million papers of full-text literature. The website provides user-friendly features such as an English interface while its Chinese journals can be easily linked to various classified English subjects. However, only the Chinese interface provides the list of all journal names.

2.4 *Publishing and Operation Mode of CNKI IAJ*

The central website and eight regional exchange service centers of CNKI IAJ are established and maintained by TKNT. Figure 3 presents the topology framework and connection methods. [7] The website has been supported by two completely identical central sites established at CERNET and China Broadband Network (CHINANET), separately. It provides services through "resource database" and "knowledge database". It also provides jointly-constructed resources and shared knowledge information. Each central website updates knowledge resources, full-text service for CNKI Knowledge Network Management Service Centers and CNKI Mirror sites in different cities through KNS5.0 (Knowledge Network Service 5.0) daily. Meanwhile, the website includes Internet retrieval service for institutions and individuals using CNKI knowledge resource and online digital submission service.

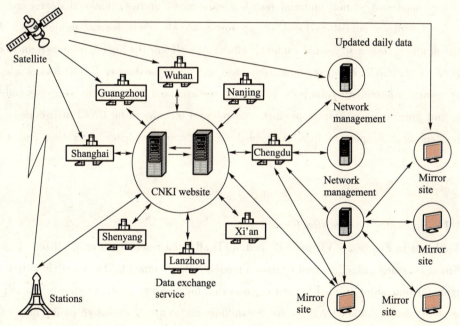

Figure 3   Topology framework of CNKI IAJ

CNKI IAJ has the following operation modes: professional customers such as universities, research institutions, public libraries, government, enterprises, secondary and primary schools purchase services by database wholesale or remote packaged database installation. The databases then established on local servers in the form of mirror sites provide service for local area network users. The subscription fee is charged per network flow, individual reader purchase and account download. The users can pay by dedicated CNKI cards, normal bank cards or pre-paid telecommunication cards. The organization also gets revenue from paid information and analysis, advertising and government support.

2.5 *CNKI IAJ's Publishing Institutions and Work Division*

TKNT, CAJEPH and Tsinghua Tongfang Optical Disc Co. Ltd. (TTOD) have worked together to deliver the CNKI project. Figure 4 shows the work division undertaken by different partners for CNKI's publishing and issuing. [8]

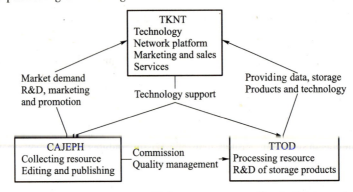

Figure 4   CNKI IAJ's publishing institutions and work division

For CNKI editing, publishing and journal distribution, CAJEPH is responsible for contacting various academic journal editorial boards, university libraries, national degree authorities and conference paper publishers to obtain approvals for electronic journal publication, discuss potential product, optimize journal content, etc. CAJEPH has the high-level copyright to editing all journal parts, CNKI full-text journal database and other databases; TTOD makes use of the content resources provided by the press to conduct research and development, improve publishing process and provide online storage products and relevant techniques for CNKI distribution; TKNT provides technical support to network publishing platform, promotes marketing and monitors sales.

3   Existing Problems of Chinese IAJs and Analysis

3.1 *Duplicated Construction Issues*

As shown in Figure 2, VIP, CNKI and WFD all fetch resources from CAJEBs. Depending on different company guidelines and operation models, they contact CAJEBs individually to obtain copyrights for publishing printed journal resources on the Internet, without known by each other. On the other hand, neither CAJEBs nor the authors are aware of exclusive policy on duplicated publishing of journals and publications, which increase the possibility that more than one IAJ publishes the journal and publication. The worse scenario is the same journal can be published simultaneously by three IAJs in this case, which causes resource repetition among the three IAJs. Investigating all printed journals collected by the three IAJs by the end of 2006, a paper[9] analyses the repetition through ISSN, journal names and serial numbers. It points out that 4,413 kinds of printed journals are collected at the same time by all the three IAJs, taking up 57%, 71% and 79% of the total journals of CNKI, VIP and WFD, respectively. Among the rest, 561,849 and 123 kinds of printed journals are collected at the same time by CNKI and VIP, CNKI and WFD, VIP and WFD, respectively. For journals which are collected only by one of the three IAJs, CNKI, VIP or WFD, the figures are 1,869, 1,119 and 170, respectively, as shown in Figure 5.

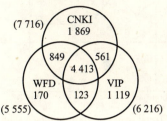

Figure 5   Repetition of resources among CNKI, VIP and WFD

The duplicated resource construction indicates that every IAJ focuses on its own business scope under different leadership or relevant superior department. There is no mutually agreed planning or overall strategy, leading to waste in journal producing, purchasing and use. From printed journals to electronic ones, each IAJ separately carries out editing, unpacking, scanning, checking and indexing, which directly causes duplicated production and waste in human resource, raw material and finance. The problem is that there are many duplicated journals as well as exclusively collected ones simultaneously. With limited funds, universitie and college libraries as the main purchasers have to spend a big amount to purchase electronic journals with a repetition rate over 50%. And users have to use more than one IAJ to improve the scope coverage which makes their burdens heavier.

3.2   *Paper "Buy and Sell" and Illegal Academic Journal Issues*

Occasionally, you may notice advertisements for buying and selling on university campus, Bulletin Board System (BBS) and instant messaging groups. Some occupations, e. g. lecturer, scientific researcher, PhD student, do receive random inquire on journal buying. Without a law over cyberspace, lawbreakers can do illegal paper dealings through the Internet. Since they follow an attractive strategy that papers can be written before money is paid and can guarantee the publishing once submitted, someone would buy "the product" and those papers are never peer-reviewed or with any academic standards. The illegal academic journal producers charge expensive fees to gain enormous profits. The issue also becomes very common among undergraduates and postgraduates. The changes in searching "paper ghostwriting" in 2008 can be observed by Google Trends, as shown in Figure 6.

The map indicates that ghost written papers increased in the first half year when undergraduates, postgraduates and doctoral students were preparing for thesis/dissertation defenses, and the demand for ghost written papers decreased sharply after they graduated. The buyers are from research institutions including universities and colleges and the papers are mainly published in illegal academic journals. On average, one illegal journal publishes 169 papers per issue. From the distribution of original authors of the 169 papers, universities and colleges are the "disaster areas" which are deceived both actively and passively. The affiliation types of these first authors are shown in Figure 6. Many of them are from key Chinese universities and colleges, as shown in Figure 7.

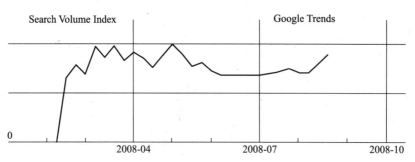

Figure 6   Search Trend map of "ghost written" Chinese journal papers

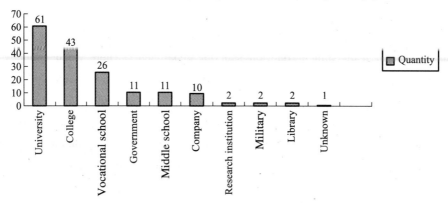

Figure 7   Statistical data on distribution of original authors

The rapid development of the Internet and communication technology has boosted paper buy and sell business, and accelerated illegal journal publishing process. A collection of anonymous users is available behind Internet shelter, and the businesses are conducted in a hidden way. Advertisements and related links of paper selling and buying are reachable pervasively over the Internet (as shown in Figure 8, with dotted line). To date, China has neither formed a strict article responsibility check system nor popularized anti-plagiarism detection software and application. The GAPP although has taken a series of measures to deal with the problems (eg., it organizes stringent activities to check journals every year) published an updating list of the illegal academic journals and punished a group of lawbreakers. These measures fail to put an end or even a temporary stop of the business. Therefore, we urge major search engines and websites to practically undertake their social responsibilities to enhance the capabilities of distinguishing between original papers and plagiarized ones for all journal publishers, to crack down or ban paper selling and buying advertisement, and to construct complete and efficient Chinese IAJ platforms.

3.3   IAJ XML Standard Problems

The standardization degree in current digital publishing industry in China is not high enough. Compared with those in developed countries, domestic digital publishing industry is far behind in terms of process establishment and implementation standards. China lacks an overall standardized protocol and even fails to establish the most basic standard system architecture, though we have introduced a variety of international standards for printing. Moreover, despite the improvement in establishment process for publication format, information-oriented publication and publication logistics, there is still some inefficiency. For example, for the publication format, comparatively systematic standards have been established only for printed books and journals, but not for audio, video products and electronic publications. Not to mention the online digital publications, the standards for the format are still to be determined and under hot debate. According to the requirements of press and publishing industry in the "11th China National Development Five-Year Plan", the research on press and publishing standard system has been listed as a key task of publishing science research. China Institute of Publishing Science has undertaken the task under the approval of the MST and has completed proving of concept by 2008. Besides, researches for Network Publishing Standards, Classified Standards for Publication Marketing and Normative Standards for Publication Logistics Procedure have already been initiated and will be finished in two to three years. [10]

The indexing resources for full-text VIP, CNKI and WFD index are text documents such as Microsoft Word documents received from CAJEBs or text documents obtained after scanning and OCR processing. The documents for displaying and download are in PDF format (with only CNKI has a unique CAJ format). When producing bibliographic information such as full-text indexes, authors, titles, affiliations, references, etc, no matter the process is conducted manually or assisted by software with manual inspection, the IAJs all choose to use different internal formats and never share with each other. Full-text reading is only limited to personal computers with PDF compatible software like Adobe Reader. Even the basic bibliographic information is only available to Internet Explorer (IE) based browsers, but does not support other browsers such as Firefox, Google Chrome or mobile Linux based browsers.

The three IAJs have experienced transition and expansion periods in aspects of scale & category collection, technical support and sales income, and have stepped into a steady development stage. How to make use of the existing successful experience in China and foreign countries to further improve and expend Chinese IAJ construction based on Extensible Markup Language (XML) along with Hypertext Markup Language (HTML) as the core, is a common problem faced by all three IAJs.

3.4 *IAJ Management and Relevant Problems*

IAJs mainly obtain their information resources from CAJEBs which have paper copyrights with control. Economic benefits are distributed only between IAJs and CAJEBs, and there is no systematic restriction or supervision mechanism to guarantee authors' financial benefits. Another problem closely related to copyright problem is that the financial benefits produced by the same paper that is published by several IAJs cannot be effectively returned to the original author and CAJEB.

According to relevant national policy, after peer review and formal collection by CAJEB before publishing, CAJEBs often charge a certain amount of money from authors in the name of page fee, publishing fee or manuscript review fee (generally called publishing fee below). IAJs completely adopt a market-oriented operation and charge libraries and information institutions in universities, research institutes, enterprises, public institutions and individuals in a variety of ways including Internet database packages, mirror site purchase, network flow, etc. After several years of operation, these IAJs show that each one operates in a reasonable status and gets a certain amount of profit annually which keeps increasing. Although IAJs such as CNKI pay copyright royalties to CAJEBs like copyright usage fees for collected articles. As a matter of fact, CAJEBs seldom provide any payment to authors. [11]

As a responsible or correspondent author of a paper, he/she has to pay a certain amount of money not only at the time of publishing, but also when reading. The subscription fee is although usually paid by the libraries or organization they work for. CAJEBs collect both of publishing fees from authors and copyright usage fees from IAJs. Every IAJ makes full use authors' academic efforts, while CAJEBs gain good financial profits, create excellent social benefit, and boost science information communication. However, concerning the profit distribution among authors, CAJEBs and IAJs is obviously unfair and improper, especially from author perspective.

4　IAJ Science Information Communication Mode based on TPA

4.1　Improvement of IAJ Communication Mode

From the view of economic scale, CNKI now gets the best enterprise benefit among the three IAJs. In 2005, its sales revenue was RMB 140 million (USD 21.5 million) with a net profit of RMB 26 million (USD 4 million), in which the overseas sales amount was more than RMB 32 million (USD 4.9 million). Its fixed assets valued RMB 190 million (USD 29.2 million) after years of accumulation. WFD ranked second and its sales revenue in 2005 was nearly RMB 200 million (USD 30.7 million) with a slightly lower net profit when compared to CNKI. Since 2003, VIP has had a steady average annual sales nearly RMB 30 million (USD 4.6 million) with around RMB 1 million (USD 0.15 million) net profit. In order to maximize the enterprise benefit, the principle of "survive the fittest" is inevitable. Under the competition mechanism of market-oriented economy, enterprises merge, combination or acquisition are normal economic activities. If WFD and VIP, both of whose net profit are relatively small and are all managed by MST, can be merged to a large-scale VIP+WFD IAJ enterprise, the new enterprise may achieve the economic benefit by size-effect which is unavailable in current state. The new combined enterprise would gather resources and techniques to compete with CNKI, and then it could also provide better services for the science information community while creating a favorable condition for its own development.

Chinese open access (OA) IAJs have had some achievements after years of construction. Science Paper Online is a good example which has included 65 kinds of OA journals. Among Chinese OA IAJs, four of them have already been indexed by Directory of Open Access Journal (DOAJ). However, the current scale cannot meet the need of Internet-based science information communications. Because domestic OA IAJs are not popular and low in influence, scientific researchers tend to submit to CAJEBs instead of OA IAJs although the publication cycles are relatively long. For example the IAJs like CNKI aimed to provide a fast track service usual cannot make a paper available online up to 2—4 months after the printed paper version. In this regard, it could be a wise model that third-party agencies finance independent OA IAJs and cooperate with CAJEBs. By learning from the operation experience of OA journals from foreign successful publishers, e. g. , Open Choice, depending on authors' objectives and financial status, after peer review approved by a CAJEB, OA IAJ fast publishing could be realized for scientific research papers. However, the authors have to pay a relatively higher fee to OA IAJs and CAJEBs in this condition. Certainly, existing IAJs including CNKI could·provide real-time fast publishing while offering other integrated services. We suggest using an improved IAJ communication mode as shown in Figure 8.

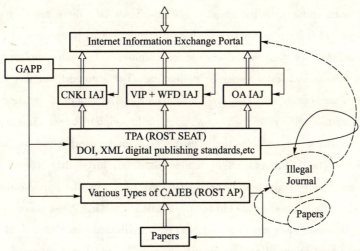

Figure 8   IAJ science information communication mode based on TPA

In this improved science information communication mode based on IAJ, the TPA is an independent, fair and non-profit organization under the leadership of GAPP. The GAPP drafts policies and instructions, conducts coordination, produces publishing contents, XML standards, copyright management and profit distribution, and supervises illegal journals. The TPA then organizes coordinates, supervises and directs the science information and it also plays a core role to improve existing science information communication mode. The major responsibilities include:

• To properly distribute journal resources among IAJs and avoid repeated collection of CAJEB resources.

• To establish relevant XML standard for IAJ for paper submission, text editing and IAJs' publishing.

• To accelerate anti-plagiarism software & application development and restrict the further spread of paper dealing activates as well as illegal journals.

Although from the very beginning the three IAJs were supported by departments and commissions of the government, they are still substantially non-state-owned IT enterprises taking sole responsibility for profits or losses. Their main commercial products are journals directed by GAPP. In order to avoid repeated journal resources collection, one of the main tasks of a third-party agency is to coordinate and allocate journal resources according to different IAJs' expertise. For journals containing interdisciplinary subjects, mathematics and computer science which may serve as tools for other subjects, university journals and comprehensive journal resources, certain degree of repeat can be helpful. For example, the subscriber can find direct academic information and relevant information within one IAJ with an improved service quality like connection speed, cost-effectiveness and user experience.

In 2007, in order to facilitate scientific researchers and IJ publishers' demand for a better XML capability, Microsoft provided an NLM DTD compatible add-in plugin[12] for Word so the users can produce XML compatible documents when using normal Word documents. The implementation makes Word documents consistent with XML standard at any stage which is convenient for publishing, storing and knowledge transfer. For the issue that there are so many CAJEBs in China while the three IAJs have distinctive pushing methods, third-party agencies should agree to establish a common XML standard for software specifications, submission implementation, format conversion and IAJ historical data resources collection. The standard enables flexible editing, paper transfer and data sharing and also lays the foundation IAJ mobile computing applications.

The paper "buy and sell" is an indirect outcome of incomplete science information communication platform,[13] which also reflects that China should make more efforts on academic ethics system construction. The IAJ management mode based on thirty-party agency should be improved, while current anti-plagiarism system (ROST AP) [14] can be applied and further developed to enhance the capabilities for all kinds of journals. The GAPP has taken a series of measures to deal with the issue. For example, it organizes dedicated professionals checking journals every year and has listed online illegal academic journals[15] to alert a group of lawbreakers and the public. However, these measures fail to put an end to paper dealing. We suggest third-party agency, together with academic institute, research related websites and search engines form an "Ally for Proper Academic Network", and jointly undertake the social responsibility for developing academic journals (ROST SEAT) [16] and cracking down the business. Law policies may be produced by organizations such as Chinese Law on Academic Norms and Global Academic Ethics to further control illegal journals.

4.2 *IAJ Copyright Management Mode Based on TPA*

The copyrights of various resources collected by IAJs are usually owned by domestic CAJEBs. IAJs must obtain rights from owners so as to legally publish these printed academic papers in IAJs.

Collective copyright management means that copyright owners including neighboring right owners authorize collective copyright management organization to manage their rights. Such an organization supervises the use of the work , negotiates the conditions of use with potential users, produces licenses, collects subscription fees and distributes the fees among copyright owners. [17] The academic paper copyright management can be regarded as one kind of CAJEBs-based collective copyright management. It facilitates flexible copyright management and realizes legal Internet variety publishing, e. g. , the same paper can be published by several publishers. It also increases science information communication channels, intensifies competition for service quality and embodies copyright collective management advantages.

The core idea of the third-party copyright management mode is that authors possess copyrights but entrust third-party copyright management organization to manage their paper ownerships and related issues. The organization gives an exclusive publishing license to CAJEB: during a certain period, other publishers are not allowed to publish the papers in any form (printed or online edition, etc), and the length of period can be changed according to factors such as publication type. The third-party copyright management organization is the only legal copyright owner of all kinds of papers (printed or online edition, etc) in terms of publishing, who takes charge of copyright management (including licenses, conditions and supervision), adjusts paper publishing priorities at CAJEBs and IAJs, and assists to establish the beneficiary payment mode of the TPA. Each IAJ must contact third-party copyright management organization to obtain a license for Internet publishing.

4.3 Third-party-based Beneficiary Payment Mode in IAJ

The essence of beneficiary payment mode is that, beneficiaries jointly pay the publishing fees for scientific research efforts and reward contributed authors. Based on beneficiary payment mode,[18] a third-party-based beneficiary payment mode has been moved forward. The following aspects are applied to boost science information communication system on both CAJEBs and IAJs:

(1) Determination of beneficiaries and beneficial degree: Authors, subscribers and IAJs are beneficiaries of published papers. For the subscribers' perspective, they may get information needed from IAJ websites directly or obtain the information from IAJ citation analysis platforms. Published papers from authors are the core resource and foundation for IAJ operations which attract users, so IAJ and authors are also beneficiaries.

(2) Payment subjects and objects: The subjects of payment are beneficiaries and objects of payment are authors and CAJEBs in the science information domain. Printed journals determine the submitted papers' academic value and claim publishing rights of authors' scientific research results. Authors first pay publication fees to CAJEB. When subscribers publish their own scientific research papers with references, the appreciation is expressed by paying the authors who are cited in references a certain amount of money. It is seen as a tribute to others' scientific research efforts and is a necessity for establishing a people-oriented scientific research environment. The use of scientific research results by enterprise customers is seldom embodied in published papers and it is hard to determine such kind of use from references. IAJs should adopt a different charging tariff for those subscribers, properly raise the use price and promote science information communication mechanisms from which they benefit more. Although IAJs do not obtain copyrights directly from authors, the fact is that authors provide the core contents. IAJs can trust CAJEBs or use other methods to manage copyrights, but it is better to bypass CAJEBs and pay authors directly to reduce administration cost.

(3) Subscription fees distribution: Authors should pay publication fees to journal editorial boards and IAJs. The fees include two parts: manuscript review fee which should not be overcharged as many potential authors may withdraw; the page processing fee which is paid after peer review, paper revision and acceptance notification. A public credible independent third-party

agency is needed to collect basic IAJ use fees from universities and colleges, research institutes, enterprises and government based on the date of use fetched from mirror sites, Internet database packing and data flow. It also collects a certain amount of use fees from authors or subscribers who cite others' literature accordingly. The payment of operations, maintenance, new technology development and some commercial profit to IAJs are based on publication contents, paper download and reference count.

The beneficiary payment mode introduction based on TPA requires a longer term follow-up and should experience academic value verification. As for all contributors, there should be a fair benefit distribution mechanism to encourage authors and at the same time to guarantee the financial interests and brand effects for publishing institutions including IAJs and CAJEBs so that a healthy operation can be maintained. We suggest that a fair, credible and independent TPA accelerate this progress to boost Internet-based science information communication. The TPA also prevents authors from becoming the vulnerable group in the chain. Please refer to Figure 9 for the beneficiary pay mode.

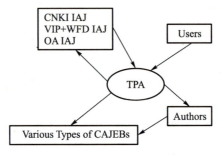

Figure 9   Beneficiary payment mode of TPA

5   Conclusion

Building Chinese Internet academic journals for science information communication based on the TPA is a systematic engineering work, for which the advance in science and technology must be accelerated through system innovation. To deepen the technological system reform and all supporting system reforms, a vigorous system model that facilitates the innovation progress should be adopted to increase productivity, embody Internet-based journals with Chinese characteristics, and conform to the technological development rule.

By learning the achievements of various Chinese IAJs and Chinese OA journal practice, several issues and operation models for digital publishing has been discussed. The benefit distribution and copyright management mode based on the TPA is proposed and studied. The future IAJs operation mode is also discussed from the view of innovative scientific research service and platform construction obstacles.

References

[1] Xu, Lifang. Digital Information Communication. Wuhan University Press, 2008. Wuhan.

[2] Willinsk, John. Proposing Knowledge Exchange Model for Scholarly Publishing. Current

Issues in Education, Vol. 3, No. 6. Available at: http://cie. asu. edu/volume3/number6/ (accessed September 18,2009).

[3] Shen, XX., Zheng, Z., Shen, C.. (2008), A Review of the Major Projects Constituting the China Academic Digital Library. The Electronic Library, Vol. 26, No. 1: 39–51.

[4] CERNET Network Center . CERNET Brief Introduction, 2008. Accessed December 12, 2009. Available at: http://www. edu. cn/cernet_jian_jie_1327/20060323/t20060323_91159. shtml.

[5] CSTNET Network Center. About CSTNET, 2008. Accessed December 12, 2009. Available at: http://www. cstnet. net. cn/about. jsp? Type = zxgk .

[6] Wang, Jiankan. Web Publishing Resources Out of a Possible Integration of the Road. China Culture Daily, October 23, 2006.

[7] CNKI. CNKI Topology for Database Exchange Service Centre. Accessed August 22, 2009. Available at: http://www. dl. cnki. ne/tgycnki/daobao/cnkidaobao4/daobao2–5. htm.

[8] CNKI. About CNKI. Accessed August 22, 2009. Available at: http://www. global. cnki. net/Grid20/Aboutus/Aboutus. htm.

[9] Soichi, Tokizane. Electronic Journal Publications in China. Journal of Information Processing and Management, 2007, Vol. 50, No. 1: 2–10.

[10] Hao, Z., et al. 2006—2007 Interpretation for Annual Report on Publishing Industry in China. China Books Press, 2007. Beijing.

[11] Chen, Shangzhi. On Copyright Protection of Journal. Journal of Zhejiang Police College, 2006, Vol. 8, No. 2: 106–8.

[12] Microsoft. Article Authoring Add-in for Microsoft Office Word. Accessed August 12, 2009. Available at: http://www. microsft. com/downloads/details. aspx? FamilyId = 09C55527–0759–4D6D–AE02–51E90131997E&displaylang = en.

[13] Shi, Guojin. On the Modern Science and the Exchange of Structure and Function of Innovation. Science and Technology Progress and Policy, 2005, Vol. 22, No. 1: 14–8.

[14] Shen, Yang, et al. Research of Anti-Plagiarism Monitoring System Model. Wuhan University Journal of Natural Sciences, 2007, Vol. 12, No. 5: 1202–9.

[15] GAPP. Illegal Journals on the List of Notification. Accessed September 12, 2009. Available at: http://218. 7. 112. 124/ Article_Show. asp? ArticleID = 627.

[16] Shen, Yang, et al. Introducing a Metadata Earch Engine – ROST SEAT. Accessed September 12, 2009. Available at: http://hi. baidu. com/whusoft/blog/item/174090168e3b771c972b432e. html.

[17] Wang, Caijie. Intellectual Property Right of Electronic Periodical in China. Shanxi Library Journal, 2007, Vol. 23, No. 1: 3–6.

[18] Ohta, T., Hayashi, K.. Innovation-oriented Publication System. Journal of Information Processing and Management, 2005, Vol. 48, No. 11: 717–22.

Authors

234

Xiangxing Shen is a professor, LIS Experimental Teaching Center, School of Information Management at Wuhan University, Wuhan, China. His research interests include digital library and experimental technology. E-mail: x. shen@ whu. edu. cn.

Dr. Xiangdong Li is an associate professor, School of Information Management at Wuhan University, Wuhan, China.

Yuan Yang is a master candidate of School of Information Management at Wuhan University, Wuhan, China.

Guanxiang Yan is an associate professor, LIS Experimental Teaching Center, School of Information Management at Wuhan University, Wuhan, China.

Chong Shen is a professor, College of Information Science & Technology at Hainan University, Haikou, China.

作者简介

沈祥兴，武汉大学信息管理学院教授，LIS 实验教学中心主任。

李向东，武汉大学信息管理学院副教授。

扬漾，武汉大学信息管理学院硕士研究生。

严冠湘，高级工程师，理学学士，武汉大学信息管理学院实验中心副主任。

沈重，教授，海南大学信息科学与技术学院。

新型学术信息交流模式的尝试

李霄

（武汉大学信息管理学院　武汉　430072）

摘要：在数字技术和网络技术发展的背景下，"中国科技论文在线"以其快捷、公开、免费的特点，对新型学术交流模式进行了有效的尝试。它通过建立首发平台、学报预印文库和学者专栏等积累了大量科技学术论文资源，并尝试出版 OA 期刊，为广大学者提供学术信息交流的平台。本文根据 2003 至 2008 年的相关统计数据和相关支柱栏目的发展情况，审视了文库在数量增长和质量控制方面所取得的成就，肯定了在线发表与开放出版的新型交流模式的尝试。

关键词：科技论文　在线发表　学术交流

New Attempts in Scholarly Information Communication

Li Xiao

（School of Information Management，Wuhan University，Wuhan，430072）

Abstract：China's scientific and technical papers online is an attempt of scholarly communication under the background that the digital technology and internet technology develop fast，having the trait like quick，openness，no charge．It accumulates a good amount of academic resources by offering a fast and real time platform，library of pre-printed，scholars column and trying to publish an OA periodical．The paper examines the columns and the development of the platform during 2003 to 2008 and talks about its achievements in online publishing．

Keywords：Scientific paper　Online publishing　Scholarly communication

1　时代背景

在数字技术和网络技术发展的背景下，全球的学术信息交流正在实现从基于印刷出版体系的传统型交流模型向数字网络的现代型交流模型转变。尤其西方开放存取运动的兴起，各国学术界都在努力为实现在线数字科技文献资料免费和快速使用，排除价格和许可两方面的障碍，使科技资源在全世界范围内自由充分的传播和利用。在中国虽然没有发生"学术期刊价格危机"，但传统学术出版生产力严重滞后于目前高速增长的学术信息交流需求，存在出版周期过长、学术交流不畅的问题，导致最新的研究成果无法及时转化为科技生产力，造成学术信息供需失衡。2004 年，中国科学院和中国自然科学基金签署了

《开放存取柏林宣言》,[1] 正式加入了这项科技信息快速共享的全球性运动, 与世界各国共同建立一种基于网络的学术无障碍交流体系。

"中国科技论文在线"是经教育部批准, 由教育部科技发展中心主办的科技论文网站。它于 2003 年 10 月 15 日开通运行, 旨在搭建一个论文发表的平台, 能够使新的科技成果和新的学术思想得到及时的交流, 同时又有效地防止论文在发表过程中的种种学风不正行为的发生, 保护作者的知识产权。经过 5 年多的运行, "科技论文在线"由最初较为单一的论文发表平台逐渐发展成集论文首发平台、高校学报预印本数据库、国内优秀学者自存档和其他类型的开放存取数据库于一体的综合型学术仓储。它是中国最早的一批的真正意义上的开放电子印本文库之一, 加上独一无二的官方背景, 致使它的发展远远快于国内其他同类文库。

2 文库结构

"中国科技论文在线"的文库资源主要来自"论文首发平台"、"学者专栏"和"科技期刊" 3 个栏目, 它们分别涵盖了国内最新的学术论文、国内优秀学者代表成果, 和近几年的高校学报刊载论文, 成为"中国科技论文在线"最重要的核心栏目, 为丰富网站的文库藏量提供数量保证。

2.1 论文首发平台

论文首发平台是网站资源库的原始积累, 自开通以来一直为用户提供在线快速发表学术论文的服务。注册用户只要根据注册—登陆—呈递—待审—打印刊载证明的发表流程, 一周内就可完成论文的发表。根据网站提供的相关数据显示, 论文的发表数量和涉及的学科数量都呈现逐年递增的趋势。如表 1 所示, 截至 2008 年 12 月 31 日, 该平台共发表28 073篇论文, 日发表量从 2003 年日平均发表不足 2 篇增长到 2008 年日平均发表 29 篇。所涉及的学科共 42 个, 其中 38 个属于自然科学类, 4 个属于社会科学类。在所有的学科中, 论文发表量过千的有 11 个学科。数量最多的几个是电子通信与自动控制技术 (3 485篇)、计算机科学技术 (2 848 篇), 和管理学 (1 804 篇), 论文数量最少的有天文学 (32 篇)、核科学技术 (53 篇)。这反映了学术界对网络发表的认知度和信任度逐渐增加。

表 1 首发平台发表论文统计

年份	2003 年	2004 年	2005 年	2006 年	2007 年	2008 年	总计
论文	116	1 304	3 405	5 644	7 051	10 553	28 073
作者	84	353	989	1 826	1 827	1 794	6 873
学科	20	39	41	41	42	42	\

表 2 作者学历背景统计

作者学历	2003 年	2004 年	2005 年	2006 年	2007 年	2008 年	总计
博士或博士在读	46	174	354	383	426	426	1 809
硕士 (或硕士在读)	32	139	509	1 155	1 235	1 150	4 220
本科 (或本科在读)	4	38	121	280	153	203	799
其他	2	2	5	8	13	15	45

网站对已发表论文的作者的学历情况进行统计。从表 2 中的数据可看出，主要的作者群中大多高等学历，其中硕士（或在读）占 62%。从增长趋势来看，网站在开通头两年以博士学历的作者居多，从 2005 年起，硕士学历的发表者迅速增长，这与网站的宣传和国内部分高校认可在校研究生在该网站发表论文为毕业达标的相关文件有关。

2.2 学者专栏

网站除了为终端用户提供发表平台，也为国内的学者打开了自我宣传和相互学习的窗口。"优秀学者"和"学者自荐"就是该网站颇具特色的两个学者专栏。

"优秀学者"是为我国优秀学者免费建立的个人学术专栏。网站成立初期就开设此专栏，旨在介绍国内优秀学者的主要学术成就，为年轻学者了解本学科的优秀学者及其研究方向提供指导。学者们在属于各自的栏目中可以提供 10 多个最具代表性的研究成果链接，并可随时更新。[2]根据网站工作人员介绍，优秀学者的基本遴选条件是候选人具备教授、博导以上的专业技术职务，在各自领域内已取得较高的学术建树，成果显著，并具有较高的学术头衔，如中国科学院院士、中国工程院院士、长江学者、国家"973"计划首席科学家、"863"项目负责人等。人数没有上限，不存在淘汰机制。优秀学者的数量每年都有所增长，据统计，截至 2008 年 12 月 31 日，已有 5 073 位优秀学者入户该专栏，53 139 篇优秀学者的研究论文收录在库。

"学者自荐"栏目于 2007 年 9 月 30 日开通，为致力于科学研究且已取得一定科研成绩的年轻学者免费建立个人学术专栏，为年轻学者展示、交流标志性成果和优秀论文提供一个便捷的网上平台，以提高年轻学者在学术界的影响力，促进学术交流与发展。学者们也可在相应的专栏中提供 10 个左右的具代表性的研究论文链接。据网站提供的数据，2008 年 12 月 31 日，自荐学者的人数已达 1 072 位，已收录论文 6 240 篇。这个数字还在继续增长。

2.3 预印本文库

"科技期刊"栏目开设于 2005 年底，集合了目前国内多所高校学报近几年刊发的论文预印本。该预印文库收录了 313 种学术期刊的论文预印本，其中 286 种来自 179 所高校主办的学报或学术期刊，27 种来自 10 多家学会及研究所。所有期刊按照名称、学科分类编排，既方便科研人员查阅又扩大了学报的影响，提高论文的引用率和期刊的影响因子。截至 2008 年 12 月 31 日，收录的文章总数高达 100 984 篇。这类集大多数国内高校学报的预印文库绝无仅有，很大程度上依赖教育部的官方背景。虽然国内 3 大期刊全文数据库中国知网、万方和维普已囊括了全国绝大多数的学术期刊，并且在所有高校和学术图书馆都可以进行信息检索，但学报预印本库更大意义上丰富了"科技论文在线"的数字资源，普及开放共享的理念传递。

3 质量控制

"中国科技论文在线"对首发论文采取的是"先发表后审评"的评定方式，经过一年多的发展，为了进一步加强文库的质量控制，于 2005 年增加同行评议的制度。

先发表后审评。据网站主编李志民介绍，根据文责自负的原则，只要作者所投论文遵守国家相关法律，为学术范围内的讨论，有一定学术水平，且符合"中国科技论文在线"的基本投稿要求，可在一周内发布。由于将论文较复杂的专业评审程序放在发表之后，因此与传统期刊相比，论文的发表速度要平均提前近一年的时间，比预印文库的发表也要快捷。[3] 此外，网站声明论文的著作权属作者本人所有，并且鼓励论文作者同时向其他学术刊物投稿，不影响作者在现存的评价体系中的任何利益诉求，从而实现最新的科技研究成果，以最快速度在国内交流，力求改变现在中国人研究出的成果争先恐后地拿到国外去评价的状况。

同行综合评议。这是该网站进行文章质量评审的工具。论文在线公布后3周内，由1—2名同行专家进行评审。评审专家主要来源于教育部博士点专项科研基金的评审专家库，该专家库由科技发展中心向国内近300所知名度较高的大学征集了57 000余名在职专家，其中教授占95%，另外部分来源于特聘专家，聘用专家全部是在该学科领域内较有影响的、具有较高学术地位的学者，并且每年都有一定程度的人员调整。

评审内容包含两部分，第一部分为论文审查的内容和综合评价意见，内容审查分别从论文题目、中文摘要、英文摘要、科学创新、研究方案、数据处理、文字表达、参考文献、学术价值9项进行打分，综合评价部分由专家对论文的整体情况进行打分，给出综合的评审意见。内容审查占总分值的40%，综合意见占总分值的60%。第二部分为专家详细修改意见，作者可根据专家的详细意见进行修改。在线评审系统根据专家打出的分值对应不同的星级，85分（包含85分）至100分对应5星，表示同行专家对该论文的综合评价为优秀；70分（包含70分）至85对应4星，表示同行专家对该论文的综合评价为良好；60分（包含60分）至70分对应3星，表示同行专家对该论文的综合评价为较好；40分（包含40分）至60分对应2星，表示同行专家对该论文的综合评价为一般；0分至40分对应1星，表示同行专家对该论文的综合评价为较差。[4]

同行评审制度加强了网站的首发论文的质量控制，增加了评审的透明度和公信度，赢得广大学者的支持和部分高校的认可。根据网站提供的相关数据，截至2008年12月31日，已有19 005篇论文被评定，占首发论文总量的58%。如表3所示，2005年至2008年已评定的论文中，3星以上的论文占大多数，其中4星论文所占比重最多，证明首发论文库的整体质量保持良好。然而，5星论文的减少和1星论文的增多也预示着最优等的论文流失和论文整体质量的下降。这种变化在2007年尤为明显，这多少与当年国内15所高校出台关于认可首发论文为研究生申请学位以及教职工工作计量有效地政策有关。同时，也充分说明在线发表论文的学术交流形式远没有获得主流学术界的认可，由此导致高质量的研究成果的流失。

表3　星级论文占评审论文的比重（单位：%）

星级	2005年	2006年	2007年	2008年
★	4	13	19	19
★★	13	20	19	18
★★★	14	15	20	20
★★★★	32	30	33	34
★★★★★	37	22	9	9

4 高校认可

随着广大科研人员逐渐认同网站的学术价值，越来越多的高校将在中国科技论文在线发表的论文认可为符合研究生毕业，或专业技术职务评聘要求的成果。在 2005 至 2008 年间，有 31 所高校颁布了关于在"中国科技论文在线"发表论文的认可文件。有 25 所高校认定为硕士研究生毕业合格成果，其中 16 所高校要求在线发表的论文等级必须达 3 星或以上为合格，1 所高校规定达 2 星以上，5 所高校不做星级要求。

根据教育部最近统计数据，目前我国有 1 983 所普通高等院校。因此，只有不到 2%的国内高校对网站首发平台表示一定程度的认可。虽然认可的学校在数量上十分有限，但是在已认可的 31 所高校中，有 12 所为教育部认定的全国"211 工程"学校。这无疑说明该网站已获得国内一些较有影响力的高校一定程度的认可，相信随着网站的发展，会获取更多高校的认可。但是，在线论文发表在本质上仍属非正式学术交流，它缺乏正式学术出版里对发表论文影响因子的评估机制和与作者利益相关的激励机制。因此，多数高校都将在线发表当作缓解研究生毕业成果问题的补充，而不会视其为替代正式出版的捷径。

5 延伸出版

随着首发论文不断增多以及评审制度的引入，产生越来越多高质量的论文，网站以在线论文进行同行专家评审后，以评出的优秀论文作为主要稿源，开办了两种连续出版物。一种是纸质的月刊《中国科技论文在线》（创刊于 2006 年 12 月），另一种是半月电子期刊《中国科技论文在线精品论文》（创刊于 2008 年 5 月）。这两种期刊均由教育部主管，教育部科技发展中心主办，具有一套严格的评审程序。前一种纸质期刊与其他学术期刊基本没有差别，审稿期 1~2 个月，并收取版面费 100 元/页，现已被国内外几种知名数据库收录，如中国知网、万方数据、波兰的《哥白尼索引》（IC）、美国《乌利希期刊指南》（UPD）、美国《化学文摘》（CA），以及美国《剑桥科学文摘》（CSA）。[5] 电子期刊实行完全免费，每期的论文将在网站中分学科全文展示，并可在中国科技论文在线网站中全文检索。

这两种期刊属于新创办的学术期刊，影响力与其他传统型学术期刊相比尚显不足。但它们的意义并非在此。这两种期刊是国内极少数真正意义上的开放存取学术期刊，它们和网站密不可分，网站为期刊提供稿源和全文检索服务，期刊为网站的学术价值争取合法的认可，使发表的论文能被引用，可谓相互补充，共同服务于学术信息交流活动。这种融合正式出版和非正式在线发表的交流模式，是学术交流处于变革时期，顺应潮流而诞生的产物，它给技术变革带来的传播方式的转变提供了缓冲期，避免造成传统学术出版由于技术和传播方式的骤然改变造成断裂，也给学者们改变交流观念和使用习惯提供了适应空间，更为传统期刊的网络化开放化提供基本模板。

6 结语

中国科技论文在线 5 年多的发展历程，使中国学术界对开放存取的各种学术交流模式有了一定程度的认识。它强大的官方背景使其具有不可比拟的政治资本和经济资本，可以迅速吸收国内各种优势资源，开展各种形式的开放存取活动，以致发展为集首发平台、预印文库、学者自存档，和开放存取期刊为一体的"百货商店"式开放文库。在这一过程中，虽然各种网络非正式交流的公开和快捷的特点受到学者们的赞誉，但它始终无法替代正式出版的合法化。这种合法化基于严格的评审程序和影响力评估机制，与学者的成果肯定、期刊的影响力、高校的竞争力息息相关。因此各种开放存取的学术交流形式的要想从非正式转为正式，这两个问题不可回避。但可以肯定的是，学术交流模式的发展日趋开放化、数字化，两种交流形式将长期并存。传播技术改变的不仅仅是学术交流的速度和效率，更坚持了对"学术自由"和"开放科学"传统的追求。

注释

［1］中国科学院网站．"我科学机构签署《柏林宣言》网络科学资源全球共享"［EB］．http://www.cas.cn/10000/10022/10006/10002/10007/2004/73150.htm.2004-05-25.

［2］中国科技论文在线．"栏目简介"［EB］．http://www.paper.edu.cn/aboutus_lmjj.php.2009-6-4.

［3］中国科技论文在线．"搭建论文发表大平台　打造学术生态新环境"［EB］．http://www.paper.edu.cn/lizhimin_jiaoyu_djlw2.php.2009-6-4.

［4］中国科技论文在线．"关于中国科技论文在线论文评审系统的说明"［EB］．http://www.paper.edu.cn/school_ack.php.2009-6-4.

［5］中国科技论文在线学报．"首页"［EB］．http://journal.paper.edu.cn/.2009-6-4.

作者简介

李霄，武汉大学信息管理学院出版科学系博士研究生。

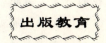
数字出版时代编辑出版专业高等教育的再思考

罗紫初　吴亮芳

（武汉大学信息管理学院　武汉　430072）

摘要：随着数字出版时代的到来，编辑出版专业高等教育也进入了数字化转型期。本文从编辑出版专业学生应具备的能力、课程体系以及培养方式三个方面对如何数字化转型进行了论述。

关键词：数字出版时代　编辑出版专业　能力　课程体系　培养方式

Revisiting of Editing and Publishing Discipline Higher Education in Digital Publishing Era

Luo Zichu　Wu Liangfang

（School of Information Management, Wuhan University, Wuhan, 430072）

Abstract：With the coming of digital publishing era, the higher education of editing and publishing discipline has entered the digital transformation period. The transformation of three aspects, i. e., the editing and publishing students' abilities, the curriculums and culturing ways have been discussed.

Keywords：Digital publishing era　Editing and publishing education　Abilities　Curriculums　Culturing methods

我国编辑出版专业高等教育自 20 世纪 80 年代起步，经过近 30 年的发展，培养了一大批优秀的出版人才。近 30 年的发展中，经历了"萌芽时期、启动时期、低谷时期、发展时期、高潮时期"[1]之后，数字出版的迅猛发展促使了编辑出版专业高等教育进入数字化转型期。

目前，"有近 40 所高校在传播学、印刷工程、编辑出版学等专业目录下开设了电子出版、数字传媒、数字印刷、数字媒体艺术、新媒体、软件工作（新媒体）等数字出版教育专业方向，每年招生 20～60 人，形成了一定的教育规模"。[2]除了武汉大学于 1997 年开设电子出版专业，北京印刷学院于 1999 年开设数字传媒专业外，"其他多数院校则是在 2004、2005 年及以后才设立相关专业方向或开设相关课程"。[3]因此，我们认为，编辑出版学高等教育随着数字出版产业的发展自 2004 年进入了转型期，由定位于传统纸介质出版运作的层面向多种介质出版运作层面发展。然而，面对数字出版时代，编辑出版学高等教育转型还处于摸索阶段，长期以来存在的培养与需求脱节的问题没有得到有效解决，甚至还越来越突出：一面是编辑出版专业的毕业生屡遭"冷遇"；一面是出版业对高素质的复合型人才，特别是数字复合出版人才求贤若渴。那么，数字出版时代，编辑出版高等教育如何迎接数字出版带来的挑战，如何抓住数字出版赐给的机遇成功转型，如何培养出版适合出版业发展需要有编辑出版人才？就此，以下从三个方面谈谈看法，以期引来众多的金玉良言。

1 数字出版时代编辑出版专业学生应具备的能力

我国出版业健康、快速、持续地发展离不开人才的支持。数字出版时代对高素质、创新型人才的渴求达到前所未有的程度，业界原有的"师徒式"人才培养模式再也无法满足出版产业的发展要求，因而培养人才的重担就由编辑出版专业高等教育来承担。那么，培养什么样的人才能够符合出版实践的需要，这是我们首先要回答的问题。出版业随着技术的发展而发展，因而出版实践对人才的需求也是不断变化的。计划经济体制下，出版业对人才的需求更多地体现为具有文字加工能力的文字编辑、校对人员以及美术编辑等人才类型；市场经济体制下，则更多地要求出版人具有市场意识、竞争意识等现代经营意识。2000 年之后，新浪、搜狐、网易三大门户网站相继上市，我国以互联网为代表的数字技术开始驶入快速发展的航道，并于 2003 年开始进入繁荣期，随着网民人数的激增而渗入社会生活的方方面面。[4]数字技术的快速发展给出版业营造了一个崭新的空间，形成了内容的数字化、编辑制作的数字化及营销、物流与消费数字化等一系列趋势。这些数字化趋势对编辑出版人才的要求又有了很大变化，不仅要求他们具有能胜任传统出版工作的能力，更重要的是要求他们具有胜任数字出版工作的能力。

当前，"复合型"、"创新型"、"立体型"等人才类型的表述，都显示了数字出版时代出版业呼唤编辑出版人才的高要求。根据数字出版时代出版业对人才的高要求，编辑出版专业高等教育也应以高求来培养学生，而对学生的培养要求应该主要体现在能力培养方面。数字出版与传统出版的不能截然分开，它"包括传统出版数字化的全部过程和结果，同时也包括新兴的数字媒体"。[5]在数字出版迅速崛起的过程中，"媒体聚合"特征将会越来越明显，行业的保护壁垒将日益消失，"大出版"、"全媒体"概念将越来越清晰。面对出版产业发展的变化与趋势，编辑出版专业高等教育应使学生具备哪些能力，才能符合数字出版时代的需求？我们认为，数字出版时代对编辑出版专业学生培养的能力结构是"多维复合型"，如图1：

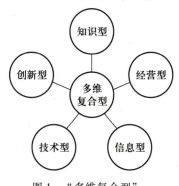

图 1 "多维复合型" 能力结构图

能力结构指"能力系统中各因素之间的耦合关系。"[6]从功能上看，它是各种符合某方面专业需要的能力组合，具体到出版工作，即编辑出版专业学生要有符合出版工作需要的能力组合。"多维"强调数字出版时代编辑出版专业学生应必备的能力之多，从图 1 可看出，数字出版时代编辑出版专业学生的"多维复合型"能力结构至少由知识型、实践型、信息型、经营型、创新型等类型组成。需要指出的是，由这些能力类型组成的结构并不是封闭的，而是呈开放状态，即随着出版新技术、新业态的不断涌现，对学生培养的能力类型也会改变。

在"多维复合型"的能力结构中：

知识型，指学习知识和应用知识的能力。数字出版时代，尽管数字技术改变了出版形态、出版流程等多方面，但仍然无法改变出版积累和传承文化的崇高使命。对从事文化事业的编辑出版人才来说，具有广博知识的要求在任何时代都不可能改变。广博知识的获得不仅需要教师的传授，更重要的是让学生具有学习知识和运用知识的能力。另外，编辑出版专业知识单一性与出版业所需学科知识多样性的矛盾，曾引发编辑出版"有学"与"无学"之争，至今都有人持编辑出版学"无学"的观点。我们认为，培养学生的知识能力是解决专业知识单一性的有效途径，正所谓"授之以鱼，不如授之以渔"。因而，培养编辑出版专业学生学习知识和应用知识的能力，不仅符合出版业的特性，也是解决编辑出版专业知识单一性与出版业学科知识多样性之间矛盾的重要对策。

创新型，指创新的能力。数字出版时代，是一个把理想变成现实的时代。"媒介聚合"给出版人提供了无限想象的空间，拥有创造力的出版人才能在激烈的出版市场竞争中游刃有余。数字出版时代，创造的范围与形式是如此多样，不仅在出版内容上创新，还可以在出版的形式上创新；不仅在出版营销上创新，还可以在出版的技术上创新；等等。

信息型，即信息能力。信息能力"指人们在社会生活及科研活动中捕获、选择、加工、传递、吸收、利用信息的能力，以及将信息物化为精神产品和物质产品的能力",[7]分为专业信息能力和普通信息。编辑出版专业学生的信息能力属于普通信息能力的范畴，包括信息识别能力、信息获取能力、信息利用能力。具有一定的信息能力不仅对其专业的学习很有帮助，而且对将来适应出版实践工作和出版业的发展都显得至关重要。

技术型，指应用技术的能力。出版技术应用能力是编辑出版专业学生将来从事出版业重要专业能力，在就业时最具竞争力的重要能力之一。以数字技术为主要特征的数字出版，要求编辑出版人才具有数字出版基础技术的应用能力是最起码的要求。具体来说，包括计算机技术、网络技术、多媒体技术、数字出版物版权技术等应用能力。

经营型，这里指驾驭出版物生产和流通的能力。出版物供求关系是构成出版市场的基本矛盾，买方市场条件下经营者需要掌握出版物供求规律，认识出版物市场的变化规律。数字出版技术的发展改变了出版的生产流程和营销手段，因而数字出版时代应主要培养学生在数字跨媒体运作和进行数字化营销的经营能力。

2　数字出版时代编辑出版专业课程体系构建

学科课程体系的建设，是高等院校专业办学的最基本的要求。编辑出版专业之所以能成为一门独立的学科，是因为它具有独特的知识体系，而这一知识体系正是通过一系列的专业课程体现出来的。通过一系列专业课程的开设，使编辑出版专业的学生具有独特的知识结构，适应出版实践的需要。从这种意义上讲，课程体系的构建，能为编辑出版专业学生创造就业条件，关系本专业毕业生的就业问题。因此，正处于转型期的编辑出版专业高等教育科学地构建适应数字出版时代编辑出版人才需要的课程体系至关重要。

2.1　数字出版时代编辑出版专业课程体系的构建要求

课程体系构建的要求由数字出版时代出版产业发展的特点与编辑出版学专业特性决定，具体体现在以下几点要求：

一是要紧紧围绕专业的培养目标来构建。1998 年，教育部颁布了新的《普通高等教育本科专业目录》，在一级学科新闻传播学之下设置了编辑出版学，并将培养目标明确为："具备系统的编辑出版学理论与技能，宽广的文化与科学知识，能在书刊出版、新闻宣传和文化教育部门从事编辑、出版、发行的业务与管理工作以及教学与科研的编辑出版学高级人才。"这是对本科层次的编辑出版学的培养目标官方表述，其中明确两层含义，即不仅要具备系统的出版学理论与技能、宽广的文化与科学知识，还要具有从事出版行业等方面的能力，最终的落脚点是要为出版业培养所需的实践应用型人才。数字出版时代，出版业的发展发生了翻天覆地的变化，但出版实践中所需要的应用型人才没有改变。因此，数字出版时代，构建课程体系时依旧要紧紧围绕专业这一培养目标，将出版业发展中的实际需要的各项专门知识列为专业课程，构成编辑出版专业的核心课程体系。

二是要充分反映出版实践所需要的能力要求。能力，意指"能胜任某项任务的主观条件"。[8]数字出版时代，编辑出版专业学生的能力培养不仅要使其具有能胜任传统出版工作的能力，更重要的是要具有胜任数字出版工作的能力。面对数字出版时代，根据"多维复合型"的能力结构要求，应主要培养学生知识和应用知识的能力、出版创新的能力、信息能力、数字出版技术的应用能力以及数字跨媒体运作和进行数字化营销的经营能力。

三是要处理好课程体系稳定性与动态性的关系。学科课程体系的建设关系专业本身的生存与发展，经过近 30 年的发展历程，开办编辑出版学专业的 100 余所高校一般都有了较稳定的课程体系，有的还根据出版业发展的需要开设了数字出版方面的课程，如武汉大学开设字数字媒体技术、网络传播、新媒体等数字出版核心课程。但我们应该看到：由于目前学科归属还没有统一，学科课程体系没有形成规范，再加上数字出版产业的蓬勃发展，编辑出版教育远远地落后于产业，脱离于产业实践的现状是不争的事实。这表明，数字出版时代，构建编辑出版专业课程体系既要吸收原有课程体系的优点，又要根据出版产业的发展需要进行及时调整，做到其构建处于稳定与动态相结合的状态中，使之更好地为出版实践提供应用型人才。

2.2　数字出版时代编辑出版专业课程体系的具体构想

学科课程体系的确立需要明确课程体系的构成结构（即由哪几个板块组成）、课程体系的核心课程以及课程体系的专业自主课程。遵循数字出版时代编辑出版专业课程体系的构建要求，以下对其构建的三大因素进行具体阐述。

（1）课程体系的结构。出版业既是具有经济性的产业，又是具有文化性的事业。由此决定了出版业从业人员应具有有别于其他行业人员的独特知识结构。我们坚持认为，"这种独特的知识结构，由三大知识模块组成：一是以编辑工作为中心的编辑业务知识及相关的文化素质类知识；二是以出版物经营为中心的市场营销知识及相关的经济学知识；三是以出版管理为中心的资源组织与行政管理知识"。[9]由此，可以确定课程体系的出版应用板块由编辑业务、出版营销和出版管理三个部分组成。需要强调的是，数字出版时代这种独特的知识结构的主体不会改变，但因数字技术的出现改变了编辑业务、出版经营与出版管理的内涵，使得其知识结构变得丰富起来。另外，出版历史、理论与技术层面的专业课也不容忽视，特别是技术层面的数字出版技术专业课程提高了前所未有的高度。由此，数字出版时代编辑出版专业课程体系的结构设计如下（见图2）：

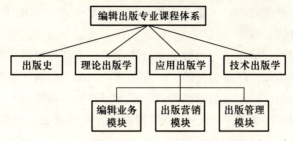

图2　编辑出版专业课程体系结构图

（2）专业核心课程。学科课程体系的结构确定后，再来决定专业核心课程。专业核心课程是指能够反映一个专业基本特征的课程，是维持课程体系稳定性的决定性因素。确定专业核心课程的依据，我们重申此观点："其一，必须是以出版业从业人员所必需的核心知识为主要内容的课程；其二，必须是具有编辑出版学专业特色的课程，也即其他学科没有开设的课程；其三，必须是课程内容的知识层次适合层次教育教学要求的课程；其四，必须是编辑出版学专业的各个专业方向都需要开设的专业普及课程。"[10]根据上述四条标准，结合数字出版时代编辑出版人才的实际需求，我们认为以下几门课程适宜作为编辑出版学专业的核心课程：出版学基础、中国出版史、编辑理论、出版物营销学、出版企业管理、出版法律基础、数字出版技术。

（3）专业自主课程。如果专业核心课程是编辑出版学专业的特质体现，需要规范与统一，那么专业自主课程则是学校办学特色化的主要标志，是不需要规范与统一的。专业自主课程承担着培养学生就业核心竞争力的重要任务，设置得科学与否将直接影响学生的就业。因此，各学校在拥有自主权的前提下，专业自主课程的设置需要遵循一定的原则：一是要以出版业发展的人才需求并结合学校的资源优势为前提；二是以自身特色的培养目标为基础；三是专业自主课程的设置必须突出学生能力培养要求。目前，在开设编辑出版学专业的100余所高校中，有部分特色鲜明，如武汉大学凭借资源优势，形成了培养发行营销管理人才的特色；华中科技大学则以学校资源为优势，形成了以培养科技编辑为主的办学特色。这些办学特色的形成为编辑出版专业高等教育发展指明方向，但需要注意的是，在特色办学的前提下还应在专业自主课程的设置上突出学生能力培养的要求。

3　数字出版时代编辑出版专业的培养方式

数字出版技术的迅速发展，从根本上改变了出版业的发展环境，对编辑出版人才也提出了新要求。这些新要求必定需要科学的培养方式，这样才能培养适合出版业发展需要的出版人才。我们认为，编辑出版专业教育可以采取以下三种培养方式。

3.1　合作式培养

合作式培养，对编辑出版学高等教育来说并不陌生。早在1983年，武汉大学与新华书店总店联合办学，在武汉大学图书情报学院创办图书发行管理学专业。这个专业的设立"不仅填补了我国高等院校专业建设中的空白，同时为院校与企业联合办学开创了一条新路"。[11]数字出版时代，合作式培养越来越突显了它的作用，不仅可以为增强高校的办学实力，如获得资金，而且可以加强高校与业界的联系，为学生创造实习条件。合作式培养的途径很多，主要有以下三种：

一是与出版企业合作培养。出版企业是编辑出版专业学生需求的主体，脱离主体需求的封闭式培养是盲目的，只会导致毕业生就业无门。从这个意义上讲，加强与出版企业的合作培养显得尤为重要。另外，与出版企业合作还可以为高校增强师资力量。师资力量与学科发展状况是相辅相成、相互促进的，一支高素质的编辑出版学师资队伍是培养优秀学生的前提与基础。然而，编辑出版学高等教育因发展较晚，师资力量薄弱一直是阻碍其发展的重要原因，特别是随着数字出版时代的到来，有些教师知识结构陈旧、缺乏实践经验、不懂数字出版技术等问题越来越突显。基于此种状况，与出版企业合作，聘请出版企业中经验丰富的出版人作为教师资源不失为一条可行的途径。

二是与政府合作。学科的建设与成长是多方力量推动的结果，其中，政府是学科发展中不可或缺的角色。当前，编辑出版专业的学科归属问题一直都没有得到有效解决，严重阻碍了学科的发展。此种情况下，更加需要政府的理解与支持。加强与政府合作办学，可以获得政府的政策支持。

三是与其他院校合作。对于起步较晚的编辑出版专业这个新兴的学科来说，需要与其他院校合作，理由有三：其一，需求借鉴其他学科培养人才的成功经验；其二，可以在一定程度上弥补编辑出版专业学生学科知识单一的缺陷；其三，可以快速地培养出具有其他学科知识背景的出版人才。我们认为，在"编辑业务模块"、"出版营销模块"以及"出版管理模式"三大知识结构中，应该鼓励学生根据自己的兴趣爱好和职业定位去选修其他院校的专业。特别是立志要当编辑的学生，更应该通过学习经济、法律、数学、外语等专业成为受业界欢迎的编辑人才。同时，编辑出版专业也可以选拔其他专业的学生学习编辑出版课程，并授予相应的学位。

四是与国外出版机构合作。全球化背景下，出版产业需要国际化人才，出版教育也需要学习国际成功的出版教育经验，并不断探索与国际出版教育接轨的人才培养模式。目前，据统计已有9所大学与国外一些有名的大学开展合作办学。然而，与国外出版企业联合办学的大学目前还极少，今后可考虑这方面的合作模式。

3.2　差异化培养

出版业是一个涉及面极广的产业，因而需要的出版人才类型也是多种多样的，这需要以差异化方式来培养。差异化培养方式，已有许多学校的编辑出版专业教育采用，并形成了自己的特色，如武汉大学出版营销管理人才，北京师范大学的中文编辑，华中科技大学的科技编辑，复旦大学的版权贸易、出版资本运营等方面的出版人才。

面对数字出版时代的到来，编辑出版专业教育更需要采用差异化培养方式，特别是针对数字出版产业所需要的出版人才培养。尽管目前部分高校也开设了关于数字出版的课程，然而所培养的学生却不太符合数字出版产业的实际需要。其原因是，各高校的专业定位大多只侧重在网络出版方面。我们知道，数字出版是出版业发展的必然趋势，其发展态势何其迅猛。2010年7月，中国出版科学研究所发布了《2010年中国数字出版年会年度报告》，报告指出，"2009年我国数字出版产业的收入达799.4亿元，比2008年增长50.6%，继续保持高增长速度"。[12]这又一次证明数字出版迅猛发展的态势。这种迅猛发展的态势对人才的需求量是显而易见的，可以说，由"著作权人—内容提供者—数字出版者—技术提供商—终端设备提供商—网络运营商—电信运营商—金融服务提供者—网络传播者—读者"[13]组成的数字出版产业链，每一个节点都在呼唤编辑出版人才。因此，编辑出版专业教育必须紧跟其步伐，针对数字出版产业链各个节点上所需要的出版人才进行差异化培养。

3.3 实践式培养

实践是提高学生动手能力最直接、最有效的手段，可以说是培养应用型、技术型人才的必由之路，也是满足出版界对人才特殊性需求的重要途径。实践式培养方式的缺位正是造成编辑出版专业教育与出版界人才需求之间矛盾的重要原因，因此，采用实践式培养方式是解决矛盾的核心和关键。

实践式培养方式主要针对本科层次的编辑出版学生，这是实现其本科层次培养目标有效途径。就武汉大学的情况而言，大学本科实习实践环节的教学，大体可分为四类："一是课程实习，这是根据课程教学需要安排的以巩固课堂学习内容为目的的实习；二是阶段实习，这是在学完几门主要专业课程后的本科学习中段安排的以实际运用这几门专业课程所学知识为目的的实习；三是毕业实习，这是在学完本专业全部专业课程后安排的以将本科阶段所学全部课程知识综合运用于实际工作的实习；四是社会实践，这是为提高学生社会适应能力而组织学生通过各种方式了解社会、接触社会的实践活动。"[14]针对出版业需要大量实践应用型人才的情况，以及编辑出版专业学生普通存在实践能力弱的现象，我们认为，加强实践式培养已势在必行了，呼吁各学校应采取有效措施加强实践式培养。

另外，需要强调的是，数字出版技术已渗透到出版产业的各个环节，数字出版时代对人才的要求更加强调实践能力。因此，编辑出版学专业的实践式培养急需要包括数字出版技术应用这方面的内容，以符合出版数字化的发展趋势。

注释

[1] 李文邦. 我国编辑出版专业研究生教育发展研究. 湖南师范大学，硕士论文，2008：9

[2] 郝振省. 2007—2008 中国数字出版产业年度报告. 北京：中国书籍出版社，2008：318

[3] 郝振省. 2007—2008 中国数字出版产业年度报告. 北京：中国书籍出版社，2008：323

[4] 肖东发，张文彦. 从"印刷文明"走向"数字时代"进程中编辑出版教育的变革. 北京联合大学学报：人文社会科学版，2007（4）：89

[5] 郝振省. 2007—2008 中国数字出版产业年度报告. 北京：中国书籍出版社，2008：3

[6] 李书慧. 能力结构浅谈. 职业时空，2009（5）：7

[7] 魏华，陈献兰. 论如何培养大学生的信息意识和信息能力. 高教论坛，2008（5）：123

[8] 中国社会科学院语言研究所词典编辑室. 现代汉语词典：第 5 版. 商务印书馆，2006：990

[9] [10] 罗紫初. 构建编辑出版学专业本科课程体系. 出版广角，2004（1）：14

[11] 谢苏. 出版教育"开放式"办学模式探索. 中国出版，2006（8）：52

［12］程晓龙，李淼. 2009 年中国数字出版产业收入达 799.4 亿元. 中国新闻出版报，
2010-07-21

［13］陈邦武. 政府与市场在数字出版中的为与不为——试论数字出版产业链建设. 出版
发行研究，2010（4）：16

［14］罗紫初. 论数字时代出版人能力之培养. 出版科学，2009（1）：33

作者简介

罗紫初，武汉大学信息管理学院出版科学系教授，博士生导师。

吴亮芳，武汉大学信息管理学院出版科学系博士研究生。

出版教育

数字出版转型期出版人才培养模式的探析

梁春芳

（浙江工商大学人文学院　杭州　310012）

摘要：在数字出版国际化的大潮中，中国出版业已进入由传统出版向数字出版的转型期，由此催生了新的产业链，新技术需要新的知识、新的技能、新的营销方法和管理手段，对我国出版教育的人才培养提出了新的、更高的要求。本文针对目前我国出版教育的现状，从构建数字出版人才培养模式为切入点，对如何培养数字出版人才进行了研究和探讨。

关键词：数字出版　出版教育　新技术　出版产业链

The Mode of Persona Training in Transformation of Digital Publication

Liang Chunfang

（School of humanities，Zhejiang Gongshang University，Hangzhou，310012）

Abstract：With digital publishing internationalized，China publishing industry has entered a period from paper publication to digital publication which puts a new industrial chain to come into being. New technology calls for new knowledge，new skills，new marketing and management methods，and thus it even requires newer and higher training for publishing persons. This essay is aimed at studying how to train publishing talents by establishing training modes of digital publication.

Keywords：Digital publication　Publishing education　New technology　Publishing industrial chain

如果说 2009 年是全球电子书的元年，那么 2010 年则是全球数字出版的元年。随着新媒体、数字技术的迅猛发展和网络的快速普及，一场席卷全球的数字出版大潮已汹涌而至，数字出版时代的到来，驱动传统出版向数字出版转型，催生了一系列新兴出版业态和新的表现形式，极大增强了出版业创造力和传播力。这是人类出版史上的一场深刻革命，不仅改变了出版业的产业结构和经济增长方式、也决定了出版业未来的走向。

1　数字出版大潮席卷全球出版业

放眼世界，距美国作家史蒂芬·金于 2000 年在亚马逊网站上发表的世界第一本电子书小说《骑弹飞行》已有 10 年时间。一些欧美国家专业出版和教育出版大型集团基本完成了数字化转型，数字出版收益在其总收益中所占比例迅猛上升，60%以上均来自数字出版及网络相关业务，数字出版商业模式转型已经基本完成。美国跨国出版集团开始运用数字出版技术开拓大众市场，亚马逊的 Kindle 在美国销售了约 50 万台，快速带动了网上书店电子图书的销售，苹果 iPad 电子阅读器开始投放国际市场，美国的电子书读者将超过1 000 万人，电子书销量将达到 1 亿册，2009 年美国电子书市场营业额同比增长 1.8 倍。德国施普林格出版集团 2009 年从数字化方面获取的收益已超过 50%；据 2010 年 6 月的调查显示，日本 53.5%的人表示"最近就会感受一下电子图书"，而在 2009 年 9 月，这一数据只有 33.2%"。长久以来一直致力于数字出版的探索与创新，被称为"数字出版的先驱之一的英国剑桥大学出版社，目前 22%的收入来自于数字出版，10 年后这个比例将达到 2/3。

纵观我国数字出版的发展，传统出版业经历了由观望—跟进—推进的历程，正处在由传统的、单一纸介质的出版向以数字技术、多媒体技术和互联网为依托的数字出版转型期，其实质也是由机械经济、工业经济向网络经济、信息经济的转变，营收效益显著。近四年来，我国数字出版产业发展一路飙升。据统计，2006 年数字出版产值 213 亿元，2007 年达 362.42 亿元，2008 年达 530.64 亿元，2009 年达 799.4 亿元，首次超过传统图书出版业产值，年均增长率超过 55%，预计 2010 年数字出版产值将突破千亿元。据中国互联网络信息中心（CNNIC）最近发布的《第 26 次中国互联网发展状况统计报告》显示，截至 2010 年 6 月，我国网民已达 4.2 亿人，已居世界首位，普及率达到 31.8%，超过了世界平均水平。手机用户超过 7.8 亿，使用手机上网的网民 2.77 亿人。《第七次国民阅读调查》数据显示，国民各类数字媒介阅读率为 24.6%，其中网络在线阅读的人数最多。可见我国数字出版、网络出版、手机出版等新兴出版业态发展势头强劲，并蕴含巨大市场潜力。新闻出版总署副署长孙寿山表示，数字出版是我国新闻出版产业发展的战略重点和未来发展方向，希望传统出版加快向数字出版转型的步伐，努力实现出版业技术升级和战略转型。

数字出版发展带来出版业态和形态的变化，需要新型出版人才提供支撑，必然带来出版人才培养的变化，但作为中国高校的出版教育，我们准备好了吗！

2　时代呼唤高素质复合型数字出版人才

新闻出版总署在《关于加快我国数字出版产业发展的若干意见》中对什么是数字出版作出了明确的界定："数字出版是利用数字技术进行内容编辑加工，并通过网络传播数字内容产品的一种新型出版方式，其主要特征为内容生产数字化、管理过程数字化、产品形态数字化和传播渠道网络化。"

从这里看出，数字出版是出版业和数字技术、网络技术的结合，带来了全新的产业格局：即传统内容出版商—数字内容制作商—信息生产商—信息提供商—信息服务商—信息运营商—终端制造商—读者。而传统出版业自身的角色、身份和功能也发生了根本的改变：即图书提供商—数字内容提供商—数字内容服务商；纸质单一形态出版—多媒体形态出版；单一渠道传播—多渠道立体传播，从而催生了新的出版产业链、新的业态和新的形态。与传统产业链相比，数字出版产业链最大的特征是产业链上的每个环节上都与新技术密切相关，宏观如多媒体技术、互联网技术、移动互联网技术、电子纸技术等；微观有出版物内容制作技术、版权保护技术；分销网站的发行技术、图书馆的管理技术、复制的即时印刷技术、读者与阅读的显示技术等。产生了数字出版的流程：即内容采集编辑—数据加工制作—内容资源管理—内容服务—内容发布—读者，它不仅改变了编辑出版工作，也改变了发布形态，纸媒不再作为唯一发布形态，网络营销、电子发行成为常态，内容出版正在向内容服务转化，出版将从销售产品转向销售服务，数据和内容的运营将成为未来赢利模式。而目前我国传统出版业中积聚的主要是纸质出版物的内容策划、编辑加工和营销人才，数字化、网络化、媒体化程度很低，不适应我国数字出版的快速发展，人才问题已成为数字出版跨越式发展战略目标的瓶颈。新闻出版总署柳斌杰署长指出："数字出版的发展具有两个显著特点：一个是以计算机技术、网络技术为支撑，没有这方面知识和技能的编辑人员将难以开展数字化的编辑出版活动。另一个是双向或多向的跨媒体交融，缺少多种媒体理论和实践的编辑人员也将难以应对跨媒体的编辑出版工作。因此，数字出版需要多方专业人员的共同协作，要求编辑人员必须是具备多方面知识和技能的复合型人才。"他多次强调"培养一批既熟悉专业出版知识，又掌握现代数字出版技术和善于经营管理的复合型出版人才，是刻不容缓的艰巨任务。"这驱动我国数字出版教育要尽快随传统出版向数字出版的转型而转型。

数字出版人才的培养较为特殊，需要多个科技行业的通力合作才能完成，这对高校编辑出版专业人才培养提出了严峻的挑战，同时也为自身的发展提供了难得的机遇。

3　构建数字出版人才的培养模式

目前，我国高等出版教育经过二十多年的发展，已初具规模，形成了专科、本科、硕士和博士等多层次、多方向培养编辑出版人才的教育体系。以立足大编辑、拓展大出版、运用大媒体、发展大文化为指导，以出版产业需求为人才培养目标，为我国出版业的快速发展输送了大批不同层次的高素质的出版专业人才。面对数字出版技术的迅猛发展，因受限于学科建设和专业审批管理制度，我国的出版教育尽管在教育教学体系上紧跟时代步伐不断探索和调整，但数字出版人才培养滞后甚至与数字出版产业发展脱节仍是不争的事实。如何通过树立新的出版理念、优化师资队伍、建立新的课程体系、加强教材和实验室建设等举措构建新的人才培养模式，为中国数字出版培养复合型人才，已成为我国出版教育人才培养学中需要迫切研究和解决的新的课题。笔者认为，应从以下几个方面构建数字出版人才培养模式。

3.1　树立大编辑、大文化、大媒体的教育理念

教育理念是人才培养的指导方针，直接影响到人才培养的质量。在传统出版向数字出版转型中，首先要建立起全新的与数字出版时代相适应的教育理念。

大编辑。编辑是文化的生产者和传承者，肩负社会责任和文化担当，同时要熟练运用纸媒、网络、手机、手持阅读器、视屏等多媒体技术进行文化传播。数字出版在经历了内容为王—渠道为王—终端为王后又回到内容为王，更凸显了大编辑的重要。

大文化。编辑不仅要有为人类文化服务和奉献的激情、精神和自觉性，还要有宽广的文化视野和深厚的文化底蕴。

大媒体。编辑要积极利用多媒体，努力实现内容传播最大化，提高文化的传播力和社会影响力，参与世界出版的竞争。

3.2　尽快组建一支精良的数字出版教师队伍

教师是实施教育的主导力量，出版教育要培养数字出版的人才，首先必须有一支适合数字出版的教师队伍。高素质的教师队伍建设是构建数字出版人才培养模式，进行教学改革，提高数字出版教学质量的重要保障。

目前全国很多高校引进师资门槛极高，非名牌大学或海归博士莫进来。数字出版是新兴学科，刚刚起步，尚无此专业的高学历、高层次的复合型专家学者，引进师资不顾现实搞一刀切，导致很多数字出版专业课程无法开设，阻碍了学科的建设。此外，由于数字出版是高科技和出版的结合，高校自身复合型知识结构的数字出版师资也严重匮乏，难以满足教育教学的要求，高校应打破现有的用人机制，将数字出版、互联网、移动互联网、多媒体制作等企业和研究院所的专家学者（包括非高学历的）请进课堂。同时开放全国各地的国家级和省市级数字出版和动漫基地，接收教师培训，还举办数字出版师资进修班或培训班等方式，解决数字出版师资匮乏的燃眉之急。

3.3　增加并强化数字出版专业相关课程

目前在全国开设数字出版专业方向的仅有北京印刷学院等为数不多的几所高校，绝大多数高校都是在编辑出版专业课程设置中增加数字出版模块，开设一些相关课程来增强学生的数字出版方面的知识和技能。开设的主要课程有：现代出版技术、电脑图文设计与制作、电子出版技术、网络出版导论、信息管理导论、网络传播学、网络信息组织与利用、网页设计与网站建设、书报刊编校软件应用、网络编辑、书业电子商务、信息资源搜集与管理等。只有极少数高校开设了动画设计与制作、广播电视制作、数字出版概论、数据库技术与应用、数字媒体技术导论、数字编辑学、多媒体采集与处理、数字版权交易、数字出版营销、移动媒体实务、数字媒体创意与策划等，而涉及网络游戏、网络广告和手机出版的课程则尚属空白。从 2009 年的统计数据显示，正是网络游戏、网络广告和手机出版产值最大，成为数字出版三巨头。各高校出版专业应根据自己培养对象的定向和媒体岗位的不同，增开并强化数字出版相关课程，增强和提高学生的数字出版理论和技能，不仅做好数字内容服务商，也可作数字技术开发商和运营商，成为适应数字出版需要的复合型人才。

3.4　加强数字出版教材建设工作

全国高校编辑出版专业开设数字出版相关课程受限原因，除了师资严重匮乏外，教材建设跟不上也是一个重要因素。由于数字出版这个新学科在我国发展还刚刚起步，很多理论和知识体系尚不系统和完备，操作实务尚待完善，给教材编写带来很大困难。一方面可由中国编辑学会教育专业委员会牵头，联系教育出版社或高校出版社等企业，根据市场需求，从数字出版较为成熟和发达的欧美国家引进教材为我所用；另一方面积极组织高校和数字出版企业及科研院所专家学者，尽快加强数字出版的理论研究和实践总结，编写和出版数字出版系列教材，使高校人才培养有"书"可教。

3.5　大力加强学校数字出版实验室建设

数字出版是一门应用学科，需要在实验室教学和操作训练。目前我国高校编辑出版专业实验室建设也参差不齐，很多实验室配备较为简单，多是装备一台多媒体教学设备，几十台电脑外加一些教学和操作软件便是全部家当，电子书出版、手机出版、即时印刷和手持阅读器等教学实训需要的硬件和软件急需投入大量资金配置。同时要优化教学计划，压缩课内学时，加大实践教学时数，增加开放性实验课程，使学生所学的数字出版理论和技能能尽快在校内实验室和实训室的平台上消化、理解和运用。鼓励学生根据出版企业和市场的需求，利用校内设施和资源，自主进行数字出版技术的研发和新项目的设计，增强学生数字化的动手能力和创新实践的能力。

3.6 开放数字出版基地和数字出版企业

新闻出版总署在"十一五"末期，将建设 4 至 15 个数字出版产业基地，形成 10 至 20 个网络出版强势企业。目前先后批准成立的上海、重庆和杭州三家国家数字出版基地涵盖了数字出版产业各个方向，云集了我国数字出版高科技人才。柳斌杰署长在如何推动我国数字出版产业发展和数字出版基地建设的要求中，特别强调基地的重点工作之一"是实施国家数字出版专业人才培养计划。国家将建立专门研发队伍，研发机构以及院校和专业，大量培养适应数字出版发展需要的高精尖人才"。

由于数字出版行业的特殊性，仅靠高校难以完成人才培养重任，必须走产学研一体化道路，在充分利用校内教学和实践资源的基础上，发挥国家数字出版基地、网游动漫基地和数字出版企业的优势，将高校数字出版人才实训纳入国家新媒体产业基地建设中，并把这项工作列入对新媒体产业基地的奖励和考核体系，和高校一起联合培养数字出版人才。高校可通过双导师制度，引导学生参与企业和社会的科研与创新活动，通过加强实践创新教育，培养数字出版产业需要的复合型人才。

3.7 导入数字出版专业竞赛和职业资格鉴定机制

为了加强编辑出版行业的学术交流，提高学生的科技创新能力和编辑职业素质，可由国家政府机构、中国编辑学会、数字出版企业、出版研究院所牵头举办不同主题不同类型的大学生数字出版创新创业大赛等活动，由高校出版专业教师组织学生积极参与。目前在学界和业界较有影响的大赛有：未来编辑杯大赛（中国编辑学会）、全国网络创业大赛（中国就业促进会）、全国大学生版权征文活动（国家版权局）等。近年来通过参与各项竞赛活动，增强了学生的自主研发和创新能力，深受学生欢迎。此外，组织高校大四学生参加国家人力资源与社会保障部主办的网络编辑资格鉴定考试和全国编辑出版职业资格考试（初级），对全面提高编辑出版专业学生的职业素质和技能不失为一项良策。

3.8 加强数字出版高层次人才培养

编辑出版专业从 1984 年创建到今天已走过 20 多年的风雨历程。据有关研究者统计数据显示，目前全国设有编辑出版专业本科的高校 52 所，有硕士点的 28 所，有博士点的 6 所，还远远不能满足作为国家出版业战略重点和未来发展方向的数字出版产业对人才的需求。

值得欣喜的是，2010 年教育部决定扩招专业学位研究生。学位办首次新增 14 所高校为出版硕士专业学位授权点。学术学位和专业学位的不同在于前者以学术研究为导向，偏重理论和研究，主要是培养大学教师和科研机构的研究人员；而专业学位以专业实践为导向，重视实践和应用，是培养具有扎实理论基础，并适应特定行业或职业实际工作需要的应用型高层次专门人才。专业学位的增设体现了国家对编辑出版学科的重视，为我国培养数字出版高层次复合型人才打开了一条绿色通道。数字出版是我国出版战略重点，也是经济发展的着力点，如果教育部能根据切实需要，将编辑出版设为一级学科，对人才培养和数字出版业发展必将产生深远的影响。

展望数字出版的未来，前景无限美好。我们将满怀豪情，努力拼搏，为建设出版强国，创造性地推动数字出版跨越式发展培养高素质、复合型优秀人才。

作者简介

梁春芳，浙江工商大学人文学院编辑出版系教授（编审）。

论全媒体语境下的出版产业
变革与专业实践教学改革

王武林

（浙江传媒学院　杭州　310018）

摘要：出版产业正在发生着重大的变革，数字化和全球化是其最基本的特征，跟踪出版产业发展趋势，改进编辑出版教育，尤其是结合学科发展前沿，对专业实践教学进行改革和探索不仅必要，而且是非常紧迫的。本文在对当前出版产业发展趋势和特点梳理的基础上，结合某些高校编辑出版专业实践教育教学的成功应变和转型事例，初步探讨了目前编辑出版专业实践教学的改革取向，并试图从专业课程设置、实践教学环节和模式创新、实践教学平台与内容改革等三个方面作为突破点，提出具体的实践教学改革与创新路径。

关键词：全媒体　出版产业　编辑出版　实践教学

Changes of Publishing Industry and Reform of Practice Teaching in the Case of Mix-media

Wang Wulin

（Zhejiang University of media and communications，Hangzhou，310018）

Abstract：Publishing industry is undergoing significant change and the digitalization and globalization is it's most basic features. It is not only very necessary but also very urgent that tracking publishing industry trends，improving education，and especially in conjunction with the frontier disciplines of editing and publishing to innovating and exploring professional practice teaching. The paper is written on the basis of the current development trends and the characteristics of the publishing industry. Combined with success stories of strain and transformation of professional practice teaching from some universities，the paper discussed the issue of professional practice teaching about reform of the orientation，and tried to look on course setting，practice teaching innovating and platform and content reforming as breakthrough point，and put forward the concrete path for reform and innovation of practice teaching.

Keywords：Mix-media　Publishing industry　Editing and publishing　Practice teaching

　　回顾编辑出版专业的教育发展历程，如果归因于未能形成系统和延续的专业教育，我们将 1947 年李次民教授已在广东国民大学中讲授编辑学课程以及 1949 年国内第一本编辑学著作出版问世二事略去不计，仅以改革开放以来，起始于 1983 年的武汉大学图书发行学教育作为现代编辑出版专业教育的发轫，时至今日，编辑出版学专业教育即将迈入而立之年。在将近三十年的教育发展历程中，出版行业发展所依赖的宏观和微观环境、所面临的内部与外部条件都曾经和正在发生着极大的变化，编辑出版专业教育亦无例外。因此，研究编辑出版教育当前所处的环境特征，并作出及时正确的应对实乃专业教育的当务之急。

1 出版产业与专业教育的局变境迁

出版产业的发展受制于宏观和微观环境的变迁，出版教育一方面需要服务于出版产业，另一方面需要在产业发展的实践中总结提升理论并积累经验和方法，因而出版教育的改进和产业发展一脉相承、相互促进。

1.1 出版产业的发展格局与趋势

从宏观上来说，当前我国出版产业的总体发展趋向是数字化、集团化和全球化，这也是现阶段出版产业最基本的特征。数字化主要体现在编辑出版流程中对数字技术的依赖与大量运用，以及数字出版形态的不断丰富和完善，数字化趋势是当前和未来出版发展的主流方向和主要特征。集团化发展是我国近年来新闻出版体制改革的最显著的外部体现形式。目前新闻出版的转企改制已经进入攻坚阶段，改革重组与集团化的进程还将持续并有待进一步深入。文化软实力作为和平年代国际间的主要竞争力，近些年常被人们所提及，大力发展文化产业是国家"十一五"规划中文化发展的主体内容，出版产业已经成为文化产业的生力军，成为国民经济中不可忽视的产业部门和重要力量，这一点从过去的2009年新闻出版业总产值突破万亿元一例亦可证明。重要的是，发展文化软实力需要"走出去"，在海外"安营扎寨"实体出版机构，抑或以版权作品和版权贸易来"攻城略地"，占领市场，同样在2009年中国作为主宾国的"法兰克福书展"上取得的丰硕成果充分说明，我们已能逐步应对全球化和国际化的出版竞争格局。

在微观上而言，出版机构内部的改革从未间断，出版业务流程的完善与整合依然在进行中，对出版形态的研究和实践不断推进，新的出版业态与赢利模式悄然涌现。总体上，出版产业的融合不断深化，不同媒体间的互动、融合和业务合作得到前所未有的加强，全媒体出版已然成为现时期出版的创新形式，内容资源多次利用、生成成本得以下降、阅读空间大大拓展。其次，数字技术持续创新，不论内容提供商还是技术提供商，在推动数字出版发展方面均有显著的表现，以许多新的搜索技术和阅读平台为主要代表。再次，产业形态逐步完善，赢利模式日渐清晰，移动阅读、网络数据库出版、网络在线出版、远程教育出版等被广泛认可和选择应用。最后，手机出版势头强劲，据第26次中国互联网络发展统计报告显示，截至2010年6月，我国手机网民达到2.77亿人，而手机阅读是主要的互联网应用项目之一，因此大量报纸与期刊开始运用手机出版方式。

1.2 编辑出版专业教育的内外部环境

前已述及，教育与产业的发展相辅相成、互为条件、互相促进，教育从产业中获取一手的实践方法与经验数据，并从中升华形成理论，反馈并指导产业实践；教育为产业发展提供合格的人才与技术支持。而产业的变革与调整影响教育的方向和内容，如果从就业角度考量，甚至对于教育的目的具有直接导向作用。

许多专家、学者和研究者在大量的专业论著中普遍谈到了本专业当前的状态，认为表现为诸如未被认可并理顺的学科关系、性质有别的院系隶属、混乱无章的课程设置、各有特色的专业偏向、层次不齐的师资配置、稳中少变的教学形式、日益尴尬的就业趋势等等，业内业外，校内校外，似乎悲观者居多，批判者居少。对此，我们应该有足够清醒的认识和更加实际的行动。一方面学校或者学院的领导者有责任对教育作出应有的变化以应对，或者教师对课程的内容和讲授的方式作出应有的调整，而不是一味人云亦云，怨天尤人；另一方面，业界的精英和管理者也有责任为教育应对产业的转变提出中肯的建议，并以实际行动来支持教育的发展，而不是在依靠从前该专业的学生打好"江山"后简单对现在的学生说不，然后漠然置之！

诚然，出版产业的变革直接引起了编辑出版教育的转型，尽管存在如此多的"共同问题"，但随着出版业的数字化、全球化、集团化进程的不断推进，近些年许多高校在编辑出版教育方面作出了及时的应对，出版产业数字化和信息化的变化趋势使得编辑出版的数字化方面的教育得以加强，不论在课程设置还是实践环节，各校都有明显的转型；高校在编辑出版学生的国际交流和版权贸易方面的课程训练，是为了应对全球化的出版产业发展趋势；对新型的出版改革体制以及非公有制出版方面的研究，意在探讨出版产业改制所带来的集团化及非公有制市场化运营等课题。另外，随着出版教育的发展和扩张，虽然没有人能提供开设出版专业学校的准确统计数据，但毋庸置疑，从 2010 年年初公布的 6 所学校新增编辑出版专业可以证明，开设的学校在逐年增加，所以为了减少激烈的就业竞争，每所学校都在考虑如何办出自身的特色，如何在同专业的竞争中能够脱颖而出、立于不败之地。

2　高校编辑出版专业实践教育的应时而变

在出版传媒呈现全媒体化趋势的当下，数字化成为一股不可抵挡的混流，推动出版产业发展的车轮滚滚向前，编辑出版教育的问题日益突出：其一，市场的细分化对编辑出版特色教育的需求日趋强烈，不同高校必须依据自身条件作出调整；其二，实践性的本质要求编辑出版教育必须作出适当应对，以满足市场对专业人才的要求；其三，出版产业的发展对教育内容的更新提出新的挑战；其四，全媒体化的趋势要求编辑出版教育就出版生产的数字化流程作出全方位、根本性的转轨。

对于本科教育而言，专业理论教育固然重要，掌握专业理论是教育的核心，但实践教育更重要，不仅在于实践能够助于理论的理解和掌握，也在于编辑出版专业实践性较强的特性。虽然各校的实践性课程差别较大，有自己的特色和侧重，但强调实践训练的重要性已经为大家所认可并付诸具体教学之中。这一点一方面从各个学校开设的课程中可以看出，另外也从实践教学环节的安排中明确体现。笔者结合对北京几所院校的实地调查和文献资料统计出了表 1 内容，表中的内容体现了在数字与新媒体出版为主要特征的今天，出版教育在教学内容和实践形式方面所作出的应时而变，其一是加强了数字类出版课程的内容和比例，其二是丰富了实践环节的训练方式。

如果说以上是各校专业实践环节的共性变化的话，基于自身特色、传统优势和文化底蕴的差异，各校在专业实践教学中形成了各具特色的培养理念。相较之下，北京大学的编辑出版学教育注重文化积淀、注重史论，在此基础上结合现代信息技术和网络多媒体技术，适当开展新媒体方面的教学和实践，而出版史和出版管理方面的实践是其优势与特色所在，该校本科生在出版管理实践基础上策划了《书香漫处显风云——北大周边的书店》一书。

表1　国内外编辑出版专业数字类课程及实践教学体系比较

学校	数字出版类课程	实践教学环节安排
武汉大学	数字出版导论、信息检索、电子与网络编辑、编校软件应用	课程实习、假期实习、专业实习
北京大学	信息检索与利用、电子出版技术、网络传播、数码艺术	课程实践、专业实习
中国人民大学	数字与传播技术应用、音频视频内容制作、出版物视觉设计、音像作品创意与制作	社会调查与研究、社会实践、社会服务、专业实习、校内媒体实习
中国传媒大学	专业软件应用、电子出版物脚本创作、数字出版物编创、网页设计与制作、非线性编辑	课程实习、假期实习、专业实习、校内媒体实习
四川大学	书籍装帧与电脑排版、多媒体与电子出版业	课程实习、假期实习、专业实习
浙江传媒学院	现代出版技术、网络出版实务、编校软件应用、非线性编辑	课程实习、学年实习、专业实习
密苏里大学	电子摄影、可视通讯、摄影	项目实习、研讨实习
纽约大学	网络出版原理与应用、网络营销与电子商务、网络科技专业出版	项目实习、研讨实习
牛津布鲁克斯大学	电子出版、桌面出版	项目实习、研讨实习

中国人民大学一直以来作为国家人文社科人才教育的摇篮，其人文底蕴厚重，人文氛围浓郁，学校各种社团主办和承办有近30种期刊报纸媒体，新闻学院学生主办有刊物《新闻周报》，被媒体称为"校园的南方周末"，在办好纸版报纸外，学生负责网站制作与网络新闻编辑。学校重视实践教学和训练，校园媒体之间的竞争也在某种程度上成为学生办好各种媒体的重要推动力和外部力量。

中国传媒大学依托自身的行业地位和优势特色，其办学理念更注重先进性和实用性，从专业角度掌握行业制高点，与国外知名高校实现接轨，共同参与实践项目，显示出教学理念和实践的前瞻性和指引性。北京师范大学出版科学研究院暂不设本科教育，但因为其有北京师范大学出版集团作为坚实的后盾，学生可以随时参与到具体的出版实践环节中去，所以其研究生的培养具有区别于其他高校院设专业所不具有的特点和优势，的确对日后高校办学具启示意义。

事实说明，尽管拥有同样的专业，但各校的理论与实践教学能够尊重传统，有效整合校内资源、发挥学校特色与优势，应时而变，从而形成了明显的办学特色。

3 编辑出版实践教学改革与探索

当前，出版的数字化已经成为潮流和趋势，产业转型成效初显，数字出版发展迅猛且形成了庞大的产业链，产业融合的加深催生了《贫民窟的百万富翁》《非诚勿扰》等全媒体出版现象，产业形态的完善加剧了包括手机报、电子图书、网络文学以及在线工具书等在内的数字出版形态的出现，数字技术的推进引起了阅读方式、检索方法及资料获取渠道的不断创新。加之，出版业界对本专业毕业生颇有微词。进行编辑出版实践教学改革显得尤为必要和迫切。以下从三个方面阐述改革实践教学的基本思路。

3.1 课程设置

课程设置是专业教育的关键，在编辑出版专业教学中，应该及时依据外部环境变化调整培养方案中的课程。当然，培养方案具有相对的稳定性，如果不作大的调整则应对课程的内容进行及时适当的修改和补充，力求突出产业变化趋势所引起的需求，如数字化环境下增加数字新媒体出版的内容，全球下背景下增加版权贸易与数字版权运作的内容。同时尽量创造条件进行相关模拟实战操作和训练，增强对内容的理解和实用性。在这方面，中国传媒大学与国外高校开展了广泛的合作交流，同时能够及时增加前沿课程，形成了办学亮点。

3.2 实践教学环节与模式探索

实践教学的环节可以突破现有形式，灵活设置课程实习、假期实习、毕业专业实习；还可以依据情况设置阶段实习，如集中一到两个星期；也可以代之以社会实践和调查；还可以采用项目驱动的方式，指定项目后，由学生自行组织人员、自行安排时间和进度，最终上交作品，进行统一评定。如浙江传媒学院的"四年一本书"项目，就是给定具体的要求，让学生自己策划、创作、组稿、排版、输出，最后完成一本完整的书刊作品。实践证明这种方式能够充分发挥学生的主观能动性，也促使他们在有效的时间内挖掘所需信息、补充相关专业知识。苏州大学研究生教学实践中的"五个一"（即初校 100 万字、三校 100 万字、责编一本书、上一次订货会、下一次印刷厂），也通过项目的形式达到了理想的效果。

实践教学的模式可以丰富和创新，融会贯通于实践和教学两个单元之中，如教学中的案例式、情景式教学法也是实践教学的重要模式，同样可以移植到实践教学模式中。实践教学中的案例式教学法也是一种示范教学法，通过具体实物的展示、数字案例的演示或者具体案例的讲解可以达到目的；其次是实验教学模式，通过具体操作和演示进行编辑、排版、校对、印刷等，让学生理解整个出版流程；其三是见习教学和见习训练，比如去网站进行网络编辑实训、去出版机构参与选题策划、组稿和校对等，可以获取一手资料，有真实的体验；其四是社会调查和社会服务，实地走访调查和服务社会有助于针对性学习和扩大视野；最后是参与竞赛和各种实操活动，如参加数字多媒体制作大赛、网络编辑竞赛、征文比赛、编校业务及排版竞赛等，这种方式可以通过自我鞭策、相互比较和借鉴，增强竞争意识，快速激发学生的创作与实践能力，进而取得良好的效果。

3.3 实践教学平台与内容改革

从实践教学平台的创设而言，可以结合各校实际，并尽量建立适应当前数字出版业务流程及专业素质培养的实践平台，然后针对不同的平台在内容上作出调整与改革。

（1）实践基地。建立实践基地是编辑出版实践教学中的基本要求。建立的方式有两种：其一是寻求企业的支持，提供实习场所和指导教师，目前此方式较为常用，如许多高校和出版机构、印刷机构之间建立了良好的合作关系。其二是与企业合作建立基地，如方正阿帕比与上海理工大学共建的数字出版产学研基地等。实践基地可以为学生提供全方位的帮助和指导，学生可以旁听选题论证会、参与策划、编辑、校对等，真实体验编辑出版的流程，或者参与版权贸易的整个过程，有助于知识的融会贯通。

（2）校园媒体。依托学校现有媒体资源，强化实践教学，是一种很好的实践教学方法。充分利用学校的各类报纸杂志、广播电视、网络媒体、出版社及书店资源平台，鼓励和支持学生进行实际锻炼是极好的实践教学途径。清华大学有每期 8 个版面的双周报《清新时报》，中国传媒大学的实践平台包括报纸《电视人》、杂志《电视人特刊》，中国人民大学新闻学院学生的实践平台更为广泛，包括报纸《新闻周报》、同名新闻网站及酝酿中的电子杂志等。而且几近真实媒体的模拟，如《新闻周报》的实战性和专业性、摄影室及演播厅的现场感与专业性，同时打破了专业界限，大家共同参与各种媒体实践，互通有无、取长补短，综合实践能力得到大力提升。《新闻周报》、《清新时报》和《电视人》分别创刊于 1982 年、2002 年和 1996 年，已逐步成为一种文化传统。浙江传媒学院历来重视实践教学和训练，为学生提供了一些实践平台，如"新闻世纪网"和《新传播》，是学生实践的重要平台。在国外，密苏里新闻学院创办报纸、电台、杂志、网站等媒体，为编辑出版专业学生提供了教学实验基地，教师担当编辑，学生直接参与编辑出版流程。

（3）实验中心。实验中心是全院学生的学习实践中心，也是实践教学的重要平台，实验中心完善的数字平台及网络条件，可为专业实践提供保障，条件允许的情况下可以对学生开放，以方便使用。实验中心一般设施比较齐全，学生在内容尤其是数字内容制作方面可以自由选择加工制作或者实训演练。

（4）工作坊。除了以上提及的平台外，利用老师或者学生创立的工作坊或者工作室进行实践教学是比较可行的方法，艺术或者美术院校的学生经常利用工作坊进行创作，在那里可以遇到志同道合的"发烧友"，技术上互相切磋学习、共同进步。目前，在我国出版行业中有许多个人文化工作室或工作坊，成员虽少，但功能兼具，而且大都运作良好、效益可观，所以从实践教学的视角出发，建立产学功能并具的工作坊不失为一种实践教学平台的选择。

一言以蔽之，出版产业发展异常迅速、日新月异，出版教育必须跟上时代潮流，特别在数字出版应用日趋广泛的未来，加强和改进编辑出版专业的实践教学必要且刻不容缓。

参考文献

[1] 邵益文. 编辑出版学专业教育迫切需要总结和提高. 山东理工大学学报（社会科学版），2005（11）

[2] 林余荫. 编辑出版专业实践性教学模式探析. 广西民族大学大学学报（社会科学版），2008

[3] 罗昕. 媒介融合时代编辑出版专业的实践教学体系建构. 中国编辑，2009（4）

[4] 李凌芳. 浅议新形势下的高校编辑出版专业教育. 当代教育论坛，2009（7）

［5］ 罗紫初. 论数字时代出版人才能力之培养.“数字出版与出版教育”论文集，2009

［6］ 2009 年新闻出版产业呈现六大特点，http://hxd. wenming. cn/xwcb/2010-07/27/con-
tent_154161. htm

［7］ CNNIC. 第 26 次中国互联网络发展状况统计报告，http://www. cnnic. net/html/Dir/
2010/07/15/5921. htm

作者简介

王武林，博士，浙江传媒学院新闻与传播学院副教授。

数字出版人才培养对策研究

艾 岚[1] 李剑欣[2]

（1. 河北经贸大学期刊部 石家庄 050061；

2. 河北经贸大学人文学院 石家庄 050061）

摘要：数字时代的来临，数字技术的广泛应用，改变了人们的阅读方式和阅读习惯，对编辑出版业人才提出了新的要求。但是，由于目前我国高校在学科定位、课程设置、师资建设等方面存有很大的不足，造成数字出版人才培养难以满足业界对数字出版复合型人才需求的局面。为此，对于培养数字出版人才的对策选择，本文指出可从以下三个方面入手：首先，国务院学位办应尽快将编辑出版专业列为一级学科，扭转学科定位不准的局面；其次，课程设置应理论与实践并重，适当减少基础理论课程的门数和学时，相应增加学生实践项目的课时，重视数字网络平台的建设，构建环境良好的数字出版实习基地；再次，加强数字出版教育师资队伍的建设，可以采取"走出去"战略，就是要求数字编辑出版知识、技能欠缺的教师通过参加全国性的数字出版教育师资队伍的培养和培训，与业界建立教师培训交流常态机制；还可采取"引进来"措施，就是将业界打拼多年已成为应用型复合人才、应用研究型复合人才、经营管理型人才等专家型职员聘任到师资力量中来，带领学生进行多种媒体的互动和融合的实战训练。

关键词：数字出版 编辑出版 人才培养

Research on Countermeasures of Digital Publication Talents Training

Ai Lan[1] Li Jianxin[2]

（1. Periodical Office，Hebei University of Economic and Business，Shijiazhuang，050061；

2. College of Humanities，Hebei University of Economics and Business，Shijiazhuang，050061）

Abstract：With the digital age's coming，the digital technique's widespread application changes people's reading way and reading custom and proposes the new request to the edition publishing industry talented person. But in present，there are very big insufficiency in our country' university in aspects of discipline localization，curriculum，teachers construction，which causes the digital publishment personnel training can't satisfy the demand of the field on the digital publication inter-disciplinary talent. Therefore，digital publication talented person's training countermeasure choices should include the following three aspects. Firstly，the State Council degree office should list the edition and publication specialization as the first-level discipline as soon as possible and reverse inaccurate discipline localization. Secondly, the curriculum should pay equal attention to the theory and the practice, reduce suitably the kind and the study period of the basic theory curriculum, increase class hours of practice project correspondingly, pay attention to the digital network platform construction, and construct digit publication practice base with good environment. Thirdly, we should strengthen the teachers' troop construction of the digital publication education by adopting "going out" strategy, which is to request teachers lack of the digital edition and publication knowledges and skills establish the teacher training exchange habit mechanism with the field through participating in the nationwide teachers' troop and training of digital publication education. We may also adopt "entering" strategy, that is appoint persons which fight many years in the field and become the application compound talented person, the applied research compound talented person and management and operation talented expert staff and so on to the teachers strength, lead the student to carry on many kinds of media interaction and fusion live operational training.

Keywords: Digital publication Editing and publishing Talents training

1　数字时代对出版业人才提出的新要求

1.1　数字时代阅读方式的转变对编辑出版人才提出新要求

中国互联网络信息中心（CNNIC）2010 年 7 月 15 日发布的第 26 次中国互联网发展统计报告显示，截至 2010 年 6 月，我国网民规模达 4.2 亿人，互联网普及率持续上升增至 31.8%，手机网民达到 2.77 亿人，10—29 年龄段的网民占 58%，周平均上网时长达到 19.8 个小时。其中，网络文学使用率为 44.8%，用户规模达 1.88 亿，较 2009 年底增长 15.7%，是互联网娱乐类应用中用户规模增幅最大的一项。[1]另外，2010 年 4 月 20 日，由中国出版科学研究所主持进行的第七次全国国民阅读调查结果显示，2009 年我国 18～70 周岁国民中接触过数字化阅读方式的国民比例达 24.6%，比 2008 年增长了 0.1 个百分点。其中，16.7% 的国民通过网络在线阅读，比 2008 年增加了 1 个百分点；14.9% 的国民接触过手机阅读，比 2008 年增长了 2.2 个百分点。[2]这一系列数据显示，青年一代业已融入以互联网和手机为标志的数字阅读时代，相当多的读者尤其是年轻人越来越习惯数字化阅读。

传统编辑出版显示的信息符号是串行顺序，信息结构固定，不论是文字、图片还是电视图像、录音录像制品，对不同的读者展现的信息都是相同的，读者识别信息必然是被作者的思维所控制。而数字化阅读由于添加了超链接，为读者从一个镜头跳转到前或后若干镜头，从一段论述链接到其他章节段落，甚至从一件作品链接到另外的作品的有关论述或镜头中提供了方便。如此情况下，"阅读同一作品时，不同的读者或同一读者在不同的阅读时段，阅读获得的信息内容结构可以不同，这种可自主选择的发散式阅读给了读者更多的选择接受不同信息组合方式的可能，给予读者阅读自主权，从而培养读者的发散式阅读思维和阅读习惯，这是数字阅读的特点。"[3]如此看来，传统阅读向数字阅读的转变，带给读者不仅仅是阅读方式的改变，最为深刻应是思维方式的改变。可以说，网络正在潜移默化地改变着读者的阅读习惯和思维习惯，产生并正在培养着数字传媒时代的阅读文化。

而传统阅读向数字阅读的这种过渡必然需要数字编辑出版活动的鼎力相助，反映到编辑出版人才素养中就是要求编辑出版者必须具备数字编辑出版所要求的各项知识背景和知识技能。

1.2 数字时代新技术对编辑出版人才提出新要求

编辑出版数字化离不开信息技术的突飞猛进，如 CTP（计算机直接制版）技术取消了出胶片、晒版等环节，实现由计算机直接到印版，不但缩短出版周期，适应快节奏的社会生活，而且降低成本提高效率；以数字文件格式储存、浏览的电子书技术，移动通信、流媒体技术，都是将文本、图片、动漫、音乐集于一体，用于手持设备上，大大提高读者阅读的便捷性、丰富性和移动性。另外，数字化内容管理技术、文件管理技术为跨媒体数字出版提供了可能，将互联网同管理信息、生产流程信息、印刷软硬件设备连接在一起，实现编辑出版生产和管理集成化，即生产系统和管理系统一体化。

一种新技术的出现往往会产生一种新的经济范式，而新的经济范式往往会涉及到新的组织形式、新的劳动技能、新的产品组合、一系列围绕关键要素使用的创新、新的基础设施的投资以及大量公司的进入、退出和大公司的集中趋势等。在数字化环境下，出版产业的发展和变化对出版人才的数量、质量都提出了新的要求。从数量方面看，出版产业的快速发展和壮大需要一大批从业人员，现有的人才的数量远不能满足出版产业大发展的需要。从质量方面看，出版印刷业技术和产业的发展需要的从业人员要具备新的技能，人才的知识结构、能力结构都要发生相应的变化，否则难以满足新的技术经济范式转变对人才的素质要求，会制约出版产业的发展。[4]

1.3 数字编辑出版人才所要达到的新要求

随着互联网的普及和数字出版技术的日新月异，新的传播方式和阅读方式"对出版观念、编辑行为、消费群多重细分、市场份额、利益重新分配、产业链重组等都产生了本质的改变，从根本上改变了出版业态，打破了传统的出版格局，催生了新的出版形态，如网络出版、移动阅读和复合出版。"[5]而在传统出版向数字出版转型的当下，为了适应数字化所带来的要求，编辑出版从业人员的知识功底、技能水平就受到了极大的关注。编辑出版人员具备了哪些新要求就可以称为数字编辑出版人才了呢？即数字出版人才所应具备的知识结构如何。

1.3.1 基础知识

一般而言，坚实而深厚的人文社科基础知识是编辑出版人才知识结构的根基。对于编辑出版人才来说，由于工作本身接触的知识面比较宽广，需要调动的知识储备也比较多，需要多学科背景的支撑，因此，某种意义上来说编辑出版人都是"杂家"，具备深厚、宽广的文化素养就成为出版人才之所以为人才所具备的最为基础的东西。数字出版人才既要懂技术、又要懂艺术，还要在新的传媒环境下，能够深刻理解数字出版产业运作规律，设计实现赢利的商业模式和产业链，因此，必须具备文理兼容、跨学科的复合型知识结构。

扎实的编辑出版专业基础知识是数字化编辑出版人才知识结构中核心部分。编辑出版基础知识是一个内容丰富，既有系统理论学说、媒介传播技术，又有广泛产业实践；既创构先进文化思想，又推动信息流整合；既有综合性、横断性又有交叉性、渗透性的学科体系。系统掌握扎实的编辑出版理论知识与业务技能，对于一个立足于长远发展的编辑出版人才而言，是绝对必不可少的知识素养。

1.3.2 技术知识

数字编辑出版就是用数字技术统领从选题、编辑、出版到营销、管理等活动的各个环节。如此看来，要成为数字编辑出版人才，除了要熟练掌握编辑出版专业知识、业务和技能外，计算机技术、计算机图形图像处理技术、网络通讯技术、数据库技术、网站编辑排版技术也要成为相关必备知识，纳入数字出版人才培养的知识体系当中。另外，根据数字出版发展特点，有学者认为出版专业人才培养需要构筑三种信息能力：一是对数字出版产业链增值环节的快速反应能力；二是对海量数字化内容的汇聚分析利用能力；三是对跨媒体内容定制放大效应的运作能力。[6]为此，数字编辑出版人才尚需掌握以下技术知识：数字内容管理技术、海量内容有效存储技术、海量内容安全快速传输技术、动画技术、三维技术、计算机辅助设计等技术。

2 数字时代高校出版人才培养存在的不足

在当下，高校毕业生招聘会上频频上演尴尬的局面：众多毕业生感叹"伯乐难遇"，而大量用人单位却直呼"将才难求"。这一渐成普遍的现象直接暴露的是我们高等教育与人才市场的需求严重脱节。具体到编辑出版专业的毕业生，普遍存在只掌握本领域的专业基础知识而缺乏多学科的知识背景，更缺乏数字化知识和技能方面素养的现象，他们很难直接从事编辑出版数字化方面的拓展。而造成编辑出版专业毕业生上述不足的主要根源在于数字时代高校出版人才培养存有不足，主要不足都有哪些呢？

2.1 学科归属的偏差

教育部于 1998 年颁布《普通高等教育本科专业目录》，对编辑出版专业的培养目标定位于"具备系统的编辑出版理论知识与技能、宽广的文化与科学知识，能在书刊出版、新闻宣传和文化教育部门从事编辑、出版、发行的业务与管理工作及教学与科研的编辑出版学高级专门人才"。这也就为各高等院校的编辑出版专业学科归属提供了不确定性，实践中大部分编辑出版专业建立在新闻传播院系之下，有些设在人文学院，还有一些设在信息管理学院或图书馆系之下。如此乱象，充分反映了我国高等教育编辑出版专业学科地位定性不够准确，即非一级学科而是挂靠在管理学或传播学等其他学科之下，本科层次的毕业生很难满足出版业对人才多样性、专业性及复合型的要求，更为甚者是在研究生教育只是作为某个专业的研究方向而存在，这已严重影响和制约了编辑出版教育层次的提升和培养目标的明晰以及我国编辑出版学科的发展和建设。这一点已在出版教育界广大研究人员中达成共识。也正是由于编辑出版专业在高校教育中的这种依托办学，导致专业难以准确定位，专业课程设置缺乏严谨性，各校差别较大，无法形成编辑出版学的科学的专业学科体系。而这也正使得课程设置和课程内容难以适应不断发展的出版产业化、数字化。

2.2 理论与实践的脱节

高等教育的创设就是为了服务于社会，担负着为社会、行业输送专门人才的职责。出版产业是实体产业，因而，数字出版人才的培养应从编辑行业出发，围绕本行业特征和需求来构建人才培养模式和课程设置。但是，从已开设数字出版专业课程的北京大学、武汉大学、北京印刷学院、浙江工商大学、河北大学等 5 所大学的具体情况来看，数字化编辑出版技术方面操作性较强的课程门类相对较少，远不能满足数字出版行业蓬勃发展的需要。

另外，编辑出版专业的实用性、可操作性的固有本性决定了其学科建设的关键要注重实践，尤其是为了满足数字化时代对编辑出版专业提出的要求，实践对于数字编辑出版人才的培养而言更具起着决定性作用。因此，科学、合理配置理论课与实践课之间的比例就成了题中应有之意。但是，各高校教学实践中理论与实践课程设置比例却很不合理，基本上遵循传统上的重理论、轻实践的指导思想。比如有学者指出，"据有关调查显示，目前我国编辑出版专业课程设置中理论课与实践课为9∶1，而国外为1∶1。"[7]造成这种局面的原因很多，既有传统习惯的思维定势，又有教师队伍缺乏出版实践经验和数字技术没有能力提供这方面的课程讲授。同时，教师所关注的研究领域及科研成果与业界所面临的急需解决的问题相脱节，出现"各说各话"、"无病呻吟"、虚假繁荣的景象，更加大了理论与实践之间的隔膜，出版专业的人才培养模式遭遇业界不信任也就成为预料之中的事。

2.3　数字编辑出版教育师资差

师资是开展各项教育的主导力量，师资的教育水平直接决定学生的教育质量。因此，数字出版人才的培育离不开既具有深厚的编辑出版基础知识又有精湛的数字技术技能复合型的高素质的师资队伍。可以说，复合型的高素质的教师队伍对于数字出版人才培养的创新模式和教学高质量都起着决定性的作用。但是，遗憾的是，各高校编辑出版教育中普遍缺乏具有编辑出版、数字技术复合型知识结构的师资队伍，多数教师的知识结构还停留在传统出版教育的培养目标层次上，难以承担起数字出版教育的重任，造成与数字出版技术相关的主要课程开设出现困难；难以实现数字编辑出版人才的培养目标，即数字出版内容编创与传达、数字出版技术应用和数字出版运营，造成与数字出版教育教学的要求相差甚远。因此，加强数字出版教育师资队伍的培养和建设已成为解除制约数字出版人才培养快速发展的法宝之一。

3　数字出版人才培养的对策选择

3.1　准确把握编辑出版专业学科定位

对于我国目前编辑出版专业科学定位不准的问题，早在2007年，一些专家学者就有所关注。尤其是李建伟教授通过对全国编辑出版专业研究生教育现状调查指出，我国现有编辑出版专业研究生办学点38个，博士点8个，分布在18个省、市、自治区的35所高校内，培养了很多硕士和博士，但目前只能挂靠管理学和传播学上培养出版人才。这也就造成目前编辑出版专业研究生教育多是依据其一级学科设置课程，而编辑出版教育最初多设在中文等文科院系，课程设置也侧重于文科。尽管后来编辑出版专业大多转到新闻传播院系，大多遵照"大传播"、"大出版"的思想进行课程设置，但是，仍不可能摆脱一级学科对编辑出版专业的制约影响，如，"不易为用人单位所接受，不利于教师开展科研，也不利于该专业的学科建设，极大地影响了编辑出版学教育的发展，更不利于我国出版产业的发展，尤其是面对跨媒体环境下的今天，近百所编辑出版学办学点也迫切需要具有硕士和博士学位的专业教师。"[8]基于此，笔者以为，作为完善而独立的学科体系的编辑出版专业完全符合国家学科专业划分一级学科的标准或条件，国务院学位办可将编辑出版专业列为一级学科。如此一来，数字编辑出版作为二级学科编辑学和出版学的专业方向的地位就会脱颖而出，名正言顺地满足"产学研"对数字编辑出版人才培养的需求。

3.2　课程设置应理论与实践并重

理论来自于实践，又指导实践，这是人类总结出的认识事物的普遍规律。当下，数字编辑出版教育理论与实践教学相脱节造成空有广阔的数字应用空间，而严重缺乏对应的数字出版人才。为了快速扭转这种状况，高等教育教学中必须抛弃只注重理论教学而轻视实践教学的传统教学模式。不过，我们不能从一个极端走到另一个极端，我们也不能只强调实践教学而忽视理论教学，因为，实践不足，难以使学生快速融入社会；理论欠缺，难以保证人才发展后劲。因此，在课程设置时，一定要科学调整两者间的比重，注意两者间学分学时的合理的比例分配。当下具体的做法就是适当减少基础理论课程的门数和学时，相应增加学生实验室课程、参观或见习编辑出版部门、独立调研等实践项目的课时，并将带领学生实践、实习的责任落实到教师当中去。比如，美国纽约大学规定出版专业的学生必须有课业实习，并结合实习的具体情况，与授课老师和出版单位实习指导老师一起选题作成功或失败的个案分析。[9]

当然，为了保证学生实践和实习的质量，一方面，各高校必须重视数字网络平台的建设，必须筹集资金加大编辑出版专业实验室的建设与改善，加大对信息采集、处理、存储、发布等功能实现的软硬件投入，实现整个信息采集加工流程的数字化，达到"按需出版"和"跨媒体出版"，最终使其与出版专业所在学院的相关信息资源系统共同构筑编辑出版学科的支撑体系。另一方面，各高校应加强与出版行业的联系，联络出版机构和前沿出版企业，为学生构建环境良好的数字出版实习基地。通过基地建设，不仅可以为研究机构、出版企业的科研人员提供教学场所，而且也可为学生提供接触数字出版的机会，在实践活动中加强知识运用能力和动手能力的培养与锻炼。比如，2008年起，北京印刷学院与中国出版科学研究所、商务印书馆、方正阿帕比公司、国际版权交易中心等一批企业科研机构共建数字出版人才培养／教育教学实践基地，取得了令人瞩目的成绩。[10]北京大学新闻与传播学院与牛津布鲁克斯大学国际出版研究中心、荷兰莱顿大学图书与出版研究所、台湾的南华大学出版事业管理研究所和新加坡南洋理工大学传播与信息学院等海外的大学或研究机构都建立了正式或非正式合作关系，鼓励博士研究生以项目合作的方式去国外学习或者进修，重点学习国外的项目管理技能和研究方法技能。[11]

3.3 加强数字出版教育师资队伍的建设

没有教师，系统教育将不复存在。因此，出版教育要培养数字出版人才，一支数字出版教育的高素质师资队伍就成为其前提。也可以说，高素质的教师队伍建设是构建数字出版人才培养模式、进行教学改革、提高数字出版教学质量的重要保障。而在数字出版复合型知识结构的高素质教师紧缺的当下，加强数字出版教育师资队伍建设就成为当务之急。那么如何快速建设数字出版教育师资队伍呢？笔者以为，可以采取"走出去"和"引进来"两种方式解决当下我国数字编辑出版教育领域高水平师资不足的问题。

"走出去"战略，就是要求数字编辑出版知识、技能欠缺的教师通过参加全国性的数字出版教育师资队伍的培养和培训，申请参加具备师资优势条件的国内外著名大学的短期访学。当然，那些具备师资优势条件和先进设备的国内著名大学有责任、有义务组织相应的培养和培训活动，提供更多接受兄弟院校青年教师申请短期访问的机会，安排资格老、技术精、专业知识深厚的专家对应提供帮助。同时，高校还可与业界建立培训交流常态机制，让教师深入出版前沿，参与编印供发各个环节，熟悉整个出版过程，定期举办沙龙或学会。

出版教育

"引进来"措施，就是将业界打拼多年已成为应用型复合人才、应用研究型复合人才、经营管理型人才等专家型职员聘任到师资力量中来，让他们将数字化出版发展的最前沿的经营管理、编辑策划、市场营销等专业知识与信息和最新数字、网络技术以及最新的国际国内数字出版成功经验和成功案例引入课堂教学，培养学生将数字出版的知识和技能转化为数字出版物，并进行多种媒体的互动和融合的实战训练，最终造就既懂出版又懂市场，又掌握现代信息技术和现代出版策略的复合型人才。

注释

[1] http://www.cnnic.net.cn/html/Dir/2010/07/15/5921.htm。

[2] 《国民阅读调查：国民阅读率总体上呈增长态势》，http://www.wenming.cn/zt/2010-04/22/content_19594796.htm。

[3] 田胜立：《数字传媒时代对编辑出版人才培养的要求》，《中国编辑》2007年第5期。

[4] 李治堂：《数字化时代的出版印刷技术发展及出版人才培养》，《北京印刷学院学报》2006年第2期。

[5] 张维娣等：《数字出版人才知识能力构成特征分析》，《北京印刷学院学报》2010年第2期。

[6] 梁春芳：《数字传媒与出版产业发展暨人才培养学术研讨会综述》，《中国出版》2007年第10期。

[7] 梁春芳：《数字传媒与出版产业发展暨人才培养学术研讨会综述》，《中国出版》2007年第10期。

[8] 肖东发，张文彦：《从"印刷文明"走向"数字时代"进程中编辑出版教育的变革》，《北京联合大学学报（人文社会科学版）》2007年第4期。

[9] 周炳娟：《数字化时代高校出版人才培养的困境与对策》，《出版与印刷》2009年第3期。

[10] 张维娣等：《数字出版人才知识能力构成特征分析》，《北京印刷学院学报》2010年第1期。

[11] 肖东发，李武：《基于"大出版"视角培养出版人才》，《中国出版》2009年第9期。

作者简介

艾岚，武汉大学新闻与传播学院博士生，河北经贸大学期刊编辑部编辑。

李剑欣，河北经贸大学人文学院副教授。

媒介融合视角下的数字出版人才培养模式研究*

陈 洁 陈 佳

（浙江大学人文学院　杭州　310028）

摘要：媒介融合亟待出版专业知识更新整合，数字化时代图书、报纸、期刊等传统分类和运作模式都深刻改变，内容、生产和表现形式的分类日趋模糊。作为一种新型的出版模式，数字出版的发展日新月异。然而编辑出版学的教学体系、课程设置却仍然在陈述一个若干年前的产业模式。本文尝试通过中外数字出版人才培养的对比分析，结合我国现状，构建多学科交叉理论支撑、全媒体应用平台的数字出版人才培养模式研究，提出综合性大学发展数字出版专业的路径和可行方案。

关键词：媒介融合　数字出版　人才培养

Research of Talent Training Mode about Digital Publishing in the View of Media Convergence

Chen Jie Chen Jia

（School of Humanities，Zhejiang University，Hangzhou，310028）

Abstract：The expertise of publishing is in urgent need of updating and integration because of media convergence. In digital age, traditional classification and mode of operation such as books, newspapers, periodicals and so on, have been deeply changed. Classification in content, production and forms become increasingly vague. As a new mode of publishing, digital publishing develops rapidly. However, the education system of publishing and its curriculum still focus on the industry model which belongs to a number of years ago. This article attempts to make a comparative analysis of talent training home and abroad, connecting the current situation in our country, building interdisciplinary support and all-media application platform about talent training mode of digital publishing, putting forward in comprehensive universities professional path and feasible plan about digital publishing.

Keywords：Media convergence　Digital publishing　Talent training

　　数字出版是出版业界和出版教育关注的前沿话题，数字出版人才培养的探讨亟待提上日程。世界各国的数字出版研究从总体上可分为技术论和经验论，主要的关注点在赢利模

* 本文为浙江省教育科学规划课题、中央高校基本科研项目成果，尚未公开发表（编号：SCG553）。

式、版权问题及不同出版类型的发展路径等具体领域。西方国家的一些专业研究杂志，如《出版研究季刊》（Publishing Research Quarterly）、《出版商周刊》（Publishers Weekly）、《学术出版》（Journal of Scholarly Publishing）等，对数字出版的概念界定、发展趋势、赢利模式等问题给予了较多关注和探讨。我国的出版研究界对于数字出版的研究和关注，相对于其他国家显得更为深入和全面。随着数字出版业界发展和学界研究的进一步深入，关于数字出版人才的培养模式成为业界、学界共同关心的新话题。武汉大学召开以数字化时代的出版专题国际会议中，专设数字出版人才培养的主题。来自北京大学、浙江大学、浙江传媒学院等高校的老师曾就培养目标作了一些论述。当前研究当中，系统的研究凤毛麟角。本文尝试以传播学的调查研究法、个案研究法为主，力图进行全景式的辨析，深入研究媒介融合视角下的数字出版人才培养模式。

媒介融合亟待出版专业知识更新整合，数字化时代图书、报纸、期刊等传统分类和运作模式都深刻改变，内容和生产和表现形式的分类日趋模糊。当前，世界传统出版业正在迅速向现代出版媒介转型，数字出版方兴未艾。作为一种新型的出版模式，数字出版的发展日新月异。然而编辑出版学的教学体系、课程设置却仍然在陈述一个若干年前的产业模式。

同时，出版单位普遍缺乏数字出版产品的研发、营销、管理专业人才，招聘职位要求一般写：需要人文、社会科学类专业大学本科及以上学历，对网络出版业务有浓厚的兴趣等。这样的职位要求实则是比较宽泛的，面对当前的数字出版人才市场，只能以这种模糊化的表述来提出人才的要求。面对数字出版新动向和业界人才新需求，高校的编辑出版学专业教育须尝试转型。

1 中外数字出版人才培养与比较研究

在高校范围内，中国的数字出版人才的培养多是在硕士生、博士生阶段才开始较为系统化地进行，本科生培养基本还停留于以传统出版理论为主、数字出版偶有涉猎的阶段。就全国而言，设置编辑出版本科学位的高等院校已经超过 200 所，设立硕士点和博士点的学校则非常稀缺，而且侧重于图书发行、出版营销和出版史等传统出版方向的研究。据了解，目前，北京大学、武汉大学、北京印刷学院等全国 100 多所院校已开设了有关数字出版的专业方向和相关课程，约 40 所院校开设了电子出版、数字传媒、多媒体出版等数字出版教育课程，形成了一定教育规模，同时，约 30 所院校设立了数字出版课程。[1] 在硕士研究生阶段设置数字出版方向的学校超过 30 所，数字出版相关的博士研究生培养也在进行之中。

一方面，我国数字出版市场越做越大，《2010 年数字出版产业年度报告》的数据表明，去年我国的数字期刊收入 6 亿元，电子书收入达 14 亿元，数字报（报纸网络版）收入达 3.1 亿元，网络广告收入为 206.1 亿元，手机出版产值则达到 314 亿元。[2] 而与之对应的数字出版人才却得不到相应的满足和补充，专业人才的培养始终滞后于数字出版行业的发展。当我们的出版教育还在过去的模式里埋头苦干时，整个出版产业已经发生了翻天覆地的变化。数字出版教育尽管已经提上日程，但是尚未形成一个系统化的学科，其重要性和迫切性还没有真正凸现出来。专门化的数字出版人才的培养尚未形成一个体系，只是附属于现有的编辑出版专业里，各大院校也是在摸索中前进。

再将我国的数字出版教育与国外的高校进行对比，两者还是有很多的异同点。以美国的纽约大学（New York University）为例，它在研究生阶段分出图书出版、期刊出版和电子出版三个方向，在电子出版的课程设计上，既有技术类（网络技术、电子文本发展），也有出版实务类（网络出版实务、网络营销与电子商务、线上期刊和学术）等类别的课程。[3] 而我国的武汉大学与其较为类似，在研究生点中设置电子与网络出版研究方向；北京印刷学院也有电子出版研究和多媒体技术等课程。台湾地区的南华大学出版事业管理研究所，也有数位出版研究、数位学习专题、电子商务与网络书店经营实务等课程。国外在本科阶段就专门开设数字出版方向的学校，数量上也比较少，典型的是英国的牛津布鲁克斯大学（Oxford Brookes University），在本科生的培养中即细分为图书出版、期刊出版和电子出版三大方向。[4]

与我国既重视数字出版实务、又紧抓数字出版理论研究的现状不同，美国的出版教育并未深入到博士生这一层次，很多西方国家的高校中也存在相同的情况。因此，西方将数字出版作为应用型极强的学科，致力于提高学生的职业技能和职业素质。

既然将其作为一门应用型性质的学科，学校就会相当重视学生的实践操作能力的培养，这在我国的教育体系之中仍是一个相对薄弱的点。比如牛津布鲁克斯大学除了常规的课堂教育外，特别设计了各种研讨班和专题讨论会，让学生与导师进行良好的互动；安排学生实地考察第一线的机构，比如印刷厂、出版社、零售书商等；大量的实习机会学生也可以充分利用。[5] 由此，学生既可时刻把握出版业的最新动态，获悉数字出版领域的前沿和发展趋势，又可与所学进行对接。当然，计算机操作能力的培养也是国外数字出版教育的重点之一。

在师资力量和构成上，国外的大学任教人员基本上都是来自于各大出版机构的专业人士，既在学校担任教授或其他学术职务，又是各级出版社的精英人士。此外，兼职和专职两种教师模式也被广泛地采用。相反，我国的师资情况则相对尴尬，业界资深人士进入高校任教得不到制度支持，而真正懂得数字出版的教师又极度匮乏。

2　媒介融合时代数字出版学的建构

2.1　数字出版学的内涵和学科体系

数字出版学是数字技术与出版理论的双重结合的学科。顾名思义，数字出版学是要专门研究数字出版领域的学科，需要注意的是，建立发展数字出版学并不是要脱离传统出版学科，相反地，数字出版学要以传统出版学科为基础，而后再注入新的元素。传统出版媒介在数字出版的环境下仍具有很高的参考和借鉴价值，数字出版学除了要强调以数字媒介为传播载体的出版新趋势之外，还应探讨数字媒介与传统媒介的融合之道。

数字出版学的内涵是与时下流行的数字出版运营模式结合，研究数字出版的赢利模式、发展现状、未来走向、多媒介的交融共荣以及现阶段遭遇的瓶颈与掣肘。它探讨的范围包括网络电子出版、手机出版、手持阅读器出版、音像出版等新型数字媒体的出版。数字出版学不是一门技术性的学科，技术只是作为一种必需的工具；它的核心目标和社会价值在于从大文化的角度，培养出能够运用数字媒体传播人类优秀文化、影响社会大众，并且把数字出版这块蛋糕越做越大的人才。

现阶段，高校的通常做法是将数字出版拆分，分流到电子出版、网站建设与开发等具体课程中去，尚未以数字出版学为中心，建立各级相关课程的体系。因此，该学科的建立旨在弥补出版教育方面的空白，将数字出版教育系统化、理论化。

学科体系的建设涵盖以下三个方面：

（1）师资队伍的建立与扩大。编辑出版学由于发展的时间性和阶段性问题，还未形成一批足够数量的专业型教师，数字出版的教育研究人才尤甚。数字出版学教师队伍的建立，应充分考虑到这一点，除了要尽可能地引进国内外的高水平理论性教学人才，更重要的是将数字出版涉及的各个领域的专家、第一线的编辑与出版人纳入师资力量中去，用他们的工作经验与战略眼光为数字出版的教育注入活力。从各大高等院校来看，教师资源存在着分配不均、集中度不高或者过高的问题，如何在全国范围内实现教学资源的共享与交流值得关注。

（2）教材体系的建设。很多高校尽管已经有意识地将数字出版作为专业教学的一部分，但是具有针对性、时代性的数字出版方面的专业教材目前仍是稀缺。与师资队伍的建立一样，教材的编写同样要取理论人才与实践工作者之长，保证数字出版学的教材兼具科学性与可操作性。

（3）实践环节的对接。数字出版是讲究实践和应用的学科，学科体系的建设应考虑到这一点。现有的开设编辑出版学专业的学校多在北京、广州、上海、武汉等新闻出版业比较发达的大城市，在与当地大型出版集团、出版社的合作方面已有一定经验。数字出版学既要与传统出版单位对接，加速其数字化的进程，又要和新媒体公司、电信运营商、手机终端商等媒体进行合作。

（4）本硕博一体的学位体制建设。正如前面所提到的，国内部分高校将数字出版纳入本科、硕士或博士的培养中去，但是已经或者正在逐步建立起本硕博一体式培养的学校几乎没有，这就导致数字出版面临着"半路出家"的窘境。因此，从高校出来的学生或者只学习了技术上的操作，掌握了一点皮毛，或者是仅仅会空谈一些传播学、社会学方面的理论，真正能够将实践操作和理论运用结合自如的人少之又少。

2.2 数字出版专业课程设置、培养目标等

从国内已开设编辑出版专业的高等院校的学科设置来看，大多归属在新闻传媒学院、信息管理学院或者人文学院之下，着重培养学生的写作能力和媒介素养，突出专业的文化性与传媒性。然而，这样的培养模式过于单一，学生的专业优势模糊，弊端十分明显，已经不能完全满足现今数字出版新趋势的需要。

数字出版专业人才的培养理应是"1+N"的新模式。"1"即传媒与文学的基本素养，不管出版的媒介发生何种改变，出版业的最终归宿仍是文化的传播与传承，因此，传媒与文学的素养始终是数字出版视角下人才培养的支撑点。文学、传播学相关课程的设置要放在突出位置，并且是专业课程的基础所在。同时，此类课程又要与社会的流行热点、特别是数字出版的新动态紧密结合，如开展对网络文学的有关研究、解析数字出版环境下大众阅读方式的变化、如何在浩如烟海的作品库中择优传播等等。"N"的范围较广，包括一定的计算机技术、管理学知识、营销学知识，甚至还要求通过辅修第二专业掌握如法律、金融、建筑等某一专门学科。在课程设置上，尤其要重点培养学生的计算机能力和出版实践能力。笔者所在的浙江大学，编辑出版专业已经开设网络文学研究、音像编辑与制作等应用性强的专业课程。再以台湾世新大学数位出版学系的课程设置来看，出版及印刷管

理、电子出版系统、字型暨版面设计等课都已纳入到专业的培养之中。数字出版是文化与技术、软件与硬件的双重结合，技术作为文化传播的载体越来越起着关键性的作用。传统编辑的分工相对明确，编辑往往只负责出版流程的某一具体环节，而数字出版模式下，编辑应同时具备选题策划、组稿审稿、人际沟通、出版发行等各个环节的专业能力。这就要求提升编辑出版专业学生的管理营销能力与人际交往素质，可适当设置公共关系学、市场营销学、管理沟通学等课程，以弥补这方面的不足。

数字出版专业的培养目标是要为出版业输送一批既有扎实的出版理论知识又有出版实务经验，特别是掌握一定数字技术、深谙出版发行营销之道的复合型专门人才。

2.3 产学研一体的全媒体应用平台构建

随着传统媒介和新媒介的并驾齐驱，全媒体这个概念正在引领当今出版行业的潮流与走向。在纸质书籍、互联网、手机、手持阅读器等出版媒介里，数字媒介毫无疑问的是重中之重，也是各单位竞争的重头。高校数字出版学学科的建立，要尽可能地能够发挥产学研一体化的优势，为全媒体应用平台的构建提出设想与解决办法。

相关的出版社、新媒体公司可与高校的数字出版专业建立长期的合作关系，设立几个固定的学生见习基地，吸收这方面的潜在资源，依托高校的教育优势。以学生为中心、数字出版教育为核心，同时进行数字出版方面的科学研究，并以市场为导向，将研究成果和教学成果应用于数字出版产业。通过产学研一体化的全媒体应用平台的构建，高校的数字出版专业能够形成一个合理的投入—产出体系。

尽管国内的高校已经陆续开展了相关的实践和实习课程，但是仍比较零碎，没有一个体制上的保证。这方面可借鉴西方国家将实践环节纳入课程体系中的做法，确保其为必修课程或者选修课程的一个环节，给予一定量的学分。

2.4 综合性大学发展数字出版专业模式

就中国而言，综合性大学一般是指文理科皆备、学科门类齐全、教学与科研并重的大学。实现多学科之间的交叉和融合，依托各学院、各科系的资源以发展自身，是在此类大学发展数字出版专业的优势所在。

与前面提到的数字出版专业课程和培养目标的有关内容的对应，数字出版专业的发展模式是以本专业为点、其他相关专业为面，点面结合、多面开花的模式。加上目前国内综合性大学呈现出的理工科实力较强的形势，数字出版专业可与计算机学院、软件学院等技术类学院开展稳定深入的合作，这些学院的技术研发实力和成果可以为数字出版所用，而数字出版专业的学生又必须具备良好的计算机操作基础；为兼顾出版的商业性与文学性的需求，还有必要与经济学院、管理学院、公共管理学院等形成良好的互动，让学生掌握社会学、管理学、营销学方面的理论知识。

由于数字出版专业属于应用型学科，有必要挖掘它对于此类高校的反哺作用。教材的数字化、立体化、音像化是目前数字出版领域的一个关注点，而综合性大学由于学科门类的齐全性程度高、学生数量大，教材以及教辅类丛书的需求量相当稳定。如果能够真正推广开去，不仅促进了高校教材体系的完善和教育质量的上升，还能够切实地为数字出版专业的学生解决就业的问题，对于数字出版专业和高校而言无疑将形成双赢的局面。业界对教材数字化的前景十分看好，普遍认为这将是一个必然的趋势，但是至今还未能找到持久的赢利模式，加上诸多不确定的因素，真正敢于"吃螃蟹"的出版社少之又少。虽然阻力重重，但教材数字化是势不可挡的潮流，高校应该致力于发挥数字出版专业的优势，做到为我所用。

与教材数字化同步的是期刊数字化，高校一般都有自己下属的学术型出版社，现在也面临着向数字化转型的过程，数字出版专业恰恰能够为其提供专业性的帮助。以浙江大学出版社为例，自 2010 年成立数字出版中心以来，现有专职人员 6 名，是在依托学校计算机、出版专业和多家信息技术公司等资源的基础之上形成了以数字出版中心为基本力量的工作团队。经过近几年的发展，浙江大学出版社已数字化的传统图书达 5 000 余种，占该社图书全品种的 70% ~ 80%。[6]

当我们的教育跟不上社会发展的现实需求，当我们的学生处处面临就业的尴尬，当我们的行业奇缺专业性的数字出版人才，如何转变现有的人才培养模式，真正地输送出一批引领出版业潮流的先锋人士，是当务之急。任重而道远，愿与同行共勉之。

注释

[1] 张淑芳. 传统出版单位如何解决数字出版人才匮乏问题. 人大复印报刊资料数据，2010-6-21

[2] 我国数字出版喜忧参半. 中国文化报，2010-7-22

[3] 张志强，万婧. 美国出版研究生教育略述. 编辑学刊，2005（6）

[4] http://www.brookes.ac.uk/studying/courses/undergraduate/2010/publishing

[5] http://www.brookes.ac.uk/studying/courses/postgraduate/2010/dp

[6] 浙大社：做数字化建设领跑者. 出版商务周报，2010-7-19

作者简介

陈洁，文学博士，浙江大学人文学院讲师。

陈佳，浙江大学编辑出版专业学生。

German Higher Education on Electronic Publishing

An Xin

(School of Information Management, Wuhan University, Wuhan 430072)

Abstract: With the rapid development of computer and network technology since the 1980s, humanity has entered the information age. Thus the publishing industry has undergone tremendous changes: from machinery printing to computer integrated printing, continued with the CD-ROM books and web publishing. Each progress is not only a technical innovation, but also a great economic benefit. According to a research report during the 2005 Shanghai Book Fair, in 2015, in China, the sales of e-book itself will reach 10 billion CNY, and even more substantial is the revenue of the other electronic publications. Even now, the sales of domestic video game had already reached 93 billion CNY. However, compared to the rapid development of the industry, the training of personnel has lagged terribly. Germany is one of the world's three printing bases, world-famous for her printing technology and machinery. In addition, German electronic communications industry is well developed (e. g. Siemens), so Germany has carried out the scientific research in the field of electronic publishing for a long time. The present worldwide-used MP3 audio encoding is developed in 1980s in Germany. Her unique training mode has also been emulated around the world, including many of our universities, and achieved good results. The main features of German electronic publishing training models are: the variety in credits, the modularization of courses, the work-based praxis and the market-oriented subjects. Thus is given an introduction to the German training model of higher education on electronic publishing, in hope of provoking discussion on Chinese training model of higher education on electronic publishing.

Keywords: Electronic publishing specialty Training model Higher education Germany

德国电子出版专业的高等教育培养模式

安 欣

（武汉大学信息管理学院　武汉　430072）

摘要：从上世纪 80 年代起，随着计算机技术和网络技术的迅猛发展，人类进入了信息时代。出版业也发生了翻天覆地的变化，从机械印刷到计算机集成印刷，再到光盘读物、网络出版，一次进步不仅是技术的革新，更带来了巨大的经济利益。2005 年上海书展期间发表的一份研究报告指出，我国在 2015 年仅电子图书的销售额就将达到 100 亿元，其他电子出版物的收益更是可观，如 2006 年国内电子游戏销售额就已达到 93 亿元。但是，和快速发展的行业相比，人才的培养却显得十分滞后。德国是世界三大印刷基地之一，印刷技术和印刷机械世界闻名。另外，德国电子通信工业十分发达（例如西门子），因此德国很早就开展了电子出版领域的科学研究。目前全球范围内广泛使用的 MP3 音频编码方式就是德国在上世纪 80 年代研制成功的。其独特的人才培养模式也被世界各国效仿，我国的许多高校就模仿其教育模式，并且取得了不错的效果。德国的电子出版专业培养模式主要特点是学分多元化、课程模块化、实践工作化，以及学科市场化。本文仅通过对德国电子出版业的高等教育培养模式的介绍，来探讨我国电子出版专业的高等教育模式，以期达到抛砖引玉的目的。

关键词：电子出版专业　培养模式　高等教育　德国

With the rapid development of computer and network technology since the 1980s, humanity has entered the information age. Thus the publishing industry has undergone tremendous changes: from machinery printing to computer integrated printing, continued with the CD-ROM books and web publishing. Each progress is not only a technical innovation, but also a great economic benefits. According to a research report during the 2005 Shanghai Book Fair, in 2015, in China, the sales of e-book itself will reach 10 billion Yuan, and even more substantial is the revenue of the other electronic publications. Even now, the sales of domestic video game had already reached 93 billion. However, compared to the rapid development of the industry, the training of personnel has lagged terribly. Thus we give an introduction to the German training model of higher education on electronic publishing, in hope of provoking discussion on Chinese training model of higher education on electronic publishing.

1　Chinese training model of higher education on electronic publishing

Generated from the digitization of the printing process, electronic publishing is closely related to pre-press process, but indirectly or do not relate to the in or after-printing process. In particular, with the development of network, the design, producing and distribution of electronic publications may need a computer to the most.

At present, most of Chinese universities put this specialty under the printing department, some of the curriculum involves a lot of courses on printing. While this helps to broaden the students' knowledge, and does train a lot of good cross-compound talents, the talents cannot escape from the traditional thinking of printing, and are in lack of creative thinking of electronic publishing.

In addition, due to the rapid development of the industry, the lack of specialized personnel of electronic publishing draws lots of professionals in computer or computer-aided art and design into this industry. They are indeed needed in the industry, but they are not the professionals in electronic publishing to the full sense. IT talents lack capabilities of designing and producing, talents of computer-aided art and design are not very proficient in technology of network or communication, the talents bearing both the knowledge of IT and designing, however, are in lack of the expertise in publishing. As a result, the work which may be fulfilled by one person has to be allocated to several individuals, thus declining the economic interests, as well as the working efficiency.

The technology of electronic publishing is a complex of the technology of computer, multimedia, network, communication, art and design, publishing and distribution, and logistics and economy, etc. Therefore, personnel of electronic publishing shall be a multi-technology professional. Hence, cultivating professionals specialized in one or two areas and proficient in a variety of technology shall be the main direction of the training of electronic publishing.

2   German training model of higher education on electronic publishing

Germany is one of the world's three printing bases, world-famous for her printing technology and machinery. In addition, German electronic communications industry is well developed (e. g. Siemens), so Germany has carried out the scientific research in the field of electronic publishing for a long time. The present worldwide-used MP3 audio encoding is developed in 1980s in Germany. Her unique training mode has also been emulated around the world, including many of our universities, and achieved good results. The main features of German electronic publishing training models are: the variety in credits, the modularization of courses, the work-based praxis and the market-oriented subjects.

2. 1   Variety of credits

Germany education has adopted the credit system; its training mode laying importance on both theory and practice are called "the dual system" (Figure 1). With the continuous development in educational philosophy, the "theory + practice" model has been updated a lot. In order to mobilize the enthusiasm for practice, and probe the actual operating capacity of the students, the practice courses are separated from the theory courses, and are attached with quite attractive credits. The practice courses are no longer the attachment of the theory courses with few or no credits. In the Electronic Publishing Department of the Media School of Stuttgart Applied Sciences University, for example, the total credits are 180, of which the theoretical courses are offered only 52%, which means that passing tests will only achieve half of the total credits. High credits for the practice courses can help to avoid a mismatch between theory and practice, and mobilize the students' enthusiasm. Students who have achieved the credits of the practical part shall become a quasi-professional on graduation.

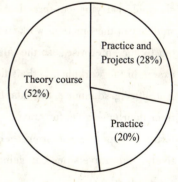

Figure   1

As well as a driving force, credit is a ruler still. The advantages of the variety in credits are obvious. German CPD is no longer simply passing the exams, but it shall include practice, praxis and project jobs. It reflects not only the theoretical level of the students, but also the comprehensive work capacity including the organization, cooperation, and interpersonal communication, and this makes it a more reasonable credit system. At present, in Chinese universities, practice time is part of the course hours. No matter how much the practice time is allocated, not directly linked to graduation, it will only result in pro forma practice and praxis, the graduates still need an adjustment period to meet the job requirements.

2.2　Modularization of courses

There are three directions in electronic publishing in Germany: production of electronic publications, computer and network technology of electronic publishing, and management of electronic publishing. In order to integrate teaching resources, facilitate teaching management and enable the students to find their future, the courses are modularized. That is to classify the courses, and to set modules of similar programs. The modules can be freely combined, any module can be the beginning, and the direction can be shifted in accordance with the interest in learning.

Students begin their study with the public programs of the three directions. If the student is very interested in the computer, he can also start from the related programs. Students fulfilling the courses will be granted certificate for Production of electronic publications.

The students can change direction into Management of electronic publishing when losing interest on the computer. Of course, students able to fulfill all parts of the courses will be granted certificates for the three directions.

The modularization of courses provides the students with possibilities to regulate actively their direction according to their interest and characteristics, and helps the university to integrate the teaching resources and carry out the teaching activities. This model of curriculum designing is an effective reference to improving the quality of our education.

2.3　Work-based praxis

Judging from the distribution of the credits, practice plays a decisive role in German education system. Besides adequate time, qualified practice is also demanded. Adequate time does not mean qualified practice; the usefulness of knowledge can only be tested by work. Therefore, alongside carrying out practice on campus, a large number of German universities settle the students to the practical work in the medium of the study. The credits for the internship is evaluated by the enterprise, so the quality of the practice can be guaranteed. Furthermore, passing the exams in the workplace, the students can guide their learning with the practical work experience. And after graduation, the adaptation period is shortened. Many graduates obtain their first job from their enterprise for praxis, which solves the problem of employment, too. As the school-enterprise cooperation is strengthened, study, research and producing can operate together effectively, the universities can gain from the businesses not only research projects but also substantial project funding.

In addition, each student must participate in a practical project, either an academic one or a technical one. Since 90% of the projects are from the businesses, the students can learn more about the needs of the businesses, and their working experience, team spirit, organizational skills and ability to innovate can be enhanced.

With praxis encoring the requirements of practical work, or going directly to the practical work, students are greatly helped in that they can consolidate the knowledge, specify learning objective, adjust the direction, and avoiding blindness and randomness of praxis.

2.4　Market-oriented subjects

An important concept of German education is that the training of personnel shall meet the demand of market. This is well applied to the electronic publishing professionals' training. A static mode of education and curriculum is sure to be eliminated. In the Electronic Publishing Department of the Media School of Stuttgart Applied Sciences University, the description of many courses only presents the framework, not the detailed programs. Such as "Programming", the course description indicates: Learn the current popular computer-aided design software. Perhaps Flash, perhaps 3DMax, or both. Reserve curriculum to cultivate professionals meeting the real demand, this is an important proof to the market orientation of the subjects.

In addition, the modularization of courses provides the necessary conditions for market-oriented subjects. When the personnel fail to meet the market demand, some modules can be adjusted to meet the new market demand.

The electronic publishing specialty was called to birth by the market demand, so when the electronic publishing industry is developing, the electronic publishing specialty must develop as well. Previous electronic publishing focuses on the audio and video products, but with the rapid development of network technology, the current focus is on the network publication. Therefore, only orienting subjects to the market can cultivate qualified competitive professionals for the market.

3 Conclusion

At present, Chinese universities are carrying out educational reform, including the electronic publishing specialty. The reforms focus on disciplinary development, subject building, training areas and teaching staff, etc. The Electronic Publishing Department of Anhui Press and Publication Technology, for example, draws on the German model and has achieved good results. There are, to meet the market demand, two directions — Production of Electronic Publications and Web Publishing of Electronic Publications. The curriculum is set into five modules: public module, network module, computer art and design module, publications management module and reserved module (adjustable according to the market). In the training area, practice is combined with certification (technical credentials, such as Adobe certification), to improve the practice effect by achieving certification. As for the teaching staff, experts in the industry are invited to participate in teaching and research, bringing information and job vacancies from the industry.

In short, Chinese higher education on electronic publishing can draw on German experience, and establish a market-oriented, practice-centered, curriculum-modularized training mode to cultivate personnel with strong sense of innovation.

References

[1] Michael Roesler-Graichen. Rechnung mit vielen Unbekannten. Börsenblatt. Das Magazin für den Deutschen Buchhandel, 2008 (175), No. 43 v. 23: 18.

[2] Michael Roesler-Graichen. Die starke Aura der E-Books. Börsenblatt. Das Magazin für den Deutschen Buchhandel, 2008 (175), No. 26 v. 2: 18.

［3］ Wir verfolgen eine offene Strategie. Ibid: 21.

［4］ Matthias Ulme Fester Rahmen fürs Digitale. Börsenblatt. Magazin für den Deutschen Buchhandel, 2008（175）, No. 40 v. 2: 14-16.

［5］ 郑霄阳等. 本科编辑出版学编辑类教材编撰研究. 出版发行研究, 2007（6）

［6］ 杨鹏. 中国编辑出版教育的危机与转机. 河南大学学报（社会科学版）, 2007（3）

［7］ 李建伟, 张锦华. 我国编辑出版专业研究生教育现状研究. 河南大学学报, 2007（2）

［8］ 蔡翔, 唐颖. 对我国编辑出版学教育的几点思考. 现代传播, 2006（3）

［9］ 刘拥军, 李宏葵. 编辑出版学专业 20 年发展回溯. 出版发行研究, 2005（2）

Author

Auxin is a doctor candidate of Information Management at Wuhan University, Wuhan, China.

作者简介

安欣, 武汉大学信管理学院出版科学系博士研究生。

河北大学编辑出版学专业本科毕业生（2001 至 2005 级）就业状况调查

金 强 闫占菁

（河北大学新闻传播学院 保定 071002）

摘要：笔者调查了河北大学（本部和新区）编辑出版学专业 2001 至 2005 级 100 余名本科毕业生的就业状况，在此基础上撰写河北大学（本部和新区）编辑出版学专业 2001 至 2005 级本科毕业生的就业调查报告，并通过对调查结果的深入分析，包括就业地域分布、职业领域分布以及影响就业的主要原因，提出了专业发展的建议：增添或删掉课程使之与工作内容紧密相关和增加实践性课程。以此希望进一步提高河北大学编辑出版学专业的办学质量。

关键词：编辑出版 河北大学 就业状况 调查

The Employment Survey Report of the Grade 2001 to 2005 Graduate in Editing & Publishing of Hebei University

Jin Qiang Yan Zhanjing

（Journalism and Communication school, Hebei university, Baoding, 071002）

Abstract: The author investigates the situation about the employment of 100 undergraduates of the grade 2001 to 2005 in Editing & Publishing of Hebei University, then makes a deep analysis on the geographical distribution of employment and writes the graduate's employment survey report. Basing on the report, the author gives some suggestions to the publishing education development, in order to further enhance the major quality of Hebei University.

Keywords: Edit and Publising Hebei University Employment Survey

1 引言

2011 年，河北大学新闻传播学院编辑出版系编辑出版专业迎来她的十周年。从 2001 级编辑出版专业招生开始，至今已经有了八届学生。目前 2006 级编辑出版专业 74 人刚刚毕业，工作状况较难统计，另外有 2007 级 93 人、2008 级 69 人在读。

本部和新校区编辑出版专业共毕业五届学生，毕业生总人数已达到 300 余人。毕业之后他们去了不同的城市，在不同的行业从事着不同的工作，但很多人的工作与编辑出版专业相关联。

笔者自 2009 年 12 月 10 日开始发放针对河北大学（本部和新区）编辑出版专业 2001 至 2005 级本部毕业生就业状况的调查问卷。此次调查的问卷[1]主要包括三个部分：毕业生个人基本信息、就业情况调查和主要针对目前仍从事编辑出版相关领域毕业生的问题调查。其中毕业生基本个人信息包括毕业生的年级、姓名、性别、班级、职务、政治面貌、籍贯、现今工作地点、工作单位名称、单位性质、工作岗位、从事工作是否与编辑或出版相关、第一份工作时间、现今工作已从事多长时间、第一份工作的月薪、现今工作的薪金范围、对大学所学专业的简单评价以及联系方式等 17 项；就业情况调查设置了 8 个基本问题，包括毕业生在就业中面临过什么样的问题、毕业生认为就业准备应该在什么时候开始、毕业生认为自己目前最欠缺的素质、毕业生认为什么对就业成败的影响最大、哪个因素是毕业生择业时需要考虑的最重要因素、毕业生认为大学中所获得的哪些知识和能力对实际工作帮助最大；第三部分主要针对目前仍在从事编辑出版相关领域工作的毕业生，包括毕业生的单位行业类型以及毕业生认为大学期间编辑出版的课程设置是否合理，主要是听取他们对于本专业以及本专业课程设置的看法和建议。

2 参与调查毕业生的总体情况说明

为了真实反映河北大学（本部和新区）编辑出版系 2001 至 2005 级本科毕业生的就业状况，笔者采用随机抽样法，调查了河北大学（本部和新区）105 名毕业生的就业状况。截至 2010 年 4 月 20 日，回收了 100 名毕业生的有效问卷。其中，2001 级本部编辑出版班 13 名毕业生接受调查，约占班级总人数的 25%。2002 级本部编辑出版班 20 名毕业生接受调查，占班级总人数的 50%。2003 级本部编辑出版班 11 名毕业生接受调查，约占班级总人数的 45%；03 级新区编辑出版班 14 名毕业生接受调查，约占班级总人数的 20%。2004 级本部编辑出版班 15 名毕业生接受调查，占班级总人数的 50%；2004 级新区编辑出版班 10 人接受调查，约占班级总人数的 30%。2005 级本部编辑出版系有 6 名毕业生接受调查，约占班级总人数的 20%；2005 级新区编辑出版系 11 名毕业生接受调查，约占班级总人数的 50%。此次抽样调查，在每班毕业生的选取上，秉承代表性和兼容性的原则，在河北大学（本部和新区）编辑出版系 2001 至 2005 级 364 名毕业生中，共选取 105 名毕业生作为调查对象。每班毕业生的就业领域基本涵盖了本次调查的全部行业分类。

此次调查依据基本的行业划分标准对接受调查的毕业生就业行业进行了划分，主要有公务员类、教育行业类、新闻行业类、企事业单位企划和宣传部门类、网络新媒体类、图书行业的图书编辑类和图书市场部门类以及读研等 8 类。其中从事公务员行业者（本调查把选调生暂列入公务员行业）3 人、从事教育行业者 5 人、从事新闻行业者 26 人、从事企事业单位企划和宣传部门行业者 39 人、从事网络新媒体者 6 人、从事图书编辑者 8 人、从事图书市场部门者 4 人、读研者（正在读研未工作的）5 人。公务员行业主要是选调生和大学生村官；教育行业主要是教师（兼学报编辑）和辅导员；新闻行业在报社、杂志社、电台、电视台都有分布，其中 3 人在中央主流级媒体（中央电视台和央视的频道栏目组），7 人在省级媒体；企事业单位企划和宣传部门者主要集中在国企、港股独资和政府部门的宣传岗位和办公室，多集中在石家庄、保定、唐山和秦皇岛；网络新媒体主要是在北京和石家庄，以有权威性的大型主流媒体为主；图书编辑主要集中在北京，大多是文化传播公司和图书工作室；图书市场部门主要集中在石家庄或保定的新华书店和北京的高校出版社；读研者主要是原学校或者其他大城市，这些大城市主要是北京、上海以及香港。

通过分析，笔者发现，接受调查的毕业生现今从事的工作并非第一份，多数毕业生都换过工作岗位，以跳槽三次者居多，跳过槽的毕业生的就业岗位多集中在大城市的民营机构。与此同时，亦有自毕业后一直从事某岗位的毕业生，这类毕业生的工作岗位多为公务员和大型事业单位岗位。

3　参与调查毕业生基本的就业信息汇总

3.1　参与调查毕业生的就业城市分布

选择就业城市是毕业生进行职业选择的第一步。毕业生先对即将就业的城市有个较为准确的定位，继而在该城市中寻找自己的工作。

笔者在本次调查中发现，提到就业，多数毕业生首先强调的是找准就业城市。是选择机会多同样也存在较强竞争的大城市（也可以叫做一线城市），还是选择压力相对较小生活相对轻松的小城市（也可以叫二线或者三线城市），是毕业生面对的首要问题。就本次调查而言，毕业生的就业城市分布主要呈现：倾向于选择大城市、去家乡所在省省会城市，以及回原籍工作等特点。具体分布情况如图 1 所示。

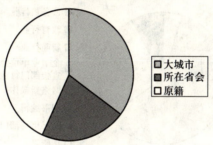

图 1　毕业生就业城市分布图

毕业生倾向于选择大城市。理论上讲，大城市的定义为经济较为发达，人口相对集中的政治、经济、文化中心。在本次调查的 100 位编辑出版毕业生中，有 34 人选择了在北京工作，占总人数的 1/3。而选择在北京工作的这些毕业生家乡多为河北和山东。本次调查的毕业生对于选择北京作为工作地点的理由主要是大城市机会多，发现空间大，况且北京又是的政治经济和文化中心，在北京工作离家还不算远。在北京工作的这 34 位毕业生中，有 25 人表示"喜欢北京，打心底里爱这座城市，在这里可以实现我的梦想"，并希望长久地留在北京，这样的毕业生比例高达 80%。这其中还有 4 位南方人，"上大学就想来北京读书，但是当时高考分数不够。之所以选择读河北大学，就是因为它在保定，离北京近，毕业后顺其自然地来到了北京工作"。另有 5 人表示"大城市可以开阔视野，年轻多出来闯闯，过几年就回家乡"。还有 4 人是因为"当时毕业之后很盲目，第一份工作签在了北京，干着还不错，就这么一直留了下去"。

毕业生选择在家乡所在省会发展。在本次调查的毕业生中，有 21 人选择了在家乡所在省会发展（河北大学编辑出版系学生本省人数占班级总人数的 80% 左右，故而这里所说的省会主要指的是河北省省会石家庄市），这占总人数的 1/5。选择省会的这些毕业生全部为河北省人，且家乡本身就在省会的毕业生为 15 人。

河北大学编辑出版学专业本科毕业生（2001 至 2005 级）就业状况调查

毕业生更倾向于回原籍工作。本次调查的毕业生中，42人选择了回原籍工作，占总人数的2/5。家乡为河北省外的毕业生选择回原籍工作的特点更加明显。家乡在河北省内的毕业生亦倾向于回所在县市工作，本次调查的100名毕业生中，有18位河北省内但非省会所在地区（即石家庄地区）的毕业生选择了回家乡所在县市工作。

3.2 参与调查毕业生的职位领域分布

就河北大学的专业设置而言，编辑出版专业隶属新闻传播学院。狭义上的编辑出版就业领域只包括报纸编辑、图书编辑以及各种出版物的出版。而广义上的编辑出版就业领域（以下称为"大出版观"就业）也包括了文字的各种相关工作，包括了各类文员与文案编辑等。按照大出版观的概念来说，本次调查的100名编辑出版毕业生90%从事了文字的相关工作。而狭义上的编辑出版就业领域即从事报纸编辑（包括记者）、图书编辑和出版工作的仅占1/3。

就业职位是毕业生所从事的具体职业。不同的就业领域对应了不同的就业职位。本次参与调查的100名河北大学（本部和新区）编辑出版学专业2001至2005级本科毕业生就业职位分布分别是：公务员行业约占3%，教育行业约占5%，新闻行业约占26%，企事业单位企划和宣传部门行业约占39%，网络新媒体约占6%，图书编辑行业约占8%，图书市场部门约占4%，读研者约占5%。如图2所示。

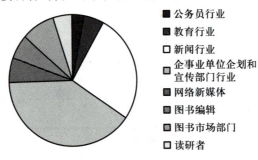

■ 公务员行业
■ 教育行业
□ 新闻行业
▨ 企事业单位企划和
  宣传部门行业
▨ 网络新媒体
▨ 图书编辑
▨ 图书市场部门
□ 读研者

图2 毕业生就业职位分布图

本次调查中，3位公务员的职位为基层乡政府组织委员、村官和镇政府办公室；在教育机构的职位是教师、学报编辑、辅导员以及师资岗位；新闻行业的主要是报社记者（或编辑）、杂志社编辑、电视台新闻节目编辑或编导、电视台某频道或者栏目组编导、广播电台记者，以及广电中心编辑等；在企事业单位中则主要从事企业形象或企业产品的宣传策划、企业或者企业产品的品牌宣传以及企事业单位的媒体关系维护工作；网络新媒体中主要从事网络编辑、网站策划与网站维护；图书编辑主要是出版社、图书工作室或文化传播公司的书籍策划、编辑与出版；图书市场部门则主要是出版社或新华书店的市场销售或市场拓展；5名读研者分别是2名河北大学在读研究生、1名国际关系学院在读研究生、1名中国政法大学在读研究生和1名香港理工大学在读研究生。

4 影响毕业生就业的主要因素

4.1 大学所读专业对就业的影响

本次接受调查的105位毕业生都是河北大学（本部和新区）编辑出版系的学生，河北大学编辑出版系隶属于新闻传播学院。河北大学新闻传播学院新闻传播系共分四个专业：新闻学、广播电视新闻专业（含播音主持专业）、广告学和编辑出版学。四个专业涵盖了媒体的主要领域：河北大学的新闻学专业分报纸新闻方向和网络新闻方向，广播电视新闻专业分为广播电视编导方向和播音主持方向，广告学专业分为广告文案方向和广告创意设计方向；编辑出版学专业分为报刊编辑方向和图书编辑方向。

笔者通过深入分析发现，大学所读专业对毕业生就业有重要的影响，甚至在一定程度上决定着毕业生的就业。具体来说，毕业生选择岗位时的首选是专业对口。本次调查中，选择与编辑出版专业相关的领域（这里指的是"大出版观"就业）来就业的毕业生占到了80%左右。但是，新闻传播学这四个方向的就业领域并不是完全分开的，表现为就业领域的相互交叉。在本次接受调查的105位编辑出版专业的毕业生中，有26人从事了新闻行业，有6人从事了网络新媒体行业，这其中还有2人在电视台工作，分别是电视台新闻节目编辑、电视台栏目组编导，另有一人从事民营机构的节目编导工作。

4.2 毕业生就业的具体影响因素

此次问卷调查的第二部分是毕业生就业的一些具体影响因素调查，设置了6个基本问题，包括毕业生在就业中面临过什么样的问题、毕业生认为就业准备应该在什么时候开始、毕业生认为自己目前最欠缺的素质、毕业生认为什么对就业成败的影响最大、哪个因素是毕业生择业时需要考虑的最重要因素、毕业生认为大学中所获得的哪些知识和能力对实际工作帮助最大等。

在"毕业生在就业中面临过什么样的问题"这一问题中，有难以确定就业方向、不了解就业市场、性别歧视、对用人单位缺乏了解、就业信息量少、缺乏工作经验、缺乏社会关系、缺乏就业技巧、升学与就业矛盾、实际岗位与期望相差悬殊、所学知识与实际差距太大、薪金状况不理想12个备选项；"毕业生认为就业准备应该在什么时候开始"这一问题有进入大学就开始、毕业前一年、毕业前半年、毕业前两个月、毕业之后5个备选项；"毕业生认为自己目前最欠缺的素质"这一问题中有解决问题的基本能力、沟通协调能力、承受压力克服困难的能力、相关工作或实习经验、编辑出版理论修养不足和学历不够6个备选项；"毕业生认为什么对就业成败的影响最大"这一问题中有成绩、学历、英语/计算机水平、工作经历、个人素质、形象包装、职业生涯规划、老师推荐、职业能力证书和社会关系10个备选项；"哪个因素是毕业生择业时需要考虑的最重要因素"这一问题中有工作地点、单位的发展前景、个人在单位的发展空间、薪水和福利、专业对口、是否能提供培训、进修等机会7个备选项；"毕业生认为大学中所获得的哪些知识和能力对实际工作帮助最大"这一问题中有专业知识、专业技能能力、外语/计算机技能、组织能力、协调沟通能力、社会活动能力和人脉的积累7个备选项。

笔者深入分析了每个选项的选择人数，并把每个问题中选项人数最多的前四个选项提炼出来，编制了一份反映毕业生认为的就业具体影响因素列表（见表1）。

表1所列问题中，"就业过程中面临过的困难"、"对就业成败影响较大的因素"和"大学所学哪些能力对实际工作帮助大"为可多选项，毕业生可单选亦可多选，各选项之间有重复。其余问题为单选项，毕业生只可选择其中一项，选项之间无交集。

4.3 毕业生就业变动的主要影响因素

跳槽现象在当今社会中屡见不鲜，而大学毕业生跳槽尤为频繁。在本次调查中，笔者发现有近70位毕业生换过工作，占本次调查总人数的70%。为此，笔者对毕业生跳槽的原因进行了深入分析，归结起来原因主要有以下几个方面。

不符合自己的爱好和专长是跳槽的主要原因。在本次调查中，跳过槽的近70位毕业生中，有近50人把跳槽原因归结为：刚毕业时不了解自己的兴趣爱好，不清楚自己的专长，第一份工作多处于自己职业生涯的试验阶段，换工作是自我探索的一部分。

要回原籍工作也是毕业生跳槽的重要原因。在本次调查跳过槽近70位毕业生中，有12位毕业生原本在北京等一线城市工作，也表示自己很喜欢第一份工作，但大城市的生活成本太高，在外面闯荡了几年之后，近而立之年还是要回到家乡安安稳稳地工作。

自主创业成为毕业生辞掉第一份工作的新理由。在本次调查中，有5名毕业生辞掉第一份工作的原因是要自主创业。这5名毕业生一致表示，当初选择就业岗位更多的是要积累自己在相关领域的经验，等到合适的时机再自主创业。

表1　毕业生就业具体影响因素

问题 ＼ 选项排名	一	二	三	四
就业过程中面临过的困难	缺乏工作经验 (70)	所学知识与实际差距太大 (54)	难以确定就业方向 (42)	薪酬状况不佳 (31)
就业准备的最佳时间	毕业前一年 (51)	毕业前半年 (25)	刚入大学时 (13)	毕业前两个月 (11)
对就业成败影响较大的因素	个人素质 (61)	社会关系 (46)	工作经历 (33)	职业生涯规划 (25)
择业时最需要考虑的因素	个人在单位发展空间 (40)	单位的发展前景 (33)	薪水和福利 (25)	单位培训和进修机会 (13)
大学所学哪些能力对实际工作帮助大	协调沟通能力 (68)	社会活动能力 (44)	专业知识技能 (20)	组织能力 (17)
目前自己最欠缺的素质	相关工作或实习经验 (49)	承受压力和克服困难的能力 (27)	编辑出版理论修养不足 (14)	学历不够 (10)

5　毕业生对专业发展的建言

5.1　毕业生对现今工作的评价

本次调查中，在"对现今工作是否满意"这一问题的回答中，有四个备选项：比较满意、满意、一般和不满意。只有不到四成的毕业生选择了满意或比较满意；五成的毕业生选择了一般；而10%的毕业生选择了不满意，并打算换一份工作。通过分析，笔者发现：选择"满意"或者"比较满意"的毕业生工作单位多为事业单位，且在中小城市；而选择"一般"的毕业生多为企业单位工作人员，即文化传播公司、图书工作室或者企业单位中企划和宣传人员，且工作地点多为大城市，其主要原因是竞争激烈、压力大且收入远远抵不上支出。

5.2 毕业生对大学课程设置的评价

本次调查的105名毕业生，全部是河北大学编辑出版系2001至2005级的学生。在调查中，多数毕业生认为编辑出版专业目前仍处于摸索阶段。在就自己的工作经历谈到编辑出版专业的前景时，有80%的毕业生对编辑出版专业的前景表示乐观。从事编辑出版相关领域的八成毕业生中，大多数人表示自己很看好这个专业，并希望可以继续从事该行业的相关工作。

同时，本次调查的105名毕业生中有90人对大学的课程设置发表了意见，调查分置的备选项目为：课程设置合理，课程设置一般和课程设置不合理。有四成的毕业生认为"课程设置合理"，这类毕业生主要集中在在教育部门、电视台或者出版社、图书制作公司工作；而有近六成的毕业生认为"课程设置一般"或者"课程设置不合理"，这类毕业生主要集中在图书市场部门和网络新媒体领域，其主要原因是课程设置陈旧，没有考虑市场和网络新媒体出版的因素。在"建议增添或者删掉的课程"一栏中，毕业生的回答呈现出了建议增添或删掉的课程与其所从事工作内容紧密相关和建议增加实践性课程两个特点。

5.2.1 建议增添或删掉课程使之与工作内容紧密相关

在深入分析毕业生对"建议增添或者删掉的课程"问题的回答中，笔者发现：毕业生建议增添或者删掉的课程类型与毕业生所从事的工作内容是紧密相关的。具体如下：从事公务员工作的3名毕业生对课程设置没有过多评价，只是强调课程设置应注重培养学生的政治修养和文学底蕴。在教育行业工作的5名毕业生认为课程设置很实际，只是要注重开发学生自己对专业的思考力。从事新闻工作的26名毕业生中有21人认为课程设置基本合理，但应该着重增加新闻评论、新闻采访与协作以及报纸编辑学等课程的分量。从事企事业单位企划和宣传工作的39名毕业生认为课程设置应该更实际一点，尤为强调的是应增加图书营销和出版社经营与管理的比重。从事网络新媒体工作的6名毕业生则认为应该增加网络编辑这门课。从事图书编辑和图书市场工作的10名毕业生则强调图书课程应深入教授。

5.2.2 建议增加实践性课程

在本次调查的100名毕业生中，有近八成毕业生强调了要增加实践性课程的比重，并强调了大学期间实习的重要性。毕业生强调增加的实践性专业课程包括现代出版技术、书籍装帧、编辑实用校对、图书选特策划以及报纸编辑学等。对于现代通讯工具的应用，近6成毕业生强调了网页制作软件、图像处理软件以及视频编辑软件的重要性。

6 结语

河北大学编辑出版系2001至2005级毕业生就自己的工作经历对在校的编辑出版学生提出了很多建议，归结起来有以下几方面。首先近七成毕业生强调了一定要学习好专业课程，不管是否喜欢编辑出版专业，不管以后是否从事编辑出版相关工作，第一要务还是要学习好专业课程。未从事编辑出版相关工作的10名毕业生也认为，学好专业课是前提。其次，毕业生强调要利用好图书馆资源，认为人文学科学生素质的培养关键在于自身的积累，而积累的主要来源是图书馆。再次，近九成毕业生强调了实习的重要性。在调查编辑出版专业学生实习得最佳时机时，近六成毕业生认为应该在大二或大三下学期实习，其原因是学生可以利用实习的经验，在大三或者大四集中学习课程设置中模块的内容，并利用大四在校时间补充自身的不足。其他没有明确指出具体实习时间的毕业生也强调了实习的重要性，寒暑假实习的机会都不可错过。

有了毕业生的积极参与、教师的理性分析及建言献策，相信编辑出版学专业会朝着更加健康的方向发展。谨以此文作为河北大学编辑出版学专业发展中的一个小小总结，更期望文中所提及之问题得到方家指点，以飨师生。

注释

[1] 本文在多处涉及并穿插该调查问卷，该问卷有部分问题包含多项选择。

作者简介

金强，河北大学新闻与传播学院编辑出版系讲师。

闫占菁，河北大学新闻与传播学院 2006 级编辑出版学专业本科生。

数字时代中美出版教育比较研究[*]

张美娟　周　瑜

（武汉大学信息管理学院　武汉　430072）

摘要：数字时代出版业的快速变化与媒体融合程度的不断提升要求更多新的知识、新的技能、新的思维方式以及新的管理手段的复合型人才，因此，数字时代更注重人才发展的动力，而人才的发展最终有赖于出版教育的发展。本文从数字时代出版人才需求的变化入手，对中美两国出版教育中的课程设置与教学方法两个方面进行比较研究，根据数字时代出版教育的需求，从中总结得出美国出版教育中的一些先进理念与方法，旨在为数字时代我国出版教育的发展提供参考。

关键词：数字时代　出版教育　比较研究

Comparative Study of Chinese and American Publication Education in Digital Age

Zhang Meijuan　Zhou Yu

（School of Information Management，Wuhan University，Wuhan，430072）

Abstract：The rapid change of publishing industry and the improvement of media integration require publishing industry has more talents with new knowledge, new skills, new thinking and new management tools, therefore, in the digital age, people pay more attention to talent development momentum, and talent development depends on the development of publication education finally. This paper presents the changing demand for publishing talents in the digital age to start, then makes a comparative study of Chinese and American publication education from two aspects of curriculum and teaching methods. According to the needs of publication education, which will figure out some American advanced publishing concepts and methods, promoting the development of publication education in China.

Keywords：Digital age　Publication education　Comparative study

* 本文是 2009 年湖北省高等学校省级教学研究项目"产业融合环境下出版人才培养与高校出版教学改革"（立项编号 2009026）的研究成果之一。

1 数字时代出版人才需求的变化

数字时代，传统出版业的组织结构、出版流程、交易形式、出版规则都发生了根本变化，这对身处其中的出版人提出了更高要求。数字时代对人才素质的要求与传统媒体时代有着鲜明的不同，不仅要求出版人才懂的各方面的知识与操作技能，而且有超前意识，能够先于读者感受到需求的变化。新形势下，适应数字出版的复合型高素质创新人才如何培养，成了出版教育的关键问题。笔者认为，当前的出版教育，在向数字化转型中更应该重视以下几个方面的内容：

（1）加强对数字出版教育

数字时代的出版教育要以大出版大传播为背景，突出对学生信息系统技术的应用技能、数字信息的抓取和知识表达能力、数字出版媒介经营管理能力的培养，使数字内容创意与表达、数字内容的经营与推广、数字技术应用都很好地融入整个出版教育。

（2）注重培养复合型管理人才

数字时代出版业的一个突出问题是复合型人才极度缺乏。这里所指的复合型人才，主要是指对传统出版流程、业务知识、数字技术及经营管理都比较熟悉或精通的人才。这样人才的产生，要求出版教育从认识阶段向实际操作与实施阶段转变，强调实践性。因此，仅仅认识到数字出版很重要已经没有意义，更重要的是要懂得如何操作、如何开发，并进而懂得如何赢利，如何适应数字出版的环境。上海理工大学出版印刷学院常务副院长楼文高说："数字时代需要复合型出版人才，他们不仅要掌握传统编辑出版流程的核心能力，即选题策划、编辑校对、市场营销能力，而且应具有创新的思维模式与丰富的计算机与网络应用能力，如网络编辑能力、信息检索与快速加工能力等。"[1]

（3）培养出版人才的信息素质

根据数字时代出版业发展特点，出版专业人才培养需要构筑三种信息能力。第一是对数字出版产业链增值环节的快速反应能力；第二是对海量数字化内容的汇聚分析利用能力；第三是对跨媒体内容定制放大效应的运作能力[2]。数字时代的出版教育应大力强化出版人才信息素养的培养，树立起数字出版人才在网络时代海量信息资源的汇聚、识别与定制出版等信息能力培养的新目标，重新构建出版教育人才培养体系，探索出版专业人才信息素养培养的新模式，从而形成具有数字化竞争力的出版专业人才培养方案，使数字时代的出版教育推动出版产业的发展。

那么，我国现在的出版教育水平和状况如何呢？笔者认为，出版课程设置和教学方法，是高校出版教育内容和基本状况的最主要和最直接的体现和反映，而美国的出版传媒业及其教育比较发达。由此，笔者拟选取中美两国比较有代表性高等院校，就其出版课程设置和教育方法进行比较分析，从中发掘对我国出版教育发展有意义的启示和借鉴。

2 中美高等院校出版课程比较分析

2.1 美国部分院校出版课程设置

据"美国新闻与世界报道"（U. S. News & World Report）网站的不完全统计，目前在美国的 993 所高校中开设有新闻、传媒或与此相关的专业。其中，爱默生学院（Emerson College）、纽约大学（New York University）及佩斯大学（Pace University）等院校比较有名气，特别是始建于 1880 年的爱默生学院，是目前全美国唯一的一所综合性传媒大学，该校现设置的专业覆盖了传媒业中的几乎所有领域，在美国传媒界及传媒教育领域都有着公认的重要地位。

因此，在美国院校出版课程设置上，笔者选取了纽约大学、佩斯大学和爱默生学院这三所院校的出版类课程，它们的课程设置各有特点。在资料获取上，笔者通过直接访问这些高校的网站，收集和整理了其课程设置的最新的一手资料，并从必修课程、选修课程和其中的数字出版课程三方面对课程设置情况进行了梳理，具体如表 1 所示。

表 1　美国三所高等院校的出版课程设置一览表

大学	必修课程	选修课程	数字出版课程
纽约大学[3]	出版简介、出版经营管理、多媒体财务分析介绍、营销和品牌介绍、出版法律：知识产权问题、互动媒体介绍	杂志编辑与管理、图书采集和编辑、多平台出版、Web 内容的创建和管理、高级营销研讨会、图书销售和分销、高级营销战略应用和案例研究、杂志消费市场和读者发展、如何使图书出版赢利、"杂志广告：印刷及在线"、数字化策略、网站编辑及印刷研讨会、网上自由出版、新产品开发的网络与移动、网络媒体、电子杂志、"从理念到帝国：新业务发展全球市场：挑战与机遇"、数字出版研讨会、博客研讨会、高级图书研讨会、高级杂志研讨会、高级管理研讨会、高级媒体研讨会、高级数字出版研讨会、高级法律研讨会、高级市场研讨会、独立研究方法	多平台出版、Web 内容的创建和管理、在线出版、数字化策略、网站编辑及印刷研讨会、网上自由出版、新产品开发的网络与移动、网络媒体、电子杂志、数字出版研讨会、高级数字出版研讨会、博客研讨会
佩斯大学[4]	出版原则、先进通信技术：研究和写作报告、专业编辑：复制和改写、图书设计与制作、杂志设计与制作、出版财务	"大众图书：收购，附属权利，推广和分发，以及出版合同"、出版信息系统、专业出版、图书销售和分销方法、出版法律、现代出版技术、图书与杂志研讨会、编辑原则与实践、杂志写作与编辑、市场原则与出版实践、杂志发行、杂志广告销售、出版商务沟通技巧、学术出版、桌面出版、儿童图书出版、高级桌面出版和图像处理/管理、电子出版、研究生研讨会	先进通信技术、现代出版技术、出版信息系统、桌面出版、高级桌面出版和图像处理/管理、电子出版
爱默生学院[5]	杂志出版概述、图书出版概述、杂志写作、杂志出版的职业道德、杂志编辑、变化的主题、编辑/作家的关系、杂志制作与生产、图书编辑、图书制作与生产	专栏写作、电子出版、桌面出版、现代出版技术、写作与出版主题的不同、多样化的图书宣传、定向研究	桌面出版、电子出版、现代出版技术

2.2 中国院校出版课程设置

国内院校的出版课程设置，笔者选择了武汉大学、南京大学、华东师范大学这三所院校。从课程设置可以看出，武汉大学的课程设置侧重发行，南京大学的课程设置侧重文献整理、华东师范大学的课程设置侧重编辑。笔者通过访问武汉大学课程中心、南京大学信息管理系、华东师范大学传播学院网站，获得了课程设置的最新资料，具体如表2所示。

表2　中国三所高等院校的出版课程设置一览表

大学	核心课程	选修课程	数字出版课程
武汉大学[6]	编辑理论研究、图书市场研究、期刊编辑研究、出版经济与出版产业、出版法制研究、传媒集团发展研究、美国出版业研究、民国时期出版经济与出版文化	出版企业人力资源管理、期刊广告与发行研究、版权贸易研究、出版业宏观管理研究、书业电子商务、数字图像处理、多媒体处理技术、电子出版物设计与制作、书业理财	网络出版研究、书业电子商务、数字图像处理、多媒体处理技术、电子出版物设计与制作
南京大学[7]	编辑出版学原理、出版物发行与营销、数字出版技术、出版经济学、出版法律与法规、中外出版史、外国出版研究	文献收集与利用、比较图书馆学、港台出版管理、出版史研究、信息咨询研究、专类工具书研究、编辑研究、中外目录学研究、外国图书管理研究、档案应用研究、编辑出版自动化研究、图书馆自动开发工具研究、数据库原理与设计、网络环境下信息开发与利用研究	数字出版技术、编辑出版自动化研究、图书馆自动开发工具研究、数据库原理与设计、网络环境下信息开发与利用研究
华东师范大学[8]	编辑学概论、编辑实务、书籍编辑学、期刊编辑学、传播学、报纸编辑学、中国编辑出版史、出版学概论、印刷基础及管理、出版发行学、书业营销学、网络出版导论、现代出版技术、出版美学、编辑美学、影视编辑、出版经营管理、出版法规概论	著作权法概论、对外图书贸易、音像电子出版物、知识产权保护、出版社管理、电视媒体研究、网站运作与编辑	网站运作与编辑、网络出版导论、现代出版技术

2.3 中美高等院校出版课程设置的异同分析

通过中美两国代表性高校出版类专业课程设置的比较，从中我们会得到如下认识[9]。

（1）中美高校在出版教育课程设置上有许多相同之处

在课程结构上，两国高校都设有各色各样的出版课程，其中包括出版业务、数字媒体技术，以及出版实物等。在课程的内容上，无论突出何种专业特色，中美高校都突出了图书出版、杂志出版、数字出版、媒体经营几个研究方向。例如佩斯大学就开设了编辑理论与实践、图书设计与制作、图书营销与实践等课程；而国内则以编辑理论研究、编辑研究、编辑与出版经营研究、编辑与作者关系等为主。总体来说，出版教育都注重培养具备出版学基本知识和基本技能的专业人才，注重培养利用现代信息技术进行出版印刷发行的应用型、复合型人才，与数字时代出版教育的发展环境比较吻合。

（2）中外高校在出版教育课程设置上亦存在明显的差异

从课程结构来看，美国注重经济管理类与出版技术类课程。纽约大学该专业的课程设置特别强调出版业的商业特点，金融、销售、统计、企业法都是必修课。近年来，出版专业直接把学生送到商学院选修有关现代企业管理、国际国内市场营销、金融会计、商业法等的各种课程。同时美国大学也更侧重技术学习，从学习的效果来看，中国多是把出版业当作文科来学习，出版技术课程比较单薄，而美国的出版技术课程更加重视学生的实践技能培训，例如纽约大学的数字出版、出版信息系统、现代出版技术、书刊研讨会、桌面出版、高级桌面出版和图像处理/管理等课程，都与计算机技术结合比较紧密。这包括Macintosh计算机的使用，诸如设计排版、图像处理、网页制作等软件的使用，都表现了强烈的技术支撑。我国大部分学校对这类课程涉及较少，尽管一些大学开设了技术类课程，也只是选修课，没有引起学生重视，实际操作与运用还远远不够，学生还不能看到行业内的应用新技术及未来市场发展的变化。

从课程设置来看，美国院校出版课程涉及多个业务环节，全面具体，课程设置细化。例如佩斯大学的课程设置从出版的图书制作、杂志出版到业务许可经营再到出版技术方面，每个方面都非常的具体，提供给学生更多的选择。纽约大学出版课程提供从原稿的评价，营销，成品销售，到图书和杂志出版以及对数字媒体各方面的深入研究。我国的院校虽各有偏重，但都比较笼统概括，专业必修课主要有编辑学、出版学、发行学、编辑出版史、编辑应用写作、图书学、出版法规、出版经营与管理、中外出版比较、新闻学概论、传播学概论等新闻传播类课程，中国文化史、汉语语言修养、汉语修辞学等文学类课程。

从理论与实践课程分配比率看，国内院校理论课程多，实践少；美国则正好相反，学生的实际操作性很强，以市场需求为导向设置课程模块。例如纽约大学的研讨会课程不仅多而且具体，涉及图书、杂志、管理、媒体、法律、市场、研究方法、数字出版多个方面。相比较而言，美国更加重视国际领域的教育与发展，爱默生学院就通过课程拓展学生多方面的能力，包括编辑，审稿，校对，内容整合，宣传，营销，图书和杂志设计生产，印刷和网络出版软件，职业道德规范等。文学课程熏陶了学生的艺术性和编辑力，在创作讲习班，培养了学生的创造力，学生也可以选择参加作文教学学院的课程或在文学社，杂志或出版社实习，专业实践性强。

3 中美高等院校出版教育的教学方法比较分析

3.1 美国出版教育的教学方法及其主要特征

美国著名出版家小赫伯特·S·贝利在其专著《图书出版的艺术和科学》中说："出版不是数学、政治、经典著作研究那样的理论性学科，而是一种活动和加工处理过程。"受这类观点的影响，即使是正规的学历教育中也很少对编辑出版理论做系统教授，而是更加注重实务，以教授可操作性的实用知识为主，从而缩短了出版教育的周期[10]。因此，美国出版教育提倡实用主义教学理念，重视博学精业的教学目标，为学生提供多种教学方法和灵活的学习方式，在数字时代背景下，更加强调数字出版教学。因此，美国的教学方法有以下特点：

（1）教学方式多样化。除了传统的教学方式以外，美国多开设讲习班、研讨会、案例教学、独立项目研究以及举办出版论坛。哥伦比亚出版研究中心的讲习班，学生有机会将出版课程讲座学到的东西加以运用，他们需要与作家、代理商，插图及广告商进行互动协作模拟。根据学生所关注的特定领域，他们会被分配到一些出版集团，负责具体的工作。哥伦比亚大学的老师会提供专业指导和意见。在每次研讨会结束时，出版界领导人仔细评估每个小组的建议，提出有建设性的批评和现实世界的反馈，在这些讲习班所掌握实践知识，经验，都能很好地运用在以后工作中[11]。

（2）重视职业资源教育与引导。学校的教师都拥有出版和媒体行业工作的丰富经验，并且一直保持着广泛的国际联系。校友遍布世界各地，因此非常注重就业指导和与校友的联系。学生可以获得职业咨询专家的建议，在网上发布出版工作求职信息及工作经验交流。大多数出版专业或培训班课程结束时，都要举行职业指导座谈会。由课程导师或邀请行业人士指导或接受咨询并召开一两次大型的工作交易会，让毕业生与出版公司直接见面。学校与毕业生保持长期的经常联系，从而广泛建立校友会。哥伦比亚大学校友事务委员就包括兰登书屋、麦克米伦出版集团、企鹅出版集团、Elle 杂志社等众多校友理事成员，职业资源非常丰富。同时学校会引导学生到牛津大学出版社、布莱克韦尔出版社、企鹅出版社、哈珀·柯林斯出版社等实习，通过实习，学生就有一个很好的就业记录，可以获得丰富的工作经验、国际实习机会、职业咨询，以及日常出版工作心得[12]。丹佛大学会将最后一周培训会的重点放在学生职业咨询，几家主要出版社和其他领域的专家如人力资源董事等会在现场回答问题并进行现场指导，提供工作机会，教会学生如何去搜索，如何准备简历。因此，学生在毕业离开丹佛大学之前，就能与出版界建立宝贵的联系[13]。

（3）与出版业紧密联系。波特兰州立大学的学生可以在自己开的 Oligan 出版社锻炼，同时丰富工作经验，进一步了解该领域的就业机会，包括编辑、市场营销、职业生涯、销售、设计以及更多的参与实习，与出版界和企业界的密切的接触。波特兰州立大学学生除了体验实际的出版经验，学生还可以找到在波特兰新闻中心的实习机会[14]。佩斯大学的学生在学习期间，会被分配到具体的项目，承担研究和分析各种活动，学生不仅可以实践更多的具体工作，而且还会研究公司和相关产业。到学期结束，学生可以根据实习发展他们的论文题目或完善基础的实习经验，并开始进行了初步研究[15]。

（4）重视数字出版教学方法。纽约大学的教学，更侧重传统媒体与新媒体的融合，努力为学生在数字出版和媒体融合时代的学习做好充分的准备。学生在平时的学习中不仅探索管理、发行、跨平台和多媒体出版的方法，而且掌握书籍、电子图书、电子期刊、博客、网站、播客、移动扩展内容以及其他格式内容的学习。传统的出版强调编辑功能，而纽约大学的出版，强调自己的核心竞争力[16]。斯坦福大学、耶鲁大学开设强化班培训，更针对出版技术、跨平台的媒体管理等进行强化训练。斯坦福大学的新媒体研讨会议就邀请硅谷企业家，思想领袖，新媒体专家参与，共同对微博客、电子阅读器、视频网络、新兴媒体工具研究。耶鲁大学的教学更加侧重新技术和内容的交付使用，未来的数字化传播等内容。学生掌握新的技能，使他们能够从未来数字出版的发展、管理过程的创新、网络营销、网络出版的深度、品牌建设等方面更有效地引导并应对转型时期出版业发生的变化[17]。

3.2 我国出版教育的教学方法及其主要特征

我国高校在出版专业教育上主要是以课堂教学为主，老师对学生授课，学生记笔记，其间夹杂一些课程讨论，但教师普遍偏重传授理论知识，不太注意结合案例指导学生综合分析、解决问题。个别学校要求学生参加实践活动，但整体来说，实践性较差，缺少鼓励学生发展个人技能、团队精神、判断力和主动参与的精神，学生动手能力、实践能力和创新能力都受到不同程度的限制，不能适应数字时代出版业发展的需要。在这样的教学方式下，虽然一个出版专业的学生所修的课程非常多，可是除了学校知识什么都不会干，能够掌握的也只是一些理论知识，更别说专业的操作技能与数字时代所需的核心能力。正所谓学非所用、用非所学。

3.3 中美出版教育的教学方法的比较分析

长期以来，受传统观念的影响，我国的出版教育仅停留于学科基础理论教育与应用技能教育，从而使得专业视野狭小，没有把视野扩大至整个传媒领域，同时也忽略了学生职业精神的培育、分析判断能力的养成，"学生在媒介生产的教育中最终只是学会完美的模仿职业化的媒介生产与制作，同时丧失掉批判分析的意识"[18]。在教学方法上，只注重理论灌输，而忽略了学生实践能力的培养。数字时代更需要出版人才的独立思考能力、对新事物的认识能力、媒介素养能力。应该学习美国出版教育中采取的讲习班、研讨会、案例教学、独立项目研究以及举办出版论坛等形式的教学，师生一起解剖，共同探讨，切实培养学生分析、解决出版问题的能力。鼓励出版发行界专家与实业家到高校举办讲座与座谈会的模式，研讨数字时代出版业发生的变化，使学生能在变化中发现并通过多种途径锻炼与提高自己的实践能力、创新能力和管理能力以及数字媒体融合技能。学生需要通过课程学习与实践所掌握的基础知识与基本技能，与数字化出版实践中各个关键领域所需要的基础知识与基本技能高度契合。同时，我们可以聘请一些专业人士任兼职教授，这些人对某一专业领域会有比较深入的研究，思路独特，实践性强，会给学生传达更多的经验知识。例如武汉大学出版科学系就聘请电子工业出版社社长敖然社长担任其兼职教授，这一形式就给学生带去了出版实践中的新鲜血液。

注释

[1] 数字出版人才培养亟待升级 [N]. 中国新闻出版报. 2008 年 11 月 13 日

[2] 梁春芳. 数字出版转型期如何培养出版人才 [J]. 数字传媒与出版产业发展暨人才培养学术研讨会综述 2008 年 1 月 2 日

[3] http://www. scps. nyu. edu/areas-of-study/publishing/professional-certificates/纽约大学出版课程，检索时间：2010 年 4 月 20 日

[4] http://www. pace. edu/page. cfm？doc_id=6624 佩斯大学出版课 2010 年 4 月 20 日

[5] http://www. emerson. edu/writing_lit_publishing/graduate/MA-in-Publishing-and-Writing. cfm 爱默生学院出版课程，检索时间：2010 年 4 月 21 日

[6] 武汉大学课程中心 http://kczx. whu. edu. cn/Able. Acc2. Web/检索时间：2010 年 3 月 20 日

[7] http://im.nju.edu.cn/南京大学资料来自南京大学信息管理系网站.检索时间：2010年3月20日

[8] http://www.comm.ecnu.edu.cn/华东师范大学资料华东师范大学传播学院网站.检索时间：2010年3月20日

[9] 罗紫初.中外高校出版类专业课程设置比较［J］出版发行研究1999年

[10] 齐骥编译.各国出版教育.新闻出版总署对外交流与合作司编 海外新闻出版实录2008［M］人民出版社.北京2009年3月

[11]［12］http://www.journalism.columbia.edu/cs/ContentServer/jrn/1175372207611/page/1165270091617/simplepage.htm哥伦比亚大学出版教育.检索时间：2010年4月25日

[13] http://mediacareers.about.com/od/classesandeducation/a/PubGradCourses.htm丹佛大学出版教育.检索时间：2010年4月26日

[14] http://www.publishing.pdx.edu/pubindex.html波特兰州立大学出版教育.检索时间：2010年4月26日

[15] http://web.pace.edu/page.cfm? doc_id=33505佩斯大学出版教育.检索时间：2010年4月28日

[16] http://www.scps.nyu.edu/areas-of-study/publishing/graduate-programs/ms-publishing/index.html纽约大学出版教育，检索时间：2010年4月28日

[17] http://publishing-course.yale.edu/耶鲁大学出版教育.检索时间：2010年5月20日

[18] 黄旦，郭丽华.媒介观念与媒介素养观念——20世纪西方媒介素养研究综述［J］.2007"传播与中国"复旦论坛

作者简介

张美娟，博士，武汉大学信息管理学院教授，博士生导师。

周瑜，武汉大学信息管理学院2009级出版发行专业硕士研究生。

教育出版的数字化模式探析[*]

丁嘉佳　贺子岳

（武汉理工大学文法学院　武汉　430070）

摘要：传统的出版业界认为，教育出版是专指那些与教材教辅相关的出版活动。然而随着数字技术的迅速发展，出版业也正进行着一场前所未有的数字革命。笔者认为在当前技术背景下，教育出版更准确地说，应该是泛指出版界为寻求更长远更广阔的发展空间而在教育领域所进行的一切旨在传播教育知识、培训知识技能等的跨媒体多形式的一系列复合出版活动。当前我国教育出版已在数字化道路上有了一定的探索和发展，大致呈现出了三种固定的运营模式：立体化教材模式、在线教育服务模式、移动教育出版模式。本文着重分析教育出版现存的这三类发展模式，并在此基础上深入探讨教育出版业如何充分利用自身的资源优势结合数字化技术，克服现有的一些不足和问题，建立具有竞争力的数字化运营模式。

关键词：教育出版　数字化出版模式　移动教育　知识服务

The digitizing mode of MA Education, Publishing

Jiajia Ding　He Ziyue

（School of Arts and Law , Wuhan University of Technology，Wuhan，430070）

Abstract：The conventional knowledge of publishing defined MA Education，Publishing as the publishing activity in connection with teaching material. However, the developing digital technology has brung the publishing industry a huge digital revolution. In this general background，the MA Education，Publishing should be newly defined as series of complex Intermedia publishing activities with the purpose of promulgating education knowleges and professional skills. This thesis emphasizes three digital modes of present MA Education，publishing circumstances. Further more，It considers the insufficiencies and the terms of settlement on that basis. In conclusion，we investigate the optimal approach of establishing essential publishing competitive forces.

Keywords：MA Education　Publishing，digital publishing mode，mobile education knowledgeservice

传统的出版业界认为，教育出版是专指那些与教材教辅相关的出版活动。因此在讨论

* 本文为教育部人文社会科学研究项目 09YJA870022 研究成果。

教育出版的时候，习以为常地局限于讨论教材教辅的开发、出版、发行上。然而随着数字技术的迅速发展，出版业也正进行着一场前所未有的数字革命。笔者认为，在当前技术背景下，教育出版更准确地说，应该是泛指出版界为寻求更长远更广阔的发展空间而在教育领域所进行的一切旨在传播教育知识、培训知识技能等的跨媒体多形式的一系列复合出版活动。当前我国教育出版已在数字化道路上有了一定的探索和发展，大致呈现出了三种固定的运营模式：立体化教材模式、在线教育服务模式、移动教育出版模式。以下逐一分析。

1 立体化教材模式

所谓"立体化教材"，不仅包括纸质的教材教辅，还包括数字化电子教案、教学课件、网络课程等，从而实现教材、教师参考书、学生指导书等不同内容出版物的横向立体化配套，以及纸质、音像、电子、网络等多种媒体出版物的纵向立体化配套。[1]

教学实践中应用立体化教材体系，在教学过程中使用动画、仿真和可视化技术的 CAI 演示课件，在线自测系统和网络视听课程等多种形式的网络化、数字化的教学支持、教学管理和教学服务的平台，可满足现代学习者个性化、自主性和实践性的要求。它依托现代信息技术和网络等多媒体手段，提供的是一套信息化课程的整体解决方案，具有灵活性、开放性、动态性、互动性、多元化、多层次、跨媒体等特征。

立体化教材模式应数字化教育方式之需求，实现了传统教材的数字化蜕变。然而，在信息泛滥的网络时代，如何为读者提供其切实所需的、有权威的、可信任的、优质的内容，让读者从"信息洪流"中找到"源头活水"，是制胜关键所在。对于教育出版业而言，不仅要求出版物形式的跨媒体多样化和传统编印发出版流程的改变，更要求从出版源头开始，就必须注重受众多样化的需求和服务，树立主动地最大化地提供个性化多元化知识服务的出版理念。复合出版这种新型的出版模式，正为教育出版商这一角色定位转变提供了契机。它不仅强调内容与形式的分离，更注重出版内容资源之间的关联。这样从实质上来说，它达到了同一内容经过结构化加工，然后分层次归类储存，最终可实现多样化表达、多媒体发布，实现最大程度的按需出版。其出版模式如图 1 所示：

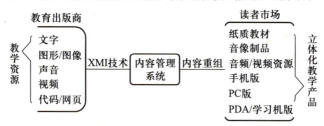

图 1 立体化教材出版模式

如图 1 所示，精选的内容经一次编辑加工后，就可根据需要在各种各样媒体终端上（包括手机），自动按适当的格式和版式展现给读者。同时为实现多样化的增值服务的提供了前提准备，利于发展多样化服务，从而推动教育出版产业转型和升级。

高等教育出版社在这方面作出了探索。高等教育出版社副总编辑吴向在第二届中国数字出版博览会上曾发言表示：高等教育出版社制定了高等教育出版社的内容结构和元数据的标准，并建立了新的数字出版流程，把精品书结构化，按照内容标准，对已经出版多媒体的出版物的资源也要进行标注，使其进入内容管理平台。与此同时还将推出门户网站集成服务。通过门户网站可以把高等教育出版社上百个课程网站都集成起来，以及跟后台的内容管理系统集成起来，为读者提供个性化的主动服务。

2 在线教育服务模式

在线教育系统是计算机技术、网络技术、数据库技术和多媒体技术相结合的现代网络在线的培训和学习的平台。它可使广大学员改变传统学习方式，不受时间、地理位置、师资水平及教学资源方面的限制，使优秀教学资源和教学方法不再受时间和空间等方面的约束，实现远程资源共享，学习者可以根据自己的学习能力和时间来布置调整自己的学习过程和学习进度，实现传统教学无法实现的针对性教学。[2]

就目前市场状况而言，为用户提供在线教学资源（包括文字、图片、视频、有声资源等）或提供资格考试培训服务的既有学校等教育部门、营利性教育培训机构，也有 IT 企业。一般专业技能类在线培训平台都是由实体存在的专业教育培训机构建立的，如新东方在线；也有的在线考试系统是授权于高校图书馆下的数据库资源，如起点考试网。它们的共同特点是资源丰富、形式多样，互动性强，并且通常采取会员注册制度，提供的是有偿信息资源或服务。但其偿付的方式多种多样，既有虚拟性的也有实币性的，还有购买特定的学习卡等。

教育出版业想分享在线教育服务这块蛋糕，除了采取上述建立在线培训、考试等网站外，更可以发挥自身的独特优势，开创更适合自身行业特点的赢利模式——基于 WEB 的在线定制出版。定制出版，也称客制出版，是一种将企业的营销目的与目标受众的信息需求结合起来的出版形态。它通过"印刷品、网络或其他媒介传递内容信息，促使接受者的行为向预期方向发展，谋求的是企业组织和定制出版商的共赢局面"。[3]定制出版充分体现了阅读的个性化需求，体现了为终端读者的服务意识，这也是教育出版的精髓所在。其简要的出版模式如图 2 所示。

图 2 在线教育定制出版模式

教育出版业发展在线定制出版有其特定的必要性和可行性，且具有符合长尾理论的"长尾"式的市场需求。它提供的并不是针对普遍化、大众化的需求产品，而是切合广泛的"分众"式需求的产品和服务。例如，对作为读者的学生而言，尤其是高校学生，通常会有因课程所需会需要买很多不同科目的教科书或专业相关书籍，然而事实上，真正用得到的知识内容往往只是书中的部分知识。这样不仅是学生经济上的浪费，也是出版物材料的一种浪费。因此，如果有定制出版，就可以向学生提供有效的内容，并由此带来相对低廉的价格，同时减少浪费。麦格劳·希尔以 primis 定制出版项目较早步入这一领域，旨在读者能够获取书中的部分章节或将不同书中的章节进行整合。此后培生、汤姆森等大型教材出版商进一步发展了定制出版。

上海伟志文化传播有限公司是新纪元教育集团下属的一家全资子公司，该公司也从教学需求分析入手在发展在线定制出版上做了一些探索和实践。他们与北大方正集团合作开发了教辅图书的数字出版平台。据了解，该平台主要由以下三个方面的核心技术组成：一是数字出版技术；二是"1+4 组卷技术"，所谓"1"就是一个高质量的题库，而"4"是四维组卷技术，即合理的知识点分布、合理的学习水平分布、合理的难度分布以及合理的时间分布；三是三维目标评估技术，分别是知识点维度的评估、学习水平维度的评估和学习目标维度的评估。按照上述三个核心技术建构而成的《教辅图书的数字出版题库》（目前被命名为"伟志智能题库"），是一个智能化、个性化的网络按需出版系统。它是一个开放的系统，会根据用户的需求信息和反馈信息，不断对产品进行整合和改进。[4]

3 移动教育出版模式

移动学习是一种全新的学习方式，它是移动通信、网络技术与教育的有机结合。移动教育产品具有更好的便利性和独特性。然而学习者需要的不仅仅是产品技术上和界面的支持性和可操作性，最实质的需求依然是对内容资源的获取。因此，教育出版要在这个市场上具备竞争力，依然要抓住自身的长处——资源的整合能力，在此前提下，提高自身为用户服务的能力。

目前市场上移动教育产品和服务的提供主要存在三种形式：一是教育机构自主研发，并在内部自主运用。二是技术服务提供商研发产品和平台，自己搜集内容资源。但这样汇集的内容资源往往鱼目混杂，很难具备真正的专业性和权威性。三是不少出版商普遍采取的模式——与技术服务提供商合作，把资源卖给技术商由他们将其发布到终端产品上。这样的结果是，如果出版商控制不好，真正的赢家便成了技术服务提供商。如此长期下去出版商便丧失了主动权。针对新的学习方式和理念，无论教育出版商最终选择何种产品服务形态，都应该坚持对核心资源的自主开发，必须把核心的内容资源控制在自己手中。在此基础上，随着产业模式的转型和升级，可试水终端平台的自主经营开发。这样一来，教育出版商更能有效地掌握终端客户资源，建立起长期的移动教育出版运营模式。

移动产品为教学打破了时间空间上的限制，使得更多人的更多知识学习都得到了新的条件支持。因此数字化的移动教育产品将成为教育产业的新型拳头产品，这势必给教育出版业带来巨大的利润空间。当前基于手机进行移动教育的研究项目开始增多起来，欧洲的"m-learning"项目、"MobileLearning"项目，北欧国家的 Erisson 公司和 Nokia 公司开发的基于手机的移动学习项目，都显示出移动学习对于某些教育应用与教育策略的有效性[5]。随着智能手机的出现，它已经被证明为很多用户手中十分受欢迎的电子书阅读器。根据尼尔森公司的研究报告，2009 年第四季度，美国无线用户中有 21% 使用智能手机，2009 年第三季度的数据时 19%，2008 年年底的数据时 14%。智能手机的市场份额将继续快速增长，尼尔森预测，到 2011 年底，美国市场上的智能手机数量将超过普通手机。考虑到目前的人口情况，这意味着，三分之二的美国中学和大学学生将在两年内用上智能手机。国内关于移动教育的研究目前还处在实验技术与理论概念的介绍上，没有发现使用手机进行移动学习的相关项目的研究文章，但有资料表明，Nokia 中国分公司使用手机进行员工培训在中国同样取得了很大的成功。[6]教育出版商可避陈推新，避开学习机这类逐渐饱和的市场，在手机这一新媒体上另辟蹊径。利用手机进行教育出版模式如图 3 所示。

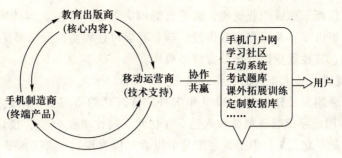

图3 移动教育出版模式

　　具体来说，教育出版可以在以下几个方面对手机媒体进行开发运用：一是建立教育出版手机门户网站，在网站上放置很多教学内容。以往普通的门户网站都主要靠点击率的累积来增加广告收入，然而在线教育的网站用户通常都是即时付费的，每增加一个用户就带来一笔实际的收入。二是进行互动教学。这里的互动不仅仅指学校教育意义上的师生之间、家校之间的互动。它更可以延伸至教育服务提供者和用户之间的信息互动和反馈。三是教材内容的延展，可以对规定标准以内的课程内容进行延伸扩展，建立相关知识链接和课外内容补充，提供更多资源、数据库的手机接入浏览，为用户主动提供更多拓展知识服务。各教育出版社都有强大的资源，只要和手机联网都可以支持这一服务方式。四是建立学习社区，利用手机 BBS、贴吧、短信群等进行学习交流。五是用手机做个性化的深度教学。六是应试辅导，手机网络同样是无限的，可以存储无数的题库。

4　教育出版在数字化道路上存在的问题

4.1　数字版权的维护问题

　　数字版权保护是很迫切需要解决的问题，做得好它能够发展成为数字版权赢利方式，而做得不好它会给数字出版带来很大困扰。传统的纸质图书产品，盗版还需要成本，而数字产品的盗版几乎是零成本，所以网络盗版问题更加泛滥。国家借助于网络发展数字化教育，无论对于教育还是出版来说，都是一次发展的契机，但值得注意的是，这一服务方式不仅与著作权人和邻接权人的复制权密切相关，而且与著作权人的信息网络传播权和邻接权人的向公众传播权直接相关，处理得不好就很容易造成侵权。

4.2　技术标准问题

　　技术标准上存在的问题首先表现在市场上现有的移动电子终端学习设备五花八门、种类繁多，却鲜有几种终端使用相同的文件传输和表现格式。这往往导致数据显示上的问题，例如某些 PC 机上的文件格式与电子产品的显示格式不兼容，要经过多重格式转换程序。这不仅加大了用户的操作难度，降低了信息的易得性，影响了受众的接受心理。此外，没有统一的格式标准，也不利于数字出版行业的整体规模化发展，增加了出版发行过程的间接成本。

4.3　产业升级中存在的问题

　　目前数字出版在国内国外来说都还不健全，包括数字出版产品的开发模式、定价模式、发行模式等都没有一个比较成熟的发展体系，大多只是在利用数字技术做传统产品的服务。所以，如何降低风险、如何架构商业模式、如何实现数字出版的行业赢利模式等是业界苦苦思索的。而数字教育出版，以其开放性、个性化、交互性等优势被认为是未来教育的趋势；但目前尚未形成产业规模，缺乏有影响力的领军企业。与传统教育出版相比，数字化的教育出版由于涉及课程内容讲授、学习者学习过程监控及结果反馈、教务管理等多种交互性活动，其性质更接近于教育服务机构。

4.4 内容提供与技术支持的合作问题

新闻出版总署副署长孙寿山在 2009 年 7 月 7 日开幕的第三届中国数字出版博览会上说，2008 年，中国数字出版业整体收入达 530 亿元，同比增长 46%，预计 2009 年数字出版业收入将超过 750 亿元。[7]但是，仔细分析以后可以发现：4 家技术平台商几乎占据了图书资源的数字化市场，4 家数据服务公司成为网络文献出版的主体，电信运营商、增值服务提供商主导着手机出版，民营网游厂商成为游戏出版的主力军。虽然 2008 年我国 578 家图书出版社中有 90% 开展了电子图书出版业务，出版电子图书 50 万种，发行总量超过 3 000 万册，收入为 3 亿元，[8]但是这些收入只有极少的一部分返回出版社，出版社大多没有从数字出版中挖到金子，未获得与内容提供主体相称的收益。

4.5 受众引导问题

今天的学生，早已适应了网络社会，在网络世界里游刃有余、如鱼得水。但不尽如人意的是，他们的老师大多还达不到这种程度，尤其是部分年长的教授更是有所欠缺。因此，对于网络教育或数字教育这种新的教学方式，以及由此而生的数字教育产品及服务的接受周期会很长。

另一方面，曾有欧洲的移动学习研究项目作出过对于移动学习者及其学习状态和效果的研究。结果表明，移动学习与传统的教育方式相比，其弱点之一在于，在移动学习过程中，由于教学内容和学习过程变得更加片段化、即时化、自由化，使教学过程的可变性增加，这在学习者的心理上造成一种随意感，由此导致学习过程中的注意力集中度不高，学习效率和效果也有所降低。

注释

[1] 禹天安，应对网络出版新对策——构建立体化教育出版体系 [J]. 印刷技术，2007/2

[2] 李天智，魏永红，张娟，李博陵. 在线学习系统的设计与实现. 河北省科学院学报，2009 年 4 月

[3] 庞远燕、叶新：《美国定制出版模式解析》，《中国出版》2007 年第 10 期

[4] 夏新宇. 教育出版的数字化转型. 江苏教育通讯. 2008 年第 02 期

[5] Clyde，L. m-Learning. Teacher Library. Vol. 32. p45-46

[6] 曾玲. 基于手机短消息服务的移动学习系统方案.《现代教育技术》，2005 年第 5 期

[7] 我国数字出版业 2008 年 2009 - 12 - 13http://tech.sina.com.cn/it/2009 - 07 - 07/11163241555.shtml.

[8] 柳斌杰在法兰克福国际出版高层论坛上作主题演讲. [EB/OL]. 2009-12-11 http://www.bookb2b.com/news/detail.php? id=9832

参考文献

[1] 刘灿姣. 我国教育出版发展现状与趋势 [J]. Publishing&Printing，2007（1），p7-9

[2] 范印哲. 教材设计与编写 [M]. 北京：高等教育出版社. 1997，p22-36

[3] 禹天安. 应对网络出版新对策——构建立体化教育出版体系 [J]. 印刷技术，2007
（2），p29-30

[4] 李天智等. 在线学习系统的设计与实现. 河北省科学院学报，2009（4），p36-38

[5] 庞远燕. 叶新. 美国定制出版模式解析. 中国出版. 2007（10），p15-17

[6] 夏新宇. 教育出版的数字化转型. 江苏教育通讯. 2008（2），p24-29

[7] Clyde，L.. m-Learning. Teacher Library. Vol. 32. p45-46

[8] 曾玲. 基于手机短消息服务的移动学习系统方案. 现代教育技术，2005（5），p55-57

[9] 我国数字出版业 2008 年. http://tech. sina. com. cn/it/2009-07-07/11163241555. shtml

[10] 柳斌杰在法兰克福国际出版高层论坛上作主题演讲. [EB/OL]. http://www. bookb2b. com/news/detail. php? id=9832

作者简介

丁嘉佳，武汉理工大学文法学院新闻传播系 2008 级研究生。

贺子岳，博士，武汉理工大学文法学院新闻传播系教授。

出版教育

中国数字出版人才培养存在问题及建议

李大玲　彭　洁　王运红

（中国科学技术信息研究所　北京　100038）

摘要：互联网技术无所不在的服务模式，为数字出版的发展提供了发展空间。本文在分析国内外数字出版的基础上，发现国内的数字出版人才培养缺乏国际视野、教师队伍由于脱离数字出版的一线工作而不能满足数字出版人才培养的需要、课程设计由于受到传统出版流程的影响而脱离数字出版实践与产业发展等问题。针对上述问题，本文提出了以下几点建议：遵循《国家中长期人才发展规划纲要（2010—2020 年)》，重视数字出版高层次出版人才培养；分析数字出版的发展趋势，开阔数字出版人才国际视野；鼓励高校出版领域师资参与数字出版第一线工作，吸引数字出版行业的精英进行高校师资培训，从而加强出版领域教师队伍建设；改善课程设置，要求数字出版人才在研究生阶段进行，要求学生有其他专业的背景，并与数字出版平台紧密联系，从而培养复合型数字出版人才。

关键词：数字出版　人才培养　教师队伍　课程设置　复合人才

Research on the Education of Digital Publishing Talent in China

Li Daling　Peng Jie　Wang Yunhong

（Institute of Scientific and Technical Information of China，Beijing，100038）

Abstract：The ubiquitous Internet provides digital publishing huge space for development. Based on the current situation of digital publishing in China and foreign countries，problems in publishing-education are explored which includes the lack of international perspective；the teachers cannot meet the need of training for the separation from the digital publishing practice；the disengagement between curriculum and the digital publishing practice and publishing industry under the influence of traditional publishing pattern. Suggestions are presented in the last part of this paper. First，we should focus on training high-qualified talent following the *National Program for long-term talent development*. Second，we can broaden international view after analyzing the future trend of digital publishing in China. Third，we also should strengthen teaching staff in the way of encouraging them to participate digital publishing practice，and attracting talents in digital publishing to train teachers in university. The last one is improving curriculum setting and training the digital publishing talents in the postgraduate stage. what's more，the talents should have an education background of another major and should be closely linked with digital publishing platform.

Keywords：Digital publishing　Publishing talents education　Teaching staff　Curriculum setting Inter-discipline talent

互联网技术无所不在的服务模式，为传统出版业带来了无限发展空间，也给传统出版业带来了巨大的挑战，促进了我国传统出版业全面向数字出版时代转移。相对于国外发达国家，我国的数字出版起步较晚，因此，我国的数字出版经历了一个探索时期。目前，我国出版界正蓄势待发，准备在数字出版领域一展宏图。但是，数字出版的发展除了依赖出版观念的更新、出版流程的再造、信息技术的应用之外，更需要数字出版人才的支撑，否则就如无源之水，难以获得长久、持续的发展。因此，需要对国外和国内的数字出版进行探讨的基础上，对我国数字出版人才培养进行思考。

1　数字出版的模式

1.1　国外数字出版模式

数字出版以其信息量大、交互性强、传播范围广、成本低、易流通、易检索、节约资源等优势，近年来在国内外迅速发展，国外发达国家的数字出版在产业链、知识产权、格式兼容等方面都取得了一些经验。

国外的数字出版产业链也较为成熟，产业链的主体包括著作权人、数字出版商、技术提供商、网络传播者和读者等，但主要的推动者是出版社。由于国外数字出版起步早，市场较为成熟，出版社（出版公司）对数字出版产业的运行较为熟悉，敢于参与数字出版。加之国外知识产权保护制度较为完善，政策法规完备，执法更为严格，因而出版社敢于将作品数字化，并通过网络扩大收益。此外，通过资本运作，发达国家形成了一些具有雄厚实力的出版集团。高度集中的出版力量较容易形成规模经济，有利于数字出版物的推广。目前，发达国家的出版社大多采用股份有限公司的形式，其中有的是上市公司。大型出版集团拥有丰富的内容资源、资金，技术实力雄厚，市场占有率高。这些集团根据市场需求和自身条件，不断推出一系列高质量的数字出版产品。他们还将产业链扩展到移动通讯、电视、电影等一系列领域。除了出书，出版集团还出售书的内容，如出售书的电影、电视版权，推销书籍的国际版权，图书的移动通信下载，电子阅读器电子书的下载等。

在数字出版的版权保护方面，1998 年美国颁布的《数字千年版权法》（DMCA）中规定，破解版权保护技术是违法行为，并定义了版权管理信息。这些版权管理信息，如作者、联系方式、授权条件、权利有效期等，不仅可以标示权利人，方便用户获得作品使用许可。还可监控用户使用情况，跟踪侵权行为的发生。这在很大程度上既杜绝了数字作品的不正当使用，又能够保证数字出版、发行、传播等环节能在合理的法律环境下有秩序地进行。针对数字出版的版权授权方式与途径。国外多采用出版社授权、通过著作权集体管理组织和专业的版权代理机构和代理人获权、集团化购买版权的方式，此外还有默许、先斩后奏、"创作共用"（Creative Commons）协议和"公民互联网授权联盟"（Citizen Internet Empowerment Coalition）的方式。

为了解决不同的文件格式之间的兼容问题，包括微软、Adobe、Spring 等近 200 家公司在内的厂商组成了 Open eBOOK[1] 组织，以商讨制定网络出版的标准。目前这个组织制定出基于 XML 的开放出版接头（OPS）、开放打包格式（OPF）、开放容器格式（OCF）[2] 行业的标准草案 EPUB，采用 EPUB 出版者可以分布式地生成和发布一个单一的数字出版物，可以为读者提供没有加密的电子书和其他出版物之间的相互操作。

1.2　中国数字出版的现状

与国外不同，我国的数字出版的驱动者不是出版商而是拥有技术和信息服务平台的集成服务商[3]。随着数字出版的发展，我国数字出版呈现出政策对数字出版的引导作用增强，监督力度正在加大，营销策略与赢利模式有所突破等特点；工信部 3G 牌照的发放，中国手机阅读用户日渐增加，为手机阅读提供了广阔的发展空间；全媒体出版初露端倪，如冯小刚的长篇小说《非诚勿扰》采用传统图书、互联网、手持阅读器、手机阅读平台等方式同步出版，开创了国内全媒体出版的先河。目前，电信运营商正在积极建设手机阅读基地，打造手机阅读产业链[4]。从 2009 年开始得到迅猛发展的微博也是一种新的数字出版形式。

在数字出版知识产权方面，网络规范与版权保护得到了政府和社会的关注与改善，新闻出版总署、国家版权局、工信部等相关部委展开治理行动，截至 2009 年 11 月末，各级版权行政执法部门及公安、工信部门共查办网络侵权案例 541 件，关闭非法网站 362 个，采取责令删除或屏蔽侵权内容的临时性执法措施 552 次。有效的措施、强大的打击力度坚定了数字出版商使用和保护正版、坚持走正版之路的信心。

传统出版集团面临数字出版的压力，纷纷涉足数字出版领域，并得到了国家政策上的支持。《国家中长期人才发展规划纲要（2010—2020 年）》[5]（以下简称"纲要"）在"建设人才工程"中提出了"文化名家工程"，提出为更好的推动宣传思想文化工作，进一步提高国家文化软实力，每年要重点扶持和资助新闻出版名家承担的重大课题、重点项目等。这些出版名家承担的重大课题和项目将会在很大程度上推动我国数字出版事业的发展。

我国数字出版产业将进入高速发展时期，数字出版产业链条将全部贯通，形成中国大型出版集团开始发力数字出版业、国内九个出版集团数字出版合纵连横发展的局面，其中万方数据股份有限公司与中国科学技术信息研究所是我国唯一的 DOI 代理，推动了行业合作和信息服务规范化，为数字出版的标准化做出了重要贡献，截至 2010 年 3 月，中文 DOI 注册数量已达 130 万，仅次于 CrossRef 位列世界第二位[6]；北京方正阿帕比技术有限公司携手投资者报推出手机报，大力发展数字出版业[7]；中国出版集团公司制定了数字出版发展战略，启动"中国数字出版网"，开始搭建数字出版平台，将与美国甲骨文公司进行深度合作，并使用其提供的 Oracle 通用内容管理解决方案打造统一的出版数字资源管理平台[8]；中国科学出版集团启动了"中国科学出版集团数字出版平台"项目，现在已经进入第二期建设，计划 2010 年为用户提供服务；广东省出版集团启动"电子书包"、教育出版数字化平台、手机出版、广东数字出版基地项目；安徽出版集团推出数字出版及新媒体业务，建立校园和社区数字网络教育系统，开通"时代"网上教育平台；江西省出版集团计划实现数字出版流程管理、数字内容管理、网络销售等，从而实现从传统出版物提供者向数字时代内容服务商转型，并与北大方正集团签署战略合作框架协议；陕西出版集团与国家图书馆签署协议，构建国内最权威、完整的"文化教育音像出版物数据库"；浙江联合出版集团计划出版资源数字化，建设全媒体出版平台，建立新的业务体系，实现数字内容的集成。

数字出版软件方面，万方数据的"全 XML 流程多样性出版服务研究"在采、编、审校、排版、出版、传播、销售、数字产权保护等数字出版全流程多环节出版过程中采用 XML 的关键技术，提高了对资源质量和编审效率，满足了多种阅读终端需求，对促进中国出版业，特别对多样性出版与应用产生了积极影响。目前国内已经出现了不少稿件管理软件系统，如方正、旗云、玛格泰克等。

2　数字出版业对人才培养存在的问题

从上面国内外数字出版模式的比较可以看出，国外的数字出版较为成熟，国内的数字出版即将进入高速发展时期，因此，高校在培养数字出版专业人才时，必须认清国内数字出版的现状，认清国内出版人才培养存在的主要问题，以及未来数字出版的趋势，培养复合型数字出版人才，从而为数字出版的高速发展提供支撑。

2.1　人才培养缺乏国际化视野

近几年来，我国出版物品种上升，销量下降，精品不多，出版贸易逆差增大，与出版机构的急功近利与经济指标决定一切的社会导向有很大的关系，但是也与出版人才的培养缺乏国际化视野，难以适应数字出版的需要有一定的联系。由于出版人才的培养相对滞后，出版从业者被培养时，数字出版的进展不明朗，缺乏对数字出版的认识，特别是对国外的数字出版与我国的数字出版的阶段性差异缺乏足够的认识，因此不能够适应数字出版的发展。

出版人才的培养现在有通才和专业化两种思路，其中通才教育要求培养出的出版人才具有多学科的背景知识和基础，不再区分编辑学、出版学、图书发行专业，是多面手；专业化出版人才强调特色化，避免模式单一。无论是通才还是专门人才，缺少国际视野将会阻碍数字出版的发展。

2.2　出版教师队伍无法满足数字出版人才培养的需求

高校是出版业从业者的主要来源，我国高校有600多个编辑出版类专业教学点，在校生10多万人，覆盖专科、本、硕、博多个教育层次，每年毕业近3万人[9]。但是，高校的培养模式跟不上数字出版对人才的需求，这是因为数字出版在中国近几年才得到较大的发展，中国的数字出版也处在探索期，数字出版的从业人员本身经验就不足，高校更是缺少具有数字出版丰富实践背景和经验的教师队伍，因此高校教育无法满足数字出版对出版人才的要求。

2.3　出版人才培养课程设置脱离数字出版实践与产业发展的要求

中国的图书出版业，从作者、出版商（编辑、印刷、发行）、分销商，再到图书馆和书店，环节较多，已经形成了成熟的经营模式，原有的出版人才培养课程设置往往遵循这一模式。此外，高校本科教学计划是提前制定的，即在学生入学之前制定专业培养计划和教学计划，在教学过程中，尽量不对教学培养计划和教学计划进行大的调整。这就造成了正在培养的和已经培养出来的人才由于课程设置不合理，脱离了数字出版实践和产业发展的要求。

另一方面，近几年数字出版技术的迅猛发展令传统出版的一般从业者有些措手不及，出版机构本身正处于一个学习、吸收和应用的阶段，大学的课程设置很难根据数字出版最新的发展立刻做出调整。

3　数字出版人才培养的建议

3.1　重视数字出版高层次人才培养

"纲要"提出人才队伍建设的主要任务是"大力开发经济社会发展重点领域急需紧缺专门人才"，具体举措中提到继续实施"四个一批"人才培养工程，加强出版领域高层次人才队伍建设。说明国家非常重视出版人才的建设，特别是高层次出版人才的建设，能够引领数字出版发展的人才是高层次出版人才中不可或缺的一部分。高层次出版人才应当包括，数字出版中的领军式经营管理人才、高水平的编辑策划人才、复合型的数字出版人才、数字时代的影响推广人才、外向型的国际出版人才，以及数字知识内容组织人才。

3.2 培养数字出版人才的国际视野

随着我国数字出版与国际日益接轨，我国出版物质量的上升，与其他国家的版权贸易的日益增长，数字出版人才必须具有国际视野，深刻理解国外数字出版的模式以及国内数字出版的现状与发展趋势，懂得国际出版市场的竞争规则，熟悉国外数字出版企业经营方式，从而能够主导国内数字出版的建设与发展。

3.3 加强数字出版师资队伍建设

人才培养不仅仅是学历教育和知识教育，更应该重视利用所学的专业和数字出版知识解决数字出版行业出现的具体问题，并把理论与实践相结合，在理论提炼与实践验证的基础上总结提炼本专业特有的方法，提高解决问题的能力。重点放在用学过的知识来解决好行业，专业的具体的问题，理论，实践。并总结出自己的方法，有效率有质量，为了实现这些目标必须加强教师队伍的建设。

高校要依托数字出版建设的主体——内容服务商和大型出版集团，聘请一线的数字出版的实践者为高校师资进行培训，并聘请其为客座教师。同时，鼓励骨干教师参与到数字出版机构的数字出版项目中去，在实践中提升对数字出版的认识和技能，系统地掌握数字出版的核心，从而增强教师的实力，为人才的培养打下夯实的基础。除了对目前的数字出版实践的参与之外，高校的出版师资队伍还要对国外的数字出版进行跟踪和研究，参考国外数字出版的情况，研究我国数字出版的未来发展趋势，研究在互联网上进行数字出版服务需要人才具有什么素质，从而提前进行准备。

3.4 改善高校出版课程设置，创新数字出版人才培养模式

在人才培养上，要满足对数字出版人才的不同层次需求，特别是对于高层次、复合型的数字出版人才的培养应当在硕士、博士阶段进行；本科阶段不设置专门的数字出版专业，数字出版硕士从其他专业学生中进行选拔。对于现有出版专业设置不能立刻改变的现状，应当要求学生辅修另一个专业的课程，并获得相应的学位方可报考数字出版专业的研究生。这样，数字出版人才首先具备了相应的专业领域知识，在研究生阶段，在对数字出版平台应用的基础上，对内容管理、全媒体出版、数字出版营销、数字出版理论四个方向均需要进行系统的学习、研究和实践，并对某个方向有所侧重。

出版基础模块主要涵盖现有出版专业能够适应数字出版时代需要的专业课程。内容组织模块是目前数字出版中的难题，包括将传统印刷的内容数字化的活动，而且对传统出版内容进行再组织，提供更小力度的知识片段的服务，它是一种依托传统和现在资源，用数字化的工具进行立体化传播的出版方式。数字出版营销模块，不仅仅是数字出版物、纸质出版物的营销，更需要建立起出版物创作者与用户之间的桥梁，把读者的阅读习惯和行为与数字内容进行连接。全媒体出版模块，主要进行传统媒体、数字媒体与出版相关的应用。数字出版理论主要对数字出版涉及的各种理论进行研究，对于新的技术从理论上进行

探索和总结。

根据上面的人才培养模式，高校出版专业课程的设置应该满足对数字资源的加工、管理及多种方式多种渠道应用的需要，能够促进读者、作者、出版社之间无障碍地进行交流和互动，从技术和原理上实现对数字出版物章节的定制，多种数字出版物组合定制的要求。

高校课程的设置，应该采取平台+模块的课程体系。平台即数字出版平台，模块即人才培养结构。在平台部分，高校通过与出版集团合作建立实习基地，模拟出版平台系统演练等多种途径来为学生提供实践的机会和体验，提高学生的动手能力和解决问题能力。

通过这种方式培养出来的人才，既解决了目前高校存在的教育弊端，又具有传统的出版知识结构和技能，对数字出版的模式、技术，以及数字出版中的知识组织与管理、数字出版的商业化等方面的知识与技能有所了解和侧重的复合型人才，又能够深入到数字出版业务链中，从而适应数字时代的发展，成长成应用型、复合型和外向型的新型出版人才。

注释

［1］ http：//www.openebook.org

［2］ http：//www.idpf.org/forums/

［3］ 贺德方. 中外数字出版现状比较给我国出版业的其实. 科技与出版，2006（5）：9-11

［4］ 李广宇. 2009 年数字出版发展状况及主要特点分析. 出版参考，2010（3）上旬刊：14-16

［5］ http：//www.hunan.gov.cn/tmzf/xxlb/ttxw/201006/P020100607340077958281.doc

［6］ 中国数字出版如何应对洋巨头冲击 http：//it.sohu.com/20100830/n274584833.shtml. ［2010-8-30］

［7］ 《2010—2015 年中国数字出版产业运行动态及前景研究报告》. http：//www.51report. com/research/detail/116056539.html

［8］ 中国出版集团牵手甲骨文抢滩数字出版. http：//tech.sina.com.cn/i/2010-05-21/ 02414213833.shtml:2010nian. ［2010-5-21］

［9］ 贺永祥. 论出版人才培养的教学困境与实践途径. 当代教育论坛，2010（3）

作者简介

李大玲，博士，中国科学技术信息研究所博士后。

彭洁，研究员，中国科学技术信息研究所资源共享促进中心主任，北京万方数据股份有限公司技术研究院副院长。

王运红，中国科学技术信息研究所资源共享促进中心课题组长。

时尚期刊网站发展 B2C 业务的 SWOT 分析

朱静雯　刘志杰

（武汉大学信息管理学院　武汉　430072）

摘要：目前，尽管中国的时尚类刊物已经全部拥有自己独立域名的网站，但仍改变不了这些网站以网络广告作为主要的赢利模式。本论文从时尚期刊网站发展 B2C 业务入手，运用 SWOT 分析法，结合当前一些时尚期刊网站在发展 B2C 业务中的优势和不足，对时尚期刊网站发展 B2C 业务的内外部环境进行分析，结合分析结果，本研究认为期刊网站发展 B2C 业务将会在为期刊网站赢利的重要构成部分，但期刊网站应当从第三方交易平台做起，并逐步发展为出售自己产品的交易平台。

关键词：SWOT 分析　期刊网站　电子商务

SWOT Analysis of B2C E-Commerce on Fashion Magazine Sites

Zhu Jingwen　Liu Zhijie

（School of Information Management in Wuhan University，Wuhan，430072）

Abstract：For the moment，although Chinese fashion publications have already had their independent domain name websites，they still cannot change the reality that these websites' major payoff mode is advertisement. The paper explores the internal and external environments of developing B2C e-commerce on the fashion magazine websites. The approach adopted in this study is known as SWOT analysis，an important strategic planning tool. In summing up it may be stated that the fashion magazine's websites have a lot of advantages to develop B2C e-commerce，and fashion magazines' publishers will generate a hefty chunk of revenue by developing B2C e-commerce on the magazine sites. But，they should start from third-party e-commerce trading platforms in the first step，and extend to sell their own products and services gradually.

Keywords：SWOT analysis　Magazine sites　B2C e-commerce

随着出版业数字化进程加快，目前，中国的时尚类刊物已经全部拥有了自己独立域名的网站，但网站的赢利模式多数还是以网络广告为主。时尚期刊如果在期刊网站上开展 B2C 业务，对期刊的赢利模式多元化具有重要意义。虽然时尚期刊涉足电子商务并不是什么新鲜事，比如昕薇、米娜等杂志的官方网站已经开始销售服饰产品，但目前学界对于时尚期刊网站发展 B2C 业务的分析还相当匮乏，本文试图通过对时尚期刊网站发展 B2C 业务的 SWOT 分析，初步阐释时尚期刊网站在电子商务方面的发展前景。

1 时尚期刊网站发展 B2C 业务的优势

1.1 时尚期刊有众多的消费能力强、品牌忠诚度高的读者，他们同时也是时尚产品的买家

电子商务网站的价值，不在于网站经营者本身销售了多少产品，而在于这个电子商务网站具有多大的消费能力，也可以说是这个网站具有多少交易机会。[1]时尚类刊物一向以化妆品和服装为主要内容，尤其是像《瑞丽服饰美容》、《时装之苑》这样的期刊，其主要内容集中于服饰和化妆品，多年来集中了具有高度忠诚度和充足购买力的受众，这些读者不仅是杂志的读者，很多还同时是服饰和化妆品的消费者，所以把受众对时尚用品资讯的关注力转化为购买力并非难事。在网络购物当中，网民更注重交易时双方的信用，期刊网站恰好具有可信度高的天然优势。以瑞丽为例，据其网络统计（如表 1 所示），瑞丽女性网拥有 2 582 000 个注册用户，这些消费者收入高，购买力强。而这些消费者中有 45% 每月至少一次网上购物，这无疑是瑞丽女性网发展 B2C 业务的最大优势。

表 1　瑞丽女性网受众调查[2]

消费行为 Behavior	周期 Period	状态或金额 Status or Amount	人数百分比 Percentage
上网时间 Net surfing	每周 every week	大于 20 小时 > 20 hours	75%
手机增值服务 Mobile Value-Added Service	每月 every month	10 元左右 around ￥10.00	61%
网上购物 Internet Shopping	每月 every month	至少一次 at least once	45%
下载瑞丽电子杂志 Rayli E-Zine Download	N/A	定期 regularly	53%
博客 Blog	N/A	1 个（超过 2 个） one（more than two）	70%（45%）

1.2 时尚期刊拥有众多时尚产品广告客户，他们同时也是时尚产品的卖家

时尚期刊的网站作为一个卖家和买家的聚集地，这个平台无可替代，所以以将广告客户的服饰和化妆品搬到期刊网站上来进行在线交易，无论对于期刊社还是广告客户，都是一件让人高兴的事情。因为作为广告主而言，他们除了希望提高自己的品牌知名度以外，更希望通过期刊的平台直接将产品出售给顾客，所以如果期刊网站与广告客户结合建立网上商城，卖家的信用和权威性不言而喻，而且此举不但可以进一步加深与广告客户的业务合作，提高广告客户对期刊的忠诚度，同时也有利于刊物对受众行为进行分析，更加清楚地了解本刊物的广告效果。国内在期刊网站发展电子商务比较成功的例子是久尚网，旗下拥有国内领先的著名女性时尚杂志《米娜 Mina》、《卡娜 Scawaii!》，专业母婴杂志《完美妈咪》。该网站除了经营自己的品牌产品外，还有和众多品牌合作，并将合作品牌产品在久尚网上销售。目前，久尚网与企业的商务合作涉及方面也非常广泛，除了广告合作以外，还包括品牌加盟、生产合作、营销合作等等。

2 时尚期刊网站发展 B2C 业务的不足

2.1 期刊社在仓储、物流配送方面短期内难以做到科学高效

期刊网站毕竟是以内容编辑为主的行业，电子商务对于期刊社来说，还是一个相对比较陌生的事物，而期刊社的物流主要是通过发行渠道来完成，而这一渠道主要是从事印刷品销售，所以期刊社的工作人员对印刷品以外物流及配送管理缺乏经验。期刊社如果发展 B2C 业务，就要有足够种类和数量的商品，这势必需要相应的仓库和科学的仓储管理。因为当订单从网上传来，就要求相应的货物配送。没有科学的管理，就会造成商品越多，配货越难，订单越多，问题越多的局面。建立一套科学高效的仓储物流系统，保证货源充足配送迅速，需要一个不断完善的过程，这对于期刊社来说也不仅要求有资金的投入还要有人力的投入，可以说是面临的最大的难题。而当前仓储物流体系的高效率运作，是电子商务得以获取优势的主要原因。以购物网站京东商城为例，尽管近年发展很快，但仓储物流的瓶颈一直制约着京东的发展壮大，尤其是春节期间订单暴增，远远超出了物流配送能力，导致订单大量延误。

2.2 客户关系管理（CRM）是一个很大的挑战

电子商务中的客户关系管理与期刊的读者信息管理有很大的不同。目前期刊社的受众信息管理是静态的，多集中于对期刊和网站内容的选择和偏好上，而 B2C 业务的客户关系管理是动态的，不仅要掌握个人信息，随时与消费者联系满足其当前的需要，还要能够让客户在线取得自己需要的信息。从目前的时尚期刊 B2C 业务来看，其客户关系管理方面尤其薄弱。以昕薇网为例，昕薇网的客服工作时间是工作日 10：30 到 17：30，周末和法定节假日休息。实际上购物是一件非常休闲的事情，很多消费者会选择休闲的时间购物，而期刊网站的工作人员休息时间也要休息，导致消费者多数情况下无法及时和客服人员取得联系。此外，对客户资料的收集与客户爱好的追踪，尽可能多地收集实际客户与潜在客户的信息，构建客户信息数据仓库，预测客户的购买行为并提供购买建议等，都是客户关系管理中的主要任务。就目前来说，更多的数据挖掘和客户关系维护，对于期刊工作人员来说是一个很大的挑战，短时间内恐怕难以做好。

3 时尚期刊网站发展 B2C 业务的外部机会

3.1 网民数量和网购市场规模增速惊人

据中国互联网信息中心（CNNIC）在 2009 年 7 月 16 日的《中国互联网络发展状况统计报告》发布中显示，截至 2009 年 6 月底，中国网民规模达到 3.38 亿人，较 2008 年年底增长 13.4%，半年增长了 4 000 万人；与网民规模持续增长相对应的，是我国互联网普及率的稳步提升。数据显示，截至 2009 年 6 月底，我国互联网普及率达到 25.5%，保持平稳上升的态势。

此外，根据艾瑞咨询统计数据显示，2008 年网络购物交易额规模突破千亿大关，达

1 281.8亿元，相比 2007 年增长 128.5%。2009 年上半年中国网购市场交易规模为 1 034.6 亿元，同比 2008 年上半年的 531.1 亿元，大增 94.8%（见图 1）。预计随着网络购物的快速增长，网购将在更多网民中普及，到 2010 年网购用户占互联网用户规模的比重有望达到 40% 以上。[3]

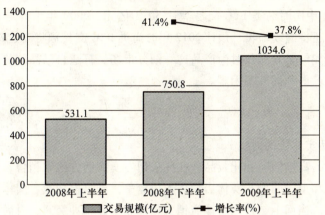

注：C2C电子商务市场规模以成交商品价值总额计算，B2C电子商务市场规模以销售额计算，两者之和为网络购物市场规模，其中暂不包括付费数字产品下载、航空客票交易、网络代缴费等商品类别的交易规模。

©2009.8 iResearch Inc.　　　　　　　　www.iresearch.com.cn

图 1　2008—2009 年中国网络购物市场交易规模[4]

与此同时，2009 年上半年，C2C 平台占比 92.1%，自主销售式 B2C 占比 5.4%，平台式 B2C 占比 2.5%，应该说，B2C 业务才刚刚起步，有很大的发展空间。在网民已购商品中，服装鞋帽类稳居第一，化妆品名列第三（见图 2）。这充分说明了时装服饰和化妆品在网购市场很受欢迎。女性时尚刊物无论是编辑内容还是广告产品都集中于服饰和化妆品行业，这无疑非常契合当前网络购物的发展方向。

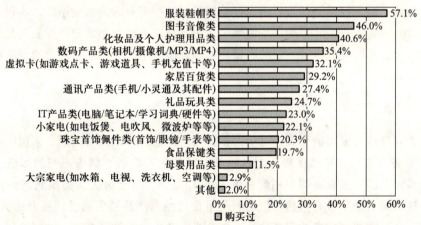

样本描述：N=26540; 2008年11—12月通过iUserSurvey在84家网站上联机调研获得

© 2009.1 iResearch lnc.　　　　　　　　www.iresearch.com.cn

图 2　2008 年网民已购商品种类排名[5]

3.2　电子商务市场的未来是细分化的市场

近几年，一些专业的电子商务平台表现抢眼，人们也逐渐开始到专业的网站购物，如京东商城、孔夫子旧书网。这些网站之所以发展得比较好，得益于它们专业的定位——不求大而全，但求专而精。从历史的发展经验来看，市场的发展总是会逐渐地细分，所以未来的电子商务市场，也必然会向着细分化和专业化的方向发展。据艾瑞咨询公布的《2009 年中国时尚商品电子商务企业竞争分析报告》显示，网上高端消费正呈爆发式增长。2009 年第一季度中国网络购物市场交易额规模达 467 亿元，同比 2008 年第一季度增长 96.7%。2008 年中国时尚类 B2C 交易额达 30.3 亿元，2009 年预计增长到 65.3 亿元，并且在未来 3 年内还将继续增长，预计 2012 年时尚类 B2C 交易额将高达 307 亿元。所以，时尚期刊网站如果能够紧紧抓住时尚产品这一细分市场，打造自己品牌的知名度，在电子商务市场中获取自己的利润并不困难。

4 时尚期刊网站发展 B2C 业务的市场威胁

4.1 时尚产品实体店的对抗

时尚产品尤其是高档服装和化妆品，往往采用专卖店的方式来销售，而当前网上销售也往往会因为价格和渠道问题与实体店销售形成竞争。到目前为止，实体店的销售仍然是时尚产品的主阵地。当网上销售和实体店销售相互竞争发生冲突时，时尚产品的供货商更可能会倾向于保护实体店的利益。前不久的雅漾事件就很能说明这一问题。2009 年 12 月，雅漾总公司、法国三大药企之一的皮尔法伯集团正式向淘宝寄送了律师函，"一刀切"地否定专柜以外的所有产品，一句"假货"的评定将网购打入谷底。同样明确不做线上渠道的还有雅诗兰黛和欧莱雅集团旗下的绝大多数中高端产品，所谓网上店铺的"官方授权"也被一一否认。[6] 如此的举动，一方面固然有厂商担心网络销售扰乱原有的价格体系，另一方面更多的是对当前专卖店形式的支持和利益的保护。所以，时尚期刊网站的 B2C 业务面对的一个很大的威胁可能是来自实体店的对抗。

4.2 同类购物网站的威胁

时尚期刊网站在发展 B2C 业务时面临竞争是不可避免的，其主要竞争对手是那些专业的时尚消费品购物网站，如抢鲜网、呼哈网等。这些专业时尚购物网站，不仅有着雄厚的经济实力，而且经过了几年的市场锤炼，无论是在产品经营和客户管理，还是在配送和售后服务方面，都已经积累了一定的经验。期刊发展电子商务之初必然会遭到这些网站的打压。

5 结论与对策

在电子商务迅猛发展的今天，对于占据消费时尚前端阵地的时尚期刊来说，在其网站发展 B2C 业务有自己独特的优势，尤其随着网民数量的激增和网购习惯的形成，时尚期刊如果能够将自己的读者资源利用起来发展 B2C 业务，对于解决当前期刊网站赢利模式不清晰的被动局面是非常有利的。但期刊网站自己经营产品销售的方式还有很大的风险，电子商务平台需要很多相应的配套体系，资金投入非常大，期刊社在这方面不仅缺乏经验而且人力、资金投入上也明显不足。对于时尚期刊网站来说，要利用自己的优势，借鉴淘宝的经验，将网站做成一个供买卖双方的交易平台，期刊社只负责网络的维护与管理，产品的销售由品牌代理商或经销商来做。这样可以避免仓储、物流等方面经验不足的劣势，同时不会因为销售广告商产品而与广告主的渠道商发生利益冲突。对于同类的购物网站或是垂直购物网站，为了避免正面的冲突，期刊网站可以考虑和这些购物网站合作，做这些购物网站的联属网站。这一点国外期刊 Parenting Group 有相对成熟的做法，该期刊集团拥有《Parenting》和《Babytalk》两本杂志和 parenting. com 网站。parenting. com 网站于 2008 年在网上开设网上销售频道，为父母提供关于玩具方面的信息和建议，通过视频展示儿童玩具，"如果家长想要购买这个玩具，他们可以点击按键到亚马逊网站上完成购买，parenting. com 网站则通过亚马逊加盟项目（Amazon's Affiliates program）得到相应的分成。"[7]

注释

[1] 杨扬. 试论我国电子商务未来的发展方向. 龙岩学院学报，2006（1）

[2] 瑞丽女性网：http://www. rayli. com. cn/2007adsite/newmedia_youshi01.html

[3] i Research China Online Shopping Research Report 2008—2009 年

[4] i Research China Online Shopping Research Report 2008—2009 年

[5] i Research China Online Shopping Research Report 2008—2009 年

[6] 日用化妆品牌的专柜与网络销售之争. http://www. hezhici. com/sort/business/hua-zhuangpinfushi/2010/0108/181558. html

[7] Joseph Galarneau. Digital Continues Upward Ascent in the American Consumer Magazine Industry. Journal of: Publishing Research Quarterly, Volume 25, Number 2（June 2009）

作者简介

朱静雯，武汉大学信息管理学院教授，博士生导师。

刘志杰，武汉大学信息管理学院出版发行系 2009 级博士研究生。

数字期刊

消费类杂志网络发行量概念初探

何 姣 刘惠婷 陈孝禹 李巧明 王晓光

（武汉大学信息管理学院 武汉 430072）

摘要：随着数字发行技术的发展和发行渠道的丰富，消费类杂志的网络发行量统计日益重要。当前正兴起的数字化发行方式主要有杂志社依托自建网站的在线发行、第三方发行商代理销售以及与移动通讯商合作开展订阅发行等几种。其衡量指标——网络发行量是指数字版杂志通过有线或无线网络实现的有效发行量。较传统发行而言，网络发行量的统计具有即时、数据细致多样及数据真实可信等特点。网络发行量的统计需要建立一套有效的、可操作的运行机制，具有参考意义的有发行商代理统计模式、协会模式和第三方认证模式。由于数字出版环境的复杂性和网络发行量本身的特性，实现这一意义重大的新型统计工作需要业界的共同努力。

关键词：网络发行量 数字出版 消费类杂志

The Preliminary Research on the Concept of Network Circulation of Consumer Magazines

He Jiao Liu Huiting Chen Xiaoyu Li Qiaoming Wang Xiaoguang

（School of Information Management，Wuhan University，Wuhan，430072）

Abstract：With the development of digital distribution technology and the enriching of distribution channels，the counting of network circulation of magazines becomes increasingly important. The increasing ways of digital distribution include the online issuing through magazine's self-built websites，the sale through distributing agents，the subscriptive issuing in cooperation with telecommunication operators，and as so on. Its indicator — network circulation refers to the effective circulation of the digital magazines which is acquired through wired or wireless network. In comparison with the traditional distribution，network circulation has lots of advantages：counting timely，the thoughtful and diverse information that statistics providing，and the authenticity of the statistics. To counting the network circulation，we need to establish an effective，workable operating mechanism. There are three ways for reference：the pattern of distributing agent，the pattern of industry association and the pattern of the third party's certification. Born in the complicated environment of digital publishing，network circulation has its own features. It also requires the efforts of relative industries to achieve this significant statistics goal.

Keywords：Network circulation Digital publishing Consumer magazines

随着网络出版的发展和用户阅读习惯的变化，消费类杂志的网络发行趋势日益明显。国际权威发行量认证机构 BPA 的统计显示，截至 2009 年 9 月开展数字发行业务的杂志出版商数量已达 338 家，比 2006 年 6 月增长了 133%，电子杂志在总发行量中所占比例在 2009 年 6 月也已达到 15.4%。这些数字表明消费类电子杂志的网络发行已成气候。

与商业类杂志不同，消费类杂志不单依靠发行量获益，更依赖于广告获取收益，所以发行量的精确统计对消费类杂志市场的健康发展至关重要。随着电子杂志网络发行量的增长，建立一套有效的电子杂志网络发行量统计标准已显得十分重要和迫切。

1　消费类电子杂志的数字发行方式

按照杂志社对杂志内容的利用形式、发行渠道、阅读载体和呈现形式，可以将消费类杂志的数字发行模式分为四种。[1]

1.1　依托自身网站在线发行

杂志社自办网站或网站群，对内容进行结构化重组利用，为读者搭建在线浏览、阅读、下载和支付平台，不仅直接向读者展示和销售原貌版、文本版或多媒体版杂志内容，同时还进行基于杂志内容的拓展性信息服务和品牌宣传。读者可以利用个人电脑、手机或移动终端阅读多种版式的杂志内容。目前，国内消费类杂志的自办网站中，已经形成品牌的网站有瑞丽系列杂志的瑞丽女性网、《中国国家地理》杂志的中国国家地理网、《财经》杂志的财经网、《青年文摘》杂志网等。

1.2　依托第三方发行商代理销售

杂志社将杂志内容直接交由第三方代理发行网站代理销售。杂志社与第三方发行商通常按照刊物的销售额度进行利润分成，代理商获权进行在线销售、销量统计和客户管理。已经形成较大影响力的第三方发行网站有 Zinio、龙源期刊网、悦读网、读览天下等网站。随着 iPad 平板电脑的流行，这些数字发行商还推出了 iPad 专用客户端软件，便于读者通过 iPad 购买杂志。

1.3　依托移动通讯商开展订阅发行

杂志社与移动通信商合作开展订阅服务也是一种常见的电子杂志发行方式。读者可以通过手机定制彩信形式的手机杂志，如中国女性时尚类手机彩信杂志发行量第一位的《手机报-瑞丽》。由于彩信形式的手机杂志读者体验较差，这种形式的电子杂志日益被读者放弃。

1.4　其他发行方式

电子杂志的发行方式创新速度很快，除了以上三种主要的发行方式外，部分电子杂志还与移动设备制造商捆绑销售，或通过苹果公司的应用商店以软件的方式直接销售，或授权给门户网站使用，等等。这些发行方式虽非主流，但也有一定的市场空间。

2　网络发行量的概念

与印刷杂志不同，电子杂志既可以整本发行，也可以按单篇文章发行，发行通道和发行方式都更加多样，所以统计电子杂志的有效发行量变得较为困难。2009 年下半年，美国杂志出版商协会（MPA）宣布，正式将杂志的网络发行量计入杂志有效发行量之中，其所定义的杂志的网络发行量是指通过网络付费发行的原貌版电子杂志的总和[2]。杂志的网络发行量的提出适应了出版业态的发展，也推动了出版业界对于发行量统计指标和赢利模式的思考。2009 年 11 月，龙源期刊网也在国内首次提出了杂志网络发行量的概念，它包括两个部分：一是用户在龙源期刊网上付费点击的杂志次数，即点击量；二是读者通过搜索引擎抓取的龙源相关页面从而进行点击的次数，即传播量。两者之和为杂志的网络发行量[3]。

龙源期刊网提出的网络发行量定义侧重于以个人电脑为载体的发行，而忽略了以手持阅读器或其他移动设备为接收载体的杂志发行。该概念将通过搜索引擎进入页面浏览杂志标题目录的传播量也并入发行量统计中，混淆了传播与发行的不同含义，并且没有明确区分单篇文章和单本杂志的差异，这不利于广告商判断杂志的广告价值。

与龙源期刊网提出的网络发行量概念相比，MPA 的网络发行量概念较为简洁和清晰。MPA 定义的网络发行量主要指电子杂志为出版商带来实际利润的付费阅读，不包括构成杂志收益主要部分的广告价值所需要的免费浏览[4]，但是 MPA 的定义忽视了免费浏览的传播功能和商业价值。

在借鉴以上两个概念的基础上，我们认为消费类杂志的网络发行量是指数字版本形式的消费类杂志通过有线或无线网络实现的有效发行量。所谓有效发行是指能够有效扩大杂志的市场占有率和社会影响力，并能带来销售和广告收益的有偿和无偿发行。当消费者直接通过电子杂志的发行平台，阅读整本杂志时，即实现了杂志的有效发行。

在我们的网络发行量定义中剔除了"传播量"的指标，这是因为传播量通常是由单篇杂志文章带来的点击量，在这种传播形式中，杂志广告往往被分割出去，所以这一指标虽然能够说明一篇文章的影响力，但对于实现一本杂志的广告价值是没有意义的。发行量统计的最重要目的是为判断广告价值服务的，所以对于这种没有意义的指标应该剔除掉。对于付费发行的电子杂志而言，有效发行量侧重于计算电子杂志单期被付费下载的次数。付费发行的电子杂志通过这种有效点击，实现了发行价值和广告价值的统一，维持了原有的杂志商业模式。对于免费发行的电子杂志，有效发行量侧重于计算杂志的免费下载量，免费下载的杂志同样具有广告价值。

3 网络发行量的监测统计模式

要使网络发行量的统计从理论走向实践，需要建立一套行之有效的操作方式和运营规则。由于电子杂志发行方式多样，其网络发行量统计也是一项复杂的工作。为实现客观、真实、权威的统计，必须充分考虑从内容提供商到终端读者的产业链各个主体的利益诉求和协调，形成一个行之有效且多方共赢的模式，才能让这一套系统得到最广泛的认可和接受。需要注意的是，在发行量监测中必须区分付费发行和免费发行。

目前，网络发行量的专业统计机构还未出现。随着电子杂志阅读量的增加，开展电子杂志网络发行量统计势在必行。在统计模式上，可以参考以下三种：

一是发行商代理统计模式。这种模式的优势是数据获取方便。如龙源期刊网从 2005 年起已连续定期发布杂志网络传播 TOP100 数据，并向各个合作刊社提供年度网络传播数据分析报告，形成了互联网时代杂志调研的有效途径，取得了一些成果。[5] 这种模式也有一定的局限性，即电子杂志通常会通过多个发行平台销售，所以要获得一种电子杂志完整的发行量必须综合多个发行平台的销售数据，而且杂志社难于监控各个发行平台上的实际发行量。

二是协会统计模式。美国杂志出版商协会担负着杂志发行调研功能，其下属的出版商信息局（PIB）正在积极开发一种新的阅读评测系统，建立阅读率统计的标准。[6]协会模式最大的优势便是集专业性与公共性于一体，数据权威性高，但受制于当前国内行业协会的管理现状，这一模式在国内实施的意义不大。

三是第三方认证模式。这种模式主要是通过对杂志社出示的具有可信价值的网络发行量数据核查，来形成权威可信的发行数据。第三方认证模式有其独具的优势：一方面将统计与审核结合起来，数据主要来自于杂志社自身，而节省了专门统计的耗费；另一方面，它相对独立的地位能更好地保证数据的真实客观性。

目前在国内具有实现电子杂志网络发行数据统计和发行平台流量监测的第三方监测功能的机构主要有，新闻出版总署在 2007 年成立的国新出版物发行数据调查中心网络出版专业委员会、国际权威认证机构 BPA 和 ABC 组织、香港出版销数公证会（HKABC）。另外一些民间调查咨询公司如艾瑞咨询集团也能提供此类调查监控和报告服务。

4　网络发行量的统计特点

电子杂志的数字产品特性克服传统印刷杂志发行量统计上的一些缺陷，在很大程度上可以避免已往统计上的难题，并具有以下特性。

第一，即时统计。电子杂志的网络发行量统计可以由计算机自动进行，读者身份也容易确定，数据可以即时更新，这便于杂志社开展实时营销活动。

第二，统计数据细致多样。电子杂志发行数据的统计不仅及时，还能细致多样。杂志商不仅可以获得每期杂志的发行量，还能知道更详细的购买者的年龄、购买时间、购买地等数据，甚至还能获得每篇文章的阅读量数据，这些细致多样的客户数据将为杂志社开展数据挖掘奠定基础。

第三，统计数据真实可信。电子杂志的网络发行需涉及杂志社、发行平台商、通讯服务商、第三方统计公司、认证机构等多个利益主体。数据统计技术的进步能够实现多方同时监控，避免了数据被篡改的可能性，因而真实可靠，容易获得广告商认可。

5　网络发行量的未来

随着电子杂志网络发行量的快速增长，开展网络发行量统计已经刻不容缓。由于"网络发行量"是个新鲜概念，统计过程、规范及标准都还有待进一步确定。一些基本的概念和认识在业界也没有达成一致，各有各家说法，但不管如何，在参考国外经验基础上结合中国的特殊情况建立一套有效的统计体系十分必要。

在数字化出版浪潮下，网络发行量概念的提出顺应了杂志业发展的趋势。尽管电子杂志发展过程中还存在很多不确定性因素，为了使电子杂志产业健康有序发展，政府部门、学界和产业界还需紧密合作建立健全电子杂志的网络发行量统计体系。

注释

[1] 王晓光等. 消费类数字化发行模式研究. [J] 出版科学，2010，（3）：84-86

[2] 李鹏. 期刊网络发行量的认定和推广. [OL] http://www.qikan.com.cn/report/2009/

script04. html,2009,11,18

[3] 李鹏. 期刊网络发行量的认定和推广. ［OL］http://www. qikan. com. cn/report/2009/
script04. html,2009,11,18

[4] 王荣. 试论报纸的"有效发行"与"无效发行". ［J］新闻大学, 2001, (3): 82–
85

[5] 李鹏. 期刊网络发行量的认定和推广. ［OL］http://www. qikan. com. cn/report/2009/
script04. html,2009,11,18

[6] 中国图书商报. 美国杂志出版商协会公布阅读评测. ［OL］http://www. cbbr. com. cn/
info_15387. htm,2008,03,14

作者简介

何姣, 武汉大学信息管理学院 2007 级本科生。
刘惠婷, 武汉大学信息管理学院 2007 级本科生。
陈孝禹, 武汉大学信息管理学院 2007 级本科生。
李巧明, 武汉大学信息管理学院 2007 级本科生。
王晓光, 武汉大学信息管理学院副教授。

让数字报刊发行实现赢利

刘玉清 杨 靓

（河北经贸大学人文学院 石家庄 050061）

摘要：中国数字报大多都是免费阅读，多数免费阅读的数字报已成为报社沉重的经济负担，为数极少的收费订阅的数字报举步维艰；数字报刊收入在数字出版产业整体收入中所占比重很小，数字报刊的创收能力还很弱。本文探讨了数字报刊之所以难以通过发行实现赢利的原因，一是由于内容缺乏原创性和渠道缺乏唯一性使数字报刊难以收费订阅，二是由于忠诚用户不足使数字报刊难以实现有效发行，三是由于采编内容屡屡被网站侵权转载使数字报刊失去赢利机会。本文还提出了数字报刊通过发行实现赢利的三个途径：建立以有效发行为核心的经营模式，以优质服务提升用户忠诚度和依赖度，加大投入以高成本谋取高回报。

关键词：数字报刊 收费阅读 有效发行 赢利

Making the Issuance of Digital Newspapers and Magazines Profitable

Liu Yuqing Yang Liang

（Department of Humanities，Hebei University of Economics and Business，Shijiazhuang，050061）

Abstract：Most of China's digital newspapers are for free reading，and have become a heavy financial burden. Very few numbers of charged newspapers are in difficult situations. The proportion of digital newspapers and magazines revenue in the whole publishing industry is still very small. Its income-generating capacity is still weak. The thesis probes into the reasons why it is difficult for digital newspapers and magazines to profit by issuance：First the lack of original content and lack of channel uniqueness which make it difficult to charge subscriptions. Second the lack of loyal user to achieve effective issuance. Third the content is illegally reprinted by other websites which makes it lost profit opportunities. The thesis also proposes the ways to achieve profit by issuance：to establish business model which effective issuance as the core；enhance user royalty and dependency through quality service；increase investment to seek high returns.

Keywords：Digital newspapers and magazines Paid reading Effective issuance Profit

由于报刊原创作品的数字化、编辑加工的数字化和发行销售的数字化需要巨大的投资，因此，所有数字报刊都期望自己的投资能够得到回报，都期望通过赢利来维持数字报刊的可持续发展。尽管数字报刊可以通过做广告、开发衍生产品等途径获得一些收入，但这些收入往往无法支撑数字报刊的正常运营。没有数字发行收入，仅仅依靠其他收入来维持数字报刊的运营是非常困难的。因此，通过数字发行营利是所有报刊经营者的共同愿望。遗憾的是很少有数字报刊依靠发行实现赢利。这里所说的"营利（seek Profits）"与"赢利（profit）"是两个概念——营利指主观上谋取利润，赢利则是指客观上获得利润。目前，如何通过发行实现赢利已经成为困扰各国数字报刊可持续发展的世界性难题。数字报刊经营者想要通过发行来赢利还有很长的路要走。

1 我国数字报刊发行现状分析

中国出版科学研究所 2008 年 11 月 20 日发布的《2007—2008 中国出版业发展报告》指出，全国已有 37 家报业集团、300 多家报社采用数字报技术在互联网上出版数字报纸，数字报刊数量由 2007 年年初不到 50 份，猛增至 2008 年 7 月底的 600 余份[1]。目前中国数字报纸大多都是免费阅读，收费订阅的数字报纸寥寥无几。在极少数收费的数字报纸中，2007 年 4 月温州报业集团旗下 4 份报纸上线发行，这是中国首份付费订阅的数字报纸。2007 年《重庆日报》数字版以每份 200 元的价格发行，2009 年《重庆日报》数字版收费发行量接近 1 万份[2]。但《重庆日报》数字版在收费两年后变回免费。2009 年 12 月 23 日，安徽日报报业集团旗下的数字报纸推出订阅收费制，订阅金额为每月 5 元。2010 年 1 月 1 日《人民日报》数字版开始收费，收费模式有三种：每月 24 元、半年 128 元、全年 198 元。此举在业界引起轩然大波，一些数字报纸正在谋划通过不同的形式进行收费。据中国出版科学研究所发布的《2007—2008 中国数字出版产业年度报告》，我国数字出版产业整体收入 2008 年达到 530 亿元。其中，数字报纸收入 10 亿元，互联网期刊和多媒体网络互动期刊收入 7.6 亿元[3]。据此推测，2008 年数字报刊收入共计 17.6 亿元，仅占整个数字出版产业的 3.3%。这说明数字报刊收入在整个数字出版产业整体收入中所占比重很小，数字报刊的创收能力还很弱。另有数据显示，2007 年传统书报刊的整体收入是 990.08 亿元，而数字化书报刊的整体收入为 19.6 亿元，仅占传统书报刊的 1.98%[4]。这说明数字书报刊在经济上对出版部门作出的贡献不大，赢利能力不强。虽然数字报刊经营的边际生产和发行成本较低，但建立和维护这套生产与发行系统的成本却是沉没成本，而且极其高昂，所以数字报刊必须不断提高赢利能力才能维持正常运营。发行是赢利的主要途径，遗憾的是少数收费订阅的数字报纸，其收费订阅收入往往只是报社总收入中的很小一部分，报纸数字化过程中巨大的开支一般难以通过发行保持收支平衡，数字报发行处于无利可图状态。而多数免费阅读的数字报则成为报社沉重的经济负担。以河北数字报为例，程栋等人对河北省 1 家省级报纸、11 家市级报纸的报业数字状况进行了问卷调查，调查结果在中国内地免费数字报中具有一定的代表性。调查显示，报社自筹经费是 12 家报纸实施数字化最主要的资金来源，占了 91.6%。从反馈的问卷来看，75% 的报纸在运营新媒体项目的过程中面临亏损，仅有 25% 的报纸赢利，但赢利水平较低，仅仅保持不亏损而已。目前河北省 12 家报纸新媒体项目的收益主要以广告收入为主，约占总收入的 72.3%，另外，对政府补贴的依赖也较强，占到了 17.2%，投资收入和其他收入总的占 10.5%[5]。此次调查结果说明，在我国报刊数字化转型进程中，急需解决的问题是如何通过发行获得利润、扭亏为盈、发展自我。报刊实施数字化转型应当与发行赢利保持同步，否则数字报刊的发行就是无利可图的。

2 数字报刊发行为何无利可图

2.1 内容缺乏原创性和渠道缺乏唯一性使数字报刊难以收费订阅

美国报业巨头新闻集团掌门人鲁珀特·默多克认为："有质感的新闻并不廉价，免费派送报纸只会削弱报业自身制作出优秀报道的能力"。[6]他主张高质量的内容应当收费阅读，收费能够促使新闻业制作优质报道。原创性是资讯质量的根本，原创的内容才是高质量的内容；原创资讯独家传播才有唯一性，这种资讯让用户在其他传播渠道无法得到，用户才会付费阅读。目前我国数字报刊大多都是免费阅读的，不是经营者不想收费，而是实在缺乏充足的收费理由。因为在同质化竞争激烈的网络世界，任何数字报刊的内容都有可能来自于其他数字媒体，轻而易举的复制与粘贴工作让传播内容丧失了原创性和唯一性，也大大降低了资讯自身的价值与含金量。所以这些传播随处可见信息的数字报刊，一旦收取阅读费用，点击率就会急转直下，用户就会转向其他数字报刊获取有关信息。而以数据库形式传播的数字化学术期刊之所以能够实现收费阅读，关键就在于这些期刊出版的学术论文具有原创性，传播渠道具有唯一性，用户想要阅读这些论文除了付费别无选择。由此可见，想要把营利愿望变成实际收入，必须要在采编内容的原创性与传播渠道的唯一性上下工夫。在信息爆炸时代，唯有采编内容具有原创性、传播渠道具有唯一性，用户才可能付费订阅。

2.2 忠诚用户不足使数字报刊难以实现有效发行

在报刊市场上，用户对报刊的忠诚程度是报刊可持续发展的重要因素，一家报刊没有一大批支撑数字报刊顺畅运营的长期稳定的用户，意味着这家报刊难以实现有效发行。所谓有效发行是指拥有数量可观的对报刊依赖程度较高的用户，能够逐步扩大报刊的市场占有率、阅读率和影响力，进而直接带来广告回报或对广告商产生吸引力的发行。在网络世界，拥有一大批长期稳定的忠诚用户是非常困难的。一方面网站数目众多，使数字报刊极易被网站的海洋所淹没，一家数字报刊很难在网络的汪洋大海中显山露水。另一方面网民转换网站极为频繁，数字报刊用户的稳定性难以保证。数字报刊发行是否能赢利取决于是否拥有数以万计的忠诚用户，缺乏数以万计的用户就不能维持数字报刊的有效发行。与此同时，忠诚用户数量不足，往往很难招揽广告。忠诚用户数量的多寡是数字报刊能不能招揽广告的决定因素。如果数字报刊办得不好，用户不满意、不买账，其结果必然是由于忠诚用户数量少不能有效地吸纳广告客户，由此而失去主要经济来源。

2.3 网站侵权转载使数字报刊失去赢利机会

目前多数数字报刊之所以想收费而不能收费，原因之一是采编内容屡屡被众多网站侵权转载，使得数字报刊失去收费机会。我国的数字报刊目前在很大程度上仍建立在纸质报刊的基础上，大部分数字报刊是将纸质报刊数字化。如果人们除了某家纸质报刊之外只能从它的数字版上看到独家资讯，这就意味着这家数字版报刊可以让用户付费阅读，数字版报刊有机会通过发行赢利。但问题是，任何一家纸质报刊采编的独家资讯几乎都可以在众多网站免费看到，这就使得数字版报刊传播独家资讯时实施收费彻底化为泡影。纸质报刊采编的资讯被其他网站肆意盗版、侵权或滥用，网站侵犯作者和出版者版权的事件屡见不鲜。有研究者深恶痛绝地说："纸媒的版权在网络世界灰飞烟灭了：批量转载，掐头去尾，乱拟标题，屏蔽作者……在大喊保护知识产权的今天，纸媒的版权成了网络的免费'奶妈'。"[7]网站考虑更多的是自身的点击率，他们很少考虑对作者和出版者版权的尊重和价值兑现。面对众多网站未经许可海量转载报刊内容但不支付报酬的现象，部分报刊社开始通过诉讼维权，此类案件数量呈逐年上升态势。北京市海淀区人民法院调研显示，2007年该院受理的纸质媒体和网络之间由于转载引起的侵权纠纷案件不到10件，2008年迅速增长到50多件，2009年截至9月上旬，已经超过了120件。海淀法院法官杨德嘉表示："网络转载纸质媒体内容是否合法，首先面临着在司法实践中界定复杂、著作权人维权成本高、获赔额度低三大难题"。[8]网站未经许可海量转载报刊内容的案件频繁发生，报刊社通过诉讼维权难上加难，这种状况不仅直接导致纸质报刊发行量持续下滑，而且还使得报刊数字版开展收费发行举步维艰。

3 如何让数字报刊发行有利可图

3.1 建立以有效发行为核心的经营模式

经营数字报刊要在每个环节都坚持"有效发行"理念，从选题策划、信息采集、编辑加工、广告招揽到阅读消费，每个环节都紧密围绕有效发行展开。要从有效发行的视角来经营数字报刊，从有助于有效发行的视角来审视数字报刊的采编发整个过程。在采编环节上，要保证采编资讯有助于报刊的有效发行，采编的资讯应具有原创性。在发布环节上，要想方设法维护传播渠道的唯一性，以便使资讯内容具有商业价值。要大胆尝试各种形式的收费阅读，不能永远停留在免费发行"赔钱赚吆喝"的状态。尝试收费阅读之初可采用以下办法：一是套餐管理。将数字报刊资源分为可供网民免费阅读的"免费餐"和需要用户付费阅读的"收费餐"两类。二是内容摘要管理。在网站摘取数字报刊内容精要，并辅之以不断更新的相关而生动的内容，以此增强对那些尚未阅读数字报刊内容的用户阅读数字报刊原创付费阅读内容的吸引力，进而促进有效发行。在广告招揽环节上，把有效发行与招揽广告工作紧密联系起来。广告与发行就像一枚硬币的两面，它们在数字报刊经营中难分难解。数字报刊应当走一条"以内容促发行，以发行促广告，以广告来赢利"的经营之路。适用于数字报刊的广告赢利路径是：编辑策划、作者制作用户需要的内容→内容吸引用户→报刊社将忠诚用户打包出售给广告商→广告商购买版面→报刊社获得收入。

3.2 以优质服务提升用户忠诚度和依赖度

尽管在网络世界拥有一大批忠诚用户不易，但我们可以通过整合优质资源、提供优质服务来逐步培育用户的忠诚度。在中国内地，数字报刊是近几年出现的新生事物，知名度往往不高，忠诚用户自然也寥寥无几。而这些数字报刊大多都是依托有长期办刊历史的纸质报刊发展起来的，因此可以借助纸质报刊的知名度和品牌影响力来培育忠诚用户。在国内，广州的《家庭医生》是期发行量超过100万份的名刊，其电子杂志两年里发行量就超过1 000万份。《家庭医生E刊》系列杂志分综合版、男性版、女性版和育儿版，把传统的纸质资源整合在一起，分别在自建网站、新浪、腾讯等发布，成为立体化信息提供平台[9]。显而易见，《家庭医生》电子杂志之所以在两年里就能吸引1 000万用户，主要依赖纸质期刊的品牌效应，还有一个重要原因就是电子系列杂志能够为用户提供优质的个性化服务。在国外，一些出版商和发行商合作，通过多年苦心经营已经培育了一大批忠诚用户，这其中甚至还包括大量中国用户。来自荷兰的爱思唯尔是世界领先的出版集团，它旗下的学术期刊涵盖了多个领域，其在线平台 Science Direct 2006 年向我国高校师生提供了3 000 多万篇下载量，占全国高校外文论文下载量的 59%。该平台的中国用户从 2000 年首批 11 家，增加到 2007 年的 200 多家，以大学为主，还有国家图书馆、中国社会科学院等。2008 年爱思唯尔宣布，今后 3 年对中国用户提价年均 15%，是至今 4 次调价中最高的一次。随后，我国一位研究人员说："我们现在用它的数据库，欲罢不能，就像吸毒上瘾，要戒掉是很难的。"Science Direct 停用后，激起了南开大学师生的怨愤："我们强烈要求校长重视这件事，我们这些搞研究的宁可学校伙食涨价，也不愿意没有资料来源。如果不能查文献了，科研真的是搞不下去了。"[10] 国外一些数字出版商悉心培养了一大批忠诚的用户，并且使这些用户对出版商的数据库产生了很大的依赖性。在掌握议价主动权的情况下，通过产品提价来牟利就变成轻而易举的事情了。因此，数字报刊经营者应当把提高用户对数字报刊的依赖程度作为营造赢利环境的重要手段。数字报刊在培育忠诚用户、提升用户依赖度过程中可遵循以下路径：免费阅读，聚敛人气，扩大影响→诱导用户频繁使用，让用户在使用中得到益处→提供用户急需的信息，让用户对信息产生依赖→尝试收费，让用户付费阅读，并随时调价。

3.3　加大投入以高成本谋取高回报

在信息传播行业，想要通过低投入、低成本实现赢利只能是痴人说梦。在网络世界，低投入、低成本采编的资讯是很难吸引用户眼球的，更不要说有用户愿意付费阅读。数字报刊出版必须走高投入、高成本的道路，只有高投入才有高回报，只有高成本才有高价位，只有高价位才有高利润。高投入可以吸引高端人才，采编优质资讯，提供优质服务，抢占高价位的市场，在激烈的竞争中处于制高点，最终获得较高回报。数字报刊的赢利门槛相当高，需要投入巨大的资金建立数字报刊生产、发行与管理平台。平台包括完善的数字报刊生产系统、发行系统，以及对数字产品版权加以保护、对侵权行为进行检测的版权控制和管理系统。以全球最大、也是最为成功的付费数字报《华尔街日报》网络版为例，它依托先进的数字报生产与发行平台，长期采用网上收费发行模式，获得令人羡慕的经济效益。目前，《华尔街日报》网络版每年向用户收取 99 美元的费用，该网站拥有 90 万用户[11]，估计每年发行收入有 8 910 万美元。毋庸置疑，正是由于舍得投入，才使《华尔街日报》网络版获得不菲的收入。作为《华尔街日报》网站群之一的 WSJ. com，其投入就达 1.3 亿美元（该网站群包括 WSJ. com、CareerJournal. com、OpinionJournal. com、StartupJournal. com、RealEstateJournal. com 和 CollegeJournal. com）[12]，整个网站群的投入更是一个惊人的数字。由此可见，数字报刊想要获得良好的经济效益，应当走"高投入、高成本→采编优质资讯、提供优质服务→制定高价位、获得高回报"之路。

注释

［1］江胜信. 报纸读者规模止跌回升　数字报刊 600 余份［N］. 文汇报，2008-11-21

［2］吴峰. 城市报业发行创新的"重庆模式"［J］. 新闻战线，2009（7）：27

［3］聂震宁. 数字出版：距离成熟还有长路要走［J］. 出版科学，2009（1）：5

［4］肖洋. 数字化语境中的出版产业思考［A］. 黄先蓉，罗紫初. 数字出版与出版教育——第二届数字时代出版产业发展与人才培养国际学术研讨会论文集［C］. 北京：

高等教育出版社，2009：222

[5] 程栋. 论地方报业数字化转型战略——以河北省为例 [J]. 新闻界，2008 (6)：19

[6] 刘霞. 优秀的新闻报道不应该廉价 [N]. 科技日报，2009-08-27

[7] 宋桂芳. 纸媒不是网络的免费"奶妈" [N]. 中国青年报，2009-4-16

[8] 王亦君，欧阳骆沙. 网站非法转载被大量起诉 [N]. 中国青年报，2009-12-10

[9] 陈兵. 论报刊业面临的挑战及数字出版战略 [J]. 中国出版，2009 (11 月下、12 月下合刊)：85

[10] 张国. 外刊依赖与学术"断粮" [N]. 文摘报，2008-06-12

[11] 刘霞. 优秀的新闻报道不应该廉价 [N]. 科技日报，2009-08-27

[12] 叶南. 《华尔街日报》网络版的赚钱秘密 [EB/OL]. http://www.people.com.cn/GB/14677/21963/22063/2975061.html[2004-11-09]

作者简介

刘玉清，河北经贸大学人文学院教授、教研室主任。

杨靓，河北经贸大学人文学院讲师。

网络期刊数字化阅读指数探析

陈 丹 周 玥

（北京印刷学院 北京 102600）

摘要：本论文以龙源期刊网为主要研究对象，试图通过对其 2005—2009 年连续 6 年的 TOP100 期刊排行榜等数据进行多角度、多侧面分析，探析目前我国网络期刊数字化阅读状况及其特征；并在此基础上提出数字化阅读指数这一概念，作为衡量网络期刊受读者欢迎程度的指标，并分析影响该指数的各种外在和内在因素，以期对目前网络内容数字化阅读行为的理论研究和实践活动提供一定的借鉴和帮助。

关键词：网络期刊 数字化阅读 阅读指数

Research on Network Periodical Digital Reading Index

Chen Dan Zhou Yue

（Beijing Institute of Graphic Communication，Beijing，102600）

Abstract：The paper intends to do an analytical and descriptive research on the TOP100 periodical rankings based on Long yuan Journal net from 2005—2010. The paper came up with the concept of Digital Reading Index（DRI）as a criterion to assess the popularity of online periodicals，and analyzed the external and internal factors which influence the index. The study may provides reference and helps to study online content consumption behavior in the digital era.

Keywords：Network periodical Digital reading Read index

1 数字化阅读概念、类型及特点

阅读是人们从符号中获得意义的一种社会实践活动和心理过程，也是信息知识的产生者和接受者借助于文本实现的一种信息知识传递过程。数字化阅读就是指通过计算机或类似设备在本地或远程读取以数字代码方式存储在磁、光、电介质上的各种信息的一种阅读方式。我们熟悉的网络阅读就是其主要的表现形式之一。数字化阅读是阅读主体（读者）与网络化数字化文本相互交流信息与知识的过程，是阅读主体借助数字化阅读工具开展实践活动与精神活动的一种体现。

根据读者对数字资源的利用方式，数字化阅读行为可以分为以下两种类型：

一是在线阅读。指读者在局域网或互联网上直接阅读所搜集到的各类网络资源，读者在阅读过程中始终"挂"在网上。

二是离线阅读。指读者将数字资源下载到另一种载体上，断开网络链接后，再进行阅读。它又可以分为两种载体，一种是以个人计算机为载体；另一种是以手持阅读器、PDA、手机等移动终端为载体。

而与传统的文本阅读相比，数字化阅读具有以下几方面的特点，即文本主题的杂合性、显示形式的多样性、阅读内容的丰富性、阅读过程的互动性、阅读环境的开放性、阅读方式的虚拟性以及阅读行为的共时性。

2　龙源期刊网网络传播排行的基础及发展历程

龙源期刊网（www.qikan.com.cn）是全球最大的中文期刊网，有将近 3 000 种网络期刊，其读者遍及海内外，每日点击者平均在 300 万人以上。龙源期刊网为用户提供了文本版、原文原貌版和语音版三种两种版本的阅读内容。

2005 年末，龙源首次将合作期刊网络传播的数据披露社会，发布了期刊网络传播亚洲和欧美的 TOP100 期刊，同时向各个合作刊社提供了年度网络传播数据分析报告，开启了互联网时代期刊调研的新渠道。此后 5 年，龙源期刊网对其在线的 3 000 多家期刊的点击和阅读状况进行统计，连续发布每年的网络传播排行数据。

本文将从不同维度对龙源期刊网 2005—2009 年发布的 TOP100 数据进行分析，以期探寻网络期刊数字化阅读的影响因素。

3　网络期刊数字化阅读指数及其影响因素分析

3.1　数字化阅读指数概念界定

阅读指数主要是对图书、期刊可读性或易读性的一个具体的衡量指标，阅读指数越高，表明某书/刊的可读性或易读性越高，其受读者欢迎程度越高；反之亦然。阅读指数可通过统计、汇总读者在一定时间内的购买量、借阅次数以及作者和读者评价，并对其进行必要的处理来得到。其表现形式可以是具体的数值，也可以是主观的评价，甚至可以是各种可视化符号。而所谓网络期刊的数字化阅读指数，是对应纸版期刊阅读指数的一个概念，它也同样反映该网络期刊的可阅读性或易读性，是该期刊（或其中的某篇文章）受读者欢迎程度的一个重要的量化指标，其具体的表现形式和衡量方法同样也有多种，目前常见的，也是较为简单、客观的一种表示方式就是该期刊或其中刊载的文章在网络上的点击率或阅读率。

前面提及的龙源期刊网 5 年来连续发布的 TOP100 数据均来源于自主开发的网络技术系统，并且经过第三方访问分析和评价系统直接生成，都是基于读者的点击率统计出来的重要数据，因此，它们在一定程度上是龙源期刊网中各上网期刊及其文章数字化阅读指数的一个量化反映。在目前，对期刊特别是网络期刊的定量研究方法还比较缺乏的情况下，数字化阅读指数无疑是衡量网络期刊受读者欢迎程度的一种简便易行的量化指标。为了更好地解析网络期刊的数字化阅读指数，本文将分析影响该指数的几个主要因素，并由此归纳出网络期刊的点击累积假说。

3.2　网络期刊数字化阅读指数影响因素分析

3.2.1　内部因素

作为传播内容的接受者，网络读者并不是被动的、孤立的存在，而是作为拥有自己价值观的社会成员，具有某种能动性。他们不会像一些人所想的那样在接触传播内容时不加辨别地全盘接受，而是更倾向于选择与自己的既有兴趣和态度一致的内容加以接触和接受，这种选择具有某种"能动性"。基于传播过程中的选择性接触机制和使用与满足理论，读者自身的条件是影响网络期刊阅读的内因。

（1）读者分布区域的影响

2009 年龙源期刊网国内用户区域分布图清晰地显示出，龙源用户分布极为不均，主要集中在北京、广东省、河南省、山东省、江苏省和四川省，这几个省和直辖市用户数都在 10 万以上，共占用户总数的 54.86%，其中北京的用户数更是达到了 623 656，居于首位，仅北京一个城市就占到了龙源网用户总数的 26.56%；其他各省、自治区、直辖市用户相对来说就比较少。

这一点与我国网民的分布地区契合度比较高，根据互联网数据分析公司 CNZZ 发布的中国互联网各地域网民的网页浏览量统计报告，截至 2009 年 8 月中国地区网民浏览量最大的是广东省，超过中国网民浏览总量的 10%。东部沿海地区（江苏、浙江、山东）的网民浏览量比其他城市浏览量大，其次网民数量较多的省市则多位于华东地区；东中西部发展差异较大，数据差距显著，东部网民网页浏览量占到了全国网民网页浏览量的 67%，超过了中西部网民浏览量总和。截至 2009 年 6 月底，北京市网民数为 1 037 万人，占总人口 61%，网民比例居中国各省市第一。

可见，读者分布区域情况对数字化阅读具有一定的影响。对于数字化阅读，读者要保证阅读的顺利进行，就必须依赖一定的阅读设备和技术。电脑、网络、上网能力是不可缺少的要素。这些要素都与读者的经济实力和区域经济发展程度有关，因此，网民集中的地区自然也成为网络期刊数字化阅读开展较好的区域。

（2）读者阅读目的影响

随着网络时代的来临，网络的便捷性、交互性和巨大的信息存储量使得阅读内容极大丰富，网络形成一个巨大的信息资源数据库，加之现代生活节奏的不断加快，读者的阅读目的也在明显转变。网络上内容资源的丰富和表现形式的生动多变使得网络阅读非常便捷和有趣，很多人进行网络阅读往往只是为了满足临时性的信息需求，或是为了打发时间、放松心情，从而网络阅读的性质也朝着享乐化和实用化的方向发展，人们的阅读深度也悄然变化。网络阅读用户对内容的深度要求降低，即所谓的"浅阅读"特征。

综合 2009 年国内、海外 TOP100 文章看，一个显著的特征是休闲娱乐性文章广受青睐，在国外尤其明显。国内榜单上，休闲娱乐作品占据 62% 的份额，国内阅读前 20 篇文章中，此类文章占 55%；国外榜单上，此类作品占到了 65%，国外阅读前 20 篇文章中，此类文章占 90%。与其他类型内容的文章相比较，休闲娱乐作品占据了压倒性优势，这说明通过阅读进行休闲娱乐活动、获得放松是国内外读者的普遍追求。

（3）读者匿名性的影响

在网上进行网络阅读时，读者在网络上是处于完全匿名的状态，在期刊网上进行登录阅读是使用用户名来进行的，而用户名只是读者自己虚构的一个代号，没有实际意义。网络读者的匿名性对网络阅读也会产生一定的影响。

分析 2009 年龙源网用户最多使用的 100 个关键词，情色小说以被搜索 26 945 次的数量位居第三；在 2009 年国内 TOP100 浏览文章中，有 6 篇文章标题涉及"性"、"色"等敏感字眼，海外 TOP100 浏览文章中，标题含有"性"、"色情"、"按摩女"等字词的文章共有 7 篇；2008 年国内阅读 TOP100 文章中有 7 篇文章涉及此类字词，海外阅读 TOP100 文章中有 5 篇文章涉及此类字词，受到了读者的关注。这说明跟传统纸质期刊阅读相比，读者在网上的匿名性使得网络阅读和读者自身的阅读行为具有一定的隐蔽性，使读者在阅读时享有更大的自由和空间，可以看更多自己感兴趣的文章，因为读者阅读一些比较敏感的文章、关键词时可以不用考虑别人的看法。

3.2.2 外部因素

（1）原刊内容的影响

① 期刊品牌（刊名）的影响

刊社是网络期刊内容的提供者，决定着刊物内容的取舍选择，是网络期刊传播活动的中心环节之一。从近三年的用户最常用搜索词 TOP100 的数据对比可以发现，2008、2009 年读者直接搜索刊物名称的次数占到了总次数的七成以上。这就说明一些用户在上龙源网时直接就会在搜索栏中搜索某本期刊再对期刊来进行阅读，因此这些用户在上龙源网之前就已经有了明确的目标——上龙源期刊网就是为了看某期刊或某栏目的，这就说明此刊的品牌在读者群中已深入人心，已经形成品牌效应，一些名牌栏目已经被读者所认可和熟知。

表 1   2005—2009 年期刊网络传播连续 5 年排名靠前的期刊

刊名	2009 年国内排名	2008 年国内排名	2007 年国内排名	2006 年国内排名	2005 年国内排名
青年文摘	1	1	1	4	9
电脑爱好者	2	4	3	7	100
意林	5	2	2	6	67
中国新闻周刊	6	5	6	24	12
刊名	2009 年海外排名	2008 年海外排名	2007 年海外排名	2006 年海外排名	2005 年海外排名
收获	8	11	11	5	16
啄木鸟	31	33	31	8	29
十月	40	7	8	4	13

从表 1 中可以看到，有几本期刊连续几年都保持了很高的点击率，例如文摘综合类中的《青年文摘》、科技网络类中的《电脑爱好者》、文学类中的《收获》、时政类的《南方人物周刊》等。其中《青年文摘》更是保持了 3 年的国内排行榜第一的成绩。这些期刊都是在与龙源网合作之前就已经是知名期刊，拥有广阔的市场和数量众多的读者。这些期刊在网络传播中，连续多年稳居排行榜前列，这显示了知名期刊的持久影响力，也确立了阅读品牌网络延伸的认知度和影响力。此外，一些新进的期刊如《故事会》，它是从 2009 年开始与龙源正式合作的，合作首年就一跃进入 TOP100 第 38 名的位置，再次证明了期刊的品牌影响力在网络上的延伸对网络阅读所产生的重要影响。

② 文章标题的影响

由于期刊网上信息繁多，登上期刊网站就会看到几十本杂志或者几百篇文章，扫描式阅读已经成为网络阅读的主要方式。读者在这种阅读环境下已经养成了对标题的"依赖感"，处在网络环境中的读者在快速扫描的过程中去发现和感受对自己有用的信息。这种阅读带有极大的跳跃性、检索性、忽略性，如果标题中没有醒目的关键词，没有清晰的提示与标识，没有引人注意的种种细节，就难以抓住读者飞速运行的眼球。

通过对 2009 年国内 TOP100 文章标题的分析和统计，有 51 篇文章在标题中有清晰、指向性明显的关键词提示，如《钱永健：登上科学巅峰的华裔才俊》（《青年文摘》）、《浅谈音乐在影视中的作用》（《琴童》）、《美元注水　全球新灾难》（《中国经济周刊》）等，这些文章在标题中都有明显的指示词，可以让读者在快速浏览时立刻明白文章内容，并点击阅读。

（2）网络期刊的表现形式的影响

根据加拿大学者麦克卢汉和英尼斯的媒介理论，传播媒介不只是传播内容的载体或者工具，它不是静态的，它可以直接影响内容的传播效果。网络的诞生把一种新的信息载体带入人们的生活中，这样就引进了一种新的尺度或者说创造了一个新的环境。我们在研究网络期刊阅读的时候，也要看到期刊与网络融合并不仅仅是把期刊放到网络上这么简单的，因为传播手段的改变，期刊的表现形式也会产生一些新的变化，从而对网络期刊的阅读产生影响。

① 网站的版式设置的影响

龙源期刊网有期刊超市、封面文章、我的阅览室三大版块（如图1所示），读者进入龙源网首先看到的就是期刊超市中向读者推荐的最新的 28 本热门期刊，读者如果有感兴趣的可以直接点击期刊封面进行在线阅读或者下载。在期刊超市中有搜索条，读者可以根据需要键入标题、刊名或作者名进行搜索，还可以打开 A-Z 期刊列表来挑选期刊。点击一本期刊进入后网站会提供刊物介绍、刊物博客和刊物官方网站，并提供本期期刊目录。

封面文章版块里有今日必读、CEO 必读两个栏目，分别针对不同人群将封面文章按类别分类，封面文章名前注有刊名，并提供简短的内容提要。在点入一篇文章后网站会提供该期刊的前六期、同类热门杂志和本期的热点文章供读者选择。

② 站内期刊的分类的影响

网页的左侧是期刊分类，主要有推荐期刊、时政人物、商业、生活、文化、文学文摘、教育与学习、专业刊物等类别，还有主编访谈、作家专卖店等栏目。在每个类别下面类别细分也十分完备，如生活类下就有旅游、游戏数码、娱乐动漫、家居装饰、老年、健康、生活家庭、情感、亲子、时尚、美食烹调、汽车、军事武器、科普、体育等小类别。方便读者按照期刊内容分类来搜索期刊，使阅读更有目标性。

龙源期刊网的这种基于网络期刊的特色表现形式，为读者的数字化阅读带来便利，一定程度上也提高了其阅读指数。

③ 期刊篇章展示方式的影响

与纸刊不同，网络期刊在龙源期刊网上的展现形式多种多样，但归根结底，其最终表现形式还是篇章化，期刊被化整为零进行传播。不管期刊是原貌版还是文本版，点击进入后用户都会看到每篇文章的链接，并且在每篇文章后都会有一些相关文章的链接，如该期

图 1　龙源期刊网首页

刊的"热点文章"、"今日必读"、"看了此文章的用户还看了"等版块。在纸质期刊发行的场合，读者可能会因为一本期刊的某一篇文章买走整本刊物，而在网络传播的场合，由于从刊到篇形式的变化，读者可以更多地关注文章质量好坏而择优阅读。

从龙源期刊网阅读 TOP100 文章的排行可以看出，这些上榜文章的来源期刊有很大差异，有不少平时名不见经传的小众期刊的文章也榜上有名，如《中国三峡建设》的《气蒸云梦泽　波撼岳阳城》、《琴童》的《浅谈音乐在影视中的作用》等文章。仅 2008 年第 11 期的《教育探索》杂志刊发的《课堂教学有效性界说偏失的现状、影响及其纠正》一文，就为杂志带来了 5 040 次的网络发行量，为《教育探索》总体点击量贡献了一半以上。

（3）网络推介方式的影响

网站信息内容组织的本质是：网站编辑在信息内容的整合和发布中，将网站信息内容的单篇层次（即单个信息内在的层次，如单条信息、照片、图表等）、单元层次（由多条信息按主题组合在一起的网站专题、栏目形成的单元）、类别层次（同单元信息按照功能组合在一块，形成一个类别如网站频道）和整体层次（目标网民定位明确的完整的网站形象）这四个层次上做好信息配置，优化信息结构。

① 延长文章的生命周期的影响

在互联网上，网络期刊阅读不存在过时的问题，网络既可以打破空间限制也可以打破时间限制。期刊的内容并不以时效性为准，而是以深度见长。因此，网络阅读克服了纸质期刊查阅、追溯不便的缺点，从而使过刊文章不再"过期"，使优质内容能在相当长的时间内发挥"长尾效应"。

以 2009 年 TOP100 文章为例，其中 2009 年发表的有 44 篇，2008 年的有 51 篇，2007 及 2007 年以前的有 5 篇；在前 10 名中，2009 年发表的只有 1 篇，排名第一的《课堂教学有效性界说偏失的现状、影响及其纠正》（《教育探索》）是 2008 年的，排名第五的《因为女人》（《当代》）是 2007 年就已经发表的，并且还是 2008 年海内外 TOP100 文章排行之首。2009 年国内阅读前五名见表 2。

表 2　2009 年国内阅读 TOP100 文章前五名

刊名	文章名	排行	年份
教育探索	课堂教学有效性界说偏失的现状、影响及其纠正	1	2008
长篇小说选刊	折腾	2	2008
青年文摘	钱永健：登上科学巅峰的华裔才俊	3	2008
人生与伴侣	你应该知道的性秘密（一）	4	2009
当代	因为女人	5	2007

因此在纸质期刊发行受到冲击的今天，网络应该是期刊涅槃重生的平台、赢得读者的利器，只要是满足读者需要、有阅读价值的文章，在网络传播中就会拥有更长的生命周期，实现长尾效应，而不会受时间因素的关系被埋没。

② 站内搜索和期刊导航的影响

龙源期刊网在页面的醒目位置，设置了针对网站收录 3 000 余种期刊的站内检索功能，包括刊名和标题检索，为读者的阅读提供方便；

另外，如读者无明确的阅读需求，只有大致的阅读倾向时，面对海量的期刊内容，运用网站提供的导航系统则为明智之举。依靠站点提供导航系统，读者可找到到达站点上其他任何信息的分级路径，回聚到因链接而发散的预定目标，完成对某一主题的完整阅读。

龙源期刊网运用后台技术，实现了较为人性化的多种形式的期刊导航，包括：清晰明确的导航条、期刊文章的导读、免费试读（前 500 字左右）、热点文章、个性推荐等，使读者能清楚地知道自己身在何处，能快速地按照自己的愿望选择自己的信息，并能准确地判断下一个目的地的位置。

（4）付费模式的影响

数字内容的收费模式一直是困扰网络运营商的一个问题，但是由于网上免费的内容仍是主流，网络期刊收费阅读势必会造成一些读者的流失。TOP100 浏览文章，是龙源期刊网唯一以点击浏览数量进行统计、排序而产生的榜单，其他 TOP100 期刊、栏目、文章等各类榜单都是以读者实际付费阅读量为依据的。在国内 TOP100 浏览文章中，涉及 24 类 85 种期刊，与实际阅读的国内 TOP100 文章涉及 17 类 45 种期刊相比，显得十分分散。海外浏览 TOP100 与付费阅读 TOP100 也出现了同样的情况。

从文章的层面上看，这个反差十分明显。国内全部 100 篇浏览量最大的文章，只有《水在时间之下》、《壹亿陆》2 篇文章出现在 TOP100 文章榜单上。海外浏览量最大的 100

篇文章中，也只有9篇《中共中央关于教育体制改革的决定出台前后》等9篇文章在付费阅读 TOP100 文章榜单中出现。海外浏览 TOP100 文章中诸如《尼康单反 D90 使用技巧》、《在澳洲买车，怎么才划算》、《教你如何刮痧》等实用性文章有 20 多篇，但在付费阅读 TOP100 中无一出现。这两类排行榜之间的巨大反差，充分说明了付费阅读导致读者的大量流失。

通过以上分析，我们发现网络期刊数字化阅读指数这一概念是由许多因子共同作用而产生。为了进一步概括数字化阅读过程中各种因素对增加读者点击率的贡献和影响，本文在此归纳总结出网络期刊数字化阅读指数公式：

$$F_{(DRI)} = f_{内(x1,x2,x3)} + f_{外(y1,y2,y3,y4)}$$

其中 $F_{(DRI)}$ ——数字化阅读指数；

$f_内$——影响数字化阅读指数内部因子；

$f_外$——影响数字化阅读指数外部因子；

x1——读者分布的区域性；

x2——读者阅读的目的性；

x3——读者阅读的匿名性；

y1——原刊内容（包括原刊刊名、标题等）；

y2——网络表现形式（包括期刊版式、分类、展示方式等）；

y3——网络推介方式（包括文章生命周期、网站搜索与导航等）；

y4——网络期刊收费情况。

可见网络期刊的数字化阅读指数由多种因素决定，提高网络期刊的数字化阅读，是一个涉及期刊读者、期刊内容、网站内容展示以及内容营销推介方式等多维度、多角度的系统工程，其中各因素对该指数的影响程度还需进一步探索和研究。

参考文献

[1]《阅读的革命，为知识增值——访龙源国际集团总裁汤潮》，中国财经报 http://cn.qikan.com/ gbqikan/view_news.asp? id＝838。

[2] 艾瑞市场咨询有限公司：《iResearch China Digital Magzine Research Report 2005》，北京，2006 年。

[3] 安结："网络期刊文献的建设和信息资源共享"，《图书馆管理与资源建设》，2003 年第 4 期，第 83～85 页。

[4] B. Shackel, The BLEND System：Programme for the Study of Some Electronic Journals, Journal of the American Society for Infor Science，Vol. 34 （1983），22.

[5] 董剑桥：《超文本与语篇连贯性》，http://www.etc.edu.cn/show/index.htm。

[6] 段伟文："网络空间的自我伦理"，《新青年》2002 年 12 月 14 日，博客网。

[7] 甘舟："期刊电子版：中国文化走向世界之路"，《中国新闻出版报》，2005 年 8 月 14 日，龙源期刊网。

[8] 何明星："将阅读变为享乐"，《传媒》，2005 年第 5 期，龙源期刊网。

[9] 黄永跃："期刊全文数据库的建设与利用"，《现代情报》，2003 年第 7 期，第 56～58 页。

[10] 姜琳：“合理选择中文电子期刊数据库”，《科技情报开发与经济》，2006年第16卷第6期，第7~8页。

[11] L. R. Garson & J. G. Howard, "Electronic Publishing: Potential Benifits and Problems for Authors, Publishers, and Libraries", *Journal of Chemical Information and Computer Sciences*, Vol. 24 (1984), 123.

[12] 雷燕：《网络电子期刊研究》，武汉大学博士学位论文，2001年3月，第4页。

[13] 李树玲：“超文本网络文学对传统文学批评的挑战”，《襄樊职业技术学院学报》，2006年第5卷第2期，第99~101页。

[14] 李志军：“中国网络杂志的岔路口 是革命还是活命?”，《经济观察报》，2006年01月04日，http://SUNMARK.CN。

[15] 刘晗：“超阅读：理念及其悖论”，《吉首大学学报（社会科学版)》，2002年第1期，第55~56页。

[16] 刘晖：《北京地区人文社科期刊数字化阅读特点分析》，2007年出版产业与文化研究年度报告，2006年12月。

[17] 龙源期刊网：《关于龙源》，网络来源：http://cn.qikan.com/gbqikan/aboutus.asp。

作者简介

陈丹，北京印刷学院出版传播与管理学院副院长，副教授。

周玥，北京印刷学院传播学2009级研究生。

数字期刊

SAGE 科技期刊网络化运营模式分析*

郑珍宇

（武汉大学信息管理学院　武汉　430072）

摘要：本文在介绍 SAGE 商业出版公司及其科技期刊的概况后，对其科技期刊的网络化运营模式展开了全面的个案分析：首先介绍 SAGE 网络期刊全文数据库及其特点；其次说明 SAGE 在线的导航功能、检索功能、链接功能以及其他功能；再次介绍了 SAGE 网络科技期刊的数字化采编系统和开放存取方案。最后文章从期刊内容来源、期刊内容组织生产、期刊经营、内容服务等方面总结其网络化运营模式的优势所在及其可借鉴之处。

关键词：SAGE 出版公司　网络科技期刊　网络运营

The Analysis of the Network Operation Models of SAGE STM Journals

Zheng Zhenyu

（School of Information Management，Wuhan University，Wuhan，430072）

Abstract：After giving a brief introduction to the SAGE Publications and its STM journals，the paper then analyzes the network operation models of SAGE online STM journals：firstly introduces SAGE online STM journals' full-text database and its characteristics；then illuminates the navigating function，searching function，linking function and other functions of SAGE journals online；thirdly presents SAGE online STM journals' digital editing system and SAGE Open．Lastly the thesis sums up the advantages of SAGE online STM journals' network operation through several aspects containing the source and production of content，the journal's management and content services．

Keyword：SAGE Publications　Online STM journals　Network operation

　　SAGE 商业出版公司（SAGE Publications）是一家独立的私有公司，1965 年成立于美国，最初以出版社会科学类学术出版物起家；1995 年开始陆续出版科学、技术、医学（STM）三大领域的文献。SAGE 出版公司自创立以来就一直定位于以学术期刊出版为主营业务，目前已经在世界各地出版了各类语言的学术杂志近千种。公司业务已经延伸到学

---

　　* 本文系 2008 年度教育部科技发展中心网络时代的科技论文快速共享专项研究资助课题"网络科技期刊出版模式研究"（项目编号：2008117）的成果之一。

术图书出版领域，目前每年出版人文、社科、哲学、传播、艺术等近 100 大类的图书 1 000 种左右。经过 40 余年的发展，SAGE 出版公司已经成为世界领先的权威学术出版公司，跻身全球前五大出版集团之列，并有遍布全球的销售与出版网络。[1]SAGE 出版的网络科技期刊在全球都享有美誉，并拥有庞大的用户群。

与其他国际大型商业出版机构相比，SAGE 出版公司发展历程并不算长，其所出版的学术期刊在数量上也不能构成规模化的竞争优势，但却形成了足以与爱思唯尔、施普林格等大型出版商角逐的重要学术出版力量，这得益于其多样化的、富有创新性的科技期刊运营模式。相较于其他大型商业出版机构，SAGE 出版公司的发展历程及其网络科技期刊运营模式对于我国期刊社的网络化发展更具借鉴意义。本文将对其科技期刊的网络化运营模式的详细介绍，并尝试总结 SAGE 网络科技期刊成功运营的几点原因及可借鉴之处。

1 SAGE 出版公司的学术期刊概况

SAGE 与全球超过 245 家专业学术协会合作出版 560 余种高品质学术期刊，每年出版 12 ~ 15 种百科全书和超过 700 种新书。SAGE 出版的学术期刊为 100% 同行评审，其中 247 种期刊收录于 2007 年 JCR（Thomson Scientific Journal Citation Report）中，占 SAGE 期刊总数的 51%，其中 183 种期刊收录于 SSCI 部分，78 种收录于 SCI 部分。30% 的 SAGE 期刊位列相应领域的前 10 位。[2]SAGE 学术期刊覆盖了人文科学、社会科学、科学技术、医学和生命科学的各个领域，包括传播媒体、教育、心理与咨询、社会学、犯罪学、城市研究与规划、政治和国际关系、商业管理和组织学、语言文学、食品科学、信息科学、数学与统计学、化学和材料科学、工程、环境科学、生命科学、护理学、健康科学与临床医学等 40 多个学科。

SAGE 出版有超过 165 种 STM 类期刊，它们中的大部分是与世界著名的学会和协会合作出版的。其科技医药类（STM）期刊主要包括四类：生命科学、临床医学、公共卫生与护理学和药理学与病毒学。

2 SAGE 科技期刊的网络化运营化模式

2.1 SAGE 网络期刊全文数据库及其特点

SAGE 全文数据库（SAGE full-text Collections）收录有由 SAGE 出版公司和与其合作的协会共同出版的最受欢迎的同行评议类期刊。SAGE 按学科类别将其旗下最受欢迎的同行评议类期刊分类组成学科论文数据库 SAGE Subject Collections，以满足不同领域专业学者的使用需求。文献内容涉及传播学、商业与管理学、政治与国际关系、心理学、社会学、犯罪学、教育学、城市研究与规划学、医学、材料科学与工程在内的十大学科领域。数据库收录有超过 395 种的期刊，178 000 篇全文、图书评论、社论等，其中的大部分带有原始的图例、表格和页数。这些全文为研究者和学生们提供一个良好的研究环境，使他们能通过轻松利用最新的研究论文信息及可追溯到第一卷第一期的过刊文献来完成研究任务。[3]全文数据库的文献均可通过 SAGE 期刊在线平台（SJO）访问。

表 1 中统计了 SAGE 数据库各个子数据库的类别、种数和所收入的学科范围。

表1　SAGE 期刊数据库[4]

学科数据库名称	种数	收录年限	学科类型
HSS Package（人文社科现刊库）	360 余种	1999 年至今	人文和社会科学
STM Package（科技医药现刊库）	150 余种	1999 年至今	科技工程，生命科学和医学
HSN Package（健康科学和护理学现刊库）	115 种	1999 年至今	生命科学，医学和护理学
CM Package（临床医学现刊库）	57 种	1999 年至今	临床医学
STM Deep Backfile（科技医药过刊库）	共计收录 354 种	从第一卷第一期至 1998 年	科技工程，生命科学和医学
HSN Deep Backfile（健康科学和护理学刊库）			生命科学，医学和护理学
CM Deep Backfile（临床医学过刊库）			临床医学

与其他国外知名的全文数据库相比，SAGE 全文数据库主要具有以下几个特点和优势：[5]

① 期刊 100% 同行评审（peer review），55% 被 JCR 所排名；

② 最多回溯约 57 年的记录；

③ 绝大部分期刊没有被其他全文数据库所收录；

④ 有引文索引链接（Cited Reference）

⑤ 与纸本期刊无捆绑销售要求；

⑥ 用户对购买期间数据拥有所有权（Perpetual Right）。

2.2　功能全面的 SAGE 期刊在线（SJO）

SAGE Journals Online（http://online. sagepub. com/）是 SAGE 全文期刊的电子访问平台，由美国斯坦福大学 HighWire 公司开发。SJO 受到科研人员及专业图书馆员的一致好评，并荣获 2007 年美国出版家协会最佳平台大奖。[6]这是基于该平台能为各类科研人员提供的领先的、功能全面的、贴心的信息服务。

导航功能：按学科分类和按刊名首字母顺序导航。SJO 还为用户提供 TopicMap 导航图功能。TopicMap 是为用户按学科浏览 SAGE 期刊所提供的一种小应用程序，使用户能通过直观的图表形式厘清上下级学科的前后关联。导航图在新的窗口运行，用户可以进行包括单击选择某一学科主题，拖动、双击主题以在原来的浏览页面显示文件列表，放大或缩小导航图页面的字体大小，重新设置检索式等便捷操作。

检索功能：①快速检索和高级检索（字段式逻辑检索），在检索结果上提供全文出处、作者、文摘、全文及参考引文链接，主题匹配等信息。②跨库检索（CrossRef Search）：可检索 45 家出版商的学术期刊全文，可检索记录：650 万条。③检索工具 MatchMaker[7]：用户选定一本期刊，MatchMaker 检索工具会提取出该期刊引文涉及的相关主题及它们的权重，并最终形成一幅包括主题权重（Topic weights）和主题名称（Topic names）的模式图。这个模式图可以用来查找相类似主题的期刊和论文。用户还可调整主题权重进行新一轮检索。

链接功能：平台支持 CrossRef 链接。与 ISI 链接，获知文章被利用情况；与 PubMed 链接，提供文章文摘信息（部分有免费全文）；与 Infotrieve 链接，付费购买单篇文章；与 Free Full Text 链接，链接至可获取免费全文的网址，获取该篇的免费全文。通过 Google 和 Google Scholar 可检索 SAGE 所有文献内容。

个性化服务：SAGE 为用户提供"我的工具（My Tools）"。注册用户可以管理个人账户，设定邮件通报服务（email alerts），管理保存的引文（Saved citations），保存检索结果（Saved searches），及选择最喜欢的期刊（My Favorite Journals）等。另外，其还提供引文管理器功能，SAGE 与 EndNote format、Reference Manager、ProCite、BibTeX 等多个引文管理器链接。

其他功能：①支持播客（podcasts）、视频流（streaming video）；②公共书签（Social bookmarking）：如 citeulike，Digg 和 Del. icio. us。③为图书馆等用户提供 COUNTER-3 兼容的统计报告。

2.3 SAGE 网络科技期刊网页

SAGE 为其各个网络期刊建立面向期刊、读者、作者、编审、广告商、合作伙伴的独立的期刊网站，以此作为信息交流平台及重要的营销平台。每个期刊主页都提供统一的、功能全面的内容模块方便各类用户获取信息。包括基本的介绍信息：期刊封面图片，期刊介绍，编委会介绍，订购信息，与论文相关的各类统计数据及帮助信息等。用户在期刊主页实现的操作：完成网上投稿，检索期刊，查看现刊，获取过刊，获得再版及其他使用授权，推荐给图书馆员及设定电子邮件通报服务等。作者还可通过在线提前出版（Online First）浏览最新的期刊论文。此外，期刊主页还是广告商宣传产品信息的平台，提供了标语广告、旗帜广告、链接广告等形式的广告服务。

SAGE 通过期刊网站实现对其网络科技期刊面向用户的发行。SAGE 还为其主要服务群体机构用户提供灵活多样的订购方案，主要包括以下五种方案：电子版和纸质版组合订购（Combined）；组合+过刊订购（Combined Plus Backfile）；电子版订购（E-Access）；电子版+过刊订购（E-Access Plus Backfile）；纸质版期刊订购（Print-Only），在此订购方案下，用户也可获得所订购期刊网络版当年及前一年的访问权。[8]

2.4 SAGE 网络科技期刊的数字化采编系统

2.4.1 在线投稿系统 SAGETRACK

SAGE 旗下每种期刊都有各自的编辑室和投稿要求。作者可通过 SAGE 的在线投稿系统 SAGETRACK 完成网上投稿过程。SAGETRACK 是一个基于互联网的同行评议与在线投稿系统。与 ScholarOne 共同合作开发的 SAGETRACK 平台能自动完成投稿流程，并且有简易的管理、编辑和审议功能，并创造个性化的界面，这些功能使得它的用户们能专注于内容而不是流程。[9]

SAGETRACK 平台的包括两大功能模块：作者中心（Author Center）和评审者中心（Reviewer Center）。在作者中心页面，作者可以实时追踪稿件所处的状态，查看所有稿件的细节。提交稿件的过程有详细的分步指导和说明。在审稿专家中心页面，审稿专家在收到编辑的审稿邀请的邮件后就可以在线完成同行评议过程。整个过程同样有详细的步骤指导和说明。界面内提供所审议文稿的详细信息和所有版本历史信息。审稿专家必须将最终的审议意见写在系统内的"评分表"上。系统还为审稿专家提供外部搜索引擎的外部链接，使他们能通过 PubMed、HighWire 和谷歌等查询作者和作品信息。

SAGE 允许作者提交包括音频、视频在内的多种格式的辅助材料。SAGE 允许作者提交的音频、视频文件的格式包括：MP3、AAC、WMA、Quicktime、MPEG、AVI 等。附件和投稿论文一起经由评审人员评议，并由期刊编辑最终决定是否同意刊载提交附件。但 SAGE 不负责审核附件内容的准确性、拼写、排版或校对，SAGE 也不为创建附件提供技术支持。

2.4.2 编辑加工和同行评议

SAGE 期刊的编辑加工过程主要有以下几步：①作者将论文提交到同行评议系统；②经由同行评议并录用文献；③文字编辑修改文稿，排版人员对论文进行排版；④PDF 格式的修改论文通过 E-mail 发送给作者和编辑；⑤作者或编辑重新审议文稿；⑥按责任编辑（Production Editor）的意见再次修改文稿；⑦责任编辑审核和校对文稿，排版人员再次排版；⑧准备付印的最终文稿以及期刊的创建（Issue Building）；⑨完成一期期刊的编辑加工，出版期刊的纸质本和电子版。

SAGE 出版的期刊 100% 为同行评议类期刊。每篇提交的投稿都由期刊编辑选择两名独立的审稿专家对稿件进行评议。同行评议的主要作用有三个：①帮助评选适合该期刊的论文；②对论文提出建设性的修改意见；③判断作品的合法性。审稿专家一般要求在四个星期之内完成稿件评议工作，并给该稿件打分，给编辑和作者提出参考建议等。

2.4.3 Online First

用户可以在 SJO 平台上通过 SAGE Online First 功能访问在线优先出版的期刊论文。Online First 功能将已经决定录用但尚未付印的期刊论文，优先在网上提供使用。这项功能使订阅者和会员能以最快的速度获取相关领域的最新论文，也缩短了作者从提交稿件到论文出版过程中的等待时间，使作者的研究成果获得更高的使用率和引用率。在线优先出版的论文都被赋予了唯一的 DOI 标识，研究人员可以直接通过标准 DOI 号引用该论文。当优先在线出版的论文被赋予卷期、期刊页面等正式出版物的信息后，这些论文就由 Online First 从论文列表中移出，这时用户就只能通过该卷期期刊来查看该论文。

2.5 SAGE 开放存取（SAGE Open）

SAGE Open 是 SAGE 公司于 2006 年推出的一种可供选择的开放存取方案。这种出版方式是由作者付费，SAGE 公司将作者论文初稿提前出版并即刻提供免费使用。这项方案的推出使作者能及时满足相关赞助机构的要求。

SAGE 出版集团一直都致力于探索富有创新性的出版模式以满足学术团体的发展需要。2007 年 11 月，SAGE 出版集团就与 Hindawi 出版公司达成协议，共同出版一系列完全供开放存取使用的期刊。SAGE 负责编辑、市场营销和新期刊的推广。后者提供技术和专业支持，负责由网上投稿，同行评议到最后出版的整个出版流程的运作。两公司出版了一系列 STM 类高品质学术期刊并且这些期刊的数量还在增加。它们都经过同行评议过程并符合相应的编辑标准。SAGE 和 Hindawi 出版公司的这次大胆的战略合作，使 SAGE 出版集团成为最大的出版有一系列高品质 OA 期刊的学术出版商。[10]

目前，SAGE 开放存取出版模式只适用于 SAGE 旗下的一些生物医学类期刊或通过合作出版方式（in a hybrid manner）出版的期刊。这种出版模式每篇文章需向作者收取3 000

美元或 1 600 英镑的费用，某些期刊还对彩印等收取额外费用或者税收费用。SAGE 开放存取出版的论文是已被相关期刊录用的文章。[11]另外，SAGE 将以作者的名义把开放存取的期刊论文送交给 PMC 和其他相关的国际部门（如 UKPMC 或 PMCI）。这使作者的文章能够在 PMC 和 SAGE 期刊页面上立刻供研究者免费使用。

3 SAGE 科技期刊网络化运营优势分析与借鉴

SAGE 在科技期刊的网络化运营模式和理念方面有其值得借鉴的优势和亮点，主要包括以下几个方面。

首先，在期刊内容来源上，SAGE 的最大特色在于 SAGE 出版集团 40 余年的发展历程中，始终与学会和协会保持良好的合作关系。如今，它已与超过 245 家的学会和协会有合作关系。与学会、协会出版的期刊约占期刊总数的三分之一，它们是 SAGE 高质量期刊的来源和保障。其旗下的多种 STM 类期刊为该领域学会的官方期刊，或者与他们共同出版的期刊。

其次，在期刊内容组织生产方面，重视信息技术的利用，通过与技术公司的合作开发在线投稿系统 SAGETRACK 实现了期刊出版全流程的数字化。SAGE 的期刊平台充分体现了网络的优势，允许用户上传数据、图表、音频、视频等多种格式的资料，并建立了编审、读者与作者之间的互动交流平台。

再次，在期刊经营上，SAGE 期刊平台除了具备强大的信息交流功能外，更是重要的网络营销平台。实现网上投稿、发布，网上订阅，网上支付，开放存取阅读及信息搜索等。通过平台直接面向用户发行成为 SAGE 网络期刊的主要的发行渠道之一。通过平台为广告商提供服务并获取收入也成为其重要的收入来源之一。

最后，在内容服务方面，SAGE 也关注和重视提升用户体验，坚持"为作者、读者及社会创建自然家园"的理念，为用户提供功能全面的期刊在线平台，提供完善的检索、导航、外部链接、互动社区及个性化服务功能。另外，其以全球化视野运作科技期刊数字出版、注重创新等特质也是其优势所在。

由此可见，对于国内学术期刊社的网络化运营而言应尽快加大技术投入，可通过与技术出版商打造功能强大的数字出版平台，实现学术期刊数字出版；打破行业和领域往来甚少的现状，通过与拥有大量优势内容资源的学、协会机构合作，加快学术期刊出版社的成长速度；找准自身定位，设计合适的赢利模式；重视创新，提升服务。

注释

[1] Company overview ［OL］. http://www. uk. sagepub. com/aboutCompany. nav［2010-02-07］

[2] CALIS 集团引进 SAGE 数据库评估报告. ［OL］. http://166.111.120.70:8000/portal/pgwj/200904SAGE. pdf［2010-02-07］

[3] SAGE Subject Collections. ［OL］. ［2010-02-07］. http://www. sagepub. com/librarians/collections/home. sp

[4] Offerings from SAGE for Library Consortia- JOURNALS ［OL］. http://www. uk. sagepub. com/librarians/purchase_consortia. sp#journals［2010-02-07］

[5] http://www.sagefulltext.com/resources/SageColl-Brochure.pdf[2010-02-07]

[6] http://www.sagepub.com/repository/binaries/consortia/SAGEPremier.pdf[2010-02-07]

[7] http://online.sagepub.com/help/pop/matchmaker.dtl[2010-02-07]

[8] http://online.sagepub.com/subscriptions/institutional-faq.dtl[2010-02-07]

[9] http://www.researchinformation.info/products/product_details.php?product_id=48 [2010-02-07]

[10] http://www.eurekalert.org/pub_releases/2007-11/sp-sah112007.php[2010-02-07]

[11] SAGE Open.[OL].http://www.uk.sagepub.com/sageopen.sp[2010-02-07]

作者简介

郑珍宇，武汉大学信息管理学院出版发行系2009级硕士研究生。

342

数字期刊

出版企业网络招聘存在的问题及优化对策

姚永春

（武汉大学信息管理学院　武汉　430072）

摘要：随着我国出版企业信息化程度不断提高，网络招聘逐渐成为出版企业招募人才的重要渠道。但是，当前出版企业的网络招聘工作基本处于招聘信息发布与应聘信息收集整理环节，网络招聘信息发布渠道狭窄，覆盖面不广，职位描述缺乏创意，网络招聘的优势未能充分发挥。出版企业需要从建立完整的网络招聘工作链，规范网络招聘工作流程，拓展网络招聘信息发布渠道，丰富招聘信息等多方面优化网络招聘工作。

关键词：出版企业　网络招聘　优化策略

Existing Problems and Optimizing Countermeasure in the E-recruitment of Publishing House

Yao Yongchun

（School of Information Management，Wuhan University，Wuhan，430072）

Abstract：E-recruitment is becoming more and more important for publishing houses to recruit talents with the improvement of informatization level of china's publishing houses. However, e-recruitment is at a low stage of development. It only includes employment information release and applicants information collection. The channels of employment information dissemination are confined to several employment websites and publishing houses' own websites. Job description is lack of creation and is unattractive to applicants. To improve efficiency of e-recruitment, publishing houses should take some countermeasures. They should develop online interview and online competence testing, standardize e-recruitment flow, and develop more channels of employment information release.

Keywords：Publishing house　E-recruitment　Optimizing countermeasure

　　网络招聘，也叫电子招聘、在线招聘，是指企业通过互联网发布招聘信息，通过电子邮件、简历数据库或搜索引擎收集应聘信息，吸引、寻找求职者以填补岗位空缺的过程。早在 2003 年左右，《财富》500 强企业中已有 88% 使用网络招聘员工[1]。我国企业自

1997 年开始运用网络渠道招聘人才，2006 年在我国的世界 500 强企业中实行网络招聘的比例已达 90%，2007 年经常采用网络招聘方式的企业也达到了 72.6%[2]。IDC 高级分析家 Marc Pramuk 指出，要想在具有卓越组织性的市场中聘请人才，就必须依赖网络招聘[3]。

随着我国出版企业信息化程度不断提高，网络招聘也逐渐成为出版企业招募人才的一条重要渠道。2005 年 12 月，上海出版行业人才中介网成功举办了我国首届新闻出版行业网络招聘会，至 2009 年，该招聘会已成功举办五届，成为上海出版企业招聘专业人才的重要平台。各类网站上出版企业的招聘信息也日渐丰富。2010 年 8 月中旬，笔者在百度以"招聘编辑"为主题词进行检索，共得到 7 713 个相关结果，信息分布于智联招聘、58 同城、赶集网等众多网站。笔者同时以北京、上海、广州、成都、沈阳为调查区域，对智联招聘、中华英才网等综合性招聘网站进行检索。在智联招聘网站，以"编辑/文案/传媒/影视/新闻"为职位类别，以"媒体/出版/影视/文化/艺术"为行业类别进行检索，共得到 372 条相关信息。在中华英才网，以"总编、副总编/美术编辑/出版/排版设计/编辑、记者"为职位类别、以"媒体、出版、文化传播"为行业类别进行检索，共获得相关信息 1 884 条。笔者又以"编辑-网络（站）编辑-视频编辑-企业内刊编辑-记者"为职位类别，限定公司性质为"国企"，不分区域在"前程无忧"网站进行搜索，获得相关信息 346 条。此外，在中国出版集团、中国科学出版集团、凤凰出版传媒、时代出版传媒等很多出版企业网站上，也有招聘信息发布。显然，出版企业已经意识到网络招聘在开发人力资源方面的价值并加以利用。但由于网络招聘对于刚刚起步的出版企业人力资源管理部门而言仍然是新生事物，因此，当前出版企业的网络招聘工作存在不少问题，需要优化与完善。

1　出版企业网络招聘存在的问题

1.1　网络招聘基本处于招聘信息发布与应聘信息收集整理环节

招聘的目的是实现人才与岗位的匹配，因此，无论是传统招聘方式还是网络招聘，在程序和内容上都应包括职位信息发布、应聘信息收集与整理、面试与测评，乃至录用与招聘工作分析等层面。对于网络招聘来说，要充分发挥网络招聘低成本、高效率、互动性强的优势，就应该建立完整的网络招聘工作链，不仅利用网络发布职位信息和收集应聘信息，而且通过在线面试与在线测评，完成人员甄选甚至作出录用决策。

但是，从目前出版企业开展的网络招聘工作来看，主要还是利用自己的网站或招聘网站发布招聘信息，通过电子邮件收集应聘信息。少数做得更深入一点的企业，如凤凰出版传媒，会利用网站发布笔试、面试及录用通知，然而也仅限于此，仍属于简单的单向信息传递。招聘工作的效率和有效性取决于招聘企业与应聘者之间的双向沟通与选择，网络招聘之所以备受关注正是源于它为企业和求职者提供了良好的互动交流平台。事实上，发布招聘信息与收集整理应聘信息只是网络招聘的序幕，通过电子邮件或在线交流方式与应聘者进行初步沟通、对应聘人员进行在线测评和面试才是网络招聘工作的中心议题。所以，从这个角度来看，目前出版企业的网络招聘工作才刚刚起步，与真正的网络招聘还存在相当大的差距。

1.2　网络招聘信息发布渠道狭窄，覆盖面不广

招聘信息的传播范围直接影响招聘工作的效果。网络招聘的信息发布渠道大体上可以分为企业自己的网站和招聘网站,后者又可以分为综合性网站、行业性网站、地方性网站、政府性网站和服务性网站等。不同网站有不同的特点和优劣势,招聘效果存在差异。企业只有根据所需人才选择合适的招聘信息发布渠道,才能扩大招聘信息的覆盖面,增强招聘信息发布的针对性。

目前出版企业常用的网络招聘信息发布渠道主要是企业自己的网站和少数几个招聘网站。一般而言,到企业网站搜寻招聘信息的人员,通常对该企业有一定的兴趣,如果能够实现与合适岗位的匹配,招聘成功的可能性很大。利用出版企业自己的网站发布信息,信息最好登载在主页显著位置。但从出版企业网站来看,由于频道和栏目设置不同,招聘信息的发布途径和传播效果不尽相同,有的很容易发现,有的需要仔细搜索。比如,凤凰出版传媒网站统一发布集团内所有成员单位的招聘信息,这些招聘信息既在首页的"专题导览"中出现,也在"出版人才分中心"频道的"招聘信息"栏目中出现,非常醒目,应聘者能够很方便地搜索到相关信息。但也有一些出版企业网站将招聘信息发布在服务频道、资讯频道或通知、公告中,需要通过多次点击才能找到,不利于招聘信息的快捷传播。招聘网站的优势在于访问量大、覆盖面广,能够吸引更多的应聘者。出版企业较为青睐两大知名综合性招聘网站——智联招聘和中华英才网,发布在这两大网站上的招聘信息远远超过其他网站。此外,在一些教育类网站如"我是应届生"、"中国教育在线"以及同城网站如"58同城"、"赶集网"上也可以见到出版企业的招聘信息。但出版企业似乎对于行业性招聘网站并不熟悉,除了出版行业人才中介网外,在别的行业网站上几乎找不到出版企业的招聘信息,比如在"行业招聘网站"的传媒人才网上没有一条相关信息。门户网站与SNS网站也没有成为出版企业发布招聘信息的选择。总体而言,出版企业网络招聘的信息发布渠道还是较为单一,覆盖面不广。

1.3 职位描述缺乏创意,细节表述不够到位

从出版企业发布在不同网站的招聘信息来看,各出版企业都比较重视职位描述和要求。无论是招聘编辑、排版等初中级岗位还是销售经理、总编室主任等高级岗位,基本都做到了详细、全面地描述岗位职责和任职资格。显然,这有助于求职者准确判断岗位是否适合自己,也有助于提高招聘成功率。但也有出版企业的招聘信息职位描述文不对题,比如有一家出版社招聘理工类策划编辑,职位描述只写了对应聘者学科专业的要求,至于这个策划编辑职位具体的职责范围只字未提。另一普遍存在的问题是职位描述相似度很高,看不出不同出版企业对该职位的特殊期待和要求。比如招聘编辑的信息,职位描述通常都是"学科+工作经验+选题、组稿、编辑加工"模式,缺乏创意。再者,有些招聘信息的细节处理略显粗糙。比如对工作经验的文字表述,"8—10年及以上"完全可以写成"8年以上"。还有任职资格与职位的匹配问题,有出版社招聘学徒工,虽然职位描述中的学历要求明确为初中即可,但在简要信息中学历要求却显示为MBA以上。这种错误可谓低级,却会严重影响企业在应聘者心目中的形象。

2 出版企业网络招聘优化策略

出版企业网络招聘工作中存在的上述种种问题,可以通过拓展网络招聘信息发布渠道及工作内容、更严谨而富于创造性的职位描述、规范网络招聘工作流程来完善和提高。

2.1 建立完整的网络招聘工作链，规范网络招聘工作流程

如前所述，网络招聘工作流程包括职位信息发布、应聘信息收集与整理、面试与测评、录用与招聘工作分析等，出版企业要充分发挥网络招聘的优势，首先应该建立完整的网络招聘工作链，规范网络招聘各个环节的工作。

对出版企业而言，要建立完整的网络招聘工作链，最急待发展的是在线人员甄选工作（包括在线笔试、在线面试与在线测评等）。在线人员甄选最能体现网络招聘的无地域限制和互动性优势[4]，有效提高招聘工作的效率，降低招聘工作的成本。目前，我国出版企业基本实现了宽带上网，QQ、MSN 等通讯工具被广泛运用于企业内部的日常工作交流及不同出版企业之间的业务联系之中。最近，随着出版企业的跨地域发展，许多出版企业已经或正在着手建设视频会议系统。这些都为出版企业开展在线人员甄选工作奠定了基础。一方面，出版企业可以通过网络素质测评测试应聘者的个性、动力因素等综合素质，获得更丰富的人员甄选信息。另一方面，出版企业完全可以利用电子邮件、聊天软件或招聘网站提供的聊天室、视频会议系统等进行在线面试。尤其是利用 QQ 视频聊天或视频会议系统面试，应聘者和招聘者之间可以像在实体空间里一样面对面沟通交流。这种在线面试，费用低、效率高、氛围轻松、信息量大，既可以用于个别面试，也可以用于小组面试或集体面试，丝毫不亚于传统面试。

规范网络招聘工作流程，制度建设是基础。出版企业要通过建立规章制度，明确网络招聘各个工作环节的主要任务和各个部门的职责分工，网络招聘的工作步骤及相互衔接。同时，要注意各个工作环节中的细节问题。比如，招聘信息中的职位名称，要通用、规范、适度。个人简历信息的收集，尽可能使用在线填写方式，以获得标准化数据，减少简历筛选的工作量。招聘信息的发布和刷新要及时，每天需要对发布在招聘网站的招聘信息进行定时刷新，如果发布时间超过一周应重新发布。处理应聘信息要快速、高效，简历筛选最好两三天内完成，对有意向的应聘者应第一时间给予回复。

2.2 拓展网络招聘信息发布渠道，巧妙利用各类招聘软件

出版企业利用网络招聘人才，要有"大渠道、大招聘"的概念。即除了在出版企业自己的网站和智联招聘等传统人才网站上发布招聘信息外，出版企业还需要将招聘信息广泛发布到符合相关职位需求的群体经常访问的综合门户或垂直门户、BBS 以及网络社区上。比如，新浪、搜狐等门户网站的首页或传媒、读书频道，中国图书商报网站、出版商务周刊网站等专业媒体网站，新闻出版总署及各地新闻出版局网站、中国出版网等行业网站，大学网站，以及出版行业人才中介网等行业性人才网站等。随着 SNS 网站的发展，网络部落化渐成趋势，一些有着共同职业或兴趣爱好的人群往往聚集到某一特定网站，如文化传媒人士偏好的豆瓣网、沃华网传媒圈 SNS 等，在这些空间里投放招聘信息，可以有效地提高信息发布的精准性。此外，如果是面向某一地区招聘人才，那么最好选择在地区门户网站或同城网站发布信息。

为提高网站竞争力，许多招聘网站开发了各类招聘软件。如前程无忧网站推出的"网才"招聘管理系统，提供与企业组织结构完全吻合的职位库管理、招聘广告自动投放管理、应聘筛选与信件自动回复、简历分析、职位考核标准及评定等一揽子解决方案，允许招聘企业建立自己的筛选标准，对求职者进行初步过滤，并对退、留邮件设置不同标记，自动回复和存档[5]。一些网站提供在线性向水平测试，并通过设置筛选标准和参数，

对应聘者进行自动筛选。一些网站可以为企业自动生成人才数据库。出版企业在选择招聘网站时，要主动了解网站能够提供的各类服务，充分利用招聘软件的优势，提高网络招聘效率。

2.3 丰富招聘信息，增强职位及企业吸引力

从目前出版企业发布的网络招聘信息来看，主要包括岗位名称、工作职责简介、任职要求、工作条件、申请投递信息等内容，比较完整，但也存在较大的改进空间。比如企业信息的传递。招聘是双向选择，不仅企业要挑选应聘者，应聘者也要挑选企业。出版企业通过在招聘信息中附带企业简介或添加企业网站链接，可以帮助求职者了解自己的企业文化、价值观、组织架构、薪酬福利等重要信息，从而增强企业对求职者的吸引力。但现在注意到这一点的出版企业并不多，只有少数几家出版社的招聘信息中有企业简介。此外，职位描述除详细全面地介绍岗位职责与要求外，也可以用来传递企业优势信息。比如，中国城市出版社在招聘健康生活编辑的信息中写道："健康版块是我们较为成熟的版块，已经先后出版了樊正伦、杨力、石原结实、孔令谦等养生大家的健康畅销书……"，这就很容易唤起求职者的兴趣。总之，在发布完整的招聘信息基础上，创造性地添加细节信息，是增强职位和企业对求职者吸引力的有效途径。

3 结语

网络招聘对出版企业而言乃新生事物，其工作流程、内容、技巧尚在摸索之中，招聘效果也有待评估。但是，随着网络招聘技术自身的完善及出版企业信息化程度的提高，网络招聘必将挟其覆盖面广、时效性强、成本低、效率高等优势，成为行进在数字化道路上的出版企业开发人力资源的重要渠道。本文对出版企业网络招聘存在问题及优化策略的探讨，仅为抛砖引玉，期待广泛的关注和探讨。

注释

[1] 马新建等. 人力资源管理与开发 [M]. 北京：石油工业出版社，2003：198

[2] 艾瑞市场咨询. 2003 年招聘企业使用的招聘方式情况 [OL]. [2008-02-27]. http://old.iresearch.com.cn/online_recruiting/detail_chart.asp?id=52239

[3] IDC：全球网络招聘 2006 年将达 157 亿美元 [OL]. [2002-05-29]. http://tech.sina.com.cn/i/w/2002-05-29/117821.shtml

[4] 如何有效实施网络招聘 [OL]. [2006-06-15]. 中国劳动咨询网，http://www.51labour.com/html/35/35617_4.html

[5] 服务声明 [OL]. [2010-09-02]. 前程无忧网，http://www.51job.com/bo/service.php

作者简介

姚永春，博士，武汉大学信息管理学院副教授。

出版社数字化转型

从市场混淆行为谈网络文学的法律规制*
——由"网络文学第一案"引发的思考

贺子岳 张 茜

（武汉理工大学文法学院 武汉 430070）

摘要：随着网络资源的繁荣，文学网站的集合化模式推动了网络文学的飞速发展，但是由于发展历时短，其产业化策略下引发的过度商业化，也导致权利人的利益不能得到合法保障，网络文学的法律保护迫在眉睫。本文以"网络文学第一案"——"罗浮"案为出发点，首先从网络文学产业化引发的竞争就"罗浮"案产生的背景做了简要论述。然后对市场混淆行为的理论进行了梳理，从我国《反不正当竞争法》第五条第二项出发，从三个方面对网络文学市场混淆行为的认定作了相关剖析。最后指出我国当前网络立法的缺失，提出了完善法律规制的建议。

关键词：网络文学 "罗浮"案 市场混淆行为 法律规制

Study on the Law Regulation of the Internet Literature in the Acts of Confusion
—— A Thinking of "The First Case of Internet Literature"

He Ziyue　Zhang Qian

（School of Arts and Law，Wuhan University of Technology，Wuhan，430070）

Abstract：With the prosperity of the network resources，the comprehensive pattern of the literature site promotes the rapid development of the internet literature. Due to the development of short duration，the industrialization strategy of this set pattern cause over-commercialization and damage the interests of rights holders. In this paper，"the first case of internet literature"——"Rover" case as a starting point，it briefly discusses the background of "Rover" case. Then，the paper gives an account of the theory of acts of confusion. From Article 5 of Anti-Unfair Competition Law，the paper analyzes the defined of the acts of confusion in Internet Literature. At last，the paper proposes some suggestions about the law regulation.

Keywords：Internet literature　"Rover" case　Confusion　Law regulation

* 本文为国家社会科学基金 10BTQ012 研究成果。

网络文学经历了十余年的发展，在主流传统文学的质疑与对抗中，已成为当前青年人情感和文学思维的主要表达方式，也成为当前文学模式中不可小觑的一股重要力量。网络文学产业模式的过度商业化，加速了互联网领域的不正当竞争，用传统立法来解决网络纠纷愈发不合时宜，网络立法的缺失使得网络版权的权利人利益难以得到保障。在被业内称为"网络文学第一案"的"罗浮"案中，知名网络写手"无罪"以不正当竞争为由，将起点中文网的经营者告上法庭。作为网络文学第一案，面对同名不同内容的知名网络文学作品，如何在传统立法基础上认定、规制网络文学的市场混淆行为，仍尚存争议。这里从"网络文学第一案"出发，从传统立法逐一予以界定，也对当前网络文学的立法规制提出了建议。

1 "罗浮"案产生的背景

1.1 网络文学的产业化

精神文化作为一种满足人类内心需求的文化，在人们心里是高高在上、照应灵魂的东西。当互联网与文学牵手构筑了文学网站这个平台时，网络文学这一概念才开始出现并逐渐在学界得以认同。网络文学的发展，改变了传统文学的发展格局和传播模式，开创了新的文学发展道路。而互联网所存在的价值性也加速了网络文学产业化进程，网络文学在带来多渠道的商业利益的同时，也带来了前所未有的挑战。

所谓产业化就是注重工业生产与管理机制运作，集中市场经营，追求价值利益的最大化。文化产业化就是利用科学技术打造现代文化的市场制度，形成独立的规模化的生产经济实体。[1]从早期名噪一时的"榕树下"到当前的起点中文网，幻剑书盟等文学网站，从最初的非产业化文学网站到如今并购之后发展较好的产业化文学网站，我们看到了经营者通过企业化的运营模式在保证网络写手创作的同时，满足了网民的精神需求，并且从中找到了与市场经济的连接点，实现了网络文学与市场经济共赢的局面。

谈到网络文学的产业化，首推盛大旗下的起点中文网，作为推行 VIP 收费制度的先驱，它以每千字三分钱的收费模式，在聚集大量优秀写手和作品及点击率的同时，也带来不菲的市场效益。VIP 的收费制度将费用以稿费的形式付给作者，作者可以得到付费阅读收入的 70% 和出版收入的 70%，这样作者的利益也得到保障。同时，起点中文网利用优秀网络文学作品的超高人气和情节素材，让我们看到网络文学产业模式下其衍生物的市场效益。在迈出网络文学市场化的第一步后，起点中文网当前着力于平台拓展，推进多层次发展的商业模式。除了推广广告之外，网络文学作品也开始与影视作品、网络游戏相衔接，随之而来相应的服装、饰品等衍生物都有待开拓。《鬼吹灯》就是起点中文网产业模式下多层次发展的一个例证。网络文学的兴起，在对传统文学和文化产业产生冲击的同时，也造就了另一个市场——掌上阅读市场，主要包括手机阅读和电子阅读器。手机作为大众的必备物品，它的随时性加速了无线增值服务的产业进程。起点中文网在学习亚马逊 Kindle 阅读器后，打造了 Bambook 电子阅读器，完善了网络文学的产业链，开创了国内网络文学阅读的新平台。

1.2 网络文学产业化背景下立法的缺失

网络文学的产业化，让我们看到其作为物质产品的一般商品属性逐渐显现，那么与传统的商品一样，网络文学作品也需要经受来自各种相关产业的竞争。当网络文学作品及其衍生物在获取大量利润的同时，我们仍要看到反方向竞争的加剧。在这个内容为王、网络立法缺失的环境下，不正当竞争将会持续影响整个网络文学体系的发展。如何应对网络文学环境下的不正当竞争，是我们必须面对的问题。就网络文学的法律规制而言，网络立法缺失，传统部门法存在空白区域等不足之处，面对各种网络侵权所显现出来的问题，不得不引起我们的思考。

纵横中文网与起点网关于"罗浮"之争，让我们看到网络文学蓬勃发展带来的反方面的问题。2010 年 7 月 12 日，知名网络写手"无罪"以不正当竞争为由，将起点中文网的经营者上海玄霆娱乐信息科技有限公司告上法庭。这一事件被业界称为"中国网络文学第一案"。争议作品为同名作品《罗浮》，纵横中文网首发时间为 2009 年 12 月 1 日，起点中文网首发时间为 2010 年 4 月 15 日。无罪的《罗浮》自首发以来，点击量累积 2 800 万，好评率为 98%。而起点中文网以 A 签形式首发的《罗浮》因购买了百度的竞价排名而在搜索结果中排名第一，导致了很多慕名无罪《罗浮》的读者在搜索阅读时将起点中文网的《罗浮》误认为是无罪的作品。即便如此，起点中文网该作品的点击量仅仅超过 10 万，读者好评率仍为零。那么，同名不同内容的网络文学作品是否构成侵权，是否构成不正当竞争，传统法律上对于作品名称，明确规定作品名称不具有著作权。同时，作者创作的任何一部作品，要将其作品的每个名称作为商标申请注册商标的可能性也不大。因此，当网络文学作品名称出现被他人做相同或近似使用时，当前只能以不正当竞争作为诉求来寻求法律保护。那么，对于"罗浮"案是否构成不正当竞争中的市场混淆行为，下面将以《反不正当竞争法》第五条第二项关于市场混淆行为的认定条文为依据做相关分析。

2 网络环境下市场混淆行为的认定

市场混淆行为也称之为商业混同行为或假冒仿冒行为，它是指经营者采用欺骗性手段从事市场交易，使自己的商品或服务与特定的竞争对手的商品或服务相混淆，以造成购买者误认或者误购之目的的不正当竞争行为。作为欺骗性市场交易行为的一种表现形式，市场混淆行为与其他欺骗性市场交易行为的主要区别在于，是否冒充特定竞争对手的商品或服务，是否损害特定竞争对手的利益。我国《反不正当竞争法》中规定了市场混淆行为的四种形式，除此之外，《商标法》、《产品质量法》、《专利法》等法律也作了相关规定。但就总体而言，我国立法上对于市场混淆行为规定的也只是现实混淆，范围狭隘，不利于实际案件的审理。为了弥补立法的不足，国家工商行政管理局《关于禁止仿冒知名商品特有的名称、包装、装潢的不正当竞争行为的若干规定》的第二条第二款对现实混淆进行了扩充，规定为"前款所称使购买者误认为是该知名商品，包括足以使购买者误认为是该知名商品"，这一规定将可能发生的混淆也归入了混淆的范畴，扩大了认定范围。

这里主要是对第五条第二项"擅自使用知名商品特有的名称、包装、装潢，或者使用与知名商品近似的名称、包装、装潢，造成和他人的知名商品相混淆，使购买者误认为是该知名商品"这一条文进行分析，根据市场混淆行为的特征，就"罗浮"案是否适用进行逐层对比，并对网络文学的市场混淆行为予以界定。

2.1 "知名商品"的理解与认定

在现代汉语词典中对于知名的解释为著名的含义。知名商品作为法律概念一般出现在反不正当竞争法中。如日本的《防止不正当竞争法》第一条第一款的第一项和第二项规定关于知名商品的定义。我国《反不正当竞争法》对知名商品既没有定义也没有作出解释性规定，只是国家工商行政管理局在《关于禁止仿冒知名商品特有名称、包装、装潢的不正当竞争行为若干规定》（以下简称《若干规定》）中第三条第一款作出相关规定，即"知名商品是指在市场上具有一定知名度，为相关公众所知悉的商品"。按照此项规定，知名商品要在相关公众中具有一定的知名度；至于相关公众，则是指与该商品有交易关系的特定的购买者。[2]因此，判断知名商品不应该以任何人对该商品是否知道为必要条件，而是以商品在相关的市场领域中有较高的知名度为条件。

根据以上标准可采用以下三个步骤来认定知名商品：第一步，考察是否存在有关商品的名称、包装、装潢被行为人假冒或仿冒的事实；第二步，如果存在以上事实，则可适用反推规则，推定行为人假冒或仿冒的商品是知名商品；第三步，结合法律规定，考察这种商品在合理界定的相关市场上是否具有较高的知名度，是否为相关的购买人和竞争对手所知悉。[3]

那么，将传统理论挪用至网络文学作品知名程度的认定上，我们可以从以下几个方面予以判定。其一，根据《若干规定》的第三条第一款的规定，只要是在市场上具有一定知名度，为相关公众知悉的，即为知名商品。这里的公众包括商品的购买者和竞争对手。那么，网络作品若为相关网民和同类文学网站竞争对手所知悉，具有较高人气和好评量的，可认定该网络文学作品在网络领域具有较高知名度，是知名商品。当然，网络作品的知名不以任何人对该作品是否知悉为必要条件，而是以该作品在相关网络文学领域中是否具有较高知名度为条件。其二，假若该网络作品的名称、内容存在被他人假冒或者仿冒的事实，也可认定该网络作品为知名商品。通过以上分析，我们可以认为无罪的《罗浮》在拥有较高点击量和好评率的情况下，在网络文学领域具有较高的知名度，为网络文学爱好者所知悉。而作为同类文学网站起点中文网对纵横网写手无罪的《罗浮》应该也存在知悉的事实。综上所述，在网络文学产业化环境下，网络文学作品已具备一般商品的属性，无罪的《罗浮》应属于网络文学市场下的知名商品。那么，对于网络文学中的知名商品，我们应称作"知名作品"，一样也贴合网络文学作品本身的内涵，笔者认为知名作品可以定义为在网络上具有一定知名度，为相关网民和同类竞争对手所知悉的作品。这类作品的知名程度可以通过其网络点击量、好评率等网络资源条件进行综合评定。

2.2 "特有"的理解和认定

国家工商行政管理局《若干规定》第三条第二款规定："本规定所称特有，是指商品名称、包装、装潢非为相关商品所通用，并具有显著的区别性特征。"所谓特有，是指足以使一个商业标识与另一个商业标识区别开来的显著特征。因此，要认定特有，就必须认清是否为"相关商品通用"，是否"具有显著特征"。

关于对"特有"的认定，有以下原则：第一，特有性与使用在先原则。特有性认定标准有两个：其一，通过其外在标准来认定的原则，即使用在先原则。《若干规定》第四条第二款规定："特有的商品名称、包装、装潢应当依照使用在先的原则予以认定。"其二，认定特有性的实质性标准即为商品所具有的显著性和区别性。第二，从标识的自然属性、社会属性来认定特有性。所谓自然属性是指标识所固有的或天然的区别性。这种自然属性一旦运用到实践中，就具有竞争意义。社会属性不是固有的或者天然的，但由于人们在社会活动中的长期使用使之具有第二涵义。

那么，针对网络中相同名称的作品，是否构成不正当竞争，就应看其名称是否具有特有性。《罗浮》案中的"罗浮"一词，从特有性和使用在先原则来看，"罗浮"二字不存在使用在先的情况，因为在其他的领域，"罗浮"早有使用。从"罗浮"的显著性和区别性看，它也不存在显著性，它不为无罪的原创，"罗浮"是中国历史上一个山名，在广东省东江北岸，为粤中游览胜地。就"罗浮"这个词，它可以为相关商品所通用。因此，"罗浮"一词不具有特有性。

当然，在近年的相关司法实务中，法院往往对特有的名称、竞争者等定义作了扩大解释。例如，台湾漫画家朱德庸诉北京电视台制作播出的《上班这点事》对其漫画作品《关于上班这件事》构成不正当竞争，法院最终认定北京电视台构成不正当竞争的行为。再如2004年，中国图书市场的"伪书门"事件。中国社会科学出版社想引进美国一本名叫《没有任何借口》的畅销书时，却发现市场上已经有一本机械工业出版社出的《没有任何借口》的书。后经查明，后者的作者名字系编造，内容也为该社自行编撰，与原作无关。"伪书门"事件被新闻出版总署高层怒斥为"奸商行为"。从传统媒体传播作品名称的相同或者近似案件，我们可以延伸至网络文学作品名称相同或者近似，但内容却不相同的案例上。《罗浮》作为网络文学第一案，虽然在名称上不具有法律理论上所认定的特有性，但是拢聚高人气和高知名度的应该是作品本身的特有内容。那么，针对网络作品，尤其是网络文学作品是否构成不正当竞争，需要一部网络立法从名称、内容、作者和经营者等多方面进行规制。

2.3 相同或近似的使用造成误认

相同使用是指完全抄袭知名商品特有的名称、包装、装潢，不作改变，比较容易认定。近似使用是指行为人使用的商品名称、包装、装潢与知名商品的特有的名称、包装、装潢相比较，并无实质性的改变。根据主要部分和整体印象相近，一般购买者施以普通的注意力会发生误认等因素综合分析判断来认定。《若干规定》第五条规定"对使用与知名商品近似的名称、包装、装潢，可以根据主要部分和整体印象相近，一般购买者施以普通注意力会发生误认等综合分析认定。一般购买者已经发生误认或者混淆的，可以认定为近似"。不难看出，我国对近似的认定采用普通注意原则。由于相同或近似的使用而造成误认分为两种，即现实的混淆和可能的混淆。所谓现实的混淆是指购买者已经发生误认，因混淆了认识而购买了相关假冒或仿冒的商品；可能的混淆则是购买者可能因为误认而在购买时发生混淆。对于这两种情形，我国《反不正当竞争法》只规定了现实的混淆，对于可能的混淆则在《若干规定》中作出规制。

对于网络文学作品，作为知名作品，它所包含的因素包括作品名称、内容、作者、经营者是否存在相似或者相近，是否会使普通网民施以普通注意力会发生误认。《罗浮》案中，广大读者慕名无罪的《罗浮》，往往通过百度进行搜索，并且习惯性点击搜索排名第一的链接，从而进入起点中文网黄鹤九曲的《罗浮》。由于在搜索的链接中通常只显示作品名称，没有作者名字，混淆了读者的认识，导致读者产生了误认，错把起点中文网的《罗浮》当作无罪的《罗浮》，大大影响了后者的点击量和作品的声誉。但是，对于链接引起的误认，它又不同于传统的商品名称、包装、装潢，"罗浮"案中除了使用了相同的作品名称（且该名称还不具有特有性），作者、内容和经营者均不相同，并不适用《反不正当竞争法》第五条第二项的关于"误认"的规定。关于"罗浮"案的网络搜索引擎导致的误认，它也不同于《反不正当竞争法》第九条关于利用广告或者其他方法，对商品做引人误解的虚假宣传。毕竟起点中文网除了以 A 签形式首发同名不同内容的《罗浮》和竞价排名购买第一的搜索结果外，其搜索引擎链接的都是真实的内容，包括作者为黄鹤九曲，内容也不同于无罪。因此，面对不存在特有性的相同或者近似名称，其他条件均不相同的网络作品，如何对链接、域名、主页等网络元素引起的误认做到明确认定，这是《罗浮》案以及同类网络不正当竞争案件给我们带来的问题。

综合以上各条具体理论概念和法律规定，从传统立法和理论上看，"罗浮"案并不具备构成市场混淆行为的要件。首先，市场混淆行为要求以竞争为目的，在本质上具有欺骗性，通过仿冒或假冒使消费者产生误认。"罗浮"案中就无罪和起点中文网单个个体而言，是否构成竞争尚未定论，搜索引擎导致网络民众产生误认也难以寻找支撑的法律依据。其次，市场混淆行为表现为对其他经营者或服务的特定商业标识的利用，这些特定的商业标识是能够将各个经营者不同的商品或服务区分开来的。"罗浮"这个名称作为无罪文学作品的名称，由于是个通用名称，不具有原创性，因此不存在名称特有性。因此，单从当前立法条例规定来看，"罗浮"案不能以《反不正当竞争法》作为判定依据。但是根据相关的司法实务和近年来一系列相似案件的判例，在不适用《著作权法》等相关法律的时候，即便理论上的构成要件存在质疑，《反不正当竞争法》仍是司法界用以定案的主要立法依据。那么，作为网络文学第一案的《罗浮》案通过不正当竞争为由寻求法律保护也并不是毫无根据的。虽然相关规定与实际案例情况存在差别，但是仍可援引之前的相似判例予以借鉴。同时，"罗浮"案又一次用网络的特殊性揭开了当前法律规制不完善的面纱，构建新的立法体系，完善相关法律规制是迫在眉睫的。

3　网络环境下市场混淆行为的法律规制

面对网络领域各种不同情形导致的不正当竞争行为，我国传统立法中的《反不正当竞争法》及其相关规定难以逐一对应。由于当前的立法并未对网络领域中的不正当竞争行为进行直接的规定，在援引相关法律法规的时候，不难看到现行立法与网络发展需要的矛盾。首先，相关法律法规及条例中对于网络版权保护的规定存在漏洞，以及空白区域。当前的网络版权纠纷大多援引《著作权法》、《反不正当竞争法》、《反垄断法》等法律法规，但是传统的法律法规不能应对网络这一特殊形式的多样性，面对一些特殊的侵权行为，很容易在法律适用形成空白区域。其次，我国并不存在针对网络版权保护的专门的网络立法，其他的网络立法多为国务院及其部委发布的规章条例，立法层次较低，效力不高。我国现行的版权保护法律基本上是一些保护条例，而缺乏具体的许可性条款和禁止性条款。专门的网络版权立法的缺失使网络版权保护处于不定之中。最后，相关法律过于概括与宏观，可操作性不强，存在滞后性。当前网络侵权形式多样，针对特定行为，网络立法上缺乏相对应的惩戒条例，只有笼统的规范。

据此，针对网络领域的市场混淆行为存在的法律漏洞提出以下建议。

第一，对《反不正当竞争法》的规制范围进行扩大和补充，针对空白领域制定专项法律法规。我国《反不正当竞争法》第五条对于市场混淆行为的规制采用的是列举性规定，而未采用例示加概括的立法形式，很难将网络领域的特殊的客体列举进来，没有充分反映《反不正当竞争法》的特点，未能起到"兜底"的保护作用。另外，反不正当竞争法在对市场混淆行为进行规范时例外条款是必不可少的。在各国或者地区立法中也作了例外条款的规定，如日本《防止不正当竞争法》第二条以及我国台湾地区的《公平交易法》第二十条均对不被视为市场混淆行为作了相关规定。首先，在完善传统立法的基础上，增加网络环境下关于文学作品引发的各类不正当竞争行为的条款，如在市场混淆行为的规制中增加"关于使用相同或者相似的特有及非特有网络文学作品名称，但作品内容具有特有性且网络知名度较高的，也可认定为市场混淆行为"，增加不被视为市场混淆行为的例外条款，如"网络作品同名不同内容，但是作品并不具有较高知名度的，可不认为是市场混淆行为"。

第二，尽快制定一部网络保护的基本法，提高其立法层次；同时，针对相关法律法规中关于网络文学作品保护内容，应适当修改加以完善。由于我国网络立法多为国务院及其部委发布的行政法规和部门规章，立法层次较低，效力不高。因此，全国人大应针对当前的网络环境制定一部关于网络信息安全的基本法，在这部网络基本法中对网络文学作品保护单独作出规定和解释，以较高的法律效力来维护网络文学作品的传播和作者的权益。

第三，结合国际的相关立法，取其精华，加以借鉴，有利于国际区域的网络文学作品的交流与合作。世界各国的网络立法主要采取两种方式，一种是偏重采用国家立法主导模式的法律规制方法，如欧盟；另一种是偏重采用行业自律的模式，如美国。这两种模式，各有特色，有利有弊，都值得我国借鉴。通过借鉴学习他国立法的长处，不断完善本国立法，并加强国际区域的网络合作。细化一系列含糊、笼统的法律法规，使其具体化，便于实际落实。由于当前关于网络文学作品的法律条文明确性较差，往往削弱了法律的适用性和可操作性。例如《反不正当竞争法》、《广告法》和《商标法》很多时候对同一内容会出现重复规定，且笼统模糊，针对网络文学的多样性，需要细化对现行网络用户、网络内容提供商、服务商等主体权利和责任的明确、第三者责任的规定等，避免不同条例或规章之间缺乏关联，出现重复、模糊之处，加强立法的系统性。

我国《反不正当竞争法》的完善还有很长的过程，在吸取他国立法优点的时候，在网络基本法尚未构建的同时，我们还应不断研究当前网络领域所暴露的一系列不正当竞争行为，完善立法体系的构建，使徘徊在法律之外的不正当竞争行为早日得到法律的规制，还网络文学一片明净的天空。

注释

[1] 傅其林. 文学网站的产业化与中国网络文学的发展［J］. 贵州社会科学，2008（10）：42-45

[2] 尹显庆：论知名产品的反不正当竞争法的保护. 载于合众法律网法律文库，http://www.forlaw.cn/Articleshow.asp? id=1171

[3] 李昌麒，刘瑞复主编：经济法［M］. 法律出版社，2004（12）：311

参考文献

[1] 种明钊. 竞争法学［M］. 北京：高等教育出版社，2002

[2] 李昌麒，刘瑞复. 经济法［M］. 北京：法律出版社，2004

[3] 朱崇实. 经济法 [M]. 厦门：厦门大学出版社，2002

[4] 傅其林. 文学网站的产业化与中国网络文学的发展 [J]. 贵州社会科学，2008
（10）：42-45

[5] 周志雄. 对原创文学网站的考察与思考 [J]. 山东师范大学学报，2009，54（4）：
92-96

[6] 陈美玲，熊彬. 论网络不正当竞争行为的法律规制 [J]. 企业经济，2009（04）：
190-1192

[7] 侯霞. 网络环境中新型不正当竞争行为的法律规制 [J]. 安徽工业大学学报，2010，
27（01）：24-25

[8] 钟静宜. 浅析网络不正当竞争行为及其法律规制 [J]. 法制与社会，2009（01）：63

[9] 温兴琦，陈曦. 网络不正当竞争：表现、特征及对策 [J]. 重庆邮电学院院报，
2004（04）：65-67

[10] 牛玉科. 网络环境下的不正当竞争及其规制 [J]. 经济与管理，2009，23（06）：
58-61

[11] 赵墅艳. 网络环境下反不正当竞争问题研究 [J]. 贵州民族学院学报，2008（02）：
92-96

[12] 段新和. 网络文学的特征及存在的问题 [J]. 武汉工程大学学报，2010（02）：72-
74

[13] 王小英，祝东. 论文学网站对网络文学的制约性影响 [J]. 云南社会科学，2010
（01）：151-155

[14] 刘丽红. 浅谈网络文学产业化的现状及发展前景 [J]. 湖南医科大学学报，2008，
10（6）：120-121

[15] 吴美霞. 网络原创文学的传播要素分析 [J]. 新闻前哨，2009（04）：43-45

[16] 姚碧风. 原创作品装点网络迪斯尼盛大娱乐内容恐遇版权难题 [J]. IT 时代周刊，
2008（16）：24-26

[17] 尹显庆. 论知名产品的反不正当竞争法的保护 [EB/OL]. 载于合众法律网法律文
库，http://www.forlaw.cn/Articleshow.asp? id=1171，[2006-03-01]

[18] 无名.《罗浮》引爆网络文学侵权第一案 [EB/OL]. 载于网络导报，http://www.
wldbs.com/template/WebRootdb/xsym.jsp? nid=100722112710213330157，[2010-07-
22]

[19] 许承光. 经济法 [M]. 武汉：武汉理工大学出版社，2004

作者简介

贺子岳，博士，武汉理工大学文法学院新闻传播系教授。

张茜，武汉理工大学文法学院新闻传播系 2008 级硕士研究生。

Effectiveness of Notification and Substantial Compliance: Threshold of Successful Claims for Digital Contributory Copyright Infringements

Wang Qing   Cong Ting

(School of Information Management, Wuhan University, Wuhan, 430072)

Abstract: The validation of take-down notification, sent by digital publishers to online service providers, depends on its substantial compliance with legislation clauses, otherwise, the legally flawed notification would not derive online service providers of qualification for the benefit of so-called Safe Harbor rules, and digital publishers doom to failure if they insist on initiating and continuing their legal proceedings against alleged online service providers.

Keywords: Digital Publishing   Takedown Notification   Substantial Compliance

移除通知书的有效性与实质性符合：成功主张数字版权共同侵权的法律门槛

王　清　丛　挺

（武汉大学信息管理学院　武汉　430072）

摘要：移除通知书内容的有效性取决于是否符合法律规定的内容，否则，该通知书并不会导致网络服务提供者丧失法律规定的避风港原则的庇护，数字出版商要求其删除或者断开与涉嫌侵犯其著作权的作品、录音录像制品的请求不仅不会满足，如果坚持诉讼，反而会招致败诉的法律风险。

关键词：数字出版　移除通知　实质性符合

1   Two Cases: Same Facts, Different Results

On May 24, 2007, two days before World Intellectual Property Day, the Beijing No. 2 Intermediate People's Court handed down repectively the judgment about Yahoo! China cases, which were brought by eleven world famous record companies, EMI Group Hong Kong, Mercury Records Limited, Sony BMG Music Hong Kong, Warner Music Hong Kong, Universal Music Hong Kong, Cinepoly Music, Go East Entertainment and Gold Label Entertainment, etc, alleging Yahoo! China had infringed their music works' copyrights by allowing its users to search, download and play pirated music on its website. The plaintiffs alleged that Beijing Alibaba Information Technology Co., Yahoo! China's parent company, had been providing auditions, links, download services of 223 Chinese and English songs, in which that they own the production right, to public via the website of its subsidiary Yahoo! China since April 10, 2006. [1]

Almost one year before these cases, another series case heard by the Beijing No. 1 Intermediate People's Court had brought attention to the liability of search engines for third party's copyright infringements in China, which was related to the biggest search engine Baidu. com in mainland China. The plaintiffs were seven of those eleven record companies worldwide mentioned above, who claimed that Baidu's act of linking songs to the public on the Internet infringed their communication right under Chinese law. In the end, the Court held that the "sampled" and "downloaded" MP3 files did not originate from Baidu; instead they originated from other web servers. Thus the Court found that the communication occurs between the users downloading the MP3 files and the website that uploaded the files. The Court clearly ruled that Baidu. com providing the links does not engage in the act of communication via the Internet under the Copyright Law of China. [2] The judgement was upheld by the appeal court. [3]

While having the almost same plaintiffs, almost same causes and nearly the same facts in these two suits, the results were completely different which caused great confusion not only to the Internet industry, but also to the intellectual property circle in China. An issue in these cases was how to define and understand the limitation of search engine's liability for third party's copyright infringments according to the statutory requirements of Takedown Notification procedure. It is therefore necessary for us to go back to understand some key principles of digital copyright law, especially *The Digital Millennium Copyright Act* (DMCA) in U. S. and *Regulations on the Protection of the Right to Network Communication of Information* (PRNCI) in China. This paper provides a broad overview to the limitations of search engine liabilities for copyright infringements, and focuses on analyzing the effectiveness of notification from complaining party, usually copyright owners or their agent, and its substantial compliance with legislation clause in the world. At last, the paper gives some proposals to Chinese digital publishers on successful claims for digital contributory copyright infringements against online service providers or Internet service providers (ISPs).

2   Legal Requirements about Takedown Notification

The evolution and development of search engines over the past ten years, poses a number of challenging legal issues to the copyright landscape all over the world. On one hand, people have the right to absorb useful sources from Internet, which are well satisfied by the technological developments and advances provided by ISPs, such search engines as Google, Baidu and Yahoo! who played a vital role in ensuring the free flow of and easier access to online information. On the other hand, ISPs may intentionally or unintentionally communicate online resources to the public by allowing users to search and illegally download files through search engine service because of the nature of search engine services. In order to provide greater certainty to ISPs concerning their legal exposure against infringements that may occur in the course of their activites and promote the prosperity of Internet, and to preserve strong incentives for ISPs and copyright owners to cooperate to detect and deal with copyright infringements that take place in digital networked environment, it is necessary for copyright law to establish the mechanism whereby balancing the different competing interests of different shareholders, the so-called safe harbor mechanism provided in U. S. and the Chinese copyright laws thus came into being, of which notice and takedown procedure is one of the key factors to determine whether ISPs could be eligible for the safe harbor limitations.

The Title II of DMCA, *Online Copyright Infringement Liability Limitation Act*, has now become a new section of the U. S. copyright law, Section 512. This Section contains limitations on ISPs' liability for five general categories of activity set forth in subsections (a) through (d) and subsection (f), i. e., digital network communications, system caching, information stored on service providers, information location tools and immunity for takedowns. As regard to limitations on the liability of qualifying ISPs providing such two services as information stored on service providers and information location tools for claims of direct, vicarious and contributory infringement, Section 512 (c) (3) sets forth procedural requirements that copyright owners or their agents and service providers must follow with respect to notifications of claimed infringement, which commonly calls for notice and takedown procedure. Pursuant to Section 512 (c) (3) (A) (i)-(vi), an effective notification should include the mandatory information, and the standard against which a notification is to be judged is within substantial compliance.

The mandatory information substantially includes: (i) a physical or electronic signature of a person authorized to act on behalf of the owner of an exclusive right that is allegedly infringed; (ii) identification of the copyrighted work claimed to have been infringed, or, if multiple such works at a single online site covered by a single notification, a representative list of such works at that site; (iii) identification of the material that is claimed to be infringing or to be the subject of infringing activity that is to be removed or access to which is to be disabled, and information reasonably sufficient to permit the service provider to locate the material; (iv) information reasonably sufficient to permit the service provider to contact the complaining party, such as an address, telephone number, and, if available an electronic mail address at which the complaining party may be contacted; (v) a statement that the complaining party has a good faith belief that the use of the material in the manner complained of is not authorized by the copyright owner, or its agent, or the law; and (vi) a statement that the information in the notification is accurate, and under penalty of perjury, that the complaining party has the authority to enforce the owner's rights that are claimed to be infringed.

Among six kinds of information above, (ii) (iii) and (iv) are essential or indispensible, just as the report of the Committee on the Judiciary of American Congress states: If notifications do not substantially comply with the requirements of subsection (c) (3), "the court shall not consider such notifications as evidence of whether the service provider has actual knowledge, is aware of facts or circumstances, or has received a notification for purposes of subsection (c) (1) (A)". [4] Besides, according to Section 512 (c) (3) (B) (ii), only these three kinds of information are included and if the service provider promptly attempts to contact the person making the notification or takes other reasonable steps to assist in the receipt of notification that substantially complies with all the provisions of subparagraph (A), the safe harbor will be available to ISPs. In other words, the information as to identification of the copyrighted work claimed to have been infringed and identification of the material that is claimed to be infringing or to be the subject of infringing activity are the key information for determing if ISPs should be liable for infringements. Without them, the complaining party makes substantive errors but not technical errors, and the notice should not has any legal binding on the ISPs.

In China, PRNCI, promulgated by the Chinese State Council on May 18, 2006, also sets forth notice and takedown procedure for ISPs providing information storage space, search engines and links to immune them from liability for the third party's copyright infringement. As for the elements of notification, Article 14 lists (i) the name, contact information and address of the owner; (ii) the title and web address of the infringing work, performance, or audio-visual recording that must be deleted or the link that must be disconnected; and (iii) preliminary materials to prove the infringement. Meanwhile, the Article also prescribes that copyright owner shall be responsible for the authenticity of this notification.

While PRNCI sets forth only three kinds of information for the notice to be included, its purpose and content actually are the same as the Section 512 of U. S. copyright law. The only difference between them is that PRNCI does not acquire the complaining party to provide the information for identification of the copyrighted work claimed to have been infringed, suggesting that PRNCI's threshold of an effective notice is lower than that of Section 512 of U. S. copyright law. Namely, only the information as to the title and web address of the infringing work, performance, or audio-visual recording suffices.

The rationale underlying the legal requirements as to the takedown notice both in U. S. and the Chinese law is that information reasonably sufficient provided by copyright owner is to permit ISPs to identify and locate the allegedly infringing material expeditiously. The rationale roots in the common awareness that confronting the huge information on Internet, imposing the duty of identifying and locating allegedly infringing materials on ISPs is an unbearable burden for them, and will restrain them from investing on online business and developing new online business services. The authors argue, it is the rationale that determines non-legal binding of ineffective notice or unsubstantial compliance with the legal requirements on disqualifying ISPs from limitations of liability under the safe harbor mechanism.

3 Judicial Judgement on Effectiveness and Substantial Compliance Of The Takedown Notice

In one of the cases as to Yahoo! China mentioned above, *Mercury Records Limited v. Beijing Alibaba Information Technology Co.*, the plaintiff sent two notices to the defendant. In the two notices, the plaintiff presented the following information to request the defendant to remove alleging infringing links: (i) the web addresses of the plaintiff's copyrighted phonogrammes; (ii) the names of music albums containing 12 songs involved in the case and theirs singers; and (iii) URL of eight songs involved in the case as exmples. According to Article 14 of PRNCI, only the latter one could help the defendant to identify and locate the allegedly infringing material expeditiously. The case record indicates that the defendant deleted the eight songs with specific URL, but didn't take any measures with respect to the other four songs without specific URLs listed. Therefore, the defendant was judged as contributory infringer who had subjective fault with indulgence to the ongoing infringements. The authors argue, the Court erred in misunderstanding the spirit of Article 14 of PRNCI, and made the madatory elements of takedown notice, especially *the title and web address of the infringing work*, *performance*, *or audio-visual recording that must be deleted or the link that must be disconnected*, are superfluous or redundant.

Now, let's turn to the series cases concerning Baidu. com. One of the most important defenses for Baidu is that such plaintiffs as Universal Music Limited, Sony BMG Music Entertainment (Hong Kong) Limited neglected of theirs duty — listing all the URLs of allegedly infringing materials in takedown notice. This defense finally won the support of the first court (Beijing No. 1 Intermediate People's Court) and the appeal court (the Beijing Municipal Higher People's Court). The adjudication, in the authors' opinion, embodies directly the spirit of PRNCI and shows the respect for the provisions of that law.

In addition to Baidu. com cases, there are many foreign cases which could support the author's opinion outlined above.

In *Perfect* 10, *Inc. v. CCBill LLC*, *et al* case,[5] the American Fourth Circuit Appeals Court found that Perfect 10 did not provide notice that substantially complied with the requirements of 512 (c) (3), and thus did not raise a genuine issue of material fact as to whether CCBill and CWIE reasonably implemented their repeat infringer policy.

In *ALS Scan v. RemarQ Communities* case[6], the Fourth Circuit considered the adequacy of a notice that simply indicated that two newsgroups consisting of many different articles infringed ALS Scan's copyrights. The plaintiff provided the defendant with such information as to (1) identify two sites created for the sole purpose of publishing ALS Scan's copyrighted works; (2) assert that virtually all the images at the two sites were its copyrighted material; and (3) refer RemarQ to two web addresses where RemarQ could find pictures of ALS Scan's models and obtain ALS Scan's copyright information. In addition, it noted that material at the site could be identified as ALS Scan's material because the material included ALS Scan's name and/or copyright symbol next to it. So, the Court believed that with this information, ALS Scan substantially complied with the notification requirement of providing a representative list of infringing material as well as information reasonably sufficient to enable RemarQ to locate the infringing material.

In Viacom v. YouTube, The Southern District Court of New York held that " [to] let knowledge of a generalized practice of infringement in the industry, or of a proclivity of users to post infringing materials, impose responsibility on service providers to discover which of their users' postings infringe a copyright would contravene the structure and operation of the DMCA", and that the "right and ability to control" first requires knowledge of such infringing activity, which again must be item-specific (i. e. , the provider must know of the particular case of infringement before he can control it). The provider needn't monitor or seek out knowledge or facts of such an activity. [7]

It follows that under DCMA, substantial compliance means substantial compliance with all of U. S. 512 (c) (3)'s clauses, not just some of them. So it is clear that substantial compliance in takedown notice is one of the key legal procedure to judge whether ISPs could exempt from liability for contributory infringement. Sometimes, a notice from a copyright owner falls short of the requirements for a proper notice. According to an estimation from Chilling Effects, a project collaborated by several Amerian law school professors and the Electronic Frontier Foundation to protect lawful online activity from legal threats, approximately 60% of takedown notices are statutorilly flawed, that is to say, nearly one out of every eleven notices existed flaws. [8] Under this circumstance, the complaining party might risk not only unsuccessfully removing or disconnecting quickly the alleging infringement materials, but also bearing damages and legal fees incurred by its further suit.

4   Conclusion

After analysis of two cases in China, there are some proposals to Chinese digital publishers with regard to copyright protection in the digital age. The most important thing for digital publishers is that they should pay much attention to legitimacy of notification. Otherwise, they will face challenge from not only the rejection of their requests for removing or disconnecting alleging infringement materials, but also compensation for damages and legal fees, just like Diebold, Inc.

In legal practices, if infringed works are found online, digital publishers should collect necessary elements of notification one by one according to the law, such as the title and web address of the infringed work, and if the ISP is a foreign one, especially a U. S. ISP. Chinese digital publishers should prepare properly theirs takedown notice pursuant to repective foreign law, i. e. , in U. S. ; information as to *identification of the copyrighted work claimed to have been infringed* should be added into theirs notice. Only that, could Chinese digital publishers be successful in safeguarding their copyrights.

Notes

[1] Record Firms Sue Yahoo! China for Copyright Infringement. http://business. highbeam. com/436093/article-1G1-161998596/record-firms-sue-baidu-china-copyright-infringement.

[2] Wang Qian, *"Direct" Decision vs. an "Indirect" Problem: A Commentary on Seven Record Labels vs. Baidu. com*, Journal of China Copyright (2007).

[3] See SONY BMG v. Baidu, No. 596 Civil Judgement, the Higher Court of Beijing, 2007.

[4] http://ipmall. info/hosted-resources/lipa/copyrights/THE% 20DIGITAL% 20MILL ENNI-

UM%20COPYRIGHT%20ACT%20DF%201998. pdf.

[5] http://www.nixonpeabody. com/linked_media/copyright_articles/perfect10_CCBill. pdf.

[6] ALS Scan v. RemarQ Communities, 239 F. 3d 619, 57 USPQ2d 1996 (4th Cir. 2001).

[7] Viacom International, Inc., v. YouTube, Inc., 2010 WL 2532404 (SDNY June 23, 2010).

[8] J. Urban & L. Quilter, *Efficient Process or "Chilling Effects"? Takedown Notices Under Section 512 of the Digital Millennium Copyright Act*, 22 *Santa Clara Computer & High Tech L. J.* 621, 674 (2006).

Author

Wang Qing, associate professor, J. D., Information Management School of Wuhan University, deputy director of Center for Advanced Research on Intellectual Property.

Cong Ting, master degree candidate, Information Management School of Wuhan University.

作者简介

王清，法学博士，武汉大学信息管理学院教授、武汉大学知识产权高级研究中心副主任。

丛挺，武汉大学信息管理学院博士研究生。

出版社数字化转型

对出版社数字化转型的思考

常韶伟

（上海交通大学出版社　上海　200030）

摘要：数字出版是当前的热点问题，数字出版产生的时间不过短短十几年，却给出版业带了前所未有的冲击，成为了未来出版业的发展趋势，面对这个趋势，作为出版业主体之一的出版社又应该如何在这样一个转型期去面对和调整成为出版业需要去思考的问题。本文从出版社为什么要进入数字出版领域，谁能成为数字出版的主体，出版社应如何应对数字出版大潮三个角度进行思考。

关键词：数字出版　传统出版　转型

Thinking on the Digitalization of Press

Chang Shaowei

（Shanghai Jiao Tong University Press，Shanghai，200030）

Abstract：Digital publishing is a hot issue nowadays. It makes such a great effection on book industry within just one decade. And the digital publishing has already formed the main trend of book industry. As one of the great subject in book industry，the press should face the trend and make the change. About this issue，this paper is designed to contemplate three questions：why enter the field of digital publishing，who can dominate the field of digital publishing and how should the press deal with the trend of digital publishing.

Keywords：Digital Publishing　Traditional Publishing　Transformation

从数字出版概念的产生，到数字出版产品的出现，再到数字出版业态的成型，只经历了短短的十几年。今天，从普通读者到专业研究人员，从技术提供商到运营商，从传统出版社到新兴的数字出版商，都在热切地谈论数字出版这个话题。对于数字出版的看法可能不尽相同，但是有一点却非常一致：数字出版作为出版业的一种新业态，最近几年获得了迅猛发展，已经成为出版业的新增长点。

广义上说，只要是用二进制这种技术手段对出版的任何环节进行的操作，都是数字出版的一部分。它包括：原创作品的数字化、编辑加工的数字化、印刷复制的数字化、发行销售的数字化和阅读消费的数字化。[1] 笔者认为从产业的角度来看，所谓数字化转型的一个明确标志是数字出版业务本身是能够赢利的，或者在一定财务周期内能够赢利。对于一个数字出版公司来说，数字出版业务能够提供主要的收入和利润，否则产业无法存在、发展。

面对数字出版风起云涌的发展，技术提供商、传统媒体、出版社纷纷高调进入数字出版领域一试身手，试图分享这一诱人的蛋糕，一时间形成了一股数字出版热潮。不少出版社都提出了向数字化转型的口号，拿出了真金白银砸向数字出版领域。面对数字出版热，作为传统出版社需要进行一系列冷静的思考。例如：为什么要进入数字出版领域？谁能成为数字出版的主体？出版社应如何应对数字出版大潮？

1 什么要进入数字出版领域

概括地说，数字出版市场潜力巨大，发展迅速，前景诱人，已经成为大势所趋。

潜在消费者数量巨大，而且仍然处于高速增长中。根据工业和信息化部提供的数据，截至 2010 年 6 月底，我国移动电话用户达 8 亿户，互联网宽带接入用户达 1.15 亿户。[2] 来自国务院新闻办的数据表明，全国网民人数达到 4.04 亿，互联网普及率达到 28.9%，使用手机上网的网民达到 2.33 亿人。[3] 这些数以亿计的消费者都是数字出版的潜在客户，而且还在高速增长中。

年轻一代的阅读习惯已经悄然改变。80 后人群是在电视机屏幕、电脑屏幕、手机屏幕前成长起来的一代人，习惯屏幕阅读，乐于接受新鲜事物，也正是目前数字出版的主力消费群体。以电子图书为例，截至 2009 年底我国有读者 1.01 亿人，其中 18 岁的以下占 20.9%，18—24 岁的占 27.5%，25—31 岁的占 28.3%。[4] 也就是说 80 后人群占据了 76.7%，显然已经成为电子图书消费的绝对主体，也就是未来相当长时间内的数字出版消费大军。

数字出版的技术条件日益成熟，设备日益完善。我国电信业在过去的 10 年里获得了突飞猛进的发展，为数字出版提供了技术支持。我国 99.1% 的乡镇和 92% 的行政村接通了互联网，95.6% 的乡镇接通了宽带，3G 网络已基本覆盖全国。[5] 终端设备功能日趋完善，台式电脑，笔记本电脑、智能手机、电子阅读器功能越来越强大，使用越来越便捷，价格越来越便宜。以电子阅读器为例，Kindle、OPPO、汉王、易狄欧、Sony Reader 等知名品牌的产品性能优越，携带方便，均能够提供良好的阅读感受。

数字出版的市场规模迅速扩大。2006 年，我国数字出版产业整体收入规模为 213 亿元，2007 年为 362.42 亿元，2008 年为 530 亿元，2009 年为 799.4 亿元。[6] 2009 年数字出版总体经济规模首次超过了传统图书出版。可见数字出版规模迅速扩大，增长速度远超传统出版。

2 谁能成为数字出版的主体

居于产业主体地位的企业，一般都处于产业的领跑地位，引领市场潮流；同时占有市场的重大份额，能够主导市场格局。就目前来看，数字出版的主体是数字技术提供商，是新兴媒体。如数字期刊领域的同方知网、维普资讯、万方数据、龙源期刊，电子书领域的方正阿帕比、书生、超星、中文在线，网络游戏领域的盛大、网易、腾讯、久游，网络广告领域的好耶、华扬联众、科思世通、腾信互动。而传统的出版社集体缺席，还处于数字化的边缘地位，尽管这两年一些大型出版集团的数字出版有发力的趋势，但是还没有形成较大的产业规模和较大的市场影响力。连一向机制灵活，充满创意的民营出版商在数字出版领域也鲜有建树。

那么是什么原因，导致了这种局面呢？笔者认为主要是传统出版业的体制机制弊端和数字出版自身的产业特性决定的。

我国出版社长期以来实行的是"事业单位企业化管理"的管理体制，所有制是单一国有制。进入新世纪以来，尽管我国的文化体制改革迅速推进，出版社纷纷转企改制，合并重组，集团化快速推进，上市融资，取得了巨大成绩，但是现代企业制度的建立和完善，市场竞争力的提升远非一蹴而就的事，需要长期的努力。国有体制下易守业难创业，普遍追求稳定回报，企业个体缺乏创新动力，缺乏市场活力。而出版业作为传统产业，有稳定的赢利模式，这也客观上导致了国有出版社、民营出版商都缺乏足够的动力去主动出击数字出版领域。数字出版是内容与技术结合的产物，技术与资本双轮驱动的特点非常明显。数字出版往往前期投入大，资金需求多，技术含量大，风险高，回收慢，还没有形成成熟的赢利模式。这些产业特性决定了数字出版产业对于风险投资的吸引力，因此在资本的驱动下以 IT 技术提供商、渠道运营商、新兴媒体快速进入，并获得了初步成功。

3　出版社如何应对数字出版大潮

出版社近几年纷纷进入数字出版领域，大型出版集团成立了数字出版中心，不少出版社成立了数字出版业务部门，但是总体上处于出版的数字化阶段，即对出版流程的数字化改造、对出版物的数字化。出版社的数字出版业务主要是围绕传统出版物展开的，比如纸质图书的数字化和数据库的研发。近几年在文化体制改革的大背景下，一部分规模大、实力强、善经营、敢创新的出版集团加大了向数字出版转型的步伐，开始探索一条适合国情的数字出版道路。

问题是出版社都需要数字化转型吗？出版社都能够数字化转型成功吗？

笔者认为不是所有的出版社都需要数字化转型。传统出版魅力依旧，市场发展空间仍然很大，产业模式清晰，利润水平稳定。作为成熟产业，传统出版业从内容生产、编辑加工、生产制作、销售推广都形成了稳定的产业链条，标准统一、规则明确、商业模式清晰，经过现代技术的提升仍然会有较大的发展。数字出版在相当一段时间内并不是简单地替代传统出版，而成为完全竞争关系，而可能互相促进，相得益彰。从总体规模来看，尽管数字出版发展迅猛，2009 年已经超过传统图书出版规模，但是仔细分析其业态构成，不难发现真正属于阅读的份额还比较少，相对于图书还是比重很小。2009 年，数字期刊收入 6 亿元，电子书收入 14 亿元，数字报（网络版）收入 3.1 亿元，网络游戏收入 256.2 亿元，网络广告收入 206.1 亿元，手机出版（包括手机音乐、手机游戏、手机动漫、手机阅读）收入 314 亿元。网络游戏、网络广告、手机出版成为数字出版的主要构成部分，而这三部分的消费者与图书消费者并不是高度重合的。因此，在传统出版领域，精耕细作，勇于创新，也不失为一种好的选择。

笔者认为不是所有出版社都能够成功数字化转型。事实上，多数出版社也还谈不上数字化转型。数字化转型是一个艰难的过程，不是喊喊口号，推出一些电子书就可以实现的，而是整个产业模式改变，收入与利润主体改变。可以说，绝大多数出版社所谓的数字化转型，就是通过社会化外包将出版物数字化推出一些电子图书、数据库、服务型网站而

对出版社数字化转型的思考

已，其收入与利润仍然要依赖传统出版业务。少数规模大、实力强、机制灵活、拥有核心资源的出版社（集团）通过机制创新、市场创新是可以成功实现数字出版转型的。

注释

[1] 新浪科技. "数字出版"概念探讨. 2006-9-29. http://tech.sina.com.cn/other/2006-09-29/16201166788.shtml

[2] 新浪新闻. 工信部：6月底我国移动电话用户达8亿户. 2010-7-20. http://news.sina.com.cn/c/2010-07-20/174517836014s.shtml

[3] 中央政府门户网站. 中国网民4.04亿网络普及超世界平均水平. 2010-5-1. http://www.gov.cn/jrzg/2010-05/01/content_1597257.htm

[4] 百度文库. 2009—2010年度中国电子图书发展趋势报告. 2010-8-15. http://wenku.baidu.com/view/1201b78a6529647d2728520f.html

[5] 中央政府门户网站. 中国网民4.04亿网络普及超世界平均水平. 2010-5-1. http://www.gov.cn/jrzg/2010-05/01/content_1597257.htm

[6] 中国新闻网. 2009年中国数字出版产业收入达799.4亿元. 2010-7-21. http://www.chinanews.com.cn/cul/2010/07-21/2416534.shtml

参考文献

[1] 黄先蓉，罗紫初. 数字出版与出版教育. 北京：高等教育出版社，2009
[2] 田胜利. 数字出版引领产业升级. 大学出版，2008（1）
[3] 徐丽芳. 数字出版：概念与形态. 出版发行研究，2005（7）

作者简介

常韶伟，上海交通大学出版社副社长。

出版企业 ERP 项目建设目标

李 彬

（东北财经大学出版社有限责任公司　大连　116025）

摘要：随着信息化进程的加快，以及行业性竞争压力的增加，出版企业管理者对信息化，尤其是 ERP 的认识已经从原来的局外旁观上升到寻求自身解决方案的层面上来。可以预测，未来一段时期内，出版企业 ERP 项目将得到长足的发展。与通常的生产企业相比，出版企业对 ERP 的功能需求与特征具有显著的不同。作为企业管理信息系统的 ERP，应与出版企业管理有机地结合在一起，以提高出版企业生产效率和经济效益。本文试图从出版企业发展信息化现状出发，并结合高校出版社的实际情况，分析说明出版企业对建设 ERP 项目的目标或期望。

关键词：ERP　出版企业　建设目标

ERP Project Construction Target of Publishing Company

Li Bin

（Dongbei University of Finance and Economics Press Limited Liability Company，Dalian，116025）

Abstract：With the speeding up of informationization and the increased pressure of industry competition，publishing business managers' understanding of informationization has risen to the level of seeking their own solutions from the spectator role level. It could be predicted that the ERP project in publishing enterprise will have a considerable development in the future. Compared to common company，the characteristic and demand of ERP's function in publishing enterprise is different. ERP which is the enterprise management information system should be organically combined with management of publishing company in order to improve production efficiency and economic benefits. This paper attempts to present development of publish enterprise and make out the goals or expectations of the informatization construction of the ERP project for publishing company and combined with the actual situation of university press.

Keywords：ERP　Publishing company　Construction target

1　前言

目前，改制是出版发行单位制度性、根本性的转变，其中包括许多繁琐、细致的工作，而重组是对企业现有业务流程及内部人、财、物等各种资源进行优化配置的一个过程，它是体制、机制和经营管理体系的重新架构，涉及企业管理运营方方面面。另外，伴随着计算机信息技术的高速发展，数字时代给出版行业的信息管理带来了新的发展机会。在竞争激烈的数字时代，为求得更大的发展空间，出版业的管理和决策显得尤为重要，如何快速、准确地获取每一种出版物的经营状况？科学规范地管理好出版社的编辑、出版、发行等业务，及时了解出版物、原材料进销存的管理状况，对数据进行有效分析，都是经营管理决策者关心的重要课题。

出版企业信息化管理的建设目标，是建成以 ERP 为核心的出版业务信息化管控系统，实现各类管理数据的实时集成，据此对经营状况进行量化分析，以期快速发现问题、处理问题，提高管理效能，促进管理水平的全面提高。

据统计，世界上最大的 10 个出版集团中，实施了 ERP 的占 80%。我国人民教育出版社的商务智能（BI）规划最初只包含财务主管领导最关心的生产销售相关的对比分析，几乎所有的查询都是围绕着财务的若干个报表来设计的。随着第一期 BI 的实现，财务领导通过已经实现的查询，分析归纳了更多深层次的要求。而负责编务、生产等其他业务的领导也从中发现了 BI 的模式带来的崭新的数据分析方式以及显著效果。负责设计、实施的信息技术人员熟练掌握数据结构以及了解领导意图后，逐步增加 BI 分析的内容。第二期 BI 系统就包含了企业从编辑、出版生产、发行销售、财务核算、部门考核等各个方面的内容，将 BI 系统在出版社全面推行开来。目前正在实施企业级的整体架构、实现图形化仪表盘关键指标监测和模拟预测的过程中。

上述资料表明，国内各出版企业从管理层到负责项目实施的技术部门信息化建设的经验并不多，对于要具体达成一个什么样的目标，怎么制定切实可行的方案，有哪些好的办法去解决信息化建设中遇到的诸多问题等，仍然认识不清。本文从分析出版企业 ERP 实际需求出发，总结 ERP 建设的实际经验，为出版企业 ERP 建设目标提供一些有价值的思考。

2   出版企业实施 ERP 管理系统现状

2.1   全面引入 ERP 管理系统的国内出版企业（见表 1 所示）

表 1   全面引入 ERP 管理系统的国内出版企业[1]

社名	信息化产品	总投资	实施周期	运行效果	服务商
高等教育出版社	德国 SAP 系统：生产管理、项目管理、应收账款等 7 个系统	软件投资 1 326 万元	历时 4 年	一般	德国 SAP
青岛出版社	和佳软件公司定制 ERP 系统	投资 400 万元	历时 4 年	良好	和佳软件公司
中国电力出版社	平章 ERP 出版综合管理系统	投资 135 万元	历时 3 个月，一期、二期上线成功，实施完成	良好	平章科技
人民教育出版社	和佳软件公司定制 ERP 系统	软件投资 1 580 万元	历时 5 年	一般	和佳软件公司

目前，我国570多家出版单位中，使用发行软件、财务软件的出版社高达97%，而使用完整出版ERP系统的仅占被调查对象的1%。

2.2 出版企业实施信息化的四种模式利弊分析（见表2）

表2 出版社实施信息化的四种可选模式及利弊分析[2]

模式	适用企业	特点	缺点	服务商
采用局部模块	小型出版社	根据自身需求，选择财务、发行等模块；上马容易	不能称作真正的ERP。如果各部门先后使用的模块的技术标准不尽相同，容易产生"信息孤岛"，造成出版社内部信息不能共享、充分流动和相互兼容	北京九州时讯网络科技有限公司北京云因科技公司南北软件
定制模式	实力比较强的大中型出版社	按出版社的要求量身定做，能够满足出版社当前对业务流程的需求，但无法应对管理发展的要求	调研开发周期相对过长，投入的人力、物力较大	北京和佳软件南北软件
德国SAP系统引进模式	大型出版社，目前只有高教社	系统研发完备，有成功的使用经验	投入成本巨大；使用过程中，隐性成本更大	德国SAP公司
成熟产品模式	众多出版社[3]	设计上借鉴成功经验，进行优化设计，引入项目管理的理念，界面友好、流程科学规范，整个系统适用、易用、好用。特别是改变了研发与实施周期长、信息共享难等弊端，且费用适中，并且可适应管理发展的要求，通过简单设置就可调整业务流程和管理模式，完全做到一次投入多年使用，免二次、三次、四次开发的老大难问题		北京平章科技发展有限责任公司

3 出版企业实施ERP管理系统所能解决的问题[4]

3.1 战略层次

（1）如何在国家推行出版单位改制过程中提高经营管理效率，加强本社的综合实力和市场竞争力？

（2）如何及时获取项目编辑出书的效益，提高出版社的整体经济效益？

3.2 经营管理层次

（1）如何调整工作流，达到高度协同办公？

（2）如何打破部门之间信息孤岛，实现资源共享和内部业务协调？

（3）如何提高图书成本核算的精确度和速度，达到明明白白出书，清清楚楚经营？

（4）如何降低出书成本和降低成品图书的库存，减少企业物流成本？

（5）如何及时、准确地获取每种图书的经营利润或销售分析数据？

（6）如何准确了解各部门、每本书（项目）的费用支出情况，如何了解近期或预测将来某一时期的收支情况？

（7）如何获取某一品种图书的发行分析数据、某一地区的发行分析数据和某一品种（或某一类出版物）在不同时间段的发行情况的比较数据？

（8）如何准确了解出版部门对纸张或其他各种出版用原材料的需求情况，调整采购计划，保证出版工作的顺利开展？

3.3 业务操作层次

（1）如何按市场的需求及时调整出版计划和资金利用率？

（2）如何及时获取各种统计分析数据，提高科学决策能力？

（3）如何及时掌握某一时间段内单品种图书的发货、回款、库存情况？

（4）如何在再版加印时掌握图书的发货、回款、社内库存、社外铺货情况？

（5）如何按市场的需求，及时调整图书加工周期，控制编辑、出版部门的工作进度，准确把握图书的出版时机？

（6）如何提高选题的质量、掌握出书的实时进度？

4 企业资源管理系统（ERP）在出版企业的建设目标

从出版社整体管理的角度看，如果采用局部信息化方案，就很难实现各业务系统的实时连接、数据资源保持统一且唯一、信息衔接实现无缝流动、决策数据充分共享等基本目的，而搭建信息化管理平台才能实现上述基本目的。

4.1 宏观层面基于 ERP 系统企业战略管理的建设目标

企业战略管理的过程实际上是一个决策执行过程，它具有多因素性、全局性、长远性和预见性。

通过实施 ERP 系统帮助高层经营管理者进行决策，已经逐渐成为当今企业实施战略管理的主流模式之一。从决策支持的观点来看，ERP 系统对决策的支持实际上是对决策者智能的延伸和对其决策活动的支持，协助管理者实现预定的组织目标。

ERP 系统对企业战略管理过程的支持[5]

战略管理是对企业未来发展方向制定决策和实施决策的动态管理过程。理论上，一个规范的、全面的战略管理过程包括战略分析与制定、战略实施、战略评价与控制三个阶段。其中，通过实施 ERP 系统能对企业战略管理提供有力的支持。

战略分析与制定阶段。实施 ERP 系统可提供战略分析过程中所需的基础数据。具体表现为：①人力资源管理模块提供管理人员数量和素质信息等；②客户服务管理模块反映了顾客对本企业产品的评价情况；③销售分析反映了本企业市场占有率的情况。

战略实施阶段。①人力资源业务在集团统一体系基础上实现适度的灵活管理；②帮助企业实行集中的财务管理模式；③逐步实现资金集中管理；④建立全面有效的预算管理体系；⑤解决人力信息由分散管理转变为集中管理；⑥优化流程，降低业务成本；⑦建立企业的人才资源管理体系；⑧实现对企业销售的量化管理；⑨实现对客户进行有效的管理；⑩实现销售统计分析功能。

战略评价与控制。战略评价与控制是战略管理的重要环节，其主要的职能是在战略实施的过程中发现问题和纠正问题。通过实施 ERP 系统能对战略评价与控制提供有力的支持：①系统实施兼顾企业长期和短期战略，制定有效系统战略评价的标准，企业战略更具有一致性、协调性、可行性和优越性；②系统实施有利于信息收集准确性、全面性和及时性，使战略评价和控制更具针对性和可靠性；③系统实施大大提高战略控制的有效性，使战略控制适度，并遵循重要性原则；④实现信息全面和精确反馈，战略控制更具适应性。

4.2 从微观层面基于 ERP 系统企业经营管理的建设目标

从微观层面看，基于 ERP 系统企业经营管理的建设目标是组织相关人员设计与实施 ERP 管理系统，并将其运用在实际编辑业务之中，依托现有支持中心的资源数据库、储运部图书库存表中的数据，在策划选题时可对潜在作者挖掘、对项目编辑和文字编辑业绩进行考核、对已有产品和未来产品进行销售、库存等深入分析。具体来讲，主要有以下四个方面：

（1）潜在作者挖掘

出版企业经营过程中会形成自己的作者和用户资源数据库。那么，如何更好地开发与利用现有的数据库资源，对企业，尤其是项目编辑来说尤为重要。通过建立 ERP 系统，在企业经营管理过程中就可以做到：

第一，维护原有作者和开发潜在作者，建立与原有作者和潜在作者之间的长久联系。比如针对高等学校，一是根据一些老师的科研方向和近期研究成果，结合自己选题策划方向可以有目的地联系这些老师成为作者。这类成功案例很多。二是根据老师所在学校选用教材数量的情况，分析判断，可以由其推荐其他有能力的老师参与编写教材。三是将一些有写作潜力，但是目前没有合适选题的目标作者作为后备作者暂时"储存"起来，以备后用。

第二，对现有的"资源库"采用动态管理的办法。由于每年积累起来的数据资料过多，加之人才流动带来的变化，有些数据无法及时得到更新，更无法有效提取出对各个编辑业务部门有用的信息。而实施了 ERP 管理系统之后，就可以迅速更新和找到所需的目标数据。

第三，为开拓目标市场服务。比如，在编辑参与学术会议或者每年参加教材推广之前可以收集相关的院校及老师的信息，有目的地进行图书推广工作。

（2）对业绩考核分析

全面建立新的绩效考核机制和薪酬管理制度，在设定了相应的指标和权重之后，可以方便、快捷地对每一位编辑工作业绩进行年中、年终的考核和打分。绩效考核的方式和方法可以随着权重的调整而改变。

（3）对产品进行分析

对产品进行分析主要表现在为不同编辑业务部门服务。以我社为例，现有经管编辑部、财会编辑部、职教编辑部、国际合作部、综合编辑室、本校教材编辑室六个编辑业务部门，通过实施 ERP 管理系统，可以对出版社的图书品种进行有针对性的分类和提取，同时产生有效信息。

（4）领导决策支持

可以在进行数据梳理和整合的基础上，形成各种统计报表和分析报表，并且对指标制订、书籍销量、印量等进行智能分析与预测。通过 WEB 挖掘技术可以搜索互联网上的商情信息，用以指导项目编辑进行选题策划。

注释

[1] 出版企业为什么要上 ERP 管理系统 [EB]. http://www.pzcp.com/admin/Html,2009-09-09.

[2] 出版 ERP：如何让出版人更轻松的报道. 出版人，2010（1）.

[3] 2004 年 10 月推出的新产品，用户有中国电力出版社、中共党史出版社、同心出版社少儿事业部、中国商务出版社、花山文艺出版社、红旗出版社、延边大学出版社、中国军事谊文出版社等。

[4] 出版企业为什么要上 ERP 管理系统. http://www.pzcp.com/admin/Html,2009-09-09.

[5] 浅谈基于 ERP 系统的企业战略管理. http://www.xbcyw.net/? thread-5895-1.html, 2009-10-31.

参考文献

电子商务环境下 ERP 的协同发展探讨 [EB]. www.lwlm.com,2009-01-14.

作者简介

李彬，东北财经大学管理科学与工程学院博士研究生，东北财经大学出版社副编审。

基于 KaaS 的数字出版特征分析及其组织实施

李 弘

（电子工业出版社 北京 100036）

摘要：本文在分析我国传统出版产业经营现状的基础上，对出版和网络环境下知识服务的关系进行了探讨；依据数字出版的特性，尝试定义了数字出版的概念，并在数字出版范畴内首次提出了"知识即服务"（Knowledge as a Service，KaaS）的思想。最后作者指出传统出版单位应该基于 KaaS 理念建立统一的知识处理流程和与之相适应的组织架构。

关键词：KaaS 数字出版 组织 流程

Study on the Digital-publish Feature and Its Implement Based on KaaS

Li Hong

（Publish House of Electronics Industry，Beijing，100036）

Abstract：Based on manage actuality of our traditional publish industry，this paper discuss the relation between the publish and the information service. Sum up the character and the concept of the digital publishing. For the first time put forward "Knowledge as a Service（KaaS）" about digital publish. In the end，the auther suggests that traditional publisher must build a organizational structure fit to knowledge treat scheme based on KaaS.

Keywords：KaaS Digital publish Organization Process

1 前言

早期的知识传播方式是将文字图形刻画于甲骨、金石、竹木、缣帛、纸张等介质上，通过刻版、拓版和印版等各种技术手段加工生产平面形态的版面媒介，它极大地突破了口口相传的语言传播的时空局限，提高了信息交流的质量，丰富了信息储存的数量，加速了人类的文明化进程。

随着人类社会进入信息化社会，传统的版面媒介在版面空间、表现形态、传播渠道及运营成本等方面面临越来越多的网络渠道和信息产品的挑战，传统出版在知识搜集、浏览服务及产品设计及提供等方面不能适应信息社会数字化和网络化的要求。作为以传播知识为己任的传统出版发行商必须在战略规划、业务流程和组织保障上作出根本的变革，以便将读者持续地"粘贴"在自己的产品和服务系统中。

2 传统出版产业的经营现状分析

特定的信息经过创作、选择、加工，构造成系统的知识体系，复制后将其广泛地传播，这就是传统出版活动中知识传播的基本过程。有一个经典的关于信息源和信息接受者的理论——香农和韦弗通信模型，如图1所示。我们如果借用这一模型，并定义作者是"信息源"，出版者是"加工者"，发行者是"传输者"，读者是"接受者"，可以简单地描述传统出版中知识信息传递的模型，这一模型客观地反映了过去几百年以来人类知识传播体的运行状态。

图1　传统出版中的知识传播模型

传统出版业经过几百年的发展形成了日趋成熟的技术应用体系，诸如激光排版和电脑分色技术、平版和转轮机印刷技术等。出版产业链也形成了自身的运动规律，例如：产业相对封闭、生产技术门槛相对较低、产品形态较为稳定并可长久保存。

在传统出版单位的产品设计与生产过程中，涉及出版物的策划、生产、发行、成本、市场、营销等管理行为和经营要素，通过为公众提供出版产品，实现知识信息的增值。我们以图1为例，来说明图书这种产品在生产和流通过程中的过多的环节及成本要素。在图2中我们可以看到，图书产品存在生产周期较长、外委加工和种次较多、生产工序繁杂、材料费用项目多、回款周期较长等特性。

目前我们并不掌握单一出版单位或单一出版物产品的经营数据，但从全行业来看，根据新闻出版总署的统计，2006—2008年度，全国共有出版社579家图书出版社，378家音像制品出版单位，电子出版物出版单位240家。全国共出版各类出版物总量情况如下面表1所示。[1]

表1　2006—2008年度全国出版物总量情况

项目	出版种数			总印数（亿册份张盒）			总定价（亿元）		
年度	2006	2007	2008	2006	2007	2008	2006	2007	2008
图书	233 971	248 283	274 123	64.08	62.93	70.62	649.13	676.72	802.45
期刊	9 468	9 468	9 549	28.52	30.41	31.05	152.23	170.93	187.42
报纸	1 938	1 938	1 943	424.52	437.99	442.92	276.09	306.53	317.96
录音录像制品	26 032	31 955	23 493	5.07	4.91	4.33	36.15	31.46	18.44
总计	271 409	291 644	309 108	522.19	536.24	548.92	1 113.6	1 185.64	1 326.27

（注：未统计电子出版物。录音录像制品的2006年总定价数为2005年度数据）

表2　2006—2008年度全国图书单品种和单册定价分析

单品种定价金额（元）			单册定价金额（元）		
2006	2007	2008	2006	2007	2008
27.744 04	27.255 99	29.273 36	10.129 99	10.753 54	11.362 93

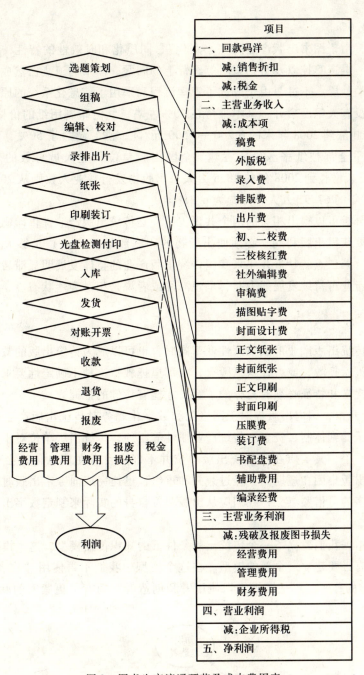

项目
一、回款码洋
减：销售折扣
减：税金
二、主营业务收入
减：成本项
稿费
外版税
录入费
排版费
出片费
初、二校费
三校核红费
社外编辑费
审稿费
描图贴字费
封面设计费
正文纸张
封面纸张
正文印刷
封面印刷
压膜费
装订费
书配盘费
辅助费用
编录经费
三、主营业务利润
减：残破及报废图书损失
经营费用
管理费用
财务费用
四、营业利润
减：企业所得税
五、净利润

图 2　图书生产流通环节及成本费用表

表 3　2006—2008 年主要图书出版经营数据变化情况

增长项	总定价	品种	印数	印张	用纸量	单品定价	单册定价
百分比	19.1%	14.6%	9.3%	8.8%	8.7%	5.2%	10.9%

　　表1—表3 的数据说明，在 2006 年至 2008 年间，单从图书一种出版物的全国出版总量情况来看，我国图书出版规模的增长动因主要来自于出版物单册定价的提高和品种数的增加，比如在图书印数和印张上分别只增长了 9.3% 和 8.8%，而定价和品种数分别增长

了 19.1% 和 14.6%。

另一方面，由于图书出版产业的"小众化"、同质化和时效性的特性，以及出版单位在供应链管理、渠道管控以及折扣策略等经营上的问题，图书的退货已然成为大多数出版单位挥之不去的梦魇。不过，由于改进了管理流程和采用了信息化系统的原因，目前全行业的退货率并没有大幅度攀升，基本维持在 20% 左右。[2]但印刷用纸的价格从 2006 年的平均 4 000 元/吨涨到 2008 年末的 6 200—6 500 元/吨，涨幅超过了 50%，在单册定价上带来的增长几乎全部被纸张涨价所吞噬。全国出版单位从业人员总数的变化不大，从 2006 年的 28 万人增长到 2008 年的 28.5 万人。出版物发行从业人数则从 2006 年的 72.22 万人降为 2008 年的 67.91 万人，降幅为 6.3%。

综合上述分析可以得出相关的两个共识，其一是传统出版产业提供印刷型出版物的经济特性在于：要获得出版利润，必须使出版物的印刷数量（产量）足够大，但受制于退货风险而不能。第二点就是近几年来我国传统出版产业的整体发展明显滞后于国民经济的整体发展，全行业可持续发展能力差，呈现滞涨或者说是相对衰落状态。

3　网络时代数字出版的特征分析

网络在对传统出版产业形成毁灭性变革同时，也可以成为传统出版的救世主。当然也有可能是先毁灭后拯救，或者在这里毁灭，在那里拯救！这种不确定性要求传统出版单位对数字出版的含义和特征必须有充分的了解，才能有稳健的把握。

从 2005 年开始，国内出版界对于网络化和数字化趋势对传统出版产业影响的认识逐渐深入。但由于受到体制、资金和传统产业惯性等制约，传统出版单位对于这种大势所趋仍然不知如何下手，其实质在于传统出版单位并不确定自身在信息化社会中的角色和定位。欧美大型出版集团在短期内，经过兼并和重组，迅速完成向数字出版时代跨越的路径在我国没有太多的可借鉴意义，我们应从出版单位自身的实际来制定数字出版组织流程和服务体系。

在上一节中，我们建立了一个传统出版条件下的知识传播模型，这个模型在网络时代就行不通了，有必要建立一个新的模型。在这个模型中我们不再使用"作者"、"读者"、"出版者"这样的称呼，这是因为知识使用者和创造者之间有了更紧密的联系。[3]如图 3 所示。

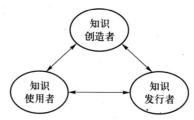

图 3　数字出版中的知识传播模型

网络技术的应用使得更多的信息资源可以得到更有效的整合，知识内容本身及其传播方式也呈现多元化、层次化和交互化的特征；知识相关者的角色、权利和需求在一定条件下会相互转换和渗透。

"数字出版"无疑已成为我国出版界最纠结的一个主题，网络环境下数字出版具有传统出版无可比拟的优势，诸如方便检索浏览、缩短生产周期、便于交流共享、降低成本消耗，等等。其经济特性区别于传统出版物：数字出版物生产成本中的固定成本（前期投入）占比较大，变动成本（后期维护）占比很小，这使得我们很难利用我们在传统出版模式下的积累的经验指导数字出版的产品及服务设计。同时，目前业界内外对数字出版的概念和逻辑也还没有一个严格的定义，很多时候我们都在"盲人摸象"式地谈论数字出版。

由于数字化的资源必须海量聚合，同时网络化使得服务模式高度发散。所以在新的知识传播模型中，所谓的数字出版必须包应含三个基本要素：一是知识创造者必须采用网络化手段对信息资源进行采集、编辑和标识。二是知识发行者必须建立数字版权保护和认证管理体系。三是知识内容必须通过信息网络与使用者建立交流和反馈。同时在数字出版模式中应将知识视为可交易的独立产品单元。

基于上述三个基本要素，可以抽象出数字化的知识在网络环境下的传播特性："知识即服务，knowledge-as-a-service，KaaS"。其含义是知识必须整合基于其之上的建议、意见、经验和解决方案，才可以获取价值提升。它的关注点是如何持续满足用户需求而不仅仅是知识本身。[4] KaaS 具有三个基本特征：以用户体验为需求模型、以解决方案为服务手段、以提升知识价值为目标。

KaaS 的组织流程是开放的、可持续的和可交互的。知识发行商不但提供知识本身，还提供对知识的描述、管理、获取和反馈等服务要素。在基于 KaaS 的数字出版模式下，知识创造者通过网络平台来生产和共享知识产品，并将其部署在知识发行者的服务器上；知识使用者按照所需的服务模式和时间通过信息网络来获取知识、支付费用。

KaaS 的基本思想是充分尊重用户对知识的个性化需求和核心价值，提供更为快捷和低成本的可扩展服务。在信息社会分工服务体系没有完整建立之前，传统出版业者应作出如下理解：数字出版即提供知识的聚合和服务！这和传统出版在工业化分工体系下的出版物的产供销经营模式（写书—编书—印书—发书）存在巨大差异。在数字出版条件下，用户通过浏览、链接和下载获取知识的过程实际上是在享受发行商提供的服务（是虚拟的产品），知识生产和服务的主体统一。也就是说，出版发行商必须提供基于知识单元的可管理的信息网络服务。

通过上述分析，我们引出对"数字出版"的定义——知识内容依托数字技术采编和标识、利用权利认证机制管理并通过信息网络进行分销和交流的过程。

3.1 知识的数字化采集、编辑和标识

由于个人计算机及字处理软件的广泛应用，作为图书产品的各种原始文档和图片都可以在计算机上来创建、修改、校对、存储和复制。应对这一趋势的关键一步是在知识创造者和知识发行者之间建立实时在线的"内容编写协同处理系统"。在该系统中，知识创造者一方面应该提供知识使用者所需的内容，还应提供该内容的服务对象及特征描述，同时须确保该内容符合一定的数字格式。而知识发行者一方面通过该系统为前者提供服务，另一方面方便自身在内容质量和商业目标等方面加以控制，有利于对知识创造者提供的信息资源进行片断解构和主题标识，以服务于知识使用者的多元化、多层化需求。

在这一过程中，需要重新确立传统出版过程中的作者和编辑的关系，编辑的责任和能力需要提高，尤其需要基于专业背景的知识解构和服务整合能力。建立基于 KaaS 的编、

审、校协同工作理念和流程，可以确保出版发行商设计开发出符合数字时代的产品和服务，重塑自己在新型信息传播体系中的核心地位。

3.2 知识的数字化版权保护和认证管理体系

计算机技术和网络技术的出现使得传统出版面临更为复杂的知识产权保护压力，互联网对传统出版最大的冲击就在于内容复制和传播的便捷性。虽然在互联网上传播的内容受到法律的保护，但互联网的倡导者和使用者从本质上反对对信息的自由传播采取任何限制措施——包括版权保护措施。

数字版权保护技术的发展有助于传统出版商开展数字出版的努力，通过访问次数、时间或者地址的限制可以有效地禁止非法使用。但在数字出版条件下知识创造者、发行者和使用者之间的权利关系肯定需要调整。

必须严肃地对待这个问题，虽然知识发行者在某些情况下会提供免费的产品及服务，但"版权"是出版产业存在和发展的基石——即使数字出版时代来临。为购买、加工和整合信息资源、建立、维护和发布知识内容等基础设施投入大量资金的知识发行者有必要采取合理的版权管理机制，用以保护自身内容资源和投资的安全，推动知识服务的可持续发展。

3.3 知识的信息网络分销和交流过程

由于信息网络具备便捷互动、时空虚拟等特征，使得知识内容聚集和整合之后的低成本传播和高效率商业应用成为可能。知识使用者可以通过互联网实现知识的消费和阅读行为，知识发行者可以自由、实时地掌握知识使用者的消费趋势和信息反馈——这一过程目前虽然深入人心，但受制于前端的知识加工手段和版权保护措施，成效甚微！在信息网络中对知识内容的分销和交流过程是知识发行者实现 KaaS 的基本途径，也是知识内容生产和传播服务实现统一的根本保证。

从出版产业的传统和现实来看，必须将知识内容的商业交易过程纳入数字出版的过程中来。虽然互联网和移动网络上拥有大量免费访问的内容和新型服务模式，诸如博客和彩信等。但如果将这些也纳入数字出版的范畴，会模糊产业的发展目标，误导公众对出版产业的正确认识，同时也会挫伤传统出版业者的数字化转型努力。

4 传统出版单位的战略和理念变革

在我国，自 20 世纪 80 年代开始，以四通公司和北大方正为代表的电子出版技术公司的微机排版系统的推广应用使得我国出版业的信息化迈入新的时代，到了 90 年代后期由于网络技术的发展使得信息采集、编排、输出的集中处理成为可能。[5]但是无论是在采编录入、校对排版、印刷输出以及最终产品的传送，我们所有出版过程信息化目的仍然是如何高效地生产和传播印刷型的出版物。这一过程的逻辑是出版物是产品，发行是服务，两者可以分离。但在 KaaS 思想下，知识的多元化、个性化生产和传播不但是出版商的产品，更是一种服务，两者必须统一。因此，传统出版单位至少应在指导思想、专业背景、编辑策划和产品形态上作出调整，以适应知识及其传播的多元性、层次性和交互性。

4.1 指导思想

传统出版单位必须制定中长期的数字出版战略，明确数字出版在出版社自身发展过程中的地位、作用和目标，用制度来保障实施上述战略的组织机构、人员和投入。对于数字出版我们不是要不要做、想不想做的问题，而是如何长期做的问题。

4.2　专业背景

用户的多元化需求成为专业和细分可以取得成功的保障。所谓专业背景是传统出版单位在建立和实施数字出版战略的过程中，必须坚持自己的专业领域和细分优势，充分利用自己在传统出版领域的品牌和市场影响力，建立新的知识服务体系。脱离自身的专业和优势来发展数字出版无疑是缘木求鱼。

4.3　编辑策划

在数字出版体系下，编辑策划的目的是为出版发行商提供一个基于产品生产和流通过程的整体性知识传播解决方案。编辑策划行为必须符合知识传播的多元性、层次性和交互性要求，也就是说我们策划的根本目的在于确保我们的知识在信息网络传播过程中满足多元用户的多层次、可交互需求，而不仅仅是提供出版物。

4.4　产品设计

结合专业背景和信息网络传播特性的数字出版产品的设计和生产对于传统出版单位来说是必须不断探索的过程。产品的设计原则仍然必须坚持开放、分层、交互、可控及基于KaaS的理念，也就是用户需求决定服务模式，服务模式决定产品价值。需求和设计高度统一，要求流程和组织必须高度统一，这样才能确保产品和服务高度统一。

5　传统出版单位的流程改造和人才培养

出版产业已有数百年的历史，传统出版仍有其存在和发展的必然性。但我们必须与时俱进，在确立数字出版战略思想和基本理念的同时，有计划分阶段改造传统出版产业的管理流程和组织架构，大力吸收和培养数字出版管理和技术人才，探索知识与服务的完美结合。从传统出版过渡到数字出版在产品形态上是一个渐进和扬弃的过程，但在服务模式上则是一场创新和变革的决战。

5.1　业务流程

出版单位的业务流程必须改革，以适应KaaS对知识生产体系的要求。编印发的传统生产流程应该变为"内容编写协同处理系统"下的策划、组稿、审稿、标识、设计和校对的知识加工体系。流程改造可以是分阶段、渐进式的，但基于内容管理的协同采编体系建设，确实是流程改造的首要任务。不如此，则无法在知识生产的源头低成本地整合知识资源。

5.2　出版组织

信息技术对传统出版的影响是全方位的，在传统的业务流程和组织体系下不会诞生数字出版的"金蛋"。信息资源的共享和交互会导致多元化的知识产品和多层次的信息服务，必须建立与之相适应的组织架构。不过组织的变革从来就不是一蹴而就的，在目前出版业体制改革和集团化发展态势下，建立符合数字出版的组织体系仍然需要不断实践。如果不能在旧的体系内改革和重组，出版单位也应该在统一的内容管理业务流程情况下，重新建立一个信息网络服务产品的生产架构。

5.3　人才培养

在KaaS模式下，知识与服务、技术与产品、组织和流程高度一体化。在数字出版体制下，技术服务可以外包或购买，但兼具技术背景、专业素养和出版实践的数字出版人才必须依靠出版单位持续稳定的培养。建立在统一内容管理业务流程下的组织必须鼓励产品和服务的创新，必须有持续稳定的资金和制度保障，确保人才的成长符合数字出版产业的发展和出版商自身的战略目标。

6 总结

计算机技术和互联网技术的发展带来社会由工业化向信息化快速转变，传统出版单位对信息资源和传播渠道的把控能力受到极大的挑战。按图书、杂志和报纸来区分信息传播的传统出版模式已经过时，他们只是用以解决信息在内容上的差异性的知识产品，"数字出版"也必须在传统意义上的出版过程中提供更多的知识重组、选择、互动和用户的感受。因为在网络时代，我们更多地会考虑知识使用者的关注度（黏性），"关注度在哪里，金钱就流向哪了"[6]。换言之，在信息爆炸、新兴事务层出不穷的网络时代，知识发行商的根本目的在于如何争夺和控制知识使用者的时间。传统的图书出版单位应该更加注意以"知识即服务"来定位自己在网络时代的角色，以最大限度地粘住读者作为其数字出版赢利模式的基础。

基于 KaaS 的知识传播体系可以使得知识发行商在网络环境下将读者、作者和出版者的关系结合得更为紧密，服务更为有效。但首先应该建立基于 KaaS 理念的"内容编写协同处理"流程以及适应此流程的组织架构。结合专业优势，加强技术储备，探索服务模式，则传统出版单位可在数字化浪潮中处变而不惊！

注释

[1] 参见 http://www.gapp.gov.cn/cms/html/21/464/200907/465083.html

[2] 任殿顺，马莹，金霞. 书业退货率不完全调查. 中国图书商报，http://www.cbbr.com.cn/

[3] 约翰·费瑟. 传递知识：21 世纪的出版业. 张志强，等，译，苏州大学出版社，2007

[4] 张红丽，吴新年. 知识服务及其特征分析 [J]. 图书情报工作，2010（3）：23-27

[5] 黄凯卿. 我国出版业信息化建设综述. 出版科学，2002 年增刊

[6] josh，Quittner. 阅读的前景. 财富（中文版），2010（5）（上半月刊）：87-90

作者简介

李弘，电子工业出版社九州时讯网络科技有限公司总经理。

论数字出版的新型内部组织结构与形态

邓红艳　尹章池

（武汉理工大学文法学院　武汉　430070）

摘要：源于管理对象的数字化，出版单位要着力调整内部部门及结构；对于中小出版社来说，比出版技术本身更重要的是建设网络型结构；出版集团要积极提升组织结构为复合研发型，转型为区域性和全国性出版平台，辐射其他中小出版社；优先建设相关数字出版部门，如数字出版物选题策划部、数字版权开发与复合出版部、数字技术开发等，并且归口整合相应的传统部门；组织结构的优化必须围绕提升核心业务、发挥资源优势、瘦身传统营销、增强竞争力等核心主题来展开。

关键词：数字出版　网络平台　组织结构

About The New Internal Organizational Structure and Form of Digital Publication

Deng Hongyan　Yin Zhangchi

（School of Arts and Law，Wuhan University of Technology，Wuhan，430070）

Abstract：From management object digitization，it is necessary for publishing units to adjust internal departments and its structure. For small and medium-sized press，the network structure is more important than publishing technology itself. Publishing group will actively promote organization structure，transforming into regional and national publication platforms and serving other small press. Construction of digital publication department is related topics，such as digital publication of planning，digital copyright development and composite publications，digital technology development，etc，and they centralize integration of traditional departments. Organizational structure optimization must revolve around the core subject which ascends the core business，plays around the traditional marketing resources advantage，thin body the traditional marketing，enhance the core competitiveness of theme.

Keywords：Figures publishing　Network platform　Organizational structure

　　数字出版已成为我国出版业发展的重要组成部分和新的经济增长点，但是数字出版面临着结构性矛盾，即传统出版社在数字出版中只是配角，新型出版单位则是主力，这一局面的改变趋势尚不明朗。目前研究过多关注数字出版技术、流程、营销与赢利模式，缺乏对传统出版社单位内部组织结构与优化的思考。组织结构是为数字出版产业服务的，但是，落后的科层制传统机构会阻碍传统出版社的数字出版发展。传统出版社应该在内部机构、数字化平台和区域性全国性的战略联盟方面有积极的动作，找到在国家数字出版产业中的定位，优化形成一个顺应数字出版的内部组织结构和形态。

1 出版单位内部组织的管理对象变化

数字出版的技术要素、产品形态、出版流程、市场营销等许多重要方面都不同于传统出版，已经对传统出版单位的组织流程及其管理等提出了新的服务要求。

1.1 出版流程的转变

数字出版基于统一、开放的数字化内容加工平台，编辑人员可以实现从选题的申报、采编计划的提出，到来稿的登记、编辑加工、校对、审批，再到稿件的发排、发布、生成纸质媒体、光介质媒体、网络媒体的全业务环节的数字化管理。相对于传统的出版流程，数字出版流程的显著特点有：一方面，出版流程简化，流通环节缩短。出版从传统的物流转变为信息流，从单向传递转变为双向互动，从以产品为主转变为以产品和服务为主。另一方面，数字技术与网络处理技术要求高。在数字出版的流程中，各个环节数字与网络处理技术相对专业化，包括出版内容的制作、编辑、内容发布以及产权保护等，都必须建立在相应的数字和网络技术的基础上，甚至包括数字阅读显示的软件和技术等。

1.2 出版单位管理重点的转变

作为一个新兴的产业，数字出版对出版单位传统的管理活动产生了巨大冲击。数字出版产业具有"二象性"的特点，其新的经济增长点主要依靠其产品特性和媒体特性。具体而言，数字出版的主要管理活动集中在两个方面：

（1）以内容管理为中心。数字出版资源储备的内容更为丰富，包括数字内容资源储备、复合型编辑以及技术人才储备、运营模式的储备，数字产品营销渠道的储备等。而且数字出版的内容具有双向性，既要求出版单位集约整合内容资源，内容资源强大使得读者拥有广阔的选择空间，甚至好的出版内容会根据读者的要求，不断延续下去。因此，对出版单位而言，内容资源强大意味着更大的市场话语权。

（2）以数字技术为依托。数字出版过程的关键在于能否以数字出版技术实现数字化的管理和控制，包括数字化的编辑出版环境支撑，数字化的编辑出版工艺流程设计，基于数字化的协同异步工作系统，在线或离线的数字生产管理模式，等等。

1.3 出版单位内部运行机制的转化

在数字出版的背景下，出版单位要实现从内容信息集成到数字出版、信息服务等各个环节的转型，首先要对出版单位内部运行机制进行转化。

（1）内容资源的整合。数字出版打破了传统出版按介质分割的限制，通过跨媒体的出版经营实现了内容资源价值的最大化。在数字出版的条件下，能充分按照主题，以最直接的阅读形式，把传统的零散的出版进行整体运作，从而真正形成整合性、系统性的连续出版。

（2）营销模式的重构。数字出版给传统出版产业带来的变革是根本性的，数字出版具有及时性、多媒体性特点，要求出版单位减少出版环节，尽量从产业链的后端向前端有效转移。数字出版对营销模式的影响是实质性的，主要表现为创造了更多营销空间和机会，而成本很低。

（3）赢利模式的重选。数字出版的赢利模式对传统出版社将是一个新的机遇，目前在个别产品上的斤斤计较可能挫伤出版社对数字出版的积极性；数字出版给予出版社创造的赢利机会和潜在价值不容置疑。

总之，传统出版社的管理对象发生了变化，负责管理和提供服务的内部组织的结构需要进行优化。出版单位的内部组织设计的合理变革，主要依据自身管理对象所发生的变化，并且要借助外部环境与技术条件。

2　适应数字出版环境的组织结构的转型方式及其定位

传统的企业组织结构形式，经历了直线型、职能型、直线职能型、直线职能参谋型等不同的形式。时至今日，国内出版单位已经基本完成企业化（除了少数公益性出版单位），但是内部机构设置仍然主要停留在职能型和事业部型这两种结构形式。职能型组织结构形式主要是通过职务专门化制定有关制度和规则，以职能部门划分工作任务，实行集权式决策，通过命令链进行经营决策；事业部制的组织结构主要是对职能部门化和产品部门化融合。这些传统出版单位的组织结构，优缺点泾渭分明，如森严的等级制造成事业单位的官僚化，职能的分割造成管理鸿沟。内部治理结构落后于现代企业体制。数字技术和网络技术的快速发展，为改进内部结构提高了新的机遇。一些有前瞻性的出版单位已经逐步优化内部组织结构，力图尽快适应数字出版产业的飞速发展。尤其是大型的出版单位如高等教育出版社在优化内部组织形态上开辟了出版的新领域。目前可供选择的内部组织形态有如下几种模式：

（1）网络型结构。当前，国内企业化之后的出版集团、发行集团和知名出版社都已经建立了基于网络运营平台的母子公司制组织结构，有的实现 ERP 管理模式，有的实现物流战略联盟，有的实现连锁经营。特别是上市出版企业的网络组织结构更成熟一些。

而中小出版社、民族出版社等公益性出版社的网络体系、组织机构及其职能尚不健全，需要予以足够重视。可以说，这些单位在传统渠道和传统组织结构方面没有大社的优势，而将网络型结构置入这些中小出版社，可以实现营销渠道的放大和增值，促进分工和专业化的发展，降低交易成本，有助于优化资源配置，充分、有效地整合有限的生产要素。

（2）扁平型结构。方正科技集团一直是扁平化渠道策略的倡导者和实践者。方正科技到最终用户之间只有一级渠道，主要通过全国的 7 个大区和 32 个区域公司直接对遍布全国的 1 500 余家代理商以及 200 余家专卖店进行管理。这种组织结构形态由于渠道层级少，方正科技集团能掌握大量一手的客户动态，对客户需求能快速响应。

传统出版社尽管企业化和内部治理这一方面有些较大的动作，但是基本上还是过去的职能制、科层制，层级过多、机制不活。数字出版部门的嵌入，如出版社网络信息中心、数字版权开发部、数字出版物选题策划与市场部等，可以极大地减少管理层次，增加管理幅度。这样就加快编辑出版速度，缩短周期，提高质量；更好地对人力资源予以组合和开发管理，有利于发挥职员的主动性和创造精神。

（3）信息控制型结构。将传统介质的内容扩展到电子格式进行传播是国际出版集团目前和长远规划的重点。荷兰沃尔特斯·克鲁维尔集团将其所有经营的产品和服务分为四类，即静态内容、动态内容、迅捷工具、定制解决方案。静态内容包括图书和散页读物，动态内容包括 CD-ROM 光盘、数据库产品以及在线产品，迅捷工具包括工作流程工具和配套应用工具，定制解决方案包括集成软件包和定制工作流程系统。通过对近几年不同种类产品的成长率和利润增长率的分析，定制解决方案的成长速度非常迅速。另外，从介质来看，电子载体产品的增长速度为 33%，而传统纸介质产品处于停滞状态，仅为 1%[1]。

国际出版集团越来越成为从事信息资源价值链和产业链的连续开发的信息集团。国内出版社在产业链整合的同时，重视建设版权信息和出版信息的组织单元，并将出版管理置于信息控制过程中，将有利于出版产业的升级换代，有利于价值链和产业链的延长，有利于保护和开发传统出版社的版权资源。

（4）复合创新型结构。现代出版机构越来越体现为学习型组织，更是基于多学科、新技术、含创意的研发型结构。如长江出版社的北京图书中心，就是一个将市场触角伸到拥有最快捷、最丰富的选题资源的北京的新型组织，还有许多出版社在全国各地的分社、分公司，以及与国外出版社驻中国办事处、民营出版社的合作开发，将文化工作室作为出版社的外设编辑机构等，都是出于选题的创意策划，借助网络技术而出现的新形态机构。

出版经营的每一本书、一个项目都是新产品，需要注入新的创意、技术和市场元素，需要保持客观、创造、研发的虔诚心态，当然，团队合作精神和研发能力却是最重要的。研发部门的功能在于，创造编辑、产品、服务及单位组织的新能量。

以上也同时反映出版单位内部组织结构的由低到高的提升顺序，较为容易的是网络型结构，有资金和技术就可以自建或加盟。而后三者需要组织内部的进一步消化、调适和创新，是对运行规则的调适、融合和完善的过程。

3 出版单位的组织结构的优化策略

3.1 数字化部门嵌入单位内部主体结构

出版社在组织结构上的创新与优化已经势不可挡，但出版组织结构变革必须遵循提升核心业务、发挥资源优势、瘦身传统营销、增强竞争力等基本原则。出版社应该把更多的资源放在内容的提供及可开发的数字化产品形式上，资源向上游内容开发集中，向终端网络客户服务集中，向数字化专业队伍培养集中。同时，对非内容创造与非信息服务部门进行瘦身和外包，比如传统营销、传统出版印刷、传统书店门面，等等。目前，至少重点建设这样三个部门：

（1）数字出版物选题策划部

数字出版的选题策划具有许多新的特点，首先数字出版物选题可以选择更多的新卖点，其次是小众化、专业化、个性化选题受到重视，再次是可以依据选题内容来选择适合它的表现形式，与传统出版物选题有很大不同。在复杂性程度上，数字出版选题足以超越传统选题方式，在管理部门归口上，也可以兼并传统纸质的图书选题部门。

（2）数字版权开发与复合出版部

以资本和技术为先行的电信产业运营商、网游企业、数字出版平台的技术型企业对版权的争夺大面积展开。以盛大公司为代表，这些公司大规模吸纳、收编作者，成立版权机构。传统出版社对于内容资源的优势不再，必须增强自主版权的保护和开发，探索出版资源挖掘与控制新模式，主动转化数字出版权。现在比较成熟的复合出版，收到了良好的市场效果。如江苏凤凰出版传媒集团以图书、互联网和数字视盘等 3 种形式，同步出版

《走进百家名村》、《非诚勿扰》、《贫民窟的百万富翁》等作品，采用了传统图书、互联网、手机阅读等多种出版方式，实现了多渠道全媒体同步出版。"全媒体出版是指图书一方面以传统方式进行纸质图书出版；另一方面以数字图书的形式通过互联网、手机、手持阅读器等终端数字设备进行同步出版。"[2]中文在线董事长兼总裁童之磊认为，全媒体出版强调多渠道的同步出版，多种载体同时发布，通过有效的全媒体整合营销，实现传播模式从单一向多元转型，从而带来版权价值最大化和信息传播广泛化。

（3）数字技术开发和信息部

目前数字出版技术系统和装备系统需要加大研发和创新，数字出版行业标准、数字出版物格式、数字出版防伪加密、数字版权保护等技术问题也都需要采取相应的措施解决。所以整合技术平台，解决数字技术问题，是发展数字出版的前提条件。同时也需要出版单位加大人才培养力度，充分发挥人才在数字出版发展中的关键作用。传统出版企业对数字出版仍缺乏足够认识，自主研发能力不够，尚未形成业界普遍认同的商业模式。要通过政策引导和重大项目实施，推动传统出版业数字化转型；加快技术创新体系建设，增强企业研发能力[3]。出版单位的内容资源、作者资源、选题资源、版权资源和人力资源等信息资源是其核心竞争力，因此应该与技术研发同步进行。

3.2 扶持建设若干个区域性或全国性出版业公共服务平台

（1）出版物流及出版市场监测平台

目前，面对经济全球化和出版市场快速变化的趋势，出版业市场监测日益成为政府加强宏观调控力度、企业提高市场响应速度的重要保证。在欧美出版业发达国家，出版供应链信息共享的基础较好，对于出版业的运行和监测发挥积极而有效的作用。我国政府和企业逐步认识到信息共享与监测的价值，建立了立足市场、面向市场的三个共享与监测系统，即北京开卷全国图书零售市场观测系统、上海中国出版物流通监测系统、新闻出版总署信息中心。存在的主要问题是当前信息的收集依然是传统的静止片面统计方法，即对零售环节的抽样统计和局部统计，忽视了某一出版物的在版、在途、在库环节状态；尽管应用了网络通信技术和POS技术，但是关于某一图书的完整数据信息就自然失真失范。这就需要若干个整合上中下游出版企业的出版供应链的数字平台，如出版集团供应链信息平台、发行集团供应链信息平台、第三方出版监测机构信息平台。政府管理部门可以观测产品供求状况、市场结构变化、产业发展趋势和行业运行格局，出版单位可以依据不断的跟踪监测结果来调整目标市场和细分市场、优化选题以及实施新的定价营销策略，等等[4]。

（2）公益性少数民族出版网络平台

现在少数民族出版社在网络基础建设方面还比较薄弱，许多民族类出版社甚至找不到其网站。这一方面表明民文出版数字化任重道远，另一方面更加凸显建立国家少数民族出版网络平台的示范意义和信息共享责任。

少数民族出版具有一般出版的共性，又具有资源特色化而产生的选题稀缺性、读者基数小而产生的市场有限性、文化保护而伴随的出版公益性、难以集团化而导致经营分散化等特殊性。建设国家少数民族网络出版平台可以聚合少数民族出版的出版资源，转化出版劣势为出版优势，示范和引导少数民族数字化出版。这个平台可提供各民族出版社在出版资源远程共享、出版政策传播研究、民文出版项目评审和监管、出版物及其版权资源的国内外贸易等方面的公共服务。

（3）版权保护和开发服务平台

数字出版产业具有"三高"性质，即内容的高度集成、技术对运维环境的高度支撑、运营模式的高度动态化。而这"三高"正是传统中小出版单位以一个出版社之力难以解决的问题。在数字出版领域有所作为并取得实质性的实效，就一定要从高端进入，即要从集团和战略联盟的层面上整体考虑，集约性地整合资源，整体性地进入，而不宜从个体的出版单位进入。如果进入层次过低，则会导致资金的无效投入、资源的无效生产和使用。这个高端首选的是版权资源及其网络平台，这是出版社的无形资产和优势资源，而这一优势正在消失，因此只有借助版权网络平台，才能挽回不利局面。出版集团具有发展为区域性版权交易平台和中心的基础，而中小出版社、民营出版社、公益性出版社则需要国家、政府的扶持，最好在国家版权局的信息中心网站建立国家版权数据库与交易子网站，优先为中小出版社提供版权保护和版权贸易的在线服务。

4 结语

出版单位内部的机构部门重置和结构优化，源于管理对象的数字化，是出版社发展数字出版的体制保障；对于中小出版社来说，比出版技术本身更重要的是建设网络型结构，还需要区域性或国家性的网络出版平台提供公共出版服务；出版集团要积极提升组织结构为复合研发型，转型为区域性和全国性出版平台，辐射其他中小出版社；主要的数字出版部门，如数字出版物选题策划部、数字版权开发与复合出版部、数字技术开发和信息部等优先建设，并且归口整合相应的传统部门，组织结构变革必须围绕提升核心业务、发挥资源优势、瘦身传统营销、增强竞争力等核心主题来展开。

注释

[1] 杨贵山. 海外书业经营案例［M］. 北京：中国水利电力出版社，2005：61-63

[2] 三石. 2010年中国出版十大预测［J］. 深圳书城，2010（6）：18-21

[3] 刘超. 数字出版带动传统出版业升级转型［N］. 中国知识产权报，2009-7-17（9）

[4] 尹章池. 基于现代出版物流中心的出版市场监测机制研究//黄先蓉，罗紫初. 数字出版与出版教育［M］. 北京：高等教育出版社2009. 4：523-529

作者简介

邓红艳，武汉理工大学2008级硕士研究生。

尹章池，博士，武汉理工大学文法学院教授，硕士生导师。

论数字出版时代的文学创作

彭 静

（武汉大学信息管理学院 武汉 430000）

摘要：数字出版强大的生命力和势不可挡的趋势在各个学科领域均有体现，文学作为出版的重要内容之一，其创作与出版正经受着一场变革。文学作为一门独立的学科发展至今，业已形成了其内在的固有的体系，稳定地沉淀在人类文化中。然而，随着数字时代的来临，数字技术渗透到各个学科中，数字出版对文学的介入，不断改变着文学的创作方式、传播媒介、表现形式、阅读方式等。数字出版对文学体系的介入主要表现在两个方面：文学管理系统和文学语言系统。数字出版时代，文学创作呈现出新的特征和问题，包括文学创作权威的消解、文学创作方法的变更。本文从数字出版对文学系统的影响和文学创作的特征两个方面对数字出版时代的文学创作加以讨论，阐释当前文学创作的转型。

关键词：数字出版 文学创作 文学系统 作者权威

Literary Creation in the Era of Digital Publishing

Peng Jing

（School of Information Management，Wuhan University，Wuhan，430072）

Abstract：Digital publishing with great vitality and unstoppable trend has reflected in various subject areas，publication of literature as an important part also suffers a revolution. Literature as an independent discipline development so far，has formed its inherent within system，steadily precipitated in human culture. However，with the advent of the digital age，digital technology penetrated into all disciplines，including literature in terms of creative ways to make literature，media，forms，ways of reading and so on. Digital publishing system involved in literature mainly in two aspects：the language of literature and literary management system. And in the digital publishing era，literature creation presents new features，including the digestion of literary authority，changes in methods of literary creation. This paper mainly makes a talk about two aspects：the impacts of the digital publishing on literature system and characteristics of literary creation，which to discuss the transformation of the current literature creation.

Keywords：Digital publishing Literary creation Literary system Authoritative

1 数字出版对文学系统的影响

文学作为一门独立的学科发展至今，业已形成了其内在的固有的体系，稳定地沉淀在人类文化中。然而，随着数字时代的来临，数字技术渗透到各个学科中，数字出版对文学的介入，不断改变着文学的创作方式、传播媒介、表现形式、阅读方式等。数字出版对文学体系的介入主要表现在两个方面：文学管理系统和文学语言系统。

1.1 文学管理系统

传统文学管理系统主要是由上游建构的，包括作者和权威机构，他们在文学系统中占据领导的地位，从文学的生产、传播到消费，都是由上游权力者全程控制，于此文学则打上了文化精英与意识形态的烙印。无论是在东方文学史还是在西方文学史上，处处可见文化精英与政府意识形态的表现，如屈原是中国诗歌史的第一位伟大的诗人，也是楚国士大夫阶层，其作品创作采用"香草美人"寓忠贞贤良之士，赞美了作为臣子为君王分忧、为国运担忧的品格，文学思想明显表现了"君为臣纲"的儒家理念。再者，传统文学管理系统强调的是一种自上而下的单向传播，没有建立良好的反馈机制，使得传播者与接受者不对等的地位，这也造成了创作集团高高在上的姿态，而不关心接受者的态度。

数字出版改变了传统信息传播过程，信息传播者地位的优劣格局被打破，传统直线型、等级划分严格而繁杂的传播模式走向扁平化，创作集团的权威被消解，创作权力不断地被下放，大众不再依赖于"精英阶层"的创作，开始自己走向创作集团。由此，文学创作表现出巨大的开放性、交互性和自由性，文学创作的意识形态属性淡化，更多体现为个体性。另外，数字出版使出版环境变得宽松，出版流程变得简捷。制度上放宽，面向广大民众而开放，出版权由精英集团分流到平民大众手上；技术上实现出版工作高效率运作和个性化服务，使文学出版走向商业化，文学创作市场化。

1.2 文学语言系统

数字出版带来的除了管理层面的影响外，还有文学语言层面的冲击。传统文学语言系统是以自然语言为主体的，包括官方语言和地方俚语，自然语言符号是历史文化的沉淀，具有较大的稳定性，其发音、形象和意义的传承性很大，历史厚重感强烈。数字出版所依赖的新媒体技术，为文学创作提供了多种语言符号。这些语言符号表现出明显的时效性、灵活性、调侃性。如渗入文学创作中的网络语言，其产生是极其偶然的，往往是一个热门事件或人物，就生产出一个新词，其来也快，其去也快，随着事件和人物的时间距离扩大，网络语言也走向冷却。

新媒体技术实现了多种语言符号的灵活排列。读者审美领域的扩宽，由文字延伸向图像、音乐等，新媒体技术迎合了读者审美对象的丰富性的同时，将各种元素分割、设计、排列，从而实现读者个性化的审美品位。随着消费社会的到来，大众对文学作品语言的越发挑剔，不喜欢严肃的、深邃的、思辨的语言风格，而倾向于口头式的、直白的、趣味的行文。新媒体技术让文本的量化生产瞬息实现的同时，也以默许的方式向创作者宣扬这种创作语言庞大的市场。传统文学创作在与市场的抗争中，滑向弱势的一方。

2 数字出版时代文学创作的特征

2.1 文学创作权威的消解

在传统文学创作体系中，作者被视为权威，作者以其知识涵养、艺术造诣，被社会认可为精英阶层，这种精英意识就往往表现在他们的行文中。数字出版时代，人人都可以是作家，人人都可以创作并出版，作者的角色从精英转向大众，作者的概念不再是文化精英的代名词，普通大众开始戴上了作者的光环。由于作者权威的消解，作者与读者呈现在平等的地位上，使得文学的创作实现了较大的开放性和交流互动性。

草根文学的出现则是最好的证明。草根文学作者作为不为人知的基层民众，以其自身的文学才能，创作并出版文学作品，实现其文学追求。文学虽然曾一度是"贵族"阶层专有的产物，但文学本质上是与人民大众分不开的，人类社会是文学创作的源泉，任何排斥某种社会文化，或将某种社会阶层踢出文学创作的范畴，都是狭隘的，这只会将文学的发展引入死胡同。数字出版时代带来了文学创作的更加自由的环境，为文学的长远发展提供了一个丰厚的土壤。

2.2 文学创作方法

创作方法是"艺术家自觉或不自觉地用来指引他们反映现实进行创作的原则和途径、精神和手法"[1]。文学理论体系提炼出了一系列文学创作方法，如写实主义、浪漫主义、印象主义等，纷繁且各具特色，反射出了文学奇葩之美。而数字出版时代的来临，其传播的快捷性、广泛性并未能使这些创作方法被广大作者所接受和应用，甚至是淹没在了创作实践中。

观当今文学创作，更多的是经验式的、情绪化的作品，作品中充斥着感性之泛滥，理性之缺失。它不以文学审美的创作目的，使文学创作流于故事的叙述，以"讲故事"的方式创作文学，过于强调故事性，突出趣味性，而忽略文字的美感。这类文学由于迎合了大众阅读口味，并借助媒介的力量，往往被打造成文学畅销书。如《明朝那些事儿》，用平白的语言，讲述历史事件与人物，在文学艺术层面上来说，手法枯燥，审美尽失，却屡屡列在文学类畅销书排行榜上，这即是文学机械化生产的结果，迎合消费文化，追求市场效益。

创作的最初形式便是模仿，并在模仿的基础上的重建，所以，一个好的模仿对象或文本，对于后来创作是有积极的引导意义的。数字出版时代使得创作的模仿更加容易，类型化、同质化创作正是在模仿中制造的。于此，应用这一渠道，将文学创作的理念与方法植入作者的创作中则是数字出版对文学创作的巨大贡献。

2.3 文学创作的问题

数字出版在提供大量的便利的同时，将花花世界呈现在创作者面前，这对创作者的心理产生负面影响，从而导致创作者的浮躁情绪，将文学作品引向了浮躁的、空洞的、功利的、娱乐的消极文学，作品的主题不再是深刻严肃的，而是调侃娱乐的；作品的用语不再是精细推敲的，而是随意粗陋的；作品的结构不再是严谨有序的，而是杂乱无章的；作品的表现手法不再是独具匠心的，而是单一效仿的，这些浮躁问题成为了优美文学创作的巨大障碍。

由于数字出版时代作者权威的消解，文学创作的开放性和自由特性，文学创作也突显出较大的随意性和文学垃圾的泛滥。文学的概念与标准、文学与非文学的界限变得模糊，文学自身体系不断发展变化，这要求作者及文学机构在文学创作和评论中，有意识地参与文学的形态和意义的建构中，一方面要坚守文学的文化阵地、摈弃粗制滥造的创作，另一方面要鼓励文学创作的百花齐放，丰富文学内涵。

注释

[1] 李泽厚. 美学论集. 上海文艺出版社. 1980。

参考文献

[1] 水明. 数字出版中的新媒体艺术语言 [J]. 西北美术，2010（1）

[2] 任璞，新媒体与艺术创作的关系浅析 [J]. 浙江万里学院学报，2004（12）

[3] 薛俊. 论网络文学与文学本质 [J]. 学术论坛，2008（4）

[4] 张才刚. 数字时代文学研究的几个基本问题 [N]. 光明日报，2010-08-01

[5] 顾祖钊. 论创作方法的理论构成 [J]. 安庆师范学院学报，1988（1）

[6] 黄鸣奋. 网络时代的许诺："人人都可成为艺术家" [J]. 文艺评论，2000（4）

[7] 李欣人，段婷婷. 权威的消解与受众的转化：数字出版时代传播关系的重构 [J]. 出版发行研究，2009（10）

作者简介

彭静，武汉大学信息管理学院出版发行专业 2009 级硕士研究生。

数字出版企业的版权危机与转机[*]

王志刚

（武汉大学信息管理学院　武汉　430072）

摘要： 数字出版的内容生产特性要求数字出版企业的发展应紧紧围绕版权资源的保护与运营来展开，而我国数字出版企业却常为一些版权纠纷所困扰。本文以同方知网、方正阿帕比和盛大文学为研究个案，分析我国数字出版企业版权现状，指出版权危机产生的原因，在此基础上提出数字出版企业应建立以版权为核心的商业发展战略，版权保护意识应从相对淡漠走向绝对重视，版权运营理念应从单纯竞争为主走向竞争与合作并重，企业版权人才储备战略应从单纯拉拢作者到建立版权人才培养机构，从而走出阻碍企业发展的版权困局。

关键词： 数字出版企业　版权危机　版权战略

Crisis and Chance of Digital Publishing Enterprises

Wang Zhigang

（School of Information Management，Wuhan University，Wu Han，430072）

Abstract： Digital publishing enterprise should be tightly on copyright protection and copyright operational as the characteristics of the content production. However，some China's digital publishing companies today often face some copyright disputes. This paper take Tongfang Knowledge Network，Apabi and Shanda Literature Limited as the major object of study to analyse the current status of copyright，and point out the causes of the copyright crisis in China. On this basis，he paper points out that the digital publishing company should establish business development strategy in which copyright as the core and go out of the dilemma of copyright. In the detail，digital publishing enterprises should highlight copyright awareness，copyright business philosophy should highlight competition and cooperation，copyright human resource reserve should highlight construction of the copyright talent training department.

Keywords： Digital publishing enterprises　Copyright crisis　Copyright strategy

版权一直是出版企业核心竞争力中最重要的元素，然而中国数字出版企业目前却处于版权困局之中：在急需原创版权来推动行业不断发展的同时也遭遇着一个接一个版权纠纷

＊本文系 2009 河南大学人文社会科学基础研究项目"数字出版企业版权战略研究"（2009YBRW036）成果之一。

的困扰。而且在众多版权官司中，数字出版企业往往成为最后的失败者，其中不乏如超星、方正、清华同方等国内知名数字出版企业。在数字出版企业方兴未艾之时，版权危机频发给数字出版企业的发展造成了严重困扰。版权危机出现的原因何在？转机何在？带着这些疑问，笔者选取代表中国数字出版业参加 2009 法兰克福图书博览会的三家数字出版商，即同方知网、方正阿帕比和盛大文学作为主要研究个案，分析其版权现状以及危机产生的原因，在此基础上提出相应的建议。调研方法主要是通过访问数字出版企业官方网站、查询司法机关在其官方网站公布的相关版权案件审判书等方式获取有效信息。

1 我国数字出版企业的版权危机

通过对我国数字出版企业的整体扫描，我们发现国内一些数字出版企业的版权获取模式可以分为两种：一是自主开发进行原创，二是通过版权许可合同实现版权资源的最大化。两种获权模式实则各有优劣，自我培养不适宜企业的大规模发展但却保证权利的绝对合法性，而本该广泛普及的版权许可模式却在实践中产生诸多问题。如同方知网、方正阿帕比和盛大文学三家企业都在不同程度地面临着版权问题的困扰，说明我国数字出版企业版权现状不容乐观，正遭遇版权危机。

同方知网在多起版权纠纷中成为被告。如 2002 年 12 月，来自成都、武汉、重庆的 22 名学术专家状告清华同方侵犯学术文章版权；2005 年 12 月，河北 32 名作者状告"中国知网"及清华同方侵权；2008 年 5 月，30 余名硕士、博士将同方股份有限公司控股的《中国学术期刊（光盘版）》电子杂志社、同方知网（北京）技术有限公司告至北京市海淀区人民法院，要求其停止侵权[1]。2008 年 9 月，104 名硕、博士论文作者一纸诉状将中国学术期刊（光盘版）电子杂志社、同方知网（北京）技术有限公司诉至北京市朝阳法院，诉由为侵犯学位论文著作权[2]。目前与同方知网相关的部分已有审理结果的版权纠纷如表 1 所示。

表 1 同方知网部分版权纠纷审结情况

审结时间	案件名称	案件结果	审理法院	备注
2006 年 3 月 17 日	樊元武与清华同方光盘股份有限公司、中国学术期刊（光盘版）电子杂志社、清华同方知网（北京）技术有限公司、上海图书馆等著作权侵权纠纷案	两审败诉	上海高院	赔付 10 200 元
2006 年 8 月 18 日	清华同方光盘股份有限公司、中国学术期刊（光盘版）电子杂志社、清华同方知网（北京）技术有限公司与蒋星煜著作权侵权纠纷案	两审败诉	上海高院	赔付 380 000 元
2006 年 12 月 25 日	范韶华诉清华同方知网（北京）技术有限公司等著作权纠纷案	原告撤诉	北京市海淀区法院	
2008 年 5 月 21 日	冯杜诉《中国学术期刊（光盘版）》电子杂志社、同方知网（北京）技术有限公司侵犯著作权纠纷案	原告撤诉	北京市海淀区法院	

我国数字出版企业的另一领军人物方正阿帕比近年来同样深陷版权危机。如继清华教授黄延复、杜昌维、苟天晓将方正电子告上法庭，称方正数字图书馆侵犯了其作品的著作权之后，2006 年 4 月 29 日，作者程汉桥又以侵犯著作权为由将方正电子再次告上法庭。公之于众的这四起案件，起因都是原告发现自己的作品在 Apabi 数字图书馆资源平台上被使用，而作为经营方的方正数字图书馆事先并未经过原告许可，也没有支付过报酬，甚至根本没有跟作者接触过就公然出售该作品的电子版本[3]。目前方正阿帕比部分已有判决结果的相关案件如表 2 所示。

表 2　方正阿帕比部分版权纠纷案件审结情况

审结时间	案件名称	案件结果	审理法院	备注
2007 年 10 月 18 日	北京书生网络技术有限公司诉北京方正阿帕比技术有限公司侵犯著作权纠纷案	一审败诉	北京海淀区法院	赔偿 1 019 元
2007 年 10 月 21 日	李昌奎与北京方正阿帕比技术有限公司侵犯著作权纠纷案	两审败诉	北京市第一中级人民法院	判决阿帕比公司赔偿李昌奎经济损失及合理开支 8 630 元，全额承担诉讼费用。
2008 年 6 月 20 日	李昌奎诉北京方正阿帕比技术有限公司侵犯著作权纠纷案	一审败诉	北京市海淀区法院	赔付 1 645 元
2008 年 10 月 10 日	北京书生网络技术有限公司诉北京北大方正电子有限公司侵犯著作权纠纷案	一审败诉	北京市海淀区法院	停止侵权，赔付 3 980 元
2008 年 12 月 25 日	北京书生网络技术有限公司诉被告北京北大方正电子有限公司侵犯著作权纠纷案	一审败诉	北京市海淀区法院	赔付 4 340 元

通过收购原创文学网站而成为数字出版重要力量的盛大文学同样也面临着版权问题的困扰。2004 年 10 月，盛大收购中国领先原创娱乐文学门户网站——起点中文网；2007 年 11 月，盛大参股文学网站晋江原创网；2008 年 3 月，红袖添香成为盛大投资公司；2008 年 7 月，盛大文学有限公司作为盛大网络旗下主要企业之一正式成立。目前，与盛大文学有关的部分版权纠纷案件审结情况如表 3 所示。

表 3　盛大文学部分版权纠纷案件审结情况

审结时间	案件名称	案件结果	审理法院	备注
2007 年 4 月 9 日	起点中文网擅自解禁签约作家作品案	一审败诉	上海市浦东新区法院	支付 12 万元稿酬
2008 年 10 月 31 日	起点中文网诉福建云霄阁网侵权案	胜诉	福建省莆田市涵江区法院	一审判处两被告有期徒刑一年半，各处罚金 10 万元

2 我国数字出版企业深陷版权困局的原因

2.1 侵权频发源于数字出版企业版权意识的淡薄

数字版权在我国法律层面的体现，主要是指作品的信息网络传播权。2001年新修订的《著作权法》，给著作权人增加了一项新的重要权利——信息网络传播权，即以有线或者无线方式向公众提供作品，使公众可以在其个人选定的时间和地点获得作品的权利。从事数字出版涉及的著作权及相关权利的法律规定，可以根据电子书的出版流程和权利分为两部分：作者享有的信息网络传播权和出版社享有的版式设计权。因此在数字出版领域要获得完整的权利，必须获得作者和出版者的授权。然而有些数字出版企业在数字版权方面缺乏严格"先授权，后传播"的意识，经常出现数字出版商宣称自己是合法授权但版权真正所有人从未授权的情况。如一些数字出版商常常采取绕过作者"取得"出版社"授权"的模式，因为这样可以避免与作者本人的一对一谈判，然而这种模式已经被证明存在法律缺陷。因为就某些图书而言，出版社根本就没有授权他人制作数字图书的权利。即使目前有权利，合同到期后若继续使用仍会引起纠纷。此外，一些数字论文出版商同样为避免与作者本人的一对一谈判，采取与学校签订一揽子合同的学位论文收录协议。但是因为部分学校的原因没有取得本校学生的授权，所以造成了对原作者数字版权的侵权。出现这些问题的重要原因就在于数字出版商不了解相关法律的规定，不了解版权的真正归属，从而使得数字版权侵权行为高发。

2.2 作者与传统出版单位的维权意识不断提高

与数字出版企业版权意识相对淡薄形成鲜明对比的是，近年来版权人开始注意运用法律武器维护自己的合法权益，因此，起诉数字出版企业侵害自身版权的相关案件此起彼伏。除了上文表1、表2、表3列举的一些版权人维权的案件，在2004年、2005年出现了郑成思等起诉书生数字公司等10余起案件。2007年7月，上海市版权局对"书香门第"网站侵犯著作权人合法权利依法作出责令停止侵权行为，罚款人民币1.5万元的行政处罚。2008年，500多名博士、硕士状告北京万方数据股份有限公司，一时间成为业内的焦点。这类案件的增多，说明广大作者的权利意识不断提高。

此外，传统出版企业也开始运用法律武器捍卫自己的版权领地。在传统出版商和数字出版商的版权之战中，传统出版商由于长期的垄断地位，拥有了大批图书版权，而这些图书版权恰恰是一些数字出版商特别是电子书出版商急需的。当一些数字出版商未经许可擅自把一些纸版书改编成电子形式时，就可能引发传统出版企业对数字出版商的版权诉讼。这种诉讼主要涉及版式设计权。如2007年中国标准出版社指控世纪超星、超星数图侵犯了该社10种图书所享有的汇编作品著作权和版式设计权，海淀法院一审判决世纪超星、世纪数图立即停止销售、使用上述10种图书电子版，并向中国标准出版社赔偿经济损失和诉讼合理支出共计16万元[4]。

2.3 恶性竞争是造成数字出版企业间版权纠纷频发的另一重要原因

数字出版企业的低门槛，使大大小小的出版商打开始进入这个领域，同时由于我国针对数字出版企业相关管理规定的相对滞后，在版权利益的驱使下，数字出版企业间出现了不同层次的恶性竞争。其主要表现可分为两种：一是疯狂盗版，二是拉拢作者争夺版权。

数字出版企业在蓬勃发展过程中遭遇到严重盗版问题的困扰。在数字领域，只要进行拷贝、粘贴就可以完成盗版，而且盗版是全方位的。据中文在线童之磊介绍，在国内1 400多个电子网站中，真正拥有版权的大概只有4.3%，大量的1 300多个网站全都是盗版[5]。盛大文学对盗版也有着较深的体会，公司法务总监陈明峰认为，大型盗版网站保守估计数量在1 万至10 万个，中小型盗版网站估计有数百万之众，几乎无法统计；对于盗版网站给起点中文网带来的经济损失，可以列举两种方式给予估算：设有1 万家盗版网站，每家平均盗版200 部作品，如果以单本作品损失2 000 元计算（目前起点中文网通过民事诉讼方式打击盗版所获得的赔偿标准约为每部5 000 至10 000 元），那么直接损失就是盗版网站、盗版作品数、单本作品损失三者的乘数，即40 亿元；如果以盗版网站每部作品盗版10 万字，每部作品浏览量1 万次，其中可能付费比例10%，每千字3 分计算，直接损失就达到60 亿元[6]。可以看出，这些网站的盗版行为严重侵害了真正拥有版权的数字出版商，形成了恶性竞争。

恶性竞争还突出体现在拉拢作者抢夺版权方面。例如在学术论文数字版权方面，中国的数字出版商一直受到版权纠纷的困扰。表面上看是由于论文授权制度不规范造成的版权纠纷，实则行业内的恶性竞争才是始作俑者。仔细分析近期发生的一些学术论文数字版权纠纷案例，由同一律师事务所代理、针对同一公司聚集1 000 余名不同专业、不同地域的论文作者，在事先不进行任何沟通和协商的情况下，直接向法院提起著作权侵权诉讼的做法折射出复杂的行业竞争生态[7]。如同方知网不仅屡屡被众多学术专家联名状告侵犯版权，而且与业内同行之间也素来不睦，相继与重庆维普、书生网都有官司事件。在网络原创文学版权争夺方面，拉拢作者争夺版权的纠纷不胜枚举。如书生电子起诉盛大文学案就是比较突出的代表。在这场版权纠纷中，盛大文学就书生读吧续写《星辰变》一事提出质疑，并发送律师函要求对方取消侵权；书生则认为《星辰变后传》是独立创作的作品，并不存在侵权问题[8]。双方针锋相对，互指对方非法竞争，展开了一场数字版权争斗。

3 数字出版企业的版权转机——以版权为核心的商业发展战略

版权危机频发给数字出版企业的发展造成了严重困扰。这种危机的产生有着宏观上国家版权战略缺失的原因，微观上更在于数字出版企业自身没有能够突出版权的战略地位。因此，应对版权危机，数字出版企业应首先从自身出发寻求转机。从数字出版本质特征和发展前景来看，数字出版企业必须制定以版权为核心的商业发展战略，从而在版权领域化被动为主动。笔者认为，这种以版权为核心的数字出版企业商业发展战略的核心在于突出版权保护意识、强调版权运营理念和重视版权人才的培养，因而能够避免侵权频发，减少企业之间在业务和人才等方面的恶性竞争。具体来讲，版权战略的建立，将使数字出版企业发生一系列积极的变化。

3.1 版权保护意识——从相对淡漠走向绝对重视

数字出版企业版权保护意识的突出体现，不仅仅是指在版权接入时要强调合法性，更在于要在整个出版过程中实现版权活动的全局性、宏观性和长远性。

突出的版权保护意识，将促使企业在版权接入时强调绝对的合法性。版权保护的目的在于鼓励文化的创造与传播，这种目的正是通过维护创作者、传播者、使用者三者利益的平衡来实现的[9]。出版工作是对版权内容进行创造性传播，版权法对数字出版企业的权利是以邻接权的形式加以保护的。因此我们在开展出版工作时一定要尊重原著作权人的权益，明确版权是数字出版产业得以生存和发展的基础，尊重与保护版权是数字出版业必须具备的法制意识。数字出版企业一定要明确应在尊重作者权利的前提下获得合法授权，也就是要确保版权接入的绝对合法性。

突出的版权保护意识，将使企业在整个出版过程都会重视版权产品的安全性。版权接入的合法确保了企业对版权产品的开发权利，也为数字出版企业在整个出版过程中对版权产品实行全方位的版权保护提供了法律基础。这种全方位的版权保护，既体现对数字出版产品的版权技术管理，如对版权产品附加时间戳（Digital Time Stamp）、防复制设备（anti-copy Devices）、数字水印等技术措施，更体现在企业有着完善的版权保护应对机制，当产生版权纠纷时相应的程序就会启动。这种对版权产品的整体保护，能够有效地从技术和机制两方面打击盗版，既维护了作者的合法权益，更为企业权益最大化提供了保障。

3.2 版权运营理念——从单纯竞争为主走向竞争与合作并重

如果说版权保护意识是数字出版企业的生存基础，那么版权运营理念就是数字出版企业做大做强的核心动力。版权运营是指将版权作为一种经营资本，对其所进行的筹划、开发、管理和交易等活动，核心思想就是要使版权效益实现最大化。数字出版产业的发展离不开版权保护，而产业的深入发展又为版权提出了新的要求，那就是版权不能止于保护，更需要经营。这是版权经济功能的重要层面，也是我国数字出版产业未来发展的重要增长点。因此，以版权为核心的商业发展战略，要求现代数字出版企业不仅要有版权保护意识，更要具有版权运营理念。

就数字出版企业而言，强调版权运营理念不仅体现在版权接入后进行的版权多元化开发，更重要的是在版权领域建立从单纯以竞争为主走向竞争与合作并重的发展模式。版权的多元化开发使得单个版权产品效益最大化，而版权领域竞争与合作并重的发展模式则使数字出版企业避免恶性竞争从而实现良性的快速发展。版权领域的合作是传统出版与数字出版共同的愿望。对于传统出版而言，随着数字出版业的飞速发展，国内传统出版商开始涉足数字出版领域，但由于经验、技术等原因使得发展并不顺利，因而产生了与成功数字出版企业进行版权合作的需求。而数字出版商由于受国内出版管理制度的限制，正苦于无法自由地出版体现自己编辑意图的纸质图书，因而也有着与传统出版业在版权领域开展深度合作的愿望。就数字出版企业内部来说，目前版权领域的恶性竞争严重阻碍了整个数字出版产业的发展，因此，必须强调竞争与合作并重的版权运营理念，改变当前数字版权领域混乱的竞争格局。

3.3 版权人才储备——从单纯拉拢作者到建立版权人才培养机构

出版企业发展的核心竞争力是人才，数字出版企业这种趋势更为突出，而以版权为核心的商业发展战略要求数字出版企业一定要重视版权人才的培养。因此要建立研究与开发机构，培养和储备优秀版权人才。

作为数字出版企业发展动力的版权人才，既包括创造数字出版产品内容的作者，同样也包括那些发现作者并维护作者权益的版权经理人。因此，数字出版企业的版权人才研发机构的主要工作目标就是建立优秀版权经理人队伍、培养优秀作者队伍并主动寻找潜在的数字出版内容资源。从战略上看，优秀版权经理人队伍的建立是数字出版企业版权人才战略实现的重要前提。因为，优秀的版权经理队伍既能有意识地培养作者，也会主动地去寻找符合企业发展目标的潜在版权资源。更重要的是，这个队伍能够在与作者的交流中具有绝对尊重作者的版权思维，无论是版权接入还是产品运作后期的版权服务，都能在作者和数字出版企业间建立充分信任的桥梁。从而为企业的发展提供稳定且不断发展壮大的内容资源，避免因急功近利而拉拢作者引发的企业纠纷。

就版权经理人队伍建设的方式而言，应该采用引进与培养并重的模式。一些实力比较雄厚的数字出版企业可以聘请资深版权经理人开展版权业务，这种引进人才的方式虽然见效比较快，但也存在着合适对象难寻、引进者忠诚度不高等问题。所以数字出版企业更应从长远考虑，从青年编辑中培养版权人才，选拔优秀人员到国外进修，这样使人才得到锻炼，并且在开展版权贸易工作过程中随着对本企业的了解，个人对企业的认同感和忠诚度将极大加强。此外，数字出版企业应主动和开设编辑出版专业的院校联系，形成合作关系，不仅能实现产学研的互动，更重要的是为企业的战略发展提供了充足的版权人才后备力量。

注释

[1] 张凤莎. 同方知网再遭侵权诉讼 ［N］. 科技日报，2008-09-23

[2] 马涛. 百名博士硕士状告同方知网侵权 ［N］. 科技日报，2008-12-01

[3] 陆学涛. 方正数字图书馆惹侵权官司版权争议成焦点 ［N］. 中华工商时报，2006-05-17

[4] 中国标准出版社与北京世纪超星信息技术发展有限责任公司侵犯著作权纠纷案 ［OL］. 北京市海淀区人民法院民事判决书，（2007）海民初字第8274号，http://www.110.com/panli/panli_88699.html

[5] 童之磊. 数字出版与版权保护 ［OL］. 人民网，2007-07-16，http://media.people.com.cn/GB/22114/79563/88707/5992730.html

[6] 辛苑薇. 网络文学盗版流失40亿盛大诉谷歌求解 ［N］. 21世纪经济报道，2009-03-05

[7] 风杉. 版权纷争成信息业"心中之痛"［N］. 中国商报，2008-11-25

[8] 任殿顺. "盛大文学" VS "书生读吧" 版权纠纷 ［OL］. 数字出版在线，http://www.epuber.com/? p=2693

[9] 王志刚. 纸质版权与数字版权相分离的成因、影响及对策研究 ［J］. 中国编辑，2009（3）

作者简介

王志刚，武汉大学信息管理学院2008级博士生，河南大学新闻与传播学院讲师。

数字时代版权代理发展对策浅析

冯广涛

（武汉大学信息管理学院　武汉　430072）

摘要：当前，随着计算机多媒体技术和网络通信技术的发展，图书出版正进入数字化时代，数字出版将成为出版业的主要业务形态。图书版权贸易领域也发生着深刻的变化，如主体、客体和法律设施等因素的变化，这些变化正对作为图书版权贸易主要环节的图书版权代理的发展提出新的挑战。面对新问题和新情况，传统出版时代的版权代理已不能适应图书贸易的需要。本文通过研究此形势下版权代理新变化的成因和主客观因素，为版权代理的发展提出新对策，希望促进版权代理的发展壮大，能有效地指导图书版权贸易的顺利实现，为图书出版行业发展奠定坚实的基础。

关键词：数字时代　版权代理　版权贸易

The Methods to Copyright Agent in the Digital Era

Feng Guangtao

（School of Information Management，Wuhan University，Wuhan，430072）

Abstract：With the rapid development of computer multimedia technology and network communication technology，book industry is entering digital era．Digital publishing will turn into the major business form of book industry．Library copyright trade field will also have profound changes，such as the change of subject，the change of object and the change of law．These changes will cause the challenges to the development of copyright agent which is the main link of library copyright trade．Face to the new problems and the new situation，it is meaningful to research the origins of these changes，and the subjective and objective factors．The aim of this article is to propose new methods to develop copyright agent，and give effective directions to library copyright trade．

Keywords：Digital era　Copyright agent　Copyright trade

改革开放以来，我国的出版业取得了飞速的发展，图书品种和图书销售总额实现连年增长。然而，著作者与出版社之间的利益矛盾始终没有消失，并因时因地对出版业的发展造成了或大或小的阻碍。出版经纪人作为著作者与出版社之间的利益协调者和润滑剂，其存在和发展对于出版业的健康、快速发展起着十分重要的作用。版权代理作为版权贸易发展的产物由此兴起。版权代理是指作者或其他著作权人，将自己享有著作权的作品委托给一个代理人或一个代理机构，由代理人或代理机构代替自己行使相关权利。版权代理是出版和版权贸易活动的重要环节，尤其是开展国际版权贸易的桥梁和纽带。通过版权代理，出版社和作者之间不仅避免了很多不必要的误会或纠纷，也节省了很多的时间和精力，可以顺畅地完成版权的转让或许可的交易。

图书出版发展到数字化时代，许多高新技术应用于出版领域，如电子投稿、编辑软件的应用、印刷的自动化、出版内容的数字化以及版权交易的网络化，这使得图书出版形式发生了前所未有的变化。出版内容新的表现形式和传播方式需要新的保护技术和配套措施，其数字过程也需要新的技术规范，这就给版权代理机制的大发展带来了新的问题和挑战。

1　数字出版时代版权代理的新问题

1.1　出版内容版权保护的难度加大，造成版权代理运作的难度随之加大

其一，由于数字出版具有网络化、全球化、开放性和即时性等特点，当出版内容以网络为中介进行在线传播时，必然会跨越国界实现全球性的传播，这就使得版权的保护工作面临巨大困难。在版权的跨国界交易难以实现之时，国际的版权代理自然无从谈起。其二就是盗版现象的猖獗。在网上检索和阅读数字内容资源时就会发现，我们可以轻易地看到许多畅销图书的电子版在网络上传播，而这些电子版有相当一部分是一些个人或网站在没有获得版权的情况下擅自制作的。由于数字版权的正当利益难以得到保障，著作权人多不愿意将作品数字化，更不愿将版权交给代理公司进行交易。其三，在数字环境下，随着复制和传播技术水平的不断提高，复制和传播所需的成本不断降低，然而版权作品的价格却没有随之降低，这不可避免地造成版权侵权现象的发生。版权供给与需求双方的利益矛盾造成版权交易的难以实现，版权代理也难以运作。

1.2　版权交易主体市场运作能力不成熟、信用缺失，制约版权代理的发展

版权交易主体是版权市场的重要组成部分，版权市场的交易主体应包括出版社、作者、版权代理机构三个部分。我国 1992 年正式加入《伯尔尼公约》和《世界版权公约》，并开始真正参与国际版权贸易，而对于数字版权贸易的工作进展缓慢，出版企业对于引进和输出数字版权的热情不高，从业人员对数字出版缺乏研究和认识，这使得出版企业的市场运作能力很低。当出版业真正进入数字化时代时，出版企业不仅会缺乏数字版权市场的竞争力，连本身的市场生存都是问题。这也相应地压缩了版权代理机构生存的空间。另外，作者与出版机构间不能明确地授权，出版机构与版权代理之间缺乏信任，经常违约，造成版权代理耗时长、成效低，给以诚信为基础的版权代理业带来很大损害，也直接影响中国出版界的版权贸易信誉和国际影响。

1.3　版权交易客体的缺乏，制约版权代理的发展

版权交易客体是指版权人所拥有的作品中的经济权利，也就是用来作为商品进行交易的知识产权。[1]开展版权贸易的目的就是要获得这种对作品进行复制、翻译等的经济权利，所以这种经济权利作为交易客体，是版权市场不可或缺的重要组成部分。目前我国版权交易客体的缺乏主要表现为符合国际市场需求的版权客体品种少、数量有限，在版权贸易上逆差严重，即版权引进远远大于版权输出，从而造成版权代理作用失衡，无法发挥正常的功能。根据新闻出版总署提供的关于 2007 年我国国际版权贸易的数据，我国引进的数字产品版权是 846 种，而输出的数字产品版权仅有 20 种。[2]造成这种情况的原因，一

是原创作品种类、数量和品质还没有达到国际市场的要求。二是因为目前国内对于著作权保护的执法力度不够，在整个社会并没有形成强烈的著作权权利意识和舆论环境，作者的数字版权极易遭到侵犯，这使得作者没有意愿实现自己版权的代理交易。

1.4 版权代理机构和版权代理人才严重缺乏，不能满足市场需求

对于传统出版社，每年出版上千种图书已经算是一个较大规模的出版机构，大可以依靠自己的力量实现版权交易，偶尔才会使用版权代理机构。而在数字化时代，数字出版企业对图书版权的需求量往往在数万乃至数十万种以上。如果 1 000 个传播者需要 100 万个著作权人的授权，哪怕每次洽谈所花费的成本（包括双方时间成本）只有区区 100 元，那社会就需要为此支付 1 000×100 万×100 元 = 1 000 亿元的交易成本。很多时候交易成本甚至比交易的版权费还高，因此，这样高昂的交易成本阻碍了大量交易的进行，使版权资源无法得到充分的应用。事实上，由于交易成本阻碍了交易的产生，国内的数字图书企业长期处于图书资源不足的状态。数量庞大的需求方与同样数量庞大的供给方之间迫切需要有沟通的桥梁，以实现集中的版权交易，避免单线交易带来的高昂交易成本，对版权代理机构的需求必然会膨胀增长。然而，目前国内只有 28 家正规版权代理机构，而且大部分人员短缺。中华版权代理公司是国家级的版权代理机构，其业务人员也不超过 8 人。上海版权代理公司的业务人员通常在 2 ~ 3 人，北京版权代理公司 12 人，算是规模最大的。[3] 有的版权代理公司甚至是有将无兵的"光杆司令"，而且人才流失现象严重。相对于全国 570 多家出版社、200 多家电子音像出版社、9 000 多家杂志出版单位和其他版权相关产业来看，中国版权贸易代理业的市场主体数量少，难以应对数字化时代每年海量的图书版权交易工作。

1.5 版权代理机构的发展受到现有体制的严重制约

版权代理机构的设立要国家版权行政机构和工商管理机构共同审查。实践表明，机制的不灵活已经严重阻碍了中国版权代理业的发展。现在市场上大多数国有版权代理机构是国有企业单位，都挂靠在地方新闻出版局或版权局，靠国家吃饭，主动性不强，效率过低，服务有待改善，不积极参与市场竞争，其不少业务属于政策性任务，由所在地出版行政部门调配业务和资源，这些版权代理机构实际上已成事业单位，一切依靠国家，少有生存危机。相对于国有版权代理公司的树大好乘凉，民营企业缺少政策资金支持，艰难地参与竞争，使很多有创造性的小版权代理公司存活不久，不能做大做强。这样的结果就是中国版权代理整体实力较弱，处于初级阶段。

2 数字时代版权代理的发展策略

2.1 通过立法和技术革新加强版权保护

国家应加强数字出版管理方面的立法，加强市场监管，严厉打击盗版、网上非法传播等侵权行为，为版权贸易提供一个健康、良序的市场环境，促进版权代理的发展。另外，国家要致力于具有数字知识产权保护功能的宽带网研究。目前基于 128 位编码技术的 IPv6 互联网协议具有强大的 ID 编码资源，就实现了数字版权保护从载体向内容加密和版权管理发展。[4] 国家在技术革新上要继续前进，如数据加密技术、数字水印技术及网上银行支付的信用保护技术等的改进和完善，加强数字版权管理，切实保护内容资源的版权利益。另外，在数字环境下，海量的信息在全球范围内自由流动，版权保护的地域性减弱，受国

际法保护的程度越来越高，国际条约成为版权国际保护的主要途径。国家要通过加入国际组织、缔结国际条约等形式与其他国家在版权保护领域开展交流与合作，积极保护版权的跨国交易。

2.2　实行版权代理人市场准入制度，加快信用体系建设

版权代理人才是版权贸易运作的基础，版权代理人才质量的好坏和数量的多寡直接关系到版权贸易的发展状况。国家版权局应设立"版权代理人资格认证制度"，统一对版权代理从业人员进行培训、管理，加快培养一批具有政治理论修养，有较好的外语水平，具备法律知识和公关交际能力和谈判能力，懂得市场经营的专业版权代理人才。面对网络时代的挑战，版权代理公司必须加速培养与知识经济相适应的、智力结构合理的版权贸易人才。高等教育机构也可设置相应专业，开设版权代理方面的课程，系统培养与市场需求相适应的高端版权代理人才，满足版权贸易工作的需要。

2.3　完善版权代理管理制度，鼓励集体授权和版权代理

数字环境下，网络被称为与传统媒体并列的"第四媒体"，海量的信息在网络上被广泛传播。我国版权法规定，以网络和全文数据库的方式出版、复制、发行、传播在著作权保护范围内的作品，必须取得出版单位和作者等有关著作权人的授权许可。在数字化时代，由于各类作品、作者数量巨大，且作者分布广泛，要求数字出版企业自身必须取得每一个著作权人的许可事实上不具有可操作性。著作权集体管理可以通过制度上的设置，将个别权利人的权利集合起来统一交给版权代理机构，以集中处理分散的权利人自身无法解决的问题。国家应努力完善版权代理管理制度，使著作权的集体管理和集体代理都能正常化、制度化和法律化，并按照市场运作方式进行，解决作者和出版机构的后顾之忧，为版权代理的发展提供良好的环境。

2.4　深化版权代理管理体制改革，调整版权代理的结构布局

国有版权代理机构应建立现代企业制度，并与主管行政单位脱钩，成为独立自负盈亏的市场主体，充分参与市场竞争。国家还应尽快出台相应法律法规，为民营版权代理机构的发展提供法律依据，放宽政策，鼓励民营资本成立版权代理公司，为其提供资金和税收方面的支持，壮大版权代理队伍，并规范对版权代理机构的市场管理和政策监管。在管理体制适应市场体制发展的情况下，版权代理机构才能实现健康、快速发展。同时，随着图书品种的急剧膨胀，市场对版权代理的需求也会快速增长，各地方的出版机构在出版规模上都有可能实现大的扩展，版权代理机构的分布也应随市场需求而有所调整，尽量实现地理分布上的平衡，不能在一个地方扎堆。

图书出版发展到数字化时代，网络传播将成为图书传播的主要方式之一，传播速度的迅捷化、传播范围的全球化和传播内容的多元化、规模化都对版权代理提出了新的要求。在发展的过程中，版权代理机构要依靠技术的进步和制度的革新，努力完善自身，应对数字出版时代的挑战。数字出版时代，版权交易的主客体都将出现大规模增长。由于可供交易的版权将是海量的，对版权代理的需求也将是巨大的，高的市场利润必将吸引众多优秀人才投身版权代理业，为版权代理注入新鲜血液。这将为版权代理的发展壮大提供前所未有的机遇。

新的时代孕育新的动力，市场经济需要市场制度与之匹配。可以预计，随着出版业进入数字时代，市场也将产生新的巨大推动力量，结果将是新闻出版行业体制改革的加快和

法律法规的逐渐完善，版权代理发展的障碍将一一消失，版权交易市场将越来越健康和规范，信用体系的建设将能很好地约束代理双方的行为，使其能够守法经营，良性运作。版权代理管理体制将更加健全，作者和出版商会乐于将版权业务交由版权代理机构代为管理和运作，自己则专司其职，集中力量发展主要业务。作者、出版社和版权代理机构良性分工协作的格局将最终得以形成，从而实现资源的节省。

在数字出版时代，图书出版业将实现前所未有的大发展，中国的版权贸易市场将是巨大的，世界版权贸易市场同样也是巨大的。市场需求的推动力是无限的，版权代理机构将迎来发展的高峰。版权代理人和版权代理机构应把握形势，培养和吸收人才，发展壮大自身力量，提高业务水平，抓住时代机遇，实现企业质的飞跃。版权交易市场必将成为文化产业领域一个大的亮点。版权代理行业也将成为新的朝阳产业。

注释

[1] 曾学民. 论版权市场的培育与版权代理的发展 [J]. 中国出版，2008（2）

[2] 新闻出版总署网站：http://www.gapp.gov.cn

[3] 姚德权，赵洁. 中国版权代理业的考量与发展 [J]. 编辑之友，2007（6）

[4] 王勤. 数字出版的十大趋势 [J]. 出版参考，2007（7）

参考文献

[1] 任凭. 经纪人及其管理 [M]. 上海：上海人民出版社，2004

[2] 肖学文主编. 经纪人与文化市场 [M]. 北京：经济管理出版社，1994

[3] 曾学民. 论版权市场的培育与版权代理的发展 [J]. 中国出版，2008（2）

[4] 姚德权，赵洁，中国版权代理业的考量与发展 [J]. 编辑之友，2007（6）

[5] 刘玲香. 英美国家的版权代理人 [J]. 出版参考，2002（22）

[6] 徐强平. 数字环境下版权保护的利益平衡 [J]. 大学出版，2005（1）

[7] 葛存山. 数字出版的概念和运作模式分析 [N]. 北京印刷学院学报，2008（5）

[8] 于永湛. 新技术与出版业的未来 [J]. 大学出版，2006（10）

作者简介

冯广涛，武汉大学信息管理学院出版发行系 2009 级硕士研究生。

细节决定编辑成败

黄秀琴

（海燕出版社　郑州　450002）

摘要：在我们的日常生活工作和学习中，细节的作用不可忽视。同样，在出版工作中，细节的作用显得尤其重要。一本图书在出版过程中，往往是一个细节注意不到，结果是全盘皆输。本文从细节小影响大，细节多莫忽略，重细节严把关等几个方面来分析细节在出版过程中的作用，同时也告诉出版同仁在多出书出好书的同时，一定要严把细节关，细节决定成败。

关键词：细节　出版

On the Importance of Details in Editing Work

Huang Xiuqin

（Swallow Press，Zhengzhou，450002）

Abstract：In our daily work and study, the importance of the details cannot be ignored. It's the same to the publishing industry where details play a more important role. In the process of publishing, if you ignore one detail, the whole book will be useless. This paper analyses the importance of details in publishing from two aspects：small details with big effects, don't ignore any details, special attention to details and strictly guarding. Mean while, it tells the colleagues of publishing that if they want to publish more and more popular books, the details must be valued. The attitude to details leads you to succeess or failuret.

Keywords：Detail　Publishing

《细节决定成败》、《细节决定命运》这类书前几年很流行。在管理学中，关于"细节"的书大多能成为热闹畅销书。在一些公关培训课上，特别强调对细节的处理，很多案例只为说明一个道理，可见细节的重要。管理无小事，忽视了一个细节，往往会导致整个系统运作的失效，造成严重的后果。得细节者得天下，对管理者如此，对编辑也是如此。

《IT 时代周刊》总编辑曹健在接受新浪网采访时说："我觉得所有的媒体，定位也好，做法也好，大同小异，关键是，谁能把这种定位这种理想做到极致，谁就能成功。大家最后拼的不是轰轰烈烈的新闻，在资讯发达的今天，谁想比别人哪怕多抢五秒钟的新闻都很难。因此，谁能够把内部的细节做得更好，更加符合读者的需求，谁就成功。而这种细节的做法就是持之以恒地去坚持把它做好。我一直强调细节，一定要把每一个细节做好，哪怕每一条线，我在《IT 时代周刊》上体现的是，每一条线，每一个标点符号和每一幅漫画、素描，你把它做细、做好，你就会成功。"

行业成就未必靠"大事"，信息时代"细节"决定成败。

1 细节小 影响大

1.1 细节可以提高读者的认可度

大作家小编辑，编辑就是为他人作嫁衣裳的。不仅要为稿件把好关，不出错误，还要为稿件润色，锦上添花。编辑注重稿子的标题改制、关键词的捕捉、规范编排包括文通字顺、标点符号正确使用，就是为了提高稿件的质量，增强读者对作品的认可度，对编辑的认可度，对出版社的信赖度。

1.2 细节可以提升品牌效应

认可的背后可能产生巨大的能量，那就是品牌效应。标题做得好，醒目传神，可以吸引读者的眼球，"逼迫"读者阅读。如果标题平淡如水或文题不符，读者的眼睛是不会光顾的。商品不能转化为效益，出版目的就不能达到。其他方面的细节也是这样的，导读的内容是稿件以外的，由编辑写成，是内容的概括，如果做得到位，可以帮忙，如果不到位，就是添乱。我觉得一个成熟的编辑都应该会写导读，一个初学编辑者应该先从写导读练起，写好了就可以从业，写不好要继续学习，直到熟练掌握。排版方面最起码不能参差不齐，文图不能相背离。

1.3 细节可以培养读者的忠诚度

"在工作中曾经遇到这样的插图：文字描绘的是在炎热的夏季里我们部队的活动，而插图里，我们的士兵还穿着厚厚的皮大衣，戴着皮帽子。炎热的夏季，我国不论什么地方都不会穿这样的衣服。仔细认真的编辑能够指出来，给予修正。我还遇到过将党旗印反、将佛的标志印成法西斯的标志等情况，都造成过不应有的事故。"（《期刊编辑工作漫议》，《中国编辑》，2003 年第 6 期）

细节对读者影响很大。有时，一个小细节可以导致读者对品牌的不利评价，甚而影响其对行业的看法，失去对品牌的信心，产生对整个行业的不满，久而久之，影响其对品牌的忠诚度。现在竞争非常激烈，忠诚度显得很重要，失去了才知道宝贵，再想培育，难度就大了。或提供的信息不完整，或者都是非常专业的术语，你能指望用户"点击"你的作品吗？标题如此，其他细节亦然。排版不好，文图乱配，导读乱写，不仅影响读者阅读作品的心情，更会导致其对品牌的负面评价，哪还有忠诚度可言呢？

2 细节多 莫忽视

"书稿是成功出版的灵魂"。儿童画家也是编辑的蔡皋在《我读松居直先生》一文中说："这全因感觉到图画书这种东西编辑的作用太重要。一本好图画书往往是作者与编辑成功合作的结果，只不过作者登台表演而编辑如导演侧身其后罢了。"编辑虽在幕后，但不能忽视细节。比如我在编辑一本书的过程中就遇到了这样一个问题：这是一本引进版图书，有一家社在我们之前引进了这本书的平装版，我们引进的是精装版。在编辑的过程中，我非常注意细节的把握，一一对照原文，发现了平装版的一个大错误，原版书中有一个篇名是 Ole Luköie，应该译成《梦神》，可在那本书中却错译成《守塔人奥列》结果是文图不符，其实这就是风马牛不相及的两篇文章。可见编辑在细节的处理上是多么重要。

2.1　内容上的细节把握

选题策划上的细节把握。蔡皋说："不仅想与作家对话，还想进一步了解编辑者的秘密，而最关紧要的秘密是想知道编辑者的人文追求，我觉得它是图画书的灵魂。没有灵魂（或曰精神）到场的图画书，无论形式如何华美，是不能令读者感动的，是不能算作'作品'的。"

新华社的一位前辈说过，作为编辑，你首先要是读者，其次才是编辑，你自己都不会过于关注不喜欢的东西，你如何能期望一般的读者去关注去喜欢呢？"挖到篮里就是菜"的做法已经 OUT 了，不管读者喜欢不喜欢，愿意不愿意读，编辑闭门造车，脱离市场，结果可想而知。

编辑在选题策划时，要有人文关怀。在少儿选题方面，尤其如此。编辑的理想、价值、人格、审美等，都要体现编辑的人文思想。思想正确，导向正确是组稿的前提，编辑要善于发现有才华的作者，有价值的作品，然后深入研究市场，根据市场进行策划。

2.2　品牌打造中的细节把握

品牌制胜，有了品牌，商品（图书）就进入良性循环，出版队伍会越来越壮大，出版社的实力会越来越雄厚。编辑应该以出版品牌为导向进行图书策划。

有研究者指出，图书策划有三大重要内容：（1）策划能创造具有品牌价值的个别图书；（2）策划能创造具有品牌价值的系列图书；（3）由所有具有品牌价值的图书形成出版品牌。零敲碎打是成不了气候的。就像革命的早期，只有开辟了根据地，巩固了根据地才能壮大队伍，形成燎原之势。要想形成有鲜明特色的品牌，就要进行图书策划，这是后续活动的基础。品牌图书多了，就形成出版品牌，树大招风，声名远播。

在策划的过程中，不仅要有自己独特的人文精神，而且要对市场进行深入考察，寻求精神和经济的切合点，去伪存真，去粗取精，进行包装设计，形成品牌。

2.3　形式上的细节把握

这方面的内容很多，只能举例说明。

一是校目录，看目录和内容是否相符；二是看导读，在内文中能不能找到；三看标题，和内容是否相符，有没有错字，转行有没有问题；四看序号有没有错误；五看文图是否相对，图上有没有错字，色彩有没有问题，有没有反季节的情况出现；其他还有作者、出版社、版权页等，都要认真看。

编辑是第一个校对，比专职校对还重要，因为编辑最熟悉情况。在送印之前，还要仔细核对图书的边边角角，图书成批装订前，再对样书进行检查。

2.4　其他细节的把握

有个老编辑说，编辑要和发行部门多沟通，不用的书稿快退，新书出来后第一时间送给作者，责任编辑不要忘记写书评等。这些都不是大事，都不难办，甚至是举手之劳，但不拘细节的编辑往往会忽略这些事情。

旧书新做的细节把握。旧书新做有两种情况：一种是做过的图书，有不尽如人意的地方，重新再做。二是图书卖得很好，供不应求，需要"补仓"。不管是哪种情况，既然重做了，就不要简单地新瓶装旧酒，仍然要像做新书一样用心地去做。

除了不合适的地方需要改正外，由于时过境迁，很多东西都变了，如果不能与时俱进，就会落伍，就会被动。新书新面貌，新包装，突出一个"新"字。

3　重细节　严把关

3.1　低调做人、高调做事

一位前辈说过，作为编辑，不要求你什么都精，却必须要什么都懂，简言之，编辑不是专家，而是杂家。低调做人，高调做事。不要认为自己是编辑高高在上，别人的话听不进去，大事做不来，小事又不做。编辑是诸多行业中的一种，也需要学习充电，关怀他人。位置摆正了，工作就好做了。

3.2　艺多不压身、艺高人胆大

编辑用心了，稿件的问题就会大大减少。

编辑是人不是神，每个人都有软肋，每个人的知识都有短板。作为编辑，不知道在工作的时候，会碰到什么样的稿子，即使是博士编辑，在同一专业中，也有不懂的地方。所以，编辑要不断地取长补短，三人行则必有我师焉，每个人都有长处，编辑应该成为杂家，不求什么都精通，但要什么都懂一些，这就要不断向别人学习，博学多思，不耻下问，时间长了就会成为通才。

读万卷书，行万里路。编辑要常去书店逛逛，看有什么新书可以借鉴，什么流行，排行榜有什么变化，读者群有什么变化，这些对编辑的工作都是有帮助的。人的记性总是有限的，工具书可以弥补人脑的不足，使用工具书，勤用工具书，显得很重要。

3.3　一夫当关、万夫莫开

编辑知识过硬，就会及时地查漏补缺，让错误无处藏身。

编辑要切实负起责来，不轻易相信作者，也不寄希望于校对，守土有责，争取在自己的工作范围里，把错误全扫光，把潜在的危险降到最低。

不轻易相信"名人"。这年头，"名人"满天飞，假名人伪名人到处都是，相信他们，只会招致错误的增加。即使是真名人，也不要完全相信，名人也有犯错误的时候。

作者简介

黄秀琴，海燕出版社策划编辑。

数字出版创新模式

饶　瑶

（武汉大学新闻与传播学院　武汉　430072）

摘要：目前我国数字出版业在快速发展的同时，也面临着版权未得到有效保护、商业模式尚不成熟、技术提供商与内容供应方之间利益分配失衡等诸多问题。我国数字出版业主要是由技术提供商推动，数字出版业作为以内容为核心的产业，内容供应方未能占据主导地位，对我国数字出版业的健康良性发展会产生不利影响。而牟利性的数字盗版和非牟利性的再传播等侵权行为也给我国数字出版业版权保护提出了难题。对此，本文试图从收费模式、经营模式、利益分配模式三个方面提出新的解决思路。创新收费模式方面，可以改进计费标准、提供在线阅读按次付费计价方式等；创新经营模式方面，可以开展互动性的内容创造、个性化的定制服务等；创新利益分配模式方面，可以考虑建立内容供应方联盟等措施。

关键词：数字出版　收费模式　经营模式　利益分配

The Innovation Patterns of Digital Publishing

Rao Yao

（Journalism and Communication School, Wuhan University, Wuhan, 430072）

Abstract: At present, China's digital publishing industry is developing fast. Meanwhile, it is also facing a lot of problems, such as lacking of effective copyright protection, immature business models, and imbalanced profit distribution between technology providers and content providers. China's digital publishing industry is dominated by technology providers rather than content providers, which is harmful to its healthy development. Both digital counterfeit and private copy raise difficulties to China's digital copyright protection. This paper attempts to put forward some new solutions from three perspectives of charge method, business model and profit distribution model. This paper suggests that we can improve charging method through modifying billing standards and providing pay-per-view pricing method, business model through interactive content creation and personalized custom services and profit distribution model through forming the syndicate of content providers.

Keywords: Digital publishing　Charge method　Business model　Profit distribution

随着互联网的迅猛发展，我国数字出版业也在快速成长，并已成为我国几大新兴产业之一。2010 年年初，新闻出版总署公布的数据显示，2009 年我国新闻出版业总产值突破1 万亿元，其中数字出版产业总产值超过 750 亿元，同比增长 42%，其发展速度远远超过传统出版业的增长水平。在大好前景的吸引下，技术提供商、内容供应商等纷纷进军数字出版业。

不过，目前我国数字出版业主要是由技术提供商推动，传统出版商多采取观望态度。由于数字出版对技术的要求，已涉足数字出版的传统出版商多是将手中已有的内容资源的数字版权卖给技术提供商，而未能在数字出版产业链中占据主导地位，从而在利益分配上受到牵制。目前我国数字出版业的利益分配格局为：技术提供商获得超过半数以上的利润额，而内容供应商还要从剩下的利润中抽出一部分支付给著作权人。数字出版业虽然传播形式不同于传统出版业，但仍然是以内容为核心的产业，这种失衡的利益分配格局会对数字出版业的良性发展产生不利影响。此外，目前也有部分传统出版商尝试自主经营数字出版业务，如部分期刊推出网络版。但不论是传统出版商与技术提供商合作，还是各自独自摸索，都面临着商业模式不成熟的发展瓶颈。

我国数字出版业面对的另一个重大课题是如何有效保护版权。一方面，一些网络运营商在没有从传统出版商和著作权人那里取得合法的数字版权与网络传播权的情况下，擅自利用这些内容进行数字出版从中牟利，严重侵害了传统出版商和著作权人的利益；另一方面，一些用户将自己获得的数字出版物公开上传至网络上供其他用户免费下载，或是发送给好友进行分享，这些再传播行为也给出版商和著作权人造成了不小的经济损失。而目前我国数字出版法律法规建设相对滞后，加上打击数字盗版、侵权行为的难度和成本较大，我国数字出版业的版权保护现状堪忧。

对于我国数字出版业面临的上述种种问题，可尝试从收费模式、经营模式、利益分配模式三个方面的创新中找到一些解决之道。

1 创新收费模式

目前我国数字出版业应对不经授权私自进行数字盗版牟利行为及用户再传播的侵权行为的主要措施是法律维权和开发应用，诸如方正阿帕比数字版权保护系统（Apabi DRM）等网络阅读防盗拷技术。事实上，在诉诸法律和应用防盗技术的基础上，可以尝试通过创新收费模式，更好地保护版权、减少出版商及著作权人的损失，并且还能带来诸多好处。现列举如下几种以供参考。

1.1 将潜在的再传播带来的损失计入收费额

数字出版物的成本包括版权费用、制作编辑费用、技术运营费用等，其计价自然是按成本加上预期利润确定的。与传统出版相比，数字出版由于省去了印刷、纸张油墨等制作成本和库存与运输成本，价格十分低廉。故可以考虑在现有价格基础上，利用相关机构的有效数据，将潜在的再传播带来的损失适当计入收费额。由于原本定价就很低，在新的定价方式中部分计入此类潜在损失，价格的升幅不会太大，从而不会对用户的消费感受产生过大影响。借助网络的海量浏览量，这种价格的微调所带来的利润增幅相当可观，可以对数字出版物售后可能发生的再传播行为造成的损失进行一定的预先补偿。

1.2 提供按次付费方式

针对数字出版物，除提供下载阅读按本计费外，还可提供在线阅读按次计费的付费方式。为确保用户利益、防止不必要的重复计费，网络运营商可设置页面阅读时长，用户在线阅读超过页面阅读时长时该页面即隐藏或被广告遮蔽；用户在未超过阅读时长情况下不慎关闭页面，可通过付费时获得的 ID 号或验证码登录，继续阅读直至时间耗尽。由于反复阅读均要计费，按次收费每次费用的定价必须明显低于按本收费，才能令用户接受。

这种收费方式的好处在于：对于有着只看一遍、之后不会重看已阅内容这种阅读习惯的用户，选择按次收费可省下很多购买成本和存储空间；而对于数字出版商而言，用户选择此种收费方式会降低其购买阅读后将电子出版物免费传阅的可能性，从而确保了出版商获得应有的收入，减少了潜在的再传播损失。

1.3 网上阅读适当收费

目前很多网络读物都是采取网上阅读免费，通过发行该内容的纸质出版物来获取赢利，较为典型的是期刊和网络原创作品。

目前很多期刊都拥有自己的网站，并将内容数字化，放到网站上供学习浏览。但此类期刊多存在数字出版严重滞后于传统出版的问题，且数字出版免费、单纯依靠传统出版赢利、数字出版附属于传统出版。事实上，数字出版相较于传统出版，实时、快捷是其最为显著的优点之一。因此，这些期刊杂志完全可以进行转型，实时更新推出数字出版物，以满足对时效性要求较高的读者的需求。由于传统出版物存在刊印、发行等环节，数字出版物必然先于传统出版物问世，出版商完全可以对数字出版物进行适当收费，摆脱目前单纯依靠传统出版赢利的局面，实现多重赢利。

除上述期刊外，很多网络读物也都采取免费在线阅读，来检验读者反响或是为已面市的传统出版物进行宣传推广。这些网络读物大可尝试采取试读免费、全文阅读收费的计费方式。对于试探市场、尚未推出传统出版物的网络原创作品，等到浏览量稳定在较大数值、反响较好时，即可采取后期阅读收费的措施。在作品全部完成后，将其制作成精美的数字出版物进行售卖，由于数字出版物可包含多媒体展现方式，不会与该作品的传统出版形式雷同，故减少了对随后推出的传统出版物的冲击，并且在创收的同时为用户提供了增值享受，可谓一举多得。

2 创新经营模式

我国数字出版业在规模迅速发展的同时，也面临着赢利模式尚不成熟的问题，主要表现为：在数字化过程中仅仅是将原有的内容简单地转化，没有进行深度开发。对此，本文从内容创造、定制服务、营销推广、关联销售等方面提出了一些创新经营模式。

2.1 互动性的内容创造

数字出版可以利用互动性的优点，在内容创造时，征询用户的意见和建议。例如，将文本的框架和梗概发布出来供试读，并根据反馈意见进行修改完善。为保证反馈机制的有效运行，数字出版机构可设置相关的激励机制，如对有效意见的提出者给予阅读购买费用优惠、会员积分、邀请试读其他新作品等奖励。同时，这些激励措施也是非常好的营销推广手段。

另外，数字出版机构除充分利用传统出版拥有的内容资源外，还应从网络上大力挖掘内容资源，例如，可根据反响较好的网络文本作品生产诸如网络游戏等其他形式的数字出版产品。数字出版机构还应努力开发利用网络用户的创造力，可尝试根据用户提出的构思进行创作，或是发展一批创造力较强、网络人气较高的用户进行网络内容资源的生产创作。

2.2 个性化的定制服务

数字出版机构可以根据用户的要求，为其提供个性化的定制服务。例如，用户可自由选择篇目和章节，组合成自己需要的出版物进行购买。数字出版机构可以对用户信息进行智能化管理，保存用户的检索历史，为用户提供即时电子通告服务，并可以根据用户信息及用户面对的实际问题，对现有信息或产品进行加工处理，为用户提供更有针对性的产品和服务。对于公司客户，数字出版机构可以利用自身优势，与公司办公自动化系统无缝对接，还可为公司提供数字内容商务计划与战略等更为专业的服务。

2.3 积极主动的营销推广

对于学术期刊的数字出版而言，除了前面所述的严重时滞、常常沦为传统出版形式的简单数字化外，目前国内已有部分学术期刊在尝试推出独立的网络版，这种尝试十分有益，但是却苦于得不到相关机构的评级认可，因此在学者和科研机构中的影响力非常小，难以获得较高质量和较大规模的投稿，处境较为尴尬。对此，学术期刊网络版的编辑应积极展开营销推广，主动与国内外较知名学者联系约稿；多参与学术研讨会、学术论坛，与学术人员、科研机构零距离接触交流，扩大影响力。只有通过积极主动的推销，才能够打破目前学术期刊网络版面临的稿源少、质量差和社会认可度低的僵局。

而对于非学术性的数字出版业务，数字出版机构可通过举办网络作品征集比赛等活动进行营销宣传，这样既有助于提升自身名气和影响力，还能够以较低的成本获得大量内容资源。

2.4 努力提升关联销售

关联销售是指向客户推荐其所购买产品的附加产品或关联产品。努力发展关联销售，有助于发掘客户的潜在需求，带动整体销售额。因此，数字出版机构应重视关联销售，在各产品推介销售页面上，巧妙地链接其附加产品或关联产品的推荐信息，以刺激用户购买欲望。以电子书籍为例，其附加产品包括配套数字音像制品、辅助性或延伸性读物，关联产品包括该作者其他作品、同类题材其他作者作品等，这些都可以向有意购买该电子书籍的用户进行有效推荐，促进销售。

3 创新利益分配模式

内容供应方缺乏技术，技术提供商缺乏内容资源，且内容供应方在利益分配格局中处于弱势，使得出版机构对数字化热情不高，这是我国数字出版业亟须解决的又一大难题。因此，有必要对目前的利益分配模式进行创新，确保数字出版各方利益得到合理满足。

由于数字出版业仍是以内容为核心的产业，故在利益分配时，应重视确保内容供应方即出版商和著作权人的利益。在此基础上，要同时将技术提供商的技术价值、品牌效应和营销举措对销售额的贡献考虑进去。要打破目前技术提供商占有过半利润的失衡局面，可采取以下措施：一是可以考虑通过政策引导来实现；二是内容供应方可结成联盟以提高议价能力，在技术条件成熟的情况下，内容供应方联盟甚至可以考虑不通过手技术供应商，自行发展数字出版业务。惟其如此，才能让我国数字出版业真正实现以"内容"为主导的合理结构。

4 小结

数字出版已成为出版业发展的必然趋势，并在国内呈现出迅猛的发展势头。对我国数字出版未来的发展走向及仍然存在的问题，业界和学界展开了热烈的讨论，提出了很多宝贵的经验和见解，为今后我国数字出版业的可持续发展进行了不懈的理论研究和实践摸索。相信我国数字出版业在时代驱使和各方努力下，会尽快进入更加成熟、更加健全的发展阶段。

参考文献

[1] 吴娜. 2009：数字出版加速发展 [N]. 光明日报，2010-02-28

[2] 刘灿姣，姚娟，刘治. 对数字出版新的商业模式的探讨 [J]. 出版发行研究，2009（9）：65

[3] 吴江文. 2009 年数字出版研究综述 [J]. 中国出版，2010（3）：37

作者简介

饶瑶，武汉大学新闻与传播学院 2009 级硕士研究生。

出版社数字化转型

传统出版社数字化环境分析与应用研究

叶姗姗

（武汉大学信息管理学院　武汉　430072）

摘要：技术是出版行业得以存在和发展的主要因素之一，在数字化的背景下，出版物的载体、形制、内容以及出版社的营销手段等都在发生巨大的变化。众多现象表明，"出版革命"的趋势是传统出版社向数字化出版社方向发展，在这次变革浪潮中，传统出版社的命运将会各自不同，决胜的关键在于谁更好地利用数字化技术以及将网络平台的商业价值与自身相连。本文尝试基于出版内容、载体、编辑过程、营销等四个方面分析传统出版社的数字化进程并结合实证分析，其中在营销数字化方面，从终端和网络社区等数字化平台出发，对传统出版社的数字化应用效果开展定性研究，试图建构合理有效的出版社数字化商业模式。

关键词：数字化　互联网　出版社

Digitalization of Traditional Publishing House: Environment and Application

Ye Shanshan

（School of Information Management，Wuhan University，Wuhan，430072）

Abstract：Technology is one of the main ingredients for the survival and development of publishing industry. Digitalization has witnessed great changes in the carrier，formation and contents of publication and the marketing methods of press. Many phenomena indicate that the trend of publishing revolution is to transfer from the traditional press to the digital one. In this transformation wave，the key point of the various destiny for the traditional press depends on the application of the digital technology and the attachment to the business value of the website. This article aiming to analyze empirically the digital process of the traditional press based on four aspects involving publishing contents，carrier，editing process and marketing. Therein，on the aspect of digital marketing，the author implements qualitative study on effect of the digital application of traditional press from the perspective of the terminal and SNS，trying to set up an effective digital business model of the press.

Keywords：Digitalization　Internet　Publishing house

从雕版印刷到铅排版再到电子排版，技术对出版行业的影响是深远的，现在已经进入以网络技术为核心的数字化信息时代，我们的出版业也随之开始了新的发展。但从现在情况来看，出版数字化大战中活跃度高的依然是技术提供商和移动运营商，传统出版社存在被边缘化的可能。本文将围绕传统出版社在数字化浪潮中的表现，研究数字化进程中出版内容、载体、编辑和营销的数字化。

1 内容的数字化

从宏观上看，传统出版社最大的优势在于多年积累下来的宝贵内容资源，即作者资源、选题资源和书号资源。但是在数字化进程中，这一优势也在慢慢消失，草根写手甚至是知名作家通过起点中文网、晋江原创文学网等一些在线文学网站可以免费或者收费的方式发布更新自己的作品；在出版市场，同样也活跃着一批个体的出版策划人，他们在庞大的网络信息中寻找适合的选题资源，并将这些有用资源最优化整合，发展前期主要是采用和传统出版社合作的方式，负责组织选题、编辑和分销环节，出版社负责审批和审读加工。通过这种方式民营出版策划人获得了发展，但是由于数字出版浪潮的兴起，潜在的商机和价值链能快速形成的特质，大批的出版策划人可能很容易转向和互联网、IT公司这些数字出版技术提供商合作。如果出版社依然在内容资源方面不走数字化之路，那么未来非常有可能因为以上原因被边缘化，失去应有的话语权。如何优化传统出版内容的数字化，高等教育出版社、作家出版社、中国出版集团等都进行了有效行动。

1.1 建立内容数据库，提供专业化在线服务

网络带来国民阅读习惯的改变，国民阅读率持续降低，网络阅读率大幅度上升。适应读者阅读倾向的变化，是占据读者市场的重要因素。将传统内容数字化，采用不同技术格式实现数字化出版内容的多样性，能够满足不同读者的阅读需求并挖掘部分潜在市场。

作为教育出版数字化建设的领军人物，高等教育出版社不断提出新的数字化建设理念并积极付之于实践，其中立体化教材和教学内容立体化的建设深受教育界人士的好评，这两者都是立足于内容资源建立的数字化服务体系，改变了传统教材和教学内容存在的形式单一、内容更新不及时和互动性不强等方面，真正以读者为中心，逐步完善依靠网络建立的全方位立体化的教学和学习环境。

1.2 拓展传统内容产品线，深度挖掘内容资源

传统出版社的核心竞争力是知识内容的生产，因此对内容进行深挖和拓展是传统出版社获得发展壮大的重要因素。易文网在这一方面做得很成功，这一网站的运营商是上海数字世纪网络有限公司，由上海世纪出版集团、上海新汇光盘有限公司和上海联合投资有限公司三方投资所建，易文网从开始运营发展到现在，已经成为中国知名度较高的专业出版门户网站并实现了赢利，网站包括图书、音像、期刊、书城、教育、听书、原创、电子书、工具书在线、历史、批发、声像、连载、印客等多个业务版块，其中原创、听书、电子书和印客版块是对内容深挖和拓展的有效性很强的业务服务。

"原创"版块主要集中发布网友用户的原创作品，这一方面满足了用户的个性化表达也丰富了出版社的稿件资源；"听书"版块将读者喜爱的图书制作成有声读物，满足了读者多方面的需求，很好地拓展了传统纸质出版物的内容表达形式；"电子书"版块是易文网与北大方正电子有限公司合作项目，充分利用出版社的优秀出版资源和品牌效应，依靠方正的技术支持，将大量已出版的图书、杂志等制作成电子书，通过在线网站提供给读者选择下载阅读；"印客"是出版社对按需印刷的初步尝试，也就是所谓的个性化定制服

务，包括个人作品的印刷定做和具有收藏价值的稀有图书的印刷定做。

1.3 实现全媒体出版，达到内容资源最优使用

传统出版社与数字技术提供商进行项目合作时，往往处于被动，仅仅是廉价的内容提供者；突破技术障碍，传统出版社自主研发数字产品，通常出现投入大与产出小的局面，并且也会分散出版社的主营业务。如何实现出版社在数字化进程中品牌优势得以延续、回归内容制胜的出版核心地位？全媒体出版是平衡传统出版和数字出版的解决之道，根据不同用户的需求快速有效形成不同形态、不同手段的产品和服务，即对同一内容资源的多形式使用，做到内容资源的最优化。

作家出版社独家引进发行、根据奥斯卡获奖影片改编的小说《贫民窟的百万富翁》在销售纸质图书的同时，采用互联网、手持阅读器数字图书、手机出版等方式同步发行，实现纸质出版、离线出版、在线出版结合的全媒体出版模式。通过相关产业的融合，实现内容资源的共享和多次利用，优化了传统纸质出版的阅读空间和阅读形式，延长了出版物的生命周期。

2 载体的数字化

传统出版和数字出版最根本的区别是载体形式的不同，以纸张作为载体的传统出版，在一定程度上都界定了内容的多少，也局限了传播范围和规模，而数字出版通过技术将优质内容附着于数字载体实现在时间和空间上无限传播。

2.1 和技术提供商、移动运营商合作，形成移动出版的规模经济

近两年，以通讯设备、手持阅读器为主的数字阅读终端产品不断升级，我国出版社在寻求机会与优秀的数字技术提供商合作。中华书局新书《孔子》在出版时选择汉王科技电纸书作为其电子版首发媒体，纸书与电子版的同步发行。电子书的定价权在出版社，据分析，如果一本书下载 1 次 1 元钱，下载 200 万次，出版社或作者可分账 160 万元，比畅销书赚钱还多，传统出版和数字出版结合的同时也给自身带来了新的赢利模式。

手机出版是发展速度最快的数字出版行业，根据新闻出版总署的一份报告指出，2007年手机出版实现近 300% 的增长速度，2008 年手机出版营业收入继续保持翻番增长，手机用户的庞大基数和不少用户已经形成通过手机收看电视、小说、游戏和上网的新阅读娱乐习惯都为手机出版物的发展提供了广阔的市场。手机出版物在印刷、库存等方面均无成本压力，同时易于通过移动运营商统计出使用人数，潜在的巨大市场前景让传统出版社以各种方式寻求与手机媒体结合，寻求新的增长空间。江苏人民出版社与手机多媒体互动平台服务商——南京掌门科技有限公司合作，将该社出版的图书制作成手机电子书，谋求纸质书籍和手机下载订阅双向赢利。

2.2 出版社在线网站建设

出版社在线网站是出版社数字化转型的关键，不仅是本版书宣传和销售的平台，也是和广大读者、图书发行销售商信息交流的平台。由中国出版科学研究所和中国出版集团公司共同发布的《出版业网站发展创新报告》数据显示：2008 年，全国 578 家图书出版社，有独立域名的网站 384 家，图书出版社建站率达三分之二；集团网站有 22 家，出版集团基本上都有自己的网站。经过随机抽样调查发现，大部分网站都设立了论坛、读者俱乐部、商品陈列、购物车等频道，但是存在众多问题，如论坛留言功能关闭，商品更新缓

慢，购物车功能无法正常使用，大部分出版社网站没有依靠其自身的资源优势开发电子出版物。

据不完全统计，目前我国互联网上有近 29 000 家各种类型的网络书店。卓越网、当当网是大众图书销售的典型代表，蔚蓝网则以其专业性在界内著称，以下是截取它们部分数据，进行分析，见表 1：

表 1　网络书店相关数据

网站	Alexa 排名	反向链接	访问速度	百度收录	百度反向链接
卓越网	896	3 956	60 分	6 520 000	433
当当网	1 153	11 037	37 分	4 710 000	381
蔚蓝网	45 999	467	46 分	1 520 000	23

一般情况下，客户对当前网页上的内容能持续保持注意的时间长度约为 10 秒钟；若系统响应时间超过 10 秒，客户会在等待计算机完成当前操作时转向其他的任务。当当网内容丰富，多媒体等资料多，导致了网站访问速度的减缓。作为专业的蔚蓝网，在教材方面的营销可以超越传统书店，很多老师和学生会在网上搜索课本的幻灯片、相关习题集等，如果专业网络书店能有效提供这些服务，显然能吸引更多的读者。

3　编辑过程的数字化

编辑过程的数字化，主要是指通过软件系统实现从选题策划、申报，到来稿的审批、登记、编辑加工、校对再到稿件的发排、发布到生成成品以及后期的信息反馈等一体化管理。

高等教育出版社从 2002 年开始分期引进 ERP 软件管理，2006 年全部上线，基本完成了对整个出版社供应链数字化管理。从上游供应商到下游的终端客户，包括主营业务的流程管理，即从选题策划、审批、合同管理、交稿计划、三审计划、排校进度、印刷进度、销售管理以及财务、人员管理等等都实现了数字化。通过实施系统软件管理的模式，高教社实现了跨部门信息集成，优化了业务流程，减少各部门的重复劳动，工作效率明显得到提高，生产管理的科学性也不断增强。

一些专业出版社利用自身的技术优势，对于编辑过程的数字化都始于自主的技术开发，如电子工业出版社自主研发了图书编辑出版管理系统（PMIS），并被多家出版社采用。

部分高校学者也积极研发相关软件，探索如何实现编辑工作的科学化。武汉大学教授沈阳设计的辅助选题分析软件，已被几家出版社试用。

4　营销的数字化

2008 年，一份由 10 多位中国数字出版领域资深专家完成的预测报告称：未来 5 年，将有超过 30% 的手机用户通过手机阅读电子书和数字报；跨媒体出版成为主流，全国 70% 的出版社将实现同步出版；全国 80% 的出版社将通过 POD（按需出版）系统为读者提供图书的按需印刷服务；全国 90% 的报社将推出数字报；由图书馆等机构用户采购的电子书、数字报的销售规模将达到 10 亿元。面对如此大的数字出版浪潮，出版社应采取积极的营销方式迅速占领市场。出版业传统的营销方式包括广告、促销、公共关系等，一旦配合个性、快速、灵活性很强的数字出版，会存在服务流程过长、服务效果差、缺乏整体性、产品形象不鲜明等问题，因此要因时制宜地制定和实行与之匹配的数字化营销方式。

4.1 手机营销

2007 年 4 月 26 日，湖南文艺出版社推广新书《野草根》，结合一些传统的营销方式外，该社还通过中国移动手机报"移动图书馆"，向 30 万手机用户发送新书彩信，将新书内容介绍传递给读者，凡将阅读意向反馈给手机报的用户，就有机会免费获得一本《野草根》。这是国内出版社较早的开展手机营销的案例。手机作为目前用户基数最大的媒体，成为了众多出版社开展新营销的载体之一，能够直接向细分受众定向和精准的传递个性化信息，逐步达到精准营销的目的。

为了进一步提升机构品牌和产品品牌的影响力，中华书局在其 2007 年出版的《马骏细解二战谜中谜》等书上尝试使用了中国移动二维码，读者无需到书店，无须用电脑，只要用手机对准书上印刷的二维码"拍照"，或者发送"中华书局"至 10658028，就可以登录到中华书局的网站。网站上的"新书预告"、"好书导读"、"读者有奖调查"等栏目，为读者提供了更个性化的阅读体验，尽管这一应用在短期内还看不出能对中华书局的图书发行量带来多大促进，其无疑是出版单位对立体营销的有益尝试。

4.2 微博营销

微博作为一种新型的网络平台，以其个体性、即时性和短消息而被网民快速接受，新浪微博 2009 年 9 月全面公测到现在，注册人数已经超过 200 万。用户活跃度和信息的广泛快速传播，都是微博营销可行性的重要条件。

笔者以新浪微博为主要研究对象，截至 2010 年 4 月 21 日，统计出与"出版"相关的微博客 245 个，经过手动删选，剔除不匹配项 136 个，最后抓取经过新浪官方实名认证的出版社微博客 41 家，非实名认证的 48 家。

4.2.1 出版机构微博现状调研

笔者调研微博共计 89 个，在累积微博数量前十出版机构中（见表 2），除两家之外其他均为新浪实名认证。在所调研的微博中，其中更新数量最多的是中信出版社，自 2009 年 9 月 16 日开通微博至 2010 年 4 月 29 日共计 1185 帖。调研微博均没有每日更新的发布频率，89 个出版微博中，几乎是几日一帖，多日不更新，当然也存在开通以来一直未更新或几月一贴的懒人微博。

表 2　出版机构微博发帖数量排行前十名

出版机构	开通时间	微博	粉丝	实名认证
中信出版社	2009.9.16	1 185	2 997	实名
神龙创意出版	2009.10.26	649	1 145	实名
新星出版社	2009.9.24	527	1 591	实名
读客图书	2009.9.24	526	2 105	实名
悦读纪	2009.9.24	249	2 004	实名
学苑出版社	2009.8.27	248	86	非实名

出版机构	开通时间	微博	粉丝	实名认证
春风文艺出版社	2010.3.9	188	12 032	实名
科学出版社大众分社	2010.3.2	177	569	非实名
华东师范大学出版社	2009.9.23	142	351	实名
山东画报老照片	2010.1.27	131	707	实名

微博粉丝数量前十的出版机构，包括春风文艺出版社、四川文艺出版社、辽宁人民出版社、江苏文艺出版社、译林出版社、重庆出版社、中信出版社、女性阅读悦读记、南京大学出版和读客图书等出版机构。从调研结果来看，四川文艺出版社的微博是作为该社官方博客的宣传平台，内容为系统自动生成的关联博客信息。中信出版的微博内容涉及面十分广泛，有观点表达，新书推介，博友互动等。读客图书较好的利用微博平台开展新书的宣传营销工作，内容包括新书介绍，新书活动，博友互动。其余出版社微博内容多为新书推介，形式多为书籍封面+一句或者几句简短书评+定价等。

表3　出版机构微博粉丝数量统计排行前十名

出版机构	开通时间	粉丝	微博	实名认证
春风文艺出版社	2010.3.9	12 032	188	实名
四川文艺出版社	2009.9.25	7 300	55	实名
辽宁人民出版社	2009.9.25	4 602	38	实名
江苏文艺出版社	2009.11.27	4 118	7	实名
译林出版社	2009.9.24	3 502	28	实名
重庆出版集团	2009.9.23	3 033	18	实名
中信出版社	2009.9.16	2 997	1 185	实名
南京大学出版社	2009.9.3	2 722	24	实名
读客图书	2009.9.24	2 106	541	实名
悦读纪	2009.9.24	2 005	251	实名

微博发帖数量前十的出版机构，包括春风文艺出版社、中信出版社、新星出版社、神龙创意出版、山东画报老照片、科学出版社大众分社、学苑出版社、女性阅读出版悦读记、华东师范大学出版社、读客图书等出版机构。这个部分剔除重复的四家出版机构外，考察结果发现除了学苑出版社的微博单纯用来作为官方博客的更新发布平台，其余发帖数量多的出版微博内容较为多样，包括新书介绍、本社活动宣传预告、博友互动等，其中华东师范大学出版社微博还兼做招聘信息的发布平台。

4.2.2　出版微博营销的可行性研究

北京读客图书有限公司出版的《我们台湾这些年》是成功利用微博开展营销的案例之一。

在这场营销革命中，出版者、作者和读者打破时间、空间的限制，在新浪微博这个平台上即时分享信息。策划方在微博上积极发布新书资讯，营造话题，向微博名人寄赠样书，与名人就该书展开讨论，利用名人的强大粉丝群，让该书的宣传范围延展至最大范围。读客还组织了网上微博书评、有奖摄影等话题活动，与读者及时沟通交流，积极解决读者提出的问题。截至 2010 年 4 月 29 日，新浪微博搜索"我们台湾这些年"，话题量达到 2 560 条，在图书营销前期，主要话题发布者是策划方，中期是策划方、业内人士加上已经购买的读者、想要购书的读者等持续发布相关话题，后期话题的发布者大部分是普通的读者，发表读后感并对未购买此书的人进行推介。读客图书公司将传统图书的营销方式融入微博网络平台，为图书营销开辟新的局面。

5　结论

综上，通过结合数字化技术和出版业传统业务，减少了出版社经营的成本。依靠简单快捷的操作流程，并利用数字化的虚拟规模优势赢得竞争强势，这就是互联网带来的全新商业模式。传统出版行业如果忽视数字化的价值，可能会遭遇失败。

参考文献

[1]　第 25 次《中国互联网络发展状况统计报告》[R]．北京：CNNIC，2010

[2]　陈飞．网络新闻评论与构建公共话语空间的多视角分析．青年记者 [J]．2007，(3-4)：81-82

[3]　Roger Fidler．媒介形态变化：认识新媒介（Media morphosis Understanding new media）[M]．明安香译著．北京：华夏出版社，2000：19

[4]　徐丽芳．数字出版：概念与形态．出版发行研究 [J]．2005 (7)：5-12

[5]　威廉·E·卡斯多夫．哥伦比亚数字出版导论 [M]．徐丽芳，刘萍译著．江苏：苏州大学出版社，2007：62-63

作者简介

叶姗姗，武汉大学信息管理学院硕士研究生。

数字环境下出版供应链
信息交流障碍与共享模式选择[*]

何国军　张美娟

（武汉大学信息管理学院　武汉　430070）

摘要：在数字环境下，出版供应链信息交流与共享改变了传统出版信息传递形式，形成新的特征和运行机制。本文通过分析数字环境下出版供应链信息交流和共享的特点和技术环境，指出了信息交流和共享在技术和协作方面的障碍，提出相应的解决对策，具体是指建立有效的信息交流和共享激励、协调、约束机制以及加强信息标准化和安全性建设。并探讨了基于数字环境的出版供应链信息交流和共享的发展模式，主要包括分散型、集中型和综合型三种类型，出版企业应该根据自己的具体情况，选择适合自己企业的供应链信息共享实现类型。

关键词：数字环境　出版供应链　信息交流与共享　障碍　模式

Information Exchange Barriers and Information Sharing
Models of Publication Supply Chain in the Digital Environment

He Guojun　Zhang Meijuan

（School of Information Management, Wuhan University, Wuhan, 430070）

Abstract: In the digital environment, information exchange and sharing have changed the traditional publishing information communication patterns, whose brand-new characteristics and running mechanism have been formed. Based on the analysis of the features and technical circumstance of the publication supply chain information exchange and sharing in the digital environment, the paper points out the barriers of the information exchange and sharing in the aspects of technology and coordination, and then presents relevant countermeasures. These countermeasures are the establishment of effective encouragement, coordination and restraint mechanism of information exchange and sharing, and the

* 本文是教育部哲学社会科学研究后期资助项目"基于供应链的出版企业物流管理：理论与实证分析"（项目批号：07JHQ0019）和武汉大学自主科研项目（新兴交叉类别）"我国出版供应链信息共享的现状、障碍与发展策略"（项目批准号：7081001）科研成果之一。

fortification of information standardization and safety build-up. The paper also discusses the development models for digital environment-based information exchange and sharing of the publication supply chain, which mainly consist of distributed, concentrated, comprehensive, all together 3 types. The publishing enterprises should select a supply chain information sharing type, which is suitable for themselves according to their own concrete situations.

Keywords: Digital environment   Supply chain of publishing   Information communication and sharing   Barriers   Models

随着我国数字网络技术的发展，生产商通过改变数字文化产品、服务和信息存在的时间和空间场所，有效满足读者对文化产品不断变化的消费需求，从而实现数字产品的文化和经济价值。这种以数字网络为载体，以数字信息为内容的产业流程构成了一条从著作权人到内容生产商、内容运营商及技术提供商，最终到图书消费者的基于数字环境的出版供应链体系。

与传统出版供应链相比较而言，数字环境下的出版供应链信息交流和共享机制发生了根本变化。如由于出版产品的内容特性，在一定程度上，一部分数字出版产品的信息流可以代替产品流，由此表现出与传统出版供应链不同的运行特性。实际上，由于与数字技术的快速更新程度不相适应，出版供应链信息交流存在发展障碍以及不同的信息共享类型选择，由此具有分析和探讨的现实必要性。本文将基于数字环境这一背景，对出版供应链信息交流特点、障碍以及发展对策、模式类型作简要分析。

1　数字环境下的出版供应链信息交流特征和技术环境

数字环境下的出版供应链具有自身的特征，体现出版数字环境对出版供应链信息交流的重要影响。同时，供应链信息交流和运行条件需要一定的技术环境，这也反映了数字技术的发展和应用程度。

1.1　出版供应链信息交流的主要特征

基于数字环境的出版供应链信息交流主要有如下鲜明特征：

（1）电子化。出版供应链数字技术日益应用和成熟，出版社已普遍构建自身的信息管理系统，经销商的图书进销存系统逐步完善，供应链信息传递运行的电子化是出版供应链信息交流的基本特征。

（2）集成化。数字化技术推动了出版供应链的信息化发展进程，供应链上的供应、生产、经销、零售等环节一体化程度不断加强，横向的协作不断深入，供应链信息交流和网络化程度不断提高，这要求供应链整合环节各方的利益和功能，具有出版供应链信息交流集成化的特征。

（3）实时化。结合即时通讯技术 IM（instant messaging）发展和应用，出版供应链信息交流借助即时通讯技术和软件支持，各要素间通过相互沟通建立起集产品展示、业务联系、企业推广和在线洽谈等多功能的通讯系统，体现了信息交流实时化的特征。

1.2　出版供应链信息交流的技术环境

数字环境下出版供应链要实现节点企业的信息传递和共享，构建适宜的信息共享模式，离不开信息技术环境的支持。数字环境下出版供应链的技术条件和环境有如下三个方面内容：

第一，基础信息技术，主要包括有：标识代码技术、自动识别与数据采集技术、电子数据交换技术（EDI）和互联网技术等。

第二，信息技术系统构成，主要包括有电子订货系统（EOS）、销售时点信息系统（POS）、企业资源计划（ERP）、制造资源计划（MRPII）、及时生产制（JIT）和计算机辅助类（CAD）等。

第三，网络和实时通讯技术，主要包括计算机辅助获取和物流支持（CALS）、实时信息系统和实时信息采集技术等[1]。

在数字环境下，出版供应链的各节点企业针对各自合作企业的不同情况，其选择和应用的信息技术策略会有所差异，其信息交流和运行的效果也相应不同。

2 数字环境下出版供应链信息交流障碍和对策分析

数字环境为出版供应链的信息交流提供了有利条件，但由于客观环境因素和节点企业主体自身的利益诉求差异，供应链信息的交流不可避免地存在障碍。为了有效解决这些问题，需要采取有针对性的方法。

2.1 出版供应链信息交流障碍

（1）客观环境方面的障碍

数字环境下出版供应链的信息交流是对供应商、制造商、批发商、零售商和最终消费者的信息进行集成管理，这对于信息技术和环境有较高的要求，其主要环境障碍主要表现在如下方面：

信息传递的准确性不足。数字环境下出版供应链中的信息往往比较复杂，包含的内容比较多。例如在基于 EDI 的供应链信息技术体系中，其所处理的信息，包括了商品的数量、品种、客户信息等各种内容，采用何种报文的形式，如何确保信息传递的完整性是客观存在的难题，信息传递的准确性不足。

信息交流的实时性不够。数字环境下出版供应链中由于环节较多，各种共享信息的迅速、及时传递和反馈便显得尤其重要，整个供应链的运作效率也依赖于共享信息及时传递，而实际中信息交流的实时性传递较难实现。

共享信息的标准化和安全性保障不充分。数字环境下出版供应链交流和共享信息的采集、存储格式、传输都应有相应的标准。同时，制定共享信息标准既要考虑我国的实际情况，又要与国际标准接轨。共享信息的标准化建设很难一步到位。在数字环境条件下，出版供应链共享信息的安全性显得尤为突出。如果在实际的交易中属于商业机密的信息外露，必将会给企业带来严重后果。而实际中信息交流安全性问题也未有效解决[2]。

（2）节点主体企业协作方面的障碍

基于数字环境的出版供应链企业的竞争不再局限于企业与企业之间，而将扩展到供应链与供应链之间。然而，供应链合作企业担心其拥有的信息，特别是自己的商业秘密的共享使其在合作中处于不利地位，失去竞争优势，因而不愿意与其他合作者进行信息共享，从而最终使供应链信息共享本身在实际操作中遇到协作方面的障碍和困难[3]。

目前，出版单位普遍建立了信息管理系统（MIS），但由于各节点企业缺乏信任和协作意识，这些系统大多用于企业内部管理，在供应链上没有形成有效的信息流。信息的分段存储和单独使用，不仅造成供应链中的功能重叠、效率低下，而且使已建成的信息系统成为一座座信息孤岛。如对需求分析的每日（周）POS 机销售数据，零售店往往将其作为商业秘密，限制流动。因此，在出版供应链中，信息流的滞塞使其无法发挥连接需求和生产的功能，供应链上信息交流和运行各个环节的相互协作成为主要发展障碍。

2.2 数字环境下出版供应链信息交流障碍的对策分析

数字环境下出版供应链信息交流存在着诸多问题，其原因就在于协调过程中出现的有效激励机制的欠缺，因此，要通过建立有效的激励协调机制，切实改善供应链企业间协作关系，保证节点企业间的信息畅通。同时，逐步解决信息交流的标准化安全性发展障碍。

（1）建立有效的信息交流和共享的激励、协调、约束机制

激励机制。为吸引出版供应链合作企业共同参与信息交流和共享的协作，应建立多阶段的、长期的供应链信息共享制度，设计出合理的激励政策和措施。在供应链合作者之间设计和签订契约时，应根据合作者贡献大小，公平合理地分配信息共享带来的利益。

协调机制。出版供应链合作企业在执行信息交流过程中会遇到许多预想不到的实际问题，如信任危机、紧急例外情况等。供应链上的合作企业之间必须在一定协调机制指导下，通过协商解决好信息共享带来的利益冲突和利润分配问题。为此，必须建立起一定的信息共享协调机制。

约束机制。出版供应链的合作者之间实现信息共享时常会出现这样的问题：与某一合作商共享信息的合作者，同时也在与该合作商的竞争对手进行合作，甚至他们之间也进行一定程度的信息共享。在这种情况下，与合作者签订信息共享契约时，要明确信息共享的层次和范围，包括对泄露共享信息的处罚及其他约束机制。同时，建立健全有效的出版供应链信息交流监督评估机制，设计合理的评价系统，并据此定期对成员企业在信息共享上的行为进行评估，形成规范化的制度监督机制，及时发现问题并作相应调整[4]。

（2）加强信息交流的标准化和安全机制建设

出版供应链信息交流的标准化，是指在供应链中使一个信息系统的信息准确顺利传达到另一个信息系统，并使其信息内容和结构等形成一个整体的标准化过程。供应链信息交流的标准化建设主要有如下三点内容：信息规范化，有统一的名称、明确的定义、标准的格式和字段要求；信息之间的关系也必须明确定义，信息的处理程序必须规范化，处理信息要遵守一定的规程；企业各部门按照统一数据库所提供的信息和处理准则进行管理决策，实现企业总体经营目标。

同时，出版供应链上的节点企业在空间上分布具有分散性和广泛性，这将要求传输和共享的信息保密。所以，共享信息在网络外部的安全对于供应链来说意义重大。在供应链管理中，信息交流和共享的安全技术主要有：防火墙技术和 VPN（Virtual Private Network，虚拟专用网）技术。这将为数字环境下出版供应链中信息交流提供技术安全保障和应用选择。

3 数字环境下出版供应链信息交流和共享模式选择

在数字环境下，出版集团化建设加快发展，发行集团连锁经营规模不断扩张，信息交流和共享的范围和程度日益复杂化。特别是出版企业对数字出版的逐步重视和加大投入，

信息交流和共享的技术和要求不断向更高层次发展。笔者认为，数字环境下出版供应链信息交流和共享主要有如下三种模式和类型：

3.1 分散型

分散型是指出版业供应链上的成员企业建立起自身的内部信息系统，供应链上的各成员企业直接把对方企业传递来的信息存放在自己的数据库中。如出版企业大多有自身的业务和财务管理系统。在这种类型中，信息直接从提供方传递给需求方，不需要经由其他数据转换，信息的提供和获取是多对多关系，即共享信息在多个信息系统间进行两两传递。这是一种信息交流和共享实现的初级模式，也是数字环境下构建出版供应链信息交流与共享的基础。

3.2 集中型

集中型是将供应链中的共享信息集中在一个公共数据库（信息平台）中，各企业根据权限对其进行操作，实现与多个合作伙伴的信息交流。按照公共数据库的提供者划分，这种模式又可分为第三方模式和信息平台模式。

第三方模式是借助第三方信息企业作为中介平台，收集、加工与供应链相关的信息，通过第三方信息公共数据库向供应链成员企业提供信息服务，该模式有一定的安全和诚信风险，需要较高的市场信用和成熟的法律环境。信息平台模式是指企业内部信息数据库和信息平台间的数据传输由计算机自动完成，其实质是用信息平台取代上述的第三方信息企业。如出版集团建立的信息中心，提供给成员出版单位作为进行出版信息交流和共享的共同平台。这种模式一般供应链成员规模不太大、数量偏多且集成程度有限。

3.3 综合型

综合型是对分散型和集中型信息交流模式的结合运用。它以一个主要信息平台为中心进行构建，对出版供应链上不同级别的成员单位信息共享采用集成的方法，建立形式多样的企业间信息综合运行模式，从而有效地满足供应链上各成员企业对共享信息不同层次的需求，这种类型一般适用于集成化程度较高的出版企业供应链。随着我国出版业整合和重组步伐加快推进，跨地域的大型出版集团将由此逐步培育和产生，这种数字环境下供应链信息交流和共享综合型模式将成为发展的必然选择[5]。

由于要考虑企业自身的资金、人才和技术设备等成本因素，基于数字环境的出版企业应根据自身供应链信息交流和共享的具体要求，科学选择适合有效的信息交流和共享模式和类型。

注释

[1] 程兆铭. 我国出版业供应链信息共享模式及技术策略研究（数字出版与出版教育）. 高等教育出版社，2009.4

[2] 张美娟. 市场一体化环境下出版供应链信息交流和共享机制. 出版科学，2010（3）

[3] 潘旭阳，张红星. 供应链中信息共享的障碍和对策分析. 商品储运与养护，2007（6）

[4] 齐二石，刘亮. 物流与供应链管理. 北京：电子工业出版社，2007.10

[5] 张美娟，出版供应链信息交流研究. 情报科学，2007（12）

作者简介

何国军，武汉大学信息管理学院 2010 级博士研究生。

张美娟，博士，武汉大学信息管理学院教授，博士生导师。

论国家少数民族出版网络平台及其公共服务模式[*]

尹章池　刘凯

（武汉理工大学文法学院　武汉　430070）

摘要：国内少数民族出版公共服务和民族图书出版的数字化现状，迫切需要建设国家少数民族出版网络平台；民文出版和网络出版的结合使得创办数字公共服务平台成为可能；确保民文出版网络平台的公益性质，它有4种运营模式；少数民族出版网络平台包含选题资源库等主要公共服务模块。

关键词：民族出版　网络平台　功能模块　公共服务

About Minority Publishing Network Platform and the Public Service Model

Yin Zhangchi　Liu Kai

（School of Arts and Law, Wuhan University of Technology, Wuhan Hubei, 430070）

Abstract：Based on current situation of Chinese minorities publication in public services and digital publishing, there is an urgent need to build national network of minority publishing platform; Integration between Chinese minorities publication and web publishing makes the founder of the combination of the number of public service platform possible; Ensuring that the people publishing the text of the public nature of the network platform, it has four kinds of operation mode; Minority publishing network platform contains major public service modules such as topics resource library.

Keywords：National publication　Network platform　Functional module　Public services

民族出版是我国民族工作的重要方面，也是我国出版工作的重要组成部分。所谓民族出版，就是指以少数民族文字出版物的出版为主，同时包含以少数民族题材为主要内容、以少数民族人民群众为主要服务对象的出版物的出版，包括少数民族类图书的出版，也包括少数民族类报刊的出版以及少数民族类电子、音像、网络和数字出版。我国民族出版是国家思想舆论平台和理论宣传工具之一，同时也是国家文化出版事业的一个有机组成部分，它被赋予了更多的社会公益性。

---

* 本文为国家社科基金项目：公益性出版单位的体制改革与发展研究（编号：08BXW012）和中央高校基本科研业务费专项资金资助项目：基于供应链管理的出版业市场监测研究（编号：2010-1b-018）的成果。

由于自身特点导致的局限性，使得民族出版的一些问题并没有得到实际改善，民族出版物具有很强的地域性和民族性，受众较少、印数低和发行量小，文化生态性强，且市场化程度低。从目前来看，文化体制的改革无疑将会促进文化事业和文化产业的快速发展。但我国民族出版业起步比较晚，资本积累少，竞争力还很弱，面临着内外市场的激烈竞争。然而今天是一个信息化的时代，网络化、数字化已经成为这个时代的重要标志，利用数字和网络技术改变传统出版模式，建立自己的网络平台，实现编辑制作数字化、办公自动化，将是所有出版社的必然选择。当今，整个出版业都身处数字化浪潮之中，我国民族出版业必然要选择数字化，而且民族出版业更加需要数字化。

1 民族出版可以利用网络将劣势转化为优势

由于民文出版的特点以及数字出版的优势，民族出版数字化是时代的必然选择。

1.1 数字出版可以克服民族出版中有语言而没有对应文字的少数民族的民族传统文化的出版困难[1]

所谓数字出版，是指以数字代码方式将图文声像等信息编辑加工之后存储在磁、光、电介质上，通过计算机或其他具有类似功能的设备读取使用。数字出版以电子（数字）形式出版和传播信息，如文本、超文本、可视图文、电子邮件、电视、广播等的制作、传递、浏览、阅读、下载、联网打印等，它建立在新兴技术手段和因特网平台的基础上，编、印、发、供等传统出版流程和环节都发生了革命性的变化，而不是哪一个环节对网络的简单借助。它是一种数字化出版，正如有人总结的那样，具有以下特征：可共享、可交互、非实物、非独占、无损消费、时效强、成本低、效率高。由此可见，数字出版具有传统出版无法比拟的便捷性，因此，可以利用图文声像处理技术以及电子出版形式，对那些有语言而没有对应文字的少数民族传统文化进行开发整理，出版发行和传播。

1.2 数字出版可以为民族文字出版节约成本

由于我国少数民族文字的书写具有很强的特殊性，所以在民族出版物的出版过程中，文字编译和排版较为困难，而且所占成本也比较高。民族出版物往往印数低、发行少，因而造成单位成本高。如果民族出版实施数字化，那么就可以大大降低民族出版物的单位成本。如蒙古文出版，按照国家规定的蒙文排版价格，仅排版一项支出就占一本书全部成本的 1/2—1/3，而如果开发采用数字技术排版就可以使排版费用在成本中的比重下降到 1/4 左右[2]。运用数字化，不仅降低了费用，而且使得信息得到共享，人力资源得到了节约，这样同时也可以避免重复选题和资源浪费，节约成本的同时提高了效率。

1.3 数字化出版适应时代要求，有利于民族出版市场的开发

当前图书阅读率持续下降，而网络阅读率则一直处于上升趋势。在电脑上阅读可以很方便地复制和粘贴，而这也是促成大量读者购买电子书的主要原因。在内容为王的今天，书籍的载体形式和形态已退居次席，读者更看重其中的内容。与此同时，我国当今已经有 4.2 亿网民，手机网民 2.77 亿，在 4.2 亿的网民数量中，宽带网民规模为 36 381 万，使用电脑上网的群体中宽带普及率已经达到 98.1%，这些数据毫无疑问证明，数字化出版在我国是有着很广的受众面，数字化阅读的读者群已经形成。这些为数字化出版创造了出版物的消费条件，当然也就为民族数字出版创造了更加广阔的读者群，也为民族出版产品开发了更大的市场。

1.4 数字出版更加适合民族出版特点，有利于民族出版内容的传播

出版行为有着很强的规模经济特性，而我国民族地区生活水平还不是很高，经济发展缓慢，教育也相对比较落后，许多民族出版物有着特定的受众，导致民族出版物具有受众少、印数少、再版少的特点[3]。除了偶尔个别比较畅销的作品外，大多数民族出版物的出版成本高收益低或者亏损。数字出版中的电子书、移动电子书、多媒体电子书、按需印刷、按页打印等新兴图书形式，可以很好地利用到民族出版的数字化中来，这样不仅有利于克服传统民族出版印数低、再版少、成本高等缺陷，而且更有利于促进民族出版内容的传播。

2 民族出版网络平台的性质和组织实施模式

民族类出版网络平台的构建，首先要明确该平台构建的性质，然后才利于组织实施策略。

2.1 民族类出版网络平台的性质

我国民族出版事业经过多年的发展，取得了很大的进步，目前全国民族文字出版社共有38家，分布在我国14个省区市，可以出版23种少数民族文字图书，年均出书5 000种，共5 000万册。在2007年，中宣部、新闻出版总署等多个部委联合发布了《关于进一步加大民族文字出版事业扶持力度的通知》，该通知指出："少数民族出版事业属公益性出版单位。中央和地方财政要按照'增加投入、转换机制，增强活力、改善服务'的方针，加大资金投入力度，增加对少数民族文字出版的财政补贴，并逐年有所增长。"该通知明确地把承担少数民族文字出版的出版社定性为公益性出版单位。因此不难看出民族类出版社网站应该是由政府支持、保护、扶持的公益性出版网站，这个平台的构建应该是以公益性为前提。

2.2 民族出版网络平台组织实施模式

现在少数民族出版社在网络基础建设方面还比较薄弱，民族类出版社许多还是局域网，有时用外网根本打不开，甚至找不到他们的主页。这一方面表明民文出版数字化任重道远，另一方面更加凸显建立国家少数民族出版网络平台的示范意义和信息共享责任。民文出版数字化不是技术问题，而是组织协调不足和原有体制、机制不活造成的。从激活民文出版市场出发，满足各民族出版社经营环境的改善，创办一个有效、持续的数字化公共服务平台刻不容缓。

目前国家民族出版网站的打造和营运至少存在以下4种模式：

（1）国家民族事务委员会的门户网站的子网

国家民族事务委员会的门户网站中设立"少数民族出版"专题，链接到"少数民族出版网络平台"。这个平台可以由国家民委信息中心组织建设。民族出版社目前属于国家民族事务委员会的委属事业单位，与其他地方民族出版社有业务指导关系，各社间形成较为固定的网络。由国家民委信息中心负责管理日常网站事务实至名归。这种模式是在原有局域网基础上的改造和升级，有承建的单位和运营基础，但后期协调和资源聚集有困难。

（2）新闻出版总署的门户网站的子网

利用民族出版专项资金创办"国家少数民族出版公共网络平台"，作为新闻出版总署的门户网站的子网。这种模式建设起点高，政策资源及后期配套效果好，资金较有保障，

但从零开始，建设周期长。

（3）民族出版社协会创办的行业网络平台

发挥协会的作用，成员单位共同出资组建，当然由若干领军理事单位出版社牵头。这种方式凝聚力和号召力强，建设出版选题数据库、版权数据库和出版人才库有先天优势，在建设资金分配和网络管理权限设置方面存在难度。

（4）独立的第三方创办的网络民文出版平台

一些非营利性组织、少数民族文化基金、信息开发商从公益目的出发，自愿开发民文图书出版网络平台，出于文化使命或企业责任的承担和坚守，这样的网站一开始规模不是很大，但只要给予政策指导和恰当的经济扶持，他们可能走得更稳、更远。

国家可以同时选择1—2中模式并行发展。

3 民族出版网络平台的功能模块与服务

在前面已经提及，大多数民族类出版社的网站都还是局域网，外网根本进不去，有的甚至还没有自己的主页。多数网站还处于简单停留在书籍介绍阶段。网页制作简单，结构也不尽如人意，网站信息发布的多位读者不感兴趣的出版社内部消息，且更新不及时，等等。

鉴于此种情况，我们认为，国家民族出版网络平台至少要包含以下功能模块，提供相应的公共出版服务。

3.1 选题资源库与合作开发

民族类出版网站的建设不应该忽视选题库资源的建设。选题资源是一个出版单位赖以生存和发展的重要资源。选题资源的开发能力和占有程度在很大程度上决定了出版单位的生存质量和发展前景。在选题资源库的建设上，民族类出版社可以借鉴辽宁出版集团的做法。辽宁出版集团是我国首家实行政企分开、政事分开的出版产业集团，拥有9家省级图书出版社，年出新书1 700余种，重版书2 500余种，代表着辽宁出版业主体实力和发展方向。历年来他们出版的图书已经具有一定的基础和相当实力的门类及知名的品牌。这主要得益于他们重视对选题资源库的建设。该集团致力于图书选题质量、品位和档次的提高，经常邀请有关学科的专家和学术带头人，组成相对稳定的专家队伍，专门化、制度化、经常化地召开专题会议，为重点选题进行论证、决策，并为长远选题建设出谋划策，重点建设自己的选题资源库。38家民族类出版社在选题上有交叉，因此重复出版现象很多，选题资源库便于各出版社在做选题时有一个共享、比较和筛选的参照蓝本。

选题资源库的建设，以各个民族类出版社的民族特色文化为主要内容，结合数字出版的特点，将各类文字与图片，视频等资源结合起来。这样建立起来的"少数民族出版选题资源库"才能真正体现中华民族文化的同根同源、丰富多彩、积淀深厚，这是建设中华民族共有精神家园的基础和源泉。少数民族优秀传统文化蕴含的民族精神、文化遗产及其传承是社会主义精神文明建设的宝贵资源、重要素材和基本途径。

3.2 出版物资源库与整合链接服务

这是对已经出版的出版物的数字化。在这点上我们以云南民族出版社为例[4]。在该出版社的首页上，有个"图书展示"区，将该社出版物分为了"文化教育"、"旅游"、"少数民族古籍"、"明信片系列"、"社科、民族、文艺"、"医药、经济、科技、农业"、

"少数民族文字"类。这样使得人们就可以对该社出版物总类一目了然。而且在"图书展示"区还建立了相应的检索系统，分为"图书查询"、"在线阅读"、"新书上架"、"分类浏览"、"阅读推荐"5个检索条目，更易于读者快速找到自己想要的书目。在出版物资源库的建设上，我国大多数民族出版社都开展了一些工作，目前需要国家民族出版网络平台进行集中或链接，当然民族类出版社网站在这块的建设上还存在的一个明显的问题，就是书目更新较慢。

3.3 版权资源库与贸易窗口服务

中国少数民族地区拥有的丰富出版资源，如蒙古文化、藏文化、彝文化、西域文化、古纳西文化已经成为国际上比较热门的研究领域，对中国民族图书感兴趣的读者越来越多[5]。其中有关民族医药、民族文化和民族风俗类的出版物最受外国读者喜爱。其中一些出版物的版权输出有很大的潜力，出版物"走出去"战略及其配套政策有利于民文图书的版权输出。"中国少数民族出版物版权资源库"可以集中各民族出版的品牌和无形资产，将零散予以集中，克服民文图书出版的分散经营、难以集团化的弊端，把无形的出版资源转化为有形的经济优势，更好地弘扬民族文化。

一些拥有与中国少数民族同族跨境而居的国家，也是少数民族出版物出口的主要市场。比如，有关蒙古族和朝鲜族的读物可以直接出口蒙古国、朝鲜和韩国这些周边国家，藏文出版物可以出口到印度、尼泊尔等国，尤其要重视这些民文图书的网络营销开发，或者与他国的合作出版。

3.4 网络书店与配送服务

谈到民族出版网络平台的构建，就应该少不了网络书店。因为现在互联网正在改变人们的生活方式和消费习惯，从而也影响了人们的消费观念和消费方式。越来越多的消费者开始在网上购物。与传统购物方式相比，方便快捷是网络购物不可比拟的优势。网络购物品种多，支持24小时下单，又辅以搜索技术，这些优势是传统零售所不具备的。[6]

网络书店突破了时空界限，可以全天候地为读者提供购书服务。读者可以在任何地方任何时间，只要能上网，就是顾客。而且网络书店的信息检索系统比浏览传统书目的方式便捷得多，有利于扩大顾客群体。不仅如此，网络书店的物流配送不断提速，随着现代交通和科技的发展，以前阻碍网购的物流配送问题也得以解决。从目前国内的电子商务环境来看，现代物流企业发展迅速，网络书店的送书和费用在大大降低。另外网络书店的支付手段更加灵活多样。虽然我国民族类出版社网站上大多都有自己的"网上购书"这个功能板块，但是目前主要存在的问题就是物流和配送的问题，因为民族类出版社大部分地处我国中西部地区，位置相对偏远，可能从发货到图书抵达购买者手中需要很长一段时间，从而影响读者的网购欲望。不过，随着交通和物流行业的发达，这个问题也将不断得到解决。

3.5 公益性项目管理与评价

2000年，国家设立了少数民族出版资金。近几年，国家下拨新闻出版发展专项资金，组织实施重点出版工程和项目，其中就有不少民族类图书。这些都是公益性项目，需要一个完善的评审、公示、实施、监督和社会评价平台，以保障资金发挥最大效益。对于这些获得资助的公益性项目的评价，其过程和指标体系应该不同于经营性项目，要提高公益性项目在出版公共服务、读者满意度和文化贡献指标等方面的权重。评价结果应当作为下一次项目申报和评审的重要依据，是信誉和资历的凭证。作为非营利的公益性民族文化单位，要始终把社会效益放到第一位。坚持为少数民族地区、民族工作服务的宗旨，贯彻党的民族政策，让发展的成果惠及少数民族读者，促进民族文化的健康发展；同时，要注重选题的针对性、可读性，努力使选题贴近群众、贴近生活、贴近实际；还要在生产上引进市场竞争机制加强管理，提高效率，使公共财政投入发挥最大的效益。[7]

3.6 网络论坛、书评与营销服务

网络论坛自从互联网诞生之初就存在了，而如今，它已经成为了一个具有很大活力的网络平台。民族出版网络平台的建设，当然不能忽略了网络论坛这一强大的宣传功能。实际上利用网络论坛进行营销具有很强的隐蔽性，往往取得意想不到的效果[8]。论坛营销除了人工费用之外，基本上不需要其他任何费用。这主要是因为公共的综合性网络论坛对任何发言者来说都是免费的，一般只需要在论坛进行会员注册。这样，既不增加出版成本，也能够缓解营销费用的压力。而且在论坛上，出版社的营销人员可以直接地和读者进行交流，对于本社出版物和服务存在的问题双方可以及时地交流和沟通。而且论坛有利于形成一个广泛的读者群体，这样有利于信息资源的收集，出版社更可以通过分析、判断，从这些信息中开发出优秀的选题，形成产品、反馈信息、新选题、新产品的良性循环。

民族类出版社网站的建设，应该重视书摘与书评这一功能模板。云南民族出版社的首页，在网页的正中央就有很醒目的一个菜单栏，其中就有书评与书摘一栏。越来越多的人已经停留于网络化的浅阅读，精心编辑的书摘可以给人留下第一眼的好印象，从而引起读者的购买欲望。民族类出版社的图书大多针对性较强，因此提供网上书摘服务，内容要有针对性。一个有效的策略是：由出版社、书商组织稿件，有计划有规模地组织实施[9]。民族类图书的书评要达到预期的作用，要保证书评具有浓缩性和解释性的特点，要具有创造性，尽量提高书评质量，使书评提供的信息不仅仅是真实、可靠的，而且具有较高的参考价值。

少数民族出版具有一般出版的共性，又具有资源特色化而产生的选题稀缺性、读者基数小而产生的市场有限性、文化保护而伴随的出版公益性、难以集团化而导致经营分散化等特殊性。数字化出版技术可以聚合少数民族出版的出版资源，转化出版劣势为出版优势，其中最重要的是建设国家网络出版平台，引导少数民族数字化出版。这个平台致力于提供各民族出版社在出版资源远程共享、出版政策传播研究、民文出版项目评审和监管、出版物及其版权资源的国内外贸易等方面的公共服务。

注释

[1] [2] 廖健太. 中国当代民族出版研究 [D]. 兰州大学民族学博士学位论文. 2008. 5：200-208

[3] 满福玺. 论民族出版物的民族性、社会性与经济性 [J]. 中央民族大学学报（哲学社会科学版），2007（5）：140-144

[4] 段波. 网络将为民族出版插上腾飞的翅膀 [J]. 今日民族，2009（7）：56-58

[5] 宝贵敏. 论民族出版的困境与出路 [J]. 中国出版，2007（4）：21-23

[6] 禹宾熙. 民族出版改革中的几个关系问题——以民族出版社为例 [J]. 出版发行研究，2009（2）：26-28

［7］ 马映红、高诚. 从网络书店的发展看网络购物的优势 ［J］. 现代经济信息，2009
（15）：41-42

［8］ 冯雁. 论坛营销——图书营销新思路 ［J］. 科技与出版，2009（7）：7-10

［9］ 梁启东. 图书的广告书评化与书评广告化 ［J］. 图书馆杂志，2010（2）：89-93

作者简介

尹章池，博士，武汉理工大学文法学院，教授，硕士生导师。

刘凯，武汉理工大学文法学院新闻传播系 2009 级硕士研究生。

出版信息交流

书业出版物信息交换标准在数字出版业的应用

庄小雪

（武汉大学信息管理学院　武汉　430072）

摘要：本文围绕为什么要建立出版物信息交换标准，出版物信息交换标准的现状，建立数字出版物可供书目，如何建立标准以及对出版物信息交换标准应用于数字出版提出的几点建议；同时分析书业出版物信息交换标准建立的必要性、现行出版物信息交换标准的运行情况，提出该标准在应对数字出版时需要做出的调整与完善。本文着重探讨信息交换标准在数字出版发行环节的应用，笔者希望通过对出版物信息交换标准的研究，来更加深入的了解数字出版的整个过程，更好的参与数字出版的细节，指导数字出版实践。

关键词：数字出版　信息交换标准　应用

Application of Book Information Exchange Standards in the Digital Publishing Industry

Zhuang Xiaoxue

（School of Information Management，Wuhan University，Wuhan，430072）

Abstract：This paper mainly talks about the reason why to establish standards of information exchange in publishing industry，and the situation，how to establish the standard，to give somes advice to application of book information exchange standards in the digital publishing industry，at the same time analyse the necessity to establish standards of information exchange in publishing industry and the operation of current standards，proposes standards in response to digital publishing and makes adjustments and maturities when necessary．This article focuses on the application of information exchange standards in distribution．the author want to know more about the book information exchange standards and the entire process，participate the digital publishing details and conduct the practice．

Keywords：Digital publishing　Information exchange standards　Application

1　为什么要建立出版物信息交换标准

1.1　信息交换在出版行业有各方需求

书业出版物信息交换是指出版行业各信息系统间的协同工作所进行的信息交换。这种信息交换要求解决异构系统的信息交换，并且是安全的、有权限区别的信息的自动交换。

行业内各部门间的信息交换需要实现信息传输网络化，通过信息的组织和提交的标准化、规范化来实现。长期以来，出版行业的信息采集部门零散，采集工作量大、渠道单一，信息的准确性没有保证。建立出版社与发行商的信息交换和共享机制，不仅可以拓宽信息采集渠道，避免重复劳动，还可以提高信息的准确性和利用率。

1.1.1　选题策划的需要

出版物的特殊属性决定了出版业是事后看效果的行业，出版物整体策划的个性化显得尤为重要。如何在日趋激烈的竞争中，把握市场脉搏，策划出符合市场要求的选题，需要得到贯穿上下游的"数据"的支持，做到"知己知彼"。可供选题论证和营销工作参考的数据有出版社的发行数据、国家新闻出版总署的 CIP 数据、出版社收集的书店数据、社店图书流通信息交换数据、第三方提供的图书数据。

1.1.2　出版物在市场上顺畅流通的需要

出版物产品的经营活动是出版活动的基本组成部分，具体表现为出版物的发行活动，是出版价值链的不可缺少的环节，它向出版物产品追加的是时间价值和空间价值。在出版产业化程度不断提升，市场竞争日趋激烈的背景下，发行活动在出版产业链中的地位逐步提升。实现信息交换，就可从多角度对发行业务进行全面分析，可按产品、按地区、按客户、按业务员、按产品分类等多角度统计发货、退货、回款、库存等相关数据，从而为管理者提供有效的分析、决策数据。针对一个单品种，可以根据当前的发货量、已发货时间及当前库存计算出理论的可发货天数，为重印、添货提供数据支持。

1.1.3　把握行业整体运行的需要

目前出版系统和发行系统基本处于各自为政的状况，各自数据不清晰，彼此数据不透明。实现信息交换，就码洋来看，横向的对比可看出各出版发行集团的高下，纵向的比较能洞察各出版物品种的起伏。从出书速度、图书进出口、图书订退货、出版社回款等方面来看，可综观全行业的运行是否顺畅，是否存在问题，哪里存在问题，是对全行业的实时监控。

1.2　实现信息交换准备不足

1.2.1　行业各系统内部信息不明确

实现信息交换的前提是交换各方的信息充足、准确、互补。粗线条的来划分行业系统可分为出版系统和发行系统。更进一步来看，又有图书储运管理系统、图书发行管理系统、图书批发销售管理系统、书目制作电子订单管理系统等项目，但系统仍不完善，信息的明确性也有待提高。比如，发行系统只能提供某种出版物的总码洋，但这些码洋是如何分摊的，主要是被哪个群体买走，都不明确，而充分了解该消费群体的年龄、职业、文化程度等具体特征对上游的出版系统而言又有重要意义。

1.2.2　系统之间未实现信息对接

国内书业信息"孤岛"现象严重。出版社手中掌握着出版物自身的基本信息，比如作者知名度、目标消费群、装帧风格、出版时间、库存信息等，发行商了解的则是出版物的发售数量、实际消费群的特点和最新市场动态，作者的优势在于熟谙出版物内容、写作风格，甚至可以把握内容上可能成为卖点的亮点。出版社与书店、作者、读者，以及其他客户之间，缺乏高效的信息流通渠道，以至出版社要聘请专门的信息员以了解各地的销售。

2　出版物信息交换标准的现状

2.1　现有出版物信息交换标准

2.1.1　《图书流通信息交换规则》

《图书流通信息交换规则》以图书流通过程为核心，明确了数据交换的内容。标准通过完整定义图书商品信息以及其在流通各环节中的信息交换内容和规则，规范图书出版发行供应链中各企业信息系统的数据接口，使企业间数据库能以标准格式相互兼容，轻易实现信息共享——每个数据库拥有者只需将自己数据库的内部格式和标准格式进行转化，就可达到供应链中各企业信息的互连，促进图书出版发行供应链之间的信息交换。标准实施以后，出版业发行供应链、信息链的数据传输大为简化。

2.1.2　七项出版物发行业标准

由全国出版物发行标准化技术委员会组织制定的《图书、音像制品、电子出版物营销分类法》、《出版物发货单》、《出版物退货单退货差错回告单》、《出版物在途查询单回告单》、《出版物物流标签》、《出版物物流作业规范第一部分：收货验收》、《出版物运输包装材料基本要求》等七项出版物发行业标准，已经由新闻出版总署批准发布。

2.1.3　MPR出版物的5项行业标准

为加快我国自主研发和具有完全自主知识产权的MPR（将多媒体数字技术与纸质印刷出版物相结合，通过阅读器将出版物对应的电子媒体文件表达出来）码技术推广应用，规范MPR码的使用，统一纸质有声出版物码制，新闻出版总署日前审核通过了MPR出版物5项行业标准：MPR码符号规范、MPR码编码规范、通用制作规范、MPR码印制质量要求及检验方法、基本管理规范。

2.2　现行出版物信息交换标准的不足

2.2.1　书号重复影响ISBN功能的发挥

书号是出版物身份的唯一标识，是出版物在流通过程中表现自身特质的重要符号，也是出版发行单位间交换出版物信息的主要依据。国际图联编制的《国际标准书目著录》（ISBN）使不同国家出版物编目数据的互换及识别成为可能。我国于20世纪80年代开始推行出版物ISBN制度，从1994年1月1日起，全国所有的出版社必须为其出版的每种新书编制国际标准书号。然而时至今日，国内出版物一号多书的现象仍比较普遍，书号的不唯一，影响了ISBN功能的发挥。

2.2.2　在版编目（CIP）数据著录不规范

CIP是印制在出版物版权页上，记录书名、作者、出版者、定价、书号等基本信息的书目数据。我国于1991年颁布国家标准《图书在版编目数据》（GB12451-90），并于1993年开始实施。目前CIP主要由各出版社自行编制，主管机构中国版本图书馆负责审核。近年来每年出版新书已超过千万种，版本图书馆实在无法胜任平均每天400多种新出版物CIP数据的审核任务。不少出版社对CIP编制工作不够重视，编目人员的业务素养参差不齐，导致CIP著录标识不符合标准，CIP数据中主题标引、分类标引不规范，出版物版权页出现排版印刷错误，在书名、著者、字母和数字等方面的误排和漏排。不规范的CIP数据影响了其作为国家标准的权威性，书店与图书馆不敢直接使用CIP数据，而是重新编制适合自己要求的书目信息，由此形成同一种出版物对应有出版社编制的CIP数据、新华书店系统编制的征订目录、图书馆编制的馆藏书目等多种不同的书目信息，从而造成人为的信息交流障碍。

2.2.3 机读书目数据交换中缺乏统一的目录格式标准

出版业信息化建设的显著特征是依托计算机和网络交流出版物信息，它要求书业企业将书目信息转化成标准的机读目录格式，以便书目信息在网络上无障碍传播和共享。美国早在20世纪60年代就研制出了比较成熟的 MARC 机读目录标准，我国也于1982年开始实施国家标准《文献目录信息交换用磁带格式》，并于20世纪90年代推出我国的文献著录标准格式 CN MARC 标准。虽然这些标准目前在图书馆与情报部门使用较普遍，但在出版界却鲜有使用机读目录格式交换数据的先例。由于目前出版业还没有统一的数据交换格式标准，所以出版社与书店开发的信息管理系统缺乏统一规划，各单位数据库的信息格式与选用的数据字段五花八门。譬如，有的系统规定书名字段著录主书名和副书名，而另一些系统则只要求著录主书名；有的单位将价格字段定义为字符型，而另一些单位却将其定义为数值型，诸如此类，不一而足。虽然各单位的计算机应用系统内的数据机读目录格式能够保持一致，但是其应用软件却无法直接识别与利用传送来的其他出版发行单位的数据，需要花费大量时间与人力专门去进行信息录入与处理，使信息化与网络化的效率大打折扣。

3 出版物信息交换标准应用于数字出版的几点建议

3.1 以书店为突破口，推广出版物信息交换标准

3.1.1 书店是信息交换标准推广后最直接的受益者

一旦实现出版物信息上下游的数据交换，书店对各家出版单位的整体实力、出版风格、竞争优势和劣势乃至各种图书的折扣都一目了然，进而对货源的确定、进货数量、进货品种等重要决策产生重大指导意义，能够有效降低书店在上游的成本。另一方面，书店自身掌握着终端市场的动态，了解市场需求，具备找到适销对路的图书的能力。从需求出发，通过透明的信息，书店能够以相对低的成本实现相对高的市场利润，规避市场风险，从而成为信息交换标准推广后出版环节中最直接的受益者，应该成为推动标准实施的强大动力。

3.1.2 以各地新华书店为试点，以点带面

在众多的书店中，新华书店当属知名度最高、信誉最好、发展最成熟、最具规模的连锁书店。新华书店在各级城市有着有成熟的发行系统，历史留下的黄金店铺，庞大的县、市及覆盖农村的发行网络。信息交换的重要基础是店社的互信，新华书店互信基础好，又有强大的政策支持，这都让新华书店具备较大优势。这也正是新华书店在传统出版向数字出版过渡的改革中有可能走在前面，对全行业的发展做出更多贡献的理由。

3.2 建立数字出版物可供书目

3.2.1 建立数字出版物可供书目的可行性分析

建立数字出版物可供书目意义重大，众望所归。可供书目，又称在版书目，现货书目，它是相对于绝版书目、售缺书目而言的，可供书目是包含预订书目、现货书目和出版社库存信息的书目体系。可供书目的目的在于介绍图书市场的供应情况，全面系统地揭示书业市场上已出版物可供信息，使书业书目信息可以有序的流动，增强购销双方信息的反

馈。书店需要动态信息，但目前不得不"看目采购"。出版社一般提供纸质书目，一年也就更新两三次，信息滞后，项目不全，一般只有书名、编号、每包的册数，缺乏简介等内容。书店不清楚出版社出了什么新书，书目上的书是否好卖，是否有货，有多少，无法根据图书的详细信息进行有重点的推广。可供书目对出版社而言，是进行选题策划的参考，有它做参照，能有效避免选题撞车、重复出版，及时了解出版策划的最新动态；对发行商而言，不仅可超越中间商信息不准确、不完整的缺陷，还直接搭建与出版社联系的桥梁，在流通领域节约资源、节省成本；对整个出版业而言，可供书目在产业链的不同环节之间传输书目数据，引导全行业逐步进入规范有序的轨道。

建立可供书目的主要瓶颈是书业信息化水平不足。随着数字出版的步伐，我国书业信息化程度正在逐步加深，传统出版向数字出版过渡正是在原有基础上建立数字出版物可供书目的重大契机。由于可供书目的建立需要耗费巨大的人力、物力、财力，书业信息化也不是单个出版单位可以独立完成的事业，需要全行业共同的努力，因而传统出版物的可供书目建设得并不理想。目前，数字出版如火如荼，各家出版单位无论是否愿意都不得不融入出版数字化的大潮，都要将传统出版物的各项信息数字化，而这正是建立数字出版物可供书目的基础。在传统出版时代实现"书业信息化"的老大难的问题，在向数字出版时代迈进的当下显得势在必行，数字出版物可供书目的建设正可以搭上这班顺风车。

3.2.2 数字出版物可供书目的建设主体

从国外经验来看，利用具有独立市场运营能力的公司实施中国可供书目建设，通过市场机制的调节，将可供书目及时准确地传递到读者面前，让读者快速获知最具价值的图书信息，可以加快图书在市场上的流通速度。中国的出版业长期处在政府的政策保护之下，如今刚刚实现转企改制，独立生存能力弱，企业秩序还未建立，可供书目的赢利模式还未探索成熟，市场上并未出现愿意专门从事可供书目建设的第三方企业，即"不愿来"。另一方面，中国的出版行业进入门槛高。出版因其在文化精神领域独特的地位，浓重的意识形态色彩，并同时肩负着引导舆论、引领思想的文化职能而备受政府部门的影响。完全市场化的运作，也是当前出版政策所不能允许的，即"不让来"。这两方面的因素共同决定，中国数字出版物可供书目的建设不能沿用外国的第三方模式。

笔者以为，由政府出面，设立出版行业的发行审查机构来担此重任，是更为可行、有效的途径。首先，政府具有强有力的宏观调控的能力，在出版业市场发展不成熟、市场秩序尚未完全建立起来的当下，宏观控制是必不可少的。另外，我国出版行业尚未出现专门的审查机构来核查各出版单位的实际出版情况，比如每年新出书品种数、某种书的发行量等统计数据，基本都是靠各出版单位自己上报，至于上报情况是否属实，并没有专门的机构来审查。设立出版业的审查机构，既是弥补了这项空白，也可以由其来具体负责数字出版物可供书目的建设。有政府在背后支撑，具体措施实施起来有保证，政府的信誉担保能够得到上游出版社的信任，从而提供真实详细的信息数据，由该审查机构出面统计，下游的发行商便于如实反馈真实的市场行情，上下游之间的沟通更加方便顺畅。

3.2.3 如何建立

第一，要各确立上下游都认可的书目信息的数据款项和数据格式，这是在搭建各种书目信息规范化、系统化的框架，有了这样的框架，书目信息才好对号入座；

第二，各出版单位要将零散的书目信息集中起来，按照框架的要求，整理分类；

第三，及时更新书目信息，确保书目信息和实际情况相吻合，对书目信息进行动态管理。

3.3 建立传统出版物信息交换标准在数字出版中的对接渠道

3.3.1 传统出版物信息数据数字化

数字出版中相当的比重来自固有内容，将传统出版物的信息数据数字化是必做的功课。与此同时一并进行的还有出版物信息数据深加工，诸如专业数据库的建立、标题信息的标引、专业分类。这项工作既可以弥补原有出版物信息缺失、遗漏等不足，又可利用时机对现有的数据进行深加工，为下一步的增值服务打下基础。

3.3.2 对虚拟数字出版物确立唯一身份识别

与传统出版物转换来的数字出版物不同，新兴的虚拟数字出版物没有实实在在的载体形式，从诞生之日起就是数字出版物的家庭成员。这种先天的特点虽然使其灵活多样，但也有明显的不足。传统出版物有 ISBN 作为其唯一身份编码，而这种先天数字出版物却没有一个类似 ISBN 的编码来表明自己的唯一身份，这为数字出版物的整理、分类工作带来了巨大的困难。给先天数字出版物一个身份，是在数字出版领域应用信息交换标准的一个前提。先天数字出版物基本是以网络为载体，因而通过网络技术对该出版物所在的位置进行准确定位也许不失为一种可行的方法。

参考文献

［1］ 书业信息化面临拐点，http://book. sina. com. cn/mediacoop/2005 - 10 - 21/ 1613191334. shtml

［2］ 书业信息化警惕"信息悖论"，http://www. guangzhi. com. cn/ViewInfo. aspx？ID = 5e6963ac–06cb–41a9–af1a–db20e077b974&categoryID = 57

［3］ http://www. cbbr. com. cn/info_3395. htm

［4］ 图书发行业信息交换有了统一标准，http://www. bjpress. cn/hyxw/2006–3–1. htm

［5］ http://qkzz. net/article/a94f3d31–5bed–4de8–baa5–209b2de0d3d1_2. htm

［6］ 总署审核 MPR 出版物 5 项行业标准发布，http://www. cnpubg. com/space8/？ action- viewnews-itemid-1103

［7］ 黄凯卿，李艳，必须加强我国出版业信息标准化建设，出版发行研究，2004（2）： 70–71

［8］ 孙万东，数字环境下可供书目信息网的建设和利用，现代情报，2006（1）：61

作者简介

庄小雪，武汉大学信息管理学院 2009 级硕士研究生。

出版信息交流

教育教学类电子出版物和电子资源（EEPER)[1]的分类原则、方法与标准浅探

王迎胜

（黑龙江大学信息管理学院　哈尔滨　150080）

摘要：虽然目前教育教学类电子出版物和电子资源的使用越来越广泛且复杂，但对其的分类原则、方法和标准进行研究仍较少。为了使教育教学类电子出版物和电子资源的开发更有针对性，使用更规范，本文尝试从教育教学过程的不同层次、类型和形式以及其他的一些特点确立了教育教学类电子出版物和电子资源的分类原则；并根据上述要素确立的参数标准确立教育教学类电子出版物和电子资源的分类方法和分类标准。

关键词：教育教学　电子出版物　分类

On the Principle, Approach and Standard of Classification on the Teaching Electronic Publication and Electronic Resource

Wang Yingsheng

（School of Information Management，Heilongjiang University，Harbin，150080）

Abstract：Although the usage of the education electronic resource is becoming more comprehensive and complicated，the scholars who probe into its principle，method，standard of classification are still inadequate．Aiming at exploiting the resource with pertinence and utilizing it with standardization，this article tries to establish the principle of classification depending on the characteristics of different arrangements，types and formats of teaching progress；and according to the parameters established by those elements，we can conclude its method and standard of classification.

Keywords：Education and teaching　Electronic publication　Classification

随着教育教学电子化、信息化程度的不断提高，教育教学类电子出版物和电子资源的使用范围越来越广泛，并且趋于复杂化。目前，专门针对这一类型的电子出版物和资源的分类原则、方法和标准进行的研究较少。为了科学地发展和利用教育教学类电子出版物和资源，笔者认为有必要为该类电子出版物和资源制定科学的分类原则、方法和标准。

教育教学类电子出版物和电子资源分类是教育信息化的现实任务之一。这种分类可以建立在几种不同标准上，一方面，按照教育类电子出版物的功能和作用，可以按照教育教学出版物的传统分类方式对 EEPER 进行分类。另一方面，也可以把传统教育教学类出版

物纳入电子出版物的范畴，对其采用电子出版物的分类原则。

对于具体的教育领域的各类电子出版物和电子资源的通用分类法是没有的。考虑电子出版物题材性质具有多样的特点，在对教育类电子出版物进行分类之前，必须明确 EEPER 电子出版物的基本特征，并以其 EEPER 的分类标准。因此特征越清楚，越有助于分类。我们首先可以根据教育层次、教育活动的类型、教育活动的形式、受教育群的特征，来确立 EEPER 的分类原则，然后根据分类原则形成分类方法，进而制定分类标准。

1　教育教学类电子出版物和电子资源的分类原则

教育教学过程具有不同层次、类型和形式的特点，针对这些特点，可以研究确立足够清晰的教育电子出版社物分类原则。教育活动的性质是教育层次分类的方法基础，如学前教育、义务教育、职业教育和继续教育，除此之外，针对肢体受限者（残疾人）的特殊教育层次。除此之外，还可以根据教育活动的类型、教育活动的形式形成分类原则。

1.1　按教育层次划分

1.1.1　按义务教育的不同阶段划分

（1）用于学前教育的 EEPER

（2）用于小学阶段的 EEPER

（3）用于初中的 EEPER

（4）用于高中的 EEPER

（5）用于其他教育形式的 EEPER

1.1.2　按职业教育的不同阶段划分

（1）用于初等职业教育的 EEPER

（2）用于中等职业教育的 EEPER

（3）用于高等职业教育的 EEPER

（4）用于大学毕业后职业教育的 EEPER

（5）用于继续职业教育。肢体受限者（残疾人）职业教育的 EEPER

1.2　按教育活动的类型划分

（1）用于全日制教学的 EEPER

（2）用于夜校教育教学的 EEPER

（3）用于函授教育教学的 EEPER

（4）用于远程教育的 EEPER

1.3　按教育活动的形式划分

（1）用于课堂讲授的 EEPER

（2）用于讨论课的 EEPER

（3）用于实践课的 EEPER

（4）用于实验课的 EEPER

（5）用于教学游戏的 EEPER

（6）用于教学科研工作的 EEPER

（7）用于教学测量和考核（考试和考查）的 EEPER

（8）用于独立教学活动的 EEPER

（9）用于学年和毕业设计的 EEPER

1.4　按受教育人群的特点划分

针对相应的教育教学层次、教学类型和教学形式的电子出版物和电子资源，作者为了某种教育层次、类型和形式而设计的具体的 EEPER，有可能也适合其他教育教学层次、类型和形式。在研制和利用 EEPER 的时候，采用现代信息技术的优势可以最大程度地改变这些电子出版物和电子资源的功能，不仅是适合教育过程的每个参加者的个性特征，而且适合整个学习群体（利用者）的特点，使研制者可以根据不同类别的受教育群体来研发 EEPER。因此，EEPER 的参数体系取决于受学习者的群体特征，根据这些具有自身群体特征的受教育群体可以确立以下划分原则：

（1）用于小学生群体的 EEPER

（2）用于中学生群体的 EEPER

（3）用于大学生群体的 EEPER

（4）用于研究人员群体的 EEPER

（5）用于行政管理人员群体的 EEPER

（6）用于教师群体的 EEPER

（7）用于家长群体的 EEPER

2　教育教学类电子出版物和电子资源的分类方法与标准

依据上述相应的教育教学类型、层次、形式等要素确定的参数标准，可以分别建立教育类电子出版物和电子资源的多层次分类体系。

一是针对教学体系，完全可以将教育教学电子出版物和电子资源划分为：

（1）附属于教育部教学大纲和教学标准的传统教学体系的 EEPER，如：教学计划、教学大纲、教育标准、教学指南等。

（2）用于深化选修课程知识的 EEPER，用于选修科目和深化课程知识的电子出版物和电子资源，在很大程度上与传统教学体系中使用的 EEPER 相似，只是在教学资料内容方面超出教育部的大纲和相关标准范围。如：教师推荐的与选修课知识体系相关的电子教材、工具书、软件。

（3）用于家庭补习的 EEPER，如：电子习题集，电子复原课堂等。

（4）用于考核和评价教学结果的 EEPER，如：学生学习、教师授课评价系统等。

（5）用于参考咨询和工具书类的 EEPER，如：电子词典、电子咨询手册、电子百科全书等。

二是用于教学目的的教育教学类电子出版物和电子资源及其组成部分可以这样分类：

（1）教学用的 EEPER（用于满足掌握教学和实践活动知识、能力和技巧和保障掌握必要层次的学习资料，如：讲义提纲、电子教材、电子教学系统、实践训练环境、教学考查/考核材料样本等）

（2）练习用的 EEPER（用于满足研发不同能力和技巧的教学系统需求和重复巩固讲授课程的内容，如：电子习题集、电子复原课堂等）

（3）考核用的 EEPER（用于满足考核、测量或掌握学习资料程度的自我考核的教学系统需求，如：电子题库、知识考核电子系统、身心测试工具等）

（4）信息检索和信息资源用的 EEPER（用于满足情报交流，形成信息分类的能力和技巧的教学系统需求，如：电子书目、信息检索系统、虚拟图书馆、互联网目录、信息检索服务）

（5）展示放映用的 EEPER（用于满足研究、学习的客体、现象和过程的影像学习需求）

（6）仿制模仿品用的 EEPER（用于满足研究结构或功能性质而进行的真实角度演示的教学需求）

（7）实验用的 EEPER（用于满足用真实实验设备进行的远程实验的教学系统需求，如：电子实验环境等）

（8）模型设计用的 EEPER（用于满足为了研究、学习的客体、现象、过程的模型设计的教学系统需求）

（9）教学——游戏用的 EEPER（用于满足创建教学情况，学习者可以以游戏的方式在该情境中完成学习活动的教学系统需求，如：发展训练的电脑游戏等）

（10）游戏用的 EEPER（用于满足组织学生业余活动，发展学生的记忆力、反应力、注意力及其他品质的教学系统需求）

（11）交流用的 EEPER（用于满足组织教师、行政管理人员、学生、家长、专家之间的个性化交流，用于满足教师和学生获得需要的信息资源的途径的教学需求）

教育教学类电子出版物和电子资源可以根据课程的组织形式进行分类，在该类课程上目的明确地采用某种类型的电子出版物和电子资源。在教学过程中，实验课、实践课、科学研究、自主培训、学年和毕业设计，考查和考试过程中所推荐采用的电子出版物和电子资源应该区别开。

三是按照上述教学内容，教育教学类电子出版物和电子资源可以按照知识形成、信息报导、能力形成、知识巩固，知识水平考核、知识能力和技巧完善、总结几个方面的进行分类。可以根据心理学上的不同认知活动阶段，对电子出版物和电子资源进行研发和分类，如：

（1）知识理解吸收阶段的 EEPER。

（2）知识深化、巩固阶段的 EEPER。

（3）形成个人经验（能力、技巧、职业直觉）的 EEPER。

（4）科学项目研究和检索活动的 EEPER。

四是教育教学类电子出版物和电子资源按照载体形式可划分为：

（1）单行本 EEPER——以一个机读设备出版、阅读的电子出版物。

（2）多"卷"本的 EEPER——由两个或两个以上部分组成，其中每一"卷"都用单独的机读设备。

（3）系列的 EEPER——以共同的宗旨、题材、目的，以同种装帧形式组合到一起的多册的系列电子出版物。

五是按照资料的叙述形式，教育教学类电子出版物和电子资源可以分为交互的、程序的、问题的和复合的。

（1）交互的 EEPER 按照传统教育，具有工具书或参考咨询性质。相关的 EEPER 能够实现教学的信息功能。

（2）程序的 EEPER 建立在"应激反应"教学理论基础上。这种出版物具有树状和线性程序的结构，主要用于学生自主学习，揭示获得知识的原理和方法，揭示这些原理和方法与职业技巧之间的相互关系。

（3）问题的 EEPER 建立在"问题学习理论"的基础上，有助于学生逻辑思维的发展，促进创造性地掌握知识。

（4）复合的 EEPER 含有以上列举的 EEPER 的所有要素。

六是教育教学电子出版物和电子资源可以按照其传播技术分类：

（1）局域性 EEPER——用于局域使用的电子出版物，以机读设备阅读的电子出版物，只供校内（单位内部）使用的 EEPER。

（2）网络 EEPER——通过远程通讯网络不限范围使用的电子出版物，主要用于远程教育教学的 EEPER。

（3）复合传播 EEPER——可以用于局域传播，也可以作为网络 EEPER 进行传播的电子出版物。

七是考虑使用者与 EEPER 相互影响程度可以分为：决定性和非决定性的教育教学电子出版物和电子资源。

（1）决定性的 EEPER——与电子出版物相互作用的参数、内容和方法由出版者决定，使用者无法改变。

（2）非决定性的 EEPER——使用者可从自己的兴趣、目的、培训水平等方面，直接或间接确定与电子出版物相互作用的参数、内容和方式，这种互动关系是在出版者所设立的运算规则的基础上实现的。

八是不同种类的教育教学电子出版物和电子资料的研制，可以根据他们的教学层次组合成 4 组：

第一组 EEPER 包括课堂教学类型的出版物——印刷材料的电子版本、数字录音、录像。印刷出版物一般包括推荐给教师和学生的教学文本形式的理论材料，以及附于文本的插图、习题集。记录的课堂讲授内容的音像出版物的教学任务是帮助学生对教学材料进行初步认识和理解。通常，第一组出版物具有初始材料的性质，以这些材料为基础来开发更有价值的材料。

第二组 EEPER 也属于教学设备类型。第二组可以包括电子教材，虚拟课堂和电脑测验系统，这一组的主要教学任务是理解、巩固和知识考核。

第三组 EEPER 可以包括虚拟练习平台，教学实验，远程实验端口及其他相关的电脑系统。在这些系统的工作中使用研究对象或研究过程的数学模型，和在进行研究规范内支持学生解决学习问题的专门系统，是这些系统的标志性特征。第三组 EEPER 的主要教学任务是形成和发展操作知识、能力、技巧，进一步认识研究对象和研究过程的特质。

第四组 EEPER 包括职业活动的电脑自动化系统或应用软件包。学生可以利用这些系统或软件在学年、毕业设计过程或实验过程中解决各种研究任务。在使用本组 EEPER 时，教学过程在自由研究的规范内进行，或以比较接近专家的职业活动形式进行。在此规范内，学生在进行科研活动时，利用远程专门实验台进行实验。

注释

[1] 这里的"电子资源"包括用于教学的各类数据库、软件、教学文件、网络系统、影像演示系统等。"教育教学类电子出版物和电子资源"缩写为英文的 EEPER，正文将以 EEPER 代替"教育教学类电子出版物和电子资源"这一名称。

作者简介

王迎胜，博士，黑龙江大学信息管理学院副教授，编辑出版学系主任、专业负责人。

出版信息交流

出版企业如何在数字出版产业链中提高议价能力

郑　倩

（武汉大学信息管理学院　武汉　430071）

摘要：数字浪潮席卷了出版行业，但是在数字出版产业链中，传统出版单位在技术提供商、平台商和运营商的狂轰滥炸中近乎"失声"，出版企业的生存压力除了来自行业内的竞争之外，还要应对来自行业外的威胁。随着行业外资本的进入，在数字出版链条中，出版企业的份额被蚕食，在此背景下，讨论提升出版企业在数字出版产业链中的议价能力非常有必要，可以从紧跟数字化潮流，精准定位，提高产品不可替代性；强化品牌建设，注重出版物内容力的提升；寻找合作伙伴，建立战略联盟等策略着手，并通过这些战略使出版企业在数字出版中逐步获得有利的地位。

关键词：出版企业　数字出版　议价能力

How to Improve the Bargaining Ability in the Digital Publishing Industry Chain

Zheng Qian

（School of Information and Management，Wuhan University，Wuhan，430071）

Abstract：The digital technology has intruded the publishing industry，but in the digital publishing industry chain，the traditional publishing companies lost their voice as a result of that the technology providers，platform providers and operators lead the trend．Publishing industry has to face the challenge both from same occupation and the company from the outside．With the capital from the other industry entering，the publishing industry has smaller and smaller part in the digital publishing chain．It is urgent to discuss how to improve the bargaining power of the publishing industry．Following is the suggestion：Keeping the pace with the digital trend and precise positioning to make sure the product irreplaceable；Strengthening brand building and focusing on the content；finding partners and establishing strategic alliances，carrying out these strategies to help the publishing companies gain a better position in the digital publishing chain gradually．

Keywords：Publishing company　Digital publishing　Bargaining power

　　新闻出版总署副署长孙寿山在 2010 年中国数字出版年会主论坛上透露："2009 年，我国广义的数字出版整体达到了 799.4 亿元，逆市增长势头强劲。"但是据出版社人士透露，在这近 800 亿元的产值中与传统出版界有关的收入不到 20 亿元，实际到出版单位手中的更是不足 2 亿元，这样的数字不禁让出版企业有些心寒。

与传统出版模式不同，在数字出版中，出版企业在产业链中所处的位置发生了变化，从曾经的连接作者和销售商及读者的中间环节转变成了单纯的内容提供商，处于作者和平台运营商中间，甚至被作者抛弃，在产业链中处于弱势地位。在这种背景下，出版企业应当如何提高议价能力，以应对来自上游作者以及下游的运营商平台上和读者，本文结合五力分析模型对此进行简要分析。

1 紧跟数字化潮流，精准定位，提高产品不可替代性

数字出版是趋势，这一点赢得了出版企业的共识。但是面对数字化转型，出版企业应当何去何的问题，传统出版企业却走向了两个极端：一个是急功近利，试图通过大投入来换取收益；另一个是无所作为，除了简单地进行一些图书电子版的转换和授权外，在其他层面上实践有限。这是导致出版企业在数字出版链条中竞争力降低主观方面的原因。从客观原因的角度分析，数字出版主要由技术提供商和运营商所主导，出版企业天然处于较弱势的地位。

五力模型中对购买者议价能力的分析告诉我们，当市场中替代品越多的时候，企业的议价能力就越多，相反，如果企业的产品具有不可替代性，那么企业就可以在竞争中掌握主动权。对于出版企业而言，就是要紧跟数字化潮流，精准定位，避免内容的同质化，提高出版物的不可替代性，从而赢得竞争的主动权。

出版企业产品的不可替代性不可能通过技术和专利上的突破来实现，而主要是在于内容的独特性，营销策划和服务的差异化来实现，而准确的市场定位就是实现差异化和不可替代性的重要手段。

对于运营商和平台提供商而言，其获得赢利最重要的就是点击率和下载量，要获得这两项，就需要拥有读者喜爱的图书内容，为了满足数字阅读用户的需求，他们没有选择的余地。在这种背景下，出版企业就应当在出版的流程中纳入数字出版的理念，即在选题的策划论证程序过程中就要充分考虑和捕捉数字阅读市场的信息，在内容设定、作者选择和相关的广告宣传、营销策划中就应当与数字出版挂钩，依此选择合适的内容和作者，争取在最大限度上满足数字阅读者的需求。以高等教育出版社为例，其在进行相关的数字出版中从最初的内容创作到加工生产再到后期的发布传播都贯穿了数字出版的理念，例如在加工生产阶段，对文字、图形、视频、音频等内容进行结构化和标准化的处理和编排，并通过在线学习平台、学术期刊发布平台和 CD、VCD 的形式发布，创造了一种与数字化生产过程相适应的利润杠杆模式。

此外，清晰准确的定位还有助于吸引针对目标读者的稿源，提高稿件质量，以增强出版企业在同业竞争者中的竞争力，从而提高议价能力。在数字出版中，能够较早根据自身优势树立数字出版理念的企业往往能够获得先机，掌握比较好的数字出版合作资源、作者资源、版权资源等，这样形成了比较系统的资源，在读者心目中也会成为一种独占资源，提升对于这些作者的议价能力。

最后，精准的定位会赢得更大范围内读者的喜爱，从而提高出版企业的议价能力。传统出版产业面临数字出版的挑战和压力归根结底是来自于读者阅读习惯的改变。越来越多

的读者接受并且非常享受这数字出版带来的生活。以 Twitter、新浪微博为代表的 "微"时代主力正在改变媒体的表达方式，也正在改变读者在新闻话语权中的弱势地位；以 Kindle 为代表的手持阅读器以及苹果公司 iPad 为代表的平板电脑在销售上获得的巨大成功都昭示着数字阅读时代正在到来。在这样的趋势中，出版企业如果能够针对数字阅读者的需求来进行策划和生产，必定会在产品差异性上更胜一筹，从而赢得读者的青睐，获得更高的议价能力。

2　强化品牌建设，注重出版物内容力的提升

窦林卿曾撰文指出："任何行业的核心竞争力的发展轨迹，最终都会是去尽浮华，还原本质。决定出版企业在数字出版时代生存问题的，正是传统出版的核心——真正具有竞争力的专业内容"。在出版行业里，最早开发电子书的并不是亚马逊而是索尼，但是亚马逊却赢得了胜利，在当前几乎成为数字出版的代名词，分析其原因，美国斯坦福大学预测师保罗·萨弗认为 Kindle 是一本真正的电子 "书"，除了硬件，它还有几十万种图书、杂志和博客的海量内容可供选择。这一案例也佐证了 "内容为王" 的观点。

当然品牌的建设不仅仅包括内容力的提升和优质化，品牌的内容更丰富，它还包括企业的外在形象、服务质量等多个方面，是一种各种优势的整合形成的。品牌会让读者形成更强的认同感和更多的信任，如果出版企业拥有一个比较好的品牌，对于作者、读者和任何一个数字出版环节的参与者来说，都有着不可忽视的吸引力，这也就保证了企业议价的能力。

首先，出版企业加强品牌建设可以增强对上游的吸引力，这里不仅仅是指作者资源，还有其他的版权贸易机构。不论是作者还是版权持有者，在选择合作出版企业时，无疑都会选择知名的、有品牌保证的合作对象。完全没有品牌知名度的出版企业在与版权持有者的进行议价的时候底气不足，不具备较强的议价能力，甚至根本不能获得议价的资格；如果出版企业本身拥有知名度，就能够利用其品牌与作者进行谈判，议价能力自然上升，从而能够获得更好的版权资源。

其次，出版企业加强品牌建设可以增强对下游企业的吸引力，主要是对运营商的吸引力加大，从而提高出版企业的议价能力。以长江文艺出版社为例，因为其本身做名人书在业内成为一种标志，金黎组合具有的号召力也非同凡响。因此国内数字出版的重要平台、全媒体出版的先行者 "中文在线" 与长江文艺出版社联手进行了《非诚勿扰》的全媒体出版运作，实现了经济效益和社会效益的双赢。也为出版社本身开创了数字出版的新方向。所以如果出版社本身具有品牌的优势就可以与数字出版下游进行议价，因为不论在何时，出版 "内容为王" 都是最重要的成功原则。

第三，出版企业通过品牌建设，可以增强对读者的吸引力。在品牌竞争的时代，拥有一个为消费者所拥护的品牌在一定程度上就获得了竞争的主动权，也对读者的议价能力上更加有发言权。数字出版产品归根结底仍然是出版物，最终决定读者选择的关键因素仍然是出版物本身的质量和品牌，因此出版企业应当加强品牌建设，这种品牌建设不光是对已有资源的品牌建设还特别要加强数字出版品牌的建设。数字出版从一定程度上来说给了出版企业一次重新洗牌的机会，出版企业应当把握机会，创造良好的品牌形成对读者的吸引力。

3 寻找合作伙伴，建立战略联盟，提高议价能力

战略联盟作为一种经营策略，通过企业之间合作，获取共同的经济利益。出版企业想要提高在数字出版链条上的议价能力，除了守住自己的核心竞争力之外，还要在产业链上延伸，主要分为向上延伸和向下延伸两种。向上延伸是解决版权问题，主要是指与作者合作；向下延伸主要是解决渠道问题，与发布平台和运营平台进行联盟。

首先说与作者进行战略合作，进行软平台的搭建。在这一方面，网络出版特别是一些文学网站有很多成功的经验，例如整合了国内众多优秀网站而建立的盛大文学，就通过与作者签约的形式形成了一个庞大的作者群，涉及各个细分领域。但是应当看到，这样建立起来的作者库"鱼龙混杂"，只适合浅阅读的模式，随着数字出版逐步融入人们的生活，对数字出版的内容要求会大幅提升，基于此，出版企业应当建立更为专业的数字出版作者群，并与之建立你中有我，我中有你的共荣竞合的关系，这样的模式在传统出版中已有成功的模式和案例，比如版税制的实施和一些作者加盟出版社成为共同的投资者和合作者等。在这种战略合作中，作者和出版社把更多的注意力放在增加图书的销售上而不是两者内部之间利益的博弈。在这种状态下，出版企业对于作者的议价能力就无形中增加了。

其次是与下游即数字出版发布平台和运营平台联盟关系的建立。在出版产业链中，版权最核心的资源，对上游的整合是为了获得更多更优质的版权资源，那么在进行下游联盟中，目的就在于通过版权获得最大的经济效益和社会效益。

数字出版并不仅仅是出版内容的数字化，更重要的是对版权资源的多层面和全方位的数字化开发和利用，其关注点在于"规模经济性"和"范围经济性"。出版企业通过向下游的联盟，可以共享技术、成本等资源，实现更为广泛的资源共享，从而使整体的成本下降。在联盟中，合作方不再是单纯的议价双方的矛盾关系，更是互惠互利的共荣关系，出版企业的议价能力自然也会得到相应的提升。

总之，数字出版是未来数字时代必然的发展方向，出版企业如何在激烈的竞争状态下和受到数字出版技术提供商、运营商和平台提供商多方夹击的形势下赢得企业的生存空间和利润成为出版企业必须考虑的问题。出版企业通过五力模型的分析，通过对象下游对象的议价能力的调整，获得更好的生存空间，捍卫出版企业在数字出版浪潮中的有利位置。

参考文献

[1] 方卿，许洁. 数字出版赢利模式设计的五要素——以高等教育出版社为例 [J]. 出版发行研究. 2009（11）：16—19

[2] 方卿，冯蓓. 出版企业如何提升议价能力 [J]. 出版发行研究. 2010（4）：19—26

[3] 窦林卿. 当出版社 PK 移动服务提供商 [J]. 出版营销. 2009（11）：83—84

[4] 常桦，迈克尔. 波特完全竞争战略 [M]. 北京：中国纺织出版社，2003

作者简介

郑倩，武汉大学信息管理学院 2009 级硕士研究生。

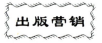
基于内容挖掘的出版社微博传播效果分析

彭 云 沈 阳

（武汉大学信息管理学院 武汉 430072）

摘要：目前注册新浪微博的大陆出版社有72家，然而真正利用微博达到了很好的信息传播效果的出版社很少。笔者总结出影响微博传播效果三个层面的因素，利用 ROST CM 等工具并结合手工分析找出了出版社传播效果不佳的原因："僵尸粉"多，更新频率不高且不稳定，更新时间不合适，内容、形式不够吸引人，与粉丝和名人的互动很少。最后笔者针对出版社特点给出了一些增强微博传播效果的建议。

关键词：出版社 微博 传播效果

The Research on Dissemination Effect of Publishing House in Micro-blog Based on Content Mining

Peng Yun   Shen Yang

（School of Information Management，Wuhan university，Wuhan，430072）

Abstract：Although 72 mainland publishing houses have registered Sina micro-blog，few of them get good communication effects from using of micro-blog. This paper summarizes factors which influence the communication effects from three aspects and points out the causes of publishing houses' bad communication effects by taking advantage of ROST CM software and hand calculation，the causes include that the large quantity of inactive fans，low updating rate，uninteresting content，monotonous expression-form and infrequent interaction between fans and the celebrities. Then considering the specific feature of publishing house，this paper gives several advices to improve the communication effect of micro-blog.

Keywords：Publishing houses Micro-blog Communication effects

微博，是基于用户关系的信息分享、传播以及获取平台，用户可以通过互联网、手机以及各种客户端组建个人社区，以 140 字左右的文字更新信息，并实现即时分享。2009年 8 月，新浪推出"新浪微博"内测版，成为国内门户网站第一家微博服务网站，而新浪微博也成为大陆最火爆的微博客。为获取最大的社会效益和经济效益，树立自己的品牌，宣传工作是出版社营销工作的重要组成部分，微博的出现为出版社提供了一个高度社会化的免费网络平台，利用好这个平台，出版社发出的信息可以轻松获得巨大读者覆盖面，极大提高宣传效率。因此怎样利用好这一平台获取最佳的传播效果对于出版营销人员至关重要。

1 出版社微博传播效果

在新浪微博中注册并被认证的出版社有 72 家，且默认按粉丝数量由多到少排列。笔者选取广西师范大学出版社、商务印书馆、上海人民出版社三家出版社，他们分别代表微博中粉丝数量最大的出版社、品牌过硬出版社、畅销书的出版社，在微博中的传播情况十分具有代表性，基本能涵盖微博中出版社的各种类型，这三家出版社注册至今的微博数、评论数、转发数、粉丝数量，及相应的平均评论率、平均转发率如表 1 所示：

表 1 三家出版社微博数据

项目	广西师范大学出版社	商务印书馆	上海人民出版社
微博数	24	34	73
评论数	101	81	74
转发数	73	56	118
平均评论率	4.2	2.4	1.0
平均转发率	3.0	1.6	1.6
粉丝数量	29 353	2 922	650

由表 1 可以看出，这三家出版社每篇微博平均评论次数分别为 4.2 次、2.4 次、1 次，平均转发次数分别为 3.0 次、1.6 次、1.6 次，考虑到这三家出版社的粉丝数量并不少，分别为 29 353、2922、650，且微博有传播速度快、互动度高的特点，这三家出版社微博评论率和转发率均低于微博评论和转发率平均值，而评论率和转发率是反映传播效果的重要指标，因此可以认为以这三家出版社为代表的全体出版社在微博中的传播效果并不好。

2 出版社微博传播效果不佳原因

为进一步了解出版社在粉丝数量较多的情况下传播效果仍然欠佳的原因，笔者将从影响微博传播效果因子的角度着手分析。影响微博传播效果的因素有三个层面：信息到达率，信息接收率和信息再生产率。笔者将从这三个层面具体分析出版社微博推送的特点。

2.1 信息到达率

信息到达率指能够到达网友页面的信息量。信息到达率由粉丝数量和粉丝的粉丝数量两方面决定。这三家出版社粉丝最少的也有 650 个，最多达 29 353 个，受众覆盖较广，因此粉丝数量在出版社传播效果评估中是正因子。

但是观察发现，出版社粉丝的粉丝的数量普遍偏低，以广西师范大学出版社为例。广西师范大学出版社是在新浪微博中粉丝最多的出版社，然而深入研究发现，其粉丝多为"僵尸粉丝"。"僵尸粉丝"即为系统自动生成的恶意注册粉丝，他们活跃度几乎为零，且没有粉丝。粉丝的粉丝越少，覆盖到的受众范围越小，"僵尸粉丝"极大地降低了出版社微博信息二次传播的概率。出版社吸引到的高质量粉丝并不多。

2.2 信息接收率

信息的接收率指能够被粉丝看到的信息量。影响信息接收率的要素主要有以下几种：

2.2.1 微博更新频率

2010年1月至8月上述三家出版社更新频率情况如表2所示：

表2 三家出版社2010年各月微博更新次数

月份	1月	2月	3月	4月	5月	6月	7月	8月
广西师范大学出版社	0	0	0	0	1	7	9	5
商务印书馆	0	0	5	2	1	2	6	10
上海人民出版社				6	1	13	1	0

从表2可以看出，三家出版社微博更新频率均偏低且无规律，微博更新无计划，随机性极大。如广西师范大学出版社连续4个月不更新微博。出版社微博信息的更新也存在扎堆现象，毫无规划可言。如商务印书馆4月29日连发2篇微博；此后整月再无任何更新。

2.2.2 微博更新时间段

三家出版社2010年1月以来各时间段微博更新次数如表3所示：

表3 三家出版社各时间段微博更新次数

时间段	8—10点	10—12点	12—14点	14—16点	16—18点	18—20点	20—22点	22—24点	0—3点
广西师范大学出版社	2	2	0	3	5	1	1	3	8
商务印书馆	2	10	3	6	9	1	1	0	0
上海人民出版社	2	3	5	6	5	0	0	0	0

由表3看出，每天14—16点和16—18点是出版社更新微博的两大活跃时间段。而《2009年中国IT网民网络行为调查分析报告》指出，每天13—17点是中国网民上网第三个波峰，与三大出版社更新微博时间段大致吻合。而微博在粉丝页面的显示完全按时间顺序排列，微博更新集中的时间段，出版社的微博被后来微博信息淹没的可能性更大，因此我们推断出版社不合适的更新时间也是导致传播效果欠佳的原因。

2.3 信息再生产率

信息再生产指评论或转发的行为，信息在被接受后，再生产率本身体现其受欢迎度。且通过再生产可以获得更好的传播效果。信息再生产率包括信息扩散性再生产率（转发率）和信息提升性再生产率（评论率）。信息再生产率受微博内容、形式等影响较大。

2.3.1 微博内容

由于出版社微博话题具有分散的特点，为提高微博话题分析准确性，笔者扩大样本，采集20家出版社共3421条微博，利用文本挖掘软件ROST CM分析得到出版社微博中出现频率最高的词语，如表4所示：

出版营销

表 4　出版社微博词频

排序	词	排序	词	排序	词
1	本书	11	先生	21	时代
2	出版	12	书店	22	丛书
3	文化	13	苹果	23	学习
4	美国	14	小说	24	问题
5	历史	15	故事	25	乔布斯
6	文艺	16	著名	26	学生
7	读者	17	作品	27	图片
8	新书	18	北京	28	开放
9	文学	19	文史	29	经典
10	研究	20	文字	30	战争

从表 4 可以看出，出版社微博具有以下特点：

① 以推介新书为主："本书"、"新书"、"丛书"等都是对新书的代称。

② 关注发达国家出版："美国"多是对美国文化和美国出版书籍的介绍。

③ 突出文化产业特征："文化"一词在出版社微博中有很高频率。

④ 关注历史和文艺："历史"、"文艺"是出版社微博的第五和第六高频词。

⑤ 关注知名人物："乔布斯"的关于互联网和移动业务的谈话多次出现在出版社微博中。

综上，三大出版社的微博话题文化氛围较浓，且均直接切入营销主题，娱乐性、故事性强的信息并不多。而根据笔者观察，传播效果良好的微博信息都具有趣味性、实用性、增值性、新闻性、哲理性的特点，且在同等质量下，原创的微博比转发的微博能给博主带来更高的人气。

对比发现，出版社微博缺乏娱乐性，同时营销目的过于明显是其致命缺点，这导致它在庞杂的微博信息中不能最迅速地吸引粉丝的注意力，自然就无法获得良好传播效果。

2.3.2　微博形式

出版社的微博通常将图书的封面或者内页放进微博，这三家出版社微博中含有图片的占总微博数的 44.3%，但是含视频的微博只占总数的 2.3%，且没有运用到音乐。微博形式并不丰富，无独特形式吸引读者眼球。

2.3.3　与粉丝互动度

这三家出版社对于粉丝的提问并不是有问必答，对问题的选择随意性强，并没有体现出对粉丝评论的足够重视。同时，对于读者在评论中分享阅读感受的，出版社也没有相应的互动。而在微博中，与粉丝互动度越高，情感交流越多，粉丝会更有兴趣评论或者转发该出版社微博，进而扩大其微博覆盖面。

2.3.4　名人效应

被知名作家转发过的微博不仅可以通过名人效应获得更高的转发率和评论率，更可以受益于名气的可传染特点获得更多粉丝。然而据笔者观察，这三家出版社关注的作家数量有限，即使关注了知名作家，跟作家之间也没有互动，并没有借助名人效应为自己的微博带来人气的意识。

综合上述对影响出版社微博传播效果的各要素的分析，我们得出结论，造成出版社微博传播效果不佳的原因是：（1）粉丝的影响力不够，僵尸粉丝过多。（2）更新频率不高且不稳定高，且容易扎堆。（3）微博更新时间恰值网友上网高峰期，部分微博信息很快被后面的微博淹没。（4）微博内容趣味性、实用性、增值性等有限，无法吸引读者注意力。（5）微博形式不够丰富。（6）出版社与粉丝和名人的互动度均不高，无法借助名人效应和粉丝互动来改善传播效果。

3　对改善微博传播效果的建议

出版社要想最大限度地利用微博为自己的业务服务，提高微博传播效果是关键。根据上文分析的影响出版社微博传播效果的因素，对出版社微博的改进工作有以下建议：

（1）派专人负责微博，提高更新频率。出版社应意识到微博在自身营销和出版信息传播中的重要价值，派专人管理微博，提高更新频率，稳定、有序的更新微博信息。

（2）选择最佳微博更新时间段。根据《2009 年中国 IT 网民网络行为调查分析报告》，每天 13 点前后及 18 点前后上网的人约占全天上网人数的 25%，为白天的人数最低时段，这个时候更新的微博信息可以在粉丝微博首页停留更长的时间，因此这个时间段是更新微博的最佳时机。上午 9 点以前上网的人也相对较少，也是更新微博的黄金时间。

（3）增强微博内容的趣味性、实用性、增值性。将书籍宣传信息或出版社活动信息用有趣委婉的方式呈献给粉丝，使粉丝在身心放松的情况下更乐于接受这些信息。出版社适当发送打折信息、赠品信息等生活实用信息，同时节选书中精彩片段、哲理知识或者提供行业知识、适当穿插生活经验类感悟等信息，会更容易吸引粉丝，提高读者的评论欲、转发欲。

（4）丰富微博形式，增加对视频和音乐的运用。微博中不仅可以发送文字，还可以发送视频和音乐。如果出版社增加更多的视频和音乐，可以在形式上吸引部分读者，增强他们评论或转发的欲望，进而提高自身微博的信息到达率和信息再生产率。

（5）增强与粉丝、名人的互动。及时回复粉丝的评论不仅可以增强交流，更可以增强粉丝的忠诚度，使其更乐于阅读该出版社发出的信息，并对今后的微博信息给予更多的关注。除此之外，出版社应特别关注那些活跃度高、信息量大、粉丝多的粉丝。利用微博分析软件，自动识别最勤奋最活跃的粉丝，多与活跃的粉丝互动，提高自己微博二次传播的概率，增加潜在受众。而与名人的互动可以借助他们的名气提高自己微博信息的到达率，以获得更多的粉丝和更多的评论。

（6）善于观察并运用微博发送中的小技巧。

（7）在微博中直接运用"@"键与某人交流，可以极大提高转发率，提高信息到达率。

参考文献

[1]　史永霞. 我国大学出版社品牌传播效果实证分析. 武汉：华中农业大学，2009：7–77

[2] 彭兰. 网络传播概论 [M]. 北京：中国人民大学出版社，2009

[3] 郭力华. 试论受众的接受心理与传播效果 [J]. 当代传播，2010（1）

[4] 尹亚辉，姬玉. 浅析媒体生态文明传播效果的优化方式 [J]. 中国出版，2010（12）

[5] 沈正赋. 突发事件报道方法与传播效果解析——2008 年我国突发事件报道研究综述 [J]. 当代传播，2009（2）

[6] 彭兰. 网络新闻传播效果评估的作用及方法 [J]. 中国编辑，2008（6）

作者简介

彭云，武汉大学信息管理学院出版发行系 2010 级硕士研究生。

沈阳，博士，武汉大学信息管理学院教授、博士生导师。

数字时代的出版物市场需求分析

邓香莲

（华东师范大学传播学院 上海 200062）

出版营销

摘要：出版业的市场需求是产业发展的风向标，而出版产值的增减则是出版市场需求的晴雨表。当前出版物市场的需求包括产品需求和服务需求，其中产品需求主要为传统出版物和数字出版物两个方面，而传统出版物和数字出版物又分别包括若干子市场，本文通过对大量数据的分析，以及对数字时代出版环境的整体把握，分别论述了数字时代下各类市场需求的现状以及发展的趋势。

关键词：数字时代 出版物 市场需求

Analysis on Market Demand of Publications in the Digital Age

Deng Xianglian

（School of Communication, East China Normal University, Shanghai, 200062）

Abstract：Publishing market demand is a windsock of the development of industry, and publishing output endorsements is the barometer of the publishing market demand. Current publications market demand includes product demand and service demand, the former can be divided into traditional product demand and digital publication, and all the traditional product demand and digital publication involve several sub-markets. Through the analysis of a great deal of dates and the whole mastery of publishing environment In the digital age, this paper describes the status and development trend of every market demand.

Keywords：Digital age Publications Market demand

出版业的市场需求乃产业发展的风向标，而出版产值的增减则是出版市场需求的晴雨表。数据显示，与 2008 年相比，2009 年全国新闻出版业总产值增长 20% 左右，图书销售增长 20% 左右，新媒体出版增长 42% 左右，网络出版、手机出版等新兴出版产业发展迅速，动漫网游出版和数字印刷等新业态发展势头强劲。2009 年，我国日报年出版总量达到 440 亿份，出版规模已连续 9 年位居世界首位，成为世界发行总量最大的报业市场；图书出版品种 27.57 万种，销售额 1456 亿元，仅次于美国；印刷复制业总产值达到 5 746 亿元，位居世界第三位；数字出版总产值达到 750 亿元，年增长 50% 以上；新闻出版业总产值已突破 1 万亿元。[1]

当前出版物市场的需求包括产品需求和服务需求，其中产品需求主要分为传统出版物和数字出版物两个方面，传统出版物市场又可细分为：印刷型出版物和音像出版物。其中，印刷型出版物又分为：图书、期刊和报纸。下面分别述之各类别当前的市场需求现状及趋势。

1 传统出版物方面

1.1 图书类市场需求

我国图书类出版物需求发展情况可以大致分为以下三个阶段。第一阶段（1978—1991年）：1991年，我国年出版图书89615种，平均每年增长14.75%；总印数61.39亿册，平均每年增长3.81%；总印张266.11亿印张，平均每年增长5.33%；第二阶段（1992—2001年）：从1992年到2001年，出版社由480家增长到562家，平均每年增长1.77%。重版率也逐年递增，以1.14%的年均增长速度由36.87%增长到40.84%；第三阶段（2002—2008年）：新出图书品种数增长率明显降低，由2003年的10.05%缩减为2007年的4.61%，2008年又有抬头的迹象，恢复到10.10%。再版率也开始回升，由2002年的10.10%增加到2008年的超过45%。图书价格开始平稳增长，由2002年的每印张1.17元的价格水平缓慢增长到2004年的每印张1.27元的价格水平，并连续4年基本保持不变。

总的说来，近年来我国图书市场的特点可以用"温和上扬"来概括。客观上讲，一方面，国民经济的不断向好为图书市场的温和上扬奠定了一定的经济基础；另一方面，全国地方出版单位和中央部分出版单位转企改制基本完成，这对于出版业重塑市场主体，增强出版企业的竞争力，起到了积极的促进作用。同时，部分出版集团正积极谋划上市，以利用资本市场的融资功能壮大企业的出版实力，再加上已经上市的出版集团，这些企业必将进一步加大对出版主业的投入，增加图书产品的供给和加大产品的营销力度。基于此，图书的市场需求和出版规模在一定程度上会相应增加。

1.2 期刊类市场需求

从表1的数据可以看出，期刊种类在2005年首次出现下降，且2005、2006、2007期刊种类数量保持不变，在2008年才开始出现增长。这反映出我国期刊市场的一个基本状态是，期刊出版种数基本稳定，期刊行业的产业结构正在不断优化。可以预计，未来几年，在期刊市场需求规模方面，期刊的总印数和总印张还会继续攀升，但需求总量不会有太大增长，渐趋饱和。随着网络对期刊市场的冲击加大，期刊业的分化和竞争会进一步加剧。

表1　1990—2008年期刊出版总量统计

年份	种数（种）	平均期印数（万册）	总印数（亿册）	总印张（亿印张）	折合用纸量（万吨）
1990	5 751	16 156	17.9	48.1	11.3
1991	6 056	18 216	20.62	54.44	12.79
1992	6 486	20 506	23.61	62.73	14.74
1993	7 011	20 780	23.51	64.21	15.09
1994	7 325	19 763	22.11	63.86	15.01
1995	7 583	19 794	23.37	67.02	15.75
1996	7 916	19 300	23.10	68.06	15.99

年份	种数（种）	平均期印数（万册）	总印数（亿册）	总印张（亿印张）	折合用纸量（万吨）
1997	7 918	20 046	24.38	73.3	17.23
1998	7 999	20 928	25.37	79.87	18.77
1999	8 187	21 845	28.46	96.78	22.75
2000	8 725	21 544	29.42	100.04	23.51
2001	8 889	20 697	28.95	100.92	23.71
2002	9 029	20 406	29.51	106.38	25.01
2003	9 074	19 909	29.47	109.12	25.64
2004	9 490	17 208	28.35	110.51	25.97
2005	9 468	16 286	27.59	125.26	29.44
2006	9 468	16 435	28.52	136.94	32.18
2007	9 468	16 697	30.41	157.93	37.11
2008	9 549	16 767	31.05	157.98	37.12

1.3 报纸类市场需求

从表2的统计数据可以看出，我国报纸种数从1997年到2004年基本上呈递减的趋势，从2005年开始，报纸种数在总量上基本趋于稳定，但总印张和总印数一直是增加的趋势。这说明我国的报业结构得到了优化，政府通过建立科学的报纸出版资源配置机制，资源配置的质量和效益有了显著的提高。报业的准入机制和退出机制相结合，实现了对报纸总量的动态调控，报纸出版业的产业机构、产品结构和地区结构正在不断优化升级，出现了一批跨地区、跨媒体的大型报业集团。需要说明的是，虽然我国现在是报业大国，但还不是真正的报业强国，随着我国经济实力的进一步增强和产业集中度的不断提升，我国报业的发展空间和市场需求规模会进一步扩大。

表2　1990—2008年报纸出版总量统计

年份	种数（种）	平均期印数（万份）	总印数（亿份）	总印张（亿印张）	折合用纸量（万吨）
1990	1 444	14 670	211.3	182.79	42.0
1991	1 524	16 393	236.51	205.77	47.33
1992	1 657	18 031	257.85	238.78	54.92
1993	1 788	18 478	263.83	287.14	66.04
1994	1 953	17 736	253.19	310.75	71.47
1995	2 089	17 644	263.27	359.62	82.71
1996	2 163	17 877	274.28	392.41	90.25
1997	2 149	18 259	287.59	459.81	105.76
1998	2 053	18 210.69	300.38	540	124.2
1999	2 038	18 632.39	318.38	636.68	146.44
2000	2 007	17 913.52	329.29	799.83	183.96

年份	种数（种）	平均期印数（万份）	总印数（亿份）	总印张（亿印张）	折合用纸量（万吨）
2001	2 111	18 130.48	351.06	938.96	215.96
2002	2 137	18 721.12	367.83	1 067.38	245.51
2003	2 119	19 072.42	383.12	1 235.59	284.18
2004	1 922	19 521.63	402.4	1 524.8	350.7
2005	1 931	19 548.86	412.6	1 613.14	379.09
2006	1 938	19 703.35	424.52	1 658.94	381.56
2007	1 938	20 545.37	437.99	1 700.76	391.17
2008	1 943	21 154.79	442.92	1 930.55	444.03

1.4 音像制品市场需求

表3 1996—2008年录音制品出版数量统计

年份	种数（种）	出版数量（亿盒/张）	发行数量（亿盒/张）	发行总金额（亿元）
1996	8 916	1.46	1.41	9.67
1997	10 872	1.49	1.51	10.5
1998	8 148	1.20	1.12	7.36
1999	8 946	1.13	1.1	7.24
2000	8 982	1.22	1.16	7.82
2001	9 526	1.37	1.16	8.42
2002	12 296	2.26	2	13.66
2003	13 333	2.2	1.96	13.25
2004	15 406	2.06	1.72	11.29
2005	16 313	2.30	1.89	15.35
2006				
2007	15 314	2.06	2.00	11.52
2008	11 721	2.54	2.49	11.21

表4 1996—2008年录像制品出版数量统计

年份	种数（种）	出版数量（万盒/张）	发行数量（万盒/张）	发行总金额（亿元）
1996	7 306	1 823.81	1 455.27	4.19
1997	11 596	5 734.08	4 764.97	7.9
1998	8 990	5 956.71	4 624.74	5.12
1999	9 721	0.64	0.5	5.13
2000	8 666	0.81	0.6	6.38
2001	11 445	1.44	1.09	9.62

年份	种数（种）	出版数量（万盒/张）	发行数量（万盒/张）	发行总金额（亿元）
2002	13 576	2.18	1.74	11.02
2003	14 891	3.54	2.6	14.3
2004	18 917	3.62	2.45	13.81
2005	18 648	3.86	3.00	20.80
2006	17 856	3.23	2.41	19.66
2007	16 641	2.85	2.36	19.94
2008	11 772	1.79	1.61	7.23

音像制品市场受新技术的冲击很大。从上面新闻出版总署相关统计数据中可以看出，无论是录音制品还是录像制品，出版种数和发行金额在 2005 年出现高峰值之后便呈下降趋势，尤其是录像制品在 2008 年下降幅度较大，出版数量、发行数量以及总金额和 2007 年相比大幅跳水。可见，随着网络的普及以及相关替代品的出现，读者的阅读和收听收看习惯已经发生了显著的改变，音像制品的市场面临着巨大的挑战。

2 数字出版物方面

在媒介融合时代，数字出版业呈现出蓬勃发展的态势。

首先，2009 年我国的数字出版业整体收入达到 750 亿元[2]，首次超过传统图书出版业的产值，与 2008 年的 530 亿元相比，预计增长 41.5%。[3] 相较于 2002 年的 20 多亿元，我国内地的数字出版产值规模在 8 年内累计增加了 35 倍以上[4]，这样的发展速度对传统出版产业而言是望尘莫及的。

其次，我国的数字出版在 2009 年实现了业态多样化，除了已在大多数出版社开展的数字化业务，用手机收看电视、上网、读报纸、读书等也已非常普遍。根据报道，75% 的报社涉足网络报，55% 的报社拥有手机报，全国手机报数量将突破 1 500 种[5]，手机已经逐渐成为人们的主要阅读终端之一。因此，手机出版作为一个新的细分市场逐渐在数字出版业崭露头角。根据中国互联网络信息中心（CNNIC）发布的《第 25 次中国互联网络发展状况统计报告》显示，通过手机阅读的人数排名第二，仅次于使用手机聊天业务，用户的比例占到总体手机网民的 75.4%[6]。

可见，数字出版的迅速发展已经成为出版业的必然趋势。这除了归功于迅猛发展的技术之外，媒介融合也是重要的推动力之一。传统出版业与网络的融合、传统出版业与手机的融合正是媒介融合下数字出版蓬勃发展的例证。

2.1 数字出版物的市场需求将会激增

2008 年，在总体市场萧条的局面下，唯有数字产品的销售却表现出繁荣之势。因此各商家纷纷加大对数字出版的投入，希望以此摆脱危机困扰，占领新媒体市场。例如，企鹅集团宣布进军手机阅读市场，发布手机版图书供 iPhone 用户购买阅读；兰登书屋免费向 iPhone 提供部分畅销书的手机版本；亚马逊推出的电子阅读设备 Kindle 更是被称作出版业的"特洛伊木马"，业内人士认为它具有改变出版行业整体格局的潜力，巴克莱资本的分析师道格·安缪斯肯定亚马逊凭借其现有商业模式在经济低迷环境中的竞争优势，并预估经济情况稳定以后亚马逊的业绩将恢复两位数的成长率。[7]

同时，受金融危机影响，传统报业广告收入下滑、传统图书销售下降，传统出版企业纷纷加快数字化的转型，期望通过寻求有效的网络出版赢利模式、协调传统发行与网络出版之间的关系来整合资源、提高回报率。尽管金融危机的蔓延在一定程度上限制了对数字出版物阅读终端技术开发资金的投入与市场推广，但从国际出版市场上看，金融危机会加快出版业数字化转型的趋势。通过推进版权的数字化开发，寻找新的利润增长点，构建新的数字出版产业链，从而加快出版产业整体格局的优化。这也是传统出版产业走出经济萧条的有效途径之一。

随着各种数字终端的普及和人们阅读习惯的改变，读者对各类数字出版物的需求将会进一步增大。而且，政府相关部门出台的支持数字出版产业发展的系列政策，也必定会进一步激发对数字出版物的市场需求，成为我国数字出版产业发展强有力的推动力。

2.2 电子图书市场规模将持续增长

截至 2005 年底，我国电子图书的数量已经达到了 21 万余种[8]，到 2006 年年底，我国电子书总量已达 53 万种，电子书的收入达到 1.5 亿元，到 2007 年，电子书总量进一步增长为 66 万种，实现销售收入 1.69 亿元。目前全国有 160 多家出版社可以同步开发电子书，而且很多出版社的电子书出版数量已经超越纸质书。[9]以北京大学出版社为例，该社 2005 年出版的电子图书相当于 7 年来出版纸质图书的总和。而高等教育出版社在 2005 年的电子书出版是当年纸质书出版的 1.64 倍，这个增长比例是传统出版社进入电子书业务力度的一个表现。[10]目前，我国一些规模较大的出版社和出版集团都已经开始深度介入网络出版。在公共教育方面，我国使用电子图书的图书馆数量已经超过 1900 家；在个人使用方面，据不完全统计，新浪、搜狐的读书频道以及阿帕比读书网、中文电子图书网站等所提供的免费电子图书下载服务，已经培养了近千万的电子图书读者，这为电子图书市场的发展奠定了良好的读者基础。[11]

2.3 手机出版势头迅猛

手机出版包括无线音乐、手机游戏和手机读物等数字出版物的出版。从发展速度来看，手机出版是增长最快的数字出版领域，其在 2007 年实现近 300% 的增长速度，2008 年手机出版营业收入继续保持翻番增长。[12]目前，传统新闻出版单位和数字内容及技术提供商纷纷推出手机出版物，各大主流媒体均推出了自己的手机报业务，如《人民日报》、《广州日报》和《北京晨报》等。一些期刊社则推出手机杂志，如《电脑爱好者》、《三联生活周刊》、《互联网周刊》、《译林》、《家庭》、《汽车族》和《时尚旅游》等。还有的出版社则着手出版手机小说，如春风文艺出版社的《城外》、江苏人民出版社的《魔幻手机》等。可以预计，随着 3G 手机的普及和三网融合时代的到来，未来手机出版势头更猛，手机出版物有着巨大的发展潜力和空间。

报纸、杂志、图书与手机的融合不仅进一步提升了互动性和灵活性，3G 技术与媒介的融合也促使移动出版的诞生和发展。手机与纸媒的融合催生了手机报，手机与广播电视的融合产生了手机广播电视，而手机与互联网的融合则推动移动互联网的发展。读者通过手机订阅，就能够获取各类手机报和手机杂志；通过上传电子书，可以随时在手机上阅读浏览；而通过手机上网，也可以获得许多由运营商提供的免费阅读服务。

有了移动出版，人们获取信息的方式更为丰富，成本也更为低廉，很多时候读者只需要拥有手机终端，就能够免费接收他们想要的信息。所以在通讯技术和网络技术高度发达的今天，随着移动通讯设备的普及，数字出版业未来会有更大的发展空间。

3　出版服务方面

在出版物市场逐步成熟和完善的过程中，产品的同质化倾向日益显现，在同等价格、同等品质的前提下，出版服务就成了出版企业实施差异化竞争战略、形成比较竞争优势的关键。这直接导致了出版企业间的竞争逐渐由产品竞争转向服务竞争，越来越多的出版企业在市场竞争中不断拓展服务的广度和深度，把现代出版服务作为重要的业务领域来拓展。

事实上，数字时代的到来以及媒介的融合使得市场对于出版服务都有了更高的要求。如何在有效满足市场需求和获取预期的回报之间找到一个平衡点，是当前出版企业应该深思的问题。

目前来看，出版增值服务是出版企业常见的赢利模式之一。数字时代的增值服务主要有两种：一是辅助传统出版，即通过数字产品的支撑提高传统产品的竞争力，为传统出版物增加新的卖点，提高市场占有率；二是在多元化服务的过程中建立强大的作者数据库和读者数据库，借此为出版物产品的选题策划和网络营销打下坚实的基础。

当前，企业直接针对读者的出版服务主要包括线上增值服务和线下读者反馈两种：①线上增值服务：利用网络连接和沟通读者，培养和维护读者忠诚度。②线下读者反馈：通常做法是，要求读者寄回读者反馈卡，每月或每一阶段抽取部分幸运读者并赠送奖品。这样一来可以调动读者购买和阅读的积极性，增加其忠诚度，更为重要的是可以掌握更详细更真实的读者信息以及他们的建议和需求，以便能更有针对性地瞄准市场改进产品与服务。

为了迎合数字时代的市场需求，立体化出版已经成为当前出版业界研究的热点之一。所谓立体化出版，其核心内容实际上是提供立体化的出版服务，利用数字技术和网络技术，使图书作为一种产品不仅仅提供其纸介质版本，还提供相关的音像制品、电子和网络出版物等立体化的产品，从而实现图书产品的增值和出版产业链的延伸。

当前出版物市场上可以实现的立体化服务至少包括以下几类：①通过制作多媒体产品，为读者提供视频和音频信息，此类服务突破传统出版物无法为读者提供音频、视频信息的局限性，以多媒体的形式向读者提供更直观、更丰富的出版物内容。②通过建立互动平台，为读者提供实时服务，它改变了传统出版物出版的单向操作流程模式，通过现代网络技术建立读者、作者、编辑之间的互动平台、专用网站或者图书专栏等，从而实现编辑、作者和读者之间的多维互动。③通过开发体验式课件，使读者积极参与体验；对于一些实践性较强的出版物，为加深读者的理解和认识，可以积极尝试开发与其相关的课件，使理论与实践相结合，促进读者动手体验，这样既能提高学习效果，也创新了出版企业为读者服务的方式。

注释

[1]　我国进入出版大国行列. http://www.gapp.gov.cn/cms/html/21/2625/201001/696377.

html. 检索时间：2010-06-04

[2] 我国进入出版大国行列. http://www. gapp. gov. cn/cms/html/21/2625/201001/696377. html. 检索时间：2010-06-05

[3] 2009 年我国数字出版铺开"新版图". http://www. chuban. cc/ztjj/pd2009/szcb/hdtp/200912/t20091223_60966. html. 检索时间：2010-06-05

[4] 2009 年我国数字出版铺开"新版图". http://www. chuban. cc/ztjj/pd2009/szcb/hdtp/200912/t20091223_60966. html. 检索时间：2010-06-05

[5] 2009 年我国数字出版铺开"新版图". http://www. chuban. cc/ztjj/pd2009/szcb/hdtp/200912/t20091223_60966. html. 检索时间：2010-06-05

[6] 今年手机阅读市场份额预计将达 6 亿元. http://www. chuban. cc/yw/201001/t20100129_63413. html. 检索时间：2010-06-05

[7] 人民网金融危机背景下的出版业发展. http://media. people. com. cn/GB/22100/54430/54431/8527172. html. 检索时间：2010-06-05

[8] 产业观察：我国数字出版产业发展规模分析. http://www. ynycwz. com/newsview. asp?typeid=1&id=6495. 检索时间：2010-06-04

[9] 电子图书移动阅读成趋势. http://news. china-b. com/itdt/20090313/861801_1. html. 检索时间：2010-06-04

[10] 张立：中国大陆地区电子图书出版——现状与趋势. http://www. chuban. cc/gj/rdjj/zhnh9/tpxw/200708/t20070803_27939. html. 检索时间：2010-06-04

[11] 产业观察：我国数字出版产业发展规模分析. http://info. printing. hc360. com/2007/11/14090870740-2. shtml. 检索时间：2010-06-04

[12] 进一步加快新闻出版业向数字化转型. http://www. gapp. gov. cn/cms/html/21/1026/200907/465018. html. 检索时间：2010-06-04

作者简介

邓香莲，博士，华东师范大学传播学院教师。

数字时代的出版物市场需求分析

微博营销：数字时代的出版营销新策略

郑　妍

（武汉大学信息管理学院　武汉　430072）

摘要：随着微博这一新型网络交互平台的兴起，微博营销发展为一种网络营销新模式。传统出版营销存在受众面窄、信息滞后等局限，微博营销以其即时性、交互性、精准性等优势为传统出版注入活力。本文试以中国新浪微博为例，分析企业、产品、个人三方面的营销案例，进而构建"出版者—读者"微博交互模型，论述微博营销在各出版环节中的应用，探讨出版企业、出版人、出版物借助微博促进营销的新策略。

关键词：微博营销　出版营销　微博　读者

Microblog Marketing: A New Publishing Marketing Strategy in Digital Age

Zheng Yan

（School of Information Management，Wuhan University，Wuhan，430072）

Abstract：With the thriving trend of microblog as a new interactive online platform，Microblog marketing has became a new pattern of online marketing. Traditional publishing marketing is limited in the narrow range of readers，the hysteresis of information，etc. The usage of microblog marketing which is instant，interactive and accurate will infuse new life into it. This paper is trying to take the microblog of SINA community in China for example，analysing three cases of marketing of enterprises，products and individuals. Then construct the model of interaction between publishers and readers，analyzes the usage of microblog marketing in each stage of publication and discuss the new strategies of using microblog to promote the marketing of publishing companies，publishers and publications.

Keywords：Microblog marketing　Online marketing　MicroBlog　Reader

1　微博营销的概念

1.1　微博与微博营销

微型博客（Micro-Blogging）简称微博，是一种基于用户关系的信息传播及获取平台，用户可通过 WEB、WAP 及各种客户端组建个人社区，实现约 140 字的信息更新与即时分享。

　　2009 年 8 月中国门户网站新浪网推出"新浪微博"内测版，成为中国门户网站中首家提供微博服务的网站。2010 年 6 月，新浪微博用户数达 4 435.8 万，成为中国最大的微博社区。

　　微博营销，是因微博的迅速推广兴起的新型网络营销，目前在业界尚无确切定义。根据其运作过程，笔者归纳如下：微博营销，是一种基于微博平台，在特定网络社区中进行信息发布、品牌展示、用户交流、客户关系管理等一系列营销行为，从而实现营销目标的网络营销方式。

　　一般地，微博营销具备以下基本要素：

　　（1）营销主体。即营销过程中的参与者，包括营销者（信息发布者）、目标客户（信息受众）及其他相关用户。

　　（2）营销对象。即所推广的事物，包括企业、产品、服务、事件、人物、体验等，本文结合出版活动主要分析企业、产品、人物三类。

　　（3）营销渠道与技术支持。微博及相关研发技术、系统。

　　（4）营销手段。包括围绕品牌发布信息、发动讨论、与受众互动交流、开展社区活动等。

　　1.2　微博营销的优势

　　通过表 1 微博营销与传统出版营销的对比可知，运用微博进行出版营销具有以下优势：

　　第一，即时发布信息，降低时间成本。传统营销的信息传播渠道存在众多中间环节，漫长的时间差降低了效率。微博的即时发布功能缩短了信息传播周期，发布者只需在主页编辑框中输入信息，即可第一时间将书讯送达读者。简短的信息也降低了读者的阅读强度，轻松的氛围更利于激发其阅读兴趣与购书愿望。

　　第二，加强读编交流，整合关系网络。传统营销以出版者单方推介为主，读者很难有机会与出版方交流，其意见得不到回应也难以作用于产品决策。微博将各种身份的人聚合在同一社区，打破了隔阂。出版方发布讯息后，读者只要登录其页面留言，即可与其交流并获得回复，也可与页面上出现的其他读者交流感想。

　　第三，提示读者需求，促进精准营销。传统读者分类体系陈旧，难以反映新形势下读者个性化的需求，微博中的热点每日更新，出版方可以通过查询热议关键词把握读者的需求动向，及时策划选题。同时，微博中有根据职业、兴趣划分群体的功能，当网友根据各自特性组成不同阵营时，在图书营销的意义上就实现了用户细分。这一个个阵营如同一个个图书市场的雏形，传递出潜在的需求。出版者只要针对特定的微博群体投放信息，即可实现信息与受众的精准匹配。

　　第四，意见领袖提升传播效力。新浪微博以汇聚名人为策略，这些用户多为现实领域中的领袖或高人气网络人物。根据"二八"理论，这 20% 的意见领袖将创造 80% 的信息，影响其他 80% 的用户，推动营销进程。

表1　微博营销与传统出版营销的对比

营销模式	信息传播					成本	侧重环节	读编交流
	信息开放度	渠道	速度	更新	影响范围			
微博营销	高，读者自由获取信息	多样化、灵活、畅通	高	方便快捷，可每日更新	广泛	低廉	信息发布、读编交流	强，方便，气氛轻松活跃
传统出版营销	低，普遍信息不平衡	有限、闭塞	低	慢，难以保证每日更新	狭窄	较高	信息发布、发行	弱，不方便，途径堵塞

2　微博营销的案例分析

2.1　企业营销案例——李开复的"创新工场"

2009年9月4日，原Google全球副总裁兼中国区总裁李开复正式辞职，当日在新浪微博上发布信息："我不加入任何公司，我会自己做一个青年创业平台。下星期会给大家更多信息。"2009年9月7日，李开复正式发布新公司"创新工场"，10月赴中国大陆招聘演讲。两个月中，他连续发布50条微博公布公司动态和招聘见闻，吸引了大量媒体、公众的目光。"创新工场"开业第一天就收到7 000封来自全国的简历，招聘演讲吸引了上万人应聘。

李开复的企业营销策略，即瞄准初创时期集中发布信息为创新工场造势，并持续发微博展示团队生活，促进公众对企业文化的了解。2009年9月4日到2010年3月4日半年内，李开复共发布微博396条，涉及创新工场的80条，占20%，平均每月13条。这些微博摆脱了企业官方网站仅报告工作动态的呆板模式，并附带照片，更多展示了团队生活化的一面。比如创业初期的奇闻轶事、员工进餐场景、圣诞聚会等。从时间上看，关于创新工场的微博的发布呈现明显的时间分布特征：9月35条，10月15条，11月4条，12月11条，1月5条，2月10条，可见宣传集中在创业头两个月，此为聚集人气的关键时期。

从表2可见，网友针对创新工场的留言数在创办的头2个月达到高峰，与李开复发布微博的集中程度一致。虽然11月降幅较大，但在12月至次年2月迅速回升并稳定在原峰值的1/2，说明关注趋于稳定。

表2　网友针对创新工厂微博的留言、转发频数

月份	留言频数	平均每条留言频数	转发频数	平均每条转发频数
9	2 532	72	1 456	42
10	2 612	174	1 010	67
11	618	154	368	92
12	1 007	91	404	37
1	1 065	213	1 164	233
2	1 547	154	963	96
合计	9 381	（平均值）117	5 365	（平均值）67

2.2 产品营销案例——图书《我们台湾这些年》

2009年11月，北京读客图书有限公司推出新书《我们台湾这些年》。上市一个月即售出30万册，蝉联畅销榜榜首，被中国图书评论学会列入"2009年度十大图书"。2009年10月1日至2010年3月31日，该书策划团队三位出版人在新浪微博上发布相关微博656条，引发500余名新浪博友的评论1 811条。该书通过微博宣传迅速走红，被业内人士称为"国内微博图书营销第一例"。

2.2.1 产品营销手段

第一，多形式、即时发布书讯。书讯内容包括四类：新书推介、文段选刊、媒体宣传、读编交流。发布者在书讯开端注明"读客早/午/晚间新闻"等标签，以区分信息、提示阅读；对有价值的博友留言予以评论并以微博形式转发；将微博与公司主页、新闻网站、作者博客设置"关联"，任一网页更新书讯将自动在微博生成链接。

第二，向业界人士赠阅。新书一出版，读客立即向微博上的公众人物（作家、媒体工作者、出版人、评论员等）寄赠样书，并利用微博交流促进他们对图书的理解。

第三，社区主题活动。营销者在微博发布公告，组织网友参与书评征集、有奖摄影、新书签售、电视节目等活动，通过微博组织网友参与主题活动，促进图书的口碑营销和品牌认知。

第四，加强读编互动与读者服务。读客利用微博开展答疑、讨论等读编交流，一方面帮助读者理解图书，激发其阅读兴趣；一方面积极采纳读者建议，加强产品建设。

2.2.2 营销阶段分期

图1统计了2009年10月—2010年3月读客主创团队发布图书信息的频数。整体上集中于2009年10月下旬至12月上旬，即上市半年中的前1/2时间。10月与11月出现了两次"大爆发"，频数为38与42。然而10月信息量很少，总频数仅99，日均3；11月信息量攀升，总频数425，日均14。12月开始骤降至总频数111，日均3.5，为11月的1/4水平。2010年1—3月总频数仅21，信息发布趋于停滞。

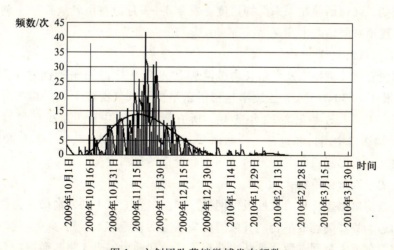

图1 主创团队营销微博发布频数

图2用四种色块表示读编交流、媒体宣传、文段选刊、新书推介这四类信息的发布频数。色块分布区域明显，表明各类微博的发布顺序和数量差别较大。半年中总频数为读编交流244、文段选刊206、媒体宣传134、新书推介57。10月中旬至11月上旬，文段选刊发布量最大（129），伴随少量读编交流与新书推介；11月中下旬，读编交流大规模聚集（196），媒体宣传次之（78），文段选刊锐减（38），新书推介频数均衡但仍最少（30）；12月上中旬，媒体宣传成为主要工作（51），读编交流骤减（13）；12月下旬至次年3月，文段选刊最多（11），其余频数皆为个位数。

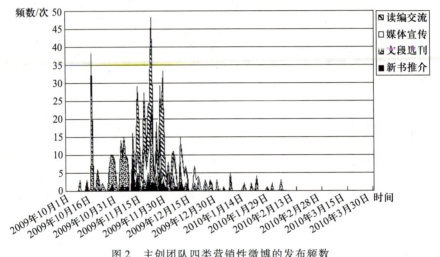

图2　主创团队四类营销性微博的发布频数

结合主创团队所发布频数与内容的时间分布，可推测其半年中的营销分期。整体上看，营销重心放在11月，中下旬达高峰。10月为品牌导入期，连续选刊文段让读者认识新书，于16日爆发刺激受众；11月为品牌成长期，一面借助广大媒体宣传造势，一面加强读编交流，把图书运作成热议话题；12月为品牌维护期，持续媒体宣传，辅以新书推介和文段选刊，确保话题在未来保持热度。次年1—3月为自由延续期，主创团队的营销目标转移，逐渐减弱话题干预。

2.3　个人营销案例——俞敏洪

新东方教育集团创始人及董事长俞敏洪从2009年9月27日开通微博至2010年9月，"粉丝"数累计1 030 375人，连续半年稳居新浪微博人气榜前十名。其微博展现的人格魅力吸引了广大网友，截至2010年3月，所有新浪博友关于（提及）俞敏洪的微博共8 880条，新浪微博中用户名包含"俞敏洪"以表达支持者共18人。他于2010年的新浪教育颁奖典礼上获得新浪网友评定的"新浪教育微博风尚大奖"。

俞敏洪的个人营销策略：

第一，微博以思想性与启发性吸引网友。与众多企业家不同，俞敏洪把微博建设成了一个启发励志、答疑解惑的平台。其微博中关于生活思考、人生励志、文化教育的言论位居发布量前三名，大量网友留言称从中获得了启示和动力。表3将其微博内容分为9类主题，各类发布频数、内容、网友的评论与转发频数如下：

表3　俞敏洪微博的频数、主题排行

主题	微博数	主要内容	留言总数	转发总数
生活动态	55	出行见闻、生活趣事、相片展示	9 401	7 319
人生励志	36	人生意义、理想、成功等话题	11 741	42 709
文化教育	33	教育体制、文化现象	4 398	4 930
为人处世	29	做人做事的智慧	11 432	42 286
闲言碎语	27	零碎的话语、回应网友	2 565	502
情趣幽默	24	转发趣味短信、调侃、生活照	6 477	24 525
社会政经	22	民主政治、国民素质、经济等	6 037	10 459
修身养性	20	心态调节、文学艺术	7 494	27 339
学习指导	12	英语学习、学习安排	1 211	2 840

　　第二，与网友建立稳定的互动机制。微博开通初期，新东方员工为俞敏洪设置了屏蔽网友评论的抗干扰项，俞敏洪使用微博后立即解除了该设置，并发微博邀请网友与自己交流。在其微博中，内容直接体现与网友交流的微博近30条，包括问候与祝福、回应或转发留言、组织在线讨论、征询意见等，获得了网友的积极回应。

3　微博营销在出版业的应用

3.1　微博营销中的角色分配

　　微博用户中涉及图书营销的角色有五类：出版者、作者、读者、业内人士、普通受众。出版者与作者构成主创团队，是图书信息的一级发布者；读者、业内人士和普通受众与前者互动，促成信息的二次传播。

　　出版者是营销信息的主要发布者；作者势单力薄，只能发布少量与本人和图书紧密相关的信息；读者包括潜在、现实两类，潜在读者多是在偶然看到信息后产生兴趣和消费倾向，他们需要信息，主要通过留言向出版者咨询。现实读者更需要交流，主要通过写读后感、对相关微博进行留言或转发等形式实现交流；一般受众是微博用户中的大多数，多数在偶然情况下看到信息并参与评论。由于职业身份的差异性、对主题的关注程度和参与动机不同，不像读者有明确的购买倾向或阅读体验，因此他们既是信息传播的最广泛受众，又是不稳定、不精准的群体；业内人士包括书评家、出版人、学者等，他们对书业营销有切身体会，因此对主题兴趣更强，形成的关注也更稳定。由于具备专业性和权威性，他们的参与将促进图书营销。

3.2　"出版者—读者"微博交互模型

　　出版者和读者是出版营销中最主要的一对主体，促进二者互动是推进微博营销的关键。

　　图3的"出版者—读者"微博交互模型由读者购书流程、图书营销示例、微博营销策略三条主线组成：中垂线的左半区描述读者的购书行为和运作流程，右半区描述出版者的策略和运作流程，读者行为与营销策略之间具有"前者由后者激发、后者依据前者展开"的关系，每一步骤都在水平方向上左右对应。中部的图书营销示例则以读者购买图

书《蜗居》为例，说明出版者如何运用微博营销策略，激发读者对图书产生关注、互动、消费、评价等一系列行为。整个模型贯穿品牌导入期、品牌成长期、品牌维护期三个营销阶段。

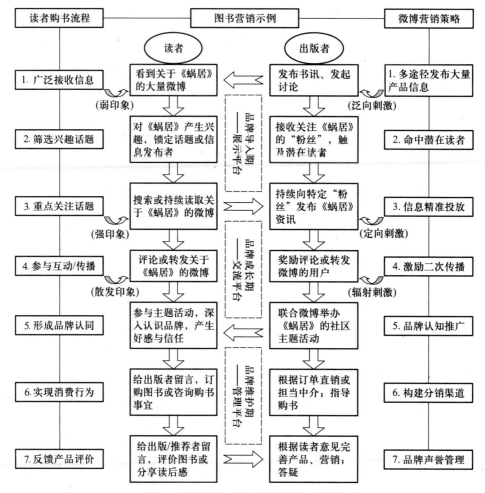

图 3　"出版者—读者"微博交互模型

（1）品牌导入期：品牌影响力弱，固定受众群尚未形成，因此要采取"广撒网"策略，向广大网友投放信息。网友对信息产生偶发性的关注并锁定感兴趣的话题，将聚合成特定信息的关注群体，成为潜在读者。出版者通过与他们建立社区关系初步确定目标受众，为精准投放信息奠定基础。这一阶段，信息与受众的匹配精度很低，因此信息对读者产生的是泛向刺激，读者对信息形成的是弱印象。

（2）品牌成长期：随着对品牌的兴趣和认知的加深，读者开始与出版者交流，甚至向亲友推荐信息，成为信息的二级传播者。出版者则通过开展社区主题活动提升品牌认知度。这一阶段，读者群逐渐成形，出版者可以针对明确的对象投放信息，因此信息与读者的匹配精度提高，信息对读者产生的是定向刺激，读者对信息产生的是强印象；同时，主动分享的读者发挥了散发印象的作用，信息对更广大的读者产生了辐射刺激。

（3）品牌维护期：出版者对读者评论进行监控和反馈，对部分读者提出的消费意向进行处理，提供直销或与沟通分销渠道，维护良好的品牌形象。

3.3 微博营销在各出版环节的应用

图书营销大致包括选题策划、编辑出版、宣传销售、售后服务等环节。微博营销可从这四个环节实现与出版营销的对接。

第一，选题策划环节，辅助市场分析。首先是定性分析，根据微博用户的阵营分布，分析读者需求的构成与分布；其次是定量分析，统计读者评论的数量，掌握各类读者需求的比例。抓住微博中的热点话题或重大事件策划选题，根据读者反应计划出版物上市的时机。

第二，编辑出版环节，根据读者意见完善产品。图书上市前可预先在微博上做一些测试，试探读者的反映，并根据读者评论完善产品。这一阶段应注意捕捉微博中的活跃人群与意见领袖，将其发展为二次传播的中坚力量。

第三，宣传销售环节，提升大众对出版社、出版物和作者的认知度。出版社可开通官方微博，发布新书资讯，提供在线订购，组织社区主题活动，加强网友对企业文化的理解；推广图书产品时，可邀请业界专家、社会名人阅读、推荐，采取激励措施发动广大网友参与图书信息的二次传播；作者可发布反映个人生活、思想情感、创作思路的微博，促进读者对作者的认知。

第四，售后服务环节，加强读者服务与读编交流。出版社的官方微博应提供读者答疑、产品评价与退换等服务，及时根据读者意见调整产品和营销策略。

本文归纳了微博营销的概念、要素与优势，通过企业、产品、个人三方面案例分析了微博营销的运作，进一步提出微博营销在出版领域的应用策略。微博出版营销目前尚处在探索阶段，如何建全机制，使微博营销规范化、更好地服务于出版事业，这是需要出版人进一步思考的问题。

参考文献

[1] Sorina Raula Girboveanu, Silvia Putu. Viral Marketing. Annals of the University of Petrosani: Economics [J], 2008 (1)

[2] Howard, Rheingold. The virtual community: homesteading on the electronic frontier. Masss: assison Wesley, 1993

[3] Hagel. J. and Armstrong, A, g, Net gain: expanding markets through virtual communities. Mass: harvard Business School, 1997

[4] Kozinets, R. V. 'I want to believe': a netnography of the X-philes' subculture of consumption. Advances in Consumer Research, 1997 (24)

[5] Preece, J. (2000). Online Communities: Designing usability, supporting sociability. Chichester, UK.: Wiley

[6] 史瑞. 论新媒体的产生、应用及其商业模式. 现代商业, 2008 (2)

[7] 王月, 蒋倩. 微博客能否成为品牌力器. 国际广告, 2009 (7)

[8] 刘玥. 微博客社会化营销新阵地——博客的前世今生. 国际广告, 2009 (7).

作者简介

郑妍，武汉大学信息管理学院编辑出版学 2007 级本科生。

出版营销

读者心理与市场营销

李 春

（湖北长江出版集团崇文书局 武汉 430070）

摘要：读者是市场营销活动中的重要因素。读者心理对市场营销的制约作用，决定了出版发行企业的市场营销活动要重视对读者心理的研究。本文试图从新书出版与读者心理、读者对价格的敏感性、畅销书与读者、广告与读者心理等方面，简述读者心理在市场营销中的作用，以期出版企业能够重视读者心理在营销活动中的作用，促进营销方式和手段的多样化。

关键词：读者心理 读者 市场营销

The Psychology of Readers and Marketing

Li Chun

（Hubei Changjiang Publishing Group, Chongwen Publishing House, Wuhan, 430070）

Abstract: Readers are the important factors in marketing activities. Reader's psychology restricts publishing groups' marketing activities, which determines that the marketing activities of publishing groups should attach importance to readers' psychology research. The paper tries to explain the influence of readers' psychology in marketing activities from the four aspects: the publishing of new books and reader's psychology, readers' sensitivity to price, best-sellers and readers, advertisements and readers' psychology. It hopes that publishing groups take readers' psychology seriously and promotes marketing mode and means of diversification.

Keywords: Readers' psychology Readers Marketing

随着出版发行体制改革的深入，图书市场更加活跃、更加繁荣，竞争也更加激烈。出版企业为了获得更多利润，对市场的关注和重视程度日趋高涨，营销理念也发生了变化，"以市场为中心，视读者为上帝"成为占统治地位的市场经营思想。鉴于读者和市场营销之间的密切关系，为使图书市场营销保持较好的水平，探索市场营销的深度和广度，就必须重视读者心理的研究。

1 读者是市场营销活动中积极的、活跃的因素

在图书市场的交换关系总体中，读者是市场的主体，是市场营销活动的中心。这是因为在市场交换中，实现商品到货币的变化，是一个惊险的飞跃。在货币与商品的对立中，

主动权总是操纵于货币所有者之手，货币所有者不愿意，这一飞跃就不能实现，再生产就会遇到阻碍。因此，出版企业的营销活动必须以读者为中心，明确读者是市场营销活动中积极的、活跃的因素。

市场读者不同于图书馆的读者，他们是具有一定阅读能力和购买能力，并有一定购买行为的社会成员，这种特殊性决定了他们对企业经营活动的影响力。出版企业通过对读者心理的探讨，为出版发行工作提供方法论的依据，为图书市场营销提供切实有效的方法，以便根据读者的需求变化和各类读者的心理特点，组织图书选题的策划和销售，取得更大的经济效益。

2 读者心理对市场营销的制约，决定了市场营销要重视研究读者心理

市场营销的策略组合包括：产品、价格、销售渠道、促销策略，等等，也可说是市场营销的手段，其中心内容始终是围绕着生产者和消费者的关系上。市场营销采取何种策略，对读者心理活动的产生、发展有着很大的影响。反过来，各类读者的心理特点和心理趋向，也对市场营销起了一定的制约作用。

2.1 新产品的开发——新书出版与读者心理

在市场营销活动中，图书是市场营销活动的物质基础，也是读者在购买活动中引起各种心理反应的客体。图书不仅具有物质属性，还有精神属性，因此，研究读者购买过程中的心理活动，除了分析读者自身的需要、兴趣、动机、个性特征及其购买行为外，还必须积极探讨客体和主体即图书与读者的心理关系。

出版企业要想有所发展，必须不断研发、策划、创新和改进新品种，要重视新产品的开发和推广，也就是要重视新书的策划和宣传。在当今这样一个信息时代，资讯高度发达，信息来源渠道多而迅捷，出版人要"嗅觉"灵敏，善于捕捉热点、亮点、卖点，做到"人无我有，人有我新"。内容创新的同时，图书的开本、版式、装帧设计等外在形式要给人耳目一新的感觉。新颖独特、美观悦目的图书，能给人以美感，激发读者的购买欲望。

当下的生活是快节奏的，读者的阅读习惯也在悄然地发生变化。对一般读者而言，紧张工作之余，他们愿意选择那些版式休闲、活泼明快、图文并茂的诸如生活指导类、知识普及类、人生感悟类的图书，出版社要善于把握这种变化，适应这种需求。对中小学生而言，教辅图书的题量大、字数多，出版社可以通过字体字号的变化，或在每单元中穿插"课外链接"或"轻松一刻"版块，使版式看起来层次分明，凹凸有致，学生们做题时会更轻松。

在新书进入市场之前，出版社要利用网络等媒体进行预告宣传，介绍新书的特点，如何独一无二与众不同，让读者知晓，引起读者注意，并展开预定。

2.2 读者对价格的敏感性

图书价格是读者购买心理中最敏感的因素，它对买卖双方都有切身的利益。对价格的不同心理反应是客观存在的。由于读者对价格的认识过程和知觉程度不同，价格心理也是不同的。图书的价格与读者的价格心理要求有时是一致的，有时却是矛盾的。往往会出现这种情形：一个从理论上认为是合理的价格，但读者从心理上不一定能够接受；相反，一个从理论上认为是不合理的价格，读者从心理上却能接受。例如，有的读者出于好奇心理

或求美心理购买某种书，其价格虽然大大高于图书的价值，但心理上还是乐于接受的。

读者对书价的认识，是从多次的购买活动中逐步体验的，并形成了对某种书价的习惯性。价格的习惯性心理对读者的购买行为有重要影响，读者往往从习惯价格中去联想和对比价格的高低涨落，以及图书的价值。在许多读者心目中，在已经形成的习惯价格的基础上，对图书价格都有一个上限和下限的概念。如果图书的价格超过上限，则认为太贵；低于下限，则会对图书品质产生怀疑。

对于出版社来说，图书定价应该从选题策划开始，就纳入该书的营销策略之中。目前出版社大多是以成本定价作为图书价格的基础，参考同类书在市场的平均价格，结合读者所能承受的心理价位，来确定书价。读者对于不同类别图书的心理价位是有差异的，一般来说，对于普通的儿童类画册，家长的心理价位在 15 元以内；对于财经等专业类图书，读者的心理价位在 20～50 元；对于大众生活类、文学类图书，读者的心理价位在 20 元左右；对于中小学教辅类图书，读者的心理价位在 15～25 元。

掌握了读者的价格心理，出版社在选题策划之初，就应有意识地控制图书的字数、页码、印张、开本、用纸、印刷工艺等，把图书成本控制在一个合理的基础上，进而定出合理的价格。

图书市场的竞争是激烈的，在价格上的体现是明显的。民营书商的图书价格低廉，缘于他们的操作模式不同于传统出版社，他们有很大的空间来压缩成本，这在出版社的体制下是难以进行的。为适应竞争，有的出版社也会定价较低，利润微薄，这主要体现在一些生活类或大批量发行的图书上。出版社借助规模化，降低前期制作成本，加大开印量，用低价位的市场策略去占领市场，从而形成某类图书在市场上的垄断与控制，以抢占市场份额，形成自己的品牌。这是出版社的营销手段之一。

2.3 畅销书与读者

任何一个畅销品种在其策划创制过程中，都必须充分考虑相关的读者群体。前些年，人民文学出版社的《哈利·波特》多次位列国内日销售榜首，并带动了魔幻图书的销售，其特定的读者对象即少年儿童。出版社抓住了少年儿童爱幻想、喜冒险、天性单纯善良的特点，连续推出多集多套，取得了巨大的成功。

出版社利用读者好奇、求新、想了解真相的心理，配合电视剧热播及重大事件发生而出书，或者请名人写书，适时包装，及时推出，并大力宣传造势，举行签名售书活动，以形成单品种的品牌效应，使图书畅销。例如，前些年电视剧《雍正皇帝》在央视一套播出，就带动了同名小说的大卖；奥巴马竞选美国总统前后，有关他的传记都很畅销；易中天在"百家讲坛"的成功，甚至让他早期的作品都跟着沾光，出现了一批"易粉"读者。

2.4 广告与读者心理

广告是经济活动中一种影响力很强的宣传方式，富于思想性、真实性、艺术性，强烈表现力和想象力的广告，能给人留下深刻印象，提高产品的知名度。

广告的载体很多，报纸杂志、广播电视、手机、网络、户外大屏、流动的车身，等等。无论采取哪种广告形式，都必须充分研究读者心理活动的特点与规律，巧妙地利用心理学原理，增强广告的表现力、吸引力、诱导力。广告中成功的信息传递，往往首先作用于读者的视觉、听觉生理，继而引发心理感应，最后导致购买行为。

由于读者在年龄、性别、兴趣、职业等方面的不同，对各类图书有不同的心理需求，广告促销也是形式多样的。例如，有一套丛书名为"疯狂阅读"的教辅图书，共 3 本，为了带动整套书的发行，出版社就在每本书的封底上印上一套三本书的封面，三书的封面设计风格一致，学生购买了"现代文阅读"，就还想购买"文言文阅读"。还有的图书在封面或封底的醒目部位，用颇具卖点的"关键词"提示本书的独特之处，以吸引读者购买。

为应对激烈的市场竞争，出版发行企业越来越重视对读者的研究，对读者心理的揣摩，越来越重视营销方式的改善和促销手段的多样化。赢得了读者的心，就赢得了市场。

作者简介

李春，湖北长江出版集团崇文书局编辑部主任。

盛大文学全版权运营模式研究[*]

邹　燕

（武汉理工大学文法学院　武汉　430070）

摘要：本文从三个方面对盛大文学的全版权运营模式进行了全面分析：一是盛大文学全版权运营的起点——微付费模式，二是全版权运营的分销，三是全版权运营的终端。在全面分析了盛大文学全版权运营模式的基础上，文章的第二部分概括了盛大文学全版权运营的成效。盛大文学的发展突飞猛进，垄断的质疑声此起彼伏，而盗版问题更是从未消停过，文章最后重点对这两大问题进行了深入分析。

关键词：盛大文学　网络文学　全版权运营　数字出版

Research on Shanda Literature Corporation's All Copyright Business Model

Zou Yan

（School of Arts and Law，Wuhan University of Technology，Wuhan，430070）

Abstract：This paper provides a comprehensive analysis on Shanda Literature Corporation's all copyright business model from three aspects：the beginning of Shanda Literature Corporation's all copyright business — micro-payment model；the distribution and terminal of all copyright business. On this basis, the second part generalizes the effects of Shanda Literature Corporation's all copyright business. Shanda Literature Corporation develops rapidly，however，it is questioned whether it is a monopoly. At the same time，the problem of piracy is never efficiently solved. At the ending part，this paper deeply analyzes these problems.

Keywords：Shanda literature corporation　Online literature　All copyright business　Digital publishing

盛大文学有限公司（以下简称"盛大文学"）是以经营网络游戏著称的盛大集团的子公司。几年来，盛大文学成功推行了网络付费阅读模式；先后收购"起点中文网"（以下简称"起点网"）、"晋江原创网"、"红袖添香"、"榕树下"、"小说阅读网"、"言情小说吧"和"潇湘书院"七家国内领先的原创文学网站；还专注于文学版权运营，为线下出

---

* 本文为武汉理工大学自主创新研究基金项目"网络原创文学出版模式研究"研究成果。

版、电影、游戏、动画等提供有版权的内容。盛大文学在实质上是新时代的数字出版公司，其发展模式有独到之处，值得深入研究。以下，笔者重点就盛大文学的全版权运营模式及目前存在的问题作一些探讨。

1　盛大文学的全版权运营模式解构

所谓"全版权"是指一个产品的所有版权，包括网上的电子版权、线下的出版权、手机上的电子版权、影视和游戏改编权，以及一系列衍生产品的版权等。盛大文学全版权运营包含两个部分：版权的生产和分销。版权的生产在盛大文学的七大原创文学网站上完成，版权的分销，则是与其他内容生产商协作完成。

1.1　全版权运营之起点

2004 年 11 月，盛大文学凭借资金优势和渠道优势，收购了起点中文网。起点网是盛大文学经营网络文学的起点，也是版权生产的起点。盛大文学从经营起点网开始，从 2004 年至 2010 年，先后收购了七家网络文学原创网站，从而使其占有市场份额超过 80%。在经营过程中，盛大文学逐渐完善了以"微付费"为特征的 VIP 网络阅读收费模式。

所谓微付费（micro-payment），也叫小额支付，是针对用户为零散内容而支付的一种模式。一般金额非常小，但是用户范围非常大。盛大在运营网络游戏的过程中，早已铺设了能达到全国近 70% 二级城市的销售推广渠道。利用这些销售渠道，盛大文学完善了起点网设计的微付费系统。这个微付费系统的独特性在于：一是对网上优秀作品进行签约，前半部供读者免费试阅，后半部需付费阅读；二是以章节为单位，按每千字 2 分钱的价格进行销售，如仅选择部分感兴趣章节，费用更低；三是作者可获得用户付费额的 50% ～ 70% 作为基本报酬，且按月结算；四是作品创作、发布、销售、反馈以分钟为间隔，作者与读者实时互动；五是尊重版权、严格准入，每个作者必须提供真实身份，对新上传作品必须声明版权所有权。

微付费模式完善了以创作、培养、销售为一体的电子在线出版机制，初步探索出了原创文学网站的赢利模式。目前，盛大文学年收入数千万元，其中付费阅读就占了 60% ～ 70%，剩下的是广告和线下版权的收入。此外，作者的总收入主要从点击率和文字数量计算。若按每千字计算，一线作者可以获得最高 500 元的稿费；二线作者，获得的稿费在 100～200 元；很多作者的稿费是按照几十元计算的。在盛大，每年能产生 10 个收入上百万元的作者，100 个收入上十万元的作者，1 000 多个收入上万元的作者。

1.2　全版权运营之分销

版权的生产主要由盛大文学旗下原创文学网站完成，版权的分销指在不同渠道将版权销售出去。图 1 以起点网为例说明盛大文学的版权分销模式：

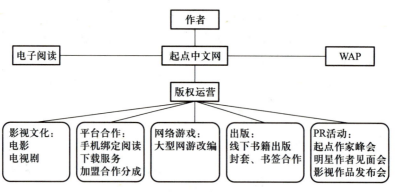

图 1　起点的版权分销模式

（资料来源：http://www.qidian.com/aboutus/ads/copyright.html）

　　盛大文学是盛大集团影视、游戏乃至音乐的版权来源。盛大投入 8 000 万元搭建推广版权衍生品的立体营销平台，邀请作家经纪人对盛大文学的签约作家进行包装和运营，探索将小说的电子版权、无线发布权、纸质版权及动漫影视改编权等统一包装、运营，打造一个以文学为核心，整合影视、版权、无线等多方资源的产业链，充分挖掘中国原创文学的文化创意产能。

　　在版权的多元化开发上，盛大文学采用的是"深挖洞"策略。"深挖洞"是指把每一个版权都运营到极致，把版权运营做精、做细、做深。把每部作品的版权、每个作者，都进行精细化的版权开发规划，把最大价值发挥出来。如，2009 年 3 月，盛大文学组织的全球写作大展启动，到 2010 年 11 月中旬截止时，共有 7 万余部文学稿件投稿，其中包括大量的长篇小说。盛大文学从中挑选出 300 多部作品，这些作品的线下出版权已经全部卖出去了，甚至有不少的影视版权也已经卖出去了。盛大文学提供的网络平台，每天都在产生无数的优秀创意、优秀剧本，补充了中国影视行业的短板。《恋爱前规则》改编自《与空姐同居的日子》，这是近年来知名度最高的网络小说之一，点击率累积超过 10 亿次。《星辰变》网络点击率超过 4 000 万，连续 40 周在百度所有关键词搜索排名中位居前列，多次名列第一，同时也是起点中文网总收藏榜排名第一名的作品，随后该作品又由线上作品变成了线下传统图书，2008 年其游戏版权以 100 万元的高价卖给了盛大游戏，并在 2009 ChinaJoy 年度优秀游戏评选中荣获"玩家最期待的十大网络游戏"第一名，其电影改编权也于 2009 年 11 月卖给了盛世影业。《鬼吹灯》出版简体中文、繁体中文及外文实体书，又配套制作了一系列动漫影视网游作品以后，版权总收入已超过 1 000 万元：在起点中文网的点击量就超过 1 000 万，实体小说销量突破 100 万本，小说 4 次加印，远销海外；2007 年 8 月 30 日起点中文网宣布将《鬼吹灯》的影视改编权以 100 万元转让给华映电影；由盛大自行研发的《鬼吹灯外传》将和同名电影同步上市；《鬼吹灯》漫画作品在 2007 年第一季度火热上市，点击量已超过 120 万。这类中国类型文学的代表一旦被拍成影视作品，对影视制作和网络文学的影响都将起到不可估量的作用。盛大文学现在已经拥有数千部当红、畅销流行小说的影视改编权，目前，已售出影视改编权的小说超过百部。

1.3　全版权运营之终端

　　盛大文学的优势在于内容，但为了进一步延伸产业链而不至于受制于终端阅读，自 2008 年开始，盛大文学便着手于无线阅读平台的优化，与中国最大的电信运营商中国移动达成战略合作协议，共同开辟无线阅读市场。为此，盛大文学专门设立了无线公司，依托于其搭建的数字版权中心，正式进军无线阅读市场。

2009 年 6 月 29 日，盛大文学与卓望信息技术达成战略合作，联手举办首届"3G 手机原创小说大展"的活动，以一字千元的高额版权金，征集优秀的手机小说创意，并打造出国内第一批手机小说家。这标志着盛大文学正式进入 3G 手机文学市场。

要立足现今中国的无线阅读市场，掌控渠道是关键，盛大文学目前已拥有两大较为稳定的自有渠道：一是 Web/WAP 网站，盛大文学旗下的三家网站拥有独立的 WAP 门户，供用户付费阅读；二是客户端（盛大书童），盛大已经与诺基亚、华为等手机终端厂商展开合作，在其手机中内置盛大文学盛大书童，并和三大运营商（中国移动、中国联通、中国电信）建立了战略合作关系。

此外，盛大文学还建立了合作渠道：其一，与梦网书城或其他文学类 WAP 网站开展内容源合作，为其提供原创文学作品；其二，与梦网书城或其他文学类 WAP 网站开展渠道合作，在其上面开辟小说专区。另外，盛大文学对电子阅读器的开发也已在紧锣密鼓中。盛大文学的渠道建设如图 2 所示。

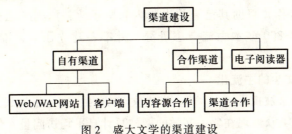

图 2　盛大文学的渠道建设

2010 年 8 月，盛大文学自产的电子阅读器 Bambook 以 999 元的价格进入正火热的电子阅读器市场。Bambook 是盛大 OPOB（One Person One Book，简称 OPOB）"一人一书"战略的一部分。该计划的核心是建立一个连接数字版权所有者、电子书硬件厂商、用户，开放云服务的大平台——云中书城，从而达到整合盛大文学旗下原创文学网站和整合全产业链的目的。云中书城（http://cloudary.sdo.com/）已经于 2010 年 8 月与 Bambook 同时上市。书城中，除了有网络原创小说外，还有大量经典原著和人文社科著作，显示盛大文学不但经营网络原创文学，而且还将向主流化方向发展。

2　全版权运营的主要成就

2.1　对数字出版赢利模式的创新

首先，VIP 网络收费阅读模式是一种全新的数字出版模式。它产生于网络环境下出版管制的灰色地带，由于内容资源的稀缺，导致对网络文学的巨大需求。原创文学网站从免费开始，逐渐探索出收费阅读模式。这种模式拥有先进的微付费系统，以及以创作、发布、销售为一体的电子在线出版制度。

其次，多维开发版权也是盛大文学的一大亮点。全版权运营模式的核心是对同一内容产品的深度开发，盛大文学在掌握了丰富的原创文学版权的同时收获了多元化的收益。目前，盛大文学旗下网站已拥有大约 85 万名作者，每天上传字数近 6 000 万字，获得近 500亿字的原创文学版权。这些版权是个巨大的资源宝库，全版权运营的关键在于附属版权的销售，即销售原创作品的改编权，通过改编创造影视、游戏、动漫等衍生作品。在这一环节中，盛大文学为其他公司提供的版权无形中已经为其创造了数次"衍生"价值。盛大通过全版权运营充分诠释了"内容为王"的含义。

2.2 初步打造数字出版全产业链

盛大文学打造了国内领先的手机产业链。盛大在这一阶段对手机产业链的打造比较全面，其内容提供，平台运营及终端渠道建设都有较大进展。现在，盛大文学已经成为中国移动手机阅读基地最大的收费内容供应商，在手机阅读领域占得先机。为了同时解决阅读障碍，丰富用户阅读体验，为3G时代的手机阅读做好全面准备，盛大文学还打造了手机小说原创平台 moga.cn，开发了"盛大书童"手机客户端软件。而随着手机上网用户即将超过 PC 上网用户，手机阅读的赢利指日可待。

OPOB 战略欲打通数字出版产业链。2010 年 3 月 10 日 14 点，盛大发布了"一人一书"的数字出版战略。OPOB 战略是要打造一条完整的数字出版产业链。目前，盛大文学在上游拥有大量的原创文学的内容资源，在中游拥有"云中书城"，在下游拥有 Bambook。现在，重点还是进一步推进上游内容资源的整合，盛大文学已经与出版传媒、北京出版集团等出版集团开展合作，帮助其已有的出版内容电子化，放到"云中书城"中。另外，盛大文学还已经汇集 800 多本主流杂志资源，并准备建立团队，准备开拓报纸的内容来源。

2.3 推动网络文学的主流化

网络原创文学历来被视为"另类"。盛大文学的内容满足了网民对大众文化的需求，使数字出版更加贴近大众。现在盛大文学的网站总计日平均访问量 4 亿次，日最高访问量 5 亿次，注册用户超过 4 300 万，分布在全球 200 多个国家和地区。

近年来，为了获得更大的用户群的认可，盛大文学积极推进主流化，为此，盛大文学采取了大量措施，如：动员传统知名作家韩寒、严歌苓、郭敬明到网络上首发自己的作品；斥资购买已经出版的图书版权，放到网上和手机频道上，方便读者阅读；盛大文学还加入"中国出版工作者协会"，从组织上融入出版产业的主流。盛大在网络文学主流化的道路上已经迈出了坚实的步伐。

另外，盛大文学积极推进网络文学的主流化，实现与传统出版的融合。《星辰变》、《鬼吹灯》等网络阅读反应良好的优秀的网络文学作品都实现了纸质图书的出版，与传统出版形成互动，线上线下相互促进，这也大大地促进了传统出版。

3　盛大文学当前存在的主要问题

3.1 遭垄断质疑

随着盛大文学在网络文学资源领域所占份额的越来越大，其面临的是否涉及垄断与不正当竞争的声音也不断传出，而且也越来越强。2008 年 10 月，读吧网运营商北京书生电子公司对盛大文学提起反垄断诉讼，控诉其利用强势地位胁迫作者停笔，违背了创作力的社会共享，这也成为了全国首例网络运营垄断案。但该案在 2009 年 12 月的终审中未获得上海高级人民法院的支持。

尽管盛大文学的市场垄断地位存在争议，但其强势地位却是不容置疑地影响到了整个网络文学生态。首当其冲的是其他竞争对手的生存问题，随着盛大文学的不断收购，用户资源几乎被盛大独占。其次，作者和读者的担忧也与日俱增。如果盛大文学形成行业垄断，那么盛大文学也就掌握了在线阅读的定价权和分成模式话语权，辛辛苦苦的网络作者和广大读者将失去原先与盛大文学平等对话的地位。

3.2 盗版困扰

盛大文学占据了国内网络文学份额的 80% 以上，但它同时也是遭受盗版危害程度最深的新媒体之一。盗版给盛大文学带来的损失，估计每年超过 10 亿元。目前，盛大文学受到的版权困扰主要有三种类型：

（1）不法网站的"盗链"。盛大文学拥有丰富的内容资源，但是更多的网民却是通过不法网站的"盗链"阅读到这些原创作品的。2008 年年底，盛大文学旗下的起点中文网赢得"国内首例网络文学侵权案"。被告"凌霄阁"网站先后刊载文学作品近 9 000 部，其中 1 300 多部"盗链"自起点中文网。最终"凌霄阁"网站两名主管都被判有期徒刑一年半并处罚金各 10 万元。[1] 在该案判决之后，盛大文学已将维权行动列为重点工作之一，筹建了国内最大的原创文学维权律师团。

（2）其他文学网站的侵权。2008 年，盛大文学旗下起点中文网上连载的《星辰变》一度走红，成为点击量最高的网络小说，作者署名"我吃西红柿"。书生公司旗下的读吧网上随后出现了署名为"不吃西红柿"的作品《星辰变后传》。因笔名相似，且沿用《星辰变》中的人物、情节、环境等要素，盛大网络要求《星辰变后传》的作者停止为读吧网创作并在起点中文网发表致歉信。2009 年元旦，读吧网的《星辰变后传》开始无法正常更新，《星辰变后传》的作者"不吃西红柿"向盛大书面致歉，并结束了在读吧网上《星辰变后传》的创作，转而到起点中文网创作新版本的《星辰变后传》。然而，读吧网则找来继任作者，仍以"不吃西红柿"为名继续更新《星辰变后传》。至此，起点中文网与读吧网的两部同名作品——《星辰变后传》均在正常更新中，作者署名也同为"不吃西红柿"。

（3）搜索引擎是盗版帮凶。继盛大拟起诉谷歌和解后，2010 年 3 月 17 日，盛大文学宣布，正式起诉百度，索赔金额达百万元。理由是百度在搜索结果及贴吧中收录了大量的网络文学盗版，这些作品侵犯了盛大文学的权益，索赔金额上百万元。[2] 目前，此案正在审理中。由于搜索引擎的特殊功能，在对其侵权行为的判定上有很大的难度。

盛大文学是一个数字化时代下的出版集团，但"网络只是盛大文学的一个鲜明特色，而非其全部特色，实际上，盛大文学在版权工业化上做了很多事情"。[3] 盛大文学的全版权运营模式已趋于成熟，值得传统出版机构在数字化改革中借鉴。至于垄断的质疑与盗版这颗毒瘤，随着对国外数字出版业发展的借鉴以及我国自身的理论研究与实践的结合，我国的数字出版产业将日趋成熟，政策与法律等行政保障体系将逐步完善。在这个进程当中，盛大文学与我国的数字出版共成长，并将以其实践经验促进我国数字出版产业的发展。

注释

[1] 盛嘉. 网络文学的盗版迷局 [J]. 产经报道，2009（4）：42-43.

[2] Ugmbbc. 盛大文学起诉百度侵权进展. 上海法院正式立案 [EB]. 中文业界资讯站，2010-03-16. http://www.cnbeta.com/articles/106320.htm. [2010-06-22].

［3］陈菁霞. 盛大文学产业链［N］. 中华读书报. http://www.gmw.cn/01ds/2009-11/04/content_1004120.htm［2009-11-04］.

参考文献

［1］盛大文学官网. http://www.sd-wx.com.cn/jtjj.html［2010-08-07］.

［2］刘世英等. 盛大传奇——陈天桥和他的"蓝海"之路. 北京：中信出版社，2007.

［3］欧阳友权. 网络文学发展简史——汉语网络文学调查报告. 北京：中国广播电视出版社，2008.

［4］盛大文学电子书战略发布会现场实录. http://www.rongshuxia.com/news/152.html［2010-08-07］.

［5］侯小强. 盛大文学的两次战略选择. http://www.chinapublish.com.cn/rdjj/09gjcblt/jbtp/200909/t20090902_54385.html［2010-08-07］.

［6］起点中文网. http://www.qidian.com/［2010-08-07］.

［7］盛大文学斥资 8 000 万介入 3G 领域. http://it.sohu.com/20090629/n264848938.shtml［2010-08-07］.

［8］盛大书童. http://www.qidian.cn/.

［9］盛大文学联合诺基亚试水移动互联网. http://tech.163.com/09/0917/04/5JCRN4TG000915BE.html［2010-08-07］.

［10］任茜. 盛大文学："让作家有钱". http://www.neworiental.org/publish/portal0/tab464/info410421.htm［2010-08-07］.

［11］陈菁霞. 盛大文学产业链［N］. 中华读书报. http://www.gmw.cn/01ds/2009-11/04/content_1004120.htm［2010-08-07］.

［12］佚名. 盛大文学连接并购文学网站. 依托版权扩张. http://media.ifeng.com/news/201002/0222_4009_1552010.shtml［2010-08-07］.

［13］陈晓平. 解读盛大 inside：为什么盛大要免费. http://tech.sina.com.cn/i/2010-04-10/00414039860.shtml［2010-08-07］.

［14］艾瑞网文学类网站排名. http://www.iwebchoice.com/Html/Class_65.shtml［2010-08-07］.

［15］侯小强揭秘盛大文学赢利之路：要价不贵多次利用. http://it.people.com.cn/GB/42891/42894/9455575.html［2010-08-07］.

作者简介

邹燕，武汉理工大学文法学院新闻传播系 2009 级硕士研究生。

小荷才露尖尖角

——论图书视频广告在中国应用的现状及发展趋势

魏丹羨 杨倩茹 詹莉波

（浙江工商大学人文学 杭州 310018）

摘要：在媒介融合时代，图书视频广告这个新兴的图书营销手段悄然兴起。因其具备了动态的传播效果，又很好地借助了网络传播的优势，图书视频广告凸显了其他传统图书宣传方式所无可比拟的优势，具有广阔的发展空间。但是作为图书营销领域的"新秀"，图书视频广告因为观念普及不够、技术人员缺乏等原因在国内未能得到广泛应用。通过对这些原因的分析，本文有针对性地提出了制作和推广视频广告的新思路、新方法、新途径和新措施，预见了视频广告将以无限的创意和鲜活的形式为图书营销市场开拓一片"蓝海"的美好前景。

关键词：视频广告 图书营销 成本 效果

The Current Development and Further Application of Book Video Advertisements in China

Wei Danti   Yang Qianru   Zhan Libo

（School of Humanities，Zhejiang Gongshang University，Hangzhou，310018）

Abstract：In the era of media convergence, book video advertisements rise as a brand new marketing strategy. Combining the dynamic effect of videos, and easy internet accesses, book video advertisements outstands from other conventional book advertisements. It has a broad space of development. But as a new strategy in the field of book marketing, video advertisements for books are not well-accepted. Together with other obstacles like the lack of technical staff, unfamiliarity among target audience, this new marketing strategy is not applied within the domestic market. In this paper, we will analyze the advantages of book video advertisements in book marketing and the obstructions that prevent book video advertisements from further application. Furthermore, in respect to the obstructions, we present a new approach of creating and applying book video advertisement, in order to promote the development of book marketing.

Keywords：Book video advertisements Book marketing Costs Effects

"到最后这一刻我才明白，我毁了你一个最初的梦想，你欠我一个本来承诺好的未来。尤瑟纳尔说，世上最肮脏的，莫过于自尊心。我突然意识到，即使肮脏，余下的这一生，我也需要这自尊心的如影相伴。每一朵乌云都镶有金边，失恋也不例外。他离开你，我陪伴你。《失恋33天》，小说或者指南，鲍鲸鲸真诚奉献，2010年1月10日温情上市。"

上述台词缘于一段流传于优酷、土豆等国内大型视频网站上的图书视频广告，意犹未尽的阐述让读者充满好奇。视频评论中有不少网友留言称赞视频，并表示对图书充满期待，亦有不少读者反馈正是通过此视频才得到了该本图书的信息，并坦言是因为对这个视频的关注引发了他们买这本书的欲望。

无独有偶，在《小时代2.0虚铜时代》强势登陆市场前，一段同样"气势磅礴"的图书视频广告首先登陆各大网站，掀起了强烈的视觉冲击风暴。

"——14家全国一级印刷厂灯火通明；
——127台高速印刷机轰然作响；
——47台胶订机器流水作业时刻不停；
——3 060名印厂工人披星戴月；
……
——370 000余家大小书店；
——2 000 000名读者持续156天的热烈期待；
——这是2009年末的超级盛宴，这是2010年开篇的文字狂欢，小时代2.0虚铜时代，郭敬明著。"

与《失恋33天》拥有故事情节的人物拍摄完全不同的是，此段视频广告利用大量不断更迭的数据，直观、形象、极具视觉冲击力地传递图书制作与销售的信息。

作为图书销售领域的新方式，图书视频广告在网上所激发的波澜引起了我们对这个图书新兴营销方式的关注。传统的图书营销方式包括发布书讯、召开作品研讨会、刊登书评、作者签售、作家访谈、巡回演讲、张贴书店海报宣传等，出版社通过各种营销手段来达到传递图书信息、引导读者购买的目的，并进而树立出版社品牌形象，增强市场竞争力。一直以来传统的图书营销方式对促进图书销售发挥了应有的作用，可谓功不可没。但是随着各种新媒体的涌现和新技术的快速发展，传统的营销方式已经无法满足媒介融合时代读者的需求，取而代之的是读者喜闻乐见的新形式。

从最近三次的全国国民阅读调查看，网络在线阅读和手机阅读等数字阅读率呈逐年上升趋势，国民对各类媒介的接触呈爆发式增长，第五次阅读调查结果显示网络媒体已成为国民依赖度排名第二的媒体，互联网阅读率已达到44.9%；第七次国民阅读调查中显示成年人中有16.7%的国民通过网络在线阅读，比2008年的15.7%增加了1个百分点，网络在线的阅读人群呈不断年轻化的态势。这些为多媒介融合时代的图书视频广告传播提供了广阔的发展空间。那么我国的图书视频广告现状如何，存在哪些亟须解决的问题，如何运用视频广告做好图书营销，其发展前景如何，将在本文中进行分析和探讨。

1 图书视频广告发展的现状

本文论述的图书视频广告，主要指在较短时间内（一般为三分钟以内）运用动态影像传递图书信息的一种营销手段。据资料显示，目前国内图书视频广告的运用比较少，甚至可以说是凤毛麟角。较有影响的例子即为上文所提到的《失恋33天》和《小时代2.0虚铜时代》的视频广告。除此之外，我们能搜索到的图书视频广告少之又少。而相对国内寥寥无几的图书视频广告状况，国外的图书视频广告则发展比较成熟，运用较为普遍，已经成为出版社图书营销的新手段。国外的图书视频广告最为常见的传播渠道是网站，且视频种类较多，主要有：录像型、幻灯片型、字幕型、电脑合成型等。多种电脑技术及拍摄手段的综合运用丰富了图书的营销手段，图书信息随着动态影像跃入读者眼中，视频广告在图书营销中为读者提供了一种新鲜的体验。

图书视频广告的营销对象是广大的读者，读者对于图书视频广告的看法显得尤为重要。为此，我们采取了在杭州各大书店实地随机问卷调查、在互联网上做问卷调查以及对读者进行随访等形式，接受调查的读者年龄分布在9~47岁，涉及人数584人。统计数据显示，目前读者获取图书信息的方式主要有实体书店海报、杂志和报纸上的书评、签售讲演、豆瓣等一系列网站的推荐、附在书或杂志中的广告、电台节目、畅销书排行榜、他人推荐等，具体数据如图1所示。其中通过杂志和报纸上的书评获取图书信息最高，占24.7%；其次是通过他人推荐，占19.2%，这个数据说明读者对图书的选择显得相对理性，他们更愿意相信口碑营销的力量；通过互联网了解图书信息的占15.1%，超过了畅销书排行榜的14.4%，由此可见互联网在图书营销领域具有较大空间和便利。此外，调查还显示，现阶段国内的图书广告确实整体呈现出一个比较低迷的状态，读者对于现行图书广告的满意度仅为37.9%。据我们了解，进入市场化运作后，传统的书评、畅销书排行榜所承载的图书信息逐渐失去其真实性和公信力，是读者对目前图书营销不甚满意的主要原因。

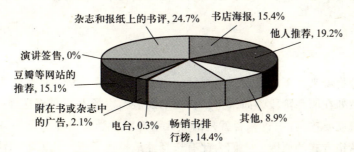

图1 读者获取图书信息方式调查数据图

我们了解到，在调查的读者中听说过图书视频广告的人占28%，听过且看过的人仅占16.1%，而互联网是其主要的获取途径。对图书视频广告，高达75.3%的人对此投出了赞成票，表示更喜欢这样一种新颖的营销方式。

在传统的图书营销方式在市场上仍占主导地位的情况下，图书视频广告尚属新生事物，读者还不甚了解，但读者对其呈现出的强烈期待和浓厚兴趣，昭示了图书视频广告发展的广阔空间。

2 图书视频广告优势分析

2.1 呈现动态传播效果

传统的图书宣传方式除电视读书节目外，主要是平面媒体，受众面相对较小，信息量有限，且受众停留在此广告上的时间也相对较少。而视频广告的画面是多种艺术手段合成的动态效果，不仅画面的冲击力强烈，信息量大，受众时间较长（一般都在半分钟以上），并直接产生感官冲击力，其效果不断增值放大。

更值得一提的是，许多视频具有故事情节性，在设计中具有可以施展无限的创新力，更容易吸引受众的注意力，引起他们的好奇心，对文艺类畅销书、少儿类畅销书甚至是科普类等图书的营销都具有突出作用。

对出版社而言，图书营销的另一目的还在于树立出版社的品牌形象，增强核心竞争力。试想，如果有出版社能推陈出新，率先采用新的营销方式，就能给读者留下深刻的印象。而我们在对读者的调查中也证实了这一点：约八成的读者认为会因为图书视频广告加深对出版社的印象。这为出版社树立"大社"、"强社"的品牌形象会起到积极的作用。

2.2 借助网络传播优势

图书视频广告的另一直观效果是拓宽了图书营销途径，加大了网络的宣传，因为网络具有其他媒介无可比拟的优势。网络广告信息量承载大，时空的跨越扩大了传播范围和受众覆盖面，双向传播的模式加强了互动性，与电视、平面广告相比，从其收到的传播效果看来，成本显得相对低廉。

图书视频广告可以充分发挥网络广告的上述优势。另外，图书与其他普通商品相比，还具有精神属性。图书视频广告定位于网络营销，可以加强受众的自主选择性：众多的口碑网、推荐网站上活跃的论坛以及多个社交网站的分享功能可以让好的图书广告在短时间内引起关注并得到受众自主传播，而链接、相关报道等网络特有的功能可以便捷地带动连锁反应，引导图书本身的信息传播，从而弱化由出版社单一推动营销所带来的过多的商业气息。

3 图书视频广告发展瓶颈

从上述的分析看来，不难发现图书视频广告独有的营销优势，但是，为什么国内的图书视频营销依然处在萌芽阶段，尚未得到长足的发展？市场上信奉着这样一句话："落后就要挨打，先进就要挨骂。"这是否就是出版社不愿意接受新的图书营销方式，一直拘泥于传统的图书营销方式的原因？我们为此有选择性地挑选了浙江几家不同性质、不同规模的出版社进行相关的调查了解，经分析得出出版社之所以较少采用图书视频广告主要有以下几个原因：

第一，出版社对图书视频广告不了解。在采访中，我们了解到出版社的一些发行人员从未听说过图书视频营销，他们仅着重于期刊、报纸等的平面媒体宣传。这个情况相信在全国范围内的出版社更为普遍。一种新事物在得到普遍认可之前总要经历一个认知的过程。

第二，技术人员的缺乏。制作视频广告不仅需要专门的设备、道具及人物，更需要掌握一定广播电视编辑能力和技术的专业人才。目前出版社现有的专业人才尚无法完成视频广告的制作和推广。

第三，对经济投入和效果产出的顾虑。作为出版社来讲，读者便是"上帝"。图书营销效果的好坏关键在于读者是否喜欢。出版社之所以不敢贸然采用视频的营销手段就是出于对读者接受能力的顾虑。面对没有效果保障的营销，出版社往往不肯轻易投入。

4 图书视频广告发展的突破口

4.1 树立新的图书营销理念

多数读者、出版发行人员甚至是出版行业的领头人，对"图书视频广告"这一概念是陌生的。所以，图书视频广告要想在我国的图书营销领域走出一条康庄大道，出版界的领军人物就必须真正发现其在图书营销中的特殊价值。在媒介融合时代，大胆尝试新技术、新形式、新手段带来的新体验和新效果。可以通过小范围的试点推广，根据效果制定下一步营销策略，在实践中发掘新事物的优势，分享新技术带来的效益。

4.2 开拓图书视频广告制作传播新路径

从上述的分析可得，阻碍图书视频广告的发展因素主要是出版社对此种新兴营销方式的成本与效果投入产出比的担忧上，一般出版业界人士都认为，视频宣传不仅制作技术复杂，难度大，且制作成本和传播成本都要明显高于平面广告。下面我们就这一问题作一分析，并从中找出解决的方法。

4.2.1 充分利用高校人才和设施资源

不可否认，相比传统的平面广告，图书视频广告的成本的确要相对高些，以调查问卷中最受欢迎的视频类型——录像型视频为例，经调查所得，一家知名广告公司制作一条30秒的录像型视频价格在50万元左右。而另一家普通广告公司的报价则是一条3分钟的录像型视频价格约为6万元。尽管相对于知名广告公司的报价，6万元已经是一个非常低的价格。但是相对于传统图书营销方式其成本依然是非常昂贵的。

出版业是考量赢利的，而并非暴利行业。那么，除了专业广告公司这条途径之外，是否存在其他可以减少成本的途径？当出版社把目光全都聚集在专业广告公司时，却忽略了一个重要领域，那就是高校的人才和设施资源。各地出版社可以与所在地高校的相关专业建立结盟合作关系——出版社可为高校提供学习实践等机会，利用高校各方面资源建立实践基地，招募相关专业的学生来制作视频。以浙江为例，多家电视台坦言，一些难度较高的片头视频都是交给拥有广播电视编辑能力的在校大学生制作的。这足以说明高校相关专业的部分学生其制作技术和水准已经得到相当的高度。而高校实践基地给出的大致价格一般一条3分钟的视频拍摄加制作费用仅6 000元。虽高校实践基地在品牌形象上比不过知名广告公司，但物美价廉，何乐而不为呢？对于出版社而言，在校大学生的想法能较好地契合当下使用网络资源最多的年轻人的思维方式，他们创意无限，制作成果奇特而生动，与图书视频广告所要呈现给读者的"新颖、新奇、时尚"等的理念不谋而合，而对于高校来说，他们可以通过这个实践基地平台培养本校学生的创新意识与实践能力。此举对出版社和高校来说，都是互利双赢、一举多得的良策。

这个图书视频广告制作的新途径对出版社具有普遍意义。在出版社为高成本的视频制作望而却步时，不妨向高校投出橄榄枝，走出合作双赢的第一步。

4.2.2 公共电视、免费网站成为营销新宠

比较常见的视频营销的途径有电视和互联网，而大众传播领域的电视由于传播成本较高，不适合图书营销，而互联网因为网站性质不同而对相应的广告收费存在很大差异，目前最常见的两种方式是按照点击数和投放时间进行收费，而根据我们收集到的资料显示，若按前者的计费方式，要想获得 50 万人的点击量至少需要支付 6 万元，而后者若按一周的投放时间为例，传播成本也在 5 万元以上。较一本图书的收益来说，这个成本仍然显得过高。

综合各因素，我们提出两种适合出版社的视频营销途径：

（1）公共电视传播。这里所要提出的公共电视指的是书店、学校内为读者、学生提供信息的电视。这两个场所所面向的人群具有明显的导向性。再则，可以通过业务上的往来与两者建立合作关系，以此降低视频传播的成本。书店本身也需要通过各种方式为本店的图书做宣传，出版社提供给书店的视频反而为书店的宣传活动提供了便利，只要一台电视机就可以随时播放，在图书展台播放宣传视频可以快速吸引目标读者，提高营销效果。而学校的电视没有明确的商业目的，一般没有需要固定播放的视频，与出版社的视频宣传不会产生冲突。出版社可以为学校的图书馆和其他信息设施定期提供的本社图书视频，使图书视频宣传深入到学校。由此看来，书店、学校的公告电视也应该是出版社重点关注的传播途径，且两者的成本在最理想的状态下有达到低投入甚至零投入高回报的可能性。

（2）免费网站传播。伴随着互联网的发展，形形色色的网站开始出现，博客、社交网站就是本文需要重点关注的两种网站。出版社可以将视频上传到自己的官方博客和其他免费的视频网站，如优酷、土豆网，走出视频宣传网络化的第一步，扩大影响力。而活跃在各个社交网站，如人人网、开心网、QQ 空间等的网友，最不缺乏对新兴传播方式的热衷，一次点击、一次分享带动的是身后无法计数的注意力——用辐射的方式不断地扩大传播面，并让接受者自发地成为下一个传播者，自发地使用属于自己的传播渠道，使之在曝光率和影响力上以指数级的速度增长。即所谓的"病毒式"网络视频广告营销策略。而这些社交网站的另一个意义还在于使用这些网站的人群本身就构成了一个相对稳定的网络社区，他们的年龄、身份差异不大，间接地为图书视频推广起到了巨大的作用。

与博客、社交网站无法计数的关注率相比，视频营销的传播成本基本为零，其中巨大的吸引力不言而喻，而出版社需要做的就是建设自己的博客网站，把视频营销放在突出的地位，以吸引和把握本社的忠实读者，并适当地培养推手，成为"病毒传播源"。

5 视频广告彰显图书营销魅力无限

图书视频广告适用于青春文艺类、绘本、科普类、少儿类、生活类图书的宣传和推广。青春文艺类图书受众多为学生和文学爱好者，对新事物接受能力较快，再加上有网络这个大环境，视频的传播效果会更强；绘本内容较为简洁，图片居多，为视频广告制作直接提供了素材，降低了制作成本；科普类和生活类图书可以直接应用图片直观地表述书中内容；少儿类图书更是可以利用可爱的动画形象来吸引小读者。

在我们对读者的调查中了解到，相对于其他图书营销方式，75.3% 的人更喜欢图书视频广告。在这个时间比金钱更珍贵的极速快餐年代，传统图书平面广告的冗长和单调已经很难激发读者的关注力和兴趣了，图书视频广告能以其生动的影像传递给观众最直观的信息。广大读者都在期待着这一创意无限、魅力无限的新型营销方式。

综上所述，在媒介融合时代，为出版业利用新技术、新产品对图书营销手段升级换代提供了广大的空间，展现了未来美好的前景。我们相信，只要出版业大胆尝试、不断完善，视频广告在图书市场竞争中将凸显巨大威力，为图书营销领域带来新的景观。

参考文献

[1] 第七次全国国民阅读调查成果，http://www.china.com.cn/news/txt/2010-04/19/content_19857743.htm.

[2] 第六次全国国民阅读调查成果，http://www.chinapublish.com.cn/ztjj/yddc/2009yd/200904/t20090422_47510.html.

[3] 第五次全国国民阅读调查成果，http://www.chinavalue.net/NewsDig/NewsDig.aspx?DigId=19385.

[4] 单文盛，戴尼耳. 浅析网络"病毒式营销"的运作模式 [G]. 湖南大众传媒职业技术学院学报，2008（7）：10-12.

作者简介

魏丹薨，浙江工商大学人文学院编辑出版系 2008 级学生。

杨倩茹，浙江工商大学人文学院编辑出版系 2008 级学生。

詹莉波，浙江工商大学人文学院编辑出版系 2008 级学生。

出版营销

长尾理论对按需印刷的影响

——以大学专业类教材为例

余　倩

（浙江工商大学　杭州　310015）

摘要：本文在已有的资料基础上，阐述长尾理论的概念及其对图书出版界的影响。从目前国内大学专业类教材的现状入手，发现国内大学专业类教材在出版、销售上存在的问题。结合国外图书按需印刷公司闪电公司以及业马逊网站对长尾图书实行按需印刷的先进经验以及国内出版社对按需印刷的实践，结合大学专业类教材的实际情况及其特点，分析目前对大学专业类教材实现按需印刷存在的一些问题，提出相应的解决方案。最后，立足本国国情，结合国外经验探讨对长尾图书实行按需印刷的发展前景，以期对长尾理论对按需印刷的影响做深入研究。

关键词：长尾理论　大学专业类教材　按需印刷　闪电资源

The Long Tail Theory on the Impact of Printing on Demand

——A Case Study of Professional Teaching Materials

Yu Qian

（Zhejiang Gongshang University，Hangzhou，310018）

Abstract：this paper explained the concept of The Long Tail theory and its impact on the publishing industry. By analyzing the current status of specialized Teaching Materials，it got to the point of specialized textbook sales problems in the publication and selling. The article is trying to analyze the issue of print-on-demand of specialized textbook for universities in China，and to come up with practical solutions，based on the investigation on the tail-demand printing of the Lighting Source，Amazon. com and press in China，and on the features of specialized textbook for universities. With discussion of the future of on the tail-demand printing based on a concentration of the environment of Chinese presses and a reference to the practice overseas，the paper tried to look into the impact of on the tail-demand printing.

Keywords：Long tail theory　Professional teaching materials　Printing on demand　Lighting source

1 绪论

2004 年，美国《连线》杂志的编辑克里斯·安德森在对在对数字公司以及亚马逊网站数据的分析中，发现了这样一个现象：那些被认为是冷门的产品在提供足够大的空间的前提下，其所产生的效益将不低于那些普遍被认为是热门的产品。安德森将获得的数据绘制成图，结果发现，曲线刚开始急剧地下降直至无限趋向于零，但是直到最右端依旧没有为零。而这些看起来是一条长长的尾巴的冷门产品加起来的总数依旧相当可观，并且其所产生的效益可与热门产品的总效益相当，这就是长尾理论。

长尾理论指出，正是这些为数巨大的处于长尾上的冷门商品，默默地贡献着新的发展机遇。随着网络书店的迅速发展，图书的销售状况也像在线音乐的零售一样，那些冷门的长尾书能够产生可与人们普遍认为的畅销书媲美的销售额。亚马逊的销售额中有 25% 左右便是由这些被传统书店所抛弃的长尾书贡献的。

大学专业类教材、学术著作、小众文学、小批量内部发行的图书，小批量的绝版书再版、脱销书加印等，都是安德森的长尾理论中的那个"长尾"。由于长尾图书本身销售周期长、库存成本高等各种问题，很大程度上阻碍了其发展。诸多原因导致长尾图书供需不平衡的现象长期存在。如何解决以上问题，以更好地实现长尾图书的利润成为当下最需要解决的关键问题。

2 长尾图书的现状分析——以大学专业类教材为例

近几年来，我国高等教育的发展一路高歌猛进。每年的招生人数都在不断地增长。有数据显示，1999—2002 年间普通高校本专科招生数平均年递增 42.4%。专业设置也适应着新形势而不断增加，大学专业类教材的需求量也不断增加。

大学专业类教材是大学教材中较为特殊的一种，不同于一般的公共课程，专业类教材的适用范围仅仅是本专业的学生，多则几个班一两百个人，少则一个班人数不过数十人。出版者出于成本与收入等诸多问题的考虑，倾向于追逐利润，导致出版社纷纷抢食公共类教材的市场份额，而对大学专业类教材则相对冷淡的情况。此外，在很长的时期内，大学专业类教材发行渠道单一。因此，总体来说，大学专业类教材的发展还比较滞后。

2.1 大学专业类教材——长尾图书的典型

大学教材的分类方法繁多，但本文根据研究需要，将大学教材分为公共类和专业类。笔者认为，大学专业类教材是指那些为某一特定专业的教学需要配套的，符合向专业学生传授本专业的发展历史、发展现状、专业原理、专业技能等的专业知识要求的教材。比如，英语是大学中所有的学生都必修的外语课程，因此《大学英语》是公共类教材；日语是特定专业的学生需要学习的课程，因此与此相关的教材即为专业类教材。以国内发展相对成熟的图书电子商务网站卓越亚马逊为例，在图书类别下，选择"教材教辅与参考书"一项，然后再选择"大学"。该网站显示出的 19 类，共计 68 989 种大学教材教辅与参考书。参见图 1。

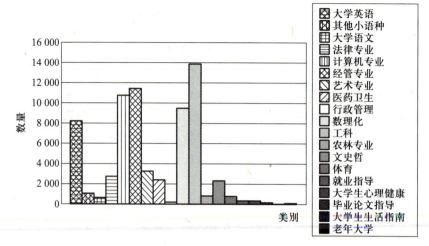

图1　卓越亚马逊网站大学教材教辅与参考书分类及品种数量情况图

由图1我们可以看出这些教材教辅的大致的品种数量对比。图书数量的高峰值出现在大学英语、计算机专业、经管专业、数理化、工科等几个种类，但是上述分类中，有些概念比较模糊，存在从属关系，比如数理化类和工科类。为研究更为直观，在此选取其中对比性较强的大学英语以及其他小语种两组数据。大学英语类作为公共类教材的典型，而其他小语种类作为专业类教材的典型。两者的对比情况能一定程度地说明公共类教材与专业类教材的情况。参见图2。

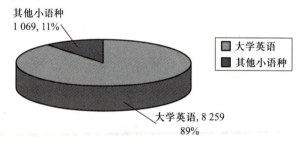

图2　卓越亚马逊大学英语与其他小语种教材教辅对比情况图

图2中，属于公共类教材的"大学英语"类有8 259种，占89%；而属专业类教材的"其他小语种"类1 069种，仅占11%，大致符合传统的20/80法则。以上的比较再次证明了大学专业类教材是一种典型的长尾图书。

2.2　大学专业类教材的现状

大学专业类教材属于长尾图书的一种是由其本身的特点决定的。由于需要配合大学专业的设置，大学专业类教材一般种类繁多，同一课程的教材有几个不同出版社的版本。而大学专业类教材受限于专业学生数量，一次性的需求量较小。考虑到种种原因，做好大学专业类教材这一长尾图书的出版在目前看来还是困难重重。

下面，分别从出版社、销售商、消费者这三个图书销售的环节对大学专业类教材的现状进行分析。

2.2.1　出版者：成本高，收益小，矛盾尖锐

随着出版社转企，对于利润的追求已成为出版社决定出什么书的一个关键问题。大学专业类教材由于种种限制，生产成本高，但收益较小。尽管做好专业类教材对于大学教育

的发展意义重大，但是许多出版社出于经济效益的考虑也宁愿选择到竞争激烈的公共类教材中去分一杯羹。总结出版者所面对的矛盾，主要有以下几点：

（1）策划、编辑环节生产周期长，耗费大

一套较好的教材需要经历较长时间的策划，出版社需要组织专家学者组成编委会，选择专业知识过硬、教学经验丰富的作者写作。对编辑的专业知识要求也相对较高，甚至需要其他专家做进一步的审稿工作。

（2）一次需求量小，易造成库存

由于大学专业类教材仅针对特定专业的少量学生和教师，一次性需求量较小。实际上，大多数大学每年的招生量为两三千人，再分到各个专业，一本专业类教材的需求量多则百本，少则几十本。传统图书由于制版、印制等生产环节成本较高，起印量一般在3 000册。面对一次性需求量小的情况，就容易造成库存问题，而库存费用是出版社不得不面对的现实问题。

（3）需求地分散，需求时间分散，运输费用较高

各地大学较为分散，尽管单位需求量小，但是运输费用难以节省。尽管目前物流业发展迅猛，但大量的小批量的运输费用累积起来，对于出版社而言也是一笔较大的支出。此外，大学专业类教材每一学年都有需要，导致图书每一年都要重复运输累积下来同样将是一笔很大的开支。

（4）读者群体较为特殊，需求量连年减小可能性大

大学生群体由于本身经济能力有限，许多人在知道书目之后，选择向学长借书。而大学图书馆资源丰富，也使得部分学生选择向图书馆借阅。此外，不可忽视的是目前校园内部网通常设有相应的二手书交易区。这些图书的循环使用分流了一部分对新教材的需求量，使得大学专业类教材的需求量年年缩减的可能性比较大，而难以保持稳定。

（5）教材更新换代成本大

有的专业的发展日新月异，为了保证向学生教授的知识紧跟专业进步进程，许多大学专业类教材需要不断修订、再版。但是一旦修订、再版，再次印刷的起印量也限制在3 000册左右，如此，出版社又陷入库存的恶性循环。

2.2.2　销售者：渠道单一，缺乏活力

目前，大学教材主要的发行方式大致有两种：一是由出版社提供图书目录给学校教材科，由教材科向任课教师推荐；二是任课教师在一定的限制下自行选择教材，上报学校教材科，由教材科统一向出版社订书。而目前后者为主要的发行方式，因此出版社处于被动地位，图书销售渠道单一且缺乏活力。

下面，对以上几种大学专业类教材的销售渠道进行详细的分析：

（1）传统书店是大部分图书发行的主要渠道，但是受陈列架限制较大，大学专业类教材这一类长尾图书难以占有一席之地

据统计，我国最近几年新出的图书已达到27万种以上，其中新出图书15万种以上，而一般的大型图书商场所能展示的图书仅为4万册左右。为了追求利益的最大化，书店必然选择将空间尽可能地让给畅销书。即使大学专业类教材能够进入传统书店，一旦销量不如意，即会被那些被认为"有卖点"的书所代替。

（2）网上书店大学专业类教材在供品种仍不理想

国内网上书店的发展速度较为迅猛，当当网在 2007 年可供图书已达 60 万种。但是不论是卓越网还是当当网，针对的都是大众读者，许多大学专业类教材依旧难觅踪迹。

（3）C2C 模式货品量少，选择面狭窄

C2C，即 Consumer to Consumer，我们可以大致理解其定义，就是个人对个人的商务活动。淘宝网就是一个典型的例子，众多个体的卖家提供商品给个人买家。大学论坛的二手书交易平台也是典型的 C2C 模式。

通过这种模式购买自己所需要的图书仅仅是消费者碰运气之举。根据定义，C2C 模式是个人对个人的自发式贸易方式，自发性强。以大学的二手书交易为例，有人在网上挂出需要的图书的目录又正好有人需要。这都是概率较小的事件。而且这种模式并不适应超过一定数量的图书销售，因为个人发起的存货量十分有限。正因为如此，这种模式下，消费者的选择面很小。

2.2.3 消费者：信息缺乏成为痼疾

大学专业类教材的主要销售渠道是任课教师指定教材，由学校教材科向出版社统一预定。在这种模式下，学生的选择面狭小。如果需要一本其他重要的专业教材作为课外的参考，就面临着缺乏信息的困境。

而尽管目前有众多图书电子商务网站以及一些新闻网站的读书频道都会定期发布畅销书排行榜，但是所针对的图书为大众类图书。大学专业类教材属于长尾图书，其性质也决定其不可能在畅销书排行榜中出现，也难以得到大众类网站的推荐。而各出版大学专业类教材的出版社的网站则更新缓慢，难以及时提供关于大学专业类教材的新信息。读者一旦有需求，就难以找到相关信息。

3 按需印刷：开拓长尾图书市场的最优方案

按需印刷，Print On Demand（简称 POD），起源于美国。目前对按需印刷的定义各有不同，但根据现有资料总结来说，按需印刷是采用数字印刷技术，根据消费者在数量、时间、内容等个性化需求，对电子化书稿进行即时印刷、装订的新型印刷方式。

3.1 按需印刷的优势

与传统印刷方式相比，按需印刷的优势明显：

（1）工序简化，生产周期大幅缩短，且生产成本降低

传统图书生产方式在"印"这一环节需要经过排版、发排、照排、胶片冲洗、拼版、晒版、印刷、装订等诸多工序，而按需印刷在数字化技术的前提下，只需要排版、印刷、装订寥寥几道工序。在此过程中，节约了大量时间和成本。

（2）不受起印量限制，适应小批量需求

传统印刷由于工序复杂，且产生的制版费用较高而需要加大印数来降低单位生产成本。而按需印刷技术由于简化了工序，节约了制版费用，不需要分摊成本，每一次印刷的成本都是一样的，因而不受制于起印数。这就适应了小批量低至一本的需求。

（3）数字化程度高，灵活度高

按需印刷的书稿都是电子化的，修改方便、灵活，不产生额外费用。在传统的印刷方式中，如果要对书稿进行修改，需要重新对相应内容出菲林以替换。修改必然产生较大费用，而若要对图书进行修订，产生的费用则更大，这也是许多出版社不愿意对一些大学专

业类教材进行再版的主要原因。而按需印刷技术则很好地解决了大学专业类教材更新换代，与时俱进的问题。

（4）先"卖书"再"印书"，降低退货风险，做到绿色出版

按需印刷，顾名思义，是有了需求，再根据需求进行印刷。这就将传统的"印书—卖书"模式转变为"卖书—印书"模式，成功地避免了退货的风险，甚至可以做到零库存。这一转变不仅降低了出版社投入，也大幅减小了纸张等资源的浪费，做到真正的绿色出版。

正由于按需印刷灵活、高效、经济等优点，解决了长尾图书的生产以及库存等方面的难题，可以说按需印刷是目前开拓长尾图书市场的最优方案。

3.2 国外按需印刷的模式分析

按需印刷技术起源于美国，因此在美国得到长足性的发展。有资料显示，在1996年，在美国，即有31%的传统印刷业务被按需印刷业务所代替。2009年，美国出版业的统计数据表明，早在2008年，美国通过按需印刷的方式生产的图书的数量已经超过了以传统的印刷方式生产的图书数量。[1]

国外按需印刷的发展时间已将近30年，有闪电资源、露露、作家解决方案公司等诸多成功地按需印刷商。而且有亚马逊这样的图书电子商务网站，在长期的发展中，已形成了较为成熟的按需印刷发展模式。其中，主要包括成熟的合作模式和赢利模式。

3.2.1 合作模式分析

目前，在国外，按需印刷主要有两种合作模式：

（1）经销商—出版商—印刷商模式

以美国著名的按需印刷公司闪电资源为例，其按需印刷的主要模式如图3所示。

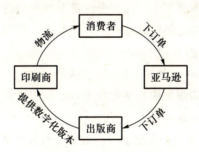

图3　经销商—出版商—印刷商模式

在这种模式下，读者在亚马逊网站上选择自己需要的图书并下订单。亚马逊没有库存，即向出版社发出购买电子版本的请求。出版社将指定图书的数字化版本发送给闪电资源公司。闪电资源公司根据所提供的数字化图书打印、装订等，并贴上亚马逊网站的标签，由物流公司传递给读者。这一过程仅需两到三天时间，读者甚至不会察觉书是经过按需印刷的方式生产的。

（2）作者（读者）—出版商（或按需印刷商）模式

这种模式也是按需印刷所广泛采用的合作模式之一，主要用于个性化的定制和出版。如图4所示。

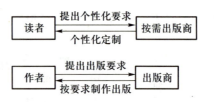

图4　作者（读者）—出版商（按需出版商）模式

这是一种个性化的出版模式。作者上传自己的文字等内容，自行排版或使用由出版者或按需印刷商提供的应用软件进行排版处理。美国按需印刷商作者解决方案公司推出的Wordclay就是一个帮助作者自己在线做出版的工具。制作完成后，将电子稿发送给按需印刷商印刷、装订。完成这些之后，作者或读者即可拿到自己所需要的书。而按需印刷商则按协议将数字化版本返还作者，以保护个人的版权。

一些出版社也有自己的按需印刷设备，可以自行进行按需印刷。比如美国纽约大学提供按需印刷的服务。有数据表明，他们每年按需印刷生产20～30本书[2]，而这些图书都是面向小众市场的，主要是学生和教师使用的材料。此外，还有国外一些图书馆，甚至书店也有按需印刷的业务，主要针对不受版权保护的、公共领域的作品，提供个性化定制。

3.2.2　赢利模式分析

由于按需印刷所涉及的图书有受版权保护的已出版图书和不受版权保护的作品或个人定制的少量的个性化产品，因此，本文针对这两种不同的按需印刷对象进行赢利模式的分析。

（1）受版权保护的已出版图书：按事先协议的比例分得利润

这种模式下，按需印刷商需要向出版者取得版权许可，然后在规定的范围内进行印刷、装订。因此，按需印刷商赢利中，需要分一部分给出版者。由于各个出版者与按需印刷商之间的协议不同，其具体比例难以估计。在上文提及的闪电资源、亚马逊网站以及出版者的合作模式，则将赢利按协议的比例分为三份。

以美国按需印刷商OnDemandBooks为例，他们与出版商达成协议，在授权范围内印制出版商的书。但需要在收到图书的数字化版本后，向出版商支付相应的版税。而印制完成后，就将数字化版本返还出版社。

（2）不受版权保护的图书或个人定制的少量的个性化产品：利润全得

不受版权保护的作品包括：法律、法规，国家机关的决议、决定、命令和其他具有立法、行政、司法性质的文件，及其官方正式译文；时事新闻；历法、通用数表、通用表格和公式；超过了著作权保护期限而进入公有领域的作品[3]。由于不受版权的限制，按需印刷商可以不必支付版税来印刷。

如美国按需印刷商诺斯希尔书店所印刷的图书中就有那些公共领域的作品。诺斯希尔书店的按需印刷定价为每页0.05～0.08美元，再加上75～100美元的其他费用，并且有偿提供各种个性化的增值服务[4]。

4　我国长尾图书按需印刷的瓶颈分析

国内早在20世纪90年代就开始应用按需印刷技术，其适应的印刷对象也是长尾图书。最早涉足按需印刷技术的是知识产权出版的专利文献，由于每种专利文献的销量不足百册，是典型的长尾图书。而当时经济实力不断上升，伴随着专利申请的数量也大大增加，专利文献的品种飙升到 40 000 种[5]。传统印刷方式中存在的起印量的限制导致这类长尾图书出现严重的供过于求的不平衡现象，造成了极大的资源浪费。在 2004 年 4 月，知识产权出版社成为引入按需印刷的"第一个吃螃蟹的人"。目前，其所有专利文献都实现了按需印刷，做到了先卖书，再印书。

尽管目前国内按需印刷发展日新月异，但仍存在着诸多问题：

4.1　应用范围狭窄，主要集中在专利、标准、期刊等小部分长尾领域

尽管接触按需印刷技术较早，但目前国内对长尾图书进行按需印刷的应用范围仍然较狭窄。引入按需印刷较早的知识产权出版社，其应用范围为专利文献出版。中国标准出版社则是应用于标准的出版领域，商务印书馆则主要将按需印刷技术应用于学术期刊的出版。总体来说，对大学专业类教材这类发展前景广阔的市场涉足较少。

4.2　规模化程度低，单位成本难以降低

目前国内对按需印刷概念的理解接受仍然处于初级阶段，按需印刷需求较为分散。很难通过将几笔订单有机连结在一起，以降低机器运行的损耗以及产生的费用。这些费用尽管远远低于传统印刷所产生的制版费用，但是需要通过加大印量来分摊成本的。

有数据显示，美国按需印刷一本 300 页的 32 开本图书，其成本约为 20 元人民币，而根据国外的图书价格，一般可以售价为 70 元人民币左右。而在国内，成本大致相当，售价却远远低于 70 元人民币，这就使得降低成本显得更为重要。

4.3　书稿电子化程度较低，且格式五花八门

我国按需印刷发展的时间较短，速度长期较为缓慢，与之相对应的是书稿的电子化程度较低。出版社只有在意识到按需印刷的优点之后，才会专门地对书稿进行电子化处理。所以，目前国内出版物的电子化程度仍然较低。

而目前所采用图书排版软件五花八门，比如方正飞腾、Indesign、Pagemaker 等。使用不同的软件其产生的排版文件的格式各不相同。以笔者了解的出版社排版情况来看，尽管目前的很多排版软件最后都可以生成 pdf 文件，但是都存在着如乱码等各种问题。如何规范相关格式将是一个亟待解决的问题。

4.4　版权制度发展滞后

目前，版权制度在国内发展仍不健全，盗版侵权现象屡禁不止，出版社对此也十分无奈。一些大学专业类图书的出版，为了防止盗版出现，出版方宁可多印一些书来满足大面积铺货需要，容易造成一定的浪费。

而在按需出版领域，版权制度的不健全所致的不利因素则更容易被放大，很大程度上地阻碍了按需印刷技术的发展。一旦按需印刷商侵权，图书的数字化版本外流，对出版社将造成不可估量的损失。目前在我国仍未建立起完善的版权信用体系，国外按需印刷的经销商—出版商—印刷商模式成立的前提就是完善的版权信用体系。而在国内，盗版侵权时有存在，出版社对于尝试按需印刷亦是步步为营，小心谨慎。因此，在按需印刷中，如何做好版权管理工作值得深入研究。

4.5　交易平台发展单一、不成熟

国内出版社在按需印刷的进程中进度不一，发展较快速的，已建立起自己的按需印刷网站，如知识产权出版社、商务印书馆。但是这些出版社的按需印刷网站仅针对自身出版

社的图书，发展模式单一。而国外的按需印刷业务有像 Amazon. com 这样的大量综合服务、交易平台，正如长尾理论所要求的那样，帮助消费者找到他们所要的商品，而且提供相应的按需印刷服务。

4.6　合作模式单一，缺乏活力，难以形成规模化效应

国内出版社引入按需印刷设备，大多仅针对本出版社的图书，并不对外。如知识产权出版社引入按需印刷设备以按需出版本出版社的专利文献。商务印书馆引入按需印刷设备以小批量再版绝版书，印制学术杂志。其主要的合作模式是作者或消费者提出要求，出版社按需定制。模式单一，且缺乏活力。

由于出版社的业务范围狭窄，业务量较小，而且零碎。按需印刷设备的使用率低，造成浪费。而闪电资源公司往往将许多笔订单组合在一起印刷，一起装订，一起运输，这就节约了很多费用。

4.7　缺乏合理的利益分配方式

按需印刷过程中，涉及经销商、出版者、印刷商等多方的利益。以国内按需印刷目前的发展状况来看，出版社走在前列，已有不少尝试；印刷商则缺乏积极性，按需印刷设备的引进费用较高，而且维护费用累积下来也将是一笔很大的支出，在目前国内按需印刷发展仍不明朗的前提下，印刷商较为被动；经销商则鲜有这方面的尝试。

按需印刷的发展总的来说还是有利可图的，闪电资源公司只印一本书也能赚钱。因此，如何将作者、出版者、印刷者的利益作为一个整体，形成三者利益分配机制，并调动各方积极性值得我们思考。

5　长尾理论启示下大学专业类教材的按需印刷发展对策

作为典型的长尾图书，大学专业类教材的出版目前看来困难重重。做好大学专业类教材的出版，要解决好出版社经济效益问题，开拓多种销售渠道，并且帮助读者顺利购买到所需，这一过程需要出版社、销售方、印刷商以及政府相关部门的共同努力。

5.1　出版社：整合现有大学专业类教材优秀资源，主动挖掘大学专业类教材"长尾"

出版社是大学专业类教材的策划者、编辑者，为按需印刷提供出版资源，是整个按需印刷过程实现的根本，提供优质的内容是出版社的主要任务。只有优秀的、经典的大学专业类教材才能会有重印、再版的需求。

5.1.1　整合现有大学专业类教材优秀资源

大多数出版大学专业类教材的出版社都有一定的发展历史，经过编辑们的辛勤工作，积累下来了不少优秀的专业类教材资源。这类专业类教材在库存销售完毕之后，还会有重印、再版的要求。出于库存成本的考虑，这类书不适合采用传统的印刷方式进行重印，而更适合采用按需印刷的新技术。针对这类大学专业类教材，出版社要整合好资源，实施按需印刷计划。

以出版学术书为主的英国剑桥大学出版社在整合现有优秀资源方面就值得学习和借鉴。作为典型的长尾图书，剑桥大学的大学专业类教材、学术著作的大部分年销售量不足500 本，其中更有90%的销售量甚至不足 50 本[6]。但是其需求在数量和时间上较为稳定，于是剑桥大学开始尝试按需印刷。

5.1.2　主动挖掘大学专业类教材的"长尾"

在做好资源的整合之外，还要做好开发。根据传统的 20/80 定律，畅销书大约只占全部图书的 20%左右，是多数出版社争夺的重点，市场竞争激烈，而 80%的长尾图书市场却鲜有出版社愿意多下工夫进行挖掘。

反其道而行之，则有可能出奇制胜。出版社可以主动策划一些精而专的大学专业类教材，主动采取按需印刷的方式生产。避开竞争激烈的畅销书市场，在"长尾"中实现利润是出版社寻求发展之路的新思维。

法国按需印刷集团 CPI 在印刷业的低谷时期进入印刷业，凭借按需印刷业务，在 2009 年发展为在欧洲的 5 个国家拥有 16 家分公司的大型企业。其秘诀就在于在竞争激烈的印刷市场中独辟蹊径，发展按需印刷，一改以往图书起印量的限制[7]。这是典型的主动挖掘"长尾"而获得成功的案例。

5.2 销售商：着力发展大学专业类教材的 B2C 商业模式，提供足够多的产品，并且帮助消费者找到所需

作为典型长尾图书的大学专业类教材，在"寸土寸金"的传统书店里难以占有一席之地，即使上架，时间也较短。因此，发展好 B2C 模式尤为重要。根据安德森的理论，长尾理论的成立需要有两个前提，在网络环境下，向消费者提供足够多的产品，并帮助消费者找到所需要的产品。这也是 B2C 模式需要努力的方向。

5.2.1 提供足够多的商品，建立强大的大学专业类教材交易平台

目前国内的两大主要书业电子商务网站，卓越亚马逊与当当网的图书品种都不足百万，相比我国每年年均出书 27 万以上的数量，显然还有一定差距。而亚马逊网站的库存达到 147 万种，可以做到畅销书的销售额与长尾图书的销售额相近。

网络环境下的虚拟库存为发展按需印刷提供了便利。有读者在亚马逊网站上购买了其并无库存的图书，但是亚马逊可以通过按需印刷公司，在短时间内按需印刷消费者所需要的图书，并从中获取利润。国内的书业电子商务所拥有的图书数量并不足以提供足够多的大学专业类教材，建立强大的交易平台显得尤为迫切。

5.2.2 帮助消费者找到自己所需要的大学专业类教材

目前的电子商务网站都可以做到这一点。比如我们在淘宝网上浏览了某种商品，下次登录时，系统会自动推荐一些同类商品。消费者在消费的过程中，总是无意识暴露出自己的消费习惯、消费倾向。B2C 环境下，通过系统记录消费者的浏览记录、购买记录，以此作为关键词，向消费者推荐其他相关产品，帮助消费者找到适合的产品。

在消费者购买大学专业类教材时，记录消费者的专业倾向，系统自动遴选出该专业的图书，并通过邮件等方式将信息传输给消费者。这有利于帮助大学专业类教材使用者方便找到相关专业其他专业类教材，并有可能促成新的销售。

5.3 按需印刷商：提升管理水平，实现规模化效应

美国闪电资源公司单笔按需印刷订单量为 1.6～1.8 本，但是仍然可以获得赢利，其秘诀就在于通过先进的管理方式。首先，将众多不同的小批量单笔印刷任务合并为大批量的印刷任务，保证设备连续运转，分摊产生的成本。其次，在物流系统上采取先进的管理方式，对图书进行分类，同一区域的订单同时出发，分摊运输成本。

在大学专业类教材的按需印刷过程中，通过先进的管理方式，分摊、降低生产成本，取得更大的利润，符合企业的利益，也有利于按需印刷的健康发展。

5.4 政府：制订大学专业类教材按需印刷的行业标准，协调各方利益

政府的宏观调控在我国按需印刷发展中起着举足轻重的作用，需要借助政策的力量，将按需印刷行业整合为一个由出版者、销售商、印刷商组成的有机整体。通过召开协调会议等方式，协调各方的利益分配促进行业健康有序地发展。此外，政府要更积极地推动企业参与发展按需印刷，发放数字印刷许可证。

上海新闻出版局在推动按需印刷发展方面就走在全国前列。2009 年年初，上海新闻出版局就推出一系列政策措施以扶持按需印刷产业的发展。这些政策的出台也的确对按需印刷业的发展起了很大的助推作用，从目前来看，上海地区的按需印刷发展也的确走在全国前列。

6 结论

在网络高速发展的今天，长尾理论的舞台越来越广阔，也为按需印刷的发展提供了新的思路，尽管目前国内按需印刷的发展状况并不成熟，可以说是问题重重，但随着 B2C 模式的发展以及敏感睿智的出版人对长尾市场的不断挖掘，相信在未来，长尾理论为按需印刷带来的启示将更好地指引出版界向新的发展模式迈进。

总而言之，为了更好地挖掘好大学专业类教材的长尾，实现长尾图书按需印刷，出版者、销售商、印刷商更应该在政府的调控下，发挥各自优势，组成有机整体。这对于避开竞争激烈的畅销书市场，在长尾市场中寻求发展的新机遇具有非常现实的意义和长远的影响。

注释

[1] 郭人杰，郁金香. 美国 POD 图书种数首次超过传统图书 [J]. 出版参考. 2009 (6)：39

[2] Robert Barth. Lulu，Publish On Demand and the Long Tail of the Demand Curve [J]. E-Business Strategy. October (12)：45

[3] 黄先蓉. 出版法规及其应用. 苏州：苏州大学出版社，2007：59

[4] 陈彦. 按需出版印刷的发展现状与展望. 数码印刷，2009 (10)：27

[5] Gwynneth Heaton. Publish or Print on Demand (POD) publishing [OL]. www. trafford. com 2010. 5

[6] 朱文秋. 按需印刷：出版的强力驱动器. 数码印刷，2009 (10)：33

[7] 安德鲁·维特考福特. 数字印刷技术对出版目前和未来的影响. 数码印刷，2009 (10)：22

参考文献

[1] 黄先蓉. 出版法规及其应用 [M]. 苏州大学出版社. 2007：59

[2] 克里斯·安德森. 长尾理论 2.0 [M]. 乔江涛，石晓燕译. 北京：中信出版社，2009

[3] 庞家驹. 科技书籍编辑学教程 [M]. 辽宁：辽宁教育出版社，1996 (1)

[4] 安德鲁·维特考福特. 数字印刷技术对出版目前和未来的影响 [J]. 数码印刷，

2009-10-22

[5] 陈双军. 浅议地图按需印刷 [J]. 数码印刷，2008 (4)：42-43

[6] 陈文革. 浅析按需印刷在出版业的应用 [J]. 数码印刷，2008 (9)

[7] 陈彦. 按需出版印刷的发展现状与展望 [J]. 数码印刷，2009 (10)：27

[8] 韩锟. 学术期刊按需印刷出版的必要性与可行性 [J]. 编辑之友，2007 (5)

[9] 贺子岳，吴梦妮. 长尾理论给网络出版带来的启示 [J]. 南阳师范学院学报，2008
(1)：81

[10] 黄孝章，张志林，王亮. 新媒体发展中的"长尾效应"探析 [J]. 北京印刷学院学
报 2008-2-21

[11] 孔辉. 基于长尾理论的图书馆服务原则 [J]. 合作经济与科技. 2009 (7)：49

[12] 李恒平. "印书—卖书"模式 PK "卖书—印书"模式 [J]. 编辑学刊. 2009 (1)

[13] 刘继和. "教材"概念的解析及其重建 [J]. 全球教育展望. 2005 (2)

[14] 柳玲. 按需印刷为何走俏中国市场. [J]. 今日印刷. 2008 (6)：41

[15] 卢军，田靓. 我国印刷市场细分调查 [J]. 今日印刷. 2008 (9)：76-77

[16] 那福忠. 按需印书：闯出一片天地 [J]. 印刷杂志. 2007 (6)：73

[17] 石蓉蓉. 在长尾巴上跳舞——长尾理论运行机制探讨 [J]. 新闻界. 2007 (10)

[18] 施萱. 按需出版搭乘数字印刷快车 [J]. 印刷杂志. 2009 (10)：21

[19] 王尚伟，李晓丽. 图书按需印刷，个性化的狂欢 [J] 中国印刷. 2006 (12)

[20] 王志华. 按需印刷的市场基因 [J]. 中国印刷. 2007 (10)：31

[21] 朱文秋. 按需印刷：出版的强力驱动器 [J]. 数码印刷. 2009 (10)：33

[22] 赵俊成，张瑞娟. 按需印刷面面观 [M]. 中国印刷，2008 (2)

[23] Gwynneth Heaton. Publish or Print on Demand Publishing [OL]. www.trafford.com

[24] Robert Barth. Lulu, Publish On Demand and the Long Tail of the Demand Curve [J].
E-Business Strategy. 2008 (12)

作者简介

余倩，浙江工商大学编辑出版系学生。

数字化背景下欧美出版企业并购的特征
及其对中国出版集团化的启示

洪九来

（华东师范大学传播学院　上海　200062）

摘要：本文主要分析了新世纪以来，在数字化背景下欧美出版集团在并购重组过程中呈现的一些新动向与特征，其主要表现为：立足于渠道的控制与品牌的融合，无意于企业规模的扩大与品种的增多；由全能型向专业化转型，大而全的集团模式已不再是热衷的目标；能否向数字化出版转型是考量的主要目标，与业外新技术类型企业的重组是主流方向，等等。文章以上述特征为评价尺度，提出中国出版企业在今后集团化改革中，应加快数字化出版的步伐，正确处理规模与效益的关系，走效益优先的有效规模之路；去除高度同质化的色彩，走分工合理的专业化出版之路；加快数字化出版的步伐，走与技术开发、信息服务相融合的出版之路。

关键词：并购　重组　数字化　集团化

The Characteristics of Mergers in European and American Publishing Industries in the Digital Era and Its Inspiration for Publishing Grouping in China

Hong Jiulai

（School of Communication，East China Normal University，Shanghai，200062）

Abstract：Since 2000，there have been a lot of mergers and reorganization activities among European and American publishing groups. This paper mainly analyses its new trends and characteristics under the digital backgrounds. Firstly，based on control of channels and combination of brands，these publishing groups have no intention of enlarging scale of enterprises and increasing variety of products. Secondly，transferring from all-around pattern to professional pattern，large and overall model is no longer the pursuit of these groups. Thirdly，changing into the digital model is the main object，and restructuring with new technical enterprises out of publishing industry is the main stream. Taking above trends and characteristics as yardstick，the paper illustrates suggestions that in the process of deepening the reform of China's publishing grouping in the future，the pace of digital publishing should be accelerated；and the relationship between scales and efficiency ought to be correctly dealt with；moreover，the professional publishing way of specializing with obvious advantages，putting efficiency first，dividing work properly and converging technology and information service is supposed to be used.

Keywords：Mergers and acquisitions　Reorganization　Digitization　Grouping

以我国第一家出版集团——上海世纪出版集团 1999 年 2 月成立为起点，中国出版企业的集团化进程已 10 年有余了。据统计，至 2009 年年底，全国已组建了 29 家出版集团公司，24 家国有新华发行集团公司，3 家期刊经营集团，49 家报业经营集团。[1]从最初有选择性的试点，到全行业的铺开，应该说 10 年来的改革成果达到了预期目标。借助企业改制与集团化重组，中国出版企业的市场主体色彩更加明确，企业的产权关系初步理顺，出现了一些规模与效益均明显增强的大型集团。随着中央部属出版社与大学出版社即将完成的全面转制，相信中国出版集团化的整合力度还会进一步增强。

毋庸讳言，自出版集团化重组以来，中国学界、业界对此也一直存在着一些争论，争论的焦点是：以政府行政力量捏合而成的集团化是否是中国出版产业做大做强的唯一途径，借助企业数量叠加而形成的规模扩容，是否必然带来中国出版业整体效益与竞争力的提高。中国出版集团化改革有一个不言而喻的参照器，就是以世界上一些出版传媒的"航空母舰"为潜在竞争目标，紧跟出版产业强国的产业发展态势。本文拟就近年来欧美出版集团在并购重组过程中呈现的一些新动向、特征加以分析，并以之为评价尺度对今后中国出版集团化改革的深化之路提出一些新的思考。

1　数字化背景下欧美出版集团在并购重组过程中呈现的一些新动向与特征

自 20 世纪 90 年代以来，受国际金融资本对出版业的渗透影响，同时伴随新技术背景下出版产业自我调整与融合的驱动作用，欧美出版业兴起了一股兼并重组的热潮，世界知名的国际出版巨头无一例外都卷入其中。这股并购潮起因于几大出版巨头对中小学教材市场份额的竞争，在形成相对均衡格局后又演变为技术投资（服务）的竞争，而且在进入新世纪后由于一些新技术"黑马"强力进入出版领域，使产业竞争的格局日渐复杂。并购活动至 2006—2007 年左右达到高潮，近几年暂趋平缓。分析欧美出版产业这一轮兼并重组的热潮，在市场化导向下进行产业重组当然还是其一以贯之的基本特色，但是在新技术背景下它也呈现出一些新的分合迹象。具体表现如下。

1.1　合：立足于渠道的控制与品牌的融合，无意于企业规模的扩大与品种的增多

近几年，国际出版企业通过兼并之路而快速占据市场的成功案例并不缺少，其中，通过兼并方式拓展企业产品线的深度、提升企业在某个领域的市场地位，这是较为主流的并购方法。最典型的是爱尔兰软件出版商瑞沃迪互动学习公司于 2006 年和 2007 年连续完成的两次震动国际教育出版界的大型并购。2006 年 12 月，瑞沃迪公司以 35 亿美元收购了美国老牌的教科书出版公司霍顿·米夫林出版公司，收购后产生的新公司更名为霍顿·米夫林瑞沃迪集团；2007 年年底，该集团又以近 40 亿美元一举完成了对英国最大的教育出版商——哈考特教育出版公司旗下三项业务的收购。通过两次并购，新公司形成了以原霍

顿·米夫林 170 年的教育内容为支撑、以原瑞沃迪互动学习公司强大的多媒体数字技术为平台、以原哈考特出版公司的评测和内容补充为支撑的三足鼎立的教育出版体系，拥有了原三家公司在全球教育产品中的巨大市场份额和强大品牌优势，市值跃升至 120 亿美元，一举成为全球最大的教育出版商之一。该并购案的成功之处在于：它没有走简单叠加同质企业，靠扩张企业人员与品种规模的旧式套路，在重组过程中甚至削减了一些重复的编辑资源，如对哈考特大众书局与米夫林的文学和辞书类选题加以整合，关闭哈考特在圣地亚哥的出版分部，甚至对整个集团的大众类图书与工具书选题规模进行一定的限制。但是在拓展各类教材产品线上则下足工夫，从满足教师与学生两个维度来丰富产品结构，提供个性化的产品与持续性的服务，打造出全方位的教育产品服务链，赢得了教育出版领域的成功地位。大股东巴里·奥卡拉汉曾对该公司的并购意图有如下清晰的解说，"当励德·爱思唯尔公司宣布其打算出售哈考特教育出版业务时，我们兴奋不已。因为，购买哈考特教育出版业务能高度提高我们在教育出版的竞争力。相比于单个品牌，合并后的公司将能够更快开发引进新产品。此次合并也将扩大和深化销售区域。"[2]

上述瑞沃迪的案例表明，通过兼并方式固然使企业在规模上扩大，但其出发点不限于自身规模，而在有效占领市场——大为形，强为神。这种战略见之于各种规模层次的出版兼并活动中。例如，2006 年初西蒙及舒斯特收购了宗教图书出版商 Howard Publishing，兰登书屋也把另一家宗教出版商 Multnoma 收至麾下。究其原因，进入 21 世纪以来美国宗教类图书的增长势头非常强劲，从 2005—2009 年的累计增长率达到 50%，远远高于一般大众书的增长幅度。而且，在 2009 年美国读者电子书阅读态度调查中，宗教类图书是所有畅销类图书中第 10 位受读者欢迎的电子书类型。[3] 上述两家出版集团就是在正确预估了市场态势后，通过并购强化自己的宗教出版计划，成功占领了相应的市场。在欧美图书发行与零售领域，也不乏这种兼并的思路。2009 年 8 月，拥有 700 多家分店的美国第一大连锁书店巴诺集团收购了巴诺校园书店。后者经营着 624 家校园书店，约为 400 万名学生和 25 万名教师供书，此前归巴诺集团的创始人莱恩·里吉欧私人所有，并不属于巴诺集团。在并购声明中，里吉欧解释了合并的原因："巴诺书店和巴诺校园书店以两家企业的形式独立运营得很好，各有自己的发行渠道和终端市场，但是，教辅书与一般书的界限已没有那么清楚，这个趋势在电子书的发行上尤其明显，因此，将这两个品牌合二为一，可以更好地向更多的顾客提供我们的纸质书和电子书。"[4] 在数字化背景下，原先异质的图书发行渠道有同质化趋向。巴诺的收购意图绝对不是想横增一条异质的销售渠道来扩大企业的产品规模，而是从优化渠道结构角度整合两个差异性愈来愈小的渠道资源，用较低的成本让自己的大众类图书快速进入校园，从而使集团在学生市场也占有优势地位。

1.2　分：由全能型向专业型转变，有所为有所不为，大而全的集团模式已不再是热衷的目标

有进就有退，有合必有分。在近年的并购活动中，许多知名集团采用分拆、转售等方式，主动放弃了一些经营多年的老牌业务，着力经营全新规划的主打业务，完成了由无所不包的"航空母舰"向轻便快捷的"攻击舰"的华丽转身。目前全球 STM（科学，技术，医学）出版的两个巨头——励德·爱思唯尔集团与汤姆森集团极其相似的转型之路就充分印证了这种趋向。

长期以来，爱思唯尔和汤姆森均视教育出版为集团不可或缺的业务板块之一，一直到

2000 年 11 月，两个集团还合作以 45 亿美元的价格兼并了在美国的竞争对手哈考特集团。其中，汤姆森集团出资 20.6 亿美元买下了哈考特大学教材和专业出版业务，而爱思唯尔得到了位居全美第二的哈考特中小学教材市场。但是，两个集团对教育出版的态度很快就发生了战略性的逆转。原因在于，随着数字化技术的不断渗透，传统出版板块在应对电子化出版时发生了明显的层分现象，像 STM、法律、金融之类的专业出版板块与新技术最先发生了充分的融合，而教育出版、大众出版等与新技术的磨合相对滞后。这对一个原先产品板块较为齐全的出版集团来说，就面临着客户群体、制作流程、营销方式等产业链因素分化的窘境。从集约化经营的要求来说，为了维护拳头产品的绝对市场地位，企业必须抓大放小，割弃与发展战略不相协调的资源。2006 年年底，两大集团先后宣布出售旗下的教育出版业务。2007 年 5 月，汤姆森教育出版集团以 77.5 亿美元被卖给加拿大的两家私投基金。同月，爱思唯尔旗下的哈考特教育集团（美国以外的市场）以 9.5 亿美元的价格出售给培生集团，而哈考特教育集团（美国本土）则经私募股权倒腾后落户上文提及的霍顿·米夫林瑞沃迪集团。汤姆森集团总裁和首席执行官 Richard J. Harrington 对集团放弃教育出版板块是这样解释的："汤姆森教育出版集团是一个运行良好的产业，但是它不符合我们长期的战略计划。在销售了汤姆森教育出版集团之后，我们的主要收入将来自电子产品和服务，这些正在高速增长的部门。同时，销售汤姆森教育出版集团可以为我们提供加速发展核心产业和拓展相关市场必需的可持续性资源，这与我们的战略保持一致。"[5]从优化资源配置、强化主业特色的角度来取舍企业的产品线与规模，而不是以多逞强、平均用力，这种并购思路无疑适用于同样卖出教育出版的爱思唯尔，用来解释买进教育出版的瑞沃迪集团的动机也是同样有效。

在此轮兼并风潮中，就每一个具体企业而言，可能面临着是分出去还是合进来、是扩张性进攻还是战略性放弃等不同的选择，但最终的目标却是高度的一致，那就是走专业化之路，追求在专业出版领域的效益最大化。究其深层原因，在一个人人自命为作者、个个充当出版商的可见将来，人类知识的质量将主要取决于个人的阅读体验，而不是来自于传统出版的"把关"作用。[6]未来作者身份与编辑角色的广泛化与模糊性，决定了出版组织的架构将是分散的、专门化的，那种包罗万象、无所不及的"通才"式出版组织模式已经没有存在的市场空间。对此，当下欧美出版界已基本达成共识，并以此为基准审视诸多出版巨人的未来前景。例如，兰登书屋是美国大众出版巨头，目前在美国拥有 9 大出版品牌（集团），共 120 多家出版社。此外，它还设有儿童出版集团、有声出版集团，以及信息出版集团等。如此庞大的组织架构与产品类型显然与出版专业化的趋势相抵牾，难怪美国许多有识之士对其前景很不乐观。兰登书屋前资深编辑 Jason Epstein 在今年年初甚至大胆预言，这个巨人五年内必然会解体。[7]兰登书屋对过于庞大的经营摊子似乎也有点难以为继，正采取措施力图压缩自己的战线。继 2009 年对旗下的矮脚鸡出版公司和双日出版公司的业务进行拆分之后，2010 年又对皇冠出版集团进行了较大规模的重组——分离出非大众出版部门，关并了若干出版社，设立统一的大众平装本图书项目等等。"我们的目的是突出强项和优势，把出版资源进行整合，促进全公司内部的团队合作。"[8]兰登书屋主席兼首席执行官马库斯·多尔解释一系列结构调整的缘由与其他并购企业之论如出一辙。

    1.3   分或合：能否向数字化出版转型是考量的主要目标，与业外新技术类型企业的

重组是主流方向

在全球出版数字化转型过程中，为什么那么多成功的"第一"，如第一家大型网上书店、第一个成熟的阅读器、最大的图书搜索引擎等，都是由出版业之外的企业完成的，而传统书业似乎有赶鸭子上架的无奈。这个弥漫在当下出版业中的迷思也许一时不会有准确的答案，因为数字化技术对人类社会带来的前景本身就充满了不确定性。但是，"数字革命席卷了媒体产业，正在重新制定图书业的规则，将行业中风行数十年老牌企业已折腾得翻天覆地。"[9]顺昌逆亡，处于危机进程中的传统出版业唯有围绕数字化战略进行结构调整，才能实现企业的现代转型。在欧美这一轮出版并购风潮中，能否融入数字出版的前行方向已成为各大公司决策时的重要考量。

同样以上述一些出版企业为例。巴诺书店曾是美国电子书的弄潮儿，但2003年它中止了自己的电子书阅读项目，给了亚马逊后来者坐大的机遇。不过巴诺勇于面对自己的决策失误，奋起直追，于2009年初收购了电子书阅读器制造商Fictionwise公司，年中推出了自己拥有70万本电子书的电子书店，年底推出了自己的阅读器Nook。由于巴诺的电子书版本能够支持大多数主流终端，用户可以在各平台直接切换阅读，比起亚马逊必须固定使用Kindle阅读器的技术已显示出一定的优势。另外，巴诺还正与Plastic Logic合作，将推出一种有弹性、可变形的新款阅读器。"零售有多强、技术就有多强"，这是书店新任CEO林奇对公司未来的描述。再如，上文中提及的霍顿·米夫林瑞沃迪集团利用先进的Riverdeep技术平台，使整个集团的数字化优势展露峥嵘。2009年，它首开向全美各州教材审查委员会提供全数字版样书的先例，单此一项就为集团节约了大量的成本。

对传统书业而言，数字化是一种具有"毁灭性"的技术，其管理系统、运作方式及赢利模式等与传统出版体系有着天然的、内在的冲突。因此，传统出版企业在转型过程中，如果试图利用旧有的管理架构进行数字化的创新努力，也许事倍功半，甚至徒劳无功。美国教育出版的两个巨头——培生与麦克劳·希尔在各自解决高校教材数字技术时，前者与市场上成熟的技术商进行合作，以购买方式为主，比较成功；而后者投资巨额进行自主研发，业界一般认为是失败的。因此，在此轮并购中，许多传统企业不仅注重与业外新技术企业的重组，而且为了保证自己的技术部门有较为独立的创新空间，在管理机制上突破传统的思路。例如，加拿大超级连锁书店英迪戈于2009年初推出电子书项目Short-Covers，市场反响很好，当年取得了百万下载量。但公司没有沾沾自喜，反而于年底把该项目从母公司实现剥离和重组，并更名为KOBO，目的就是使其尽量远离现行管理机制的束缚，为公司打造一个全新的"臭鼬工程"（skunk works）。美国业界预测，一些目前较为"另类"的新技术出版企业，如社交网络媒体、开放式网络书店、自费出版服务商、移动阅读技术商等等，将是下一轮并购活动的宠儿。

2 中国出版企业集团化改革的发展之道

通过以上初步梳理可以发现，欧美出版产业并购的基本规律是：产品专业化是调整的重要手段，效益优先化是追求的现实目标，向数字化转型是前行的必然方向。尽管中国当下的出版集团在市场化程度上与发达国家相比还存在着差距，另外中国出版集团化的制度背景也有自己独特的地方，但他山之石，可以攻玉，作为后来者的中国出版业完全可以借鉴欧美产业并购中的一些基本规律与成功方法，破解当前集团化过程中形成的一些制约瓶颈，跨越式地融入扑朔迷离的全球化数字出版大潮中。具体而言，可以从以下几个方面进一步完善中国出版集团化的发展之道。

2.1 正确处理规模与效益的关系，走效益优先的有效规模之路

欧美的经验显示，出版集团正从原先多元化的经营渐渐剥离其他业务，退回到出版主业之中；在经营主业时，也从原先无所不及的全能型向有选择性的专才型转变，出版产业的发展趋势是精深化、分拆化，对有限市场的绝对占有量与控制能力将是企业追求的第一要务。由于行政捏合的原因，中国现有的大部分出版集团都属于大而全的聚合体，在整合内部资源链与品牌价值链、形成有效出版规模上有着先天的不足，一些集团内部的经营效益未能出现 1+1>2 的效果，甚至少数集团的经营资产比例有主业弱化、次业上升的情况。因此，中国的出版集团在规模膨胀化之后必须有一个塑身健体的自我强化疗程，借助关停并转等猛药进行内部消化治理，从而达到市场占有率与赢利水平"双高"的改革预期。对即将完成改制的部属出版社与大学出版社而言，要避免重蹈大而全的单一模式，引导其在市场化导向下进行跨地区、跨所有制形式、股权方式多样化的重组，在市场选择中或分或合。

2.2 去除高度同质化的色彩，走分工合理的专业化出版之路

中国现有出版集团的同质化现象，一是体现为地域分布的行政化现象，基本上是各个省市级出版发行集团划地为王、以行政区块平均配置出版资源；二是体现为产品结构的同构化现象，各个集团不管规模大小、实力强弱，产品线大多雷同（如多属全覆盖型），企业的赢利点也相似（如大多依赖中小学教材的出版发行）。要破解这个计划经济体制遗留的结构瓶颈也要从两方面着手：一是政府层面要进一步加大出版要素市场的开放力度，割断地方保护主义的现实利益链，从而使出版产业在地域分布上向资源配置更为优化的产业集群转变；二是企业层面要有所为有所不为，力戒贪大求全的非理性竞争方式，根据资源优势与发展定位选择自己欲进入的产品市场，通过内涵式的发展使现有的集团完成向专业化方向的再转型，诞生出一批有一定影响力的中国 STM、财经、教育、大众等出版品牌集团。

2.3 加快数字化出版的步伐，走与技术开发、信息服务相融合的出版之路

或许受益于国家对文化产业一定的保护措施，中国出版业对传统出版已经面临的危机程度还缺少足够的忧患意识，甚至认为当下发生在欧美教育、大众等出版领域的危机与我们的国情还不尽一致，自己还有 5~10 年的时间去从容应付，等等。故此，中国现有出版企业的整体数字化程度不高，一些大型出版企业满足于传统的规模扩张，置数字化战略于边缘地位；还有少数企业投入人力物力进行数字化的闭门尝试，试图在现有企业的管理架构中实现自我创新。总之，在目前数字出版产业链中，传统的内容提供商与技术开发商、平台服务商之间存在着观念与利益上的多种隔阂，产业的融合状况非常松散。欧美经验已经表明，数字出版对传统出版而言是一种颠覆性的革命，旧出版之"体"已经无法容纳新出版之"用"。只有断然另立创新门户，或欣然接纳他人加盟，传统企业才能免于不被淘汰的命运。因此，中国出版企业须在增强数字转型紧迫感的同时，还要在与新技术（企业）融合的观念与方式上借鉴他人成功的经验，勇于尝试，才能在未来的竞争中立于不败之地。

国际出版

注释

［1］柳斌杰. 鼓励新闻出版企业跨媒体跨所有制并购重组. 光明日报，2010-1-4

［2］彭致. 美米弗林收购哈考特教育子公司. 中国新闻出版报，2007-8-2

［3］Book Industry Study Group, Inc. Consumer Attitudes Toward E-book Reading, Report 1. P12（Jan 2010）www. bisg. org

［4］Barnes & Noble College Booksellers To Become Part of the World's Largest Bookseller. （Aug. 10, 2009）http://www. bncollege. com/about_news. aspx

［5］Thomson Announces Strategic Realignment of Operations：Company to Sell Education Businesses. （Oct. 25. 2006）http://thomsonreuters. com/content/press_room/corp/corp news/139161

［6］Jason Epstein. Publishing：the Revolutionary Future. The New York Review of Books, Volume 57（March 11, 2010）

［7］这个观点是 Jason Epstein 先生在 2010 年 2 月 4 日美国 pace 大学出版系的一个讲座中公开表示的

［8］Leon Neyfakh. Massive Reorganization at Random House. The New Yorker Observer, （Dec. 3, 2008）

［9］Jeffrey A. Trachtenberg. E-Books Rewrite Bookselling. WSJ,（May 21, 2010）

作者简介

洪九来，博士，华东师范大学传播学院副教授，传播学系系主任，美国 Pace 大学出版系访问学者。

美国期刊数字化创新探析

丛 挺

（武汉大学信息管理学院 武汉 430060）

摘要：目前，国内传统期刊业面临着期刊发行量萎缩、广告收入下滑等严峻挑战，各方都意识到数字化趋势不可逆转，数字创新势在必行；但从实践层面来看，数字出版与传统出版仍处于相互对立的不利局面，两者仍存在诸多无法融合的现实障碍。与此同时，作为期刊出版业的先进代表，美国期刊业尽管同样面临着上述挑战，然而其在数字出版发展上通过积极的创新，已取得突破性进展。本文立足美国期刊数字化的整体发展状况，依据 2009 年美国出版商协会（MPA）公布的期刊数字化创新实例，从内容编辑、广告经营、发行订阅三方面筛选出具有代表性的创新举措，对其进行针对性分析，结合国内期刊数字化发展需求，探讨值得中国期刊业借鉴的经验和启示，包括专注目标用户，加强内容定制服务，深化纸网融合。

关键词：期刊数字化 数字化创新 内容定制

The Analysis of Digital Initiatives of American Magazine Publishing

Cong Ting

（School of Information Management, Wuhan University, Wuhan, 430060）

Abstract: Nowadays, Chinese traditional magazine industry is facing serious challenges, such as the decline in circulation drop and advertising revenues. Every parties of magazine industry realizes that the digital trend is irreversible. As a matter of fact, digital publishing and traditional publishing are still opposed but not connected to each other from practical perspective. At the same time, as the advanced example of magazine industry, some breakthroughs have been made through digital innovation in the American magazine industry. According to the current situation of the development of digital magazine industry in the United States, the author sums up the magazine digital initiatives which announced by Magazine Publishers of America in 2009, analyses them from content editing, advertising operation and subscription, points out some important experience and enlightenment for Chinese magazine industry, such as focusing on target audience, strengthening customized service and improving the relationship between paper and online publishing.

Keywords: Digital magazine Digital initiative Customized content

1 发展状况

在最近的几年中，美国纸质期刊收入出现着较大幅度的下滑。2008 年上半年，美国期刊报摊销售与 2007 年相比整体下跌 6.3%，美国报摊销售量排名首位的《大都会》（*Cosmopolitan*）销量下降了 6%。[1]在全球经济危机的大背景下，仅靠纸质版收入的期刊面临着较大的生存压力。创刊近 30 年的 *PC magazine* 就从 2009 年第二期开始停发纸质印刷版，转为全数字发行。更多期刊由周刊改为月刊，加大网络期刊发行。与纸质期刊整体略显疲态相比，数字期刊呈现相对较好的发展态势。据美国杂志出版商协会（MPA）2009 年发布的报告显示[2]，美国期刊网站数量 2009 年达到 15 204 个，数字化比例超过 65%（见图 1）。截至 2009 年第一季度，期刊网站的用户访问量达到 7 580 万，较 2007 年上升 20%。另据 BPAW2009 年 6 月统计显示[3]，旗下出版商中有 338 个发行数字期刊，较 2008 年增长 18.2%，较 2006 年增长 133%（见图 2）。

Number of Magazines
with Websites 2005–2009

year	total	consumer only
2005	10,131	4,712
2006	10,818	5,395
2007	11,623	5,950
2008	13,247	6,453
2009	15,204	7,473

Source:MediaFinder,2009(data as of March,2009)

图 1　2005—2009 年美国期刊网站数量情况

图 2　2006—2009 年 BPAW 中数字期刊出版商数量情况

目前，美国期刊数字化主要有以下几种形态：以内容资源整合为主的网站形态，借助数字发行平台的电子杂志形态，借助手机、电子阅读器等移动媒体发布的期刊形态，传统期刊嵌入数字技术的新型纸质期刊形态等。在数字化发展过程中，大型出版商建立了相对完善的数字化形态，其网站一般都包括垂直搜索服务，丰富的视频资源，并向读者提供个性化定制服务，如《时代》、《赫斯特》、《娱乐周刊》等知名期刊往往包含了以上列举的多种形态。不少中小型出版商，尤其是 B2B 类出版商则由于建设成本、短期回报率低等原因限制其数字化发展，数字期刊仅仅是纸质期刊的翻版，如 *Small Magazine* 内容方面仅包含简单的目录信息，订购页面仅仅是让读者发送电子邮件。

2 数字化创新举措

据美国出版商协会（MPA）调查显示，旗下的大众期刊在 2009 年第一季度共推出 76

项数字化创新，同比上升10%。[4]在这些数字化创新中，包括嵌入纸质期刊的视频广告，通过在线活动加强读者互动，利用twitter实现订阅服务，整合营销活动以及在线社区活动，等等。值得说明的是，随着2010年4月平板电脑iPad的发布，在美国期刊出版商中引发了一阵基于iPad等移动终端的应用软件的开发热潮，就在2010年MPA期刊数字化创新列表中，有超过半数的出版商在iPad平台上开发了期刊应用。数字技术与商业应用之间快速而紧密的结合已成为近两年来美国期刊业发展的显著特征。

对于期刊业来说，数字创新的核心目标在于长期价值回报，进而实现可持续的商业模式。因此，面对层出不穷的创新项目，我们试图沿着内容编辑、广告经营、发行订阅的脉络梳理出具有代表性的创新个案，从中发现隐藏在创新现象背后的惊喜。

2.1 内容编辑创新

内容编辑方面以《时代周刊》（*Times*）为代表。2009年3月，美国《时代》周刊创办为读者量身定制的"自助"杂志《我的》。读者可从《时代》周刊、《体育画刊》、《美食与美酒》、《返璞归真》、《金钱》、《型时代》、《高尔夫》和《旅游+休闲》8种杂志中任选5种，挑出自己感兴趣的栏目重组成一本36页的杂志免费订阅，总共有56种选择方式。该杂志每期将发行23.1万份，有纸质和电子两个版本，仅有排在前3.1万名的读者能获得纸质版本，其余20万名读者能获得电子杂志。除时代华纳公司外，美国媒体新闻集团也向旗下报纸读者提供"自助"定制报纸服务，读者能通过关键词、作者和题目自由选择文章订阅。一直以来，加强出版者与读者之间的互动性是活跃期刊内容，扩大期刊影响力的关键要素，数字环境给予两者交互以广阔的发展空间。《时代周刊》读者自行组装期刊栏目的创新项目便是读者参与编辑的初步尝试，为今后读者深层次嵌入编辑流程的运行模式提供了重要参考。

2.2 广告经营创新

广告经营方面以《娱乐周刊》（*Entertainment Weekly*）为代表。美国《娱乐周刊》，在2010年9月18日出版的纸质期刊中嵌入一个超薄LCD液晶屏和一个迷你扬声器，用户一打开杂志，视频广告的图像和声音就会自动通过媒体播放器播送出来。由于使用了迷你播放器，《娱乐周刊》当期每本杂志的成本从12美元激增到30美元[5]，而这种视频广告的费用还在保密阶段。值得注意的是，嵌入视频广告的纸质期刊只面向纽约和洛杉矶的订阅者。《娱乐周刊》嵌入视频广告的创新提高了纸质期刊的互动性，扩充了期刊广告的实际容量。从某种程度上讲，正如美国《广告时代》周刊记者布莱恩·施泰因贝格所说，"这是传统媒体运作模式变革的又一个范例。"另一方面，《娱乐周刊》这一特刊选择纽约与洛杉矶订阅者作为发行对象，固然有创新试验的现实考量，但是否会成为今后行业期刊受控发行的新思路同样值得思考，即针对特定对象发行含有视频广告的纸质期刊。

2.3 发行订阅创新

发行订阅方面以赫斯特（*Hearst*）为代表。赫斯特推出针对订阅者的电子邮件新闻订阅业务，收到电子邮件新闻的读者可以通过点击"绿色网站"（TheDailyGreen. com）进行回复。在这个网站上，《美丽家居》的订阅者可以获取如何节省家庭开销的信息，《大众机械》的订阅者可以查阅"2008年10大最省油汽车的信息"。通过这种的方式，期刊订阅者顺利转化为"绿色网站"的流量，据悉2008年4月纸质期刊订阅者的访问量占了该网站整体流量的1/4。这种订阅方式一方面扩大期刊网站流量，提供订阅者相关增值服务，为实现网络营收打下基础；另一方面通过发送账单、提供续订服务等方式，与订阅者建立长期稳定的联系，进一步巩固纸质期刊的订阅。

3 借鉴与启示

其实，新媒体技术的发展无论对于美国还是中国，都是一个新的课题。抛开两国媒介制度方面的差异，中美期刊业在数字化创新发展过程中会面临许多相似的问题，因此分析美国期刊数字化创新中的一些规律和经验，对中国期刊业具有一定的借鉴意义。

3.1 专注目标读者，实现中小期刊的特色生存

美国期刊业在数字化领域马太效应明显。以 B2B 期刊为例[6]，近三成小出版商 2007 年的利润率为 5% ~9%，而只有 15% 的小出版商去年的利润率超过 30%。而对于大出版商来说，大部分表示杂志的利润在 20% ~30% 之间，极少数表示去年没有赢利。对于正处在投资阶段的数字化领域，大小出版商资金、技术、人才等方面的差距都意味着这是一场不对等的竞争。从新技术投资来看，大出版商的平均投资额是小出版商的 10 倍。投资最终反映到收益上，从新媒体业务收益来看，只有极少数大出版商表示他们的在线业务 2007 年没有赢利，不过对于小出版商来说，这一比例接近 15%。中国期刊业的马太效应其实也很明显，以《时尚》、《财经》、《汽车族》为代表的传统期刊领域的知名刊物同时也是数字期刊的排头兵，它们网站的广告经营取得了不菲的业绩，而小型期刊出版商则在拓展网站流量、吸引网络广告方面面临更大的困境。有专家认为新媒体证愈来愈沦为"富人间的游戏"。

当然，马太效应的存在并不意味着中小出版商就没有生存较好的可能。一些优秀的中小出版商充分利用"船小"的优势，在危机情况下专注目标读者群，打造特色内容，同时精确预算成本，借助新媒体进行创新营销，实现公司的良性运营。以《烹调画报》（COOK'S ILLUSTRATED）为例，该杂志采取独特的数字化经营策略，为了保证推荐的公正性，其网站不设置任何广告，同时以 35 美元的价格向数字期刊订阅者收取年费，目前该杂志数字订阅者数量已达到 26 万，较 2008 年上升 30%。究其成功的原因，其实就是在期刊同质化的竞争中，突出自身内容特色，他们没有涉足时下流行的食物品鉴等内容，而是将有限的精力投注到所擅长的家庭烹饪方面，利用数字技术更好地为目标读者服务。例如，杂志对提供的每一种菜谱都精心挑选，反复测试，通过网络视频的方式生动地向读者呈现菜肴制作过程。COOK'S ILLUSTRATED 网站上有一句对其杂志定位与品质的形象描述"如果 COOK'S ILLUSTRATED 推荐一款酪乳，那它的编辑一定已经尝过 45 遍。"[7]

与国外类似，国内中小出版商数字化发展同样受其本身资源的限制，正因为如此，制定数字化策略方面才更需要明确的定位，借助数字技术在呈现方式、读者互动、口碑营销等方面的优势，以加强自身在目标读者心目中的形象与定位。只有这样，数字化才不会是盲目的跟风热潮，而成为中小出版商应对危机实现更好发展的利器。

3.2 深化编辑理念，加强内容定制服务

当前，编辑与读者之间的深度互动已成为期刊业的一种潮流，如何更好地挖掘读者在期刊编辑中的参与性，加强内容定制的创新，将有可能会给出版商带来新的利润增长点。

期刊数字化背景下，读者可以参与内容编辑，甚至直接生成内容，传统的编辑理念被

重新打散和解构，并以大众需求为导向进行有效组合，这里就包括为读者提供完善的定制服务。个性定制是数字出版的必然选择，现在的问题是如何使这种定制服务从心理体验、实际效果、支付成本等方面更加贴近读者。美国《时代》周刊创办的读者自行组合内容的编辑模式虽然只是简单的一步，但却体现个性定制的核心理念，即赋予读者在内容选择上的主动权，使其阅读更具个性化。由于读者是从五本杂志中选取自己喜欢的栏目进行组合，在成本方面同样具有一定的吸引力。

另一方面，这种用户组合内容模式打破了传统期刊按份阅读的习惯，逐步转向单篇阅读、多篇组合的阅读方式，可能对今后大众类与行业类的数字期刊的定价模式产生影响。比如采取灵活的栏目定价方式，根据读者对不同栏目的需求情况，设置相应的栏目文章价格，对提升期刊栏目内容具有一种激励作用。另外，借鉴学术期刊数字化定价模式，大众类与行业类期刊可以推出编辑精心设计的订阅套餐，给予读者更大的订阅优惠，鼓励读者参与订阅。

深化编辑理念，加强内容定制服务不仅是适应期刊数字化发展中读者个性需求的必然选择，更是传统期刊突破数字化赢利瓶颈的关键所在，这方面美国期刊业给予我们很大的启发。

3.3 扎实布局，探求纸网双赢新途径

探求纸质期刊与数字期刊的双赢是这些年来美国期刊业关注的焦点。出版商在数字化方面进行的许多创新尝试反映了一种趋势，即追求务实的数字化战略，一方面消减传统期刊与数字技术的对立态势，积极寻求两者的融合；另一方面，不将单纯的高科技使用程度作为评判期刊数字化发展状况的指标，而更看重创新的回报率与可操作性。

在当前的各种媒体中，无论从用户花费时间，还是信任感等维度来看，期刊都是广告传播效果最好的媒介载体，《娱乐周刊》选择在纸质期刊中嵌入视频广告或许正是基于这一点考量。从形式来看，这种创新模式实现了纸质期刊的多媒体传播，而从结果来看，它使广告接受度最高的期刊读者群进一步接受长达40分钟的广告推送。当然，这种创新依然不排除事件营销的因素，只是在吸引眼球之外，这类创新更提供了具有潜在赢利空间的运作思路，这也正是传统期刊与数字技术融合的价值所在。

寻求纸网双赢还包括建立纸质期刊与期刊网站之间的联动机制。期刊网站是目前期刊数字化的一种主要形式，从网站访问量可以判断该网络期刊受欢迎程度，但对于广告商来说，数字期刊用户与数字期刊订阅者是有明显差别的，在美国很多广告商直接言明如果提供数据仅是网站流量将不予采用。因此，如何获得有价值的期刊网站流量是实现网络营收的重要一步。赫斯特针对纸质期刊订阅者所进行的电子邮件营销为其网站带来1/4的流量增长，这部分流量的意义在于其用户是赫斯特的忠实读者，其特征是清晰可描述的，这就为针对这部分用户数字环境下的消费需求提供增值服务打下了基础，形成纸网联动的双赢局面。

另外，把握传统阅读与数字阅读的特征差异也是实现纸网双赢的重要方面，比如性别差异。艾瑞公司曾在2007年针对全美23家大型月刊网站用户进行了在线阅读偏好的调查[8]（见图3），结果显示有近90%的男性网络用户只阅读在线数字杂志，而女性对在线阅读的热情低于男性，只有83%的女性网络用户只阅读在线数字杂志。尽管在传统期刊领域，女性读者无论在数量还是阅读热情上都占据绝对优势，但在数字期刊领域，至少从

参与热情来看，男女之间比例已发生逆转。这意味着抓住男性读者市场在数字环境下有可能带来更加理想的回报，而简单地将纸质版挪到网站显然不能适应这种读者结构的变化。除此之外，年龄结构、职业特点、收入水平等因素的差异都要求出版商在实际运作中既注重纸网联动，又必须充分体现内容呈现方式的差异性。

	只阅读的在线数字杂志	同时还阅读印刷版杂志
按性别		
男性	90%	10%
女性	83%	17%
按年龄		
18-44岁	82%	18%
45岁及以上	85%	15%
Source:Nielsen//NetRatings, 2007.6		
©2007.8 iResearch Inc.		www.iresearch.com.cn

图3   2007 年美国数字杂志读者对在线阅读的偏好情况

4   小结

综上所述，随着数字技术在期刊业的广泛渗透，如何打造符合自身特点的数字化战略成为各方关注的焦点。面对数字化转型的大趋势，美国出版商进行了许多有益的创新和尝试，并在打造特色内容，深化编辑理念，探求纸网联动等方面留下宝贵的经验，值得国内出版商借鉴学习。然而，任何经验和方法的借鉴都必须与现实国情相结合，对于正处在体制创新与技术创新的双重驱动下的中国出版业来说，只有抱着客观务实的态度，深刻地理解技术创新背后所蕴含的价值目标，才能打造出具有中国特色的数字化创新战略。

注释

［1］ 罗昕. 美国杂志品牌延伸的新媒体转向［J］. 中国编辑. 2009．1：80

［2］ The magazine handbook2009/10［OL］. ［2010-07-15］. http://www. magazine. org/advertising/handbook/Magazine_Handbook. aspx

［3］ More print publishers finding value in electronic editions［OL］. ［2010-07-15］. http://www. marketwire. com/press-release/Bpa-Worldwide-1054862. html

［4］ Magazine Digital Initiatives Help Drive Growth to Publishers' Websites［OL］. ［2010-07-15］. http://www. magazine. org/association/press/mpa_press_releases/magazine-web-traffic-digital-initiatives-q1-2009. aspx

［5］ 传统媒体创新，杂志嵌入视频［OL］. ［2010-07-15］. http://news. sina. com. cn/w/2009-08-27/142818524255. shtml

［6］ 李鹏. B2B 杂志开源不截流［OL］. ［2010-05-10］. http://www. cbbr. com. cn/info_17105_2. htm

［7］ How Cook's Illustrated thrives while others are dying［OL］. ［2010-07-15］. http://37signals. com/svn/posts/1518-how-cooks-illustrated-thrives-while-others-are-dying

［8］ 2007 年美国男性比女性更偏好在线阅读数字杂志［OL］. ［2010-07-15］. http://

作者简介

丛挺，武汉大学信息管理学院出版发行学 2009 级硕士研究生。

欧美国家数字出版发展态势探析

赵树旺

（河北大学新闻传播学院　保定　071002）

摘要：欧美出版集团持续关注数字出版的现状与趋势、观念与技术，在商业模式上体现出一些全新的发展态势，如形成专业化发展、向信息服务商转化、内容与技术日趋融合、移动出版和离线阅读正在成为出版业的未来等。笔者从四个方面对欧美国家数字出版态势进行了深入的探析，旨在对欧美当下数字出版的状况有一个系统的了解，进一步来指导我国的数字出版实践，使我国的数字出版跟上国际化的步伐。

关键词：欧美国家　数字出版　发展态势

The Present Situation and Tendency of Digital Publishing in European and America

Zhao Shuwang

（College of Journalism & Communication，Hebei University，Baoding，071002）

Abstract：The publishing groups in European and America pay attention to the present situation and tendency, the idea and technology of the digital publishing continually, and manifest some brand-new present situation and tendency in the business model, such as the form of specialized development, transforming to the information service providers, the integration of the content and technology, mobile publishing and off-line reading's becoming the future of the publishing industry, and so on. the author research the present situation and tendency of digital publishing in European and America, so that know more about the European and America digital publishing。

Keywords：Europe and America　Digital publishing　Present situation and tendency

　　欧美出版产业的数字化发展已经有十几年的历史了。欧美出版集团持续关注数字出版的现状与趋势、观念与技术、战略布局与运营格局、赢利模式与竞争优势等。近几年，经过一系列抛售、兼并和重组，欧美大型出版集团正迅速完成向数字出版时代的跨越。作为一个新兴的产业，数字出版所表现出的强劲发展势头和巨大产业潜力不容忽视。相对的，传统出版业也由此面临数字化技术带来的巨大挑战。传统出版业如何依靠数字化信息和数据占领未来市场、谋求新赢利和发展模式，成为摆在传统出版商面前的重大问题。

　　但是，数字出版并不等同于数字出版物。数字出版物是运用数字技术对图书出版的综合开发。而数字出版的外延已远远超越数字出版物，是不仅包含数字出版物、更包括了由数字出版物所衍生的一系列服务的出版生产过程和商业模式。

从运营角度看，"内容"概念在数字化"处理"中已经被赋予全新内涵。从纸介质到高阶数据库，要经历一次次创造性的"内容处理"。大型编辑与信息管理技术平台的开发与设计，是一项复合型工程，需要外部资源高效整合才能择期、有效完成。更为重要的是，现代数字技术的发展，为大规模定制提供了可能，由此掌握更多的内容资源便成为传统出版人创造新的商业模式的关键。

如，尼尔森国际传媒集团公司、约翰·威立-布莱克维尔出版集团公司、麦格劳·希尔教育出版集团公司、培生教育出版集团公司、哈泼·柯林斯出版集团公司、桦榭出版集团美国公司、牛津大学出版社纽约公司、圣智教育出版集团公司（原汤姆森学习出版集团）等8家出版集团均倾全力建设数字化的基础设施，不仅早已完成了文本的数字化，建立了数字化的图书仓库，把已经出版的图书转换成 PDF 格式放到网上，把已经出版的期刊转换成 FLSH 格式放到网上。但不止于此，它们还普遍建立了各种类型的大型数据库和在线编辑平台、在线教育平台以及各种数字产品和工具。[1]

传统出版向数字出版转化最大的难点并不在于技术和资金，而在于能否把握数字出版的本质和特点，进而建立起相应的商业模式。欧美各大出版集团在商业模式上受制于不同出版类型和需求模型，体现出一些全新的发展态势。

1   形成专业化发展

欧美出版集团经过多年的产业运作，通过专业特色的形成和对优质资源的占有，基本完成产业运作的高度提升。目前，欧美出版商主要以数据库在线出版、E-learning（在线学习）出版、期刊和电子书在线出版3种模式开展数字出版业务，很多大的专业出版公司已赢利。美国的主要传媒集团在从传统出版向数字出版的转型中均迈出了第一步：汤姆森与路透合并后，在法律、金融和科技医疗信息服务方面形成了难以撼动的优势；从汤姆森分离出来的圣智学习出版集团，作为全球领先的电子数据和教育出版商，通过推进各种类型的大型数据库和在线平台的建设步伐，开发了各种类型的数字产品，其旗下的 Gale 创建并维护着 600 多个数据库，服务于图书馆、学校和商业领域，提供精确、权威的参考文献、报刊、杂志内容[2]

在哈考特集团被培生、霍顿·米夫林等公司"分食"以及威科集团出售教育出版的过程中，资源的细分、整合也遵循着专业化的规律，大家各自拆取有用的同类关联资源，以获得更大规模的资源集中。

数字出版对传统出版的冲击毕竟无法避免，纸张百科全书已经差不多消失了，字辞典产业也感受强烈的竞争，许多数据库形式的内容产业，例如法律判例库、医学药品库等，在店销书业者尚未知觉之际，就已经离开纸张媒体，直接进入数字时代了。在新科技的冲击下，不同类型的出版商重新回溯读者背后的心理动机，把单一形式重新解放为更进一步的专业化。如：电子辞典商满足了快速查生字的需求，因此占有比传统字典商更大的市场；传统地图商转型为 GPS 行车系统，因此顺利转型为高科技厂商；还有数字服务对传统图书出版社的重大挑战，博客搜索引擎 Technorati 投入的新公司（非常指南 Offbeat Guides）就瞄准了庞大的旅游指南市场。"非常指南"透过网络服务，为个人提供量身打造的专属旅游指南。他们直接挖掘网上的旅游信息（从文化、天候到汇率），为个人的行程建立最实时的独家指南，并且可印制成册。

2　向信息服务商转化

产业融合的加剧，使得出版业与媒体产业、信息服务产业变得更为紧密，也让单纯的对于出版业务销售收入的统计变得更加困难。前 10 名的出版大鳄们之间的兼并重组在 2007、2008 年中表现得较为活跃，并表现出回归服务化的鲜明特点。无论是以金融、法律等信息服务为主的新兴传媒企业，还是以期刊、STM（科学、技术、医学）出版为代表的传统出版企业，都朝着以规模经济为基础的信息服务商方向发展，他们大量并购同一类型资源的基础数据库，以满足用户日益增长的大规模定制的需求。

2007—2009 财年，欧美一些大型出版集团数字出版的收益继续上升，据各家年报显示，汤姆森集团、励德·爱思唯尔集团、培生集团等均有半数以上收入直接或间接来自其数字化产品及相关网络业务。不过，当仔细分析其数字化产品收入结构时，我们会发现其中诸多数字化业务距离我们所理解的传统出版已经渐行渐远。如麦格劳·希尔集团旗下的标准普尔指数（Standard Poor），完全就是金融标准服务商；爱思唯尔所属的律商联讯（LexisNexis），也主要提供法律咨询、商业信息服务。

内容行业正逐渐被纳入更为宏观的服务业范畴，由数字化浪潮所带来的产业融合正使得出版、传媒、教育等行业的界限被打破；而内容领域的出版、信息、网络等原本严格区分的行业边界愈发模糊。

早在 20 世纪七八十年代，以传统传媒业务起家的传媒集团已经纷纷开始拓展关联业务，如道琼斯集团旗下的《华尔街日报》、培生集团旗下的金融时报集团、麦格劳·希尔集团旗下的标准普尔指数公司以及励德·爱思唯尔所属的律商联讯等，早已经从单纯的传媒企业变身为金融、财经信息服务企业，向用户提供媒介信息以外的增值服务。

虽然较汤姆森和爱思唯尔而言，培生更像一个传统图书出版商，但其数字化产品和服务所创造的收入也大幅增长，特别是在教育出版和测评考试市场，趋势十分显著。2007 年，培生共有超过 10 亿美元的收入来源于新技术产品和服务。

结合媒体的特有属性，信息服务变成了许多企业的首选。爱思唯尔这一以传统出版业务起家的出版传媒集团，抛售旗下以广告和会展为基础的传统传媒业务，进而转换经营模式，集中发展增长更快的信息服务业务。如今，爱思唯尔集团的定位已经是"Information solutions for professionals"，意为"为专业人士提供信息解决方案"；培生的宣传语则是"live and learn（生活与学习）"，在服务学习之外，培生也为人们的生活服务。爱思唯尔的重大调整，也带动着许多以传统出版业务起家的大型出版集团纷纷转型。一些集团以数字化出版为目标，而像爱思唯尔、EMAP 等公司，则全面转向信息服务，离传统的出版越行越远。

从汤姆森集团的发展历程来看，汤姆森集团根据时代特征和市场状况，不断调整自己的经营管理策略，汤姆森集团的业务结构发生了很大的变化，1995 年占比重最大的旅行和报纸被汤姆森在调整中舍弃，"做自己最擅长的"成为汤姆森最大的经营策略，即便占收入比重最大的业务也不惜舍弃。事实证明汤姆森集团在放弃旅行和报纸之后，迅速收购了在欧美考试和教育评估方面具有领先地位的 Prometric，为汤姆森集团在教育方面巩固领先地位奠定了基础。除了多元化的经营理念、以人为本的服务理念，为了适应时代的进步和要求，积极应用信息技术，提供各类电子解决方案，积极拓展国际市场，成为汤姆森集团重要的发展理念。汤姆森集团在 2007 年将业绩良好、以教育出版为主的汤姆森学习集团售出，集中发展以专业出版（STM）领域的数字化产品。汤姆森公司认为，如果继续持有旗下教育业务部门汤姆森学习出版集团，将影响到整个集团的战略和发展方向。汤姆森集团在 2008 年并购路透，汤姆森和路透的整合后，全球资讯提供商"三足鼎立"的格局形成——汤姆森路透、彭博和励德·爱思唯尔。新公司汤姆森路透集团对图书出版业务范围进行了重新界定。这使得原来相对独立的图书出版业务在结构上转变成更加强调专业化的部门，在赢利划分上也采用了新的计算方式。如今的汤姆森路透集团，已从传统出版商蜕变为数字出版商，或称数字内容服务商——其大部分收入都来自于电子产品和信息服务，法律、税收、财会、金融服务、科学研究以及健康保健是汤姆森的主要方向，汤姆森路透集团希望整合新闻信息、财经服务、投资管理等业务，继而成为全球最大金融信息服务提供商。从上面提及的业务领域我们可以看出，积极应用电子信息技术是汤姆森集团未来发展的重要理念，

3 内容与技术日趋融合

产业融合的加剧使得出版业与 IT 业、互联网业的边界越来越模糊，这也意味着内容和技术、服务之间变得越来越紧密。人工智能，这一被誉为计算机发展史上的下一座里程碑的理念，也必将对内容的生产形式产生影响，使得个性化内容成为可能。

比如，亚马逊网会记录读者购买过的图书，并通过人工智能向读者推荐他/她可能喜欢的图书，亚马逊还会为某位读者提供可能与他/她兴趣相仿的人购买的图书（alsobuy 功能）。随着人工智能技术的进一步发展，数字化时代基于读者需求的个性化内容提供将成为可能。

"在图书里放广告"是亚马逊的另一种新尝试。由于数字出版物可零成本广泛传播的特点，在数字出版物中插入广告将会获得意想不到的效果，这无疑为广告模式提供了良好的基础。就是在这个环境下，亚马逊开始为"在图书里插广告"申请专利。可以说，亚马逊盯牢了图书这块市场，并为所有可能的商业模式做了一切准备：向读者收费，向读者免费而向广告商收费。[3]但亚马逊可能需要承担来自众多传统出版商的压力。

亚马逊同时还从云计算中获益。亚马逊的云计算系统被称为"弹性计算云"，可以提供"现购现付"的服务，包括计算能力和数据存储。2001 年，当亚马逊建设了基于自己零售体系的全球最大的 IT 系统后，意识到自身的服务器、数据中心等闲置的 IT 资源还能为其他用户所用。一些个人开发者、程序员、中小型企业、大型企业租用亚马逊的存储服务器、带宽、CPU 资源开发应用，运营公司业务。尽管亚马逊没有对外透露云计算的收入，但有分析师预测其年收入为 5 000 万到 1 亿美元。[4]

美国出版集团在推进数字化的进程中，对于新技术的采用更多的是通过与 IT 企业合作或收购 IT 企业的方式来进行的。哈泼·柯林斯是通过与 Newstand 合作并拥其 10% 股权来完成其数字化基础设施建设的。而桦榭美国公司则是通过收购 Jumpstart 来完成其网上广告销售的。Jumpstart 是一家拥有数字平台广告销售经验的企业。桦榭公司在收购 Jumpstart 后迅速地推动了其所属期刊品牌网站的建设，优化了对搜索引擎的敏感度，大幅度地

提高了网站的访问流量。

与谷歌、微软等大型 IT 企业合作更是许多出版集团开展数字化业务时的一种重要的选择。例如大多数出版集团均在利用谷歌的搜索引擎来拓展自身的业务。谷歌的图书搜索不仅能帮助读者搜索到其所需要的图书，而且还能帮助读者快速地就近购买到图书。谷歌、微软等 IT 企业依靠其强大的信息技术力量已经在很大程度上进入了数字出版市场并建立了可持续赢利的商业模式，并有利于形成转型中内容提供商和技术供应商合作共赢的局面。[5]

4　移动出版、离线阅读正在成为出版业的未来

早在上世纪末，人们就开始想象在未来世界里图书会变成什么样子。如今，当亚马逊 Kindle、索尼 Reader、iRex iLiad 等一批琳琅满目的电子阅读器已经大行其道，苹果 iPad 也已经加入战团。就像当年 iPod 拯救唱片业一样，电子阅读器有可能改变并拯救整个出版业，新型的商业模式可能为出版业带来福音。种种迹象都表明，移动出版、离线阅读或许就是出版商的未来。像传统的出版方式一样，数字出版物也可以通过直接出售来赢利。亚马逊网上书店（Amzon. com）已经在这个领域做出诸多尝试，并展示了一个美好的远景：人们会像购买传统的纸质书一样，购买电子版的书籍。

电子书阅读器作为融合内容产业、IT 产业、电信产业等多个领域的新生产物，其产业链和价值链构成较为复杂，上游联着内容提供者（作者、出版社、报社、杂志社等），中游有虚拟运营商（亚马逊等）、电信运营商，下游为硬件和内容的消费者，电子书阅读器连接典型的"多边市场"，并正在改变传统出版的商业模式。

各种阅读器推出了不同的"订阅模式"、下载模式、无线连载或是"本月图书俱乐部"，读者因为互联网而与图书有些疏远的关系或许通过订阅重新密切起来。阅读器为内容资源增添了新的发布渠道，虽然仍有不少出版商还是担心其会对传统图书造成冲击，但数字化的大趋势已不可逆转。随着优质内容的嵌入和嫁接，不少人士都对阅读器以及出版业的前景持乐观态度。

同时，手机阅读方式也早引起了欧美出版商的注意，为了应对电子阅读器的发展，很多电子书产品瞄准了手机用户，苹果的 iPhone 持有者可以利用一款名为 Stanza 的免费阅读软件，下载并浏览成千上万的电子书。2008 年 12 月初，另外两大跨国出版巨头企鹅和兰登书屋也宣布了各自的手机图书计划，而已经启动手机图书项目的大出版商还有哈泼·柯林斯、霍顿·米夫林和哈考特，以及西蒙和舒斯特等。企鹅集团将旗下书库中的 5 000 种图书数字化，同时，企鹅还展开了与致力于免费数字图书的"古腾堡计划"的合作，后者现有约 2.4 万种经典书目，供免费下载。[6]多形式的电子阅读方式有利于传统出版模式的换代升级。

注释

[1]　陈昕、王一方：美国数字出版考察报告：一样的斜坡一样的跋涉，http://www. allchina. cn/AdConsult/news_center_23604. html

[2]　陈昕：从美国数字出版现状看出版新趋势，http://www. china. com. cn/book/txt/ 2008-01/20/content_9559211_3. htm

［3］海猫：亚马逊为"在图书里放广告"申请专利，数字出版在线，http：//www.epuber.com/?p=4353

［4］刘佳：亚马逊：从卖书到卖"云"，http：//www.epuber.com/?p=2835

［5］陈昕、王一方：美国数字出版考察报告：一样的斜坡　一样的跋涉，http：//www.allchina.cn/AdConsult/news_center_23604.html

［6］王胡：2009年将成划时代"电子书年"？，http：//www.epuber.com/?p=2540

参考文献

［1］任殿顺，王艾：50强称霸2008全球出版业《出版人》，2009年8月

［2］任殿顺：2008上半年亚马逊国际市场销售成绩斐然，http：//hi.baidu.com/allirra/blog/item/c0344d5472ebfc52564e0091.html

［3］刘佳：亚马逊：从卖书到卖"云"，http：//www.epuber.com/?p=2835

［4］陈昕、王一方：美国数字出版考察报告：一样的斜坡　一样的跋涉，http：//www.allchina.cn/AdConsult/news_center_23604.html

［5］加拿大汤姆森集团简介，http：//wiki.mbalib.com/wiki/%E5%8A%A0%E6%8B%BF%E5%A4%A7%E6%B1%A4%E5%A7%86%E6%A3%AE%E9%9B%86%E5%9B%A2

［6］陈昕：从美国数字出版现状看出版新趋势，http：//www.china.com.cn/book/txt/2008-01/20/content_9559211_3.htm

［7］海猫：亚马逊为"在图书里放广告"申请专利，数字出版在线，http：//www.epuber.com/?p=4353

［8］王睿：iPad破冰世界电子书江湖，出版人，2010年3月合刊

［9］李燕然：Kindle，硬件的软利润，商界评论，2010年4月13日

［10］王胡：2009年将成划时代"电子书年"？，http：//www.epuber.com/?p=2540

作者简介

赵树旺，河北大学新闻传播学院副教授。

美国电子杂志产业发展现状与趋势观察

缪　婕

（武汉大学信息管理学院　武汉　430000）

摘要：近年来，电子杂志产业在许多国家和地区快速发展，而美国凭借雄厚的传统杂志产业发展基础和先进的技术，成为行业发展的典型代表。本文通过收集近几年来的最新数据，分析电子杂志的生产和运营，在内容、形式以及经营等多方面的状况，通过一系列数据和图表的分析，更加具体和详细地了解美国现阶段电子杂志产业的运作。笔者在总结电了杂志产业出现的重要现象，分析美国电子杂志产业的发展现状，发展模式以及发展趋势的同时，希望能够在美国电子杂志产业的研究上有所突破和创新。

关键词：电子杂志　美国电子杂志产业

The Situation and Trend of American Digital Magazine Industry

Miao Jie

（School of Information Management，Wuhan University，Wuhan，430072）

Abstract：In recent years，digital magazine industry developed very papidly in many countries and regions．With a solid foundation of traditional magazines and advanced technology，the U. S. digital magazine industry become a outstanding Model．By collecting the latest data in recent years and summing up the important Phenomenon of publishing industry，analyse the function of the digital magazine industry，the contents，the form and the circulation．By analysing the data and the chart to know more about the function of the American digital magazin industry．the author will analyze the present situation and Trend of U. S digital magazine industry．

Keywords：Digital magazine　U. S. digital magazine industry

1　电子杂志现状概览

近年来，电子杂志产业正在经历快速上升期。作为杂志产业最发达的国家，美国电子杂志发展极快，尤以消费类与 B to B 杂志为甚。根据美国杂志出版商协会（MPA）和媒体发行认证公司 BPA 的统计，过去几年来，杂志电子版的订阅用户增加了六倍。[1] 2008 年年底，仅由美国四大数字技术提供商统计的数据看，其记录在案的电子杂志已有 2 718 种，比 2005 年的 585 种有了大幅增长。[2] 而业界普遍认为该数据还远不够全面，许多大型独立运营商的没有包含在内，如灯塔数统（Beacon Digital Strategies）的总裁 Steve Paxhia 就表示现今美国的电子杂志数量至少在 6 000 种以上，发行量在 2 500 万份左右。[3] 而在 2009 年第一季度，美国有 76 种消费类杂志宣布发行电子版，这一数字比去年同比增长 10%。[4]

同时，人们对发行有电子版的杂志关注度不断增加。BPA 的尼尔森在线数据统计显示，其登记在案的 476 种（截至 2009 年第一季度）有电子版的消费类杂志在 2009 年第一季度网站平均每月访问量达到 7 580 万，比去年同比增长 7.2%，是美国第一季度网民增长（3.2%）的两倍多；美国的网民中登录过杂志网站的人由 2008 年的 43.4% 增加到 45.1%，消费者在杂志网站上花费的时间则比去年增加了 1.3%。[5] 2009 年 5 月，Texterity 发布了由 BPA 认证的第四次电子报刊年度调查，结果显示 90% 的电子版读者对电子杂志表示满意。[6]

电子杂志的发展也引起了官方的关注和肯定。2009 年 10 月，象征美国杂志出版商最高荣誉的国家杂志奖（ASME）宣布将增设覆盖网络媒体的 12 个新奖项，包括移动媒体，新闻报道，互动工具，播客，视频和社区等。ASME 还特别增加了一个将印刷版和网络版最佳结合杂志的奖项，将其评为年度杂志。[7]

2 电子杂志的生产与运营

2.1 电子杂志的生产

随着新技术的出现和读者要求的提高，传统的忠实于印刷版的 PDF 电子杂志已经在走向没落，强调互动性、独立性、多元性的电子杂志正在兴起，完成这一工作需要各种复杂的技术支持，而专业的数字出版技术提供商则在其中扮演了重要角色。

美国最有影响的三大技术提供商为 Texterity、NXTbook Media 及 Olive Software。

Texterity 在美国电子杂志技术提供商中占有着举足轻重的地位，主要提供将出版商现有的原始 PDF 文件转化为网络通用的浏览内容的技术。其他技术支持包括使电子杂志符合 Adobe 的数字版标准，使其适用于 Zinio 平台，以及基于网络浏览的 Flash iPaper 转换方案。长期客户包括 News Corporation（新闻集团），O'Reilly Media，T & L Publications，Time Inc.（时代集团），Vibe Media Group，Worldwide Inc.，Morris Communications Corporation 等。

NXTbook Media 是唯一进入世界 500 强的数字出版技术提供商，为电子杂志和其他电子出版物提供制作、发行、追踪服务。Nxtbooks 以 Adobe Flash 和 XML 为主要技术标准进行在线和离线的电子杂志的制作，并以利用丰富的声像多媒体技术见长。其主要客户有 Advanstar Communications，Hewlett-Packard，Reed Business Information 等。

Olive Software 是美国一家大型的出版业数字化应用方案供应商。力求用数字化技术使报纸，杂志和其他内容的出版商削减印刷和发行成本，提高网络流量，创造新的市场和收入来源。主要杂志出版商客户为 Bassmaster，LNG Publishing，Reed Business Information，Time Inc. 等。

2.2 电子杂志发行模式

美国现今电子杂志的发行主要有两种形式，纯电子版杂志（Digital-Only magazine）一般在自己的网站上提供电子版本的订阅。有印刷版的杂志出版商大部分只在自己的网站上提供纸质版订阅，而把电子版交给各种大型"数字报刊亭"（Digital Newsstand）或电子杂志提供商（Digital edition provider）网站合作发行。

美国较有影响力的三大杂志发行平台为 Zinio、Qmags 及 Issuu：

Zinio 是美国现今最大的电子杂志发行平台，同时也是重要的电子杂志技术提供商。它集合了全球超过 1 500 种杂志的数字版，并有大量电子书，如与麦格劳希尔高等教育公司合作发行的电子版教科书。Zinio 有英特尔等大型企业的投资，并有多家优秀杂志公司与其合作，如 Business Week，Harvard Business Review，Science，PC Magazine，U. S. News & World Report，Reader's Digest 等。其中，少量过刊和杂志样本提供免费下载。

Zinio 提供的杂志以 PDF 为技术内核，以在线阅读为主，离线阅读需下载杂志并安装专有阅读器 Zinio Reader 进行读取。

Qmags 平台的杂志直接采用 PDF 格式，十分便捷。相对于以大众类为主的 Zinio，Qmags 平台的杂志以专业杂志和特殊兴趣杂志为主，如 MotorHome Magazine，Industrial Laser Solutions，Electric Light & Power，Fire Engineering Magazine 等。网站上有部分杂志提供注册后免费下载。Qmags 自身还出版一份名为《Digital Magazine News》的免费双月刊，其内容涵盖出版物数字发行的诸多方面，这份杂志本身也以电子版形式发行。

Issuu 是一个注重阅读审美的电子出版物发布平台，也是一个专业的在线 PDF 文档分享服务网站，其口号是"Making digital publishing beautiful"，提供的电子杂志主要以平面和视觉摄影类为主，并且很多可以免费浏览。Issuu 极其强调与普通用户的互动，通过 Issuu，网民可以上传分享自己的 PDF 文档，也可以通过 Issuu 提供的服务在你的网站或 Blog 分享 PDF 文档，方便地将自己的 PDF 做成可翻页的电子书或电子杂志。Issuu 的新兴互动社区模式吸引了大量平面爱好者，如今每月流量在 600 万以上，并被时代杂志评为 2009 年最好的 50 个网站之一。[8]

2.3　电子杂志的经营

在中国，电子杂志至今还没有找到一种稳定的赢利模式，因为中国的网民习惯于免费获得来自于网络的内容，不愿意为电子杂志付出订阅费用。但美国的电子杂志订阅较为成熟，一般模式是电子杂志平台在读者付费后，通过电子邮件将杂志的观看或下载地址发给读者。杂志发布平台通过为内容提供商发行杂志和联营广告与其进行利益分成，技术提供商则以提供电子化服务赢得利润。

不论是印刷版杂志还是电子杂志，广告都是其主要收入来源。与中国电子杂志市场广告集中，大部分杂志投放效果不理想不同，美国电子杂志广告效果已经得到了大众的认可，并且效果也比较明显。Texterity 最近发布的 2009 电子报刊年度调查显示，91% 的电子杂志读者在阅读广告后会采取包括与他人讨论，浏览广告商网页等行动。[9] 同时根据 Zinio 的数据，其 2008 年发行杂志超过 200 万份，Zinio 的调查还显示，85% 的 Zinio 用户表示会将 Zinio 介绍给其他人，而 79% 的用户会点击杂志中提供的广告。[10]

当然，杂志内部投放的广告并不一定是唯一的广告收入来源。随着电子杂志产业的逐渐规模化，网络搜索也在不断发生变革。在解决了图书搜索上复杂的版权纠纷以后，Google Book Search 在今年又首次引入了基于电子杂志的内容搜索功能。在读者搜索到杂志内容后，旁边会出现 Google 设置的相关广告，由于搜索带来的流量增加和广告效益所获得的利润将由 Google 和杂志出版商按协议分成。[11]

3 电子杂志的发展趋势

3.1 电子杂志内容与形式发展趋势

3.1.1 内容为王，开发适应网络方式的独占性内容

出版物的最重要的功能就是为读者或者消费者提供读者喜闻乐见的内容。在电子杂志中，由于多媒体的使用便利性，图片、动画、甚至许多互动的媒体应用将会使文字的内容显得似乎不那么重要了。但是我们不能忘记，一个杂志最赖以生存的还是内容，所有的技术和媒体表现形式都只是一种工具和手段。

当杂志已经具有了优秀的内容时，是不是就可以肯定其电子版也会受欢迎呢？笔者认为不一定。在现阶段，有纸质版的电子杂志内容安排大致有两种方式，一种是传统杂志的电子翻版，如 Reader's Digest、ELLE、Business Week 等，这些杂志的网络版是纸质期刊的忠实还原，页码、内容都和印刷版毫无二致，只是增加了部分超链接。另一种则是与印刷版在篇幅或内容上有所区别的专门网络版。如老牌周刊 U. S. News & World Report 由于广告收入下降改版为月刊，但为了延续其时效性和满足老读者的需求，其发行了配套电子杂志 U. S. News Weekly，印刷版仍然致力于教育和健康问题的深入报道，电子版则以报道白宫和华盛顿的最新消息为主。著名户外杂志 Outside 的附属杂志 Outside's Go 则把电子版作为印刷版的延展，电子版提供与印刷版完全不同的额外内容，免费发送给愿意提供邮箱地址的订阅者。[12]笔者认为，后一类杂志更能代表将来电子杂志的发展趋势。由于载体和介质的不同，人们在网络阅读中难以像传统阅读那样保持持久的耐心，也容易受到其他因素的干扰，并且人们在网络阅读中倾向于一次性而不是反复消化杂志的内容。这就要求电子杂志具有更吸引人的标题，更精练、更简洁，甚至是与印刷版不同的内容。

3.1.2 界面友好，减少技术壁垒

Texterity 发布的 2009 电子报刊年度调查显示，电子杂志的主体读者是"喜爱电子化资源并重视多媒体价值，常常使用网站、大众媒体、电邮、博客、维基、博客的网络爱好者"[13]由此可以看出，除了行业杂志和专业杂志读者平均年龄可能较高外，消费类电子杂志的读者偏向年轻群体。对于一般产业来说，高消费能力是被市场期待的第一特质，而高消费能力通常意味着高收入，高教育程度及较高年龄段的人群。这些人除本职之外的知识构成相对陈旧，阅读习惯传统保守，时间宝贵。但是，网络杂志现有的获取和阅读方式要求消费人群付出昂贵的技术成本和时间成本。不管是美国还是中国现有的几大网络杂志发行平台都使用了自身的数字版权管理（DRM，digital right management）技术对杂志的PDF 文档进行封装，其结果就是在读者进行部分在线阅读和绝大部分离线阅读时都要求专门下载和安装专门的阅读器或对浏览器进行特定设置。实际上，大部分 40 岁以上的人宁愿购买一本印刷杂志而不愿忍受各种古怪网络技术名词的困扰，毕竟对于高消费能力的人群来说，更新知识比付出金钱要困难得多。

这就意味着，电子杂志想要获得更多更稳定的受众，必须以友好易用的界面与最低限度的技术要求呈献给读者。[14]网站运营者应该要千方百计降低技术的使用门槛。特别是在一个内容资讯特别易得的时代，更应该化繁为简，而不是相反。

笔者认为，虽然一些读者都会更偏爱将电子杂志下载下来，享受真正拥有杂志的感觉，但电子杂志很可能朝在线阅读的形式发展，在线阅读将为读者提供更方便、更快捷、

国际出版

更安全的阅读方式，而且基于网页和浏览器能够形成一种较为统一兼容的技术标准，而在线阅读方式也是 Zinio，Qmags 等平台默认并且正在倡导的。

3.1.3 多平台推广与格式兼容相统一

近年来，电子杂志正在突破电脑这一平台，向多种掌上媒体发展。电子阅读器（E-Readers）成为人们的热门关注点之一，当亚马逊 Kindle 阅读器上市后，立刻引发了人们的热烈追捧。随后，其他阅读器纷纷出世，形成了激烈的竞争态势。在 Kindle 上市后不久，Sony 公司推出的 Sony Reader 很短时间内成为了人们新的焦点。巴诺公司的 Barnes & Noble's nook；Plastic Logic 公司的 QUE；Spring Design 公司的 "Alex" 也都各有特色[15]。在阅读器大潮中，苹果公司也不甘示弱，其最新推出的掌上平板电脑 iPad 一出现就成为了业界的焦点。

同时，手机、MP4 播放器也正在成为极受欢迎的阅读平台，这其中又尤以 iPhone 和 iPod Touch 风头最盛。电子杂志技术提供商 Texterity 已经为 Apple 公司系列产品打造了电子杂志平台，Zinio 也推出了 iPhone 和 iPod Touch 版本的应用，并免费为 iPhone 用户提供每月销量最好的电子杂志，包括《大众机械师》、《花花公子》及其他家居、汽车和时尚杂志。[16]许多大型出版商为旗下杂志制作了专门的 iPhone 版本。2009 年 10 月，Nxtbook Media 也宣布要推出一个适用于 iPhone 和 iPod Touch 的电子杂志平台 Digital Magazines News Wire，给读者提供在手机上阅读杂志的新体验[17]。这些平台的发展是否能够成熟和成功现在尚不得而知，但电子杂志如果想要充分利用起这些由于便携和操作简易而受到读者欢迎的新型平台，就必须发展灵活美观且兼容性强的通用格式，与这些产品形成相互促进的良好循环。

3.2 电子杂志经营发展趋势

3.2.1 发行：发展多渠道与特色推广

在零售行业里，多渠道的销售模式具有单一销售模式不可比拟的优势。多渠道销售因为可以共享购买的后端流程和管理流程，平均下来的服务成本更低，而且可以针对不同的客户群实现针对性销售，长期的回报是非常可观的。

就现阶段来看，美国电子杂志的发行渠道和中国一样是比较单一的，几大大型电子杂志平台几乎垄断了全国电子杂志的发行。但同时值得注意的是，美国的几家大型电子杂志发行平台虽然都很有实力，却并没有出现杂志雷同，重复发行的情况，具有各自的经营特色。这对发行平台重复陈列杂志、恶性竞争的中国电子杂志产业很有借鉴意义。笔者认为，走特色化的发行渠道之路更有利于电子杂志的发展。

除了通过大型平台进行杂志发行，电子杂志还应该积极通过其他方式进行渠道拓展。如传统杂志在与内容相关的场所陈列售卖的经验就是可以借鉴的。美国著名的大型家居与妇幼商品贩卖网站 Target（http://www.target.com）在 2009 年 10 月与 Zinio 联营开始开展电子杂志业务。在贩卖商品的同时发行以女性、家居杂志为主的电子杂志，如 Elle，Dwell 和 Woman's Day，也兼顾娱乐、流行和特殊兴趣类杂志。读者可以直接通过 Target 平台电子杂志上的链接到达 Target 的商品页面。[18]笔者认为这是一种很好的经营思路。也许在将来，读者们可以在专卖户外和摄影产品的网站上订阅电子版的《国家地理》，也可以在化妆品及服饰网站上订阅到各种时尚杂志。这种一站式的服务与针对性极强的广告方式也许会是电子杂志广告发展的新方向之一。

另外，电子杂志的发展也为著名杂志创造了让读者进一步了解自己历史的机会，保存为 DVD 盘片成为拥有较长历史的杂志满足收藏者愿望的新选择。2007 年，Playboy 与 Bondi Digital 公司合作出版了杂志集成 DVD 礼盒，每套以年代分隔，包括从 1954 年到 2007 年的全部过刊，还包含编辑特别设计的精美礼品画册。这种收藏版电子杂志受到 Playboy 忠实读者的欢迎。[19] 历史悠久的 National Geographic 同样推出了电子杂志历史集合，并且是 120 年的 6 片 DVD 大礼盒，售价 59.95 美元。这种专属收藏电子杂志绝不只是纸质的翻版，其具有许多炫目的效果，还有知识测试等附加功能。这种数据库化的电子杂志也许会成为消费类杂志新发行渠道之一。

3.2.2 定价：灵活实际，提供附加价值

由于具有良好的信用体系和付费传统，美国的电子杂志绝大部分都需付费订阅。如何进行合理的定价是杂志出版商和发行平台需要共同考虑的重要问题。

一些传统出版商认为电子杂志的价格应该为印刷版的价格减去印刷或配送成本。如一本 Playboy 的单本价格 5.99 美元，而电子版本是 4.99 美元；全年的 Playboy 订阅价格 15.96 美元（其中 12 美元订阅费加 3.96 美元邮递费），而订阅全年的 Playboy 电子版只需要 12 美元。

另外一些出版商则采用更有选择性的定价方式，并大幅降低电子版的价格。如 O'Reilly Media 为读者提供 do-it-yourself 功能，做出了三种订阅选择：订阅印刷版，订阅印刷版和电子版，只订电子版。订阅全年印刷版需要 34.95 美元，而只订电子版则只需要 26.95 美元。奥普拉的"O"杂志印刷版全年封面价 36 美元，纸板订阅价 18 美元，而电子版 12 美元。事实上，在网络读者的心中，电子杂志的心理价位是远低于印刷版的，因为在他们看来，电子杂志的成本比印刷杂志低得多，所以更多的出版商为了满足读者的心理需要和推广电子版为电子版制订了很低的价格。O'Reilly 的数字部总监认为，任何价格的制定都要以订阅者和广告商愿意支持的心理价位为基础。[20]

当然，电子杂志比印刷杂志便宜也不是一种必须遵循的定律。纯电子版女性杂志 VIVmag 就找到了适合于自己的定价方式，订阅全年的 VIVmag 需要 36 美元（价格较高，全年的 ELLE 电子版只需 12 美元），但 VIVmag 保持着每期 35 万份的发行量，并拥有忠实的读者群。原因是 VIVmag 的电子杂志订阅包括了会员服务，其特权包括可被邀请参加特约广告商和合作商举办的大型活动，直接与编辑进行专属邮件联络等。而 Playboy 在开发与印刷版内容不同的电子版时定价策略也相当灵活。虽然普通的单期电子杂志定价 4.99 美元，但增加了附加内容的特别版定价为 7.99 美元，过刊专题珍藏版需 9.99 美元。Playboy 近期将几年前的 50 周年纪念刊做成电子版售卖，定价为 25 美元，仍售出近 2 000 份。通过提供独占性的附加价值和灵活定价，电子杂志能够在赢利和读者满意度上找到良好的平衡。

3.2.3 服务：注重细节与个性化，提供定制

个性化的定制服务的发展是由来已久的，期刊的读者和受众的细分就是一个表现形式，而随着竞争的加剧，电子期刊领域的定制化服务也将成为一种趋势，期刊市场正在从面向大众化的市场化阶段过渡到面对目标读者群的小众化阶段。

　　个人定制服务在许多与互联网相关的领域已经有了应用，比如说 Google 和百度的信息定制，博客的 RSS 定制阅读服务。而在期刊行业，定制服务方兴未艾。2009 年 3 月，美国时代集团推出了一项允许读者定制个人杂志的服务。读者可从时代集团所属杂志中挑选感兴趣的内容可集结成"我的杂志"（Mine.），并以定期接收电子版的方式阅读。读者可从《时代》、《体育画报》、《美食与美酒》、《精致生活》、《金钱》、《型时代》、《高尔夫》和《旅游与休闲》8 本杂志中选出 5 本，并且加起来不超过 36 页。此外，每期定制杂志包括电子版和印刷版在内限量供应 25.1 万份，读者可以在 10 周时间内每 2 周收到 1 份。[21] 从小众化服务的趋势我们可以预测到，在读者需求针对性日益提高和电子期刊的个性化服务和平台日益完善的趋势下，定制化的服务会更加细分，例如将杂志解析到文章和栏目，作者可以针对自己感兴趣的文章和栏目进行选购，反过来也可以促进电子期刊的内容更加符合读者的需要和兴趣。这样，随着个人定制化服务的发展，媒体出版行业按需生产的时代也即将到来。

注释

［1］ Digital Magazine Trend Watch. http：//www. foliomag. com/whitepapers/2007/digital-magazine-trend-watch,2009-10-22.

［2］ The State of Digital Magazine Delivery，2008. Folio. http：//www. foliomag. com/2008/state-digital-magazine-delivery-2008,2009-11-10.

［3］ Looking Ahead at Digital Publishing Strategies. http：//www. foliomag. com/2009/looking-ahead-digital-publishing-strategies,2009-11-07.

［4］［5］ Magazine Digital Initiatives Help Drive Growth to Publishers' Websites. http：//www. magazine. org/association/press/mpa_press_releases/magazine-web-traffic-digital-initiatives-q1-2009. aspx,2009-11-14.

［6］ Profile of the Digital Edition Reader. Fourth Annual Business and Consumer Digital Magazine and Newspaper Reader Survey. May 2009. Texterity. Inc. Page5 见图一

［7］ Digital Media To Be Eligible For Awards As Magazines. New York Times，2009-10-14.

［8］ Making digital publishing beautiful. http：//issuu. com/about/about,2009-11-10.

［9］ Profile of the Digital Edition Reader. Fourth Annual Business and Consumer Digital Magazine and Newspaper Reader Survey. May 2009. Texterity. Inc. Page8 见图二

［10］ Zinio Systems，Inc. Raises $8. 4 Million in Financing. http：//img. zinio. com/corporate/pr12. html,2009-11-10.

［11］ Google Building Digital Archives of Magazine Content. Digital Magazine News. Qmags. http：//www. digitalmagazinenews. com/News/Jan09/Google. Asp,2009-11-10.

［12］ Print/Digital Combo Strategies：New Dynamics，New Solutions. Digital Magazine News. http：//www. digitalmagazinenews. com/News/Jan09/ValueAdded. asp,2009-11-10.

［13］ NEW 2009 Research：Who is the Digital Reader?. Folio. http：//texterity. foliomag. com/node/133,2009-11-10.

［14］ Designing a Reader-Friendly Digital Edition. http：//www. foliomag. com/2009/designing-reader-friendly-digital-edition,2009-11-08.

[15] What E-Readers Mean for Digital Magazines. http://www.foliomag.com/2009/what-e-readers-mean-digital-magazines,2009-11-15.

[16] 基于 iPhone / iPod 电子杂志体验视频. 数字线出版在线. http://www.epuber.com/?p=422,2009-11-05.

[17] Jason Fell. Nxtbook tweaks editions for iPhones, iPod Touch. Folio. http://www.foliomag.com/2009/digital-magazines-news-wire-10-29-09.

[18] Target Launches Digital Newsstand. Folio. http://www.foliomag.com/2009/target-launches-digital-newsstand,2009-11-16.

[19] Playboy Makes Digital Archive Free. http://www.foliomag.com/2009/playboy-makes-digital-archive-free

[20] Pricing Digital Editions: Finding the Sweet Spot. Folio. http://www.foliomag.com/2009/pricing-digital-editions-finding-sweet-spot-0, 2009-11-03.

[21] Time Inc.'s new made-to-order magazine lets readers tailor content. http://ca.news.finance.yahoo.com/s/18032009/2/biz-finance-time-inc-s-new-made-order-magazine-lets.html,2009-11-08.

作者简介

缪婕，武汉大学信息管理学院出版科学系 2009 级硕士研究生。

国际出版

英、美教材数字化道路探索

张洪艳

（武汉大学信息管理学院　武汉　430072）

摘要：近几年有关出版业数字化发展的讨论声此起彼伏，但涉及教材数字化发展的探讨并不多。我国出版业的数字化发展整体来说落后于发达国家，教材数字化方面更是刚刚起步。本文选取英、美两国的主要教材出版商为观察对象，总结出两国教材数字化发展的多种模式，分析了教材的数字化出版所具有的优点和缺陷。本文还探讨了英、美大多数出版社正在从事的三种教材数字出版形式之间的差异和各自的优缺点，得出教材数字化发展的趋势所向。

关键词：教材　数字化　出版集团

To Explore the Road of British and American Digital Textbook

Zhang Hongyan

（School of Information Management，Wuhan University，Wuhan，430072）

Abstract：In recent years，the sound of the development of digital publishing industry after another，but little about the textbook. In the whole，China's digital publishing industry lags behind developed countries，not to mention the development of the digital textbook. This paper selects the major British and American publishers for the observation，summarizes various models of the development of digital textbook，and analyzes the advantages and disadvantages of digital publication of textbook. The thesis not only probes into the difference between three textbook digital publishing forms that major British and American publishers are utilizing，but also their merits and defects. The paper obtains the trend to the digital textbook in the last.

Keywords：Textbook　Digital　Publishing group

随着社会的发展，人类已经步入了"数字化"时代。具体到出版业，"数字出版"则成为当下最热门的话题。引用威廉·E·卡斯多夫（William E. Kasdorf）的一句话来说，"几乎所有的出版都在某种程度上数字化了，无论最后它是以电子的方式还是印刷的方式来传播内容。但是具体到每一类出版，则有它自己数字化的方式与道路。像学术期刊出版商和参考资料出版商，它们已经在电子出版的道路上走得很远，几乎要开始放弃印刷出版了；其他的，如大众杂志出版商和商品目录出版商，它们更加关注数字化生产技术；还有报纸出版商，它们则集中精力整合印刷出版和网络出版的工作流程。电子书具有很强的优势，这一点对教科书出版商和学术出版商来说尤其如此，但它仍然处于实验阶段。"[1]这句话概括出了数字出版的现状，并指出，在教材领域，数字出版仍然处于实验阶段。但在出版巨头云集的英美两国，对数字化教材的探索已经初现规模。

1　三种主要的数字化形式

1.1　"无书包"模式

所谓"无书包"模式即将教材内容电子化，制作成为多媒体光盘或电子书等形式。学生和教师可以通过各种终端阅读器进行阅读，而不需要再携带课本出行。多媒体光盘和电子书模式在大众出版领域已经得到了广泛的应用，但在教材出版领域，尚处于实验阶段。爱丁堡大学出版社认为，专业类和学术类市场对电子书的需求将会非常高，尤其是在图书馆方面。2006 年，爱丁堡大学出版社就率先推出了 PDF 格式的电子教材。到目前为止，爱丁堡大学出版社 50% 的教材已实现了数字化，并且销售状况良好。汤姆森公司也曾表示，希望通过将中小学教材数字化，并通过各种阅读终端来进行上传作业，从而减轻学生的负重，更为深远的效果是可以缓解美国某些州正在面临的经济危机问题。培生集团作为全球最大的教育出版商，曾在 2006 年向美国加利福尼亚州有关政府部门提交了一份数字化课程的建议，内容涉及到历史和社会学科等学科。到目前为止，培生教育集团已经斥资过 2 000 万美元，来开发自己的数字化资源。麦格劳-希尔集团称其名下 90% 的教材已经有了电子版本。同时，麦格劳-希尔教育与亚马逊合作，将其名下的 100 种最畅销的高等教育图书在亚马逊的 Kindle DX 阅读器上发行。[2]

基于数字化教材制作的灵活性，不少出版社适时地引入了大众出版界"按需印刷"的思想。大多数知名教育出版集团纷纷对数字化资源采取按需制作，按需购买的模式。培生教育集团利用其自主开发的"培生选择"项目，使老师和学生可以自行选择所需内容，并进行定制。通过培生的 Audible. com 网站，学生自行选择下载有声教科书和相关资料，以便在电脑、手机或其他阅读器上随时使用。麦格劳·希尔、汤姆森学习集团也都已将最畅销的教材制成电子书，供订购或按章节购买。[3]"无书包"模式工作流程如图 1 所示。

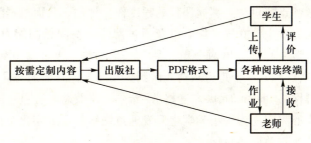

图 1　"无书包"模式

1.2　"无校园"模式

网络的便捷性，使用户需求多样性达到最大化。通过前期的尝试，越来越多的出版集团意识到，"无书包"模式并不是真正意义上的数字出版，它仅仅是传统教材出版向数字出版转变的过渡。更多的出版集团将目标放在了教育整体数字化上，从整体教学过程出发，开发与数字化教材相配套的在线学习工具和在线教学流程，这就随即产生了"无校园"模式。

所谓"无校园"模式是指学生可以在家中，或者其他任何地方与教师直接沟通，接收学校教育。得益于政府对教育投资的加大，英美中小学教育领域的"无校园"模式发展成果颇丰。培生集团早在 2006 年就明确表示已经做好了迎接"无校园"模式的准备。2007 年，培生集团注资 4.77 亿美元收购了在线学习软件公司 ecollege，其在线产品实力和服务的水平有了很大的提高。在高教领域，大约有至少 450 万名美国的大学生在使用培生集团的某一个在线学习项目，其中有 230 万左右的人注册使用培生的网上家庭作业 My Lab 进行在线学习。在美国高等教育出版最大的三个学科领域中的两个，即心理学和经济学领域，培生成功地为首次出版即畅销的教材——西克雷利（Cicarrelli）的《心理学》和哈伯德（Hubbard）的《经济学》，开发了配套的"我的心理学实验课"网上学习项目及"我的经济学实验课"在线课程，此举不仅提高的学生学习效率，同时也起到了促进纸质教材销售的作用。[4] 另外，培生集团的 My Course Compass 系列还可以提供在线教学活动。培生集团从 1994 年就开始了数字化学习平台 My Course Compass 的建设。他们以网络教学平台技术为核心，结合自己的数字化资源与网络课程，为高等学校提供教学支持服务。教师和学生可以直接登录到 My Course Compass 开展教学活动。这种服务模式被称为"应用服务提供商"（Application Service Provider，ASP）。第一、第二代 my course compass 是免费为教师提供服务的（前提是要购买培生的教材），第三代开始部分收费，第四代产品开始集成第三方的一些产品以增加服务内容。更高层次的收费服务，主要针对那些有旺盛需求的特定学科，如数学、经管等。My Course Compass 的后台是数字化资源的内容管理平台 WPS（Web Publishing System）。WPS 前端设计多种模版，并为编辑提供数字资源的收集、整理的工具，通过审核资源入库，最终将数字内容发布到 My Course Compass 上供教师和学生使用。[5] 培生集团还多次表达将继续开拓数字化发展道路，以帮助低收入家庭和行动不便的学生接受良好的教育。

对此，麦格劳-希尔教育出版集团也迅速作出反应，宣布为中小学学生创建了兼具在线互动及在线学习功能的数字创新中心。研发中心的成员由曾担任教师、工程师和软件开发人员的集团员工组成，根据美国各州标准以及学区、师生的需求开发个性化的数字平台。这个平台将使教师迅速对学生掌握课程的程度作出评估，从而根据学生的需求及时调整授课，同时也可培养学生独立思考能力以及通过网络解决问题的能力。该平台以语言、数学和科学课为主。该中心已推出两个新产品：一个是兼具 Web 2.0 特征及师生共建社群网特征的 CINCH 项目，另一个是为从幼儿园到 3 年级学生开辟的与同伴进行线上游戏、完成学习目标的社群网络 Planet Turtle。麦格劳-希尔主席兼总裁特里·麦格劳表示，该集团开发的这个研发中心将率先为中小学学生开发通过网络打通数字化交往与学习障碍的方式，帮助师生和家长实现共同的目标。[6]

圣智学习出版集团也推出了一种个性化的教学软件，即根据各个学校不同的情况，在获得学校许可的情况下，把有差别的内容放在软件上，以供读者选择使用。一方面，教师和学生们能接触到尽可能多的教学内容，既包括圣智学习集团提供的庞大的内容资源，也包括名校的资源，如哈佛商学院提供的教学内容；另外也增加了扩展性的教学内容，这些内容可以是哈佛商学院提供的内容，也可以是圣智集团的图书馆项目 Galer 提供的内容。教师、学生和教学机构都可以在这个平台上测试学生的成绩。每门课程都包括核心阅读材料、互动和多媒体材料。[7]

约翰·威立自主开发的 e Grade Plus，不仅提供教学资源，还可以帮助教师创建课程内容、安排作业和跟踪学生的学习进度。"无校园"模式的工作流程如图 2 所示。

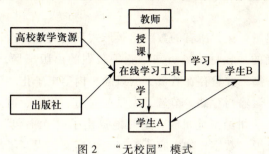

图 2 "无校园"模式

1.3 "无教师"模式

回顾教材数字化发展简短的历史不难发现，目前被普遍采用的数字化发展方式都是对课堂教学的一种模仿，它并没有能把学生放在主动地位上，忽略了学生的参与性与主动思考性。实力雄厚的出版社大多已意识到这个问题的存在，并努力通过合作提高教学和服务质量。反映到具体行动上则表现为：对教材内容进行深入挖掘加工，提供教育培训服务，提供高附加值的增值服务。在这种模式中，学习者可以自主独立地完成学习，不需要教师的参与，因而被称为"无教师"模式。

培生集团作为这一模式的开拓者，拥有 My PHLIP，My Course Compass，Prentice Hall Web CT，Companion Website，Prentice Hall Black Board 五种支持工具、资源库和网络教学支持。培生集团利用自主开发的朗文互动英语学习平台来进行远程教育，每年惠及十几万人。2006 年 1 月培生集团旗下 VUE 公司收购了 Promissor 公司，将 Promissor 公司在房地产、保险、按揭贷款、承包、招聘和医疗保健等行业提供的知识测评服务运用到教育界，提高了培生集团的教育测试能力，使得使用培生产品的学习者可以主动地参与，准确地寻找出学习盲点，巩固所学内容。2009 年 9 月 8 日培生集团正式宣布推出新一代基于计算机的英语水平考试——PTE 学术英语考试（PTE Academic）。这是基于培生完备的自动评分系统而推出的一种可以准确测量非英语本族语考生的英语听、说、读、写能力的测评系统。在整个学习过程中，培生集团的各项产品整合在一起，完全达到了教师在学生学习中所起的重要作用。

麦格劳-希尔教育也在逐渐从一个简单的教材出版商向教育服务提供者转变。相对于培生集团来说，麦格劳-希尔更侧重于关注学习者，从学习者的角度出发，尽最大的可能提供一切可以为学习者提供方便的产品。所以，麦格劳-希尔不仅提供了范围广泛的测评产品，更推出了面向大学的 McGraw-Hill Connect TM 之类的产品。这类产品通过将数字化的教材、教案和测评工具形成及时有序的互动，使学习者可以体验到坐在课堂里的逼真学习环境。

2 三种数字化模式比较

三种数字化道路目前均是数字化道路在教育领域的牛刀小试。对于哪种出版方式更好目前我们还不能下结论。每一种出版方式都存在着其独特的优点，同时也不可避免地存在一些缺点。但是概括来说，这三种数字出版方式可以理解为是一脉相承的，其是按照"传统出版——局限于内容电子化的主流数字出版——为电子教材提供在线学习工具和在线教学服务的延伸数字出版——提供内容深度挖掘加工和高附加值的增值服务的深入数字出版"的路线来循序渐进和突破创新的，但作为数字出版的不同形式，它们之间也存在着一些共性。

与传统纸质教材出版相比，所有的数字出版形式都具有经济性、便捷性和环保性的特点，这一点是毋庸置疑的。教材市场历来是竞争激烈的出版市场，纸质出版物印刷成本高，运输和存储费用更高，并且存在着极大的风险。内容电子化之后，出版社不再需要印刷纸质教材，也不需要运输与存储，节省了大量的人力、物力、财力，也降低了风险。汤姆森集团就是在美国某些州经济危机时，适时地提出了"无书包"运动，且受到大力推广。对于学生与老师来说，数字化的内容不但表现力丰富，提高了教学效果，同时也减轻了书包的重量，当条件达到时，学生和老师完全可以不携带任何教材。定制教材的出现更是方便了老师和学生的学习。有时候学生们需要的仅仅是一本书中的某几章，或者是几本书中的某几章来进行辅助学习，借助定制教材，读者可以不用为对自己无用的内容买单。而且作为出版社，数字化的教材让教材定制操作起来也非常方便，这在纸质教材时代完全是不可想象的。2006 年，在美国中小学教材出版业整体下滑 9% 的背景下，培生教育集团教材出版业务收入上涨了 3%，这主要得益于培生的个性化数字服务项目收入的增加。

当然，与传统纸质出版相比，教材的数字化出版并不是完美无缺的，首先急需解决的就是版权的问题。网络时代的到来使得版权问题越来越引起人们的重视。盗版纸质图书的成本微乎其微，盗版的数字出版物的成本几乎为零。针对纸质出版物，各国都已经制定了具体可靠的法律政策予以规范，但对于数字出版物这种新生事物还没有做到细致规范。这会严重地影响教材出版行业的积极性。其次，定制出版的流行，会带来版本不一致的问题。教材的篇章顺序可能会不同，书籍的页码各不相同。假设数字化教材完全取代了传统纸质教材，在给新创作的文献进行参考文献标注时，将会有很大的麻烦。个性化越强，带来的不便越多。另外，人类多年来的学习习惯问题也是阻碍数字出版发展的另一大障碍。纸质书籍仍然被很多人认为是最方便的阅读工具，相对于各种阅读终端来说，纸质书籍让人感觉更像是在阅读，也更健康。而各种阅读终端都或多或少地存在辐射或者损害视力的问题，而且受客观条件限制较多。

但是忽略所有的数字出版的普遍特征，我们也可以发现，英、美大多数出版社正在从事的三种教材数字出版形式之间也存在一些差异性。

与局限于内容电子化的教材出版模式相比，为电子教材提供在线学习工具和在线教学服务的数字出版方式，可以说是教材出版的进一步延伸，它不仅可以将教材内容完全数字化，还将教学过程延伸到了课堂外，提出了一种全新的"无课堂"理念。学生可以利用在线学习工具与老师和其他学生进行直接交流互动，甚至做课堂测试，一方面可以监督学习过程，另一方面可以增强学习效果。由于国外大学费用普遍较高，这一数字化出版方式给行动不便的残疾人和低收入者带来了很大的便利。但比起提供内容深度挖掘加工和高附加值的增值服务的深入数字化教材出版来说，这些优点显然算不了什么稀奇。"无课堂"理念虽然淡化了教室存在的意义，但在教学模式方面，依然是老师授课、学生听课、课堂讨论和测评的形式。高附加值的增值服务简单来说就是让学生占据主动地位，淡化老师的力量，即"无学校"理念。出版社掌握着众多学习资源，当出版社可以与学生之间展开直接沟通时，学校就没有了存在的必要。在这种模式中，学生占据主动地位，它充分地开发了学生的积极思考和主动参与的能力。学习过程不仅涉及文字材料，其中的教案讲解、甚至实验模拟都能给学生带来身临其境的感觉。当然，这是数字化教材出版的趋势所在。以目前的水平，生化、医学等学科的实验还无法达到实验室的效果，但对于类似语言类的学习来说，这种效果是完全可以实现的。上述三种教材数字化模式的比较如图3所示。

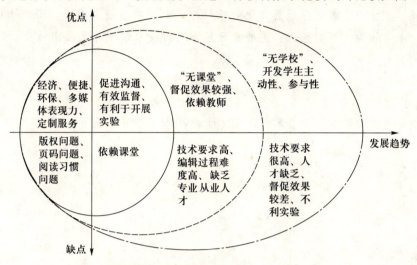

○ 局限于内容数字化的教材数字出版
○ 为电子教材提供在线学习工具和在线教学服务的延伸数字出版
○ 提供内容深度挖掘加工和高附加值的增值服务的深入数字出版

图3　三种教材数字化模式比较

　　当然，事物总是存在两面性的，局限于内容数字化的出版方式，虽然在很大程度上只能起到辅助课堂教学的作用，但对于监督学习效果，督促实验的完成是很有好处的。人类的沟通过程从"面对面"进化到现在通过网络联系世界各地，许多社会问题也随之出现，如自闭，沟通障碍症等。现在的社会学家大多鼓励人们多与他人进行面对面的交流，这样更有利于身心健康。教材内容数字化不仅可以在一定程度上节省出版教材的成本，也可以在课堂外辅助学生巩固知识，更可以促进人与人之间的沟通交流，促进学生的健康成长。对于提供在线学习工具和在线教学活动的出版方式，编辑流程是整个工作的重中之重，这需要惯于文字编辑的出版从业人员要具备编辑在线学习工具的能力，即要求从业人员不仅能够懂得教材所覆盖的知识内容，更要懂得怎么用数字化的手段去最有效地表达它。教材的内容及制作方法是决定教材能否成功面市的根本，这就要求从业人员需要专业知识及数字技术知识双重能力。"无学校"的数字化教材出版模式对数字技术的要求就更高了。除此之外，"无学校"出版方式对学生的要求过高，主动权完全掌握在学生手中。其实越自由方便，越会存在更大的隐患，这不由得会让人们担心教学效果。

　　目前英、美教材的数字化发展在世界范围内仍然处于领先水平，但远远没有开发出教材数字化发展的潜力。在技术飞速发展的今天，出版界已经发生了许多翻天覆地的变化，教材数字化发展的明天，我们将拭目以待。

注释

[1] 威廉·E·卡斯多夫. 哥伦比亚数字出版导论 [M]. 徐丽芳，刘萍译著. 苏州：苏

州大学出版社，2007

[2] 渠竞帆. 从国外传媒巨头 07 年报管窥欧美书业 ［N］. 中国图书商报，2008-04-22

[3] 彭文波，赵晓芳. 未雨绸缪：国际出版集团新媒体发展策略 ［J］. 编辑之友，2007（4）

[4]．[6] 渠竞帆. 电子教材时代到来了？［N］. 中国图书商报，2009-07-17

[5] 覃文圣，周立军. 教育出版数字化的新形态 ［N］. 出版商务周报，2009-03-23

[7] 陈昕. 数字出版中西对话五：圣智学习集团随新技术改变与重塑出版业 ［N］. 出版商务周报

作者简介

张洪艳，武汉大学信息管理学院出版发行系 2009 级硕士研究生。

国外科技期刊订阅平台研究[*]

邹　莉

（武汉大学信息管理学院　武汉　430072）

摘要：在数字出版时代，网络科技期刊日益迅猛发展，适应这种趋势的科技期刊订阅平台的作用也日渐重要。它们不仅给生产者提供良好的产品展示和销售，也帮助使用者高效便捷地使用最新的内容服务。本文介绍了国外三大主要科技期刊订阅平台（EBSCO Information Services，Swets，Publishing Technology）的概况及其主要功能。通过系统分析这些具代表性的订阅平台的一些基本功能和特色，指出其问题，为我国科技期刊订阅平台发展提供参考和借鉴。

关键词：订阅平台　出版商　科技期刊

A Study on the Subscription Platform of Foreign Scientific Journals

Zou Li

(School of Information Management, Wuhan University, Wuhan, 430072)

Abstract: At the age of digital publishing, network scientific journals are enjoying their prosperity. The scientific journals subscription platform which adapts to this trend is playing an increasingly important role. Through the platform, academic publishers can increase their overall range of exposure and gain more revenue, at the same time; the users can use the latest content. This article describes the profile and main function of the three major scientific journals subscription platforms: EBSCO Information Services, Swets, and Publishing Technology. Through systematic analysis of these representatives of the subscription platform, this article analyzes the status and problems of the subscription platform, and gives some suggestions on how to develop the scientific journals subscription platform in China.

Keywords: Subscription platform　Publisher　Scientific journals

科技期刊订阅平台是适应数字化信息交流的必然要求，它作为出版商和用户之间的沟通桥梁，其自身功用正日趋强大，当网络科技期刊日益迅猛发展之时，订阅平台的价值更

＊ 本文系 2008 年度教育部科技发展中心网络时代的科技论文快速共享专项研究资助课题"网络科技期刊出版模式研究"（项目编号：2008117）的成果之一。

是得到了进一步凸显。它们大多都是兼具信息集成和传播双重功能，而不仅仅是提供订阅服务的简单电子商务平台。这些平台更好地实现了信息资源的集成和有效整合，不仅给生产者提供良好的产品展示和销售，也帮助使用者高效便捷地使用最新的内容服务。本文旨在通过对国外知名科技期刊订阅平台的调查，系统了解其发展现状，以期较为全面地展示目前国际上主要期刊订阅平台的状况，为我国科技期刊订阅平台发展提供参考和借鉴。

1 订阅平台基本概况

国外期刊订阅平台发展由来已久，但目前为止，其数量已经从 100 多家锐减到只有 10 多家主要的订阅平台，许多著名的订阅平台，如 SMS，Hills，Faxon，Dawson 都被收购。本文只选取现今发展态势良好的三个主要订阅平台展开研究，其中：Swets 是典型的期刊订阅代理，侧重提供期刊印刷版和网络版的订阅服务；Publishing Technology 则可以划归为期刊平台供应商，侧重于为纸质期刊网络化提供以技术支持为主的相关服务；EBSCO Information Services 也是全球著名的期刊订阅代理，而其特殊则因为其隶属的 EBSCO. Inc 是图书馆和出版商之间最大的中介结构，且其诸多分支机构也在期刊发行方面卓有建树：EbscoPublishing 公司是集成商，EBSCO Online 是其网络科技期刊的门户，它又有 Metapress 公司来为其他出版商提供网络出版平台[1]，这些机构与 EBSCO Information Services 形成合力，从而更加全面有效地服务于期刊订阅发行。下面对上述三个订阅平台概况进行具体介绍。

1.1 EBSCO Information Services

EBSCO Information Services 隶属于 EBSCO. Inc，它是美国的一家私人集团公司。公司创建于 1944 年，其名称是由创始人 Elton B. Stephens 名字首字母加公司（company）前两个字母缩写而成，是全球最早推出全文在线数据库检索系统的公司之一，专门经营纸本期刊、电子期刊发行和电子文献数据库出版发行业务。作为其子公司，EBSCO Information Services（EIS）专门经营印刷本期刊和电子期刊发行以及电子文献（全文和摘要）数据库的出版发行业务。作为一站式文献服务机构，它为全球文献收藏者提供了完整的文献服务解决方案，包括：期刊订购服务，参考文献数据库、电子期刊服务、图书订购服务以及与其相关的文献订购、服务和管理平台。目前，该公司在全球 23 个国家设立了 31 家分公司，负责 200 多个国家的产品运营，代理发行全球 79 000 个出版商的 300 000 种出版物，拥有 50 多个全文期刊数据库，50 多个文摘型数据库，近 10 000 种电子期刊，其中近 8 000 种可以检索到摘要或全文，并可连接到全文。此外，它还代理发行许多世界知名出版商出版的广为使用的二次文献数据库。EIS 又下设 EBSCO Subscription Services（ESS）和 EBSCO Publishing（EP）。ESS 的主要业务是代理全世界 4 万余个出版社、26 万余种印刷本期刊及近 4 000 种电子期刊的发行。EP 的主要业务是出版、发行自己的电子文献数据库（全文、摘要及目次）及代理发行其他出版社的电子文献数据库。

1.2 Swets

Swets Information Services 隶属荷兰皇家 Swets & Zeitlinger 公司，创建于 1901 年，现已成为世界首屈一指的期刊订购服务与信息服务商。分支机构遍及六大洲 20 多个国家，获得了 160 多个国家的 6 万多个客户的认可，其中包括许多世界著名的研究机构图书馆以及《财富》全球 500 强中超过 40% 的企业，年营业额超过 10 亿美元。Swets 独有全球 65 000

个出版社的信息，并拥有 300 000 种期刊以及 180 000 种电子书的查询与订购目录，每年处理 180 万份期刊订单。100 多年来，Swets 致力于向图书馆提供订阅、获取、管理信息的解决方案，是名副其实的"长尾"发电站，能提供综合、尖端的电子商务平台。Swets 已连续两年被 E-Content 杂志评为 100 家最有影响力的数字资源产业公司之一，并被 FEM Business 杂志评定为荷兰顶级 500 强企业。值得一提的是，Swets 还是全球唯一连续 10 年通过 ISO9001：2000 质量认证的订阅服务公司。[2]

除了为图书馆等机构用户和个人用户提供期刊订阅服务外，Swets 还为多个学、协会出版社提供在国内的电子期刊推广服务，如：IWA 国际水协会出版社（英国）、CSIRO 澳大利亚科学与工业研究院（澳大利亚）等。此外，Swets 非常关注中国市场，目前 Swets 的电子期刊服务于中国 100 余所高校及科研机构，与 JALIS，CALIS 和 NSTL 建立了排他性的协议，这些突破性的协议也让 Swets 与中国市场建立了稳定和可信的联系。2009 年 8 月 17 日，Swets 在北京设立了办事处，以便在中国深度拓展市场。[3]

1.3 Publishing Technology

Publishing Technology 的前身是 Ingenta 学术信息平台，Ingenta 于 1998 年建成，随后，其收购了巴斯大学的一个数字服务巴斯网络图书馆。在随后几年的发展中，该公司先后兼并了多家信息公司，并合并了这些公司的数据库。2001 年，Ingenta 公司兼并了 Catchward 公司，并将两家公司的信息平台整合为一体。在整合之前，用户可分别从 Ingenta.com 和 Catchward.com 查询对方提供的全部信息。2007 年 2 月，Ingenta 宣布与 Vista 国际公司合并组建一个新公司——Publishing Technology 出版技术公司，它已经在伦敦证券交易所的另类投资市场上市。[4]目前，Publishing Technology 在英国和美国多个城市设有分公司，拥有分布于世界各地的 350 多个出版商用户，25 000 个图书馆机构用户以及 2 000 多万个个人用户，Publishing Technology 的 IngentaConnect 平台拥有 30 000 种学术专业出版物，每月拥有 450 万的访问者和 1 200 万的页面浏览量。Publishing Technology 着重于提供技术解决方案，它与世界上最大的八个出版商合作，是出版业最大的技术和相关服务的提供商。它为出版商提供了包括数据转换、在线托管、访问控制、分销和营销服务和信息电子商务系统等在内的全套服务，使出版商的内容产品增值；对于普通用户、图书馆员和相关专业人员，Publishing Technology 则为其提供了全面的网上内容访问和订阅服务，并保证为用户提供更好的对文献信息的管理。

2 订阅平台的功能分析

菲利普·安德森和艾琳·安德森认为订阅平台能够在 9 个方面实现增值效应，包括期刊购买者，销售者，产品或者服务，规模经济，范围经济，安排合适的时间和地点，减少影响质量的不确定因素，保存信息，对所提供的产品进行再加工[5]，如图 1 所示。

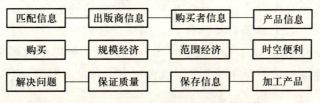

图 1 订阅平台如何在网上实现价值增值

首先，订阅平台能够匹配信息。提供销售商、购买商、商品之间的信息，并对其进行匹配，使商品的使用价值和价值均实现最大化。具体而言，订阅机构拥有图书馆信息，出版商可以据此提供更加合理的增值服务。在现有的商业模式下，订阅平台可以在许可协议方面产生更大的价值，当订阅平台代表许多图书馆时，他们可以一次和许多出版商或者其他中间机构谈判，图书馆则能从中获取更大利益。

在匹配信息基础之上，则能从更经济的角度、更经济的范围，实现信息产品在时间和空间上的最大利用，使订购价值增值。作为一个"服务中心"，顾客在此预置订单，订阅平台将信息汇聚，并将此提供给出版商、集成商以及在线聚合平台等。消费者和供应商一起形成了一个服务产业链条，在此基础上，订阅平台能够创造经济规模效益。订阅平台的"中心"角色能提高工作效率，并将间接紧密联系出版商和图书馆等订阅客户。订阅平台提供的 ERMS 管理系统如 SwetsWise、EBSCOhost EJS Enhanced 则很好地实现了技术和规模经济效益之间的平衡，拓展了订阅平台的服务和价值。此外，订阅平台与 ILS 机构的工作拓展了图书馆系统的功用，从而也进一步强化了其规模效益价值。其经济效益则是从由可以经由一个平台生产多种产品得以体现，比之于以前的一个平台只产出一种产品来说，成本减少，而效益增加，以上表述也可以通过一个简单的数学公式得以体现：$AC(X,Y) < [AC(X,0)]$，其中，X，Y 代表产品，而 AC 则是生产它们的平均费用。当网络期刊市场的发展日益迅猛，获取经济效益对于订阅平台的发展已经至关重要，只有订阅平台提供更多便捷的服务，并且代表图书馆机构的角色去集团购买产品，图书馆在网络期刊的获取和管理费用才会得以有效消减；而对于出版商，其产品想通过一个端口传达至多个购买者，也是需要订阅平台深度价值的拓展。此外，在其基本价值功能之上，其提供的诸多服务功能，能够实现用户保证和产品质量的确定，同时，也能对资源信息进行保存，在产品加工和服务的双效功用下完善产业链上中下游各方功能。

下面，即通过 EBSCO、Swets、Publishing Technology 的具体功能对其价值体现进行具体分析。

2.1 内容构建

在期刊内容产品的构架上，订阅平台与大型出版商、学会、科技社团的网络出版平台相比，虽然在形式上都旨在提供在线数字期刊，但基于订阅平台本身功能的特殊性，在具体操作层面，与其他网络出版平台仍存在很大区别。

首先，订阅平台本身并不出版任何原创文章，它也不生产、拥有或授权内容。它与集成商的功能类似，只是致力于征集许多纸本期刊并将其全文数字化，是帮助出版商进行期刊在线出版销售的技术提供者，其工作重点一方面是将印刷期刊的全文电子化，另一方面则是通过该平台顺利实现期刊目标客户群体销售。在此大前提下，订阅平台不收录作者自投稿，其期刊均来自于出版社已经通过审核的期刊，因此平台上的期刊均为经过同行评议的期刊，且不再允许作者修改。与此相对应，网络科技期刊出版平台不可或缺的统一编辑政策在订阅平台上也没有得到体现，相反，它们是在最大程度上保留期刊印刷版的本色。如 IngentaConnect 平台，充分考虑各个出版主体的不同风格定位，依靠其自身强大的技术支撑能力，为 200 多个出版机构制定了自身的网站方案，真正实现了特色化小众服务。

各个订阅平台所收录的期刊产品品种都很丰富，学科范围也都基本涵盖，从而保证用户多方面多层次的存取需要。Swets 收录了全世界 400 多个出版社的 20 000 余种期刊的篇名目次（TOC）信息，是基本的网间连接器，其中全文期刊有 9 800 多种。期刊学科覆盖范围广泛，有理、工、医、农、人文社会各类学科。截至 2009 年 5 月 4 日，该平台共有 1 万多种 OA 期刊，3 000 多种 OA 电子书。Publishing Technology 收录期刊已超过 13 530 种，拥有期刊文章索引（或文摘）4 547 834 篇[6]，广泛覆盖了自然科学与社会科学领域的各个学科。基于单篇文献而言，平台提供的目次信息包括文题、作者姓名、卷、期、页码、学科分类、出版日期、分类号等，点击作者姓名、摘要、参考文献、论文辅助信息等则可以链接到更多相关信息。在期刊论文的出版格式上，一般都提供 PDF 和 HTML 两种比较常用的格式。其中，HTML 便于文章中的关键词检索链接，PDF 格式则能保证阅读清晰，方便用户离线阅读，而 EBSCO 还提供 XML 格式的文档，这样就可以检索系统所提供的目录、文摘。此外，获得授权的用户还能通过订阅平台获得包括篇名目次、文摘和索引、纸本和电子期刊三个层次在内的文献信息访问权，从而有效提高信息获取能力。而利用动画、立体图像等多媒体格式也在进一步的开发中。

在作品版权问题处理上，作为托管商，其不具有版权所有者的权利也不能把权利转移给其他用户，文章的著作权等相关权利仍然是属于原来的版权所有者。若有关于网络期刊论文版权的疑问，作为第三方机构，它们也仅是通过平台所提供的图书或期刊主页的出版机构信息，让用户直接与出版机构联系，自身并不参与其中。

再次，考虑订阅平台上的在线预出版和出版时滞以及开放存取政策等，可以得知，其开放存取力度并不大，如 EBSCO 平台上的绝大多数期刊是需要付费才可以阅读的，共有 3 993 种，完全意义上的开放存取期刊尚不存在。IngentaConnect 平台上的大多数出版机构都能在第一时间提供资料以便集成到平台上，因此其内容都可以及时更新，但有时由于出版机构出版周期发生问题，也会影响到期刊内容的正常提供。IngentaConnect 平台上的期刊或者文章前方会有不同的标识符，如 **F** 表示 Free Content，则其内容是可以免费获取的；**N** 表示其内容是最新发表的，有利于用户搜索最新出版的期刊或者文章；**S** Subscribed Content，表示该期刊是属于订阅者才能获取的；**T** 表示该期刊内容在一定时期内可以免费获取；**H** 表示该期刊属于图书馆机构所有。在这其中，**F** 所提供的期刊多为过刊，滞后性一般长达 4 至 5 年，但也有部分期刊在其出版几个月内即提供印刷版的网络免费获取。因此，总体而言，订阅平台为了保证出版商的利益，其开放存取的力度还不够明显。

2.2　服务支持

内容产品的构建和深度开发利用离不开服务项目的支持，基于内容的服务措施展开能够使产品价值最大化，从而最终与基于用户的服务深度融合。下面分别通过各个平台的检索服务、导航服务、引文链接服务、通报服务以及其他特色服务对其进行分析。

2.2.1　检索服务

对于用户而言，平台检索功能、检索技术、文献输出形式以及其所提供的个性服务等对于用户文献使用以及对平台产生顾客忠诚具有重要影响。各订阅平台期刊检索系统比较如表 1 所示。

表 1　订阅平台期刊检索系统比较表

网站	SwetsWise	IngentaConnect	EBSCOhost
网址	http://www.swetswise.com	www.ingentaconnect.com	http://search.ebscohost.com http://search.epnet.com
期刊内容检索	文章检索，出版物检索，出版商检索	关键词，论文标题，摘要，出版物检索	关键词检索，出版物检索，公司简介，主题辞典检索，索引浏览，引用参考检索
检索结果处理	在线浏览，下载（多种文件格式选择），电子邮件传递，多层链接，个人图书馆，TOC Alert，Search Alert	在线浏览，打印，链接，接收电子邮件通讯，书签，管理个人账户，通报服务	存盘，打印，Email 输出，收入个人文件夹，检索通报服务

　　具体而言，EBSCO 公司的检索系统功能最为强大，特别是其引文检索和图片检索能够帮助读者对文献资源进行深度利用，Swets 则是根据用户权限的不同，能够使用的检索功能也会不同。此外，在检索途径的利用上，EBSCO 也是独具一格，包括关键字、出版物、辞典、索引、参考文献、图像等信息，可以保证用户对系统资源的全方位深度利用，但是也可以看出，订阅平台在多媒体信息资源的利用上还是不如传统强大的出版平台，截词检索、位置检索等使用率不高，超文本链接功能和排序输出功能等需要进一步拓展。另外，优选期刊（内容质量）的完整性和同步性也需要加强。

2.2.2　导航服务

　　对于订阅平台而言，导航服务主要从网站、出版物以及单篇文章三个层面展开，较好的导航服务能够帮助用户迅速了解平台使用路径、熟知构架，从而深度挖掘资源。

　　首先，在网站层面，三个平台皆通过网站地图（site map）或者是网站目录（site index）提供树状基本导航，对网站的构架进行基本解构，方便读者获取网站的全部功能信息。在期刊出版物层面，平台具有按学科分类导航和按刊导航的基本导航功能。其中，EBSCO Information Service 的导航功能最为强大，该公司自己开发了名为"A-to-Z"的刊名目录及导航服务系统，为图书馆馆员和读者提供了一个功能完善的期刊目录（电子期刊和纸本期刊）。A-to-Z 将图书馆拥有的所有期刊资源集中到一个一目了然的目录中，无论这些资源是出版社的套订期刊、单独的电子期刊或是各种数据库，甚至是图书馆订购的纸本期刊，都被囊括在这个客户定制的目录中。A-to-Z 由 EBSCO 公司每天实时更新（包括 URL 的更新），这使得它与其他类似的服务相比更为准确、及时，而且可以最大限度地减少图书馆员的工作量。这项服务不但帮助馆员追踪馆藏的利用情况，而且使这些资源更容易被读者获得，从而得到更好的利用。而 Swets 系统则有 SwetsWise title bank 对期刊刊名进行导航，整合纸本馆藏、数据库期刊、电子期刊，从而帮助读者获知某种期刊本馆的馆藏信息，获取某个学科领域本馆的期刊馆藏信息。相较而言，Ingenta 出版物层面的导航功能则显得比较单薄，但也较为便捷，它按统一主题分为 15 个学科大类，125 个子类，在其首页右边"subject area"中按字母顺序列出了这 15 个大类的类名。点击类名，显示该类目中包含的子类名称。每一栏目下列有相关信息资源的站点名称及其超链接，使用起来极为便捷。针对单篇文章的导航服务，目前三个平台的特色都不突出。

2.2.3 引文链接服务

引文链接包括平台内部链接和跨平台链接，平台内部链接能够实现平台内部资源的有效整合和利用，而跨平台链接则可以实现内部资源和外部资源的相互关联，从而扩展内部资源的使用价值。三个平台皆有效地实现了内部资源的有效链接，充分保障了用户的使用权益。然而，与各种外部在线资源的链接能力则更能凸显平台自身价值。在外部链接上，EBSCOhost 数据库和 EJS 都能使用定制链接（由图书馆指定的链接，例如：到 OPAC 的链接）和智能链接（预先完成使用权审查并提供给读者的链接，如：从 EBSCOhost 的文摘连接到 EJS 的全文）。在 A-to-Z 中，也可以建立定制链接，通过 EBSCOhost 的连接服务器（Link Source）可以连接到 50 余家全球知名的文献出版和发行公司的数据库，或者从 20 余家知名公司的数据库中连接 EBSCOhost 和 EJS。如 EBSCOhost 可同时链接到 PsycINFO、AGRICOLA、American Humanities Index、Applied Science &Technology Abstracts、Art Abstracts、ATLA、ATLAS Full Text Plus、Biological Abstracts、BIOSIS Previews、CINAHL、CommSearch、Environmental Policy Index、ERIC、INSPEC、MEDLINE、MLA International Bibliography、PsycARTICLES 等二次文献数据库，充分扩展自身系统资源，整合利用知识信息。

对于 Swets 而言，其资源链接 Linker 能够方便读者更有效地链接到全文，它是一个 OpenURL 连接分解器，拥有来自于 2 700 多家出版社 90 000 份以上电子期刊与 1 200 个以上的内嵌馆藏目次，涵盖顶尖的电子期刊收集器，为最终读者创造一个精密的检索环境。联邦检索 Searcher 使用用户检索多元化电子资源，并且利用单一的检索查询快速地获得相关检索结果，直接连接到电子资源出处。从目录到数字资源、电子期刊、内部资料库和网际网路，全面搜索相关资源并去除重复内容、重新排序。由此可以看出，二者在文献信息的深度服务上皆卓有建树，而 Publishing Technology 因为专注于技术支持，在内容服务方面明显落后于前者。

2.2.4 通报服务

通报服务主要包括专题通报、期刊通报、最新目次通报、检索通报、引文通报、RSS 订阅等。通过这些通报服务，用户可以在第一时间获知需求信息的出版动态，并得到相关信息的链接地址。如 EBSCO Information Service 提供专题通报服务和期刊通报服务，读者在系统内设定相关服务功能，每当数据库更新数据时，系统会根据读者设定的执行时间和频率自动将所设期刊新增文献通过 Email 发送给读者，读者只要点击 Email 信件中的链接，即可直接阅读文献全文。在通告服务的邮件格式上，EBSCO 还允许用户输入多个收件人地址，并可设定邮件主题，以及是否包含检索式等。在通告服务的有效期上，EBSCO 允许用户自设有效期，最长不超过一年。这样做有两个好处。其一，防止过度占用资源。当用户课题结束，不再需要通告时，应该把服务资源让出来。其二，保护数据版权。当注册用户身份变化，不再是合法用户时，有效期可以阻止其通过通告服务继续享用数据库信息。

IngentaConnect 平台所提供的通报服务主要包括刊物出版通报和检索策略新知通报两种，用户可以通过 Email 的方式获取据此获取 IngentaConnect 平台上出版物的最新出版信息，但最多只能建立 5 种出版物的新知通报信息。5 条以上的新知出版信息则需要付费才能获取。此外，用户还可预先存一些检索策略（最多包括 5 个检索式），一旦有新的文章被该系统收录时，系统将自动执行预先准备好的检索策略，并把检索结果发到用户的电子信箱中。

Swets 也具有目录通告和检索通告服务，通过这些快速精准的通告服务，能够加速用户使用，但在通告内容的设置上，订阅平台仍有其局限性，一般出版平台比较常用的引文通报，即当其他用户引用该文章时则向定制用户发送通告的服务则没有得到较好体现。如此，则不利于文献使用者之间的互动交流。

2.2.5　特色服务

除了必备基本功能，各个平台还具有一些特色服务功能，这些个性化的服务能够拓展平台使用价值，是内容产品极好的支撑要件。如 Ingenta 提供管理个人账户的功能，个人用户可以借此管理个人信息（个人联系信息）、订阅信息，以及交易信息等。通过管理个人信息，可以修改个人的联系信息等；管理订阅信息，则可以通过其获取全文出版物；管理交易信息，可以方便快捷地购买需要支付费用的期刊。为了增强订阅平台的互动性，订阅平台也都设有常见问题解答版块，对个人用户、出版商和图书馆用户群体最常询问的问题进行解答，帮助用户解决一些平台的基本问题，而 Ingenta 还提供了 Ingenta Labs，Ingenta Blog 版块与个人用户、出版商、图书馆用户等进行信息的交流，从而加强了彼此的互动联系。在培养用户忠诚度方面，Swets 还开展了用户培训活动以及相关的目录服务等，加强与客户交流，及时推介平台产品，帮助用户（出版商）服务用户（图书馆），从而更好实现平台价值。Swets 与其出版商一起开发出了能够将电子内容发送到手机终端上的服务，这样，通过用户名、IP 地址等设置，用户就能在自己手机上阅读所订阅的期刊最新内容资讯。该项服务的开展无疑是学术期刊手机阅读模式拓展的前驱。

2.3　交易模式

订阅平台的交易模式，即平台通过何种商业模式提供用户访问权限从而回收先期投入，它也是资金和内容或者注意力交换的过程，订阅平台借此完成发行使命。对于订阅平台交易模式的考察，可以从用户进入平台的访问方式到用户付费结算完成消费这一完整电子商务过程的两端展开。总体而言，订阅平台皆采用了多种访问控制方式，如 IP 地址控制，用户名+密码登陆等。其中，IP 地址控制主要面向机构用户，隶属于该机构的成员则可以通过 IP 地址控制从而使用机构订阅的产品服务；通过用户名和密码的访问方式则多是针对个人用户，它们皆无并发用户数量限制，也不需要下载其他插件或客户端软件，用户访问较为方便。Swets 即是采用该种方式，而 Publishing Technology 则是通过 Athens 和口令的方式登陆，EBSCO 主要通过用户名+密码的方式登录，由此，图书馆机构外的用户可以借由此获取图书馆所订购的资源。

在付费结算方面，国外的三个订阅平台皆体现了即时结算的便捷性，这一方面是由于国外网上强大支付系统以及用户个人稳定成熟的网上消费习惯的支持；而另一方面则是由于用户小众化需求的逐渐攀升，每篇文章、每页、甚至每字节都可以成为一个单独出售的产品要素，而这在以"刊"为单位销售的传统科技期刊领域则是不可实现的。而网上订阅平台的出现恰能帮助传统 STM（科学、技术、医学）出版商实现期刊产品的"解构化"销售，创造出传统订阅之外的额外利益。如读者还可以通过查看 IngentaConnect 平台上该篇文章的主页，来判断这篇文章的递送是通过电子，还是传真或者 Ariel 方式。对于

SwetsWise 平台上的期刊则可以通过在线订购，用信用卡支付的方式完成国内读者认为非常复杂的订阅程序，EBSCO 也是如此。由此可见，方便快捷的网上支付方式为期刊订阅发行的顺利开展提供了先决保障。而国内订阅平台主要通过充值卡方式实现期刊产品销售，交易方式稍显复杂。

3 讨论

通过以上分析，我们可以了解国外科技期刊订阅平台的发展状况，不管是在内容组织建设，抑或为图书馆出版商等用户提供的功能服务，这些订阅平台皆具备了专业成熟化的运作模式，帮助出版商更多更好更快实现期刊销售，提供给图书馆等机构更好的资源利用整合方案，从而从根本上实现科技期刊交流的本质。基于此，订阅平台在科学信息交流方面的作用也将在网络化的今天得到更进一步的拓展。

反观国内，其科技期刊订购服务主要由中国教育图书进出口公司报刊电子文献进口部（CEPIEC）和中国图书进出口（集团）总公司报刊电子出版物部（CNPIEC）等负责。如中国图书进出口（集团）总公司下设报刊电子出版物部，其经营范围涵盖 110 多个国家和地区 1 万余家出版机构的各类载体报刊出版物。可向客户提供 160 多个国家和地区出版的 10 万多种各类载体报刊出版物的目录信息，并通过集团设在美、英、德、日和俄等国家和地区的分支机构，构建庞大的采购网络，以此保证客户订单及时准确的执行。[7]它代理购买/租用世界上各个国家和地区正式发行的不同类型、不同学科的全部光盘数据库、网上数据库，承担数据库全国集团购买的组织、引进和使用工作，并且还向国内个人用户提供单篇文献的电子版的服务等。中国教育图书进出口公司下的内容服务平台 CSP 也面向广大个人和机构用户提供优惠且灵活的订购服务，是国内首个集电子出版物引进、导航、订购、集成管理于一体的电子商务平台。[8]虽然目前上述国内订阅平台均取得了一定进展，但在实力和功能方面皆无法与国外同类机构对比。而这也是与我国目前高速发展的科技期刊出版与科技期刊消费需求相矛盾的，从更深意义上讲，也在一定程度上影响了国内科技界与国外科技同行的学术信息交流。因此，从各个方面考虑，国内科技期刊订阅平台加快发展迫在眉睫。

此外，基于订阅平台自身如何在数字环境下实现长久发展，也依然面临许多挑战，网络技术的发展和网上发行给传播和获取信息带来了新的发展机遇，但它也从根本上改变了传统的信息产业链模式，信息产业发展的环境更加复杂：更多的供应商，更多的文本格式，更多的关系类型，更多的平台，更多的价格和许可模式，新的购买和销售信息的方式，新的获取信息的方式（集团购买，单篇文章购买、大宗购买），不断变动的网络科技产品供应（技术、成本、价格），等等。对于大多数人而言，现有订阅模式和期刊的现有形态的未来发展仍不清晰。网络技术和网上发行带来的新的信息处理、管理要求已经对传统订阅模式提出了挑战。不管怎样，订阅平台的发展被提上了更加重要的位置，它们在日趋复杂的网络环境下扮演着信息中间商的角色，为信息创造者和图书馆等使用者提供更好的帮助。

注释

[1] 徐丽芳. 网络科技期刊发行模式研究 [J]. 出版科学，2010 (1)

［2］http：//www. swets. com/web/show/id＝44472/langid＝42

［3］http：//www. swets. com/web/show/id＝46021/langid＝42/contentid＝432

［4］http：//www. ingenta. com/corporate/company/profile/［2009－12－10］

［5］http：//chinesesites. library. ingentaconnect. com/［2009－12－10］

［6］Philip Anderson，Erin Anderson. The New E-Commerce Intermediaries，*MIT Sloan Management Review* 43，No. 4（Summer 2002）：53

［7］http：//periodical. cnpeak. com/AboutUs/［2009－12－28］

［8］http：//csp. cepiec. com. cn/ns. aspx?did＝4［2009－12－28］

作者简介

邹莉，武汉大学信息管理学院出版发行系 2009 级硕士研究生。

美国电子出版的发展历史及行业变革

杨状振

（河北大学新闻传播学院　保定　071000）

摘要：本文通过对从"谷登堡计划"开始实施到当今美国各出版公司相继推出电子书阅读器，并以各种方式开拓电子图书市场这一阶段的简要回顾，描述了当今美国电子图书市场的现状。在此基础上分析了美国电子出版对传统市场造成的冲击，以及美国出版机构为应对这种冲击所采取的措施。最后，提出了对电子出版发展中所面临的盗版盛行和人们阅读能力可能降低等问题的思考。

关键词：美国电子出版　发展历史　冲击　问题

The Development History and Industry Innovation of the American Electronic Publication

Yang Zhuangzhen

（School of Journalism & Communication, Hebei University, Baoding, 071000）

Abstract：The article briefly reviewed the history which from the beginning of Project Gutenberg to today when several American companies produce sorts of e-Book Reader and use any other means to explore electronic books market, show the current situation of today's American Electronic Books Market. Based on this, the paper analyzed the impact which caused by the development of the American Electronic Publication on the traditional publication market, and the measures which the American publishers had taken to cope with the impact. In the end, the author thought the problems that come with the development of the American Electronic Publication, such as the problem of pirate and the possibility of the reduction of people's reading abilities.

Keywords：American electronic publication　Development history　Impact　Problem

1　美国电子出版的发展历史

"电子出版既不是先前人们所认为的金矿，也不是如今很多人所害怕的雷区。无论人们对它有何怀疑，电子出版仍是现在和今后出版业所必须面对的最重要的课题之一。"[1]对于美国的电子出版来说，其发展历程在某种程度上，实际上就是美国国内个人电脑和互联网技术发展历史的缩影。1971 年 7 月，在个人电脑尚处于萌芽状态的时候，美国伊利诺伊大学学生迈克尔·哈特（Michael Hart）就以 100 万美元的启动资金，实施了把因版权过期而进入公有领域的图书转化为电子文本（e-Book）的"古登堡计划"（Project Gutenberg）。这一计划事实上成为了世界上第一个大规模的免费数字图书馆项目。随着个人计算机用户和互联网技术 20 世纪 80 年代后期以来的迅速发展，古登堡计划在 2003 年时已经拥有了 10 000 册以上的在线流通书量，内容涵盖 25 个语种，月上线新书 380 余种。部分美国电子图书馆网址和主办者如表 1 所示。除了以在线方式提供图书的检索阅读功能之外，这一计划还把其中的部分图书制作成 DVD 光盘，进入实体流通领域上市销售，这也成为了今天美国电子图书市场上的代表性运营方式之一：实体销售和网络传播并存，免费阅读和有偿购买同行。随着个人电脑储存能力、手持阅读器及相关操作软件的持续升级和价格调整，电子图书的出版发行也被媒体和学者们赋予了越来越多的期望。

表 1 美国部分电子图书馆

网址	主办者
http：//library. wustl. edu/subjects/life/books. html	Washington University
http：//wwwlib. umi. com/cr/utexas/main	University of Texas-Austin
http：//ymtdl. med. yale. edu/ETD–db/ETD–search/search	Yale University Library
http：//etd–gw. wrlc. org/ETD–db/ETD–search/search	The George Washington University
http：//www. lib. ncsu. edu/ETD–db/ETD–search/search	North Carolina State University
http：//www. library. njit. edu/etd/index. cfm	The New Jersey Institute of Technology's Electronic Theses & Dissertations
http：//library. umsmed. edu/free–e_res. htm#Journals	University of Mississippi Rowland Medical Library
http：//www. ohiolink. edu/etd/search. cgi	Ohio State University
http：//etda. libraries. psu. edu/ETD – db/ETD – search/search	Pennsylvania State University library
http：//web. uflib. ufl. edu/etd. html	University of Florida
http：//www. lib. usf. edu/cgi – bin/ETD–db/ETD–search/search	University of South Florida

1995 年，美国诺沃媒介公司（Nuvomedia）推出了首款屏读"火箭电子书阅读器"（e-Book Reader），专门用于电子图书的阅读、批注与编辑，但其售价却多在 1 000 美元以上，昂贵的价格令绝大多数消费止步于实质性消费之外。为了开拓市场，1999 年 11 月，诺沃媒介公司将阅读器价格调降至 199 美元，并同时借助互联网为电子图书的发行大力宣传，美国电子出版商协会（Association of Electronic Publishers）也在网上同步推出了火箭电子书排行榜，希望以此带动电子出版和电子阅读器的发展与普及。尽管如此，在 2000 年斯蒂芬·金的电子小说《骑乘子弹》出版之前，美国电子图书的市场影响力仍极为有限，并没有引起传统出版商和广大受众的真正重视。2000 年 3 月，斯蒂芬·金出版的电子小说《骑乘子弹》改变了这一现状：1.6 万字的篇幅，2.5 美元的低廉价格，50 多万人

次的下载量和 100 多万美元的销售收入，迅速引发了传统出版机构对投资电子出版市场的极大兴趣，并纷纷介入这一领域。

这期间，兰登书屋先后成立了电子重印出版社 AtRandom、现代丛书重印出版社 The Modern Library imprint，并收购了数字出版社——希伯里斯和"声频"（Audible）公司的股份，大规模介入电子图书市场的实质性运营，并以提供版权进入公有领域的知名作家的原版电子图书和各种经典文学作品，而迅速成为美国电子出版市场上具有较大影响力的传统出版机构之一。时代华纳公司也在此期间推出了名为 iPublish.com 的出版网站，专门经营小说和其他非虚构性电子图书。巴诺连锁书店和微软公司的战略结合，是这股风潮中最具有代表性的事件之一。2000 年 4 月，巴诺书店为方便读者以多终端形式下载图书，在自己的销售系统中推出了微软公司的清晰型版式软件图书，这一举措也使微软公司很快进入到美国电子图书出版大户行列。与此同时，巴诺公司还向电子书重印业务领域跨步，推出了自己的印刷出版业务，年营业额达到 1.5 亿美元。直到 2003 年巴诺书店退出这一经营领域为止，其在网上开设的电子图书超市，都一直致力于电子书目的出版与发行工作。在此前后，微软公司还与西蒙—舒斯特、兰登书屋、时代华纳等展开合作，在内容提供、传播平台和销售系统的联动共享上，推动了电子出版业务的发展与成熟。而微软公司还对电子图书市场的发展进程进行了预测，如表 2 所示。

表 2　微软公司预测的电子图书市场进程

年度	标志性事件
2001 年	电子教科书出现
2002 年	屏幕显示将比印刷品更好
2003 年	电子书阅读器重 16 盎司，售价 100 美元
2004 年	出现用于书写桌上个人计算机
2005 年	图书、报刊电子书销售上升至 10 亿美元
2009 年	电子书比纸质书卖得更好
2010 年	电子书重 8 盎司，拥有百万种书
2018 年	最后的纸质版报纸出版
2019 年	90% 的新书发行电子版

在阅读软件的改进方面，软件开发商 Adobe 和电子书出版商"玻璃书公司"（Glassbook）联合开发了影响深远的 Adobe Acrobat Reader，这成为阅读可携式电子文件 PDF（Portable Document Files）最广泛使用的阅读软件之一。2003 年，美国出版行业协会（AAP）发布了对美国图书出版市场的销售调查数据，认为美国电子图书在市场上的单月销售额已经突破了 90 万美元，虽然所占市场比例仍然不大，但其 268% 的增速却成为美国图书市场上增长最强劲的力量之一。[2] 面对这一形势，有专家预测，美国电子图书出版市场在 5 年内贸易额将增加 10～30 亿美元，到 2020 年时，人们的阅读种类中将有 50% 是以电子图书的形式出现，随着电子图书使用的日益方便，新一代数字读者群体也必将随之形成，以此为依托，电子图书市场也可望在未来 5 年内实现跨越式增长。[3]

2　美国电子出版对传统市场造成的业态冲击

在 2008 年金融危机风暴的袭击下，美国书业研究集团的统计数字表明，美国图书总销售量 31.3 亿册，销售总额 403 亿美元，环比下降了 1.5%，其中成人读物下降尤其明显，销量与收入下降幅度均超过了 2%。但与以上总体发行趋势遭遇困境形成对比的则是，随着索尼电子书阅读器（支持掌上阅读和 BBeB 电子书、PDF/JPEG/MP3 等显示格式，一次可连续阅读 7 500 页内容，并具有折叠印刷产品的视觉稳定性，分辨率 SVGA 800×600）和新款 Kindle DX 电子书阅读器（主要用于支持教育类书籍和学生电子书包项目，可以显示教科书和报纸上各种式样的复杂图表，并具有签名功能和更大的存储空间）的推出，电子出版市场显现出空前的发展空间与市场活力。根据亚马逊网络书店创办人兼首席执行官杰夫·贝索斯的描述，目前亚马逊书店的电子书销售额，已占到了书店 12.5 万种可供图书销售量的 6% 左右；在教育出版和专业出版领域，一些在数字化方面走在前列的出版商如爱思唯尔集团和施普林格集团等，也都利用电子书的出版发行抢占了美国国内 23 亿美元的教科书出版市场。再加上美国经济减速及严重金融危机所带来的印刷成本价格上涨等因素，电子图书的价格优势得以凸显，并由此迎来出版发行的又一个高峰时期。

与传统出版行情相比，同一本书消费者使用 Kindle 阅读器下载的电子版价格是 10 美元，而其纸本书的价格却在 15 美元以上，并且还有可能因临时缺货而无法及时取得所购书籍；与图书相比，电子杂志则更为便宜，通过电子阅读器下载的 ZINIO 网站的知名杂志，全年 12 期，售价仅有 20～30 美元。面对这一发行局面的变化，长尾理论提出者安德森、全球最大数字文件共享平台 Scribd 网站创始人弗里德曼，以及《纽约时报》网络专家比尔顿，也都纷纷向出版商呼吁，要求这些出版机构更新产品概念，适应新传播环境下的技术变革及内容需求。为拯救美国报业日益困顿的经营危机，《纽约时报》、《波士顿邮报》和《华盛顿邮报》也陆续宣布与亚马逊网站合作，在 2009 年夏天通过其 Kindle 阅读器将内容低价销售给读者，从而结束网上免费读报时代。在中小学教育用书领域，为了更加适应网络时代成长起来的学生的学习习惯，亚利桑那州立大学、普林斯顿大学、弗吉尼亚大学、凯斯西储大学、里德学院等高校，也在各自校园内纷纷推出了电子出版阅读计划。在电子出版和数字化运营的大趋势下，默多克（Rupert Murdoch）掌管下的新闻集团和赫斯特集团也开始关注并介入电子图书出版领域，其集团不但参与了 2007 年电子媒体的市场并购活动，而且还在 2008 年正式进军电子阅读器研发领域，以期为集团在电子出版领域的未来发展创设下良好的技术基础和资源优势。

3　美国电子出版发展中所面临的问题

电子出版搅乱了美国传统出版市场的生态结构和稳定布局，也由此引发了作者和出版社之间的争议与分歧。源于对出版社包揽版税率、印数和促销计划等过程的抵触，作者普遍要求出版社调高图书版权的发行收益，而出版社则认为作者根本不了解出版市场残酷的竞争现实和按需出版的发展趋势，要求作者在出版协议中以最低收入条款取代最低库存条款，作为收回版权的约定协议，以利于出版社更好地开发图书版权，补偿其在数字开发领域的资金投入。如兰登书屋就认为，新技术的出现已经让以最低库存作为指标的版权收回条款过时了，作者需要给予出版机构以足够的版权支配时间和开发信任，在此情况下，出版机构可以考虑与作者就电子出版的纯营利收入实现对半分成。

除此之外，电子出版发展还必须正视的另外一个问题是盗版现象的盛行与相关遏制方法的完善建设。随着读者对电子图书需求量的增加，大量未经授权的纸质图书的电子版流入下载网站和文档共享平台上，如科幻作家厄修拉·K·勒吉恩的《黑暗的左手》、J·K·罗琳的《诗翁彼豆故事集》等，都曾遭遇过被电子书网站侵权盗用的情况。为了应对盗版盛行的现象，"版权世界网"（Rightsworld.com）、"版权中心网"（Rightscenter.com）等数字版权管理商，向出版社推出了提供编码和其他系统服务的措施，以保护出版社的图书内容不受盗版侵扰，并获取正当的版权收益；受到指责的网站则被要求设置上传过滤器，以甄别上传或下载的作品其版权是否受到保护。数字版权清理中心 2000 年开发的数字版权管理系统，目的即在于通过提供电子内容传输的即时许可，减少经互联网传输内容的侵权现象，并为出版社提供测定用户下载量和为用户提供信用卡付费等便利功能。

电子出版所带来的另外一个问题或说怀疑，是人们对电子出版所可能造成的阅读能力降低的忧虑。美国《经济学家》描述说，与互联网和电子出版发展相同步，美国的阅读率自 1985 年以来持续下滑，传统图书消费在美国人的娱乐开支中也下降了 7 个百分点。互联网与电子出版不仅改变了人们的阅读方式，也影响到了人们的思维方式，甚至是自我能力的认同。电子出版以及由它所带来的阅读方式，正越来越多地让人们的思维呈现出"碎读"式特性，深度思考和长时间阅读能力逐渐降低，"过去我们是深海潜水者，现在则好像踩着滑水板，从海面上飞驰而过。"塔夫茨大学的心理学家玛雅妮沃尔夫甚至担心，将"效率"和"直接"置于一切之上的阅读风格，将会使人们沦为单纯的"信息解码器"，从而流失掉原有阅读习惯所形成的理解文本的能力及丰富的精神联想活动。对于电子出版市场的长远、健康发展来说，这或许才是人们和出版机构最感到担心，并需要得到恰当解决的关键问题。

注释

[1] 杨贵山、种晓明. 海外出版业概述 ［M］. 苏州大学出版社，2007：23
[2] 杜若岩. 美国电子图书销售逆市上扬 ［J］. 中华读书报，2003（7）
[3] 曲阳. 举步维艰的美国电子书 ［J］. 出版参考，2005（4）

作者简介

杨状振，博士，河北大学新闻与传播学院讲师。

国际出版

日本数字内容产业政策研究*

吕　睿

（武汉理工大学文法学院　武汉　430070）

摘要：日本以动漫产业为代表的数字内容产业的快速发展受到世界关注，政府出台的一系列政策与法规成为其迅猛发展的助推手。本文从日本数字内容产业的兴起入手，阐述了数字内容产业的内涵及其在日本的发展过程，重点介绍了几个重要的政策与一部具有里程碑意义的法规，并分析了其未来的发展趋势。最后，通过对比提出了对于我国数字内容产业发展的几点思考。

关键词：数字内容产业　产业政策　政策调整

Research of Policy about Digital Content Industry in Japan

Lü Rui

（School of Arts and Law，Wuhan University of Technology，Wuhan，430070）

Abstract：The rapid development of Japanese digital content industry which represented by animation industry has received worldly attention. A series of policies and regulations unveiled by government became the pushing hand of the rapid development of Japanese digital content industry. This paper starts with the rising of Japanese digital content industry. Then it describes the connotation of digital content industry and its development process，emphasizes on several important policies and a landmark legislation and analyzes the developing tendency in the future of its digital content industry. At last，this paper proposes several considerations of our country's digital content industry's development through a comparison with Japan's digital content industry's development.

Keywords：Digital content industry　Industrial policy　Policy change

1　日本数字内容产业的兴起

《火影忍者》、《灌篮高手》、《足球小子》、《名侦探柯南》等这些动漫作品对很多中国的动漫爱好者来说耳熟能详，这些动漫作品已经深深地影响到一些年轻人的兴趣爱好与职业发展。这就是日本令人骄傲的动漫产业，而它只是日本数字内容产业的一部分而已。

---

* 本文为教育部人文社会科学研究项目09YJA870022研究成果。

在日本，权威部门日本财团法人数字内容协会对内容产业定义如下：在各种不同媒介中流通的影像、音乐、游戏、书籍等，通过动画、静止画、声音、文字、程序等表现要素构成的信息的内容。[1]欧盟对内容产业做了如下定义：内容产业的主体定位为那些制造、开发、包装和销售信息产品及其服务的企业，内容产业的范围包括各种媒介上的印刷品、音像电子出版物、音像传播以及用于消费的游戏。[2]而同样的意思在不同国家有着不同的说法，例如：英国叫创意产业，法国叫文化产业，美国叫版权产业或娱乐产业，韩国叫文化内容产业等。随着数字化在内容产业中的不断发展，数字内容逐渐形成产业化集群，而数字内容产业就是内容产业中以数字化作为记录形式的那一部分产业。

根据上述定义可知，内容产业的发展是与数字化的进程相关联的，是通过各种媒体形态将内容产品进行加工制作及传播的一个过程。因此，可以从内容产品和媒介形态两方面对内容产业进行分类，日本《数字内容白皮书》将内容产品划分为：影像、音乐、游戏、图文四大类，内容流通的媒介形态为：光碟出版、互联网流通、手机流通、电影院、卡拉OK、卫星电视以及有线电视等的流通。而数字内容产业由于内容产品的数字化，流通的媒介形态有所变化，主要以光碟出版、互联网以及手机流通等为主。

2 日本数字内容产业的发展

日本数字内容产业起步于 20 世纪初，且发展十分迅速，虽然近年来所占 GDP 的比重有所下降，但是日本数字内容产业的规模巨大，产业额仅次于美国排在世界第二位，其中动漫产业为数字内容产业带来的收益相当可观。日本政府也十分重视对其动漫产业国际化的推广。

根据统计，2009 年 8 月 27 日正式发行的日本《数字内容白皮书》显示，2008 年日本整个内容产业的市场规模同比减少了 2.6%，从整体上看呈下降趋势。这是由于受经济形势恶化的影响，内容产品在市场中的竞争日趋白热化，面对琳琅满目的内容产品受众的选择性更多，从而造成产品销路受到影响，因而持续增长的内容产业开始出现下滑。

然而暂时的低落并不能掩盖日本内容产业在 21 世纪初强劲的增长势头，2002 年内容产业生产总值为 129 861 亿日元，2003 年为 130 952 亿日元，增长率为 0.8%，2004 年为 133 362 亿日元，增长率为 1.8%，2005 年为 138 316 亿元，增长率为 2.3%，此时日本内容产业增长达到顶峰，从此以后出现拐点，2006 年为 137 823 亿元，增长率为 0.3%，2007 年为 138 180 亿元，增长率为 0.3%。[3]而数字内容产业由于数字技术革命带来的强大推动力，以及互联网、手机、便携式阅读器等媒介形态的多样性，数字内容产业持续增长，且增长率高于整个内容产业。按日本数字内容产业协会的统计，日本 2003 年数字内容产业的实际总产值为 22 215 亿日元，2004 年为 24 685 亿日元，比 2003 年增长 11.1%，2005 年实际为 25 275 亿日元，比 2004 年增加 11.8%，2006 年为 28 892 亿日元，比 2005 年增加 14.3%。[4]数字内容产业保持 7% ~10% 的年增长速度，而内容产业只有 2% ~4% 的年平均增长速度，因此数字内容产业必然会引起重视，也将成为各国内容产业增长的主力军。在数字内容产业的快速增长中，以网络传输和手机传输为载体的数字内容产业增长迅速，持续保持超过 20% 的年均增长率。互联网和手机用户逐年增加并普及，我们的生活已经被互联网和手机传输网络所包围。如果没有互联网和手机传输，人们的工作及生活将受到巨大影响。目前日本数字内容产业已经从光碟制品向互联网和手机媒体转移，日本使用手机上网用户达到 80%，而美国只有 8%。以互联网和手机传输作为支撑及中心的数字内容产业将成为今后内容产业发展的主流。

3　日本数字内容产业相应政策与法规

3.1　日本政府发展数字内容产业之政策促进

内容产业及其数字内容产业已经成为日本经济增长的支柱产业和新兴产业，日本政府为了更好地促进内容产业大规模商业化，为此制定了一系列有利于内容产业及数字内容产业发展的政策，发展数字内容产业也逐渐成为国家战略。日本政府主要从产业结构调整入手，比如 1998 年底日本通产省修订了"经济结构的改革和创造行动计划"，重点突出与信息通信产业相关联的内容产业。

20 世纪 90 年代日本经济整体低迷，但是其内容产业与数字内容产业却显现出了极强的生命力，稳定大幅增长，为此日本政府于 21 世纪初期制定了一系列有利于内容产业和数字内容产业发展的政策。2002 年 3 月，召开了由内阁总理、11 名阁僚大臣及 11 名业界名人参加的旨在及早建立和推进国家知识财产战略的"知识财产战略会议"。2003 年 3 月，日本政府组建了由总理大臣挂帅及 20 名内阁及业界名人组成的"知识财产战略本部"，下设"内容产业专业调查会"。在日本经济决策中占据重要地位的日本经济团体联合会同时也成立了文娱内容产业部会，开始研究内容产业政策问题。2003 年 12 月，振兴内容产业议员联盟成立，开始了支持有关振兴内容产业的相关立法问题的研究。2004 年 3 月，知识财产战略本部完成了研究报告《振兴内容商务政策》。2004 年 4 月，内容产业专业调查会发表了题为《内容产业振兴政策——软力量时代的国家战略》的报告；此报告具有很强的影响力和导向作用，它针对内容业界现代化与合理化要求、社会及经济领域评价有待提高、海外市场及国内新市场展开不足等三方面问题，提出了业界合理化等三项目标和拓展海外市场等七项基本措施。2008 年 6 月 18 日，日本的"知识财产推进计划 2008"，在 2003—2006 年前两个时段成果的基础上提出了第三个时段的目标与任务。[5]

3.2　日本政府发展数字内容产业之立法扶持

仅有政策还不能完全对产业界进行强有力的监督和约束，立法可以解决政策执行力度不足问题，使产业界生产、制造及保护内容产品更具规范化，为此日本政府出台了几部扶持内容产业及数字内容产业发展的法律。2001 年 11 月出台了《文化艺术振兴基本法》，2002 年 11 月出台了《知识财产基本法》，2004 年 6 月日本国会通过了一项重要法案——《关于促进创造、保护和活用内容的法律》（以下简称"促进法"）。此法案是日本在数字内容产业领域最权威、最完整的法案，确定了促进内容产业发展的基本政策方向和框架。并推动了日本政府的相关机构陆续出台实施大量具体的政策，作为促进内容产品的创造、保护以及充分利用的法案，振兴内容产业的根本政策依据从此诞生。

"促进法"共有四个章节，第一章和第四章主要是概述与总结部分，具体的措施集中在第二章和第三章。第二章提出了关于内容制品的创造、保护和充分利用的一般性政策措施：（1）提出以人才培养为基础通过高端技术促进内容产业的发展；（2）明确指出采取有效手段切实保护知识产权，维护知识产权所有者的权利不受到侵害，缓和互联网等传播媒体的多样性对知识产权保护带来的冲击；（3）要加强对内容产品的流通及在流通中内容产品的保存。第三章主要阐述了促进内容产业发展的政策措施：（1）强调要尽快建立起完整的融资体系，政府要采取多种措施及渠道来保证资金筹集到位；（2）加大对动漫和游戏等日本特色内容产品的宣传力度和出口力度；（3）确定保护制作者、承包者的利益，以及委托、代理之间，大企业和展销企业之间的公平交易。

3.3 日本数字内容产业政策与法规调整趋势

日本数字内容产业的发展并不是一帆风顺的，日本正处于人口老龄化和少子化十分严重的时期，数字内容产业国际化面临十分严峻的挑战，为此日本政府在政策上也作出了相应调整，强调以内容为中心继续增加创造文化产业的投入。虽然日本数字内容产业的规模比较大，但是在整个 GDP 中的比重又相对较小，因而日本政府需要继续加大对数字内容产业的投入和支持，走产业化道路。2004 年以前，知识财产战略本部《知识财产推进计划》以"内容产业的飞跃性扩大"为题，关注"内容产业振兴"，2005 年以来，《知识财产推进计划》立足"打造文化创造型国家"，着眼"内容振兴"。[6] 由此可见日本政府关于数字内容产业的政策调整将有如下趋势：（1）继续推进数字化进程。数字化水平是发展数字内容产业的基础，应提高产业结构的数字化适应性。利用 3G 网络平台，强调科技立国，进行一场通信与网络传播革命。（2）加强专业性人才的培养。特别对于少子化严重的日本来说，培养精英人才是一个行业持续发展的基础。（3）实施内容产业国际化战略。内容产业的长期快速发展离不开国际化道路，特别是其动漫产业在世界上的影响力非凡，更应加强国际化战略。

4 对我国数字内容产业政策的几点思考

我国数字内容产业是在文化产业、信息产业、传媒产业相互融合的基础上，在网络技术和数字技术飞速发展的背景下应运而生，虽然起步较晚，但发展较快。但是由于国情不同，我国的数字内容产业发展不平衡，也存在一些不足，需要我国政府主要从以下几方面在政策上给予大力扶持和改进。

第一，促进产业融合。数字内容产业融合了内容产业与信息技术产业的特征，在我国，技术商由于较早地进入了这一领域并拥有强大的技术优势从而主导了数字内容产业的发展。同时，由于内容产业在我国的特殊性和重要性，我国政府对其实行严格的准入制监管，技术企业无法兼并内容企业，这就在一定程度上阻碍了二者的融合，也不利于数字内容产业的发展。为此，从促进数字内容产业发展的角度出发，建议允许二者在一定程度上可以实现兼并重组和战略联盟。

第二，加大知识产权保护的力度。数字内容产业是专门以信息资源为劳动对象，提供文化形态的产品和服务，随着信息通信技术（ICT）的应用，所有的内容产品均可以数字化。因此，数字内容产业大量交易的背后实际上是交易知识产权。如果知识产权保护不利，会严重影响到整个行业的运作环境，特别是容易破坏整个产业链的形成。目前我国数字内容产业市场上盗版、侵权现象严重，亟须政府在法律层面加强调控以加大知识产权的保护力度。

第三，增强我国数字内容产业的国际竞争力。数字内容产业的发展得益于数字化技术的提高，而数字化正是国际化的核心内容，国际化是数字化的表述方式。因此，发展数字内容产业离不开国际化进程，而我国的数字内容产业在国际竞争力上还需要提高。正如日本将本国特色内容产业动漫业推向世界一样，我国作为一个有着悠久历史和灿烂文化的发展中大国，也应该将自身的优势内容推向国际市场。

注释

［1］财团法人デジタルコンテンツ协会．デジタルコンテンツ白書 2009［M］．日本：日本经济产业省商务情报政策局，2009．（8）

［2］赵子忠．内容产业论［M］．北京：中国传媒大学出版社，2005（2）．

［3］［4］数据来源于 2003 年至 2009 年日本财团法人数字内容协会编写的《数字内容白皮书》．

［5］于素秋．日本内容产业的市场结构变化与波动［J］．现代日本经济，2009（3）

［6］陈红梅．从内容产业振兴到内容振兴［J］．电影艺术，2008（6）

作者简介

吕睿，武汉理工大学文法学院新闻传播系 2008 级硕士研究生。

中日手机出版发展比较研究

秦洁雯

（武汉大学信息管理学院　武汉　430000）

摘要：随着当今时代数字出版的飞速发展，手机出版不仅在其中占据重要地位，其速度更是一日千里，成为数字出版的亮点。日本作为手机出版大国，在手机出版上有众多值得学习和借鉴的地方，不管是在管理方式，机制体制还是整个手机出版的运作上。本文着重从中日手机出版规模、中日手机出版物开发、中日手机出版赢利模式、中日手机出版利益分成及中日手机出版用户需求等五个方面对中日两国手机出版的发展进行了比较研究，系统地就中日手机出版进行了提炼和研究，笔者希望本文的研究对手机出版领域有所创新，从中得到一些关于手机出版产业的启示，提出一些有建设性的想法，特别是在中日手机出版的比较上，它们之间的异同和联系，并以此来指导中国手机出版的发展。

关键词：中日　手机出版　比较研究

Comparative Studies of Sino-Japanese Mobile Publishing Development

Qin Jiewen

（School of Information Management，Wuhan University，Wuhan，430000）

Abstract：As the rapid development of the present era of digital publishing，the mobile publishing，not only occupies an important position，developing with high speed，but also been a bright spot in digital publishing. Japan，as a mobile phone publishing country，has many worthy aspects for the development of Chinese mobile phone. This article focuses on the following five aspects：the mobile phone publishing，the scale of the development of Sino-Japanese mobile publications，the publishing profitable model of Sino-Japanese mobile phone，the interests allotment of the Sino-Japanese mobile phone and the users' needs between the Chinese mobile phone publisher and the Japanese one. By comparing the publishment of the mobile phone development in China and Japanese，the author hopes this paper will have some reference for Chinese mobile publishment.

Keywords：Sino-Japanese　Mobile publishing　Comparative study

　　纵观当今数字出版的发展，手机出版是其亮点和强劲生命力的体现。手机出版发展的实现当以手机的普及以及实现手机上网为前提。据日本总务省 2009 年 6 月公布的统计数据，日本手机用户达 1.08 亿，约占总人口（约为 1.2 亿）的 85.1%，几乎人手一部手机。一半以上的手机用户已经使用定额的浏量支付行为。据中国互联网络信息中心（CNNIC）发布的《中国手机上网行为研究报告》显示，至 2008 年年底，中国手机用户已超过 6.4 亿，而通过手机上网的用户数量已超过 1.176 亿，较 2007 年增长了 133%。随着手机普及率及上网率的逐年提高，手机出版对传统出版已造成重大影响。因此，对两国手机出版发展进行比较有其必要。一般认为，只要是经过了手机这种传输渠道到并供手机用户阅读的数字作品就是手机出版。手机出版产品主要包括手机阅读（手机报、手机期刊、手机小说、手机书、手机原创文学、手机动漫）、手机音乐（彩铃）、手机游戏、手机电视、手机电影等。本文着重从中日手机出版规模、中日手机出版物开发、中日手机出版赢利模式、中日手机出版利益分成、中日手机出版用户需求等五个方面进行比较，希望对中国的手机出版业发展有借鉴意义。

1 中日手机出版规模比较

数字出版是近年日本出版业的热点，增长速度非常快。如表 1 所示，从 2003 年（20亿日元销售额）到 2008 年的 5 年间，总量增长了 20 余倍，年均增长率接近 200%，但已出现了放缓趋势，其发展正逐步走向平稳。数据表明：同比 2006 年，2007 年日本数字出版市场增长率为 195%；而同比 2007 年，2008 年的增长率已经下降至 131%。但仍然保持的 100% 以上的速度增长。日本作为手机出版强国，在手机持有量方面，已经发展到几乎人手一部手机的地步。[2]

表 1 中日手机出版收入规模比较

国家	手机出版收入（2008 年）	手机付费阅读收入（2008 年）	年均增长率（2006—2008 年）
日本	402 亿日元（约 26.8 亿元人民币）	21.44 亿元	131%（数字出版）
中国	150 亿元（含彩铃、游戏、动漫）[1]	3030 万元	300%（手机出版）

在中国，随着手机价格和上网费用逐渐下降，以及 2008 年初 3G 网络开通，智能机、大屏幕适宜阅读的手机开始大量普及，手机阅读人数迅速增长。从 2007 年的 5.9% 增长到 2008 年的 6.3%。虽然手机阅读人数增长比例不大，但是手机阅读市场收入是有显著增长的。手机阅读市场收入由 2007 年的 650 万猛增到 2008 年的 3 030 万，所占比例由3.8% 增长到 13.4%，发展速度极为强劲。[3]

从销售收入来看 2008 年中日手机出版规模，日本手机出版销售收入 402 亿日元（约26.8 亿元人民币），中国手机出版收入达 150 亿元。乍一看，中国的手机出版似乎较日本手机出版规模大很多，然而两国手机出版实际发展情况和统计情况各有特点，日本数字出版主要集中在漫画、小说、写真集和时尚杂志这四个领域，且 2008 年，手机出版占日本数字出版的 86%，手机出版是数字出版发展的主要力量。而且手机阅读占手机出版收入的 80% 以上，2008 年日本手机出版 26.8 亿元的收入中，有 21.44 亿元是手机阅读，可见，日本手机阅读是手机出版甚至可以说撑起了数字出版发展中的天空。在中国手机出版

150 亿元的收入统计中是包含了手机彩铃、手机游戏、手机动漫等手机出版业务的，其中手机阅读收入只有 3 030 万元，在手机出版中所占份额极小。从传统出版业主体角度来看，要包括手机报、手机期刊、手机小说、手机书、手机原创文学、手机动漫产品的手机阅读发展规模是手机出版规模中是最具代表性的类别。因此，我们就手机阅读的收入进行对比，2008 年日本手机阅读的收入为 21.44 亿元，中国手机阅读的收入为 3 030 万元，日本手机出版规模都远远大于我国手机出版规模。

通过对以上对中日手机出版发展规模的比较发现，日本手机出版在数字出版中占绝对优势，且发展中心突出，主要在传统阅读基础上发展起来的手机阅读，可以知道传统出版主体在手机出版甚至数字出版中大有作为。同时，日本手机出版市场发展已趋于饱和，进入平稳发展阶段。在中国，手机出版有着其强劲的发展势头，手机出版特别是手机阅读发展规模还是很小的，其销售收入在手机出版销售收入统计中的份额很小，但是凭借手机阅读在手机出版中 13.4% 的迅猛增长速度，手机阅读有着很大的发展空间，传统出版主体在手机出版发展中一定能发挥越来越重要的作用。

2　中日手机出版物开发比较

手机出版不管是在内容上还是在形式载体上都与传统出版有着很大区别。一般来讲，传统出版主要包括纸质书、报、刊的出版。而手机出版主要包括手机阅读（手机报、手机期刊、手机小说、手机书、手机原创文学、手机动漫）、手机音乐（彩铃）、手机游戏、手机电视、手机电影等。

手机等新媒体的互动功能使得读者和作者的界限越来越模糊，普通读者有了成为作者的可能。日本每年通过手机网络和有线互联网收集的图书选题稿件数量，已经大大超过了每年的图书出版数量。如今利用手机或普通有线网络的文学互动社区及网站来选择作品，已成为了出版业进行选题开发的新渠道。一些业余写手也不断创造出人气作品，并被正式出版。[4] 当作品作为手机小说热卖后，将会同时以手机动漫、手机游戏、手机电影或纸质书等多种形式进行出版。这样不仅对阅读受众的多样化需求具有针对性，同时能够在最大程度上实现了作品的价值。在 2007 年东贩发表的畅销书（文艺类）排行榜的前 10 位中有 5 部是手机小说，且前三位均为手机小说。另外，日本出版机构开始尝试利用同一品牌创造完全不同的内容模型。例如，讲谈社的手机版《星期五》杂志上发布的内容与其纸质《星期五》杂志上出版的内容不同，获得了经营上的成功。在出版界产生很大影响并被效仿。

在内容来源方面，中国手机阅读市场也是以网络原创作品居多，传统出版社所占份额很小。中国有 500 多家出版社，现在只有 40 多家和中国移动通信公司的手机阅读基地进行合作。[5] 但中国手机出版也已经形成了门类齐全、灵活多样的手机出版物格局，供读者选择。出版社也开始关注电子阅读市场，利用手机等新媒体的力量进行产品或品牌的宣传推广。但中国的手机出版还主要集中在手机阅读、手机动漫领域，各种手机出版业务间没有形成紧密衔接的链式结构。值得高兴的是在 2008 年，天津科技出版社、中国对外翻译出版公司和方正阿帕比公司进行合作，全媒体出版两本新书，在国内开创了纸书、电子书、手机书同步出版的先河。

通过对中日手机出版的内容及形式开发的对比可以发现，中日手机出版在内容方面，普通读者的参与性高，互动性强，传统出版社的参与积极性还有待提高，一些好的作品还没有利用起来。形式开发方面，日本手机出版的各种业务、形式共同发展，相互配合，并与其他媒体互动，形成了良好的发展格局。而中国的传统手机出版业务还只是在有限的领域发展，与运营商和内容服务商的合作还谈不上互动，在适应市场的步伐方面还比较慢。因此，中国手机出版可以发挥后发优势，学习日本手机出版先进的运作方式，同时联动传统出版单位，促进中国出版业的繁荣发展。

3 中日手机出版赢利模式比较

手机出版的赢利模式目前主要有三种：一是收取包月订阅费；二是学习传统出版物的赢利方式，在出版物内插入广告收取广告费；三是收取出版物使用费。发展得最好的是前两种模式，而且目前也早已不再是早期单纯的完全付费模式了，越来越多的出版社采取了免费与付费相结合的方式，即利用部分免费模式吸引用户，了解和研究读者的需求偏好，以指导付费内容的开发。

实现手机阅读需要支付的费用包括手机上网费和出版物订阅费两部分。手机上网资费有按流量和包月两种方式。如表2所示，日本手机上网的收费采用弹性制度，并与通话费用及手机款式相结合。上网资费实行手机单向收费，按流量计算为 0.84 日元/KB，极低的资费使得日本手机上网人数超过了电脑上网人数。在订阅资费方面，日本的手机小说下载、手机包阅读也采用包月收费的方式，提供摘要免费阅读，爱友公司提供每月 4 410 日元的网络包月套餐。日本网络技术正处于从 2G 转换为 3G 的末期，通信市场竞争激烈，运营商积极采用新技术，移动通信公司为争夺客户，只有不断降低手机资费，消费者成为最大的受益者。

表2 中日手机出版赢利模式比较

国家	上网费（有包月和按流量两种方式）	收取包月订阅费	收取广告费	收取出版物使用费
日本	爱友公司的780日元月租的套餐规定，按流量计算为 0.84 日元/KB；套餐有 1 000 日元、1 600 日元、2 600 日元、4 000 日元和 7 000 日元等。	一般是免费阅读摘要；爱友公司提供每月 4410 日元的网络包月套餐。	9亿美金，成长率超过50%	只要每个月交 315 日元（1美元约合 117 日元）会费，就可在角川书店旗下的读书网站阅读 100 多部作品。
中国	按流量 0.03 元/KB，套餐有 5 元包 10 兆、20 元包 50 兆、100 元包 800 兆、200 元包 2 000 兆的套餐。	中国移动提供两种方式：2 元包月只有一个精品区，而 5 元包月包括 5 个频道。	受技术等的限制，还很少，多为文字广告	按一本书单独计费，费用包括 5 元/本，3 元/本不等，也可以按照章节计费，资费标准为为 0.04 元/千字。

日本数字出版业多采取不开放的直接收益方式，即让读者直接利用各种方式付费购买内容，以便内容销售方控制产品流和信息流。但以谷歌为代表的数字技术服务商则普遍采用的是开放性的后期收益模式，即前期提供免费服务，再通过广告、后期增值服务或延伸技术领域获取收益。两种模式之间的巨大差异严重影响了数字出版业的发展。据日本行业代表 DeNA 公司的 Moriyasu 在"2009 年全球移动互联网大会"上提到，日本手机的广告

市场这两年成长非常快，尤其 2007 年、2008 年成长率超过 50%。2008 年已经成为 9 亿美元的市场，个人电脑互联网的广告市场大约为 50 亿美元。虽然手机广告市场份额还比较小，但有着很好的发展，预计在 2011 年的时候，手机广告市场规模会成长为 25 亿美元市场规模。所以在日本手机出版的手机广告比手机内容的赢利成长更加迅速。另据翔飞日本留学网的报道，《朝日新闻》全部广告中的出版类广告就占了 16.4%。除传统媒体之外，日本出版业还充分利用了电影、电视、广播、交通、户外等新媒体。广告和出版的发展相互促进，形成了良好的互动。

在中国通信市场上主要是中国移动、中国联通和中国电信等三家企业占据市场主导地位。手机上网资费比较贵，实行双向收费，并且资费信息时常变动混乱。归结起来主要有包月和按流量计算两种方式，即使是包月的也有流量限制。尽管通信运营商不断降低相关费用，但对比日本来说，还是比较高的。因此在我国，虽然很多用户有手机上网的需求，但较高的上网费用对手机上网的发展产生了阻碍，同时也决定了手机阅读在中国的普及还需要时间。

和日本的内容收费模式一样，我国数字出版基本都靠订阅方式的前向收费，即通过用户购买来实现赢利。随着技术发展，用户能够通过越来越多的渠道获得其所需要的资料，加上盗版力量的夹击，我国数字出版的发展境地艰难，手机出版的赢利模式尚不明确。目前，手机出版商还无法像传统媒体一样将手机建成一个完整的营销平台来承载丰富的广告信息。如受手机容量所限，彩信手机报的内容一般只能容纳 7 000～10 000 字的图文信息，只能包含二十多条四百字左右的新闻内容，没有足够的广告空间。因此只能靠订阅费用来满足运营商和内容提供商之间的利益分配。但是可以看到中国的移动运营商在努力进行阅读平台建设。如中国移动在浙江组建的手机阅读基地，出版社、原创网站、数字出版商及软件厂商、终端设备厂商等纷纷介入，积极开发和创新手机阅读产品形态，进行技术革新，共同推动手机阅读产业链的建设。然而在产业不断融合的同时，我们不难看到，出版业为数不多的利润在技术创新及免费模式的双重夹击下继续流失。

将中日手机阅读资费情况进行对比可以看到，中国手机阅读费用明显高于日本手机阅读费用。究其原因有市场发展缓慢，部分企业一家独大，没有实现很好的竞争。但随着通讯业及手机出版行业的发展和充分竞争，中国手机上网资费一定会适应广大用户的需求而进行调整。通过对中日手机出版赢利模式的对比发现，日本手机出版技术发展成熟，赢利模式多样。日本手机出版的广告市场潜力巨大，出版与广告相辅相成，相互促进。而在我国受制于经济因素，对出版类的广告投入还比较少；受制于技术因素，在手机出版产品中植入广告的能力还有限，使得手机出版的赢利模式更加单一。学习和引进先进的技术，成为我国手机出版创新赢利模式的关键。

4 中日手机出版利益分配比较

表 3　中日手机利益分配比较

国家	内容提供商利益分成	电信运营商、服务提供商利益分成
日本	7/10	3/10
中国	3/10	7/10

　　日本电信行业是由日本电信控股公司、软银电信和日本电报电话公司三极共存，共同领导市场。成立了 I-MODE 研发中心控制和整合手机生产商、内容服务商及通讯公司，打通了手机出版产业链条，实现资源的有效分配。日本手机出版是在电信运营商和内容服务商积极推动下发展。据专家介绍，在日本，内容提供商与电信运营商、服务商的分成比例是 7：3，内容提供商获得手机出版的绝大部分收益，电信运营商取得 9%[6]。以内容提供商为主导的格局，合理的利益分配，调动了各方面的积极性，扶持了手机出版产业的发展。

　　中国手机阅读用户的日渐增多，手机上网速度的不断提升，为手机阅读提供了广阔的发展空间。中国移动、中国联通和中国电信等三大运营商都非常看重移动阅读市场。中国移动在浙江建设手机阅读基地，要通过各方的努力和营销打造传统阅读的新型发行渠道。中国联通和中国电信对于手机阅读这个庞大的市场也在作积极准备。目前，我国内容提供商与电信运营商、服务商的分成比例是 3：7。[7]可以看到，运营商由于其依托的用户资源以及对网络资源的控制，优先占据了主动权。

　　通过中日手机出版利益分成的对比，可以发现稳定的市场格局，合理的产业链对行业的迅速发展极为有利。获利太低，导致传统出版业对手机出版的发展不太积极。中国手机出版要实现迅速发展，一方面要承认内容为王，支持内容提供商的地位；另一方面需要电信运营商转变观念，扶持新产业的发展。

　　手机不只个头小，而且功能多样，能满足通信、阅读，看电视、看电影等各种需求，加上日本人喜爱小东西的心理，可以说手机完全适应日本人的需求。2008 年 4 月，日本公募指南社（公募ガイド社）在全国范围内针对年龄处于 10～70 岁之间的 6 272 个人进行了《关于手机小说的问卷调查》的采访了。其中值得注意的问题："如果出版有趣的手机小说会购买吗？"，回答"是，会购买"的竟高达 77.1%。[8]日本的手机服务比较完善，用户只要注册缴费，服务方就会提供大量的内容供用户直接下载。新潮社的中村说，自 2002 年以来，日本出版界在探索手机小说的赢利模式过程中作出了很多努力。最初出版商尝试直接将纸质小说转变成手机阅读的方式，但是销路并不好，因为习惯纸质书的读者并不认可用手机看那书本上已经存在的内容。接着，出版商尝试用手机提供黄色内容，结果也失败了，因为大多数的手机小说读者是女性。据日本出版社 ALLMEDIA 统计，电子书店中漫画作品占了 60%，读者多为日本年轻女性。经过一系列的失败，出版商渐渐对手机小说的市场有了更深入的了解。他们发现，内容为神话和浪漫故事的手机小说卖得很好，而且故事情节还不能过于缠绵和拖泥带水。[9]随着手机小说市场的迅速扩大和竞争加剧，出版商持续不断的创新经营模式，畅销的手机小说被作为纸质书、电影、电视剧、动漫出版并获得成功。

　　据中国互联网络信息中心（CNNIC）发布的《中国手机上网行为研究报告》显示，目前移动互联网用户以男性用户为主，占到 74.6%。与此同时，女性用户的比例正在逐年增长。80 后群体成为移动互联网的主体用户，占手机网民总数的 70.8%。主要行为是娱乐应用，特别是手机音乐，其活跃用户约 660 万。手机电视、手机博客等的手机网民数正蓬勃发展，活跃用户数量达 250 万。移动互联网公司的强势市场，仍然是一些具有技术针对性的领域，如手机阅读、手机电视等。由于年轻人对新事物的敏感，以及通信商推出的"动感地带"等在年轻人中应用普遍的通讯套餐中包含了上网费用，各种移动阅读功能在手机上网中能够方便地运用，有力地推动了年轻人使用手机阅读模式的普及。据第23次中国互联网络发展状况统计报告，学生以及体力工作者有明显的手机上网倾向，是手机上网的主要群体。年轻受众是手机出版上最具发展潜力和消费潜力的群体，如图1所示。因此，对年轻受众消费心理的研究是手机出版受众研究中的重点。

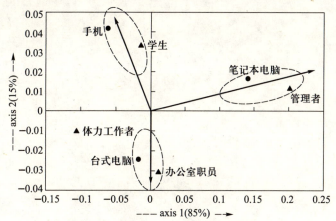

图1　网民身份与上网设备对应分析

（图表来源：2009年1月《第23次中国互联网络发展状况统计报告》）

通过对中日手机出版受众及其需求的分析，我们可以知道，日本手机出版市场需求的得出是经历了市场发展的检验的，年青女性是手机出版的主要读者，主要集中在手机漫画方面，手机小说的内容主要是简洁的神话和浪漫的爱情故事。而通过调查研究知道，中国的手机出版市场需求主要是以男性用户市场为主的年轻受众，主要在娱乐应用方面。消费需求还有待市场检验，手机阅读等虽然是移动互联网公司强势的市场，还有待发展。当然，我们也可以根据这些读者特征，结合手机出版灵活、自由、互动性强等特点，指导手机出版内容的开发，加强手机出版的针对性和精准性，实现手机出版的飞速发展。

注释

[1] 中国出版科学研究所，《2007—2008中国数字出版产业年度报告》

[2] 日本的数字及动漫出版状况调查，出版发行研究考察团，出版发行研究，2009年9期

[3] 2008年度中国电子图书发展趋势报告，2009-04-20，http://news.du8.com/html/67/n-88667.html

[4] 日本的数字及动漫出版状况调查，出版发行研究考察团，出版发行研究，2009年9期

[5] 传统出版商应全面参与数字出版，中国图书商报，2010-06-04

[6] 手机出版兵临城下惠天灵，方志，出版参考，2008年6月下旬刊

[7] 手机出版兵临城下惠天灵，方志，出版参考，2008年6月下旬刊

[8] 佚名，携带小説に関するアンケート，2008-6-13，http://www.koubo.co.jp/contents/publication/index.html

[9] 手机旋风劲吹日本出版业，《中华读书报》，2007-7-18

作者简介

秦洁雯，武汉大学信息管理学院出版发行系硕士研究生。

移动出版的发展模式及其评价[*]

李镜镜[1] 张志强[2]

（1. 南京大学信息管理系　南京　210093；2. 南京大学出版科学研究所　南京　210093）

摘要：随着网络的发展和技术的不断进步，知识和信息的传播发生了巨大的变化，以手机出版和电子书阅读器为代表的移动出版和移动阅读异军突起，我国移动出版产业链上的各大网络运营商、技术商、平台服务商和出版企业开始了产业控制权的争夺战，造成了现在产业链各方"争霸"的局面。基于国内移动出版发展现状和发展趋势的判断，本文首先总结出现阶段我国移动出版产业中四种主流发展模式，即内容提供商主导型、平台服务商主导型、网络运营商主导型、终端制造商主导型，然后分别归纳了这四种发展模式的发展现状和特色，并对其进行评价和利弊分析，最后预测了移动出版产业的发展趋势。

关键词：移动出版　手机出版　电子书阅读器

Analysis and Evaluation on the Development Mode of Mobile Publishing

Li Jingjing[1]　Zhang Zhiqiang[2]

（1. Department of Information Management, Nanjing University, Nanjing, 210093；

2. Institute of Publishing Science, Nanjing University, Nanjing, 210093）

Abstract：With the increasing development of the network and technology, great changes have taken place in the communication of the knowledge and information, the handset publishing and e-book reader, which stands for the mobile publishing and mobile reading industry, has risen as the new force. The network operators, technology providers, platform providers and the publishers in the mobile publishing industry chain of our country have started the competition of the industry controlling power, making every side of the industry chain strive for supremacy. Based on the estimation of the status and development trends of the domestic mobile publishing, this paper summarizes four kinds of development modes of the domestic mobile publishing at the present stage, namely, the content provider-oriented mode, platform provider-oriented mode, network operator-oriented mode, terminal manu-

* 本文系江苏省六大人才高峰项目（07-H-006）、江苏省333工程科研资助项目（2009-81）阶段性成果之一。

facturers-oriented mode. And then it concludes their development status and distinguishing features as well as weighing their advantages and disadvantages respectively. At last, it forecasts the development trends of mobile publishing industry.

Keywords: Mobile publishing　Handset publishing　E-book reader

移动出版与电子书刊

近几年来，随着手机出版在日韩风生水起，亚马逊 Kindle 横空出世，苹果 iPhone、iPad 如火如荼，以手机出版、手持阅读器为代表的移动出版和移动阅读异军突起。进入 2010 年，移动出版持续升温，产业前景被业界普遍看好，甚至被视为数字出版的重要拐点。国内各大网络运营商、技术商、平台服务商和出版企业均对移动出版表现出了极大的热情和兴趣，在移动出版领域动作频频：4 月中国出版集团推出自己的第一款电子书阅读器，盛大集团 3 月 10 日正式发布电子书战略，中国移动浙江移动阅读基地 5 月 5 日正式启用，汉王科技与中国文学著作权协会 5 月 10 日签订合作协议。

移动出版是将图书、报纸、杂志等内容资源进行数字化加工，运用数字版权保护技术（DRM），通过互联网、无线网以及存储设备进行传播，用户在移动阅读设备上通过阅读软件实现阅读或听书等功能，实现随时随地的阅读。[1] 进入 21 世纪以来，随着网络的发展和技术的不断进步，知识和信息的传播也发生了巨大的变化，面对海量的信息、资讯和知识，人们需要比传统阅读更加方便、快捷、精准、个性化的阅读方式。移动阅读以其移动性、私密性、快捷性、贴身性、智能性、无线上网等优势，成为一种越来越受现代人追捧的阅读方式。移动出版的出现，终于克服了数字出版内容不能随时随地阅读的缺陷，使纸质图书便于携带的特点也用到了数字图书上。

随着中国 3G 时代的到来和数字出版的深入发展，移动出版得到了数字出版产业链上各方的重视。基于对移动出版业发展现状的认识和其发展趋势的判断，并借鉴国外移动出版发展的经验，我国现阶段移动出版分成四种主要的发展模式，即内容提供商主导型、平台服务商主导型、网络运营商主导型、终端制造商主导型。这四种发展模式各有其利弊。

1　内容提供商主导型

内容提供商主要包括出版社、杂志社、报社、原创文学网站等，它们为移动出版提供出版的内容或服务。如果说此前掌握着数字出版核心资源的内容提供商由于体制、观念、技术等方面的原因对于数字出版的态度总因担忧而显得欲纳还拒的话，如今，随着移动出版的风生水起，内容提供商再也不甘于自己总是处于产业利益分配不利和被人"忽悠"的位置，在发展思路、自身定位、战略构想上开始转变，对移动出版表现出了极大的兴趣，开始主动出击。如读者集团研发并于 2010 年 5 月推出专属阅读器，社会大众可以用该阅读器读到新一期的《读者》杂志和创刊近 30 年来的精选文章，并通过专属格式下载各类数字图书[2]；上海世纪出版集团 2010 年 3 月 30 日正式推出了全球首款由出版机构出品的电子书阅读器；2010 年 5 月江苏凤凰出版传媒集团与元太科技在深圳文博会上签订合作协议，将联手针对教育市场推出"凤凰电子书包"。

内容提供商为主导的移动出版发展模式是指内容提供商凭借着自身较为雄厚的资金实力，依托移动出版核心的内容资源，与产业链下游的平台、运营、终端等合作。它们已经开始不满足于仅仅把自己定位为内容提供商，而是将上游的优势不断放大并将这一优势扩展到下游，开始自己做技术、做平台、做终端。如中国出版集团将移动出版作为集团2010年的重点和主攻方向，在构建完整移动出版产业链上频频发力：牵手国际软件巨头甲骨文公司采用 Oracle 通用内容管理解决方案打造统一的出版数字资源管理平台；开通集原创、版权、销售、供需为一体的电子商务平台——中国数字出版网；成功获得"增值电信业务经营许可证"，能够独立地在全国进行增值电信业务的经营；发布第一款自主品牌电子书阅读器。[3]在内容提供商主导型发展模式下，内容提供商能够将自身旗下的众多内容资源进行整合，将手中丰富、优质、严谨内容资源优势发挥到极致，坐拥移动出版的定价权。

但是，这种发展模式也存在不少问题。首先，构建数字出版或者移动出版的平台难度较大，很难将其他实力雄厚的内容提供商的优质内容资源整合到平台上来，试想江苏凤凰出版传媒集团会愿意把自己的优质内容资源给中国出版集团吗？其次，也有人认为，技术并非没有门槛，"内容企业向下兼容"的难度比"技术企业向上兼容"的难度大。[4]网络运营做不过网络运营商、终端做不过做纯硬件的；最后，由于内容提供商在前一阶段移动出版发展中错失先机，在移动出版产业中属于后进入者，对于移动出版的赢利模式、支付手段、用户需求等还有待进一步的探索。

2　平台服务商主导型

平台服务商为消费者和内容商提供平台服务。如美国的亚马逊和国内的盛大、方正。平台服务商一直以来都在数字出版中发挥着非常重要的作用。它们具有非常敏锐的市场嗅觉，往往能够最早捕捉到商机和行业发展趋势，是移动出版实践的先驱者和开拓者。但是随着产业链各方的不断发力，平台服务商的先发优势受到挑战。在平台服务商主导的发展模式下，平台服务商拥有先进和优质的技术资源和开发能力，能为移动出版提供一揽子的硬件和软件解决方案；它们还拥有丰富的数字出版经验和相对较为成熟的赢利模式、版权保护能力和支付体系；长期聚集积累的较为丰富的内容资源也为其移动出版平台的整合提供了有利条件。

国内平台服务商凭借自身移动出版的先发优势，靠长期积累和聚集的内容资源和优质先进的技术服务资源，构建移动出版的技术和服务平台，左携内容提供商、右拥阅读终端，意图效仿亚马逊打通移动出版上下游。如盛大集团就采取了发布"一人一书"电子书战略，构建开放的移动出版资源平台——云中图书馆，开放渠道和营销体系，成立盛大创新院等一整套硬件软件解决方案等措施；方正集团则成立了致力于移动阅读解决方案和阅读终端的方正飞阅传媒有限公司，发布最新版电子书阅读器终端"文房"，推出"番薯网"整合庞大的数字图书和报纸资源等。

但是，国内这类企业的实力和号召力还远没有大到能在较大范围内整合内容资源，构建统一完善移动出版平台的地步，内容话语权仍然牢牢掌握在传统出版商的手中；而且构建平台的前期成本较高，以盛大、方正为代表的这一类平台服务商要想发展成为"内容+平台+终端"的亚马逊模式还有很长的路要走。

3 网络运营商主导型

网络运营商是指提供和控制移动网络服务的厂商。如中国的中国移动、中国联通和中国电信，外国的 SK Telecom、NTT 等大型移动网络运营商。2009 年伊始，工业和信息化部分别为中国移动、中国电信和中国联通发放 3G 牌照，而随着三大运营商相继放号商用，中国正式步入 3G 时代。在这样一个媒介大融合的时代，商机无处不在，作为目前 3G 统治力量的运营商，显然不会甘于沦为"通道"。[5] 面对移动出版和移动阅读产业这块"肥肉"，网络运营商们纷纷加大对移动出版和移动阅读的开发力度。

它们挟雄厚的资金、技术和网络优势"以命诸侯"，凭借它们无与伦比的控制力，开始整合移动出版产业链：构建自己的内容资源平台，并将触角延伸至终端，开始各自制订电子阅读下载的专有格式，这些专有格式连同移动阅读器软件与终端设备绑定，以保证内容的版权和计费，将自己打造成一个集内容、平台、通道、终端为一身的移动出版超级航母。比如中国移动除了此前着力打造的梦网书城之外，最近在移动出版领域动作频频：先是联合包括汉王、华为、大唐电信、方正及美国 Firstpaper 公司在内的 5 家终端厂商，推出定制电子书阅读器，用户可以"不换卡，不换号，不登记"，即可使用该服务；然后是积极与传统内容出版商合作，建立中国移动浙江移动阅读基地，全面打造移动阅读内容平台。另外两家网络运营商中国电信和中国联通也丝毫不敢松懈，紧跟其后，纷纷准备建立类似于中国移动的移动阅读基地，显示出全面进军移动阅读市场的决心。

在这种移动出版的发展模式下，网络运营商资金技术实力雄厚，并且垄断了网络通道，对于终端厂商和内容提供商具有强大的号召力和吸引力，具备整合产业链的实力；拥有庞大的用户群，并且移动阅读所具备的随时随地的特性以及图文并茂的展现方式，也将进一步提升用户使用黏性并有效扩大用户群；[6] 网络运营商通过在阅读器或者手机上面绑定自己的手机卡，可以很好地解决支付方式的难题。

虽然网络运营商不断缩短自己与产业链上游与下游的差距，企图主导整个移动出版产业，但是内容资源一直都是它们的短板，尤其是传统出版商的优质严谨内容，虽然中国移动建立了移动阅读基地，但是与之签约合作的内容提供商还是少数，传统出版商出于对盗版、定价权等方面的顾虑，不敢将内容轻易放手；另外产业链上平台服务商、内容提供商也不想轻易将行业主导权让给网络运营商，定价主导权的竞争异常激烈。

4 终端制造商主导型

终端制造商是提供终端阅读设备的厂家，如国内的汉王。这类发展模式是以终端为主，兼顾平台建设。与亚马逊依托于自身丰富的内容资源（亚马逊拥有全球最大的在线零售书店）崛起不同，国内的电子书阅读器市场一开始便是由一批汉王之类的专注于终端的企业预热的。这些企业都是先做硬件再考虑内容，在移动出版和移动阅读消费市场还未真正激发的阶段，这类企业利用自己的先发优势和强势的市场宣传不仅培育了消费市场而且抢占了移动出版和移动阅读的先机，目前汉王电子书阅读器的销售已经取得了电子书阅读器全球市场销售前三甲的成绩[7]。

在终端制造商主导的发展模式中，终端制造商走的是一条开放终端阅读平台的道路，其开发的阅读器能够支持尽可能多的格式，最大限度发挥阅读器的兼容性；凭借其在终端研发、终端推广上面的实力，在成功占得阅读器市场先机之后，着力打造内容资源平台，企图采用"终端+内容"的模式整合移动出版的上下游资源。比如汉王在坐稳了国内电子书阅读器市场头把交椅之后，凭借自己是上市企业，有资金、有技术、有市场，着力打造汉王电子书城，不仅与传统出版社、媒体报刊业合作获得电子书、电子报、电子杂志等内容资源，还开拓与网络文学网站的合作，努力构建移动阅读内容平台。

终端制造商主导型的移动出版发展模式下，终端制造商们不断改进产品特性，创新商业模式，满足读者需求。它们在终端产品设计和推广上具有无可比拟的优势，在中国当前移动出版和移动阅读消费市场缺乏成熟的消费文化需求的前提下，从终端做起更适合当前产业的发展现状。

但是，终端制造商一直以来在移动出版产业链中影响力不够，资源整合及版权问题是终端制造商主导型发展模式下最大的发展瓶颈，由于我国版权保护意识较差，作为内容掌握源头的出版商不愿意把内容资源授权给硬件厂商；同时随着移动阅读市场的持续火爆，包括惠普、戴尔、联想、华为、方正、长虹、华硕在内的近百个品牌都计划涉足电子书阅读器市场，再加上中国平安子公司以及外资品牌的进入，这意味着移动终端制造将进入战国纷争的时代，终端制造商的竞争将更加残酷。[8]

5　结语

可以看出，目前的中国移动出版产业呈现出一种"跑马圈地""群雄争霸"的战国纷争局面。移动出版和移动阅读产业链的利益各方，都不想在市场刚刚培育的初期放弃这样一个发展前景被普遍看好的产业，都想能占得先机、赢得主动，都想在移动出版的产业链中占据主导地位。不管是内容提供商、平台服务商、网络运营商还是终端制造商，均不满足于自己在产业链中扮演的单一角色，均不愿失去定价权和主导权，于是拼命整合资源将触角延伸到整个产业链的上下游。这样一个"混战"的局面和产业链各方"争霸"的模式，是由当前我国移动出版发展的现状和移动阅读消费市场和消费环境所决定的，是移动出版产业发展的一个阶段，所以这些模式在一段时间内还将继续存在，接受市场的竞争和淘汰。

虽然移动出版是传统出版商转型的重要方式，是平台服务商深入发展的重要途径，是网络运营商增值服务的重要内容，是终端制造商跨越发展的重要动力，能够主导产业赢得话语权固然重要，但是移动出版产业链上各方不能够也不应该盲目扩张。这种盲目扩张反而容易忽视自己的核心资源，导致核心竞争力的降低。一个成熟的、健康的、有生命力的产业应该是产业链上各方各司其职、利益各方能够得到合理分配，而不是上下游通吃、独大垄断。未来中国移动出版产业的发展趋势应该是内容提供商、平台服务商、网络运营商、终端制造商通过打造自己的核心竞争力，各司其职、合作竞争、利益均衡发展。

注释

[1]　朱音. 移动阅读点亮出版未来 [J]. 中国出版，2008（6）：59

[2]　仵树大.《读者》电纸书即将量产上市 [EB/OL]. http://finance.sina.com.cn/roll/20100414/09237746650.shtml，2010-05-24

[3]　栎风，苏磊."云出版"的实践者——中版集团数字传媒有限公司总经理刘成勇访谈

录 [J]. 科技与出版, 2010 (6): 4-6

[4] 任殿顺. 阅读器产业四大阵营. [EB/OL] http://www. epuber. com/? p=5596,2010-05-20

[5] 任殿顺. 运营商暗夺移动阅读话语权 [EB/OL]. http://hi. baidu. com/allirra/blog/item/1417ed245f7199084d088d7d. html, 2010-05-22

[6] 金朝力, 吴辰光, 张晓东. 电子书产业链竞合拉开序幕? [EB/OL]. http://www. bbtn ews. com. cn/nbbtnews/sd/channel/sd91432. shtml, 2010-05-22

[7] 新浪科技. 汉王电纸书销售总监: 目前全球第三将来要第一 [EB/OL]. http://tech. sina. com. cn/e/2009-07-10/14043253155. shtml. 2010-05-20

[8] 中国新闻网. 华为分羹电子阅读器市场折射产业融合大势 [EB/OL]. http://www. chinanews. com. cn/it/it-itxw/news/2010/01-29/2099485. shtml, 2010-05-24

作者简介

李镜镜, 南京大学信息管理系 2007 级本科生。

张志强, 南京大学信息管理系教授、博士生导师, 南京大学出版科学研究所所长。

汉王电纸书产品策略之分析与思考

安小兰

（中央财经大学文化与传媒学院　北京　100081）

摘要：中国汉王科技股份公司生产的"汉王电纸书"系列是国内知名的电子阅读器产品，有了一定的销售量，但总体来说这些业绩距市场普及还有一段距离。文章从产品策略角度对其原因进行了分析，认为汉王电纸书的产品策略为品牌形象差异化策略、产品组合多样化策略和预装书策略。文章对这三个方面的策略进行了深入分析，并对其不足提出了一些建议，认为汉王产品策略还可以进行以下改进：1. 加大技术研发的力度，改进产品功能，提升产品的性价比；2. 减少同质性较强的版本的推出，专注于打造几款优质产品；3. 取消或使用更为灵活的预装书模式。

关键词：汉王电纸书　产品策略　品牌形象差异化　产品差异化

Analysis on the Product Strategy of Hanvon E-reader

An Xiaolan

（School of Cultural and Media, Central University of Finance and Economics, Beijing, 100081）

Abstract: Hanvon E-reader is a famous brand in China. But it has a long distance towards to market popularization. We try to give an analysis on the product strategy of Hanvon e-reader in this paper. The paper points out that, brand differentiation and high end brand image, product differentiation and variety of products, built-in e-books are the main product strategies of Hanvon e-reader. Based on the analysis, we also give some further improvement suggestions to Hanvon product strategies which include putting more effort on R & D and increasing Price/performance ratio, releasing less homogenize versions of e-reader and focusing on several main products, designing more flexible built-in e-books model.

Keywords: Hanvon E-reader Product strategy Brand differentiation Product differentiation

2008 年，美国亚马逊专用电子书阅读器（Dedicated e-book readers）kindle 的火爆销售，改变了全世界对于电子书市场的认识，巨大的商业前景使得越来越多的企业开始进入这个市场。中国汉王股份科技敏感地把握到了阅读器电子书市场的先机，从 2008 年起，开始将电子书产品列为公司的"一号工程"，[1] 目前，汉王已经向市场推出了十几款名为"电纸书"（即专用电子阅读器）的产品，并展开了铺天盖地的广告攻势。显然，汉王的目标是做中国的亚马逊。

笔者对于专用阅读器电子书的未来深信不疑，也深为汉王意欲占领阅读器电子书产业市场的胆识和雄心而感动。就目前情况来看，汉王电纸书在海内外市场上已经有了广泛的知名度。也有了一定的销售额。据报道，自 2008 年 10 月份上市至 2009 年上半年，汉王电纸书共销售了 10 万台，[2] 2010 年第一季度，汉王销售量达到 16.45 万台，占国内市场阅读器销售额的 66.04%。[3] 这些数据令人振奋，但另一方面，与中国庞大的人口基数比起来，这些数字还不能说令人满意。此外，汉王电纸书有很大一部分是以行业采购，即商务礼品等的形式售出的，也就是说，普通消费者中购买阅读器的数量还要低于这个数字。可以说，汉王电纸书距离普及还有很长的路要走。

笔者认为，这种情况的出现，在很大的程度上是与汉王的产品策略的某些不足有关的。因此，本文即将对汉王目前的产品经营策略进行观察和分析，并在此基础上谈一些建议。

1 汉王电纸书产品策略简析

产品策略是指企业为了在激烈的市场竞争中获得优势，在生产、销售产品时所运用的一系列措施和手段，包括产品组合策略、产品差异化策略、新产品开发策略、品牌策略以及产品的生命周期运用策略等。由于产品是企业经营理念和形象的载体，消费者要通过产品来理解、感受企业并获得实际利益，因此，产品策略的好坏对企业的成败有非常直接的作用。汉王在向市场推出电纸书时，采取了一些产品策略，虽然汉王并未对外直接公布这些策略的内容，但我们可以根据现有材料和产品来进行分析。汉王科技副总裁、电纸书事业部总经理王邦江在谈到汉王电纸书的经营策略时曾说："汉王的策略是分三步走的，现在先用硬件培养用户，当用户数量和内容都累积到一定程度的时候，内容也将会成为一个重要的收入来源。"[4] 如此，则汉王目前为止的基本策略还是在培养硬件用户，扩大阅读器销售方面。因此，我们将把论题集中在电纸书硬件产品的策略分析方面。笔者经过观察和分析，认为其有如下策略：

（1）品牌形象差异化策略，走高端品牌之路。即通过产品的品牌和形象实现产品差异化。具体做法是：通过高促销、高价格的策略进入市场，打造高端品牌形象，并在此基础上获得差异化的优势。

（2）品种多样化策略。从 2008 年 6 月推出第一款产品 N510 到现在，汉王共推出十几款产品，最主流的则是 N516、N517、N518、D20、D21、F21 等。这些产品在品质、外形、商标、包装、功能、价格等上都有差别。例如，D21 是学生版，N518、F21 则是商务版。显然，汉王在产品组合方面采用多样化策略，目的在于为不同人群提供不同的产品。

（3）预装书策略。汉王在推出产品时，采取了一项非常独特的推广策略，即预装书策略。在汉王的电纸书中，预装了大量正版书籍，从最初的 300 册到后来的 1 500 册不等，旨在弥补目前中国电子图书内容的不足，增加消费者的购买动力。

2 对汉王电纸书产品策略的分析和建议

2.1 品牌形象差异化策略分析和建议：提高性价比

产品形象的差异化策略，是现代企业常用的、行之有效的策略之一。从 2008 年开始，为了推动市场，汉王斥资 1 亿元在互联网、报纸、期刊、电视台、户外广告等各种媒体进行轰炸式的市场启蒙和宣传，与之相配合，汉王在产品价格上也走的是高端路线。根据电子书经销商百战网的报价，汉王电纸书主流产品的基本定价在 3 000 元左右，优惠价为 2 900 元左右，较早的第一代产品定价是 1 350 元。怎样理解这个价格呢？我们不妨做一比较，如表 1 所示。

表 1　各品牌主流型号电纸书比较

品牌	汉王	翰林	易博士	EDO	Kindle	上网笔记本
价格	2 800 ~ 3 000 元	2 250 元	2 000 元	2 550 元	1 700 元	2 000 ~ 2 700 元
性能及主要优势	5 寸屏；内置 1 500 册书；支持常见格式；手写识别。	6 寸 e-ink 屏；支持常见格式。	翻页速度快；5 寸屏；全反射 TFT 屏；支持 WIFI 无线上网；支持常见格式。	6 寸 E-INK 阅读器；二代屏；手写、wifi；可直连 EDO 书城。	附带的 3G 无线上网功能（免收网费）；6 寸屏幕；外观优美；质量上乘。	支持无线上网；阅读、写作；具备笔记本电脑的功能。

由于阅读器的技术指标较多，这里仅就各款机器中最有特点的地方进行罗列。从中可以看到，与国内外同类产品比起来，汉王电纸书最大的强项在于手写识别功能（可以方便读者做注记、摘要、圈点）和内置大量书籍（这一策略后文将专门论述），而在无线上网，屏幕大小等方面上均无优势。与网本比起来，汉王电纸书功能单一，只适宜阅读。再具体分析一下价格：

（1）与国内同类产品比较。目前中国生产电子阅读器的厂家主要有天津津科翰林、广州金蟾易博士、上海易狄欧 EDO 等。翰林主流型号 V3 的价格为 2 250 元，易博士的主流型号 M218B 价格为 2 000 元，EDO 主流型号的价格为 2 550 元。

（2）与亚马逊的阅读器相比较。亚马逊第一款 Kindle 的上市价格是 359 美元，后一款产品的上市价格为 299 美元，不久再次下调价格至 259 美元，后更降至 189 美元，约合人民币 1 300 元。

（3）与其他电子产品比较。目前一台 Dell、HP 或三星上网笔记本电脑的价格约在 2 700 元左右，国产的神舟等上网笔记本电脑的价格则在 2 000 元以下。

比较之下，汉王电纸书无论与国内外同类产品相比，还是与其他电子产品相比，价格都是偏高的。综合比较看起来，其性价比在各种产品中并不算高。

显然，汉王采取这一高价策略的目的是希望在消费者中树立高品质的形象。一般来说，高价格产品的基础是优良的性能和形象。那么，汉王的产品性能如何？

汉王在进入市场时，采取的是典型的快速撇脂价格策略，即所谓高促销、高价格策略。一般来说，企业采用快速撇脂价格策略的基本思路是：消费者对此款产品不了解，生产者希望在短时间内通过高密集宣传将产品迅速推出，使大众了解，并快速扩大销售量，通过高价格迅速收回成本。这一策略的基本假设是，产品的质量和形象能够支持产品的高价格，而且潜在消费者也有能力支付高价格。汉王具有较强的资金和技术实力，采取这一策略，本是无可厚非的，但汉王在采用这一策略时也有明显的失误。由于汉王电纸书并没有明显的性能优势，在一些关键技术和功能上与其他同类产品差别不大，因此形成了广告与产品、质量和价格的落差，与消费者期望有些差距。事实上，广告只是营销的一种看得见的手段，是浮在水面上的冰山，而冰山之下的内功修炼——技术研发、对消费者持久的关心等看不见的东西才是决定企业成功的根本因素。

基于以上论述，笔者认为汉王在今后的发展中，应该将重点放在技术研发、改进产品上。而这种改进必须要建立在对电纸书特质深刻理解基础之上。所谓电纸书，简而言之就是一种专门代替书籍的电子产品，其所以称为专用，是因为其设计的主要用途是为了替代纸质书，向人们提供更好的阅读体验。它的特征是，既具有传统纸质书的阅读感觉，又有纸质书不具备的优势。具体来说，这种产品至少应具有如下两个特征：其一，与纸质书近似的特点，如较大的屏幕、电子墨技术等；其二，优于纸质书的特点，如书签、笔记、可变字体和样式、电池持续时间长、朗读等功能以及内置字典、巨量储存、轻便、便携等。人们之所以在手机、电脑、掌上游戏机等都可以阅读的情况下依旧选择购买阅读器，其根本原因就是看重上述两种特征。让阅读器尽量贴近纸质书的阅读感觉并优于纸质书，这是其独特的价值所在。

汉王董事长刘迎建曾说，他们要生产的是电纸书，而不是电子阅读器。这句话显示出他对电纸书的特点有深刻的理解。汉王在产品设计和改进中，尽力体现了这些理解，但也有不足，即在汉王的产品中，对一些并不十分重要的因素，比如，手写笔的外观等有较多的重视。而事实上，对那些最能体现专用阅读器的特征和优势的、消费者真正关心的因素进行升级改进才是至关重要的。汉王目前的产品基本技术指标是：使用国际通用的电子墨技术、几千本书的内存容量、持久的电池续航能力、支持常见电子文件格式 TXT（HTXT）、DOC、HTML、PDF、PNG、JPG、MP3、WMA、WAV 等，这些已经是当今专用电子阅读器的必须具备的特征。在笔者看来，要使电纸书成为真正的"书"而不是一般的电子阅读器，以下几个方面是至关重要的：①做大屏幕，至少是 6 寸屏。汉王目前的产品都是 5 寸屏，仅略大于一个大屏幕的手机，整个机子与口袋书大小一致，远远达不到纸质书的效果。②内置书要有封面、页码、出版社等。缺乏这些，数字内容将只是一些电子格式的文件，而不是真正的书籍。③应有强大的检索功能。由于电子阅读器存储量大，读者对于这个功能的需求是必然的。④翻页速度要快。⑤整体设计应精致、美观。⑥系统升级，加强 CPU 的功能，避免死机等现象出现。⑦支持无线上网。无线上网可以为读者提供随时随地上网找书的服务，极大地提高产品的附加价值，因此它是未来电纸书发展的必然趋势，但由于这项技术受制于中国整体的电信运营环境，并涉及收费制度，因此需要时间来完成。总之，只有在上述技术和功能都有了长足提升的情况下，汉王的产品才能够真正以高品质独秀于电子阅读器领域之中，其高端形象才有了扎实的基础。

2.2　关于汉王电纸书多样化策略的分析和建议：减少款式、做精技术

产品实施差异化的根本目的，在于为不同消费者提供不同的产品，以满足消费者差异化的需求。汉王电纸书从面世起就面向学生、商务人士及一般消费者不断推出新款，旨在涵盖多级、多类目标市场的需求。对此，刘迎建也有说明："我们基本上是两个月推出一款新的模具，再加上衍生产品，差不多是一个月一款新品……汉王的产品可以满足不同用户的使用需求……每款产品在外观和功能方面都有不同，就连每个产品的手写笔都是不一样的。"[5]那么，这种差异化到底如何？我们不妨以两款电纸书来进行对比，如表 2 所示。

表 2 两款汉王电纸书比较

产品型号	产品规格	显示屏	支持格式	功能
D21 (学生版)	173 mm×117 mm× 10.3 mm	8 阶灰度 5 寸电子纸显示屏（EPD）；比例为 4：3；分辨率 800×600	TXT（HTXT）、DOC、HTML、PDF、PNG、JPG、MP3、WMA、WAV 等	预装海量图书、内置五大权威词典：《朗文当代高级英语辞典（英英·英汉双解）》第三版，《大英百科》，《英汉词典》，《新华词典》，《古汉语词典》，即时取词、同步查询、全文显示、双语阅读
F21 (商务版)	173 mm×117 mm× 10.3 mm	8 阶灰度 5 寸电子纸显示屏（EPD）；比例为 4：3；分辨率 800×600	TXT（HTXT）、DOC、HTML、PDF、PNG、JPG、MP3、WMA、WAV 等	预装 1 500 余本正版书籍。另增地理词典、科学教育、医学字典、网络词汇四本词典。朗读机内所有英汉文。完美 3D 音效，超强反应速度。

为了便于论述，我们对一些基本技术指标，如电子墨技术、接口、电池续航能力等没有罗列在内。大体看上去，这两款机器虽然是过去产品的升级版，但在一些关键技术和功能上却几乎没有改进。D21 与 F21 版的区别，只是学生版更类似学习机，比商务版的多了双语阅读和生词本功能，而商务版比学生版多了几本词典。事实上，商务人群和学生人群是两个完全不同的群体，其需求差异十分巨大。生产者在设计产品时至少应该考虑以下几个问题：

（1）这两组人群购买电纸书的真正目的何在？电纸书对他们有什么用？

（2）两组人群的阅读范围是什么？

（3）两组人群的价格承受能力是多少？

所有这些，在这两款产品中都没有得到体现，其技术指征近乎一致，价格也一致，换言之，D21 与 F21 并没有真正区分学生人群和商务人群的不同需求是什么，并依据这些不同来设计产品功能。以学生版来说，电纸书确实可以做成学生用品，但它的设计必须紧紧切合学生群体的身份。我们不妨引用一些消费者对于学生版的意见来进行说明：

超强待机，黑白类纸屏互眼阅读是电纸书的长项，这是其他任何设备都做不到的，在此基础上，再加上以下几个方面的功能，电纸书就可以做成电子课本：①局域无线互联的功能：在某种意义上有传统多媒体教室的功能，比如一对多的作业与试卷发送，教师主机的判卷，成绩统计分析，学生之间互评等功能。②本机智能判卷系统：学生自己本机做题之后，可以判断过程与答案是否正确。③在实现无线互联的基础上，可以实现 5 天×10 小时每天的持续使用。如果电力做不到，那么也要做成可方便更换的充电电池，以方便班级统一为学生更换电池，而不是设计很多电源线。④要预置电子版的教材，练习册等，不需要学生另行购置纸的课本。[6]

以上消费者的意见是颇有见识的。学生版具备了上述功能，才能真正体现学生这个消费群体的真正需求，才能够和商务版有实质上的区别。目前，汉王推出了十几款机器，虽然名目较多，在一些细节上有所不同，总体来说大同小异，针对性不强，并没有体现出不同人群的不同需求。这种没有区分消费者需求的多样化，反而会产生两个问题：其一，产品型号凌乱，使消费者不知所从；其二，过快的更新换代使产品的保值度降低，从而使消费者宁愿处于观望状态而不去购买。

实行产品多样化，企业就要投入大量的资金、人力、物力对每一款产品进行研发，这对企业的实力是一个巨大的考验。基于此，笔者认为，汉王电纸书目前还是应在提高产品性能方面下工夫，减少名目繁多的款式，集中精力将电纸书的关键技术做精、做透，做出适合所有阅读人群的、可以替代纸质书的阅读器，在此基础上再进行差异化产品设计与开发。

2.3 关于预装书策略的分析和建议：使用灵活的预装书策略

汉王以模式识别技术起家，在手写、语音、OCR、生物特征等方面拥有多项国际领先的核心技术和自主知识产权，在技术研发与硬件制作方面有很强的实力。正因如此，汉王在进入阅读器市场后很自然地将自己定位为终端机生产者的形象，也就是说，汉王希望在电纸书市场所扮演的，是硬件供应商而非图书零售商的角色。刘迎建曾说过，他相信电纸书必将和个人电脑、手机一样进入千家万户，成为人手一台的电子产品，他希望汉王做阅读器市场的诺基亚。[7]然而手机与阅读器也有质的不同，手机是一种通讯工具，与内容供应无关，而阅读器则离不开数字内容的提供。如果没有足够的数字内容供读者选择阅读，则阅读器将失去存在的价值。汉王在决定进入阅读器市场时，为了满足消费者对内容的需求，实行了预装书策略。即在书中捆绑预装一些书籍，具体数字各种版本不同。

笔者认为其预装书策略也有不足，具体如下：其一，汉王电纸书大致分为畅销作品、名家名作、外国名著、英文名著、经管文化、法律法规、生活百科、国学经典等几类。这些书看起来包括万象，内容很丰富，但对于大多数读者来说，其中大部分的书可能不是自己需要读的，价值并不大。须知，读者购买阅读器的目的，不是为了看免费书，而是为了看自己想看的书，不是为了拥有一个公共图书馆，而是为了拥有一个自己可携带的图书馆。其二，这些预装书内容大多陈旧，不少可在网上免费下载，汉王花费如此大的价钱购买版权，所起到的作用最多只是减免了读者上网寻找下载的麻烦，而并没有成为消费者购买产品的助推器。事实上，对于自己喜欢的书，读者往往并不在乎花时间上网寻找，假如价格低廉，质量很好，他们也不会在乎花钱购买。其三，这些书虽然是正版，质量也有令人不满的地方。笔者翻阅了国学经典的一些书，其中不乏错字、别字，所选底本也非上佳。但应该看到，汉王选择哪些出版社的书可能受制于各种因素，比如，目前国内很多出版社数字化出版程度还较低，无法为汉王提供较好的数字出版物，数字版权的购买成本较高；汉王本身对出版业也不够熟悉等。但无论如何，对于消费者来说，书的质量肯定是影响购买决策的重要因素之一。其四，加大了成本，提高了电纸书价格，影响了销售。据刘迎建介绍，"汉王在电纸书的研制过程中，版权投入所捆绑的成本已经占总价值的第二位，内容占到整个产品价格的15%左右。"[8]如果按照一台汉王电纸书的价格为3 000元计算，15%即相当于450元左右。也就是说，如果没有这些预装书，汉王电纸书的价格可以直接降到2 500~2 600元，而价格则直接影响到销量。

基于以上论述，笔者认为，汉王的预装书策略可实行更为灵活的模式，可做以下调整：

（1）除了几本字典，其他书均不必预装。

（2）提供裸机价格，即不带预装书的电纸书价格。

对于那些已经购买了版权的电子图书，汉王可以制定不同的价格，消费者可自由选择，按需求来购买其电子图书。如此，就兼顾到了生产商和读者双方的需求和利益。

3 余论

以上我们从三个方面对汉王电纸书的产品策略进行了分析，并提出了建议。笔者认为，尽管国内专用电子阅读器市场还受到一些因素的制约，比如，整体的商业环境和体制的不够成熟、数字内容供应不足、民众版权意识不够浓厚等，但国内电子阅读器厂商也具有很大的优势，比如大众对电子书阅读器已经有了认识、亚马逊 Kindle 等国外主流阅读器尚未正式进入中国市场、中国本土的同类产品也尚未出现占据绝对优势的领先者等，因此这个市场还是大有可为的。国内阅读器厂家只要树立消费者第一的观念，并在深刻理解行业特征和市场逻辑基础上，勤练内功，建立良好的经营策略，就一定能建立自身的竞争优势，在竞争激烈的市场中脱颖而出。本文提出的建议只是一得之见，也许不够全面。笔者真心希望中国的电子书阅读器产业能够快速进入良性的发展轨道之中，有更好、更宽阔的前景。

注释

[1] 刘迎建. 将电纸书产品列为一号工程 ［OL］. http：//tech. sina. com. cn/it/2009－05－08/18103076468. shtml. (2010－06－25 访问)

[2] 程晓龙. 第三届中国数字出版博览会在京召开. 出版参考. 2009 (7)：10

[3] 张亚男. Q1 中国电子阅读器销量达 24.9 万部 汉王超半壁江山 ［OL］. http：//news. cyzo ne. cn/news/2010/05/12/150563. html

[4] 猛发飙！汉王首款手写电纸书高调宣言 ［OL］. http：//mouse. zol. com. cn/134/1349079. html(2010－06－25 访问)

[5] 专注成就大汉王科技董事长刘迎建专访纪实 ［OL］. http：//www. hw99. com/news/news view－689. htm(2009－06－25 访问)

[6] 汉王电纸书 D21－百战测评 ［OL］. http：//bbs. baizhan. com. cn/thread－76364－1－1. html. (2010－06－25 访问)

[7] 汉王董事长刘迎建：电子书价格明年有望大幅下降 ［OL］. http：//tech. sina. com. cn/it/2009－09－18/11343449627. shtml. (2010－06－25 访问)

[8] 郑春峰. 汉王董事长敲桌子痛斥：山寨电纸书横行如强盗. 南方日报，2009-9-22

作者简介

安小兰，博士，中央财经大学文化与传媒学院副教授。

移动出版与电子书刊

从亚马逊模式看国内电子书阅读器的现状与发展趋势[*]

肖　洋[1]　张志强[2]

（1. 华东师范大学传播学院　上海　200062；

2. 南京大学出版科学研究所　南京　210093）

摘要：全球电子书阅读器正在汇成东、西方两大中心市场，美国市场有亚马逊、索尼、苹果等为代表，而中国市场已形成汉王、方正等多极竞争的格局，且几乎所有国内电子阅读器厂商都将亚马逊的电子书阅读器 Kindle 作为标杆。本文对亚马逊在电子阅读器市场的四个关键产业链环节形成的独有的接通与延伸模式进行了剖析，认为亚马逊模式在国内短期内无法复制，国内各电子书阅读器厂商需要在整条产业链中重新寻找到自己的定位，并在自身的领域形成足够的规模才是出路。

关键词：亚马逊模式　电子书阅读器　延伸产业链

Look From Amazon Mode of Domestic E-book Viewer of the Present Situation and the Development Trend

Xiaoyang[1]　Zhang Zhiqiang[2]

（1. School of Communication，East China Normal University，Shanghai，200062；

2. Institute of Publishing Science，Nanjing University，Nanjing，210093）

Abstract：The global markets of e-book reader have been merging into two centers. The western central market is American，with Amazon，Sony，Apple etc. as the representative. As the eastern central market，China has formed a multi-polar pattern of competition with Hanvon，Founder，and so on. And almost all domestic manufacturers of e-book reader take Amazon e-book reader Kindle as a benchmark. This paper carries out an analysis of the linkage of industrial chain and extension of industrial chain mode that are formed uniquely in the four key industrial chain links of Amazon e-book reader's market.

Keywords：Amazon mode　E-book reader　Extension of industrial chain

＊ 本文系华东师范大学教学建设特色实验项目"网络与电子出版"（项目号 52160123）、江苏省六大人才高峰项目（07-H-006）、江苏省 333 工程科研资助项目（2009-81）的阶段性成果之一。

数字技术的繁荣，让我们越来越深刻感受到数字出版的全球移动阅读时代悄然而至。也许这个时代是被 Kindle "点亮"，却被证实是一个市场硝烟纷飞的时代。传统出版商正在回味亚马逊创始人和首席执行官杰夫·贝佐斯（Jeff Bezos）那句"书籍是互联网时代最后一个没被攻破的城堡"的名言时，2007 年 11 月 19 日，亚马逊推出 Kindle 第一代电子书阅读器，挂在官网上 5 个半小时后被抢购一空。2009 年 2 月，花旗集团根据 Kindle 的无线服务提供商 Sprint 所激活的 Kindle 数量推测，2008 年亚马逊 Kindle 销量为 50 万台[1]。截至 2009 年 12 月，Kindle 在全球累计销量达到 300 万台，亚马逊成为全球最大电子书终端供应商[2]。业内人士断言，1995 年杰夫·贝佐斯在西雅图一间车库里为亚马逊网站发出第一本书的行动看起来只是一个铺垫，12 年后他的电子阅读器 Kindle 才是攻击"城堡"的第一颗炮弹[3]。不同的是，前者试图重新定义"书店"，后者则重新定义"书籍"。

不可否认，电子书取代纸质书的优势地位已经进入倒计时，电子书的诞生是对传统出版业的一次颠覆。2009 年法兰克福书展"是否需要将所有纸质书都数字化？"主题论坛上，哈珀·柯林斯英国及全球 CEO 维多利亚·巴恩斯利，布鲁姆斯伯里出版社执行总监理查·德查金，数字图书出版商 O'Reilly 传媒数字创新部副总裁安德鲁·萨维卡斯以及 MV8 营销公司管理总监罗纳德·施尔德这四位全球数字出版先锋人物的发言不再讨论数字出版与传统出版取代与否的关系问题，而是将论坛内容建立在认定数字出版必将取代传统出版的基础上，直接就电子书定价、发行模式、数字版权保护等一系列业界颇有争议的话题进行讨论。电子书阅读器，作为一种便携式手持电子设备，具备大屏幕的显示器，能模仿纸书显示效果，不伤眼睛，可以让人舒适地长时间阅读图书。因电子书阅读器便携、存储容量大的特点非常适合数字时代的移动阅读，加上数字版权贸易和网络技术的发展，用户可以通过更低的价钱方便快速地购买到更多的图书，电子书阅读器自然就成为出版业数字化的关键要素，也引发了电子书市场的繁荣和激烈对抗。

全球电子书阅读器正在汇成东、西方两大中心市场，美国市场有亚马逊、索尼、苹果等为代表，而中国市场已形成汉王、方正等多极竞争的格局。美国市场研究公司 iSuppli 预计，2010 年全球电子书的销量将达到 1 200 万台，中国市场的销量将达 300 万台，占全球市场的 25%，到 2015 年中国有望超过美国成为全球最大的电子书市场[4]。良好的市场前景正吸引国内外企业纷纷进军中国电子书市场，一场中外电子书产业的大战即将打响。汉王、翰林、方正、龙源、盛大、上海世纪出版集团、中国移动等各路诸侯纷纷进军电子阅读器市场。几乎所有国内电子阅读器厂商都将亚马逊的电子书阅读器 Kindle 作为标杆，然而要借鉴亚马逊的成功，得全面梳理其产业模式，否则画虎不成反类犬，陷入茫然和被动的境地。

1 亚马逊模式的关键要素

亚马逊是一个成功的网上书店，在网络售书方面积累了许多成功的经验[5]。亚马逊 Kindle 作为出版业数字化的成功典范，得益于它在电子阅读器市场的四个关键产业链环节形成了独有的接通与延伸模式。

1.1 平台服务商

亚马逊作为平台服务商，在推出 Kindle 前已在图书零售业有着超过 10 年的积累，在品牌、渠道、产业认知度和用户需求调研方面具备了相当的积淀，强大的内容供应能力让亚马逊被有关媒体认为是"网络售书"的代名词，给予了"不是内容提供商，胜似内容提供商"的定位。在亚马逊 Kindle 上市之初，就拥有包含畅销书在内的近 90 000 种图书提供下载，至 2010 年 3 月已经超过 480 000 种，其中涵盖《纽约时报》畅销书榜单前 112 部中的 105 部。通过收购 Audible.com，进一步扩充数字内容资源，拓展音频书籍业务。亚马逊网站还提供包括《纽约时报》、《卫报》、《每日电讯》、《泰晤士报》、《经济学人报》、《福布斯》、《时代周刊》等超过 1 000 家主流报纸杂志的付费或免费下载。如此强大的内容服务是亚马逊不可替代的优势，也是 Kindle 能够顺利推出的必要基石。

1.2 硬件生产商

作为阅读器的硬件生产商，亚马逊开发 Kindle 的项目从酝酿到实施，花了 3 年时间。项目初期，杰夫·贝佐斯从苹果公司招揽设计师，专门成立 Lab126 设计公司，反复论证如何"模仿"实体书的问题，如使用多大的屏幕，采用何种字体与多大的间距，才符合传统阅读习惯。在确定使用显示屏生产商 E-Ink 的电子屏幕技术与 32 开本大小后，亚马逊又将提供 EVDO 网络技术支持的 Sprint 公司的技术整合进来，以提供快速的下载服务。2007 年 11 月，引领全新电子阅读体验的亚马逊 Kindle 阅读器诞生了。在市场的激烈竞争中，亚马逊也一直不断追求设计细节完善和功能的改进。从 Kindle 1 的布满键盘的设计，到 Kindle 2 的五向导航控制按键；从 Kindle 1 的 4 级灰度显示屏提升到 Kindle 2 的 16 级灰度显示屏；从 Kindle 2 的 6 英寸屏幕到 Kindle DX 的 9.7 英寸屏幕；增加电池续航时间，提高翻页速度，增加读文本功能，支持 Facebook 和 Twitter……亚马逊在扮演生产商角色时一直保持着数码产品的时尚性与专注于传统阅读感官的思考，其产品 Kindle 阅读器的设计追求人性化，以期给读者带来更为愉快的阅读感受。

1.3 内容提供商

亚马逊经营的努力目标一直是为消费者提供尽量多样的品种，这种渠道角色让亚马逊与各类出版社建立了广泛的合作关系，在获取电子书销售授权方面具有得天独厚的优势，其拥有的电子书的资源首屈一指。尽管美国一些大型出版社拥有自己的电子书零售网站，但他们仍然会将其中一部分内容资源放进亚马逊，亚马逊的电子书库拥有 1 000 余种兰登书屋、西蒙·舒斯特的书，3 000 多种麦格劳-希尔的书；一些零售力量偏弱的中小出版社则更愿意与亚马逊合作实现双赢。Kindle DX 在新闻内容资源上也得到《纽约时报》、《波士顿环球报》和《华盛顿邮报》等内容提供商的支持。同时 Kindle 借助格式转化等新业务与新途径，扩大可供阅读的内容范围，如免费公益数字图书馆、下载网站的书，甚至 Word、html 等常规格式文档，开辟更为广阔的内容资源空间。

1.4 网络运营商

如果说，无可匹敌的海量书籍内容服务与媲美纸书的阅读体验优势足以让亚马逊 Kindle 领先于电子阅读器市场，那么独立存在的网络服务则是确立其绝对霸主地位的辅弼良臣。独立的网络服务，让 Kindle 的价值超越一本电子书阅读器的个体局限，而是拥有一个便携的海量图书馆。亚马逊构建独立的免费网络，通过与美国电信运营商 Sprint 合作，在 Kindle 内建 3G EV-DO 模块，让内容和硬件之间实现无缝的网络链接，类似于 iTunes 音乐商店的平台 Whisper-net，基于 EVDO 无线宽带服务技术，随时随地从亚马逊的平台下载正版电子书。Kindle 的网络浏览器同时可便捷地浏览最新的新闻、天气，阅读报纸和博客内容，不用再去支付任何费用。使用者可通过预订方式，亚马逊会每天把博客内容发送到 Kindle 设备上，读者就能及时阅读这些内容。

2　国内电子书阅读器的市场现状

国内电子书阅读器市场是在 2008、2009 年亚马逊 Kindle 阅读器取得市场巨大成功的强烈刺激下催生的，加上 2009 年汉王科技对电子书阅读器的高调回归，中国的电子书阅读器市场开始出现巨大波动，汉王、翰林、方正、龙源、盛大等来自产业链不同环节的企业纷纷涉足市场。

有研究指出，目前国内很难有一家公司能拥有亚马逊或者苹果那样的创新能力和足够的号召力，意味着国内的电子书阅读器市场无法在一个产业形成规模前提前完成布局。模仿或者说是恶性竞争的结果，只会导致原本不大的市场蛋糕分割更加严重，让更多的充满期待的商家吃不饱。

亚马逊模式在国内短期内无法复制。从产业链的角度来看，目前国内电子书阅读器市场有如下特点：

（1）以内容提供商的角色进入电子书阅读器市场

传统出版社如上海世纪出版集团、中国出版集团公司，拥有内容资源，通过定制电子书阅读器，试图掌控内容平台的主动权，如上海世纪出版集团推出辞海电纸悦读器，中国出版集团公司与中国移动合作推出中国出版集团公司移动阅读器。出版行业开始把握数字出版的主导权和主动权，然而技术并非没有门槛，掌握资源去做工业设计，其潜力无法与硬件生产商竞争，做平台的难度又比方正要大，而且内置自家正版书的做法在兼容性方面的考虑是否会引发更多的出版社跃跃欲试，开发自己的阅读器，其结果让人担忧。国内原创网络文学的行业巨擘——盛大文学，其"锦书"已列入盛大公司的产品序列中，产品拟将整合"起点中文网"、"晋江文学城"、"红袖添香"、"榕树下"、"小说阅读网"、"潇湘书院"等内容资源，通过内容资源优势构建"中国版"的亚马逊模式。然而盛大文学在多种内容资源的整合及产业链上下游的协调方面能力稍显不足，同时会受制于中国电信等网络运营商，阻碍其后续移动阅读的发展。

（2）以平台服务商的角色进入电子书阅读器市场

标榜"全球最大的中文数字出版技术提供商和内容运营商"的方正集团属于产业链中的内容平台服务商。旗下子公司方正飞阅与中国移动旗下卓望信息于 2009 年 10 月联合推出可提供图书、新闻、股票等综合资讯服务的掌控电子阅读器文房（WeFound）。从成立方正阿帕比公司，到建立阿帕比数字图书馆，再到 2009 年 7 月打造番薯网的平台，方正集团一直以先驱者的姿态介入数字出版。根据番薯网的数据来看，虽然图书总量突破了180 万种，不过在正版电子书的描述上仅用"数以万计"含糊带过[6]，其数量与亚马逊所能提供的 48 万种相去甚远。且前期集团高层透露的硬件加三年不限流量的 3G（TD-SCDMA）套餐服务加正版畅销书免费下载三年（只限前 1 万名）打包销售 4 800 元左右的高价位，让用户的购买意愿着实受到影响。

与方正不同的是，汉王、EDO、易万卷等企业是以硬件生产商的身份转向内容平台服务商角色。但想在短期把平台做大，难度非常大。汉王自己开发汉王书城提供电子书免费下载服务，明显试图复制"亚马逊+Kindle"的商业模式。但对于汉王而言，"罗马不是一天建成的",更应该看到亚马逊在推出 Kindle 之前在图书零售业的 10 年积累。而且汉王的主要精力还是投入在技术研发方面,与其费神费力构建平台,不如转向提供接口,让用户自由连接开放平台。在汉王书城上读者每下载一本电子书到阅读器,汉王就会向相关出版社支付 2 元钱的电子书使用费用。这种无法从平台建设中直接获利的商业模式也使得汉王难以在平台建设上做出强势的改进,平台沦落成附属品,无法形成"大而全"的规模。

（3）以网络运营商的角色进入电子书阅读器市场

2009 年 5 月 7 日,中国移动在北京宣布"手机阅读"业务正式商用上市,并表示已经做好手机阅读业务"三年不挣钱"的打算,将为用户补贴相关的数据流量费用。移动手机阅读业务定位于"打造全新的图书发行渠道",是以手机终端和移动电子书为主要形态,与具备内容出版或发行资质的机构合作,整合阅读内容,满足客户随时随地阅读需求的一项业务。中国移动以网络运营商的角色,通过自有的传统服务来推手机阅读电子书,让用户获得实惠,在潜移默化中认可运营商的收费模式。中国移动的高层也表示,中国移动不仅要引入 iPhone 手机,商谈在下一代的 iPhone 装入 TD-SCDMA 3G 模块,还要引入 iPad 平板电脑。中国联通、中国电信也计划采购电子阅读器。作为网络运营商,它们具备渠道、用户、合作伙伴以及对数字产业链掌控能力方面的先天优势,也具备较强的内容资源整合能力,但定价偏低的策略和其他因素在一定程度上也会影响内容提供商参与的积极性,而且网络运营商发展电子书阅读器终端的商业模式不明晰,长远发展的局势前途未知。

（4）以 IT 企业的角色进入电子书阅读器市场

这是一股单纯进军电子书阅读器硬件市场的力量,有津科、艾利和、三星以及众多山寨品牌……作为典型的 IT 企业角色进入电子书阅读器市场,对于产业链认识很"清晰":就是卖终端,卖时尚数码产品,给内容提供充分的接口和显示渠道。尽管媒体一再强调"电子书没有内容无以成书",但国内网络小说盗链严重,专门提供盗链小说的网站非常多,这为电子阅读器提供了大量、免费且与受众品味吻合的内容资源,因此在当前我国知识产权保护环境下,这类企业仍然有巨大的生存空间。当然,由于缺少其他产业链环节提供的服务,这种"单纯"的阅读器仅依靠"优质阅读体验"对多数读者而言,吸引力很有限,无法进入电子书阅读器的主流市场。

当然,电子书阅读器产业的未来存在很大的不确定性,各厂商需要在整条产业链中重新寻找到自己的定位,并在自身的领域形成足够的规模才会有出路。

3　电子书阅读器的发展趋势

3.1　产品走向

3.1.1　多元的感官体验

目前的汉王电纸书已经可支持多种文本类、图片类、音频类格式,拥有 3D 环绕立体声播放模块,既可录音也可播放音乐,且可将音乐设置为背景播放,实现边看电子书边听音乐的惬意享受,国际领先的 TTS 识别核心,可朗读各种英文、中文小说,边看边听,并有下划线显示当前朗读进度。未来的电子书阅读器将提供更丰富的多媒体的感官享受,集图、文、声、像于一体,在一部彩色的电子书阅读器上可以读文字,可以查看相关图片,看累了可以听朗读,可以欣赏影音视频。同时可以自定义字体、字号,在电子书上随意地进行圈圈点点、批注、添加书签或者信手涂鸦，圈点重要信息，留下阅读的痕迹。

3.1.2 便携的产品形态

当前市售的电子书阅读器造型大同小异，均与 Kindle 的大小形状相仿。一些追逐电子书形态的先行者，如台湾纬创资通公司正在研发一款采用可弯曲电子纸显示技术的 5～6 英寸的手持设备，该设备采用和先前 Polymer Vision 公司的 Readius 可折叠电子书类似的设计。将来我们就能看到可卷曲屏幕的电子书阅读器，可以随意折叠卷曲，不用担心显示屏被挤压扭损，占用空间小，携带方便，随时都可阅读[7]。

3.1.3 集成的终端服务

如今电子书阅读终端品类繁多，除专业的阅读器外，手持游戏机、MP3 播放器、手机均可阅读电子书，谁都不愿意携带一大包数码设备出行。2010 年 1 月，北京万物青科技有限公司联手 E-INK、EPSON 公司在京推出国内首款能打电话的电子阅读器"毕升 1号"。在支持电子阅读功能的同时，不仅可以打电话、发短信，支持 GSM、WIFI、3G 无线上网，还可支持 MP3 播放、收音机等功能，且待机时间超过普通手机。可以预见，将来的电子书阅读器将会集阅读功能、手机功能、音乐功能、游戏功能、学习功能、相机功能、上网功能于一体，用户只需携带一部设备即可享有所有功能。

3.1.4 复本数销售模式

电子书的"复本数"模式已在国外应用广泛。复本数是表述同一种文献收藏数量的概念。图书馆或其他文献情报机构为满足众多读者的需求常收藏多册（件）同一版次及版式的同种文献，其中的一册（件）被称为正本或保存本，其余的都称复本。从国外电子书产业的发展来看，"复本数"模式同样得到了广泛应用。在"复本模式"与"单本模式"的背后，是电子书价值链上利益的调整与分配。这种沿袭了纸质书模式的"复本数"模式，严格有效地控制电子图书的低廉价格或免费的大面积传播，保护了新的出版产业链条上各方利益，使数字出版产业能够进行可持续性的发展。

在国内，方正电子有限公司多年来一直提倡并实行"复本数"模式销售电子书。方正阿帕比利用自主研发的数字版权管理（DRM）技术实现对电子书版权的保护，卖给图书馆的电子书都是可计数的，图书馆像纸质书那样将电子书分册借给读者阅读，并在借阅时间到期后自动收回，杜绝了图书破损、丢失、到期不还等现象。未来的电子书阅读器将推行"复本数"的销售模式，电子图书的相关销量、版税得到保障，才能更好地保护著作权人的利益，激发内容生产者的积极性，促进电子书产业的良性循环。

3.2 产业布局

未来合理的电子书阅读器产业布局将建立在今天产业竞争主体对产业的优势整合之上。以出版社、报社、杂志社、盛大等为主要力量的内容提供商，其努力方向应该是追求精品内容的生产和加工，依靠电子书的销售分成获得收益。以方正、龙源期刊网等为主要力量的平台服务商，其努力发展的方向应该是巩固自身平台优势，扩大平台规模，完善数字版权管理，提高绑定式阅读器的竞争力，提出低廉的网络连接方案，与其他环节对接，从电子书的销售分成及绑定式阅读器获得收益。以中国移动、中国联通、中国电信为主要力量的网络运营商，其努力方向是保持与平台的良好合作关系，提供低价网络解决方案，以优质的网络服务实现与平台和硬件的对接，以向内容平台和阅读器使用者出售无线网络服务作为利润来源。以汉王、津科、艾利和、三星等为主要力量的硬件生产商，其努力方向是提高技术的竞争力，不断强化阅读器功能，扩展与网络、平台与兼容 DRM 体制的对接，依靠出售电子阅读器产品本身获取利润。

4 结语

综上所述，虽然在国内市场照搬亚马逊模式成功概率不高，但其运营模式和成长思路却值得业内厂商借鉴。尽管随着盛大文学、中国出版集团公司、上海世纪出版集团等强大的内容提供商在电子书阅读器市场的强势进入，市场的竞争格局已经和即将进一步发生变化，依托内容资源优势，有利于中国版亚马逊模式的构建与诞生。但现有市场的竞争较为激烈，内容资源的平台化运营成为必然趋势，须多方力量共同努力，各司其职，构建合作、开放、共赢的内容运营平台，一方独领市场的可行性不大。当务之急，在被称作电子书阅读器井喷之年的 2010 年，国内相关厂商应冷静思考自身定位，加强产业链各环节的交流与合作，避免同质化竞争，在积累整合内容资源的基础上，进一步加大技术和应用的研发投入，面向市场需求不断推动技术进步和产业升级，共同促进我国电子书阅读器产业的快速、健康发展。

注释

[1] Peter Kafka. Citi Says Amazon Sold 500,000 Kindles Last Year；$1.2 Billion Business-NextYear. [EB/OL]. [2009-2-3]. http://mediamemo. allthingsd. com/20090203/citi-says-amazon-sold-500000-kindles-last-year-12-billion-business-next-year/.

[2] 徐楠，张晓东. 电子书大战一触即发 [N]. 北京商报. 2010-3-15（C6-C7）.

[3] 杨樱. 为颠覆而生 [J]. 第一财经周刊，2009-6-18.

[4] JULIET YE. Outlook for electronic books in China appears bright — once big hurdles are cleared. [N]. The Wall Street Journal. 2010-1-5.

[5] 杜亭，张志强. 网上书店中的信息流与图书的宣传及销售——"亚马逊模式"剖析 [J]. 科技与出版，2007，（8）.

[6] 番薯网——关于我 [EB/OL]. [2010-6-15]. http://www. fanshu. com/other/about. html.

[7] 可卷屏弯曲电子书 Readius 预计明年上市 [EB/OL]. [2009-11-15]. http://tech. sina. com. cn/digi/2009-11-15/21481133362. shtml.

参考文献

[1] 郝振省. 2007-2008 中国数字出版产业年度报告 [M]. 北京：中国书籍出版社，2008.

[2] 安小兰，谭云明. 亚马逊电子书经营模式分析 [J]. 出版发行研究，2009，（6）.

[3] 王晓光. 电子书市场的双边结构及其定价策略研究 [J]. 出版发行研究，2009，（7）.

[4] 王艾，魏凯. 从 2009 法兰克福书展看全球数字出版未来 [N]. 中国新闻出版报. 2009-11-13.

[5] 宁良春. 中外电子书大战三年内爆发 [N]. 经济参考报. 2010-2-23（A06）.

[6] 吕文龙. 电子书融冰 [J]. 互联网周刊, 2010, (3).

[7] 清科研究中心. 2010 年中国电子阅读器市场投资研究报告 [R]. 2010-5.

[8] 亚马逊观察. http://www.amazonly.com/.

[9] 数位之墙. http://blog.donews.com/ladios/.

作者简介

肖洋, 博士, 华东师范大学传播学院讲师。

张志强, 博士, 南京大学信息管理系教授, 博士生导师, 南京大学出版科学研究所所长。

移动出版与电子书刊

对中国博客书发展瓶颈的探析

潘蓓开

（浙江工商大学编辑出版系　杭州　310018）

摘要：本文以中国博客书出版为研究对象，在分析了博客书出版现状的基础之上，归纳了博客书出版具备的四大优势：即发展空间广阔，读者需求的多样性能促进博客书质量的提升，更加贴近作者和内容资源丰富。通过总结日本博客出版的三大成功经验，分析中国博客书出版中存在的过分追求名人效应、过分看重博文点击率、连续的有故事性的博文尚待发掘、未能反映社会热点以及博客圈的资源尚未引起编辑关注等问题，指出中国博客书出版应从内容、全媒体开发和开发草根文化三个方面为突破口，发掘出更多的具有"双效益"的博客书。

关键词：博客　博客书　中国出版　日本出版

The Analysis of Bottleneck for the Development of the Chinese Blook Publication

Pan Beikai

（Editor and Publishing Department，Zhejiang Gongshang University，Hangzhou，310018）

Abstract：This article analyses the situation of the blook publication，and then concludes that the blook publication has four advantages，such as has a wide development space，the diversity of readers' requirements can promote the quality of blook，closer to the readers and has abundant content resources. The paper summarizes three successful experiences of Japan blook publication，analyses the problems of China blook publication，such as excessively seek celebrity charm，pay too many attention to the hits，the blog posts are lack of continuous story and don't reflect the society reality，the editors pay no attention to the resources of blog circles. Further more，the paper points out that China blook publication should emphasize on the contents，the development of Omnimedia and the exploitation of grassroots culture so as to publish more blooks which have both good social and economic benefits.

Keywords：Blog　Blook　China publish　Japan publish

1　博客书出版现状

博客书在今天的图书市场上已经不是一个新话题，从 2004 年在中国出现以来，博客书一直是出版界想要做好但是却总是力不从心的一个领域。似乎中国出版界总是没有找到一个好的途径把出现在博客中那些具备市场价值的内容出版成书。当出版社踌躇满志把那些在网上被网友疯狂点击的文章变成一本本实在的书籍推向市场的时候，也总是意外地遭遇冷落。从 2004 年开始，相继出现周轶君的《上帝最近》、乔乔的《乔乔相亲记》、董事长的《特别内向》、北京女病人的《病忘书》、梅子的《恋人食谱》，再到被称为"博客年"的 2006 年，徐静蕾的《老徐的博客》、郑渊洁的《博客郑渊洁》、潘石屹的《潘石屹的博客》等名人博客书的出版，博客书在中国已经有了 6 年的历史，尽管其中部分博客书也在当时受到了一定的追捧，但是至今在中国仍未出现一部引起轰动，甚至带动全媒体效益的博客书。博客书如一条小河，始终无法汇入出版界的大海。经过几次失败，国内的出版人已经对博客书持较为保守的态度。

纵观世界博客书出版市场，以日本成功案例最为典型，日本也是博客群最为活跃的国家，已经出现了像中野独人的《电车男》、白石昌的《生协的白石先生》、Kazuma 的《鬼妻日记》此类畅销博客书，《电车男》和《鬼妻日记》还通过全方位的媒体开发，获得了巨大的市场价值。而在欧美，全球博客图书奖在 2006 年首次顺利评出年度的优秀博客书——朱莉·鲍威尔的《朱莉和朱莉娅：365 天，524 道菜，一间狭小的公寓厨房》，平民化的博客书受到社会的关注。

2 博客书出版优势分析

2.1 网络传播力为博客书提供广阔的空间

互联网如今已经成为很多人生活中必不可少的部分，据艾瑞咨询集团发布的 2010 年第一季度网民形态核心数据显示，2010 年中国网民月度数量已突破 3 亿，其中网页搜索和博客的普及度在所有网络应用中名列前茅，部分博客中整合了休闲交友的游戏功能，2009 年 3 月浏览时间达 12.7 亿小时，环比增长 235%。[1] 此外，从第七次全国国民阅读调查中得到的数据我们可以发现，2009 年，我国 18—70 周岁国民中接触过数字化阅读方式的国民比例达 24.6%，比 2008 年的 24.5% 增长了 0.1 个百分点。网络阅读成为很多人特别是年轻人的选择。

博客产生于网络，网络的传播力远较传统媒介广泛和快速，在网络传播的基础上，好的博客本身已经具备了相当数量的关注群，也就是说如果具备出版成书价值的博客，出版图书有可行性就是因为图书在上市之际就拥有大批的"潜在购买者"。

2.2 读者的阅读需求为博客书质量的提升提供动力

丰富的网络资源已经在很大程度上开阔了中国网民的视野，很多以前看不到不知道的知识如今可以轻而易举地在网络搜索中获得。博客阅读的火爆也反映了网民对阅读的多项需求，博客汇聚了中国各个阶层的人，有专家学者，有白领商人，有作家，当然，更多的是表达个人思想情感的普通人。尽管博客对个人来说是在网络上的私人空间，但是大部分人还是希望能够得到其他人的关注，而博客内容就是吸引他人最为重要的因素，只有写出与他人不同的、有思想有内容的博客文章，才能够获得关注。读者多样化的阅读需求就是不断推动博客书质量提升的动力。

2.3 及时沟通的优势让作品更加贴近读者

博客作为博主发表个人言论的阵地，不仅成为个人与外界沟通一个独特的桥梁，也成为个人表达自己思想的一个重要平台。而互动性强让浏览者可以直接与作者进行沟通，你可以了解别人对当今世界上所发生的事情的了解和看法，也可以对陌生人与自己契合的言论进行评论和品味。如潘石屹的《潘石屹的博客》一书中，就摘录了 3 万多字网友最精彩的评论。这种贴近读者的方式总是较容易写出更加贴近读者需求的文章。

2.4　丰富的内容为出版提供大量的资源

借助网络这个平台，博客已经发展出一种典型的"平民文化"。发表一篇博文没有文笔的要求，也可以不必考虑市场的需要，随意性高，无需成本。在数量庞大的博客群中，存在很多有思想但是尚未被发现或是未成系统的博文，这就需要有心的编辑去发掘。当然，在博客这个原生态的文化圈中，还存在着很多低俗的博文，是否会成为书籍流向市场就需要编辑把关。

3　日本畅销博客书出版成功模式借鉴

与中国的博客书市场低迷相比，日本的博客书市场出现了许多备受追捧的博客书，并利用多种媒介进行全方位开发，创造了巨大的经济效益和良好的社会效益。

在刘义军、资明霞的《博客出版：日本出版界的宠儿》一文中就提到："博客新媒体的出现弥补了书籍和杂志期刊的缺乏互动的短处。近年来，博客的兴起在日本受到了广泛关注与欢迎，日本大众利用博客表达自我心中的愿望，讲述各种传奇的故事，把博客空间打造成社会关注的公共空间，成为大众讨论的话语空间。出版商为了抓住受众眼球，迅速组织出版优秀博客中书写的传奇故事，捕捉了出版界的新动向。"[2]

说到博客书，就不得不提日本的超级畅销博客小说《电车男》，这本书可以说是日本甚至是世界出版的一个奇迹，先后推出了小说、漫画、电影和电视剧、舞台剧、朗诵剧。小说《电车男》一问世，在短短 7 个月创下了 100 万册的超高销售纪录。这部博客小说还被翻译成中文、英文、韩语、泰语和意大利语等版本走向世界。于 2005 年搬上银幕的电影版《电车男》，为电影公司 TOHOCO 创收了 3 000 万美元的收入。总之，一切与之相关的文化产品推向市场后都获得了巨大的成功，给低迷的日本出版业带来了新希望。同时也让人看到，优秀博客与书籍、漫画、电影、电视剧、舞台剧等形式的融合，能够创造出不计其数令人艳羡的价值。

《电车男》的成功给了我国的博客书出版几个重要的启示。

第一，有新意的原创文学作品更能吸引读者的眼球。

《电车男》是来自网络的一个真实故事，讲述的是一位不通世事的网名为"电车男"的男子与"爱马仕"小姐的爱情故事，从"电车男"和"爱马仕"小姐的相遇、相知、相恋到结婚，都与网友的关注和为"电车男"指点迷津息息相关，这些互动性极强的真实博文最终形成一个完整动人的爱情故事，为出版提供了一个极好的素材。

第二，多媒体融合能够互相促进，实现利益的最大化。

《电车男》算是典型的多媒体互动的成功案例，与网络文学相同，作为网络文学的一个分支的博客文学同样能够实现全媒体应用的利益最大化。具有完整故事情节的文学性博客书书可通过与电影、电视剧、舞台剧等多种形式的互换，以书带动电影票房，电视剧收视率的提高。反过来，以电视剧、电影这种更加广泛、快捷的方式提升书的知名度，从而带动书的销量。

第三，优秀出版物的外文输出可获得更加广阔的市场。

《电车男》通过多国语言翻译后从日本走向世界图书市场，获得了较好的收益。好的作品就要向全世界传播，这不单单是指博客书的出版，中国的出版业如今还是缺少一种"世界观"，纵观世界出版市场，来自中国的优秀出版物寥寥无几。这是我们所有编辑出版人应该思考的问题。

第四，关注社会现象、探讨社会热点问题的书才是时代的好书。

《电车男》除了故事本身的趣味性和真实性能够吸引人之外，潜藏在背后的是一个新的社会问题，那就是日本社会近年来出现的"御宅男"次文化族群现象。这些自我封闭沉迷在自我世界的青年男子，对外面的世界有一定心理上的排斥和畏惧，不懂得如何去适应这个社会，这是一个令人担忧的社会现象。《电车男》就适时地将目光转向这样一个群体，让人们对"御宅男"的关注提上一个高度。

关注社会现象，多媒体融合，面向世界的行销策略从而获得的版权收益，《电车男》真正实现了效益的最大化。

4 中国博客书出版存在问题分析

4.1 过分追求名人效应

与美国关注的平民博客书出版不同，中国一度掀起一股名人出版博客书的热潮，大部分出版社也都将目光锁定到名人博客上，主要是想借助名人在社会上的影响力来带动销售。最典型的要算徐静蕾的《老徐的博客》一书了。在这种情况下，出版方会转向对作者的关注而将内容处于次要地位。名人不一定都是好的作者，过分追求名人效应可能会造成博客书质量的下降，也不利于创造出更好的社会效益。

4.2 过分看重博文点击率

在出版徐静蕾的《老徐的博客》之前，出版社对徐静蕾博客的点击量能够带动图书销售持乐观的态度，过千万的点击量必然有不计其数的潜在读者购买群，首印10万册也看出出版社的过于乐观。尽管点击率可以大致看出市场走向和需求，但是，点击率不能完全代表购买意向，很多博文的性质是属于博主的个人简单体验，随意性较大，出版成书之后内容稍嫌琐碎，对于博客文章来说，要达到优秀出版物的要求尚有距离。所以，片面关注点击率是无法判断能否出版成一本好的博客书。点击率只能说明被看过，而不能就以此说明网民很喜欢。出版了《不要联想》的博客作者王小峰明言："网络跟现实是有差距的。起哄是一回事，偷窥是一回事，掏钱买书又是一回事。"[3]

4.3 新鲜的引人关注的连续性故事博文尚待发掘

《电车男》、《鬼妻日记》就是在博客的基础上发展起来的完整故事，通过博主在博客上对一件事情的连续地诉说和网友的热烈反应，最后以小说的形式面市，并且集合了畅销小说适合的开发模式，电影、电视剧等多种形式也不断地互相推动。博客书是网络书的一种，又与网络书有一定的差别，博客相比其他发表文章的网站，更加私人化，碎片化，很多时候只是博主个人心情的发泄，并不像我国已出现的如《鬼吹灯》、《盗墓笔记》、《明朝那些事儿》等网络小说目的性强和连贯。博客文章则更多讲述的是个人故事，但是在平凡人身上也可以发生很多不凡事，这就为出版提供了很多好选题。

4.4 博客书对于社会热点还未能最大程度地反映

博客是一个很好的针砭时弊的平台，很多优秀的畅销书甚至是长销书都是因为以一种良好的方式反映了社会问题。博文是时刻更新着的文章，很多都契合当今读者对这个社会心理的一种反映。如果只是千篇一律的碎碎念和个人心事，那样对这个书业市场的发展也会起到消极的影响。只有出好书，才能带动读者购书的欲望，才能使书业市场繁荣起来。

4.5　博客圈的资源尚未引起出版社编辑的关注

经过几次博客书出版的失败，中国的出版界普遍不看好博客这个领域，但是在日本，众多博客书的成功让出版商瞄准了博客这个巨大的市场，甚至还专门成立了针对博客的出版社——AmebaBooks，全心全意搜罗网络上的优秀博文。在中国，书籍出版还是一直走一个较为传统的选题——约稿——出版的路子，所以博客书的出版才会很大程度上的依赖名人效应和点击率。当然并不是否认这种出版方式，这是出版优秀出版物的可靠路径。但是，我觉得出版界应该适应今日网络时代的发展，将更多的关注目光转向网络，用心去发现网络上值得出版的资源。

5　中国博客书的突破口

5.1　内容为王，关注社会

一本书能够吸引读者眼球并让读者真正愿意掏钱买下并吸引更多读者，内容是起决定性作用的，特别是在今天这个网络资源丰富和共享的时代，读者不一定非要通过买书才能够阅读，书籍在某种程度上已经成为一种收藏。而能够具备收藏价值的，是能够让读者不断品读的，内容肯定是居首要位置。所以博客书的出版要重视出版内容，以内容为第一。只有那些原创的、富有深刻内涵的、贴近人们生活的、贴近社会主题的、丰富读者知识面的书籍才能够真正让人关注。

一本书能否被称为好书，好的社会效益必不可少，如日本的《电车男》关注了御宅男这个社会现象，《鬼妻日记》以诙谐的手法反映日本新型家庭关系、颠覆日本男女性传统形象。《生协的白石先生》打出温情励志牌，日本当代大学生的彷徨和苦闷进行了解答和安慰，也获得了众多的支持。只有立足当下，关注社会，才能够做出好的书。博客就是反应当下社会现状的一个重要平台，只要潜心发现，总能找到符合中国社会、中国人心理的好文章。

5.2　资源融合，全面开发

如同《电车男》一样，好的书籍是可以通过全方位的媒体开发来带动书籍的销量。反过来，畅销的书籍也能够带动其他媒体的开发。博客书本身已经具备了网络的优势，传播快、影响范围广、互动性强，懂得适宜地利用多种媒体，才能做出畅销书。

5.3　不过分追求名人效应，发展优秀的草根文化

博客的备受关注本来就是一种草根文化的兴起，如果只把目光放在名人的身上，也就显得太狭隘了。其实，放开所谓名人的名气，专心去关注一些真正有出版价值的平凡人写的不凡事，而非名人写的平凡事，博客书的内涵可以更上一个层次。在博客中，有很多各个领域的专家学者发布博客文章，为国人答疑解惑，为社会问题开剂良方，他们的深刻和权威之作如果能够变成一本本实在的书流传下去，相信一定是我们这个社会不可多得的精神财富。

任何一本好书都是来之不易的，任何一个好的选题都不是偶然的，潜心关注我们社会的种种问题，细心留意在我们身边的篇篇好文，我们会发现，其实做一本好的博客书没有

那么难，难的是我们没能用心去看、去发现优秀博文的优秀之处。

因此，面对博客的丰富内容资源，需要编辑沉下心来，少点急功近利，拨开被点击率、名人光环遮罩住的表面，挖掘真正有价值的内容资源，肯定能够在做出更多具备文化价值和社会意义的博客书。

注释

[1] 参见艾瑞咨询公司官方网站 http://www.iresearch.com.cn/coredata/2010q1_6.asp

[2] 刘义军，资明霞. 博客出版：日本出版界的宠儿. 编辑之友，20099（4）

[3] 王小峰，媒体资深人士，现任《三联生活周刊》杂志主笔，曾出版博客书《不许联想》

作者简介

潘蓓开，浙江工商大学编辑出版学系本科生。

移动出版与电子书刊

电子书出版的版权维护探讨

马小媛

（浙江工商大学人文学院　杭州　310018）

摘要：本文以数字出版中的重要产出物——电子书为媒介，在剖析其经营模式、对比分析与传统图书出版的版权差异的基础上，结合我国现状，提出了一次性完全购买方式、建立版权信息交易平台、采用公告制度、构建数字版权监督机构、增添出版合同内容等电子书版权保护的解决之路。

关键词：数字出版　电子书　版权　解决方法

Maintenance of E-book Publishing Copyright

Ma Xiaoyuan

（School of Humanities，Zhejiang Gongshang University，Hangzhou，310018）

Abstract：In this paper，an important output of digital publishing—E-books is taken as the medium．Base on the analysis of their business model and comparative analysis on copyright protection with the traditional book publishing，then combining with our current national situation，this paper puts forward the following E-book publishing copyright protection proposals such as the one-time complete purchase，the establishment of copyright information trading platform，taking notice system，setting up digital rights monitoring bodies，adding content of publishing contracts and so on．

Keywords：Digital publishing　E-book　Copyright　Solution

1　电子书及其经营模式

电子书是数字出版的重要产品形态，随着国内外越来越多有实力的企业加入电子书出版市场，其发展前景为业界一致看好。但是版权保护问题制约了电子书出版的进一步发展，版权制度若无法完善，电子书出版必将陷入泥潭，甚至会导致产业链的崩溃。为了更好地分析和研究电子书出版的版权维护问题，本文先对电子书的概念及其经营模式进行概述。

1.1　电子书

目前社会各界初步认定为：电子书代表人们所阅读的数字化出版物，从而区别于以纸张为载体的传统出版物，是利用计算机技术将一定的文字、图片、声音、影像等信息，通过数码方式记录在以光、电、磁为介质的设备中，并借助于特定的设备来读取、复制、传输。

它由三要素构成：①电子书的内容，又称电子图书，主要以特殊的格式制作而成并可以通过互联网或终端阅读器读取。②电子书的阅读器，它包括桌面上的个人计算机、个人手持数字设备、专门的电子设备等，如翰林电子书。③电子书的阅读软件，如 Adobe 公司的 AcrobatReader、Glassbook 公司的 Glassbook、微软的 MicrosoftReader、超星公司的 SReader 等。本文研究的主要是电子图书的版权保护问题，因而下文除非有特殊说明，文中的电子书一般均指的电子图书。

1.2 电子书经营模式

传统的图书出版是"六个主体"，即作者、出版社、印刷厂、图书发行商、书店和读者。作者将作品提供给出版社加工后，由出版社交往印刷厂印刷再进行发行，发行的图书经发行商销售到读者的手中。

而电子书的出版有很大不同，主要是"三个主体"，即数字版权人、数字出版商和用户。其中又分为三种主要的经营模式。一是作者将作品提供给经营数字内容的网站，网站通过加工编辑制作成各种格式的电子书，再通过网站在线售卖电子书，读者支付一定费用即可在线阅读或下载，整个过程都只在虚拟环境中进行。二是出版社将原有的资源，重新加工制作成电子书后，交给出版物网络发行商，按 POD（按需出版）方式销售。三是基于 web2.0 的概念，作者的作品可在个人网页上直接与读者交流，直接将内容传递给读者。

2 版权差异与存在问题

2.1 传统图书出版与电子书出版的版权差异

传统出版，虽然有其出版周期长、需求量难以准确估计、成本高等缺点，但在维护作者的版权上却比电子出版简易得多。对出版社而言，一方面其与各大图书经销商的关系是密切的，对图书的销量也能得到较为准确的反馈；另一方面，销售收益可观和资金的回笼速度快，这些对作者、出版社、经销商都是有利的。对于读者而言，大部分读者在选择传统纸质图书时更倾向正版图书，因为盗版图书的质量是不能与正版图书相比的。此外，不法分子对图书进行盗版也有相当难度。同时，传统纸质图书的分享范围是有限的，甚至是狭小的，因此绝大部分的读者需要通过购买图书才能进行阅读，并且向书店和零售商购买基本上是唯一途径。这表示着传统出版经营模式是一条单一流水线型的产业链，规范的流程让作品经过出版社的审核，为读者去粗存精，统一的末端出口又能保证了作者的版权。

但由于电子书属于数字化信息，脱离了物质载体而独立存在，可以在计算机上无限复制，还可以通过邮箱互寄、在网站上发表等方式传播，所以在维护作者的版权时相当困难。版权受到侵犯通常的表现为：作品在未经作者授权时被任意使用，导致了作者在版权方面的经济损失。这种版权侵犯一般来源于两个方面：一是数字版权人与数字出版商之间的利益争端；二是数字版权人与某些读者之间的利益争端。数字版权人拥有大量的内容资源，因此成为数字出版商的主要承揽对象。出版商一般采取每卖一本电子书就按比例分给作者相应版税的方式得到网络传播权，但这里存在着很大的不确定性：没有一个权威的机构能证明电子出版商卖出了多少本电子书，作者对电子出版商抱着不信任的态度，但是对电子出版商提供的销售数据又无可奈何。另一方面，如果读者在看完电子书后就随意地复制传播，也会造成电子书的销售量大跌，需求变小，导致作者的权益无法得到保护。像如今互联网中强大的百度、谷歌之类的搜索工具和超链接功能，使读者想要免费检索作者的劳动成果变得更为容易。

2.2 版权侵犯所带来的多方面影响

不管数字技术怎么发展，版权的基本原则没有改变，就是先授权后使用。版权侵犯所带来的影响是恶劣的，它所波及的区域是多方面的。一方面数字出版商会容易因为版权问题受到作者的起诉，从而在电子书的发行上面束手束脚，这样就满足不了读者对电子书的阅读需求；另一方面，出版单位若因为各种原因未获得作者的逐一授权，却将版权授予数字出版商，就会增加作者对出版单位的不信任，甚至导致作者与出版单位关系破裂；更重要的是，版权的侵犯直接伤害作者利益，挫伤了作者的创作积极性。

2010 年 5 月 27 日，龙源期刊网的总裁因侵犯作者被法院行政拘留，起因是湖南师范大学副教授起诉该网未经授权擅自刊登其 58 篇文章，法院判决该副教授胜诉。此事件引起社会广泛的关注。实际上龙源期刊网已与 3 000 多家杂志社签约，被允许制作期刊的电子版并进行网络销售代理，该网获得收益后向杂志社支付约定的版税和收益，并委托杂志社向作者支付稿酬。但是按照《信息网络传播条例》的规定，该网只有获得了所有作者的逐一授权才可使用相关文章，即使付给作者稿酬也不能洗脱侵权罪名。[1]

而出版单位如今一致认为由于许多作家使用笔名，有些作家行踪不定，有些作家已故或难以联系等等原因，逐一获得作家授权十分困难。在向数字出版商转让版权的时候，往往畏首畏尾，无法给予合适的交代。

此外，电子书的内容是凝聚了人类创造性劳动的"知识产品"，知识的生产者需要得到适当的利益回报和保护，如果不对电子书内容的使用加以限制，就会挫伤作者的积极性。假设作者版权受到侵害时，首先是挫伤了创作积极性，就写不出令人满意、有价值的作品。而一旦"作者"这一产业链的源头出现了问题，与其紧密相连的出版商、运营商等都将没法正常运作，而读者同样就也不会有电子书可供阅读或下载。作者为了自身的权益不被侵犯只能又回到传统出版产业链上来，例如许多作者在网络上免费写作赚取知名度，而后却又寻找出版社为其出书获利。这种现象与社会数字出版的发展趋势相违背，是现阶段的行业的运营模式和法律法规不够成熟所导致的停滞。

数字网络技术并不应该让版权被削弱，而是应当强化版权，因为版权制度无法完善，数字出版产业必将陷入泥潭。让数字版权人真正从数字出版中获得利益，这应当是数字出版商首先要考虑的问题。互利和共赢是产业壮大繁荣的基础，否则产业注定是短命的。因此，版权维护问题，这个电子书发展的瓶颈需要尽快解决，如无法有效解决版权问题，势必限制数字出版向前发展，甚至会导致数字出版产业链的崩溃。

3 电子书版权保护解决方法

结合我国电子书出版的实际，本文提出以下几点电子书版权保护的解决之道，以供参考借鉴。

3.1 合理定价，采用一次性购买方式

通过一次性合约的方式来买卖知识产品其实是一种有效的方法。拥有版权的作者或者出版单位可以根据国家出版部门制定的稿酬政策，从本人或者本单位的实际情况出发，估

量自己作品的价值，制定出合理的价格，将网络传播版权卖给数字出版商。进行交易的过程中要严格地按照法律程序进行，定制合同，双方主要负责人签订协约。

3.2　区分概念，建立版权信息交易平台

由于法律意识淡薄和对本行业的相关法规不够了解，很多时候数字出版商或者出版单位侵犯作者的版权利益是一种不经意的行为。因此有必要由行业协会、版权管理机构、运营商协会共同搭建一个版权信息交易平台，通过各种方式让出版相关人士和作者聚集，分享版权交易的经验和研究维护版权的办法，解决海量信息、海量作者、海量授权的问题。此外，更有必要让相关人士了解电子出版、电子发行和电子传播等概念。

3.3　建立数字版权监督机构

随着数字出版业的迅猛发展，建立数字版权监督机构或者类似性质的数字出版机构是势在必行的事情。整个数字出版业需要接受一个专门的机构的监督，从而规范自己的行为。这个机构必须是规范、公正、权威的，是受到数字出版行业各个方面人士尊重和信任的。这样，在售卖电子书方面，数字版权监督机构对每一季度或每一年度各个数字出版公司的电子书售卖情况进行统计和记录，向社会公示，使其透明化。这样即使数字出版商不是一次性买断数字版权人的知识产品，而是采用分期按销量给数字版权人利益回馈的方法，也不会出现太大的问题：因为此权威机构提供的售卖记录清晰而准确，一方面赢得了数字版权人的信任，另一方面数字出版商也不能虚构销售数字。

3.4　增添出版合同内容

几千年来，纸质书籍一直都是人们的主要阅读载体，出版单位与作者签订的出版合同中也只会涉及到纸质出版的相关明细。但随着网络的发展和各种科技产品的日新月异，增添出版合同内容已经势在必行。出版合同应该要增添数字出版和网络出版权利等相关内容，可以许诺若有数字出版和网络出版的情况则给予作者一定的经济报酬。或者出版单位对外刊登投稿声明，即一旦向本出版单位投稿则视为同意授予数字出版和网络传播的权利。这种做法，一开始就为防止侵犯作者版权打了一剂强心针，比较简单可行。需要在整个出版行业、作者领域形成自律和共识。

3.5　采用公告制度

可以创立一个新的公告制度，即一些具有数字出版资质的出版单位，若有想出版成电子书形式的作品，可以采用公告制度告知版权人和大众。一方面数字出版单位拟定信函给可以联系上的作者或者版权人，告知其想出版的文章和拟定支付的报酬。另一方面通过公告告知想出版的作品、作品的作者以及拟定支付的报酬标准（这项有时可以不公示）。如果公告发出30日内作者不同意出版的，数字出版单位便不得出版，如果公告发出后30日后，公告期算结束，作者没有提出异议的，出版单位便可以进行数字出版，并按公告拟定的支付报酬标准进行支付。如果找不到作者的，必须支付给中国作家协会。作家协会每年统计这笔资金的数额，无论大小，年末必须捐献给国家慈善机构。

3.6　建立第三方操作部门

数字出版商的出版也讲究时效性，将畅销的书籍和文章第一时间赶制出来，传递给读者，才能获取最高的利润。所以如何快速、有效地拿到作者的作品授权，对数字出版商和出版单位来说，都是非常重要的。我们可以通过建立第三方操作部门来实现这个设想，第三方部门是一个中间部门，在"作者——第三方操作部门——数字出版商/出版单位"这

一链条中起到将作者与数字出版商或出版单位联系起来的桥梁的作用。只要数字出版商愿意合法使用和合理付费就可以联系第三方操作部门，第三方部门则以最快的速度联系作者，依据出版单位或数字出版商开出的条件代表它们与作者协商，争取到作品的版权，并拟定详尽的责任和权利，签订相关合同。这也就对第三方操作部门提出了较高的要求：只要有出版作品的作者，都必须在它们的登记下，这种登记还包括联系方式和所有出版作品；它必须清楚了解与出版相关的所有法律法规；必须能和作者保持良好联系，以最快的速度联系上作者并且进行商谈。

3.7 完善法律法规，宣传使用正版的意识

数字出版行业正在蓬勃发展中，关于这个行业的法律也必须建立和完善起来。从法律上规范整个产业的行为的效果应该是明显有效的。例如网站经营商在引用或链接其他通过正规购买方式得到相关内容的网站时，应该自觉付费，如果不遵守这项规则，在被揭发或者检查出后必然要受到法律的惩罚。而对于擅自传播、提供链接造成作者版权受到侵犯的行为，作者可以通过法律的方式依法要求获得赔偿，相关法律在这方面必须给予支持。

同时，政府部门应该向公众大力宣传使用正版的好处和使用盗版所带来的危害，使公众从心理上认可正版的必要。虽然改变旧有观念非常艰难，但是依旧要贯彻实施，并且应该从娃娃抓起，从小就培养大家使用正版的意识，这样才能规范电子出版的产业环境，也许带来的更多是整个国民素质的提升。

3.8 改变现有运营模式的某些环节

传统图书的一些优势是值得借鉴的。电子书出版的营销形式，应该像传统出版一样形成良好有序的、统一标准的产业链，使其整个产业划分清晰、格式统一，沟通上简单明确。另外，传统图书的二维码识别技术使得图书的销售量能有效标记、易于识别，那么对于电子书，也可以采用类似的标记法。即在加工制作的过程中，为每本电子书加入电子码（以下称为 KEY）的概念，相信随着科技的进步，KEY 会得到应用。可以让每本书在下载后便有一个独一无二的 KEY，每个 KEY 只能绑定一台电子书阅读器。这样既使得出版的电子书数量可以衡量和记录，又能限制读者未经许可地向外传播。

另外对于手机作为阅读平台的情况，也可以采取收费的方式。手机平台读者在阅读的时候，手机运营商可以收取手机读者的流量费，与此同时，因为电子出版商提供的内容增加了手机用户的流量使用量，所以手机运营商应该适当给予电子出版商一些回扣。另外电子运营商可以通过在电子书内容中插入广告的方式，从广告商处获得利润。而 PC（个人电脑）读者的阅读收费方式只适合插入广告这一做法，广告商通过电子书把自己的商品宣传出去，可以适当给予电子出版商回扣。但是非常值得注意的是，在电子书中插入广告的做法要恰当，广告相对来说要能具有可读性和审美价值，不能让读者在阅读的时候产生反感情绪。

电子书出版作为数字出版的重要组成部分和一个正在蓬勃发展中的行业，保证其健康持续发展对数字出版产业的发展都有重大意义，为此，必须重视版权保护问题。无论政府、业界还是读者都应该积极参与其中，为其创造良好的发展环境。

注释

[1] 程华. 数字时代版权保护亟待破题 [J]. 出版商务周报，2010，6

作者简介

马小媛，浙江工商大学人文学院编辑出版系 2008 级学生。

移动出版与电子书刊

运用钻石理论浅析大众手机报竞争力的提升

李 茜 杨 威

（武汉大学信息管理学院 武汉 430072）

摘要：被誉为"第五媒体"的手机报，从一问世就以其随时、随地、随身等特点受到了大众欢迎。本文运用钻石理论，从生产要素、需求条件、相关产业和支持产业的表现、企业的战略、结构、竞争对手的表现、机会及政府六个角度对大众手机报产业进行分析。笔者认为，数字时代，大众手机报展现出极大的发展潜力，但在内容质量、受众需求、传播渠道和赢利模式等方面仍存在问题，本文亦针对性地提出解决措施，力求提升大众手机报竞争力。

关键词：大众手机报 钻石理论 竞争力

Enhancing Competitiveness Methods of the Mass Mobile Newspaper Based on the Diamond Model

Li Qian   Yang Wei

（School of Information Management，Wuhan University，Wuhan，430072）

Abstract：As known as "the Fifth Media"，Mobile Newspaper continued to gain popularity with "anytime，anywhere，carry" since it was born．This paper analyzes the mass mobile newspaper by using Michael Porter's "Diamond Model" from factor conditions，demand conditions，related and supporting industries，firm strategy，structure and rivalry，government，chance．We reach such conclusions：In the digital age，the mass mobile newspaper has a huge developing potentiality．But simultaneously，it also suffers from the problems of content quality，audience demands，transmission channel，and profit-making model，etc．This paper also puts forward solutions，and strives to enhance the competitiveness of mass mobile news-paper．

Keywords：Mass mobile newspaper Diamond model Competitiveness

数字时代快速推进，手机报展现了迅猛的发展速度与巨大的发展潜力。但目前国内大众手机报仅为在传统报纸基础上开辟移动数字平台通路，与传统报纸相比，只改变了传播载体和表现形式，内容等并没有发生实质性转变，相反易造成手机报之间、与传统报纸间的竞争力提升障碍。

钻石模型是由美国哈佛商学院著名的战略管理学家迈克尔·波特在其代表作《国家竞争优势》一书中提出的。波特的钻石模型用于分析一个国家某种产业为什么会在国际上有较强的竞争力。波特认为，决定一个国家的某种产业竞争力的有四个因素（如图所示）：

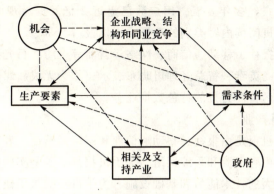

钻石模型结构图

生产要素：包括人力资源、天然资源、知识资源、资本资源、基础设施。

需求市场：主要是本国市场的需求。

相关和支持性产业：这些产业和相关上游产业是否有国际竞争力。

企业：企业的战略、结构、竞争对手的表现。

在四大要素之外还存在两大变数：政府与机会。机会是无法控制的，政府政策的影响是不可漠视的。

虽然钻石模型是针对国家某种产业的竞争力提出的，但在商业实践中，钻石模型往往被应用于产业或企业的中观或微观分析。

1　基于钻石模型的大众手机报竞争优势分析

1.1　生产要素

先进的技术支撑。互联网技术、计算机技术和通信技术结合使手机实现了从人际沟通向大众媒体跨越。时代的要求和技术的发展也促使纸媒业纷纷将眼光投向数字出版。从2004年第1份手机报诞生至今6年间，手机报已成为最主要的手机阅读方式之一。截至2009年底，全国报业已推出手机报约1 800种，用户达1.5亿，付费用户达7 000万。

充足的信息资源。作为传媒产品，手机报的生产过程是信息创造和利用过程，信息资源奠定了手机报的内容、市场等各方基础。其一，传统纸媒在新闻采编、读者群等方面资源可为其所属手机报所利用。其二，数字时代，内容与媒体逐步分离，手机报内容采集不再局限于专业人员，读者、运营商等都可成为内容提供方。其三，数字技术发展，信息资源实现跨媒体共享成为可能。

充足的人才储备。传统纸媒拥有一批富有经验的报业人才，移动通信、互联网络等新媒体及相关行业从业者数量也随着数字时代推进急剧壮大。国家新闻出版总署《全国报纸出版业"十一五"发展纲要》（下简称《纲要》）就明确提出"黄金一代"创新型人才培养行动计划，为手机报业在内容生产、渠道构造、安全保障等流程所需人才培养提供了条件。

1.2　需求市场

庞大的需求人群。据中国互联网信息中心（CNNIC）发布《第26次中国互联网络发展状况统计报告》统计：截至 2010 年 6 月，中国手机网民用户达 2.77 亿，手机网民成为拉动中国总体网民规模攀升主要动力，手机报潜在用户群愈加庞大。作为方便实用快捷的手机报也受到极大青睐，经多年发展，用户数已逼近 2 亿。据易观国际数据显示，2010年移动互联网用户对手机阅读内容类别的选择中手机报占 56%。

扩展的需求市场。报社、移动通信商、网络运营商等纷纷将目光投向手机报业。中国最大的无线新媒体服务商英泰利智总经理屠晓东表示，作为无线新媒体的典型代表，手机报如今已成为国内三大运营商力推的特色数据业务。

1.3 相关和支持性产业

三方密切联系。手机报是由报社、移动通信商和网络运营商三者共同构建的信息传播模式。报社拥有庞大的内容资源和采编网络，为手机报打下了坚实的内容基础。移动通信商、网络运营商具备强大的技术能力和基础设施，为手机报提供了便捷、互动、稳定的传输系统。并且手机报产业链各环节也正突飞猛进发展，相互联系迅速加强。

传统纸媒发展。手机报是数字化技术与传统纸媒结合的产物，传统纸媒的发展对其有极大影响。如今数字化建设已成为各报业集团关注焦点，从采、编、发的全面计算机化，到实现新闻信息的数字化存储，再发展到内部的网络建设及信息共享，报业集团的信息化建设也推动着手机报发展。

1.4 企业

手机报行业壮大。"两型社会"思想兴起，作为数字时代新兴产品的手机报较传统纸媒更符合资源节约型、环境友好型社会的要求，通过投入思想文化、智力创意等"轻资产"，结合基本采编传输接收设备，即可实现数字信息的高效传播。因此受到了政府大力支持、读者广泛青睐。目前，手机报正从短信、彩信阶段朝 WAP 及流媒体阶段发展，突破了单一文字和图文传输表现形式，大量融入文本、音频、Flash、视频技术，为用户提供了丰富多彩的视听体验。同时高度综合新闻、网络、通信等各多个媒体，手机报业产业链的建设更为完善，发展前景更为长远，手机报行业蒸蒸日上。据统计，2010 年 1 季度中国手机阅读市场总营收达 5.99 亿元，其中 5.49 亿元为手机报贡献。在"2010 年新媒体业态发展"的调查中，八成以上受访者表示 2010 年将是手机报业黄金之年。

1.5 政府和机会

新技术、新动力。数字技术的飞速进步为手机报的发展提供了强大的推动力。例如，随着 2009 年初 3G 牌照的发放，移动互联网基础设施不断建设完善，就为手机报发展打下了坚实的硬件基础。据工信部资料显示，截至 2010 年 7 月底，全国 3G 用户达到 2 808万户，到 2011 年将达 1.5 亿户。3G 是未来通讯业难以阻挡的流行趋势，据《中国 3G 现状调查报告》结果显示超半数被调查者愿意选择 3G 手机。这将为手机报的发展提供了市场、技术等多方面机遇。

新政策、新机遇。国家近年出台的一系列新闻出版和数字出版相关政策也为手机报的发展提供了宽松、广阔的发展环境。例如《纲要》明确提出了 14 项具体行动计划，经 5年发展已逐步实现，尤其是"行业信息资源平台"发展计划、"数字报业实验室"计划、"7/24 数字信息架构"发展计划等直接服务于手机报业的发展。更加值得关注的是，2010年 6 月国家正式启动三网融合工作，预计到 2015 年，我国电信网、广播电视网、互联网将形成一条全新双向的信息高速公路。手机、电脑、电视将实现互联互通互融，资源共享、优势互补，为用户提供多样化、多元化、个性化服务。使手机报多媒体化、个性化、互动化等的实现成为了可能。

2 大众手机报竞争力提升的障碍

2010 年 6 月，笔者就湖南省内三家大型大众手机报进行了跟踪调查，基本情况如下表所示。

2010 年 6—7 月湖南地区三家大众手机报基本情况

手机报	湘江手机报	潇湘晨报手机报	三湘手机报
基于报刊/网站	长沙晚报/星辰在线	潇湘晨报/红网	三湘都市报/湖南在线
模式	彩信	彩信	彩信
发布周期/时间	周一至五早晚各一报 公务员版 07：30—08：30 新闻版 17：00—18：00 周末一报 10：30	周一至五早晚各一报 早报 07：30—08：30 晚报 17：00—18：00 周末一报 10：30	每日一报 周一至周五 07：30—08：30 周末 10：00 周一增发财富周刊 17：30 周五增发双休刊 17：30
大小 资费	45K 左右 3 元/月	40K 左右 3 元/月	45K 左右 5 元/月
专刊 增值服务	高考特刊 南非世界杯特刊 用户俱乐部：电影券、礼品、团购、旅游等	晨报招考高考版	

同时结合相关资料可以总结出目前大众手机报竞争力提升障碍主要表现在以下四个方面：

2.1 内容质量

内容同质严重。大众手机报之间，以及与所基于的传统纸媒、网站之间，内容同质化非常严重。从对三份手机报的调查来看，三份手机报新闻内容几乎全部依附于同集团下的报刊和网站，仅是对内容做精选、改写、缩编处理。并且三份手机报之间的内容和栏目设置也大同小异。这造成极大的资源浪费，同时也削弱了手机报的竞争力。

信息容量缺乏。手机报的信息量仍无法与所基于的传统纸媒和网站匹敌。从所调查的手机报来看，其均基于彩信服务，大小普遍在 40K～50K，4～5 千字，不及传统报纸新闻版两版字数，丰富度更无法匹敌。手机单屏容量有限导致手机报内容易过度精炼、片面化，而大众手机报的内容覆盖面需求广与手机信息单条容量小的矛盾，也易造成手机报内容过度整合成摘要，碎片化，降低了可读性。而手机屏幕大小限制也导致手机报图片清晰度不高。并且虽然手机视频音频技术已成熟，但受手机内存和信息传输接收速度限制，目前仍无法在手机报中广泛使用。

2.2 受众需求

阅读习惯限制。大多数用户需重新适应手机报的翻页式、扫描式阅读方式。一是阅读需要大量翻页。目前手机屏幕普遍在 2~3 寸，每屏可显示字数为 100 字左右，阅读一份彩信手机报需翻 50 页左右；WAP 版则需不停缩放、移动页面，阅读存在极大不便；二是长篇专题报道、评论等缺失，造成习惯阅读深度新闻的用户流失。而目前手机报难长期保存、无法进行剪辑等也带来阅读困扰。

订阅服务障碍。从性价比来看，传统报纸是按订阅日开始计费，而手机报是按订阅月开始计费，订阅成本每日逐渐增高，甚至超过传统报纸。从支付方式看，传统报纸可采用传统缴费、收费方式，也可采取电话支付、移动支付、电子支付等，业务办理查询方便。但大部分手机报采取的仅是移动支付中的手机支付，业务办理查询需依赖移动设备或前往柜台。

细分需求矛盾。目前大众手机报仍是将传统报纸内容浓缩拷贝后进行普遍传播。从调查来看，三份手机报内容仅是将每期传统报纸精华摘录形成一份几千字的大杂烩，这其中可能仅百余字为用户所需。信息发展趋势在于需求细分化和内容专业化，手机报用户时常处于移动状态，无安坐品报时间，若手机报业无法在最短时间内为特定用户提供最有价值的信息将很难提升其竞争力。

2.3 传播渠道

接收性能不稳。手机报发布接收稳定性受通讯基础设施、手机终端设备等多方影响，易出现漏发、误发、错发。从彩信、WAP 两种主流传播模式看，彩信容量小，只支持特定格式内容，且须依靠彩信模式传输阅读，笔者在调查期曾尝试停机半日，复通后三份手机报全出现网络连接失败、无法接收现象；且接收时间均有三天限制，超时接收也失败。而 WAP 模式排队等待页面显示耗时长，受通信信号影响非常大，容易出现断线。

安全性能难保。手机报的传输接收是基于用户提供的手机号，私密性的资料将不可避免被传送到无线信息平台公开、广泛传播。这直接导致个人隐私被破坏，也易为他人利用，传送垃圾、病毒信息而损害用户利益，也造成手机报的大众传播功能和手机私人通讯功能的矛盾。例如工信部宣布从 2010 年 9 月 1 日起正式实施的手机用户实名登记制度对手机报用户隐私的负面影响值得重视。

2.4 运营方式

三方地位失衡。据调查显示，手机报经营全国模式的利润分成比例为报社 18%、移动通信商 40%、网络运营商 42%；地方模式中由移动通信商兼后者，报社与移动通信商一般是五五分成或四六分成。三方利润分成比例悬殊，且手机报的价格高低与否、发行通畅与否等几乎为后两者操控，报社没有话语权，这势必削弱作为内容提供商的报社参与积极性。

多头管理失调。手机报内容属新闻宣传部门管理，移动通信和网络运营却属信息产业部管辖，可能导致管理部门间意见不一和管理程序复杂，降低行政管理效率，甚至产生新的矛盾与问题。

行业沟通障碍。目前大部分手机报都是各自为政，手机报间信息沟通存在障碍，很难交流融合、互利进步，内容、技术等方面提升滞后。且不少大众手机报为丰富内容，大量转载网络和其他纸媒信息，如监管不严，易造成虚假新闻再传播、版权纠纷等弊端。

2.5 赢利模式

手机报一般采取以下三种模式赢利：一是对短信、彩信定制用户收取包月订阅费；二是对 WAP 网站浏览用户采取流量计费；三是采取发布广告赢利。

订阅收入为主。目前手机报仍以订阅费和流量费为主营收入，而调查三份手机报则均采取订阅制。手机报市场还处于拓展期，靠订阅费和流量费的利润十分有限。且从内容来说，手机报之间，手机报与其他媒体内容同质非常高，加上互联网普遍免费提供形式，手机报订阅群难稳定，这一定程度制约了订阅费和流量费的利润提升。

广告赢利较低。一是广告数量少，手机报靠广告赢利份额低。所调查三份手机报每期广告均在 2—3 种，都为单一图片格式，且广告位赢利收入较弱，无法与传统纸媒广告匹敌。二是广告投放缺乏针对性。所调查的三份手机报广告均采取订户全覆盖来实现广告目标，缺乏针对性，对于非需求订户这是垃圾信息，而对于广告商，广告费用也白白浪费。

增值收入缺乏。增值服务是手机报作为新媒体能大展身手的一亮点，也是手机报一大潜在利润点，既可获得定制收益，也可得到商家支持，还能建立稳定用户群。但从调查的三份手机报来看，其优势并没有得到显现，仅《湘江手机报》通过用户俱乐部提供电影券、旅游信息、团购等增值服务。

3　提升大众手机报竞争力的途径

3.1　生产要素：把握内容为王

内容挖掘手段灵活，牢握创新源头。大众手机报信息可通过现场采集、平面及立体媒体转载多方获得。但创新却是手机报建设强势品牌的核心：灵活挖掘资源，增加独家新闻比例；对信息进行交互性、可选性等二次改造，提升内容吸引力；利用手机媒体的优势，借助多媒体资源强化视听，增强新闻表现形式。

内容制作团队独立，加强人才储备。目前大部分大众手机报制作团队仍未与纸媒团队分离，因此，只有建立独立专业的采编制作团队和运作管理体系，才能改变大众手机报为传统报纸附属品的现状，获得健康快速发展。从调查看，《潇湘晨报》已率先在时尚生活方面成立了专业手机报制作团队。

内容服务模式个性，打造服务基础。个性服务是提升大众手机报竞争力的有力面。大众手机报，可利用手机媒体快捷迅速特点，尝试全天滚动播报，实现新闻实时更新；可根据所在地域、用户阶层等，提供相关出行、购物、餐饮等方面生活资讯服务，例如《湘江手机报》就从最初单一的"公务员版"发展到"公务员版"、"新闻版"和"周末版"，随时穿插大量便民咨询；在高考、2010 年足球世界杯期间不定时提供系列专题报道。

3.2　需求市场：力求读者至上

提高互动性。采用多元的互动模式，实现手机报与用户紧密联系，发掘潜在赢利点：为用户提供参与新闻进行评论、爆料突发新闻的平台，从而得到及时独家的新闻素材；鼓励用户对手机报内容制作等各方面进行好用度反馈，从中获得改进意见建议，发掘读者需要，及时更改。例如《湘江手机报》建立了"自由联盟、互动专区"，时刻跟进读者需求。与订户互动实现双赢成为可能。

细分用户群。进行市场细分、精准营销。菲利普·科特勒在《营销管理》一书中提到："市场细分"最终层次是"细分到个人"、"定制营销"和"一对一营销"。因此，在内容个性服务的基础上，可对手机报内容进行针对性的整合分类，为用户提供栏目选择权，采用短信或在线方式进行定制，将用户选择的各项服务进行重组，形成一份量身定制的手机报。真正实现新闻内容、风格等方面个性化展现，体现手机媒体自身特色，提升用户忠诚度，更可为广告商提供需求信息数据库，实现与广告商的互动，构建手机报核心竞争力。

灵活定价法。赢利模式应多元化发展，3G 时代，手机传输和容量等技术逐渐突破瓶颈，以广告增值收益为主、订阅费为辅的手机报赢利模式将成为主流。适当在手机报中增加广告和增值服务、提高定制功能：通过为广告商提供更多平台从中获得广告位收益；通过有针对性地为特定用户提供定制资讯，提升定制收入。增加增值服务、按定制收费利于提升用户阅读价值，也利于广告商精准宣传，更有利于手机报独特价值体现以及读者群的稳定扩大，使得其赢利最大化。

3.3　相关和支持性产业：建立优势网络

内部三方协作。报社、移动通信商、网络运营商是一个统一利益体，三方应树立协作共赢的"统一战线"思想，在明确各自角色定位的同时，整合资源、协调运作，形成稳定高效、完善合理的手机报产业链，提升手机报综合竞争力。例如为满足市场需求，报社应强化内容建设，不断贴近市场需求，确保内容及时、准确、合法；跟进多元化渠道和多样化终端发展步伐，适时推出增值服务。移动运营商应关注渠道建设管理，强调用户隐私保护，保证手机报传输接收稳定性，降低内容失真率和误差值；不断降低成本，以优惠价格服务用户，获得更广阔读者群。网络运营商应重视建设与维护手机报系统平台、保障网络安全，与其他两方保持沟通联系，对反映的投诉和故障问题及时处理。

对外与纸媒互补。作为新媒体的手机报诞生，并不代表传统纸媒的消亡。大众手机报兼容了纸媒与移动设备共同优势。纸媒在内容采集、制作、服务等拥有成熟模式，拥有稳定用户群和专业人才资源。纸媒也可通过借鉴新技术、新业态、新经验进行多元化发展。纸媒对新闻的把握及处理能力，以及整个新闻网络资源的价值在新媒体时代仍然十分重要。因此手机报可以参考传统纸媒已有模式，利用强大的采编技术基础，借助读者和人才资源基础进行创新发展。

3.4　企业：实现媒体"共赢"

手机报间合作。手机报行业在良性竞争同时需重视合作，构建行业信息资源平台，紧跟国家政策，适时调整发展策略，积极进行渠道优化、硬件革新等，开发多层次、多形态的内容产品和增值服务业务，共同向手机报产业链深度开拓。在推进手机报发展的同时，促进数字出版的进步。例如，在新闻资源利用上，通过构建共享平台，实现新闻资源一次采集、多方多元利用。在简化流程、提升效率、便于管理、节约资源的同时，有效提升新闻资源的附加值。

多媒体间融合。3G 时代，短信、彩信手机报将成为过去，WAP 及未来集成视听、综合多平台、具有交互功能的流媒体模式手机报将成为主流，未雨绸缪，需要多媒体间相互沟通合作，共同打造 3G 时代手机报畅通发展平台。但是大众手机报相较其他手机报受众更为广泛，面对的接收载体、读者素质等参差不齐。因此不应一味追求技术发展而忽视技术适应性，例如，在础设施不完善、人们购买力低下的偏远地区，手机报高端传输显示模式无法适用。

3.5　机会：抓住时代脉搏

借助技术机遇。利用前沿的通信技术、网络技术、多媒体技术等进行手机报创新改造，不断适应社会需求。如今 3G 建设方兴未艾，利用 3G 平台，手机报实现多媒体信息高速、稳定、大规模传输成为可能。但并且 3G 技术弊端也不容忽视。例如：据人民网通信频道 2010 年 6 月所做"阻碍 3G 普及因素"调查显示，"资费过高"、"终端不丰富"是目前阻碍 3G 发展的两大瓶颈，占调查者比例达 80.21%、74.77%，这也是制约 3G 手机报发展的障碍。因此在抓住 3G 发展机遇同时，也需高度重视、警惕发展阻碍因素，扬长避短，使手机报用户实现低资费、稳定高速上网、获取高质量多媒体实时信息。

3.6 政府：影响不可漠视

完善监管，重视版权。不断加强手机报业及其相关产业政策研究，及时出台相关政策，明确内容提供商、移动运营商和技术供应商三方的权利与义务，协调三方面的利益，鼓励良性竞争、限制过度集中；设立专门的监管机构，建立完善的手机报准入审查和质量审核制度，监管和规范手机报的内容，保障质量和传输安全，确保手机报业繁荣有序，健康快速发展；积极修订适合数字时代发展环境的相关法律法规，协调各方利益。积极建立中国报业信息网络传播权保护联盟，设立许可和付费等制度，加强手机报内容的知识产权保护，提倡创新、打击盗版侵权、畅通申诉渠道，保护手机报参与者合法利益。

重视教育，培育人才。大力培育数字时代所需的数字出版、网络技术、通信行业人才，与国外数字出版人积极交流、沟通、借鉴，提高手机报从业人员的素质。通过树立人才兴业、人才强业思想，培养高技能、多元型领军人才投入行业发展，强化手机报内容的实用性、多元性，提升手机报传输的时效性、安全性，推动手机报社会效益、经济效益"双丰收"，促进数字出版产业发展。

参考文献

[1] 迈克尔·波特，李明轩，邱如美. 国家竞争优势 [M]. 北京：华夏出版社，2002

[2] 匡文波. 手机媒体概论 [M]. 北京：中国人民大学出版社，2006

[3] 陈昕. 美国数字出版考察报告 [M]. 上海：上海人民出版社，2008

[4] 菲利普·科特勒，梅清豪. 营销管理 [M]. 上海：上海人民出版社，2007

[5] 苏兴秋. 报业如何应对新媒体的挑战 [M]. 广州：南方日报出版社，2007

[6] 郝振省. 2007—2008 中国数字出版产业年度报告 [M]. 北京：中国书籍出版社，2008

[7] 赵子忠. 内容产业论—数字新媒体的核心 [M]. 北京：中国传媒大学出版社，2005

[8] 李松岭. 传媒经济理论研究 [M]. 湖南：湖南大学出版社，2008

[9] 董璐. 媒体营销—数字时代的传媒动力学 [M]. 北京：北京大学出版社，2009

[10] 田中阳，王海刚. 3G 时代湖南手机报发展对策研究——湖南手机报市场调查报告 [J]. 湖南师范大学社会科学学报，2009，(6)：130-135

[11] 小竹. 一项调查显示：受惠国家产业政策 手机报发展进入黄金期 [J]. 中国出版，2010，(7)

[12] 武文颖. 手机报未来发展趋势探讨 [J]. 新闻战线，2009，(2)

[13] CNNIC. 第 26 次中国互联网络发展状况统计报告 [R]. 北京：中国互联网络信息中心，2010

[14] 易观国际. 2010 年第 1 季度中国手机阅读市场季度监测 [R]. 北京：易观国际，

2010

[15] 易观国际. 2010 年移动互联网用户对手机阅的内容类别的选择 ［R］. 北京：易观
国际，2010

[16] 中华人民共和国新闻出版总署. 新闻出版业"十一五"发展规划 ［EB/OL］.
http://www.gapp.gov.cn/cms/html/41/571/200711/449958.html. 2007-11-12

[17] 中华人民共和国新闻出版总署. 全国报纸出版业"十一五"发展纲要 ［EB/OL］.
http://www.gapp.gov.cn/cms/html/285/2236/200608/667871.html. 2006-8-11

作者简介

李茜，武汉大学信息管理学院 2009 届本科毕业生。

杨威，武汉大学信息管理学院 2009 级硕士研究生。

手机杂志的 SWOT 分析及发展对策

许斐然

（武汉大学信息管理学院　武汉　430072）

摘要：本文就在简要介绍了手机杂志的含义、阅读方式和发展现状等一些情况之后，运用 SWOT 分析法，探讨和分析了手机杂志从内容到服务的自身优势和劣势、发展中面临的宏观和微观的生态环境、可利用的机会和威胁，并根据分析与考察，从行业规范、产业链整合、杂志内容设计和赢利模式等方面提出相应的发展对策与建议。

关键词：SWOT 分析法　手机杂志　发展对策

The SWOT Analysis of Mobile Magazine and Development Countermeasure

Xu Feiran

（School of Information Management，Wuhan University，Wuhan，430072）

Abstract：This paper probes into the Strengths，Weaknesses，Opportunities and Threats of Mobile magazine with SWOT analysis．The author gives some suggestions to development of Mobile magazine．

Keywords：SWOT analysis　Mobile magazine　Countermeasure

1　手机杂志及其发展现状

随着无线网络技术的进步，3G 时代的到来，手机智能化的应用，手机杂志开始越来越多地被认识和了解。所谓手机杂志，就是用手机看的杂志，它是应用无线网络技术，以手机为载体，接收由服务商定期发布的集"图、文、音频、视频"等多媒体内容，可供用户在线或离线阅读的电子杂志，它也是传统杂志的数字化形式之一。据有关统计，目前国内手机杂志已超过 300 种，其中多数为传统杂志的手机数字版，另外还有一些服务商制作发行的专门的手机杂志。目前，用手机阅读杂志的方式主要有：一、通过手机登录杂志网站在线阅读；二、用户订阅，由代理服务商定期发送杂志到用户的手机上；三、用手机连接互联网，下载杂志在手机上离线阅读；四、安装专门的阅读软件进行阅读。现阶段，手机杂志的目标用户基本是 20—45 岁的白领阶层，常订阅的手机杂志的内容主要集中在时尚类、生活资讯类、时政财经类等，阅读手机杂志已经成为现在都市生活的一种时尚。

2 手机杂志的 SWOT 分析

SWOT 分析法，又称为态势分析法，是欧美国家在战略管理和规划领域广泛应用的主流分析工具。各字母的含义是：S 指企业内部的优势因素；W 指企业内部的劣势因素；O 指企业外部环境的机会因素；T 指企业外部环境的威胁（挑战）因素。这种分析方法是将与研究对象密切相关的各种主要内部优势、劣势、机会和威胁等列举出来，进行全面系统的分析、评价和考察。

2.1 优势分析（S）

2.1.1 阅读便利

手机杂志是以手机为载体和接收终端的，手机媒体自身所具备的贴身性、轻巧、携带方便等特性，在成就了手机杂志可随时随地阅读的便利性的同时，也致使手机杂志内容呈现的"短小精悍"，又正是这种信息编辑的简短方便性，便于用户及时地、有效地获取所需要的信息，保证了获取信息的便利。这种阅读与获取信息的便利性，也使得手机杂志的阅读可以突破时间的限制，用户可以利用碎片时间实现阅读。这也正是手机阅读的最大优势，即突破传统阅读在时间上的较高要求，使用户能进行轻松、随意的阅读。

2.1.2 内容具有多媒体特征

相比于传统纸媒介只能承载文字和图形，手机这种媒介则具备可以承载动画、音频、视频等多媒体内容的优势，手机阅读能够借助多媒体，如有声文学、Flash、动漫等形式提升客户的阅读体验。现阶段，手机杂志内容的实现是依托传统媒体及现有互联网媒体为主要内容源，针对手机杂志特点及用户细分需求进行内容的二次加工和开发。得益于手机智能化和 3G 的多种应用，使得手机杂志的内容可以集成文字、图像、声频、视频多媒体信息，在给用户带来生动阅读体验的同时，也体现了手机杂志内容所具备的多媒体特征。

2.1.3 阅读成本的相对低廉和阅读效率的相对高效

传统杂志尤其是高端时尚杂志的价格普遍较高，而随着电信资费的价格水平不断降低，手机阅读的成本也不断降低。以 3G 门户网站为例，5 元/月就可以享受 100MB 网络流量，这个流量足以实现手机在线阅读至少 5 本 10 万字的小说。同时手机阅读还精简了一些发行中间环节，有效地降低了成本。另一方面，现在的智能手机手机都具备搜索和内容定制功能，用户可以根据自己的需要自主定制杂志内容和信息，并可利用手机搜索随时获取所需，极大提高了人们的阅读效率。

2.1.4 互动性强及服务个性化

手机杂志阅读的平台搭建是基于无线网络的开放、互动性，所以手机杂志服务商就可以组建互动阅读社区，也可以实现杂志栏目作者与读者的互动交流。同时基于这种良好互动性，手机杂志可以根据客户的个性特征一对一地发送各种有针对性的内容，用户也可自主选择和定制杂志的栏目和内容。手机杂志服务商也可以根据用户个性信息，提供杂志社区，自主定制内容等个性化服务。

2.1.5 用户接受度高

现阶段的手机杂志大多是传统杂志的手机版，或是通信运营商特制的信息服务式杂志，而原有杂志出版商大多也是为读者所熟悉的，通过手机发布的杂志内容也是据同名纸质杂志的摘选或全部使用，这也就使手机杂志具有原有杂志的品牌特性，可信度也就相对较高，易于被用户接受。

2.2 劣势分析（W）

2.2.1 阅读门槛高

手机杂志是集成多媒体信息一种 3G 应用，它要求作为载体的手机必须支持无线上网和彩信服务，这也就把很多手机用户挡在了门外。再者，任何一种用手机阅读杂志的方式，都必然要求用户支付两种费用，即杂志的阅读许可费和无线上网流量费。这些因素都无形中提高了手机杂志阅读的门槛。

2.2.2 手机媒体自身属性的限制

虽然手机媒介具备便利、精准传播等优势，但它自身属性的一些限制也给依赖于它的手机杂志带来了劣势。主要有：①手机屏幕的尺寸相对较小，限制了手机杂志的内容页面大小，使手机杂志内容呈现碎片化，手机杂志阅读也因此成为快餐式的浅阅读；②手机杂志的显示效果受手机分辨率和一些功能上的限制；③手机容量的大小限制了手机杂志内容的大小和用户可保存杂志的多少，这也使手机杂志很难具有收藏价值；④手机型号与配置的不同对手机杂志格式提出了不同的要求，影响了手机杂志格式标准的统一。

2.2.3 手机杂志广告容量低，对广告创意要求高

由于无线网络带宽和手机媒体在功能上的一些限制，使手机杂志自身在内容上就有一定量的限制，嵌入在其中的杂志广告就必然会受到内容容量的约束。适应手机媒体特点的手机杂志在大小、内容、效果等方面的一些限制也向手机杂志广告的创意提出了很高的要求，只有适合手机传播效果又满足手机杂志内容要求的广告创意才能达到较好的传播效果。

2.3 外部机会（O）

2.3.1 政策

国家对新媒体持鼓励政策，手机媒体作为新媒体的重要组成部分也受到国家政策的鼓励和保护。国家高度重视 3G 网络建设和《电信法》的制定及推进工作，积极营造利于手机媒体发展的基础产业环境，这些都使依托于手机媒体的手机杂志受到很大帮助。

2.3.2 技术

2009 年 1 月 7 日工业和信息化部为中国移动、中国电信和中国联通发放了三张 3G 牌照，宣告了我国 3G 元时代的开启。3G 时代的展开，高速网络宽带与无线网络技术的不断发展，各种智能手机的兴起，都预示着手机媒体在逐渐成为集通信、互联网应用、娱乐等功能于一体的多媒体接收终端。更大、更清晰的屏幕、更长的待机时间、更强大的数据传输能力都必将极大提高手机杂志的表现能力，可以说技术的不断进步在为手机杂志提供着越来越有利的发展条件。

2.3.3 用户规模

据我国工信部最新数据显示，中国手机用户已经达到 6.4 亿，中国互联网信息中心（CNNIC）于 2009 年 8 月进行的调查显示，中国手机网民占到整体手机使用人数的34.2%，总规模达到 1.8 亿，并且还保持着持续的增长之势。6.4 亿手机用户及近 2 亿的手机网民为手机杂志提供了广泛的潜在用户资源。根据艾瑞咨询公司发布的报告显示，手机杂志已经成为了手机用户最常订阅的内容，在运营商资源的有效推广下，2010 年手机杂志用户预计将突破 9 000 万。

2.3.4 阅读需求与阅读习惯

时代的进步，技术的发展，促成了新媒体势力的迅速扩张。人们的阅读习惯也随着阅读环境而改变，快节奏的生活也使得人们对资讯的即时需求不断上升。特别是年轻一代新兴消费群体的兴起，他们追随新技术新媒体的脚步，崇尚个性化、互动式的轻松阅读体验。这样的群体正是具备多媒体功能的手机杂志的服务对象，为他们带去丰富的阅读体验，他们较强的付费阅读意愿也为手机杂志应用的扩展创造了机会。

2.3.5 服务商的推动

手机杂志媒体价值的显现，促使了服务商的参与，而各服务商的推动也为手机杂志的进一步发展创造了机会。作为内容提供商的传统媒体，其优质的内容源为满足用户对手机杂志的细分阅读需求提供了保障；强势的移动运营商以资费下调和套餐服务的方式，为手机杂志带来了阅读的便利和成熟的收费系统；而平台技术服务商则通过各种阅读软件的升级，为手机杂志的发布提供着良好的平台环境；手机终端厂商也通过研制和开发更加智能化的手机，为手机杂志提供硬件支持。

2.4 外部威胁（T）

2.4.1 市场有待完善

手机杂志是在手机阅读兴起的大势之下有所发展的，受到关注的时间还不是很长。目前，只是少量的传统杂志涉足，更多的是一些阅读软件的开发商在推动，杂志出版的通用标准和规范还都没有形成，软件商也是各自为政，有待规范。手机杂志固定的读者群也还没有完全形成，现在的用户多是从手机上网用户中分流出来的一部分。手机杂志的市场还处在培育期，市场规范、竞争机制等都还有待建立和完善。

2.4.2 产业链尚未构建完全

手机杂志的产业链相对复杂，有内容提供商、移动运营商、平台开发商、手机终端厂商等主体。移动运营商原有的用户、资金、运营经验、传播渠道和结算优势都有助于其成为产业链上的领导者。但手机杂志同时又是内容为王的应用，内容提供商发挥关键作用。而在产业发展初期，平台开发商依靠阅读软件聚集了大量内容，已经占据了先发优势。还有终端厂商也在通过各种手段增加其在手机阅读市场的竞争力。目前，各方主体都还出于自身利益的考虑，未能形成有序统一的产业链。

2.4.3 赢利模式尚不清晰

当前适用的手机杂志的赢利模式主要有个人收费模式和广告模式，但由于多数用户付费习惯还未形成，据易观国际的调查，用户可接受的收费的手机应用中，手机阅读仅占8.8%，这就使向用户收费模式受到限制。而广告模式也受到广告主投放意愿不强，广告占用用户阅读流量等的限制。另外，由于产业链的不够完备统一，对其他有效赢利模式的开发还处在探索阶段。

2.4.4 版权问题

很多传统杂志的电子版在互联网上可以从多种渠道获取，而手机杂志也类似于此，未经过授权就发布的不占少数，这些资源被平台开发商利用，一些传统杂志也因其宣传广告效应而没有严格追究版权问题。而市场监管上的不力，也助长了这些问题的存在。但随着手机杂志市场的发育，版权意识的增强，这些遗留问题必将成为未来发展的隐患，容易引起版权纠纷。

2.4.5　安全、文化问题

手机具有很强的私人性，包含个人真实信息的记录，手机杂志用户在参与社区互动的时候，或是链接杂志上的电子商务在线支付的时候，都会涉及用户隐私和信息安全的问题。另外，有可能会因为手机杂志的下载而导致手机病毒的传播，威胁手机安全使用。手机杂志作为一种阅读型的应用，它也具备着一定的社会责任，但其传播的互动性，用户发布内容的个性化等，都会在不同程度上影响所传播内容的文化性，阅读环境的健康程度也会受到威胁。

在综合分析了手机杂志的优劣势、机会与威胁因素的基础上，构建 SWOT 分析矩阵，如表 1 所示。

表 1　手机杂志 SWOT 分析矩阵

	优势（S）	劣势（W）
内部条件	1. 阅读便利 2. 内容具有多媒体特征 3. 阅读成本相对低廉与阅读效率相对高效 4. 互动性强服务个性化 5. 用户接受度高	1. 阅读门槛高 2. 手机媒体自身属性的限制 3. 手机杂志广告容量低，对广告创意要求高
	机会（O）	威胁（T）
外部环境	1. 技术 2. 政策 3. 服务商 4. 阅读需求与阅读习惯 5. 用户规模	1. 市场有待完善 2. 产业链尚未构建完全 3. 赢利模式尚不清晰 4. 版权问题 5. 安全、文化问题

3　手机杂志的发展对策

通过对手机杂志进行 SWOT 分析，我们可以看到，虽然手机杂志发展面临的机会和威胁几乎对等，但手机杂志自身的优势明显多于劣势，可以采取以下对策利用机会、发挥优势，克服劣势、回避威胁。

3.1　制定适用的市场规范和标准

手机媒体作为一种新兴媒体广受社会关注，手机杂志作为以手机为载体的应用，其市场规范和发布标准等是可以以手机媒体出版的相关规范运行的。政府应在市场规范的过程中发挥引导作用，并由行业协商制定各方共赢的市场规范和相关标准。从而规避因手机杂志阅读软件开发商各自为政、标准不一而造成的市场混乱，保障市场的有序合理。还应对手机杂志的内容进行一定的约束，以保证传播内容的健康；另外还需制定相关条例保证用户隐私和信息安全。良好的标准和规范是规避风险，应对安全、市场不完善的威胁的行之有效的对策。

3.2　整合和完善手机杂志产业链

产业链整合是应对当前产业链不完善，产业主体间不合作状况而应采取的对策。在产业链整合过程中，应以合作共赢为基本原则。产业链各方应突出差异化优势，通过战略联营，为用户提供更好的产品和服务。最终用户才是产业价值链的终点，手机杂志只有满足用户的需求，拥有持续的竞争力，才能更好地为用户所接受。通过产业链的整合，内容提供商与应用服务商间的授权合作，才可以规避不必要的版权纠纷，降低经营风险。

3.3 灵活计费，实现多元化赢利模式

赢利模式是服务商的利润来源，也是产业得以维持的最重要因素，探索和创新赢利模式就必然是手机杂志刻不容缓的发展对策。移动运营商应为用户提供如按本、按次、会员制、免费服务专区等灵活多样的支付方式，来改进内容收费模式。对广告模式而言，应通过多样化的，既能提升广告效果又易于用户接受的广告形式与有针对性的营销将信息传递给受众。通过对现有赢利模式的改进，开创新的赢利点。除了这两种模式之外，手机杂志可采取的赢利模式还有电子商务，通过手机杂志上显示商品的链接，实现手机首销，从中获得利润分成。另外还可以通过互动业务的开展，调动用户主动参与的积极性，逐渐培养他们运用手机媒体主动选择信息、娱乐的消费习惯。

3.4 完善内容设计，克服自身限制，体现个性化优势

作为一种阅读性的应用，在手机杂志的发展中，内容是关键。手机媒体的自身属性成就了手机杂志的相对优势，也带来了一些不足，所以就需要通过对手机杂志内容进行个性化设计来弥补这些不足。手机的数字化技术将有助于满足用户对更为个性化的信息的需求，通过充分利用现有技术，完善手机杂志内容的设计，打造量身定做的，符合手机特点和用户特征的杂志内容。采用多媒体的表现形式，增加杂志的可读性，以更加个性化的内容吸引用户，丰富其阅读体验。

参考文献

[1] 匡文波，王权. 手机媒体发展的三大趋势 [J]. 传媒. 2010 (5)：59

[2] 李姗姗. 论 3G 时代下手机杂志之生态环境 [J]. 新闻世界. 2010 (1)：168–169

[3] 罗创东. 手机：方寸之间开辟媒介新天地 [J]. 信息科技. 2009 (10)：34

[4] 马凌，丁琳. 基础创新扩散理论的手机杂志发展策略 [J]. 出版发行研究. 2010 (2)：22–23

[5] 陈旭. 手机杂志：广告营销价值新高地 [J]. 传媒. 2009 (12)：58–59

[6] 艾瑞咨询集团. 2009 中国手机媒体价值研究报告 [EB/OL]. 2009.06

[7] 高娟. VIVA CEO 韩颖："手机杂志"将成 3G 业务亮点应用 [EB/OL]. [2010–02–27]. http://www.cww.net.cn/zhuanfangjian/html/2009/4/28/200942894806964.htm

[8] 国内手机杂志发展：核心竞争是技术 [EB/OL]. [2010–3–2]. http://www.chinairn.com/doc/70310/202310.html

[9] 贺世铭，孙运凡. 手机杂志的未来猜想：人人皆媒体 [J]. 传媒. 2009 (12)：57

[10] 项立刚. 2009 中国手机媒体的元年 [J]. 信息系统工程. 2009 (2)：25

[11] 中国手机媒体研究报告. 中国互联网研究中心. 2008.12

[12] 程洁. 新数字媒介论稿 [M]. 上海：上海三联书店，2007

作者简介

许斐然，武汉大学信息管理学院出版发行学硕士研究生。

出版集团应对电子阅读器产业兴起的六个策略

李新祥

（武汉大学信息管理学院　武汉　430072）

摘要：电子阅读器作为一种新型阅读媒介，目前还存在诸多缺陷和限制，但作为一种产业，其兴起却已经成为事实并代表着一种发展趋势。本文认为，为应对电子阅读器产业的兴起，以出版传统纸质图书为主业的我国出版集团可采取六个策略：管理创新策略、人才建设策略、产品整合策略、新品开发策略、搭建平台策略和掌握定制策略。

关键词：出版集团　电子阅读器　出版产业

The Coping Strategy of the Rising of E-reader Industry for Publishing Group

Li Xinxiang

（Information Management School, Wuhan University, Wuhan, 430072）

Abstract: Although e-reader still exist some defects and limitations, e-reader industry's rising has already become a reality and represents a trend. This paper discusses six strategies for publishing groups in China which adhere to the traditional p-book industry to take in order to deal with the rising of e-reader industry, including management innovation, talent training, product integration, new-product development, platform building, terminal customization.

Keywords: Publishing group　E-reader　Publishing industry

　　电子阅读器作为一种新型阅读媒介，目前还存在诸多缺陷和限制，但作为一种产业，其兴起却已经成为事实并代表着一种发展趋势。2009 年全球大约有 400 万电子图书阅读器出售。美国市场情报公司 iSuppli 预计，2010 年电子阅读器的销量将达到 1 200 万台，2012 年达到 1 800 万台。而据研究公司 DisplaySearch 最近一份报告的预测，2010 年中国的电子阅读器销量将从 2009 年的 80 万台跃升至 300 万台，达到全球市场的 20%。该公司进而预测，中国将借助其人口规模，在 2015 年之前超过美国成为世界最大的电子阅读器市场。[1] 据美国消费电子协会数据显示，电子阅读器市场 2009 年收入增长 265%，是发展速度最快的产品之一。NextGen 公司发布的最新报告显示，从 2008 年到 2013 年，全球电子阅读器市场将保持 124% 的年复合增长率，并将在 2013 年底突破 25 亿美元规模。[2] 对此，以出版纸质图书为主业的我国出版集团应采取哪些策略呢？本文拟就这一问题作些探讨。

1 管理创新策略：更新理念，再造业务流程

人类出版史的发展规律显示，出版技术革新是出版事业发展的核心力量。电子阅读器作为数字出版技术发展的结晶，使得数字出版拥有了巨大的阅读需求和消费潜力，这无疑会对传统纸质图书出版的生产、制作、复制、发行、消费、阅读各个环节产生了革命性的影响，对传统印刷出版造成巨大的冲击。以出版纸质图书为主业的我国出版集团不得不谋求转型。首要策略是实现管理创新，只有出版集团的管理机制能够顺应新媒介的发展，才有可能在发展中赢得主动权。

第一，更新出版理念。出版理念作为指导出版机构和出版人的准则、信念和哲学纲领，是最能代表一个出版机构外在形象的精髓，是其整个出版活动的灵魂。[3]出版集团应该明确"转变发展方式、突破增长极限"的发展主线，改变传统出版"简单扩张规模、高退货、高库存、低效益"的粗放发展模式，积极探索基于数字技术的新业务领域和形态，集团的增长重心应该转到以传统出版为基础的数字出版领域。上海世纪出版集团近几年的发展经验验证了这种理念转变的重要性。[4]

第二，再造业务流程。使用电子阅读器作为阅读终端的出版物，其出版模式将发生革命性转变，不再受到印刷（复制）、发行等环节的制约。因此，出版集团应对业务流程进行信息化、数字化、网络化的系统改造，进而向出版数字化转型。建立数字化工作流程，实现网上选题决策、网上收发稿、网上编辑等，并通过网络技术实现内外信息交流。

2 人才建设策略：内培外引，重构应对能力

人才是产业发展的根本，出版集团想适应并引领阅读器产业的发展，需要培养并储备一批复合型人才。这些人才除了具备传统的出版从业技能外，还要了解数字阅读产品的市场需求特征，并掌握制作、传输数字阅读产品的技术。具体而言，包括懂得电子阅读产品版权确认和处理的法律人才，有敏锐市场意识和操作能力的数字阅读产品项目的设计和管理人才，掌握上网检索资料和整合、加工信息的能力，熟练处理文本、照片、图表、音频、视频等数字阅读产品所必需的各种信息元素的人才，熟练运用相关软件编辑电子阅读产品的内容和形式的人才等。

培养方法主要有两种：内部培养和外部引进。内部培养，即选拔一批本单位专业素质较高的人员进行培训；外部引进，即从高等院校和其他社会机构招聘专业人才。人才队伍建设，可谓重构出版集团适应阅读器产业发展能力的核心策略。

3 产品整合策略：掌握版权，整合内容资源

当前电子阅读器产业发展遇到的瓶颈就是内容受限，内容供给还满足不了读者的阅读需求。多年的传统图书出版业务的开展，使得出版集团自然地在阅读器产业链中首先应该定位于内容提供商。既有图书产品无疑是出版集团的资源宝库，也是有效参与产业链竞合的重要"家当"。数字版权保护的糟糕现状，无疑是降低出版集团参与阅读器产业热情的重要因素。但在数字化浪潮扑面而来的当下，出版集团只能积极面对，不可消极等待。做好既有产品的有效整合，演好内容提供商的角色，是出版集团的第一选择。

第一，掌握既有产品的版权。出版集团应该积极地与其他阅读器产业链主体共同推动尽快建立和完善适用于数字出版领域版权保护的相关制度。比如，应制定统一的数字版权保护标准，尝试建立著作权补偿金制度等。更为重要的是，即便是在现有法律框架下，出版集团也应该做好既有图书产品的数字版权的确认工作。哪怕与作者补签合同所费精力较大，也不应该轻易放弃既有产品内容的数字版权。电子阅读器产业刚刚兴起，出版集团直接提供既有内容尚没有很好的赢利预期。但不可否认，这些既有产品是阅读器产业成熟之后的宝贵资源，是一座有待开发的金矿。

第二，提高内容的数字化水平。出版集团应将所有图书进行数字化处理，为今后进一步开发电子书、手机阅读等各类数字阅读产品做好准备。在现有内容资源数字化的基础上，建立数字资产管理系统，加强多媒体内容的开发工作。出版集团应该以拥有自主知识产权的内容资源积极开发数字化数据检索服务平台，占领专业用户市场。比如，上海世纪出版集团就开发了系列数字阅读产品，包括在线普教系统、在线工具书编纂平台和若干大型数据库（如辞海、英汉大词典、牛津英语大词典、"SKY"标准生物医药资源数据库、历史文献知识库等）。

出版是以内容为基础的文化产业，无论是数字出版还是传统出版，谁掌握了内容，谁就掌握了竞争的主动权。出版集团在长期的发展中积累了丰富的内容资源，但必须看到，这些资源现有的数字化水平和开发程度还远远不能适应电子阅读器产业发展的需要。出版集团要想在即将到来的内容产业时代继续保持主导地位，就必须做好既有内容资源的整合。[5]

4 新品开发策略：把握特征，创新阅读产品

目前国内的阅读器生产企业大多都欠缺内容资源的支持，如果缺少了畅销的正版图书资源支持，电子阅读器产业就会深陷产业链断层的困境。[6]这的确是一个事实。但出版集团如果就此认为阅读器生产企业"终究会求上门而守株待兔"，那无异于自欺欺人。因为，电子阅读器作为一种新型出版物媒介，绝不只是纸质图书的升级，而是对以往所有出版物媒介的融合和创新。"把电子阅读器称作电纸书，将其定义为'看书'的终端，本身就是一种狭隘的理解。除了书籍，新闻、股市行情、市场报价、教材，甚至公文和考试试卷，都存在随时随地阅读的需求。这些需求所带来的市场空间，甚至可能超过书籍阅读。"[7]因此，出版集团应该在做好既有内容资源整合的基础上，摒弃出版物的既定形态的观念，着力研究并把握电子阅读器的媒介特征，着力开发新型数字阅读产品。

出版集团面对阅读器的发展趋势，应主动调整自己的定位，从传统出版物提供商转型到数字内容服务提供商。可以通过出版电子图书、增加数据业务、开展网络营销等方式充分发挥自身的内容整合优势，积极应对阅读器产业的兴起。不再把业务范围仅仅局限在纸介质上，主动求变、积极转型，形成跨媒体出版体系。可以充分利用书刊等传统介质的优势与电子媒体的优势，将书刊的传统纸介质和光盘、互联网等电子媒体捆绑结合起来，将一个主题作品用不同的媒体形式表现，增加出版物的价值，更好地满足读者的需求。具体说来，出版集团可以借助阅读器开展四方面的工作：一是建立具备一定规模的数字资源库，提供基于互联网的学术出版、文献与信息服务；二是开展优秀读物的复合出版，即纸质与数字同时出版；三是开展按需出版和定制出版业务；四是开展个性化的信息服务、知

5 平台搭建策略：合纵连横，参与产业联盟

根据《2009 电子（纸）阅读器测试报告》分析，国产电子（纸）阅读器注重功能丰富和对开放资源的适应性，而国外品牌更注重对资源平台的建设，并围绕其资源平台设计开发产品。2003 年，日本电器、出版、印刷业界等 19 家公司代表共同创立了"电子图书商业财团"，财团划分成若干功能小组广泛展开研究和实践，最终形成电子图书产业模式：图书电子数字化数据存储于超级容量数据库（平台）→网络传输、有偿下载→电子图书阅读器限时阅读。美国 Kindle 阅读器获得成功，根本原因在于亚马逊公司拥有庞大的资源平台。电子阅读产业的竞争最终将是平台和平台的竞争，这个平台以海量咨讯、精准、精确互动、辅助决策为一体。只有建立高智能化的平台，出版集团才能在电子阅读器产业链中站稳脚跟。而光靠一个出版集团进行平台建设，还不足以支撑整个电子阅读器产业的需求。平台搭建需要出版集团采取合纵连横的策略，构建产业联盟。

合纵，是指出版集团与作家、运营商、硬件厂商和技术提供商等产业链上的参与者结成联盟，共同研究解决基于中文的格式标准、版权保护标准、定价原则，由联盟来推动政府进行立法和提供资金扶持，形成一个各参与者共赢的商业模式。连横，则指出版集团与出版社、出版集团及其他内容提供商结成联盟，搭建内容更为丰富的资源平台。

最近，国内酝酿成立了多个类似的产业联盟。北京出版集团发起成立数字出版产业联盟，广东数字出版企业共同发起成立数字出版产业联合会，盛大文学推出 OPOB（One Person，One Book）战略。对出版集团而言，对此类联盟的态度应该是积极参与，而不是消极旁观。电子阅读器产业是一个需要长期发展的产业，大家联手形成合力，方能共享发展成果。

6 终端定制策略：推出阅读器，打通产业链

由出版集团主导研发电子阅读器，而非由设备制造商推出，意味着出版集团可以突破行业壁垒，以内容的优势打通行业产业链，将数字出版从"技术引领"转向"内容主导"。应该说，拥有完整的产业链是数字阅读产业决胜的关键，谁整合了完整产业链，谁就掌握了行业未来。

目前已有多家出版集团试水，推出了自己的电子阅读器。上海世纪出版集团推出"辞海电纸悦读器"，并将开发出大屏幕阅读器、平板电脑、"电子书包"、电脑辞典等不同载体形式的系列产品。辽宁出版集团推出了大屏幕彩色阅读器、"掌上书房"黑白显示阅读器、"电子书包"和"电子乐谱"等四种阅读产品。此外，甘肃读者出版集团推出"读者电纸书"、中国出版集团也成立了关于电子阅读器技术的子公司。

当然，终端技术是出版集团的短板，定制终端会加大运营成本。目前出版集团定制电子阅读器时机是否成熟还需市场进一步考察。[9]不过，对于那些志在做大做强并拥有内容优势的出版集团来说，定制终端无疑是一种正确的策略选择。

总之，整个电子阅读器产业的源头是数字阅读产品的内容。"当前，服务平台、网络运营商、终端都开发出了金矿，只有产业链条中最重要的内容创造者收益最少。"[10]出版集团应采取合理的策略，积极参与，共同实现电子阅读器产业的美好愿景。

注释

[1] Juliet. 中国电子阅读器市场前景看好 [EB/OL]. http://blog. sina. com. cn/s/blog_5db68bfd0100h08b. html. 2010-01-18.

[2] 吴刚. 电子书"翻开"商机无限 [EB/OL]. http://www. 21cbh. com/HTML/2009-12-24/159233. html. 2009-12-24.

[3]《中国大百科全书》总编委会. 中国大百科全书（第3卷）[M]. 北京：中国大百科全书出版社，2009：574.

[4] 陈熙涵. "电纸辞海"为数字出版树标杆 [N]. 文汇报，2010-04-10（1）.

[5] 祁庭林. 传统出版该如何应对数字出版的挑战 [J]. 编辑之友，2007（4）：6.

[6] 霍光. 缺少畅销正版资源，电子阅读距黎明还差一步 [EB/OL]. http://www. done-ws. com/it/201005/93606. shtm. 2010-05-24.

[7] 宗仪. 电子书市场烽烟四起 [N]. 大连日报，2010-04-18：B01.

[8] 祁庭林. 传统出版该如何应对数字出版的挑战 [J]. 编辑之友，2007（4）：6.

[9] 易观. 出版社不应急于进入电子阅读器市场 [EB/OL]. http://www. enfodesk. com/SMinisite/index/articledetail-type_id-1-info_id-4519. html. 2010-05-13.

[10] 刘扬. 电纸书新赛季喜忧参半 [EB/OL]. http://tech. sina. com. cn/i/2010-04-01/14254012464. shtml. 2010-04-01.

作者简介

李新祥，武汉大学信息管理学院 2009 级出版发行学专业博士研究生，浙江传媒学院新闻与文化传播学院编辑出版系副教授。

移动数字阅读：走差异化竞争之路

张 炯

（湖北第二师范学院文学院　武汉　430205）

摘要：移动数字阅读是一种创新的阅读形式，吸引了众多企业和消费者的目光。本文对移动数字阅读的产品类型进行了区分，将其分为电子阅读器、手机终端和其他终端，并对各种产品类型的国内市场现状做了简要介绍。文章从用户、价格、内容和技术四个方面的竞争入手，论证了移动数字阅读走差异化竞争之路的必要性，并提出了针对不同产品类型的差异化竞争构想，即电子阅读器的专业化之路、手机阅读的大众化之路和其他阅读终端的个性化之路。

关键词：数字阅读　移动终端　差异化竞争

移动出版与电子书刊

Portable Digital-reading: Differential Marketing Competition Strategy

Zhang Jiong

（School of Liberal Arts, Hubei University of Education, Wuhan, 430205）

Abstract: Portable digital-reading is a new way of reading in the society, absorbs many corporations and consumers. This paper divides the portable digital-reading products into e-book reader, mobile phone and other terminals, then briefly introduces the current domestic market situation of every products. The article analyzes the competition of four aspects including users, price, contents and technology, which demonstrates the necessity of differential marketing competition strategy. Then the author give several specific strategies, such as the specialization strategy for the e-book reader, the popular strategy for the mobile phone reading and the personalization strategy for the other terminals reading.

Keywords: Digital-reading Mobile terminal Differential marketing competition

数字出版产业是一个朝阳产业，也是我国今后将重点发展的五大文化产业之一。移动数字阅读作为数字出版产业的新业态，正以迅猛的速度开拓市场，无论是图书还是报纸杂志，都可以通过数字化终端一手掌握。这种创新的阅读形式，不仅让读者享受到随时随地、方便快捷的阅读乐趣，而且也吸引了众多的关注目光。短短几年时间，国内外包括出版商、网络书店、通信运营商、IT企业等在内的一大批机构纷纷涉足该领域，数字出版产业出现群雄逐鹿的局面。

1　移动数字阅读的产品类型

数字化阅读是未来的发展趋势，便携式、可移动的数字阅读产品是推动这一进程的重要动力。目前，可以实现移动数字阅读的产品有电子阅读器、手机、MP4 播放器、PDA、PSP 游戏机等，它们凭借各自的优势在数字出版市场一争高下。

电子阅读器，又名掌上阅读器或手持阅读器，是电子书的主要终端产品。自亚马逊的 Kindle 点燃电子阅读器市场以来，中国的电子阅读器制造商为占领市场制高点而展开了激烈的争夺。2009 年全球大约有 400 万电子阅读器售出，而据研究公司 DisplaySearch 最近一份报告的预测，2010 年中国的电子阅读器产品销量将跃升至 300 万台，达到全球市场的 20%。[1] 作为国产电子阅读器的代表，汉王、翰林、易博士等电子阅读器将在 2010 年继续显露峥嵘，而包括方正、联想、华为、纽曼、华旗等在内的一大批 IT 企业也将蜂拥而入，正式推出各自的电子阅读器产品。

手机是移动数字阅读的另一大终端，从《第 25 次中国互联网络发展状况统计报告》的数据中我们看到，截至 2009 年 12 月底，手机网民规模为 2.33 亿，占网民总体的 60.8%。而在手机应用方面，手机阅读仅次于手机在线聊天服务，占到总体手机网民的 75.4%，手机小说、手机报等业务已经成为手机网民的最重要应用之一。[2] 由此可见，手机终端在移动数字阅读中发挥出越来越重要的作用。

除了专门的电子阅读器和智能手机，能够阅读电子书的终端还有 MP4 播放器、PDA、PSP 游戏机等，它们将电子阅读功能作为产品的功能之一，开拓更广阔的用户市场。随着科技的进步，终端的类型会更加多样化，例如方正于 2009 年 8 月推出的业内首款创新型个人便携电子书系统——"U 阅迷你书房"，该产品采用 U 盘形式，内置电子书与阅读器，并首次将 DRM 数字版权保护技术引入移动设备，使读者摆脱固定电脑的束缚，可以在任何设备上阅读海量正版电子图书。

2　移动数字阅读走差异化竞争之路的必要性

在数字化阅读成为时髦的今天，移动数字阅读产品的开发成为一块利润丰厚的新"蛋糕"，竞食者如潮水般涌入，产业开始风生水起。随着市场竞争的加剧，抢占市场份额成为焦点，用户之争、价格之争、内容之争及技术之争日渐白热化。

2.1　用户之争

2009 年 12 月 27 日，美国亚马逊公司宣布，其电子书销量首次超过实体书的销量。这暗示着，数字阅读的用户在数量上已经超过了纸质阅读。在我国，虽然数字阅读的用户比例不及美国，但用户基础庞大，潜力非凡，近几年也出现了几何级数的增长。其中，城市白领、时尚人群是目前电子阅读产品的主要消费群体，对他们而言，可以用来阅读电子书的设备存在太多选择，从台式个人电脑（PC）到上网本（NetBook），从 MP4 播放器到 PSP 游戏机，抑或功能强大，抑或价格诱人。总之，任何一种产品想要统领市场都不是一件容易的事。

相对于用户的增长速度，各方力量吸引用户的努力更是惊人。电子阅读器经过数次更新换代，产品功能更加强大，除了基本的书籍阅读、字体缩放、翻页跳转等功能外，还具备手写批注、即时翻译、关键字检索等辅助功能，因此拥有了一批专业"书虫"。手机在电子阅读方面的功能虽说比较单一，但当阅读功能与通话、上网、娱乐等功能融为一体的时候，手机自然也获得了一部分用户的青睐。MP4 播放器、PSP 游戏机等设备也同手机一样，凭借其多媒体功能吸引了部分用户。

如果从性别、年龄、职业等角度细分用户群的话，电子阅读器、手机和 MP4 播放器等设备的用户目标将更加明确。以手机为例，中国互联网络信息中心（CNNIC）的研究表明，手机网民的男性用户更多，达到 56%；在年龄上，10 岁到 29 岁年龄段的用户分布最为集中，占到 73.2%。与整体网民相比，手机上网更多地吸引了年轻群体，在学生、公司职员、打工者中有更高的使用比例。

2.2 价格之争

随着近几年数字出版的火爆，市场竞争者越来越多，尤其是"山寨"军团加入以后，价格战可谓是一触即发。

电子阅读器之所以历经数年而未能成为大众消费的主流，价格昂贵是其主要原因。据了解，目前国内市场上大多数电子阅读器的价格都在 2 000 元以上，有的甚至高达 5 000元。相比之下，亚马逊的 Kindle 阅读器在美国的售价为 260 美元，而索尼公司最小的一款电子书阅读器售价只有 200 美元。我国电子阅读器的价格偏高的主要原因在于成本问题，包括技术成本与硬件设备成本。虽然随着市场规模的扩大，不少品牌的电子阅读器呈现降价的趋势，但与同时期市场上主流手机或者 MP4 播放器的价格相比，电子阅读器仍不占优势。

而且，国内大多电子阅读器厂商都采取了"预装图书"的方式，这实际上是将购书款转移到了产品售价中，导致价格居高不下。而手机或 MP4 播放器往往使用的是免费的网络资源，不需要向内容提供商支付任何费用，因此成本大大降低，售价更具"亲和力"。

2.3 内容之争

"数字出版看上去诱人，实际上难啃。"北京磨铁图书有限公司总裁沈浩波表示，硬件厂商们急吼吼地进场，如同没有电影票的观众先进场占座位。电影票就是电子书的内容，读者要看的是机器里的书。

虽然电子纸显示屏是电子阅读器的核心部件，但电子阅读器的灵魂在于内容。随着移动数字阅读的飞速发展，合法的数字内容将成为电子阅读器厂商竞争力的决定因素。[3] 目前，国内的正版数字资源正处于发展阶段，尽管一些电子阅读器厂商通过与出版商合作，拥有了一定数量的电子书，而且还不定期地增加资源，但却远远不能满足读者的需求。我国不少电子阅读器采取的是"终端+内容"的商业模式，其中"内容"依赖于内容供应商，即出版社。出版社有权决定将自己的数字版权卖给这家，或是那家，也有权决定电子书销售的数量及品种。针对有限的数字资源，电子阅读器厂商们必定竭力争取。以汉王为例，在汉王书城中，电子书由内容提供商定价，收入的八成归内容商，汉王仅收取二成。[4] 汉王如此斥巨资购买电子书的目的就在于用内容吸引用户，为其终端的销售打下基础。

2.4 技术之争

对于电子阅读产品来说，阅读的舒适性至关重要。随着 E-ink（电子墨水）技术的发展，电子阅读器在显示效果上已经和传统图书相似，加上手写电磁屏技术的应用，在屏幕上书写、勾画等操作也都能轻松实现。的确，电子墨水屏具有节能环保、强光可看、全视角阅读等优点，但也存在一些不足，比如只支持黑白显示、抗压性差、刷新速度慢等[5]。而手机和 MP4 播放器等设备采用的是液晶显示屏，因此避免了电子墨水屏的缺陷，但同时，手机等设备又面临着无法添加批注、无法全文检索以及功耗高等问题。

除了硬件之争，软件之争也在所难免。以数字阅读产品的格式为例，电子阅读器支持的格式多达数十种，包括常用的 TXT、HTML、PDF、DOC 等，可以实现字号的无限缩放和版式的切换。手机等设备支持的电子书格式有 TXT、UMD、JAR 等，在阅读功能上不及电子阅读器，但在其他多样化功能上更胜一筹。

针对电子阅读器的功能单一化问题，现在也有不少厂商进行了大胆创举。例如 2009 年 9 月，汉王科技推出了一款 3G 阅读器，可以接入中国移动的网络，使用户能够上网下载图书。2009 年 10 月，方正集团推出了一款与 Kindle 相似的阅读器，包含了手机接入功能，并安装了方正自己的电子图书软件。除了这些产业巨头，一些新成立的公司也不甘示弱，2010 年初，一家名为"万物青"的公司推出全球首款能打电话的电子书"毕升1"。

从这些技术之争我们可以看出，不同产品间的差异性是厂商开展竞争的前提，而这种优劣互补正好促进了数字出版市场的繁荣。

3 移动数字阅读走差异化竞争之路的构想

3.1 电子阅读器——走专业化之路

电子阅读器的用户往往是阅读量较大的读者，譬如教师、学者、研究人员等，这是一个成熟的消费群体，拥有较高的学历和稳定的收入，对知识的需求要高于一般人。所以，电子阅读器在订购数字内容时要分清大众、分众和小众市场，在提高文化类、历史类图书质量的同时，适当增加教育类、专业类图书的品种和数量，使其成为用户名副其实的随身图书馆。

企业商务人士是电子阅读器的另一大用户，他们需要的不仅有休闲类书籍的阅读，还需要将电子阅读器作为一种移动办公工具使用，比如机密性的企业内部文件、高附加值的研究报告、专属性质的报价文件等数字内容，都应该可以由电子阅读器来满足阅读、说明、收藏及保密的需求。这就要求电子阅读器厂商开发出更好的工具性软件和功能性软件，让电子阅读器成为更多企业高管、商界精英的随身锦囊。

电子阅读器的专业化还可以选择和机构团体合作，例如与图书馆合作，最大限度地开发图书馆资源，提高图书馆的服务能力；与学校合作，预装相关的教学教辅资料，用轻便的电子书包替代沉重的传统书包。如果电子阅读器推行电子书包计划，则需要增加更具人性化的设计，比如不仅能存储大量的教科书、学习参考书，还要能保存多媒体讲义，完成习题及考试。另外，作为学生学习的得力助手，它还应该具备翻译和点读的功能。

3.2 手机阅读——走大众化之路

随着中国手机网民的增长，用手机阅读电子书、电子报的人越来越多。手机进入数字出版领域的门槛很低，从技术的层面上讲，手机阅读利用的是已有的液晶显示屏；从内容上讲，手机不必为用户预装图书，利用的是免费的网络资源。这些都为手机阅读的低价亲民提供了保障。

目前手机用户的主流人群是学生、上班族和打工者，作为年轻群体，他们需求的信息以休闲娱乐为主，具有多样性和多变性。手机为阅读功能所作的贡献，就是能够在线阅读和随时下载更新，满足用户对这类信息的需求。相对于电子阅读器、PSP游戏机等设备，手机在农村市场有更大的优势，覆盖率更广。随着3G网络的普及和手机上网资费的调整，手机阅读的现象将在农村更加普遍。

同时，面对海量的网络原创作品，手机还需解决阅读软件的问题，包括格式的兼容、操作的简易等。目前，常见的手机阅读软件有百阅、Qreader、熊猫看书、掌上书院等，均能支持多种电子书格式。

3.3 其他终端——走个性化之路

对于其他电子类产品，阅读功能只是其众多功能中的一种，起的是锦上添花的作用，并非用户考虑购买与否的决定性因素。正因如此，许多MP4播放器和掌上游戏机厂商并未将研发设计的重点放在电子阅读功能上。但是，随着市场竞争的加剧，电子类产品功能的趋同，这类产品若想继续生存和发展，就必须技高一筹，走个性化之路。

以索尼公司的PSP游戏机为例，它最初就是为娱乐功能而诞生的，对于玩游戏、看视频的人来说，其屏幕的大小及质量显得尤为重要。阅读同样需要高质量的大屏幕，索尼PSP3000拥有4.3英寸16∶9宽屏液晶，响应速度8毫秒，抗反射技术可使用户在明亮的室外清晰地阅读；所安装的eREAD软件在阅读时可以自然切换背景，文字大小随意调换，还能欣赏漫画、写真，各类图片自由缩放，画面移动流畅自然，阅读完全不受屏幕尺寸限制。

现阶段，移动终端的阅读对象主要集中在图书和报纸，杂志相对而言对色彩的要求更高。针对目前电子阅读器不能显示彩色效果的缺陷，以及手机屏幕太小的问题，PSP游戏机完全有潜力去开发杂志阅读这块市场。杂志的数字版权一方面来自于传统的杂志社，另一方面则是新兴的网络杂志平台。倘若能与Zcom、Xplus等网络杂志平台合作，势必吸引更多的年轻读者，拥有更广阔的发展前景。

无论是哪一种数字阅读产品，都有自身的弱势和强势，走差异竞争之路是为了扬长避短，既能满足不同用户的需求，又能确保自己不被其他具有相同功能的产品所取代。

注释

[1] 中国电子书市场前景看好 但竞争将更为激烈. 参见搜狐 IT. http://it.sohu.com/20100105/n269394213.shtml(2010-01-05 访问)

[2] 李雪昆. "数"说中国互联网 2009. 参见中国新闻出版网 http://www.chinaxwcb.com/index/2010-01-19/content_187691.htm(2010-01-19 访问)

[3] 杨洪. 电子阅读器显露峥嵘. 中国新闻出版报, 2009 (12)

[4] 焦立坤. 电子书产业链集体躁动. 北京晨报, 2010 (1)

[5] 李淼, 杨海鹏. "电子书"走近大众要过几道坎. 中国新闻出版报, 2009 (11)

作者简介

张炯，湖北第二师范学院文学院讲师。

电子杂志的优越性浅析

杨 欢

（武汉大学信息管理学院 武汉 430072）

摘要：电子杂志作为一种数字信息时代出版产业的新兴品种，近年来不断发展壮大，并逐渐呈现主流化趋势。本文针对声情并茂、动静结合的页面设计；互动设计的艺术化两方面对艺术性进行探讨，并总结认为电子杂志在功能性、艺术性和广告价值三个方面具有不可取代的优势。

关键词：电子杂志 功能性 艺术性 广告价值

The Advantages of E-magazine

Yang Huan

（School of Information Management，Wuhan University，Wuhan，430072）

Abstract：As a new variety of the publishing Industry in digital information age，E-magazine has grown in strength in recent years and gradually becomes the mainstream. This paper discusses E-magazine's artistic quality through web page design and interaction design. In this paper，the functionality，artistic quality and advertising value of E-magazine will be analyzed to explain the irreplaceable advantages of E-magazine.

Keywords：E-magazine Functionality Artistry Advertising value

电子杂志目前处于实验、发展和变化的阶段，各种尝试和设想层出不穷。虽然我们无法断言十年后电子杂志的面貌，却可以清晰地看到和切身地感觉到现阶段电子杂志不可替代的优越性。

1 电子杂志的功能性

区别于与传统杂志，电子杂志有三种特性：一是采用先进的 P2P 技术发行，集 Flash 动画、视频短片和背景音乐、声音甚至 3D 特效等各种效果于一体，内容丰富生动，如同给传统杂志披上一件绚丽而自由的数字外衣；二是实现了读者通过界面与编者、广告主及其他读者互动；三是以互联网为主要传播途径。美国马萨诸塞州理工大学的浦尔教授曾提出"媒介融合"的概念，他认为媒介融合是指各种媒介呈现出多功能一体化的趋势，数码电子技术的发展是导致历来泾渭分明的传播形态聚合的原因。可以说，电子杂志正是

"媒介融合"的产物。[1]

1.1　多媒体互动

多媒体电子杂志能针对不同用户做阅读分析，并得到及时更新的阅读反馈，从而为内容制作和广告投放提供参考。

多媒体电子杂志能够实现用户细分。用户可以根据自己的喜好和需求来下载和或线阅读各类杂志，后台服务器能够精确地计算出点击率，统计哪些栏目受欢迎，为后期内容制作提供了针对性的参考。

多媒体电子杂志与电子商务同步，点击广告商品的同时可以继续查询、搜索其详细功能并通过第三方购买商品，一步到位。

1.2　使用便捷

提供多种多样的阅读模式，可在线或离线阅读、直接通过网页浏览器打开或独立可执行文件等，有些网站需要下载官方提供的阅读器进行阅读。例如，在 Zcom 阅览电子杂志前就需要下载 Zcom 杂志订阅器。文件按照内容的不同大小从几兆到上百兆不等，但比起目前电脑硬盘的容量来说不足挂齿，使用非常便捷。这样只要电脑在手，可以充实闲暇时间，比起厚实的纸质刊物方便得多。

1.3　低成本、低门槛

电子杂志的制作、发行、订阅和读者反馈都通过互联网进行，大大降低了成本。一本100 页 80 克铜板印刷的纸质杂志，成本需要大约 8 元人民币，而发行电子杂志的边际成本接近于零，只需支付制作设计费和服务器费用。

电子杂志的制作其实并不只有专业公司才能制作，只要对 Flash 有一定的了解，再加上专业电子杂志制作软件，完全可以制作出风格各异的电子杂志。网上提供专门的素材库、模板、制作软件下载。无论是企业还是个人，只要拥有电脑并能联网，就能够制作出自己的电子杂志。

1.4　内容表现形式丰富

数据显示，相对于传统杂志，电子杂志的优势排序为：内容表现形式丰富、阅读便捷、免费阅读、信息量丰富、种类全面、适合年轻人、定势阅读、互动性强。[2]

1.5　环保性

电子杂志不需要实际的介质和印刷，因此不存在浪费资源和环境污染的问题，符合当今提倡的环保主题，与时俱进。

2　电子杂志的艺术性

心理学认为，人对对象的认知和把握过程是一种"心物场"心理运动过程，"心物场"的建立要考虑如何在要素间实现动力交互作用，构建整体有效的思维模型，更为有效地促进信息传递。[3]电子杂志在界面视野中通过视频、声音等元素及虚拟现实技术，以更为直观的方式让阅读者在相对短的时间内完成对文本意义的大概认知，从而完成感情的交流。这种融合了诸多感官体验的阅读方式，更容易让读者感受到电子杂志的超感觉艺术性，带给读者个性化、沉浸式和互动性的阅读体验。

2.1　声情并茂，动静结合的页面设计

"视觉是人类最为复杂、高度发展的重要感觉。是光照射到眼睛，在视网膜上成像并

发生能量转换最终传输入大脑而产生。"[4]电子杂志的多媒体视觉是受到读者欢迎的关键所在，在一个页面中可以不受限制的编排大量的图片，并以各种各样有趣的形式展现，读者可以用鼠标点击后逐一放大浏览，实现了图片数量与质量的共赢。

"听觉是人类仅次于视觉的重要感觉。是声音通过外耳收集到达鼓膜，通过鼓膜震动将声波传输到内耳的听觉感受器发生能量的转换最终传输入大脑而产生。"[5]电子杂志中的声音有多种表现形式，说白、音乐、音效等，无论是哪种表现形式，都能起到表现主题、渲染气氛，提供画面的艺术感染力的作用，给读者带来轻松、愉悦的心境。

电子杂志中的"视觉"与"听觉"是可以相互补充的，例如在音乐杂志中，对音乐的介绍仅靠音频来完成会显得单薄无力，结合了文字、图像、视频等视觉元素就显得生动有力。

电子杂志中的"视觉"与"听觉"是可以相互转换的。美国音乐学家马利翁曾说："声音是听得见得色彩，色彩是看得见的声音。"[6]当读者看见银幕上绚丽多彩的画面时，听觉会产生愉悦感，犹如听见了悦耳的音乐。反之亦然。例如《瑞丽妆》第41期，杂志中介绍了很多妆容的画法，阅读"可爱妆"的页面时，有活泼的韩国音乐与之匹配；阅读"冷艳装"的页面时，有时尚奔放的欧美音乐与之匹配，给读者营造出身临其境的感觉。

2.2　艺术化互动设计

2.2.1　艺术性的互动内容

艺术性的互动内容能够给读者提供美感的享受，优秀的互动设计能够引起读者的参与兴趣。在名人电子杂志《开啦》中，第47期的第4页展示并介绍了三星最新款手机，流动的画面让读者对此款手机产生了强烈的了解欲望，点击手机图画可以链接到另外一个网页中，此网页有这款手机的具体介绍，还有在线购买业务，即使不买也可以了解到了最新电子产品的一些新功能，开阔了眼界。在一些旅游杂志中，要想吸引读者最达到最终的目的，互动内容尤为重要，介绍某一城市的同时，可以在页面中增加一些互动环节，介绍该城市的名吃，娱乐、游玩的地方，不仅丰富了杂志的内容，还提高了杂志的艺术性。

2.2.2　互动形式的艺术化

电子杂志页面沿用了传统杂志的外观形式，由封面、封底、目录和内页组成。页面与页面之间的切换、正文的展开与滚动阅读、视频的播放等互动环节的设计和排版尤为重要，只有充分运用统一与变化、对比与和谐、节奏与韵律等形式法则，将内容与形式完美相融才能创造最佳的艺术效果。《开啦街拍》第21期第50页，是介绍一个搜包的主题，展示了一些街头潮人的背包并有详细的文字介绍，在人物与文字介绍直接有两个小圈圈图片吸引读者的眼球，把鼠标放上去马上显示出放大的图片，展示这些潮人们背包里面装的所有东西，这种互动形式不但新颖，而且具有很好的艺术形式感，能够给读者留下非常深刻的印象。

3　电子杂志的广告价值

据资料显示，我国互联网用户70.54%集中在经济较为发达地区，64%家庭人均月收入高于1 000元，85.8%年龄在18岁到35岁之间，83%受过大学以上教育。因此，网络广告的目标群体是目前社会上层次最高、收入最高、消费能力最高的消费群体。这一群体的消费总额往往大于其他消费层次之和。与电视广告相比，网络广告表现为受众关注度高，调查显示，电视观众40%的人同时在阅读，21%的人同时在做家务，13%的人在饮食，12%的人在玩赏它物，10%在打电话或玩手机；而网上用户55%的人在使用计算机时不做任何其他事，只有6%的人同时在打电话，5%在饮食。

电子杂志继承了传统杂志的诸多优势，电子杂志最具突破性的特点是非强迫性的广告行为，其广告策划原则是"提升快乐指数"。以娱乐性、互动性的表现形式，让读者潜移默化地接受企业品牌。

3.1 广告的形式绚丽多姿

采用多媒体的形式，集动画、视频短片和背景音乐，甚至3D特效等各种效果于一体，这种声画并茂的多感官、多通路的广告集群，将有效地提高广告的表现力和感染力，产生"1+1>2"的放大效应，深得广告商的喜爱。

3.2 广告互动性强

电子杂志强调分享与参与，鼓励双向沟通。广告商更重视的是读者看了广告后是否理解和愿意讨论这则广告并分享自己的观点，通过话题讨论、互动游戏等方式使得广告信息与杂志内容水乳交融。

3.3 广告的效果可以被衡量

广告大师约翰·沃纳梅克面对传统广告媒体时曾说过："我在广告上的投资有一半是无效的，但问题是我不知道是哪一半。"电子杂志的用户管理后台具有对读者的地域定位、时间定位以及行为定位的检测系统，读者的各种有效信息都可以反馈给广告主，使得广告针对性更强，投放更精准。

3.4 形象宣传

对于政府而言，可以有效利用多媒体电子杂志进行政府形象宣传，推广途径是政府综合服务大厅的触摸平台，或者制作成光盘，赠送给百姓，从而使政府和百姓有效的沟通，向服务型政府转变。对于企业而言，用多媒体电子杂志可以更加生动形象的表现企业文化和产品，从而提升企业文化内涵的专业程度。企业可以在展会、客户来访参观、赠送客户资料时运用多媒体电子杂志，这样可以有效提升企业形象，而且多媒体的形式更容易让人接受。[7]

注释

[1] 宋昭勋. 新闻传播学中 Convergence 一词溯源及内涵 [J]. 现代传播，2006（1）

[2] 考夫卡. 心理学流派格式塔学派代表人物.《格式塔心理学》

[3]《中国传媒产业发展报告（2007—2008）》

[4][6] 曹方,《视觉传达设计原理》，江苏人民出版社，2005 年

[5] 张春兴,《现代心理学—现代人研究自身的科学》，上海人民出版社，1994 年

[7] 百度百科. 电子杂志. http://baike.baidu.com/view/9365.htm

作者简介

杨欢，武汉大学信息管理学院出版发行专业硕士研究生。

汉王电纸书产业链建设与运营模式探析

阮 静

（武汉大学信息管理学院 武汉 430072）

摘要：本文以汉王电子书为例，在系统描述我国电子阅读器产业链构成的基础上，分析汉王电纸书在产业链上所处的角色。并且，本文详细介绍汉王电纸书以终端为依托，构建出"终端+内容"的运营模式，并将指出目前这种运营模式存在的问题。希望通过这些分析能对汉王电子书以及其他的电子阅读器的产业链建设与运营模式的建立提供有益的参考。

关键词：汉王电纸书 产业链 运营模式

An Analysis on Industry Chain and Operation Mode of Hanvon Electric Paper Books

Ruan Jing

（School of Information Management, Wuhan University, Wuhan, 430072）

Abstract：This paper will take the Hanvon as example and analyze how it function to the chain, which is based on the description of composition of the industrial chain of e-readers. Secondly, this paper will introduce the Hanvon's terminal + content business model which relies on the terminal. And it also points out the problems of this business model. This analysis aims to give some suggestion for the construction of the industrial chain and the establishment of the business model of the Hanvon and other electronic readers.

Keywords：Electric paper books Industry chain Operation mode

电子阅读器作为专业数字内容如电子图书、电子报纸等的承载终端，以其类纸显示屏技术和低耗电等核心性能在中国发展已久。2009 年，中国的电子阅读器市场似乎才迎来其高速发展的黄金期，不仅各类电子阅读器终端品牌纷纷涌入，内容提供商、电信运营商业也加入到市场的角逐中。但是，我国目前尚未建立成熟的移动阅读产业链，这影响了电子阅读器市场的深度发展。汉王电纸书在我国的移动阅读终端销售市场上一直处于领先地位。"据清科研究中心的最新数据显示，2010 年中国电子阅读器市场销量达 24.91 万部。其中汉王电子阅读器销量约为 16.45 万部，比例高达 66.04%，销量优势绝对领先。"[1]本文以汉王电子书为例，对其产业链建设与运营模式进行分析，从而对中国电子阅读器的产业链建设进行一些有益的思考。

1 汉王电纸书产业链建设现状

1.1 我国电子阅读器产业链构成

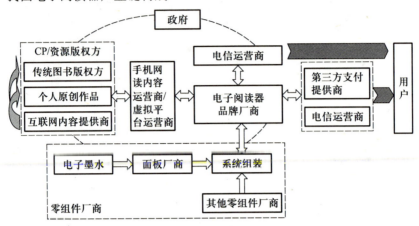

中国电子阅读器产业链结构图[2]

如上图所示，我国电子阅读器产业链条上大致有五个部分，首先是居于产业链上游的零部件组装厂商，主要由电子墨水厂商、面板厂商、其他零部件厂商以及系统组装厂商组成。第二个部分是掌握数字出版内容资源的内容提供商。它们凭借其独特的内容资源优势，在整个电子阅读器产业链中有一定话语权。第三个部分是内容平台运营商，也称虚拟平台运营商，由内容提供商、终端厂商及第三方支付提供商组成。汉王科技为了服务自己的终端阅读器的销售而打造的"汉王书城"就是属于这种内容平台运营商。第四个部分是品牌终端厂商，也就是本文的主体——汉王电纸书所扮演的角色。目前，中国市场上的电子阅读器品牌终端厂商众多，包括汉王、方正、翰林、大唐、艾利和、索尼、大唐、易博士、润唐等。此外，一些传统的 IT 厂商如联想、华硕、同方、爱国者、LG 等也相继推出电子阅读器终端。这些厂商共同组成了中国电子阅读器市场的重要推动力量之一。第五个部分是电信运营商。中国三家电信运营商：中国移动、中国电信、中国联通将先后加入电子阅读器市场的角逐。最先做出反应的是中国移动，电信运营商在整个产业链条上有着天然的主导力量，因此当 2009 年中国移动做出一系列动作时，对整个中国的移动阅读市场带来了不小的冲击。最后，产业链当然还包括广大的终端用户，但是目前电子阅读器的价位还是偏高，超过大多数用户的经济承受能力，加上数字阅读的资源相对稀少，广大用户对电子阅读的认识不足，导致整个中国的电子阅读器市场的购买力还是处于相对偏低的状态。

1.2 汉王电纸书在电子阅读器产业链中的角色分析

如前文所述，汉王电纸书在中国电子阅读器终端的销售市场上处于领先地位，有一定的品牌影响力。"汉王电纸书"上市仅五个月就销售五万多本，带动公司的业绩在 2008 年翻了一番。正因为如此，2008 年汉王科技将公司的重心完全转向了电子阅读器市场，试图通过电子阅读器的崛起让汉王转入主流市场。

但是，汉王电纸书在整个电子阅读器产业链条上到底是处于什么位置，通往行业绝对领军位置的道路是否如设想的那样顺畅？

正如业内大多数人所承认的那样，中国电子阅读器产业链是不成熟的，整个产业链条亟须整合。汉王电纸书在电子阅读器产业链中影响力不足，受制于产业链中上游，面临诸多困境，具体可表述为以下几个方面：

首先，产业链上游零部件厂商存有技术壁垒，直接影响汉王电纸书终端的赢利空间。电子阅读器生产的核心技术在于电子纸基材和面板。目前生产电子纸基材的厂商有三家：E-Ink（电子墨水）、SiPix 以及 Bridgestone（普利司通），其中 E-Ink 公司是商业化最成功、市场占有率最大的，也是唯一一家能够量产的公司，以汉王电纸书为首的众多国内厂商，以及亚马逊、索尼等主流品牌均采用 E-Ink 的电子纸基材，除此之外，SiPix 公司的 Micro-cup 技术同样具有一定的竞争能力。而电子面板厂商则主要集中在中国台湾地区，处于领导地位的是元太科技与友达光电，元太科技更是占据全球 80% 的市场份额。2009 年年底，元太科技宣布并购美国 E-Ink 公司，整合了电子书电子纸基材和面板技术，从而一统电子纸技术江湖，而友达光电也通过收购 SiPix 公司的部分股份而进入电子纸行业。[3] 在电子阅读器的硬件成本中，电子纸基材和面板所占的比例高达 35% ~ 50%，而这些技术目前掌握在少数生产厂家手中，这也是造成电子阅读器相较于其他电子类科技产品价位长期居高不下的主要原因。此种情况下，必然形成诸如汉王电纸书等电子阅读器终端长期依靠高价位赢利的模式。

当然，这种现象终将得到改变，更多新的显示技术将陆续登场，比如美国苹果公司的 iPad 实力非凡，刚一登场就对 E-Ink 造成重大冲击。更多技术的投入会加剧市场的竞争，价格战不可避免，电子阅读器终端价格的必定会持续走低，汉王电纸书必须寻求新的突破，弥补其赢利空间因为上游零部件厂商的竞争格局变化缩减而带来的损失。

其次，内容提供商是汉王电纸书的潜在致命缺陷。现阶段，汉王电纸书的赢利前景比较乐观，但是随着阅读器终端价格下滑，它将会受到内容资源匮乏的挑战。读者使用电子阅读器自然会将它与传统的阅读相区别，会希望从电子阅读器中读取的信息是丰富和便捷的。要获取出版社热门的畅销书需要花费巨大代价，很多出版社会担心出版资源数字化会影响到他们原有的纸质图书的发行和赢利，而那些知名的出版社和网络文学网站更是不在乎一点蝇头小利。内容提供商与阅读器终端厂商的利润分成模式不确定，电子书的运营和支付平台也不成熟，很多中国的用户购买了电子阅读器后还是很难接受内容付费的模式。因此汉王电纸书自建的"汉王书城"平台还是依靠电纸书内置图书加上免费下载，其图书资源有限，以经典读物特别是那些版权保护期限到期，无需交付版权费的图书为主。

最后，电信运营商对电子阅读器终端厂商有强大的号召力和吸引力。"运营商的支付模式非常成熟，与国外需要通过信用卡或者点卡支付不同，运营商可以在电子阅读器上面绑定自己的 SIM 卡，通过手机话费和流量计费。终端厂商和内容提供商如果和电信运营商取得合作，让读者通过电子阅读器随时随地连接到高速数据库网络下载期刊，或者订阅网站新闻博客，他愿意接受更灵活的合作模式，比如免费提供附带少量杂志广告的内容。"[4] 2009 年，中国移动推出 G3 阅读器，建立一个以电子书为核心的资源运营平台，汉王、华为等四家企业成为了首批的电子阅读器的定制厂商，中移动向这四家终端厂商提供补贴，明确由中移动负责采购、招标和销售。中国移动试图通过这个资源网络运营平台，整合各个出版集团和网络原创网站，统一阅读器上的文件格式，并降低无线下载的费用，这样各家终端阅读器企业就要发挥各自本领，拓展市场。

总的说来，包括汉王电纸书在内的各家电子阅读器品牌厂商几乎都处于产业链不顺畅的不利境地之中，中国电子阅读器产业链亟需整合。

2 汉王电纸书运营模式探讨

2.1 我国电子阅读器的三种典型运营模式

我国电子阅读器市场上的厂商在竞争中主要形成了三种运营模式：

第一种是"终端+内容"的运营模式。这其中还要分为两种方式，一是以终端为市场切入点，逐渐构建以终端为主的"终端+内容"模式，汉王电纸书就是这类模式的典型代表；二是以内容为切入点，逐渐构建成以内容为主的"内容+终端"模式，这一模式的典型代表是"盛大文学"。本文将重点分析汉王电纸书的发展模式，但是无论是"汉王电纸书"还是"盛大文学"，实质是殊途同归，电子阅读器的核心竞争优势终将还是内容。

第二种是完全硬件的运营模式。

第三种是电信运营商深度定制终端的运营模式。前文提到的中国移动推出 G3 阅读器，打造资源运营平台就是这种模式。[5]

2.2 汉王电纸书以终端为依托，构建"终端+内容"的运营模式

在汉王电纸书发展前期，因为终端的定价高，利润大，将发展重心放在终端市场是明智的。但是随着产业链上游技术壁垒的逐渐打破，众多厂商涌入电子阅读器市场，终端市场的利润必然会减少。因此，进入发展的现阶段，汉王电纸书以终端为依托，侧重内容资源整合与内容平台的构建，形成"终端+内容"的运营模式是正确的。汉王电纸书从终端与内容双向入手，为用户打造"汉王书城"，定位于平台服务提供商，通过与出版社、报社、互联网内容提供商分别展开合作，获得优质而丰富的内容资源，努力实现产业链整合。

2009 年汉王与湖北、上海等地的传媒集团展开渠道和版权方面的深度合作，还考虑在未来将重点放在独家买断优质文化产品的版权上。2010 年与《新京报》、《京华时报》签订数字内容合作协议，这两家都市报纸的内容将正式登陆汉王书城。汉王书城已经有包括《环球时报》、《文汇报》、《新京报》、《京华时报》等在内的 50 多份报纸和 4 万种图书。2010 年 6 月汉王科技副总裁王邦江在接受《北京商报》采访时表示："汉王今年在内容资源购买上的花费将达 3 000 万元"。汉王通过上市募集来的资金很大部分用于汉王书城资源部的人员招聘上，以求快速提升汉王书城的图书资源内容。此外，汉王还与易博士、翰林等终端厂商以及中国出版集团数字传媒有限公司、万榕书业等出版机构联合番薯网一起打造全行业合作的"云阅读"平台，使终端用户能有更多选择，"用户能够在任何时间、任何地点、应用任何媒介阅读电子书。"

汉王依靠终端优势而逐渐发展构建"终端+内容"的运营模式与亚马逊的 Kindle 模式十分相似，但是，汉王电纸书的这种发展中模式中还有一个问题没有得到很好的解决，那就是阅读收费方式的问题。要知道，电子阅读器的运营模式中要解决的主要问题就是要处理好资源提供和阅读收费的关系。汉王与出版社、报刊、互联网站等内容提供商的合作实行的是利润二八分成，考虑到中国消费者的习惯和心理预期，以及目前内容平台上读者基数还不够大，汉王将首要目标还是放在平台搭建上，而后才会更多去考虑利润分成和收费方式的问题。

3 基于汉王电纸书产业链建设与运营模式现状的思考

正如前文所分析的那样，中国电子阅读器产业链是不成熟的，整个产业链条亟须整合。但是同时我们也要认识到，电子阅读器产业链条上每一个环节都很重要，它们都有自己专注的领域，各要素要各司其职，协调各自的利益和关系，形成整体优势，企图依靠一家垄断是不可能将整个行业做大做强的。

汉王电纸书受到产业链上其他环节的限制较多，只有在其占据整个市场优势地位的情况下，认识到自身不足寻求突破，才能获得长远发展。在今后的发展过程中，汉王电纸书一方面要抓住与包括中国移动在内的电信运营商的合作机会，通过与电信运营商打造的内容平台的对接，提升汉王电子书的市场影响力，扩大销量。另一方面，还是要加大自身"汉王书城"内容平台的建设力度，广泛开展与广大中小内容提供商的合作，扩充"汉王书城"的内容资源。

注释

［1］［2］清科研究中心．2010 年中国电子阅读器市场投资研究报告，2010 ［OL］http://wenku.baidu.com/view/90e1d5b069dc5022aaea001e.html#

［3］［5］联合证券有限责任公司研究所．电子书——大规模应用即将启动，2010 ［OL］http://files.laoqianzhuang.com/upload/154488.pdf

［4］张小洁．谁能整合电子阅读 ［J］．IT 经理世界，2009 （6）

作者简介

阮静，武汉大学信息管理学院 2009 级硕士研究生。

移动出版与电子书刊

数字出版物长期保存的要求与方法

张婵娟

（武汉大学信息管理学院　武汉　430070）

摘要：此论文简要分析了数字出版物长期保存的主体、要求及方法，希望对做好我国数字出版物长期保存的工作，最大限度地保存和利用有价值的数字资源有所帮助。

关键词：数字出版物　长期保存　保存对象　保存要求　保存方法

The requirements and ways of digital publications' long-term preservation

Zhang Chanjuan

（School of Information Management，Wuhan University，Wuhan，430070）

Abstract：This paper briefly analyzes who should be responsible for long-term preservation of digital publications，the requirements and the ways of digital publications' long-term preservation. I hope these will be useful for the long-term preservation of digital publications and using valuable digital resources in our country.

Keywords：Digital publication　Long-term preservation　The objects of preservation　The ways of preservation　The requirements of preservation

网络化时代，数字资源爆炸性增长，数字资源在海量产生的同时也在大量丢失，由于数字资源的出版和保存都与传统的纸质资源有着很大的不同，其更新速度非常快，许多资源稍纵即逝，如果不注重保存，很可能就无法再找到信息资源的内容。数字出版物长期保存成为亟待解决的问题。开展数字出版物长期保存涉及保存对象、保存主体、保存策略等一系列问题。

1　数字出版物长期保存的概念

所谓数字出版物长期保存，即是对目前社会所拥有和使用的数字形态的出版物进行有效保存，是为保证数字形态的出版物可长期维护和其内容可长期获取的必要管理活动。这里有两层含意，一是长期存储，二是长期可获取。

2　数字出版物保存的对象

在海量的数字出版物中应该保存那些容易丢失的、与未来有关联的、有重要价值的数字资源，保存重要的科学数据，特别是"原始数据"。保存的数字出版物的内容具体来说，应该主要包括以下几个方面：

2.1　数字出版物的来源

即数字出版物的出处，能证实该信息的来源与历史，有助于确认该信息是真实、完整和可信的。

2.2　数字出版物存储介质

通过对数字出版物存储介质的保存或迁移，确保存储其中的物理数字数据能被准确完好地读出。

2.3　数字出版物的功能性

数字出版物具有远远超出传统信息的功能性，它可以包含多媒体成分；可以以超文本存在；还可以含有由数字存储器自动产生的动态成分。另外，数字信息还具有导航功能，如工具栏、关键词或内容交互式表格等。这些截然不同于传统信息的功能性，要求能完整地保存下来。

2.4　数字出版物的技术信息

通过保存有关数字出版物编码、格式、标记、结构、压缩、加密等方面的技术方法信息，确保能够识别和解析数字出版物的内容。

2.5　数字出版物的管理手段

包括数字出版物的内容校验、身份认证、版本演变、知识产权管理机制、信息安全机制等。这样做的目的是为了确保能可信、可靠和合法鉴别、使用被保存的数字信息。

3　数字出版物长期保存的主体

在数字出版物长期保存活动中，内容资源的提供方、保存方和使用者形成了利益共同体，存在一个权益平衡的问题，他们对这些数字资源都负有保存责任，都属于数字资源长期保存的主体。这些责任主体包括：数字出版物的生产者、出版发行者、图书馆档案机构、政府机构等。

3.1　生产者和出版商

数字出版物只有在其生产的环境中加以保存才是最经济、最可行的，这也是维护其长期保存的可靠方式，因此数字出版物的生产者和出版者对数字资源的长期保存负有主要责任和最初责任。如果在数字资源生产的初期就关注和保存就会减少成本，方便后期的共享和存取。

3.2　图书馆和档案馆

图书馆、档案馆等传统保存机构的职责是传承人类文明、保存人类文化遗产，在数字时代，他们依然负有这个使命，即保存各种形式的数字信息资源。世界各国的很多图书馆、档案馆都积极投身于数字信息长期保存的研究与实践中，成为数字信息保存的主力军。除了国家图书馆、国家档案馆，还有很多大学、科研机构的图书馆和信息保存中心及专业档案馆等数字保存机构也开展了数字信息的长期保存活动。

3.3　软硬件技术开发者

数字出版物的长期保存首先要设计出能够制作完全相同并具有一定稳定性的数字产品的可靠系统和程序。这就需要软硬件开发者进行专门开发，以满足数字出版物长期保存的系统的特殊需求。

3.4 政府机构

政府加入到数字出版物长期保存活动中可以尽可能多地整合社会各种力量，扩大合作的范围；可以增强数字出版物保存的社会影响力，提高公众意识，营造良好的社会氛围；为数字出版物长期保存活动提供政策、法律、经济等方面的保障；探索并建立国家级保存机构与地方级保存机构组成的数字出版物归档系统；加强国际合作和互助，更好地保存自己的数字资源并使其得到持续不断的利用。

4 数字出版物长期保存的要求

4.1 载体应具有较长和稳定的存储寿命

数字出版物是存储在各种类型的物理实体上的。它既可以脱机存储在磁带、磁盘、光盘上，也可以联机存储在网络服务器上。相对于传统纸介质，数字出版物存储实体容易变质，易受阳光、尘埃、磁场、温度、湿度的影响。可见，数字资源载体抵抗外界环境的能力及其寿命将直接影响数字出版物的长期保存。不同的数字媒体对数字资源长期保存的影响也不同，常见的数字媒体有光盘、硬盘。软驱、磁带等，它们在容量、速度、耐久性等方面各有优劣。因此，数字出版物的长期保存需要提高存储载体的稳定性和延长其寿命以减少存储成本。

4.2 拥有可靠的格式转换及迁移技术

目前，我国的数字出版物存取技术缺乏广泛接受的标准。因此，各种存储机构在存储和利用数字资源时，生产者、提供者和维护者各自为政，随意采用各种系统和技术，其结果必然导致数字资源在以后的存取和信息共享过程中面临多种困难。由于数字出版物的保存标准不统一，严重影响数字资源的交流和共享。这是制约数字出版物长期保存的首要瓶颈。从数字出版物对其产生的环境的依赖性可以看出，要保持数字出版物的长期可存取性，只有将其依存的软硬件设备长期保持不变。但是，技术的发展是不可避免的，当软件或硬件的规范发生变化时，软件与硬件就不再匹配，信息就无法读出，对于多媒体产品而言，这种情况会更严重。目前，计算机软件、硬件及信息处理方式大约 2～5 年就要更新换代，这使得记录、存储与检索数字信息的手段与产品也要迅速随之发生变更。这就使得掌握可靠地数据迁移技术变得尤为重要。

4.3 具备较强的抵御风险能力

数字出版物的服务大多集中在计算机网络上，而网络本身固有的特性，导致计算机网络的安全性降低，不安全因素增加，如计算机病毒、黑客入侵等都使数字出版物面临着前所未有的安全问题，数字出版物一旦受到病毒的侵蚀和黑客的破坏都将可能在瞬间化为乌有。加上人为操作失误、保存环境变化、硬盘故障、电压不稳定、停电、备份制度以及各种自然灾害等都可能会造成服务器损毁、系统瘫痪、信息数据丢失的问题，造成无法挽回的损失。可见，安全问题已经成为严重威胁数字出版物能否长期保存的问题。

4.4 具有足够的资金支持

第一，信息技术是发展最快、竞争最激烈的领域。技术的进步必然导致软件升级、硬件更新；存储实体的寿命和使用中因磨损需要重新拷贝信息内容，数据格式变化带来格式转换，技术升级导致信息的迁移；原有设备的维护，已淘汰设备因信息存取的需要而进行的保存等都需要相应的费用。

第二，数字出版物的维护需要有高素质的人力资源，并应随着技术的发展随时对人员进行必要的培训，这是一笔不可忽视的长期的费用。

4.5　具有相关的国家政策和法规的支持

数字出版物长期保存过程中的资源获取、提供服务和存储管理几个环节都涉及相应的知识产权问题，法律因素影响数字出版物的长期保存。一方面数字出版物长期保存是一项影响人类文明传承，需要国家层面支持的行动，因此法律上的保证必须解决；另一方面，相关法律的制定和变更需要许多程序，时间周期很长，相对于数字出版物保存的紧迫性，这种周期是一个很严重的问题。数字出版物的保存需要对相关法律如知识产权法进行修改和完善，对于保存机构的保存责任的法律例外非常需要，只有当相关的法律例外获得承认，真正的数字出版物保存计划才能够全面推行。

5　长期保存的策略

5.1　鉴定数字出版物的价值

数字出版物的内容比较广泛，难免良莠不齐，因而要对海量的数字出版物全部保存是没有必要的。或许有人会说利用得多的就保存，利用得少的就不保存，这未免有点武断，有的内容因为其的冷门性而不被大量关注，但是其内容却有可能是十分有价值的。所以应拟定一个数字出版物选择与决定是否保留的策略，并请专家对其价值进行评定，将有保存价值的数字出版物确定下来加以长期保存。

5.2　延长载体寿命

通过技术研究，改进物理载体的稳定性、存储能力和使用寿命。目前，有些光盘的设计寿命已长达 100 年之久，其寿命已超过了读取信息所用软、硬件设备的寿命。尽管如此，还是要提高存储载体的稳定性和寿命以减少存储成本。

5.3　数据迁移

迁移是目前实际运行中使用比较成熟和频繁的方法。为保证当前存储的数字信息总能被当前系统读取，采用数据迁移的方法，持续地将数字信息从旧的软硬件环境转换到新的计算机环境，从而保证数字资源可以在发展的环境中被识别、使用和检索，以进行数字信息的长期保存。迁移主要有两种情况，一是把数字信息从种类繁多的格式下迁移到当前广泛使用的几个标准格式中。二是将数字信息从稳定性低的媒体迁移到稳定性更高的媒体上，从对软硬件环境依赖强的格式迁移到对软硬件环境依赖程度低的格式下，等等。

5.4　完善标准

我国的数字出版物存取技术缺乏广泛接受的标准，由于数字出版物长期保存技术发展快，标准不统一，严重影响数字资源的交流和共享。这是制约数字出版物长期保存的首要原因。针对其目前的现状，应该尽快制定数字出版物长期保存的通用技术标准与组织管理协议，以尽量减少数字出版物在新旧平台的转换的难度。作为被保存的数字资源应当采用最稳定的技术与通用的标准归档，与相关行业标准及国际标准相互兼容，这也是首先应考虑解决的问题。我们需要一个标准化的、长期使用的规范，以达到资源最大限度的共享、最低成本的保存。在标准制定方面，数字出版物长期保存的标准应是通用性、兼容性的，能与国际标准和行业标准兼容。

5.5　加大经济投入

数字出版物保存的经费开支主要包括几个方面：一是基础设施建设，如信息存储设备等，这部分开支数目巨大，需要专项资金支持；二是数字出版物保存过程中所需的开支，包括软件升级、专业人员培训、设备消耗等费用；三是对保存的数字出版物管理的开支，数字出版物的保存要求持续不断地投资，并且要对资源进行积极地管理。为解决资金短缺的问题，保存机构首先应努力争取政府的支持，扩大资金来源，加大宣传力度，使政府机构和主要上级领导意识到数字出版物长期保存的重大意义，在政策上和资金上给予大力支持，并保证各级政府投入的稳定性和连续性；其次是通过接受民间捐赠，按照共同投入、共同开发和共同受益的原则，鼓励企业和个人投资，多渠道、多形式地利用民间资金，逐步形成多元化的投入体系，使之获得持续的资金支持。

5.6　订立与完善相关的法律法规

5.6.1　加强相关法律法规的订立工作

数字出版物长期保存过程涉及的知识产权和版权是一个不可忽视的问题，在长期保存过程中会涉及到权利的转让、重新界定（如格式转换后导致的权限改变）等一系列问题，这也就涉及数字资源的处置、利用权限问题。为了最大限度减少或避免由此产生的相关产权纠纷，有必要加快数字出版物长期保存中的知识产权立法建设，对数字资源的复制、下载、传播、转换、迁移等相关行为所涉及的权限问题进行界定，对数字产品的知识产权、版权和发行权等问题制定专门的法律法规。

5.6.2　加强与版权人的协商

虽然我们可以通过对合理使用制度的修订来解决一些数字出版物长期存取中的知识产权问题，但是因为法律对合理使用的适用条件有着严格的限制，所以图书馆等机构需要长期保存的许多数字资源无法适用合理使用。例如，法律规定合理使用只能针对馆藏作品，但是对于图书馆所购买的一些在线出版物，图书馆对其拥有的仅仅是使用权而不是所有权，因此它们不是传统意义上的馆藏作品，从而不能利用合理使用来进行长期保存。因此，图书馆对于那些具有重要使用价值的数字资源，最可行的办法就是通过和版权人协商，应在采购谈判时就提出长期保存权利，获取其授权来解决数字资源的长期存取问题，增加永久性保存条款。

5.6.3　与国际法协调的问题

数字出版物保存不仅在内容方面要与有关国际法协调，而且归档数字资源一旦在互联网上传播，还会有许多与国际法相关的新问题产生，这也是需要认真研究解决的。因此，数字出版物保存行为的法律体系中应该包括国际条约、协定，在制定相关法律、法规、规章时必须充分考虑怎样有机地融合与容纳国际条约、协定的宗旨和精神，特别是那些我国政府已经签署参加的国际公约、协定，从而使法规体系建设更加科学、完备。

5.6.4　完善数字出版物缴送制度

（1）规范数字出版物缴送格式

应该加快数字出版物的格式规范化和标准化工作，提倡和鼓励出版者以标准化格式出版和呈缴。出版机构应以比较常用的标准化格式生产和呈缴数字出版物，以确保数字出版物的长期保存和有效利用。

（2）建立出版商补偿机制

基于更好的长久保存的目的，受缴单位一般被允许有权复制送缴的数字出版物，但是对用户"合理使用"这些数字信息的权限应该有一个明确的规定，以免用户毫无限制地使用这些数字资源，影响到出版商的利益进而影响到出版商呈缴的积极性。还可以建立比较行之有效的补偿机制，可以尝试通过国家补偿、读者补偿和协议补偿等方式来提高出版机构送缴数字出版物的积极性，便于数字出版物被更好地保存和利用。

5.7 加强合作

数字出版物的长期保存是一项艰巨复杂的系统工程，它需要解决经济、标准、技术、法律法规等多方面的难题。数字出版物长期保存工作是一项庞大的工程，单独某个机构、单靠技术手段无法解决其长期保存中的问题，必须走协调合作的道路。目前我国在数字出版物长期保存方面还缺乏统一的合作网络，相关单位进行保存都是独立进行，不仅造成了人力、物力的浪费，还很可能造成资源的重复建设，因此有必要制定一个统一的规划和完整的整合共享方案来合作完成数字出版物的长期保存项目。

6 结语

当前，国内对于数字出版物长期保存的研究和实践还处于起步阶段，我们可以结合数字出版业的实际情况，更多地借鉴国外数字出版物长期保存的经验，做好我国数字出版物长期保存的工作，最大限度地保存有价值的数字资源，为子孙后代可持续利用、为传承人类文明作出自己的贡献。

参考文献

[1] 宋育贤. 电子出版物长期保存问题的探讨［J］. 国外油田工程，2003（3）：53-54

[2] 杨淑萍. 关于数字资源长期保存风险管理问题的探讨［J］. 图书馆学研究，2007（7）：83-87

[3] 黄旭，毕强. 国内外数字资源长期保存研究现状与进展［J］. 图书馆学研究，2009（1）：25-28

[4] 袁丽华，包平. 国国外数字资源长期保存及我国的发展策略［J］. 新世纪图书馆，2009（2）：9-11

[5] 韩丽. 国外数字信息资源合作保存及我国的发展策略［J］. 现代情报，2007（9）

[6] 于嘉. 数字信息长期保存的策略探讨［J］. 河南图书馆学刊，2005（3）

[7] 李文. 试论数字资源的长期保存问题［J］. 惠州学院学报（社会科学版）2005（2）

[8] 王萍. 数字信息资源长期保存策略探析［J］. 湖南第一师范学报，2009（4）：136-138

[9] 杨小云，魏鑫，吴玉玲. 数字资源长期保存存在的问题及对策［J］. 农业图书情报学，2009（11）：30-33

作者简介

张婵娟，武汉大学信息管理学院硕士研究生。

郑重声明

高等教育出版社依法对本书享有专有出版权。任何未经许可的复制、销售行为均违反《中华人民共和国著作权法》，其行为人将承担相应的民事责任和行政责任；构成犯罪的，将被依法追究刑事责任。为了维护市场秩序，保护读者的合法权益，避免读者误用盗版书造成不良后果，我社将配合行政执法部门和司法机关对违法犯罪的单位和个人进行严厉打击。社会各界人士如发现上述侵权行为，希望及时举报，本社将奖励举报有功人员。

反盗版举报电话　（010）58581897　58582371　58581879
反盗版举报传真　（010）82086060
反盗版举报邮箱　dd@hep.com.cn
通信地址　北京市西城区德外大街4号　高等教育出版社法务部
邮政编码　100120